Computational Modeling and Simulation of Intellect:

Current State and Future Perspectives

Boris Igelnik
BMI Research Inc., USA

Senior Editorial Director: Kristin Klinger
Director of Book Publications: Julia Mosemann
Editorial Director: Lindsay Johnston
Acquisitions Editor: Erika Carter
Development Editor: Joel Gamon
Production Coordinator: Jamie Snavely
Typesetters: Jennifer Romanchak and Michael Brehm
Cover Design: Nick Newcomer

Published in the United States of America by
Information Science Reference (an imprint of IGI Global)
701 E. Chocolate Avenue
Hershey PA 17033
Tel: 717-533-8845
Fax: 717-533-8661
E-mail: cust@igi-global.com
Web site: http://www.igi-global.com/reference

Library of Congress Cataloging-in-Publication Data

Computational modeling and simulation of intellect: current state and future perspectives / Boris Igelnik, editor.
p. cm.
Includes bibliographical references and index.
Summary: "This book confronts the problem of meaning by fusing together methods specific to different fields and exploring the computational efficiency and scalability of these methods"--Provided by publisher.
ISBN 978-1-60960-551-3 (hardcover) -- ISBN 978-1-60960-552-0 (ebook) 1. Machine learning. 2. Adaptive control systems. I. Igelnik, Boris, 1940-
Q325.5.C654 2011
006.3'1--dc22
2010054438

British Cataloguing in Publication Data
A Cataloguing in Publication record for this book is available from the British Library.

Peter Sarlin, *Stockholm University, Sweden*
Dan Simon, *Cleveland State University, USA*
Janusz Starzyk, *University of Ohio at Athens, USA*
Marco Vannucci, *Scuola Superiore Santa Anna, Italy*

Table of Contents

Foreword 1 xviii

Foreword 2 xix

Preface xxi

Acknowledgment xxix

Section 1
Application of AI and CI Methods to Image and Signal Processing, Robotics, and Control

Chapter 1
Image Processing for Localization and Parameterization of the Glandular Ducts of Colon in Inflammatory Bowel Diseases 1
Stanislaw Osowski, Warsaw University of Technology & Military University of Technology, Poland
Michal Kruk, University of Life Sciences, Poland
Robert Koktysz, Military Institute of Medicine, Poland
Jaroslaw Kurek, University of Life Sciences, Poland

Chapter 2
The Kolmogorov Spline Network for Image Processing 25
Pierre-Emmanuel Leni, University of Burgundy, France
Yohan D. Fougerolle, University of Burgundy, France
Frédéric Truchetet, University of Burgundy, France

Chapter 3
Intelligent Information Description and Recognition in Biomedical Image Databases 52
Khalifa Djemal, University of Evry Val d'Essonne, France
Hichem Maaref, University of Evry Val d'Essonne, France

Detailed Table of Contents

Section 1
Application of AI and CI Methods to Image and Signal Processing, Robotics, and Control

Stanislaw Osowski, Warsaw University of Technology & Military University of Technology, Poland
Michal Kruk, University of Life Sciences, Poland
Robert Koktysz, Military Institute of Medicine, Poland
Jaroslaw Kurek, University of Life Sciences, Poland

In medicine the inflammatory bowel disease (IBD), for example Crohn's disease and ulcerative colitis, form a group of inflammatory conditions of the large and small intestines. The important problem is to diagnose the beginning of the illness, i.e. the point, when the glandular ducts are attacked by the human defense system. As a result of such attack the shape and other parameters describing the geometry of ducts are changing. The important consequence of this attack is the appearance of the liquid in the stroma of the tissue, extension of the area between the neighboring glandular ducts as well as beginning of the division process of the glandular ducts. These facts may be discovered in the image of the biopsy of the colon tissue. Analyzing such image the authors of this chapter are trying to extract the knowledge of IBD that is contained in it, especially to associate different stages of IBD with the location, shapes, geometry and parameters of the ducts.

This chapter focuses on the presentation of Igelnik and Parikh's Kolmogorov Spline Network (KSN) for image processing and details two applications: image compression and progressive transmission. In compression, the reconstruction quality, using univariate functions containing only a fraction of the original image pixels, is studied. The images of details are obtained by wavelet decomposition in order to improve the reconstruction quality. The authors combine the KSN and wavelet decomposition into the JPEG 2000 encoder, and have show that this combination of methods improves JPEG 2000 compression scheme, even at low bit rates. In progressive transmission, a modification of the generation of the KSN is proposed. The results of the simulation of a transmission over packet-loss channels are presented.

This chapter presents the intelligent information description techniques and the mostly used classification methods in an image retrieval and recognition system. A multicriteria classification method applied for sickle cells disease image databases is given. The recognition performance system is illustrated and discussed.

This chapter describes a number of machine learning algorithms for autonomous navigation in vegetative environment. Specifically we focus on the task of generalization and classification of a great number of high-dimensional feature vectors. For this purpose we consider such machine learning algorithms as k-nearest neighbor algorithm, multilayer perceptron and support vector machine.

The authors of this chapter consider an application of the principles of Adaptive Dynamic Programming (ADP) to the control of a quadrotor helicopter platform flying in an uncontrolled environment and subject to various disturbances and model uncertainties. The ADP is based on reinforcement learning. The chapter is perfectly organized, combining the rigor of mathematics with deep understanding of practical issues.

Perception, cognition, and higher cognitive abilities of the mind are considered here within a neural modeling fields (NMF) paradigm. Its fundamental mathematical mechanism is a process from "vague-fuzzy to crisp", called dynamic logic. The chapter discusses why this paradigm is necessary mathematically, and relates it to a psychological description of the mind. Surprisingly, the process from "vague to crisp" corresponds to Aristotelian understanding of mental functioning. Recent fMRI measurements confirmed this process in neural mechanisms of perception. After an overview of NMF the authors describe solutions to two important problems: target tracking and situation recognition. Both problems can be solved within the NMF framework using the same basic algorithm.

This chapter presents an application of a newly developed evolutionary algorithm called biogeography-based optimization (BBO) for tuning a PID control system for real-world mobile robots. The BBO algorithm can be also used for the purpose of solving general global optimization problems. The authors have obtained impressive results in reducing the tracking error cost function.

Section 2
Application of AI and CI Methods to Medicine and Environment Monitoring and Protection

Uncertain reasoning is closely associated with the pertinent analysis of data where there may be, imprecision, inexactness and uncertainty in its information content. In computer modelling, this should move any analysis to be inclusive of such potential uncertainty, away from the presumption of perfect data to be worked with. The nascent Classification and Ranking Belief Simplex (CaRBS) technique, employed in this chapter, enables analysis in the spirit of uncertain reasoning. The operational rudiments of the CaRBS technique are based on the Dempster-Shafer theory of evidence, affording the presence of ignorance in any analysis undertaken. An investigation of Total Hip Arthraplasty (THA), concerned with hip replacements, forms the applied problem around which the uncertain reasoning based analysis using CaRBS is exposited. The presented findings include the levels of fit in constructed models, and the contribution of features within the models. Where appropriate, numerical calculations are shown, to illustrate this novel form of analysis.

This chapter introduces a novel Levenberg-Marquardt like second-order algorithm for tuning the Parzen window σ in a Radial Basis Function (Gaussian) kernel. In this case each attribute has its own sigma parameter associated with it. The values of the optimized σ are then used as a gauge for variable selection. In this study Kernel Partial Least Squares (K-PLS) model is applied to several benchmark data sets in order to estimate the effectiveness of the second-order sigma tuning procedure for an RBF kernel. The variable subset selection method based on these sigma values is then compared with different feature selection procedures such as random forests and sensitivity analysis. The sigma-tuned RBF kernel model outperforms K-PLS and SVM models with a single sigma value. K-PLS models also compare favorably with Least Squares Support Vector Machines (LS-SVM), epsilon-insensitive Support Vector Regression and traditional PLS. The sigma tuning and variable selection procedure introduced in this chapter is applied to industrial magnetocardiogram data for the detection of ischemic heart disease from measurement of the magnetic field around the heart.

Due to its inherent robustness, artificial neural network models have proved to be successful and have extensively been used in biological wastewater treatment applications. However, only recently, with the scientific advancements made in biological waste – gas treatment systems, the application of neural networks has slowly gained the practical momentum for performance monitoring in this field. Simple neural models, after vigorous training and testing, are able to generalize the results of a wide range of operating conditions, with high prediction accuracy. This chapter gives a fundamental insight and overview of the process mechanism of different biological waste – gas (biofilters, biotrickling filters, continuous stirred tank bioreactors and monolith bioreactors), and wastewater treatment systems (activated sludge process, trickling filter and sequencing batch reactors). The basic theory of artificial neural networks has been explained with a clear understanding of the back propagation algorithm. A generalized neural network modelling procedure for waste treatment applications has been outlined, and the role of back propagation algorithm network parameters has been discussed. Anew, the application of neural networks for solving specific environmental problems is presented in the form of a literature review.

Section 3
Concepts

The author of this chapter describes the motivated learning (ML) method that advances model building and learning techniques for intelligent systems. The
chapter addresses: 1) critical limitations of the reinforcement learning (RL) in coordinating a machine's interaction with an unknown dynamic environment by maximizing the external reward; 2) and the ML method that overcomes deficiencies of the RL by dynamically establishing the internal reward. ML is favorably compared with RL in an example, using a rapidly changing environment in which the agent needs to structure its motivations as well as to choose and implement the goal in order to succeed.

The authors of this chapter address the role of the hippocampus in the physiological and cognitive mechanisms of topological space representation in humans and animals. The have shown that using only the times of spikes from hippocampus place cells it is possible to construct a topological space. The authors argue as well that the hippocampus is specialized for computing a topological representation of the environment. The chapter discusses a possibility of a constructive neural representation of a topological space.

This chapter suggests a cognitive model of human conceptualisation on the basis of a cognitive theory of information processing and a Peircean theory of signs. Two examples are demonstrated related to a conceptualisation by an individual and to an elicitation by a team of participants. The results of experiments, conducted I these examples, to some degree justify the use of the cognitive model in various fields of human-computer interfacings such as computer aided problems solving and elicitation problem.

The author of this chapter focuses on the application of the discovery of association rules in approaches vague spatial databases. The background of data mining and uncertainty representations using rough set and fuzzy set techniques is provided. The extensions of association rule extraction for uncertain data as represented by rough and fuzzy sets are described. Finally an example of rule extraction for both types of uncertainty representations is given.

This chapter describes a method of feature selection and ranking based on human expert knowledge and training and testing of a neural network. Being computationally efficient, the method is less sensitive to round-off errors and noise in the data than the traditional methods of feature selection and ranking grounded on the sensitivity analysis. The method may lead to a significant reduction of a search space in the tasks of modeling, optimization, and data fusion. The structure of ranking procedure refutes the common belief that neural networks are black box models.

A computational modeling can help to solving the problem how neurons code information about stimulus, in addition to experimental research. This chapter discusses the spiking neural network architectures for visual, auditory and integrated audiovisual pattern recognition and classification. A spiking neural network, suggested by the authors, uses time to first spike as a code for saliency of input features. The system is trained and evaluated on the person authentication task. The authors conclude that the time-to-first-spike coding scheme may not be suitable for this difficult task nor for auditory processing. Other coding schemes and extensions of this spiking neural network are discussed as the topics of the future research.

The author of this chapter suggests to model the intellect from a coordination of actions point of view, a balanced perspective that recognizes both social and individual aspects. He argues that coordination is made possible by certain innate dispositions called (by the author) activity modalities: contextualization, spatialization, temporalization, stabilization, and transition. Consequently, a central task for modeling the intellect is to understand how perceptions received through sensory modalities are related to the activity modalities. The author proposes a research program for modeling the intellect, based on the concept of "activity" (introduced in the Russian Activity Theory) and the activity models. Provisional arguments for the relevance of the activity modalities are discussed in three different realms associated with the intellect: the social, conceptual, and neural ones. The chapter is concluded with some preliminary research questions, pertinent for the research program.

Chemical reaction-diffusion media represent information processing means fundamentally different from contemporary digital computers. Distributed character and complex nonlinear dynamics of chemical reactions inherent in the medium is the basis for large-scale parallelism and complex logical operations performed by the medium as primitives and equivalent to hundreds of binary fixed-point operations. Photosensitive catalysts controlling dynamics (modes of functioning) of the medium enable to easily perform input of initial data and output of computational results. It was found during the last decades that chemical reaction-diffusion media can be effectively used for solving artificial intelligence problems, such as image processing, finding the shortest paths in a labyrinth and some other important problems that are at the same time problems of high computational complexity. Spatially non uniform control of the medium by physical stimuli and fabrication of multi level reaction-diffusion systems seem to be the promising way enabling low cost and effective information processing devices that meet the commercial needs. Biological roots and specific neural net architecture of reaction diffusion media seem to enable simulating some phenomena inherent in the cerebral cortex, such as optical illusions.

A Modified Learning Vector Quantization (MLVQ) algorithm is presented in this chapter. MLVQ determines the learning constant parameter and modifies the terminating condition of the LVQ algorithm so that convergence can be achieved and easily detected. Experiments on the MLVQ algorithm are performed and contrasted against LVQ, GLVQ and FCM. Results show that MLVQ determines the number

These research results make it possible to solve complicated problems more simply and efficiently with 1-n-1 complex-valued neural networks. In particular, an application of the 1-n-1 type complex-valued neural network to an associative memory is presented.

Foreword

To understand how the human beings perceive the world around them, and reason about it has been on the agenda of many fields of science for years. The most ambitious and popular approaches developed in that area belong to the field of artificial intelligence. Over the years, and many ups and downs this field has gone through, it has become clear that the data-oriented and, recently, human-oriented methods and techniques are vital for the achievement of goals set for artificial intelligence. These may be viewed as part of a broader paradigm that involves areas such as "computational intelligence" or "intelligent computing", and is also well characterized by the concept of a "computational modeling and simulation of intellect" referred to in the title of this volume.

These efforts are inspired by the ability of animate systems, meant both as individuals and groups of individuals, to solve complex decision problems. This broadly meant field, in addition to the traditional, heavily symbolic computing based artificial intelligence, includes such disciplines as soft computing, fuzzy logic, granular computing, intelligent database systems, information retrieval, information fusion, intelligent search (engines), data mining, cluster analysis, unsupervised learning, machine learning, intelligent data analysis, (group) decision support systems, decision theory, collective intelligence, case-based reasoning, intelligent agents and multi-agent systems, artificial neural networks, genetic algorithms, evolutionary computation, particle swarm optimization, artificial immune system, knowledge-based systems, approximate reasoning, knowledge engineering, expert systems, imprecision and uncertainty handling, human-computer interface, internet computing, semantic web, electronic commerce, e-learning and Web-intelligence, cognitive systems, distributed systems, intelligent control, advanced computer modeling and simulation, bioinformatics, etc. Thus, this paradigm is meant to cover the areas of interest of the traditional artificial intelligence as well as many other related topics, notably those inspired by attempts to mimic the biological systems and those which have emerged with the development of advanced IT.

The current volume edited by Dr. Boris Igelnik provides a superb perspective on this vast new field. The papers collected deal with both fundamental theoretical problems as well as with specific practical problems including the vital areas of medicine and environmental protection. Some of them provide very valuable state-of-the-art surveys of important subfields. The reader can get a deeper understanding of some already traditional approaches and learn about new ones.

Dr. Igelnik has been very active in the field for many years and has participated in its development with many important contributions. Thanks to his excellent work and vision the volume will be a valuable reference and source of information on the fields concerned for researchers, graduate and postgraduate students as well as practitioners.

Sławomir Zadrożny
Warszawa, Poland, August 2010

Foreword

Explorations and insights into how humans think and reason have been of intense interest of researchers for centuries – in fact, they can be traced back to the origins of humanity. However, only in recent decades not only the computational modeling, but also simulation of intellectual capabilities of humans has become a reality. This was a direct consequence of the massive increase in computational power. It can also be credited to proliferation of hardware for inexpensive and easily searchable data storage.

Modeling and simulation of intellect can explore different approaches and can dwell on a variety of inspirations. The approaches presented in this volume are rooted in biology-inspired computing techniques. These techniques, based on efforts to understand and model the nature offer a wide range of insights, solutions and opportunities. They bridge the gap between the traditional, anthropocentric view of intellect with the modern computational metaphor that allows mimicking of intellect with computational models and tools.

The main thread of this publication is biologically-inspired intellect modeling and simulation in various fields, such as digital signal processing, image processing, robotics, systems biology, and their applications to areas of finances, business, management, defense, national security, medicine and new drug research. The book presents a wide spectrum of diverse approaches to the problems in these different areas. Altogether, the book reflects an interdisciplinary perspective of intellect modeling and simulation. It also tackles the issue of possible fusion of presented methods, as well as their computational efficiency, and their scalability.

The book consists of four sections with 22 chapters covering applied topics in image and signal processing, robotics and control (Sect. 1, 7 chapters), applications in biomedicine and environmental science (Sect. 2, 3 chapters), general concepts (Sect. 3, 9 chapters), and applications of these methods to learning (Sect. 4, 4 chapters).

Three papers of Sect. 1 discuss the biomedical image processing technique applied to specific disease recognition (inflammatory bowel disease), intelligent information characterization of biomedical images, and theoretical approaches to image compression and transmission. Three papers to follow cover distributed sensing, processing, communication and navigation of robots or unmanned vehicles. Adaptive linear programming applied to helicopter flying in an uncontrolled environment subject to various disturbances, and model uncertainties are also discussed.

Sect. 2 features two papers covering reasoning and detection methods based on uncertainty analysis, and specifically on classification and ranking with belief simplex technique in hip replacement treatment and diagnosis; and covers analysis of magnetocardiograms for detection of ischemic heart disease from measurements of magnetic field around the heart. The third paper is concerned with artificial neural networks for modeling of waste-gas and wastewater treatment.

Sect. 3 discusses general concepts of learning. It opens with the chapter on motivated learning, which makes use of the goals, rewards, advanced perception and motor skills to achieve desired cognitive properties. The chapter to follow introduces a constructive neural representation of a topological space in the brain's hippocampus. Discussion in the next chapters of intelligence augmentation in individual and teamwork and related cognitive models, and discovery of associations from vague spatial data bring another contribution to intellect analysis.

The two remaining chapters of this section cover an important aspect of feature selection and of their ranking in the classification process, and discuss how spiking neurons look for salient features in the person authentication task. Next, the modeling of intellect based on the concept of activity is presented from the coordination perspective. Finally, the chapter on information processing by chemical reaction-diffusion media postulates this approach for better solutions of fundamental artificial intelligence problems.

The final Sect. 4 addresses the concept of learning based on artificial and computational intelligence paradigms. Discussion of learning vector quantization for improved centering of fuzzy membership function is followed by the mathematical modeling and associated demonstrations of outlier detection in linear regression. The following chapter offers a survey of techniques dealing with unbalanced datasets in real-life applications. The closing chapter of the volume explores how complex-valued neural networks can learn to perform transformations and produce associative memories.

This interesting and ambitious book will assist researchers, users, developers and designers of the information and management systems. It will also offer a comprehensive overview of computational and artificial intelligence issues to graduate students and other learners, who want a gentle but rigorous introduction to the computational modeling and simulation of intellect.

I do hope that the readers will find this volume interesting and that it will contribute to the further development of research in the exciting area of natural computing.

Jacek M. Zurada
University of Louisville, USA
September 8, 2010

Preface

The methods of computational modeling and simulation of intellect have been developing in various fields, such as digital signal processing (Haykin, 2002, 2007; Swanson, 2002; Richaczek & Hershkowitz, 200; Mars, Chen, Nambiar, 1996; Katz, 1996), image processing (Batchelor & Whelen, 1997; Pratt, 2007; Lillesand & Kiefer, 1999; Jain, 1989), robotics (Bekey, 2005; Bekey et al, 2008; Haykonen, 2003, 2007; Mataric, 2007), control (Hunt et al, 1995; Simon, 2008), systems biology (Alon, 2007; Boogerd, 2007; Priami, 2009; Wilkinson, 2009), molecular computing (Adamatzky, 2001, Sienco et al, 2003), cognitive neuroscience and cognitive modeling (Anderson, 2007; Feng, 2004; O'Reilly & Munakata, 2000; Davis, 2005; Polk & Seifert, 2002; Thelen & Smith, 1998; McLeod, Planket, Rolls, 1998; Perlovsky & Kozma, 2007), cognitive informatics (Wang, 2009), computational neuroscience (Trappenberg, 2002; Lutton, 2002), general artificial intelligence Goertzel & Pannacin, 2007), knowledge engineering (Cloete & Zurada), knowledge based neurocomputing (Kolman & Margaliot, 2009), multi-agent systems (Gorodetsky et al, 2007; Khosla, Dillon, 1997), semiotics (Gudvin & Queros, 2007), neural-symbolic learning systems (Garses, Broada, Gabbay, 2002), social networks (Bruggerman, 2008), bioinformatics (Zhang, Rajapakse, 2009), data mining (Taniar, 2004), computational intelligence (Reisch, Timme, 2001; Schwefel, Wegener, Weinert, 2003, Zurada, Marks, Robinson, 1994), neural networks (Haykin, 1994; Kasabov, 1996; Perlovsky, 2001), etc. There were published several interesting books on what we call below "concepts", for example, Freeman, (2000), Kitamura (2001), Minsky (1986), and Gardenfors (2000). The topic is of great importance for information and management science and technology, both currently and in future. This book presents a number of diverse methods and approaches to the problem of modeling and simulation of intellect, currently existing in the different areas, their perspectives, and targets a possible fusion of these and coming methods as well as computational efficiency and scalability of these methods.

The main themes of the publication are: the problem of meaning; fusion of methods specific to different fields; computational efficiency and scalability of the methods. Researchers, instructors, designers of information and management systems, users of these systems, and graduate students will acquire the fundamental knowledge needed to be at the forefront of the research and to use it in the applications.

With progress in science and technology, humans experience increasing difficulties in processing huge amounts of high-dimensional data, extracting information from it, and eventually finding a meaning in the structured data. While computers definitely play a positive role in obtaining large databases, their current ability to make sense of the data is at best questionable. On the other hand, humans and their forerunners had millions years of experience (multiplied by billions of individuals) in information and technology exchange, and have developed an astonishingly efficient capability of extracting meaning from data. Facing tremendous difficulties in using computers for solving this task, the designers of information and management systems have started thinking: how do we do it? The complete answer to this question is still unknown, but attempts to make it using diverse computational methods and approaches have been emerging in many areas of science and technology. Therefore, it is useful to summarize this variety of methods and approaches in a discipline, which might be called COMPUTATIONAL MODELING AND SIMULATION OF INTELLECT. It is equally important and useful to describe a future development of these and coming methods and to target their fusion, computational efficiency, and scalability.

I came to the idea of this book while reviewing some of existing approaches to this discipline, which were actually based on a combination of the genetic, environmental, and social foundations in the different proportions. It is impossible to expect that there exists a unique approach best suited for the solution of the problem of modeling and simulation of intellect, just due to its giant complexity. Therefore, it is essential to fuse the knowledge contained in different approaches. The proportion of different foundations in an approach is also of great importance. I prefer to shift attention more to environmental and social foundations than to its genetic base, and I have the long-term goal to implement the learning of intellect by a dynamic combination of the exchange data and knowledge first among humans, next among humans and computers, and next among the computers. This process of learning is supposed to evolve in time with the increasing role of interactions among computers. In my opinion, in the current, early period of development of the discipline, making a preference for social and environmental bases of intellect may save time in obtaining some practical results, while the methods of molecular and systems biology will be moving to a deeper understanding of the genetic foundations of the intellect. As was mentioned above, no general approach or idea (including my own) can be a panacea in the attempts to find a method for computational modeling and simulation of intellect.

ORGANIZATION OF THE BOOK

The book is divided into four main sections: Application of AI and CI Methods to Image and Signal Processing, Robotics, and Control (Chapters 1-7), Application of AI and CI Methods to Medicine and Environment Monitoring and Protection (Chapters 8-10), Concepts (Chapters 11-18), and Application of AI and CI Methods to Learning (Chapters 19-22).

A brief description of each of the chapters follows below.

- **Chapter 1** analyzes the images of colon in inflammatory bowel diseases (IBD) for localization and parameterization of the glandular *ducts* in order to extract the knowledge of IBD that is contained in it, especially to associate different stages of IBD with the location, shapes, geometry and parameters of the ducts.
- **Chapter 2** focuses on the presentation of Igelnik and Parikh's Kolmogorov Spline Network (KSN) for image processing and details two applications: image compression and progressive transmission. In compression, a combination the KSN and wavelet decomposition into the JPEG 2000 encoder is presented. In progressive transmission, a modification of the generation of the KSN is proposed. The results of the simulation of a transmission over packet-loss channels are demonstrated.
- **Chapter 3** presents the intelligent information description techniques and the mostly used classification methods in an image retrieval and recognition system. A multicriteria classification

method applied for sickle cells disease image databases is given. The recognition performance system is illustrated and discussed.

- **Chapter 4** describes a number of machine learning algorithms for autonomous navigation in vegetative environment. Specifically it focuses on the task of generalization and classification of a great number of high-dimensional feature vectors. For this purpose such machine learning algorithms as k-nearest neighbor algorithm, multilayer perceptron and support vector machine are considered.
- **Chapter 5** consider an application of the principles of Adaptive Dynamic Programming (ADP) to the control of a quadrotor helicopter platform flying in an uncontrolled environment and subject to various disturbances and model uncertainties. The ADP is based on reinforcement learning. The chapter is perfectly organized, combining the rigor of mathematics with deep understanding of practical issues.
- **Chapter 6** describes an application of a neural modeling fields (NMF) paradigm to solution of two important problems: target tracking and situation recognition. It is shown that both problems can be solved within the NMF framework using the same basic algorithm.
- **Chapter 7** presents a newly developed biogeography-based optimization (BBO) algorithm for tuning PID control system for real-world mobile robots. The BBO algorithm can be also used for the purpose of solving general global optimization problems.
- **Chapter 8** employs the nascent Classification and Ranking Belief Simplex (CaRBS) technique that enables analysis in the spirit of uncertain reasoning. The operational rudiments of the CaRBS technique are based on the Dempster-Shafer theory of evidence, affording the presence of ignorance in any analysis to be undertaken. An investigation of Total Hip Arthraplasty (THA), concerned with hip replacements, forms the applied problem around which the uncertain reasoning based analysis using CaRBS is exposited.
- **Chapter 9** introduces a novel Levenberg-Marquardt like second-order algorithm for tuning the Parzen window σ in a Radial Basis Function (Gaussian) kernel. The Kernel Partial Least Squares (K-PLS) model is applied to several benchmark data sets in order to estimate the effectiveness of the second-order sigma tuning procedure for an RBF kernel. The variable subset selection method based on these sigma values is then compared with different feature selection procedures such as random forests and sensitivity analysis. The sigma-tuned RBF kernel model outperforms K-PLS and SVM models with a single sigma value. K-PLS models also compare favorably with Least Squares Support Vector Machines (LS-SVM), epsilon-insensitive Support Vector Regression and traditional PLS. The sigma tuning and variable selection procedure introduced in this chapter is applied to industrial magnetocardiogram data for the detection of ischemic heart disease from measurement of the magnetic field around the heart.
- **Chapter 10** gives a fundamental insight and overview of the process mechanism of different biological waste – gas (biofilters, biotrickling filters, continuous stirred tank bioreactors and monolith bioreactors), and wastewater treatment systems (activated sludge process, trickling filter and sequencing batch reactors). The basic theory of artificial neural networks has been explained. A generalized neural network modeling procedure for waste treatment applications has been outlined, and the role of back propagation algorithm network parameters has been discussed. Anew, the application of neural networks for solving specific environmental problems is presented in the form of a literature review.

- **Chapter 11** describes the motivated learning (ML) method that advances model building and learning techniques for intelligent systems. The chapter addresses: 1) critical limitations of the reinforcement learning (RL) in coordinating a machine's interaction with an unknown dynamic environment by maximizing the external reward; 2) and the ML method that overcomes deficiencies of the RL by dynamically establishing the internal reward. ML is favorably compared with RL in an example, using a rapidly changing environment in which the agent needs to structure its motivations as well as to choose and implement the goal in order to succeed.
- **Chapter 12** addresses the role of the hippocampus in the physiological and cognitive mechanisms of topological space representation in humans and animals. The have shown that using only the times of spikes from hippocampus place cells it is possible to construct a topological space. The authors argue as well that the hippocampus is specialized for computing a topological representation of the environment. The chapter discusses a possibility of a constructive neural representation of a topological space.
- **Chapter 13** suggests a cognitive model of human conceptualisation on the basis of a cognitive theory of information processing and a Peircean theory of signs. Two examples are demonstrated related to a conceptualisation by an individual and to an elicitation by a team of participants. The results of experiments, conducted in these examples, to some degree justify the use of the cognitive model in various fields of human-computer interfacings such as computer aided problems solving and elicitation problem.
- **Chapter 14** focuses on the application of the discovery of association rules in approaches vague spatial databases. The background of data mining and uncertainty representations using rough set and fuzzy set techniques is provided. The extensions of association rule extraction for uncertain data as represented by rough and fuzzy sets are described. Finally an example of rule extraction for both types of uncertainty representations is given.
- **Chapter 15** describes a method of feature selection and ranking based on human expert knowledge and training and testing of a neural network. Being computationally efficient, the method is less sensitive to round-off errors and noise in the data than the traditional methods of feature selection and ranking grounded on the sensitivity analysis. The method may lead to a significant reduction of a search space in the tasks of modeling, optimization, and data fusion. The structure of ranking procedure refutes the common belief that neural networks are black box models.
- **Chapter 16** discusses the spiking neural network architectures for visual, auditory and integrated audiovisual pattern recognition and classification. A spiking neural network, suggested by the authors, uses time to first spike as a code for saliency of input features. The system is trained and evaluated on the person authentication task. The authors conclude that the time-to-first-spike coding scheme may not be suitable for this difficult task nor for auditory processing. Other coding schemes and extensions of this spiking neural network are discussed as the topics of the future research.
- **Chapter 17** suggests to model the intellect from a coordination of actions point of view, a balanced perspective that recognizes both social and individual aspects. A research program for modeling the intellect, based on the concept of "activity" (introduced in the Russian Activity Theory) and the activity models, is proposed. Provisional arguments for the relevance of the activity modalities are discussed in three different realms associated with the intellect: the social, conceptual, and neural ones. The chapter is concluded with some preliminary research questions, pertinent for the research program.

- **Chapter 18** describes use of chemical reaction-diffusion media as the information processing means fundamentally different from contemporary digital computers. Distributed character and complex nonlinear dynamics of chemical reactions inherent in the medium is the basis for large-scale parallelism and complex logical operations performed by the medium as primitives. It was found during the last decades that chemical reaction-diffusion media can be effectively used for solving artificial intelligence problems, such as image processing, finding the shortest paths in a labyrinth and some other important problems that are at the same time problems of high computational complexity. Spatially non uniform control of the medium by physical stimuli and fabrication of multi level reaction-diffusion systems seem to be the promising way enabling low cost and effective information processing devices that meet the commercial needs. Biological roots and specific neural net architecture of reaction diffusion media seem to enable simulating some phenomena inherent in the cerebral cortex, such as optical illusions.
- **Chapter 19** presents a Modified Learning Vector Quantization (MLVQ) algorithm. Experiments on the MLVQ algorithm are performed and contrasted against LVQ, GLVQ and FCM. Results show that MLVQ determines the number of clusters and converges to the centroids. Results also show that MLVQ is insensitive to the sequence of the training data, able to identify centroids of overlapping clusters and able to ignore outliers without identifying them as separate clusters. Results, using MLVQ algorithm and Gaussian membership functions with Pseudo Outer-Product Fuzzy Neural Network using Compositional Rule of Inference and Singleton fuzzifier (POPFNN-CRI(S)) on pattern classification and time series prediction, are also provided in order to demonstrate the effectiveness of the fuzzy membership functions derived using MLVQ.
- **Chapter 20** has made a discussion of the most well-known and efficient outlier detection techniques with numerical demonstrations in linear regression. The chapter will help the readers interested in exploring and investigating an effective mathematical model. This chapter is self-contained, maintaining its general accessibility.
- **Chapter 21** surveys the problem of classification tasks in unbalanced datasets. The effect of the imbalance of the distribution of target classes in databases is analyzed with respect to the performance of standard classifiers such as decision trees and support vector machines. The main approaches to improve the generally not satisfactory results obtained by such methods are described. Finally two typical applications coming from real world frameworks are introduced and the use of the techniques employed for the related classification tasks is shown in practice.
- **Chapter 22** demonstrates the behavior of the 1-n-1 complex-valued neural network that has learned a transformation on the Steiner circles is demonstrated, The relationship between the values of the complex-valued weights after training and a linear transformation related to the Steiner circles is clarified via computer simulations. Furthermore, the relationship between the weight values of the 1-n-1 complex-valued neural network learned 2D affine transformations and the learning patterns used is elucidated. These research results make it possible to solve complicated problems more simply and efficiently with 1-n-1 complex-valued neural networks. In particular, an application of the 1-n-1 type complex-valued neural network to an associative memory is presented.

Boris Igelnik
BMI Research Inc., USA

REFERENCES

Adamatzky, A. (2001). *Computing in nonlinear media and automata collectives*. Bristol, UK: Institute of Physics Publishing. doi:10.1887/075030751X

Alon, U. (2007). *An introduction to systems biology: design principles of biological circuits*. London, UK: Chapman & Hall/CRC.

Anderson, J. R. (2007). *How can the human mind occur in the physical universe*? New York: Oxford University Press.

Batchelor, B. G. & Whelan, P., F. (1997). *Intelligent vision systems for industry*. New York: Springer.

Bekey, G. A. (2005). *Autonomous robots: from biological inspiration to implementation and control*. Cambridge, MA: The MIT Press.

Bekey, G. A. et al. (2008). *Robotics: state of the art and future challenges*. Hackensack, NJ: World Scientific Publishing.

Boogerd, F. C., et al (Eds.). (2007). *Systems biology. Philosophical foundations*. Amsterdam, Netherlands: Elsevier.

Bruggerman, J. (2008). *Social networks. An introduction*. London & New York: Routledge, Taylor & Francis Group. Cloete, I. & Zurada, J., M. (Eds.). *Knowledge-based engineering*. Cambridge, MA: The MIT Press.

Davis, D. N. (Ed.). (2005). *Visions of mind. Architectures for cognition and affect*. Hershey, PA: Information Science Publishing.

Feng, J. (Ed.). (2004). *Computational neuroscience: a comprehensive approach*. Boca Raton, FL: Chapman & Hall/CRC.

Freeman, W. J. (2000). *How brains make up their minds*. New York: Columbia University Press.

Garcez, A. S., A., Broada, K., B., Gabbay, D., M. (2002). *Neural-symbolic learning systems. Foundations and applications*. London, UK: Springer.

Gardenforc, P. (2000). *Conceptual spaces. The geometry of thought*. Cambridge, MA: The MIT Press.

Goertzel, B., & Pennacin, C. (Eds.). (2007). *Artificial general intelligence*. Berlin, Heidelberg: Springer-Ferlag. doi:10.1007/978-3-540-68677-4

Gorodetsky, V. (Eds.). (2007). *Autonomous intelligent systems: agents and data mining*. Berlin, Heidelberg: Springer-Ferlag. doi:10.1007/978-3-540-72839-9

Gudvin, R., & Queiroz, J. (Eds.). (2007). *Semiotics and Intelligent Systems Development*. Hershey, PA: Idea Group Publishing.

Haikonen, P. O. (2003). *The cognitive approach to conscious machines*. Charlottersville, VA: Imprint Academic.

Haikonen, P. (2007). *Robot brains. Hoboken, NJ.* O.: John Wiley & Sons, Inc.

Haykin, S. (1994). *Neural networks. A comprehensive foundation*. New York: Macmillan College Publishing.

Haykin, S. (2002). *Adaptive filter theory* (4th ed.). Upper Saddle River, NJ: Prentice Hall.

Haykin, S. (Eds.). (2007). *New directions in statistical processing: from systems to brain*. Cambridge, MA: The MIT Press.

Hunt, K. J., Irwin, G., R., and Warwick, K. (Eds). (1995). *Neural network engineering in dynamic control systems*. New York: Springer.

Jain, A. K. (1989). *Fundamentals of Digital Image Processing*. Englewood Cliffs, NJ: Prentice-Hall.

Kasabov, N. K. (1996). *Foundations of neural networks, fuzzy systems, and knowledge engineering*. Cambridge, MA: MIT Press.

Katz, R. A. (Ed.). (1996). *Chaotic, fractal, and nonlinear signal processing*. Woodbury, NY: AIP Press.

Khosla, R., & Dillon, T. (1997). *Engineering intelligent hybrid multi-agent systems*. Norwell, MA: Kluwer Academic Publishers.

Kitamura, T. (Ed.). (2001). *What should be computed to understand and model brain function? From robotics, soft computing, biology and neuroscience to cognitive philosophy*. Singapore: World Scientific.

Kolman, E., & Margaliot, M. (2009). *Knowledge-based neurocomputing: a fuzzy logic approach*. Berlin, Heidelberg: Springer-Ferlag.

Lillesand, T. M. and Kiefer, R. (1999). *Remote sensing and image interpretation*. New York: Wiley.

Lytton, W. (2002). *From computer to brain. Foundations of computational neuroscience. New York*. W.: Springer-Verlag.

Mars, P., & Chen, J. R., R. Nambiar. (1996). *Learning algorithms. Theory and applications in signal processing, control and communications*. Boca Raton, FL: CRC Press.

Mataric, M. J. (2007). *The robotics primer*. Cambridge, MA: The MIT Press.

McLeod, P., & Planket, P. K., Rolls, E., T. (1998). *Introduction to connectionist modeling of cognitive processes*. Oxford, UK: Oxford University Press.

Minsky, M. (1986). *Society of minds*. New York: Simon and Schuster.

O'Reilly, R. C., & Munakata, Y. (2000). *Computational explorations in cognitive neuroscience*. Cambridge, MA: The MIT Press.

Perlovsky, L. I. (2001). *Neural networks and intellect. Using model-based concepts*. Oxford: Oxford University Press.

Perlovsky, L. (2007). Symbols: integrated cognition and language . In Gudvin, R., & Queiroz, J. (Eds.), *Semiotics and intelligent systems development*. Hershey, PA: Idea Group Publishing.

Perlovsky, L. I., Kozma, R. (Eds.). (2007). *Neurodynamics of cognition and consciousness*. Heidelberg: Springer.

Polk, T. A. and Seifert, C., M. (2002). *Cognitive modeling.* Cambridge, MA: The MIT Press.

Pratt, W. K. (2007). *Digital image processing, Fourth edition.* Hoboken, NJ: John Wiley & Sons, Inc.

Priami, C. (2009). Algorithmic systems biology. *Communications of the ACM, 52*(5), 80–88. doi:10.1145/1506409.1506427

Reusch, B., & Timme, K.-H. (Eds.). (2001). *Computational intelligence in theory and practice.* Heidelberg: Phisica-Verlag. doi:10.1007/3-540-45493-4

Rihaczek, A. W., Hershkowitz, S., J. (2000). *Theory and practice of radar target identification.* Norwood House: Artech House.

Schwefel, H.-P., Wegener, I., & Weinert, K. (2003). *Advances in computational intelligence. Theory and practice.* Berlin: Springer.

Sienco, T., Adamatzky, A., Rambidi, N., & Conrad, M. (Eds.). (2003). *Molecular computing.* Cambridge, MA: The MIT Press.

Simon, D. (2006). *Optimal state estimation. Kalman, H_∞, and nonlinear approaches.* Hoboken, NJ: Wiley& Sons.

Swanson, D. C. (2002). *Signal processing for intelligent sensing systems.* New York: Marcel Dekker.

Taniar, D. (Ed.). (2004). *Research and trends in data mining technologies and applications.* Hershey, PA: Idea Group Publishing.

Thelen, E., & Smith, L. B. (1998). *A dynamic systems approach to the development of cognition and action.* Cambridge, MA: MIT Press.

Trappenberg, T. P. (2002). *Fundamentals of computational neuroscience.* Oxford: Oxford University Press.

Wang, Y. (Ed.). (2009). *Novel approaches in cognitive informatics and natural intelligence.* Hershey, PA: IGI Global.

Wilkinson, D. J. (2006). *Stochastic modelling in systems biology.* Boca Raton, FL: Chapman & Hall/CRC.

Zang, Y.-Q., & Rajapakse, J. C. (Eds.). (2009). *Machine learning in bioinformatics.* Hoboken, NJ: J. Wiley & Sons, Inc.

Zurada, J. M., Marks II, R., J., Robinson, C., J. (Eds.). (1994). *Computational intelligence. Imitating life.* New York: IEEE Press.

Acknowledgment

The editor would like to acknowledge the help of Prof. Tohru Nitta for his advices in many aspects of organization the development process for this book

All the authors of the chapters included in this book, Prof. Fredric M. Ham and Dr. Peter Sarlin served as referees for chapters written by other authors. Thanks go to all of them.

Special thanks also go to the publishing team at IGI Global, whose contributions throughout the whole process from inception of the initial idea to final publication have been invaluable. In particular to Mr. Joel Gamon, who continuously prodded via email for keeping the project on schedule and to Ms. Kristin M. Klinger and Ms. Erika Carter, whose enthusiasm motivated me to initially accept their invitation for taking on this project.

Special thanks go to the members of the Editorial Advisory Board for this book project for their helpful supports.

To my wife Nelli, and our sons Mark and Michael for their support.

I wish to thank all of the authors for their insights and excellent contributions to this book.

Boris Igelnik
BMI Research Inc, USA
August 2010

Section 1
Application of AI and CI Methods to Image and Signal Processing, Robotics, and Control

Chapter 1
Image Processing for Localization and Parameterization of the Glandular Ducts of Colon in Inflammatory Bowel Diseases

Stanislaw Osowski
Warsaw University of Technology & Military University of Technology, Poland

Michal Kruk
University of Life Sciences, Poland

Robert Koktysz
Military Institute of Medicine, Poland

Jaroslaw Kurek
University of Life Sciences, Poland

ABSTRACT

This chapter presents the computerized system for automatic analysis of the medical image of the colon biopsy, able to extract the important diagnostic knowledge useful for supporting the medical diagnosis of the inflammatory bowel diseases. Application of the artificial intelligence methods included in the developed automatic system allowed the authors to obtain the unique numerical results, impossible for achieving at the visual inspection of the image by the human expert. The developed system enabled the authors to perform all steps in an automatic way, including the segmentation of the image, leading to the extraction of all glandular ducts, parameterization of the individual ducts and creation of the diagnostic features, as well as characterizing the recognition problem. These features put to the input of SVM classifier enable to associate them with the stage of development of the inflammation. The numerical experiments have shown that the system is able to process successfully the images at different stages of development of the inflammation. Its important advantage is automation of this very difficult work, not possible to be done manually, even by a human expert.

DOI: 10.4018/978-1-60960-551-3.ch001

INTRODUCTION

In medicine the inflammatory bowel disease (IBD), for example Crohn's disease and ulcerative colitis, form a group of inflammatory conditions of the large and small intestines (Carpenter & Talley, 200), (Carter et al. 2004). The important problem is to diagnose the beginning of the illness, i.e. the point, when the glandular ducts are attacked by the human defense system. As a result of such attack the shape and other parameters describing the geometry of ducts are changing. The important consequence of this attack is the appearance of the liquid in the stroma of the tissue, extension of the area between the neighboring glandular ducts, as well as beginning of the division process of the glandular ducts (Carpenter & Talley, 2000).

These facts may be discovered in the image of the biopsy of the colon tissue. Analyzing such image we are trying to extract the information of IBD that is contained in it, especially to associate different stages of IBD with the location, shapes, geometry and parameters of the ducts. Especially challenging is to associate the stage of development of IBD with some parameters of ducts. Knowing this association we will be able to build an automatic system supporting the medical expert in his diagnosis.

Figure 1 presents the image of the biopsy of the colon tissue at different stages of the IBD. Figure 1a corresponds to the individuals with full remission of disease (no clinical and endoscopic signs of IBD). The ducts are clearly visible. Most of them are of regular elongated shape, placed parallel to each other. The space between ducts are filled in by the stroma, representing the background of the image. At the beginning of the illness corresponding to initial acute stage (Figure 1b) we can observe the changes in the shape of ducts. Some of them are split into separate parts. Figure 1c presents the moderately advanced active phase of illness. The most characteristic symptom of it is further split of the ducts into many separate small size parts, not connected into compact regions. In the heavy state of IBD (Figure 1d) most of the fragmentary parts of ducts have disappeared and are hardly visible in the image. Their place has been taken by the uniform liquid of the stroma.

It is evident that the advancement of IBD is strictly connected with deformation of the shapes of the glandular ducts in the image. The parameters of these shapes may be treated as a measure of advancement of the illness. However it is impossible to determine these parameters by the visual inspection. We have to employ the computer aided image processing, aimed in discovering and recognizing the essential parts of the image and parameterize them. Hence there is a need for development of a specialized computer program able to preprocess such images in order to localize, extract and parameterize the glandular ducts, and in its final stage to classify the analyzed image into appropriate class corresponding to the development stage of IBD. Up to now there are no such systems used in the hospital practice.

This work is concerned with the automatic extraction and parameterization of the glandular ducts existing in the microscopic image of the biopsy of the colon tissue. The computer program should mimic the human intelligence to find out the characteristic features of the image, use them to extract the appropriate parts of interest (the ducts), and then characterize each duct with the proper set of geometrical parameters. These parameters or the features defined on their basis will be used as the input information to the neural classifier, which is responsible for the recognition of the development stage of IBD. In this way the human intelligence is included in the computer program extracting the fragments of the image that contain the most important part of information regarding the inflammation stage and associating them with the recognition of IBD.

As a result of fully computerized analysis of the image we get the main parameters of the glandular ducts, on the basis of which the automatic neural classifier decides what is the intensity of the inflam-

Figure 1. The images of the biopsy of the colon tissue at different stages of IBD illness: (a) full remission of disease, (b) initial acute stage, (c) moderately advanced stage of illness, (d) heavy advanced state of IBD

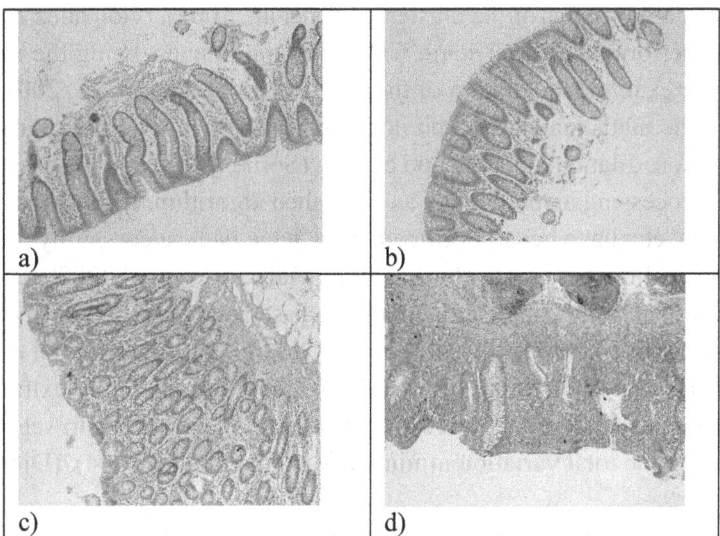

mation. In this way the results of the work may be of great help for medical staff in the process of undertaking the diagnosis of the patients suffering from IBD.

RELATED WORKS

The heart of the proposed solution is the image recognition system, able to perform the successful segmentation and labeling of the individual segments (ducts). The individual segments are transformed into numerical features, which are then associated with the appropriate development stage of the illness through the classification system. Although this particular task defined for the glandular ducts have not been developed yet, there are some related works concerning other biomedical images.

Segmentation of the image is the crucial step in most image recognition systems, especially these devoted to the medical problems. The segmentation of medical images belongs to the most challenging problems due to a large variability in topologies, the complexity of medical structures and poor image modalities such as noise, low contrast, artifacts, etc. Different methods of segmentation have been developed up to day. The most basic are related on edge detection (Duda et al., 2003), (Gonzalez & Woods, 2005), using either approximation of gradient (Sobel, Canny, etc. methods) or the second derivative Laplacian (Kimmel & Bruckstein, 2003).

Thresholding plays also very important role in the segmentation process. The crucial point in thresholding is the proper adjustment of the threshold value. One of the most efficient is the Otsu method (Otsu, 1979), assuming the threshold value separating two classes in a way to minimize the intra-class variance, defined as a weighted sum of variances of the two classes. Another approach is to apply sequential thresholding at different threshold values. This approach is needed at very complex images subject to segmentation. The successful application of this strategy has been developed for segmentation of cells in the image of breast cancer (Markiewicz et. al., 2009).

The segmentation of the image is also possible at application of K-means algorithm. In this approach the task of segmentation is transformed to the classification of different pixels on the basis of their distance to the representative center of the cluster (Duda et al., 2003), (Gonzalez & Woods, 2005). The segmentation may be performed also on some features of the images, being the results of some other preprocessing steps, for example the texture of the image (Markiewicz et. al., 2009).

More efficient are the mathematical morphology approaches, relying the segmentation process on such operations as erosion, dilation, opening and closing (Soille, 2003). On the basis of these operations more complex image processing methods such as watershed algorithm, filling the holes, morphological gradient, reconstruction, etc. have been developed. They have been successfully applied in many solutions regarding biomedical images (Kruk et al., 2007), (Markiewicz et al., 2009).

A popular technique in medical image segmentation is based on a class of deformable models, referred as level set or geodesic active contours (Vasilevskiy & Siddigi, 2002), (Kimmel & Bruckstein, 2003). Recently the variational level set method followed by window-based feature extraction based on PCA and SVM have been proposed (Li et al., 2006). There are also approaches to segmentation combined with denoising, based on the total variation minimization (Chambolle, 2004), (Djemal 2005), (Chan et al., 2006).

After segmenting the image we get the set of objects that are of interest in further image recognition problem. The most important task at this stage is to develop the efficient set of features describing the object in a most discriminative way. In generating features we usually try to follow the human expert by stressing the details, on the basis of which the recognition will be done. In the case of our problem, where the ducts are represented by black and white objects, the most important are the details describing the geometry of these objects (glandular ducts). Among them we may mention the area, perimeter, radius, compactness, concavity, distances between neighboring objects, and the relative coefficients comparing different features (Kruk et al., 2007), (Osowski et.al.2007). These features should characterize the image in a way suppressing the differences within the same class and enhancing them for objects belonging to different classes.

In the case of color medical images many different descriptors may be applied in practice. Among them are the colorimetric descriptors, histograms or texture (Osowski & Markiewicz, 2005), statistical Hu and Zernike moments, 2-D Fourier or wavelet transformation, etc. (Bankman, 2008), (Gonzalez & Woods, 2005). The source of other characterization methods may be found in the books devoted to the pattern recognition (Marraval & Patricio, 2002), (Duda et al., 2003).

The characterization of an image by numerical descriptors results in many features of different quality. Good feature should be stable for samples belonging to the same class (the smallest possible variance) and at the same time it should differ significantly for different classes. The feature assuming similar values for different classes has no discriminative power and may be treated as the noise from the classifier point of view. To get highest possible recognition ratio we have to rely the decision on the most stable and robust features, strictly correlated with the recognized classes. Hence the selection of features is very important on this stage. Many different selection methods have been developed up to day. To the most popular belong principal component analysis, projection pursuit, correlation existing among features, correlation between the features and the classes, analysis of mean and variance of the features belonging to different classes, Fisher LDA. mutual dependence characterization, application of linear SVM or nonlinear feature ranking, etc. Good source of these techniques may be found in (Guyon & Elisssef, 2003), (Lin & Motoda, 2008)

The last step of image recognition is application of an automatic classifier fed by the set of selected features. There are many different solutions of classifier systems used in practice. The simplest Bayesian and KNN classifiers are now pushed out by different types of neural solutions, such as multilayer perceptron (MLP), radial basis function (RBF) networks, neuro-fuzzy networks or Support Vector Machine (SVM). Good review and comparison of these solutions are to be found in excellent textbooks (Haykin, 1999), (Scholkopf & Smola, 2002), (Bishop, 2004). According to the present state of art the most efficient in the classification problems are solutions based on SVM. The structure of SVM is similar to RBF, however its learning algorithm, transforming the problem to the quadratic optimization task is much more efficient and provides better generalization ability (Markiewicz & Osowski, 2005).

The results of all these steps put together in a pipeline fashion create the computer aided diagnosis system, able for the automatic analysis of biomedical images. Although it looks like the universal solution, each case of image analysis has its own peculiarities and needs to treated very carefully. The size of the objects under interest, variability of topologies or poor image modalities force the application of special approach, which guarantee the best possible accuracy of the image recognition.

THE PROPOSED AUTOMATIC SOLUTION FOR DUCT EXTRACTION

The starting point is a microscopic digitized image of the biopsy of the colon tissue at the total magnification equal 100x. The image is saved in the form of a bitmap file. The first step of processing is the extraction of the glandular ducts through the segmentation process connected with the elimination of the other small size elements. The problem is rather complicated, since it should be effective for very different images. Application of linear filters is not efficient due to poor image modalities (low contrast, artifacts and fuzzy character of images). On the other side the level set methods are not directly suitable for clinical image segmentation due to high computational cost, complicated parameter settings and the fact that the convergence of these methods is sensitive to the placement of initial contours (Vasilevskiy & Siddigi, 2002), (Li et al., 2006). One of the possible segmentation solution is also the application of self-organization of pixels on the basis of distances between actual pixels and their prototypes representing either duct or background. However the problem are significant changes of pixels within the duct area.

On the basis of this analysis we have decided to apply the nonlinear image processing, associated with the morphological operations (Gonzales & Woods, 2005), (Soille, 2003), like opening, closing, hole filling, etc. Is known fact, that morphological image processing is successful in segmentation processes (Kruk et al., 2007), Soille, 2003). We have used the morphological operations organized in the pipeline system, applying many times such operations as opening, closing, hole filling and reconstruction. As a result we get the transformed image composed of separate regions containing the separated ducts. Figure 2 presents the general algorithm of extraction of ducts.

The first step is the equalization of the histogram, which emphasizes the details of the image. The equalization is performed by simple rescaling each pixel at the position (x,y) of the original intensity $L(x,y)$ into equalized $L'(x,y)$ according to the equation

$$L'(x,y) = \frac{L(x,y)-1}{L_{\max} - L_{\min}}\left(L(x,y) - L_{\min}\right) \quad (1)$$

Figure 2. The diagram illustrating the algorithm of ducts extraction

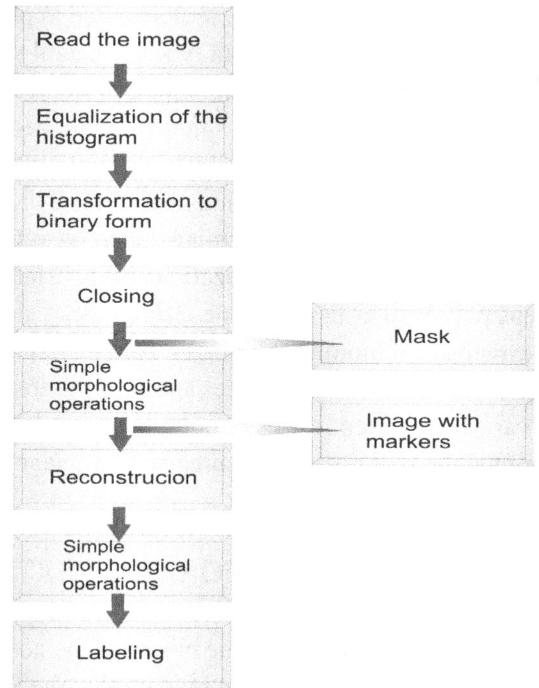

Figure 3. The equalization of the image (a) original image, (b) equalized image

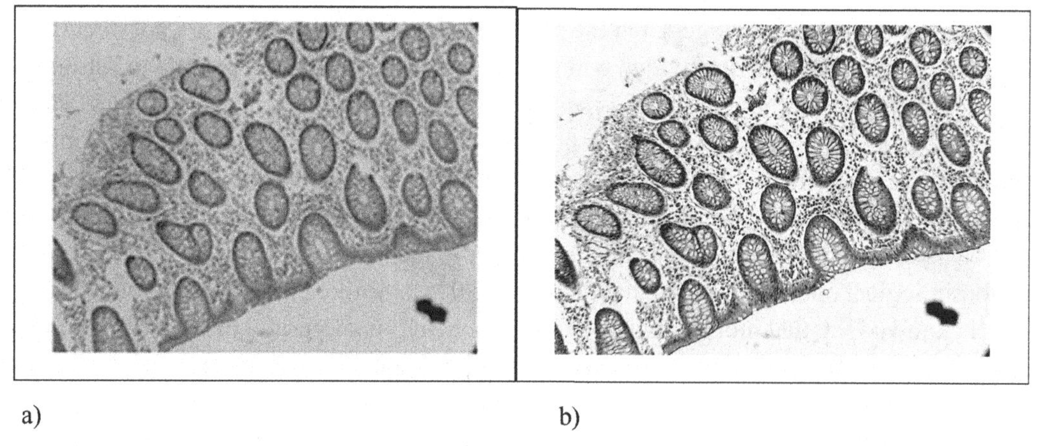

a) b)

where L_{min} and L_{max} represent the minimum and maximal intensity of all pixels. Figure 3 illustrates the original and equalized image of the ducts.

The next operations (the transformation of RBG into binary representation and morphological closing) form the binary mask of the image. In the transformation of the image from RGB to binary we have applied very effective Otsu algorithm (Otsu, 1979), determining the optimal value of bias automatically. To eliminate all tiny elements (the defense cells, the artifact elements of stroma of the tissues, etc.) existing in the image we have applied morphological closing (forming the binary mask) followed by the

Figure 4. The mask (a) and marker form (b) of the transformed image

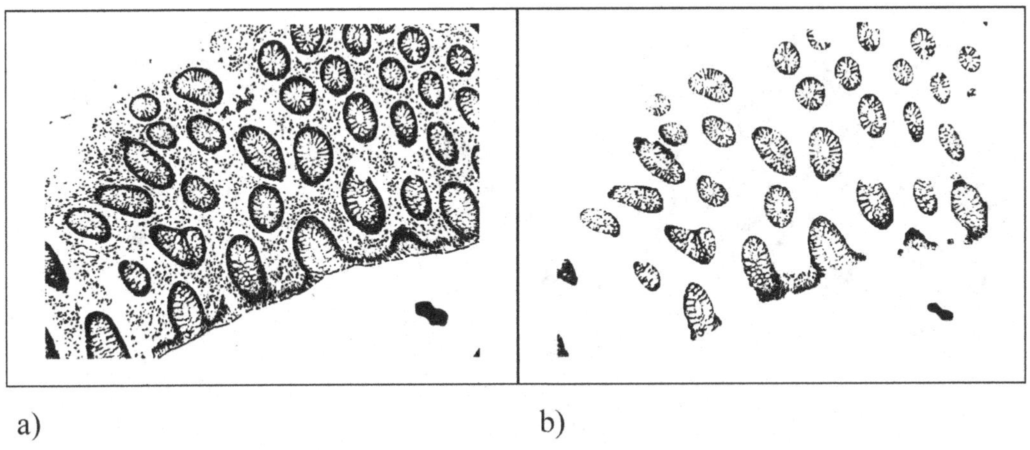

a) b)

hole filling and opening (the marker image). The closing and opening operations were performed by applying the disc structuring element of different sizes: 3 for closing and 7 for opening.

Figure 4 presents the image containing the binary mask (Figure 4a) and marker form (Figure 4b). The markers represent the positions of ducts in the image, on the basis of which we are able to reconstruct full shapes of the ducts.

The mask and markers take part in the next operation called reconstruction (Soille, 2003) of the ducts. This operation recovers the real shape of the ducts while eliminating all small size elements outside them. The next operations consist of series of simple morphological operations performed on the reconstructed image: closing, hole filling and opening. As a result we get the resulting image containing fully filled shapes of discovered ducts, separated from each other. Figure 5 illustrates the reconstructed image (Figure 5a) and the final binary image of duct shapes denoted by different colors (Figure 5b). After labeling each duct we save them as the separate images for further processing.

After segmentation of the image each glandular duct represents the individual image, which must be further processed for creation of its numerical descriptors. In medical diagnosis the most important are the geometrical parameters of these ducts and especially the distances between the nearest glandular ducts. Among the geometrical parameters the most interesting are:

- the real area (A)
- the convex area covered in the polygon circumscribed on a duct (A_c)
- the real perimeter (P)
- the convex perimeter (P_c) defined as the perimeter of the polygon circumscribed on a duct
- the longest (L_l) diameter
- the shortest (L_s) diameters.

The area (A) is the real area covered by the glandular duct (given in pixels). Diameter is the quantity defined in two mutually perpendicular directions. We recognize the long diameter L_l and the short one L_s. The long diameter is the distance (in pixels) between two most distant pixels belonging to the same duct. The short diameter is determined by finding the longest perpendicular line to the long diameter. It

Figure 5. The reconstructed image containing the ducts (a) and the final form of cleaned ducts shapes (b)

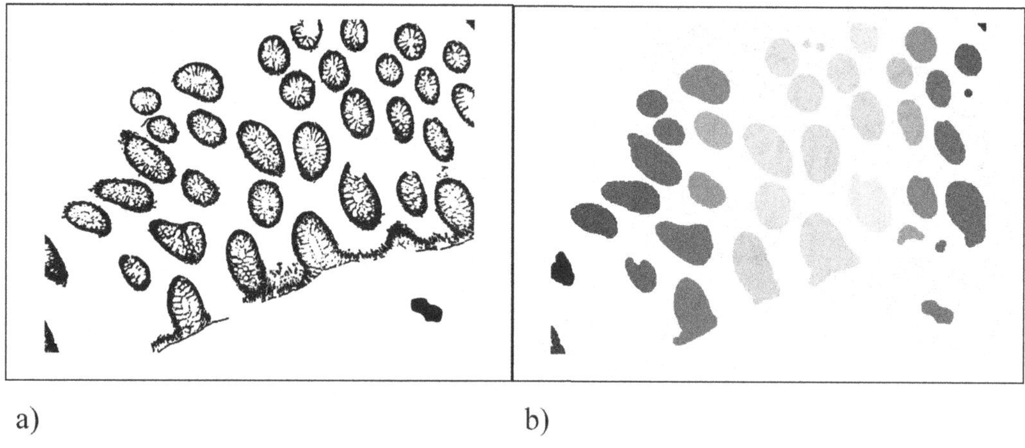

a) b)

is also given in pixels. The real perimeter P is the number of pixels placed on the periphery of the duct (in pixels). The convex perimeter P_c is the perimeter of the polygon circumscribed on a duct. Convex area A_c is the area of the polygon circumscribed on a duct. All of them can be easily computed in an automatic way for each duct, for example using Matlab (Matlab, 2007).

Especially important in the diagnosis are the distances between the neighboring ducts. At the inflammation these distances are higher, because of the liquid appearing in the stroma. To compute automatically these distances between the neighboring glandular ducts we had to develop special algorithm. Once again the human intelligence has been translated into artificial intelligence. The algorithm for distance computation may be presented as following.

- The first step is to find the long diameter of each glandular duct. Its position represents the most important information characterizing the orientation of it in the image.
- After getting the long diameter we draw the series of lines perpendicular to it with the distance of 5 pixels.
- If the perpendicular line intersects the long diameter of the other neighboring glandular duct the distance between the boundary pixels of both ducts are saved.
- Then the mean distance and standard deviation of these distances between the closest neighboring ducts are computed. Standard deviation characterizes the diversity of all distances taken into account in the estimation process. Small value of standard deviation denotes high parallelism of two neighboring ducts.
- The obtained results in the form of the distances between the closest neighboring ducts, the mean distances between them and corresponding standard deviations are saved in the database.

Figure 6b illustrates the applied method of the computation of distances between the neighboring ducts corresponding to the colon tissue image of Figure 6a. The components taken into account at computation of the mean distances between the glandular ducts are visible as the lines between the long diameters. For the purpose of diagnosis only the smallest value of the mean distance between the succeeding ducts and their closest neighbors should be taken into account and saved on a disc.

Figure 6. The illustration of the procedure of computation of distances between the neighbouring glandular ducts: (a) the image of a colon tissue, (b) the extracted duct areas found by the algorithm (labeled by the numbers from 1 to 15) and the lines used in determination of distances between ducts.

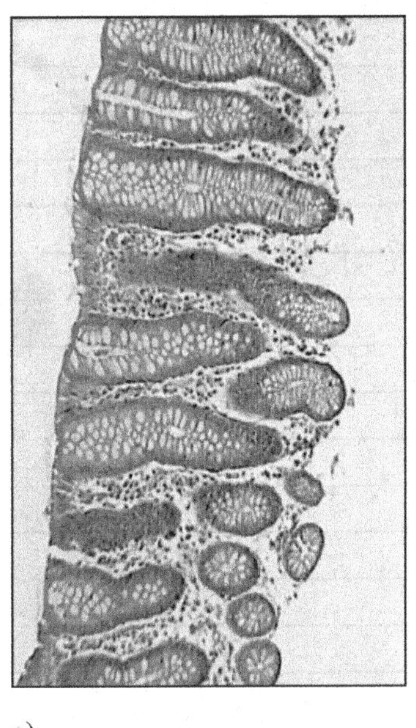

a)

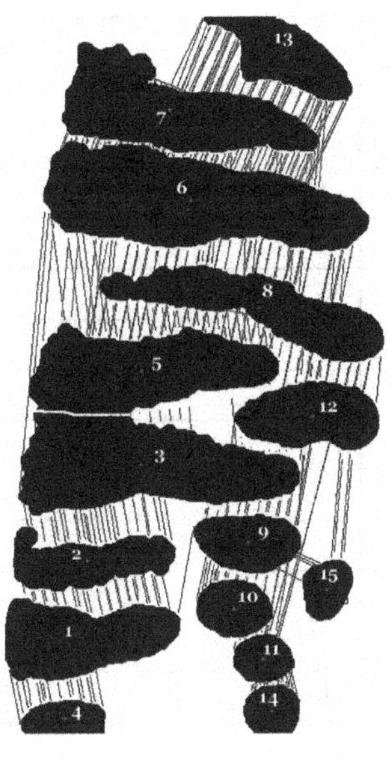

b)

Note that the neighbors of the glandular ducts may vary. For example the closest neighbor for duct No 1 is the duct No 2 and vice versa. However it is not the general rule. For example the closest neighbor of duct No 8 is duct No 12, but for duct No 12 the closest neighbor is duct No 5. Note that neighbors are selected on the basis of the average distances for all lines connecting two ducts. This is the reason, why the ducts No 3 and 5 are not the closest neighbors, although on a short section they are very close to each other.

Table 1 presents the numerical values of the distances and standard deviations between the closest neighboring ducts corresponding to Figure 6. For each glandular duct the mean value of this distance and standard deviation are given. We can see that highly parallel ducts, for example 1 and 2 have very small values of std/mean ratio.

In general the mean values of distances between the neighboring ducts averaged over all pairs of ducts provide the important information of the general inflammation state of the intestines. On the other side the standard deviation characterizes the diversity of all distances that have been taken into account at the estimation process. Small value of standard deviation denotes high parallelism of two neighboring ducts.

Actually all stages of analysis of the image, leading to the extraction and parameterization of glandular ducts are done automatically by the computer and the numerical results are saved in Excel file. The time of full image analysis is very short. For the average image it takes only few seconds on a PC. The developed computerized system of automatic image analysis written in Matlab (Matlab, 2007) is able to do the following steps (Kruk et al., 2007):

Table1. The distances between the glandular ducts

Glandular duct	Neighbouring duct	Mean distance	Std of distances
1	2	121,71	24,76
2	1	121,71	24,76
3	12	83,88	14,28
4	1	160,79	31,28
5	12	71,57	24,37
6	7	62,88	22,11
7	6	62,88	22,11
8	7	97,48	19,62
9	5	162,28	34,89
10	11	123.17	29,13
11	10	123.17	29,14
12	5	74,57	22,54
13	10	84,04	18,79
14	13	137,04	27,82
15	11	120,09	25,42

- reading and saving the whole image of biopsy on the disc
- segmentation and extraction of all glandular ducts appearing in the image
- measuring the distances between the neighboring ducts
- determination of the other geometrical parameters of the ducts mentioned in the text
- saving the results of parameterization on the disc in the form of Excel file
- putting the binary images of the ducts in the archive graphical files for future use.

The developed system is able to do all these steps automatically (without intervention of the human operator) for the images corresponding to the first step of illness development. In the case of more advanced stages the automatic interpretation of the image may be difficult and sometimes there is a need for intervention of the human operator (to cut some connection of the ducts with the stroma of the tissue, not properly segmented by the automatic system). This operation is also supported by the handy graphical user interface developed by us.

THE AUTOMATIC SYSTEM FOR CLASSIFICATION OF THE DEVELOPMENT STAGE OF IBD

After extraction and parameterization of the ducts it is possible to build an automatic classification system able to recognize among three mentioned stages of illness. The idea is to develop some set of numerical descriptors based on the estimated geometrical parameters of the ducts that well characterizes different stages of IBD development. Two tasks should be solved at this stage.

- Definition of the most representative descriptors (features) that are able to separate different classes of illness.
- Application of automatic classification system of highest possible efficiency, able to recognize patterns characteristic for different stages of illness.

To get good results of recognition we have to develop the features well representing the patterns characteristic for each stage of illness. On the basis of them the classifier will generate its most accurate decision concerning the final recognition. Good feature should be very stable for samples belonging to the same class (the smallest possible variance) and at the same time it should differ significantly for different classes. To distinguish between these classes, the positions of means of feature values for the data belonging to different classes should be separated as much as possible. The feature of the standard deviation value much higher than the distance between two neighboring class centers is useless for these two particular classes recognition, since it does not distinguish between them. It has no discriminative power and may be treated as the noise from the classification point of view. Thus the main problem in classification is to find out the efficient methods of selection of features according to their importance for the problem solution (Duda et al., 2003), (Guyon & Elisseff, 2003). In our solution we have applied Fisher measure, since it directly incorporates our demand for the separation of features describing different classes. For two classes *A* and *B* Fisher discrimination coefficient of the feature *f* is defined as follows

$$S_{AB}(f) = \frac{\left| c_A(f) - c_B(f) \right|}{\sigma_A(f) + \sigma_B(f)} \tag{2}$$

In this definition c_A and c_B are the mean values of the feature *f* in the class *A* and *B*, respectively. The variables σ_A and σ_B represent the standard deviations determined for both classes. The large value of $S_{AB}(f)$ indicates good potential separation ability of the feature *f* for these two classes. On the other side small value of it means that this particular feature is not good for the recognition between classes *A* and *B*. In the case of many classes recognized by application of the same set of feature, the usefulness of each of them may be measured by the sum of S_{AB} over all pairs of classes (*A,B*).

After determination of the most important features the next problem is to chose the most effective automatic classifier, which would be able to recognize the class on the basis of these features. Among many existing classifiers, like Bayes, distance classifiers, classical neural networks and support vector machines (SVM). The SVM is commonly regarded as the most effective solution (Haykin, 1999), (Scholkopf & Smola, 2002). This is the reason why we have chosen SVM as the classifying tool.

The learning problem of SVM is formulated as the task of separating learning vectors $\mathbf{x}_i$ (i=1, 2,..., p) into two classes of the destination values either $d_i=1$ (one class) or $d_i=-1$ (the opposite class) with the maximal separation margin (Scholkopf & Smola, 2002), (Vapnik, 1998). Applying the Lagrangian approach this primary task is transformed to the so called dual problem of maximization of the quadratic function $Q(\pm)$ with respect to the Lagrange multipliers α_i, defined in the way (Scholkopf & Smola, 2002)

$$\max \quad Q(\alpha) = \sum_{i=1}^{p} \alpha_i - \frac{1}{2} \sum_{i=1}^{p} \sum_{j=1}^{p} \alpha_i \alpha_j d_i d_j K\left(\mathbf{x}_i, \mathbf{x}_j\right) \tag{3}$$

with the constraints

$$\sum_{i=1}^{p} \alpha_i d_i = 0 \qquad (4)$$
$$0 \le \alpha_i \le C$$

In this formulation C is the regularization constant, defined by the user, p - the number of learning data pairs $(\mathbf{x}_i, d_i)$ and $K(\mathbf{x},\mathbf{x}_i)$ is the kernel function fulfilling Mercer conditions (Vapnik, 1998). As it is seen the learning task is transformed to the solution of the quadratic optimization problem, which has many, very efficient implementations. In practice we have applied the modified sequential programming algorithm (Hsu & Lin, 2002), (Scholkopf & Smola, 2002).

The important point in designing SVM classifier is the choice of kernel function. The simplest linear kernel was inefficient due to the lack of linear separability of the data. The polynomial kernel checked in the introductory experiments was found also useless, since high degree of polynomial was needed and the system had become badly conditioned. The most often used is the Gaussian kernel defined in the form $K(\mathbf{x},\mathbf{x}_i) = \exp\left(-\gamma \left\|\mathbf{x}-\mathbf{x}_i\right\|^2\right)$, where γ is the hyperparameter chosen by the user. In our experiments we have applied this kernel.

The regularization coefficient C determines the balance between the complexity of the network, characterized by the weight vector **w** and the error of classification of learning data. Low value of C means smaller significance of the learning errors in the adaptation stage. For the normalized input signals the value of C is usually much bigger than one. Its optimal value is usually determined after a series of experiments via the standard use of the validation test set. For normalized data the typical value of C is in the range (100, 1000). The process of optimizing the values of C and γ is done together. Many different values of C and γ combined together in the learning process have been used in the learning process. Their optimal values are those for which the classification error on the validation data set (small part of learning set) is the smallest one.

The decision function of the classifier associating the input vector **x** with a class is relied on the output signal y(**x**) of the SVM, where this signal is determined by (Scholkopf & Smola, 2002)

$$y(\mathbf{x}) = \sum_{i=1}^{N_{sv}} \alpha_i d_i K(\mathbf{x}_i,\ \mathbf{x}) + b \qquad (5)$$

N_{sv} is the number of support vectors (the vectors $\mathbf{x}_i$ for which the Lagrange multipliers are different from zero). The positive value of the output signal $y(\mathbf{x})$ is associated with the first class and the negative with the opposite one. To deal with a problem of many classes we have used one against one approach (Hsu & Lin, 2002). In this approach the SVM networks are trained to recognize between all combinations of two classes of data. For M classes we have to train $M(M\text{-}1)/2$ individual SVM networks. In the retrieval mode the vector **x** belongs to the class of the highest number of winnings in all combinations of classes.

RESULTS OF EXPERIMENTS

Using the developed system we have checked 197 images of the intestine biopsies prepared for the patients of different stages of development of IBD. Among them 26 belonged to individuals in remission phase in which the patients underwent biopsy due to other diseases, 61 – initial acute stage, and the highest number (110) to the advanced active stage of IBD development. These were the number of patients available to date in the data base of the hospital. Especially small is the group of individuals with full remission of disease, since this group of people is generally not subject to such investigation. As a result of all image preprocessing we have extracted 2944 glandular ducts. Only in the most difficult cases corresponding mainly to the heavy advancement of illness the manual intervention of human operator was needed in the extraction process. However such images represented not more than 5% of all images in the data base. All extracted ducts have been labeled and saved on the disc.

The applied image processing has resulted in two kinds of outcome. The first one is in the graphical form of extracted ducts and the second - in the numerical forms of geometrical parameter values associated with each extracted ducts. The numerical data have been saved in Excel file. Further analysis of these parameters using SVM classifier has allowed to associate them with the stage of development of IBD.

Graphical Form of Output

The graphical results of image processing correspond to all investigated stages of IBD. Figure 7 presents three examples of images processed fully automatically by our processing system (without any intervention of the human operator). They cover all stages of IBD development.

As it is seen all glandular ducts have been extracted practically in a perfect way. All of them have been labeled automatically by our system and saved on a disc in the form of a graphical file.

Figure 8 presents the set of images, where some intervention of the human operator in the processing of the image was needed. The main difficulties in automatic analysis of these images were either the changes of illumination of some parts of the image (the upper image) or advanced stage of inflammation causing the stroma and defense cells create the structure resembling the ducts (the middle and lower images of Figure 8).

The quality of an automatic extraction of ducts was satisfactory from the medical point of view. Their quantity found in the image as well as the shape of each duct were in good agreement with the human expert assessment. This means that the graphical results may stand good basis for further medical investigations directed to the parameterization of the ducts.

Parameterization of Ducts

The medical researchers are looking for the numerical measures that are strictly associated with the advancement of IBD. To these measures belong first of all the geometrical parameters of the ducts. They form the potential diagnostic features. To get reliable recognition system we should search for the reasonably large set of them, characterizing the problem from different points of view. Sufficiently high number of features provides perspective of good characterization of the process of image recognition. However among automatically generated features there might be some not well discriminating different classes, and hence useless from the recognition point of view. Note that the features assuming the same

Figure 7. The examples of images processed automatically by our system without intervention of the human operator: left column – the original image, right column – the extracted glandular ducts generated by the system. The images in the middle row represent the initial acute stage of IBD and the other images – the advanced active phase.

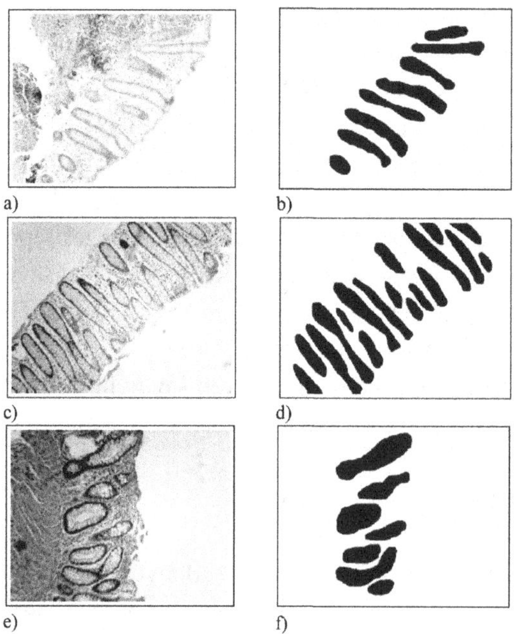

Figure 8. The examples of images processed semi-automatically with some help of human operator (all of them belonged to advanced active phase of IBD): left column – the original images, right column – the extracted glandular ducts.

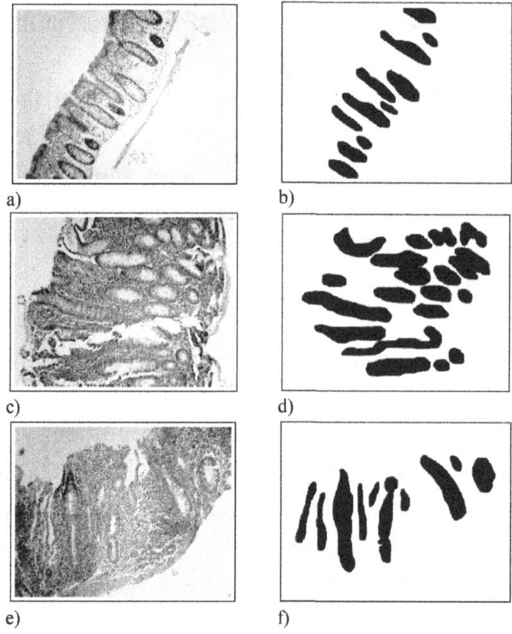

values for different classes have no discriminative properties. The same could be said about the features of the values interlacing for different classes or are largely dispersed.

The digital image processing tools developed in the form of the computer program allow to find the candidates for diagnostic features in an automatic way. The easiest way of assessing the class discriminative abilities of the individual features is to study their mean and standard deviation for the particular class. Table 2 presents the results of determination of the distances D between the neighboring ducts (one of the most important factors checked by the medical expert) and the basic geometrical parameters (the real area A, compact area A_c, the perimeter P, the convex perimeter P_c, long diameter L_p and short diameter L_s) for three chosen patients belonging to three representative groups: class 1 - individuals with full remission of disease, class 2 – the initial acute stage and class 3 - the advanced active phase. We present the mean values and standard deviations (std) for all ducts existing in the image corresponding to each patient (all expressed in pixels)

The analysis of these results can deliver quite important information for supporting the medical diagnosis. First of all we can see that the mean distances between the neighboring ducts are generally larger at more advanced stages of illness. Besides this the values of the standard deviation are less stable at the advanced stage of IBD. These particular results of the mean distances confirm good correlation of the averaged mean distances between the neighboring ducts and the stage of development of the inflammation for the chosen individuals. It means that the information regarding the mean distances between

Table 2. The mean values and standard deviations (std) of the geometrical parameters of all ducts in the image calculated for three kinds of patients: class 1 - individuals with full remission of disease, class 2 – the initial acute stage and class 3 - the advanced active phase

Patients			D	A	A_c	P	P_c	L_l	L_s
Class 1	P332	mean	69.3	41831	43352	732	626	348	141
		std	15.00	29233	31024	321	300	172	30
	P331	mean	73.4	43652	45442	749	600	337	162
		std	17.02	18175	20695	208	178	102	33
	P327	mean	76.2	44930	52219	870	681	393	142
		std	20.08	29062	38263	351	300	187	27
Class 2	P326	mean	92.4	37451	39502	724	590	318	149
		std	19.96	16423	18490	229	218	108	46
	P330	mean	87.1	63058	73250	1122	997	521	152
		std	23.03	32540	39927	420	406	216	44
	P325	mean	80.57	21267	22115	507	377	208	133
		std	12.65	10832	11582	154	137	86	18
Class 3	P328	mean	133.1	107421	130113	1413	1233	678	214
		std	45.01	62965	91720	697	671	349	31
	P323	mean	112.5	78198	90157	1360	1233	673	137
		std	25.80	31969	38965	415	414	216	32
	P329	mean	107.4	65434	69290	981	839	461	172
		std	24.01	46081	50829	473	422	266	44

the neighboring ducts may be a good indication of the stage of inflammation of the intestines and provide the important factor at the assessment of the stage of illness.

The other geometrical parameters presented in Table II for the same representatives of these three groups of patients are not so easily conclusive. There is a large variety of these values, which change greatly for patients belonging to the same group and also between groups. Note also large values of standard deviations of these parameters (usually half or even more of the mean). These large values are the evidence of high variability of parameters of the individual ducts existing in the analyzed images.

To confirm these observations we have performed the same calculations for all patients belonging to these three groups of interest (class 1 - 26 individuals, class 2 – 61 individuals, class 3 - 110 individuals). Table 3 presents the statistics of these investigations in the form of mean values and standard deviations of these parameters.

Looking at these statistical results we can see quite large variability of most of the statistical parameters, undermining their usefulness in the diagnosis process. The most stable are only the results concerning the average distances between the neighboring ducts (parameter D), making this parameter very important in the diagnosis. Moreover most of the average parameters (except D) characterizing each group of patients are very close to each other. It means that these parameters are not appropriate for recognition of the stage of advancement of illness.

Analyzing the detailed numerical results of parameterization for the whole set of images of patients belonging to these three classes we have tried to find another, more stable characterization of patients, relying on the ratio of some of them. Close analysis of the details of results concerning the data base of parameters has enabled to reveal some other more stable descriptors in the form of appropriate ratios, that are defined on the basis of the crude values obtained from the parameterization. We have introduced the following descriptors defined in the form of the ratio of the appropriate geometrical parameters:

circularity factor F_c

$$F_c = \frac{4\pi A}{P} \tag{6}$$

factor of convex circularity F_{cc}

$$F_{cc} = \frac{4\pi A_C}{P_C} \tag{7}$$

homogeneity factor F_h

$$F_h = \frac{P^2}{A} \tag{8}$$

factor of convex homogeneity F_{ch}

Table 3. The mean values and standard deviations (std) of the geometrical parameters of all ducts in the image calculated for the whole population of investigated patients forming the group of 3 classes

Group of patients		A	A_c	P	P_c	L_l	L_s	D
Class 1	mean	85501.37	87338.30	1259.22	1198.33	448.90	176.18	87.08
	std	34375.66	37579.30	285.88	263.98	143.21	44.28	28.06
Class 2	mean	91959.45	108684.27	1450.17	1134.70	522.72	189.01	103.70
	std	46137.06	53353.85	341.66	286.84	154.67	62.19	38.39
Class 3	mean	101359.44	149697.75	1608.01	1166.66	505.72	185.03	160.42
	std	27175.90	37378.06	351.13	200.64	176.05	15.06	30.56

$$F_{ch} = \frac{P_c^2}{A_c} \tag{9}$$

corrugation factor F_{cr}

$$F_{cr} = \frac{P_c}{P} \tag{10}$$

factor of ruggedness F_r

$$F_r = \frac{A}{A_c} \tag{11}$$

number N of ducts in the image of the normalized size

They represent the potential features used in the recognition of the stage of advancement of illness. In Table 4 we present the statistical results (means and standard deviations) concerning these features calculated for the whole data base of the analyzed images.

Comparing the values of the mean and standard deviation of these descriptors we can observe the significant improvement. The mutual distances between their means corresponding to three stages of development of IBD are now much larger, while the standard deviations of the feature within the same group is smaller.

To assess the discrimination ability of the developed descriptors in a most objective way we have used the Fisher measure described by (2).This measure is defined for each feature f and for each pair of classes under recognition: $S_{12}(f)$, $S_{13}(f)$ and $S_{23}(f)$. Table 5 presents the values of Fisher measure for each of the candidate features: D, F_c, F_{cc}, F_h, F_{ch}, F_{cr}, F_r and N, at recognition of two class problems. The first row of results corresponds to recognition of the first two classes, second row – the classes 1 and 3 and the third row – classes 2 and 3. Since the same features will be taken into account in assessment of each image we have to rely in our choice on the sum of Fisher measures concerning all compared pairs of

Table 4. The mean values and standard deviations (std) of the relative factors characterizing of all ducts in the image calculated for the whole population of investigated patients forming the group of individuals with full remission of disease (class 1), initial acute stage (class 2) and the advanced active phase of IBD development (class 3)

Group of patients		D	F_c	F_{cc}	F_h	F_{ch}	F_{cr}	F_r	N
Class 1	mean	87.08	853.25	915.87	18.54	16.44	0.95	0.97	15
	std	28.06	112.21	102.87	3.78	3.32	0.11	0.14	5
Class 2	mean	103.70	796.86	1203.63	22.86	11.84	0.78	0.84	18
	std	38.39	116.76	132.54	4.23	2.79	0.09	0.11	7
Class 3	mean	160.42	792.10	1612.43	25.51	9.09	0.72	0.67	6
	std	30.56	176.65	234.76	4.78	2.21	0.09	0.07	3

Table 5. The values of Fisher measure of the discrimination ability for the set of features at recognition of pairs of classes.

	D	F_c	F_{cc}	F_h	F_{ch}	F_{cr}	F_r	N
$S_{12}(f)$	0.2501	0.2463	1.2224	0.5393	0.7529	0.8500	0.5200	0.2500
$S_{13}(f)$	1.2511	0.2117	2.0631	0.8143	1.3291	1.1500	1.4286	1.1250
$S_{23}(f)$	0.8226	0.0162	1.1130	0.2941	0.5500	0.3333	0.9444	1.2000
Sum	2.3238	0.4742	4.3985	1.6477	2.6320	2.3333	2.8930	2.5750

classes. Hence in the fourth row we show the total discrimination power of each descriptor expressed as the sum of elements in the appropriate column.

It is seen now that the best descriptor (corresponding to the largest value of the summed Fisher measures) is the factor of convex circularity F_{cc}. Its total value 4.3985 is almost twice higher than the next one. Moreover it is almost equally good for recognition between each pair of classes. Evidently the worst one is the circularity factor F_c, which seems to be useless at recognition of any pair of classes (very small value of Fisher measure for all pairs of classes). On the basis of this analysis we have decided to exclude this descriptor from the applied feature set used in automatic recognition of the state of inflammation. So the input vector to the classifier is composed of 7 remaining features.

Automatic Recognition of the Intensity of Inflammation

In the next experiments we have checked how the selected features are efficient in automatic recognition of the stage of IBD development. Many different solutions of classification system may be applied. Nowadays the most effective are the neural like classifiers, such as MLP, RBF, neuro-fuzzy or SVM. According to our experience and very detailed comparisons made by researchers (Meyer et al., 2003) the most effective classifier is SVM. The PCA analysis of distribution of features has shown, that the data are not linearly separable, thus the nonlinear kernel SVM is needed. The SVM classifier of Gaussian kernel function was selected. This kind of solution is very similar to RBF with respect to the structure,

Table 6. The average confusion matrix of the IBD stage recognition (in relative terms) corresponding to 20 trials

Class	1	2	3
1	94.1%	2.63%	3.27%
2	3.35%	92.26%	4.19%
3	0	2.63%	97.37%

but of absolutely different principle of learning algorithm. The detailed comparison of it with RBF (Markiewicz & Osowski, 2005) has shown the superiority of SVM.

The important step in learning is the choice of hyperparameters C (the regularization constant) and γ (the parameter of Gaussian function). These hyperparameters have been adjusted by trying the limited set of predefined values and choosing the values corresponding to best results on the validation set (20% of the learning data). The optimal values of them were found as follows C=200 and γ=0.01. To get the most objective results of testing we have applied the cross validation approach. From the available data 2/3 of the set have been used in learning of SVM and the remaining 1/3 were left for testing purposes. The learning stage of SVM is extremely quick. The average time of learning the SVM classifier system was about 3 seconds. The experiments of learning and testing have been repeated 20 times at random choice of both subsets. As the vector **x**, applied to the input of the SVM classifier we have assumed the seven element vector containing the most important features $\mathbf{x}=[F_{cc}, F_r, F_{ch}, N, F_{cr}, D, F_h]$, chosen according to summed Fisher measures gathered in Table 5.

Table 6 presents the average results of recognition of each class on the testing data not taking part in learning. The results are in the form of confusion matrix representing the average values of recognition ratio obtained at 20 runs of experiments in cross correlation mode. The diagonal entries of this matrix represent right recognition of the class and the off diagonal – the misclassification ratios (all expressed in percentage). The row presents how the particular class has been classified. The column indicates which class has been classified as the type mentioned in this column. The results of Table 6 point directly what was the accuracy of recognition of each class and what is the average misclassification ratio.

The average accuracy of recognition of the first class among all other cases was equal 94.1%, for the second class - 92.26% and of the third one - 97.37%. If we calculate the relative error as the ratio of the number of all misclassifications to the total number of cases we get the mean value in all experiment equal 4.59% at standard deviation of 2.68%. For comparison we made similar experiments with other neural classifiers. At application of MLP of the optimal structure 7-8-3 the total misclassification rate on the same data base was equal 6.27%. Application of RBF resulted in the total relative error equal 5.92%.

The most striking observation is the relative high value of misclassification of the samples belonging to the first class (full remission of disease). This is due to the small number of learning data of this class used in experiments (most of the investigated patients were ill). The population of the representatives of three investigated classes was highly unbalanced (only 26 samples representing the first class in comparison to 110 of the third one). However notice, that none of the patients in an advanced stage (class 3) was misclassified with class one (full remission of disease).

FUTURE RESEARCH DIRECTIONS

The research presented in the chapter has shown the way of automation of the process of recognition of different stages of IBD. However a lot of additional research should be done before applying it in the medical practice.

- Much larger data base of cases should be collected in the hospital and used in testing to find the most objective assessment of the real efficiency of the proposed system. Extending the data base we should take care of balancing the cases belonging to different classes.
- Additional attention should be paid to find another diagnostic features of good class separation ability. At large number of such features the selection of the best features should be done as an additional step. As a selection tools we may apply not only Fisher measure but also more advanced algorithms, for example application of SVM.
- The next direction is to apply many classifiers arranged in an ensemble. It is well known that efficiency of the ensemble is higher than individual classifier. These classifiers may be build on the basis of Gaussian kernel SVMs by applying as input information to each of them the limited number of diagnostic features selected randomly from the whole set of best features.
- The additional research problem is the optimal integration of the ensemble. The classical majority voting, weighted majority voting, different forms of naïve Bayes approaches, principal component approach, as well as Kullback-Leibler divergence methods are the examples of solution that might be applied.

CONCLUSION

The work has presented the computerized system directed to extracting the important diagnostic knowledge contained in the medical image of the colon biopsy. In creating it we have mimicked the way the human expert assesses the image. Application of the artificial intelligence included in the developed automatic system allows to obtain the unique numerical results, not possible for achieving at the visual inspection of the image by the human expert.

The system is able to extract the ducts at different stages of development of the inflammation. Its important advantage is automation of this very difficult and responsible work, not possible to be done manually by the human expert. The developed system has been applied to the analysis of 197 medical images corresponding to different stages of IBD. In most investigated cases the system was able to extract the ducts automatically and there was no need for human operator to intervene. Only in the case of heavy advancement of illness the human intervention in the image processing was sometimes needed to obtain the accurate results of extraction.

The most important results are concerning the numerical characterization of the glandular ducts, enabling to apply them as the input information for automatic neural type classifier, able to recognize the stage of advancement of the illness. The numerical experiments performed at the application of SVM as a classifier have shown very encouraging results, confirming the hope to develop an efficient tool for supporting the medical diagnosis of IBD.

The developed system allows to analyze the colon images in a very short time, delivering the readable results in a very convenient form. Thanks to this it may present very efficient tool for medical scientists involved in investigation of hundreds of cases of IBD, enabling to accelerate the research in this important medical area.

REFERENCES

Bishop, C. (2006). *Pattern recognition and machine learning*. Singapore: Springer.

Carpenter, H., & Talley, N. (2000). The importance of clinicopathological correlation in the diagnosis of inflammatory conditions of the colon. *The American Journal of Gastroenterology*, *95*, 234–245. doi:10.1111/j.1572-0241.2000.01924.x

Carter, M., Lobo, A., & Travis, S. (2004). Guidelines for the management of IBD for adults. *British Society of Gastroenterology*, *53*, 1–16.

Chambolle, A. (2004). An algorithm for total variation minimization and applications. *Journal of Mathematical Imaging and Vision*, *20*, 89–97. doi:10.1023/B:JMIV.0000011321.19549.88

Chan, T., Esedoglu, S., & Nikolova, M. (2006). Algorithms for finding global minimizers of image segmentation and denoising models. *SIAM Journal on Applied Mathematics*, *66*, 1632–1648. doi:10.1137/040615286

Djemal, K. (2005). *Speckle reduction in ultrasound images by minimization of total variation*. International Conference on Image Processing, Sousse, Tunisia.

Duda, R. O., Hart, P. E., & Stork, P. (2003). *Pattern classification and scene analysis*. New York, NY: Wiley.

Gonzalez, R. C., & Woods, R. E. (2005). *Digital image processing*. Reading, MA: Addison-Wesley.

Guyon, I., & Elisseeff, A. (2003). An introduction to variable and feature selection. *Journal of Machine Learning Research*, *3*, 1158–1182. doi:10.1162/153244303322753616

Haykin, S. (1999). *Neural networks-a comprehensive foundation*. New York, NY: Macmillan.

Hsu, C. W., & Lin, C. J. (2002). A comparison method for multi class support vector machines. *IEEE Transactions on Neural Networks*, *13*, 415–425. doi:10.1109/72.991427

Bankman, I. N. (Ed.). (2008). *Handbook of medical image processing and analysis*. Boston, MA: Academic Press.

Kimmel, R., & Bruckstein, A. M. (2003). Regularized Laplacian zero crossings as optimal edge integrators. *International Journal of Computer Vision*, *53*, 225–243. doi:10.1023/A:1023030907417

Kruk, M., Osowski, S., & Koktysz, R. (2007). Segmentation and characterization of glandular ducts in microscopic colon image. *Przeglad Elektrotechniczny*, *84*, 227–230.

Li, S., Fevens, T., & Krzyzak, A. (2006). Automatic clinical image segmentation using pathological modeling, PCA and SVM. *Engineering Applications of Artificial Intelligence*, *19*, 403–410. doi:10.1016/j.engappai.2006.01.011

Liu, H., & Motoda, H. (2008). *Computational methods of feature selection*. London, UK: Chapman.

Markiewicz, T., Wisniewski, P., Osowski, S., Patera, J., Kozlowski, W., & Koktysz, R. (2009). Comparative analysis of the methods for accurate recognition of cells in the nuclei staining of the Ki-67 in neuroblastoma and ER/PR status staining in breast cancer. *Analytical and Quantitative Cytology and Histology Journal*, *31*, 49–63.

Markiewicz, T., & Osowski, S. (2005). *OLS versus SVM approach to learning of RBF networks*. International Joint Neural Network Conference, Montreal, (pp. 1051-1056).

Marraval, D., & Patricio, M. (2002). Image segmentation and pattern recognition. In Chen, D., & Cheng, X. (Eds.), *Pattern recognition and string matching*. Amsterdam, The Netherlands: Kluwer.

Meyer, D., Leisch, F., & Hornik, K. (2003). The support vector machine under test. *Neurocomputing*, *55*, 169–186. doi:10.1016/S0925-2312(03)00431-4

(2007). *Image Processing toolbox - Matlab user manual*. Natick, MA: MathWorks.

Osowski, S., & Markiewicz, T. (2007). Support vector machine for recognition of white blood cells in leukemia. In Camps-Valls, G., Rojo-Alvarez, J. L., & Martinez-Ramon, M. (Eds.), *Kernel methods in bioengineering, signal and image processing* (pp. 93–123). Hershey, PA: Idea Group Publishing. doi:10.4018/9781599040424.ch004

Otsu, N. (1979). A threshold selection method from grey-level histograms. *IEEE Transactions on Systems, Man, and Cybernetics*, *9*, 62–66. doi:10.1109/TSMC.1979.4310076

Schölkopf, B., & Smola, A. (2002). *Learning with kernels*. Cambridge, MA: MIT Press.

Soille, P. (2003). *Morphological image analysis, principles and applications*. Berlin, Germany: Springer.

Vasilevskiy, A., & Siddigi, K. (2002). Flux maximizing geometric flow. *IEEE Transactions of PAMI*, *24*, 1565–1578.

Vapnik, V. (1998). *Statistical learning theory*. New York, NY: Wiley.

ADDITIONAL READING

Bartlett, P., & Traskin, M. (2008). AdaBoost is Consistent. *Journal of Machine Learning Research, Vol.*, *9*, 2347–2368.

Corani, G., & Zaffalon, M. (2008). Learning Reliable Classifiers From Small or Incomplete Data Sets: The Naive Credal Classifier 2. *Journal of Machine Learning Research*, *9*, 581–621.

Demirkaya, O., & Asyali, M. H. (2009). *Image processing with Matlab application in medicine and biology*. London: CRC.

El-Naqa, I., Yang, Y., Wernick, M. N., Galatsanos, N. P., & Nishikawa, R. M. (2002). A support vector machine approach for detection of micro calcifications. *IEEE Transactions on Medical Imaging*, *21*, 1552–1563. doi:10.1109/TMI.2002.806569

Gonzalez, R. C. Woods R. E, & Eddins S. L. (2009). *Digital Image Processing Using MATLAB.* Upper Saddle River, Prentice Hall.

Guyon, I., Weston, J., Barnhill, S., & Vapnik, V. (2002). Gene selection for cancer classification using Support Vector Machines. *Machine Learning, 46*, 389–422. doi:10.1023/A:1012487302797

Heijmans, H. J., & Roerdink, J. B. (1998). *Mathematical Morphology and its Applications to Image and Signal Processing* (eds). Dordrecht, Kluwer Academic Publishers.

Heijmans, H. J. (1999). Connected Morphological Operators for Binary Images. *Computer Vision and Image Understanding, 73*, 99–120. doi:10.1006/cviu.1998.0703

Kotsiantis, S. B., & Pintelas, P. E. (2004). Combining bagging and boosting. *Intern. J. of Computational Intelligence, 1*, 324–333.

Kruk, M., Osowski, S., & Koktysz, R. (2009). Recognition and Classification of Colon Cells Applying the Ensemble of Classifiers. *Computers in Biology and Medicine, 39*, 156–165. doi:10.1016/j.compbiomed.2008.12.001

Krupka, E., Navot, A., & Tishbt, N. (2008). Learning to select features using their properties. *Journal of Machine Learning Research, 9*, 2349–2376.

Kuncheva, L. (2004). *Combining pattern classifiers: methods and algorithms.* New Jersey: Wiley. doi:10.1002/0471660264

Liu, H., & Motoda, H. (2008). *Computational methods of feature selection.* London: Chapman & Hall/CRC.

Liu, Y. (2004). A Comparative Study on Feature Selection Methods for Drug Discovery. *Journal of Chemical Information and Computer Sciences, 44*, 1823–1828. doi:10.1021/ci049875d

Mitra, S., & Acharya, T. (2003). *Data mining.* New York: Wiley.

Muthu, R. K., Pal, M., Bomminayuni, S. K., Chakraborty, C., & Paul, R. R. (2009). Automated classification of cells in sub-epithelial connective tissue of oral sub-mucous fibrosis—An SVM based approach. *Computers in Biology and Medicine, 39*, 1096–1104. doi:10.1016/j.compbiomed.2009.09.004

Najarian, K., & Splinter, R. (2005). *Biomedical Signal and Image Processing.* London: Taylor & Francis.

Nixon, M., & Aguado, A. S. (2008). *Feature Extraction & Image Processing.* London: Academic Press.

Osowski, S., Siroić, R., Markiewicz, T., & Siwek, K. (2009). Application of Support Vector Machine and Genetic Algorithm for Improved Blood Cell Recognition. *IEEE Trans. Meas. and Instrum, 58*, 2159–2168. doi:10.1109/TIM.2008.2006726

Schurmann, J. (1996). *Pattern classification, a unified view of statistical and neural approaches.* New Jersey: Wiley.

Semmlow, J. L. (2004). *Biosignal and Medical Image Processing.* New York: Marcel Dekker.

Spyridonos, P., Cavoura, D., Ravazoula, P., & Nikiforidis, G. (2002). Neural network based segmentation and classification system for automatic grading of histologic section of bladder carcinoma. *Analytical and Quantitative Cytology*, *24*, 317–324.

Stork, D., & Tov, E. Y. (2004). *Computer Manual in MATLAB to Accompany Pattern Classification*. New Jersey: Wiley.

Sugiyama, M. (2007). Dimensionality Reduction of Multimodal Labeled Data by Local Fisher Discriminant Analysis. *Journal of Machine Learning Research*, *8*, 1027–1061.

Tan, P. N., Steinbach, M., & Kumar, V. (2008). *Introduction to data mining*. New York: Pearson.

Young, I. T. (1996). Quantitative Microscopy. *IEEE Engineering in Medicine and Biology*, *15*, 59–66. doi:10.1109/51.482844

Zhang, Y. J. (2008). *Image Engineering - Processing, Analysis, and Understanding*. Hongkong, Cengage Learning.

Chapter 2
The Kolmogorov Spline Network for Image Processing

Pierre-Emmanuel Leni
University of Burgundy, France

Yohan D. Fougerolle
University of Burgundy, France

Frédéric Truchetet
University of Burgundy, France

ABSTRACT

In 1900, Hilbert stated that high order equations cannot be solved by sums and compositions of bivariate functions. In 1957, Kolmogorov proved this hypothesis wrong and presented his superposition theorem (KST) that allowed for writing every multivariate functions as sums and compositions of univariate functions. Sprecher has proposed in (Sprecher, 1996) and (Sprecher, 1997) an algorithm for exact univariate function reconstruction. Sprecher explicitly describes construction methods for univariate functions and introduces fundamental notions for the theorem comprehension (such as tilage). Köppen has presented applications of this algorithm to image processing in (Köppen, 2002) and (Köppen & Yoshida, 2005). The lack of flexibility of this scheme has been pointed out and another solution which approximates the univariate functions has been considered. More specifically, it has led us to consider Igelnik and Parikh's approach, known as the KSN which offers several perspectives of modification of the univariate functions as well as their construction. This chapter will focus on the presentation of Igelnik and Parikh's Kolmogorov Spline Network (KSN) for image processing and detail two applications: image compression and progressive transmission. Precisely, the developments presented in this chapter include: (1) Compression: the authors study the reconstruction quality using univariate functions containing only a fraction of the original image pixels. To improve the reconstruction quality, they apply this decomposition on images of details obtained by wavelet decomposition. The authors combine this approach into the

DOI: 10.4018/978-1-60960-551-3.ch002

JPEG 2000 encoder, and show that the obtained results improve JPEG 2000 compression scheme, even at low bitrates. (2)Progressive Transmission: the authors propose to modify the generation of the KSN. The image is decomposed into univariate functions that can be transmitted one after the other to add new data to the previously transmitted functions, which allows to progressively and exactly reconstruct the original image. They evaluate the transmission robustness and provide the results of the simulation of a transmission over packet-loss channels.

INTRODUCTION

The Superposition Theorem is the solution to one of the 23 mathematical problems conjectured by Hilbert in 1900. Hilbert suggested that solutions to high order equations were at least bivariate functions. This hypothesis was proven wrong by Kolmogorov in 1957 when he showed that continuous multivariate functions can be expressed as sums and compositions of univariate functions as

$$f\left(x_1,\cdots,x_n\right)=\sum_{q=0}^{2n}\Phi_q\left(\sum_{p=1}^{n}\psi_{q,p}\left(x_p\right)\right). \tag{1}$$

Our goal is to investigate some aspects of this decomposition for images by considering a gray level discrete image as a sample of a continuous bivariate function. To achieve such decomposition, the univariate functions Φ_q and $\psi_{q,p}$ must be constructed. The functions Φ_q are called outer or external functions, and the functions $\psi_{q,p}$ are called inner or internal functions.

A construction method has been proposed in (Sprecher, 1996) and (Sprecher, 1997). Sprecher provides an explicit and exact computation algorithm for the values of the univariate functions at a user defined precision. The Kolmogorov superposition theorem, as reformulated and simplified by Sprecher, can be written as

$$f\left(x_1,\cdots,x_n\right)=\sum_{q=0}^{2n}g_q\left(\sum_{i=1}^{n}\lambda_i\psi\left(x_i+bq\right)\right). \tag{2}$$

We have implemented Sprecher's algorithm, using the improvements proposed in (Braun and Griebel, 2007) to guarantee the monotonicity of the internal function ψ, and tested it on image decomposition in (Leni *et al.*, 2008). In this algorithm, the univariate functions can be exactly computed for any coordinates of the definition space of the multivariate function at a given precision, but no analytic expression exists. One of the main drawbacks of this approach is that the univariate function definitions cannot be modified without completely modifying the overall pipeline of this method. This issue has led us to consider Igelnik and Parikh's approach, known as Kolmogorov Spline Network (KSN), that approximates the univariate functions as well as offers a greater flexibility on several parameters of the algorithm (*i.e.*, univariate function constructions, number of layers, tile size, and so on).

We present in detail the original KSN introduced by Igelnik and Parikh, then we propose some modifications for two compression and progressive transmission.

In the KSN, a multivariate function *f* is approximated by

$$f(x) = f(x_1, \cdots, x_n) \approx \sum_{q=1}^{N} a_q g_q \left(\sum_{i=1}^{n} \lambda_i \psi_{q,i}(x_i) \right) = \sum_{q=1}^{N} a_q g_q (\xi_q(x)). \tag{3}$$

The functions $\xi_q(x)$ play the role of hash functions, as illustrated in Figure 1, are mapping functions from $[0,1]^d$ to $\mathbb{R}$, and are used to evaluate the argument of the external functions $g_q(.)$.

In this formulation, the number of layers is now variable, and the function ψ is no longer unique: a function $\psi_{q,i}$ is associated for each layer q along each dimension i. The algorithm for the construction of a KSN is divided into two parts: a construction step, in which the univariate functions are interpolated by cubic splines, and a second stage, in which the spline parameters and the weights of the layers a_n are optimized to ensure the convergence of the approximation to the function f. A comparison between KSN and Sprecher's algorithm can be found in (Leni *et al.*, 2008). To construct the functions g_q and $\psi_{q,i}$, a tilage over the definition space of the multivariate function to be approximated is constructed. By construction, the tiles are disjoint; therefore, in order to cover the entire space, several tilage layers are generated. The internal and external univariate functions are built and associated with each tilage layer, and the superposition of these layers constitutes what is called a network. One network contains several various parameters, such as the spline parameters and the layer weights that are further optimized to improve the reconstruction accuracy. Consequently, using Igelnik and Parikh's approximation scheme, images can be represented as a superposition of layers, *i.e.*, a superposition of images with a fixed resolution.

Most of image processing tools are extensions of 1D signal processing tools. Two approaches are generally considered: the 1D tools can be mathematically extended to 2D; or the image is converted into a 1D signal, often by concatenating the lines or columns of the image. The KSN decomposition offers radically different approach: the image is converted into 1D functions with various characteristics

Figure 1. Kolmogorov spline network: example of a 5-layer network

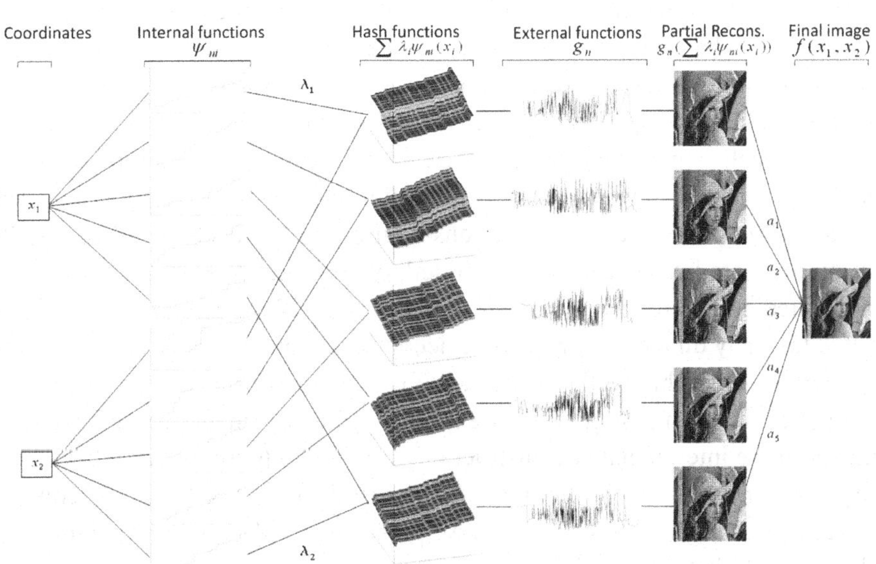

(step-increasing for the internal functions; chaotic, noisy for the external functions) without preserving the pixels neighborhood. Therefore, the KSN decomposition offers new and promising perspectives for image processing, such as through the application of 1D tools that can hardly be converted to higher dimensions. In this chapter, we present applications for compression and progressive transmission, using the characteristics of the 1D functions and the function networks obtained from the image decomposition.

For compression tasks, the representation of multivariate functions through KSN offers several degrees of freedom. More precisely, the network can be modified to contain only a fraction of the pixels of the original image; the smaller are the tiles, the larger is the quantity of information. We study the reconstruction quality as a function of the number of pixels contained in the network: the univariate functions can be defined with only a fraction of the original image pixels. First results showed that the reconstruction quality rapidly decreases when the number of pixels utilized to define the network is reduced. To improve the reconstruction quality, we apply this decomposition to detail images obtained through wavelet decomposition. In this case, the external functions corresponding to detail images can be simplified with better reconstruction quality than larger tile sizes and the sweeping orientation of the image can be globally controlled to match the orientations of the images of details. Moreover, when considering sparse data, the approximation errors of the network are decreased. This method has been introduced in (Leni *et al.*, 2009a) and (Leni *et al.*, 2009b). We present various results of compression applied to classical images. This approach is introduced as a new step in the JPEG 2000 encoder. The results of the modified encoder are presented and compared to the original JPEG 2000.

The second aspect we investigate concerns the modifications and the improvements of the KSN to provide a spatial scalable scheme for progressive image transmission. In the original algorithm, the image is approximated by compositions and superpositions of univariate functions. More precisely, the univariate functions are constructed and associated to disjoint tilages with identical tile sizes for every layer. All the layers are then superposed and the external univariate functions are composed to reconstruct the original image. Every layer corresponds to an approximation of the image slightly translated and seen through a disjoint tilage, and provides a partial reconstruction of the original image using only its associated univariate function. We modify the generation of the tilage and the construction of the univariate functions to obtain different tilage densities, one for every layer, and progressively construct the external functions. Thus, for each layer, an image that represents the original image at a lower resolution can be computed. The original image is decomposed into several univariate functions, built at different resolutions that can be transmitted one after the other to progressively reconstruct the original image. Each function adds new data to the previously transmitted functions, which limits the quantity of data transmitted at each step. In other words, the original image can be progressively reconstructed up to its original resolution, without error, and only a limited quantity of data is required to increase the resolution between intermediate reconstructions. Our algorithm is characterized by its flexibility: any number of intermediate images can be transmitted, of any resolution, and with an almost constant quantity of transmitted data to reconstruct the original image without any error. Moreover, the reader should note that data of any dimensionality can be decomposed and progressively transmitted with this method. Our contributions in this section include the presentation of a new modification of KSN for progressive image transmission that provides flexibility and exact image reconstruction: the quantity and the resolutions of the intermediate reconstructions can be freely modified. We study the transmission of the univariate functions and present the influence of data loss on the final reconstruction. More precisely, a packet-loss channel is simulated, and we present the PSNR of the final image as a function of the packet-loss probabilities and packet sizes.

BACKGROUND

From the Kolmogorov Superposition Theorem to the Kolmogorov Spline Network

In literature, most of the theoretical contributions related to the Kolmogorov superposition theorem focus on its representation, improvements through neural networks, and the computability of the monovariate functions. Hecht-Nielsen, in 1987, first drew attention on the Kolmogorov superposition theorem for neural network computation by interpreting the theorem as a feed-forward neural network with one input layer, one hidden layer, and one output layer. Unfortunately, the internal functions he proposed are highly non-smooth and the external functions cannot be expressed in a parameterized form. More precisely, the internal functions are defined using infinite series of functions, which cannot be computed. This fundamental issue led Girosi and Poggio (1989), to consider the Kolmogorov superposition theorem to be irrelevant for neural network computing. This hypothesis was rejected by Kurkova (1991, 1992), who demonstrated that the neural network could be implemented by approximating the monovariate functions. This approach relies on Sprecher's work (1965), who proposed to replace the original internal functions $\psi_{q,p}\left(x_p\right)$ by one unique function $\lambda_p\psi\left(x_p + bq\right)$ for every dimension p and layer q.

Other constructive approaches using approximation can be found in (Nees, 1993) and (Nakamura, 1993) that also features an historic of the Kolmogorov superposition theorem in neural network computing. Among the most remarkable contributions to this field, Sprecher proposed in 1996 and 1997 a complete algorithm to compute the internal and external functions. Sprecher presents a detailed algorithm to explicitly evaluate the monovariate functions that can approximate the decomposition of the multivariate functions at a given precision. Braun (2007) improved this approach by changing the definition of the internal function to ensure the continuity and the monotonicity of the inner function. Brattka (2004) has demonstrated that the continuous functions mentioned in the superposition theorem could be replaced by computable functions (functions that can be evaluated by a Turing machine), and therefore validates Sprecher's algorithm for practical implementation.

As already mentioned before, Köppen (2002, 2005) has applied Sprecher to decompose grey level images, proposing one of the few applications of the KST to image processing so far. We have also presented the application of Sprecher's algorithm to grey level images in (Leni *et al.*, 2008). Unfortunately, the lack of flexibility of this approach has been pointed out and remains a major issue for the exploration of possible applications of the Kolmogorov supersposition theorem in image processing.

Igelnik and Parikh (2003) have proposed an approximating algorithm, known as the KSN. It relies on the approximation of the monovariate functions and its implementation using neural networks. The monovariate functions are interpolated by cubic splines, that are further included in a network for the approximation optimization. The spline interpolations ensure the continuity of the monovariate functions and the convergence of the algorithm.

The work presented in this chapter is built upon the results of Igelnik and aims at exploring the potential of the KSN for image processing, namely image compression and progressive transmission.

Image compression has been intensely studied for the past decades, and has led to various techniques and standards that are commonly separated into two families: lossy and lossless compression. Lossless compression approaches are well-known, widely used (Salomon, 2007), and include: the Run-length encoding, Predictive Coding, Entropy encoding, Adaptive dictionary algorithms, and Deflation. The lossy compression techniques include the reduction of the color space (Papamarkos, 2002), Chroma subsampling (Chen, 2009), and Fractal compression (Barnsley, 1993). Most of recent approaches, such as JPEG 2000 or SPIHT (Set Partitioning In Hierarchical Trees), rely on Transform coding to reduce the energy into only few coefficients. Depending on these coefficients encoding, these approaches can lead to lossy or lossless compressions. SPIHT has been proposed by Said (1996) and takes advantage of the correlation between the wavelet coefficients amongst the decomposition levels to propose efficient lossy or lossless compression. The JPEG 2000 standard (Taubman, 2001), relies on wavelet decompositions, and provides lossy and lossless compression as well. In addition, extra features, amongst other advantages, can be mentioned, such as: progressive recovery of an image by pixel accuracy or resolution, superior low bit-rate performance than existing standards, and good resilience to transmission errors.

Chee (1999) proposes to classify the methods for progressive image transmission in four different categories (nonexclusive): Successive Approximation (the precision of the coded data of the image is progressively increased), Multistage Residual Coding (the error between the original image and the reconstructed image is progressively minimized), Transmission-Sequence-based Coding (the data are separated into different transmission groups and the order is rearranged before transmission), and Hierarchical coding (the image is separated and transmitted into different hierarchical levels). Most of recent works propose Successive Approximation approaches, based on wavelet decomposition (such as in (Chang, 2008)): bits of encoded wavelet coefficients are transmitted progressively. This approach is also often combined with a Hierarchical coding as in (Garcia, 2005), or such as for SPIHT (including error correction (Hwang, 1999)) and JPEG 2000.

The techniques for progressive image progressive transmission frequently include compression and aim at providing a progressive bitrate transmission while reconstructing the image with the best accuracy, whereas our method focuses on the spatial progressivity of the image reconstruction. Our approach shares the advantage of multiscale (hierarchical) coders, *i.e.*, in non homogenous display environments, the image can be accessed at different resolutions; and Multistage Residual Coding, *i.e.*, the final image is exactly reconstructed. More generally, it is comparable to the "naïve" approach of a progressive image transmission (transmit one pixel over four, then one pixel over two and so on), except that the progressive transmission is not performed from the pixels, but from the external univariate functions, which implies a fundamentally different behavior.

The Kolmogorov Spline Network

The Kolmogorov Spline Network has been introduced by Igelnik and Parikh (2003). The algorithm has two main steps to construct the inner and outer univariate functions. The first step of the construction of the internal functions is the definition of a disjoint tilage over the definition space $[0,1]^d$ of the multivariate function *f*. To entirely cover the space, several tilage layers are generated by constant translation of the first layer, as illustrated in Figure 2. For a given tilage layer *n*, the internal functions ψ_{ni} are generated, one per dimension, independently of the function *f*. The functions ψ_{ni} are step functions, with randomly generated step heights, such as the function is increasing. To ensure the continuity of the inner functions ψ_{ni}, their values are interpolated by cubic splines. The convex combination of the internal functions ψ_{ni} with real values λ_i corresponds to the functions $\xi_n(x)$, and is the argument of the external functions g_n. Finally, the external functions are constructed, using the *a priori* known values of the multivariate function at the centres of the hypercubes of the disjoint tilage. By construction, one couple of internal and external functions is associated with each tilage layer. We refer to the set constituted by all parameters defining the internal and external monovariate functions as a network. To optimize the network construction, each layer is weighted by coefficients a_n and summed to approximate the multivariate function *f*. Figure 1 presents an overview of a network constituted of five tilage layers. The tilage is then constituted of hypercubes H_n (the tiles) obtained by the Cartesian product of the intervals $I_n\left(j\right)$, defined as follows:

$$\forall n \in \left[\!\left[1, N\right]\!\right], j \geq -1, I_n\left(j\right) = \left[\left(n-1\right)\delta + \left(N+1\right)j\delta, \left(n-1\right)\delta + \left(N+1\right)j\delta + N\delta\right], \tag{4}$$

where δ is the distance between two intervals I of length $N\delta$, such that the oscillation of function *f* is smaller than $\frac{1}{N}$ on each hypercube *H*. Since we focus on the study of bivariate functions, the hypercubes *H* are squares. The index *j* identifies the position of an interval along one dimension, the first interval being obtained for $j = 0$ or $j = -1$, depending on the current layer *n*. Values of the index *j* are defined such that the previously generated intervals $I_n\left(j\right)$ intersect the interval [0,1], as illustrated in Figure 2(a). Considering this condition, the equation (4)becomes:

$$\forall n \in \left[\!\left[1, N\right]\!\right], \left(n-1\right)\delta + \left(N+1\right)N\delta + N\delta \geq 0 \Leftrightarrow j \geq \frac{1-n-N}{N+1} \geq -1. \tag{5}$$

According to the construction, the size of the tiles is constant for all the layers, but the tilage is translated for each layer, thus ensuring that any point in [0,1] is located on at least one interval I_n for $N-1$ layers; see Figure 2(b).

Figure 2. Kolmogorov spline network: construction of the tilages. (a) Cartesian product of intervals to define a disjoint tilage of hypercubes H. (b) Superposition of translated disjoint tilages

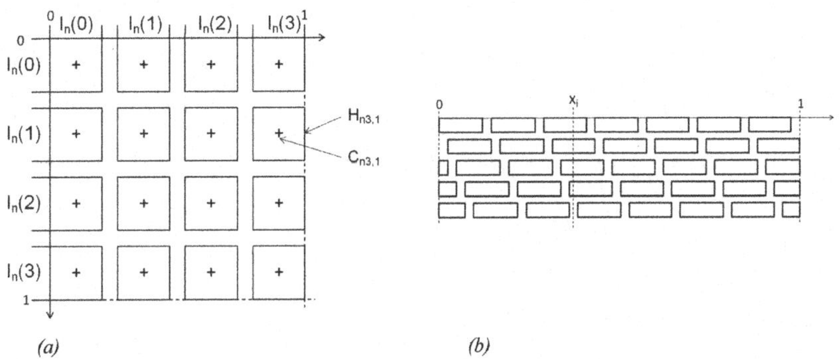

A. Construction of the Internal Function ψ_{ni}

At every interval $I_n(j)$, the internal functions ψ_{ni} have constant values y_{nij}, called plateaus, as illustrated on Figure 3(a). The intervals *I* are disjoint, so are the plateaus. To construct a continuous internal function, sampling points are computed using existing values of plateaus y_{nij} and random values between two consecutive plateaus. The sampling points are then interpolated by a cubic spline. Specifically, each function ψ_{ni} is defined as follows:

- Generate a set of *j* distinct numbers y_{nij}, between Δ and $1-\Delta$, $0<\Delta<1$, such that the oscillation amplitude of the interpolating cubic spline of ψ on the interval δ is lower than Δ.
- The index *j* is detailed in equation (4). $j \in \mathbb{Z}, j \geq -1$.
- The real numbers y_{nij} are sorted, *i.e.*: $y_{nij} < y_{nij+1}$. The image of the interval $I_n\left(j\right)$ by function ψ is y_{nij}.

Figure 3. KSN: construction of the internal functions ψ (a) Random construction of the plateaus (b) Regular sampling

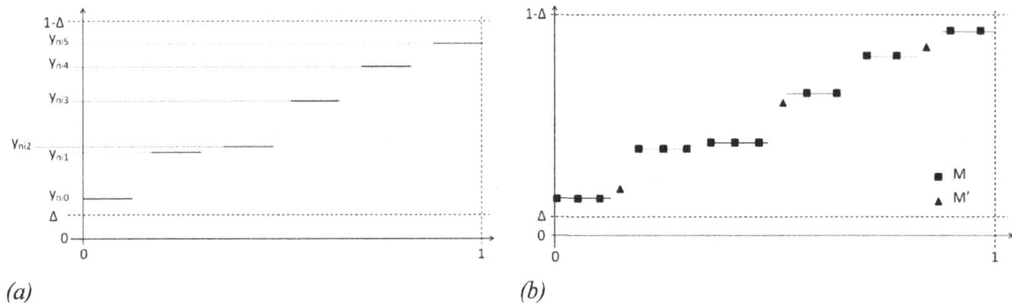

Figure 4. Example of internal function sampled by 1000 points after spline interpolation

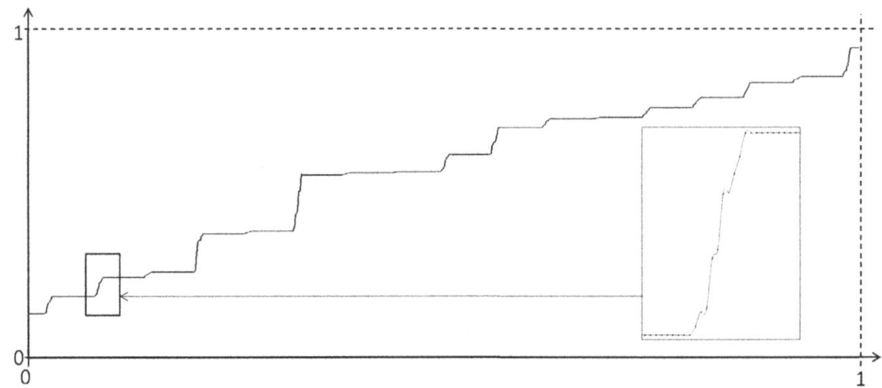

Then, ψ is sampled along regularly spaced points. We obtain two sets of points, namely, the points M located on plateaus over intervals $I_n(j)$, and the points M' located between two consecutive intervals $I_n(j)$ and $I_n(j+1)$, which are randomly chosen in the interval $]y_{nij}, y_{nij+1}[$, as illustrated in Figure 3(b). These sampling points are then interpolated by a cubic spline to obtain a continuous and increasing function, as illustrated in Figure 4. One algorithm of cubic spline interpolation can be found in (Moon, 2001). The choice of a cubic spline is to ensure the convergence of the algorithm, as demonstrated in (Igelnik, 2003). The coordinates of points M' are optimized during network construction using a stochastic approach (Igelnik, 2003). The optimization of these points is a key aspect because it decreases the reconstruction error of the network and ensures the convergence of the approximation to the function *f*.

Once the functions ψ_{ni} are constructed, the argument of external function g_n, *i.e.* the value of the function ξ_n, can be evaluated. On hypercubes $H_{nj_1,\cdots,nj_d}$, the function ξ_n has constant values $p_{nj_1,\cdots,nj_d} = \sum_{i=1}^{d} \lambda_i y_{nij_i}$. Every random number y_{nij_i} generated verifies that the generated values $p_{nj_1,\cdots,nj_d}$ are all different, $\forall i \in [\![1,d]\!], \forall n \in [\![1,N]\!], \forall j \in \mathbb{Z}, j \geq -1$. The real numbers λ_i must be chosen linearly independent, strictly positive, and such that $\sum_{i=1}^{d} \lambda_i \leq 1$. The coordinate vector of the centre of the hypercube $H_{nj_1,\cdots,nj_d}$ is denoted $C_{nj_1,\cdots,nj_d}$.

B. Construction of the External Functions g_n

One external function g_n is defined per tilage layer of index *n*. First, a set of points is computed: the abscissas of each point are the images of the associated function ξ_n, *i.e.*, real values $p_{nj_1,\cdots,nj_d}$ that uniquely identify a hypercube $H_{nj_1,\cdots,nj_d}$ from the tilage layer. The ordinates of each point are the images of the multivariate function *f* for the centres of the hypercubes $C_{nj_1,\cdots,nj_d}$. Then, to obtain a continuous function, these points are connected with nine-degree splines and straight lines to define a continuous function g_n. Specifically, each function g_n is constructed as follows:

- For every real number $t = p_{nj_1,\cdots,nj_d}$, $g_n(t)$ is equal to the Nth of the value of the function *f* at the centre of the hypercube $H_{nj_1,\cdots,nj_d}$: $g_n\left(p_{nj_1,\cdots,nj_d}\right) = \frac{1}{N} f\left(C_{nj_1,\cdots,nj_d}\right)$, denoted as points $A_k = \left(t, g_n(t)\right), k \in \mathbb{N}$.
- The definition interval of function g_n is extended to all $t \in [0,1]$ as follows:
    - Two points B_k and B_k' are randomly placed in A_k neighbourhoods, such that $t_{B_k} < t_{A_k} < t_{B_k'}$. The placement of points B_k and B_k' in the neighbourhood of A_k must preserve the order of points: $\cdots, B_{k-1}', B_k, A_k, B_k', B_{k+1}, \cdots$; *i.e.*, the distance between B_k and A_k or A_k and B_k' must be smaller than half of the length between two consecutive points A_k and A_{k+1}.

- Points $B_k^{'}$ and B_{k+1} are connected with a line of slope r.
- Points A_k and $B_k^{'}$ are connected with a nine degree spline, noted s, such that: $s\left(t_{A_k}\right) = g_n\left(t_{A_k}\right)$, $s\left(t_{B_k^{'}}\right) = r$, $s^{(2)}\left(t_{B_k^{'}}\right) = s^{(3)}\left(t_{B_k^{'}}\right) = s^{(4)}\left(t_{B_k^{'}}\right) = 0$.
- Points B_k and A_k are connected with a similar nine-degree spline. The connection conditions at points A_k of both nine degree splines yield the remaining conditions.

This construction ensures the functions continuity and the convergence of the approximation to *f* as shown in (Igelnik, 2003). Figure 5 illustrates this construction.

The complex shape of the external function is related to the global sweeping scheme of the image Sprecher and Draghici (2002) have demonstrated that sweeping curves can be defined as a mapping of the functions g_n. The linear combination of the internal functions associates a unique real value with every couple from $[0,1]^d$. Sorting these values defines a path through the tiles of a layer, which corresponds to a sweeping curve. Figure 6(a) illustrates an example of such a curve: the pixels are swept without any neighbourhood property conservation.

As a remark, the question of the local control of the sweeping remains open. This could provide information repartition between internal and external functions. The preferential sweeping direction can be controlled through constants λ_1 and λ_2 used in equation 3. Figure 6 presents two scanning functions using different constants λ_1 and λ_2; (b) is obtained with $\lambda_1 \simeq 0.00004$ and $\lambda_2 = 0.95$, and (c) is obtained with $\lambda_1 \simeq 0.95$ and $\lambda_2 = 0.00004$. Note that this tends toward classical column-per-column (line-per-line, respectively) image sweeping.

C. Network Stochastic Construction

One can remark that between two consecutive tiles, the monovariate function values are not generated according to the multivariate function *f*. To decrease the approximation error of the constructed network,

Figure 5. Construction of the external functions g_n. Points B, A and B' are connected by a nine degree spline. Points B' and B are connected by straight lines

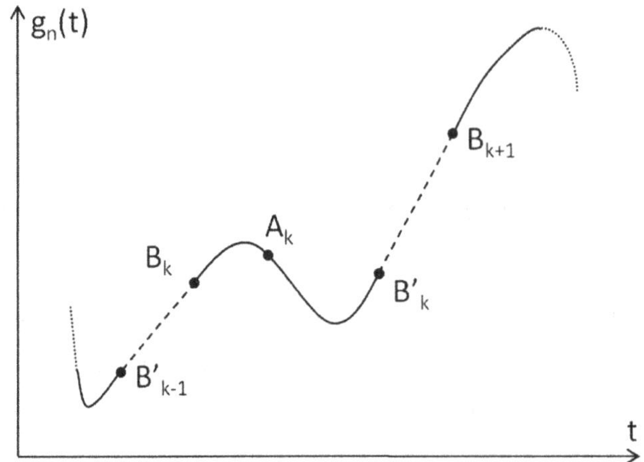

several optimizations are necessary. The construction of the univariate functions requires some parameters to be optimized using a stochastic method known as ensemble approach, see Igelnik (1999). This includes the weights a_n associated with each layer and the placement of the sampling points M' located between two consecutive intervals of the internal functions. To optimize the network, three sets of points are used, namely, a training set D_T, a generalization set D_G, and a validation set D_V. N layers are successively built. To add a new layer, K candidate layers are generated with the same plateaus y_{nij}, which yields to K new candidate networks. The difference between two candidate layers is the set of the randomly chosen points M' located between consecutive intervals. We keep the layer from the network with the smallest mean squared error that is evaluated using the generalization set D_G. The weights a_n are obtained by minimizing the difference between the approximation given by the network and the values of function f at points of the training set D_T. The algorithm is iterated until N layers are constructed. The validation error of the final network is determined using the validation set D_V, *i.e.*, by applying the approximated function to D_V. Figure 7 presents the network construction steps. To determine the coefficients a_n, the difference between f and its approximation $\tilde{f}$ must be minimized:

Figure 6. Example of sweeping curves obtained from Igelnik's approximation scheme. (a) with $\lambda_1 = 0.55$ *and* $\lambda_2 = 0.4$. *(b) with* $\lambda_1 = 0.00004$ *and* $\lambda_2 = 0.95$. *(c) with* $\lambda_1 \simeq 0.95$ *and* $\lambda_2 = 0.00004$

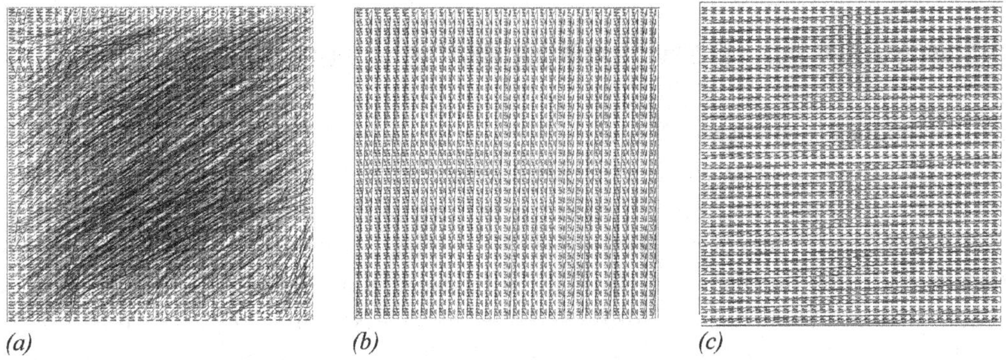

Figure 7. Network construction steps

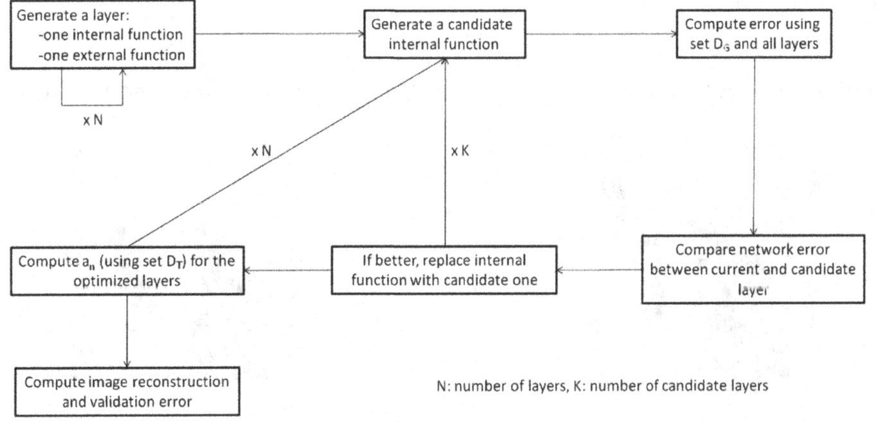

$$\left\| Q_n a_n - t \right\|, noting\ t = \begin{bmatrix} f\left(x_{1,1},\cdots,x_{d,1}\right) \\ \vdots \\ f\left(x_{1,P},\cdots,x_{d,P}\right) \end{bmatrix}, \tag{6}$$

where Q_n is a matrix of column vectors q_k, $k \in [\![0,n]\!]$, that corresponds to the approximation $\tilde{f}$ of the kth layer for the set of points $\left(\left(x_{1,1},\cdots,x_{d,1}\right),\cdots,\left(x_{1,P},\cdots,x_{d,P}\right)\right)$ of D_T:

$$Q_n = \begin{bmatrix} \left[\tilde{f}_0\left(x_{1,1},\cdots,x_{d,1}\right)\right],\cdots,\left[\tilde{f}_n\left(x_{1,1},\cdots,x_{d,1}\right)\right] \\ \vdots \\ \left[\tilde{f}_0\left(x_{1,1},\cdots,x_{d,P}\right)\right],\cdots,\left[\tilde{f}_n\left(x_{1,1},\cdots,x_{d,P}\right)\right] \end{bmatrix} \tag{7}$$

The algorithm to compute the pseudo-inverse Q_{n+} of matrix Q_n and to evaluate the solution $Q_{n+}t = a_n$ is proposed by Igelnik (1999). The coefficient a_l of the column vector $\left(a_0,\cdots,a_n\right)^T$ is the weight associated to the layer $l, l \in [\![0,n]\!]$.

KOLMOGOROV SPLINE NETWORK FOR IMAGE COMPRESSION

We present a technique to adapt the KSN construction, *i.e.* the internal and external functions, to achieve lossy image compression. The parameters that are adjusted are the size of the tiles and the number of pixels used during the learning step. Compression is performed in two different manners. A first strategy consists in reducing the number of pixels used to build the external function by increasing the tiles size. Unfortunately, using this approach, the PSNR dramatically decreases. Figure 8 presents several reconstructions obtained using between 100% and 40% of the pixels from the original image. We can observe that the reconstruction quality rapidly decreases. As a remark, our approach provides equivalent results to nearest neighbour methods, but bicubic interpolation provides better reconstruction quality, as PSNR is at least improved by 4 dB. Results show that the PSNR of the reconstructed image is below 30dB with only a 40% compression, which means that this decomposition cannot be directly used for satisfying compression rates.

Figure 8. Image reconstruction, using 80% (a), and 40% (b) of the original image pixels

(a)

(b)

To improve this approach, we combine KSN with wavelets: the network approximation can be improved by adjusting the global sweeping orientation of the images, and the reconstruction is more accurate when working on spare images. The original image is first represented in the wavelet space, *i.e.*, it is represented as an approximation image and three detail images. The approximation image and the three detail images are then separately represented by distinct Kolmogorov Spline Networks.

Once all the networks are built, the external functions associated with detail images are simplified by removing the pixels used in the learning step. Our goal is to decompose the detail images using small tiles, and, taking advantage of the limited contrast, to replace the values in the external functions to reduce the number of pixels from the original image required for the construction of the external functions as if larger tiles were used. Additionally, the preferential direction of sweeping is adjusted for the vertical, horizontal, and diagonal details by modifying the coefficients λ_1 and λ_2.

This approach uses a fixed tilage size and is applied during the construction of the external functions. The first step of this construction is the generation of points corresponding to the pixels located at the centre of the hypercubes. The simplification is then applied to decrease the number of pixels retained for the network construction. The mean value of each external function is computed, and the points located at a distance from the mean value smaller than the standard deviation are replaced by the mean value of the external function. In other words, the mean value μ_n and the standard deviation σ_n of the external function are computed, and every value such that $K \in \mathbb{N}^*, | g_n - \mu_n | < \frac{\sigma_n}{K}$ is replaced by μ_n. The constant K can be adjusted: the smaller, the more points are simplified. With this method, the pixels located at the centres of the hypercubes and used to compute these points are no longer required after simplification. Figure 9 illustrates such a simplification: (a) presents the original external function, and (b) the external function after simplification. Specifically, a small tile size is utilized to decompose a detail image, and is reduced up to only 15% of pixels after external function simplification. In terms of transmission, a compression is realized, since the quantity of pixels needed to reconstruct the original image is decreased.

To characterize the compression of our approach, we represent the PSNR of the reconstructed image as a function of the number of pixels of the original image that are contained in the network by training the network with a 384x384 pixel image to reconstruct a 384x384 pixels image. Figure 12 illustrates both compression approaches, using the combination of KST decomposition with wavelets, and shows that the simplification of the external functions provides better results than using larger tiles to decrease the number of pixels used for construction. Figure 13 presents the compression rate and the associated reconstruction PSNR for five images. The PSNR of the reconstructed images is higher at above 40dB for an up to 65% compression rate for these images. Figure 14 presents the results obtained on these five images with two external function simplifications (*i.e.*, at high and low compression rates). We observe that the reconstruction is not visibly altered. The irregular repartition of the measures is due to the external function simplifications; the simplification of the external functions obtained is image-dependent, so is the compression ratio.

The behavior of our compression scheme is different from other compression approaches. In our approach, the image is decomposed using wavelets, and the wavelet coefficients are decomposed using univariate functions that are simplified. After this simplification, only few wavelet coefficients are retained to be able to later build the KSN to approximate the original wavelet decomposition. In other

Figure 9. External function simplification. (a) Original function. (b) External function after simplification

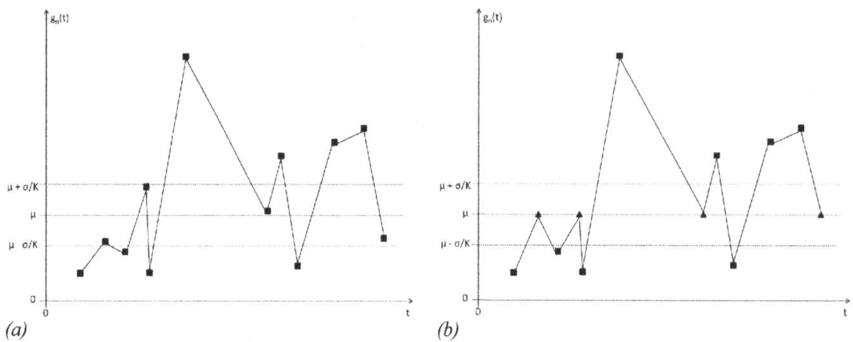

Figure 10. JPEG 2000 overview, including additional KSN decomposition

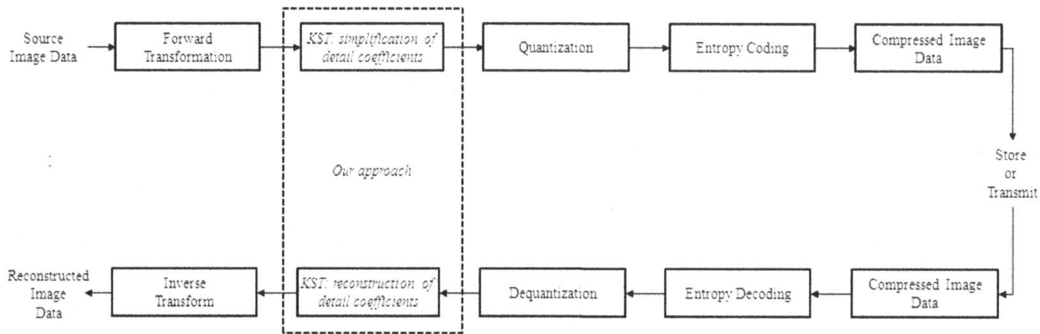

Figure 11.(a) Detail image after simplification (b) 1D representation (c) "Defragmented" detail image

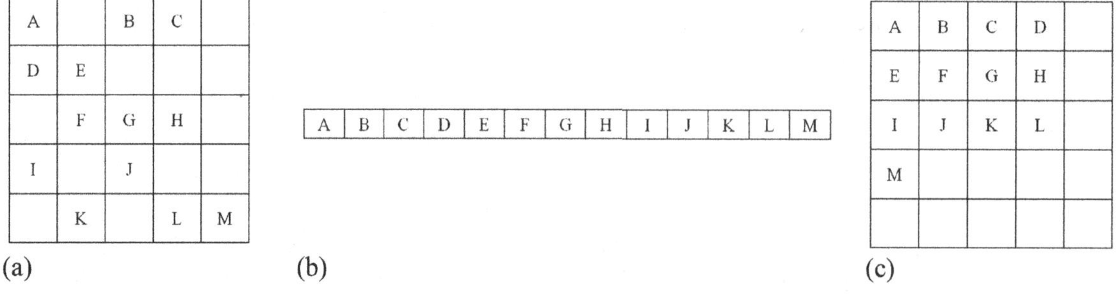

words, the "compressed" image contains holes (see Figure 11(a)), as a result of univariate function simplifications.

To compare this approach to modern image compression approaches, we integrate this method into the JPEG 2000 compression scheme. JPEG 2000 is one of the most widely used and recognized compression standards, and relies on wavelet decomposition, which makes it adequate to be combined with

Figure 12. PSNR of image reconstruction using wavelets as a function of the number of pixels utilized to define external functions

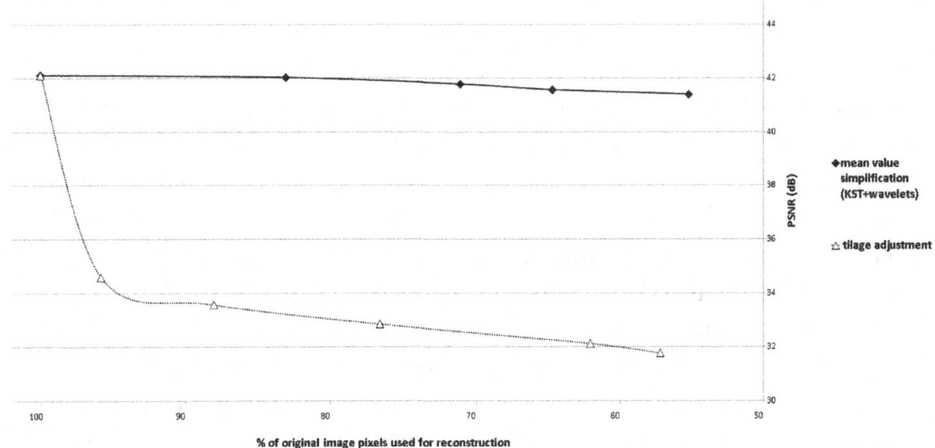

Figure 13. Evolution of the PSNR in function of the percentage of pixels used for the reconstruction

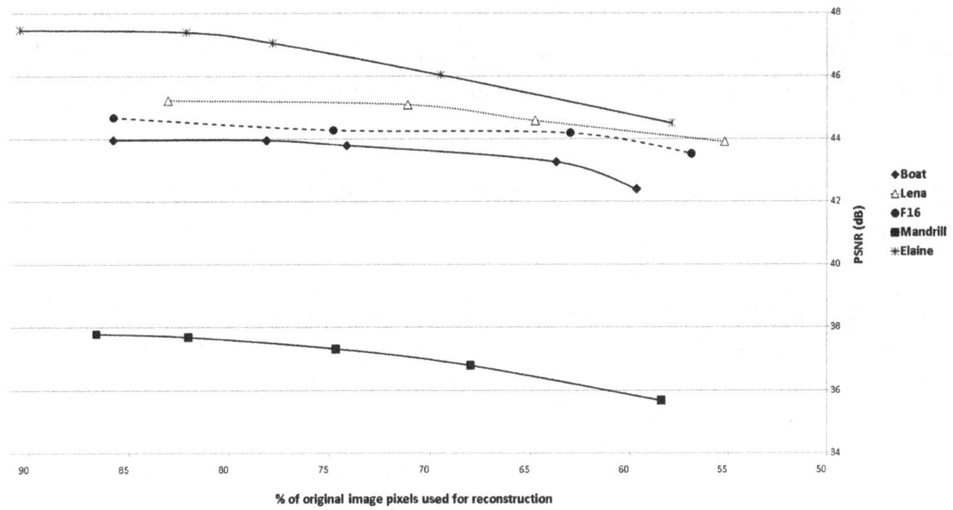

Figure 14. Reconstructions of Lena (a), F16 (b), Boat (c), Elaine (d), and mandrill (e), using about 55% of the original image pixels

(a) (b) (c) (d) (e)

our approach. We briefly describe several steps in the JPEG 2000 encoding and decoding algorithm, in depth explanations can be found in (Taubman, 2001) and (Skodras, 2001). The first step is the decomposition of the image into components, and optionally into tiles. Then, the wavelet transform is applied. Two wavelet families are implemented: Le Gall 5-3 for reversible transform (lossless compression) and Daubechies 9-7 for irreversible transform (lossy compression). The decomposition levels are subdivided into subbands of coefficients (tiles). These subbands are then quantized and converted into code blocks before being entropy encoded into bit planes. Lastly, the code stream is generated and a header is computed to describe the original image and the various decomposition and coding parameters that have been used.

We insert the KSN compression approach as a new step, after the wavelet transform and before the subdivision of wavelet coefficients for quantization, as illustrated on Figure 10.

As previously mentioned, the number of coefficients retained to build the KSN network after the univariate function simplifications is decreased. The remaining coefficients can be re-assembled to form smaller subbands. To do so, a binary table of same size as the original image is utilized to memorize, for each position, whether a pixel has been simplified. Remaining coefficients are read line by line to obtain a 1D representation (see Figure 11(b)) and then reorganized to fill the image block per block (see Figure 11(c)). These subbands can then be imported into JPEG 2000 and processed as the result of the wavelet decomposition of a smaller image.

Table 1 presents the results of a JPEG 2000 compression of Lena with and without using our additional step. We can note that the PSNR is improved by at least 0.5 dB and up to more than 2dB. As shown in Figure 15, no visual artifacts are generated by our approach.

KOLMOGOROV SPLINE NETWORK FOR PROGRESSIVE IMAGE TRANSMISSION

We present our modifications and improvements to Igelnik and Parikh's algorithm to provide a spatial scalable scheme for progressive image transmission. The key idea here is the determination of a strategy to construct external functions at different resolutions, such that any external function at a given

Table 1. PSNR after JPEG 2000 Compression and JPEG 2000+KSN

Bitrate(bpp)	JPEG 2000-PSNR(dB)	JPEG2000+KSN-PSNR(dB)
2,7	49,7	50.2
2.5	48.5	49.7
2,2	46,9	47.9
1,7	44,5	46.3
1,3	42,2	44.9

Figure 15. Lena reconstruction after JPEG 2000+KSN compression at 1.3bpp

resolution can be built from the external functions at lower resolutions. In the original algorithm, all of the layers are superposed and the final univariate functions are composed to reconstruct the original image. Every layer provides a partial reconstruction of the final image using only its associated univariate functions. This corresponds to an approximation of the image slightly translated and seen through a disjoint tilage. We modify the generation of the tilage and the construction of both the inner and outer functions using different tilage densities, one for every layer, in order to progressively reconstruct the final univariate functions.

The first step is the generation of the highest density tilage, *i.e.* one tile per pixel, and its associated external function. Intermediate layers, corresponding to lower resolutions, are then generated using larger tiles, such that the external functions obtained are sub-samples of the initial external function generated for the image at the highest resolution. To build the sub-samples of the initial external functions, the internal functions associated to the intermediate layers have to be constructed using the values of the plateaus generated for the internal functions associated to the highest density tilage. This realizes the sub-sampling of the internal functions and ensures that the real value associated to a position of the 2D space is the same for all layers. Then, transmitting the external functions associated to each intermediate layer allows for the progressive reconstruction of the original external function associated to the full resolution image. With each intermediate external function, partial reconstruction of the image can be computed, progressively increasing the resolution of the reconstructed image. Moreover, the quantity of data per layer can be adapted by modifying the tilage density, as well as the number of intermediate layers. Each external function adds new data to the previously transmitted external functions, which limits the quantity of data transmitted at each step. In other words, the original image can be progressively reconstructed up to its original resolution, without error, and a limited quantity of data is enough to increase the resolution between intermediate reconstructions. This approach is comparable to the "naïve" approach of a progressive image transmission where one transmits one pixel over four, then one pixel over two, and so on, except that the progressive transmission is performed from the values of the external function instead of the values of the pixels. Our algorithm is characterized by its flexibility: any number of intermediate images can be transmitted, at any resolution, and with an almost constant quantity of transmitted data to finally reconstruct the original image without any error. Moreover, using this algorithm, the original data are converted into univariate functions that are eventually transmitted. The reader should note that data of any dimensionality can be decomposed and progressively transmitted with this method.

The network is modified for progressive transmission as follows: one tilage is generated per layer n with an increasing density: the size of the tiles decreases when n increases. The internal functions are constructed such that a position in the 2D space has the same real value for any layer. Thus, transmitting the layers one after the other, the external functions are progressively constructed to finally contain all of the data required to reconstruct the original image. Figure 16 presents an overview of such a modified network.

The definition of the tilage is modified and takes into account the layer number n. The tilage is obtained by the Cartesian product of the intervals $I_n(j)$, defined as follows:

$$\forall n \in [\![1, N]\!], j \geq -1, I_n(j) = \left[(N+1)j\delta_n, (N+1)j\delta_n + N\delta_n\right]. \quad (8)$$

Figure 16. Overview of a 5-tilage layer network modified for progressive transmission. The external function is progressively reconstructed by adding points from the previously constructed external functions, and the internal functions are adjusted for the increasing number of tiles by adding the corresponding steps.

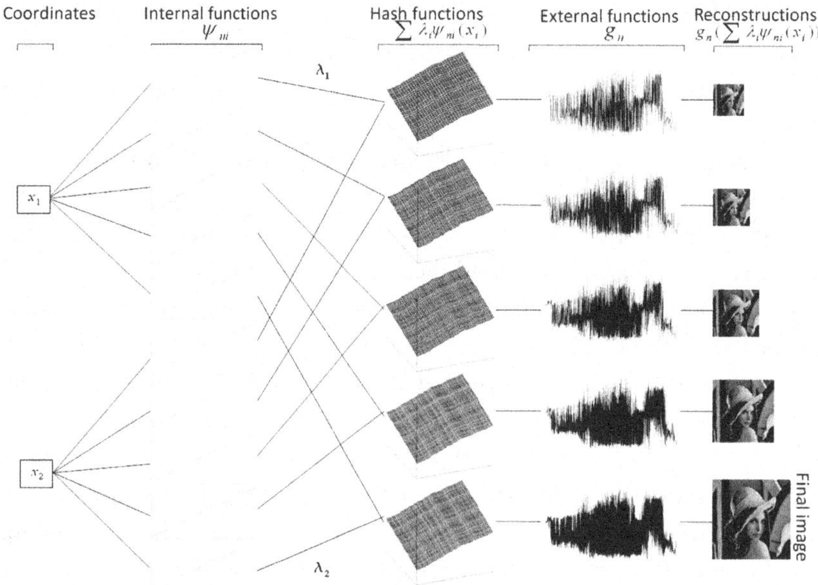

One can note that δ has been replaced by δ_n, which means that the distance between tiles changes for each layer. The term $(n-1)\delta$ corresponding to the translation between the layers is removed. Using this definition, the intervals sizes can be modified for each layer. Specifically,

$$\forall n_1, n_2 \in [\![1, N]\!], n_1 < n_2 \Rightarrow \delta_{n_1} > \delta_{n_2}, \tag{9}$$

i.e., starting from large tiles, the tilage densities will increase with the number of layers, ending with a tilage covering each pixel of the image. Figure 17 shows the superposition of the generated layers.

Figure 17. Superposition of disjoint tilages with size variation according to layer number

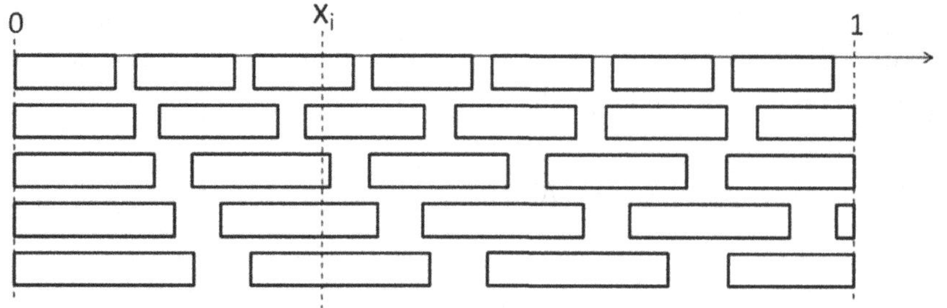

A. Construction of the Internal Functions ψ_{ni}

We detail in this section the modifications for the generation of the steps y_{nij} of the functions ψ_{ni}. With the previous modifications, the length of the plateaus of the functions ψ_{ni} will decrease as *n* increases. The internal functions associated to the latest layer *N* are first constructed using a tilage for which one tile corresponds to one pixel. The internal functions associated to the intermediate layers ($n < N$) are generated by sub-sampling the internal functions of the layer *N* as follows: to each interval $I_n(j)$, associate a real number y_{nij} that will be the image of the interval $I_n(j)$ by the function ψ_{ni}. From the layer *N*, find the index j', such that the center of the interval $I_n(j)$ belongs to the interval $I_N(j')$, which can be written as

$$\left(N+1\right)j\delta_n + \frac{\delta_n}{2} \in I_N\left(j'\right), \tag{10}$$

which implies $y_{nij} = y_{Nij'}$. Then, each function ψ_{ni} is sampled along regularly spaced points that are further interpolated by a cubic spline, as stated in the original algorithm. The function ξ_n is evaluated as in the original algorithm.

B. Construction of the External Functions g_n

Concerning the functions g_n, only the construction of the original set of points using the centres of the hypercubes is modified: the values of the external functions g_n at the hypercube centres are defined as

$$\forall i \in [\![1,d]\!], \forall n \in [\![1,N]\!], \forall j \in \mathbb{Z}, j \geq -1, \quad g_n\left(p_{nj_1,\ldots,j_d}\right) = f\left(x_{C_{nj_1,\ldots,j_d}}, y_{C_{nj_1,\ldots,j_d}}\right). \tag{11}$$

The definition interval of the function g_n is extended to all $t \in [0,1]$ as in the original algorithm. No further optimization is performed, and this concludes the construction of the network for the progressive transmission.

We detail the various parameters that can be adapted, that is, the number of intermediate reconstructions as well as their resolutions. We show various step-by-step examples of the external monovariate functions and the quality of the final reconstructed image. Considering the transmission of the network, the internal functions are randomly generated and thus, are not required to be transmitted because we can assume that the emitter and the receiver can use the same random generator. On the contrary, the points in the external functions have to be transmitted.

Figure 18 illustrates a progressive construction of the external function for a 3-layer network. For the first layer, 3 points are sent and a first external function is computed (a). With the second layer, 4 points are added (triangles) to the existing construction (circles), and the external function is updated to a new one (b). Finally, 5 points are sent for the last layer (triangles), and the final external function is computed (c). One can note that new points are added at any position, not necessarily between already transmitted points, and no points are duplicated.

Figure 18. Progressive reconstruction of the external function. The new points are represented by triangles. (a) External function reconstructed from the first layer. (b) External function reconstructed from the first and second layers. (c) External function reconstructed from the three layers.

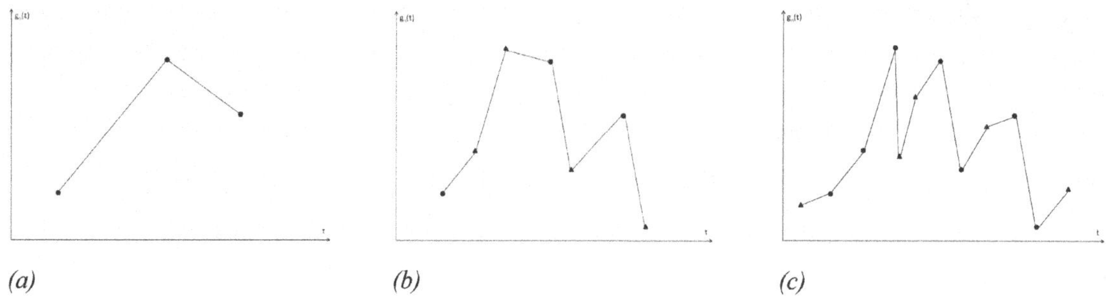

(a) (b) (c)

Figure 19. Progressive reconstruction. Left column: External function. Right column: associated reconstruction

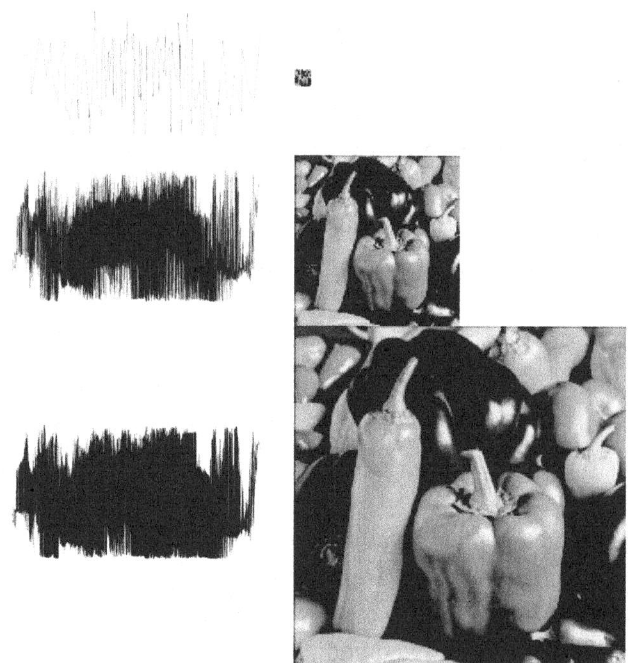

Figure 19 details three successive external functions and the reconstructed image for a 200×200 pixel image. The original image is reconstructed after all three layers have been transmitted. One can note than the number of points contained in the external function increases after each transmitted layer along with the resolution of the reconstructed image, but the total number of transmitted points is constant for any number of intermediate reconstructions/resolutions.

Figure 20. Progressive reconstruction using a 3-layer network

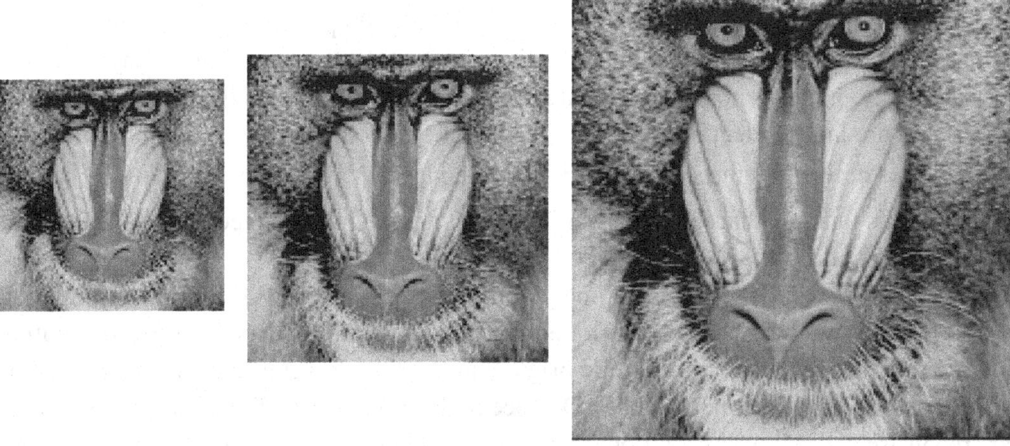

Figure 21. Progressive reconstruction using a 6-layer network

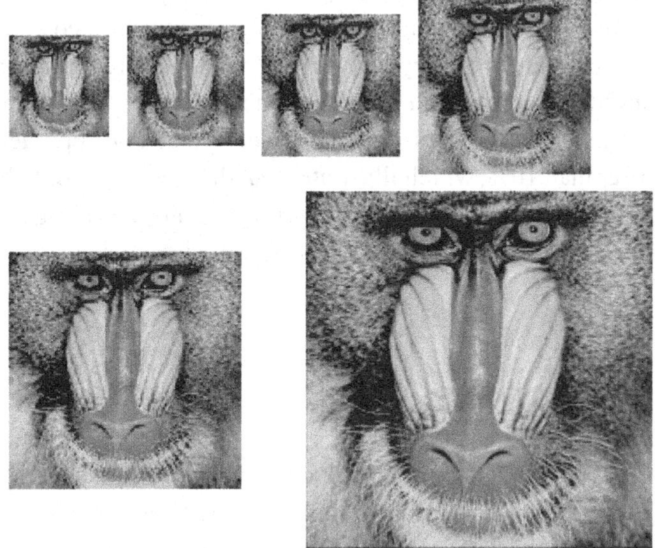

Figure 20 and Figure 21 present two examples of spatial scalability for progressive image transmission, which illustrates the flexibility of our approach. The first results in Figure 20 are computed using a 3-layer network. The first layer corresponds to the reconstruction of a 100×100 pixel image, the second layer corresponds to 133×133 pixels, and the original 200×200 is built using all three layers. The results in Figure 21 present the images reconstructed with a 6-layer network. No visible artifact is introduced by this method and the reconstruction is perfect (the mean squared error is null). The final reconstructed image is the same, but the quantity of data has been adapted from two large transmitted sets in the first example to several small and almost identical sets.

Table 2 details the influence of the number of layers on the number of points required for each external function, and the overall number of points required to be transmitted to reconstruct the image with its original resolution. The measures are realized using a 200×200 pixel image. For any number of intermediate layers of any resolution, the total quantity of data to be transmitted is always the same, and the reconstruction is optimal as no data is missing. These properties are related to the univariate function constructions and are independent of the size of the image: the total number of points contained in the external function is defined by the size of the tilage of the layer *N*. The $n, n \in [\![1, N-1]\!]$ layers define subsamplings of this function that can be transmitted one after the other to reconstruct the external function associated to the layer *N*.

Most of the approaches for progressive image transmission are based on a multiresolution decomposition, and progressively transmit the encoded coefficients obtained from the transformation, thus generating intermediate reconstructions of the original image with lower accuracy. In our approach, the progressive transmission is performed in the 1D-space of the monovariate functions, so the intermediate images are reconstructed at lower resolutions than the original image, using the already transmitted data. Therefore, the comparison with the original image or with the intermediate reconstructions from other approaches is not possible. Nevertheless, we propose a measure of the transmission robustness to allow a comparison with existing progressive transmission approaches. We simulate the transmission of the monovariate functions over a packet-loss channel: the points contained in the external functions are split into various packet sizes. Each packet is transmitted independently with a fixed probability of being lost and is replaced by noise (random values of grey level). We do not use any error correction or detection algorithm, but a 3×3 median filter is applied on the reconstructed images. Table 3 presents the obtained PSNR for various packet sizes and loss rates. We can observe that our approach is not sensitive to packet sizes or loss rates lower than 10%, which illustrates that the approach could be adapted to various kinds of transmission channels. More generally, as shown by Figure 22, the general image aspect is preserved for loss rates lower than 10%. For a 20% loss rate, the image can still be reconstructed, but with some visible artifacts.

FUTURE RESEARCH DIRECTIONS

The combination of the KSN and wavelets for image compression offers several promising research directions. We have limited our choice to the Haar wavelets, but further works could be dedicated to the study of other wavelet families and their impact on the reconstruction quality. Additionally, the simplification of the external functions remains very simple and more intelligent and efficient techniques should

Table 2. Influence of the intermediate layers on the quantity of information

number of new points in external function (×10³)										
N	40x40	44x44	50x50	57x57	67x67	80x80	100x100	133x133	200x200	total
9	1.7	1.9	2.4	2.8	3.7	4.8	6.3	8.0	8.8	40.4
7	/	/	2.6	3.1	3.8	5.1	7.0	9.5	9.3	40.4
5	/	/	/	/	4.5	5.8	7.6	11.3	11.2	40.4
3	/	/	/	/	/	/	10.2	13.5	16.7	40.4

be considered. A challenging research direction consists in studying the potential of our approach: more precisely, the integration into JPEG 2000 remains experimental and not optimal.

Another promising research perspective is related to the encryption and the transmission of multivariate functions represented by KSNs. We have focused on the proposal of a very flexible and simple algorithm for adaptable and progressive image transmission, but the nature of the decomposition itself may lead to innovative encryption or watermarking algorithms. As we have seen previously, the internal functions are required to rearrange the values of the external functions in order to reconstruct the image. One can imagine an encryption algorithm where the key would be constituted by the internal functions used as a signature. The data sent would only be the values of the external functions which would be impossible to rearrange without the appropriate internal functions. Moreover, such encryption approach could be combined with the proposed progressive transmission to provide a novel approach for progressive transmission of encrypted images. Eventually, taking advantage of the continuity of the external functions, some values could be inserted within the external functions to develop watermarking algorithms.

At last, we have modified and applied the KSN to represent images, as samples of bivariate functions, but one can think about the extension of the approach to represent iso-values, and no longer the complete function, of multivariate functions in higher dimensions, which may open new research fields for 3D mesh representation and processing.

Table 3.PSNR (dB) of the reconstructed image as a function of packet sizes (points) and packet loss probabilities

Loss prob. Packet size	**0.01**	**0.02**	**0.05**	**0.1**	**0.2**
50	28.28	28.26	27.63	27.32	25.38
100	28.27	28.12	27.52	27.24	24.53
200	28.03	27.98	27.76	27.38	23.71

Figure 22. Reconstruction after a 3×3 median filter. (a) corresponds to the best transmission channel (packet size=50pts, loss rate=0.01), whereas (b) corresponds to the worse one (packet size=200pts, loss rate=0.2)

(a)

(b)

CONCLUSION

We have proposed two adaptations of the KSN algorithm introduced by Igelnik and Parikh (2003), for image compression and progressive image transmission. Both approaches take advantage of the fundamental contribution of Igelnik and Parikh (2003), who provide an efficient technique to explicitly construct internal and external continuous functions to approximate any multivariate function. We show that the combination of KSN, wavelets, and elementary simplifications of such external functions can lead to efficient compression rates, and we illustrate the strength of our approach on various images. We also present an experimental integration of our approach into JPEG 2000 and the results provided by this new compression approach, which improves JPEG 2000 compression even at low bitrates. We have presented a second modification of the algorithm, where we adjust the size of the tilages used in the construction of the internal functions to propose a simple and flexible algorithm for progressive image transmission. We illustrate the robustness to packet-loss, and we show that our approach preserves the image integrity even with high rates of packet losses.

The originality of our work lies in the fact that the processing (simplification, transmission, etc) is now performed on the values of the external functions or the lengths of the plateaus of the internal functions, which is a fundamental difference with other well known approaches using basis functions or local pixel neighbourhoods, for example. As illustrated previously, the way the image is swept using this technique is fundamentally different from classical line per line scanning, which implies the loss of local neighbourhood when spanning the external functions. Both approaches belong to the very few works using Kolmogorov superposition theorem and, most importantly, applying it to image or signal processing, such as (Lagunas *et al.*, 1993), (Köppen, 2002), and (Köppen & Yoshida, 2005). Our approach clearly illustrates that, accordingly to Kurkova (1991), Kolmogorov superposition theorem is definitely relevant, applicable, and proposes several promising research directions, such as the extension of KSN to 3D mesh processing, image encryption, or watermarking.

REFERENCES

Barnsley, M. F., Hurd, L. P., & Anson, L. F. (1993). *Fractal image compression*. AK Peters Massachusetts.

Brattka, V. (2004). *Du 13-ième problème de Hibert à la théorie des réseaux de neurones: aspects constructifs du théorème de superposition de Kolmogorov*. Paris, France: Editions Belin.

Braun, J., & Griebel, M. (2007). On a constructive proof of Kolmogorov's superposition theorem. *Constructive Approximation, 30*(3), 653–675. doi:10.1007/s00365-009-9054-2

Chang, C.-C., Li, Y.-C., & Lin, C.-H. (2008). A novel method for progressive image transmission using block wavelets. *International Journal of Electronics and Communication, 62*(2), 159–162. doi:10.1016/j.aeue.2007.03.008

Chee, Y.-K. (1999). Survey of progressive image transmission methods. *International Journal of Imaging Systems and Technology, 10*(1), 3–19. doi:10.1002/(SICI)1098-1098(1999)10:1<3::AID-IMA2>3.0.CO;2-E

Chen, H., Sun, M., & Steinbach, E. (2009). Compression of Bayer-pattern video sequences using adjusted chroma subsampling. *IEEE Transactions on Circuits and Systems for Video Technology*, *19*(12), 1891–1896. doi:10.1109/TCSVT.2009.2031370

Garcia, J. A., Rodriguez-Sanchez, R., & Fdez-Valdivia, J. (2005). Emergence of a region-based approach to image transmission. *Optical Engineering (Redondo Beach, Calif.)*, *44*(6). doi:10.1117/1.1928268

Girosi, F., & Poggio, T. (1989). Representation properties of networks: Kolmogorov's Theorem is irrelevant. *Neural Computation*, *1*(4), 465–469. doi:10.1162/neco.1989.1.4.465

Hecht-Nielsen, R. (1987). Kolmogorov's mapping neural network existence theorem. *Proceedings of the IEEE International Conference on Neural Networks,* (pp. 11-13). New York.

Hwang, W.-J., Hwang, W.-L., & Lu, Y.-C. (1999). Layered image transmission based on embedded zero-tree wavelet coding. *Optical Engineering (Redondo Beach, Calif.)*, *38*(8), 1326–1334. doi:10.1117/1.602174

Igelnik, B., Pao, Y.-H., & LeClair, S. R. (1999). The ensemble approach to neural-network learning and generalization. *IEEE Transactions on Neural Networks*, *10*(1), 19–30. doi:10.1109/72.737490

Igelnik, B., & Parikh, N. (2003). Kolmogorov's spline network. *IEEE Transactions on Neural Networks*, *14*(4), 725–733. doi:10.1109/TNN.2003.813830

Igelnik, B., Tabib-Azar, M., & LeClair, S. R. (2001). A net with complex weights. *IEEE Transactions on Neural Networks*, *12*(2), 236–249. doi:10.1109/72.914521

(2009). Kolmogorov's spline complex network and adaptative dynamic modeling of data. InIgelnik, B., & Nitta, T. (Eds.), *Complex-valued neural networks: Utilizing high dimensional parameters* (pp. 56–78). Hershey, PA: Information Science Reference Publishing.

Köppen, M. (2002). *On the training of a Kolmogorov network.* (LNCS 2415), (pp. 140-145).

Köppen, M., & Yoshida, K. (2005). Universal representation of image functions by the Sprecher construction. *Soft Computing as Transdisciplinary Science and Technology*, *29*, 202–210. doi:10.1007/3-540-32391-0_28

Kurkova, V. (1991). Kolmogorov's theorem is relevant. *Neural Computation*, *3*, 617–622. doi:10.1162/neco.1991.3.4.617

Kurkova, V. (1992). Kolmogorov's theorem and multilayer neural networks. *Neural Networks*, *5*, 501–506. doi:10.1016/0893-6080(92)90012-8

Lagunas, M. A., Pérez-Neira, A., Najar, M., & Pagés, A. (1993). *The Kolmogorov signal processor.* (LNCS 686), (pp. 494-512).

Leni, P.-E., Fougerolle, Y. D., & Truchetet, F. (2008), Kolmogorov superposition theorem and its application to multivariate function decompositions and image representation. In *Proceedings of IEEE Conference on Signal-Image Technology & Internet-Based System* (pp. 344–351). IEEE Computer Society Washington, DC, USA.

Leni, P.-E., Fougerolle, Y. D., & Truchetet, F. (2009b). *Kolmogorov Superposition Theorem and wavelet decomposition for image compression.* (LNCS 5807), (pp. 43-53).

Moon, B. S. (2001). An explicit solution for the cubic spline interpolation for functions of a single variable. *Applied Mathematics and Computation*, *117*, 251–255. doi:10.1016/S0096-3003(99)00178-2

Nakamura, M., Mines, R., & Kreinovich, V. (1993). Guaranteed intervals for Kolmogorov's theorem (and their possible relation to neural networks). *Interval Computations*, *3*, 183–199.

Nees, M. (1993). Approximation versions of Kolmogorov's superposition theorem, proved constructively. *Journal of Computational and Applied Mathematics*, *54*, 239–250. doi:10.1016/0377-0427(94)90179-1

Papamarkos, N., Atsalakis, A. E., & Strouthopoulos, C. P. (2002). Adaptive color reduction. *IEEE Transactions on Systems, Man, and Cybernetics*, *32*(1), 44–56. doi:10.1109/3477.979959

Said, A., & Pearlman, W. A. (1996). A new fast and efficient image codec based on set partitioning in hierarchical trees. *IEEE Transactions on Circuits and Systems for Video Technology*, *6*(3), 243–251. doi:10.1109/76.499834

Salomon, D. (2007). *Data compression: The complete reference*. New York, NY: Springer-Verlag.

Skodras, A., Christopoulos, C., & Ebrahimi, T. (2001). The JPEG 2000 still image compression standard. *IEEE Signal Processing Magazine*, *18*(5), 36–58. doi:10.1109/79.952804

Sprecher, D. A. (1965). On the structure of continuous functions of several variables. *Transactions of the American Mathematical Society*, *115*(3), 340–355. doi:10.1090/S0002-9947-1965-0210852-X

Sprecher, D. A. (1996). A numerical implementation of Kolmogorov's superpositions. *Neural Networks*, *9*(5), 765–772. doi:10.1016/0893-6080(95)00081-X

Sprecher, D. A. (1997). A numerical implementation of Kolmogorov's superpositions II. *Neural Networks*, *10*(3), 447–457. doi:10.1016/S0893-6080(96)00073-1

Sprecher, D. A., & Draghici, S. (2002). Space-filling curves and Kolmogorov superposition-based neural networks. *Neural Networks*, *15*(1), 57–67. doi:10.1016/S0893-6080(01)00107-1

Taubman, D., & Marcellin, M. (2001). JPEG2000. In *Image compression fundamentals, standards and practice*. Kluwer Academic Publishers.

ADDITIONAL READING

Adams, M. D. (2001). *The JPEG-2000 Still Image Compression Standard*. University of British Columbia.

Bodyanskiy, Y., Kolodyazhniy, V., & Otto, P. (2005). Neuro-Fuzzy Kolmogorov's Network for Time Series Prediction and Pattern Classification. *Lecture Notes in Computer Science*, *3698*, 191–202. doi:10.1007/11551263_16

Cheng, H., & Li, X. (1996), On the application of image decomposition to image compression and encryption, *in proceedings of Communications and Multimedia Security II, IFIP TC6/TC11 Second Joint Working Conference on Communications and Multimedia Security*, Vol. 96, 116-128.

Coppejans, M. (2003). On Kolmogorov's representation of functions of several variables by functions of one variable. *Journal of Econometrics*, *123*, 1–31. doi:10.1016/j.jeconom.2003.10.026

Ismailov, V. E. (2008). On the representation by linear superpositions. *Journal of Approximation Theory, 151*(2), 113–125. doi:10.1016/j.jat.2007.09.003

Kolodyazhniy, V., & Bodyanskiy, Y. (2004). Fuzzy Kolmogorov's Network. *Lecture Notes in Computer Science*, 764–771. doi:10.1007/978-3-540-30133-2_100

Lamarque, C. H., & Robert, F. (1996). Image analysis using space-filling curves and 1D wavelet bases. *Pattern Recognition, 29*(8), 1309–1322. doi:10.1016/0031-3203(95)00157-3

Liu, Y., Wang, Y., Zhang, B. F., & Wu, G. F. (2004),Ensemble algorithm of neural networks and its application, *in Proceedings of 2004 International Conference on Machine Learning and Cybernetics*, Vol. 6.

Ozturk, I., & Sogukpinar, I. (2004), Analysis and Comparison of Image Encryption Algorithms, *in proceedings of ICIT 2004: International Conference on Information Technology*, 38-42.

Pednault, E. (2006), Transform regression and the Kolmogorov superposition theorem, *Proceedings of the Sixth SIAM International Conference on Data Mining*, Society for Industrial Mathematics, 35—46.

Perez-Freire, L., Comesana, P., Troncoso-Pastoriza, J. R., & Perez-Gonzalez, F. (2006). Watermarking security: a survey. *Lecture Notes in Computer Science, 4300*, 41–73. doi:10.1007/11926214_2

Vecci, L., Piazza, F., & Uncini, A. (1998). Learning and approximation capabilities of adaptive spline activation function neural networks. *Neural Networks, 11*, 259–270. doi:10.1016/S0893-6080(97)00118-4

Chapter 3
Intelligent Information Description and Recognition in Biomedical Image Databases

Khalifa Djemal
University of Evry Val d'Essonne, France

Hichem Maaref
University of Evry Val d'Essonne, France

ABSTRACT

There is a significant increase in the use of biomedical images in clinical medicine, disease research, and education. While the literature lists several successful methods that were developed and implemented for content-based image retrieval and recognition, they have been unable to make significant inroads in biomedical image recognition domain. The use of computer-aided diagnosis has been increasing. It is based on descriptors extraction and classification approaches. This interest is due to the need for specialized methods, which are specific to each biomedical image type, and also due to the lack of advances in image recognition systems. In this chapter, the authors present intelligent information description techniques and the most used classification methods in an image retrieval and recognition system. A multicriteria classification method applied for sickle cells disease image databases is given. The recognition performance system is illustrated and discussed.

INTRODUCTION

To understand the influence of the images database on the description method and the appropriate classification tool, it is more convenient to subdivide the image databases into two categories. The first category consists of image databases usually heterogeneous. In this context, the objective of images

DOI: 10.4018/978-1-60960-551-3.ch003

recognition system is to assist the user to intelligently search in images database a particular subject adapting to the subjective needs of each user. The system seeks to be as flexible as possible, for example, offering the user to refine his request for a more precise result. The second category concerns specific image databases. In this context, the images are most often a uniform semantic content. The concerned applications are generally professional. To index these image databases, the user must integrate more information defined by the expert to develop a specific algorithm. The objective is to optimize system efficiency and its ability to respond as well as the expert. Image retrieval in such databases is a specific problem of image recognition in biomedical image database. This categorization is taken into account when developing any content image retrieval system. Indeed, to obtain satisfactory results, the choice or development of new description methods must be appropriate for the considered type of images database. This is due simply to the great difficulty in obtaining a universal description algorithm.

Biomedical images also play a growing role, often central in many aspects of biomedical research, particularly in the field of genomics and biotechnology for health, but also in pharmaceutical research. These biomedical images provide anatomical information, functional, and even physical tissues and organs with spatial and temporal resolutions on the increase. Quantitative analysis of these data provides an unparalleled source of information for the development and testing of new drugs and new therapeutic approaches. Finally, better use of biomedical images absolutely requires the development of new methods for analyzing such images. Joint approaches to description, analysis, and classification algorithms appear to be perfectly suited to address this problem description and content image retrieval in large image databases.

Image recognition systems require two essential steps: the images description and their classification. The choice of descriptors is mainly due to their capacity to describe images and the combination made by the fusion of this set allows to achieving a better description. On the classification, the kernel based classifiers such as RBF and SVM, and multicriteria approach are often chosen. This choice is justified by the qualities they offer in terms of speed, precision and response time.

The study of content based image recognition has led us to experiment different description techniques and methods of classification. The objective is to evaluate these techniques while studying the influence of selected descriptors and their contribution in terms of image recognition efficiency. To this end, several tests were performed by using several samples of images. In this chapter, the results are presented and discussed in relation with the used images database, the selected descriptors and classification techniques. The different sections of this chapter recall and present the importance and the influence of the description and classification in image content recognition system. Indeed, in section 3 different description methods and two classification approaches are presented and discussed. We illustrate the principle and obtained results of these methods on sickle cells disease application in sections 4 and 5.

RELATED WORKS

The image recognition system consists of extracting from a database all the similar images to a request image chosen by the user. Indeed, the system has attracted research interest in recent years. Principal difficulties consist on the capacity to extract from the image the visual characteristics, the robustness to geometrical deformations and the quantification of similarity concept between images. Indexation and recognition are given from classification methods accomplished on image descriptors.

We find several choices of active descriptors from the low level to high level: shape, geometry, symbolic features, etc. The basic goal in content-based image retrieval and recognition is to bridge the gap from the low-level image properties. Consequently, the users can directly access to the objects in image databases. For example, color histograms (Stricker & Swain, 1994), (Swain & Ballard, 1991), are commonly used in image description and have proven useful, however, this global characterization lacks information about how the color is distributed spatially. Several researchers have attempted to overcome this limitation by incorporating spatial information in the descriptor. (Stricker & Dimai, 1997), store the average color and the color covariance matrix within each of five fuzzy image regions. (Huang et al., 1997), store a color correlogram that encodes the spatial correlation of color-bin pairs. (Smith & Chang, 1996) store the location of each color that is present in a sufficient amount in regions computed using histogram back-projection. (Lipson et al., 1997) retrieve images based on spatial and photometric relationships within and across simple image regions. Little or no segmentation is done; the regions are derived from low-resolution images. In (Jacobs et al., 1995), authors use multiresolution wavelet decompositions to perform queries based on iconic matching. Some of these systems encode information about the spatial distribution of color features, and some perform simple automatic or manually-assisted segmentation. However, none provides the level of automatic segmentation and user control necessary to support object queries in very large image databases. Carson et al. see image retrieval ultimately as an object recognition problem and they proceed in three steps (Carson et al., 2002). Firstly, the image is segmented into regions which generally correspond to objects or parts of objects. These regions are described in ways that are meaningful to the user. The proposed system allows access to these region descriptions, either automatically or with user intervention, to retrieve desired images. In this approach the features do not encode all the important information in images and the image retrieval is obtained without classification, which can pose a problem of recognition in large image databases. (Antania et al., 2002) present a comprehensive survey on the use of pattern recognition methods which enable image and video retrieval by content where the classification methods are considered. Research efforts have led to the development of methods that provide access to image and video data. These methods have their roots in pattern recognition. The methods are used to determine the similarity in the visual information content extracted from low level features.

Many indexation and recognition systems were developed based on image content description and classification in order to perform image recognition in large databases. These systems use low level features such as the colors and orientation histograms, Fourier and wavelet transforms. In spite of these acceptable results, the classification based on a similarity distance computing is not enough robust to manage great dimensions of the extracted feature vectors. To resolve this problem, other proposed systems calculate a characteristics vector for each pixel of an image. This vector contains the components associated with the color, the texture and position descriptors, which gives a better description of the image. But the performances of the image description remain to be improved. Moreover, several works were based on the wavelet tools. The authors in (Serrano et al., 2004) have enhanced their image representation by the use of the texture features extracted by wavelet transform. A new extraction technique of rotation invariants is proposed in (Sastry et al., 2004), this method offers satisfactory results, taking into account the rotation features. For more precision and representativeness of images, a new transform called Trace transform is proposed in (Kadyrov & Petrou, 2001). This transform offers at the same time a good description of image and is invariant to rotation, translation and scaling. After the features extraction, classification is made by the means of a classifier, such as KNN classifier (Smith & Chang, 1996). But this classifier is slow considering its incapacity to manage great dimensions of feature vectors. A more effective method based on a Bayesian approach (Sclaroff & Pentland, 1995), which consists in concatenation of feature blocks, gave better results. The methods of computational intelligence (artificial neural networks (ANN), genetic algorithms, etc) were also used in the field of the image classification. Their broad use is due to the facilities which they offer to the level computing time and their performances in term of classification. Indeed, we find many works based on the ANN. The obtained results show a great capacity thanks to the speed offered by the ANN and the simplicity of their implementation (Takashi & Masafumi, 2000), (Egmont-Petersen et al., 2002). In (Djouak et al., 2007), a combination of features vectors is proposed. These vectors are obtained by a visual search based on the colors histograms, the geometrical and texture features. The rotation invariants and texture features are given using wavelet transform. In addition, the Trace transform is introduced in order to obtain more invariance. A good compromise between effectiveness and computation simplicity is obtained using RBF classification technique.

The content-based image retrieval that we have just described above has attracted the increase development. Indeed, there has been growing interest in indexing large biomedical images by content due to the advances in medical imaging and the increase development of computer aided diagnosis. Image recognition in biomedical databases is critical assets for medical diagnosis. To facilitate automatic indexing and recognition of large biomedical image databases, several methods have been developed and proposed.

(Antani et al., 2004) present the challenges in developing content-based image retrieval of biomedical images and results from our research efforts. This research focuses on developing techniques for hybrid text/image query retrieval from the survey text and image database. The obtained results show that the techniques for effective and efficient combination of features need to be developed. In the same way, (Lim & Chevallet, 2005) propose a structured framework for designing and learning vocabularies of meaningful medical terms with associated visual appearance from image samples. These VisMed terms span a new feature space to represent medical image contents. After a multi-scale detection process, a medical image is indexed as compact spatial distributions of VisMed terms. (Liu et al., 2004) present their work on volumetric pathological neuroimage retrieval under the framework of classification-driven feature selection. The main effort presented in this work concerns off-line image feature space reduction for improved image indexing feature discriminating power as well as reduced computational cost during on-line pathological neuroimage retrieval. The results show that the feature selection and feature dimension reduction remain an open problem in biomedical image recognition systems. A multi-level semantic modeling method is proposed in (Lin et al., 2006), which integrates Support Vector Machines (SVM) into hybrid Bayesian networks (HBN). SVM discretizes the continuous variables of medical image features by classifying them into finite states as middle-level semantics. Based on the HBN, the semantic model for medical image semantic retrieval can be designed at multi-level semantics. To validate their method, a model is built to achieve automatic image annotation at the content level from a small set of astrocytona MRI (magnetic resonance imaging) samples. Indeed, multi-level annotation is a promising solution to enable medical image retrieval at different semantic levels. Experiment results show that this approach is very effective to enable multi-level interpretation of astrocytona MRI scans. This study provides a novel way to bridge the gap between the high-level semantics and the low-level image features.

A software framework and database system for biomedical image related to Chinese human genetic resources was proposed and implemented based on web database technique and sevice-oriented architecture (Liguang et al., 2008). In this work, the implemented image characterization and storage are well adapted with the conceived database system. The customized imagery retrieval methods and the metadata retrieval approach were introduced. Finally, the image visualization was carried out based-on open source software development environment properly. With this implementation the authors show the usefulness for computer-assisted diagnosis system.

Image recognition for computer aided diagnosis systems as we have noted above was devised to automatically analyze biomedical images. Each research provides improvements in one or more steps of these systems which are images enhancement, pathologies detection, description and classification using different approaches. These diagnosis systems essentially aim to detect pathologies and to classify them into different categories. To improve breast cancer recognition system in mammographic image databases, we have developed previously different methods and techniques. In (Cheikhrouhou et al., 2007), authors have presented an automatic breast abnormalities recognition method for mammographic images diagnosis. To reach classification, many steps are prepared in advance. We start by filtering radiographic images by an adapted PDE using minimization of total variation in order to eliminate noise and to preserve contour (Djemal, 2005). The restored image is thereafter segmented aiming to extract all suspicious zones: microcalcification, opacity or architectural distortion. Segmentation algorithm is based on level set formulation using geometrical active contour model (Djemal et al., 2002), (Djemal et al., 2006). Then, we try to build a complete description of abnormalities. So, we extract shape and textural features for characterizing at better the behavior of malignant and benign forms. These features are used as inputs in Radial Basis Function neural network classifier. RBF output is used for making diagnosis. The obtained result provides a second opinion to radiologists and helps them in making decision. In other works, authors have focused on breast masses description (Cheikhrouhou et al., 2008), indeed, new mass description dedicated to differentiate between different mass shapes in mammography has been presented. This discrimination aims to reach a better mammography classification rate to be used by radiologists as a second opinion to make the final decision about the malignancy probability of radiographic breast images. Therefore, we have used geometrical features which focus on mass borders by discriminating circumscribed from speculated shapes. Their performance was evaluated one by one before collecting them for mammography classification into the four standard categories. For classification, we have used Support Vector Machine (SVM) with Gaussian kernel as classifier for its higher performance. In the same way we have introduced a sickle cells disease recognition system based on Fourier descriptors and neural networks RBF classifier (Djemal et al., 2005). In this work, an automatic diagnosis method on temporal sequences has been presented. Through the obtained results the performance of the presented method is discussed where the invariant problems are highlighted.

After the most recent works presentation, one differentiates two important stages in an image recognition system, the content description and the classification according to the developed descriptors. Indeed, we describe these two stages in sections 3 and 4 by itemizing some methods of description and classification. Sections 5 and 6, deal respectively with the sickle cells disease description and a multicriteria classification method. Proposed approach allows the development of an automatic diagnosis system through biomedical image databases.

Image Description

Many image indexing and recognition systems have been developed in various fields, the developed algorithms can be divided into several stages of treatment, where the two most important are: information extraction and description, and classification. Indeed, to achieve effective recognition, one must be able to extract from an image some regions of interest. The performance of detection should approach 100%

in terms of quality, where each important information is taken into account. Each region of interest is characterized by number of descriptors. There is a wide variety of description methods, some offering a comprehensive representation of objects, for example from the greyscale of the image, others taking into account the shape of regions of interest, as their size, volume, regularity of their contour, etc.

In this section, we present the two important steps which generally compose an image recognition system, the information description and classification. Knowing that, the descriptors of regions or entire image are given as input to a classification method, which provides a decision about recognition.

Information Description

The descriptors should be robust, especially invariant by dilation, translation and rotation. We associate to each object a number of characteristics calculated by these descriptors. There are different types of shape descriptors, the techniques called Global, which are the general appearance of shapes, using the area, perimeter, width, moments, etc, and these characteristics provide information on the elongation or the circularity of the object. Global descriptors such as invariant moments can also be used on the entire image, for example, indexing of heterogeneous image databases. The techniques called local provide infomations on specific parts of the shapes, such as corners or vertices (position, angles...), segments (position, length...), facets or regions (position, size, color, texture...). Other techniques can be classified into one or other of these categories, as the study of the skeleton or the contour regularity.

The different descriptors tend to respond to a fundamental problem: determine if two objects are similar, independently of their pose in the image. We consider here the invariance to translation, rotation and dilation. These invariants descriptors must satisfy certain criteria including robustness towards small changes in shape and numerical approximations, and simplicity for the calculation in real time. The extracted descriptors by the Fourier-Mellin Transform and the theory of algebraic moments are widely used in current systems of indexing and search images by content. For an image request, the reference models are sorted according to a similarity measure. The image of the database that minimizes the difference of description is chosen. We describe in this section the Hu moments, Zernike moments, Fourier descriptors and descriptors of Fourier-Mellin Transform.

Hu Moments

Hu invariants are obtained from quotients or powers of moments. A moment is a sum over all pixels of the image model by weighted polynomials related to the positions of pixels. Let $I(x,y)$ the grayscale of a pixel in the image I, we define the moment of order $(p+q)(p,q>0)$ of an image I by:

$$m_{p,q} = \int_{R^2} x^p y^q I(x,y)dxdy \tag{1}$$

Let (x_0,y_0) be the centroid coordinates of the function I and the centered image $I_T(x,y)=I(x+x_0,y+y_0)$ is invariant by translation. The central moment of order $(p+q)$ of the function I is written as follows:

$$v_{p,q} = \int_{R^2} x^p y^q I(x+x_0, y+y_0)dxdy \tag{2}$$

The central moments are invariant by translation. We introduce the normalized moments as follows:

$$\mu_{p,q} = \frac{v_{p,q}}{v_{0,0}^{(1+(p+q)/2)}} \tag{3}$$

These moments are invariant to translation and scale changes. Hu moments are calculated from normalized moments and are invariant by translation, rotation and change of scale:

$$\varphi_1 = \mu_{2,0} + \mu_{0,2}$$

$$\varphi_2 = (\mu_{2,0} - \mu_{0,2})^2 + 4\mu_{1,1}^2$$

$$\varphi_3 = (\mu_{3,0} - 3\mu_{1,2}^2 + (3\mu_{2,1} - \mu_{0,3})^2$$

$$\varphi_4 = (\mu_{3,0} + \mu_{1,2})^2 + (\mu_{2,1} + \mu_{0,3})^2$$

$$\varphi_5 = (\mu_{3,0} - 3\mu_{1,2})(\mu_{3,0} + \mu_{1,2})[(\mu_{3,0} + \mu_{1,2})^2 - 3(\mu_{2,1} + \mu_{0,3})^2] + (3\mu_{2,1} - \mu_{0,3})(\mu_{2,1} + \mu_{0,3})$$
$$[3(\mu_{3,0} + \mu_{1,2})^2 - (\mu_{2,1} + \mu_{0,3})^2]$$

$$\varphi_6 = (\mu_{2,0} - \mu_{0,2})[(\mu_{3,0} + \mu_{1,2})^2 - (\mu_{2,1} + \mu_{0,3})^2] + 4\mu_{1,1}(\mu_{3,0} + \mu_{1,2})(\mu_{2,1} + \mu_{0,3})$$

$$\varphi_7 = (3\mu_{2,1} - \mu_{0,3})(\mu_{3,0} + \mu_{1,2})[(\mu_{3,0} + \mu_{1,2})^2 - 3(\mu_{2,1} + \mu_{0,3})^2] - (\mu_{3,0} - 3\mu_{1,2})(\mu_{2,1} + \mu_{0,3})$$
$$[3(\mu_{3,0} + \mu_{1,2})^2 - (\mu_{2,1} + \mu_{0,3})^2]$$

The Zernike Moments

Zernike polynomials were first proposed in 1934. The formulation of these moments is very popular. We study here the original formulation of the orthogonal invariant moments. They are constructed using a set of complex polynomials which form a complete orthogonal set on the unit disk with $(x^2+y^2) \leq 1$:

$$A_{m,n} = \frac{m+1}{\pi} \int_x \int_y I(x,y)[V_{mn}(x,y)]dxdy \tag{4}$$

where *m* and *n* define the order of the moment and *I(x,y)* the grayscale of a pixel in the image *I* on which we calculate the moment. Zernike polynomials $V_{mn}(x,y)$ are expressed in polar coordinates:

$$V_{m,n}(r,\theta) = R_{mn}(r)e^{-jn\theta}, \tag{5}$$

where $R_{mn}(r)$ is the orthogonal radial polynomial:

$$R_{mn}(r) = \sum_{s=0}^{\frac{m-|n|}{2}} (-1)^s \frac{(m-s)!}{s!(\frac{m+|n|}{2}-s)!(\frac{m-|n|}{2}-s)!} r^{m-2s} \tag{6}$$

The moments A_{mn} are invariants by rotation and change of scale.

The Fourier Transform

The Fourier Transform of two-dimensional function with complex values is defined by:

$$z(u,v) = \int_{R^2} I(x,y) e^{-2i\pi(ux+vy)} dxdy \tag{7}$$

Its kernels $k(u,v,x,y)=e^{-2i\pi(ux+vy)}$ are invertible. The module of the Fourier Transform, called spectral density is invariant by translation on the function I. We define the Fourier Transform for a circular periodic function of period 2π as follows:

$$I_l(r) = \frac{1}{2\pi} \int_0^{2\pi} I(r,\theta) e^{-il\theta} d\theta \tag{8}$$

where $I(r,\theta)$ is a function expressed in polar coordinates and $I_l(r)$ is a function of radius. The generalized Fourier descriptors are defined by:

$$D_I(\lambda) = \frac{2\pi}{\lambda} \int_0^{2\pi} \left|\hat{I}(\lambda\cos\theta, \lambda\sin\theta)\right|^2 \lambda d\theta, \tag{9}$$

where $\hat{I}$ is the Fourier Transform of the function I.

The Fourier-Mellin Transform

Fourier-Mellin Transform of two-dimensional function with complex values is defined by:

$$z(u,v) = \int_0^{+\infty} \int_0^{+\infty} I(x,y) x^{iu-1}.y^{iv-1} dxdy \tag{10}$$

The 2D module of the Fourier-Mellin Transform is invariant by change of scale of an axis of I. The analytic Fourier-Mellin Transform of the function I, described in polar coordinates relative to its inertia center is given by ($\sigma>0$):

$$\forall(k,v) \in Z * R, M_{I_\sigma}(k,v) = \frac{1}{2\pi}\int_0^\infty \int_0^\infty I(r,\theta)e^{\sigma - iv}.e^{-ik\theta}\frac{dr}{r}d\theta \tag{11}$$

It is possible to derive a complete family of invariant descriptors. It is possible to obtain translation invariance through the Fourier Transform, and the rotation and change of scale using the Fourier-Mellin Transform.

Specific Shape Descriptors

For recognition of known geometric shapes, as application presented in this chapter about sickle cell disease (section 4), we can define adapted descriptors to a prior knowledge that we have on the type of objects to recognize, or we can also adapt others from known descriptors. So we have seen above the different ways to characterize the shapes of objects in an image. This information will help to build models of objects for the recognition and indexing in a database. To properly accomplish this task, we need a classification system able to categorize all objects and images in a database from their description.

Classification

We call automatic classification, the algorithmic categorization of the objects. This one is to determine in which class or category we can "store" each object, based on similarities criteria. Many classification or learning methods have been developed (Bay, 1999), and used in a wide spectrum of applications: diagnosis (Moreno et al., 1994), bioinformatics (Polat & Günes, 2006), speech recognition, etc. Learning algorithms can be categorized according to the type of learning that they employ.

- The supervised learning: An expert is used to correctly label objects. The learner must then find or approximate the function to assign the correct label to these objects. The linear discriminator analysis or Support Vector Machines (SVM) are typical examples and are most commonly used for classification (Vapnik, 1998).
- Unsupervised Learning: No expert is available. The algorithm must discover by itself the data categorization. The clustering method in (Bay, 1999) is an example of unsupervised learning.

There are many methods of classification, used in many works. For example, to segment medical images, is to give a certain class to certain regions in the image. These techniques can be named the classification. (Li et al., 2006), present a segmentation method, where the descriptors are extracted on the regions of the image, and on which we apply a principal component analysis to reduce the size of the data. A Support vector machines classifier is used on reduced data in order to assign a class for different regions. We present two kinds of classifiers. First the support vector machines, and then another type of classification techniques, the multicriteria approach. The support vector machines is a discrimination technique. It is used to separate two (or more) sets of points by an hyper-plane. From the distribution of samples, the performance of an SVM can be superior to those of a neural network or a Gaussian mixture model (Moreno et al., 1994), (Polat & Günes, 2006), the SVM seems a little less fast, requiring in some cases to reduce the descriptors space.

Classification Principle by Support Vector Machines

This method of supervised classification was published by Vapnik (Vapnik, 1998). An SVM is a supervised learning algorithm allows to define a separator between classes. We have a finite set of separated vectors of R^n, as part of a binary classification into two groups, or two classes. Learning to a group is defined by an associated label to each vector, which is inscribed group 1 or group 2. Find a separator is equivalent to reconstruct a function that takes a vector from a set of samples and can say what group it belongs. However, it expects the SVM good generalization properties, i.e. if a new vector is introduced and it was not in the set of database, the SVM will say which group it probably belongs.

The linear separator is the lower part of the SVM, that is a relatively simple problem, and that allows later on to the SVM providing some well more powerful separators. We saw that we started from a finite set of labelled vectors. We say that all the labelled vectors that we give are the set of samples noted S, which contains p elements.

$$S = (\vec{x}_l, y_l)_{1 \leq l \leq p} with \forall l, y_l \in \{-1, 1\} \tag{12}$$

The scalar product of two vectors is noted where is $\langle \vec{x}, \vec{y} \rangle$, we can then define the linear separator $f_{\vec{w},b}$ by the following equation:

$$f_{\vec{w},b}(\vec{x}) = \langle \vec{w}, \vec{x} \rangle + b \tag{13}$$

This separator does not provide valid values only -1 or 1, but we assume that the result when $f_{\vec{w},b}(\vec{x})$ is positive, then the vector is of the same class as samples of label 1, and the result when $f_{\vec{w},b}(\vec{x})$ is negative, the vector belongs to the class of examples labelled -1. The equation $f_{\vec{w},b}(\vec{x}) = 0$ defines the border between the two classes. This boundary is an affine hyper-plane in the case of linear separator.

Separability and Margin

We suppose that S is linearly separable. The basic idea of SVM is to separate samples of each class, but it is also necessary that the hyper plane passes as possible between the two classes. It is to define this

Figure 1. A separator that the margin is not maximized, have less good generalization properties than that which the margin is maximized

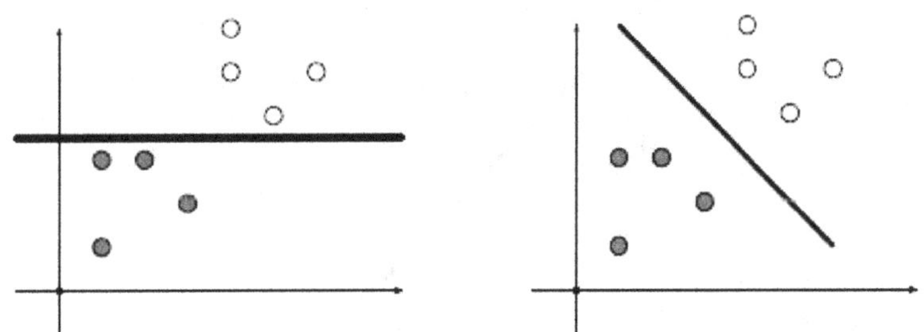

notion that we introduce the margin. The margin is the minimum distances of each sample to the hyper plane (Figure 1).

The aim of the SVM, in case where *S* is separable, is to give separator *S* whose margin is maximal, while ensuring that properly separates the samples with label -1 and the samples with label 1. The maximum margin separator is such that, the smaller sample has a margin wider than the sample of the smallest margin of the other possible separators. In fact, there are really at least two samples of smaller margin, a class 1 and class -1. They force this margin, and the border of separation passes between them (Figure 2). These are the only samples that force the margin, and remove all other samples of the database does not change the separator. These samples are called support vectors, hence the name of the method.

General Case

For the general case where *S* is not separable, the solution is to allow some samples to have a lower margin than the margin chosen as the smallest margin or even negative. However, the solution of the problem may be very bad if too many samples are allowed to have a small margin. The idea is to add value margins lower than the maximum margin in the expression to minimize. This avoids that the margins are too low, which limits the samples that do not respect the separability through a separator solution of optimization problem. This is a problem of quadratic convex optimization, i.e. an optimization problem that admits no local optimum, but only one optimum, thus overall. This is crucial because the convexity of the problem is a guarantee of convergence to the SVM solution.

The interest of the kernel functions is that they allow using what we just presented on the linear separation to the non-linear separations. Let *S* a set of samples labelled by 1 or -1 depending on the class to which they belong, which is not at all linearly separable. The method we have seen works in this case but may give poor results, and many samples became support vectors. The idea of using kernels comes from the assumption that if a set is not linearly separable in the descriptors space, it can be in a space of higher dimension. A better way to separate the samples is to project them into a different space, and perform a linear separation in this space, where this time it should be more adapted. The kernel functions can achieve this projection, and must check a number of properties to ensure the effectiveness of this

Figure 2. The separator which should maximize the margin

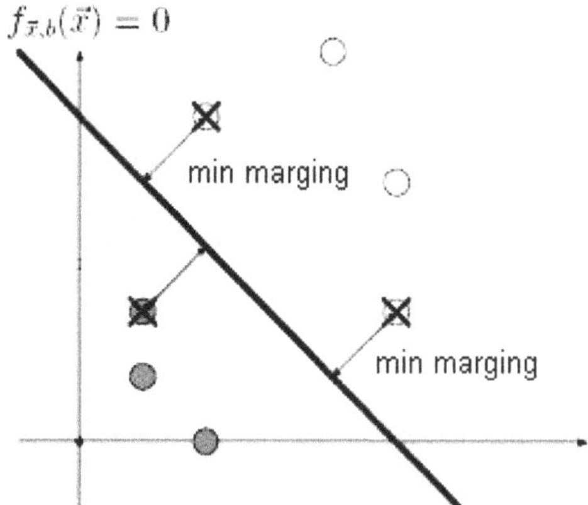

technique, so we do not have to make calculations in very large dimensions. With the kernel functions, we can work in very large dimensions (Scholkopf & Smola, 2002). However, a linear separation, and a linear regression is facilitated by the projection of data in a space of high dimension. Projecting in the space of descriptors and using an algorithm to maximize the margin, SVM managed to get a severability retaining good generalization capacity, is the central idea of SVM.

Multicriteria Classification Approaches

The classification is a process widely used in many applications, we have seen, and a research area in constant evolution. Many methods, including SVM we have described above, usually make a classification in the descriptors space, even in a space of higher dimension. This space is composed of the descriptors considered relevant to the recognition of one or more objects.

Descriptors are more numerous, we have seen, we can develop more accurate models of the shapes that we want to recognize. The space of features (descriptors) is usually very large. Intuitively, it is natural to realize that such a monolithic treatment (Giacinto et al., 2003), generally applied to very heterogeneous database, is not necessarily adapted. It may be difficult for a single classifier to deal efficiently with very different descriptors. In this case, the fusion of multiple classifiers using a different representation of data can be more effective than an approach based on large vectors representing all the available descriptors. The fusion of information is in fact the basis of any classification system. Indeed, a single vector is composed by a variety of information obtained in different ways, which is a fusion of information in terms of descriptors. This is represents the concatenation of several descriptors. However, we have seen, this fusion is a little naive, and a fusion at from different classifiers may be a little more judiciously. It must find an effective fusion technique between the responses of several different classifiers, respecting certain fusion rules established in advances. For much information on descriptor values fusion, the readers can refer to the book of Kuntcheva (Kuntcheva, 2004).

We have presented in this section two important steps that constitute an image recognition system by content in large databases, the description and classification. We have detailed the principles of the information description contained in an image and the importance of robustness. Two classification approaches were presented, explaining the principle of use and their importance in an image recognition system.

SICKLE CELLS DISEASE APPLICATION

Description and Evaluation

Sickle cell anaemia is a genetic disease that causes a lack of oxygenation of blood by the sickling of red blood cells. This serious inherited disease particularly affects people from Black Africa, North Africa and Latin America. The particularly high frequency of occurrence of this disease in some of these regions requires the establishment screening from birth. Several tests exist, like chemical, genetic, but also visual tests on the apparent quality of red cell observed under the microscope. In our work, we focus on this latter type of test. It appears that this method, although it is not sufficient to establish a definitive diagnosis, is the most easily generralizable, and has low cost equipment that requires this technique. Considering the particular form of blood with sickle cell disease, it seems interesting to make this automatic testing procedure, for providing a faster processing, thus to deal more patients, and also have an objective treatment of microscopic images, with the prior information of an expert. In this section, we present an adapted descriptors improved for sickle cells disease. The developed descriptors are evaluated before using them for a classification system. In section 5, a multicriteria classification method will be presented and compared to an SVM classifier.

For sickle cells disease, a database with some hundreds of images, represents in reality some thousands in terms of cells that can be treated. Figure 4 and Figure 5 are images of different patients with sickle cell disease. Indeed, the sickled cells are characterized by their elongated shapes and the healthy cells tend to be circular. The sickling process of cells is represented in Figure 6.

After the pre-processing of images and segmentation of regions of interest (Li et al., 2006), the description of these segmented regions and the classification are achieved. For pre-processing, we have

Figure 3. Architecture of multicriteria classification method

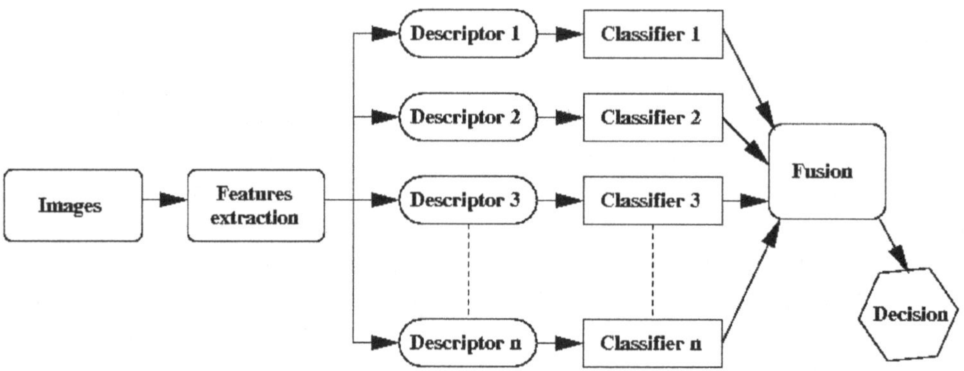

Figure 4. Segmentation result obtained by deformable active contour, (a) original image, (b) initialization step with level set function, (c) the convergence of the level set function, (d) the extracted contours corresponding to the zero level set function.

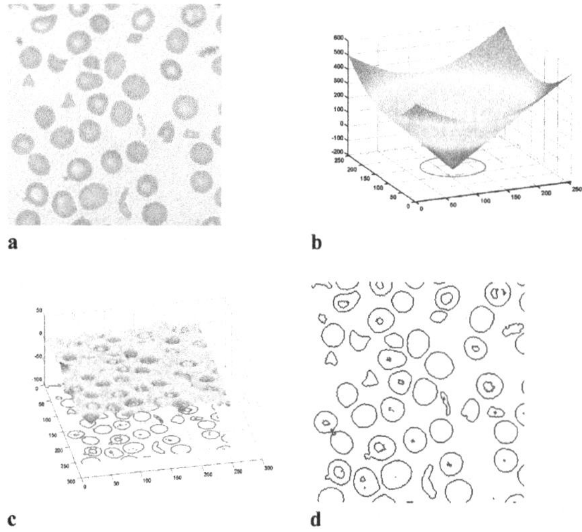

used an adapted method to the microscopic images (Djemal, 2005). The regions of interest and their shapes are obtained by a segmentation method using deformable active contours (Djemal et al., 2006). An example of the segmentation results is presented in Figure 4. In this case, the description of the regions of interest representing the sickle cell disease is a crucial step (Djemal et al., 2005), (Moreno et al., 1994), in fact, a good description would get a better recognition rate.

Descriptors Evaluation

As we have mentioned, a number of geometric invariants descriptors have already been used in the literature. The choice of our used descriptors is adapted according to specific characteristics of sickle cell disease (Figure 6). In this application, we have chosen to implement 11 descriptors, including 7 Hu invariants (Ghorbel et al., 2006), (Cao et al., 2008), and 4 improved geometric invariants descriptors introduced by (Shouche et al., 2001). To simplify the understanding of these methods, we present obtained results from 76 properly selected cells. These 76 cells compose 22 sick and 54 healthy. In the Table 1, we present a mean and standard deviation values for the two first Hu (Hu_1 and Hu_2) descriptors and four geometric descriptors (d_1, d_2, d_3, and d_4).

Hu Invariants Evaluation

Centred and normal moments, described in section 3, are calculated using the surface of each cell, from these moments, we calculate the seven Hu invariants. We can observe in the Table 1 the first invariant

Figure 5. Types of microscopic images from sickle cells disease database

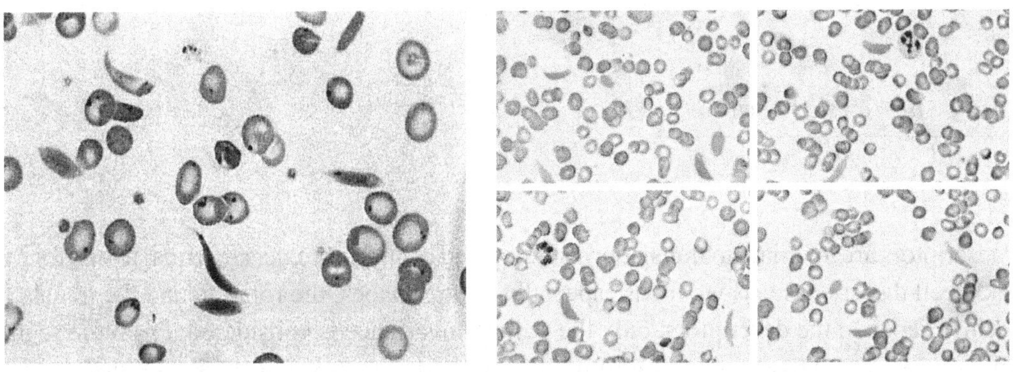

Figure 6. Sickling process of a sickle cell blood

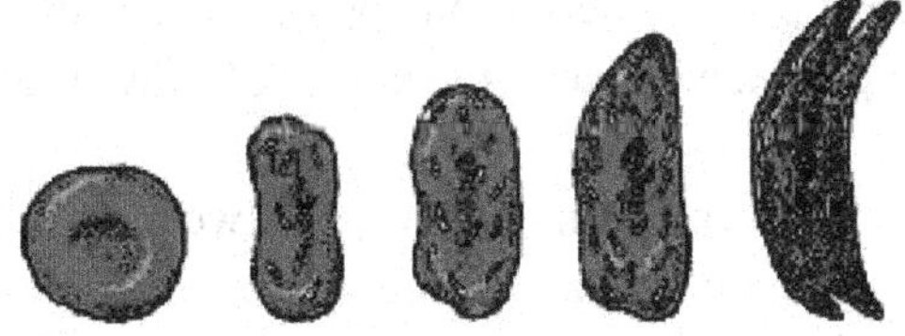

Table 1. Mean and standard deviation obtained by each descriptors evaluated by Fisher measures

		Hu_1	Hu_2	d_1	d_2	d_3	d_4
Healthy	**mean (μ_H)**	0.0011	3.12E-08	1.3239	0.5549	1.4173	0.9009
	Std (σ_H)	0.0005	5E-08	0.0670	0.1116	0.0771	0.0472
Sick	**mean (μ_S)**	0.0021	3.16E-06	0.9128	0.1057	3.4666	0.4033
	std (σ_S)	0.0013	3.56E-06	0.2064	0.0824	1.2078	0.1129
Fisher Criteria (FC)		0.5555	0.8667	1.5036	2.3154	1.5949	3.1080

Hu, it does not seem really invariant. Indeed, the Fisher measure shows that the second Hu invariant is more discriminating. Despite the apparent non-invariance of the first Hu descriptor, we find that these invariant moments are a good way to differentiate healthy of sick cells.

Geometric Invariants

As it has been noted, a number of geometric invariants descriptors are used in the literature. We chose to use descriptors according to characterize that we know on cells:

isoperimetric:

$$d_1 = \frac{4 \times \pi \times area}{(perimeter)^2} \tag{14}$$

elongation:

$$d_2 = \frac{area \quad of \quad circleinscribed}{area \quad of \quad circlecircumscribed} \tag{15}$$

Both descriptors are invariant to translation, rotation and change of scale, and equal to one for a circle. In the sickle cell disease case, as we focus especially on the shapes, the rotation and the translation do not imply invariance of the descriptors, only the scaling invariance is considered. From the segmented images of cells, we can extract different information necessary to descriptors calculation.

The perimeter is the number of elements that we have in the table having recovered all the pixels forming the contour of the red cell. The area is obtained by counting the number of black pixels, which represents the total surface of a cell. The ray of circumscribed and inscribed circles are in turn calculated by considering the center of gravity of the cell, calculated using the algebraic moments, as the center of the circles. This simplification appears to be a good approximation of the real rays. The radius of the inscribed circle is the minimum distance between the center of gravity of the cell, and all points of its contour.

The radius of its circumcircle is the maximum distance between the center of gravity and all points of the contour of the cell. Areas are calculated accordingly. Two other geometric descriptors were used, introduced by (Shouche et al., 2001), we have improved the two descriptors where becomes:

$$d_3 = \frac{(major \quad axis)^2}{area} \quad \text{and} \quad d_4 = \frac{area}{\left(\frac{major \quad axis}{2}\right)^2 \times \pi} \tag{16}$$

However, we have noticed exploring the values that take these descriptors for all 76 cells that we described above, they were not all invariants to change of scale. Indeed, calculations have revealed that they were both increased by a dilation factor k.

In their work, (Shouche et al., 2001), use different descriptors. The automatic recognition system applied to digital images using a specific protocol, always at the same scale. It was not mandatory for authors to have descriptors invariant to changes of scale. We have therefore improved the descriptor d_3, to make it completely invariant. The descriptor is not dependent on a scale factor k. There are also in table 1 not only that this descriptor has real qualities of invariance, but the values it gives to the healthy cells are also all very close. They approach the value $4 / \pi \approx 1.27$, given by the descriptor for circular shapes.

There is also the d_4, descriptors that have good properties of invariance, from the values that are relatively close to healthy cells. These values to healthy cells approaching 1, given by the descriptor for circular shapes.

From real evaluation of these descriptors on images database properly chosen, we have determined descriptors able to provide same values (decision) for cells of the same aspect (shapes). The most recognizable cells are healthy cells. Indeed, we know that they are circular, with no other options, while the sick cells have certain heterogeneity. According to our assumptions, we can say that the three most effective descriptors and invariants are d_2 (Eq.15), d_3 and d_4 (Eq.16). Indeed, their respective values on the used cells database seem to be very homogeneous for healthy cells, and well-differentiated sick cells. Descriptors d_1 (Eq.14) and the 7 Hu invariants, even if they are relatively successful, did not appear as homogeneous. Once these descriptors chosen, it remains to establish models of healthy and sick cells. These models are useful to create a good learning cells database which is necessary for suitable classification.

In order to evaluate the performances of the descriptors, we use the Fisher measure criteria noted FC described by:

$$FC = \frac{|\mu_H - \mu_S|}{\sigma_H + \sigma_S} \tag{17}$$

where μ_H and μ_S are the mean values of descriptors for healthy and sick classes, respectively. σ_H and σ_S are the standard deviation values for the same corresponding classes.

Table 1 presents mean and standard (std) values of the characteristics obtained by each descriptor calculated for healthy and sick cells. The last row shows the Fisher measure for each descriptor. We can observe that these measures justify our descriptors choice.

MULTICRITERIA CLASSIFICATION OF SICKLE CELLS DISEASE

In this section we develop a multicriteria method for sickle cells disease classification for a possible lack of precision in the responses provided by kernel classifiers like Neural Network and SVMs. Indeed, blood cells are gradually taking a sickle shape, depending on the conditions under which they evolve. This evolution implies intermediate cell shapes (Figure 6), which introduce difficulty in classification step. Our approach considers that each descriptor is a criterion. As a first step, we define a classifier able to give relevant information from each descriptor. In a second step, we have determined a fusion model allows to obtaining a final decision from the results of all criteria (Giacinto et al., 2003).

Assumptions and Modeling

For each criterion, during the model calculation, from the learning database, the average values of this criterion are recorded for healthy and sick cells. Healthy cells have theoretically the same shape, i.e. they are almost circular. The sick cells can have a variety of shapes, which affects the values of standard deviations. During classification, for a cell of unknown shape, the desired criterion is calculated, and then the cell is assigned to one of the classes according to the proximity of the criterion value against one or the other averages. This was done for each cell and for each criterion. Indeed, for a descriptor δ_i we compute the three following informations:

- $\overline{x}_{\delta_i}^{healthy}$: is the average value of the descriptor for healthy cells;
- $\overline{x}_{\delta_i}^{sick}$: is the average value of the descriptor for sick cells;
- $\sigma_{R_{\delta_i}}^{healthy}$: is the relative standard deviation value of healthy cells.

Descriptor for each image gives an answer about the health of the red cell. We have therefore, for 11 descriptors, 11 answers. According to our assumptions and the considered distribution (Figure 7), we used the weighted sum rule as fusion model. Hence, it seemed ideal to take into account the relative effectiveness of some classifiers over others. This model allows, by setting the weights properly, to give greater weight to some than to other descriptors. In our approach, we determine the weight in two steps during the learning stage for all images database, and then some of these weights are determined dynamically during the recognition (generalization step).

Our goal is to assign a greater weighting to a descriptor that makes fewer mistakes than a descriptor that does more. One notes that the error rate increases when the descriptors are vague, and where the curves of healthy and sick cells overlap (Figure 7). We must therefore assign a high weight to a descriptor where the standard deviation of the curves is small as possible, and the average distribution of healthy and sick cells is farthest possible. With the aim of normalization, we consider the relative standard deviation rather than the standard deviation, which is actually the standard deviation divided by the mean. For descriptor δ_i, , with value x_i, we use relative standard deviation defined as follows:

$$\sigma_{R_{\delta_i}}^{healthy} = \frac{\sigma_i^{healthy}}{\overline{x}_i^{healthy}} \tag{18}$$

with $\sigma_i^{healthy}$ is the standard deviation of descriptor δ_i for healthy cells, and $\overline{x}_i^{healthy}$ is the average of descriptor δ_i for healthy cells. We consider the assumption that the greater relative standard deviation is low, the descriptor is more discriminating. The weight for each descriptor is defined as follows:

whereas the descriptor δ_i, with value x_i for cell C_1, and average value of sick and healthy cells, respectively x_i^{sick} and $x_i^{healthy}$, if the classifier with single criterion says that the cell C_1 is sick for this descriptor, the considered weight is as follows:

$$w_{x_i}^{sick} = \frac{\left|x_i - \overline{x}_i^{healthy}\right|}{\left|x_i - \overline{x}_i^{sick}\right|} \tag{19}$$

whereas the descriptor δ_j, with value x_j for cell C_2, and average value of sick and healthy cells, respectively x_j^{sick} and $x_j^{healthy}$, if the classifier with single criterion says that the cell C_2 is healthy for this descriptor, the considered weight is as follows:

$$w_{x_j}^{healthy} = \frac{\left|x_j - \overline{x}_j^{sick}\right|}{\left|x_j - \overline{x}_j^{healthy}\right|} \tag{20}$$

For cell C, consider the descriptor δ_i, with value x_i, we have the final weighting in the fusion model:

Figure 7. Example of densities of probability distribution for all values of one descriptor

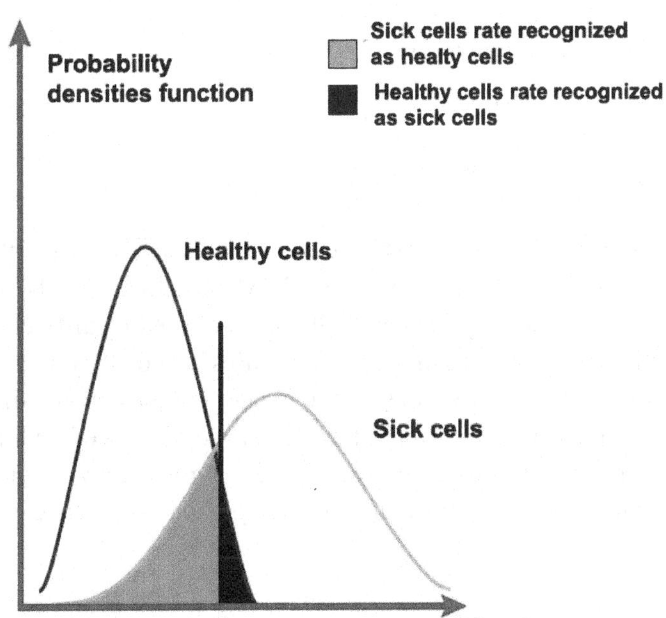

if the classifier with single criterion says that the cell C is sick then:

$$W_{x_i}^{S} = \frac{1}{\sigma_{R_{\delta_i}}^{healthy}} \cdot \frac{\left|\overline{x}_i^{sick} - \overline{x}_i^{healthy}\right|}{\left(\frac{\overline{x}_i^{healthy} + \overline{x}_i^{sick}}{2}\right)} \cdot w_{x_i}^{sick} \tag{21}$$

if the classifier with single criterion says that the cell C is healthy then :

$$W_{x_i}^{H} = \frac{1}{\sigma_{R_{\delta_i}}^{healthy}} \cdot \frac{\left|\overline{x}_i^{sick} - \overline{x}_i^{healthy}\right|}{\left(\frac{\overline{x}_i^{healthy} + \overline{x}_i^{sick}}{2}\right)} \cdot w_{x_i}^{healthy} \tag{22}$$

The first term (Eq. 22) is the inverse of the relative standard deviation, given that over the relative standard deviation of normal cells is low, the more we want this descriptor has a large weight.

The second term is an indicator of the proximity or remoteness of the averages of healthy cells and sick to handle the descriptor δ_i, i.e. the distance between the averages of healthy cells and sick, normalized by the average of averages. These first two weighting factors are the fixed part of the weight, determined for each descriptor. Finally, the third term represents the approximation on the description results obtained by study cell and compared to the class that was assigned. This is the part of the weight that varies with each classified cell. The final decision is obtained in the following equation:

$$Decision = \sum_{i=1}^{N} W_i \cdot \delta_i , \tag{23}$$

with $W_i = W_{x_i}^{S}$ or $W_i = W_{x_i}^{H}$ according to the response of the classifier with single criterion.

The architecture of the multicriteria classification method is described in Figure 3.

Classification Results and Comparison

In this section, we present the different used tests to evaluate the performance of the developed method. The obtained results are analyzed and compared to the SVM classifier. Models of SVM classifiers and multicriteria are obtained from learning database. This is composed of different cells extracted from microscopic images. Each cell is classified as shown in Figures 9, and 10 by a bar showing the score, or the response of the classifier. If this score is positive, it means that the cell classification belongs to the sickle cell disease class. If it is negative, this implies that the cell is placed with the healthy cell class. The recognized cells, as sickle cell disease, are represented in green color (Figures 9, and 10). Those whose classification is considered by the milticriteria method as intermediate cells are indicated by a black arrows.

Learning Tests

The training database includes 3228 cells, with 2291 healthy and 937 sick cells. From the extracted features, we carry out SVM learning using concatenated features as input. The obtained and computed model is a hyper-plane which represent separation border between the two clusters according to the resulting feature vector. The multicriteria model is obtained by following the proposed approach explained in the previous section. By training the model in the same database, the training cells are divided in to correctly classified and misclassified. The training classification rate of the models and for each class healthy or sick can be given by the correctly classified cells divided by the number of cells in each considered class.

Table 2 presents the global classification rates for the two classifiers SVM and Multicriteria in the learning stage tests. The first learning test is carry out with all learning cells. The recognition rate obtained by the SVM is 87%.

With our proposed approach, the Multicriteria classifier obtains comparable rate 88%. Any other test is achieved with selected cells, SVM obtains 96% as global classification rate, with 86% for sick cells, and 100% for healthy cells. Considering only the signs of the return values, the multicriteria classifier, obtains 97% of classification performance rate, with 90% for sick cells, and 100% for healthy cells. The multicriteria method considers the intermediate shapes (figure 8), this advantage make its results comparable to the SVM classifier.

Generalization Tests

Among several generalization tests, we show and discuss two examples of classifications. Discussed cases are achieved on different extracted cells from microscopic images.

The first generalization is performed on 35 extracted cells, containing two clearly cells recognizable with sickle cell disease. It also contains many cells with intermediate shapes, which make it interesting to study the reaction of each classifier in relation to these cases. The classification results are shown in figure 9.

Table 2. Classification rates obtained in learning stages, the test are carryout on all learning cells database and on selected cells

		SVM		Multicriteria	
		Each class	**Global classification rate**	**Each class**	**Global classification rate**
Learning test with all learning cells database *3228 cells*	Test with all Healthy cells (2291)	96%	87%	95%	88%
	Test with all Sick cells (937)	81%		83%	
Learning test with selected cells *76 cells*	Test with selected Healthy cells (54)	100%	96%	100%	97%
	Test with selected Sick cells (22)	86%		90%	

Figure 8. Example of cells of the learning database whose classification is close to zero for the multi-criteria classification method

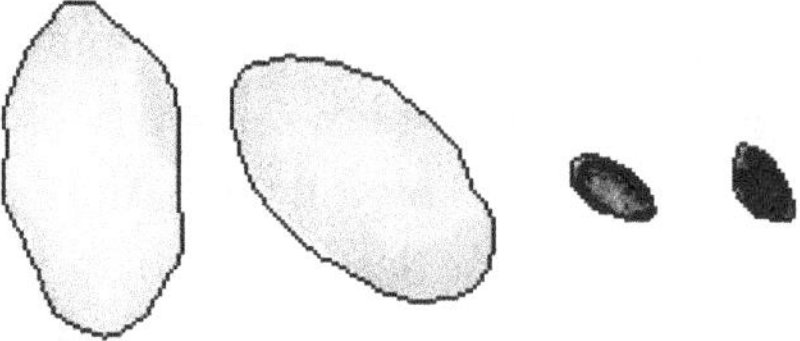

Figure 9. Generalization results: left, with SVM classifier, and right with multicriteria classifier method

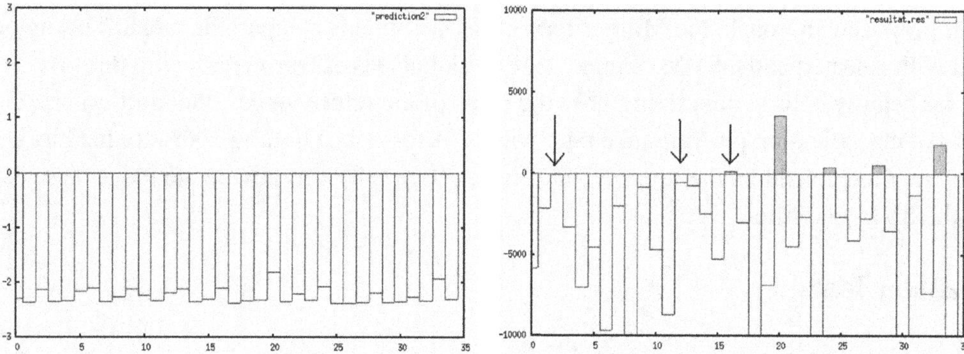

SVM classifier presents difficulties to classify sickle cells in this case. However, the multicriteria classifier recognizes perfectly the two cells with sickle cells disease and especially the intermediate cells are close to zero (indicated by black arrows).

The second test is performed with 115 cells suitably chosen. The classification results of this test are presented in Figure 10. All sickle cells are recognized by both classifiers. The SVM classifier has two cases of cells whose classification is not clearly specified (Figure 11, left). The multicriteria classifier recognizes with success the sick cells, but presents some others misclassified cells (Figure 11, right).

Considering the two ambiguous cells for SVM, the first cell is classified as healthy by the multicriteria classifier, the second is considered sickle cell. Indeed, these cells are intermediate shapes and taking them into account for classification is very difficult. Analysis of these results shows that it is always necessary to improve and develop new description methods appropriate to different types of cells.

The generalization tests are performed on a Pentium 4 machine, CPU 2.80 GHz and with 512 MB of RAM. Without the learning stages, the time of classification (recognition stage) is comparable. Indeed, considering the second generalization test using 115 cells, the computation time is respectively 1 mn 38 seconds for SVM and 1 mn 14 seconds for multicriteria classifier. Of course, these computation times take into account the feature extraction stage of test cells.

We present in Table 3, the two confusion matrixes corresponding to the results obtained by the SVM and our proposed multicriteria method. These matrixes represent the average recognition values obtained after 15 experiments with testing cells not taking part in learning stages. The two classifiers obtain good recognition results for healthy cells, 97.24% for SVM and 98.31% for Multicriteria. For the sick cells,

Figure 10. Generalization results: left, with SVM classifier, and right with multicriteria classifier method.

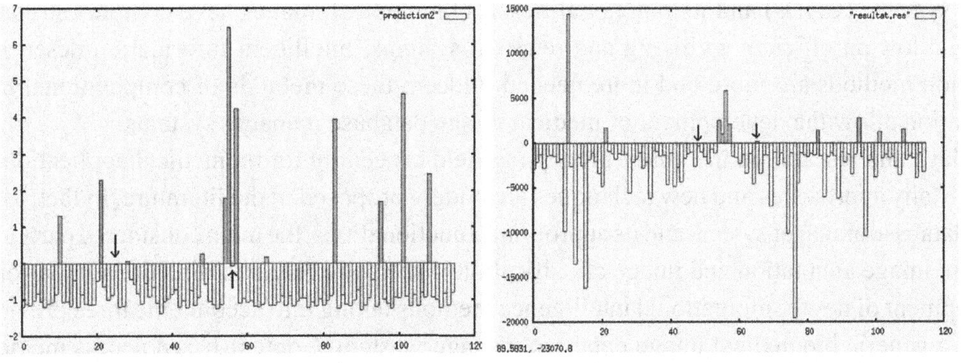

Figure 11. Ambiguous classification: left, with SVM classifier, and right with multicriteria classifier method

Table 3. Confusion matrixes of the recognition rate obtained by the two classifiers SVM and Multicriteria

SVM			**Multicriteria**		
Class	Healthy	Sick	**Class**	Healthy	Sick
Healthy	97.24%	2.76%	Healthy	98.31%	1.69%
Sick	4.64%	95.36%	Sick	3.77%	96.23%

the Multicriteria classifier presents the advantage in taking into account the intermediate shapes, where it leads to 96.23% as recognition rate.

These two presented classification methods are relatively efficient compared to sickle cell disease recognition problem. Indeed the two classifiers give interesting results from a qualitative point of view. Their results may be complementary in some cases, particularly for determining that a cell cannot be assigned to a class, due to its shape, or really sick/healthy. The multicriteria appears for these cases can give results close to zero, that facilitates the recognition of healthy and sick cells without intermediate shapes.

FUTURE RESEARCH DIRECTIONS

Image processing methods are ones of the main application fields within Biomedical Informatics. Biomedical image processing is widely needed by professionals and researchers and may require important computation capabilities to reach satisfactory results. Therefore, the use of computational intelligence methods in different biomedical image processing stages is especially appropriate for Computer Aided Diagnosis systems (CADs) and its functionalities. As biomedical images have complex structures and in order to allow an efficient archiving and retrieval systems, intelligent information description and classification methods are more and more needed. Indeed, these methods of computational modeling and simulation allow the development of medical image database manager systems.

Nowadays, the research in the image processing field especially for biomedical applications is very intensive. Many approaches and new techniques are widely proposed in the literature. In fact, to develop an image database manager system and its appropriate functionalities, the main considered parts are image description, image annotation and image classification. The future research directions in our opinion is the development of new computational intelligence methods taking into account the three previous parts leading to a generic biomedical image database manager system. Content-based access methods have an enormous potential when used in the correct way. It is now the time to create appropriated medical applications and to use this potential for diagnosis and decision, research and teaching.

CONCLUSION

In this chapter, we have presented the different stages of an image recognition system dedicated to computer aided diagnosis in biomedical domain. Indeed, the information description and classification constitute the two important steps which are detailed. Two classification approaches were presented, explaining the principle of use and their importance in the image recognition system.

Through the sickle cells disease application, presented and improved descriptors are invariant and give homogeneous values for healthy cells and permit to differentiate sick cells. We have proposed multicriteria classification method adapted to studied disease application. Compared to the SVM classifier, and without an intermediate shapes, the proposed multicriteria algorithm can give results close to zero and facilitates the healthy and disease cells recognition. Indeed, the two classifiers give interesting results from a qualitative point of view and their results may be complementary in some cases.

In the other hand, to obtain satisfactory recognition results, the choice or the development of new description methods must be appropriate to the type of the considered images database. This is due to the great difficulty to obtain a universal description algorithm. Furthermore, a good compromise between efficiency, representation of images and satisfactory computation time are required.

Searching digital biomedical images remain a challenges problem. Indeed, the biomedical domain has been unable to take advantage of image recognition methods and systems in spite of their acknowledged importance in the face of growing use of image databases in medical practice, research, and education. The challenging type of images to be treated and the lacking of suitable systems have hindered their acceptance. While it is difficult to develop a single comprehensive system, it may be possible to take advantage of the growing research interest and several successful systems with developed techniques for specific image databases. In addition, to develop intelligent information extraction, description and recognition methods, the automatic biomedical image categorization needs also interfaces allowing to the specialist intervention to perform their diagnosis.

REFERENCES

Antani, S., Long, L. R., & Thoma, G. R. (2004). Content-based image retrieval for large biomedical image archives. In *Proceedings of 11th World Congress on Medical Informatics (MEDINFO)*, (pp. 829-833).

Antania, S., Kasturi, R., & Jain, R. (2002). A survey on the use of pattern recognition methods for abstraction, indexing and retrieval of images and video. *Pattern Recognition*, *35*(4), 945–965. doi:10.1016/S0031-3203(01)00086-3

Bay, S. D. (1999). Nearest neighbor classification from multiple feature subsets. *Intelligent Data Analysis*, 3.

Cao, F., Lisani, J.-L., Morel, J.-M., Musé, P., & Sur, H. (2008). *A theory of shape identification*. (LNCS 1948). Springer.

Carson, C., Belongie, Se., Greenpan, H., & Jitendra, M. (2002). Blobworld: Image segmentation using expectation-maximization and its application to image querying. *IEEE Transactions on Pattern Analysis and Machine Intelligence*, *24*(8). doi:10.1109/TPAMI.2002.1023800

Cheikhrouhou, I., Djemal, K., Masmoudi, D. S., Derbel, N., & Maaref, H. (2007). Abnormalities description for breast cancer recognition. *IEEE International Conference on E-medical Systems*, (pp. 199-205). October, Fez, Morocco.

Cheikhrouhou, I., Djemal, K., Masmoudi, D. S., Maaref, H., & Derbel, N. (2008). *New mass description in mammographies. IEEE International Workshops on Image Processing, Theory, Tools and Applications (IPTA08), November 23*. Tunisia: Sousse.

Djemal, K. (2005). *Speckle reduction in ultrasound images by minimization of total variation*. IEEE International Conference on Image Processing, ICIP'05, Volume 3, (pp. 357–360). September, Genova, Italy. ISBN: 0-7803-9134-9

Djemal, K., Bouchara, F., & Rossetto, B. (2002). *Image modeling and region-based active contours segmentation*. International Conference on Vision, Modeling and Visualization VMV'02 (pp. 363-370). November, Erlangen, Germany. ISBN: 3-89838-034-3

Djemal, K., Chettaoui, C., & Maaref, H. (2005). *Shapes description for cells sickle illness recognition*. IEEE International Conference on Systems, Signals & Devices, Communication and Signal Processing, volume 3, March, Sousse, Tunisia.

Djemal, K., Puech, W., & Rossetto, B. (2006). Automatic active contours propagation in a sequence of medical images. *International Journal of Image and Graphics*, *6*(2), 267–292. doi:10.1142/S0219467806002252

Djouak, A., Djemal, K., & Maaref, H. (2007). Image recognition based on features extraction and RBF classifier. *Journal Transactions on Signals, Systems and Devices. Issues on Communication and Signal Processing*, *2*(3), 235–253.

Egmont-Petersen, M., de Ridder, D., & Handels, H. (2002). Image processing with neural networks-a review. *Pattern Recognition*, *35*(10), 2279–2301. doi:10.1016/S0031-3203(01)00178-9

Ghorbel, F., Derrode, S., Mezhoud, R., Bannour, M. T., & Dhahbi, S. (2006). Image reconstruction from a complete set of similarity invariants extracted from complex moments. *Pattern Recognition Letters, 27*(12), 1361–1369. doi:10.1016/j.patrec.2006.01.001

Giacinto, G., Roli, F., & Didaci, L. (2003). Fusion of multiple classifiers for intrusion detection in computer networks. *Pattern Recognition Letters.*

Huang, J., Kumar, S. R., Mitra, M., Zhu, W.-J., & Zabih, R. (1997). Image indexing using color correlograms. In *Proceedings of IEEE Computer Society Conference on Computer Vision and Pattern Recognition,* (pp. 762–768).

Jacobs, C., Finkelstein, A., & Salesin, D. (1995). Fast multiresolution image querying. In *Proceedings of SIGGRAPH.*

Kadyrov, A., & Petrou, M. (2001). *The trace transform and its applications. IEEE Transactions on Pattern Analysis and Machine Intelligence* (pp. 811–828). PAMI.

Kuncheva, L. (2004). *Combining pattern classifiers: Methods and algorithms.* New Jersey: Wiley. doi:10.1002/0471660264

Li, S., Fevens, T., & Krzyzak, A. (2006). Automatic clinical image segmentation using pathological modeling, PCA and SVM. *Engineering Applications of Artificial Intelligence, 19*(4). doi:10.1016/j.engappai.2006.01.011

Liguang, M., Yanrong, C., & Jianbang, H. (2008). Biomedical image storage, retrieval and visualization based-on open source project. *IEEE Congress on Image and Signal Processing, 3*(27-30), 63-66.

Lim, J.-H., & Chevallet, J.-P. (2005). *A structured learning approach for medical image indexing and retrieval.* In CLEF Workhop, Working Notes Medical Image Track, Vienna, Austria, 21–23 September.

Lin, C.-Y., Yin, J.-X., Gao, X., Chen, J.-Y., & Qin, P. (2006). *A semantic modeling approach for medical image semantic retrieval using hybrid Bayesian networks.* Sixth International Conference on Intelligent Systems Design and Applications (ISDA'06), vol. 2, (pp. 482-487).

Lipson, P., Grimson, E., & Sinha, P. (1997). Configuration based scene classification and image indexing. In *Proceedings of the IEEE Computer Society Conference on Computer Vision and Pattern Recognition,* (pp. 1007–1013).

Liu, Y., Lazar, N., Rothfus, W., Dellaert, F., Moore, A., Schneider, J., & Kanade, T. (2004). Semantic based biomedical image indexing and retrieval. In *Trends and advances in content-based image and video retrieval.*

Moreno, L., Piñeiro, J., Sanchez, J., Mañas, S., Merino, J., Acosta, L., & Hamilton, A. (1994). Using neural networks to improve classification: Application to brain maturation. *Neural Networks, 8*(5).

Polat, K., & Günes, S. (2006). Automated identification of diseases related to lymph system from lymphography data using artificial immune recognition system with fuzzy resource allocation mechanism (fuzzy-airs). *Biomedical Signal Processing and Control.*

Sastry, C. S., Pujari, A. K., Deekshatulu, B. L., & Bhagvati, C. (2004). A wavelet based multiresolution algorithm for rotation invariant feature extraction. *Pattern Recognition Letters*, *25*, 1845–1855. doi:10.1016/j.patrec.2004.07.011

Scholkopf, B., & Smola, A. (2002). *Learning with kernels*. Cambridge, MA: MIT Press.

Sclaroff, S., & Pentland, A. (1995). Modal matching for correspondence and recognition. *IEEE Transactions on Pattern Analysis and Machine Intelligence*, *17*(6), 545–561. doi:10.1109/34.387502

Serrano, N., Savakis, A. E., & Luo, J. (2004). Improved scene classification using efficient low-level features and semantic cues. *Pattern Recognition*, *37*, 1773–1784. doi:10.1016/j.patcog.2004.03.003

Shouche, S. P., Rastogi, R., Bhagwat, S. G., & Sainis, J. K. (2001). Shape analysis of grains of Indian wheat varieties. *Computers and Electronics in Agriculture*, *33*(1). doi:10.1016/S0168-1699(01)00174-0

Smith, J. R., & Chang, S. F. (1996). Tools and techniques for color image retrieval. *In SPIE Proceedings. Storage and Retrieval for Image and Video Databases*, *2670*, 426–437.

Smith, J. R., & Chang, S. F. (1996). VisualSEEk: A fully automated content-based image query system. *Proceedings of ACM Multimedia,* Boston MA, (pp. 87–98).

Stricker, M., & Dimai, A. (1997). Spectral covariance and fuzzy regions for image indexing. *Machine Vision and Applications*, *10*(2), 66–73. doi:10.1007/s001380050060

Stricker, M., & Swain, M. (1994). *Capacity and the sensitivity of color histogram indexing.* (Technical Report, 94-05, University of Chicago).

Swain, M., & Ballard, D. (1991). Color indexing. *International Journal of Computer Vision*, *7*(1), 11–32. doi:10.1007/BF00130487

Takashi, I., & Masafumi, H. (2000). Content-based image retrieval system using neural networks. *International Journal of Neural Systems*, *10*(5), 417–424. doi:10.1016/S0129-0657(00)00032-6

Vapnik, V. (1998). *Statistical learning theory*. Wiley-Interscience.

ADDITIONAL READING

Bankman, I. N. (Ed.). (2008). *Handbook of Medical Image Processing and Analysis*. Academic Press, Series in Biomedical Engineering.

Berry, E. (Ed.). (2007). *A Practical Approach to Medical Image Processing, Series in Medical Physics and Biomedical Engineering*. CRC Press.

Chany, H., Sahiner, B., Petrick, N., Helvie, M., Lam, K., Adler, D., & Goodsitt, M. (1997). Computerized classification of malignant and benign microcalcifications on mammograms: texture analysis using an artificial neural network. *Physics in Medicine and Biology*, *42*, 549–567. doi:10.1088/0031-9155/42/3/008

Chen, C. M., Chou, Y. H., Han, K. C., Hung, G. S., Tiu, C. M., Chiou, H. J., & Chiou, S. Y. (2003). Breast Lesions on Sonograms: Computer-aided Diagnosis with Nearly Setting-Independent Features and Artificial Neural Networks. *Radiology*, 504–514. doi:10.1148/radiol.2262011843

Chena, D. R., Changb, R. F., Chenb, C. J., Hob, M. F., Kuoa, S. J., & Chena, S. T. (2005). Classification of breast ultrasound images using fractal feature, *Journal of Clinical Imaging. Elseiver*, *29*, 235–245.

Egerton, S., Ling, T. C., & Ganapathy, V. (2009). A Semantic SLAM Model for Autonomous Mobile Robots Using Content Based Image Retrieval Techniques. *In 16th International Conference on Neural Information Processing. Lecture Notes in Computer Science*, *5864*, 93–106. doi:10.1007/978-3-642-10684-2_11

Güld, M. O., Thies, C., Fischer, B., & Lehmann, T. M. (2007). Ageneric Concept for the implementation of medical image retrieval systems. *International Journal of Medical Informatics*, *76*(2–3), 252–259. doi:10.1016/j.ijmedinf.2006.02.011

Hersh, W., Mailhot, M., Arnott-Smith, C., & Lowe, H. (2001). Selective Automated indexing of findings and diagnoses in radiology reports. *Journal of Biomedical Informatics*, *34*, 262–273. doi:10.1006/jbin.2001.1025

Hsu, W., Antani, S., Long, L. R., Neve, L., & Thoma, G. R. (2009). SPIRS: A Web-based image retrieval system for large biomedical databases. *International Journal of Medical Informatics*, *78*, 13–14. doi:10.1016/j.ijmedinf.2008.09.006

Jain, A. K., Dvin, R. P. W., & Mao, J. (2000). Statistical Pattern Recognition: A Review. *IEEE Transactions on Pattern Analysis and Machine Intelligence*, *22*(1), 4–37. doi:10.1109/34.824819

Khapli, V. R., & Bhalachandra, A. S. (2008). CBIR system for biomedical images: challenges and open issues. *In IET Conference on Wireless, Mobile and Multimedia Networks,* pages: 85–88.

Lam, S. Y., & Hong, Y. (2006). Blood vessel extraction based on Mumford Shah model and skeletonization. *In Proceedings of the Fifth International Conference on Machine Learning and Cybernetics,* pages: 4227–4230.

Lehmann, T. M., Güld, M. O., Thies, C., Fischer, B., Keysers, M., Kohnen, D., et al. (2003). Content-based image retrieval in medical applications for picture archiving and communication systems, *In Proceedings of the SPIE Conference on Medical Imaging,* Vol. 5033, SanDiego, CA, USA, 2003.

Müller, H., Michoux, N., Bandon, D., & Geissbuhler, A. (2004). A review of content-based image retrieval systems in medical applications-clinical benefits and future directions. *International Journal of Medical Informatics*, *73*(1), 1–23. doi:10.1016/j.ijmedinf.2003.11.024

Müller, H., Squire, D. M. & Pun T. (2004). Learning from user behavior In image retrieval: application of the market basket analysis, *Int. J. Comput. Vis. (special issue on content-based image retrieval),* Vol. 56(1-2), pages: 65—77.

Pun, T., Gerig, G., & Ratib, O. (1994). Image analysis and computer vision in medicine. *Computerized Medical Imaging and Graphics*, *18*(2), 85–96. doi:10.1016/0895-6111(94)90017-5

Qian, X., & Tagare, H. D. (2005). Optimal embedding for shape indexing in medical image databases, *In Proceedings of the International Conference on Medical Image Computing and Computer Assisted Intervention,* Vol. 8(2), pages: 377–384.

Rangayyan, R., & Desautels, J. (2005). Content-based retrieval and analysis of mammographic masses. *Journal of Electronic Imaging, 14*(2),.

Serjeant, G. R., & Serjeant, B. E. (2001). *Sickle cell disease* (3rd ed.). Oxford University Press.

Tavares, J. M., & Natal, J. R. M. (Eds.). (2009). *Computational Vision and Medical Image Processing.* CRC Press. doi:10.1007/978-1-4020-9086-8

Vannier, M. W., Staab, E. V., & Clarke, L. C. (2002). Medical image archives-present and future, *In H. U. Lemke, M. W. Vannier, K. Inamura, A. G. Farman, J. H. C. Reiber (Eds.), Proceedings of the International Conference on Computer-Assited Radiology and Surgery (CARS2002)*, Paris, France.

Wang J. Z. (2000). Region-based retrieval of biomedical images. *In eighth ACM international conference on Multimedia,* pages: 511–512.

Wei, L., Yang, Y., Nishikawa, R. M., & Jiang, Y. (2005). A Study on Several Machine-Learning Methods for Classification of Malignant and Benign Clustered Microcalcifications. *IEEE Transactions on Medical Imaging, 24*(3), 371–380. doi:10.1109/TMI.2004.842457

Xu, X., Lee, D., Antani, S., & Long, L. R. (2008). A spine X-ray image Retrieval system using partial shape matching. *IEEE Transactions on Information Technology in Biomedicine, 12*(1), 100–108. doi:10.1109/TITB.2007.904149

Yang, S., Wang, C., Chung, Y., Hsu, G. C., Lee, S., Chung, P., & Chang, C. (2005). A Computer Aided system for mass detection and classification in digitized mammograms. *Biomedical Engineering Applications. Basis and Communications, 17*(5), 215–228. doi:10.4015/S1016237205000330

KEY TERMS AND DEFINITIONS

Biomedical Image Databases: These databases contain specific medical images describing special disease or heterogeneous biomedical images which can represent different diseases.

Classification: From image databases, the classification methods try to categorize it in classes using learning methods and similarity criterions.

Feature Extraction: Consists in developing methods able to extract features describing the totality or a part of image content.

Image Recognition: Generally, the image recognition consists in objects identification in an image. In CBIR systems, the image recognition term is also used to represents the classification rate obtained form a set of query images.

Intelligent Information Description: Consists in modelling or defining intelligent descriptors which represent image content.

Multicriteria Approaches: These approaches use criteria for each used classifier. The final classification decision is obtained by the fusion model based on different obtained results by all classifiers.

Sickle Cells Disease: A genetic blood disease due to the presence of an abnormal form of hemoglobin, namely hemoglobin S. Hemoglobin is the molecule in red blood cells that transports oxygen from the lungs to the farthest reaches of the body.

Chapter 4
Machine Learning for Visual Navigation of Unmanned Ground Vehicles

Artem A. Lenskiy
University of Ulsan, South Korea

Jong-Soo Lee
University of Ulsan, South Korea

ABSTRACT

The use of visual information for the navigation of unmanned ground vehicles in a cross-country environment recently received great attention. However, until now, the use of textural information has been somewhat less effective than color or laser range information. This chapter reviews the recent achievements in cross-country scene segmentation and addresses their shortcomings. It then describes a problem related to classification of high dimensional texture features. Finally, it compares three machine learning algorithms aimed at resolving this problem. The experimental results for each machine learning algorithm with the discussion of comparisons are given at the end of the chapter.

INTRODUCTION

Literature Overview

The area of autonomous driving on- and off-road vehicles is expanding very rapidly. A great deal of work has been done developing autonomous navigational systems for driving along highways and roads in an urban environment. The autonomous navigation in determined and rigid urban environment with lanes, road markers and boards is relatively easier than the off-road autonomous navigation. In off-road navigation the significantly changing environment with fuzzy or no roads creates a new complexity for navigational issues. Only recently has cross-country navigation received appropriate attention. A good example is The Grand Challenge which was launched by the

DOI: 10.4018/978-1-60960-551-3.ch004

Defense Advanced Research Projects Agency (DARPA) in 2003. The original goal of the project was to stimulate innovation in unmanned ground vehicle navigation. Two years later an unmanned ground vehicle (UGV) named Stanley was able to navigate a 132-mile long off-road course and complete it in 6 hours 53 minutes (Thrun, et al., 2006).

UGVs are usually equipped with multiple sensors to operate in a variety of cross-country environments (Figure 1). This equipment along with sophisticated algorithms serves to solve navigational problems such as map building, path planning, land mark detection, position estimation and obstacle avoidance. In this chapter we focus on the visual terrain segmentation task. The terrain segmentation allows the robot to detect obstacles and select the optimal path. Based on the information obtained by means of terrain segmentation, the robot is able to avoid unnecessary stops caused by traversable tall patches of grass. The segmentation information also allows adjusting traversal velocity depending on the terrain slippery factors.

There are multiple ways to segment a cross-country scene image, depending on what image characteristics are taken into account. Regardless of what characteristics are used, the final goal is to separate spatial image regions on the basis of their similarity. In the terrain segmentation task, image characteristics as color (Manduchi, 2006; Rasmussen, 2002), texture (Castano, Manduchi, & Fox, 2001; Sung, Kwak, & Lyou, 2010) and range data(Dahlkamp, Kaehler, Stavens, Thrun, & Bradski, 2006; Lalonde, Vandapel, Huber, & Hebert, 2006) are commonly utilized. The best terrain segmentation results are obtained when all characteristics are incorporated in the segmentation process. Nevertheless, in this chapter texture information is applied for cross-country scene segmentation. Depending on the terrain type, some image characteristics are more distinctive than others. Particularly, color information is useful in distinguishing classes such as sky, dry or green vegetation. However, there are a number of shortcomings associated with color segmentation algorithms. Compared to texture, color based segmentation algorithms are less robust to brightness changes caused fluctuations in natural illumination or shadows. Another demerit is that red, green, and blue color components that constitute color space are less discriminative than multidimensional texture features. Finally, color segmentation does not work at night, while texture segmentation can be applied to IR images captured at night. Nevertheless, adaptive color segmentation algorithms are useful especially in combination with other types of features. The off-road scene segmentation algorithm implemented in Stanley (Dahlkamp, et al., 2006; Thrun, et al., 2006) (the DARPA Grand Challenge winner) did not take into account texture information. There are likely two

Figure 1. An unmanned ground vehicle

reasons for this. Texture features are usually computationally expensive to extract, and until now the performance of texture features was quite unsatisfactory compared to other scene characteristics.

Rasmussen (Rasmussen, 2002), provided a comparison of color, texture, distance features measured by the laser range scanner, and their combination for the purpose of cross-country scene segmentation. The segmentation was the worst when texture features were used alone. In the case when 25% of all features were used for training, only 52.3% of the whole feature set was correctly classified. There are two probable explanations of this poor result. One is related to the feature extraction approach. The feature vector consisted of 48 values representing responses of the Gabor filter bank. Specifically, it consists of 2 phases with 3 wavelengths and 8 equally-spaced orientations. The 48-dimensional vector appears to have enough dimensions to accommodate a wide variety of textures. However, besides the feature dimensionality, the size of texture patches also influence the segmentation quality. The size of the patch was set to a relatively small constant value equal to 15x15, which led to poor scale invariance. Furthermore, features' locations were calculated on the grid without considering an image content. Another reason of the problematic segmentation results is in the low classifier's capacity. As a classifier, the author used a neural network with only one hidden layer with 20 neurons. A one layer feed-forward neural network is not capable of partitioning concave clusters, while terrain texture features are very irregular.

Sung et al. (Sung, et al., 2010) instead, used a two-layer percpetron with 18 and 12 neurons in the first and second hidden layers correspondingly. The feature vector was composed of the mean and energy values computed for selected sub-bands of two-level Daubechies wavelet transform, resulting in 8 values. These values were calculated for each of three color channels resulting into 24-dimensional feature vector. The experiments were conducted in the following fashion. First, 100 random images from the stored video frames were selected and used to extract training patches. Then among them ten were chosen for testing purposes. The average segmentation rate was 75.1% when two-layer perceptron and 24-dimensional feature vectors were applied. Considering that color information was not explicitly used and only texture features were taken into account, the segmentation rate is promising, although there is still room for improvement. Similarly to Rasmussen (Rasmussen, 2002), the wavelet mean and energy were calculated for fixed 16x16 pixel sub-blocks. Consider a resolution of input images of 720x480 pixel, the sub-block of 16x16 pixels is too small to capture texture characteristics, especially at higher scales, which leads to poor texture scale invariance.

Castano et al. (Castano, et al., 2001) applied Gabor features extracted as described in (Manjunath & Ma, 1996) with 3 scales and 4 orientations. Two statistical texture models were analyzed. The first classifier modeled the probability distribution function of texture features using mixtures of Gaussian and performed a Maximum Likelihood classification. The second classifier represents local statistics by marginal histograms over small image squares. Comparable performances were reached with both models. Particularly, in the case when half of the hand segmented images were used for training and the other half for testing, the classification performance on the cross-country scene images was 70% for mixtures of Gaussian and 66% for histogram based classifiers. Visual analysis of presented segmentation results suggests that the wrong classification happens due to the short range of scale independence of Gabor features.

There are two major directions for algorithmic improvement: features extraction and machine learning. In this chapter we focus on comparison of the following machine learning algorithms: nearest-neighbor algorithm (NNA), multi-layer perceptron (MLP) and support vector machine (SVM). We also analyze the influence of changing the dimension of feature vectors on the quality of feature classification.

Problem Statement

The majority of papers related to texture segmentation consider homogeneous textures which usually lack real-world problems, when appearance of the same texture greatly changes. Cross-country segmentation brings immense complexity into the texture segmentation task due to high inter- and intraclass variation. For instance, in the example of tree textures, there is a broad variety of trees to consider. Secondly, even for the same type of trees the appearance of their texture patches changes drastically with the changing distance to the camera. When a camera is close enough it is possible to distinguish branches and single leaves so the texture patch has one set of properties; when the camera is further away the tree looks like a green spot, resulting in completely changed properties. The intraclass variation comes from the similar appearance of different texture classes. Textures from different classes may look similar depending on factors such as their distance from the camera, weather conditions and the time of day (Figure 2).

To be able to account for all these possibilities and correctly segment input images, a high-dimensional feature space with a great number of features is needed. That is where data analysis plays a great role. We consider two mutually related machine learning problems. The first one is the generalization problem accounting for transforming the training set in to a more compact and generalized form. The second one is a classification problem; an algorithm learns to predict positions of each class vectors.

Let $S = \{(x_i, y_i) \mid i = 1..n\}$ is a training set, where $x \subset \boldsymbol{R}^d$ is a feature vector and $y = \{1, \ldots, m\}$ is a feature's label, *m* corresponds to the number of classes. It is often useful to take into account information on how likely a feature was classified to a particular class. Therefore, to allow us to represent non-mutually exclusive classes we code output vectors as *m* dimensional vector, with $y \subset \boldsymbol{R}^m$. The goal is to find a transform *f* such that $f(x) \sim y$ and, in the least mean squares sense we look for a transform minimizing the following loss function:

$$\varepsilon(f) = \sum_{i=1}^{n} \left(y_i - f(x_i)\right)^2 \tag{1}$$

Figure 2. Texture similarity in between classes and dissimilarity within a class

It is easy to see that the simplest approach to make the criterion (1) equal to zero is by forcing *f* to pass through all training samples. Lazy-learning algorithms are good examples of this principle. Although this approach is easy to implement, it has two disadvantages. When a training set contains a great number of samples it becomes time and memory consuming to simply store all samples in the knowledge base. The second disadvantage is related to overfitting of noisy data contained in the training set. On the other hand, inappropriate reduction of the number of training samples would lead to poor generalization and classification. Our goal is to compare and find an appropriate machine learning algorithm which suits a vast amount of high-dimensional vectors by not only minimizing the loss function (1) but also minimizing the computational time and memory demands for classification.

Cross-Country Scene Segmentation System Overview

Depending on the view point the scene segmentation system can be divided into sub-systems or functioning stages. From the machine learning perspective the system consists of two stages: the learning stage and the recognition stage. In the learning stage, the training set is transformed into a compact and generalized form suitable for classification. The result of the learning stage is some form of knowledge base which depends on a machine learning algorithm. From the other point of view, the system consists of three subsystems. The first subsystem deals with image preprocessing and texture features extraction. The second subsystem depending on the learning or recognition stage is responsible for supervised learning or features classification. The last subsystem segments the input image using the classification results.

The main focus of this chapter is the learning as well as recognition stages.

THE TRAINING DATA PREPROCESSING

Our terrain segmentation system is designed to recognize five different terrain types. The list of terrains includes grass, gravel, trees, dirt/mud and sky. The training data is selected from prerecorded video sequences. The total number of images is 2973, with every 100th being hand segmented. The hand segmentation process itself is a challenge. It is often the case when terrains of different types are mixing up so, it makes difficult to distinguish a region containing only one type of terrain (Figure 2). In this case the region is segmented to the class that pixels are the most represented in the region. Another problem we face during hand segmentation is that terrains residing far away from the camera lack strong textures and are usually blurred; they therefore look similar to one another. In this case very blurred regions are avoided due to their insignificancy for the training set and also due to the fact that the priority of the UGV is to recognize nearest environment rather than distant.

We overall selected and segmented 29 images. Ten of them were selected for the testing purpose and 19 for training. Each training image pair was processed with the subject to extract salient features. Salient features are sorted up into five matrices according to their labels (Figure 3). As for salient features, we chose speeded-up robust features (SURF) (Bay, Ess, Tuytelaars, & Gool, 2008). Each feature consists of two vectors. The first vector contains information of the feature's location, scale and strength, and the second vector is a descriptor characterizing the region around its location.

The SURF algorithm consists of three stages. In the first stage, interest points and their scales are selected. The features' locations and scales are selected by finding the maxima of the determinant of the Fast-Hessian matrix calculated in scale space. In the second stage, features' orientations are estimated.

At this stage Haar wavelet responses are calculated for both x and y directions surrounding the interest point and the dominant orientation is estimated by calculating the sum of all responses within a sliding orientation window. This direction is then used to create a rotated square around the interest point. Finally, to build the descriptor, an oriented quadratic grid with $n \times n$ square sub-regions is laid over the interest point. For each square, the vertical d_y and horizontal d_x Haar wavelet responses are computed from 5×5 samples. Then, the wavelet responses d_y and d_x and their absolute values $|d_x|$ and $|d_y|$ are summed up over each sub-region forming the description vector.

In our system we experimented with the SURF algorithm as well as with an upright version of the SURF (U-SURF). The latter is a rotation dependent version of the SURF. It skips the second stage and as a result it is faster to compute. We also experimented with two different numbers of sub-regions $n = 4$ and $n = 3$.When $n = 4$, the total number of the feature's dimensions is 64, and in the case of $n = 3$, the number of dimensions is 36.

The number of features detected by the SURF algorithm greatly depends on the predefined blob response threshold and the image content. If the threshold is too high than just a few features are detected, if the image is monotonic then the number of detected features is small too. On the other hand if the threshold is low and the image consists of not monotonic regions, then the number of detected features is high. To limit the number of detected features from the top and at the same assure that the number is not too small; we set the blob response threshold to low and then reduce the number of detected features as follows. The first, image is partitioned into boxes with the size of 20×20 pixels, then the feature with the highest strength is selected among all features fallen into each box (Figure 4). Therefore, if the image resolution is 640×480 pixels and the box size is 20×20 pixels, then the maximum number of features equals 768. The advantage of this approach versus those mentioned in the introduction is that the number of features and as well as features' locations are automatically adjusted depending on the image content. Moreover, instead of a fixed window size used in previous approaches, it is automatically adjusted by the SURF algorithm.

Extracting features from all of 19 training images results in 11394 labeled features.

This great number of accumulated features consequently leads to a high time demanding classification procedure and thus the training data should be intelligently processed.

Figure 3. An schematic representation of features extraction from a training pair

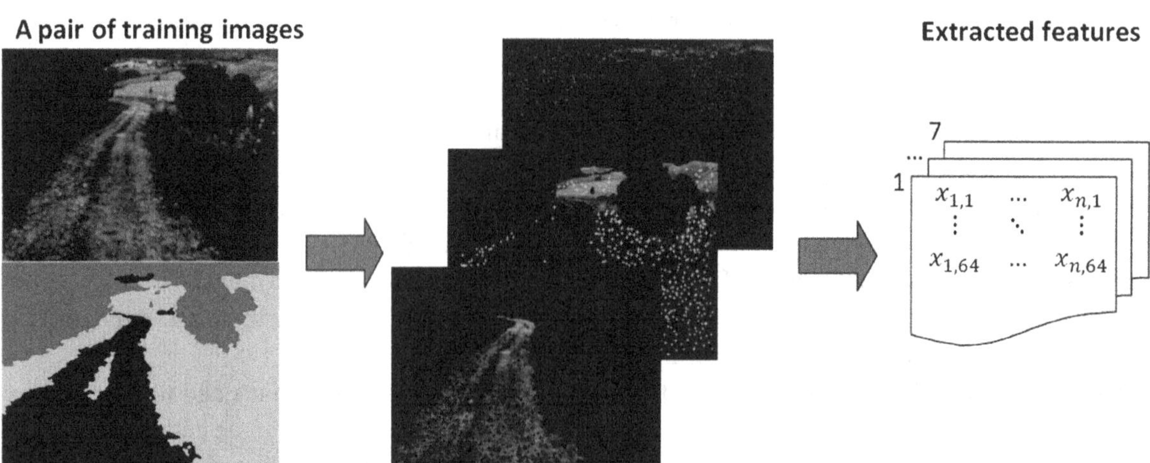

Among extracted features some are outliers that either were by accident wrongly hand-segmented, or are non-informative and represent statistically very improbable patches of texture. To omit these outliers, features from each terrain class are processed as follows:

Calculate distance matrix D, which contains distances between all pairs of descriptors:

$$D = \begin{bmatrix} d_{1,1} & \cdots & d_{N,1} \\ \vdots & \ddots & \vdots \\ d_{1,N} & \cdots & d_{N,N} \end{bmatrix} \tag{2}$$

Sort up each row of matrix D and add up first *k* elements with lowest values:

$$D^{/} = \mathrm{sort}\left(D\right) \tag{3}$$

$$\text{¼}_j = \sum_{i=1}^{k} e^{-\frac{D^{/\,2}_{j,i}}{\text{Ã}}} \tag{4}$$

Eliminate 5-20% of total number of descriptors with smallest μ.

After eliminating 10% of the features in each class, the total number of remained features is 10746.

Before we proceed with the description of machine learning algorithms, it is useful to visualize feature space. This visual information allows us to understand how features of different classes are scattered, which is useful for parameters selection in classification routines. A number of approaches have been proposed to visualize high dimensional data. One of them is based on dimension reduction techniques. High-dimensional feature vectors are transformed into vectors with three components, so they can be plotted in the three dimensional space. We applied two approaches to reduce feature space dimensions

Figure 4. (a) Red points represent centers of detected features, green circles are selected features; (b) Circles corresponding to selected features, circles' radii are proportional to features' scales.

that do not take into account the information on features' labels. The first one is a linear technique based on principal component analysis (PCA). PCA performances linear mapping in a way that variance of the data in the dimensionally reduced space is maximized. The reduced feature space is shown in Figure 6a. Another approach for feature dimension reduction consists in applying a multi-layer perceptron (MLP) with a bottle neck principle. The number of input units and neurons in the output layer are set equal to the number of feature dimensions. The number of neurons in the hidden layer is set to a desired lower number, which represents the dimension of the reduced feature space. In our case the MLP structure is 64-3-64. The MLP learns to compress the data from 64 to 3 and then back to 64 dimensions. After the training process is finished, the outputs of neurons in the hidden layer represent new low-dimensional feature vectors (Figure 5d). For further analysis we separate a feature set, in the original 64-dimensional, space into two subsets. The first subset combines features whose *N* nearest neighbors are features of the same class (Figure 5b, 5e), and the second subset contains the remaining features (Figure 5c, 5f).

Points from the first subspace are located deep inside clusters, far from cluster boundaries and therefore are less informative. The algorithm that separate one subset from the other can be summarized in the list of steps as follows:

1. Calculate distance matrix D, which contains distances between all pair of descriptors;
2. Sort up each row of matrix D and choose first N nearest neighbors;
3. If all of them belong to the same class, then the feature is placed into the subset with dense features otherwise it is placed in the subset with non-dense features.

When $N = 5$, 39% of features fell in the first dense subset, and the remaining 61% is within the second subset. This ratio supports the assumption that there is an underline structure presented in the features space, meaning that features corresponding to similar textures are also located in close proximity. Furthermore, it can be seen from Figure 6 that both linear and non-linear dimension reduction techniques generate very similar feature distributions. Therefore the data can be separated by a function with much

Figure 5. Reduced feature space using PCA (a) full set, (b) dense features subset, (c) non-dense features subset, and using MLP (d) full set, (e) dense features subset, (f) non-dense features subset.

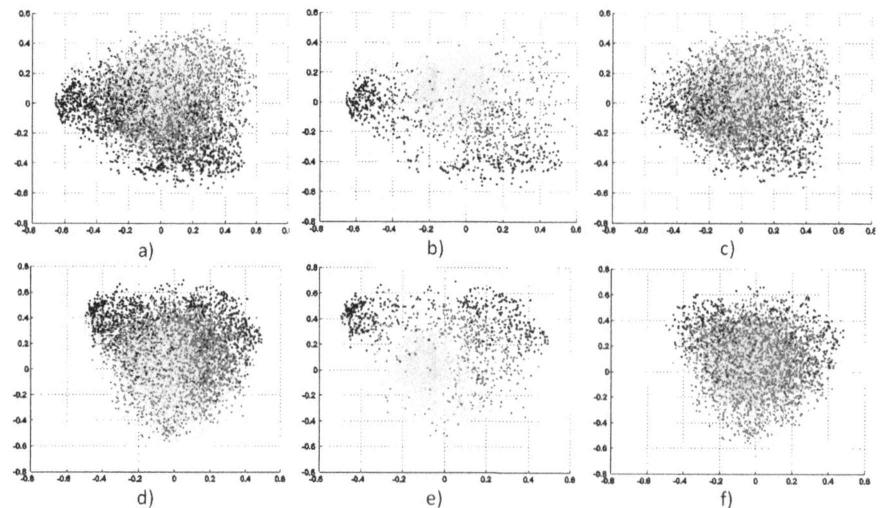

less parameters than the number of features in the training set. It is interesting to notice that blue features representing trees are distributed in two groups. This fact is due to two visually different groups of tress. The first group contains trees with crowns, so that textures of leaves are distinguishable. The second group is trees without a crown, so that tree branches are visible. Difference in appearance of leaves and branches leads to two separable clusters.

MACHINE LEARNING ALGORITHMS

Visual analysis of Figure 5 suggests that some features are more discriminative than the others. It is crucial to select those features which contribute to class partitioning more and omit those which are less informative. The benefits are a lower system complexity and less storage requirement. Moreover, it improves the classifier performance and reduces computation time.

In the next sections we consider three supervised classifiers. The purpose of a classifier is to predict or estimate the likeliness of class label of an input feature vector after having seen a number of training examples. A broad range of classifiers have been proposed. We consider the following widely used classifiers: *k*-Nearest Neighbor Algorithm, Multilayer Perceptron and Support Vector Machine.

k-Nearest Neighbor Algorithm and Kernel Method

In this section we discuss a modified lazy-learning algorithm which is based on the combination of two non-parametric estimators. The first is called the *k*-nearest neighbor algorithm and the second is the Parzen window method. Both algorithms are similar although with some differences. *k*-Nearest Neighbor is well developed machine learning algorithms with a long history (Cover & Hart, 1967). The algorithm is based on the assumption that feature vectors of the same class located in close proximity to each other. Then an unclassified vector can be classified by observing the class labels of nearest neighbors. It was

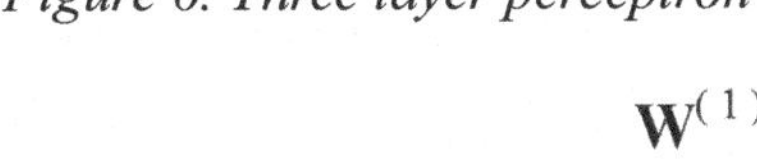

Figure 6. Three layer perceptron

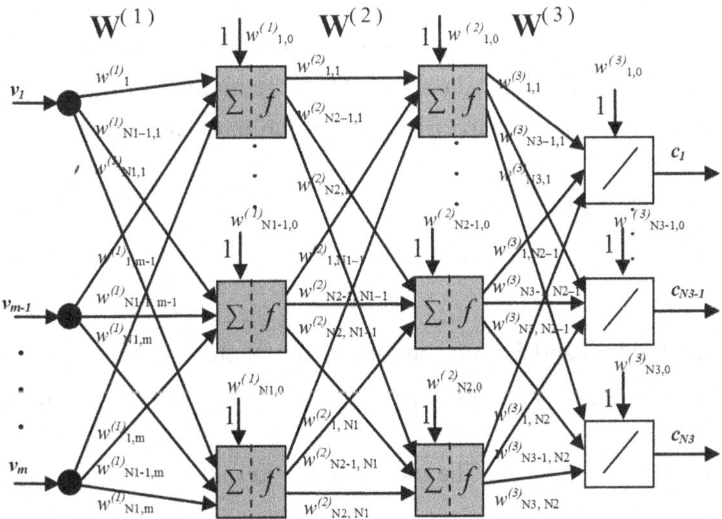

shown that *k*-nearest neighbor is guaranteed to approach the Bayes error rate, for some value of *k*, where *k* increases as a function of the number of data points.

Let among *k* nearest vectors k_m are from class $c^{(m)}$ and let the total number of vectors in class $c^{(m)}$ be n_m. Then the class conditional probability $\hat{p}\left(x|\,c^{(m)}\right)$ is

$$\hat{p}\left(x|\,c^{(m)}\right) = \frac{k_m}{n_m V}, \tag{5}$$

V is a volume centered at a point *x*, and the prior probability $p(c_m)$ defined as

$$\hat{p}(c^{(m)}) = \frac{n_m}{n}, \tag{6}$$

$$n = \sum_{m=1}^{M} n_m \tag{7}$$

The class of an unclassified point *x* is determined using the following rule:

$$c = \arg\max_{\mathrm{i=1..M}} \hat{p}(c^{(i)} \mid x) \tag{8}$$

Or applying Bayes' theorem,

$$c = \arg\max_{\mathrm{i=1..M}} \left(\frac{k_i}{n_i V} \cdot \frac{n_i}{n} \right) \tag{9}$$

It can be easily seen from (9), that *x* is assigned to the class with the largest number samples among *k* nearest neighbors.

In the Parzen method (Parzen, 1962) instead of fixing the number of nearest neighbors the algorithm fixes the volume around the vector to be classified. Then the number of neighbors residing within the volume is counted and the class probability $\hat{p}\left(x|\,c^{(m)}\right)$ is estimated as:

$$\hat{p}\left(x|\,c^{(m)}\right) = \frac{1}{n_m h^p} \cdot \sum_{i=1}^{n_m} K\left(\frac{x - x_i^{(m)}}{h} \right) \tag{10}$$

Where *K* is a kernel function and *h* is the smoothing parameter. To make $\hat{p}(x)$ satisfy properties of probability density function $p\left(x\right) \geq 0$ and $\int p\left(x\right) dx = 1$, kernel *K* should conform to the following conditions: $K\left(z\right) \geq 0$ and $\int_{R^p} K\left(z\right) = 1$. The most popular kernel is the Gaussian kernel:

$$K\left(z\right)=\frac{1}{\left(\sqrt{2\cdot\pi}\right)^{p}}\cdot\exp\left(-\frac{x^{T}x}{2}\right), \tag{11}$$

where p is a number of dimensions.

With estimated class PDFs the following classification rule can be used to classify a new feature:

$$c=\arg\max_{\mathrm{i=1..M}}\hat{p}\left(x|\,c^{(m)}\right). \tag{12}$$

The algorithm we use in our experiments is based on Parzen window method the difference is that it estimates local probability density function by taking into account only *k*-nearest neighbors. This approach allows us to save time on computing many Gaussian kernels in dense regions or to take into account *k*-nearest neighbors in sparse regions.

k-Nearest Neighbor as well as Parzen window methods are both classified as instance-based learning algorithms. Instance-based learning algorithms delay their generalization process until the classification stage. This aspect leads to large memory requirements due to the necessity of storing all training samples. A consequence of large training sets is high computational demands related to calculating distances to each training sample. Another disadvantage particularly related to *k*-NN and Parzen methods is a requirement of choosing the similarity function as well as *k* or *h* parameters.

Multi-Layer Perceptron

Another approach to decrease calculation time and increase generalization of the segmentation system consists in applying a classifier based on a multilayer feed-forward neural network or more specifically on the multilayer perceptron(MLP). A classifier based on MLP has a few advantages against the lazy learning algorithms discussed early. Instead of computing distances between an input vector and all features from the training set, the MLP learns to transform training vectors into matrices of interlayer weight coefficients. The total number of coefficients is usually substantially less than the number of training samples multiplied by the number of components in a feature vector. As a consequence fast computation can be achieved with less memory requirement.

The training process consists in turning coefficients of interlayer W^{Hi} and output W^{O} matrices. In our experiments we used a neural network with two hidden layers. It has been proved that an MLP with one hidden layer with sigmoid activation functions is capable of approximating any function with multiple arguments to arbitrary accuracy (Cybenko, 1989). However, for classification purposes, an MLP has to have two hidden layers to be able to separate concave domains. The decision function of an MLP with two hidden layers with sigmoid activation functions and with linear action function in output neurons (fig. 6) can be written as follows:

$$y_{l}=\sum_{i=0}^{N3}w_{l,i}^{(3)}f\left(\sum_{j=0}^{N2}w_{i,j}^{(2)}f\left(\sum_{k=0}^{N1}w_{j,k}^{(1)}x_{k}\right)\right) \tag{13}$$

x is an input SURF vector and f is a sigmoid function. We used the following hyperbolic sigmoid function:

$$f(x) = \frac{2}{\left(1 + e^{-2 \cdot x}\right)} - 1 \tag{14}$$

The training set contains pairs of input x and known target vectors t. The number of network inputs corresponds to the number of dimensions of a SURF vector and the number of outputs is equal to the number of classes. The target vector is filled with -1 for all elements except the one $\hat{p}$ representing the class of input vector which equals 1. A feature vector v is classified by simply choosing the class c with maximum output:

$$c = arg\left(max_{1 \le l \le 5}\left(y_l\right)\right) \tag{15}$$

Our image segmentation algorithm takes into account not only the class label but also the likeliness of belonging to that as well as to other classes. Therefore, in the image segmentation process the whole vector y is used. Although negative output vector components are set to zero.

The goal of the learning procedure is to find weights W that minimize the following criterion obtained by substituting (3) into (1):

$$\varepsilon\left(w\right) = \sum_{m=1}^{M}\left[\sum_{i=0}^{N3} w_{l,i}^{(3)} f\left[\sum_{j=0}^{N2} w_{i,j}^{(2)} f\left[\sum_{k=0}^{N1} w_{j,k}^{(1)} x_k\right]\right] - t_m\right]^2 \rightarrow min \tag{16}$$

The most popular method for learning in multilayer networks is called Back-propagation. The idea behind the learning algorithm is the repeated application of the chain rule which allows finding how much each of the weights contributes to the network error (17):

$$\frac{\partial \varepsilon}{\partial w_{i,j}} = \frac{\partial \varepsilon}{\partial f_i}\frac{\partial f_i}{\partial u_i}\frac{\partial u_i}{\partial w_{i,j}}, \tag{17}$$

Then according to calculated errors modify each weight (18) to minimize the error:

$$w_{i,j}\left(t+1\right) = w_{i,j}\left(t\right) - \mu\frac{\partial \varepsilon}{\partial w_{i,j}}(t). \tag{18}$$

The ordinary gradient decent by back propagation is slow and often ends far from the optimal solution. To improve the quality of minimum search a number of modifications have been proposed. One is called RPROP, or 'resilient propagation' (Riedmiller & Braun, 1993). The idea behind the algorithm is to introduce for each weight its individual update-value $\Delta_{i,j}$ which determines the size of the weight-update. Every time the partial derivative of the corresponding weight $w_{i,j}$ changes its sign, which indicates that the last update was too big and the algorithm has jumped over a local minimum, the update-value $\Delta_{i,j}$ is decreased by the factor μ^{-}. If the derivative retains its sign, $\Delta_{i,j}$ is slightly increased in order to accelerate convergence in shallow regions. After all update-values are adapted, neural weights are adjusted as follows:

$$\Delta w_{i,j}(t) = \begin{cases} -\Delta_{i,j}(t) & if \frac{\partial \varepsilon}{\partial w_{i,j}}(t) > 0 \\ +\Delta_{i,j}(t) & if \frac{\partial \varepsilon}{\partial w_{i,j}}(t) < 0, \\ 0 & else \end{cases} \tag{19}$$

$$w_{i,j}(t+1) = w_{i,j}(t) - \Delta w_{i,j}(t). \tag{20}$$

Probably the most successful and widely used learning algorithm is the Levenberg–Marquardt algorithm (Martin Hagan & Menhaj, 1994). The quasi-Newton methods are considered to be more efficient than gradient decent methods, but their storage and computational requirements go up as the square of the size of the network. Levenberg–Marquardt algorithm (LMA) is taking advantages of both Gauss–Newton algorithm and the method of gradient descent.

If error function is simply written as

$$\varepsilon(w) = \sum_{m=1}^{M} \left(e_m(w)\right)^2 \tag{21}$$

and

$$e_m(w) = y_i(w) - t_i \tag{22}$$

then using the following notation:

$$e(w) = \begin{bmatrix} e_1(w) \\ e_2(w) \\ \cdots \\ e_M(w) \end{bmatrix}, \; J(w) = \begin{bmatrix} \frac{\partial e_1}{\partial w_1} & \frac{\partial e_1}{\partial w_2} & \cdots & \frac{\partial e_1}{\partial w_n} \\ \frac{\partial e_2}{\partial w_1} & \frac{\partial e_2}{\partial w_2} & \cdots & \frac{\partial e_2}{\partial w_n} \\ \cdots & \cdots & \cdots & \cdots \\ \frac{\partial e_M}{\partial w_1} & \frac{\partial e_M}{\partial w_2} & \cdots & \frac{\partial e_M}{\partial w_n} \end{bmatrix} \tag{23}$$

Gradient vector and Hessian approximation corresponding to (21) defined as

$$g(w) = \left[J(w)\right]^T e(w), \tag{24}$$

$$G(w) = \left[J(w)\right]^T J(w) + R(w), \tag{25}$$

where $R(w)$ contains Hessian components of higher order derivatives.

The main idea of the LMA consists in approximating $R(w)$ with regularized parameter $v_k I$, so that Hessian is approximated as follows:

$$G(w_k) = [J(w_k)]^T J(w_k) + v_k I. \tag{26}$$

Then at the beginning of learning procedure, when w_k is far from the optimal solution, v_k is substantially higher than eigenvalues of $[J(w_k)]^T J(w_k)$. In this situation the Hessian matrix is replaced with:

$$G(w_k) = v_k I, \tag{27}$$

and minimization direction is chosen using the method of gradient descent:

$$p_k = -\frac{g(w_k)}{v_k}. \tag{28}$$

However, while the error is reducing the parameter v_k is reducing too and therefore the first component in (26) start contributing more and more. Then v_k is close to zero, the equation (26) is turning into the Gauss–Newton algorithm.

One of the advantages of the LMA is that it converges in less number of iterations than when resilient propagation is used.

Support Vector Machine

Support Vector Machines are relatively new machine learning algorithm (Vapnik, 1995). They transform a classification problem into quadratic programming problem, which always allows us to find an optimal solution. An advantage of SVMs consists in a good ability to separate very complex domains due to their ability of nonlinearly transforming data into a higher dimensional space, where hyper planes can separate already lineralized data (Figure 7). Another advantage is that SVMs selects only those vectors which are located close to the class boundary (support vectors) and therefore reduce the number of features.

The decision function for the Kernel-SVM is:

$$f(x) = \sum_i \alpha_i \mathrm{K}(x_i, x) + \mathrm{b} \tag{29}$$

$\mathrm{K}(x_i, x)$ is the kernel function of the following form:

Figure 7. (a) Block scheme of the SVM decision function, (b) illustration of nonlinear transform from 2D to 3D space, bold circles highlight support vectors.

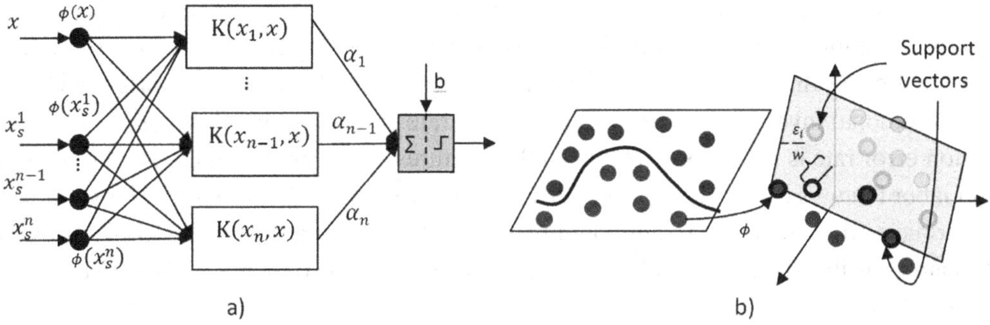

$$K\left(x_i, x\right) = \Phi(x_i) \cdot \Phi\left(x\right) \tag{30}$$

To tune the SVM parameters the following optimization problem should be solved:

$$min_\alpha D\left(\alpha\right) = \frac{1}{2}\sum_{i,j} \alpha_i \alpha_j \Phi\left(x_i\right) \cdot \Phi\left(x_j\right) - \sum_i y_i \alpha_i \quad s.t. \begin{cases} \sum_i \alpha_i = 0 \\ 0 \le y_i \alpha_i \le C \end{cases} \tag{31}$$

As a kernel function we used RBF kernel:

$$K\left(x, x^{/}\right) = \exp\left(-^{3} x - x^{/2}\right) \tag{32}$$

For multi-class classification we followed one-against-one approach, when $k(k-1)/2$ binary classifiers are constructed and each one trains data from two different classes. To decide to which class an input vector belongs to, each binary classifier is considered. A vector is classified as the class with the maximum number of assignments among $\frac{k\left(k-1\right)}{2}$ classifiers.

There are two parameters C the upper bound and γ the Kernel's width which greatly influence the classification accuracy. To select the optimal parameters we ran a set of experiments for different values of C and γ. We calculated classification accuracy for each pair of the parameters. The classification accuracy is calculated as follows:

$$Accuracy = \frac{\#\, correctly\, predicted\, data}{\#\, total\, data} 100\% \tag{33}$$

Parameters that yield the best accuracy are selected for the model construction.

In our image segmentation algorithm it is necessary to know the probabilities of an input vector belonging to each class. The probabilities are estimates as described in (Chang & Lin, 2010).

EXPERIMENTS AND DISCUSSION

The experiments were conducted for the training and testing datasets. First we started with the lazy learning algorithm and applied it to a set of different salient features. We tested the classifier on two datasets, one constructed of 64-dimesnional SURF features and the second consists of upright SURF features i.e. without rotational invariance. Comparing the error rates for these two datasets, and found that the segmentation error rate is much lower for U-SURF features. This result coincides with the results obtained for Gabor features in (Castano, et al., 2001). Gabor features without rotational invariance showed better performance than those with rotational invariance. The advantage of U-SURF features compared to SURF features is that the former is faster to compute and they also increase class distinctivity, while maintaining robustness to rotation of about $\pm 15^{\circ}$. Therefore, for further analysis only variations of U-SURF features are considered. To decrease memory demands and decrease computation time we looked into feature vector reduction. One approach to reduce dimensionality is to use separately sums of either d_y and d_x (USURF32) or of their absolute values $|d_x|$ and $|d_y|$ (USURF32abs). In this case, the feature's dimension reduces by half and equals to 32. Another way consists in reducing the quadratic grid laid over the interest point from 4×4 to 3×3. Then, the number of dimensions reduces to 36. Among these three dimensionally reduced features, the best performance is achieved with 36 dimensional vectors. Surprisingly, the 36-dimension version of U-SURF performs much better on the test data than in the case of 64-dimension U-SURF descriptors. For that reason in further experiments we use the upright version of SURF features with 3×3 quadratic grid. We also experimented with different numbers of neighbors, specifically with $k = \{1,2,3,4,5\}$. The parameter k did not greatly influence the error rate for the training data set as well as the testing data, although when the parameter k=3 the algorithm performed slightly better. Finally, we divided the U-SURF36 set into the subsets of dense and non-dense features as discussed earlier and then estimated error rates for both of them for $k = 1$ and $k = 3$. The total number of features was 2823 and 7922 for dense and non-dense feature subsets correspondingly. The error rates of dense features data significantly increased, however for non-dense features the results are comparable to the above discussed feature sets for both training and testing image sets.

We conducted three experiments with the classifier based on a neural network. In the first and second experiments we applied the Levenberg–Marquardt learning algorithm for two network structures. In both cases the training set consisted of U-SURF 36 dimensional vectors. Half of the set was used for training, a quarter for testing, and another quarter for validation. The structure of the first network was 36-40-40-5 and of the second was 36-60-60-5. In the third experiment the latter network structure was used; however, the learning algorithm was switched to resilient propagation. The experimental results show that a neural network with the structure of 36-40-40-5 is less effective than the network with 36-60-60-5. Among learning algorithms, the network trained with LMA shows the lowest error rate. It is worth noting that in terms of memory and computation requirement neural network substantially outperforms lazy learning algorithms. In the case when the network with a structure of 36-60-60-5 is used, the number of coefficients stored in the network is (36×60 + 60) + (60×60 + 60) + (60×5 + 5) = 6185, but in the case when lazy learning is used the number of coefficients is 10746 x 36 = 386856 for all training vectors and 7922×36 = 285192 for only none-dense vectors. So the number of coefficients necessary for classification is based on neural network constitutes for (6185/386856) * 100% = 1.6% of the whole training set and (6185/285192) * 100% = 2.1% for non-dense features. Nevertheless, a neural network classifier achieves comparable results.

The last classifier we experimented with was an SVM. The choice of parameters for the SVM greatly impacts the classification accuracy. Performing parameters selection procedure as discussed early in Table 1, we found that the best accuracy is achieved for $^{3} = 8$ and $C = 4$. For these parameters 8101 support vectors were selected. Which constitutes for 8101/10746 * 100% = 75% of the entire training set.

The error rates for all the above discussed classifiers and salient features are presented in Tables 2 and 3. In the left column an abbreviation for classifier and type of salient features are given. SURF and USURF stands for rotationally variant and invariant features. The number followed after SURF indicate vectors dimension. NN1 to NN5 stands for abbreviation of nearest number and the number correspond to the number of neighbors which were considered during the classification. DF and NDF stands for dense and non-dense feature sets. MLP40, MLP60 stands for multilayer perceptron with 36-40-40-5 and 36-60-60-5 structures trained with LMA and MLP60RP is MLP trained with RPPROP. In the central parts error rates for ten images are given. The right column contains an average error rate among 10 images and its standard deviation.

Some examples of terrain segmentation are shown on Figure 8. The same training image as well as the same test image for each classifier is shown for comparison purposes.

CONCLUSION

Among all the experiments we conducted, non-rotationally invariant 36-dimensional vectors significantly outperformed the 64-dimensional version of SURF. Among the experiments with various classifiers on

Table 1. Parameters selection. Star sign indicates that particularly pair of parameters was not checked.

$\gamma \setminus C$	2^{-1}	2^{0}	2^{1}	2^{2}	2^{3}	2^{4}	2^{5}	2^{6}	2^{7}
2^{-4}	62.73	64.39	65.44	66.12	66.49	*	*	*	*
2^{-3}	64.50	65.55	66.25	66.79	68.65	*	*	*	*
2^{-2}	65.89	66.55	67.33	67.86	68.65	*	*	*	*
2^{-1}	67.02	67.90	68.55	69.38	69.80	70.89	71.54	72.03	*
2^{0}	68.30	69.12	69.80	71.02	71.74	72.28	72.63	72.52	*
2^{1}	69.46	70.78	71.42	72.49	73.07	73.19	72.54	71.84	*
2^{2}	*	72.18	73.14	73.6	73.43	72.35	71.51	70.82	*
2^{3}	*	73.45	74.08	**74.12**	73.02	72.53	72.48	72.49	72.49
2^{4}	*	72.87	73.97	73.56	73.59	73.62	73.62	73.62	73.62
2^{5}	*	*	65.51	65.1	65.1	65.53	65.53	65.43	65.53

Table 2. Experimental results conducted on training dataset

SURF64	6.03	4.78	3.90	4.61	4.10	7.74	6.10	6.33	6.50	5.20	5.53±1.21
USURF64	6.77	4.90	4.03	4.86	4.34	8.27	6.88	6.61	6.28	5.38	5.83±1.34
USURF32	6.40	4.95	3.82	4.81	4.69	7.39	6.90	6.511	6.44	5.29	5.72±1.15
USURF32abs	9.09	5.89	6.45	6.35	5.62	10.08	7.25	9.11	8.36	6.12	7.43±1.59
USURF36NN1S1	5.39	4.82	3.73	4.55	4.12	6.90	5.79	6.03	6.03	21.08	6.84±5.09
USURF36NN1	5.73	4.84	4.01	4.57	4.08	7.27	6.90	6.43	6.67	5.27	5.58±1.19
USURF36NN2	5.93	4.89	4.08	4.57	4.20	7.33	7.85	6.63	6.86	5.25	5.76±1.35
USURF36NN3	6.05	4.95	4.07	4.84	4.23	7.48	8.86	6.80	7.01	5.44	5.97±1.54
USURF36NN4	6.10	5.07	4.13	4.96	4.24	7.66	10.03	7.00	7.16	5.64	6.20±1.81
USURF36NN5	6.20	5.14	4.19	5.04	4.30	7.93	11.27	7.27	7.29	5.87	6.45±2.12
USURF36DF1	24.34	21.70	15.54	14.54	13.59	25.01	32.93	20.37	18.46	22.00	20.85±5.81
USURF36DF3	26.49	22.25	16.42	14.53	14.83	26.48	33.53	21.96	18.85	23.07	21.84±5.98
USURF36NDF1	6.27	4.79	4.24	4.85	4.28	7.22	7.16	7.24	6.82	5.80	5.87±1.23
USURF36NDF3	6.08	4.86	4.19	4.98	4.32	7.39	9.08	7.28	7.05	6.24	6.15±1.57
USURF36MLP40	23.83	24.53	18.94	13.45	12.20	23.01	32.08	21.02	22.29	21.49	21.28±5.64
USURF36MLP60	21.40	20.65	14.11	12.32	10.60	23.21	29.53	18.75	16.55	19.69	18.68±5.59
USURF36MLP6RP	25.83	22.81	17.28	13.82	12.40	24.83	31.22	18.93	19.25	21.41	20.78±5.69
USURF36SVM	7.05	6.02	3.64	4.90	4.65	7.89	13.57	7.351	7.13	6.70	6.89±2.71

Table 3. Experimental results conducted on testing dataset.

SURF64	15.61	23.91	18.20	20.21	23.31	25.13	20.23	17.80	19.16	19.49	20.31±2.98
USURF64	16.03	31.60	22.39	21.68	26.09	32.44	25.12	20.29	21.97	25.57	24.32±5.02
USURF36NN1S1	11.28	19.93	15.75	17.27	19.04	19.34	17.12	16.61	18.48	22.17	17.70±2.92
USURF32	16.96	24.61	19.18	22.46	21.89	24.60	22.66	19.94	21.38	23.38	21.71±2.43
USURF32abs	20.94	29.06	23.08	21.79	28.69	33.46	26.77	25.56	24.08	20.35	25.38±4.17
USURF36NN1	13.31	19.53	16.32	17.45	20.18	20.66	18.42	17.66	18.66	17.55	17.97±2.11
USURF36NN2	12.42	19.70	15.55	16.23	18.66	19.31	18.40	17.34	17.73	17.75	17.31±2.14
USURF36NN3	12.48	19.76	15.24	15.91	18.09	19.22	18.63	17.69	17.57	18.15	17.27±2.17
USURF36NN4	12.70	19.63	15.09	15.79	17.98	19.32	18.90	18.02	17.41	18.53	17.34±2.18
USURF36NN5	13.13	19.75	15.03	15.74	17.85	19.58	19.29	18.35	17.33	18.91	17.50±2.20
USURF36DF1	26.89	23.52	18.37	16.36	19.95	25.10	23.58	23.65	20.10	25.56	22.31±3.42
USURF36DF3	27.77	24.72	19.33	16.52	20.46	26.44	24.13	24.05	20.28	25.87	22.96±3.61
USURF36NDF1	15.30	22.20	19.06	19.59	22.71	21.67	19.18	19.07	20.97	19.35	19.91±2.13
USURF36NDF3	13.51	21.07	16.79	16.91	19.78	19.37	18.63	18.08	18.24	19.15	18.15±2.07
USURF36MLP40	30.59	23.56	14.50	16.50	22.71	24.97	22.68	24.35	21.67	21.53	22.31±4.43
USURF36MLP60	25.46	23.30	15.61	14.38	20.17	23.67	21.62	22.39	20.40	22.32	20.13±3.50
USURF36MLP6RP	23.25	21.49	15.54	14.23	22.73	24.42	21.52	22.49	18.05	22.31	20.60±3.44
USURF36SVM	14.76	20.43	12.45	14.09	17.42	18.06	19.95	18.35	18.08	19.01	17.26±2.63

Figure 8. Example of cross-country segmentation using SVM a), b), kNN with 3 neighbors c),d) and MLP with 60 neurons in each hidden layer e), f). The images a),c),e) are from the training image set and b),d),f) are from the testing set.

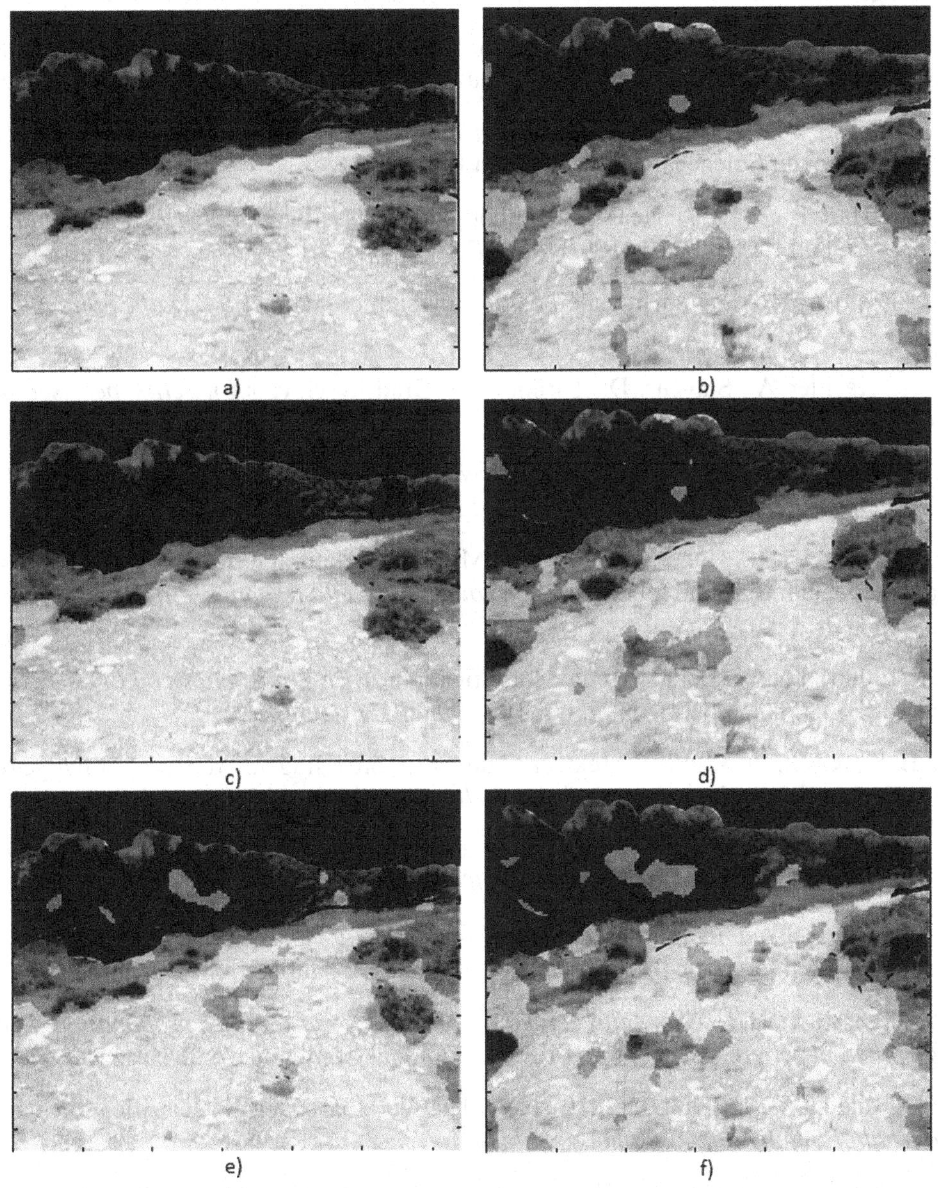

the testing dataset, the lowest error rate was achieved with the SVM classifier and with *k*-NN classifier, when *k*=3. However, the number of support vectors smaller than in the complete training dataset, make the SVM more suitable for terrain segmentation. Multi-layer perceptron trained with LMA, showed higher error rates, although if we consider that only 50% of the training sets were used for training and the other half for validation and testing, the error segmentation rate of 20.13% is respectable compared to the 17.26% for SVM. Moreover, as it was mentioned above the number of coefficients needed for classification is almost 100 times less than in the case of the SVM classifier.

REFERENCES

Bay, H., Ess, A., Tuytelaars, T., & Gool, L. V. (2008). Speeded-Up Robust Features (SURF). *Computer Vision and Image Understanding*, *110*(3), 346–359. doi:10.1016/j.cviu.2007.09.014

Castano, R., Manduchi, R., & Fox, J. (2001). *Classification experiments on real-world texture.* Paper presented at the Third Workshop on Empirical Evaluation Methods in Computer Vision, Kauai, Hawaii.

Chang, C.-C., & Lin, C.-J. (2010). *LIBSVM: A Library for Support Vector Machines*. Taipei, Taiwan: Department of Computer Science, National Taiwan University.

Cover, T. M., & Hart, P. E. (1967). Nearest neighbor pattern classification. *IEEE Transactions on Information Theory*, *13*(1), 21–27. doi:10.1109/TIT.1967.1053964

Cybenko, G. (1989). Approximation by superposition of a sigmoidal function. *Mathematically Controlled Signals. Systems*, *2*, 303–314.

Dahlkamp, H., Kaehler, A., Stavens, D., Thrun, S., & Bradski, G. (2006). *Self-supervised monocular road detection in desert terrain.* Paper presented at the The Robotics Science and Systems Conference.

Hagan, M., & Menhaj, M. (1994). Training feedforward networks with the Marquardt algorithm. *IEEE Transactions on Neural Networks*, *5*(6), 989–993. doi:10.1109/72.329697

Lalonde, J.-F., Vandapel, N., Huber, D., & Hebert, M. (2006). Natural terrain classification using three-dimensional ladar data for ground robot mobility. *Journal of Field Robotics*, *23*, 839–861. doi:10.1002/rob.20134

Manduchi, R. (2006). Learning outdoor color classification. *IEEE Transactions on Pattern Analysis and Machine Intelligence*, *28*(11), 1713–1723. doi:10.1109/TPAMI.2006.231

Manjunath, B. S., & Ma, W. Y. (1996). Texture features for browsing and retrieval of image data. *IEEE Transactions on Pattern Analysis and Machine Intelligence*, *18*(8), 837–842. doi:10.1109/34.531803

Parzen, E. (1962). On estimation of a probability density function and mode. *Annals of Mathematical Statistics*, *33*, 1065–1076. doi:10.1214/aoms/1177704472

Rasmussen, C. (2002). *Combining laser range, color, and texture cues for autonomous road following.* Paper presented at the International Conference on Robotics & Automation, Washington, DC.

Riedmiller, M., & Braun, H. (1993). *A direct adaptive method for faster back propagation: Learning the RPROP algorithm*. Paper presented at the IEEE International Conference on Neural Networks (ICNN).

Sung, G.-Y., Kwak, D.-M., & Lyou, J. (2010). Neural network based terrain classification using wavelet features. *Journal of Intelligent and Robotic Systems.*

Thrun, S., Montemerlo, M., Dahlkamp, H., Stavens, D., Aron, A., & Diebel, J. (2006). Stanley: The robot that won the DARPA grand challenge. *Journal of Field Robotics*, *23*(9), 661–692. doi:10.1002/rob.20147

Vapnik, V. (1995). *The nature of statistical learning theory*. Springer-Verlag.

KEY TERMS AND DEFINITIONS

Unmanned ground vehicle: It is a robot capable of operating outdoors with minimal or no human assistance.

Unmanned vehicle navigation: A problem of autonomously controlling a vehicle in a variety of environments.

Machine learning algorithms: A variety of algorithms designed for features selection, classification, clustering, etc with the purpose of extracting novel knowledge from a dataset.

Salient features: In computer vision, salient features are distinctive patches of an image. They are used for image matching, object recognition and 3D reconstruction.

Feature extraction: In computer vision, a number of transforms are applied to find invariant under various deformations features. In data analysis, feature extraction is a synonym for features selection or dimensionality reduction.

Image segmentation: It is a problem of dividing an image into sub regions based on a predefined similarity measure.

Terrain segmentation: It is a task of segmenting an image into regions of different types of terrains, such as gravel, tress, bushes and grass.

Chapter 5
Adaptive Dynamic Programming Applied to a 6DoF Quadrotor

Petru Emanuel Stingu
University of Texas at Arlington, USA

Frank L. Lewis
University of Texas at Arlington, USA

ABSTRACT

This chapter discusses how the principles of Adaptive Dynamic Programming (ADP) can be applied to the control of a quadrotor helicopter platform flying in an uncontrolled environment and subjected to various disturbances and model uncertainties. ADP is based on reinforcement learning. The controller (actor) changes its control policy (action) based on stimuli received in response to its actions by the critic (cost function, reward). There is a cause and effect relationship between action and reward. Reward acts as a reinforcement signal that leads to learning of what actions are likely to generate it. After a number of iterations, the overall actor-critic structure stores information (knowledge) about the system dynamics and the optimal controller that can accomplish the explicit or implicit goal specified in the cost function.

INTRODUCTION

There is currently a dichotomy between optimal control and adaptive control. Adaptive Control algorithms learn online and give controllers with guaranteed performance for unknown systems. On the other hand, optimal control design is performed off line and requires full knowledge of the system dynamics. In this research we designed Optimal Adaptive Controllers, which learn online in real-time and converge to optimal control solutions. For linear time-invariant systems, these controllers solve the Riccati equation online in real-time by using data measured along the system trajectories. These results show how to approximately solve the optimal control problem for nonlinear systems online in real-time, while

DOI: 10.4018/978-1-60960-551-3.ch005

simultaneously guaranteeing that the closed-loop system is stable, i.e. that the state remains bounded. This solution requires knowledge of the plant dynamics, but in future work it is possible to implement algorithms that only know the structure of the system and not the exact dynamics.

The main focus of this chapter is to present different mechanisms for efficient learning by using as much information as possible about the system and the environment. Learning speed is crucial for a real-time, real-life application that has to accomplish a useful task. The control algorithm isn't usually allowed to generate the best commands suitable for exploration and for learning, because this would defeat the purpose of having the controller in the first place, which is to follow a designated trajectory. The information gathered along the trajectory has to be used efficiently to improve the control policy. There is a big amount of data that has to be stored for such a task. The system is complex and has a large number of continuous state variables. The value function and the policy that corresponds to the infinite number of combinations of state variable values and possible commands have to be stored using a finite number of parameters. The coding of these two functions is made using function approximation with a modified version of Radial Basis Function (RBF) neurons. Due to their local effect on the approximation, the RBF neurons are best suited to hold information that corresponds to training data generated only around the current operating point, which is what one can obtain by following a normal trajectory without exploration. The usual approach of using multilayer perceptrons that have a global effect suffers from having to do a compromise between learning speed and the dispersion of the training samples. For samples that are concentrated around the operating point, learning has to be very slow to avoid deteriorating the approximation precision for states that are far away.

Two very important characteristics of learning are generalization and classification. The amount of information gathered by the system corresponds only to particular state trajectories and particular commands. Still, the value of being in a certain state and of using a certain command has to be estimated over an infinite continuous space. The RBF neurons are able to interpolate between the specific points where data samples are stored. They don't provide a global solution, but they certainly cover the space around the states likely to be visited in normal conditions.

The neural network structure is adaptive. Neurons are added or removed as needed. If for a specific operating point the existing neurons can't provide enough accuracy to store a new sample, then a new neuron is added in that point. The modified RBF neurons are created initially with a global effect in all dimensions. It is only on the dimensions where there is a need to discern between different values of the state variable that the effect is local. This mechanism allows neurons to partition the state space very efficiently. If some state variables do not affect the value function or the control policy corresponding to a certain region of the state space, then the neurons in the vicinity of that region are global on those dimensions. This organization of the RBF network falls in line with the idea that if the function to be approximated is not very complicated, then a reasonably small number of parameters should be sufficient to achieve a small error even if the number of dimensions of the input space is large. This applies to smooth and nice behaving functions. In the worst case, the number of parameters needed grows exponentially with the number of inputs. For the current implementation, the total number of neurons is kept at a reasonable value by pruning the ones in regions that have been visited in the distant past and thus diluting the approximation precision in those regions.

Background

Quadrotor helicopters have become popular for research in UAV control due to their relatively simple model and the low-cost involved in operating the experimental platforms. They are inherently unstable and need well-designed controllers for successful flight. Our goal is to implement control algorithms that can adapt well to uncontrolled environments and unexpected conditions. Many groups were successful in developing autonomous quadrotor vehicles. Until only a few years ago, good results were obtained exclusively by using tethers or motion guides, or by having precise external sensors to track the attitude and position (Castillo, 2004), (Park, 2005), (Valenti, 2006). Today there are projects that are able to do autonomous indoor or outdoor flight using only on-board sensors for attitude estimation and without needing any motion-constraining device. The project in (Guenard, 2005) uses a commercially-available remote-controlled vehicle on which an IMU and a DSP board were installed. Only the attitude is controlled as there is no mechanism to measure the position of the quad-rotor. Quaternion representation is used for the attitude and backstepping techniques are applied to drive the error quaternion to zero. The OS4 project (Bouabdallah, 2007) uses integral backstepping for full control of attitude, altitude and position on a custom platform. The attitude is sensed using an IMU, the altitude using an ultrasound range sensor and the horizontal position using an external vision system. Finally, the vehicle developed by the STARMAC project (Hoffmann, 2007)] has the ability to fly outdoor. A comprehensive model was developed that includes the induced air velocity and the effects of blade flapping in translational flight. Neural networks were used to design an adaptive controller in (Nicol, 2008) and to learn the complete dynamics of the quadrotor online and to stabilize the platform using output feedback by (Dierks, 2010).

All these projects and many others use various techniques to stabilize the quadrotor, but they can't reach optimal performance. On-line ADP has a great potential in this direction, while also maintaining the adaptability and robustness of other algorithms. Still, the scale of the problem seems too big for standard ADP algorithms that are usually applied to systems with two or three states. Even more, we try to solve a trajectory tracking problem, not the regulation problem. A compromise has to be made. Instead of having overall optimality, the control algorithm is split around three smaller loops with similar behavior: translation, attitude and motor/propeller control. A global critic is maintained, but the overall behavior only converges to some correlated local optimums.

Physical analysis of dynamical systems using Lagrangian mechanics, Hamiltonian mechanics, etc. produces system descriptions in terms of nonlinear ordinary differential equations. Particularly prevalent are nonlinear ODEs in the state-space form

$$\dot{x} = f(x, u)$$

with the state $x(t) \in \boldsymbol{R}^n$ and control input $u(t) \in \boldsymbol{R}^m$ residing in continuous spaces. Many systems in aerospace, the automotive industry, process industry, robotics, and elsewhere are conveniently put into this form. In addition to being continuous-state space and continuous-input space systems, in contrast to Markov decision processes (MDP) which have discrete states and actions, these dynamics are also continuous-time (CT) systems. For nonlinear systems, the policy iteration (PI) algorithm was first developed by Leake and Liu (1967). Three decades later it was introduced in (Beard, Saridis, and Wen, 1997) as a feasible adaptive solution to the CT optimal control problem.

The bulk of research in ADP has been conducted for systems that operate in discrete-time (DT). Although the quadrotor model is a continuous-time model, all other signals outside the robot are sampled in discrete time. Therefore, we develop DT ADP control algorithms. Some clarification is required regarding the indices used to show the current time step and the signals available at each time step. Some of the existing literature does not necessarily consider what happens on a real sampled system and ignores the fact that signal propagation through the system and the algorithm computation require a certain amount of time. For simulations this issue is not very important, but for real-time applications things have to be defined very clearly.

At time step k the following two events take place at the dynamic system $\dot{x} = f(x,u)$: the state x_k is sampled, and the command u_k is presented to the system. There is a zero-order hold for the command, so u_k remains constant for the whole time interval $[k, k+1]$. Because u_k must be available concurrently with the sampling of x_k, there is no time left for the control algorithm to calculate u_k as a function of x_k. For a practical sampled system subjected to communication and data processing delays there is a delay of at least one sample period between the measurements and the commands.

There are standard methods for sampling or discretizing nonlinear continuous-time state space ODEs to obtain sampled data forms that are convenient for computer-based control [Lewis and Syrmos 1995]. The resulting systems unfold in discrete time and are generally of the state-space form

$$x_{k+1} = F(x_k, u_k) \tag{1}$$

with k the discrete time index. These systems satisfy the 1-step Markov property since their state at time $k+1$ only depends on the state and inputs at the previous time k. For good precision in estimating x_{k+1} , a Runge-Kutta algorithm can be used to find a solution to the ordinary differential equation $\dot{x} = f(x,u)$ with initial condition x_k and constant input u_k for the time interval $T = t_{k+1} - t_k$. If precision is not needed, the first-order approximation may be preferred:

$$x_{k+1} = x_k + Tf(x_k, u_k). \tag{2}$$

Quadrotor Model

We have selected a quadrotor as an implementation platform. The quadrotor is unstable, and so makes an excellent platform for testing the suitability and effectiveness of control algorithms. Its dynamics are nonlinear, but relatively simple so that nonlinear control schemes can be designed and compared. Yet the quadrotor has enough nonlinearities to pose a meaningful challenge to controller design methods. Quadrotor is highly susceptible to wind gust disturbances, so that disturbance rejection capabilities of proposed controllers can be tested.

A good quadrotor model has to use theory usually applied for helicopters. Having four rotors in close proximity complicates the problem even further. There are interactions between the wakes produced by the rotors and the fuselage, and also between individual rotors. Except for hover, the expression for the rotor wash induced velocities cannot be obtained in closed-form, creating difficulties when the model is used to design certain types of controllers.

Figure 1. The axes definitions for the quadrotor model

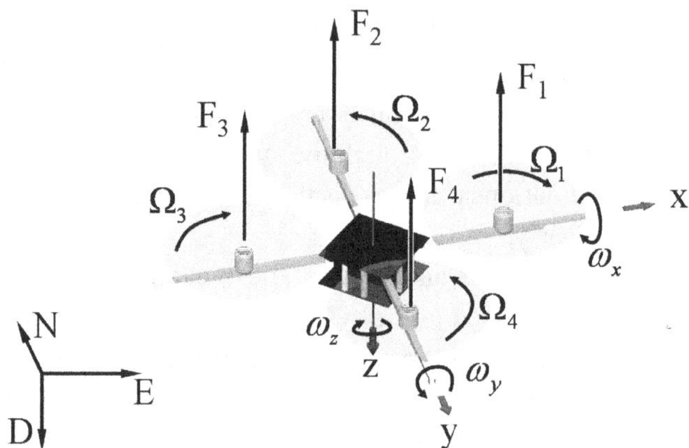

The derivation of the nonlinear dynamics is performed in the North-East-Down (NED) inertial coordinates and in the x-y-z body-fixed coordinates (Figure 1). Variables resolved to the inertial axes are denoted by an *e* subscript and the ones resolved to the body axes have the *b* subscript. The attitude is represented using quaternions. Most equations are derived from [Dreier 2007].

The model has 17 states: body angular velocities, attitude quaternion, linear velocity, position, rotor speeds.

$$\mathbf{x} = \begin{bmatrix} \omega_b & \mathbf{q} & \mathbf{V}_b & \mathbf{P}_e & \Omega \end{bmatrix}^T$$

All the states are available to the control algorithm. Some are directly measured and others are obtained using estimators. The inputs into the model are the four motor voltages:

$$\mathbf{u} = \mathbf{V}_{mot}$$

Nomenclature

ω_b angular velocity resolved to body frame $(rad\ /\ s)$
q attitude quaternion
$\mathbf{V}_b$ velocity in body frame $(m\ /\ s)$
$\mathbf{P}_e$ position in the inertial frame (m)
$\mathbf{I}_{nb}$ moment of inertia tensor $(kg \cdot m^2)$
F total force that acts at the center of gravity (N)
M total moment that acts at the center of gravity $(N \cdot m)$
m total mass of the quadrotor (kg)
$F_1 - F_4$ thrust force for each rotor (N)
τ_{mot}, τ_{rot} motor and rotor torques $(N \cdot m)$

$\mathbf{R}_{ROT-CG}$ vector of rotor placement relative to the center of mass (m)
Ω_i rotation speed of the rotors (rad / s)
R rotor radius (m)
b number of blades for each rotor
I_{flap} moment of inertia tensor for blade flapping $(kg \cdot m^2)$
$\mathbf{V}_{mot}$ motor voltages (V)
R_{mot} winding resistance for the motors (Ω)
K_T, K_V mechanical and electrical constants of the motors
ρ air density (kg / m^3)
c rotor blade chord (m)
a_0 linear lift-curve slope
C_L lift coefficient
D_D drag coefficient
d rotor wash velocities (m / s)

Solid Body Dynamics

The kinematic and dynamic equations model the vehicle as a rigid body under the influence of the Earth gravity and the thrust forces produced by the rotors.

$$\dot{\omega}_b = \mathbf{I}_{nb}^{-1}\left(\begin{bmatrix} M_x \\ M_y \\ M_z \end{bmatrix} - \omega_b \times \left(\mathbf{I}_{nb}\omega_b\right)\right) \tag{3}$$

$$\dot{\mathbf{q}} = \frac{1}{2}\mathbf{q} \otimes \bar{\omega}_b \tag{4}$$

$$\dot{\mathbf{V}}_b = \frac{1}{m}\begin{bmatrix} F_x \\ F_y \\ F_z \end{bmatrix} + \mathbf{q}^* \otimes \begin{bmatrix} 0 \\ 0 \\ g \end{bmatrix} \otimes \mathbf{q} - \omega_b \times \mathbf{V}_b \tag{5}$$

$$\dot{\mathbf{P}}_e = \mathbf{q} \otimes \mathbf{V}_b \otimes \mathbf{q}^* \tag{6}$$

$$\mathbf{M} = \mathbf{M}_{FUSE} + \sum_{i-1}^{4} \mathbf{M}_{Ri} \tag{7}$$

$$\mathbf{F} = \mathbf{F}_{FUSE} + \sum_{i=1}^{4} \mathbf{F}_{Ri} \tag{8}$$

where

$$\bar{\omega}_b = \begin{bmatrix} 0 \\ \omega_b \end{bmatrix} \tag{9}$$

Motor and Rotor Rotation Dynamics

$$\tau_{mot\ i} = \frac{K_T}{R_{mot}} V_{mot\ i} - \frac{K_T}{K_V R_{mot}} \Omega_i \tag{10}$$

$$\dot{\Omega}_i = \frac{1}{bI_{flap}} \left(\tau_{mot\ i} - \tau_{rot\ i} \right) + \left(-1\right)^i \dot{\omega}_{bz} \tag{11}$$

Rotor Aerodynamics

The rotors are modeled as rigid propellers. Blade flapping and wake interaction are ignored. The *a* subscripts indicate aerodynamic velocities, *w* wash velocities and *i* inertial velocities.

$$\mathbf{V}_a = \begin{bmatrix} V_{xb} \\ \left(-1\right)^i V_{yb} \\ V_{zb} \end{bmatrix} - \begin{bmatrix} V_{xw} \\ \left(-1\right)^i V_{yw} \\ V_{zw} \end{bmatrix}$$

$$\omega_a = \begin{bmatrix} \left(-1\right)^i \omega_{xb} \\ \omega_{yb} \\ \left(-1\right)^i \omega_{zb} \end{bmatrix} - \begin{bmatrix} \left(-1\right)^i \omega_{xw} \\ \omega_{yw} \\ \left(-1\right)^i \omega_{zw} \end{bmatrix}$$

$$\mathbf{V}_i = \begin{bmatrix} V_{xb} \\ \left(-1\right)^i V_{yb} \\ V_{zb} \end{bmatrix} - \begin{bmatrix} V_{xw} \\ \left(-1\right)^i V_{yw} \\ V_{zw} \end{bmatrix} + \begin{bmatrix} d_x \\ \left(-1\right)^i d_y \\ d_z \end{bmatrix}, \quad i = 1..4$$

$$B_T = 1 - \frac{\sqrt{2\left|C_z\right|}}{b}$$

$$\sigma = \frac{bc}{\pi R}$$

$$\bar{C}_L = \frac{-6F_{za}}{\sigma}$$

$$C_D = \delta_0 + \delta_1 \bar{C}_L + \delta_2 \bar{C}_L^2$$

$$\varepsilon_0 = \frac{C_D}{a_0}$$

$$\Omega_a = \Omega - \omega_{za}$$

$$V_{Ta} = \Omega_a R$$

The following variables are resolved in the wind-mast coordinates. This new reference system has the same vertical axis as the vehicle body, but it is rotated such that the new x coordinate points in the direction of the lateral aero velocity. All the aerodynamic expressions have a simpler form in this co-ordinate system.

$$V_{xa|WM} = \sqrt{V_{xa}^2 + V_{ya}^2}$$

The body angular velocities are also expressed in wind-mast coordinates:

$$\omega_{xa|WM} = \frac{V_{xa}}{\sqrt{V_{xa}^2 + V_{ya}^2}}\omega_{xa} + \frac{V_{ya}}{\sqrt{V_{xa}^2 + V_{ya}^2}}\omega_{ya}, \quad \omega_{ya|WM} = -\frac{V_{ya}}{\sqrt{V_{xa}^2 + V_{ya}^2}}\omega_{xa} + \frac{V_{xa}}{\sqrt{V_{xa}^2 + V_{ya}^2}}\omega_{ya}$$

The non-dimensional velocities are defined as

$$\mu = \frac{V_{xa|WM}}{V_{Ta}}, \quad \lambda_a = \frac{V_{za}}{V_{Ta}}, \quad \lambda_w = \frac{V_{zw}}{V_{Ta}}, \quad \lambda_i = \frac{V_{zi}}{V_{Ta}}$$

$$\hat{p}_a = \frac{\omega_{xa|WM}}{\Omega_a}, \quad \hat{q}_a = \frac{\omega_{ya|WM}}{\Omega_a}.$$

From the following expressions for the force and torque coefficients it can be seen that they strongly depend on the vertical (λ) and the lateral (μ) velocities. This creates a strong coupling between the inertial dynamics and the aerodynamics.

$$C_{x|WM} = \frac{\sigma a_0}{2}\left[\begin{array}{l} -\left(\frac{B_T^2\mu}{2}\right)\varepsilon_0 + \left(\frac{B_T\mu}{2}\lambda_a\right)\theta_0 + \left(\frac{B_T^2\mu}{4}\lambda_a\right)\theta_T + \\ +\left(\frac{B_T^3}{6}\theta_0 + \frac{B_T^4}{8}\theta_T + \frac{B_T^2}{2}\lambda_a\right)\hat{p}_a \end{array}\right] \tag{12}$$

$$C_{y|WM} = \frac{\sigma a_0}{2}\left[\left(\frac{B_T^3}{6}\theta_0 + \frac{B_T^4}{8}\theta_T + \frac{B_T^2}{2}\lambda_a\right)\hat{q}_a\right] \tag{13}$$

The following three equations may create an implicit dependence between the thrust force and the self-induced wash velocity. A dynamic model of the rotor wake is used. Normally the wake has its own dynamics and a good model has to consider it, but this adds extra states to the already complicated model, and even worse these states can not be measured in real applications. For precise simulations the dynamics can be kept and updated along with the main model. One of the advantages of the extra states is that the relation between the thrust force and the wash velocity becomes explicit. For normal modeling it is simpler to iterate locally through equations (14)-(16) until steady-state is reached and use those values for C_z and λ_w for the rest of the model.

$$C_z = -\frac{\sigma a_0}{2}\left[\begin{array}{l} \left(\frac{B_T^3}{3} + \frac{\mu^2 B_T}{2}\right)\theta_0 + \left(\frac{B_T^4}{4} + \frac{\mu^2 B_T^2}{4}\right)\theta_T + \\ +\left(\frac{B_T^2}{2} + \frac{\mu^2}{4}\right)\left(1+\varepsilon_0\right)\lambda_a + \left(\frac{B_T^2\mu}{4}\right)\left(1+\varepsilon_0\right)\hat{p}_a \end{array}\right] \tag{14}$$

$$\frac{4k^3}{3}\dot{\lambda}_w = -2\sqrt{\mu^2 + \lambda_a^2}\,\lambda_w - C_z \tag{15}$$

The dimensionless aero velocity takes the self-induced rotor wash into account:

$$\lambda_a = \lambda_i - \lambda_w \tag{16}$$

$$C_{mx|WM} = \frac{\sigma a_0}{2}\left[-\left(\frac{B_T^3\mu}{3}\right)\theta_0 - \left(\frac{B_T^4\mu}{4}\right)\theta_T - \left(\frac{B_T^2\mu}{4}\right)\lambda_a - \left(\frac{B_T^4}{8}\right)\hat{p}_a\right] \tag{17}$$

$$C_{my|WM} = \frac{\sigma a_0}{2}\left[-\left(\frac{B_T^4}{8}\right)\hat{q}_a\right] \tag{18}$$

$$C_q = \frac{\sigma a_0}{2}\left[\begin{array}{l} \left(\frac{B_T^4}{4} + \frac{B_T^2\mu^2}{4}\right)\varepsilon_0 - \left[\left(\frac{B_T^3}{3}\right)\theta_0 + \left(\frac{B_T^4}{4}\right)\theta_T + \left(\frac{B_T^2}{2}\right)\lambda_a\right]\lambda_a + \\ +\left(-\frac{B_T^3\mu}{6}\theta_0 - \frac{B_T^4\mu}{8}\theta_T - \frac{B_T^4}{8}\hat{p}_a\right)\hat{p}_a + \left(-\frac{B_T^4}{8}\hat{q}_a\right)\hat{q}_a \end{array}\right] \tag{19}$$

$$\tau_{rot} = \rho\pi R^3 V_{Ta}^2 C_q \tag{20}$$

The x and y force and moment coefficients are resolved back to the body axes:

$$C_x = \frac{V_{xa}}{\sqrt{V_{xa}^2 + V_{ya}^2}} C_{x|WM} - \frac{V_{ya}}{\sqrt{V_{xa}^2 + V_{ya}^2}} C_{y|WM}$$
$$C_y = \frac{V_{ya}}{\sqrt{V_{xa}^2 + V_{ya}^2}} C_{x|WM} + \frac{V_{xa}}{\sqrt{V_{xa}^2 + V_{ya}^2}} C_{y|WM}$$
$$C_{mx} = \frac{V_{xa}}{\sqrt{V_{xa}^2 + V_{ya}^2}} C_{mx|WM} - \frac{V_{ya}}{\sqrt{V_{xa}^2 + V_{ya}^2}} C_{my|WM}$$
$$C_{my} = \frac{V_{ya}}{\sqrt{V_{xa}^2 + V_{ya}^2}} C_{mx|WM} + \frac{V_{xa}}{\sqrt{V_{xa}^2 + V_{ya}^2}} C_{my|WM}$$

Rotor Forces and Moments at the C.G.

$$\mathbf{F}_R = \rho\pi R^2 V_{Ta}^2 \begin{bmatrix} C_x \\ (-1)^i C_y \\ C_z \end{bmatrix} \tag{21}$$

$$\mathbf{M}_R = \begin{bmatrix} 0 \\ 0 \\ (-1)^i \tau_{mot} \end{bmatrix} + \rho\pi R^3 V_{Ta}^2 \begin{bmatrix} (-1)^i C_{mx} \\ C_{my} \\ 0 \end{bmatrix} + bI_{flap}\Omega \begin{bmatrix} (-1)^i \omega_{yb} \\ \omega_{xb} \\ 0 \end{bmatrix} + \mathbf{R}_{ROT-CG} \times \mathbf{F}_R \tag{22}$$

Rotor Self-Induced Velocity and Wash Interaction

The Glauert model is used for the propellers seen as actuator disks. The induced wash velocity depends on the thrust force:

$$\mathbf{d} = \frac{-1}{2\rho\left|\mathbf{V}_a\right|} \begin{bmatrix} 1/\pi R^2 & 0 & 0 \\ 0 & 1/\pi R^2 & 0 \\ 0 & 0 & 1/\pi R^2 \end{bmatrix} \mathbf{F}_R \tag{23}$$

The only place where wind appears in the model is here. Wind is included in the wash velocity after it is resolved to body coordinates. Wash velocity affects the aerodynamic velocity, so wind appears in most aerodynamic equations implicitly.

$$\mathbf{V}_w = \mathbf{d} + \mathbf{q}^* \otimes \mathbf{V}_{wind} \otimes \mathbf{q} \tag{24}$$

There is no rotating wake modeled.

$$\boldsymbol{\omega}_w = \begin{bmatrix} 0 & 0 & 0 \end{bmatrix}^T$$

The variable i is odd for clockwise rotor rotation and even for anti-clockwise rotation; τ_{mot}, τ_{rot}, Ω are always positive and independent of the direction of rotation.

Dynamic Inversion

The dynamic representation of the quadrotor system can be written as

$$\dot{\mathbf{x}} = \begin{bmatrix} \dot{\omega}_b \\ \dot{\mathbf{q}} \\ \dot{\mathbf{V}}_b \\ \dot{\mathbf{P}}_e \\ \dot{\Omega} \end{bmatrix} = \begin{bmatrix} f_\omega\left(\boldsymbol{\omega}_b, \mathbf{q}, \Omega\right) \\ f_q\left(\boldsymbol{\omega}_b, \mathbf{q}\right) \\ f_V\left(\boldsymbol{\omega}_b, \mathbf{q}, \mathbf{V}_b\right) \\ f_P\left(\mathbf{q}, \mathbf{V}_b\right) \\ f_\Omega\left(\Omega, \boldsymbol{\omega}_b, \mathbf{q}, \mathbf{V}_b, \mathbf{V}_{mot}\right) \end{bmatrix} \tag{25}$$

From the equations of the quadrotor model it is possible to obtain some approximate inverse functions for f_ω, f_V and f_Ω. These functions are of interest:

$$\begin{aligned} \mathbf{V}_{mot} &= f_\Omega^{-1}\left(\dot{\Omega}_{des}, \boldsymbol{\omega}_b, \mathbf{q}, \mathbf{V}_b\right) \\ \Omega &= f_\omega^{-1}\left(\dot{\boldsymbol{\omega}}_{b\ des}, \mathbf{q}\right) \\ \mathbf{q} &= f_V^{-1}\left(\boldsymbol{\omega}_b, \dot{\mathbf{V}}_{b\ des}\right) \end{aligned} \tag{26}$$

Figure 2. The three subsystems of the quadrotor model

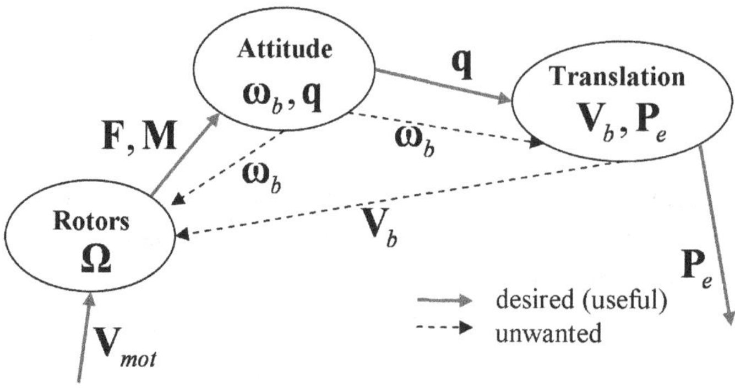

1. Solve for F_z and $\mathbf{q}$ given a_N, a_E, a_D and Ψ

Condition for having F_z parallel to the acceleration vector: $F_x = 0, F_y = 0$. The effect of the $\boldsymbol{\omega}_b \times \mathbf{V}_b$ term is ignored.

$$\dot{\mathbf{V}}_b = \frac{1}{m}\begin{bmatrix} 0 \\ 0 \\ F_z \end{bmatrix} + \mathbf{q}^* \otimes \begin{bmatrix} 0 \\ 0 \\ g \end{bmatrix} \otimes \mathbf{q} = \mathbf{q}^* \otimes \begin{bmatrix} a_N \\ a_E \\ a_D \end{bmatrix} \otimes \mathbf{q}$$

$$\frac{1}{m}\begin{bmatrix} 0 \\ 0 \\ F_z \end{bmatrix} = \mathbf{q}^* \otimes \begin{bmatrix} a_N \\ a_E \\ a_D - g \end{bmatrix} \otimes \mathbf{q}$$

$$F_z = m\sqrt{a_N^2 + a_E^2 + \left(a_D - g\right)^2}$$

The necessary attitude $\mathbf{q}$ is obtained by calculating the yaw and the tilt configurations separately as rotations around the vertical (D) axis and around an axis in the horizontal plane that will make the z axis parallel to the desired acceleration vector:

$$\mathbf{q}_\Psi = \begin{bmatrix} \cos\frac{\Psi}{2} \\ \sin\frac{\Psi}{2}\begin{bmatrix} 0 \\ 0 \\ 1 \end{bmatrix} \end{bmatrix} = \begin{bmatrix} \cos\frac{\Psi}{2} \\ 0 \\ 0 \\ \sin\frac{\Psi}{2} \end{bmatrix}$$

$$\mathbf{r} = \begin{bmatrix} 0 \\ 0 \\ -1 \end{bmatrix} \times \begin{bmatrix} a_N \\ a_E \\ a_D - g \end{bmatrix}$$

$$\alpha = \operatorname{arctan}_2\left(\frac{\sqrt{a_N^2 + a_E^2}}{-\left(a_D - g\right)}\right)$$

$$\mathbf{q}_\alpha = \begin{bmatrix} \cos\frac{\alpha}{2} \\ \sin\frac{\alpha}{2} \cdot \frac{\mathbf{r}}{\left|\mathbf{r}\right|} \end{bmatrix}$$

$$\mathbf{q} = \mathbf{q}_{\alpha} \otimes \mathbf{q}_{\Psi}$$

2. Solve for $\Omega_1, \Omega_2, \Omega_3, \Omega_4$ given $\dot{\omega}_x, \dot{\omega}_y, \dot{\omega}_z, \dot{V}_z$

There is no closed-form solution to this problem because the thrust force and the induced velocity of the rotors depend on each other in equations (14)-(16). A Newton-Raphson algorithm is used to trim the quadrotor model for the desired accelerations and to obtain the necessary rotor speeds. To calculate a starting value for Ω, hover conditions are assumed (i.e. no horizontal or vertical speed). Some terms cancel in equation (14) and for simplicity $B_T = 1$ and $\varepsilon = 0$. Using the Glauert momentum model the relation between the induced velocity and thrust is

$$w = \frac{T}{2\rho A \left\| V \right\|}.$$

Because at hover the total velocity $V = w$ and $F_z = -T$ (by definition the thrust T points upwards, but F_z is positive downwards) it is easy to see that

$$w_{hover} = \sqrt{\frac{-F_z}{2\rho A}}$$

and λ_a can now be calculated from w_{hover}. In (14) Ω_{start} is the solution of a second-order equation that depends on F_z. The acceleration $\dot{V}_z$ includes the effect of g (i.e. $\dot{V}_z = 0$ means hover) so

$$F_z = \min\left\{ (\dot{V}_z - g_z)\frac{m}{4}, 0 \right\}$$

Where g_z is the projection of the gravitational acceleration on the z axis:

$$g_z = \begin{bmatrix} 0 & 0 & 1 \end{bmatrix} \left(\mathbf{q}^* \otimes \begin{bmatrix} 0 \\ 0 \\ g \end{bmatrix} \otimes \mathbf{q} \right)$$

The general form of the quadrotor model is $\dot{\mathbf{x}} = f(\mathbf{x}, \mathbf{u})$. During the Newton-Raphson iterations, all the states $\mathbf{x}$ are kept constant and equal to their values at the current operating point, except for the states $\Omega_1, \Omega_2, \Omega_3, \Omega_4$ which are used as inputs. Only the $\dot{\omega}_x, \dot{\omega}_y, \dot{\omega}_z, \dot{V}_z$ components of the function f are considered as outputs. Instead of running the full model, from equation (25) it can be seen that f_ω and f_V are sufficient. Numerical perturbation on the Ω inputs is used to construct the Jacobian matrix J. The solution for $\mathbf{\Omega} = \begin{bmatrix} \Omega_1 & \Omega_2 & \Omega_3 & \Omega_4 \end{bmatrix}^T$ is found after a few iterations:

$$J_k = \begin{bmatrix} \frac{\partial f_{\omega x}}{\partial \Omega_1} & \cdots & \cdots & \frac{\partial f_{\omega x}}{\partial \Omega_4} \\ \frac{\partial f_{\omega y}}{\partial \Omega_1} & & & \frac{\partial f_{\omega y}}{\partial \Omega_4} \\ \frac{\partial f_{\omega z}}{\partial \Omega_1} & & & \frac{\partial f_{\omega z}}{\partial \Omega_4} \\ \frac{\partial f_{Vz}}{\partial \Omega_1} & \cdots & \cdots & \frac{\partial f_{Vz}}{\partial \Omega_4} \end{bmatrix}_{[\Omega_{1..4}]=\mathbf{\Omega}_k} \quad \text{and } \mathbf{\Omega}_{k+1} = \mathbf{\Omega}_k - J_k^{-1}\left(\begin{bmatrix} \dot{\omega}_{x\ k} \\ \dot{\omega}_{y\ k} \\ \dot{\omega}_{z\ k} \\ \dot{V}_{z\ k} \end{bmatrix} - \begin{bmatrix} \dot{\omega}_{x\ ref} \\ \dot{\omega}_{y\ ref} \\ \dot{\omega}_{z\ ref} \\ \dot{V}_{z\ ref} \end{bmatrix}\right)$$

3. Solve for $V_{mot1}, V_{mot2}, V_{mot3}, V_{mot4}$ given $\dot{\Omega}_1, \dot{\Omega}_2, \dot{\Omega}_3, \dot{\Omega}_4$:

The following equations are written without the motor index for simplicity.

The electro-mechanical system is described by

$$\tau_{mot} = \frac{K_T}{R} V_{mot} - \frac{K_T}{K_V R} \Omega$$

$$V_{mot} = \frac{R}{K_T} \tau_{mot} + \frac{1}{K_V} \Omega$$

The inertial dynamics of the motor and propeller is

$$\dot{\Omega} = \frac{1}{b I_{flap}} \left(\tau_{mot} - \tau_{rot} \right) + \left(-1\right)^i \dot{\omega}_{bz}$$

$$\tau_{mot} = b I_{flap} \dot{\Omega} + \tau_{rot} - b I_{flap} \left(-1\right)^i \dot{\omega}_{bz}$$

Finally the motor voltage necessary to achieve a certain rotation acceleration is

$$V_{mot} = \frac{R}{K_T} \left[b I_{flap} \dot{\Omega} + \tau_{rot} - b I_{flap} \left(-1\right)^i \dot{\omega}_{bz} \right] + \frac{1}{K_V} \Omega$$

Reference Model

For each subsystem, a reference model is introduced. The reference model generates reference accelerations ($\dot{\mathbf{\Omega}}_{ref}$, $\dot{\boldsymbol{\omega}}_{b\ ref}$, $\dot{\mathbf{V}}_{b\ ref}$) needed for tracking. A NN-based actor augments this signal and compensates for imprecision in the inverses of the f_ω, f_V and f_Ω functions. The reference models are similar for the three loops. The one for the translation subsystem is given by:

$$\mathbf{a}_{c\ ref} = K_P\left(\mathbf{P}_c - \mathbf{P}_{ref}\right) + K_D\left(\mathbf{V}_{e\ c} - \mathbf{V}_{e\ ref}\right)$$
$$\dot{\mathbf{V}}_{e\ ref} = \mathbf{a}_{cref} - \mathbf{a}_{aw}$$
$$\dot{\mathbf{P}}_{e\ ref} = \mathbf{V}_{e\ ref}$$

The purpose of the $\mathbf{a}_{aw}$ variable is to prevent the reference model from demanding tracking if the inner loop actuators are saturated or if the inner loop dynamics is too slow. The actor does not see $\mathbf{x}_{ref}$ values that have no effect on the inner loop because of saturation or slow dynamics. The learning process can thus continue even during saturation. The gains in the reference model can be tuned manually in order to provide certain handling qualities to the vehicle, or can be obtained using an optimal algorithm. Saturation for the velocities can be introduced in the following manner:

$$\mathbf{a}_{c\ ref} = K_D\left[\max\left(\min\left(\frac{K_P}{K_D}\left(\mathbf{P}_c - \mathbf{P}_{ref}\right), \mathbf{V}_{\max}\right), \mathbf{V}_{\min}\right) + \left(\mathbf{V}_{e\ c} - \mathbf{V}_{e\ ref}\right)\right]$$

Approximate Dynamic Programming

An actor-critic structure is used for implementing efficient reinforcement learning (Figure 4).

Most ADP algorithms solve regulation problems. The quadrotor is designed to follow a certain trajectory and not just to hover. The ADP algorithm has to be modified to include an additional reference signal $\eta_k \in \boldsymbol{R}^n$ that is provided from outside the model. The tracking error is defined as

$$z_k = x_k - \eta_k. \tag{27}$$

The actor, or the control policy is

$$u_k = h(x_{k-1}, z_{k-1}). \tag{28}$$

Figure 3. Control structure for the translation subsystem

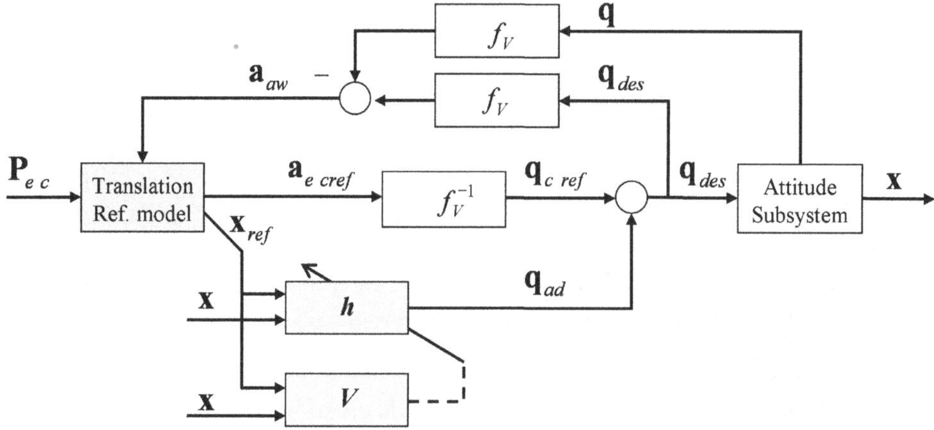

Figure 4. Generic ADP structure

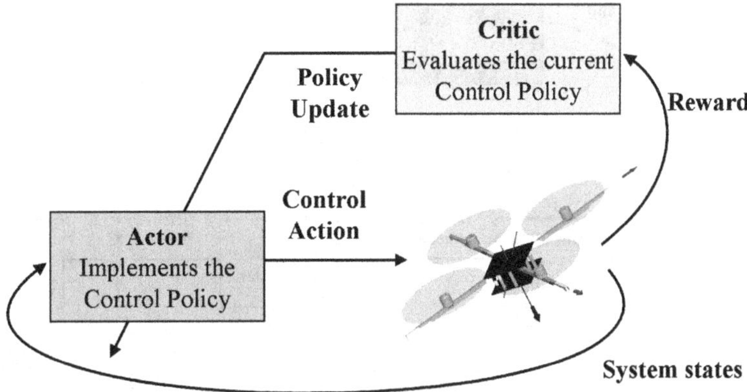

It is important to observe that the command u can only be calculated as a function of previous states. This is a consequence of the fact that the sampling of the state variables and of the command is synchronous. Also note that u_k in this section represents a vector that contains the following signals:

$$u = \begin{bmatrix} \mathbf{q}_{ad} \\ a_{z\ ad} \\ \mathbf{\Omega}_{ad} \\ \mathbf{V}_{mot\ ad} \end{bmatrix}$$

The quadrotor has 17 states and only 4 control inputs ($\mathbf{u} = \mathbf{V}_{mot}$), thus it is very under-actuated. Three control loops with dynamic inversion are used to generate the 4 control signals. Some learning is forced to reside locally by splitting the actor into local actors for each of the three loops. Each actor works with a reduced set of states. The critic is global:

The weights of the NN-based actors are set to generate known stable PD controllers at the initialization phase of the algorithm. They will depart from this configuration while training takes place.

The control policy is distributed in the three subsystems of the quadrotor: translation, attitude and motor/propeller control (Figure 5):

$$h(x_k, z_k) = \left[h^{1T}(x_k^1, z_k^1), h^{2T}(x_k^2, z_k^2), h^{3T}(x_k^3, z_k^3)\right]^T$$

where the variables x^i, z^i, u^i are subsets of the state vector, the tracking error vector and the command vector that are used for the control policies in each of the three loops.

The key idea of reinforcement learning generally and of dynamic programming in particular is the use of value functions to organize and structure the search of good policies. The notion of goal-directed optimal behavior is captured by defining a performance measure or value function

Figure 5. Distributed ADP structure for the quadrotor

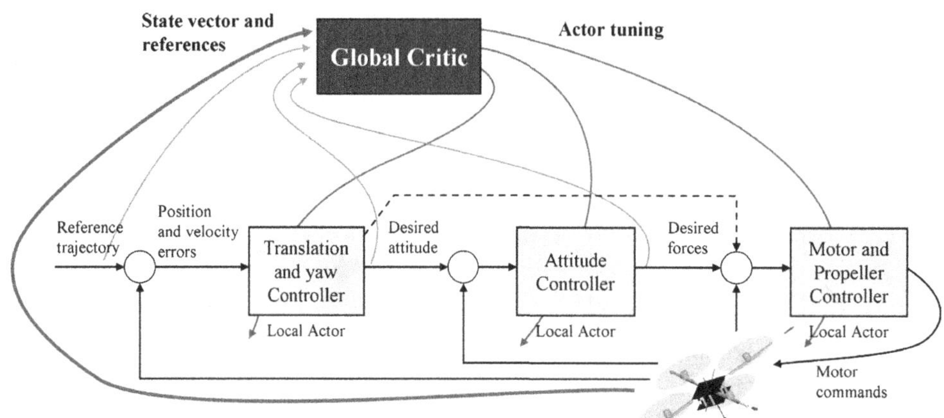

$$V_h(x_k, z_k) = \sum_{j=k}^{\infty} \gamma^{j-k} r\left(x_j, z_j, u_j\right) \tag{29}$$

with $0 < \gamma \leq 1$ a discount factor and $u_k = h(x_{k-1}, z_{k-1})$ a prescribed feedback control policy. This is known as the cost-to-go associated to the policy h and is a sum of discounted future costs from the current time k into the infinite horizon future if the policy h is used at every step. The discount factor reflects the fact that we are less concerned about costs acquired further into the future.

Function $r(x_k, z_k, u_k)$ is known as the utility, and is a measure of the one-step cost of control. For the tracking problem it is defined in the following manner (Marsili-Libelli, 1981), (Park, 1996), (Zhang, 2008):

$$r\left(x_k, z_k, u_k\right) = z_k^T Q z_k + \left(w_{k+1} - w_k\right)^T R\left(w_{k+1} - w_k\right) + \left(u_k - u_{ek}\right)^T S\left(u_k - u_{ek}\right) \tag{30}$$

where Q, R, S are positive definite matrices, w_k is the deviation from the expected control

$$w_k = u_k - u_{ek}$$

and the expected control u_{ek} is the command given in optimal conditions with perfect tracking when the nominal subsystem in equation (2) is considered:

$$\eta_{k+1} = \eta_k + Tf(\eta_k, u_{ek})$$

$$u_{ek} = f^{-1}\left(\eta_k, \frac{1}{T}\left(\eta_{k+1} - \eta_k\right)\right). \tag{31}$$

The objective of optimal control is to select the policy that minimizes the cost to obtain

$$V^*(x_k, z_k) = \min_h \left(\sum_{j=k}^{\infty} \gamma^{j-k} r\left(x_j, z_j, h\left(x_{j-1}, z_{j-1}\right)\right) \right) \tag{32}$$

which is known as the optimal cost, or optimal value. Then, the optimal control policies are given by

$$h^*(x_k, z_k) = \arg\min_h \left(\sum_{j=k}^{\infty} \gamma^{j-k} r\left(x_j, z_j, h\left(x_{j-1}, z_{j-1}\right)\right) \right). \tag{33}$$

By writing (29) as

$$V_h(x_k, z_k) = r\left(x_k, z_k, h\left(x_{k-1}, z_{k-1}\right)\right) + \gamma V_h(x_{k+1}, z_{k+1}), \quad V_h(0) = 0 \tag{34}$$

instead of evaluating the infinite sum (29), one can solve the difference equation to obtain the value of using the current policy $u_k = h(x_{k-1}, z_{k-1})$. This is a nonlinear Lyapunov equation known as the Bellman equation. Evaluating the value of a current policy using the Bellman equation is the first key concept in developing reinforcement learning techniques. Bellman's optimality principle (Bellman, 1957) states that "an optimal policy has the property that no matter what the previous decisions have been, the remaining decisions must constitute an optimal policy with regard to the state resulting from those previous decisions". This gives the Bellman optimality equation or the discrete-time Hamilton-Jacobi-Bellman (HJB) equation:

$$V^*(x_k, z_k) = \min_h \left(r\left(x_k, z_k, h\left(x_{k-1}, z_{k-1}\right)\right) + \gamma V^*(x_{k+1}, z_{k+1}) \right). \tag{35}$$

Determining optimal controllers using these equations is considerably easier since the optimum value is inside the minimization argument.

Since the optimal policy must be known at time $k+1$ to use (35) to determine the optimal policy at time *k*, Bellman's principle yields a backwards-in-time procedure for solving the optimal control problem. This is by nature an off-line planning method and full knowledge of the system dynamics $f(x_k, u_k)$ is needed. We prefer to avoid using the system dynamics whenever possible to allow for adaptation to changing dynamics, and we also need on-line methods.

Approximate Dynamic Programming will be used to do on-line reinforcement learning in real-time for solving the optimal control problem by using data measured along system trajectories (Sutton & Barto, 1998). Q learning, introduced by Watkins (1989) provides an alternative path to take partial derivatives with respect to the control input that does not go through the system, allowing optimization without the knowledge of the system dynamics. The quality function *Q* associated with the policy *h* is defined as

$$Q_h\left(x_k, z_k, u_k\right) = r\left(x_k, z_k, u_k\right) + \gamma V_h\left(x_{k+1}, z_{k+1}\right). \tag{36}$$

The policy $u_k = h\left(x_{k-1}, z_{k-1}\right)$ has to be admissible, meaning that it must be stabilizing and it must yield a finite cost $V_h\left(x_k, z_k\right)$. That is why the RBF neural networks that approximate the policies h^1, h^2, h^3

are initialized at the beginning with the necessary structure and the weights corresponding to known stabilizing PD controllers. The optimal Q function is defined as

$$Q^*\left(x_k, z_k, u_k\right) = r\left(x_k, z_k, u_k\right) + \gamma V^*\left(x_{k+1}, z_{k+1}\right). \tag{37}$$

In terms of Q^* the Bellman optimality equation can be written in the very simple form

$$V^*\left(x_k, z_k\right) = \min_u\left(Q^*\left(x_k, z_k, u\right)\right) \tag{38}$$

and the optimal control as

$$h^*\left(x_k, z_k\right) = \arg\min_u\left(Q^*\left(x_k, z_k, u\right)\right) \tag{39}$$

In the absence of control constraints, the minimum value if obtained by solving

$$\frac{\partial}{\partial u} Q^*\left(x_k, z_k, u\right) = 0. \tag{40}$$

A RBF neural network is used to approximate the Q function. It has the general form

$$Q_h(x, z, u) = W^T \phi(x, z, u). \tag{41}$$

Temporal-difference learning uses experience to solve the prediction problem. Prediction error is introduced in terms of the Bellman equation as

$$e_{k-1} = r\left(x_{k-1}, z_{k-1}, h\left(x_{k-2}, z_{k-2}\right)\right) + \gamma W^T \phi\left(x_k, z_k, u_k\right) - Q\left(x_{k-1}, z_{k-1}, u_{k-1}\right) \tag{42}$$

If the Bellman equation holds, $e_{k-1} = 0$ and the equation above can be solved for the Q function:

$$Q\left(x_{k-1}, z_{k-1}, u_{k-1}\right) = r\left(x_{k-1}, z_{k-1}, h\left(x_{k-2}, z_{k-2}\right)\right) + \gamma W^T \phi\left(x_k, z_k, u_k\right).$$

Once the value of the Q function at $(x_{k-1}, z_{k-1}, u_{k-1})$ is known, a backup of it is made into the RBF neural network by adjusting the weights W and/or by adding more neurons and by reconfiguring their other parameters. This is a separate process that just needs to know the $\left(x, z, u\right)$ coordinates and the new value to store. The method is available in [Li, Sundararajan and Saratchandran 2000].

$$\begin{aligned} Q\left(x_{k-1}, z_{k-1}, u_{k-1}\right) = {} & W^T \phi\left(x_{k-1}, z_{k-1}, u_{k-1}\right) + \\ & + \alpha\left[r\left(x_{k-1}, z_{k-1}, h\left(x_{k-2}, z_{k-2}\right)\right) + \gamma W^T \phi\left(x_k, z_k, u_k\right) - W^T \phi\left(x_{k-1}, z_{k-1}, u_{k-1}\right)\right] \end{aligned} \tag{43}$$

which means $Q_{stored} = Q_{old} + \alpha\left(Q_{new} - Q_{old}\right)$ with $0 < \alpha < 1$. As it can be seen, the update of the Q value is not made completely towards the new value. This slows down the learning, but adds robustness.

The policy update step is done by simply solving

$$\frac{\partial}{\partial u} Q\left(x_k, z_k, u\right) = 0 \tag{44}$$

after the new Q value was stored. The value for $h(x_k, z_k) = u$ is stored into the actor RBF neural network using the same mechanism as before:

$$h\left(x_k, z_k\right) = U^T\sigma\left(x_k, z_k\right) + \beta\left[u - U^T\sigma\left(x_k, z_k\right)\right]. \tag{45}$$

Faster learning and improved robustness can be obtained by extending the learning process back in time and also into the future. Based on the new values for the Q function, training can be done again for a list of previously visited states. The algorithm maintains a fixed-size buffer of past values for (x, z, u). Equations (43)-(45) are applied in order for the time indices $k-2, k-3, \ldots, k-d-1$ where d is the depth of the buffer. If this mechanism is used, the α and β constants must have lower values. Simulation into the future can be made using the system model in equation (2) to obtain the future states likely to be reached. If the model is precise, a longer horizon can be chosen. Equations (43)-(45) are applied this time for the time indices $k, k+1, k+2, \ldots$. This mechanism allows the pre-training of the ADP neural networks for states that have not been visited before. The system model might not be very precise, but it can still provide better information than a completely untrained neural network. To prevent the model from affecting data that was already learned well, only the neurons with an old update timestamp could be trained.

Global vs. Local Learning

At any moment in time, for the quadrotor in normal operating conditions only training data from near the operating point is available. There is no way of doing NN training based on samples from the entire state space because a very long time has to be spent collecting them. NN with global activation functions can only be trained reliably using batch methods with samples that cover the entire input domain. If training is attempted using samples concentrated into a specific region, the NN will adapt to that region and will *forget* what it has learned for the other regions of the input domain. That is why the learning algorithms for these networks either:

- Are very slow in order to do only small changes along the state-space trajectory.
- Require very big amplitudes for the probing noise to guarantee that every region of the state space is visited often.

Sampling the entire state-space for learning can be computationally expensive and impossible to realize with a real system due to time and energy constrains and also because the system has to do something useful like following a designated trajectory. In the short term, sampling along the system trajectory generated by the policy focuses learning to the states that are actually commonly occurring. In the long term, learning can suffer because the value function for these states is already very close to the optimal value and further learning does not help, and on the other hand there is not enough information for less common states. In Figure 6 the state space is not fully explored and there are long periods of time when the velocity only resides in a limited zone of the state space. This behavior does not follow the two requirements above and neural networks with global activation functions can't be trained with this data.

One important requirement for efficient learning is the following: optimizing for the current operating point should not lose information stored in the past for the other operating points. When the system reaches a previously visited operating point, it should not have to re-learn everything again. RBF neural networks allow local training with data taken from a restricted region of the state space. Training can be done at every sample or in batches. Every time only a few neurons that have a significant output for the current operating point are affected by learning. Data learned in the past for other operating points is preserved and immediately available when needed. This is very useful for cases when the operating point has a sudden jump due to severe disturbances. An algorithm that only has information around the current operating point would fail immediately when such a situation occurs.

The Curse of Dimensionality

The actor acts as a nonlinear function approximator. Normally we have

$$u_{k+1} = h(x_k)$$

In the quadrotor case, because the reference is not zero and the system is nonlinear, we need

$$u_{k+1} = h(x_k, z_k)$$

or even better for learning

Figure 6. Local activation functions

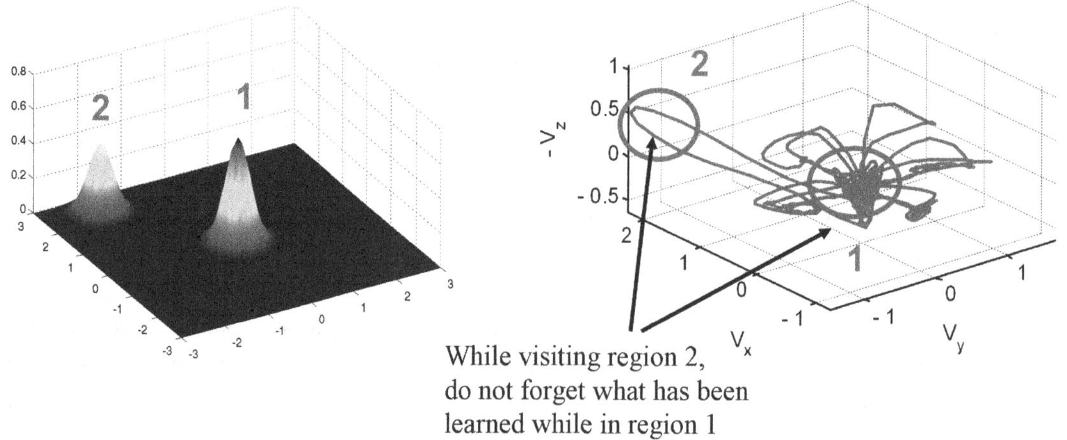

2
1
- V_z
V_x
V_y
While visiting region 2, do not forget what has been learned while in region 1

$$u_{k+1} = h(x_k, z_k - x_k)$$

For each of the position, attitude and motor/propeller loops the state vector includes the local states and the external states that have a big coupling effect on the loop performance. It is easy to see that this way the input space can easily have n=14 or more dimensions. A RBF neural network with the neurons placed on a grid with N elements in each dimension would require N^n neurons. For $N = 5$ and $n = 14$, $6 \cdot 10^9$ are required. Placing neurons on a grid is no better than a look-up table. The solutions to reducing the number of neurons are the following:

- preprocess the states to provide signals with physical significance as inputs
- combine multiple states into a lower dimension signal
- map multiple equivalent regions from the state-space into only one

One simple example of removing a dimension is presented next. From the aerodynamic equations it can be seen that it is not the V_x and V_y velocities that directly affect the rotor forces, but their sum. If all the three velocities are inputs to the actor NN, the locus of a certain lateral velocity is a cylinder. Every time that specific velocity is reached, a different neuron close to the cylinder may be updated.

Learning can be made much faster by concentrating it from a cylinder to a line. This way a dimension can be removed from the input space of the NN.

Input processing for the neural networks can also speed up and concentrate learning. The usual approach of expressing the attitude by using with Euler implies that yaw error is an angle in the Earth horizontal plane (around the Down axis) and tilt error is expressed as pitch and roll error angles. The errors are resolved to Earth coordinates and this adds nonlinearities and couplings. Furthermore, the errors are dependent on the attitude of the vehicle relative to the Earth. This is very bad for learning because a certain amount of tilt error can have an infinite number of parameterizations.

In the current approach yaw error is an angle ψ in the *x-y* plane of the vehicle (around the *z* axis) and tilt is expressed as a tilt direction γ_H in the *x-y* plane and a tilt amount α_H. The attitude errors are

Figure 7. Removing a dimension from the NN input

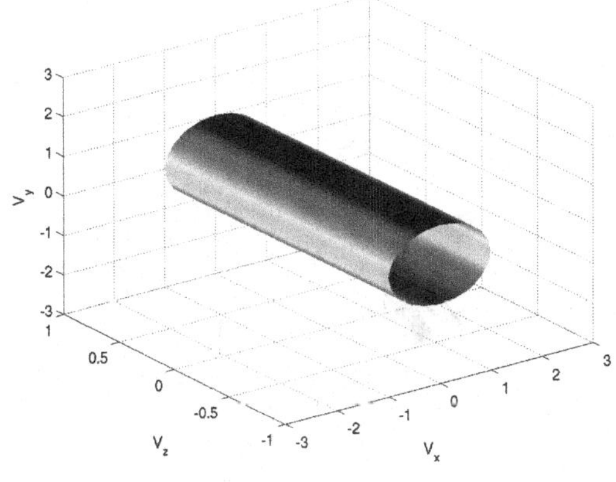

V_x, V_y, V_z as inputs to the NN

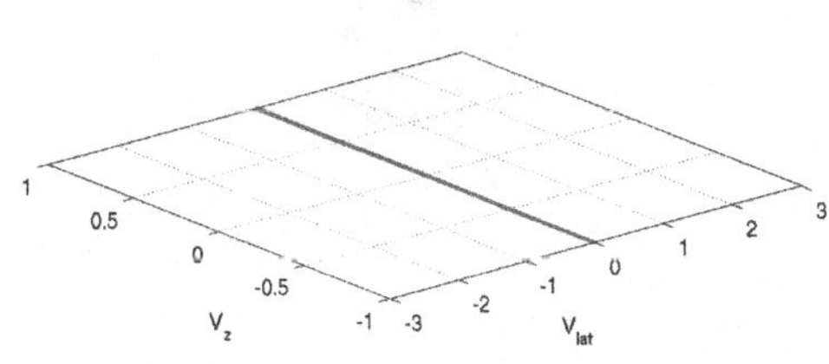

$\sqrt{V_x^2 + V_y^2}$, V_z as inputs to the NN

resolved to body coordinates and this makes them independent of the attitude of the vehicle relative to the Earth. Learning can be much faster and focused because a certain amount of tilt error is always parameterized the same way. They also have better physical significance because they express directly what corrective movements the vehicle has to make in its own coordinate system, allowing for a direct mapping to the actuators.

RBF Neural Networks for Function Approximation

The actor neural network starts with a low number of wide RBF neurons that model a PD controller. The neurons are set to have infinite width on the dimensions where the input does not influence the output. This makes the quadrotor able to fly without any initial learning. Every time a training procedure is started, for any operating point, the algorithm tries to tune only the neurons that are active for that operating point. Each neuron has a linked list with its neighbors for fast real-time searching. If tuning the existing neurons can't offer enough precision, one more is added at the current operating point.

Each neuron has a time value associated with it from when it was last updated. The ones with the oldest values are eliminated if by taking them out and retraining the neighbors the precision doesn't go below a certain limit. This mechanism of adding neurons where needed and pruning the old ones without diluting the precision too much allows good function approximation for recent data and reasonable approximation for old data that might be slightly outdated anyway.

EFFICIENT LEARNING:

Exploration vs. Exploitation

For a real-time system that can crash at the first mistake, learning has to be very efficient. For a practical system, there is a conflict between learning and doing a useful job (Figure 9).

An algorithm that requires persistence of excitation is not exciting for people in the industry. They work hard to make things smooth and use minimum energy. Under these conditions learning has to use

Figure 8. Standard and new error parameterization

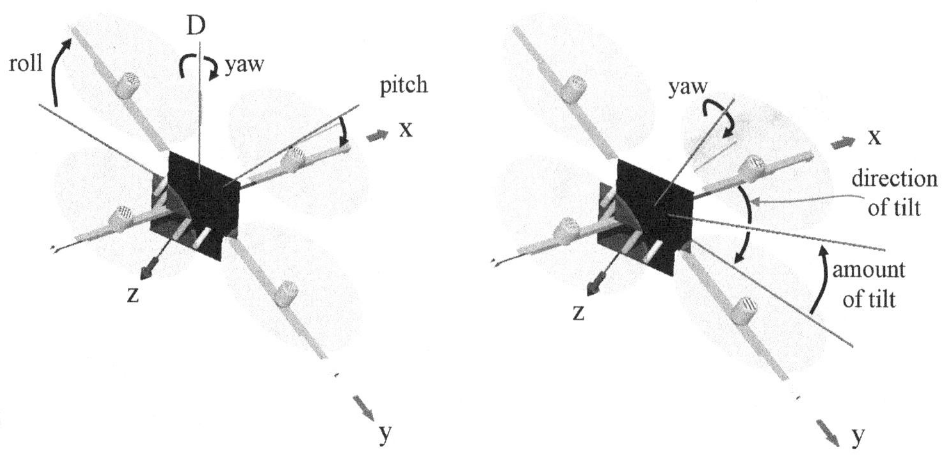

Figure 9. Exploitation versus exploration

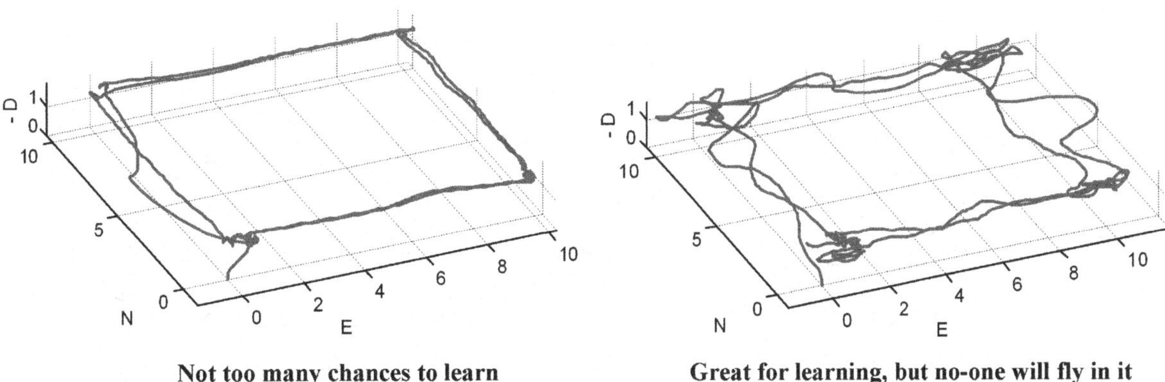

Not too many chances to learn | **Great for learning, but no-one will fly in it**

whatever data is available during the normal operation of the vehicle. Having limited information for learning and limited freedom in deviating from the prescribed trajectory means that some information has to be obtained from another source. The best one is the actual system model. This seems to exclude from the start the model-free ADP algorithms. Other reasons are that they need to explore the whole state space numerous times. This can be done with simple systems that have 2 or at most 3 states. But what can be done for an under-actuated system with 17 states (with only 14 that have to be explored – North, East, Down do not matter)? Extensive exploration is time-consuming. Large deviations from the prescribed operating point are not desired or allowed. Unnecessary maneuvers increase energy consumption and chances of failure. Learning is also usually too slow for practical applications. There is another question: how does one place an under-actuated system that he doesn't know yet how to control in different representative points of the state space?

Model-based ADP algorithms can be made to only need local exploration around the nominal operating point. The exploration space is reduced by a few orders of magnitude. The amplitude of the probing noise can be smaller. Learning can be guided and it becomes much faster and more focused. Reasonable modeling errors can be also accommodated.

Simulation Results

The control algorithms are implemented in Simulink and run directly in the Matlab environment in normal or accelerated mode (Figure 10), allowing an instant transition between design and experiments. The same model can run a simulation or can control a real quadrotor. A special S-function block was created to allow the Simulink model to receive sensor data from the quadrotor and to send back the motor commands. The block communicates via USB with a base-station module connected to the computer. Simulink generates and compiles C code for the model and is able to run it in real-time.

The simulation is done in the presence of either disturbing wind, weight imbalance and both at the same time. The quadrotor flies in a loop in the shape of a 10 x 10 meters square two times for 160 seconds. The wind has 5 m/s in the North direction and 5 m/s in the East direction. The ideal trajectory is a square formed by the points (0,0)-(0,10)-(10,10)-(10,0) meters. In Figures 11 and 12 the trajectory is shown first without adaptation and then with adaptation. Only two or one dimension are selected for plotting for the NN weights. When both wind and weight imbalance are present, the quadrotor becomes

Figure 10. Simulink implementation for simulation and experiments

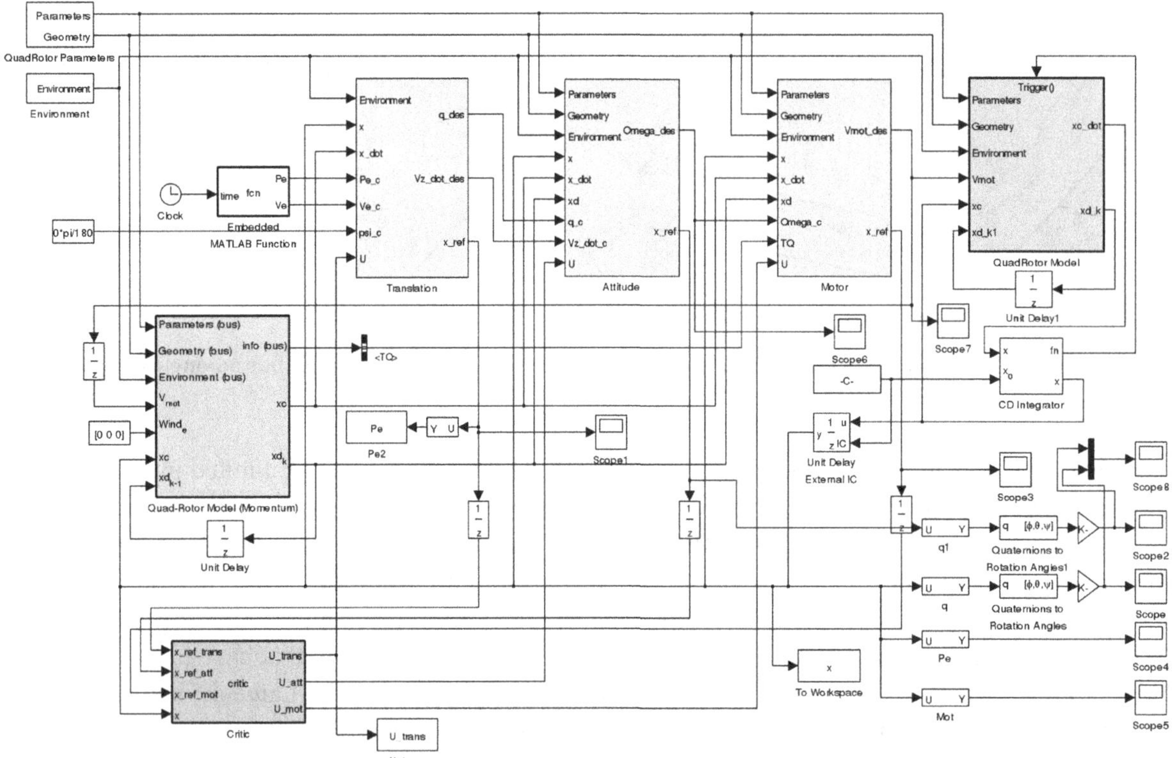

unstable without adaptation. In Figure 13 it is easy to observe the consequences of poor exploration of the state space. The adaptation only affects a few neurons corresponding to the states and the references that have been visited or applied.

FUTURE RESEARCH DIRECTIONS

Model-based ADP algorithms do not converge to the optimal solution when the model is not fully known or when its parameters deviate from the nominal values. In this case model-free algorithms are needed. Unfortunately, model-free ADP algorithms can not be used on complex systems directly. They can be considered only after enough information about the system and the environment has been acquired and stored in the neural networks using other methods. They can further refine the learning, but are not suitable for coarse learning from the beginning. A future implementation of a control algorithm for a quadrotor that allows the model to change and still converge to the optimum control policy would have to follow these steps:

1. Model the system and the environment with what precision is possible.
2. Use on-line or off-line model-based ADP to train the Actor and Critic NN. The NN should be able to store information for any operating point, not only for the nominal operating point.

Figure 11. Wind disturbance

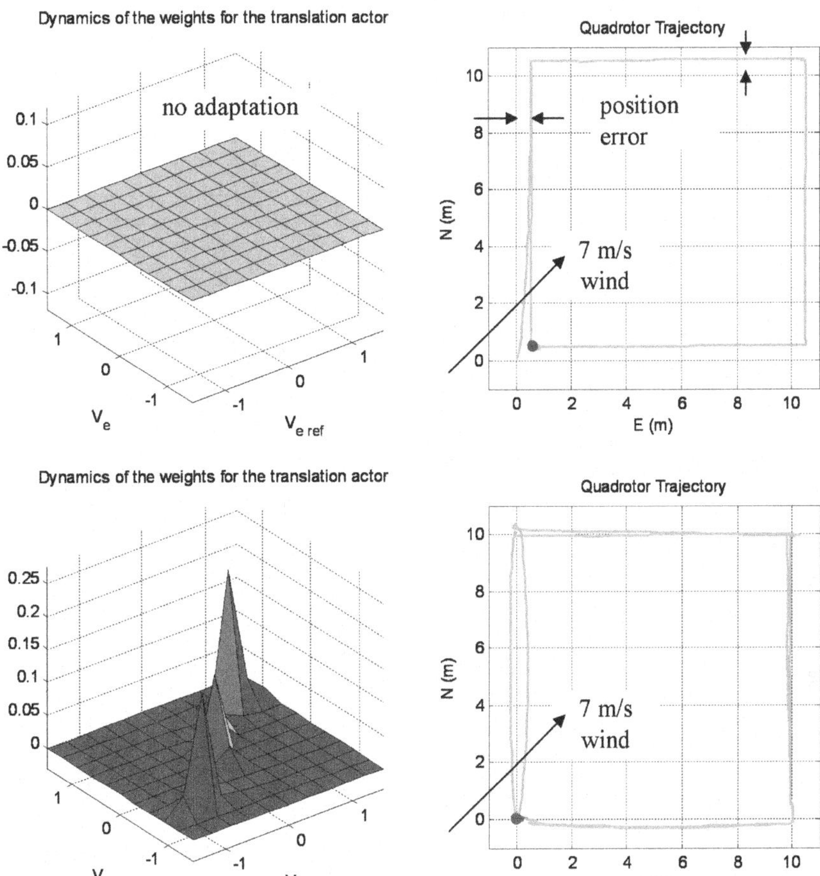

3. Use the on-line model-free ADP algorithm with the pre-trained NN. Only local exploration would be sufficient for reaching optimality even if the model starts departing from nominal values.

CONCLUSION

This chapter presented the development of on-line ADP reinforcement learning algorithms in suitable format for implementation on a quadrotor platform. A formulation for reinforcement learning was developed that consists of focused learning on subsystems of the quadrotor, with each subsystem having its own control actor yet all subsystems having a globally defined utility function. An objective was to formulate a realistic structure for ADP for practical implementation, that also relates to standard control system structures such as PID and nonlinear algorithms.

Figure 12. Weight imbalance

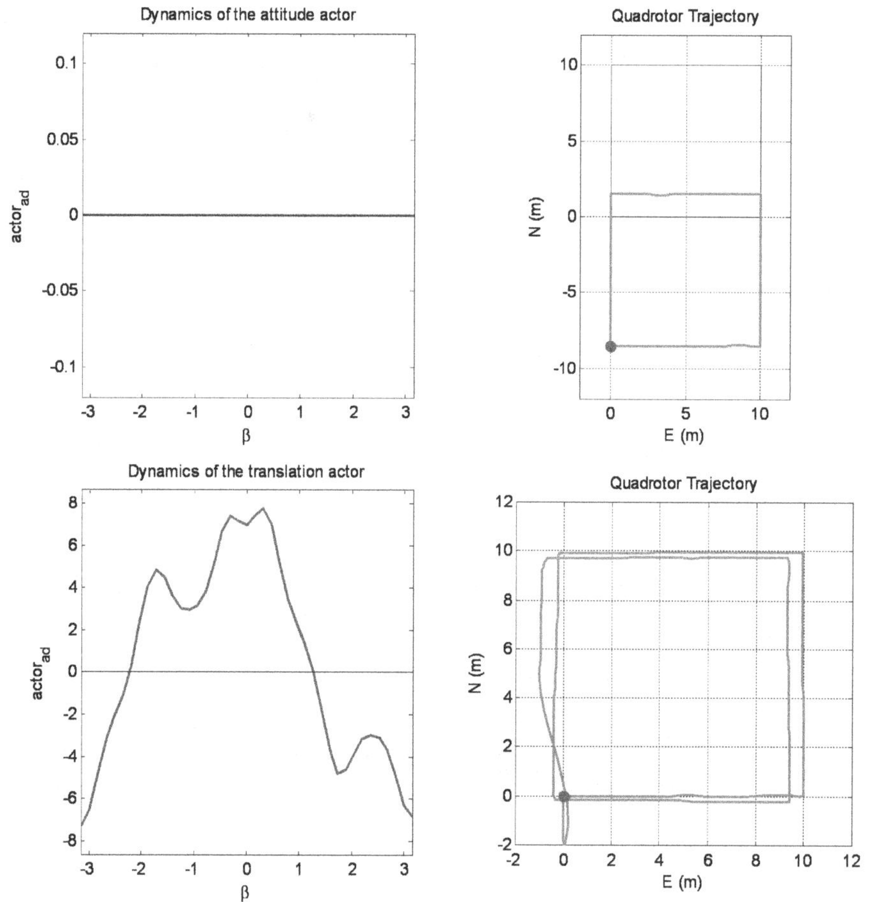

Figure 13. Adaptation to both wind and weight imbalance

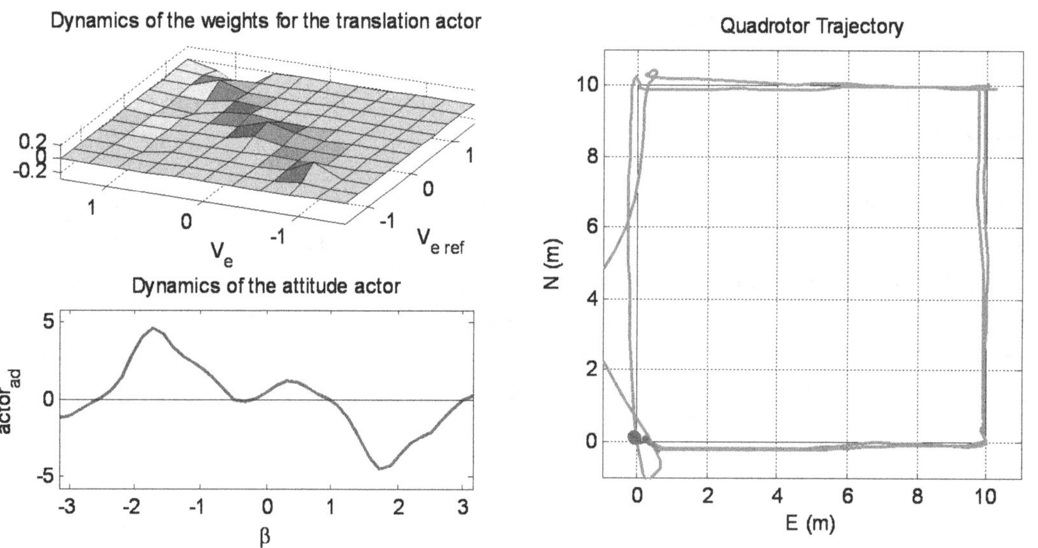

REFERENCES

Beard, R., Saridis, G., & Wen, J. (1997). Approximate solutions to the time-invariant Hamilton-Jacobi-Bellman equation. *Automatica, 33*(12), 2159–2177. doi:10.1016/S0005-1098(97)00128-3

Bellman, R. E. (1957). *Dynamic programming*. Princeton, NJ: Princeton University Press.

Bouabdallah, S., & Siegwart, R. (2007). *Full control of a quadrotor*. IEEE/RSJ International Conference on Intelligent Robots and Systems, (pp. 153–158).

Castillo, P., Dzul, A., & Lozano, R. (2004). Real-time stabilization and tracking of a four-rotor mini rotorcraft. *IEEE Transactions on Control Systems Technology, 12*(4), 510–516. doi:10.1109/TCST.2004.825052

Dierks, T., & Jagannathan, S. (2010). Output feedback control of a quadrotor UAV using neural networks. *IEEE Transactions on Neural Networks, 21*(1), 50–66. doi:10.1109/TNN.2009.2034145

Dreier, M. E. (2007). *Introduction to helicopter and tiltrotor flight simulation. AIAA Education Series*. AIAA.

Guenard, N., Hamel, T., & Moreau, V. (2005). Dynamic modeling and intuitive control strategy for an X4-flyer. *International Conference on Control and Automation, 1*, 141–146.

Hoffmann, G. M., Huang, H., Wasl, S. L., & Tomlin, C. J. (2007). *Quadrotor helicopter flight dynamics and control: Theory and experiment*. AIAA Guidance, Navigation, and Control Conference.

Leake, R. J., & Liu, R. W. (1967). Construction of suboptimal control sequences. *SIAM Journal on Control and Optimization, 5*(1), 54–63. doi:10.1137/0305004

Lewis, F. L., & Syrmos, V. (1995). *Optimal control* (2nd ed.). New York, NY: Wiley.

Li, Y., Sundararajan, N., & Saratchandran, P. (2000). Analysis of minimal radial basis function network algorithm for real-time identification of nonlinear dynamic systems. *IEE Proceedings. Control Theory and Applications, 147*(4), 476–484. doi:10.1049/ip-cta:20000549

Marsili-Libelli, S. (1981). Optimal design of PID regulators. *International Journal of Control, 33*(4), 601–616. doi:10.1080/00207178108922945

Nicol, C., Macnab, C. J. B., & Ramirez-Serrano, A. (2008). *Robust neural network control of a quadrotor helicopter*. IEEE Canadian Conference on Electrical and Computer Engineering, (pp. 1233–1238).

Park, S., Won, D. H., Kang, M. S., Kim, T. J., Lee, H. G., & Kwon, S. J. (2005). *RIC (robust internal-loop compensator) based flight control of a quad-rotor type UAV*. IEEE/RSJ International Conference on Intelligent Robots and Systems, (pp. 3542–3547).

Park, Y.-M., Choi, M.-S., & Lee, K. Y. (1996). An optimal tracking neuro-controller for nonlinear dynamic systems. *IEEE Transactions on Neural Networks, 7*(5), 1099–1110. doi:10.1109/72.536307

Sutton, R. S., & Barto, A. G. (1998). *Reinforcement learning: An introduction (adaptive computation and machine learning)*. The MIT Press.

Valenti, M., Bethke, B., Fiore, G., How, J. P., & Feron, E. (2006). *Indoor multi-vehicle flight testbed for fault detection, isolation, and recovery*. AIAA Guidance, Navigation and Control Conference.

Watkins, C. (1989). *Learning from delayed rewards*. Unpublished doctoral dissertation, Cambridge University, Cambridge, England.

Watkins, C., & Dayan, P. (1992). Q-learning. *Machine Learning*, *8*, 279–292. doi:10.1007/BF00992698

Zhang, H., Wei, Q., & Luo, Y. (2008). A novel infinite-time optimal tracking control scheme for a class of discrete-time nonlinear systems via the greedy HDP iteration algorithm. *IEEE Transactions on Systems, Man, and Cybernetics. Part B, Cybernetics*, *38*(4), 937–942. doi:10.1109/TSMCB.2008.920269

Chapter 6
Cognitive Based Distributed Sensing, Processing, and Communication

Roman Ilin
Air Force Research Laboratory, USA

Leonid Perlovsky
Air Force Research Laboratory, USA

ABSTRACT

Perception, cognition, and higher cognitive abilities of the mind are considered here within a neural modeling fields (NMF) paradigm. Its fundamental mathematical mechanism is a process "from vague-fuzzy to crisp," called dynamic logic. The chapter discusses why this paradigm is necessary mathematically, and relates it to a psychological description of the mind. Surprisingly, the process from "vague to crisp" corresponds to Aristotelian understanding of mental functioning. Recent fMRI measurements confirmed this process in neural mechanisms of perception. After an overview of NMF, the chapter describes solutions to two important problems: target tracking and situation recognition. Both problems can be solved within the NMF framework using the same basic algorithm. The chapter then discusses the challenges of using NMF and outlines the directions of future research.

INTRODUCTION

The greatest challenge to modern sensor processing is computational complexity and limited communication bandwidth. Consider a multi sensor distributed image communication system for real time situation monitoring. An example of such system would be security video surveillance consisting of multiple cameras covering a certain area. Image sequences from the cameras provide multiple views of the same

DOI: 10.4018/978-1-60960-551-3.ch006

area from different vantage points. The timing of the images is not synchronized. Human operators are usually overwhelmed by the amount of visual information that has to be processed in real time. There is a strong need for automated detection of events of interest and bringing them to operator's attention.

The challenges for such automation are (1) information fusion, (2) object detection, classification, and tracking, and (3) situation classification. Information fusion associates the data from different cameras that originated from the same object (Hall & Llinas, 2001). This task is difficult due to multiple objects in the view, asynchronous image sequences, and the presence of a large number of irrelevant objects. A brute-force algorithm for testing all possible combinations of data points from each camera results in exponential computational time. Object detection and classification is often difficult due to high noise, occlusions by other objects, variations in size, shape, color, and other characteristics of objects falling within the same class (Bishop, 2006). Object tracking, similarly to information fusion, is challenging due to the data association problem (Bar-Shalom & Fortmann, 1988). Finding correspondences between image points that belong to consecutive images may require exponential computational time. Finally, situation classification requires consideration of multiple objects, their spatial relationships, and time evolution. Due to the large number of irrelevant objects in the images this task could not have been automated. Each of the aforementioned challenges is an area of active research. The importance of systems meeting all of the above challenges can hardly be overstated.

Cognitive modeling shows promise in overcoming these challenges based on the evidence from neuroscience and psychology. The brain is known to perform information fusion from various senses, object tracking and recognition, and situation recognition in efficient manner. In fact, the term situational awareness is used almost exclusively to describe human ability to understand the meaning of current perceptions and predict the future events (Endsley, 1995). It seems that building an artificial agent capable of situational awareness will involve going beyond modeling the perceptual abilities of human beings, such as vision, touch and smell. In what follows we argue that successful cognitive modeling has to include such attributes of the mind as instincts, emotions, and language. All of these components of the mind find their place within the Neural Modeling Fields theory (NMF) of the mind. The objectives of the chapter are to provide an overview of NMF, examples of usage of NMF, and outline the directions of future research within this exciting area of cognitive modeling.

Background

How the mind works has been a subject of discussions for millennia, from Ancient Greek philosophers to mathematicians to modern cognitive scientists. Words like mind, thought, imagination, emotion, concept present a challenge: people use these words in many ways colloquially, but in cognitive science and in mathematics of intelligence they have not been uniquely defined and their meaning is a subject of active research and ongoing debates (for the discussions and further references see: (Grossberg S., 1988), (Albus, 2001), (Perlovsky, 2001). Standardized definitions come after completion of a theoretical development (for instance "force" was defined by Newton's laws, following centuries of less precise usage). In this section we are outlining the direction for a future brain-mind theory. Such a theory has to correspond to the everyday usage of the words "mind," "emotions" as well as the new scientific findings. We use a dictionary definition of the mind as a starting point. According to the dictionary definition of the mind includes conscious and unconscious processes, thought, perception, emotion, will, memory and imagination, and it originates in brain (The American Heritage College Dictionary, 2000). These constituent notions will be discussed throughout the chapter. Specific neural mechanisms in the brain "implementing" various mind functions constitute the relationship between the mind and brain. We will discuss possible relationships of neural structures in the brain and the proposed mathematical models.

The problem addressed in this chapter is developing a mathematical technique suitable to describe higher cognitive functions. Such a technique could serve two purposes. First, it would lead to the development of intelligent sensor processing with thousands of applications. Second, it would help to unify and clarify complex issues in philosophy, psychology, neurobiology, and cognitive science. Achieving the two purposes, of intelligent computers and mind theory will require the collaboration of many people.

A broad range of opinions exists about the mathematical methods suitable for the description of the mind. Founders of artificial intelligence, including Allan Newell (Newell, 1983) and Marvin Minsky (Minsky, 1988) thought that formal logic was sufficient and no specific mathematical techniques would be needed to describe the mind. An opposite view was advocated by Brian Josephson (Josephson, 1997) and Roger Penrose (Penrose, 1994), suggesting that the mind cannot be understood within the current knowledge of physics; new unknown yet physical phenomena will have to be accounted for explaining the working of the mind. This chapter develops a point of view that there are few specific mathematical constructs, "the first principles" of the mind. Several researchers advocated this view. Grossberg (Grossberg S., 1988) suggested that the first principles include a resonant matching between bottom-up signals and top-down representations, as well as an emotional evaluation of conceptual contents (Grossberg & Levine, 1987). Zadeh (Zadeh, 1997) developed the theory of granularity; Meystel (Meystel, 1995) developed the hierarchical multi-scale organization; Edelman suggested neuronal group selection (Edelman & Tononi, 1995), and Perlovsky (Perlovsky, 2001), suggested the knowledge instinct, aesthetic emotions, and dynamic logic among the first principles of the mind.

This chapter presents neural modeling fields theory (NMF), a mathematical 'structure' that we propose is intrinsic to operations of the mind, and dynamic logic, governing its temporal evolution. It discusses specific difficulties encountered by previous attempts at mathematical modeling of the mind and how the new theory overcomes these difficulties. We argue that the theory is related to an important mechanism behind workings of the mind, which we call "the knowledge instinct" as well as to other cognitive functions. We discuss neurobiological foundations, cognitive, psychological, and philosophical connections, experimental verifications, outline emerging trends and future directions.

NEURAL MODELING FIELDS

Complexity and Logic

The act of object perception involves signals from sensor organs and internal representations of objects. According to contemporary understanding (Grossberg S., 1988), perception involves the matching of top-down and bottom-up neural signals. The buttom-up signals are coming from sensors. The top-down signals originate from the mental representations of the objects and events. During perception, the brain associates subsets of bottom-up signals corresponding to objects with object mental representations. This recognition activates brain signals leading to mental and behavioral responses, which are important for the phenomenon of understanding.

Developing mathematical descriptions of the very first recognition step in this seemingly simple association-recognition-understanding process has not been easy as a number of difficulties have been encountered over the last fifty years. These difficulties were summarized under the notion of combinatorial complexity (CC). CC refers to multiple combinations of various elements in a complex system. For example, recognition of a scene often requires concurrent recognition of its multiple elements that could be encountered in various combinations. CC is prohibitive because the number of combinations is very large: for example, consider 100 elements (not too large a number); the number of combinations of 100 elements is 100^{100}. No computer would ever be able to compute that many combinations.

The problem was first identified in pattern recognition and classification research in the 1960s and was named "the curse of dimensionality" (Bellman, 1961). It seemed that adaptive self-learning algorithms and neural networks could learn solutions to any problem 'on their own' if provided with a sufficient number of training examples. The following thirty years of developing adaptive statistical pattern recognition and neural network algorithms led to the conclusion that the required number of combinations often itself was combinatorial. Self-learning approaches encountered CC of learning requirements.

Rule-based systems were proposed to solve the problem of learning complexity. An initial idea was that rules would capture the required knowledge and eliminate a need for learning. However, in the presence of variability the number of rules grew. Rules depended on other rules, combinations of rules had to be considered and rule systems encountered CC of rules. Beginning in the 1980s, model-based systems were proposed. They used models that depended on adaptive parameters. The idea was to combine advantages of learning-adaptivity and rules by using adaptive models. The knowledge was encapsulated in models, whereas unknown aspects of particular situations were to be learned by fitting model parameters. Fitting models to data required selecting data subsets corresponding to various models. The number of subsets, however, is combinatorially large. A general popular algorithm for fitting models to data, multiple hypotheses testing (Singer, 1974) is known to face CC of computations. Model-based approaches encountered computational CC (N and NP complete algorithms).

CC is related to formal logic underlying various algorithms and neural networks (Perlovsky L., 1998). Formal logic is based on the "law of excluded middle," according to which every statement is either true or false and nothing in between. Therefore, algorithms based on formal logic have to evaluate every variation in data or models as a separate logical statement (hypothesis). A large number of combinations of these variations result in combinatorial complexity. Multivalued logic and fuzzy logic were proposed to overcome limitations related to the law of excluded third (Kecman, 2001). Yet the mathematics of multivalued logic is no different in principle from formal logic, "excluded third" is substituted by "excluded n+1." Fuzzy logic encountered a difficulty related to the degree of fuzziness. If too much fuzziness is specified, the solution does not achieve the required accuracy, if too little, it becomes similar to formal logic. Complex systems require different degrees of fuzziness in various elements of system operations; searching for the appropriate degrees of fuzziness among combinations of elements again would lead to CC. The problem of CC remains unresolved within logic.

Instincts, Emotions, and Concepts

As it became clear from the previous section, logic does not work, but the mind works. So let us turn to the mechanisms of the mind. Possibly, we will find inspiration for developing mathematics needed for intelligent computers and decipher mechanisms of higher cognitive functions. Mechanisms of the mind, essential for the development of a mathematical theory of intelligence in this chapter include: instincts, concepts, emotions, and behavior. The full discussion of these mechanisms is outside of the scope of this chapter. Here we only summarize aspects of these mechanisms important to our purpose to relate mathematics to psychology and neurobiology of the mind.

Instincts are innate capabilities, aptitudes, or behavior, which are not learned, complex, and normally adaptive. Instincts are different from reflexes, a word used for more simple immediate mechanisms. In humans and higher animals, instincts are related to emotions. Psychoanalysts equated instincts with human motivational forces (such as sex and aggression); today these are referred to as instinctual drives. Motivation is based on emotions, on the search for positive emotional experiences and the avoidance of negative ones.

We will use the word "concept" to designate a common thread among words like concept, idea, understanding, thought, or notion. Different authors use these words with subtle differences. A common thread among these words is an abstract, universal psychical entity that serves to designate a category or class of entities, events, or relations. A concept is the element of a proposition rather in a way that a word is the element of a sentence. Concepts are abstract in that they omit the differences of the things in their extension, treating them as if they were identical. Concepts are universal in that they apply equally to everything in their extension. Plato and Aristotle called them ideas or forms, and considered them the basis for the mind understanding of the world. Similarly, Kant considered them a foundation for the ability for understanding, the contents of pure reason. According to Jung, conscious concepts of the mind are learned on the basis of inborn unconscious psychic structures, archetypes. Contemporary science often equates the mechanism of concepts with internal representations of objects, their relationships, situations, etc. Ray Jackendoff (Jackendoff, 2002) considers terms *representation* or *symbol* as too loaded with "thorny philosophical problem of intentionality," and uses the word *model.*

Emotions refer to both exaggeratedly expressive communications and to internal states related to feelings. Love, hate, courage, fear, joy, sadness, pleasure, and disgust can all be described in both psychological and physiological terms. Emotion is the realm where thought and physiology are inextricably entwined, and where the self is inseparable from individual perceptions of value and judgment toward others and ourselves. Emotions are sometimes regarded as the antithesis of reason; as is suggested by phrases such as "appeal to emotion" or "don't let your emotions take over." A distinctive and challenging fact about human beings is a potential for both opposition and entanglement between will, emotion, and reason. It has also been suggested that there is no empirical support for any generalization suggesting the antithesis between reason and emotion: indeed, anger or fear can often be thought of as a systematic response to observed facts. What should be noted, however, is that the human psyche possesses many possible reactions and perspective in regard to the internal and external world—often lying on a continuum—some of which may involve the extreme of pure intellectual logic (often called "cold"), other the extreme of pure emotion unresponsive to logical argument ("the heat of passion"). In any case, it should be clear that the relation between logic and argument on the one hand and emotion on the other, merits careful study. It has been noted by many that passion, emotion, or feeling can add backing to an argument, even one based primarily on reason—particularly in regard to religion or ideology, areas of human thought which frequently demand an all-or-nothing rejection or acceptance, that is, the adoption of a comprehensive worldview partly backed by empirical argument and partly by feeling and passion. Moreover, it has been suggested by several researchers that typically there is no "pure" decision or thought, that is, no thought based "purely" on intellectual logic or "purely" on emotion—most decisions and cognitions are founded on a mixture of both.

An essential role of emotions in working of the mind was analyzed by many researchers, from various perspectives: philosophical - Rene Descartes (Descartes, 1989); Immanuel Kant (Kant, 1943); Jean Paul Sartre (Sartre, 1984); analytical psychology - Carl Jung (Jung, 1971); psychological and neural - Stephen Grossberg and Daniel Levine (Grossberg & Levine, 1987), Andrew Ortony (Ortony

& Turner, 1990), Joseph Ledoux (Ledoux, 1998); philosophical-linguistic - P. Griffiths (Griffiths, 1998); neuro-physiological - Antonio Damasio (Damasio, 1995); and from the learning and cognition perspective by Perlovsky (Perlovsky L., Emotions, Learning, and Control, 1999). Descartes attempted a scientific explanation of passions. He rationalized emotions, explaining them as objects and relating them to physiological processes. According to Kant, emotions are closely related to judgments about which individual experiences and perceptions correspond to which general concepts and v.v. The ability for judgment is a foundation of all higher spiritual abilities, including beautiful and sublime. Kant's aesthetics is a foundation of aesthetic theories till this very day (we will continue this discussion later). Sartre equated emotions, to significant extent, with unconscious contents of psyche; today this does not seem to be adequate. Jung analyzed conscious and unconscious aspects of emotions. He emphasized undifferentiated status of primitive fused emotion-concept-behavior psychic states in everyday functioning and their role in psychoses. He also emphasized rational aspect of conscious differentiated emotions. Ortony explains emotions in terms of knowledge representations and emphasizes abductive logic as a mechanism of inferencing other people's emotions. Ledoux analyses neural structures and pathways involved in emotional processing, especially in fear. Griffiths considers basic emotions and their evolutionary development within social interactions. According to Damasio, emotions are primarily bodily perceptions, and feelings of emotions in the brain invoke "bodily markers". Grossberg and Levine consider emotions as neural signals that relate instinctual and conceptual brain centers. In the processes of perception and cognition, emotions evaluate concept-models of objects and situations for satisfaction or dissatisfaction of instinctual needs.

Behavior is comprised of many mechanisms. Behavior is controlled by the endocrine system, and the nervous system. The complexity of behavior of an organism is related to the complexity of its nervous system. In this chapter we refer only to neurally controlled behavior; it involves mechanisms of negative feedback (e.g., when reaching an object with a hand) and positive feedback (e.g. when making a decision). The first does not reach consciousness, a second, is potentially available to consciousness (Grossberg S., 1988).

Explaining basic mind mechanisms requires no mysterious assumptions, each can be described mathematically. Among the mind cognitive mechanisms, the most directly accessible to consciousness are concepts. Concepts are like internal models of the objects and situations in the world; this analogy is quite literal, e.g., during visual perception of an object, a concept-model in our memory projects an image onto the visual cortex, which is matched there to an image, projected from retina (this simplified description will be refined later).

Concepts serve for satisfaction of the basic instincts, which have emerged as survival mechanisms long before concepts. We have briefly mentioned current debates of the roles of instincts, reflexes, motivational forces, and drives. Often, inborn, less adaptive, unconscious, and more automatic functioning is referred to as instinctual. This lumping together of various mechanisms is inappropriate for the purposes of this chapter – the development of mathematical description of the mind mechanisms. We follow proposals (see (Grossberg & Levine, 1987) for further references and discussions) to separate instincts as internal sensor mechanisms indicating the basic needs, from "instinctual behavior," which should be described by appropriate mechanisms. Accordingly, we use "instincts" to describe mechanisms of internal sensors: for example, when a sugar level in blood goes below a certain level an instinct "tells us" to eat. Such separation of instinct as "internal sensor" from "instinctual behavior" is only a step toward identifying all the details of relevant biological mechanisms.

How do we know about instinctual needs? We do not hear instinctual pronouncements or read dials of instinctual sensors. Instincts are connected to cognition and behavior by emotions. Whereas in colloquial usage, emotions are often understood as facial expressions, higher voice pitch, exaggerated gesticulation, these are outward signs of emotions, serving for communication. A more fundamental role of emotions within the mind system is that emotional signals evaluate concepts for the purpose of instinct satisfaction. This evaluation is not according to rules or concepts (like in rule-systems of artificial intelligence), but according to a different instinctual-emotional mechanism, described first by Grossberg and Levine (Grossberg & Levine, 1987), and described below for higher cognitive functions. *The emotional mechanism is crucial for breaking out of the "vicious circle" of combinatorial complexity.*

A mathematical theory described in the next section leads to an inevitable conclusion: humans and higher animals have a special instinct responsible for cognition. This conclusion is drawn from the basic knowledge of the mind operations as described in thousands of publications. Clearly, humans and animals engage into exploratory behavior, even when basic bodily needs, like eating, are satisfied. Biologists and psychologists discussed curiosity in this regard (Berlyne, 1960). However, it was not mentioned among 'basic instincts' on a par with instincts for food and procreation. The reasons were that it was difficult to define, and that its fundamental nature was not obvious. The fundamental nature of this mechanism is related to the fact that our knowledge always has to be modified to fit the current situations. One rarely sees exactly the same object: illumination, angles, surrounding objects are usually different; therefore, adaptation-learning is required. A mathematical formulation of the mind mechanisms makes obvious the fundamental nature of our desire for knowledge. In fact virtually all learning and adaptive algorithms (tens of thousands of publications) maximize correspondence between the algorithm internal structure (knowledge in a wide sense) and objects of recognition. As discussed in the next section, concept-models that our mind uses for understanding the world are in a constant need of adaptation. Knowledge is not just a static state; it is in a constant process of adaptation and learning. Without adaptation of concept-models we will not be able to understand the ever-changing surrounding world. We will not be able to orient ourselves or satisfy any of the bodily needs. Therefore, we have an inborn need, a drive, and an instinct to improve our knowledge. We define it as *the knowledge instinct*. Mathematically it is described as a maximization of a similarity measure between concept-models and the world.

Emotions evaluating satisfaction or dissatisfaction of the knowledge instinct are not directly related to bodily needs. Therefore, they are 'spiritual' or aesthetic emotions. We would like to emphasize that aesthetic emotions are not peculiar to perception of art; they are inseparable from every act of perception and cognition. Conceptual-emotional understanding of the world results in actions in the outside world or within the mind. In the next section we describe a mathematical theory of conceptual-emotional recognition and understanding. As we discuss, in addition to concepts and emotions, it involves mechanisms of intuition, imagination, conscious, and unconscious. This process is intimately connected to an ability of the mind to think, to operate with symbols and signs. The mind involves a hierarchy of multiple layers of concept-models, from simple perceptual elements (like edges, or moving dots), to concept-models of objects, to relationships among objects, to complex scenes, and up the hierarchy… toward the concept-models of the meaning of life and purpose of our existence. Hence the tremendous complexity of the mind, yet relatively few basic principles of the mind organization go a long way explaining this system.

To summarize, for the purposes of developing the mathematical description, concepts or mental representations are described as models, instincts as sensor type mechanisms indicating the essential needs to the organism, emotions as neural signals connecting the instinctual parts of the brain with the concepts. We consider only one type of behavior – learning and understanding.

Mathematical Description

Neural modeling field is a multi-layer, hetero-hierarchical system (Perlovsky 1987), (Perlovsky, 2001). The mind is not a strict hierarchy; there are multiple feedback connections among several adjacent layers, hence the term hetero-hierarchy. NMF mathematically implements mechanisms of the mind discussed above. At each layer there are concept-models encapsulating the mind's knowledge; they generate top-down signals, interacting with input, bottom-up signals. These interactions are governed by the knowledge instinct, which drives concept-model learning, adaptation, and formation of new concept-models for better correspondence to the input signals.

This section describes a basic mechanism of interaction between two adjacent hierarchical layers of bottom-up and top-down signals (fields of neural activation). Sometimes, it will be more convenient to talk about these two signal-layers as an input to and output from a (single) processing-layer. At each layer, output signals are concepts recognized in (or formed from) input signals. Input signals are associated with (or recognized, or grouped into) concepts according to the models and the knowledge instinct at this layer. This general structure of NMF corresponds to our knowledge of neural structures in the brain; although this is true about mathematical description in the following sub-sections, however, it is not mapped to specific neurons or synaptic connections. How the actual brain neurons "implement" models and the knowledge instinct is a subject for future research. The knowledge instinct is described mathematically as maximization of a similarity measure. In the process of learning and understanding the input signals, models are adapted for better representation of the input signals so that similarity between the models and signals increases. This increase in similarity satisfies the knowledge instinct and is felt as aesthetic emotions.

At a particular hierarchical layer, we enumerate neurons by index n =1... N. These neurons receive bottom-up input signals, X(n), from lower layers in the processing hierarchy. X(n) is a field of bottom-up neuronal synapse activations, coming from neurons at a lower layer. Each neuron has a number of synapses; for generality, we describe each neuron activation as a set of numbers, $X(n) = \{X_d(n), d = 1,... D\}$. Top-down, or priming signals to these neurons are sent by concept-models, $M_h(S_h,n)$. We enumerate models by index h=1..H. Each model is characterized by its parameters, S_h. The models are encoded in the neuron structure of the brain by the strength of synaptic connections. Mathematically, we describe them as a set of numbers, $S_h = \{S_{ah}, a = 1... A\}$. Models represent signals in the following way. Suppose that signal X(n) coming from sensory neurons is activated by object h, characterized by parameters S_h. These parameters may include position, orientation, or lighting of an object h. Model $M_h(S_h,n)$ predicts the value X(n) of a signal at neuron n. For example, during visual perception, a neuron n in the visual cortex receives a signal X(n) from retina and a priming signal $M_h(S_h,n)$ from an object-concept-model h. A neuron n is activated if both bottom-up signal from lower-layer-input and top-down priming signal are strong. Various models compete for evidence in the bottom-up signals, while adapting their parameters for better match as described below. This is a simplified description of perception. The most benign everyday visual perception uses many layers from retina to object perception. The NMF premise is that the same laws describe the basic interaction dynamics at each layer. Perception of minute features, or everyday objects, or cognition of complex abstract concepts is due to the same mechanism described below. Perception and cognition involve models and learning. In perception, models correspond to objects; in cognition models correspond to relationships and situations. Input signals, models, and other parts of the learning mechanisms at a single processing layer described below are illustrated in Fig. 1.

Learning is an essential part of perception and cognition, and it is driven by the knowledge instinct. It increases a similarity measure between the sets of models and signals, L({**X**},{**M**}). The similarity measure is a function of model parameters and associations between the input bottom-up signals and top-down, concept-model signals. For concreteness we refer here to an object perception using a simplified terminology, as if perception of objects in retinal signals occurs in a single layer.

In constructing a mathematical description of the similarity measure, it is important to acknowledge two principles. First, the exact content of the visual field is unknown before perception occurred. Important information could be contained in any bottom-up signal; therefore, the similarity measure is constructed so that it accounts for all input information, **X**(n),

$$L(\{X\},\{M\}) = \prod_{n=1}^{N} l(X(n)) \tag{1}$$

This expression contains a product of partial similarities, l(**X**(n)), over all bottom-up signals; therefore it forces the mind to account for every signal (even if one term in the product is zero, the product

Figure 1. For a single layer of NMF bottom-up input signals are unstructured data {X(n)} and output signals are recognized or formed concepts {h} with high values of similarity measures. Top-down, "priming" signals are models, $M_h(S_h,n)$. Conditional similarity measures $l(X(n)|h)$ and association variables $f(n|h)$, eq.(3), associate data and models. They initiate adaptation and concept recognition. The adaptation-learning cycle defined by this structure and equations (3), (4), and (5) maximizes similarity measure (1). Psychologically, it satisfies the knowledge instinct; changes in similarity (1) correspond to aesthetic emotions. New data coming from sensors, if they do not match exactly existing models, reduce similarity value, do not satisfy the knowledge instinct, and produce negative aesthetic emotions. This stimulates the constant renewal of adaptation-learning cycles.

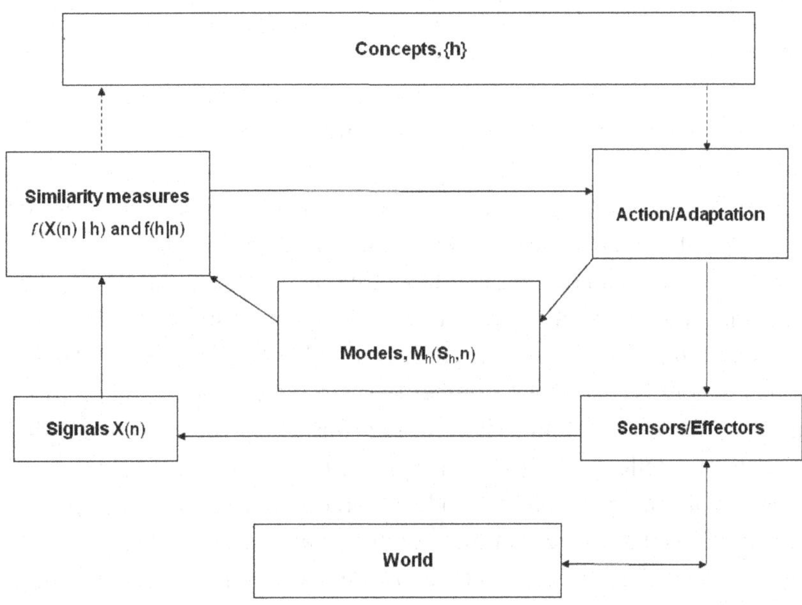

is zero, the similarity is low and the knowledge instinct is not satisfied); this is a reflection of the first principle. Second, before perception occurs, the mind does not know which retinal neuron corresponds to which object. Therefore a partial similarity measure is constructed so that it treats each model as an alternative (a sum over models) for each input neuron signal. Its constituent elements are conditional partial similarities between signal **X**(n) and model $\mathbf{M}_h$, l(**X**(n)|h). This measure is "conditional" on object h being present, therefore, when combining these quantities into the overall similarity measure, L, they are multiplied by r(h), which represent the measure of object h actually being present. Combining these elements with the two principles noted above, a similarity measure is constructed as follows.

$$L(\{X\},\{M\}) = \prod_{n=1}^{N}\sum_{h=1}^{H} r(h)l(X(x) \mid h) \qquad (2)$$

The structure of (2) follows standard principles of the probability theory: a summation is taken over alternatives, *h*, and various pieces of evidence, *n*, are multiplied. This expression is not necessarily a probability, but it has a probabilistic structure. If learning is successful, it approximates probabilistic description and leads to near-optimal Bayesian decisions. The name "conditional partial similarity" for l(**X**(n)|h) (or simply l(n|h)) follows the probabilistic terminology. If learning is successful, l(n|h) becomes a conditional probability density function, a probabilistic measure that signal in neuron *n* originated from object *h*. Then L is a total likelihood of observing signals {**X**(n)} coming from objects described by models $\{\mathbf{M}_h\}$. Coefficients r(h), called priors in probability theory, contain preliminary biases or expectations, expected objects *h* have relatively high r(h) values; their true values are usually unknown and should be learned, like other parameters $\mathbf{S}_h$.

Note that in probability theory, a product of probabilities usually assumes that evidence is independent. Expression (2) contains a product over *n*, but it does not assume independence among various signals **X**(n). There is a dependence among signals due to models: each model $\mathbf{M}_h(\mathbf{S}_h,n)$ predicts expected signal values in many neurons *n*.

During the learning process, concept-models are constantly modified. From time to time a system forms a new concept, while retaining an old one as well; alternatively, old concepts are sometimes merged or eliminated. This mechanism works as follows. In this chapter we consider a case when functional forms of models, $\mathbf{M}_h(\mathbf{S}_h,n)$, are all fixed and learning-adaptation involves only model parameters, $\mathbf{S}_h$. More complicated structural learning of models is considered in (Perlovsky L., Integrating Language and Cognition, 2004) and (Perlovsky L., Symbols: Integrated Cognition and Language, 2006). Formation of new concepts and merging or elimination-forgetting of old ones require a modification of the similarity measure (2); the reason is that more models always result in a better fit between the models and data. This is a well known problem, it can be addressed by reducing similarity (2) using a "penalty function" p(N,M) that grows with the number of models M, and this growth is steeper for a smaller amount of data N. For example, an asymptotically unbiased maximum likelihood estimation leads to multiplicative $p(N,M) = \exp(-N_{par}/2)$, where N_{par} is a total number of adaptive parameters in all models (this penalty function is known as Akaike Information Criterion, see (Perlovsky & McManus, 1991) (Perlovsky L., Mathematical Concepts of Intellect, 1996) for further discussion and references).

The learning process consists in estimating model parameters **S** and associating signals with concepts by maximizing the similarity (2). Note that all possible combinations of signals and models are accounted for in expression (2). This can be seen by expanding a sum in (2), and multiplying all the terms;

it would result in H^N items, a huge number. This is the number of combinations between all signals (N) and all models (H). Here is the source of CC of many algorithms used in the past. For example, multiple hypothesis testing algorithms attempts to maximize similarity L over model parameters and associations between signals and models, in two steps. First it takes one of the H^N items that is one particular association between signals and models and maximizes it over model parameters. Second, the largest item is selected (that is the best association for the best set of parameters). Such a program inevitably faces a wall of CC, the number of computations on the order of H^N.

Modeling field theory solves this problem by using *dynamic logic.* An important aspect of dynamic logic is matching vagueness or fuzziness of similarity measures to the uncertainty of models. Initially, parameter values are not known, and uncertainty of models is high; so is the fuzziness of the similarity measures. In the process of learning, models become more accurate and the similarity measure more crisp, the value of the similarity increases. This process "from vague to crisp" is the mechanism of dynamic logic.

Mathematically it is described as follows. First, assign any values to unknown parameters, $\{\mathbf{S}_h\}$. Then, compute association variables f(h|n),

$$f(h \mid n) = r(h)l(X(n) \mid h) \,/ \sum_{h'=1}^{H} r(h')l(X(n) \mid h') \tag{3}$$

Eq.(3) looks like the Bayes formula for a posteriori probabilities; if l(n|h) in the result of learning become conditional likelihoods, f(h|n) become Bayesian probabilities for signal *n* originating from object *h*. The dynamic logic of the Modeling Fields (MF) is defined as follows,

$$\frac{\partial f(h \mid n)}{\partial t} = f(h \mid n)\sum_{h'=1}^{H}[\delta_{hh'} - f(h' \mid n)]\frac{\partial \ln l(n \mid h')}{\partial M_{h'}}\frac{\partial M_{h'}}{\partial S_{h'}}\frac{\partial S_{h'}}{\partial t} \tag{4}$$

$$\frac{\partial S_h}{\partial t} = \sum_{n=1}^{N} f(h \mid n)\frac{\partial \ln l(n \mid h)}{\partial M_h}\frac{\partial M_h}{\partial S_h} \tag{5}$$

where

$$\delta_{hh'} = \begin{cases} 1\, if \quad h = h' \\ 0 \quad otherwise \end{cases} \tag{6}$$

Parameter t is the time of the internal dynamics of the MF system (the number of internal iterations). A more specific form of (5) depends of the similarity function l(n|h) specific to a particular application. In most of all our applications we use the conditional pdf of the data element n given model h as the measure of similarity. Other similarity measures are possible.

The following theorem was proven (Perlovsky, 2001).

Theorem. Equations (3) through (6) define a convergent dynamic NMF system with stationary states defined by $\max_{\{Sh\}}L$.

It follows that the stationary states of an NMF system are the maximum similarity states satisfying the knowledge instinct. When partial similarities are specified as probability density functions (pdf), or likelihoods, the stationary values of parameters $\{\mathbf{S}_h\}$ are asymptotically unbiased and efficient estimates of these parameters (Cramer, 1946). A computational complexity of the NMF method is linear in N.

The theorem means that dynamic logic is a convergent process. It converges to the maximum of similarity, and therefore satisfies the knowledge instinct. If likelihood is used as similarity, parameter values are estimated efficiently (that is, in most cases, parameters cannot be better learned using any other procedure). Moreover, as a part of the above theorem, it is proven that the similarity measure increases at each iteration. The psychological interpretation is that the knowledge instinct is satisfied at each step: a modeling field system with dynamic logic *enjoys* learning.

In summary, the mathematical procedure described in this section is interpreted in behavioral terms as follows. The dynamic logic iterations model the behavior of learning, which is inseparable from every act of perception and cognition. The similarity models instinct for knowledge, with small similarity corresponding to strong need for knowledge and large similarity corresponding to minimal need for knowledge. The change in total similarity from one iteration to the next corresponds to the aesthetic emotion resulting from learning the right concepts.

Hierarchical Structure

Mathematical apparatus described in the previous section can be extended to hierarchical systems. In terms of the mind, the hierarchy refers to the increasing level of abstraction in concepts. The lower levels are concerned with physical objects, whereas the higher levels operate concepts that involve complex groupings and relationships between lower level concepts. An example of such abstraction is recognition of situations. In a simplified manner we can say that any situation involves recognition of certain objects being present in the sensor input. A lecture is characterized by a teacher, students, chairs, whiteboard, etc. A bank robbery is characterized by certain objects and relationships observed by the surveillance system operator. Situation recognition is a difficult problem because it involves the recognition of objects, which is combinatorial by itself as explained in the previous section, and the recognition of situation as a combination of objects and their relationships, in the presence of many irrelevant objects.

Fig. 2 illustrates the main components of an intelligent system capable of situational awareness. Note that the bottom layer of this hierarchy receives inputs from multiple distributed sensors, whereas the higher layers are centralized and receive inputs from the bottom layers. In the case of surveillance system the bottom layer corresponds to low level sensor processing of camera images and their sequences. The higher layers are concerned with the meaning of the results coming from the layers below. Top layers provide the feedback to the bottom creating an attention mechanism necessary to focus on interesting events detected by the bottom layers.

Each layer in Fig. 2 is described by the single layer dynamics (3)-(5). The inputs into the higher levels of the hierarchy are given by the activation levels of the models from the lower level, given by the quantities f(h|n). In the simplest form of hierarchical processing there is one way communication from the lower to the higher level. We should note that a more biologically plausible architecture will include feedback mechanism focusing the system's attention on models that are more relevant to the higher layers. It is also plausible that all layers process the signals simultaneously. Combined with the feedback loops this creates a new type of dynamics more complex than single layer, which is the subject

Figure 2. Diagram of multilayer system for situation monitoring. The top layer function is usually performed by human operator.

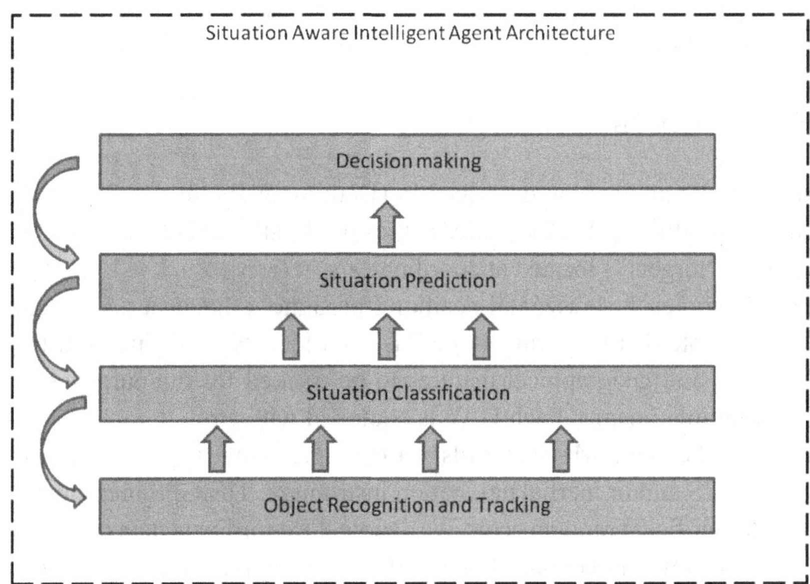

of future research. In this chapter we demonstrate the usage of single layer of NMF which builds the foundation of the multi-layered system.

The example applications describe how the single layer mathematics is used to solve problems in tracking and in situation recognition. These problems are performed daily by our minds. The attempts to solve them mathematically are plagued by combinatorial complexity of data association, which can be overcome by the use of NMF.

The first example of the next section touches upon another important aspect of sensor data processing: the distributed nature of the sensory network. Multiple aircraft performing surveillance of the same geographical area provide sensor data that needs to be combined in exact and efficient manner. Such data fusion capabilities can be easily implemented within the NMF framework. Let us emphasize that the ability of the mind to fuse information from multiple senses again provides the encouragement for using cognitive based methods.

APPLICATIONS

NMF has been successfully applied to the tasks of simultaneous detection and tracking and target characterization (Deming, Sept. 14-17, 1998), (Deming & Perlovsky, 2007), (Deming, Schindler, & Perlovsky, April 30 – May 3, 2007), (Deming, Schindler, & Perlovsky, April 17-20, 2007), (Deming, Schindler, & Perlovsky, 2009), (Perlovsky & Deming, 2007). In the following examples we focus on problems relevant to new directions of NMF research concerned with the development of distributed hierarchical systems mimicking the mind in its efficiency and diversity of applications. Each example is developed is a uniform fashion using the following steps.

1. Define the observable input data,
2. Define the models and their parameters,
3. Derive specific form of dynamic logic equations (3)-(5) for the NMF iterations
4. Run computer simulations.

Multiple Platform Tracking

This section is based on the application described in (Deming & Perlovsky, 2007). The details of the problem are the following. Multiple UAVs located at the coordinates $\mathbf{X}_j = (X_j, Y_j, Z_j)$, $j = 1,2,...,J$, are flying over a group of objects ("targets") located at coordinates $\mathbf{x}_k = (x_k, y_k, z_k)$, $k = 1,2,...,K$, where z denotes the elevation and (x,y) denotes the horizontal position (throughout the discussion, vector quantities are indicated in bold type). Note that the term "target" is used loosely, referring both to potential threats and simply to landmarks and geographical features to be tracked for the purposes of navigation and registration between multiple images. Each UAV is equipped with an

optical sensor (a digital camera which records, for example, a matrix of visible or infrared information) and, optionally, a GPS and/or inertial navigation instrument. The GPS measures the UAV position directly, although with significant random error. We denote the coordinate data output by the GPS as $\mathbf{X2}_j = (X2_j, Y2_j, Z2_j)$. Figure 3 shows a diagram of one of the UAVs flying over the group of targets.

The targets are considered to be point reflectors. The sensors on the UAVs record replicas of three dimensional scenes onto two-dimensional images, for example mapping an object located at $\mathbf{x}_k = (x_k, y_k, z_k)$ to a (horizontal + vertical) position (a,b) on the camera's focal plane. Because the mapping goes from 3D to 2D, we cannot reverse the mapping to compute a target position uniquely from a single image, even if we know the UAV position. However, from multiple views of the same target it would be possible to triangulate the position, and this illustrates an advantage of having a swarm of sensors. In fact, the problem of localizing objects in 3D based on their image locations in a set of spatially separated photographs is well studied, and is discussed in detail in standard treatments of "photogrammetry" (Thompson, 1966). Of course, when performing the process automatically, the difficulty lies in enabling a computer to associate a target signature from one digital photograph with its counterparts in the other photos acquired by other UAVs. This problem is especially acute when the photos contain many targets, some partially obstructed and significant clutter. This "association problem" is addressed using the NMF framework, as we will discuss.

Following the discussion in (Thompson, 1966, Sections 2.3.1 and 2.3.2), the mapping from the 3D world coordinate $\mathbf{x}_k = (x_k, y_k, z_k)$ to the 2D focal plane coordinate (a,b) of a camera located at $\mathbf{X}_j = (X_j, Y_j, Z_j)$ is given by the well known pair of photogrammetric equations

$$a = d_f \frac{(x_k - X_j)m_{11} + (y_k - Y_j)m_{12} + (z_k - Z_j)m_{13}}{(x_k - X_j)m_{31} + (y_k - Y_j)m_{32} + (z_k - Z_j)m_{33}} \tag{7}$$

and

$$b = d_f \frac{(x_k - X_j)m_{21} + (y_k - Y_j)m_{22} + (z_k - Z_j)m_{23}}{(x_k - X_j)m_{31} + (y_k - Y_j)m_{32} + (z_k - Z_j)m_{33}} \tag{8}$$

Figure 3. A single UAV flying over a group of targets

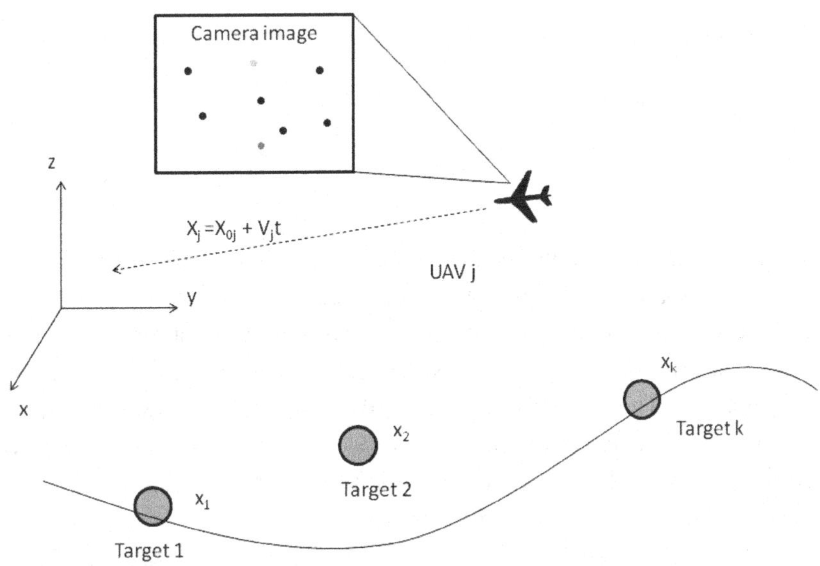

where d_f is the camera focal distance, and the quantities m_{rs} are the elements of the 3 · 3 direction cosine matrix **M** relating the global coordinate frame to the coordinate frame local to the camera on the UAV. Explicitly, the direction cosine elements are given as follows

$$M = \begin{pmatrix} \cos\varphi\cos\kappa & \cos\omega\sin\kappa + \sin\omega\sin\varphi\cos\kappa & \sin\omega\sin\kappa - \cos\omega\sin\varphi\cos\kappa \\ -\cos\varphi\sin\kappa & \cos\omega\cos\kappa - \sin\omega\sin\varphi\sin\kappa & \sin\omega\cos\kappa + \cos\omega\sin\varphi\sin\kappa \\ \sin\varphi & -\sin\omega\cos\varphi & \cos\omega\cos\varphi \end{pmatrix} \tag{9}$$

where (ω, φ, κ) are the rotational angles (yaw, pitch, and roll) for the coordinate frame of the camera. For simplicity, we will assume these angles can be measured precisely using onboard sensors, although the method can be extended in a straightforward manner to include estimation of (ω, φ, κ) along with the other parameters. If we define the vectors $\mathbf{M}_i = (m_{i1}, m_{i2}, m_{i3})$, we can rewrite Eqs. (7) and (8) using the compact notation

$$\begin{bmatrix} a \\ b \end{bmatrix} = d_f \begin{bmatrix} M_1 \\ M_2 \end{bmatrix} \frac{(x_k - X_j)^T}{M_3 (x_k - X_j)^T} \tag{10}$$

where T denotes the vector transpose. As the jth UAV flies, it captures image frames at intervals along its path, and we wish to combine the information from these frames and from the sets of frames from the other UAVs. Models for the UAV flight trajectories will facilitate this task. Let us assume that UAV j flies at a constant velocity $\mathbf{V}_j$ so that its equation of motion is

$$X_j = X_{0j} + V_j t \tag{11}$$

Using this motion model we can rewrite (10) as

$$\begin{bmatrix} a \\ b \end{bmatrix} = d_f \begin{bmatrix} M_1 \\ M_2 \end{bmatrix} \frac{(x_k - X_{0j} - V_j t)^T}{M_3 (x_k - X_{0j} - V_j t)^T} \tag{12}$$

The position (a,b) of a target signature in the image is only one piece of the data collected by the cameras. The other piece is the target signature itself, i.e., the array of pixel intensities (red, blue, and green) in the vicinity of the target's image on the focal plane. Most automatic target recognition algorithms make use of a preprocessing step in which a manageable set of classification features are computed from the signature. These features are specially designed to allow signatures from threats to be automatically separated from signatures of clutter objects. In our case, the features will also help in the association problem, as we will discuss. We assume that a set of features $\mathbf{f} = (f_1, f_2, \ldots, f_d)$ has been computed at multiple locations within each image frame.

The data from each target signature include the set of classification features **f** plus the signature location (a,b) on the focal plane. Thus, the information from an image frame is reduced to a set of data samples $(a_{jn}, b_{jn}, \mathbf{f}_{jn})$, where n = 1,2,...,N is the index of the sample and j = 1,2,...,J denotes which UAV acquired the image. Each of these samples was produced by a particular object (target or clutter).

Also recorded with each sample is the time t_{jn} at which the corresponding image frame was acquired. In addition to the data from the camera, we have the data $X2_{jn}$ from the GPS (to make things simple, we assume a GPS data point is acquired simultaneously with each photo). Therefore, the total set of data is contained in the set of samples $w_{jn} = (\mathbf{X2}_{jn}, a_{jn}, b_{jn}, \mathbf{f}_{jn})$ and their corresponding times t_{jn}. Since the rotational angles of each UAV change with time, we will henceforth indicate this dependence in the directional cosine vectors using the notation M_i^{jn}.

At this point we are ready to cast the problem in terms of NMF. The data is given as follows

$$w_{jn} = (X2_{jn}, a_{jn}, b_{jn}, f_{jn}), j = 1..J \quad n = 1..N \tag{13}$$

Each data point originates either from some target or from clutter. Thus we need to define two types of models and identify their parameters.

The target model specifies the conditional pdf of the data point w_{jn} coming from target k as follows.

$$p(w_{jn} \mid k) = p_1(X2_{jn}) p_2(a_{jn}, b_{jn} \mid k) p_3(f_{jn} \mid k) \tag{14}$$

Here the total pdf is broken down into the product of pdf's for the GPS position, the camera coordinates, and the features. This is possible since given the kth target these components of the data vector (13) are independent. We use Gaussian pdf to model sensor errors and thus the three components of the target pdf are expressed as follows.

$$p_1(X2_{jn}) = \frac{1}{(2\pi)^{\frac{3}{2}} \sigma_g^3} e^{-\frac{1}{2\sigma_g^2}(X2_{jn} - MX2_{jn})(X2_{jn} - MX2_{jn})^T} \tag{15}$$

Where $MX2_{jn}$ is the expected value of the GPS data given by (11) and σ_g is the GPS error standard deviation. The pdf for camera coordinates is

$$p_2(a_{jn}, b_{jn} \mid k) = \frac{1}{(2\pi)\sigma_a^2} e^{-\frac{1}{2\sigma_a^2}\left[(a_{jn} - Ma_{jnk})^2 + (b_{jn} - Mb_{jnk})^2\right]} \tag{16}$$

where Ma_{ijk} and Mb_{ijk} are the expected values of the camera coordinates computed using (12), and σ_a is the standard deviation of the error in signature position. Finally, the pdf for the feature data is

$$p_3(f_{jn} \mid k) = \frac{1}{\sqrt{(2\pi)^d \left|C_{fk}\right|}} e^{-\frac{1}{2}(f_{jn} - MF_k) C_{fk}^{-1} (f_{jn} - MF_k)^T} \tag{17}$$

where C_{fk} is the covariance matrix of the features and d is the number of features. MF_k is the expected value of the feature.

The clutter model is simpler as it describes data points uniformly distributed across the camera focal plane. The model is thus Gaussian over the features and uniform over the other data components. We use the model index k=0 for the clutter model and express the pdf as follows.

$$p\ (w_{jn} \mid 0) = \frac{1}{\sqrt{(2\pi)^d \left|C_{f0}\right|}} e^{-\frac{1}{2}(f_{jn} - MF_0) C_{f0}^{-1} (f_{jn} - MF_0)^T} \tag{18}$$

Going back to the general definition of the NMF process (3)-(5) we can now specify all the components of the solution for this problem. They are given in Table 1.

The derivatives of the pdf's with respect to all the parameters are obtained using regular calculus. The derivations can be found elsewhere (Deming & Perlovsky, 2007). The results of computer simulations are now presented to demonstrate the algorithm.

Throughout these simulations the cameras were assumed to point directly downward. We first considered two examples having four targets distributed within the ground coordinate ranges [$-20 \le (x_k, y_k) \le 20$], and vertical coordinate [$0 \le z_k \le 10$], and three UAVs distributed within the ranges [$-30 \le (X_{0j}, Y_{0j}) \le 30$] and [$15 \le Z_{0j} \le 20$]. The UAV velocities were distributed within the ranges [$-10 \le (dX_j/dt,\ dY_j/dt) \le 10$] and [$-2 \le d\,Z_j/dt \le 2$]. The full sensor model given by Eq. (12) was used to calculate the data at time samples t = (0, 1.5, 3) (frame times). For example, in a realistic close-range scenario, all time units might be in seconds and all position units in m.

We randomly generated 1600 clutter samples per frame having a single classification feature f with mean MF_0=0 and variance C_{f0}=0.75. The target features were also randomly drawn from distributions having variance C_{fk} = 0.75 and means of MF_k = [5.5, 7.5, 9.5, 11.5], respectively for k = 1,2,3,4. The K-factor is a commonly used quantitative measure of the degree of separation between two distributions having equal variances. If σ^2 is the variance and ΔM is the separation between the means, then $K = \Delta M / \sigma$. Thus, for this example the K-factors of each of the four targets vs. the clutter are roughly K = [6, 9, 11, 13]. Also, the standard deviations of the GPS and signature position errors were set to σ_g = 4 and σ_a = 0.1, respectively. Fig. 4a–d shows the results of the simulations, plotted over the space of the

Table 1. Components of NMF solution for tracking ground targets with multiple UAV's

Component	Description	Symbols for Variables/Parameters
Data	GPS position, camera coordinates, image features	$X2_j$, a_{jn},b_{jn}, $\mathbf{f}_{jn}$
Clutter Model	Gaussian feature, Uniform position	C_{f0}, MF_0
Target Model	Gaussian feature, Gaussian GPS, linear motion with Gaussian noise	x_k, X_{oj}, V_j, MF_k, C_{fk}
Known parameters	GPS error and camera alignment error, prior probabilities of target	σ_g, σ_a, r(h)

UAV 1 sensor focal plane. In (a) the distribution of preprocessed feature data is shown. Here the high values of the target classification features show up as relatively dark pixels over a lighter, speckled, clutter background. For display purposes, the target signatures from all three frame times are shown superimposed onto a single frame of clutter, thus for each of the four targets there are (potentially) three dark pixels corresponding to the three time instances. In (b) the initial, randomly selected, estimates for target signature positions are shown as symbols connected by lines; three symbols for each of four targets. The large circles around signature positions indicate the high initial uncertainty in the estimates.

Plots (c) and (d) show the evolution of the signature position estimates at iterations 10 and 50, respectively. Here, the radii of uncertainty shrink with increasing iterations as the data association becomes less ambiguous. In (d), the data has been properly associated, and the signatures for all four targets have been identified at all frame times.

We generated Monte Carlo results to study the effects of the clutter level on algorithm performance. The error distributions were chosen as in the preceding examples, and target and UAV positions and UAV velocities were generated randomly within the ranges specified above. Figure 5 plots the errors in estimated target and UAV positions as function of the number of UAVs in the swarm. The vertical axis in these plots indicates the average in radial error, normalized by GPS error, and averaged over 100 Monte Carlo iterations for each data point. From these plots it is apparent that both target and UAV position errors increase roughly linearly with decreasing S/C. Also, the errors decrease as roughly $1/\sqrt{J}$, as J ranges from 2 to 8, where J is the number of UAVs in the swarm.

This example illustrates how a complex problem of target detection and tracking can be solved by NMF. NMF allows to easily combine data coming from different elements of the distributed sensor network, in this case a swarm of UAV's. The solution converges within a limited number of iterations avoiding combinatorial complexity of data association inherent in multiple tracking.

Tracking Extended Objects

Our next example also concerns tracking multiple objects in sequences of video frames. This time we make the problem more complex by tracking targets of unknown size. As we will see, this only introduces additional parameters into the solution without changing the overall methodology. For simplicity we consider a single stationary optical sensor.

Consider Figure 6. This is a fragment of a gray scale image frame with one object and the corresponding model $\mathbf{M}_h$ describing it. The object shape is approximately elliptical and we model it as solid. There

Figure 4. Results from the low-clutter example, UAV 1, of 3 total. In (a) the preprocessed feature data is shown distributed over the sensor focal plane. Here the high values of the target features show up as relatively dark pixels over a lighter, speckled, clutter background. In (b) the initial, randomly selected, estimates for target signature positions are shown as symbols connected by lines; three symbols (corresponding to three different time instances) for each of four targets. The large circles around signature positions indicate the high initial uncertainty in the estimates. Plots (c) and (d) show the evolution of the signature position estimates at iterations 10 and 50, respectively. Here, the radii of uncertainty shrink with increasing iterations as the data association becomes less ambiguous.

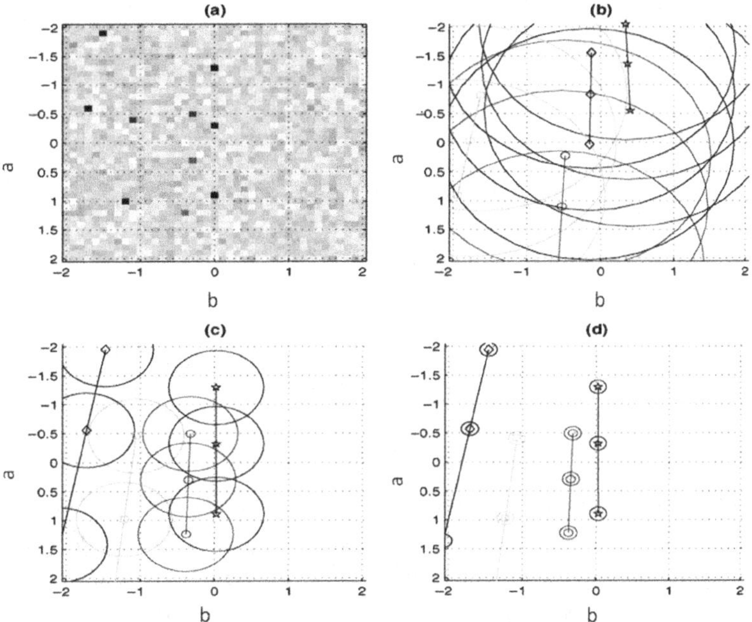

are several clutter pixels. We denote a point inside the object corresponding to its center by $\mathbf{x}_c$. Object center is a location on the frame roughly corresponding to object's center of mass.

Since we assume that the objects are rigid, the object model can be specified relative to its center. Let's focus on pixel $\mathbf{x}_n$. This pixel is represented by two position coordinates (row, column), intensity value $\mathbf{y}_n$, and time stamp t_n. The event "$\mathbf{x}_n$ belongs to object $\mathbf{M}_h$" can be decomposed into three simultaneous events: (1) coordinates of $\mathbf{x}_n$ fall within the borders of the object model, (2) center $\mathbf{x}_c$ of the object model coincides with the current object position on the track model, and (3) intensity $\mathbf{y}_n$ corresponds to the current object intensity model. This is expressed by the following product of PDF's.

$$p(n \mid h) = p_{obj}(n \mid h) p_{feat}(n \mid h) p_{mot}(n \mid h) \tag{19}$$

The three factors correspond to the object model, feature model, and motion model. We model all three factors with the following Gaussian densities.

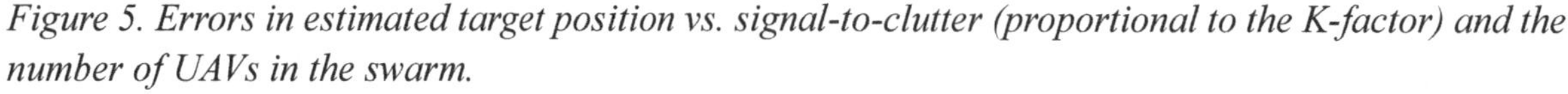

Figure 5. Errors in estimated target position vs. signal-to-clutter (proportional to the K-factor) and the number of UAVs in the swarm.

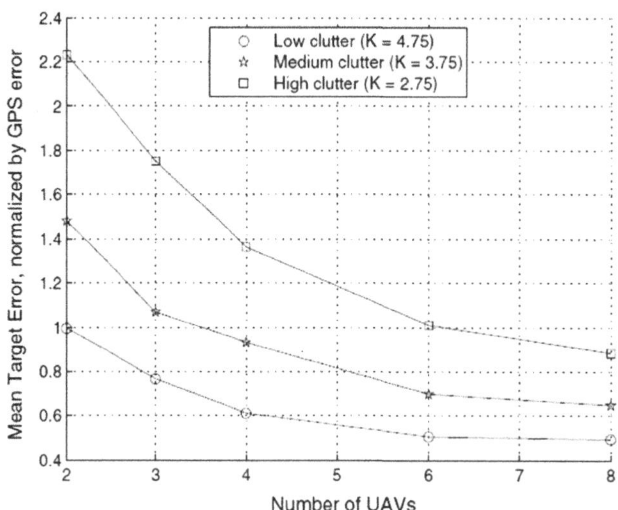

Figure 6. Elements of track model on top of an image fragment. The dashed ellipse and the dashed arrow show the true location and direction of motion of the moving object. The solid ellipse is the current estimate of the object shape and the dot-dashed ellipse and the solid arrow show the current estimate of the object's trajectory. Upon convergence the estimate of the center of the object xc and the estimate of the object's position x_k will move close to each other and to the true object's center

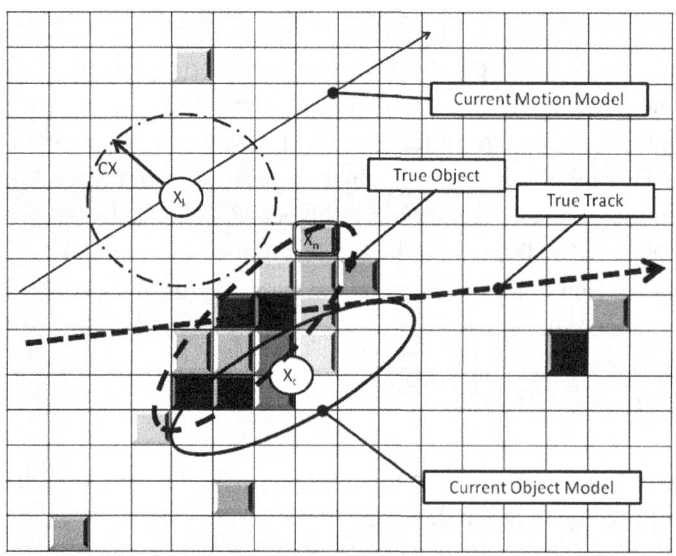

$$\begin{cases} p_{obj} = \dfrac{1}{\sqrt{(2\pi)^2 \left|CO_h\right|}} e^{-0.5(x_n - xc_{hn})CO_h^{-1}(x_n - xc_{hn})^T} \\ p_{feat} = \dfrac{1}{\sqrt{(2\pi)^d \left|CY_h\right|}} e^{-0.5(y_n - Y_h)CY_h^{-1}(y_n - Y_h)^T} \\ p_{mot} = \dfrac{1}{\sqrt{(2\pi)^2 \left|CX_h\right|}} e^{-0.5(xc_{hn} - X_{hn})CX_h^{-1}(xc_{hn} - X_{hn})^T} \end{cases} \tag{20}$$

The full PDF is the product of the first three expressions in (20). The object model uses the fact that most of the data lies within 2 standard deviations from the mean of a Gaussian pdf. Thus an elliptical object is modeled by a Gaussian pdf with covariance matrix CO_h, which determines the size of the object. The motion model describes our hypothesis about object trajectory. As in the previous example we use the assumption of linear motion with constant velocity. Such assumption works well when tracking objects over short sequences of frames. Other model could be used as well within the same methodology. The linear trajectory is described by two parameters: initial position and velocity. Thus the estimate of the mean value of object center position is given as follows.

$$X_{hn} = X0_h + V_h t_n \tag{21}$$

This equation clarifies the use of subscript n in and. This expression needs to be substituted into (3) before derivatives are taken. The pixels within the same frame have the same time stamp and therefore the number of distinct object centers equals to the number of frames and not the number of pixels. We do not, however, introduce a new index for frame since the time stamp of the pixel indicates which frame it belongs to.

We use the background model with uniform position distribution and Gaussian feature distribution. The likelihood of a pixel given the background model is as follows.

$$p(x_n, y_n, t_n \mid h = background) = \frac{1}{A} \frac{1}{\sqrt{(2\pi)^d \left|CY_h\right|}} e^{-0.5(y_n - Y_h)CY_h^{-1}(y_n - Y_h)^T} \tag{22}$$

Here A is the area of the image measured in squared pixels. The factor is the probability of pixel's position, which is constant in this simple model. The feature model is the same as in the case of extended object. Correspondingly, the parameters of the clutter model can be estimated using (15).

At this point we have the expressions for all three models, summarized in Table 2. Note that the center positions xc_{hn} have to be treated as parameters along with the mean estimates since they are not part of the data and were introduced to separate the motion model from the object shape model.

The results of simulation are shown in Figure 7. We generated a series of images with 3 objects of different size moving in different directions. The images contain a number of clutter objects appearing in various locations.

Table 2. Components of NMF solution for tracking extended objects

Component	Description	Symbols for Variables/Parameters
Data	Pixel positions, brightness, and timestamp	x_n, y_n, t_n
Clutter Model	Gaussian feature, Uniform position	Y_h, CY_h
Target Model	Gaussian feature, Elliptical shape, linear motion with Gaussian noise	xc_{hn}, X_{hn}, CO_h, Y_h, CY_h, XO_h, V_h, CX_h

Figure 7. Operation of tracking algorithm on a sequence of 5 images with 3 targets and 10 clutter objects in each frame

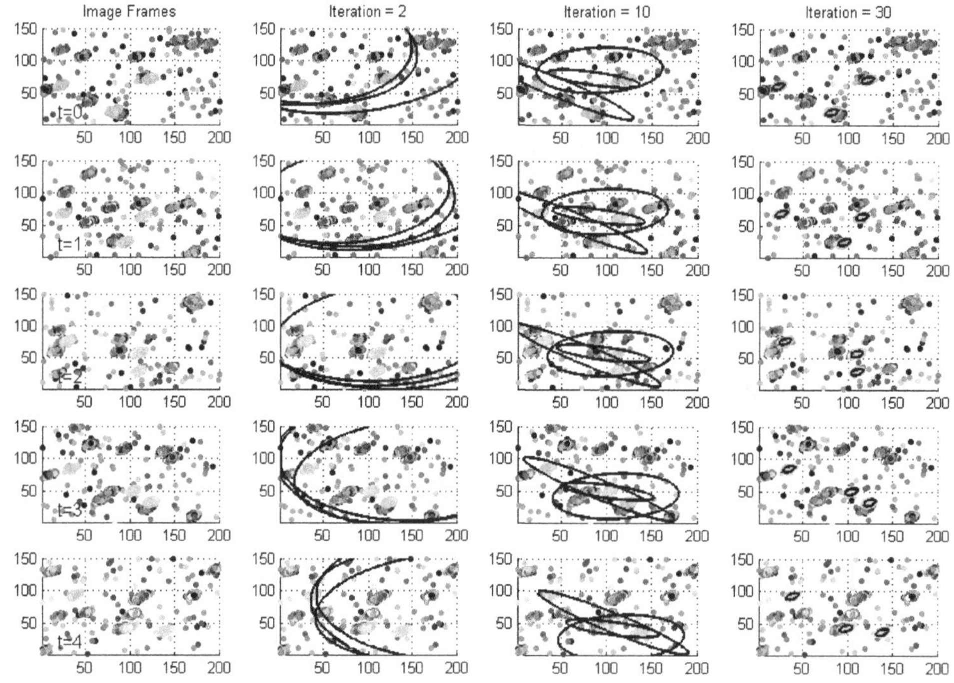

Learning Situations

Our final example shows how NMF can learn more abstract concepts by considering the problem of situation recognition. This section is based on (Ilin & Perlovsky, 2010). In a simplified problem statement, situations are characterized by the presence of certain objects or object configurations. In the urban warfare, for example, the situation "city" is characterized by the presence of buildings, paved roads, public transportation, etc. The situation "village" is characterized by the presence of small houses, unpaved roads, large domesticated animals, etc. In this contribution we assume that the problem of object recognition has been addressed by means of image analysis. For our purposes, a situation is defined as a set of objects. We do not consider the relationships between objects, for example their relative positions.

A trainee learning to identify situations is informed about the situation at the time he perceives the objects at the scene. However he is not explicitly taught which subset of the observed objects is essential for this particular situation. For example, the presence of trees and bushes in the city is not essential. As the trainee is exposed to the same situation many times, his understanding of what constitutes a particular situation improves. The nonessential objects are filtered out and the essential ones are used to conceptualize and recognize the situation. The trainee may also be informed of a situation when it is not present. For example he may hear somebody talking about a village without being there. Not knowing what a village is, he may assume that he is seeing a village. After learning to identify the essential parts of the village the mistake will be corrected.

Suppose that D is the total number of objects that exist in the world. This is a large but finite number, which is one of the simplifications that are employed in this work. Suppose that our agent can perceive N_p objects in the scene. This is a much smaller number compared to D. Each situation will be characterized by the presence of N_s objects where N_s is less or equal to N_p. The sets of objects that constitute different situations are allowed to overlap, with some objects being essential to more than one situation. We assume that each object is encountered in the scene only one time. This simplification is not unacceptable if we agree to consider sets of similar objects as a new object type. For example, "book" is an object type and "books" is another object type referring to more than one book. If necessary, a new object type – "lots of books" - can be introduced to refer to a large collection of books as such object may be essential for situations like "library" or "archive".

Perception of a scene can be represented as a binary vector $x_n = (x_1 \dots x_i \dots x_D)$. If the value of x_i is one the object i is present in the situation and if x_i is zero, the corresponding object is not present. Since D is a large number, x_n is a large binary vector with most of its element equal to zero. We introduce a situation model as a vector of probabilities $p_h = (p_{k1 \dots} p_{hi \dots} p_{hD})$. Here p_{hi} is the probability of object i being part of the situation k. Thus a situation model contains D unknown parameters. We assume that the elements of vector p_h are independent. The conditional probability of vector x_n representing a situation h is then given by the following formula.

$$prob(x_n \mid h) = \prod_{i=1}^{D} p_{hi}^{x_i}(1 - p_{hi})^{(1-x_i)} \tag{23}$$

This is the total probability of the binary vector x_n when the probabilities of individual components are given by p_{hi}. We will use this probability as the measure of similarity between the binary vector and its model p_h.

The components of NMF solution are summarized in Table 3. The derivatives of the pdf (4) with respect to parameters p_{hi} can be easily obtained and substituted into the general NMF iteration (3)-(5). We show the results of numeric simulations below.

We set the total number of objects in the world equal to 100 (D=100). The total number of objects perceived in the scene N_p is set to 10 in the first set of experiments and to 15 in the second. The number of essential objects is set to 5 (N_s=5) in both sets. The number of situations to learn is set to 10. Note that the true identities of the objects are not important in this simulation so we simply use object indexes varying from 1 to 100. The situation names are also not important and we use situation indexes.

The data is generated by first randomly selecting 10 groups of 5 objects, allowing some overlap between the groups. Next we add 5 or 7 more randomly selected objects to each group. We also generate

Table 3. Components of NMF solution for situation recognition

Component	Description	Symbols for Variables/Parameters
Data	Binary strings indicating presence of objects in situations	$x_n = (x_1 \ldots x_i \ldots x_D)$.
Clutter Model	Every object has 50% chance of being present in situation	
Target Model	Bernoulli distribution	P_{hi}, i=1..D
Known parameters	Total number of objects	D

10 more groups of 12 randomly selected objects to model random perceptions that do not correspond to repeated situations. We generate 25 data samples for each situation resulting in the total of 500 data samples. The input data is visualized in Figures 8 and 9.

Figure 10 shows the operation of the algorithm by displaying the values of p_{hi} for each model. After one iteration most of the probabilities are high meaning that each model includes many possible objects. As the algorithm progresses only the probabilities of the relevant objects remain high. The solution converges within few iterations to the true probabilities for each situation. As the results indicate, the NMF overcomes the combinatorial complexity of the problem and arrives at the solution after only a few iterations. This is accomplished by the dynamic logic process "from vague to crisp."

Figure 8. Visualization of the binary data input for the experiments with N_p=15. The object index is shown along the vertical axes and the situation index along the horizontal axes. For each column in this image, bright squares represent presence of an object in a situation and dark squares represent the absence of the object. Each column contains 15 bright squares. The data is sorted by situation index

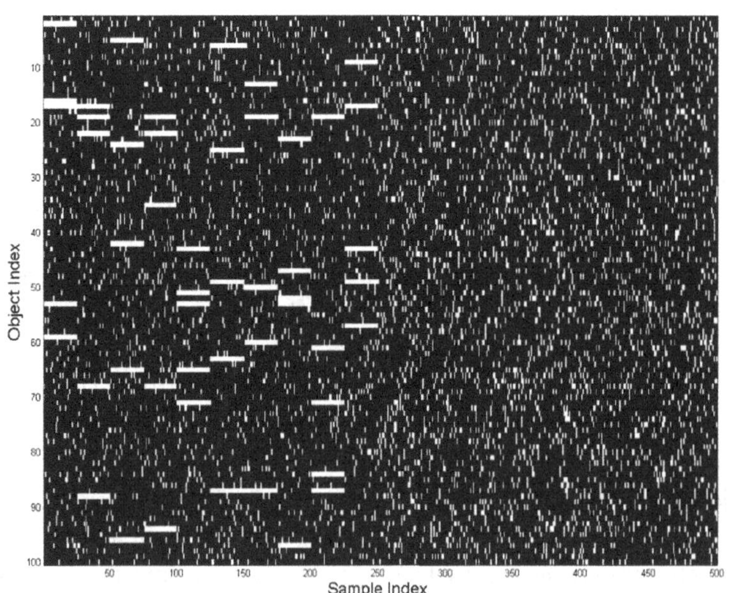

Figure 9. The same data as in Figure. 8 with randomly permuted situation indexes

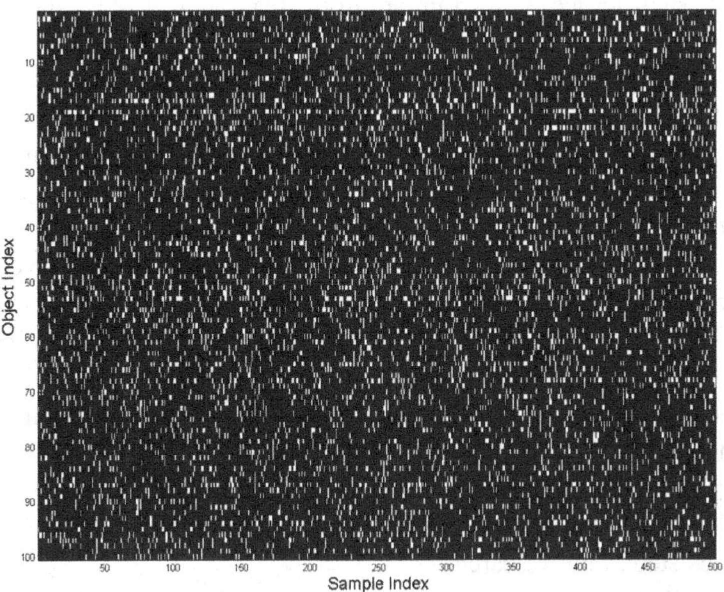

Figure 10. First four iterations of the dynamic logic "vague-to-crisp" process with un-supervised initialization mode. Each image displays the values of probabilities for each of the 20 models. As the iterations progress the essential object probabilities increase and the other objects' probabilities decrease.

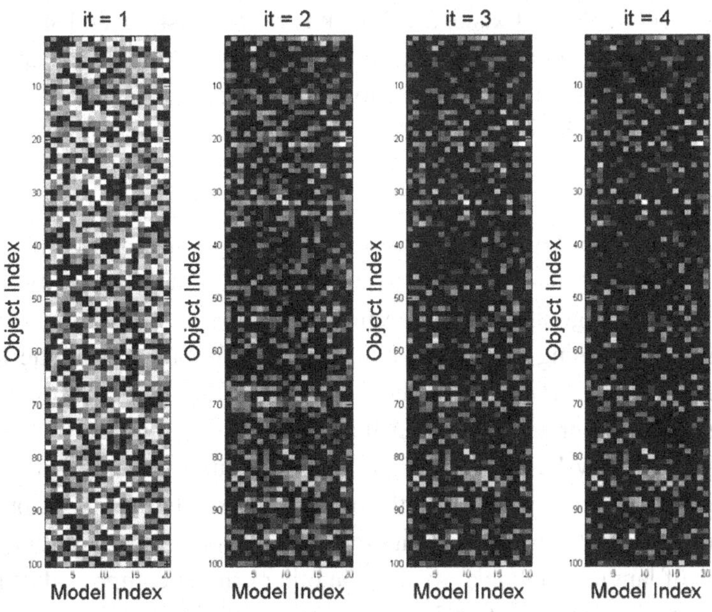

FUTURE RESEARCH DIRECTIONS

Let us now discuss the significance of the examples from the previous section and outline the directions of future research. We started this chapter by describing the challenge of combinatorial complexity encountered by all computational intelligent paradigms and the fact that the brain is the only known computational devise able to overcome this challenge. We proposed a theory of the mind-brain governed by the dynamic process "from vague to crisp" as a possible explanation to how the mind-brain overcomes this challenge. We expressed this idea mathematically in the form of an iterative process of dynamic logic (3)-(5) and tied the components of our mathematical model to the elements of the mind: concepts, instincts, and emotions. We propose to model the mind as a hierarchy of NMF layers each governed by dynamic logic process "from vague to crisp".

We believe that cognitive modeling is crucial for creating efficient large scale distributed processing. The examples in the previous section demonstrate how the same basic NMF algorithm can be applied to difficult problems in tracking and situation recognition. Consider an implementation of the situation recognition layer on top of the layer capable of tracking extended objects. The shape of the objects can be made more complex modeling real world objects. The model parameters and association weights from the object tracking layer will become the inputs into the situation recognition layer. The two layer architecture in the next step of this research.

Relating in details NMF to brain mechanisms is a subject of ongoing and future research. General neural mechanisms of the elementary thought process are similar in NMF and ART (Carpenter & Grossberg, 1987) and have been confirmed by neural and psychological experiments. These include neural mechanisms for bottom-up (sensory) signals, top-down imagination model-signals, and the resonant matching between the two (Grossberg S., 1988),. Adaptive modeling abilities are well studied with adaptive parameters identified with synaptic connections (Koch & Segev, 1998), (Hebb, 1949); instinctual learning mechanisms have been studied in psychology and linguistics (Piaget, 1981), (Chomsky, 1981), (Jackendoff, 2002), (Deacon, 1998). Existence of the knowledge instinct and specific emotions related to knowledge have been demonstrated experimentally (Perlovsky, Bonniot-Cabanac, & Cabanac, Curiosity and pleasure, 2010). Dynamic logic "vague to crisp" process, a specific mechanism of matching bottom-up and top-down signals in NMF, proceeds from vague to crisp models (mental representations); this was demonstrated in neuroimaging experiments to model the actual brain processes in human perception (Bar et al, 2006).

Ongoing and future research will confirm, disprove, or suggest modifications to specific mechanisms considered in this chapter: model parameterization and parameter adaptation, similarity measure as a foundation of the knowledge instinct and aesthetic emotion, relationships between psychological and neural mechanisms of learning on the one hand and, on the other, aesthetic feelings of harmony and emotion of beautiful. For example, it has been suggested that object recognition might be based on *sets* of features, similar to our eq.(23), rather than on *statistical* models of features, similar to our eq.(17) (Barsalou, 1999; Perlovsky & Ilin, 2010). Specific neural systems will have to be related to mathematical descriptions on one hand and, on the other, to psychological descriptions in terms of subjective experiences and observable behavior. Ongoing research addresses evolution of cognitive models jointly with evolution of language models, which is another crucial component of the mind (Fontanari & Perlovsky, Evolution of communication in a community of simple-minded agents., 2005),; Perlovsky & Ilin, Neurally and Mathematically Motivated Architecture for Language and Thought, 2010); joint research with D. Levine addresses relationships of NMF and the knowledge instinct to issues of behavioral psychology and to specific brain areas involved in emotional reward and punishment during learning (Levine & Perlovsky, 2008). We will have to develop differentiated forms of the knowledge instinct, which explains the infinite variety emotions perceived in music (Perlovsky, Musical emotions: Functions, origin, evolution. 2009). Future experimental research needs to study in details the nature of hierarchical interactions: to what extent the hierarchy is "hardwired" vs. adaptively emerging; what is a hierarchy of differentiated learning instinct? We will have to develop further interactions between cognitive hierarchy and language hierarchy (Perlovsky L., Integrating Language and Cognition, 2004). Experimental verifications are required for the developed explanations of higher cognitive functions, music and the beautiful (Perlovsky, 2009, 2010).

The existence of the mechanism "from vague to crisp" in the brain found support in a recent study (Bar, et al., 2006). It has been demonstrated that the object recognition by human subjects occurring in the temporal cortex is facilitated by the low spatial frequency top-bottom signals originating in the orbitofrontal cortex. These initial top-down signals coming from models/representations are therefore vague is accordance with the Dynamic Logic mechanism.

CONCLUSION

This chapter introduced the principles of brain modeling with NMF and dynamic logic. The mathematical formulation of the theory has been explained and examples of its usage were given. We outlined the directions of ongoing and future work in this area.

REFERENCES

Albus, J. M. (2001). *Engineering of mind: An introduction to the science of intelligent systems.* New York, NY: Wiley.

Bar, M., Kassam, K., Ghuman, A., Boshyan, J., Schmid, A., & Dale, A. (2006). Top-down facilitation of visual recognition. *Proceedings of the National Academy of Sciences of the United States of America, 103*, 449–454. doi:10.1073/pnas.0507062103

Bar-Shalom, Y., & Fortmann, T. (1988). *Tracking and data association.* San Diego, CA: Academic Press, Inc.

Barsalou, L. W. (1999). Perceptual symbol systems. *The Behavioral and Brain Sciences, 22*, 577–660.

Bellman, R. (1961). *Adaptive control processes.* Princeton, NJ: Princeton University Press.

Berlyne, D. E. (1960). *Conflict, arousal, and curiosity.* New York, NY: McGraw-Hill. doi:10.1037/11164-000

Bishop, C. M. (2006). *Pattern recognition and machine learning. Springer Science + Business Media.* LLC.

Carpenter, G., & Grossberg, S. (1987). A massively parallel architecture for a self-organizing neural pattern recognition machine. *Computer Vision Graphics and Image Processing*, *37*, 54–115. doi:10.1016/S0734-189X(87)80014-2

Chomsky, N. (1981). Principles and parameters in syntactic theory. In Hornstein, N., & Lightfoot, D. (Eds.), *Explanation in linguistics: The logical problem of language acquisition*. London, UK: Longman.

Damasio, A. (1995). *Descartes' error: Emotion, reason, and the human brain*. New York, NY: Avon.

Deacon, T. (1998). *The symbolics species: The co-evolution of language and the brain*. W.W. Norton & Company.

Deming, R. (1998). Automatic buried mine detection using the maximum likelihood adaptive neural system (MLANS). *Proceedings of the 1998 IEEE ISIC/CIRA/ISAS Joint Conference*. Gaithersburg, MD.

Deming, R., & Perlovsky, L. (2007). Concurrent multi-target localization, data association, and navigation for a swarm of flying sensors. *Information Fusion*, *8*(3), 316–330. doi:10.1016/j.inffus.2005.11.001

Deming, R., Schindler, J., & Perlovsky, L. (2007). *Concurrent tracking and detection of slowly moving targets using dynamic logic*. 2007 IEEE Int'l Conf. on Integration of Knowledge Intensive Multi-Agent Systems: Modeling, Evolution, and Engineering (KIMAS 2007). Waltham, MA.

Deming, R., Schindler, J., & Perlovsky, L. (2007). *Track-before-detect of multiple slowly moving targets*. IEEE Radar Conference 2007. Waltham, MA.

Deming, R., Schindler, J., & Perlovsky, L. (2009). Multitarget/multisensor tracking using only range and doppler measurements. *IEEE Transactions on Aerospace and Electronic Systems*, *45*(2). doi:10.1109/TAES.2009.5089543

Descartes, R. (1989). *The passions of the soul: Les passions de lame*. Indianapolis, IN: Hackett Publishing Company.

Edelman, G. M., & Tononi, G. (1995). *A universe of consciousness: How matter becomes imagination*. New York, NY: Basic Books.

Endsley, M. R. (1995). Toward a theory of situation awareness in dynamic systems. *Human Factors*, 32–64. doi:10.1518/001872095779049543

Fontanari, J. F., & Perlovsky, L. I. (2007). Evolving compositionality in evolutionary language games. *IEEE Transactions on Evolutionary Computation*, *11*(6), 758–769..doi:10.1109/TEVC.2007.892763

Fontanari, J. F., & Perlovsky, L. I. (2008). How language can help discrimination in the neural modeling fields framework. *Neural Networks*, *21*(2-3), 250–256. doi:10.1016/j.neunet.2007.12.007

Griffiths, P. E. (1998). *What emotions really are: The problem of psychological categories*. Chicago, IL: University Of Chicago Press.

Grossberg, S. (1988). *Neural networks and natural intelligence*. Cambridge, MA: MIT Press.

Grossberg, S., & Levine, D. (1987). Neural dynamics of attentionally modulated pavlovian conditioning: Blocking, inter-stimulus interval, and secondary reinforcement. *Psychobiology*, *15*(3), 195–240.

Hall, D. L., & Llinas, J. (2001). *Handbook of multisensory data fusion*. CRC Press LLC.

Hebb, D. (1949). *Organization of behavior*. New York, NY: J.Wiley & Sons.

Ilin, R., & Perlovsky, L. (2010). Cognitively inspired neural network for recognition of situations. *International Journal of Natural Computing Research.*

Jackendoff, R. (2002). *Foundations of language: Brain, meaning, grammar, evolution*. New York, NY: Oxford Univ Press.

Josephson, B. (1997). *An integrated theory of nervous system functioning embracing nativism and constructivism*. International Complex Systems Conference. Nashua, NH.

Jung, C. (1971). Psychological types. In *The collected works, v.6, Bollingen Series XX.* Princeton, NJ: Princeton University Press.

Kant, I. (1943). *Critique of pure reason (trans. J.M.D. Meiklejohn)*. New York, NY: Willey Book.

Kecman, V. (2001). *Learning and soft computing: Support vector machines, neural networks, and fuzzy logic models (complex adaptive systems)*. Cambridge, MA: The MIT Press.

Koch, C., & Segev, I. (1998). *Methods in neuronal modeling: From ions to networks*. Cambridge, MA: MIT Press.

Ledoux, J. (1998). *The emotional brain: The mysterious underpinnings of emotional life*. New York, NY: Simon & Schuster.

Levine, D. S., & Perlovsky, L. I. (2008). Neuroscientific insights on biblical myths: Simplifying heuristics versus careful thinking: scientific analysis of millennial spiritual issues. *Zygon. Journal of Science and Religion*, *43*(4), 797–821.

Meystel, A. (1995). *Semiotic modeling and situational analysis*. Bala Cynwyd, PA: AdRem.

Minsky, M. (1988). *The society of mind*. Cambridge, MA: MIT Press.

Newell, A. F. (1983). Intellectual issues in the history of artificial intelligence. In *The study of information*. New York, NY: J. Wiley.

Ortony, A., & Turner, T. (1990). What's basic about basic emotions? *Psychological Review*, *97*, 315–331. doi:10.1037/0033-295X.97.3.315

Penrose, R. (1994). *Shadows of the mind*. Oxford, UK: Oxford University Press.

Perlovsky, L. (1987). *Multiple sensor fusion and neural networks*. DARPA Neural Network Study.

Perlovsky, L. (1996). Mathematical concepts of intellect. *Proceedings, World Congress on Neural Networks* (pp. 1013-16.). San Diego, CA: L. Erlbaum Assoc.

Perlovsky, L. (1998). Conundrum of combinatorial complexity. *IEEE Transactions on Pattern Analysis and Machine Intelligence*, *20*(6). doi:10.1109/34.683784

Perlovsky, L. (1999). Emotions, learning, and control. *Proceedings of the International Symposium on Intelligent Control, Intelligent Systems & Semiotics*, (pp. 131-137). Cambridge, MA.

Perlovsky, L., & Deming, R. W. (2007). Neural networks for improved tracking. *IEEE Transactions on Neural Networks*, *18*(6), 1854–1857. doi:10.1109/TNN.2007.903143

Perlovsky, L. I. (2004). Integrating language and cognition. *IEEE Connections*, *2*(2), 8–12.

Perlovsky, L. I. (2006). Symbols: Integrated cognition and language. In Gudwin, R., & Queiroz, J. (Eds.), *Semiotics and intelligent systems development* (pp. 121–151). Hershey, PA: Idea Group. doi:10.4018/9781599040639.ch005

Perlovsky, L. I. (2009). Musical emotions: Functions, origin, evolution. *Physics of Life Reviews*, *7*(1), 3–31.

Perlovsky, L. I. (2010). (in press). Intersections of mathematical, cognitive, and aesthetic theories of mind. *Psychology of Aesthetics, Creativity, and the Arts*. doi:10.1037/a0018147

Perlovsky, L. I., Bonniot-Cabanac, M.-C., & Cabanac, M. (2010). *Curiosity and pleasure*. IEEE World Congress on Computational Intelligence (WCCI'10), Barcelona, Spain.

Perlovsky, L. I., & Ilin, R. (2010). (in press). Neurally and mathematically motivated architecture for language and thought. *The Open Neuroimaging Journal*.

Perlovsky, L. I., & McManus, M. M. (1991). Maximum likelihood neural networks for sensor fusion and adaptive classification. *Neural Networks*, *4*(1), 89–102. doi:10.1016/0893-6080(91)90035-4

Perlovsky. (2001). *Neural networks and intellect.* New York, NY: Oxford Univerity Press.

Piaget, J. (1981). *The psychology of the child (trans. H. Weaver)*. Basic Books.

Sartre, J. P. (1984). *Existentialism and human emotions.* Citadel Press, Reissue edition.

Singer, R. S. (1974). Derivation and evaluation of improved tracking filters for use in dense multitarget environments. *IEEE Transactions on Information Theory*, *20*, 423–432. doi:10.1109/TIT.1974.1055256

(2000). *The american heritage college dictionary*. Boston, MA: Houghton Mifflin.

Thompson, M. (1966). *Manual of photogrammetry*. Falls Church, VA: American Society of Photogrammetry.

Zadeh, L. (1997). Information granulation and its centrality in human and machine intelligence. [Gaithersburg, MD.]. *Proceedings of the Conference on Intelligent Systems and Semiotics*, *97*, 26–30.

ADDITIONAL READING

Carpenter, G. A., & Grossberg, S. (1987). A massively parallel architecture for a self-organizing neural pattern recognition machine. *Computer Vision Graphics and Image Processing*, *37*, 54–115. doi:10.1016/S0734-189X(87)80014-2

Damasio, A. R. (1995). *Descartes' error: emotion, reason, and the human brain*. Avon, NY, NY.

Deacon, T. W. (1998). *The symbolic species: the co-evolution of language and the brain*. W.W. Norton & Company.

Deming, R., Schindler, J., & Perlovsky, L. (2009). Multitarget/multisensor tracking using only range and doppler measurements. *IEEE Transactions on Aerospace and Electronic Systems*, *45*(2), 593–611. doi:10.1109/TAES.2009.5089543

Deming, R. W., & Perlovsky, L. I. (2007). Concurrent multi-target localization, data association, and navigation for a swarm of flying sensors. *Information Fusion*, *8*, 316–330. doi:10.1016/j.inffus.2005.11.001

Fontanari, J. F., & Perlovsky, L. I. (2008). *A game theoretical approach to the evolution of structured communication codes*, Theory in Biosciences, **127**, pp.205-214; e-version http://dx.doi.org/10.1007/s12064-008-0024-1

Grossberg, S., & Levine, D. S. (1987). Neural dynamics of attentionally modulated Pavlovian conditioning: blocking, inter-stimulus interval, and secondary reinforcement. *Psychobiology*, *15*(3), 195–240.

Hameroff, S. (1994). *Toward a scientific basis for consciousness*. Cambridge, MA: MIT Press.

Ledoux, J. (1998). *The emotional brain: the mysterious underpinnings of emotional life*, Simon & Schuster, New York, NY.Fontanari, J.F. and Perlovsky, L.I. (2004). *Solvable null model for the distribution of word frequencies*. Physical Review **E 70**, 042901 (2004).

Chapter 7
Biogeography-Based Optimization for Robot Controller Tuning

Paul Lozovyy
Cleveland State University, USA

George Thomas
Cleveland State University, USA

Dan Simon
Cleveland State University, USA

ABSTRACT

This research involves the development of an engineering test for a newly-developed evolutionary algorithm called biogeography-based optimization (BBO), and also involves the development of a distributed implementation of BBO. The BBO algorithm is based on mathematical models of biogeography, which describe the migration of species between habitats. BBO is the adaptation of the theory of biogeography for the purpose of solving general optimization problems. In this research, BBO is used to tune a proportional-derivative control system for real-world mobile robots. The authors show that BBO can successfully tune the control algorithm of the robots, reducing their tracking error cost function by 65% from nominal values. This chapter focuses on describing the hardware, software, and the results that have been obtained by various implementations of BBO.

1. INTRODUCTION

The purpose of engineering is to find feasible or optimal solutions to problems in the world. As engineering challenges have become larger, more complex, and more multidisciplinary, evolutionary algorithms (EAs) have become attractive optimization methods for problems that are not amenable to traditional, analytic algorithms (Rao, 2009). For example, EA research is being used for smart highway systems

DOI: 10.4018/978-1-60960-551-3.ch007

to solve traffic problems (Baluja, 2001), and for medical diagnosis (Brameier & Banzhaf, 2001). The prevalence of optimization problems has created an explosion in the development of EAs, especially in the last decade.

The idea and the origin of EAs can be traced to the 1950's and the works of Bremermann, Friedberg, Box, and others. The scientific community was mostly unaware of the field of EAs for its first three decades due to lack of computer power. Since then, many EAs have been devised, each being named according to its specific emphasis or the model from which it was derived. These works slowly started to be published in the 1970's. The fundamental works of Holland, Rechenberg, Fogel, and Schwefel began in that decade. The basis for most EAs can be traced to one of three separate and independent approaches: genetic algorithms, evolutionary programming, and evolution or mutation strategies (Bäck, Hammel, & Schwefel, 1997).

Powerful computers became more accessible in the early 1980's, which facilitated more research in EAs. Since 1985, worldwide conferences have been established with workshops focusing specifically on EAs (Bäck, Hammel, & Schwefel, 1997). The advantages of these algorithms relative to traditional optimization approaches are their flexibility and their adaptability. They are designed for solving complex optimization problems. EAs explore a large search space to find optimal solutions using specific evolutionary techniques.

There are several main topics in the forefront of evolutionary robotics. They can be broken down into two groups: off-line tuning and on-line tuning. Off-line tuning means that the EA optimizes the system from the outside, whereas on-line tuning means that the EA is built into the system. The simplest and most common off-line application of EAs to robotics is the use of EAs to tune robot controller parameters. EAs have been applied this way many times in the past. Robot control tuning can be used as a real-world benchmark test for EAs (Iruthayarajan & Baskar, 2009).

There are several on-line applications of EAs to robotics: on-line controller tuning; automatic controller building (Fleming & Purshouse, 2002); and evolutionary robotics, which is composed of training phase evolution and lifelong adaptation by evolution (Walker, Garrett, & Wilson, 2006). On-line control parameter tuning is useful for situations in which a human cannot tune a controller or compensate for changes in the system. With EA-based tuning software on-line, a robot is able to improve its actions over time without human intervention. Control tuning can occur in real time, or it can be performed before the controller starts, during a less risky training phase (Fleming & Purshouse, 2002). However, the controller may fail while the EA explores the search space. For instance, if an EA is tuning the control parameters in an industrial robot, the EA may choose a poor solution that causes the robot to fail at its task, which can be expensive or dangerous. This is a significant problem with on-line controller tuning.

Automatic controller building is often used in applications where the physical system to be controlled is complicated, hard to model, or hard to define. In these cases an EA can be used to build a control system out of predefined parts. For instance, a robot that performs functions analogous to a human will have many parts, and without a control system optimized for the problem it may not have the ability to complete its tasks (Fleming & Purshouse, 2002).

In evolutionary robotics, training phase evolution and lifelong adaptation by evolution are distinct from each other. Training phase evolution is an initial step in which the EA searches through a wide range of safe conditions before robotic operation begins. Lifelong adaptation by evolution is a method in which an EA continuously optimizes the controller in order to adapt it to changing conditions. Both of these approaches may use on-line parameter tuning or automatic controller building, and both may be performed and applied to the real world, a simulation, or a combination of the two (Fleming & Purshouse, 2002). The training phase approach helps reduce controller failure by narrowing the search space before taking any risky actions, and lifelong adaptation helps the robot adapt to changing conditions throughout its life.

Previous simulation-based research has shown that a new EA called biogeography-based optimization (BBO) works well in a noisy environment. However, simulations cannot fully match real-world complexity, and sometimes they can actually be misleading (Mataric & Cliff, 1996). Simulations are good for preliminary studies but they are not conclusive. This is why we have made the focus of this research the application of BBO to optimize the control parameters of physical robots. The hardware that we use is based on previous work (Churavy, et al., 2008). In our research, these robots were reconstructed to make them suitable for the use of BBO to tune their control parameters. This work is the first implementation of BBO in a physical system.

This work focuses on the application of BBO to robot controller tuning, and on distributed implementations of BBO. In distributed optimization, a central processor is not in control of the optimization process, but rather individual candidate solutions to the optimization problem communicate directly with each other. As the optimization generations proceed, the subsets of communicating candidate solutions change. This obviates the need for a centralized communication structure at the expense of performance.

In Section 2, an overview of standard centralized BBO, and distributed BBO (DBBO) is presented. The robot hardware is described in Section 3. In Section 4 the operation and structure of the robots' controller is explained. Section 5 discusses the robot simulations and experiments, and presents results.

2. BIOGEOGRAPHY-BASED OPTIMIZATION (BBO)

2.1 Centralized BBO

BBO is a new EA based on the migration of species across habitats, a study which is referred to in the biology literature as *biogeography* (Lomolino, Riddle, & Brown, 2009), (Whittaker, 1998). Mathematical models of biogeography were first published in the 1960s, and were first applied to optimization with the introduction of BBO in 2008 (Simon, 2008). BBO terminology uses the following terms from the theory of biogeography: *habitats*, which are analogous to problem solutions; *habitat suitability index* (HSI), which is analogous to fitness in other EAs; and *suitability index variables* (SIVs), which are the independent variables (the domain) of the optimization problem.

Migration is reciprocal—there is both immigration and emigration between habitats. Their respective rates, λ and μ, are determined by the HSI of a habitat; a habitat with a high HSI will have a low immigration rate and a high emigration rate. This is based on natural biogeography in which a habitat with a high HSI already hosts a large number of species and thus cannot accept many immigrants. Conversely, a habitat with a low HSI has a high immigration rate and a low emigration rate. Again, this is based on biogeography in which a habitat with a low HSI has a low number of species and thus is a more likely destination for the immigration of newcomers. Algorithm 1 gives an outline of the BBO algorithm.

In BBO, migration is an evolutionary operator which plays the same role as recombination in a genetic algorithm (GA). The reciprocal nature of BBO's migration is what makes it different from crossover philosophies. In GAs, parents contribute their genetic information to an offspring and die at the end of the generation (Goldberg, 1989), whereas the solutions in BBO share their information with each other at each generation and continue to survive.

Algorithm 1. One generation of a centralized BBO algorithm

```
For each solution H_i
For each solution feature s
Select solution H_i for immigration with probability proportional to λ_i
If solution H_i is selected then
Select H_j for emigration with probability proportional to μ_j
If H_j is selected then
H_i(s) ← H_j(s)
end
end
next solution feature
Probabilistically mutate H_i
next solution
```

BBO also features the mutation operator, which acts to increase the diversity of a population of solutions. Mutation is also featured in many other EAs. In GAs mutation has traditionally been a background operator. However, in other algorithms, like evolutionary programming, mutation has a more significant role (Fleming & Purshouse, 2002). In BBO, a mutation probability parameter is specified with a range of zero to one, which gives a 0% to 100% chance of mutation occurring for each independent variable in each candidate solution. BBO's default mutation scheme replaces the selected solution features with randomly generated ones within the specified domain.

In order to retain the best solutions, elitism can be applied to BBO. Elitism has been used for a long time in other EAs to prevent the loss of desirable information. An elitism parameter which is coded into BBO specifies the number of solutions that the algorithm considers elite for each generation. At the end of each generation, the poorest solutions are replaced by the previous generation's elite solutions.

2.2 Distributed BBO

In this section, we introduce a distributed implementation of BBO. Distributed BBO is in distinction to the standard BBO algorithm discussed in the previous section, which we refer to as centralized BBO. In BBO, GAs, and many other EAs, solutions represent independent candidate solutions to some optimization problem, but the evolution of these candidate solutions is controlled by a centralized processor. In a situation where an EA's individuals correspond to autonomous entities, such as robots that make their own decisions in real time, the EA may need to be implemented in a distributed manner in order to retain the independence of each individual from the group. This means that the EA algorithm must be performed by the EA individuals rather than by a centralized processor. In our case, the candidate solutions are robot control parameters, and in our initial experiments, the robots were used to generate cost function data for a standard, centralized BBO algorithm as depicted in Algorithm 1. However, for situations that are incompatible with a centralized optimization approach, a distributed implementation must be used. The constraints that may force a distributed implementation include the case when the solution entities cannot always be within proximity of a centralized computer.

We propose a distributed BBO (DBBO) implementation which is inspired by peer-to-peer (P2P) networks (Oram, 2001). In DBBO, the solutions are thought of as peers; for each generation, a few randomly-selected solutions are chosen to be peers, which interact with, and only with, each other. Although there is no simple analog to mutation in P2P networking, mutation is an important part of an EA, so we consider it necessary to include in DBBO. For each generation in DBBO, each peer has a probability of mutation. This results in the number of mutation opportunities being equal to the number of function evaluations, which is the same as mutation in centralized BBO. It is difficult to conceptualize an elitism scheme for DBBO, and since elitism is considered a second-order effect in EAs, we do not implement elitism in DBBO. An outline of a single generation of the DBBO algorithm is shown in Algorithm 2.

The DBBO implementation depicted in Algorithm 2 can still be implemented in a centralized processor. Therefore, depending on its implementation, it may not provide autonomous optimization. However, it still simulates the logic of the interactions that each robot would have with each other in a distributed optimization algorithm. This method of implementing DBBO reduces the complicated communication structure that is required in centralized BBO. Distributed BBO will be useful for systems in which each individual must learn from a subset of the entire population, such as industrial robots on an assembly line that communicate only with a subset of their peers.

2.3 Performance Evaluation

We used a set of 13 popular benchmark functions (Simon, 2008) to gauge the performance of DBBO versus BBO. We optimized each of the benchmarks with BBO and three versions of DBBO (with the number of peers set to 2, 4, and 6). For each algorithm, we used a population size of 50, a problem dimension of 20, and a mutation probability of 1% per independent variable per generation. We did not use elitism. We used a function evaluation limit of 500,000. Table 1 shows the mean of the best costs from 50 Monte Carlo simulations of each of these benchmarks for each BBO algorithm. We use the geometric mean to represent the overall performance of each algorithm since the geometric mean provides a better indication than the mean of the order of magnitude of a set of data.

Algorithm 2. One generation of a distributed BBO algorithm.

Initialize n as the number of peers
Randomly select a group of n peers $\{P_i\}$
For each peer P_i
Update each peer's estimate of the best and worst cost in the population:
$P_i(\max) \leftarrow \max_i\{ \max[P_i(\max), \text{Cost}(P_i)] \}$
$P_i(\min) \leftarrow \min_i\{ \min[P_i(\min), \text{Cost}(P_i)] \}$
next peer
For each peer P_i
Set each peer's relative immigration and emigration probabilities:
$\mu_i \leftarrow [P_i(\max) - \text{Cost}(P_i)] / [P_i(\max) - P_i(\min)]$
$\lambda_i \leftarrow 1 - \mu_i$
next peer
For each peer P_i
For each solution feature s
Select solution P_i for immigration with probability proportional to λ_i
If solution P_i is selected then
Select P_j ($j = 1, \ldots, n$) for emigration with probability proportional to μ_j
If P_j is selected then
$P_i(s) \leftarrow P_j(s)$
end
end
next solution feature
next peer
Probabilistically mutate each peer

One can see from Table 1 that for the same number of function evaluations, DBBO obtains worse results than BBO. However, DBBO can be used to obtain suboptimal performance results in cases where full communication between population members is not possible or not practical. Figure 1 shows typical centralized and distributed BBO results for the Ackley benchmark.

In order to further examine the relative performance of BBO and DBBO, we use a *t*-test. The *t*-test was developed by William Sealy Gosset and published under the pseudonym *Student* (Zabell, 2007). The *t*-test can be used to determine the probability that two sample means come from the same distribution. This allows one to determine how similar two sets of data are (Fisher, 1925). We use the *t*-test to

Table 1. Results of 50 Monte Carlo benchmark simulations

Benchmark Function	Mean of the Best Costs of 50 Monte Carlo Runs			
	BBO	DBBO (2 peers)	DBBO (4 peers)	DBBO (6 peers)
Ackley	8.44E-03	2.25E-01	2.03E-01	2.16E-01
Fletcher	4.39E+03	8.97E+05	8.58E+05	8.45E+05
Griewank	1.00E+00	4.54E+01	3.92E+01	3.45E+01
Penalty #1	7.13E-04	1.64E+07	1.17E+07	1.17E+07
Penalty #2	1.05E-03	3.94E+07	3.02E+07	3.40E+07
Quartic	8.01E-04	4.12E+00	3.33E+00	3.60E+00
Rastrigin	3.01E-04	1.10E+00	1.58E+00	8.35E+00
Rosenbrock	1.48E+01	6.62E+02	5.84E+02	5.92E+02
Schwefel 1.2	5.71E-02	4.51E+02	4.36E+02	4.90E+02
Schwefel 2.21	8.34E+01	1.87E+04	1.76E+04	1.63E+04
Schwefel 2.22	1.91E-04	6.85E+06	8.31E+01	2.65E+04
Schwefel 2.26	4.98E-01	1.48E+01	1.21E+01	1.09E+01
Sphere	5.70E-04	1.13E+01	1.09E+01	1.11E+01
Geometric Mean	**5.29E-02**	**1.49E+03**	**5.66E+02**	**1.01E+03**

Figure 1. Typical centralized and distributed BBO results for the Ackley benchmark function. The distributed BBO simulation results shown here uses two peers.

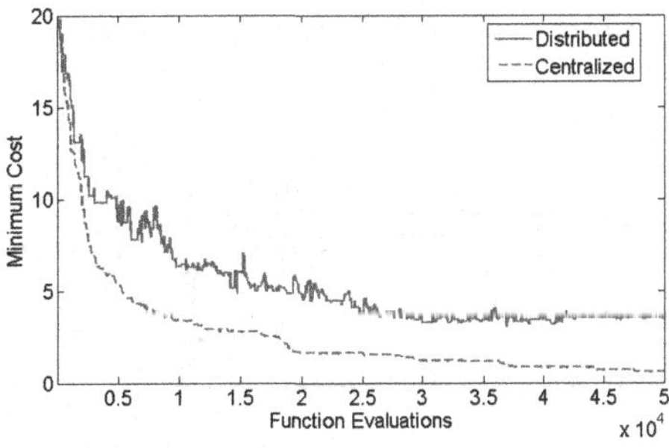

compare BBO and DBBO, and also to compare DBBO with different numbers of peers (parameter n in Algorithm 2).

With the cost data from the 50 Monte Carlo simulations, we computed t-values and their respective probabilities using Microsoft Office Excel®. Table 2 contains the geometric mean of the t-test probabilities that each algorithm results in a performance difference that is statistically significant from the other algorithms.

As before, we used the geometric mean to represent the probabilities because it provides an appropriate average of the order of magnitude of a set of data. When using the t-test to compare BBO with DBBO, regardless of the number of DBBO peers, the probability value is very low, as seen in the first row and first column of Table 2. This indicates that these data definitely did not come from the same distribution, and thus, BBO provides optimization results that are significantly better than DBBO. This provides a statistical corroboration of our earlier observations on the cost data; our DBBO implementation performs very differently from the original BBO. The probability values from the t-tests between DBBO with different numbers of peers are much greater, and range from 5% to 29%. These values are large enough that the differences between the groups of DBBO data may not be statistically significant (Eberhart, Kennedy, & Shi, 2001).

3. HARDWARE

3.1 Assembly

Figure 2 is a photo of one of the robots. Each robot is built for easy access to its components. Electronics such as a microcontroller, voltage regulators, and H-bridges, are mounted and soldered on a two-layer printed circuit board (PCB). The robot electronics are mounted on thin plastic boards separated by aluminum standoffs. Two geared DC motors are attached with brass brackets. Two AA battery packs, which each hold eight rechargeable batteries, supply power to the motors and PCB separately.

A Microchip PIC18F4520 microcontroller is used in this work. Of its peripherals, the pulse width modulation (PWM) modules and hardware universal asynchronous receiver/transmitter (UART) are used for motor control and communication with the base station (via wireless radio) respectively. The base station is a personal computer running MATLAB® which controls the BBO algorithm to optimize the control parameters in each robot.

Table 2. Geometric means of the t-test probabilities of each algorithm versus the others for all 13 benchmarks

t-test results	Geometric mean of probabilities			
	BBO	**DBBO (2 peers)**	**DBBO (4 peers)**	**DBBO (6 peers)**
BBO	N/A	8.7E-18	3.7E-21	5.2E-18
DBBO (2 peers)	8.7E-18	N/A	1.2E-1	4.8E-2
DBBO (4 peers)	3.7E-21	1.2E-1	N/A	2.8E-1
DBBO (6 peers)	5.2E-18	4.8E-2	2.8E-1	N/A

Figure 2. One of the robots

Two voltage regulators are used to provide a steady 5 V power supply--one for the microcontroller and one for the motors. We use two separate voltage regulators to ensure that inductive loads such as motors cannot draw all the current from the microcontroller and cause it to reset. The SN754410NE quad H-bridge is used to amplify the signal from the microcontroller to drive the motors since the PIC outputs can only provide 25 mA.

Each robot is equipped with a MaxStream 9Xtend radio, which is used to communicate with the base station computer. The base station can transmit commands to each robot, update robot control parameters, and receive robot tracking data. The radio can transmit with an output power of between 1 mW and 1 W as configured by the user, and has a maximum outside range of 40 km. It uses a serial interface that can operate at several baud rates. The radio ($200 US) is the most expensive device on each robot.

Each robot has two digital ultrasonic range finders. The robots use these as inputs to the motion controller. The range finders are mounted on the left side of the robots as shown in Figure 2. Since they are mounted above one of the motors, the ultrasonic noise from the motors interferes with the sensor readings. At first, the cause of the ultrasonic sensor noise was unclear. We tried several things to reduce this noise, such as using styrofoam as sound insulation, and soldering capacitors onto the motors to reduce back EMF, but these methods did not solve the problem. Finally, we raised the range finders further away from the motors, which reduced the noise to a level at which the robots could function consistently.

3.2 Operation

Once the robot is ready to follow the wall, an acknowledgment ping is requested by the base station PC. The ping returns from the robot to the base station to indicate that the robot's radio and hardware is intact and ready for the next command. The next step is to transmit randomly generated K_p and K_d controller parameters wirelessly from the BBO algorithm (which executes in the base station) to the robots and store them in microcontroller EEPROM. Once that step is complete, the command is sent from the base station telling the robot to drive forward using PD control and to collect tracking data with range finders. As the robot runs, it saves one data point (tracking error) every 0.1 seconds to flash program memory. The robot stops after it records 200 data points, which takes 20 seconds. When the robot completes its run, it stops and waits for the next radio command from the base station. The base station then sends a message to the robot requesting tracking data, and the robot responds by sending its tracking data to the base station. We used six robots for our initial experiments, which means that the BBO population was comprised of six individuals. Once the base station has received the tracking data for all six robots, it

Figure 3. Conventional feedback control system, adapted from (Araki, 1996).

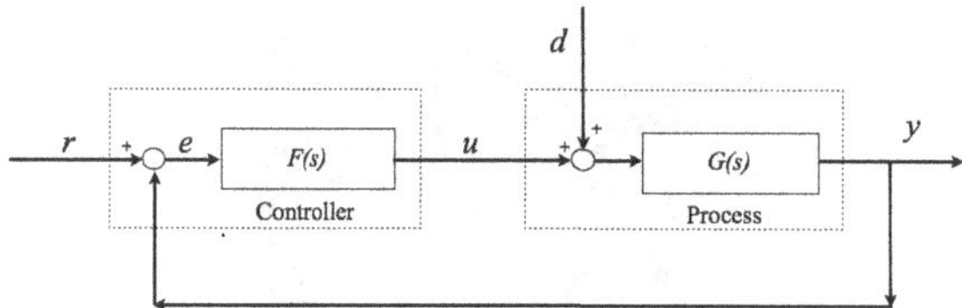

runs one generation of the BBO algorithm to generate new K_p and K_d parameters for each robot in the next generation. The process then repeats for the next BBO generation.

4. ROBOT CONTROLLER

4.1 PID

PID (proportional, integral, derivative) control is a feedback algorithm that has been in use for almost 100 years and has been applied in virtually every area of control engineering (Araki, 1996). In spite of many advances in control theory, PID is still one of the most widely used controllers today because of its ease of use. The proportional gain is referred to as the *P* gain, the integral gain as the *I* gain, and the derivative gain as the *D* gain. An investigation performed in 1989 in Japan indicated that more than 90% of the controllers used in process industries are PID controllers and their variants (Araki, 1996).

The basic structure of conventional feedback control systems is shown in Figure 3. In this figure, the process *G(s)* is the system being controlled by the controller *F(s)*. The purpose of control is to make the process output variable y follow the set-point value r. To achieve this purpose, the manipulated control variable u is determined by the controller. As an example of a process that needs to be controlled, consider a mobile robot following a wall and trying to maintain a desired distance from the wall by adjusting the speed of its two direct-drive wheels. The distance from the wall is measured by range finders that are mounted on the side of the robot. The process output variable y is the distance of the robot from the wall, and the manipulated control variable u is the signal determined by the controller. The disturbance is any factor other than the manipulated control variable that influences the process. Figure 3 assumes that only one disturbance is added to the manipulated variable. However, this does not mean that only one disturbance exists. Most simulations can be adjusted to add external and unpredictable noise to the simulation of a control system. The error e is defined by $e = r - y$. The controller *F(s)* is the computational rule (PID in our case) that determines the manipulated control variable u based on its input data, which is the error e.

A PID controller has the following transfer function from the tracking error (controller input) to the process input (controller output):

$$F(s) = K_p + \frac{K_i}{s} + K_d s \tag{1}$$

where s is the Laplace transform variable. The proportional term K_p determines the amount of control signal which is proportional to the error. A proportional gain that is high results in a large controller output. If the proportional gain is too high, the system becomes unstable. If the proportional gain is too low, it results in a small output response to a large input error, which results in a sluggish controller. A larger K_p value typically gives a faster response.

The integral term K_i accelerates the movement of the process output towards the desired reference value and eliminates the steady-state error that may result from a proportional-only controller. A large K_i parameter eliminates steady state errors more quickly but the tradeoff is larger overshoot, and possibly instability.

The derivative term K_d decelerates the rate of change of the controller output. Therefore, derivative control is used to reduce the amount of overshoot created by the proportional and integral terms and improve controller stability. A large K_d value will decrease overshoot but slow down the response time. One potential danger of derivative control is that measurement noise may be amplified in the differentiation of the error, and this can lead to instability.

4.2 Robot Control Implementation

The function of each of our robots is to follow a wall. The purpose of the robot controller is to maintain a fixed, specific distance from the wall. The angle between the robot orientation and the wall orientation is calculated as follows. First, the difference between the distances read by the two ultrasonic range finders is obtained. This provides one minor leg of a right triangle (d_1-d_2). Second, the distance between the two sensors themselves is used as another leg of the right triangle (d_b). Finally, the arctangent of the first leg over the second leg provides the desired angle:

$$\theta = \arctan\left(\frac{d_1 - d_2}{d_b}\right) \tag{2}$$

This gives an angle which tells the robot which way it is moving. The tracking error is calculated as

$$e(t) = y_{ref} - \frac{d_1 + d_2}{2}\cos(\theta) \tag{3}$$

where y_{ref} is the desired tracking distance between the robot and the wall. The controller output

$$\Delta u(s) = F(s)e(s) \tag{4}$$

is the change in the square wave PWM duty cycle which is applied to the motors. In this case we use the duty cycle of the PWM waveform to approximate an analog voltage. The PWM value that we apply to each motor is an unsigned 8-bit integer which is translated by the H-bridge driver to ±5 V for application to the motors. Therefore, motor voltage resolution is (10/255) V. The PWM value 128 corresponds to 0 V; values below 128 correspond to negative voltages. The controller output is used to change the motor voltages as follows:

$$u_r = u_{ref} - \frac{1}{2}\Delta u(s) \tag{5}$$

where u_r is right wheel PWM value, u_l is left wheel PWM value, and u_{ref} is the nominal duty cycle, which is equal to 192 (3/4 of the maximum duty cycle). The robot's maximum wheel velocity is 0.22 m/s at 60 RPM under normal robotic load, with a wheel diameter of 0.07 m.

Figure 4 depicts a robot tracking toward the reference line, $y = y_{ref}$. The dotted line represents the oscillatory path that the robot takes. This is a qualitatively typical response generated by our robots' PD controllers. This figure also provides a geometric representation of many of the quantities that we discussed in the previous paragraphs.

The derivative contribution to the control signal is the rate of change of error multiplied by the derivative gain. The rate of change of error is calculated by subtracting the error at the previous time step from the error at the current time step, and then dividing the result by the sampling time. This provides information about how fast the error is changing with respect to time. The rate of change of error depends on the heading angle of the robot. If the robot is moving parallel to the wall then there will be no derivative error, but if the robot is at an angle with respect to the wall, then there will be a nonzero derivative error. The larger the angle, the larger the magnitude of the derivative error, which will result in a larger contribution to the control signal.

In a PID controller there is also an integral term which is used to remove steady-state error by generating a contribution to the control signal which is proportional to the integral of the error. The robots used in this work exhibited little steady-state error, so the added complexity of the integral component was not needed.

5. BBO ROBOTICS EXPERIMENTS

5.1 Experimental Setup

This section details the infrastructure of the proof-of-concept BBO robotics experiment. The base station is a PC connected to a radio module via a serial port and a level-shifting integrated circuit. The base

Figure 4. Depiction of the robot's path and related quantities

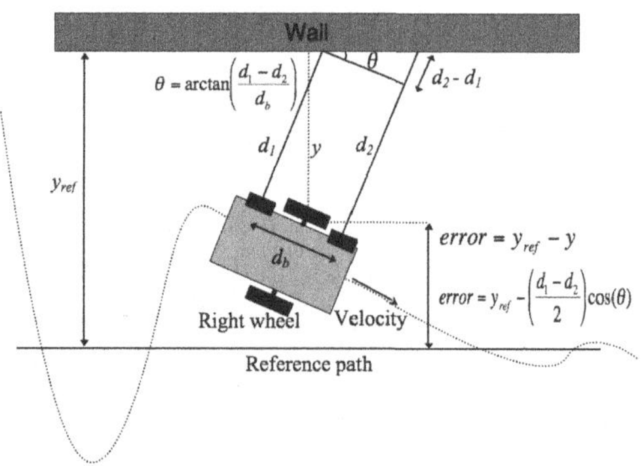

station's software was written in MATLAB. We chose MATLAB for the base station software because the generic BBO code was originally written in MATLAB, which made it easy to adapt to this research. We took advantage of MATLAB's built-in graphical-user-interface development environment (GUIDE) to create a GUI to simplify experimentation, and its serial port capabilities for communication with the robots through a radio module. Figure 5 provides an illustration of the procedural flow of the experiments, which is controlled by the GUI on the PC.

When the user presses the "Run BBO" button on the GUI for the first time, initialization code will execute and the first BBO generation will start; on subsequent presses of the "Run BBO" button, a new generation will start. When the user presses the "Begin Run" button on the GUI, the PC transmits the appropriate command to the robots, and they start tracking the wall and taking distance measurements. For a BBO fitness evaluation of the robot control algorithm in each robot, the robot takes 200 distance measurements, with each measurement taken about 1/10 second apart. After the robot finishes taking 200 distance measurements, execution on the robot's microcontroller enters an idle loop, during which the robot waits until it receives another command from the base station. The user then presses the "Get Data" button on the GUI, which sends an appropriate radio command to the robots that tells them to

Figure 5. A flow chart of the experimental procedure

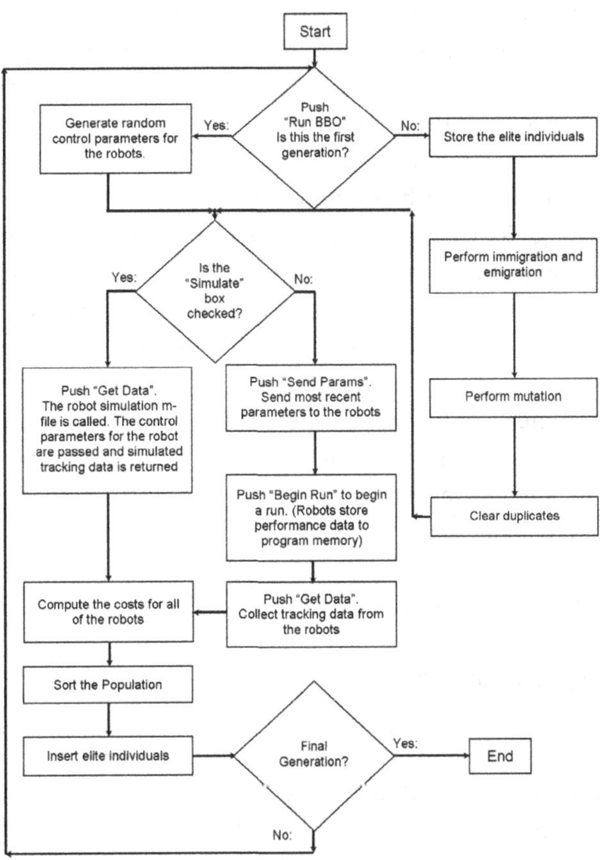

transmit their tracking distance array to the base station. Finally, when the user presses the "Compute Costs" button on the GUI, the BBO algorithm on the PC computes a cost value for each array of tracking data (i.e., for each robot), concludes the current generation, and displays results for that generation in the GUI.

We established a simple communication protocol to transmit commands and data between the robots and the base station. We programmed the robots to transmit only in response to a command from the base station. If the base station communicates with several robots, it will do so sequentially in order to prevent radio interface and in order to allow for the use of a single radio channel. Our protocol is inspired by machine code, so we consider a packet to be a command, which is composed of an 8-bit opcode, a context-specific variable-length operand, and a 16-bit termination word (0x00FF). The variable-length operand with a terminator was chosen over a fixed-length operand for flexibility. Each of the robots' radios has its own unique 16-bit radio address. The base station must switch its radio address (which is done by holding the radio's command pin high and then sending commands to its transmission pin) to that of one of the robots to communicate with it. Radio addresses enable the base station to communicate with one robot at a time, and make sure that the robots do not communicate with each other.

The control parameters, K_p and K_d, are stored in each robot's microcontroller as single precision floating-point values. Since the control parameters are generated in MATLAB on the base station PC, they are inherently represented on the PC in the IEEE 754 floating-point format (IEEE, 1985). We wrote a simple routine for the robots to convert these floating-point values to Microchip's format, which involves changing the location of the sign bit from to the left of the exponent to between the exponent and the mantissa. Also, the d_b variable (see Figure 4) is different for each of the robots, since each of the robots is slightly different. The d_b, K_p, and K_d values are stored to EEPROM in each robot's microcontroller so that these values can be retained even if the power is interrupted.

All of the trigonometric functions in the robot code are implemented as lookup tables, which use less than 5% of the microcontroller's flash program memory, while the required ANSI C library functions use 10% of flash. Although lookup tables usually take up more space than computational methods, lookup tables are generally much faster than real-time computation (Parhami, 2000). Since we do not need to evaluate any of the trigonometric functions on large domains, we were able to decrease the size of the tables considerably. For example, we only needed to evaluate the inverse tangent of a function in the range [-35°, 35°], since the robots' sensors become very inaccurate at angle magnitudes greater than 35°. The sign of the argument for the inverse tangent function determines only the sign of the final value, not the magnitude. Because of this, we only need to store values for inverse tangent in the range [0°, 35°]. We also needed to compute the cosine of this angle. Since cosine is an even function, we only need to store the values on the domain [0°, 35°].

5.2 Simulation Results

5.2.1 BBO, DBBO, and GA Simulations

For both our simulation and hardware experiments we used a population size of six robots with two control parameters each (proportional and derivative gain). The probability of random mutation was set to the unusually high value of 20% to help increase the diversity of solutions because of the small population size of six robots. No elitism was used in the simulation experiment since no elitism scheme has been developed for DBBO. The ranges of K_p and K_d values for this experiment were [0, 2] and [0,

10] respectively. These ranges were chosen because they are broad and are useful for preliminary study. The optimization cost function was a weighted sum of the controller's rise time and the integral of the magnitude of error:

$$Cost = k_1 \int |e(t)| dt + k_2 r \tag{6}$$

where k_1 and k_2 are weighting constants, *e(t)* is the tracking error, and *r* is the controller's rise time, which is the length of time that it takes the robot to reach 95% of the reference tracking distance. For our experiments, k_1 was set to 1 and k_2 was set to 5. These values were chosen to make the orders of magnitude of typical rise time and integral of absolute error values the same, so that they make approximately equal contributions to the costs. The values for k_1 and k_2 are not important, it is the ratio of k_1 to k_2 that is meaningful, since cost is unitless and the absolute range of costs is arbitrary. This weighted sum cost function was chosen over a multiobjective method (Fleming & Purshouse, 2002) to reduce the complexity of the optimization problem.

Before implementing the PD control in our robots, we first wrote a simulation to do some preliminary examination. By approximating the conditions that our real robots would undergo, we were able to find a suitable range of K_p and K_d values that we could use for subsequent work. We also used the robot simulation to compare the performance of centralized BBO, a standard GA, and distributed BBO. Figure 6 depicts the costs versus number of generations for BBO, DBBO with the number of peers set to two and four, and a GA.

As seen from Figure 6, BBO outperforms the GA. In addition, centralized BBO performs better than distributed BBO. As the number of communicating peers in DBBO decreases, performance becomes worse. We also collected results for distributed BBO with 6 peers; however, these were almost identical to the results with standard BBO. We suspect that DBBO with the number of peers equal to the population size is operationally identical to standard BBO.

5.2.2 Manual PD Tuning

The first methods developed for tuning PID controllers were manual methods. The simplest of these are ad-hoc methods, in which the parameters are varied without any clear systematic approach. These

Figure 6. Cost values versus number of generations. The plots show the minimum cost at each generation, averaged over 1000 Monte Carlo simulations.

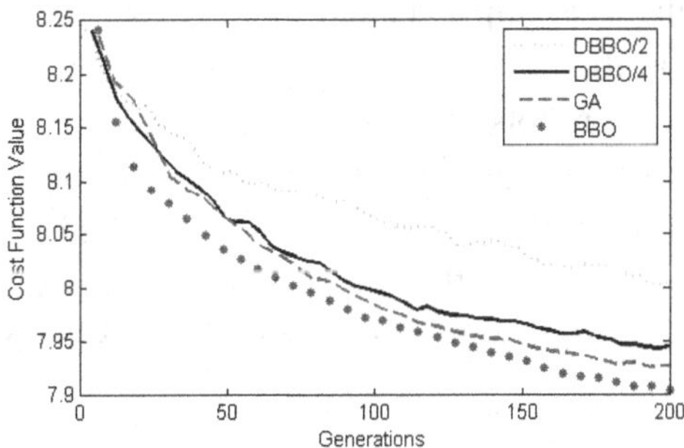

methods are the most time consuming and rarely produce optimal results, but can be used by people with little to no familiarity with control systems.

One of the most common manual tuning methods for PID is the Ziegler-Nichols method.

In this method, all of the parameters are set to zero, then K_p is increased until the system becomes unstable. This point of instability is called K_{MAX}, and the frequency of oscillation at the point of instability is called f_0. The method then sets K_p to a predetermined fraction of K_{MAX} and sets K_i and K_d as a function of f_0 (Ellis, 2000).This method is useful because it is easy to perform and does not require any extra hardware or software, other than a way of changing the parameters.

We tuned our PD robot controller using a method similar to the Ziegler-Nichols method (Ellis, 2000). K_d is set to zero and K_p is slowly increased to the point of instability. However, instead of setting the other parameters to constants, we held K_p constant at the point of instability and raised K_d until the overshoot was minimized. Performing this method took about 20 minutes using MATLAB. We ran the robot simulation with different K_p values in increments of 0.0005 and different K_d value in increments of 0.05. The parameters we selected were $K_p = 0.039$ and $K_d = 1.4$, and the cost (using the same cost function as the previous simulations) produced by this combination of parameters was 12.18. This cost is 4.28 units higher than the lowest cost produced by BBO (see Figure 6), so BBO produces more optimal results.

Considering that 1000 Monte Carlo simulations with four optimization algorithms depicted in Figure 6 took about an hour of computer time, one run of BBO took about one second (3600 s / 4 / 1000). Therefore, BBO optimized our robot controller about 1000 times faster than manual tuning. These are rough estimates, but they reflect the fact that automated optimization algorithms can perform much faster than a human operator.

5.3 Experimental Hardware Results

The conditions for our hardware experiments are essentially the same as the simulations (Section 5.2) but with the following exceptions. One elite value was stored between generations, which guaranteed that the best solution was retained in the BBO population. For the physical robots the ranges of K_p and K_d values were [0.01, 0.10] and [4.0, 6.0] respectively. These ranges were chosen with previous simulation and hardware experimentation in mind; the robots were shown to function poorly outside of these ranges.

Figure 7a is an illustration of the robot's improvement over 10 BBO generations, represented by the best and mean costs for each generation. Figure 7b illustrates the decrease in tracking error from the first generation of BBO to the 10th generation of BBO on a single robot. The integral of absolute error decreased from 28,907 in the first generation to 10,204 in the 10th generation, a decrease of 65%.

In order to be sure that BBO resulted in a statistically significant improvement in the robots' tracking ability as measured by the cost function, we take the standard deviation of the costs from a sample of several runs and compare it to the total improvement in cost from the first generation to the last generation. The total improvement in the best cost is 12.7 (as shown in Figure 7a), the highest standard deviation of the cost out of all of the robots for a single (K_p, K_d) combination is 5.2, and the average of all of the robots' standard deviations of cost for a single (K_p, K_d)combination is 2.6. Because the cost improvement due to BBO is significantly greater than even the highest cost standard deviation for a single robot, we can say with confidence that this improvement is not caused by random variation. Thus, BBO has resulted in a statistically significant improvement in tracking performance.

Figure 7. (a) BBO's performance in the proof-of-concept run. (b) Reduction in tracking error after 10 generations of BBO.

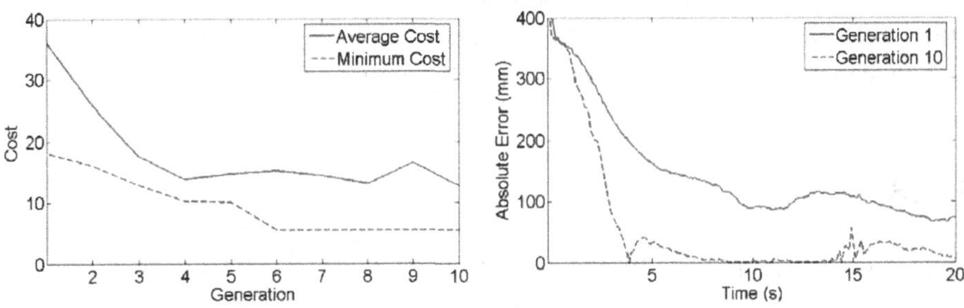

6. CONCLUSION

Our results have shown that BBO is capable of optimizing robot control parameters in a real experimental system. Further work will include a quantitative analysis of the performance of BBO. This will include running BBO with different settings (e.g., different mutation probabilities and elitism options), or comparing BBO to other EAs for this problem.

Future work will also include reducing the noise in the robot's tracking data. We are pursuing noise reduction by testing analog infrared (IR) range finders for suitability in our research. Since IR range finders use light instead of sound for range finding, they will not be susceptible to sonic noise created by the motors; however, analog components are inherently more susceptible to electrical noise than digital components. Error due to noise in a digital signal will corrupt the information encoded into it to some extent, but as long as the noise in an analog signal does not cause a change the corresponding digital state, the digital signal's encoded information will remain intact. By experimenting with IR range finders, we will either reduce the tracking noise in the robots, which would mean that the noise in the ultrasonic tracking data has been propagating sonically, or we will narrow down the source of the tracking noise by verifying that the noise is not sonic in nature. It may also be useful to try hardware or software filters for noise reduction.

Also, we want to design new printed circuit boards (PCBs) for our robots. New PCB design is important because the current robot PCBs were designed for ultrasonic range finders and thus cannot be used with the IR range finders that we are proposing for future work. When designing these new PCBs, we will also be able to add hardware filters and other capabilities. The current robot PCBs have headers connected to general purpose input-output pins on the microcontroller, but these are designed for adding specific peripherals like switches and sensors.

The distributed BBO implementation that we discuss in this chapter is a preliminary one. It may be possible to create different implementations of DBBO that produce results as quickly as and more optimally than the distributed BBO presented in this chapter. Also, we have yet to explore different mutation schemes and elitism possibilities for DBBO. Should we mutate every solution or just the selected peers? Should we examine each individual for elitism, or only the peers?

Several modifications to BBO are being examined in other work; these modifications include immigration refusal (Du, Simon, & Ergezer, 2009) and opposition-based learning (Ergezer, Simon, & Du,

2009). It may be fruitful to apply those modifications to the robot control optimization problem. Also, we plan to code an on-line, distributed BBO that executes on the robots themselves instead of on a centralized computer. If this is done, then no centralized computer will be needed.

Some auxiliary material related to this work, including supplemental reading, raw data, and MATLAB and C source code, can be found at http://embeddedlab.csuohio.edu/BBORobotics.

REFERENCES

Araki, M. (1996). Stability concepts - PID control. In H. Unbehausen (Ed.), *Control systems, robotics, and automation.* Kyoto, Japan: Encyclopedia of Life Support Systems (EOLSS).

Bäck, T., Hammel, U., & Schwefel, H.-P. (1997). Evolutionary computation: Comments on the history and current state. *IEEE Transactions on Evolutionary Computation*, *1*(1), 3–16. doi:10.1109/4235.585888

Baluja, S., Sukthankar, R., & Hancock, J. (2001). Prototyping intelligent vehicle modules using evolutionary algorithms. In Dasgupta, D. (Ed.), *Evolutionary algorithms in engineering applications* (pp. 241–258). New York, NY: Springer.

Brameier, M., & Banzhaf, W. (2001). A comparison of linear genetic programming and neural networks in medical data mining. *IEEE Transactions on Evolutionary Computation*, *5*, 17–26. doi:10.1109/4235.910462

Churavy, C., Baker, M., Mehta, S., Pradhan, I., Scheidegger, N., Shanfelt, S., et al. (2008). Effective implementation of a mapping swarm of robots. *IEEE Potentials*, 28-33.

Du, D., Simon, D., & Ergezer, M. (2009). *Oppositional biogeography-based optimization.* IEEE Conference on Systems, Man, and Cybernetics (pp. 1035-1040). San Antonio, TX: IEEE.

Eberhart, R. C., Kennedy, J., & Shi, Y. (2001). *Swarm intelligence.* San Mateo, CA: Morgan Kauffman.

Ellis, G. (2000). *Control system design guide.* San Diego, CA: Academic Press.

Ergezer, M., Simon, D., & Du, D. (2009). *Oppositional biogeography-based optimization.* IEEE Conference on Systems, Man, and Cybernetics (pp. 1035-1040). San Antonio, TX: IEEE.

Fisher, R. A. (1925). *Statistical methods for research workers.* Edinburgh, UK: Oliver and Boyd.

Fleming, P. J., & Purshouse, R. C. (2002). Evolutionary algorithms in control systems engineering: A survey. *Control Engineering Practice*, 1223–1241. doi:10.1016/S0967-0661(02)00081-3

Goldberg, D. (1989). *Genetic algorithms in search, optimization, and machine learning.* Reading, MA: Addison-Wesley.

Hedar, A.-R., & Fukushima, M. (2003). Minimizing multimodal functions by simplex coding genetic algorithm. *Optimization Methods & Software*, *18*(3), 265–282.

IEEE. (1985). (IEEE standard 754-1985 for Binary Floating-point Arithmetic). *SIGPLAN*, *22*(2), 9–25.

Iruthayarajan, M. W., & Baskar, S. (2009). Evolutionary algorithms based design of multivariable PID controller. *Expert Systems with Applications*, 9159–9167. doi:10.1016/j.eswa.2008.12.033

Lomolino, M. V., Riddle, B. R., & Brown, J. H. (2009). *Biogeography*. Sunderland, MA: Sinauer Associates.

Mataric, M., & Cliff, D. (1996). Challenges for evolving controllers for physical robots. *Robotics and Autonomous Systems*, 67–83. doi:10.1016/S0921-8890(96)00034-6

Oram, A. (2001). *Peer-to-peer: Harnessing the power of disruptive technologies*. Sebastopol, CA: O'Reilly Media.

Parhami, B. (2000). *Computer arithmetic: Algorithms and hardware designs*. Oxford, UK & New York, NY: Oxford University Press.

Rao, S. (2009). *Engineering optimization: Theory and practice*. New York, NY: Wiley.

Simon, D. J. (2008). Evolutionary biogeography-based optimization. *IEEE Transactions on Evolutionary Computation*, *12*(6), 702–713. doi:10.1109/TEVC.2008.919004

Walker, J. H., Garrett, S. M., & Wilson, M. S. (2006). The balance between initial training and lifelong adaptation in evolving robot controllers. *IEEE Transactions on Systems, Man, and Cybernetics*, *36*(2), 423–432. doi:10.1109/TSMCB.2005.859082

Whittaker, R. (1998). *Island biogeography*. New York, NY: Oxford University Press.

Zabell, S. L. (2007). On student's 1908 article 'The probable error of a mean'. *Journal of the American Statistical Association*, *103*(481), 1–7. doi:10.1198/016214508000000030

ADDITIONAL READING

Brueckner, S. A., & Parunak, H. V. D. (2005). *Engineering Self-Organizing Systems: Methodologies and Applications*. New York, NY: Springer.

Buford, J., Yu, H., & Lua, E. K. (2008). *Networking and Applications* (p. 2P). San Fransisco, CA: Morgan Kaufmann.

Burbidge, R., Walker, J. H., & Wilson, M. S. (2009). Grammatical evolution of a robot controller. *2009 IEEE/RSJ International Conference on Intelligent Robots and Systems* (pp. 357-362). St. Louis, MO: IEEE.

Camponogara, E., & de Oliveira, L. B. (2009). Distributed optimization for model predictive control of linear-dynamic networks. *IEEE Transactions on Systems, Man, and Cybernetics*, *39*(6), 1331–1338. doi:10.1109/TSMCA.2009.2025507

Camponogara, E., Scherer, H. F., & Moura, L. V. (2009). Distributed optimization for predictive control with input and state constraints: preliminary theory and application to urban traffic control. *Proceedings of the 2009 IEEE International Conference on Systems, Man and Cybernetics*, 11-14. Piscataway, NJ: IEEE.

Cantu-Paz, E. (2003). *Genetic and Evolutionary Computation - GECCO 2003 Part II* (1st Edition ed.). New York, NY: Springer.

Choset, H. (2005). *Principles of Robot Motion: Theory, Algorithms, and Implementations*. Cambridge, MA: The MIT Press.

Coello, C. A., Christiansen, A. D., & Aguirre, A. H. (1998). Using a new GA-based multiobjective optimization technique for the design of robot arms. *Robotica, 16*, 401–414. doi:10.1017/S0263574798000034

Craig, J. J. (2004). *Introduction to Robotics: Mechanics and Control* (3rd Edition ed.). Upper Saddle River, NJ: Prentice Hall.

Guivant, J., & Nebot, E. (2001). Optimization of the Simultaneous Localization and Map Building Algorithm for Real Time Implementation. *IEEE Transactions on Robotics and Automation, 17*(3), 242. doi:10.1109/70.938382

Jazar, R. N. (2010). *Theory of Applied Robotics: Kinematics, Dynamics, and Control* (2nd Edition ed.). New York, NY: Springer.

Jian, Z., & Ai-Ping, L. (2009). Genetic algorithm for robot workcell layout problem. *Proceedings of the 2009 WRI World Congress on Software Engineering* (pp. 19-21). Xiamen, China: IEEE.

Kuntschke, R. (2008). *Network-Aware Optimization in Distributed Data Stream Systems*. Saarbrücken, Germany: VDM Verlag.

Malanowski, K. (1996). *Modelling and Optimization of Disributed Paramenter Systems* (1st Edition ed.). New York, NY: Springer.

Nolfi, S., & Floreano, D. (2004). *Evolutionary Robotics: the Biology, Intelligence, and Technology of Self-Organizing Machines*. Cambridge, MA: The MIT Press.

Roy, P., Ghoshal, S., & Thakur, S. (2010). Biogeography-based optimization for economic load dispatch problems. *Electric Power Components and Systems, 38*(2), 166–181. doi:10.1080/15325000903273379

Siegwart, R. (2004). *Introduction to Autonomous Mobile Robots* (Edition, I., Ed.). Cambridge, MA: The MIT Press.

Sundaram, R. K. (1996). *A First Course in Optimization Theory*. New York, NY: Cambridge University Press.

Takashi, E. G. (2001). *Evolutionary Robotics: From Intelligent Robotics to Artificial Life*. New York, NY: Springer.

Tan, L., & Guo, L. (2009). *Quantum and biogeography based optimization for a class of combinatorial optimization. ACM/SIGEVO Summit on Genetic and Evolutionary Computation* (pp. 969–972). New York, NY: ACM.

Thrun, S., & Burgard, W. (2005). *Probabilistic Robotics*. Cambridge, MA: The MIT Press.

Wan, Y., Wang, G., Ji, S., & Liu, J. (2008). A survey on the parallel robot optimization. 2008 Second International Symposium on Intelligent Information Technology Application (pp. 655-659). Shanghai, China: IEEE.

Wang, L. (2006). *Evolutionary Robotics: From Algorithms to Implementations*. Hackensack, NJ: World Scientific Publishing Company.

Watanabe, K., & Hashem, M. M. A. (2004). *Evolutionary Computations*. New York, NY: Springer.

Yu, X., & Gen, M. (2010). *Introduction to Evolutionary Algorithms*. New York, NY: Springer.

KEY TERMS AND DEFINITIONS

An Evolutionary Algorithm (EA): A population-based optimization approach that includes candidate solutions which evolve over time to produce an optimal solution to some problem.

Biogeography-Based Optimization (BBO): An evolutionary algorithm based on the migration of species between islands.

T-Test: A statistical test that provides information on the relationship between the means of two sets of data.

Distributed BBO (DBBO): An algorithm that is distributed among the individuals. A centralized processor is not used in DBBO.

Centralized BBO: A BBO implementation in which a single computer controls the algorithm.

Peers: A randomly chosen subset of the DBBO population which interacts during a given generation for the purpose of migration.

Migration: The sharing of solution information among BBO individuals.

PID: Proportional/integral/derivative (PID) control is a widely used feedback control method in which the control signal is proportional to the tracking error, its integral, and its derivative.

Section 2

Application of AI and CI Methods to Medicine and Environment Monitoring and Protection

Chapter 8
An Exposition of Uncertain Reasoning Based Analysis:
An Investigation of Total Hip Arthroplasty

Malcolm J. Beynon
Cardiff University, UK

Cathy Holt
Cardiff University, UK

Gemma Whatling
Cardiff University, UK

ABSTRACT

Uncertain reasoning is closely associated with the pertinent analysis of data where there may be imprecision, inexactness, and uncertainty in its information content. In computer modelling, this should move any analysis to be inclusive of such potential uncertainty, away from the presumption of perfect data to be worked with. The nascent Classification and Ranking Belief Simplex (CaRBS) technique employed in this chapter enables analysis in the spirit of uncertain reasoning. The operational rudiments of the CaRBS technique are based on the Dempster-Shafer theory of evidence, affording the presence of ignorance in any analysis undertaken. An investigation of Total Hip Arthraplasty (THA), concerned with hip replacements, forms the applied problem around which the uncertain reasoning based analysis using CaRBS is exposited. The presented findings include the levels of fit in constructed models, and the contribution of features within the models. Where appropriate, numerical calculations are shown, to illustrate this novel form of analysis.

DOI: 10.4018/978-1-60960-551-3.ch008

INTRODUCTION

Uncertain reasoning is closely associated with the pertinent analysis of data where there may be, imprecision, inexactness and uncertainty in its information content (Cortes-Rello & Golshani, 1990; Barnden, 2001). In computer modelling, this moves any analysis to be inclusive of such potential uncertainty, away from the necessity/presumption of perfect data to be worked with. Uncertain reasoning, within computer modelling, can be considered part of the wider research area of artificial intelligence (AI), which perhaps itself has an open domain, and includes the many directions that uncertainty may be apparent in an intended analysis.

With regard to the positioning of AI in the legal domain, Barnden (2001, p 117) offers a 'state of play' position of how uncertainty could be viewed in analysis (see also Allen, 2001):

"Indeed, the legal domain provides good illustrations of why AI accounts of mental-state reasoning need to incorporate a powerful treatment of uncertainty. Unfortunately, the research in various disciplines on mental-state reasoning has largely skirted the question of uncertainty of reasoning, at least when it comes down to detailed technical proposals. But in practical applications – notably including law – conclusions generally do not follow with complete certainty from premises."

There are a number of points to come from this statement, namely the notion of mental-state reasoning, put simply, this relates to analysis where there is a level of modelling with subjective data (or perhaps where there is subjective uncertainty about the impact of the data), and the specific mention of how conclusions 'in reality' do not offer certainty in their findings. Hence in computer modelling, there should be the allowance for such uncertainty to be present in analysis and importantly any findings.

Amongst the general methodologies closely associated with uncertain reasoning is the Dempster-Shafer theory (DST) of evidence, introduced in Dempster (1967) and Shafer (1976). Often described as a generalisation of the well-known Bayesian theory (Shafer and Srivastava, 1990; Lucas & Araabi, 1999), DST has a close association with the ability to undertake analysis in the presence of ignorance (Safranek, Gottschlich & Kak, 1990). It is worthwhile to stress that other techniques exist which purport to undertake analysis in an uncertain environment, for example, Kim and Nevatia (1999) describes uncertain reasoning with two other analysis techniques, namely neural networks (Russell & Norvig, 1995) and Bayesian networks (John & Langley, 1995).

The nascent Classification and Ranking Belief Simplex (CaRBS), introduced in Beynon (2005a, 2005b) and Beynon, Jones and Holt (2006), is the main analysis technique presented in this chapter. With its operational rudiments based on DST, the evidence from the features describing objects, which contribute to a formulated binary classification of the objects, is expressed through belief functions (Daniel, 2006). Throughout this chapter, a real application is considered, namely the investigation of the differences in gait features resulting from total hip arthroplasty (THA), in layman's terms, it is looking at the variation in motion functions of subjects (the objects here), who may or may not have had one or two forms of hip replacement surgical procedures.

According to the NHS in Britain, at least 50,000 THA procedures are carried out in Britain each year, where worn and painful hips are replaced with an artificial joint. The two commonest surgical approaches used in THA, involve accessing the joint from the side (lateral) or behind (posterior) the joint. Each surgical approach compromises different muscles and static constraints surrounding the hip, resulting in varying post-operative stability and control of the new joint. Despite the success of the operations, gait (motion including walking) does not always return to normal (Madsen *et al.*, 2004; Whatling *et al.*, 2008). The employed surgical technique is a potential contributing factor to the level of gait function achieved post-operatively and is investigated here using the CaRBS technique.

Biomechanical gait data from patients (subjects) with THA, collected using motion analysis techniques was used in the analyses. In this investigation, 14 subjects had received THA via the McFarland-Osborne - direct *Lateral Approach* (LA) (McFarland and Osborne, 1956) and 13 subjects via the Moore - southern exposure *Posterior Approach* (PA) (Moore, 1959). There were also 16 subjects with hips with no-pathology (NP) considered, forming a control group. A significant challenge to the clinical use of gait information is the successful analysis of the data (Chau, 2001a). A common difficulty is not only the vast amount of data yielded but its variability which can be difficult to interpret subjectively (an issue of subjective uncertainty about the impact of data). Jones, Beynon and Holt (2006) and Jones, Holt and Beynon (2008) have introduced a similar CaRBS based technique to classify healthy and osteoarthritis knee function using objective classification and subsequently to assess outcomes and explore the return of healthy function for the patients who have then undergone total knee replacement surgery (see also Jones and Holt, 2008).

In this chapter, the CaRBS technique is applied to the THA problem, to exposit an understanding of the effectiveness of each surgical approach and discerning the significant clinical appeal of gait features associated with the two approaches to THA. At the technical level, three separate analyses are undertaken, which look at the discerning of pairs of subject types (LA against PA, LA against NP and PA against NP), with descriptions of level of fit and feature contribution presented. With each analysis presented necessitating the configuration of a CaRBS system, here described as a constrained optimisation problem. It follows, in this chapter the constrained optimisation is performed using trigonometric differential evolution (Fan & Lampinen, 2003), a nascent development on the recently introduced differential evolution (Storn & Price, 1997).

For the reader of this chapter, it is clear uncertain reasoning in itself is an interesting way forward in terms of computational modelling, and this chapter furthers its elucidation. Barnden (2001, p. 149) placates the importance of this furthering of its understanding:

"Uncertainty is inherent in important inference techniques such as default reasoning, abduction and case-based/analogy-based reasoning, and agents that are being reasoned about may use these techniques; also, any reasoning about people's mental states or processes is fraught with uncertainty since we do not in fact have access to their minds."

Overview of Dempster-Shafer Theory, Classification and Ranking Belief Simplex and Trigonometric Differential Evolution

This section of the book chapter covers technical details later used, namely the three topics: Dempster-Shafer theory (DST) of evidence - the general uncertain reasoning methodology underpinning the analysis undertaken, Classification and Ranking Belief Simplex (CaRBS) - the nascent classification technique employed in the analysis (whose operations are based on DST), and Trigonometric Differential Evolution (TDE) - the constrained optimisation technique used in the operations to configure CaRBS systems.

Dempster-Shafer Theory

The operational rudiments of the CaRBS technique later described are based on the Dempster-Shafer theory of evidence - DST (Dempster, 1967; Shafer, 1976). Support for the use of DST in uncertain reasoning based analysis is strongly supported in the study by Cortes-Rello and Golshani (1990, p. 17), who states:

"While there exists several methods for management of uncertainty in expert systems, the Dempster-Shafer approach proves superior for a number of reasons. Compared to ad hoc techniques, this technique is more desirable because of its rigorous mathematical underpinning. Compared with other probability-based methods such as Bayesian, the Dempster-Shafer theory is more powerful since it can work with probability of sets of points instead of probability of just individual points. In addition it can handle contradictory evidence in a satisfactory manner."

Formally, DST is based on a finite set of p elements $\Theta = \{s_1, s_2, ..., s_p\}$, collectively called a frame of discernment (Θ). A *mass value* is a function m: $2^\Theta \rightarrow [0, 1]$ such that $m(\varnothing) = 0$ ($\varnothing$ - the empty set) and $\sum_{s \in 2^\Theta} m(s) = 1$ (2^Θ - the power set of Θ). Any proper subset s of the frame of discernment Θ, for which $m(s)$ is non-zero, is called a focal element and the concomitant mass value represents the exact belief in the proposition depicted by s. The notion of a proposition here being the collection of the hypotheses represented by the elements in a focal element. The collection of mass values (and the focal elements) associated with a piece of evidence is called a body of evidence (BOE)

To further understand the DST and to demonstrate the properties of using the DST over the Bayesian approach, an example, which considers the question "which type of hip replacement surgical procedure did Mrs Jones have?", is expounded, adapted from Beynon, Curry and Morgan (2000) and Jones, Beynon and Holt (2006). It is known that the replacement hip surgical procedure is either Lateral Approach (LA) or Posterior Approach (PA). Thus, the frame of discernment Θ contains the elementary hypotheses "the surgical procedure is lateral approach", {LA} and "the surgical procedure is posterior approach", {PA}; i.e. Θ = {LA, PA}. A theatre assistant believes with 80% certainty that the surgeon undertook the lateral approach. This gives a mass value of 0.8 to the focal element {LA}, i.e. $m(\{LA\}) = 0.8$. Using DST, in contrast to the Bayesian approach, no presumptions are made about the remaining mass and so it is assigned to the entire Θ (= {LA, PA}), i.e. $m(\{LA, PA\}) = m(\Theta) = 0.2$.

Classification and Ranking Belief Simplex (CaRBS)

The CaRBS technique was introduced in, Beynon (2005a, 2005b) and Beynon, Jones and Holt (2006), as a novel technique able to perform classification and ranking based analysis. The reader is encouraged to read through these research studies for a fuller understanding of this technique.

The aim of the CaRBS technique, when undertaking binary classification (using DST), and described here using terms closely associated with the THA problem later considered, is to construct a BOE for a variable/feature (feature BOE), defined $m_{j,i}(\cdot)$, which quantifies that feature's evidential support for the classification of a subject o_j to a hypothesis ($\{x\}$), not-the-hypothesis ($\{\neg x\}$) and ignorance ($\{x, \neg x\} = \Theta$), see Figure 1. To have in mind when reading through these technical details, Barnden (2001, p 117-118) considers deductive reasoning and includes mention of hypotheses:

"In short, straightforward use of standard deductive reasoning is of limited interest, and one must allow for levels of uncertainty in hypotheses, and, relatedly, for retractability (defeasibility) of tentatively established hypotheses when evidence mounts against them."

Here, it is the inclusion in CaRBS for evidence to support a hypothesis, not-the-hypothesis and ignorance.

In Figure 1, stage *a*) shows the transformation of a feature value $v_{j,i}$ (say from j^{th} subject, i^{th} feature) into a confidence value $cf_i(v_{j,i})$, using a sigmoid function with control variables k_i and θ_i. This process transforms a feature measurement to a value on a scale of 0 to 1. The confidence value represents a level of confidence in (or not in) the support that a feature measurement offers between one subject type against another (in the THA problem - LA against PA, LA against NP and PA against NP).

Stage *b*) transforms a $cf_i(v_{j,i})$ into a *feature* BOE $m_{j,i}(\cdot)$, made up of the three mass values $m_{j,i}(\{x\})$, $m_{j,i}(\{\neg x\})$ and $m_{j,i}(\{x, \neg x\})$, defined by (from Safranek *et al*., 1990 and Beynon, 2005a);

$$m_{j,i}(\{x\}) = \max\left(0, \frac{B_i}{1-A_i} cf_i(v_{j,i}) - \frac{A_i B_i}{1-A_i}\right), \; m_{j,i}(\{\neg x\}) = \max\left(0, \frac{-B_i}{1-A_i} cf_i(v_{j,i}) + B_i\right) ,$$

and $m_{j,i}(\{x, \neg x\}) = 1 - m_{j,i}(\{x\}) - m_{j,i}(\{\neg x\})$, (1)where A_i and B_i are two further control variables. Stage *c*) shows a feature BOE $m_{j,i}(\cdot)$; $m_{j,i}(\{x\}) = v_{j,i,1}$, $m_{j,i}(\{\neg x\}) = v_{j,i,2}$ and $m_{j,i}(\{x, \neg x\}) = v_{j,i,3}$, can be represented as a simplex coordinate ($p_{j,i,v}$) in a simplex plot (equilateral triangle). In the simplex plot, the point $p_{j,i,v}$ exists such that the least distance from $p_{j,i,v}$ to each of the sides of the equilateral triangle are in the same

Figure 1. Stages in CaRBS for a single feature value $v_{j,i}$ to formulate a feature BOE and its subsequent representation in a simplex plot

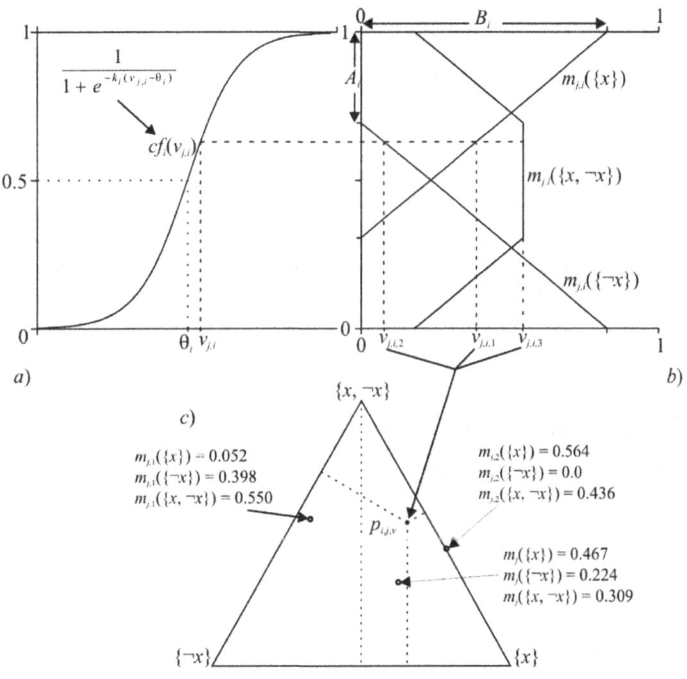

ratio as the mass values, $v_{j,i,1}$, $v_{j,i,2}$ and $v_{j,i,3}$. Briefly, the nearer a simplex coordinate is to a specific vertex the more association the evidence in the BOE has to that subset of the Θ. Illustrative evaluations of the mass value equations in (1) are given in the applied analysis later undertaken.

With a subject described by a series of n_C features, Dempster's rule of combination can be applied iteratively to combine the associated series of feature BOEs, producing a *subject* BOE. The combination of two BOEs, $m_{j,i}(\cdot)$ and $m_{j,k}(\cdot)$, defined $[m_{j,i} \oplus m_{j,k}](\cdot)$, results in a combined BOE whose mass values are given by (in terms of a newly created BOE made up of three mass values):

$$[m_{j,i} \oplus m_{j,k}](\{x\}) = \frac{m_{j,i}(\{x\})m_{j,k}(\{x\}) + m_{j,k}(\{x\})m_{j,i}(\{x,\neg x\}) + m_{j,i}(\{x\})m_{j,k}(\{x,\neg x\})}{1-(m_{j,i}(\{\neg x\})m_{j,k}(\{x\}) + m_{j,i}(\{x\})m_{j,k}(\{\neg x\}))},$$

$$[m_{j,i} \oplus m_{j,k}](\{\neg x\}) = \frac{m_{j,i}(\{\neg x\})m_{j,k}(\{\neg x\}) + m_{j,k}(\{x,\neg x\})m_{j,i}(\{\neg x\}) + m_{j,k}(\{\neg x\})m_{j,i}(\{x,\neg x\})}{1-(m_{j,i}(\{\neg x\})m_{j,k}(\{x\}) + m_{j,i}(\{x\})m_{j,k}(\{\neg x\}))}, \quad (2)$$

$$[m_{j,i} \oplus m_{j,k}](\{x,\neg x\}) = 1-[m_{j,i} \oplus m_{j,k}](\{x\}) - [m_{j,i} \oplus m_{j,k}](\{\neg x\}).$$

The ability to explicitly write out the combination of two characteristic BOEs (rather than the original combination rule - Dempster, 1967; Shafer, 1976), is due to a binary frame of discernment being considered (the hypotheses x and $\neg x$ only). To illustrate this method of combination using (2), two example BOEs, $m_{j,1}(\cdot)$ and $m_{j,2}(\cdot)$, given in the vector $[m_{j,i}(\{x\}), m_{j,i}(\{\neg x\}), m_{j,i}(\{x, \neg x\})]$ as, [0.564, 0.000, 0.436] and [0.052, 0.398, 0.550], are next combined,

$$[m_{j,1} \oplus m_{j,2}](\{x\}) = \frac{m_{j,1}(\{x\})m_{j,2}(\{x\}) + m_{j,2}(\{x\})m_{j,1}(\{x,\neg x\}) + m_{j,1}(\{x\})m_{j,2}(\{x,\neg x\})}{1-(m_{j,1}(\{\neg x\})m_{j,2}(\{x\}) + m_{j,1}(\{x\})m_{j,2}(\{\neg x\}))},$$

$$= \frac{0.564\times 0.052 + 0.052\times 0.436 + 0.564\times 0.550}{1-(0.000\times 0.052 + 0.564\times 0.398)},$$

$$= \frac{0.029 + 0.023 + 0.310}{1-(0.000 + 0.224)} = \frac{0.362}{0.776} = 0.467,$$

$$[m_{j,1} \oplus m_{j,2}](\{\neg x\}) = \frac{m_{j,1}(\{\neg x\})m_{j,2}(\{\neg x\}) + m_{j,2}(\{x,\neg x\})m_{j,1}(\{\neg x\}) + m_{j,2}(\{\neg x\})m_{j,1}(\{x,\neg x\})}{1-(m_{j,1}(\{\neg x\})m_{j,2}(\{x\}) + m_{j,1}(\{x\})m_{j,2}(\{\neg x\}))},$$

$$= \frac{0.000\times 0.398 + 0.550\times 0.000 + 0.398\times 0.436}{1-(0.000\times 0.052 + 0.564\times 0.398)}$$

$$= \frac{0.000 + 0.000 + 0.174}{1-(0.000 + 0.224)} = \frac{0.174}{0.776} = 0.224,$$

$$[m_{j,1} \oplus m_{j,2}](\{x, \neg x\}) = 1 - [m_{j,1} \oplus m_{j,2}](\{x\}) - [m_{j,1} \oplus m_{j,2}](\{\neg x\}),$$

$$= 1 - 0.467 - 0.224 = 0.309$$

It follows, in vector form, the combination of $m_{j,1}(\cdot)$ and $m_{j,2}(\cdot)$ is evaluated to be $m_C(\cdot) = [0.467, 0.224, 0.309]$. This combination process is graphically represented in Figure 1*c*, where with there being less ignorance associated with the $m_{j,1}(\cdot)$ BOE, so a simplex coordinate position nearer the base of the simplex plot, the resultant BOE $m_C(\cdot)$ is nearer $m_{j,1}(\cdot)$ BOE. It is also nearer the base of the simplex than either constituent BOEs, demonstrating as evidence is combined (BOEs combined), there is a reduction in the concomitant ignorance in the resultant BOE.

The CaRBS technique is governed by the values assigned to the incumbent control variables k_i, θ_i, A_i and B_i. The process of assigning values to these control variables is termed the configuration of a CaRBS system. The effectiveness of a configured CaRBS system is measured by a defined objective function (OB). Using the equivalence classes $E(x)$ and $E(\neg x)$ of subjects, with the optimum solution being to maximise the difference values $(m_j(\{x\}) - m_j(\{\neg x\}))$ and $(m_j(\{\neg x\}) - m_j(\{x\}))$, respectively (from $E(x)$ and $E(\neg x)$), where optimisation is minimisation with lower limit zero, the OB is given by (Beynon, 2005*b*):

$$\text{OB} = \frac{1}{4}\left(\frac{1}{|E(x)|} \sum_{o_j \in E(x)} (1 - m_j(\{x\}) + m_j(\{\neg x\})) + \frac{1}{|E(\neg x)|} \sum_{o_j \in E(\neg x)} (1 + m_j(\{x\}) - m_j(\{\neg x\})) \right), \quad (3)$$

in the limit, $0 \leq \text{OB} \leq 1$. It is noted, for example, maximising a difference value $(m_j(\{x\}) - m_j(\{\neg x\}))$ for the subjects in $E(x)$, minimises classification ambiguity but only indirectly the associated ignorance. The utilisation of the objective function OB in (3) in the configuration of the CaRBS system is to directly minimise the level of ambiguity present in the classification of subjects to their association to $\{x\}$ and $\{\neg x\}$, but not the concomitant ignorance ($\{x, \neg x\}$). The configuration process is so termed enabling binary classification with ignorance using CaRBS.

Trigonometric Differential Evolution (TDE)

A configured CaRBS system is governed by the values assigned to the control variables, k_i, θ_i, A_i and B_i, $i = 1,.., n_C$ (so $4n_C$ control variables), which enable the construction of feature BOEs and their subsequent combination to subject BOEs. The mass values of the respective subject BOEs $m_j(\cdot)$ $j = 1,.., n_O$ (number of subjects), are used in the objective function OB measuring the level of fit in the constructed model. The assignment of values to the control variables, producing an optimum fit in terms of OB value, is formulated here in terms of a constrained optimisation problem (Brest, Žumer and Maučec, 2006).

The constrained optimisation problem formulated here, in the configuration of a CaRBS system, is solved here using Trigonometric Differential Evolution (TDE) (Storn and Price, 1997; Fan and Lampinen, 2003). The domain of TDE is the continuous space made up of the $4n_C$ control variable values needed to be assigned values (in the THA problem). For an alternative configured system, its series of control variable values are represented as a point in this continuous space (parameter/target vector). In TDE, a population of *NP* parameter vectors, $\overrightarrow{y_h^G}$, $h = 1, \ldots, NP$, is considered at each generation G of the progression to an optimum solution, measured through a defined objective function (the OB in this chapter).

Starting with an initial population, TDE generates new parameter vectors by adding to a third member the difference between two other members (this change is subject to a crossover operator with parameter *CR*). If the resulting vector yields a lower OB value then a predetermined population member takes its place. More formally, a parameter vector $\overrightarrow{y_h^G}$ is made up of the values $y_{h,k}^G$, $k = 1, \ldots, 4n_C$ in the Gth generation. In the next generation the possible change in a value $y_{h,k}^G$ to a mutant vector value $z_{h,k}$ is given by;

$$z_{h,k} = y_{r_1,k}^G + F(y_{r_2,k}^G - y_{r_3,k}^G), \tag{4}$$

where $r_1, r_2, r_3 \cdot [1, NP]$, are integer and mutually different, with $F > 0$ and controls the amplification of the differential variation. This construction of a trial vector $\vec{z_h}$ is elucidated in Figure 2, where an example two dimensional (X_1, X_2) case is presented.

In Figure 2, the effect of the 'vector' difference between $\overrightarrow{y_{r_2}^G}$ and $\overrightarrow{y_{r_3}^G}$ on the constructed mutant vector $\vec{z_h}$ from $\overrightarrow{y_{r_1}^G}$ is elucidated. A further operation takes into account the OB values associated with the three vectors $\overrightarrow{y_{r_1}^G}$, $\overrightarrow{y_{r_2}^G}$ and $\overrightarrow{y_{r_3}^G}$ chosen, used to perturb the trial vector according to the following formulation;

$$z_{h,k} = (y_{r_1,k}^G + y_{r_2,k}^G + y_{r_3,k}^G)/3 + (p_2 - p_1)(y_{r_1,k}^G - y_{r_2,k}^G)$$
$$+ (p_3 - p_2)(y_{r_2,k}^G - y_{r_3,k}^G) + (p_1 - p_3)(y_{r_3,k}^G - y_{r_1,k}^G), \tag{5}$$

Figure 2. Example of an OB with contour lines and process for generation of the new vector $\vec{z_i}$

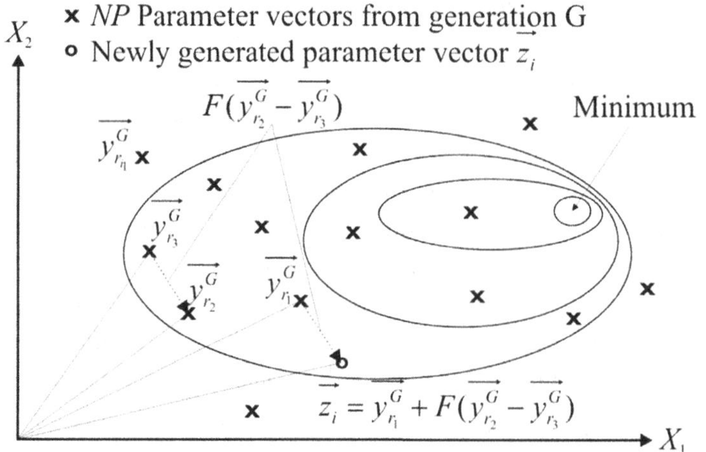

where $p_1 = \text{OB}(\overrightarrow{y_{r_1}^G})/p_T$, $p_2 = \text{OB}(\overrightarrow{y_{r_2}^G})/p_T$ and $p_3 = \text{OB}(\overrightarrow{y_{r_3}^G})/p_T$ with $p_T = \text{OB}(\overrightarrow{y_{r_1}^G}) + \text{OB}(\overrightarrow{y_{r_2}^G}) + \text{OB}(\overrightarrow{y_{r_3}^G})$. This trigonometric operation, which is the development in TDE (Fan and Lampinen, 2003) from the original differential evolution (Storn & Price, 1997), on occasions, takes the place of the original mutation (see (4)) using a 'trigonometric mutation probability' parameter M_t, where a random value less than M_t implies the use of the trigonometric mutation. A crossover operator then combines the mutant vector $\vec{z}_h = [z_{h,1}, z_{h,2}, \ldots, z_{h,4n_C}]$ with the target (old) vector $\overrightarrow{y_h^G} = [y_{h,1}^G, y_{h,2}^G, \ldots, y_{h,4n_C}^G]$ into a trial vector $\overrightarrow{y_h^T} = [y_{h,1}^T, y_{h,2}^T, \ldots, yh_{i,4n_C}^T]$ according to;

$$y_{h,j}^T k = \begin{cases} z_{h,k} & \text{If rand}(j) \leq CR, \\ y_{h,k}^G & \text{If rand}(j) > CR, \end{cases} \tag{6}$$

where rand(j) · [0, 1] is a random value and CR is the defined crossover constant. It follows, if $\text{OB}(\overrightarrow{y_h^T}) < \text{OB}(\overrightarrow{y_h^G})$ then replacement takes place and the progression continues. The progression of the construction of new generations continues until a satisfactory OB value is achieved. This may mean a required level has been attained or a zero decrease in the OB value is identified (over a number of generations). The necessary operating parameters used throughout this paper with TDE, were (Fan & Lampinen, 2003): amplification control $F = 0.99$, crossover constant $CR = 0.85$, trigonometric mutation probability $M_t = 0.05$ and number of parameter vectors $NP = 200$.

CaRBS Analysis (and Description of Total Hip Athroplasty)

The main thrust of this chapter is the elucidation of the CaRBS technique in a pertinent application. The application considered is concerned with expositing the level of gait function associated with subjects known, or not known, to have had one of two approaches to hip replacement, called the total hip arthroplasty (THA) problem.

This section of the chapter first describes the THA problem, followed by three CaRBS based analyses investigating the difference between subjects types considered in the THA problem (the first of which gives intermediate 'tutorial' calculations when using CaRBS).

Description of Total Hip Arthroplasty (THA) Problem

Patients with movement disorders are occasionally referred to clinical motion-analysis laboratories, where a wealth of biomechanical data relating to the functional abnormality of a patient is collected, for example, range of movement, walking speed, etc. However, the reality is, it is extremely difficult to objectively analyze and gain conclusions from such a wealth of data. Benedetti *et al.* (1998, p. 204) commented, "it is often not easy for the clinician to examine so much data without a systematic and rigorous approach".

Chau (2001a; 2001b) presented extensive reviews of the techniques applied to the "formidable task" of gait-data analysis. Such techniques include multivariate statistics, fuzzy methods, wavelet analysis, fractal analysis, and artificial neural networks (see for example the references contained in Chau, 2001a;

2001b). These and other methods have been developed to manipulate and interpret data that use the various characteristics of an object (patient) to aid in their classification to a particular category.

Hip osteoarthritis is treated by replacing the diseased joint with artificial components in a procedure called Total Hip Arthroplasty (THA). Whatling *et al.* (2008, p. 897) succinctly describe the reasons for THA,

"Total hip arthroplasty (THA) is a common procedure for the treatment of hip osteoarthritis and is successful in reducing pain and improving function and patient quality of life."

THA is routinely performed to effectively relieve the pain and disability associated with hip osteoarthritis (Ritter *et al.*, 1995). Despite the success of a THA, hip biomechanics during level gait does not always return to what is typically quantified as normal (Madsen *et al.*, 2004, Whatling *et al.*, 2008).

There are two main surgical approaches to THA (see Whatling *et al.* (2008), and references contained therein). These are the direct lateral approach (LA) where the hip is accessed from the side of the joint and the posterior approach (PA) where the joint is accessed from behind (see McFarland and Osborne, 1956; Moore, 1959). There are understood advantages and disadvantages of the employment of LA or PA, with comparisons between the surgical approaches undertaken, based on a variety of gait function features, see for example, Downing *et al.* (2001) and Jolles and Bogoch (2004).

The level of function restored by the new joint may be influenced by the choice of surgical approach. It is important to establish whether this is an influential factor on patient recovery, as currently there is no common consensus on the best surgical approach. In this chapter, subject specific features from gait analyses (see Table 1) were selected from three subject types, broken down to, 14 LA subjects, 13 PA subjects and 16 subjects with no hip pathology (NP), the latter forming a control group (see Whatling *et al.*, 2008).

In this exploratory study, only four features are considered, describing different aspects of the gait function of subjects, see Downing *et al.* (2001), Jolles and Bogoch (2004) and Whatling *et al.* (2008) for fuller descriptions of similar subject based features.

To offer some indication on the underlying diversity existing in the subject based features, descriptive statistics of the feature values over the different subject types are briefly considered, see Table 2.

Table 1. Descriptions of subject based features, C1, C2, C3 and C4

Label	Description	Contribution
C1	A Principal component of the hip flexion-extension waveform during level gait. The Principal component represents hip extension from initial foot contact to early terminal stance and from initial swing until the end of the gait cycle	Magnitude of the principal component score decreases with an increase in hip extension.
C2	A Principal component of the pelvic obliquity (pelvic position in the frontal plane) waveform. The Principal Component represents pelvic obliquity during early loading response, from mid-stance to terminal stance and from the end of the terminal stance to the end of the gait cycle	Magnitude of the principal component score increases with an increase in pelvic obliquity
C3	A Principal component of the hip power waveform in the frontal anatomical plane, during the stance phase of gait. The Principal component represents frontal hip power during four periods of the stance phase	Magnitude of the principal component score increases with a decrease in frontal plane hip power
C4	A Principal component of the frontal hip moment waveform during the stance phase of gait. Principal component representing frontal hip moment from late loading response to mid pre-swing phase.	Magnitude of the principal component score increases with an increase in frontal plane hip moment

Table 2. Descriptive statistics of the subject based feature values associated with different subject group types

	C1	C2	C3	C4
LA	[−16.64, 3.26, 18.00] 8.06	[−17.17, −0.92, 17.97] 9.10	[0.27, 4.53, 12.67] 3.50	[−24.60, −5.13, 5.06] 8.62
PA	[−9.88, 0.37, 12.19] 7.40	[−11.43, −2.26, 4.62] 4.87	[−10.65, 0.95, 8.71] 4.86	[−10.09, 3.38, 13.30] 7.13
NP	[−13.86, −3.16, 3.78] 6.16	[−5.29, 2.64, 12.65] 6.47	[−15.83, −4.73, 2.96] 4.98	[−7.49, 1.74, 9.27] 5.00

In Table 2, for each feature, and a specific subject type, the minimum, mean and maximum feature values are presented, with the concomitant standard deviation values shown below them. A brief inspection of these values shows, in most cases, an overlap of sub-domains of values. However, some trends are noticeable, for example, for the feature C3, working down the table, considering LA, then PA and then NP, there is a general decrease in the associated values (the minimum, mean and maximum values all decrease in value as the different subject group types are considered).

In the subsequent sub-sections of this section the CaRBS technique is employed to discern between pairs of subject group types (LA against PA, LA against NP and PA against NP).

CaRBS Analyses of THAs

The CaRBS analyses in this section, following its description previously, includes a discussion an exposition of the levels of fit of the different models investigated (configured CaRBS system), as well as insights into the contribution of the considered features describing the gait of subject types associated with total hip arthroplasty (LA, PA and NP in this analysis).

Discerning between Subject Types LA and PA

The first model considered, with intermediate calculations included, is on the discernment of LA (considered the hypothesis (x = LA) here and assigned value 1 in analysis) and PA (considered the not-the-hypothesis ($\neg x$ = PA) and assigned value 0). This analysis compares against the gait function of subjects known to have had a hip replacement, using either of the lateral and posterior surgical approaches for THA (it is not taking into account the control group NP).

To configure a CaRBS system through the minimisation of the respective OB, the subject based feature values were initially standardised (using the descriptive statistics similar to those presented in Table 2), prior to the employment of TDE (see later), allowing consistent domains over the control variables incumbent in CaRBS, set as; $-6 \leq k_i \leq 6$, $-3 \leq \theta_i \leq 3$, $0 \leq A_i < 1$ and $B_i = 0.7$ (see Fan & Lampinen, 2003; Beynon, 2005b). The upper bound on the B_i control variables ensured a predominance of ignorance in the evidence from individual characteristic values (in the concomitant feature BOEs next constructed - see Beynon, 2005b), so reduced over-conflict during the combination of the pieces of evidence (combination of feature BOEs).

The TDE method was employed, based on the previously defined TDE-based parameters, and run five times, each time converging to an optimum value, the best out of the five runs being OB = 0.265

Table 3. Control variables values associated subject based features, when discerning between subject types LA and PA, using OB in the configuration of CaRBS system

Feature	C1	C2	C3	C4
k_i	6.000	−6.000	6.000	−6.000
θ_i	−0.484	−1.306	−0.649	0.602
A_i	0.668	0.833	0.360	0.186

(there was little difference in the control variable values found over the different runs as previously found in Storn & Price, 1997). A reason for the OB value being away from its lower bound of zero is related to the implicit minimum levels of ignorance associated with each feature BOE (fixing of the B_i control variable values), possibly also due to the presence of conflicting evidence from the different features.

The resultant CaRBS associated control variables found from the best TDE run are reported in Table 3. A brief inspection of these results, with referral to Figure 1, shows the uniformity in the absolute values of the k_i control variables, but with the directions of influence of the four features split, with two, C1 and C3 showing positive relationship (going from PA to LA - see later) and the other two, C2 and C4, showing negative relationship (going from PA to LA). This exhibits the attempt to offer most discernment between the types LA (the hypothesis x in this case) and PA (not-the-hypothesis $\neg x$ in this case), in the evidence from the subject based features (see Figure 1 and definition of confidence factor $cf_i(\cdot)$). The role of these defined control variable values is to allow the construction of feature BOEs and their subsequent combination to formulate a series of subject BOEs for the 27 subjects considered (total of subject types LA and PA).

The construction of a feature BOE is next demonstrated, considering the subject S_9 and the subject based feature C4. Starting with the evaluation of the confidence factor $cf_{C4}(\cdot)$ (see Figure 1*a*), for the respondent S_9, C4 = 30.889, when standardised, it is $v_{9,C4} = 0.509$ (see Table 4 presented later), then;

$$cf_{C4}(0.509) = \frac{1}{1+e^{-(-6.000)(0.509-0.602)}} = \frac{1}{1+0.572} = 0.636,$$

using the control variables in Table 3. This confidence value is used in the expressions making up the mass values in the characteristic BOE $m_{9,C4}(\cdot)$, as given by (1), namely; $m_{9,C4}(\{LA\})$, $m_{9,C4}(\{PA\})$ and $m_{9,C4}(\{LA, PA\})$, found to be;

$$m_{9,C4}(\{LA\}) = \max(0, \frac{0.7}{1-0.187}0.636 - \frac{0.187\times 0.7}{1-0.187}) = \max(0, 0.547 - 0.160),$$

$$= \max(0, 0.387) = 0.387,$$

$$m_{9,C4}(\{PA\}) = \max(0, \frac{-0.7}{1-0.187}0.636 + 0.7) = \max(0, -0.547 + 0.7),$$

$$= \max(0, 0.153) = 0.\ 153,$$

Table 4. Feature values and feature BOEs for the subjects, S_9 and S_{15}, when discerning between subject types LA and PA, using OB in configuration of CaRBS system

BOE	C1	C2	C3	C4
S_9 (actual)	2.186	2.922	5.421	3.546
S_9 (standardised)	0.040	0.606	0.572	0.509
$m_{9,i}(\{LA\})$	0.613	0.000	0.699	0.387
$m_{9,i}(\{PA\})$	0.000	0.700	0.000	0.153
$m_{9,i}(\{LA, PA\})$	0.387	0.300	0.301	0.460
S_{15} (actual)	11.197	−1.559	1.361	6.553
S_{15} (standardised)	1.183	0.001	−0.316	0.843
$m_{15,i}(\{LA\})$	0.700	0.000	0.570	0.004
$m_{15,i}(\{PA\})$	0.000	0.698	0.000	0.536
$m_{15,i}(\{LA, PA\})$	0.300	0.302	0.430	0.460

$m_{9,C4}(\{LA, PA\}) = 1 - 0.387 - 0.153 = 0.460.$

For the subject S_9, this feature BOE is representative of all the associated feature BOEs $m_{9,i}(\cdot)$, presented in Table 4 (using standardised feature values), along with those for the subject S_{15}. These feature BOEs describe the evidential support from all the perceived subject based feature values, associated with a subject (S_9 and S_{15} are known to be of subject types LA and PA respectively).

In Table 4, for the evidence from the features to support correct classification of the subject S_9, in this case to the subject type LA ({LA}), it would be expected for the $m_{9,i}(\{LA\})$ mass values in the feature BOEs to be larger than their respective $m_{9,i}(\{PA\})$ mass values, which is the case for the features, C1, C3 and C4, whereas the feature C2 offers more evidence towards the subject being associated with subject type PA. The predominance of feature BOEs supporting correct classification (of those giving evidence), is reflected in the final subject BOE $m_9(\cdot)$ produced (through the combination of all the feature BOEs for this subject using (2)), which has mass values $m_9(\{LA\}) = 0.769$, $m_9(\{PA\}) = 0.179$ and $m_9(\{LA, PA\}) = 0.052$. This respondent BOE, with $m_9(\{LA\}) = 0.769 > 0.179 = m_9(\{PA\})$, suggests the subject S_9 is more associated with subject type LA, which is the correct classification in this case.

For the subject S_{15}, the evidence from the subject based features is more conflicting, with two features, C1 and C3, offering evidence towards the subject being associated with the subject type LA, and the other two C2 and C4 offering evidence towards its association with subject type PA. The combination of the concomitant features BOEs produces a subject BOE $m_{15}(\cdot)$, with $m_{15}(\{LA\}) = 0.487$, $m_{15}(\{PA\}) = 0.442$ and $m_{15}(\{LA, PA\}) = 0.072$, which indicates slightly more association to LA ({LA}), which is in-correct in this case since it is known to be associated with subject type PA.

For further interpretation of the feature and subject BOEs associated with the subjects, S_9 and S_{15}, their graphical representations as simplex coordinates in a simplex plot are reported in Figure 3.

Figures 3a and 3b, offer a visual representation of the evidence from the four subject based features to the classification of the subjects, S_9 and S_{15}, as to whether they are of subject types LA and PA. In each simplex plot the dashed vertical line partitions the regions in a simplex plot where either of the mass values assigned to {PA} (to the left) and {LA} (to the right) is the larger in a BOE (feature or

Figure 3. Simplex coordinates of feature and subject BOEs for the subjects, S_9 and S_{15}, when discerning between subject types LA and PA, using OB in configuration of CaRBS system

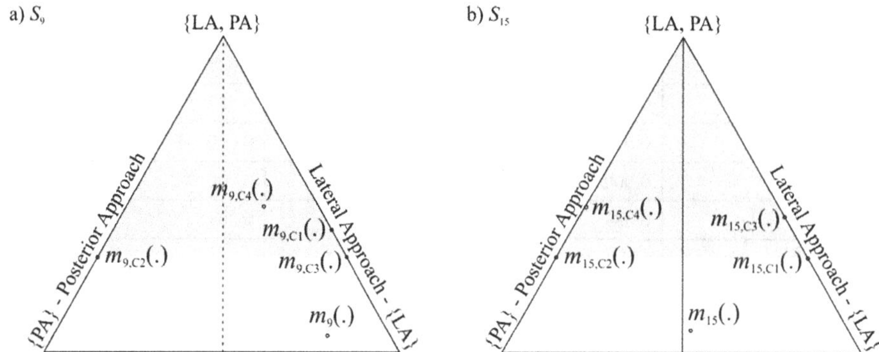

subject BOE). The grey shaded sub-regions show the domains where the feature BOEs can exist (due to the bounds on B_i control variables).

Inspection of these simplex plots, with referral to Table 4, clearly elucidates the contribution of the evidences from the different subject based features. For example, in the case of the subject S_{15} the conflict in the evidences from the features is clearly shown, along with the ambiguity of the final classification of this subject (the subject BOE $m_{15}(.)$ is near the vertical line in the simplex plot in Figure 3b).

The predicted association of each of the 27 considered subjects can be similarly made, representing the subject BOEs as simplex coordinates in a simplex plot, to the lateral (LA) and posterior (PA) approaches to THA, see Figure 4.

Figures 4a and 4b partition the presentation of the subjects' subject BOEs between those subjects known to be associated with having lateral (4*a*) and posterior (4*b*) approaches to THA, where each subject BOE is labelled with a circle and cross, respectively. Based on their subject BOEs' simplex coordinate positions either side of the vertical dashed lines in the simplex plots in Figure 4 (correct side denoted by the grey shaded regions), it was found 14 out of 14 (100.00%) and 9 out of 13 (69.23%) LA and PA subjects, respectively, were correctly classified as having the hip replacement approach they actually had. This combines to a total of 85.16% classification accuracy.

Figure 4. Simplex plot based representation of final subject BOEs for subject types LA and PA, using OB in configuration of CaRBS system

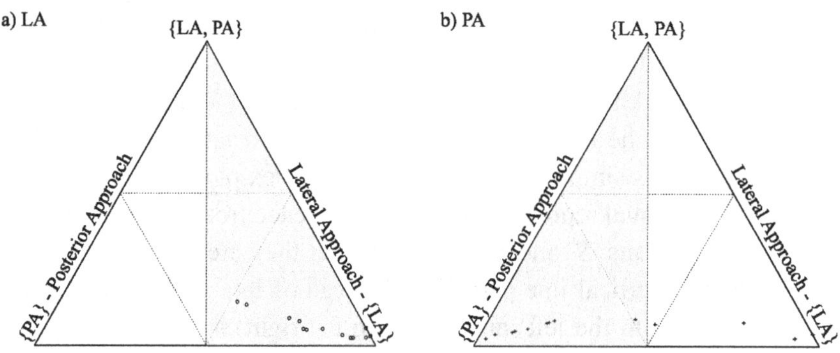

Beyond the level of fit of the CaRBS based model, consideration of the contribution of the individual respondent perceived subject based features can be graphically gauged from combining stages *a* and *b* in Figure 1, for the individual subject based features C1, C2, C3 and C4, see Figure 5.

In Figure 5, each graph shows the direct evidential contribution of the feature values of the considered subject based features. To elucidate, for the case of feature C1, in Figure 5a, as the feature values moves up from the sample minimum value of near −16.64 there is a gradual nonlinear decrease in the evidence supporting the a subjects association to being of subject type PA ($m_{j,\mathrm{C1}}(\{\mathrm{PA}\})$ decreases), down to zero near the value −2.86, with a corresponding increase in the level of ignorance associated with the evidence from this feature ($m_{j,\mathrm{C1}}(\{\mathrm{LA, PA}\})$ increases). Between the feature values −2.86 to −1.12, there is only total ignorance in the evidence from this feature ($m_{j,\mathrm{C1}}(\{\mathrm{LA, PA}\}) = 1$). As the feature value increases from near −1.12 upto its sample maximum value near 18.00, there is an increase in the evidence associating a subject to subject group type LA ($m_{j,\mathrm{C1}}(\{\mathrm{PA}\})$ increases), there is a corresponding decrease in the level of ignorance in the evidence ($m_{j,\mathrm{C1}}(\{\mathrm{LA, PA}\})$ decreases).

In summary, for the subject based feature C1, as the feature value increases from the sample minimum of near −16.64 upto the sample maximum of near 18.00, there is a move away from evidence to PA to evidence towards LA, here termed a positive relationship (also indicated by the positive number 6.00 for the k_1 control variable in Table 3). For the other features, C2, C3 and C4, in summary, they exhibit negative, positive and negative relationships with respect to evidence moving away from PA to LA.

The next two analyses briefly consider the equally important issue of how discerning each of the gait patterns of the each of the groups of subjects having had total hip replacement are with those subjects with no pathology (have not undertaken total hip replacement).

Discerning between Subject Types LA and NP

This section considers the ability to discern between gait functions, through subject based features, of subject types, LA (lateral approach to THA and considered the hypothesis x = LA - assigned value 1 in

Figure 5. Contribution diagrams showing the levels of exact belief in evidence towards subject types LA and PA over the different feature domains

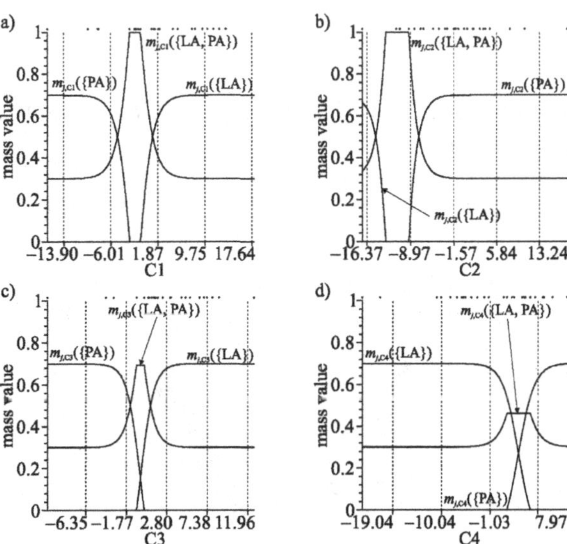

the analysis) and NP (no THA and considered the not-the-hypothesis $\neg x$ = NP - assigned value 0). In total there were 30 subjects in this analysis, with 14 and 16 subjects associated with subject types LA and NP, respectively. The analysis in this sub-section (and next) does not include example calculations in the construction of feature BOEs etc. (as in the previous section).

The TDE method for constrained optimisation was again employed, using the previously defined TDE-based parameters, and run five times, each time converging to an optimum value, the best out of the five runs being OB = 0.153 (again there was little difference in the control variable values found over the different runs as previously found in Storn and Price, 1997). The resultant CaRBS associated control variables found from the best TDE run are reported in Table 5.

The results in Table 5, concentrating on the k_i control variables values indicates the same directions of relationships as in the previous analysis (the same 6.000 and −6.000 values). That is, when discerning from NP to LA subject types, there are positive, negative, positive and negative directions of contribution from the subject based features, C1, C2, C3 and C4, respectively.

Concentrating on the level of fit of the configured CaRBS based model, the final subject BOEs are considered, in terms of their simplex coordinate positions in simplex plots, see Figure 6.

In Figure 6, the two graphs, Figures 6*a* and 6*b*, partition the presentation of the subjects' subject BOEs between those subjects known to be associated with having lateral approach to THA (6*a*) and no pathology (6*b*) (where each subject BOE is labelled with a circle and cross, respectively). Based on their simplex coordinate subject BOE positions either side of the vertical dashed lines in the simplex plots in Figure 1 (correct side denoted by the grey shaded regions), it was found 13 out of 14 (92.86%) and 16 out of 16 (100.00%) subjects were correctly classified as having the hip replacement approach they actually had. This combines to a total of 96.67% classification accuracy.

Table 5. Control variables values associated subject based features, when discerning between LA and NP, using OB in the configuration of CaRBS system

Feature	C1	C2	C3	C4
k_i	6.000	−6.000	6.000	−6.000
θ_i	0.140	−0.212	0.054	0.583
A_i	0.897	0.968	0.298	0.337

Figure 6. Simplex plot based representation of final subject BOEs for subject types LA and NP, using OB in configuration of CaRBS system

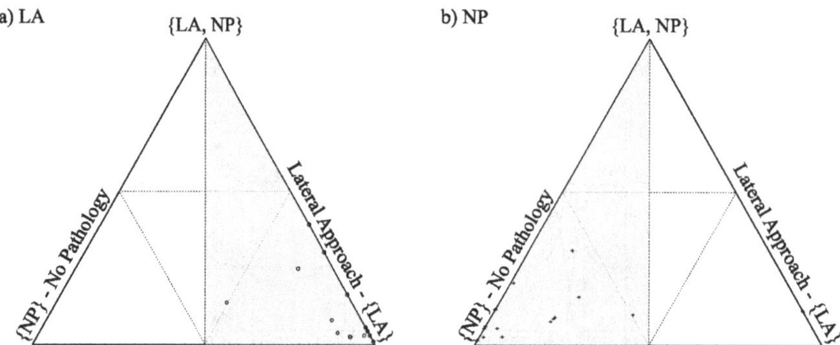

This accuracy result is larger than in the previous case (LA against PA), inspection of the respective simplex coordinates of subject BOEs presented in Figures 4 and 6, show, for certain subjects in Figure 6, there are higher levels of ignorance (simplex coordinates nearer top $\{x, \neg x\}$ vertex), which may have allowed for the better accuracy results.

Beyond the level of fit of the CaRBS based model, consideration of the contribution of the individual respondent perceived subject based features can be graphically gauged from combining stages *a* and *b* in Figure 1, for the individual subject based features C1, C2, C3 and C4, see Figure 7.

Concerning the results in Figure 7, for the features, C1, C2, C3 and C4, in summary, they exhibit positive, negative, positive and negative relationships with respect to evidence moving away from NP to LA (following the results surrounding Table 5).

Discerning between Subject Types PA and NP

This section considers the ability to discern between gait functions, through subject based features, of subject types, PA (posterior approach to THA and considered the hypothesis x = PA - assigned value 1 in the analysis) and NP (no THA and considered the not-the-hypothesis $\neg x$ = NP - assigned value 0). In total there were 29 subjects in this analysis, with 13 and 16 subjects associated with subject types PA and NP, respectively. The analysis in this sub-section (and next) does not include example calculations in the construction of feature BOEs etc. (as in the previous section).

The TDE method for constrained optimisation was again employed, using the previously defined TDE-based parameters, and run five times, each time converging to an optimum value, the best out of the five runs being OB = 0.253. The resultant CaRBS associated control variables found from the best TDE run are reported in Table 6.

Figure 7. Contribution diagrams showing the levels of exact belief in evidence towards subject types LA and NP over the different feature domains

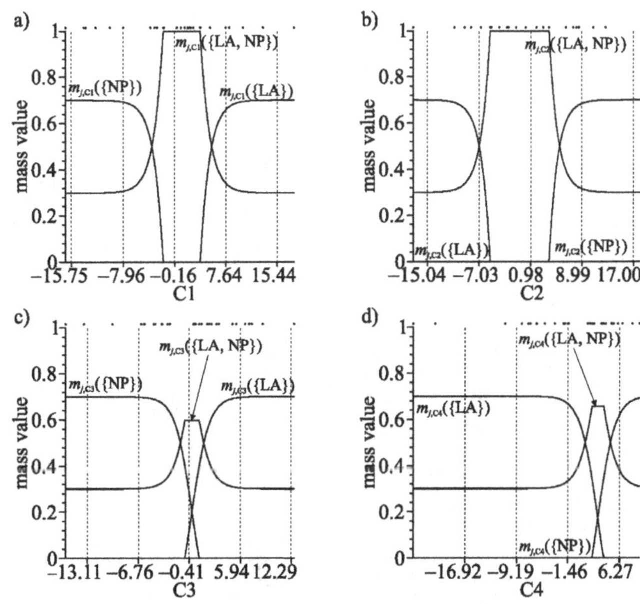

The results in Table 6, concentrating on the k_i control variables values indicates a variation of directions of relationships between the subject based features and subject types PA and NP. That is, when discerning from NP to PA subject types, there are negative, positive, negative and negative directions of contribution from the subject based features, C1, C2, C3 and C4.

Concentrating on the level of fit of the configured CaRBS based model, the final subject BOEs are considered, in terms of their simplex coordinate positions in simplex plots, see Figure 8.

Based on their simplex coordinate subject BOE positions either side of the vertical dashed lines in the simplex plots in Figure 1 (correct side denoted by the grey shaded regions), it was found 11 out of 13 (84.62%) and 13 out of 16 (81.25%) subjects were correctly classified as having the hip replacement approach they actually had. This combines to a total of 82.76% classification accuracy.

Beyond the level of fit of the CaRBS based model, consideration of the contribution of the individual respondent perceived subject based features can be graphically gauged from combining stages *a* and *b* in Figure 1, for the individual subject based features C1, C2, C3 and C4, see Figure 9.

Concerning the results in Figure 9, for the features, C1, C2, C3 and C4, in summary, they exhibit negative, positive, negative and negative relationships with respect to evidence moving away from NP to PA (following the results surrounding Table 5).

Table 6. Control variables values associated subject based features, when discerning between PA and NP, using OB in the configuration of CaRBS system

Feature	C1	C2	C3	C4
k_i	6.000	−6.000	6.000	4.974
θ_i	1.134	0.887	−0.005	−0.706
A_i	0.099	0.206	0.154	0.999

Figure 8. Simplex plot based representation of final subject BOEs for subject types PA and NP, using OB in configuration of CaRBS system

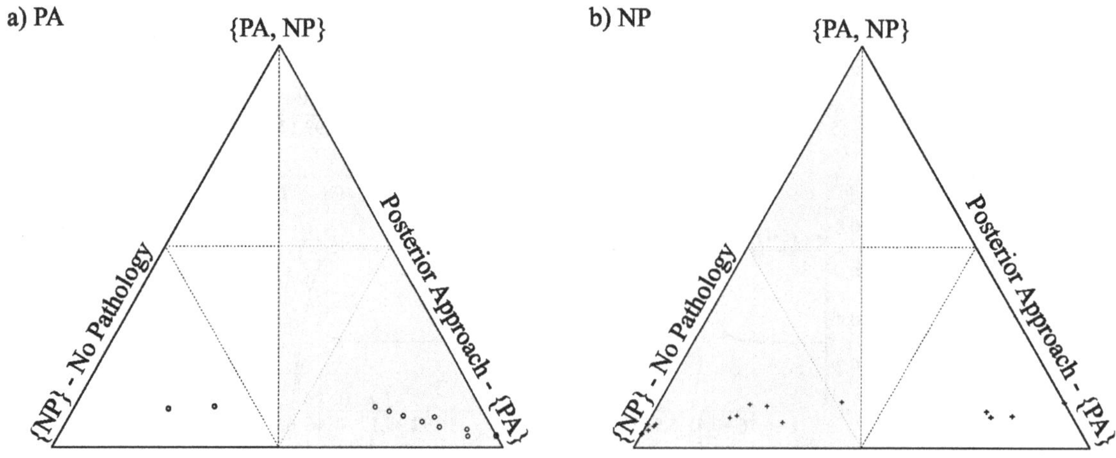

Figure 9. Contribution diagrams showing the levels of exact belief in evidence towards subject types PA and NP over the different feature domains

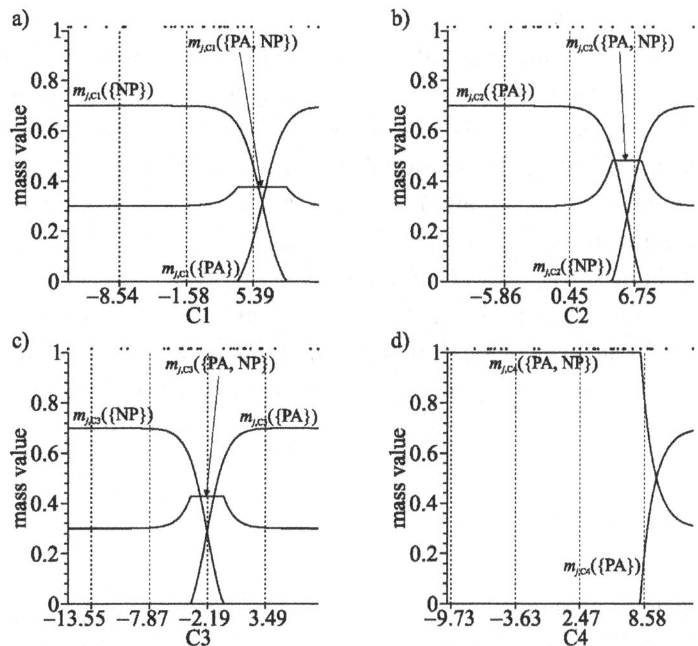

Future Research

As with any nascent technique the directions its development will take may be varied. The biomedical area of total hip arthroplasty, for example, has its own concerns on what it requires from a technique, further discussions with more practitioner-based individuals will identify the technical directions pertinent to their requirements.

There is a so far unconsidered issue worth mentioning, concerned with the often encountered problem of analysing incomplete data (with missing values present). That is, with the allowance for ignorance in the evidence a feature value may contribute, a missing value, when using the CaRBS technique, can be considered a totally ignorant piece of evidence and retained in the analysis, so not requiring any external management of the incomplete data. Within computer modelling, this issue regarding missing values demonstrates the new directions that analysis has to think about when considering the environment of uncertain reasoning.

Clearly, the CaRBS technique, being nascent in nature, will become an increasingly practical tool for analysis as it becomes more easily employed. For this to happen, there will have to be a concerted effort to produce this analysis tool in easily-usable software.

CONCLUSION

The elucidation of classification analysis is an important issue in many areas of work, including business, engineering and medicine. As a computational modelling problem, there is the need to look beyond the regularly identified model fit, at other issues that need to be considered. These further issues include the presentation or results, a noted issue in medical oriented problems, and the contribution of features in a performed classification analysis.

In terms of presentation of results, a significant emphasis when using the CaRBS technique is the ability to present findings using the simplex plot form of data representation. This form of representation can be adopted for both the final classification of subjects (their subject BOEs) as well as the influence of feature values to the classification of individual subjects (their feature BOEs). It is believed, in the future, with familiarisation, such presentation of results could become a standard form for the understanding of classification results, such in medical diagnosis etc.

In terms of the contribution of features (variables) in any models, the notion of uncertain reasoning is clearly shown. That is, for sub-domains of a feature it may offer total ignorance in the evidence it is contributing (unlike only the zero value in regression based approaches such as logistic regression). Ironically, it is uncertain, but exciting how uncertain reasoning may impact on the way computer modelling is thought about.

REFERENCES

Allen, R. (2001). Artificial intelligence and the evidentiary process: The challenges of formalism and computation. *Artificial Intelligence and Law*, *9*, 99–114. doi:10.1023/A:1017941929299

Barnden, J. A. (2001). Uncertain reasoning about agents' beliefs and reasoning. *Artificial Intelligence and Law*, *9*, 115–152. doi:10.1023/A:1017993913369

Benedetti, M. G., Catani, F., Leardini, A., Pignotti, E., & Giannini, S. (1998). Data management in gait analysis for clinical applications. *Clinical Biomechanics (Bristol, Avon)*, *13*(3), 204–215. doi:10.1016/S0268-0033(97)00041-7

Beynon, M., Curry, B., & Morgan, P. (2000). The Dempster-Shafer theory of evidence: An alternative approach to multicriteria decision modelling. *OMEGA - International Journal of Management Science, 28*(1), 37–50.

Beynon, M. J. (2005a). A novel technique of object ranking and classification under ignorance: An application to the corporate failure risk problem. *European Journal of Operational Research*, *167*, 493–517. doi:10.1016/j.ejor.2004.03.016

Beynon, M. J. (2005b). A novel approach to the credit rating problem: Object classification under ignorance. *International Journal of Intelligent Systems in Accounting Finance & Management*, *13*, 113–130. doi:10.1002/isaf.260

Beynon, M. J., Jones, L., & Holt, C. A. (2006). Classification of osteoarthritic and normal knee function using three-dimensional motion analysis and the Dempster-Shafer theory of evidence. *IEEE Transactions on Systems, Man, and Cybernetics. Part A, Systems and Humans*, *36*(1), 173. doi:10.1109/TSMCA.2006.859098

Brest, J., Žumer, V., & Maučec, M. S. (2006). *Self-adaptive differential evolution algorithm in constrained real-parameter optimization*. IEEE Congress on Evolutionary Computation, Vancouver, BC, Canada

Chau, T. (2001a). A review of analytical techniques for gait data, part 1: Fuzzy, statistical and fractal methods. *Gait & Posture*, *13*(1), 49–66. doi:10.1016/S0966-6362(00)00094-1

Chau, T. (2001b). A review of analytical techniques for gait data, part 2: Neural network and wavelet methods. *Gait & Posture*, *13*(2), 102–120. doi:10.1016/S0966-6362(00)00095-3

Cortes-Rello, E., & Golshani, F. (1990). Uncertain reasoning using the Dempster-Shafer method: An application in forecasting and marketing management. *Expert Systems: International Journal of Knowledge Engineering and Neural Networks*, *7*(1), 9–18. doi:10.1111/j.1468-0394.1990.tb00159.x

Daniel, M. (2006). On transformations of belief functions to probabilities. *International Journal of Intelligent Systems*, *21*, 261–282. doi:10.1002/int.20134

Dempster, A. P. (1967). Upper and lower probabilities induced by a multiple valued mapping. *Annals of Mathematical Statistics*, *38*, 325–339. doi:10.1214/aoms/1177698950

Downing, N., Clark, D., Hutchinson, J., Colclough, K., & Howard, P. (2001). Hip abductor strength following total hip arthroplasty: A prospective comparison of the posterior and lateral approach in 100 patients. *Acta Orthopaedica Scandinavica*, *72*(3), 215–220. doi:10.1080/000164701528465 01

Fan, H.-Y., & Lampinen, J. (2003). A trigonometric mutation operation to differential evolution. *Journal of Global Optimization*, *27*, 105–129. doi:10.1023/A:1024653025686

John, G. H., & Langley, P. (1995). Estimating continuous distributions in Bayesian classifiers. In *Proceedings of the 11th Conference on Uncertainty in Artificial Intelligence*.

Jolles, B., & Bogoch, E. (2004). Posterior versus lateral surgical approach for total hip arthroplasty in adults with osteoarthritis. *Cochrane Database of Systematic Reviews*, *1*, CD003828.

Jones, L., Beynon, M. J., & Holt, C. A. (2006). An application of the Dempster-Shafer theory of evidence to the classification of knee function and detection of improvement due to total knee replacement surgery. *Journal of Biomechanics*, *39*(13), 2512–2520. doi:10.1016/j.jbiomech.2005.07.024

Jones, L., & Holt, C. A. (2008). An objective tool for assessing the outcome of total knee replacement surgery. *Proceedings of the Institution of Mechanical Engineers (IMechE), Part H: J. Engineering in Medicine*, *222*(H5), 647–655. doi:10.1243/09544119JEIM316

Jones, L., Holt, C. A., & Beynon, M. J. (2008). Reduction, classification and ranking of motion analysis data: An application to osteoarthritic and normal knee function data. *Computer Methods in Biomechanics and Biomedical Engineering*, *11*(1), 31–40. doi:10.1080/10255840701550956

Kim, Z. W., & Nevatia, R. (1999). Uncertain reasoning and learning for feature grouping. *Computer Vision and Image Understanding*, *76*(3), 278–288. doi:10.1006/cviu.1999.0803

Lucas, C., & Araabi, B. N. (1999). Generalisation of the Dempster-Shafer theory: A fuzzy-valued measure. *IEEE Transactions on Fuzzy Systems*, *7*(3), 255–270. doi:10.1109/91.771083

Madsen, S., Ritter, M. A., Morris, H. H., Meding, J. B., Berend, M. E., Faris, P. M., & Vardaxis, V. G. (2004). The effect of total hip arthroplasty surgical approach on gait. *Journal of Orthopaedic Research*, *22*, 44–50. doi:10.1016/S0736-0266(03)00151-7

McFarland, B., & Osborne, G. (1956). Approach to the hip: A suggested improvement on Kocher's method. *The Journal of Bone and Joint Surgery. British Volume*, *36*(3), 364–367.

Moore, A. T. (1959). The Moore self-locking Vitallium prosthesis in fresh femoral neck fractures: A new low posterior approach (the southern exposure). In: *AAOS. Instructional Course Lectures*, *16*, 309–321.

Ritter, M. A., Albohm, M. J., Keating, E. M., Faris, P. M., & Meding, J. B. (1995). Comparative outcomes of total joint arthroplasty. *The Journal of Arthroplasty*, *10*(6), 737–741. doi:10.1016/S0883-5403(05)80068-3

Russell, S., & Norvig, P. (1995). *Artificial intelligence: A modern approach*. New York, NY: Prentice–Hall.

Safranek, R. J., Gottschlich, S., & Kak, A. C. (1990). Evidence accumulation using binary frames of discernment for verification vision. *IEEE Transactions on Robotics and Automation*, *6*, 405–417. doi:10.1109/70.59366

Shafer, G., & Srivastava, R. (1990). The Bayesian and belief-function formalisms: A general perspective for auditing. In Shafer, G., & Pearl, J. (Eds.), *Readings in uncertain reasoning*. San Mateo, CA: Morgan Kaufman Publishers Inc.

Shafer, G. A. (1976). *Mathematical theory of evidence*. Princeton, NJ: Princeton University Press.

Storn, R., & Price, K. (1997). Differential evolution–a simple and efficient heuristic for global optimization over continuous spaces. *Journal of Global Optimization*, *11*, 341–359. doi:10.1023/A:1008202821328

Whatling, G. M., Dabke, H. V., Holt, C. A., Jones, L., Madete, J., Alderman, P. M., & Roberts, P. (2008). Objective functional assessment of total hip arthroplasty following two common surgical approaches: The posterior and direct lateral approaches. *Proceedings of the Institution of Mechanical Engineers (IMechE), Part H: J. Engineering in Medicine*, *222*(H6), 897–905. doi:10.1243/09544119JEIM396

ADDITIONAL READING

Bohren, B. F., Hadzikadic, M., & Hanley, E. N. (1995). Extracting knowledge from large medical databases: an automated approach. *Computers and Biomedical Research, an International Journal*, *28*, 191–210. doi:10.1006/cbmr.1995.1013

Breiman, L. (2001). Statistical modelling: The two cultures. *Statistical Science*, *16*(3), 199–231. doi:10.1214/ss/1009213726

Csöndes, T., Kotnyek, B., & Szabó, J. Z. (2002). Application of heuristic methods for conformance test selection. *European Journal of Operational Research*, *142*(1), 203–218. doi:10.1016/S0377-2217(01)00284-3

Deluzio, K. J., Wyss, U. P., Costigan, P. A., Sorbie, C., & Zee, B. (1999). Gait assessment in unicompartmental knee arthroplasty patients: Principal component modeling of gait waveforms and clinical status. *Human Movement Science*, *18*, 701–711. doi:10.1016/S0167-9457(99)00030-5

Gioftsos, G., & Grieve, D. W. (1995). The use of neural networks to recognize patterns of human movement: Gait patterns. *Clinical Biomechanics (Bristol, Avon)*, *10*(4), 179–183. doi:10.1016/0268-0033(95)91395-U

Holzreiter, S. H., & Köhle, M. E. (1993). Assessment of gait patterns using neural networks. *Journal of Biomechanics*, *26*(6), 645–651. doi:10.1016/0021-9290(93)90028-D

Pandey, B., & Mishra, R. B. (2009). Knowledge and intelligent computing system in medicine. *Computers in Biology and Medicine*, *39*(3), 215–230. doi:10.1016/j.compbiomed.2008.12.008

Schubert, J. (1994). Cluster-based specification techniques in Dempster–Shafer theory for an evidential intelligence analysis of multiple target tracks. M.S. thesis, Department of Numerical Analysis and Computer Science, Royal Institute of Technology, Stockholm, Sweden.

Winter, D. A. (1987). *The Biomechanics and Motor Control of Human Gait*. Ontario: University of Waterloo Press.

Wu, W.-L., & Su, F.-C. (2000). Potential of the back propagation neural network in the assessment of gait patterns in ankle arthrodesis. *Clinical Biomechanics (Bristol, Avon)*, *15*(2), 143–145. doi:10.1016/S0268-0033(99)00037-6

KEY TERMS AND DEFINITIONS

Body of Evidence: From a piece of evidence (data value), a series of mass values and associated focal elements.

Confidence Factor: A function to transform a value into a standard domain, such as between 0 and 1.

Equivalence Class: Set of objects considered the same subject to an equivalence relation (e.g. those objects classified to x).

Evolutionary Algorithm: An algorithm that incorporates aspects of natural selection or survival of the fittest.

Focal Element: A finite non-empty set of hypotheses.

Mass Values: A positive function of the level of exact belief in the associated proposition (focal element).

Objective Function: A positive function of the difference between predictions and data estimates that are chosen so as to optimize the function or criterion.

Simplex Plot: Equilateral triangle domain representation of triplets of non-negative values which sum to one.

Uncertain Modelling: The attempt to represent uncertainty and reason about it when using uncertain knowledge, imprecise information, etc.

Total Hip Arthroplasty: General term associated with a common procedure for the treatment of hip osteoarthritis.

Trigonometric Differential Evolution: Constrained optimisation technique used in operations to configure CaRBS systems.

Chapter 9
Sigma Tuning of Gaussian Kernels:
Detection of Ischemia from Magnetocardiograms

Long Han
Rensselaer Polytechnic Institute, USA

Mark J. Embrechts
Rensselaer Polytechnic Institute, USA

Boleslaw K. Szymanski
Rensselaer Polytechnic Institute, USA

Karsten Sternickel
Cardiomag Imaging, Inc., USA

Alexander Ross
Cardiomag Imaging, Inc., USA

ABSTRACT

This chapter introduces a novel Levenberg-Marquardt like second-order algorithm for tuning the Parzen window σ in a Radial Basis Function (Gaussian) kernel. In this case, each attribute has its own sigma parameter associated with it. The values of the optimized σ are then used as a gauge for variable selection. In this study, the Kernel Partial Least Squares (K-PLS) model is applied to several benchmark data sets in order to estimate the effectiveness of the second-order sigma tuning procedure for an RBF kernel. The variable subset selection method based on these sigma values is then compared with different feature selection procedures such as random forests and sensitivity analysis. The sigma-tuned RBF kernel model outperforms K-PLS and SVM models with a single sigma value. K-PLS models also compare favorably with Least Squares Support Vector Machines (LS-SVM), epsilon-insensitive Support Vector Regression and traditional PLS. The sigma tuning and variable selection procedure introduced in this chapter is applied to industrial magnetocardiogram data for the detection of ischemic heart disease from measurement of the magnetic field around the heart.

DOI: 10.4018/978-1-60960-551-3.ch009

BACKGROUND OF SIGMA TUNING

This chapter introduces a novel tuning mechanism for Gaussian or Radial Basis Function (RBF) kernels where each attribute (or feature) is characterized by its own Parzen window sigma. The kernel trick is frequently used in machine learning to transform the input domain into a feature domain where linear methods are then used to find an optimal solution to a regression or classification problem. Support Vector Machines (SVM), Kernel Principal Component Regression (K-PCR), Kernel Ridge Regression (K-RR), Kernel Partial Least Squares (K-PLS) are examples of techniques that apply kernels for machine learning and data mining. There are many different possible kernels, but the RBF (Gaussian) kernel is one of the most popular ones. Equation (1) represents a single element in the RBF kernel,

$$k(i,j) = e^{-\frac{\left\|x_i - x_j\right\|^2}{2\sigma^2}} \tag{1}$$

where x_i and x_j denote two sample data. Traditionally, most machine learning approaches use a single value σ in the RBF kernel (as indicated in the equation above), which then needs to be tuned on a validation or tuning data set. In this paper each attribute is associated with a different σ value which is then tuned based on a validation data set with the aim to achieve a prediction performance that is an improvement over the one achieved by the RBF kernels with a single σ. The expression for a single RBF kernel entry becomes,

$$k(i,j) = \prod_{l=1}^{m} e^{-\frac{\left\|x_i^l - x_j^l\right\|^2}{2\sigma_l^2}} \tag{2}$$

where m is the number of attributes in the sample data. There are several advantages of using an automated tuning algorithm for a vector of σ rather than selecting a single scalar variable:

- Manual tuning for multiple σ-values is a tedious procedure;
- The same automated procedure applies to most machine learning methods that use an RBF kernel;
- The values of the optimized σ can be used as a gauge for variable selection (Specht, 1990).

LITERATURE OVERVIEW

Automated tuning of the kernel parameters is an important problem, it could be used in all different scientific applications: such as image classification (Guo, 2008; Claude, 2010) and time series data forecasting (He, 2008; Rubio, 2010), etc. A number of researchers have proposed algorithms for solving it, especially in the context of SVMs. Related work includes Grandvalet et al. (Grandvalet, 2002), which introduced an algorithm for automatic relevance determination of input variables in SVMs. Relevance is measured by scale factors defining the input space metric. The metric is automatically tuned by the minimization of the standard SVM empirical risk, where scale factors are added to the usual set of parameters defining the classifier. Cristianini et al. (Cristianini, 1998) applied an iterative optimization scheme to estimate a single kernel width hyper-parameter in SVM classifiers. In its procedure, model selection and learning are not separate, but kernels are dynamically adjusted during the learning process to find the kernel parameter which provides the best possible upper bound on the generalization error. Chapelle et al. (Chapelle, 2002) extend the single kernel width hyper-parameter to multiple-sigma parameters for solving the same problem in SVMs in order to perform adaptive scaling and variable selection. An example of this method is extended to Gaussian Automatic Relevance Determination kernel via optimization of kernel polarization (Wang, 2010). A further extension includes a multi-Class feature selection in the application of text classification (Chapelle, 2008). Chapelle et al's method has the advantage that the gradients are computed analytically as opposed to the empirical approximation used in this paper. The algorithm proposed in this paper is very similar to the one proposed by Chapelle et al. However, the approach in this study is different in the sense that we use a Levenberg-Marquardt-like optimization approach, which uses a λ parameter that gradually changes the algorithm from a first-order to a second-order. In addition, we use a Q^2 error metric which shows more robustness on unbalanced data sets and a leave-several-out validation option for improved computing time, and, finally, we apply the algorithm to K-PLS rather than SVMs.

Kernel Partial Least Squares

Partial Least Squares (PLS) (H. Wold, 1966) was introduced by a Swedish statistician Herman Wold for econometrics modeling of multi-variate time series. Currently PLS has become one of the most popular and powerful tools in chemometrics and drug design after it was applied to chemometrics in the early eighties (S.Wold, 2001). PLS can be viewed as a "better" Principal Components Analysis (PCA) regression method, where the data are first transformed into a different and non-orthogonal basis and only the most important PLS components (or latent variables) are considered for building a regression model (similar to PCA). The difference between PLS and PCA is that the new set of basis vectors in PLS is not a set of successive orthogonal directions that explain the largest variance in the data, but are actually a set of conjugant gradient vectors to the correlation matrix that form a Krylov space (Ilse, 1998), a widely used iterative method for successfully solving large system of linear equations in order to avoid matrix-matrix operations, currently available in numerical linear algebra. PLS regression is one of the most powerful data mining tools for large data sets with many variables with high collinearity. The NIPALS implementation of PLS (H.Wold, 1975) is elegant and fast.

Linear Kernel Partial Least Squares (K-PLS) was first described in (Lindgren, 1993) and applied to spectral analysis in the late nineties of twentieth century (Liu, 1999). Instead of linear K-PLS, Rosipal introduced K-PLS in 2001 (Rosipal, 2001) as a nonlinear extension to the PLS. This nonlinear extension of PLS makes K-PLS a powerful machine learning tool for classification as well as regression. K-PLS can also be formulated as a paradigm closely related (and almost identical) to Support Vector Machines (SVM) (Vapnik, 1998; Boser, 1992; Bennett, 2003). In addition, the statistical consistency of K-PLS is recently proved from theoretical perspective (Blanchard, 2010).

Applications of Kernel Partial Least Squares

Since K-PLS was introduced in 2001, researchers in chemometrics has gradually switched from PLS to K-PLS as a standard tool for the data mining (Embrechts, 2007; Tian, 2009). Meanwhile, K-PLS has been attracted by other researchers for different industrial applications such as face recognition (Štruc, 2009) and financial forecasting (Huang, 2010). In the specific domain (electrocardiogram, echocardiogram, and angiogram, etc) where signal is retrieved through sensor, machine learning has become a crucial tool for the signal analysis. PLS combining with different signal preprocess techniques are applied in different research projects. Partial least squares logistic regression was used for electroencephalograms for early detection of patients with probable Alzheimer's disease (Lehmann, 2007). Chen et al. (Chen, 2009) conducted partial least squares with Fourier transform in the near infrared reflectance spectroscopy to analyze the main catechins contents in green tea. In this paper, a sigma tuning of Gaussian kernel is applied on the magnetocardiogram for the diagnosis of ischemia heart disease. The sigma tuning procedure is implemented for a K-PLS model. The justification here for using K-PLS is that there is generally no significant difference in performance between K-PLS and other kernel-based learning methods such as SVMs (Han, 2006).

PERFORMANCE METRICS

A common way to measure error in regression modeling is via the Least Mean Square Error (LMSE), which is defined as the average value of the squared error between predictions for responses and target values according to:

$$LMSE = \sqrt{\frac{\sum_{i=1}^{n}(y_i - \hat{y}_i)^2}{n}} \tag{3}$$

Where y_i is the response value, $\hat{y}_i$ is its corresponding prediction value, and n is the number of samples. However, the LMSE is dependent on how the response variable is scaled. In order to overcome the scaling effect, two additional metrics are introduced here: r^2 and R^2. The first metric, r^2, is the square of coefficient of correlation between predicted and target values.

$$r^2 = \frac{(\sum_{i=1}^{n}(y_i - \bar{\hat{y}})(y_i - \bar{y}))^2}{\sum_{i=1}^{n}(y_i - \bar{\hat{y}})^2 \sum_{i=1}^{n}(y_i - \bar{y})^2} \tag{4}$$

Where $\bar{\hat{y}}$ and $\bar{y}$ are mean value for predictions, $\hat{y}$, and target values, y, respectively. r^2 is used for assessing the general quality of the trained model. Usually, a higher value for r^2 corresponds to a better trained model. An obvious drawback of r^2 as an error metric is that r^2 only measures a linear correlation, indicating how well the predictions, $\hat{y}$, follow a line if they are plotted as a function of y. While one might expect a nearly perfect model when r^2 is close to unity, this is not necessarily the case. For that reason, a second and more powerful error metric will be used: the so-called "Press R^2 squared", or R^2, which is commonly used in chemometric modeling. R^2 is defined as (Embrechts, 2004; Golbraikh, 2002):

$$R^2 = 1 - \frac{\sum_{i=1}^{n}(y_i - \hat{y}_i)^2}{\sum_{i=1}^{n}(y_i - \bar{y})^2} \tag{5}$$

The R^2 metric is usually very close to the r^2 metric, but is considered a more meaningful error metric than r^2 because it accounts for the residual error as well. The higher the value of R^2 is, the better is the model. However, it should be noted that in certain cases, the R^2 metric can actually become negative. For similar purposes, two related metrics are introduced to assess the performance of validation data or test data: q^2 and Q^2. They are defined as $1 - r^2$ and $1 - R^2$, respectively. They are only used in validation and tuning, and only on test data (never on training data).

In addition to the above error metrics, the area under the Receiver Operating Characteristic (ROC) Curve (Swets, 2000; Fawcett, 2001; Fawcett, 2003), AUC (Bradley, 1997), will be used for binary classification problems. The same algorithm will also be applied to regression data for comparative purposes, even though a physical interpretation of the AUC in that case is not obvious. For binary classification problems the balanced error (BE) will also be reported. The balanced error is defined as the average of the correct classification rate between the positive cases and the negative cases.

SIGMA TUNING ALGORITHM

In this part, the sigma tuning algorithm will first be explained. Metric Q^2 is chosen as an error metric, denoted as $E(\sigma)$, which depends on the vector σ. Leave-One-Out (LOO) K-PLS is used to obtain an initial Q_0^2 value based on an initial starting guess for the sigma-vector denoted as σ_0. A second-order gradient descent method is utilized to minimize the objective function $E(\sigma)$ and find the optimal choice for σ. The search process starts from the initial point $\mathrm{E}(\sigma_0) = Q_0^2$. The value of σ is updated based on the minimization of the leave-one-out (or alternatively, leave several out) tuning (or validation) error, rather than directly minimizing the training error (Figure 1). According to Newton's rule for finding a minimum in a multi-dimensional space, the relation between $E(\sigma)$ and σ at the minimum can be written as:

$$\sigma = \sigma_0 - \mathbf{H}^{-1} \bullet \nabla E(\sigma_0) \tag{6}$$

Where **H** is the Hessian matrix. $\nabla E(\sigma_0)$ is a vertical vector, as expressed by:

$$\nabla E(\sigma_0) = \nabla E(\sigma)\big|_{\sigma=\sigma_0} = \begin{pmatrix} \frac{\partial E}{\partial \sigma_1}\big|_{\sigma=\sigma_0} \\ \vdots \\ \frac{\partial E}{\partial \sigma_m}\big|_{\sigma=\sigma_0} \end{pmatrix} \tag{7}$$

After rearranging, the equation can be reorganized as

$$\mathbf{H} \bullet \Delta\sigma = -\nabla E(\sigma_0) \tag{8}$$

Figure 1. Process flow for sigma tuning

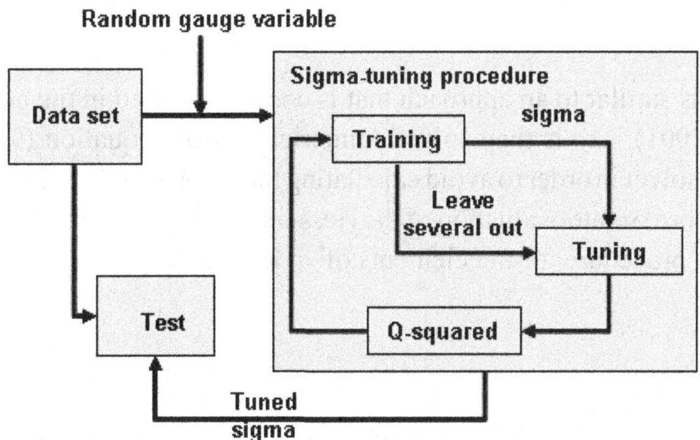

where $\Delta\sigma = \sigma - \sigma_0$. In order to efficiently proceed towards a converged solution, a Levenberg-Marquardt approach will be utilized. This is achieved by adding a small scalar λ to the diagonal elements in the Hessian **H**, as expressed by:

$$(\mathbf{H} + \lambda\mathbf{I})\bullet\Delta\sigma = -\nabla E(\sigma_0) \tag{9}$$

In this approach, the algorithm starts out as a first-order approach and gradually proceeds towards the second-order approach outlined below. We will solve equation (9) for $\Delta\sigma$.

Note that each element $\frac{\partial E}{\partial \sigma_i}|_{\sigma=\sigma_0}$ in the right side of equation (7) will be computed by numerical perturbation as shown below:

$$\frac{\partial E}{\partial \sigma_i}|_{\sigma=\sigma_0} \approx \frac{\Delta E}{\varepsilon}|_{\sigma=\sigma_0} = \frac{E(\sigma_i + \varepsilon) - E(\sigma_i)}{\varepsilon}|_{\sigma=\sigma_0} \tag{10}$$

where ε is a small perturbation value acting on the ith component in σ. $E(\sigma_i)$ is the performance metric Q^2 obtained from the change in the ith component of σ only.

A second approximation will be introduced before solving the above equations. Because the elements of the Hessian are expensive to evaluate, we will introduce a fast and efficient approximation for the Hessian matrix. Each element in the Hessian matrix is originally defined by:

$$\mathbf{H}(i,j) = \frac{\partial^2 E}{\partial \sigma_i \partial \sigma_j} \tag{11}$$

In principal, the second partial derivatives can be numerically calculated. However, in order to speed up the calculation process, the second-order partial derivatives are approximated by:

$$\frac{\partial^2 E}{\partial \sigma_i \partial \sigma_j} \approx \frac{\partial E}{\partial \sigma_i} \frac{\partial E}{\partial \sigma_j} \tag{12}$$

This approximation is similar to an approach that is commonly used in the neural network literature (Masters, 1995; Ham, 2001). $\Delta\sigma$ is then solved numerically from equation (9) with a fast conjugate gradient based equation solver in order to avoid calculating the inverse of the Hessian matrix, **H** (Suykens, 2003). Because of the approximate evaluation of the Hessian, a heuristic coefficient α will be introduced in the iterative updating procedure for the elements of σ leading to:

$$\sigma = \alpha\Delta\sigma + \sigma_0$$

The value of α is set to 0.5 which turns out to be a robust choice based on hundreds of experiments with this algorithm on different data sets. A more detailed description for the implementation of the algorithm is shown in Figure 1 and the sigma tuning algorithm is illustrated in the following:

1. Start with an initial guess σ_0 and calculate the initial Q^2 error metric from a leave-one-out K-PLS model and estimate $E(\sigma_0)$. Start with $\lambda = 1$.
2. ΔE Calculation: For each scalar σ_i calculate the corresponding element in ΔE by perturbation.
3. $\Delta\sigma$ Calculation: Solve equation (9) for $\Delta\sigma$ by using a fast conjugate gradient-based equation solver.
4. λ Adjustment: If the Q^2 error gets smaller, update σ and decrease $\lambda = 0.93\lambda$; otherwise, make no change for σ and increase $\lambda = 3.5\lambda$. If $\lambda > 1$, cap λ to unity.
5. Iterate the process: Use the new solution as a new starting point and go to step 2. If the error cannot be improved or the process reaches the iteration number limit, halt the procedure.

Note that both coefficients 0.93 and 3.5 are empirical values based on many experiments on different data sets.

VARIABLE SELECTION

Dimensionality reduction is a challenging problem for supervised and unsupervised machine learning for classification, regression, and time series prediction. In this section we focus on variable selection for supervised classification and regression models. The taxonomy of variable selection has two branches: variable ranking and subset selection (Blum, 1997; Guyon, 2003). Variable subset selection can be further divided into (i) wrappers, (ii) filters, and (iii) embedded methods. The pros and cons of different variable selection methods vary depending on the specific domain problem, computational expense, complexity, and Robustness (Guyon, 2003). In this study, a natural ranking of input variables is proposed based on the values of tuned Parzen window parameters, σ.

The original variables are ranked corresponding to the sigma ranking (from low to high σ values). Bottom-ranked variables, i.e., variables corresponding to a higher σ value correspond to features that do not contribute much to the calculation of the RBF kernel entry and are therefore less important. Some of the bottom-ranked variables can therefore be eliminated. The elimination phase can (i) proceed iteratively, where a few variables are dropped at a time, or (ii) proceed in a single-step greedy fashion. A random gauge variable (Embrechts, 2005; Bi, 2003) can be introduced to avoid discarding possibly significant variables. This random variable can either be uniform or Gaussian. Only features that rank below the random gauge variable will be eliminated (during a single step).

After the variable selection stage, a new K-PLS learning model is built based on different bootstraps with bagging in order to evaluate the performance of the sigma tuning based feature selection. Two benchmark data sets illustrate this procedure on a regression and a classification problem. Furthermore, the final predictive models are compared with alternate variable selection procedures based on (i) Random Forests (Han, 2006). Random Forests variable selection with PLS was introduced in (Han, 2006). For each variable subset, a PLS or K-PLS model is used for training and validation. For each variable, a score is based on the Q^2 metric for the model in which this variable participated. Finally, variables are ranked according to the average score of each feature. (ii) Sensitivity Analysis (Embrechts, 2005). The hypothesis of Sensitivity Analysis is that variables that change the output more when tweaked are more sensitive and therefore more important. Sensitivity Analysis can easily be implemented as follows: once a model is built, all features are frozen at their average values, and then, one-by-one, the features are tweaked within their allowable range. The features for which the predictions do not vary a lot when they are tweaked are considered less important, and they are slowly pruned out from the input data in a set of successive iterations between model building and feature selection (Embrechts, 2005). (iii) A simple linear kernel PLS model with Z-scores. Z-scores are a linear statistical method for selecting the important variables in a regression or classification problem (Hastie, 2003).

EXPERIMENTAL RESULTS

Benchmark Data

Sigma tuning based variable selection with K-PLS was benchmarked with two data sets: South African Heart Data (SAheart) and the Boston housing market data. The SAheart is a subset from a larger data set (Rousseauw, 1983) which defines an almost linear classification problem. It describes a retrospective sample of males in a high-risk heart-disease region of the Western Cape in South Africa. There are roughly two controls per case of Coronary Heart Disease (CHD). It consists of one response and nine variables: systolic blood pressure (sbp), cumulative tobacco consumption (tobacco), low density lipoprotein cholesterol level (ldl), adiposity, family history of heart disease (famhist), type-A behavior (typea), obesity, alcohol, and age. A total of 462 samples are included in this data set.

The Boston housing data is a standard benchmark regression data set from the UCI data Repository for Machine Learning (Merz, 1998). This benchmark data set has 506 samples with 12 continuous and one binary variable: per capita crime rate (CRIM), proportion of residential land zoned (ZN), proportion of non-retail business acres (INDUS), Charles River dummy variable (CHAS), nitric oxides concentration (NOX), average number of rooms (RM), proportion of owner-occupied units (AGE), weighted distances (DIS), index of accessibility (RAD), full-value property-tax rate (TAX), pupil-teacher ratio (PTRATIO), B value (B) and a percentage of population with low status(LSTAT) and one response variable: median value of owner-occupied homes (MEDV) in \$1000 and capped at \$50,000.

For each data set, 350 instances are randomly selected for training data, the remaining data are used as test data. We use normalization scaling to pre-process the data for both data sets.

During the sigma tuning stage, a leave-several-out K-PLS model with (tuned) 5 Latent Variables (LVs) was evaluated to calculate a Q^2-error metric from the training data. For both benchmark data sets, 70 data instances were randomly selected for a single leave-several-out validation case. 200 sigma tuning iterations were sufficient for a stable set of σ values. The starting value for σ_0 for the Boston Housing data is initialized to 2, a relatively low value. For the South Africa Heart, the initial value for σ is set to 30, because this data set is known to lead to linear machine learning models.

Before comparing different variable selection methods on the benchmark data, the results of a sigma-tuned K-PLS model are compared with those obtained from other machine learning methods include (i) Least Squares Support Vector Machines (LS-SVM), (ii) ε-insensitive Support Vector Regression (Chang, 2004) (ε-SVR), and (iii) PLS. The prediction results shown in Table 2 indicate that sigma-tuned K-PLS outperforms K-PLS with a single sigma value. The K-PLS results also outperform or are close to the other machine learning models. For the metrics presented in this table, the models were built by bagging all the models obtained from a leave-one-out training procedure.

For the variable selection based on sigma tuning, two criteria are used. One criterion is based on rejecting variables that correspond to larger σ; the second criterion aims to retain at least a similar performance metric between models with all the variables and models with a reduced set of variables. Based on the relative variable importance metric for the SAheart data, the variables "alcohol" and "obesity" were dropped from these data. Likewise, two variables, "CRIM" and "CHAS", are discarded from the original variables in the Boston housing data. Furthermore, when we continue to dropping the third variable, "ZN", the model with the remaining variables still maintains a similar prediction performance (Figure 3). Note that for both data sets only a few features are eliminated in order to maintain a prediction performance similar to the models without variable selection.

The results of variable reduction for both benchmark data sets are shown in Figure 3. Notice that the σ-tuning based feature selection results are better than the results obtained from the other two feature selection methods. Note also that by using leave-one-out modeling, the performance metrics have a low variance.

Figure 2. Experimental results with all variables

Data sets	q2	Q^2	AUC	LMSE	BE	Comments
Boston (σ Kernel-PLS)	0.127*	0.133*	-	3.882	-	LVs = 12
Boston (K-PLS)	0.129	0.135	-	3.904	-	LVs = 12, σ = 4
Boston (LS-SVM)	0.129	0.134	-	3.811	-	σ = 4
Boston (ε-SVR)	0.133	0.135	-	3.903	-	σ = 4
Boston (PLS)	0.260	0.278	-	5.607	-	-
SAheart (σ Kernel-PLS)	0.750	0.756	0.797	0.422	67.8	LVs = 3
SAheart (K-PLS)	0.760	0.766	0.790	0.426	68.8	LVs = 5, σ = 30
SAheart (LS-SVM)	0.730*	0.748*	0.812	0.421	68.8	σ = 30
SAheart (ε-SVR)	0.750	0.834	0.794	0.445	71.4	σ = 30
SAheart (PLS)	0.749	0.755	0.797	0.423	67.9	σ = 30

Notes: The * indicates the best performance

Figure 3. Experimental results with reduced set of variables

Data sets	q2	Q²	AUC	LMSE	BE	Comments
Boston (σ Tuning)	0.131*	0.136*	-	3.927	-	"crim", "chas"
Boston (RF)	0.134	0.142	-	4.008	-	"zn", "age"
Boston (Z-scores)	0.138	0.146	-	4.071	-	"age", "indus"
Boston (SA)	0.133	0.138	-	3.900	-	"zn", "indus"
SAheart (σ Tuning)	0.714*	0.721*	0.810	0.413	69.6	"obesity", "alcohol"
SAheart (RF)	0.762	0.768	0.793	0.426	69.6	"sbp", "alcohol"
SAheart (Z-scores)	0.762	0.768	0.793	0.426	69.6	"sbp", "alcohol"
SAheart (SA)	0.785	0.793	0.770	0.433	68.8	"sb", "ldl"

Notes: The * indicates the best performance

Figure 4. Left: the Magnetocardiograph, installed in a hospital room, without magnetic shielding. The figure shows the operator adjusting the subject's position and sensor head level above the torso. Right: Relative positions of the heart and the nine sensors (small circles) inside the cryostat housing at four consecutive positions over the body surface.

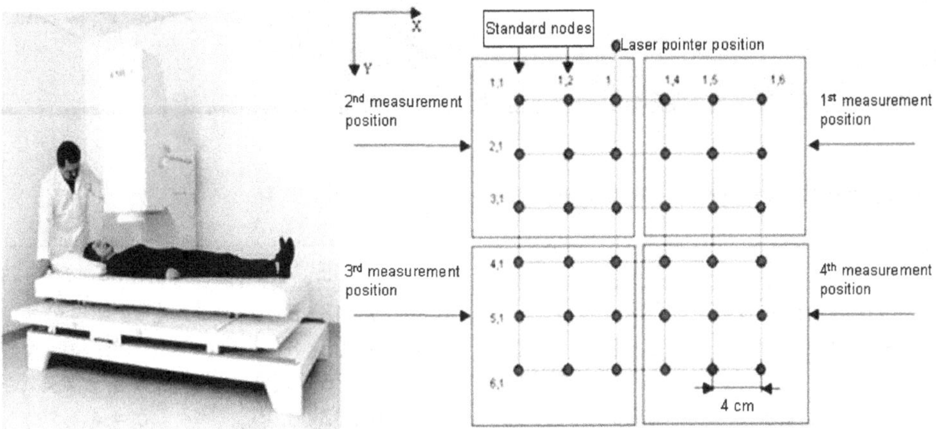

Classification of Magnetocardiograms

The aim of Magnetocardiogram (MCG) based cardiology is to rapidly identify and localize the onset of heart disease from measuring the magnetic field of the heart. In this application we are interested in detecting myocardial ischemia, i.e., a cardiac condition in which there is a restriction in blood supply to the heart. Figure 5 illustrates an MCG system (Model CMI-2049, CardioMag Imaging, Inc., Schenectady, NY) which collects cardiac magnetic field data at 36 points spread over the torso in four sequential measurements in mutually adjacent positions. Data acquisition at 1 kHz for 90 seconds per position results in 36 individual time series of 90,000 samples each. These data are filtered and averaged to produce average cardiac cycles at each of the 36 measurement points. Additional post-processing of the T-wave portion the average cardiac cycles yield a set of 74 variables. The 74 variables are related to delay behaviors of the individual signal traces in the T3-T4 region. 325 patients sample data were collected for the automated detection of ischemic heart disease. There are two response classes: negative and positive.

Figure 5. Left: Filtered and averaged temporal MCG Trace for one cardiac cycle in 36 channels (the 6x6 grid). Right Upper: Spatial map of the cardiac magnetic field generated at an instant within the ST interval. Right Lower: T3-T4 sub-cycle in one MCG signal trace.

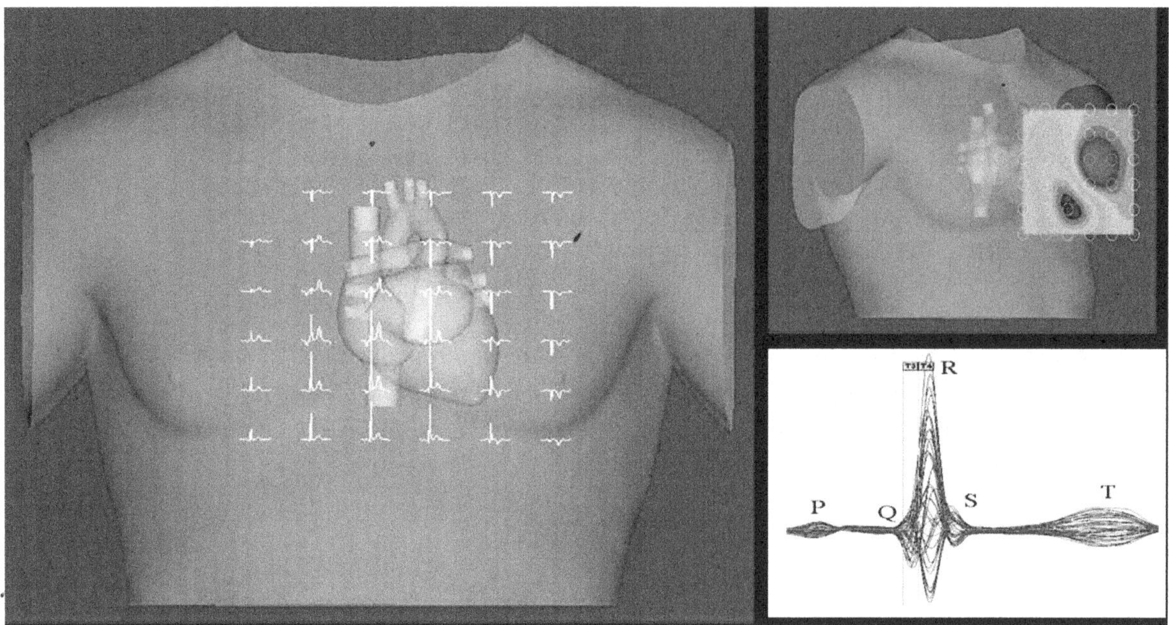

Figure 6. Experimental results for MCG data with all variables

Data sets	q2	Q²	AUC	LMSE	BE	Comments
MCG (σ Kernel-PLS)	0.542*	0.560*	0.884	0.743	81.0	LVs = 5
MCG (σ Kernel-PLS)	0.617	0.623	0.856	0.785	81.7	LVs = 5, group σ
MCG (K-PLS)	0.595	0.611	0.855	0.776	82.5	LVs = 5, σ = 4
MCG (LS-SVM)	0.607	0.622	0.845	0.783	82.5	σ = 4
MCG (ε-SVR)	0.626	0.651	0.838	0.801	81.7	σ = 4
MCG (PLS)	0.805	0.957	0.761	0.972	73.3	-

Notes: The * indicates the best performance

The MCG data are normalized and 241 instances are randomly selected as training data; the remaining 84 samples are used as test data.

For MCG data, five Latent Variables (LVs) were used. Deleted variables are listed in the last column of Figure 7. Figure 7 shows that Random Forests results outperform Z-scores ranking and they are close to those obtained from Sensitivity Analysis.

In this study, two experiments were conducted for these data that utilize the sigma tuning algorithm introduced in this study. In one case, three sets of variables are associated with three different Parzen window σ's, because each variable in one of these three sets has a very similar physical meaning. In the other case, each of the 74 variables is characterized by a different Parzen window σ. The sigma tun-

Figure 7. Experimental results for MCG data with reduced set of variables

Data sets	q2	Q2	AUC	LMSE	BE	Comments
MCG (σ Tuning)	0.551*	0.565*	0.880	0.747	80.7	7 vars deleted
MCG (RF)	0.611	0.621	0.852	0.782	81.7	7 vars deleted
MCG (Z-scores)	0.627	0.637	0.848	0.793	78.3	7 vars deleted
MCG (SA)	0.592	0.604	0.859	0.772	83.3	7 vars deleted

Notes: The * indicates the best performance

ing procedure is carried with 5 latent variables out in a leave-several-out model, where 50 data are left out from 241 with 120 iterations. The starting value for σ_0 is initialized to 2 as well.

For the experiment with three group σ's, the results illustrate a stable convergence of the sigma tuning algorithm. The last two features (#73 and #74) can be discarded from the model because of their large σ value. After discarding these two features, we still obtain undiminished prediction performance. 200 iterations are used for the second case experiment. Experimental results indicate that the variable ranking is relatively robust over the number of iterations. In the final model, as shown in Figure 7, the seven variables with the highest σ values are discarded, maintaining a similar Q^2 and q^2 performance as for the original 74 variable model. The final predictions for the test data are shown in Figure 8. Two probability density functions are generated based on the prediction results for each class. Note that the balance error depends on the setting of threshold. The threshold value for the results shown in Figure 8is set at zero. The corresponding confusion matrix is also illustrated in Figure 8.

Figure 8. Prediction results for the MCG data set with relative probability densities for the positive and negative classes

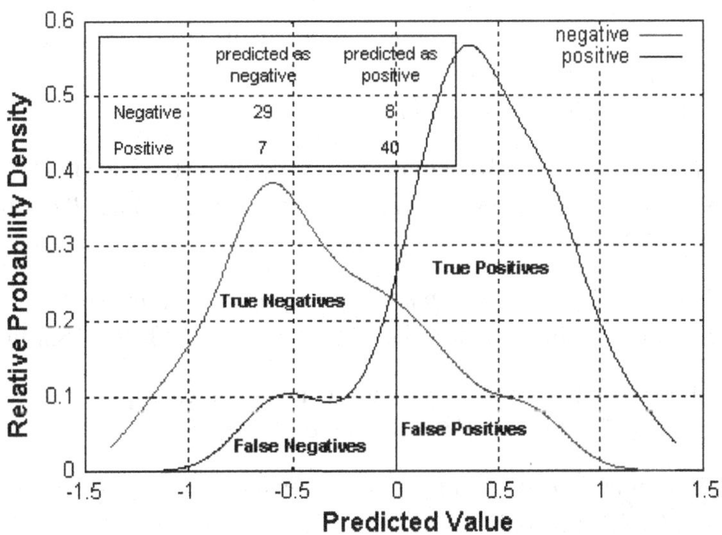

CONCLUSION

We introduced a novel Levenberg-Marquardt like second-order algorithm for tuning the Parzen window sigmas in a RBF kernel. The effectiveness of this algorithm was demonstrated with K-PLS. After tuning the sigmas, we then introduced a novel variable selection procedure by (iteratively) discarding variables with larger associated sigmas. Benchmark comparisons showed the effectiveness of the tuning procedure and the sigma tuning based variable selection method.

FUTURE RESEARCH DIRECTION

The sigma tuning procedure outlined in this chapter could only proceed in a timely matter by introducing a heuristic approximation for the second-order derivatives in the Hessian matrix. Further research will compare this approach with a more accurate way of calculating the second-order derivatives based on a numerical perturbation approach. Further research is also needed to assess whether the Mercer condition (Cristianini, 2000) is satisfied with the sigma-tuned kernels used in this chapter. Of course, we can always consider the revised kernel function as a data transformation technique similar to DK-PLS (Bennett, 2003) and then still apply K-PLS. In extension to the current implementation of single response, a multiple response sigma tuning algorithm can be investigated for the future work.

In the application of the MCG data analysis, we realized the bias in the samples, where the number of patients having positive is less than the number of patients having negative. Using the current objective function in the K-PLS will put less weight on negative samples and lead to bias in the model calibration. It would be better to use a different loss function rather than quadratic loss to catch the bias in the samples. A further research is to generalize K-PLS so that it can be applied to all different loss functions, including entropy loss function for the biased samples.

REFERENCES

Bennett, K., & Embrechts, M. (2003). An optimization perspective on kernel partial least squares regression. In J. Suykens, G. Horvath, C. M. S. Basu, & J. Vandewalle (Eds.), *Advances in learning theory: Methods, models and applications*, volume 190 of *NATO Science III: Computer & Systems Sciences* (pp. 227–250). Amsterdam, The Netherlands: IOS Press.

Bi, J., Bennett, K., Embrechts, M., Breneman, C., & Song, M. (2003). Dimensionality reduction via sparse support vector machines. *Journal of Machine Learning Research*, *3*, 1229–1243. doi:10.1162/153244303322753643

Blanchard, G., & Krämer, N. (2010). *Kernel partial least squares is universally consistent.* Thirteenth International Conference on Artificial Intelligence and Statistics (AISTATS), Sardinia, Italy.

Blum, A., & Langley, P. (1997). Selection of relevant features and examples in machine learning. *Artificial Intelligence*, *1-2*, 245–271. doi:10.1016/S0004-3702(97)00063-5

Boser, B., Guyon, I., & Vapnik, V. (1992). *A training algorithm for optimal margin classifiers*. 5th Annual ACM Workshop on COLT, Pittsburgh, PA, ACM Press.

Bradley, A. (1997). The use of the area under the ROC curve in evaluation of machine learning algorithms. *Pattern Recognition*, *30*(7), 1145–1159. doi:10.1016/S0031-3203(96)00142-2

Chang, C., & Lin, C. (2003). *LIBSVM: A library for support vector machines*. Retrieved on 5 September, 2004, from http://www.csie.ntu.edu.tw/~cjlin/libsvm

Chapelle, O., & Keerthi, S. (2008). Multi-class feature selection with support vector machines. *Proceedings of American Statistical Association.*

Chapelle, O., & Vapnik, V. (2002). Choosing multiple parameters for support vector machines. *Machine Learning*, *46*(1-3), 131–159. doi:10.1023/A:1012450327387

Chen, Q., Zhao, J., Chaitep, S., & Guo, Z. (2009). Simultaneous analysis of main catechins contents in green tea (Camellia sinensis) by Fourier transform near infrared reflectance (FT-NIR) spectroscopy. *Food Chemistry*, *113*(4), 1272–1277. doi:10.1016/j.foodchem.2008.08.042

Cristianini, N., & Campbell, C. (1998). Dynamically adapting kernels in support vector machines. *Proceedings of the 1998 conference on Advances in neural information processing systems,* vol. 11.

Cristianini, N., & Shawe-Taylor, J. (2000). *Support vector machines and other kernel based learning methods*. Cambridge, UK: Cambridge University Press.

Embrechts, M., Bress, R., & Kewley, R. (2005). Feature selection via sensitivity analysis with direct kernel PLS. In Guyon, I., & Gunn, S. (Eds.), *Feature extraction*. New York, NY: Springer.

Embrechts, M., & Ekins, S. (2007). Classification of metabolites with kernel-partial least squares (K-PLS). *Drug Metabolism and Disposition: the Biological Fate of Chemicals*, *35*(3), 325–327. doi:10.1124/dmd.106.013185

Embrechts, M., Szymanski, B., & Sternickel, K. (2004). Introduction to scientific data mining: Direct kernel methods and applications. In Ovaska, S. (Ed.), *Computationally intelligent hybrid systems: The fusion of soft and hard computing* (pp. 317–362). New York, NY: John Wiley.

Fawcett, T. (2003). *ROC graphs: Notes and practical considerations for data mining researchers*. (Technical Report HPL-2003-4, Hewlett Packard), Palo Alto, CA.

Fawcett, T., & Provost, F. (2001). Robust classification for imprecise environments. *Machine Learning Journal*, *42*(3), 203–231. doi:10.1023/A:1007601015854

Fillion, C., & Sharma, G. (2010). Detecting content adaptive scaling of images for forensic applications. In N. Memon, J. Dittmann, A. Alattar & E. Delp III (Eds.), *Proceedings of SPIE-IS&T Electronic Imaging,* vol. 7541.

Golbraikh, A., & Tropsha, A. (2002). Beware of q2! *Journal of Molecular Graphics & Modelling*, *20*, 267–276. doi:10.1016/S1093-3263(01)00123-1

Grandvalet, Y., & Canu, S. (2002). Adaptive scaling for feature selection in SVMs. *Proceedings of the 2002 conference on Advances in neural information processing systems*, vol. 15.

Guo, B., Gunn, S., Damper, R. I., & Nelson, J. (2008). Customizing kernel functions for SVM-based hyperspectral image classification. *IEEE Transactions on Image Processing, 17*(4), 622–629. doi:10.1109/TIP.2008.918955

Guyon, I., & Elisseeff, A. (2003). An introduction to variable and feature selection. *Journal of Machine Learning Research, 3*, 1157–1182. doi:10.1162/153244303322753616

Ham, F., & Kostanic, I. (2001). *Principles of neurocomputing for science and engineering*. New York, NY: McGraw Hill.

Han, L., Embrechts, M., Szymanski, B., Sternickel, K., & Ross, A. (2006). Random forests feature selection with K-PLS: Detecting ischemia from magnetocardiograms. European Symposium on Artificial Neural Networks, Bruges, Belgium.

Hastie, T., Tibshirani, R., & Friedman, J. (2003). *The elements of statistical learning: Data mining, inference, and prediction*. New York, NY: Springer.

He, W., Wang, Z., & Jiang, H. (2008). Model optimizing and feature selecting for support vector regression in time series forecasting. *Neurocomputing, 72*(1-3), 600–611. doi:10.1016/j.neucom.2007.11.010

Huang, S., & Wu, T. (2010). Integrating recurrent SOM with wavelet-based kernel partial least squares regressions for financial forecasting. *Expert Systems with Applications, 37*(8), 5698–5705. doi:10.1016/j.eswa.2010.02.040

Ilse, C., & Meyer, C. (1998). The idea behind Krylov methods. *The American Mathematical Monthly, 105*, 889–899. doi:10.2307/2589281

Lehmann, C., Koenig, T., Jelic, V., Prichep, L., John, R., & Wahlund, L. (2007). Application and comparison of classification algorithms for recognition of Alzheimer's disease in electrical brain activity (EEG). *Journal of Neuroscience Methods, 161*(2), 342–350. doi:10.1016/j.jneumeth.2006.10.023

Lindgren, F., Geladi, P., & Wold, S. (1993). The kernel algorithm for PLS. *Journal of Chemometrics, 7*, 45–49. doi:10.1002/cem.1180070104

Liu, S., & Wang, W. (1999). A study on the applicability on multicomponent calibration methods in chemometrics. *Chemometrics and Intelligent Laboratory Systems, 45*, 131–145. doi:10.1016/S0169-7439(98)00097-5

Masters, T. (1995). *Advanced algorithms for neural networks: A C++ sourcebook*. New York, NY: John Wiley & Sons.

Newman, D., Hettich, S., Blake, C., & Merz, C. (1998). *UCI repository of machine learning databases*.

Rosipal, R., & Trejo, L. (2001). Kernel partial least squares regression in reproducing kernel Hillbert spaces. *Journal of Machine Learning Research, 2*, 97–128. doi:10.1162/15324430260185556

Rousseauw, J., du Plessis, J., Benade, A., Jordann, P., Kotze, J., Jooste, P., & Ferreira, J. (1983). Coronary risk factor screening in three rural communities. *South African Medical Journal, 64*, 430–436.

Rubio, G., Herrera, L., Pomares, H., Rojas, I., & Guillén, A. (2010). Design of specific-to-problem kernels and use of kernel weighted k-nearest neighbors for time series modeling. *Neurocomputing, 73*(10-12), 1965–1975. doi:10.1016/j.neucom.2009.11.029

Specht, D. F. (1990). Probabilistic neural networks. *Neural Networks, 3*, 109–118. doi:10.1016/0893-6080(90)90049-Q

Štruc, V., & Pavesić, N. (2009). Gabor-based kernel partial-least squares discrimination for face recognition. *Informatica, 20*, 115–138.

Suykens, J., Gestel, T., Brabanter, J., Moor, B., & Vandewalle, J. (2003). *Least squares support vector machines*. Singapore: World Scientific Publishing Company.

Swets, J., Dawes, R., & Monahan, J. (2000, October). Better decisions through science. *Scientific American*, 82–87. doi:10.1038/scientificamerican1000-82

Tian, H., Tian, X., Deng, X., & Wang, P. (2009). *Soft sensor for polypropylene melt index based on adaptive kernel partial least squares*. Control and Instruments in Chemical Industry.

Vapnik, V. (1998). *Statistical learning theory*. New York, NY: John Wiley & Sons.

Wang, T., Huang, H., Tian, S., & Xu, J. (2010). Feature selection for SVM via optimization of kernel polarization with Gaussian ARD kernels. *Expert Systems with Applications, 37*(9), 6663–6668. doi:10.1016/j.eswa.2010.03.054

Wold, H. (1975). Path with latent variables: The NIPALS approach. In Balock, H. M. (Ed.), *Quantitative sociology: International perspectives on mathematical and statistical model building* (pp. 307–357). New York, NY: Academic Press.

Wold, H. (1996). Estimation of principal components and related models by iterative least squares. In Krishnaiah, P. (Ed.), *Multivariate analysis* (pp. 391–420). New York, NY: Academic Press.

Wold, S., Sjōlstrōm, M., & Erikson, L. (2001). PLS-regression: A basic tool of chemometrics. *Chemometrics and Intelligent Laboratory Systems, 58*, 109–130. doi:10.1016/S0169-7439(01)00155-1

ADDITIONAL READING

Bennett, K., & Embrechts, M. (2003). An optimization perspective on kernel partial least squares regression. In J. Suykens, G. Horvath, C. M. S. Basu, & J. Vandewalle (Ed.), *Advances in learning theory: methods, models and applications*, volume 190 of *NATO Science III: Computer & Systems Sciences* (pp. 227–250). Amsterdam: IOS Press.

Chapelle, O., & Vapnik, V. (2002). Choosing multiple parameters for support vector machines. *Machine Learning, 46*(1-3), 131–159. doi:10.1023/A:1012450327387

Cristianini, N., & Shawe-Taylor, J. (2000). *Support vector machines and other kernel based learning methods*. Cambridge: Cambridge University Press.

Embrechts, M., Bress, R., & Kewley, R. (2005). Feature selection via sensitivity analysis with direct kernel PLS. In Guyon, I., & Gunn, S. (Eds.), *Feature extraction*. New York, NY: Springer.

Embrechts, M., Szymanski, B., & Sternickel, K. (2004). Introduction to scientific data mining: Direct kernel methods and applications. In Ovaska, S. (Ed.), *Computationally intelligent hybrid systems: The fusion of soft and hard computing* (pp. 317–362). New York, NY: John Wiley.

Embrechts, M., Szymanski, B., Sternickel, K., Naenna, T., & Bragaspathi, R. (2003). Use of machine learning for classification of magnetocardiograms. Proceeding of IEEE Conference on System, Man and Cybernetics, Washington DC.

Han, L., Embrechts, M., Chen, Y., & Zhang, X. (2006). Kernel partial least squares for Terahertz radiation spectral source identification. IEEE World Congress on Computational Intelligence.

Rosipal, R., & Trejo, L. (2001). Kernel partial least squares regression in reproducing kernel Hilbert spaces. *Journal of Machine Learning Research, 2*, 97–128. doi:10.1162/15324430260185556

Schōlkopf, B., & Smola, A. (2002). *Learning with kernels*. Cambridge, MA: MIT Press.

Shawe-Taylor, J., & Cristianini, N. (2004). *Kernel methods for pattern analysis*. Cambridge: Cambridge University Press.

Szymanski, B., Han, L., Embrechts, M., Ross, A., Sternickel, K., & Zhu, L. (2006). Using efficient SUPANOVA kernel for heart disease diagnosis. Proceeding of ANNIE 2006, Intelligent Engineering Systems Through Artificial Neural Networks, St. Louis, MO, ASME, New York, NY.

Vapnik, V. (1998). *Statistical learning theory*. New York, NY: John Wiley & Sons.

Wold, H. (1975). Path with latent variables: The NIPALS approach. In Balock, H. M. (Ed.), *Quantitative sociology:International perspectives on mathematical and statistical model building* (pp. 307–357). New York, NY: Academic Press.

Wold, H. (1996). Estimation of principal components and related models by iterative least squares. In Krishnaiah, P. (Ed.), *Multivariate analysis* (pp. 391–420). New York, NY: Academic Press.

KEY TERMS AND DEFINITIONS

Kernel Partial Least Squares: A kernel function to replace the linear kernel matrices XX^T in the PLS methods. PLS can be viewed as a "better" Principal Components Analysis (PCA) regression method, where the data are first transformed into a different and non-orthogonal basis and only the most important PLS components (or latent variables) are considered for building a regression model.

Gaussian Kernel: or Radial Basic Function (RBF) kernel, is most widely used. Each kernel entry is a dissimilarity measure through using the square of Euclidean distance between two data points in a negative exponential. The σ parameter contained in the entry is the Parzen window width for RBF kernel.

Variable Selection: or feature selection, is a technique in the machine learning or statistics to select a subset of relevant features for building a robust learning model.

Ischemic Heart Disease: mayocardial ischaemia, is a disease caused by reduced blood supply to the heart muscle. It is more common in men and those whose close relatives have ischaemic heart disease.

Levenberg-Marquardt Algorithm: is an algorithm in mathematics and computing to minimize a function by providing a numerical solution. It is a popular alternative to the Gauss-Newton method.

Chapter 10
Artificial Neural Network Modelling for Waste:
Gas and Wastewater Treatment Applications

Eldon R. Rene
University of La Coruña, Spain

M. Estefanía López
University of La Coruña, Spain

María C. Veiga
University of La Coruña, Spain

Christian Kennes
University of La Coruña, Spain

ABSTRACT

Due to their inherent robustness, artificial neural network models have proven to be successful and have been used extensively in biological wastewater treatment applications. However, only recently, with the scientific advancements made in biological waste gas treatment systems, the application of neural networks have slowly gained the practical momentum for performance monitoring in this field. Simple neural models, after vigorous training and testing, are able to generalize the results of a wide range of operating conditions, with high prediction accuracy. This chapter gives a fundamental insight and overview of the process mechanism of different biological waste gas (biofilters, biotrickling filters, continuous stirred tank bioreactors and monolith bioreactors), and wastewater treatment systems (activated sludge process, trickling filter and sequencing batch reactors). The basic theory of artificial neural networks is explained with a clear understanding of the back propagation algorithm. A generalized neural network modelling procedure for waste treatment applications is outlined, and the role of back propagation algorithm network parameters is discussed. Anew, the application of neural networks for solving specific environmental problems is presented in the form of a literature review.

DOI: 10.4018/978-1-60960-551-3.ch010

INTRODUCTION

General

Environmental pollution control strategies and regulations have focused on the acute effects of air and water pollutants on human health and natural environment. In the past fifty years, however, advances in medical and environmental sciences have led to a better understanding of other deleterious effects of these pollutants. Well known industrial air pollutants like benzene, toluene, styrene, hydrogen sulphide (H_2S), ammonia (NH_3), dichloromethane, hexane, and water pollutants like pharmaceutical drugs, pesticides, synthetic dyes, nitrates and phosphates could frequently enter into the natural environment through improper handling and disposal practices, ineffective treatment procedures, leakage during storage and transportation and disposal of petroleum by – products. The potential health effect caused by an accidental release depends on the total exposure time of the species with the released chemical and its concentration level, usually expressed as ppm or g m^{-3}. For example, exposure to volatile organic compounds (VOCs) like benzene, toluene, ethyl benzene and xylenes (BTEX) can easily cause dizziness, staggering gait, bone marrow suppression, respiratory arrest, lassitude and other dyspeptic disorders. Chronic exposures can lead to leukaemia and deflating dermatitis. It has been reported that, in workers exposed to benzene concentrations of 450 to 2000 mg m^{-3}, the incidence of leukaemia is at least two times higher than those found in the general population (Infante et al., 1977). The presence of VOCs in the ambient atmosphere leads to ozone layer depletion and climate changes through its direct toxicity and reactivity.

The finite nature of fresh water and its declining trend due to rapid industrialization and the propping up of small – scale industrial parks has repercussions on natural ecosystems. The water quality is continuously degrading as a result of the free flow of contaminants like suspended solids (SS), organic wastes, bacteria, nitrates, phosphates and other recalcitrant chemicals. For example, as point – source pollution, excessive amount of nitrates – bearing wastewaters are generated from pulp and paper, ammunition manufacturing facilities, besides being generated enormously as non – point source run – offs from the over application of nitrogen rich fertilizers. When ingested, nitrate is converted to nitrite, which then reacts with haemoglobin in blood to form methemoglobin, a condition that severely affects the oxygen transport mechanism in blood.

Waste Gas and Wastewater Treatment Processes

Both physico – chemical and biological treatment systems have been successfully implemented in industrial facilities for environmental management, as an end – of – pipe treatment step. The implementation and use of biological techniques, *viz., aerobic and anaerobic*, for treating toxic odorous compounds and hazardous chemicals present in waste – gases and wastewater is exponentially growing at the industrial level, especially considering the degree of treatment accomplished at a low cost. During aerobic biotreatment, the microorganisms present in these systems demand a steady supply of organic material as a carbon source and O_2 as a terminal electron acceptor for complete metabolism of the contaminant (Kennes & Veiga, 2001). Ideally, the organic pollutant serves as the sole energy and carbon source to the microbes, and complete mineralization leads to the formation of CO_2, H_2O, biomass and some amount of heat. This is given by equation (1) described herein;

$$\text{Organic pollutant} + O_2 \xrightarrow{\text{Microorganisms}} \underbrace{CO_2 + H_2O}_{\text{Innocuous End products}} + \text{Heat} + \text{Biomass} \quad (1)$$

(Substrate) (Electron acceptor) (Exothermicity) (Residue)

On the other hand, anaerobic systems have also proven to be effective in treating high – strength wastewaters. In this process, the organic substrate is degraded in the absence of oxygen to CO_2 and methane. Apart from the economics gained in terms of methane produced, anaerobic treatment offers many operational advantages, such as less biomass produced per unit of substrate consumed, and the biotreatment of high organic loads without experiencing problems of oxygen limitations. This chapter will focus more on the different aerobic treatment systems for waste gas and wastewater treatment, though in some cases, anaerobic steps have been mentioned due to the inherent process strategy of the system.

Scope for Artificial Neural Network Models in the Biological Treatment of Effluents

Neural Networks are able to learn non – linear static or dynamic behaviour exclusively by measuring data. Since the knowledge of internal procedure is not necessary, the modelling can take place with minimum previous knowledge about the process through proper training of the network. The impetus of employing artificial neural networks (ANNs) to model dynamic biological waste gas and wastewater treatment systems is due to their inherent advantage over other non – linear modelling paradigms, that can be summarized as follows;

(i) usefulness in solving data – intensive problems where the algorithm or rules to solve the problem are unknown (Zhang & Stanley, 1997), (ii) the ability to detect all possible interactions between predictor variables, (iii) less formal statistical training, (iv) ability to implicitly detect complex nonlinear relationships between dependent and independent variables, (v) ability to generalize and find relations in imperfect data as long as they do not have enough neurons to over – fit data imperfections (Chen, Jakeman & Norton, 2008), and (vi) the availability of multiple training algorithms (Tu, 1996).

Besides, ANNs can be easily applied to solve seven categories of problems: pattern classification, clustering, function approximation, prediction, optimization, data retrieval and process control (Jain, Mao & Mohiuddin, 1996). Livingstone, Manallack and Tetko (1997) nicely describe ANNs as ‘ ’*Data modelling with neural networks is certainly not ‘an answer to the maiden's prayer’, but neural networks do offer a number of advantages over some of the more traditional methods of data – modelling and should be viewed as an useful adjunct to these techniques*”. Hussain (1999) reasons that ‘*the versatility in structure and application of neural networks enables them to be utilized in the middle – ground between conventional model – based approaches and black – box approaches for solving many classes of problems*’.

In this chapter, the application of ANNs for predicting the performance parameters in waste gas and wastewater treatment systems has been explored. Recently, several mathematical and empirical models have been proposed by researchers, some of them however fail to predict the data of other researchers as they were originally developed and validated with the experimental data from a particular system.

Besides, changing biofilm kinetics, along with other physico – chemical and biological factors such as packing media in packed bed reactors, type of microorganism, the composition of the effluents (whether individual or a mixture of different pollutants having different biodegradation rates), and the persistence of uncertainty due to unexpected shock loading conditions affect the performance characteristics of any biological process, that makes some of the conventional model parameters difficult to predict (Kennes & Veiga, 2001; Rene, Veiga & Kennes, 2009).

Contents of the Chapter

The contents of this chapter will highlight the typical biological processes used for waste gas and wastewater treatment, with more detailed information on the more commonly used biofilter (BF), sequencing batch reactor (SBR) and activated sludge process (ASP). Anew, the parameters of prime importance to assess the performance in real – time operation will be discussed under each section, together with the conventional design equation and phenomenological model used. The later part of the chapter will focus in depth on ANNs, the guidelines to select the best network topology, and the routine followed to develop a particular ANN model waste gas and wastewater treatment systems. A detailed literature review is done and information pertaining to the use of ANN to model such systems, as performance indicators, and as bioprocess monitoring and control device, is provided.

ARTIFICIAL NEURAL NETWORKS (ANNS)

General

ANNs are one of the modelling techniques developed originally from the fundamental concept of artificial intelligence (AI), that attempt to simulate the operation of the human brain and nervous system. They contain a series of mathematical equations that are used to stimulate the learning and memorizing process. ANNs learn '*by example*' in which an actual measured set of input variables and the corresponding outputs are presented to determine the rules that govern the relationship between the variables. The input and the output variables are interconnected by neurons present in a hidden layer and these neurons receive specific command in the form of a weight function. As the interconnections between the neurons are not well understood, numerous neural network models have been developed by researchers and many are yet to come. These networks are generally classified as feed – forward and recurrent types. Of considerable interest, in this chapter, is the feed forward network, where signal from one neuron to other flows only in the forward direction. Some of the common network models developed are perceptron, adaline and madaline, back propagation networks, radial bias function networks, modular neural networks, etc (Haykin, 1994). Many ANN topologies have been proposed, amongst which many of them have found to be suitable for practical applications (Hopfield, 1982; Feldman & Ballard, 1982; Widrow & Sterns, 1985; Rumelhart, Hinton & Williams, 1986; Kohonen, 1988). Each differs in the number and character of the processing nodes, their connections, training procedures and on whether the input/output values are continuous or discrete.

Multilayer Perceptron and Back Error Propagation Algorithm

Multilayer perceptron (MLP) belongs to the class of supervised feed – forward networks in which the processing elements are arranged in a multi – layered structure (Figure 1a). The network topology and the internal mathematics behind different algorithms used in MLPs have been discussed by many researchers. As mentioned previously, the structure of MLPs consists of an input layer, one or more hidden layers and an output layer. The input from each processing element (PE) in the previous layer is multiplied by a connection weight (W_{ji}). These connection weights are adjustable and may be linked to the coefficients in statistical models. At each PE, the weighted input signals are summed and a bias value is added or subtracted. This combined input is then passed through a non – linear transfer function to produce the output of the PE. The output of one PE provides the input to the PEs in the next layer.

Rumelhart, Hinton and Williams (1986) proposed the back error propagation (BEP) training algorithm in which the error function is minimized with respect to the connection weights only. Hence when a training vector sample is presented to the network, the global error function (E) can be calculated by using equation (2), as;

$$E = \frac{1}{2}\sum (O_d - O_p)^2 \tag{2}$$

Where, E is the global error function, O_d is the desired output and O_p is the output predicted by the network.

The back propagation algorithm uses the gradient descent technique to adjust the weights in which the global error function, E, is minimized by modifying the weights using the following equation,

$$\Delta W_{ji} = -\eta \frac{\partial E}{\partial W_{ji}} \tag{3}$$

Where, Δw_{ji} = weight increment from node i to node j; and η = learning rate, by which the size of the step taken along the error surface is determined.

The weights between the hidden layer and the output layer are adjusted first, followed by the weights between the hidden layer and the input layer. Rumelhart, Hinton and Williams (1986) described a process to solve the above problem without leading to any discrete oscillations during training. This process simply adds a momentum term to the weight adjustment that is proportional to the amount of the previous weight change. The momentum term may be considered to increase the effective step size in shallow regions of the error surface (Hassoun, 1995) and can speed up the training process by several orders of magnitude (Masters, 1993). Once an adjustment is carried out, it is saved and used to modify all subsequent weight adjustments. This means that the weight change of the current step should carry some momentum of the weight change from the previous step. The modified adjustment of the delta weight, Δw_{ji}, is given by equation (4);

$$\Delta W_{ji}(t) = \sum_{N=1}^{\varepsilon} -\eta \frac{\partial E}{\partial W_{ji}} + \mu \Delta W_{ji}(t-1) \tag{4}$$

Figure 1. (a) Schematic of a three layer neural network, (b) log – sigmoid, tanh and linear transfer functions, and (c) typical examples of local minima and variations of error during training, testing and validation

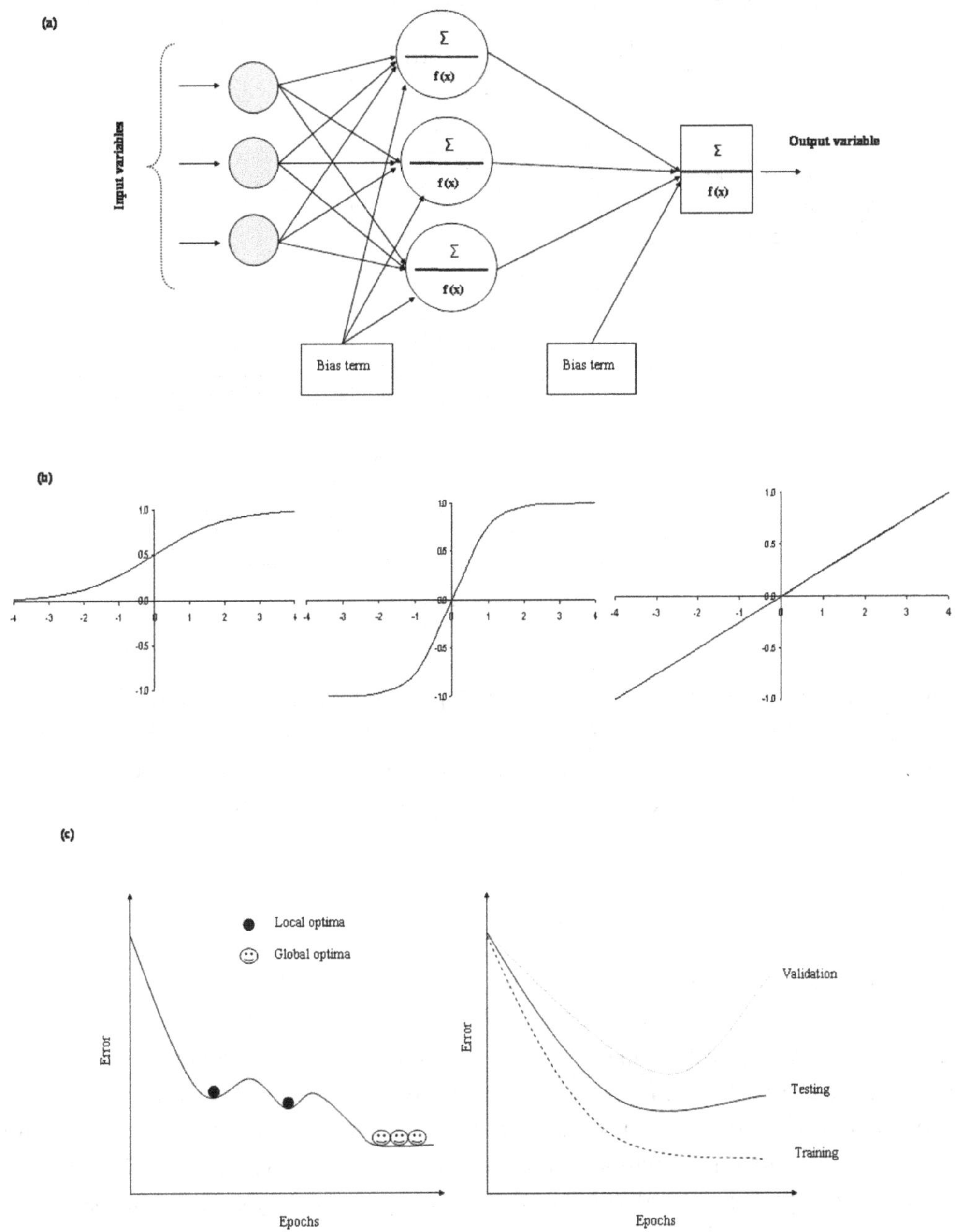

Where, N is the training sample presented to the network, and μ is the momentum term.

The above process is repeated, which propagates the error term needed for weight adjustment until the network can obtain a set of weights that result in the input/output mapping. Once the network is properly trained, validated and tested, the developed ANN model can be deployed and used in practice.

Figure 2. Generalized neural network procedure for modelling environmental systems for prediction purposes

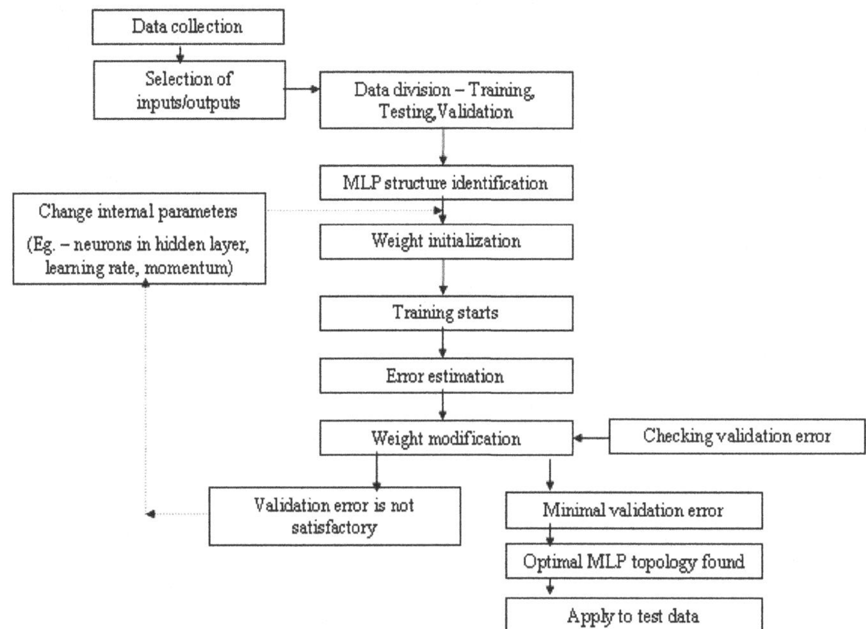

The step – wise procedure that is followed to develop an appropriate neural model for waste gas and wastewater treatment applications is illustrated in Figure 2. The other sections described herein give suitable information on data selection and analysis, important network parameters and their usefulness, methods to be followed to avoid over – fitting and interpretation of connection weights.

Data Selection

To get more meaningful results from an ANN model, it is important to select input variables that are likely to play a major role in influencing the desired output (variable to be modelled). When the available data set has high dimensions, it is necessary to select a subset of the potential input variable to reduce the number of free parameters in the model in order to obtain good generalization with finite data (Fernando, Maier & Dandy, 2009). Different strategies have been adopted for variable selection, these include; forward inclusion, backward elimination, multiple linear regression models, mutual information technique, and partial mutual information technique (Livingstone, Manallack & Tetko, 1997). Pruning techniques with the help of specific algorithms aim to prune unnecessary connections between neurons and some of the neurons inherit the ability to prune themselves until all their connections are severed. These algorithms are either based on the direct analysis of neuron weights, or based on the network error following the elimination of the connections. Data refining can also be performed to eliminate all outliers, transposition errors due to improper input of data, which are considered to be unusual points. Refining can be done by removing measurements that are not within the range of $\pm 3\sigma$, standard deviations around the group. For some specific cases, statistical manipulations can be performed in order to decrypt trends in the data series, using conventional smoothing techniques (Mjalli, Al – Asheh & Alfadala, 2007). Principal component analysis (PCA) can also be used as a tool to identify linear correlations between random state variables aiming at data dimensionality reduction (Choi & Park, 2001).

Influence of Internal Network Parameters of the BEP Algorithm

The process of developing the best network architecture involves a number of network specifications to be optimized; the number of neurons in the hidden layer, the learning rate, epoch size, momentum, the processing element activation function and the training count of the network.

Epoch Size

The epoch size refers to the number of training samples presented to the network when connection weights are updated during training. It has been suggested that this value should be kept equal to the size of the training data set, as it forces the search to move in the direction of the true gradient at each weight update (Maier & Dandy, 2001).

Initial Connection Weights

At the beginning of the training process, the weights are initialized to some zero – mean random values, mostly specified by the software used for modelling. However, care should be taken to choose adequate upper and lower boundary values for connection weights. If the initial weights are too large, the nodes would prematurely stagnate, and this could easily affect the training process.

Learning Rate

The amount of a particular weight connection changed is proportional to the learning rate, η which in turn affects the size of steps taken in weight space (Maier & Dandy, 1998a). If η is too low (say 0.01), the network learns the pattern very slowly. On the contrary, a high η value (0.99) makes the weights and objective function diverge, so there is no learning at all. Most learning functions have some provisions to change the η and this value remains fixed during the training process (Warner & Misra, 1996). η can be different for the connections between the network topology, i.e., η between the input layer – hidden layer (η_{ih}) and the η between hidden layer – output layer (η_{ho}). These terms are usually positive and vary between 0 – 1. If this value is more than 1, it is easier for the learning algorithm to overshoot in correcting the weights and one would notice more oscillations in the error surface. Hence, sufficient care should be taken in choosing this parameter.

Momentum Term

The momentum term μ accelerates the convergence of the error during the learning process and is the most popular extension of the back propagation algorithm. This term simply adds a fraction of the previous weight update to the current one and is often related to the η. High η and μ values can rush convergence towards a local minimum with huge steps, whereas small η values with high μ can lead to divergent behaviour during training (Maier & Dandy, 1998a; 1998b; 2001). This value ranges from 0 – 1 and is normally determined by trial and error for a given network (Dai & Macbeth, 1997).

Activation Function

The activation function denoted by $f(x)$, defines the output of a neuron in terms of the induced local field x. Three basic types of activation functions are normally envisioned during the development of networks for prediction purposes; linear, hyperbolic tangent and sigmoid (Figure 1b). The most commonly used activation function within the neurons is the logistic sigmoid function, which takes the form as shown in equation (5);

$$f(x) = \frac{1}{1 + e^{-x}} \tag{5}$$

The hyperbolic tangent function takes the form;

$$\tanh(x) = \frac{e^{x} - e^{-x}}{e^{x} + e^{-x}} \tag{6}$$

For specific applications, and for noisy, non – linear data, transfer functions like radial bias transfer function, polynomial, rational function and Fourier series have been used.

Data Division and Normalization

The data are normally divided as training (70%), test (20%) and validation data set (10%). It is important to understand the statistical properties of the data to ensure that optimal model performance is achieved.

The data are also normalized and scaled to the range of 0 to 1, according to equation (7), so as to suit the transfer function in the hidden (sigmoid) and output layer (linear).

$$\hat{X} = \frac{X - X_{min}}{X_{max} - X_{min}} \tag{7}$$

Where, $\hat{X}$ is the normalized value for the variable, X_{min} is the minimum value of the variable, and X_{max} is the maximum value of the variable.

Network Architecture

The minimum number of neurons (nodes) in the hidden layer can be equal to or greater than the number of inputs to the network. However, the optimum number of neurons is generally estimated by trial and error. Roger and Dowla (1994) gave an empirical relationship between the number of training samples and network size (equation 8), to determine the upper limit for the number of hidden layer neurons.

$$N_H \leq \frac{N_{Tr}}{N_I + 1} \quad (8)$$

Where, N_H is the number of hidden layer neurons, N_I is the number of inputs to the network and N_{Tr} is the number of training samples.

A lot of effort has been put forward in the recent years to develop procedures that automatically adjust the number of neurons during network training, so as to determine the smallest network that is capable of capturing the relationships between parameters. For many biological waste treatment systems, ANN model with one hidden layer can approximate any function, given that sufficient degrees of freedom, in terms of connection weights, are provided. The use of more than one hidden layer would provide more flexibility to approximate the given function, with lesser weight adjustments, but if data – points are less, the network would fail to generalize. The ratio between the number of training samples and the number of connection weights should be > 1 (Maier & Dandy, 1998a; 1998b).

Stopping Criterion and Methods to Avoid Over – Fitting

It is important for the user to estimate the best network topology by carrying out a vigorous trial and error task during training. However, the criterion used to decide when to stop the training also depends on user, because of the fundamental knowledge gained from initial trials. Maier and Dandy (2000) suggest that '*even though the error obtained using the test set might not increase at some stage during training, there is no guarantee that it will not reach lower levels at a later stage even if training were continued*'. In some cases, training can be stopped when the training error goal is reached, while in other cases, cross – validation using a separate data set has been used as a stopping criterion (Amari, Chen & Cichochi, 1997). Livingstone, Manallack and Tetko (1997) observed that, back propagation networks have the tendency to find local minima (Figure 1c), presumably because the fitting error surface has a complex structure due to the large number of adjustable parameters, like connection weights, and these minima are often closer in value. There are several ways proposed in the literature to escape local minima, viz., (i) increasing/decreasing the η and μ values, (ii) adding a small amount of random noise to the input patterns to shake the network from the line of steepest descent, (iii) adding more hidden nodes and, (iv) relocating the network along the error surface by randomizing the initial weights and re – training (Sietsma & Dow, 1988).

Over – fitting or over – training refers to the condition where the neural network attempts to map all the irregular peaks and plains of the training data set, resulting in a poor performance for the external test data. Over – fitting can be stopped in three ways, (i) by limiting the number of hidden nodes, (ii) by adding a penalty term to the objective function for large weights, and (iii) by limiting the amount of training using cross – validation (Tu, 1996). 'Early stopping' is another well known training strategy in neural network modelling. This involves the use of a control set to monitor network training and training is continued until the control set error begins to rise, and this however requires a further set to function as an independent test set (Livingstone, Manallack & Tetko, 1997).

Importance of Connection Weights

The connection weights obtained from a developed ANN model, after training, can be thought of as 'β' coefficients in a regression model. At each hidden node, a weighted linear combination of the inputs is summed with the bias term, to determine the net output to that node and then this result passes through the activation function. Estimating these connection weights in an optimal way is important to improve model performance. The connection weights can also be used to estimate the relative importance of various input variables on the output variable (Garson, 1991). The relative importance (I_j) of the 'j'th input variable on the output variable can be determined using equation (9);

$$Ij = \frac{\sum_{m=1}^{m=N_h}\left(\left(\frac{\left|W_{jm}^{ih}\right|}{\sum_{k=1}^{N_i}\left|W_{km}^{ih}\right|}\right)\times\left|W_{mn}^{ho}\right|\right)}{\sum_{k=1}^{k=N_i}\left\{\sum_{m=1}^{m=N_h}\left[\left(\frac{\left|W_{km}^{ih}\right|}{\sum_{k=1}^{N_i}\left|W_{km}^{ih}\right|}\right)\times\left|W_{mn}^{ho}\right|\right]\right\}} \tag{9}$$

where, N_i and N_h are the input and hidden neurons, respectively, W is the connection weight, superscripts '*i*', '*h*', '*o*' denote the input, hidden and output layers, respectively, and subscripts '*k*', '*m*' and '*n*' refer to input, hidden and output neurons, respectively.

In majority of the published research papers, these connection weights are not provided, because they might be prohibitively large and difficult to interpret. Nevertheless, it is important for an end – user to understand the importance of these connection weights, so as to interpret the results in a systematic manner (Tu, 1996).

Sensitivity Analysis of the Model

The strength of the relationship between the output variable and input variable is normally estimated by carrying out a sensitivity analysis, i.e., a small change in the input variable could have a very large impact on the output variable. The sensitivity is calculated by summing the changes in the output variables caused by moving the input variables by a small amount over the entire training set. The sensitivity of each input can be estimated using equation (10);

$$Sensitivity = \frac{\%\ Change\ in\ output}{\%\ Change\ in\ input}\times 100 \tag{10}$$

The Absolute Average Sensitivity (AAS) is the average of the absolute values of the change in the output. This value is then divided by the total amount of change for all input variables to normalize the values. The Average Sensitivity (AS) is calculated in the same way as the AAS variable except that the absolute values are not taken. If the direction of the change in the output variable is always the same, then both these sensitivity values would be identical. The absolute value average sensitivity matrix ($S_{ki,abs}$), can be calculated according to equation (11);

$$S_{ki,\ abs} = \frac{\sum_{p=1}^{P} \left| s_{ki}^{(p)} \right|}{P} \tag{11}$$

where, P is the number of training patterns presented to the network.

Error Indices

There are different ways to express the error term during model development, i.e., estimating the error between the measured and the model fitted values. Some of the most commonly used expressions and their significance are mentioned here.

The accuracy factor (A_f) is a simple multiplicative factor that represents the spread of results from the prediction. A_f can be estimated using equation (12);

$$A_f = 10^{\left(\sum \frac{\left| \log\left(\frac{Y model}{Y meas} \right) \right|}{N} \right)} \tag{12}$$

An accuracy factor value of 1 means the perfect agreement between the model fitted and the measured variable, and the larger the value of A_f, the less accurate are the model fittings.

The Aikaike information criterion (AIC) is defined as;

$$AIC = N \log\left(\frac{1}{N} \sum_{i=1}^{n} (Y_{meas} - Y^{*}_{pred}) \right) + 2N_I \tag{13}$$

where, Y^*_{pred} is the mean value of the predictions.

The Nash – Sutcliffe coefficient of efficiency (NSC) can be defined by:

$$NSC = 1 - \frac{\sum_{i=1}^{n} (Y_{model} - Y_{meas})^2}{\sum_{i=1}^{n} (\overline{Y} - Y_{meas})^2} \tag{14}$$

$\overline{Y}$ is the average value of the measured parameters, *Ymodel* and *Ymeas* are the model predicted and measured values, respectively. NSC values are usually less than 1, and = 1, when the predictions are equal to the measured value of the variable (Nash & Sutcliffe, 1970).

The mean absolute percentage error (MAPE) is calculated as follows;

$$MAPE = \frac{1}{N} \sum_{i=1}^{n} \left| \frac{Y_{meas} - Y_{model}}{Y_{meas}} \right| \times 100 \tag{15}$$

The mean absolute error (MAE), mean squared error (MSE) and root mean square error (RMSE) are calculated as follows;

$$MAE = \frac{\sum_{i=1}^{n} \left| Y_{meas} - Y_{model} \right|}{N} \tag{16}$$

$$MSE = \frac{\sum_{i=1}^{n} \left(Y_{meas} - Y_{model} \right)^2}{N} \tag{17}$$

$$RMSE = \sqrt{\frac{\sum_{i=1}^{n} \left(Y_{meas} - Y_{model} \right)^2}{N}} \tag{18}$$

Total root mean squared error ($RMSE_t$) can also be used as an indicator of improving the developed model, with all the constraints of variability in the observed data. $RMSE_t$ is estimated using equation (19), as shown below;

$$RMSE_t = \left[\frac{\sum_{i=1}^{N} (Y^{R}_{model} - Y_{meas})^2}{RMSE} \right]^{0.5} \tag{19}$$

where, Y^{R}_{model} is the estimation of the predictions yielded by the least – squares regression line of $Y^{R}_{model} = a \times Y_{meas} + b$, where 'a' and 'b' are the slope and intercept. For a perfect model, a = 1 and b = 0 (Elias et al., 2006). Typical $RMSE_t$ values are usually < 0.4.

The standard deviation (SD), error and average relative error (ARE) terms can be estimated using the following equations;

$$SD, \% = \left[\frac{\sum_{i=1}^{N} \frac{(Y_{meas} - Y_{model})}{Y_{meas}}}{N - 1} \right]^{0.5} \times 100 \tag{20}$$

$$Error, \% = \frac{(Y_{meas} - Y_{model})}{Y_{meas}} \times 100 \tag{21}$$

$$AVE,\ \% = \frac{\sum_{i=1}^{N} Error}{N} \times 100 \tag{22}$$

BIOLOGICAL WASTE GAS TREATMENT SYSTEMS

The implementation and use of biological techniques for VOC removal at industrial scale is growing exponentially (Kennes & Veiga, 2001). The most commonly used biological waste gas treatment techniques include bioreactor configurations (Figure 3) such as biotrickling filter (BTF), biofilter (BF), bioscrubbers (BS), and bioreactors based on air diffusion through suspended growth (often activated sludge) reactors. Other systems such as the membrane bioreactors and the monolith bioreactor are still at the development stage, before any possible industrial use (Jin, Veiga & Kennes, 2006a; Jin, Veiga & Kennes, 2008). Though the mode of operation for all these configurations is very similar, they are distinguished by the behaviour of the liquid phase (continuously moving or stationary) and by the location of the microorganisms (freely dispersed or immobilized). However, while choosing an appropriate treatment technique, focus is placed on the operational and control requirements needed to ensure an optimal chemical and physical environment for mass transfer and biodegradation of the pollutant in order to achieve high removal efficiencies (Waweru et al., 2005).

Typical operational and performance parameters of waste gas treatment systems can be estimated by the following equations;

Volumetric Loading Rate:

$$VLR = \frac{Q}{V}, [\ h^{-1}] \tag{23}$$

Mass Loading Rate:

$$MLR = \frac{Q \times C_i}{V}, \left[g\ m^{-3}\ h^{-1}\right] \tag{24}$$

Figure 3. Schematic of different waste gas treatment systems, (a) biofilter, (b) biotrickling filter, and (c) continuous stirred tank bioreactor

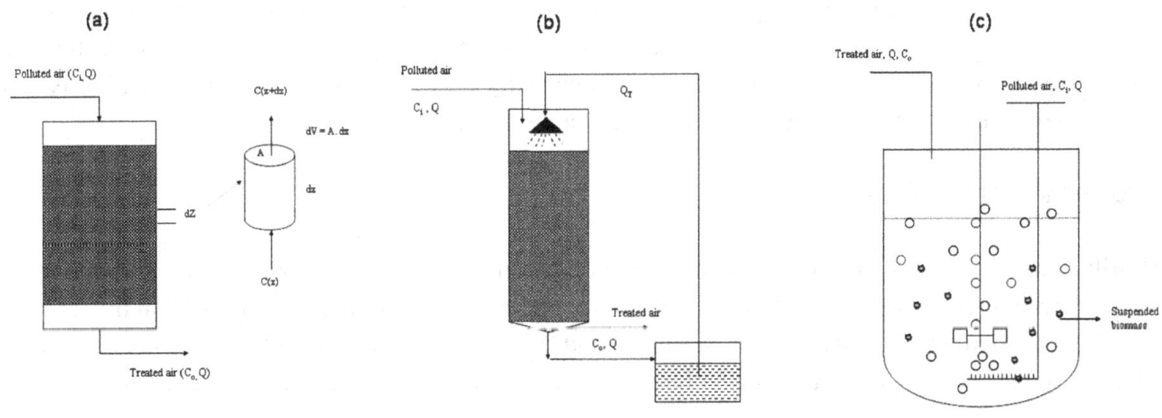

Elimination Capacity:

$$EC = \frac{Q \times \left(C_i - C_o\right)}{V}, \left[g\ m^{-3}\ h^{-1}\right] \tag{25}$$

Removal Efficiency:

$$RE = \frac{\left(C_i - C_o\right)}{C_i}, \left[\%\right] \tag{26}$$

Carbon dioxide Production Rate:

$$P_{CO_2} = \frac{Q \times \left(CO_{2,\ out} - CO_{2,\ in}\right)}{V}, \left[g\ m^{-3}\ h^{-1}\right] \tag{27}$$

where, Q is the gas – flow rate ($m^3\ h^{-1}$), V is the volume of the filter bed or aqueous medium (m^3), C_i and C_o are, respectively, the inlet and outlet pollutant concentrations ($g\ m^{-3}$), $CO_{2,in}$ and $CO_{2,out}$ are the inlet and outlet CO_2 concentrations of the bioreactor ($g\ m^{-3}$).

Biofilters

Biofiltration utilizes a support matrix for microbial growth to remove odors and contaminants from air streams. A typical BF (Figure 3a) consists of a packed bed containing microorganisms. The solid support matrix consisting typically of compost, peat moss, wood chips and synthetic materials provides adequate nutrients required for the activity of the microorganisms. An ideal packed bed should have a long working life and offer low pressure drop for the gases to pass through. The humidified contaminated air is pumped through a distributor placed at the top or the bottom of the filter bed. The contaminants in the air stream are absorbed and metabolized by the microbial flora. Treatment begins with the transfer of the contaminants from the air stream to the water phase (Devinny, Deshusses & Webster, 1999; Kennes, Rene & Veiga, 2009). The treated air is discharged into the atmosphere through an outlet at either the top or the bottom of the BF, depending on whether air is fed in either upflow or downflow mode. Most BFs that are in operation today can treat odors and VOCs effectively with efficiencies greater than 90%. Typical examples for maximum elimination capacity (EC_{max}) envisioned in different bioreactor configurations used for waste gas treatment are given in Table 1.

Process Mechanism

Biofiltration is a two – phase process consisting in the transfer of the compounds from the air phase to the water phase and oxidation of the absorbed compound by the microorganisms present in the BF. The dissolved contaminant is transported by diffusion and by advection in the air. When air flows around the particle there is continuous mass transfer between the gas – phase and the biofilm (Figure 4).

Table 1. Typical gas – phase pollutants treated in waste gas treatment systems and their corresponding EC values

Pollutant	Packing Material	MicroOrganism	Reactor Type	EC_{max}, g m^{-3} h^{-1}	References
Benzene	GAC	Mixed culture from waste-water treatment plant	BF	20.1	Kim, 2003
Toluene	Perlite	*Paecilomyces variotii*	BF	60	Estévez, Veiga & Kennes (2005)
TEX	Perlite	2 bacteria + 1 fungi	BF	>120	Veiga & Kennes (2001)
Styrene	Perlite	*Sporothrix sp.*	BF	336	Rene, Veiga & Kennes (2010)
DCM	Lava rock	*Hyphomicrobium sp.*	BTF	160	Bailon et al. (2009)
HS-P-M	Pall rings + perlite	*Ophiostoma sp.,* + autotrophic bacteria + *Candida boidinii*	BTF+BF	HS – 45 P – 138 M – 894	Rene et al. (2010a)
Toluene	Ceramic particles	*Bacillus cereus*	BtF	152	Li et al. (2008)
Styrene	Celite pellets	Mixed culture	BTF	62	Sorial et al. (1998)
Styrene	Ceramic monolith	*Sporothrix sp.*	MB	67.4	Rene et al. (2010b)
DCM		*Hyphomicro-bium sp.*	CSTB	117	Bailon et al. (2009)

Note: GAC – granular activated carbon, TEX – toluene, ethyl benzene and xylene mixture, HS-P-M – mixture of H_2S+ α – pinene + methanol, DCM – dichloromethane, BF – biofilter, BTF – biotrickling filter, MB – monolith bioreactor, CSTB – continuous stirred tank bioreactor, EC_{max} – maximum elimination capacity

The contaminant as it passes through the filter bed will adsorb onto either the filter medium or the biomass itself. The effectiveness of this mechanism depends on the characteristics of the filter bed, microbial heterogeneity, toxicity of the pollutants, availability of nutrients and oxygen, temperature, bed pressure drop, and pH ((Devinny, Deshusses & Webster, 1999). Generally the degradation rate for various chemicals depends on their chemical complexity. Biodegradation is influenced by a mixed microflora of degraders, competitors and predators that are at least partially organized in a biofilm. This active biofilm supplies essential nutrients for biological activity, maintains an aqueous environment for microbial growth, acts as the air/water interface for mass transport and as recipient of various by – products of the reaction (Kennes et al., 2009).

Microbial Aspects of BFs

The elimination of organic substrates by microorganisms results from the fact that these organisms generally use organic compounds as their sole energy (catabolism) and carbon source (anabolism) (Ottengraf & Diks, 1991). A prior knowledge of the species that are present, their densities, their metabolic transformations and their interactions with the environment is useful to biofilter operation. Typical bacteria include the following; *Pseudomonas putida*, *Coryneformic* bacteria, *Bacillus sp.*, *Methylobac-*

Figure 4. Schematic of pollutant removal mechanism in the biofilm attached to the filter bed of waste gas treatment systems (C_g is the gas – phase pollutant concentration)

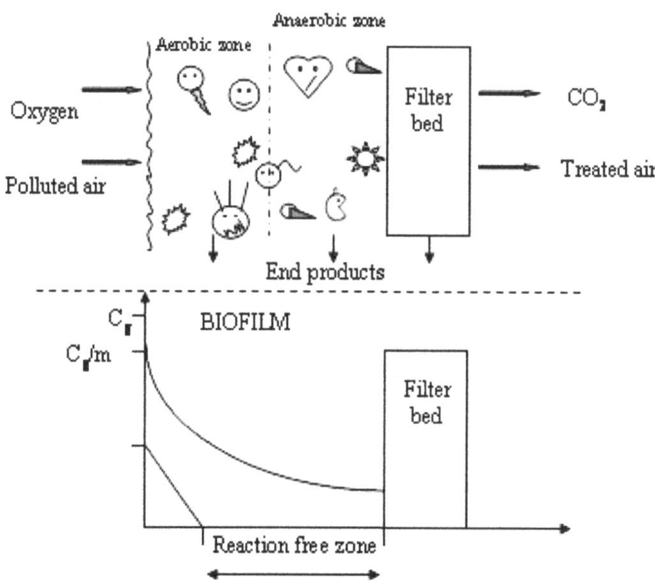

terium, *Mycobacterium sp.*, and *Pseudomonas fluorescens,* amongst others. Among fungal cultures, the most extensively studied organism belongs to the genus *Exophiala*, although strains of *Scedosporium*, *Fusarium*, *Paecilomyces*, *Cladosporium*, *Cladophialophora*, *Pleurotus*, *Trametes*, *Bjerkandera* and *Phanerochaete* have also been detected in BFs or used to treat gas – phase VOCs (Kennes & Veiga, 2004; Kennes, Rene & Veiga, 2009; Kennes et al., 2009).

Biotrickling Filters

The schematic of a BTF is shown in Figure 3b. The packing is generally made of chemically inert materials such as a plastic support, polyurethane foams, activated carbon, lava rock, pall rings, etc. that can be either arranged in a random or structured manner (Maliyekkal et al., 2004). These materials offer no nutrients to the microorganisms. Hence, nutrient medium is continuously trickled from the top of the reactor. The liquid phase and gas – phase flow can be fed co –or counter currently through the bed depending on the convenience of the user. The trickling solution contains inorganic and other trace nutrients for sustaining microbial activity in the biofilm. It can also act as a buffer, especially for compounds that are difficult to degrade or for compounds that generate more acidic metabolites (Oh & Bartha, 1997). The advantages of BTFs compared to BFs include; (i) better process control (ii) smaller footprints (iii) treatment of high concentration of VOCs, (iv) treatment of hot gases and acid producing contaminants and (v) good adaptation capacity of biomass (Devinny, Deshusses & Webster, 1999; Kennes & Veiga, 2001). The factors affecting pollutant removal are, among others; (i) composition and concentration of the waste –gas stream, (ii) structural configuration of the packing material, (iii) flow pattern, (iv) nutrient composition, (v) residence time, (vi) pH, and (vii) temperature (Sorial et al., 1995; Weber & Hartmans, 1996; Chou & Huang, 1997; Chou & Wu, 1999; Cox & Deshusses, 2001; Jin, Veiga & Kennes, 2007).

Air Diffusion through Suspended – Growth Bioreactors

Removal of air pollutants by means of diffusion through suspended – growth bioreactors is often done in completely mixed – type reactors (CSTB or completely stirred tank bioreactors), with constant aeration (Figure 3c), where microbes are kept in suspension in a nutrient rich aqueous phase. However, CSTBs for waste gas treatment often use the gas – phase pollutant as their sole carbon and energy source, preferably hydrophilic or slightly hydrophilic pollutants. As these systems are designed for aerobic biodegradation of the contaminants, mass transfer can be optimized for specific contaminants and both mass transfer and oxygen requirements would be the driving force for good reactor design (Bielefeldt, 2001). The efficiency of the CSTB depends on the following factors: (i) the hydraulic retention time (HRT), (ii) concentration and characteristics of the gas – phase pollutant, (iii) the presence of inhibitory metabolites within the system, and (iv) the gas hold – up. The major challenge regarding its long term operation in industrial facilities is reducing biomass growth and disposal. A few methods have been suggested for reducing biomass accumulation in CSTBs; (i) increasing the mean cell residence time so that the requirement for maintenance energy increases, and/or (ii) decrease efficiency of energy generation for biomass growth by limiting nutrient supply. The advantages of this process include; better temperature and pH control, simple construction, good process control, adaptability to fit reactor configurations such as two – stage systems, better control of different phases, example – addition of an oil phase for increasing pollutant solubility, easy maintenance and low operating costs. CSTBs have been tested under lab scale conditions for removing trichloroethylene (TCE) and dichloromethane (DCM), among others (Lee, 2003; Baílon et al., 2009).

BIOLOGICAL WASTEWATER TREATMENT SYSTEMS

Microorganisms play a major role in oxidizing the dissolved and particulate carbonaceous organic matter present in wastewater to acceptable forms that can make the ultimate disposal mode simpler. Aerobic microbes are particularly suitable for the removal of organic matter in the concentration range between 50 to 4000 mg l^{-1}, as biodegradable chemical oxygen demand (COD).

The oxidation of organic matter by microorganisms present in a waste stream containing nutrients like NH_3 and PO_4^{3-} usually occurs according to this stoichiometric equation;

$$Organic\ matter\ +\ O_2 + NH_3 + PO_4^{3-} \rightarrow new\ cells\ +\ CO_2 + H_2O \tag{28}$$

Biological treatment systems can be classified as suspended growth processes and attached growth processes, and choosing an appropriate system depends on the wastewater composition and the desired level of treatment. However, biological wastewater treatment systems can be either modified or integrated with other systems to provide high biochemical oxygen demand (BOD) removal, carbonaceous COD removal, nitrification, denitrification, color removal, phosphorous removal and for the treatment of other high – strength wastewaters. In this section, the sequencing batch reactor (SBR) (Figure 3e) and activated sludge process (Figure 3f) are discussed as representative suspended growth reactors, while the operation of trickling filters (Figure 3g) has been given as an example for attached growth process.

Sequencing Batch Reactor

A SBR unit can be modified to provide secondary advanced treatment, simultaneous nitrification, and denitrification, in one reactor configuration (Figure 5a). SBRs have also been used extensively for COD, phosphate and nitrogen removal from both industrial and domestic wastewaters (Dangcong et al., 2004; Ganesh, Balaji & Ramanujam, 2006). It consists of time sequence steps of various operations in which the reactor is filled with the wastewater during a discrete period and operated in batch mode. The same reactor can be provided to accomplish equalization, aeration and classification in time sequences. The operation consists of aerobic, anaerobic and anoxic conditions to enhance the desired microbial activity.

Activated Sludge Process

The activated sludge process is a versatile bioreactor configuration for removing soluble organic components (BOD) present in wastewater using an aerobic suspension of microbes. The basic schematic of this process is shown in Figure 5b. The process consists of an aeration tank followed by a clarifier. The name 'activated' arises from the fact that, earlier, during its initial stages of process development, these systems were operated in batch mode. At the end of each aeration period, SS present in the reactor were left to settle and the clear supernatant was withdrawn in batch modes. During the next batch mode, this settled sludge was activated by aeration and fresh supply of incoming wastewater, thus increasing the growth of viable microbial cells inside the system.

The pollutant laden wastewater (primary influent) enters the aeration tank and is aerated for a specified length of time. The activated sludge present in the aeration tank uses the available organic matter as the carbon source, leading to more SS and more new cells. The SS then become a part of the existing activated sludge, and this sludge together with the wastewater reaches the next stage, the clarifier section, where the floc particles (50 to 200 μm) are separated from treated water. More than 95% of SS can be removed in the clarification step (Metcalf & Eddy, 2003). In some instance, to maintain the required concentration of mixed liquor suspended solids (MLSS), the solids are returned to the aeration

Figure 5. Schematic of different wastewater treatment systems, (a) sequencing batch reactor, (b) activated sludge process, and (c) trickling filter

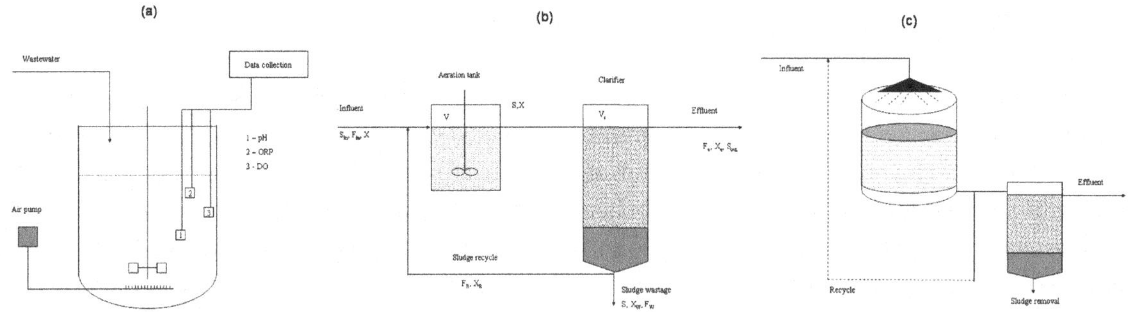

tank together with the influent (sludge return), and also periodically the excess solids and organisms are removed from the system (sludge wastage). Some of the most influential parameters that affect the operation and performance of an ASP are; temperature, sludge return rate, oxygen concentration, amount of organic matter, pH and aeration time.

A wide variety of microorganisms have been reported to be present in the activated sludge. These include; heterotrophic bacteria such as *Pseudomonas sp., Achromobacter sp., Citromonas sp., Flavobacterium sp.*, and *Zoogloea sp.*, (Jenkins, Richard & Daigger, 1993). These microbes obtain their energy from the carbonaceous matter present in wastewater. Autotrophic bacteria may also be present in the activated sludge and these are specific forms of bacteria that are able to synthesize their own food from inorganic substances. These bacteria may obtain their energy by oxidizing ammonia nitrogen to nitrate nitrogen in a two – stage conversion process known as nitrification when such nitrogen compounds are present in the wastewater. However, as very little energy is derived from these oxidization reactions, besides their own energy requirement to convert carbon dioxide to cellular carbon, nitrifying bacteria represent a small percentage of the total population of microorganisms in activated sludge. Typical examples of nitrifying bacteria are *Nitrosomonas* and *Nitrobacter*. The process of nitrification can be represented as follows;

$$55NH_4^+ + 76\ O_2 + 109\ HCO_3^- \rightarrow 5H_7O_2N\ +\ 54\ NO_2^- + 57\ H_2O\ +\ 104\ H_2CO_3 \tag{29}$$

$$400\ NO_2^- + NH_4^+ + 4H_2CO_3 + HCO_3^- + 195\ O_2 \rightarrow C_5H_7O_2N\ +\ 3H_2O\ +\ 400\ NO_3^- \tag{30}$$

Besides, protozoa have also been reported to be present in the activated sludge. These include, *Vorticella microstoma, Opercularia coarcta, Carchesium polypinum, Chilodonella uncinata, and Aspidisca costata* (Curds & Cockburn, 1970).

Trickling Filters

The trickling filter is one of the oldest type of water treatment system developed originally for treating municipal wastewater (Figure 5c). It consists of a filter bed made of either rock or plastic material over which wastewater is passed continuously. A uniform layer of biofilm is present over this rigid support that actively takes part in the pollutant removal process. The wastewater is passed uniformly over the filter material with the help of a distributor, and treatment occurs as soon as the water gets in contact with the biofilm. The distribution system consists of long arms (up to 60 m in length), fitted with unevenly spaced nozzles. An under drain and proper oxygen supply system is provided at the bottom of the unit. In some cases, the collected wastewater is recycled back to the system to dilute the strength of the influent, and to maintain the required moisture level in the filter. Two different types of trickling filters are commonly used in practice, and they are classified according to their organic loading rates, as low – rate and high – rate filters. Low – rate filters can produce an effluent of consistent quality within an influent of varying strength, i.e., fluctuating loading characteristics. In such filters, the dosing tanks are small, with only a 2 min retention time based on twice the average flow, so as to minimize intermittent dosing. As this type of filters are prone to stratification in terms of the biological characteristics, i.e., different microbial population at different bed heights due to irregular wetting, the lower portion is over populated with nitrifying bacteria that oxidize ammonia nitrogen to nitrates and nitrites. High – rate filters are usually designed for two – stage processes, and operated with recycle. Recirculation permits higher loadings, higher dosing rates on the filter and improves liquid distribution and oxygen supply to the system. This type of trickling filter can easily remove 60% to 85% of the organic load and are usually used in large – scale municipal facilities.

Dosing rate and adequate air flow are critical factors that are to be taken care of during the design stage of trickling filters. Dosing rate represents the depth of liquid discharged on top of the packing for each pass of the distributor. For higher distributor rotational speeds the dosing rate is lower. At high dosing rates, large volume of water is being discharged per revolution that in turn affects the formation of the biofilm, i.e., thinner biofilm. Hence the dosing rate has to be optimized to control biofilm thickness, and one way to solve this problem is to include a flushing dose periodically to the system. A steady supply of air is needed for the efficient operation of a trickling filter, and to prevent odors. It has been suggested that a forced ventilation system using low – pressure fans would provide a reliable and more controlled airflow (Metcalf & Eddy, 2003).

The microorganisms present in the trickling filter are, aerobic and facultative bacteria, fungi, algae and protozoans. Usually, facultative bacteria are predominantly present in trickling filters, which together with aerobic and anaerobic bacteria are able to utilize the organic material present in the wastewater. Fungal species like *Fusazium*, *Mucor*, *Penicillium*, *Geotrichum* and *Sporatichum* have also been identified (Higgins & Burns, 1975).

TYPICAL DESIGN EQUATIONS AND MODELS FOR WASTE GAS TREATMENT SYSTEMS: ATTACHED GROWTH PROCESSES

A prior knowledge about bio – kinetic parameters is essential to model waste gas treatment systems. According to the model reported by Jin, Veiga & Kennes (2006b), for the biofiltration of α – pinene using the fungus *Ophiostoma sp.*, the kinetics for cellular systems can adequately be described by the Monod type kinetics, that takes the form,

$$\mu^{\bullet} = \frac{\mu^{\bullet}_{\max} S}{K_s + S} \tag{31}$$

Where, S is the gas – phase pollutant concentration, g m $^{-3}$, K_S is the half – velocity constant (g m $^{-3}$) and is equal to the concentration of the rate limiting substrate when the specific growth rate ($\mu^{\bullet}$, h $^{-1}$) is equal to one half of its maximum value. This can be represented as $K_S = S$, when $\mu^{\bullet} = (1/2)\ \mu^{\bullet}_{max}$.

The specific microbial growth rate and the substrate consumption rate in the biofilm can be described as follows;

$$r_s = -\frac{dS}{dt} \tag{32}$$

$$= \frac{\beta\ \mu^{\bullet}}{Y_{X/S}} \tag{33}$$

$$= r_{s,\ \max} \frac{S}{K_S + S} \tag{34}$$

where, $r_{s,max}$ is the maximum substrate degradation rate corresponding to $\beta\mu^{\bullet}/Y_{X/S}$, $Y_{X/S}$ is the biomass yield coefficient based on the substrate (g cell g substrate $^{-1}$) and β is the biofilm density, g cell m $^{-3}$.

By considering a small segment of the BF with height 'z' (Figure 3a), and doing a mass balance for the pollutant, one can derive the following equation;

$$- \int_{C_i}^{C_o} \frac{K_S + S}{S}\ dS = r_{s,\max} \frac{A}{Q} \int_0^H dz \tag{35}$$

After integration over the entire bed height, we get;

$$Left\ \ side = (C_i\ \ -\ \ C_o) \left[1 + \frac{K_S}{(C_i\ \ -\ \ C_o) / \ln \frac{C_i}{C_o}} \right] \tag{36}$$

But, V/Q = Ci – Co /r_s, thus the right side of equation (35) becomes;

$$Right\ \ side = r_{s,\ \max}(C_i - C_o) = (C_i\ \ -\ \ C_o) \left(1 + \frac{K_S}{\overline{C}} \right) \tag{37}$$

where, $\overline{C} = C_i - C_o/\ln (C_{i/}C_o)$. $r_{s,max}$ and K_S can easily be obtained by non – linear regression of the experimental data, at different flow rates.

The volume of the BF (V) can also be calculated from the inlet gas concentration (C_i), the gas – flow rate (Q) and the required outlet concentration after biotreatment (C_o), represented as;

$$V = \frac{Q}{r_{s,\max}} \left[(C_i - C_o) + K_S \ln \frac{C_i}{C_o} \right] \tag{38}$$

The rate of mass transfer depends on the concentration gradient across the bulk – gas liquid interface (Figure 4), and can be defined as;

$$Mass\ \ flux = K_L \left(\frac{C_i}{\mathrm{H}} - C_L \right) \tag{39}$$

where, K_L is the mass transfer coefficient, C_L is the concentration of pollutant in the biofilm phase, and H is the Henry's constant (dimensionless).

The overall elimination rate of the pollutant in the biofilm can be reaction limited or diffusion limited, depending on the characteristics of the biofilm. Thus, the relationship between gas – phase pollutant concentration and the height of the bioreactor under reaction limitation condition can be represented by;

$$\frac{C_o}{C_i} = 1 - \left[\frac{k_o A_S \delta\ h}{Q\ C_i}\right] \tag{40}$$

where, k_o is the zero – order reaction constant (g m $^{-3}$ h $^{-1}$), A_S is the biofilm interfacial area per volume of packing material (m^2 m $^{-3}$), δ is the biofilm thickness (mm), and h is the height of the filter bed (m).

On the other hand, for diffusion limitation conditions, the theoretical dependence of inlet concentration on the filter bed height can be modelled by;

$$\frac{C_o}{C_i} = \left(1 - \frac{A_S H}{Q}\sqrt{\frac{k_o D_{eff}}{2C_i H}}\right)^2 \tag{41}$$

where, D_{eff} is the effective diffusion coefficient (m^2 h $^{-1}$).

TYPICAL DESIGN EQUATIONS FOR WASTEWATER TREATMENT SYSTEMS: ACTIVATED SLUDGE PROCESS

In 1982, the IAWPRC (International Association on Water Pollution Research and Control) initiated the task of developing mathematical models to represent the behaviour of ASPs in field situations. This led to the development of four well – known models using the fundamental biokinetics of the process, viz., ASM1 that includes nitrogen removal, ASM2 that includes biological phosphorous removal, ASM2d that includes denitrifying PAO's and ASM3 that simplifies the previous ASM biokinetics (Gujer et al., 1999).

Mass Balance Equations

A simple mass balance equation can be given by considering the ASP as a single – substrate, single – biomass system (Baruch et al., 2005). Besides, it is assumed that the aeration tank is completely mixed and that the concentration of each component is spatially homogenous (Figure 3f). Thus, the mass balance to the bioreactor can be expressed in terms of the biomass concentration, X(t), and substrate concentration, S(t), as follows;

$$X(t) = \left(\mu^A(S) - \frac{F_{in}(t) + F_R(t)}{V} - c_d(t)\right) X(t) + \frac{F_R(t)}{V} X_R(t) \tag{42}$$

$$S(t) = -\frac{1}{Y}\mu^A(S)\ X(t) + \frac{F_{in}(t)}{V} S_{in} - \frac{F_{in}(t) + F_R(t)}{V} S(t) \tag{43}$$

Where μ^A is the specific growth rate (h^{-1}), F_{in} is the influent flow rate (h^{-1}), F_R is the recycle flow rate (h^{-1}), C_d is the decay rate parameter, V is the volume of the bioreactor (aeration tank, m^3), X_R is the biomass concentration in the recycle stream ($g\ m^{-3}$).

The dynamics of microbial concentration in the clarifier section (settling tank), can be described by the following mass balance equation;

$$X_R(t) = \left(\frac{F_{in}(t) + F_R(t)}{V_s}\right) X(t) + \left(\frac{F_W(t) \ + \ F_R(t)}{V_S}\right) X_R(t) \tag{44}$$

where, F_W is the waste flow rate (h^{-1}) and V_S is the volume of the settler (m^3).

Estimating Oxygen Requirements

Dissolved oxygen (DO) concentration is one of the most important parameters to control in an ASP, because of its significant impact on the process efficiency and the energy saving related to aeration (Mingzhi et al., 2009). The quantity of oxygen required could be calculated as the ultimate COD and NH_4^+ of the waste less the ultimate COD and NH_4^+ discharged in the effluent and in the sludge flow. The theoretical amount of air required can be calculated as;

$$Q_{air,th} = \frac{\left[T_u\left(COD_{in} - COD_{out}\right)Q_{in} + T_N\left(NH_4^{+}{}_{in} - NH_4^{+}{}_{out}\right)Q_{in}\right]}{K_{la} \times P_o \times \rho_{air}} \tag{45}$$

where, T_u is the typical ratio of oxygen demand for removing unit mass of COD ($T_u = 1.1$), T_N is the typical ratio of oxygen demand for removing unit mass of NH_4^+, K_{la} is the coefficient of mass transfer, P_o is the percentage weight of oxygen in air, and ρ_{air} is the density of air.

Biokinetic Expressions in Activated Sludge Process

The biomass growth rate is proportional to the substrate utilization rate by the synthesis yield coefficient (Y), and biomass decay is proportional to the amount of biomass present (Metcalf & Eddy, 2003). Thus, the net biomass production rate ($r_{g,}$ g VSS $m^3\ d^{-1}$) can be modelled by;

$$r_g = \text{-}Yr_{su} \text{ - } K_d X \tag{46}$$

$$= Y\frac{kSX}{K_S + S} \text{ - } K_d X \tag{47}$$

Dividing both sides by biomass concentration (X), we get,

$$\mu^A = \frac{r_g}{X} = Y\frac{kS}{K_S + S} - K_d \quad (48)$$

where, r_{su} is the substrate utilization rate (g COD m $^{-3}$ d $^{-1}$), Y is the synthesis yield coefficient (g VSS g COD $^{-1}$), k_d is the endogenous decay coefficient (g VSS g VSS d $^{-1}$), and μ^A is the specific biomass growth rate (g VSS g VSS d $^{-1}$).

The oxygen uptake rate (r_o, g O_2 m $^{-3}$ d $^{-1}$) can be defined by the relationship;

$$r_o = -r_{su} - 1.42r_g \quad (49)$$

The effect of temperature on the reaction rate of a biological process can be modelled by the Arrhenius type equation, given as;

$$k_T = k_{20}\theta^{(T-20)} \quad (50)$$

where, k_T is the reaction rate coefficient at temperature T, °C, k_{20} is the reaction rate coefficient at 20 °C, θ is the temperature activity coefficient, and T is the temperature, °C.

The average SRT in the aeration tank can be defined as;

$$SRT = \frac{VX}{(F_{in} - F_w)F_e + F_w X_R} \quad (51)$$

The food to microorganism ratio (F/M) ratio is defined by;

$$\frac{F}{M} = \frac{F_{in}S_{in}}{VX} = \frac{S_{in}}{\tau X} \quad (52)$$

where, F/M has the unit g BOD or COD g VSS d $^{-1}$, F_{in} is the influent wastewater flow rate (m^3 d $^{-1}$), V is the aeration tank volume (m^3), X is the biomass concentration in the aeration tank (g m $^{-3}$) and τ is the hydraulic retention time of the aeration tank (d).

ANN BASED MODELLING FOR WASTE GAS TREATMENT SYSTEMS

Though the working mechanism of a waste gas treatment system such as a BF looks simple, it is bound by certain interdependent processes such as absorption, adsorption, biodegradation, apart from being influenced by other physico – chemical factors (Kennes et al., 2009). Simple mathematical models have been developed, as mentioned in the previous sections, and simple protocols to monitor the performance under lab – scale conditions have been stated. However, there are difficulties to use these protocols in field conditions. Applying the concepts of ANNs to model waste gas treatment systems was initiated only recently, in the mid 2000's, when a BTF and BF were modelled for their performance (Rene et al.,

2006; Elias et al., 2006; Rene, Veiga & Kennes, 2009). Elias et al. (2006) obtained start – up, intermittent fluctuation, steady – state and shut – down data from a lab – scale BF packed with pig manure and saw dust, handling H_2S vapours. Data division was done using cluster analysis in combination with a genetic algorithm, and the data were divided as training (50%), testing (40%) and validation (10%). Inlet H_2S concentration and unit flow values (Q/V, h^{-1}) were used as the input to the model, for predicting the removal efficiency of the BF (RE, %). The best MLP was decided by trial and error, by testing nearly 10,000 different combinations of MLPs, and it was observed that a 2 – 2 – 1 network architecture was able to predict RE well with relatively high R^2 values (0.92). Results from sensitivity analysis showed the influence of flow rate in affecting the BF performance, and these findings were similar to the actual experimental data collected from the BF during 3 years of operation. Rene, Veiga & Kennes (2009) modelled the performance of a BF (RE, %) using a back propagation algorithm for a reactor inoculated with a mixed culture taken from the wastewater sludge of a petrochemical refinery and treating gas – phase styrene. A log – sigmoid transfer function was used with inlet styrene concentration and unit flow as the inputs, and the best network topology obtained through trial and error was found to be 2 – 4 – 1. During regular experiments, greater than 92% styrene removal was achievable for loading rates up to 250 g m^{-3} h^{-1}, and the critical load to the system was found to depend highly on the gas – flow rate, i.e., EBRT. A sensitivity analysis, in terms of absolute average sensitivity (AAS) was carried out for the developed model, to estimate the most influencing input parameter for the model, and it was observed that these values were 0.5250 and 0.4249 for unit flow and inlet styrene concentration, respectively. This higher AAS value for unit flow suggested that the BF performance highly depended on the flow rate, and that the effects due to the pollutant, gas – phase styrene, was only minimal. The results were further interpreted in terms of contour plot to envisage the safe operating regime for the BF (Figure 6a). An attempt was also made to model the performance of a CSTB, treating gas – phase styrene, inoculated with the fungus *Sporothrix variecibatus*, by choosing unit flow, inlet styrene concentration and biomass concentration as the input variables. A 3 – 5 – 1 topology best described the styrene removal efficiency of the system. The internal network parameters of the back propagation algorithm, namely η and momentum term and training count were varied in a series of trial and error steps to obtain high predictions for gas – phase styrene removal. Through sensitive analysis, it was envisaged that the most influential parameter for the CSTB was inlet concentration. The biomass concentration in the CSTB remained relatively constant after a few weeks of operation. In biological waste gas treatment systems, the most influential parameter affecting the performance of the system could easily change depending on the operational characteristics of the system. The contour plot shown in Figure 6b reveals the influence of inlet styrene concentration and biomass concentration on the removal efficiency. As evident, for achieving high RE in the system, inlet styrene concentrations should be maintained below 2 g m^{-3}. In the case of a CSTB, a suspended growth system, mass transfer plays a major role in contaminant transfer from the gas – phase to the liquid phase, while in the case of a BF (attached growth system), mass transfer limitations occur during contaminant transfer from the bulk gas – phase to the biofilm attached onto the porous carrier material. The hydrophobic nature of the pollutant (styrene) affected the mass transfer in the former case, and thus inlet concentration was shown to be the major influential parameter for its removal (non – published data).

Krasnopolsky & Chevallier (2003) suggest a regular re – assessment of any developed ANN model and hinted out that '*ANNs obviously provide powerful solutions for the simulation of environmental processes, but like any other parameterization, their relevance needs to be regularly re-evaluated with respect to the particular computational and scientific contexts where they are developed and used*'.

ANN BASED MODELLING FOR WASTEWATER TREATMENT SYSTEMS

Model for SBR

Nutrient concentrations in SBRs are generally monitored regularly by routine chemical analysis, yet, these procedures are time consuming. In order to achieve a well – timed adaptive process control for SBRs, accommodating influent fluctuations and other disturbances, a more precise timely control device is needed. Under such conditions, an online ANN based software sensor for nutrients with auto – regressive and exogenous inputs has been suggested (Hong et al., 2007). In that study, a fill – and – draw SBR was operated in 8 h cyclic mode and each cycle consisted of 2 h anaerobic, 4 h 30 min aerobic, 1 h 30 min settling and drawing phase. SRT was maintained by periodically wasting MLSS at the end of the aerobic stage. Multi – way principal component analysis (MPCA) was used for analysis for the whole

Figure 6. Contour plots illustrating, (a) the effect of unit flow and styrene concentration on the removal efficiency of a BF, and (b) effect of styrene concentration and biomass concentration on the performance of a CSTB

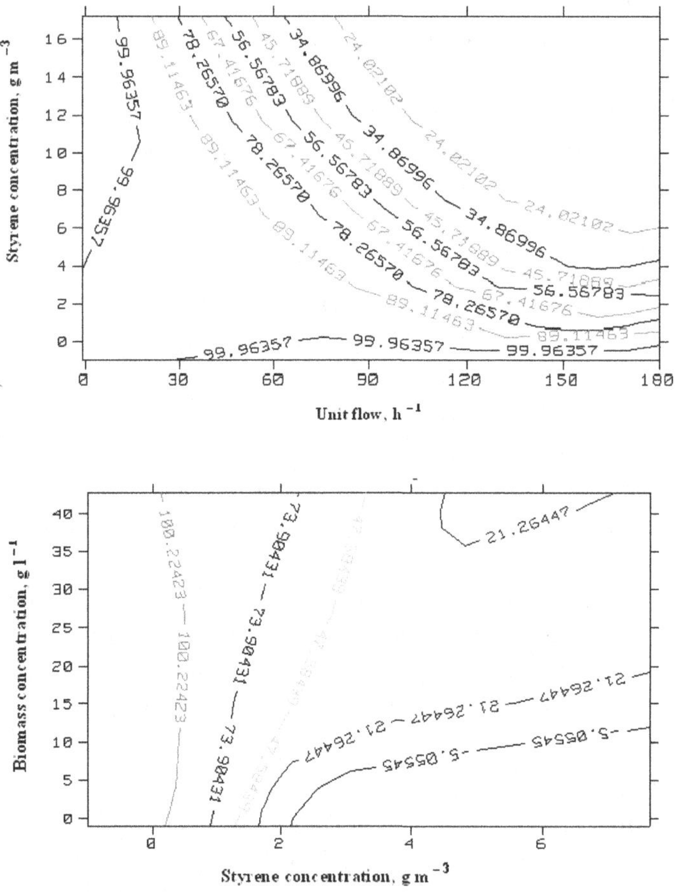

process data consisting of 24 batches. MPCA was used to compress the normal batch data and extract the important information by projecting the data onto a low – dimensional space that summarizes both the variables and their time trajectories. Easily available online measurements such as pH, ORP and DO were taken as inputs, while the nutrient concentrations, viz., NH_4^+, NO_3^- and PO_4^{3-}, were considered as the outputs (Figure 7a). By assigning the target online monitoring interval as 5 min, specific neural models were developed for the anaerobic and aerobic phases. The results showed that, for normal batch operations, excellent monitoring capability could be obtained. However, for abnormal batch operations, the software sensor showed poor monitoring ability, which was attributed to the range of data contained in the training set, i.e., the developed neural models were not good at extrapolating the state variables. SBRs have also been tested for their ability to perform under saline – rich conditions, typically those arising from fish processing industries. Rene, Kim & Park (2008) operated a SBR at different C/N ratios (3 – 6), aeration times (4 – 10 h) and salt concentrations (0.5 – 2%) to estimate the COD and nitrogen removal efficiencies. The results suggested that, COD removal efficiencies under steady state operation were consistently greater than 80%, while nitrogen removal efficiencies (10 to 98%) were inhibited by high salt concentrations. Back propagation neural network was applied to model these experimental data using influent COD, influent nitrogen, salt concentration, aeration time, MLSS concentration and C/N ratio as the inputs to predict the performance parameters, viz., COD removal efficiency (COD-RE), total nitrogen removal efficiency (T-RE), $NH_4 – N$, $NO_3 – N$ and $NO_2 – N$ produced in the SBR, according to the topology shown in Figure 7b. The appropriate internal network parameters were selected using the 2^k – full factorial design of experiments, and ANOVA results gave statistical significance of the effect of these parameters on the response, i.e., correlation coefficient values. The appropriate network topology for this system (6 – 12 – 5) was selected by estimating the best correlation coefficient (R^2) value (>0.84) achieved during prediction of the testing set.

Aguado et al. (2009) operated a bench – scale SBR under anaerobic / aerobic (A/O) conditions for enhanced biological phosphorous removal (EBPR). The SBR was operated with four 6 – h cycles per day and each cycle consisted of the five general stages of SBR operation. Phosphorous (P) concentration in each cycle was considered to be very important to evaluate the overall treatment performance, and thus a ANN model was developed to predict P – concentrations using pH, electrical conductivity, oxygen reduction potential (ORP), temperature and DO concentration as inputs to the model. The developed neural model enabled to develop a soft – sensor for monitoring laboratory – scale SBR operated for EBPR. Besides, ANN also acted as an automatic tool to optimize the length of the stages within each reaction cycle.

MODEL FOR ASP

Moral, Aksoy and Goksay (2008) explored the versatility of ANN based modelling strategy for a real wastewater treatment plant located in Iskenderun, Turkey. The treatment system composed of coarse and fine screens, grit removal, primary sedimentation tanks, activated sludge aeration tanks and secondary sedimentation tanks. The plant was designed to handle wastewater at the rate of 57,000 $m^3 d^{-1}$. The plant was monitored continuously as a function of SRT, influent flow rate, influent pH, water temperature, influent COD, MLSS, effluent COD, effluent TSS, sludge volume index (SVI) and sludge production rate. ANN was applied to model these data so as to predict the effluent COD (COD_{eff}). The above – mentioned variables, alone or as combinations were used as input to the model, and it was observed that TSS

Figure 7. Network architectures developed for wastewater systems from literature sources, (a) Hong et al. (2007) model for SBR, (b) Rene, Kim & Park (2008) model for SBR, and (c) Pu & Hung (1995) model for trickling filter

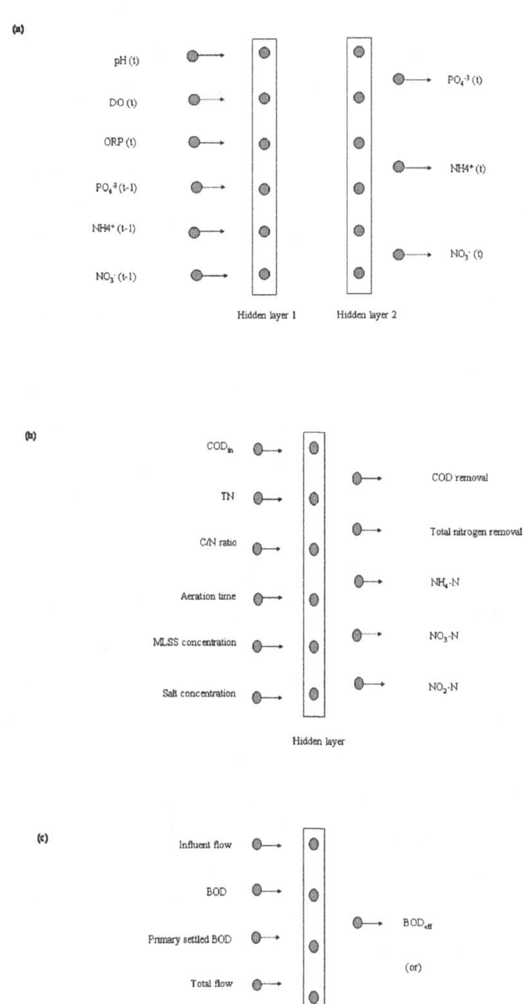

concentrations as the sole input approximated effluent COD (COD_{eff}) better than other combinations. The advantages of using ANNs for ASPs include; (i) the possibility to develop scientific models that would consider local operating conditions, and (ii) the flow rate, TSS concentration and MLSS concentration can be monitored very easily every day, and hence it can be possible to have a continuous estimate of the effluent COD concentrations. Besides, ANN models have also shown to minimize the operational costs and assess the stability of an actual wastewater treatment plant. Mjalli, Al – Asheh & Alfadala (2007) used neural networks with one and two hidden layers, BOD, SS and COD values to monitor the performance of a wastewater treatment plant (Doha, Qatar), that had the following characteristics; flow rate – 54,000 m^3 d^{-1}, peak flow – 183,000 m^3 d^{-1}, BOD – 300 mg l^{-1}, TSS – 300 mg l^{-1}. The input parameters to the ANN model were TSS, BOD and COD values from the crude stream, used in 12 different combinations, both as alone and as ternary mixtures, to predict TSS, BOD and COD of the secondary treatment effluent. A graphical user interface, developed using MATLAB was designed for implementing the neural model for the wastewater treatment plant, where the user had the choice of predicting any plant output using different plant input variables.

Model for Trickling Filter

The relationship between operating parameters such as, food to microorganism (F/M) ratio, influent BOD concentration, mean cell residence time are not fully understood in full – scale trickling filters. ANN has shown to functionally map the relationship between these variables, by using influent flow rate, total flow to the trickling filter, recirculation flow, SS, primary settled BOD, raw BOD, and primary SS concentration as the input variable, and effluent BOD and effluent SS concentration as the output variable (Figure 7c) for data collected from a wastewater treatment plant located in Solon, Ohio (Pu & Hung, 1995). The plant had an average daily flow of 13,600 m^3 d^{-1}, and a peak daily flow of 34,000 m^3 d^{-1} and for modelling purpose, daily data for the above – mentioned parameters for 3 consecutive years were used. Pu and Hung (1995) observed that, the number of input variables as well as the number of nodes in hidden layer did not appear to have a definite effect on the prediction error, but, the prediction efficiency was found to depend highly on the most influential input parameter, namely, influent flow rate, settled BOD, total and recirculation flow.

OTHER APPLICATIONS

Dellana and West (2009) compared linear and non – linear approaches for predictive modelling in wastewater treatment systems and after a review of existing literature, they have reported that '*Many researchers have come to realize that there is no single best model to use in all wastewater and watershed situations*'.

Estimation of K_La in CSTR

The successful operation of a CSTR depends on the volumetric mass transfer coefficient (K_La), which is one of the most important parameters in reactor design and scale – up. The values of K_La depend on factors such as viscosity and surface tension of the liquid, the geometry of the vessel and stirrer, sparger type, superficial gas velocity and other operational conditions. Garcia – Ochoa & Castro (2001) developed a hybrid ANN model by combining ANN and empirical equations representing the estimated parameter values. The best network topology was 8 – 5 – 1, and this hybrid model was able to predict the correct influence of geometric parameters of the vessel on the K_La values. The model was also used as a simulator to predict the influence of operating conditions on K_La.

Exploring Fuzzy Systems and ANN Together

ANNs coupled with fuzzy systems have also been used in wastewater treatment processes. One of the advantages of fuzzy neural network modelling is its ability to learn relationships through the data itself rather than assuming the functional form of the relationship. Fuzzy neural networks can be used as emulator and controller in process control systems. The fuzzy emulator is trained off – line and then used to simulate the dynamics of the process, while the controller is trained by the data of a real system inputs, operating results and control parameters. Mingzhi et al. (2009) modelled the complex unit operations in a paper mill wastewater treatment facility using a combined fuzzy system and ANN model. In that study, an adaptive fuzzy neural network was developed to model relationships between pollutant removal rates and chemical additive dosages (coagulant), and the dosage required for transient influent conditions were adequately forecasted. The results showed that the coupled system was able to provide satisfactory predictions based on previous dosage information.

Physico – Chemical Wastewater Treatment Processes

A simple MLP was developed using the back propagation algorithm to estimate the dye decolorization efficiency (Aleboyeh et al., 2008). In that study, photochemical decolorization of Acid Orange 7 solution by a combination of UV and H_2O_2 was investigated in an annular photochemical reactor. Initial dye concentrations, H_2O_2 dosage, pH and operating time were assigned as model inputs, while decolorization efficiency was the output for the ANN model. The relative importance of the input variables were estimated using Garson's method (1991), and it was concluded that, H_2O_2 concentrations (48.9%) had a strong influence in affecting the performance of the photoreactor. Syu & Chen (1998) applied the Fenton's method (chemical oxidation of waste in water followed by coagulation of suspended particles after oxidation) to oxidize the organic compounds in wastewater. They developed a neural network structure for online control of the system, by training the network in a dynamic mode during online operation. A moving window method was adapted, i.e., a fixed number of training data was provided at a given time, and when a new data was added, the oldest data was removed. This method was found to be efficient in terms of saving training time and also in terms of periodic update of the existing data, besides being carried out online. A back propagation neural network with the topology 7 – 4 – 1, to predict COD at time 't', was found to be efficient when the model acted as a learner/predictor, and on the other hand, when the network was switched to be a controller, the input element of COD (t) was replaced by the set – point of 90 ppm, which is the discharge limit for COD.

Other Bioreactors for Wastewater Treatment

A novel pulsed plate immobilized cell bioreactor was modelled by ANN for the biodegradation of phenol using *Nocardia hydrocarbonoxydans* (Shetty, Nandennavar & Srinikethan, 2008). Flow rate (ml h^{-1}), influent phenol concentration (mg l^{-1}), and vibration velocity (s^{-1}) were chosen as the inputs to predict the phenol removal efficiency, using the standard back propagation algorithm. Though limited data points were used from experimental investigation (24), as training, and 3 data points for testing the network, the model showed high prediction efficiency, with correlation coefficient values >0.99.

Up – flow anaerobic sludge blankets (UASB) are used in full scale water treatment applications for handling domestic wastewater. The up – flowing wastewater travels through a zone containing a large number of sludge particles held under suspension in the reactor, thus providing large surface area for attachment of organic matter undergoing biodegradation. Singh et al. (2010) modelled the performance of an UASB, based in Kanpur, India, using linear and non – linear approaches. BOD, COD, NH_4 – N and TKN were used as inputs to predict effluent COD/BOD ratio in one model (one output), and effluent COD and BOD in the other model (2 outputs). Among the three modelling procedures adapted, viz., multivariate linear, low – order non – linear and ANNs, the low – order non – linear and the ANN models were able to statistically perform better than the multivariate linear model.

The concept of modelling and real – time control strategy of wastewater treatment systems has significant implications in real time processes. Programmable logic controllers (PLCs) and expert systems for process fault diagnosis have also been used successfully in ASP. Miller et al. (1997) used a simplified hybrid neural net to model and analyze the chemical wastewater treatment plant in Mizushima, Japan. The prime aim was to reduce the occurrences of overflow in the clarifier caused by filamentous bulking and thereby increase wastewater treatment capacity.

Apart from their extensive use in the field of biological waste treatment, ANNs have also been widely used as a control tool for chemical processes like, (i) CSTR, (ii) distillation column, (iii) polypropylene – propane splitter, (iv) anaerobic digestion systems, (v) feed pre – heater systems, and (vi) neutralization tanks (Hussain, 1999). Their ability to forecast future time series makes them a popular tool in the field of medicine, finance, power generation, telecommunication, risk assessment, applied hydraulics, air quality management, and other branches of engineering sciences.

CONCLUSION

An overview of the current biological waste gas and wastewater treatment methods, their salient features for enhanced performance, and the related phenomenological design equations has been presented. The emerging computational resources have led to the development of a large number of newer techniques based on the fundamental concept of artificial intelligence. Among them, neural networks appear to be more effective compared to the classical modelling and control techniques, as evident from their successful implementation to model, design and control wastewater treatment systems. Neural networks are able to model the behaviour of any biological waste treatment process with limited information on their biokinetic parameters. In most of the cases, a three layered feed forward neural network has shown to approximate the working mechanism of these processes with an input, hidden and output layer. Based on the extensive literature that was reviewed, it is quite apparent that the application of ANN to model bioreactors for waste gas treatment is still at its early stages of development and is slowly gaining popularity. Environmental modelling research should also focus more on developing neural models for waste gas treatment systems, so that online control of state variables becomes much simpler and faster. Online sensors coupled with programmable logic controllers and neural networks can efficiently be used to monitor the plant performance during steady state and transient state operations.

ACKNOWLEDGMENT

The authors thank the Spanish Ministry of Science and Innovation (Project: CTM2007 – 62700/TECNO), and the European FEDER for providing financial support. Eldon R. Rene thanks the Ministry of Science and Innovation for his post doctoral research contract (JCI-2008-03109). The PhD research work of M. Estefania López is being supported by the Environmental Engineering group at the University of La Coruña.

REFERENCES

Aguado, D., Ribes, J., Montoya, T., Ferrer, J., & Seco, A. (2009). A methodology for sequencing batch reactor identification with artificial neural networks: A case study. *Computers & Chemical Engineering, 33*, 465–472. doi:10.1016/j.compchemeng.2008.10.018

Aleboyeh, A., Kasiri, M. B., Olya, M. E., & Aleboyeh, H. (2008). Prediction of azo dye decolorization by UV/H_2O_2 using artificial neural networks. *Dyes and Pigments, 77*, 288–294. doi:10.1016/j.dyepig.2007.05.014

Amari, S., Chen, T., & Cichocki, A. (1997). Stability analysis of learning algorithms for blind source separation. *Neural Networks, 10*, 1345–1351. doi:10.1016/S0893-6080(97)00039-7

Bailón, L., Nikolausz, M., Kästner, M., Veiga, M. C., & Kennes, C. (2009). Removal of dichloromethane from waste gases in one-and two-liquid-phase stirred tank bioreactors and biotrickling filters. *Water Research, 43*, 11–20. doi:10.1016/j.watres.2008.09.031

Baruch, I. S., Georgieva, P., Barrera-Cortes, J., & de Azevedo, S. F. (2005). Adaptive recurrent neural network control of biological wastewater treatment. *International Journal of Intelligent Systems, 20*, 173–193. doi:10.1002/int.20061

Bielefeldt, A. R. (2001). Activated sludge and suspended growth bioreactors. In Kennes, C., & Veiga, M. C. (Eds.), *Bioreactors for waste gas treatment* (pp. 215–254). Dordrecht, The Netherlands: Kluwer Academic Publisher.

Chen, S. H., Jakeman, A. J., & Norton, J. P. (2008). Artificial intelligence techniques: An introduction to their use for modelling environmental systems. *Mathematics and Computers in Simulation, 78*, 379–400. doi:10.1016/j.matcom.2008.01.028

Choi, D. J., & Park, H. (2001). A hybrid artificial neural network as a software sensor for optimal control of a wastewater treatment process. *Water Research, 35*, 3959–3967. doi:10.1016/S0043-1354(01)00134-8

Chou, M.-S., & Huang, J.-H. (1997). Treatment of methylethylketone in air stream by biotrickling filters. *Journal of Environmental Engineering, 123*, 569–576. doi:10.1061/(ASCE)0733-9372(1997)123:6(569)

Chou, M.-S., & Wu, F. H. (1999). Treatment of toluene in an air stream by a biotrickling filter packed with slags. *Journal of the Air & Waste Management Association, 49*, 386–398.

Cox, H. H. J., & Deshusses, M. A. (2001). Biotrickling filters. In Kennes, C., & Veiga, M. C. (Eds.), *Bioreactors for waste gas treatment* (pp. 99–131). Dordrecht, The Netherlands: Kluwer Academic Publisher.

Curds, C. R., & Cockburn, A. (1970). Protozoa in biological sewage-treatment processes-I. A survey of the protozoan fauna of British percolating filters and activated-sludge plants. *Water Research, 4*, 225–236. doi:10.1016/0043-1354(70)90069-2

Dai, H., & MacBeth, C. (1997). The application of back-propagation neural network to automatic picking seismic arrivals from single-component recordings. *Journal of Geophysical Research*, *102*, 105–113. doi:10.1029/97JB00625

Dangcong, P., Yi, W., Hao, W., & Xiaochang, W. (2004). Biological denitrification in a sequencing batch reactor. *Water Science and Technology*, *50*, 67–72.

Dellana, S. A., & West, D. (2009). Predictive modelling for wastewater applications: Linear and nonlinear approaches. *Environmental Modelling & Software*, *24*, 96–106. doi:10.1016/j.envsoft.2008.06.002

Devinny, J. S., Deshusses, M. A., & Webster, T. S. (1999). *Biofiltration for air pollution control*. Boca Raton, FL: Lewis Publisher.

Elías, A., Ibarra-Berastegi, G., Arias, R., & Barona, A. (2006). Neural networks as a tool for control and management of a biological reactor for treating hydrogen sulphide. *Bioprocess and Biosystems Engineering*, *29*, 129–136. doi:10.1007/s00449-006-0062-3

Estévez, E., Veiga, M. C., & Kennes, C. (2005). Biodegradation of toluene by the new fungal isolates *Paecilomyces variotii* and *Exophiala oligosperma*. *Journal of Industrial Microbiology & Biotechnology*, *32*, 33–37. doi:10.1007/s10295-004-0203-0

Feldman, J. A., & Ballard, D. H. (1982). Connectionist models and their properties. *Cognitive Science*, *6*, 205–254. doi:10.1207/s15516709cog0603_1

Fernando, T. M. K. G., Maier, H. R., & Dandy, G. C. (2009). Selection of input variables for data driven models: An average shifted histogram partial mutual information estimator approach. *Journal of Hydrology (Amsterdam)*, *367*, 165–176. doi:10.1016/j.jhydrol.2008.10.019

Ganesh, R., Balaji, G., & Ramanujam, R. A. (2006). Biodegradation of tannery wastewater using sequencing batch reactor-respirometric assessment. *Bioresource Technology*, *97*, 1815–1821. doi:10.1016/j.biortech.2005.09.003

Garcia-Ochoa, F., & Castro, E. G. (2001). Estimation of oxygen mass transfer coefficient in stirred tank reactors using artificial neural networks. *Enzyme and Microbial Technology*, *28*, 560–569. doi:10.1016/S0141-0229(01)00297-6

Garson, G. D. (1991). Interpreting neural-network connection weights. *Artificial Intelligence Expert*, *6*, 47–51.

Gujer, A., Henze, M., Mino, T., & van Loosdrecht, M., & IAWQ Task Group on Mathematical Modelling for Design and Operation of Biological Wastewater Treatment. (1999). Activated sludge model no. 3. *Water Science and Technology*, *39*, 183–193. doi:10.1016/S0273-1223(98)00785-9

Hassoun, M. H. (1995). *Fundamentals of artificial neural networks*. Cambridge, MA: MIT Press.

Haykin, S. (1999). *Neural networks: A comprehensive foundation*. Pearson Prentice Hall.

Higgins, I. J., & Burns, R. G. (1975). *The chemistry and microbiology of pollution* (pp. 55–105). London, UK: Academic Press.

Hong, S. H., Lee, M. W., Lee, D. S., & Park, J. M. (2007). Monitoring of sequencing batch reactor for nitrogen and phosphorus removal using neural networks. *Biochemical Engineering Journal, 35*, 365–370. doi:10.1016/j.bej.2007.01.033

Hopfield, J. (1982). Neural networks and physical systems with emergent collective computational abilities. *Proceedings of the National Academy of Sciences of the USA, 9*, (p. 2554).

Hussain, M. (1999). Review of the applications of neural networks in chemical process control–simulation and online implementation. *Artificial Intelligence in Engineering, 13*, 55–68. doi:10.1016/S0954-1810(98)00011-9

Infante, P. F., Rinsky, R. A., Wagoner, J. K., & Young, R. J. (1997, July 9). Leukemia in benzene workers. *Lancet*, 76–78.

Jain, A. K., Mao, J., & Mohiuddin, K. M. (1996). Artificial neural networks: A tutorial. *IEEE Computer, 29*, 31–44.

Jenkins, D., Richard, M. G., & Daigger, G. T. (1993). *Manual on the causes and control of activated sludge bulking and foaming*. Boca Raton, FL: Lewis Publishers.

Jin, Y., Veiga, M. C., & Kennes, C. (2006a). Development of a novel monolith bioreactor for the treatment of VOC–polluted air. *Environmental Technology, 27*, 1271–1277. doi:10.1080/09593332708618744

Jin, Y., Veiga, M. C., & Kennes, C. (2006b). Performance optimization of the fungal biodegradation of α-pinene in gas-phase biofilter. *Process Biochemistry, 41*, 1722–1728. doi:10.1016/j.procbio.2006.03.020

Jin, Y., Veiga, M. C., & Kennes, C. (2007). Co-treatment of hydrogen sulphide and methanol in a single-stage biotrickling filter under acidic conditions. *Chemosphere, 68*, 1186–1193. doi:10.1016/j.chemosphere.2007.01.069

Jin, Y., Veiga, M. C., & Kennes, C. (2008). Removal of methanol from air in a low–pH trickling monolith bioreactor. *Process Biochemistry, 43*, 925–931. doi:10.1016/j.procbio.2008.04.019

Kennes, C., Montes, M., Lopez, M. E., & Veiga, M. C. (2009). Waste gas treatment in bioreactors: Environmental engineering aspects. *Canadian Journal of Civil Engineering, 36*, 1–9. doi:10.1139/L09-113

Kennes, C., Rene, E. R., & Veiga, M. C. (2009). Bioprocesses for air pollution control. *Journal of Chemical Technology and Biotechnology (Oxford, Oxfordshire), 84*, 1419–1436. doi:10.1002/jctb.2216

Kennes, C., & Veiga, M. C. (2001). Conventional biofilters. In Kennes, C., & Veiga, M. C. (Eds.), *Bioreactors for waste gas treatment* (pp. 47–98). Dordrecht, The Netherlands: Kluwer Academic Publisher.

Kennes, C., & Veiga, M. C. (2004). Fungal biocatalysts in the biofiltration of VOC polluted air. *Journal of Biotechnology, 113*, 305–319. doi:10.1016/j.jbiotec.2004.04.037

Kim, J. O. (2003). Degradation of benzene and ethylene in biofilters. *Process Biochemistry, 39*, 447–453. doi:10.1016/S0032-9592(03)00093-1

Kohonen, T. (1988). *Self organization and associative memory*. Berlin, Germany: Springer-Verlag.

Krasnopolsky, V. M., & Chevallier, F. (2003). Some neural network applications in environmental sciences. Part II: Advancing computational efficiency of environmental numerical models. *Neural Networks*, *16*, 335–348. doi:10.1016/S0893-6080(03)00026-1

Lee, E. Y. (2003). Continuous treatment of gas-phase trichloroethylene by Burkholderia cepacia G4 in a two-stage continuous stirred tank reactor/trickling biofilter system. *Journal of Bioscience and Bioengineering, 96*, 572–574. doi:10.1016/S1389-1723(04)70151-6

Li, G., He, Z., An, T., Zeng, X., Sheng, G., & Fu, J. (2008). Comparative study of the elimination of toluene vapours in twin biotrickling filters using two microorganisms Bacillus cereus S1 and S2. *Journal of Chemical Technology and Biotechnology (Oxford, Oxfordshire)*, *83*, 1019–1026. doi:10.1002/jctb.1908

Livingstone, D. J., Manallack, D. T., & Tetko, I. V. (1997). Data modelling with neural networks: Advantages and limitations. *Journal of Computer-Aided Molecular Design*, *11*, 135–142. doi:10.1023/A:1008074223811

Maier, H. R., & Dandy, G. C. (1998a). The effect of internal parameters and geometry on the performance of back-propagation neural networks: An empirical study. *Environmental Modelling & Software*, *13*, 193–209. doi:10.1016/S1364-8152(98)00020-6

Maier, H. R., & Dandy, G. C. (1998b). Understanding the behaviour and optimising the performance of back-propagation neural networks: An empirical study. *Environmental Modelling & Software*, *13*, 179–191. doi:10.1016/S1364-8152(98)00019-X

Maier, H. R., & Dandy, G. C. (2000). Neural networks for the prediction and forecasting of water resources variables: A review of modelling issues and applications. *Environmental Modelling & Software*, *15*, 101–124. doi:10.1016/S1364-8152(99)00007-9

Maier, H. R., & Dandy, G. C. (2001). Neural network based modelling of environmental variables: A systematic approach. *Mathematical and Computer Modelling*, *33*, 669–682. doi:10.1016/S0895-7177(00)00271-5

Maliyekkal, S. M., Rene, E. R., Swaminathan, T., & Philip, L. (2004). Performance of BTX degraders under substrate versatility conditions. *Journal of Hazardous Materials*, *B109*, 201–211. doi:10.1016/j.jhazmat.2004.04.001

Masters, T. (1993). *Practical neural network recipes in C*. San Diego, CA: Academic Press.

Metcalf & Eddy Inc. (2003). *Wastewater engineering: treatment and reuse* (4th ed.). New York, NY: McGraw-Hill.

Miller, R. M., Itoyama, K., Uda, A., Takada, H., & Bhat, N. (1997). Modelling and control of a chemical waste water treatment plant. *Computers & Chemical Engineering*, *21*, 947–952.

Mingzhi, H., Ma, Y., Jinquan, W., & Yan, W. (2009). Simulation of a paper mill wastewater treatment using a fuzzy neural network. *Expert Systems with Applications*, *36*, 5064–5070. doi:10.1016/j.eswa.2008.06.006

Mjalli, F. S., Al-Asheh, S., & Alfadaza, H. E. (2007). Use of artificial neural network black-box modelling for the prediction of wastewater treatment plants performance. *Journal of Environmental Management*, *83*, 329–338. doi:10.1016/j.jenvman.2006.03.004

Moral, K., Aksoy, A., & Gokcay, C. F. (2008). Modelling of the activated sludge process by using artificial neural networks with automated architecture screening. *Computers & Chemical Engineering, 32*, 2471–2478. doi:10.1016/j.compchemeng.2008.01.008

Nash, J. E., & Sutcliffe, J. V. (1970). River flow forecasting through conceptual models part 1 — a discussion of principles. *Journal of Hydrology (Amsterdam), 10*, 282–290. doi:10.1016/0022-1694(70)90255-6

Oh, Y.-S., & Bartha, R. (1997). Removal of nitrobenzene vapors by trickling air biofilter. *Journal of Industrial Microbiology & Biotechnology, 18*, 293–296. doi:10.1038/sj.jim.2900384

Ottengraf, S. P. P., & Diks, R. M. M. (1991). Promising technique-process technology of biotechniques. *LUCHT, 4*, 135–144.

Pu, A., & Hung, Y. (1995). Use of artificial neural networks: Predicting trickling filter performance in a municipal wastewater treatment plant. *Environmental Management and Health, 6*, 16–27. doi:10.1108/09566169510085126

Rene, E. R., Kim, S. J., & Park, H. S. (2008). Experimental results and neural prediction of sequencing batch reactor performance under different operational conditions. *Journal of Environmental Informatics, 11*, 51–61. doi:10.3808/jei.200800111

Rene, E. R., López, M. E., Veiga, M. C., & Kennes, C. (2010a). Steady- and transient-state operation of a two-stage bioreactor for the treatment of a gaseous mixture of hydrogen sulphide, methanol and α-pinene. *Journal of Chemical Technology and Biotechnology (Oxford, Oxfordshire), 85*, 336–348. doi:10.1002/jctb.2343

Rene, E. R., López, M. E., Veiga, M. C., & Kennes, C. (2010b). Performance of a fungal monolith bioreactor for the removal of styrene from polluted air. *Bioresource Technology, 101*, 2608–2615. doi:10.1016/j.biortech.2009.10.060

Rene, E. R., Maliyekkal, S. M., Swaminathan, T., & Philip, L. (2006). Back propagation neural network for performance prediction in trickling bed air biofilter. *International Journal of Environment and Pollution, 28*, 382–401. doi:10.1504/IJEP.2006.011218

Rene, E. R., Veiga, M. C., & Kennes, C. (2009). Experimental and neural model analysis of styrene removal from polluted air in a biofilter. *Journal of Chemical Technology and Biotechnology (Oxford, Oxfordshire), 84*, 941–948. doi:10.1002/jctb.2130

Rene, E. R., Veiga, M. C., & Kennes, C. (2010). Biodegradation of gas-phase styrene using the fungus *Sporothrix variecibatus*: Impact of pollutant load and transient operation. *Chemosphere, 79*, 221–227. doi:10.1016/j.chemosphere.2010.01.036

Rogers, L. L., & Dowla, F. U. (1994). Optimization of groundwater remediation using artificial neural networks with parallel solute transport modelling. *Water Resources Research, 30*, 457–481. doi:10.1029/93WR01494

Rumelhart, D. E., Hinton, G. E., & Williams, R. J. (1986). Learning internal representations by error propagation. In D. E. Rumelhart, J. L. McClelland & the PDP Research Group (Eds.), *Paralled distributed processing. Explorations in the microstructure of cognition. Volume 1: Foundations*, (pp. 318-362). Cambridge, MA: The MIT Press.

Shetty, K. V., Nandennavar, S., & Srinikethan, G. (2008). Artificial neural network model for the prediction of steady state phenol biodegradation in a pulsed plate bioreactor. *Journal of Chemical Technology and Biotechnology (Oxford, Oxfordshire)*, *83*, 1181–1189. doi:10.1002/jctb.1892

Sietsma, J., & Dow, R. J. F. (1998). *Neural net pruning - why and how?* In IEEE International Conference on Neural Networks (ICNN - 1988), 1, (pp. 325-333).

Singh, K., Basant, N., Malik, A., & Jain, G. (2010). Modelling the performance of up-flow anaerobic sludge blanket reactor based wastewater treatment plant using linear and nonlinear approaches—a case study. *Analytica Chimica Acta*, *658*, 1–11. doi:10.1016/j.aca.2009.11.001

Sorial, G. A., Smith, F. L., Suidan, M. T., Biswas, P., & Brenner, R. C. (1995). Evaluation of trickle bed biofilter media for toluene removal. *Journal of the Air & Waste Management Association*, *45*, 801–810.

Syu, M. J., & Chen, B. C. (1998). Back-propagation neural network adaptive control of a continuous wastewater treatment process. *Industrial & Engineering Chemistry Research*, *37*, 3625–3630. doi:10.1021/ie9801655

Tu, J. (1996). Advantages and disadvantages of using artificial neural networks versus logistic regression for predicting medical outcomes. *Journal of Clinical Epidemiology*, *49*, 1225–1232. doi:10.1016/S0895-4356(96)00002-9

Veiga, M. C., & Kennes, C. (2001). Parameters affecting performance and modeling of biofilters treating alkylbenzene-polluted air. *Applied Microbiology and Biotechnology*, *55*, 254–258. doi:10.1007/s002530000491

Warner, B., & Misra, M. (1996). Understanding neural networks as statistical tools. *The American Statistician*, *50*, 284–293. doi:10.2307/2684922

Waweru, M., Herrygers, V., Langenhove, H. V., & Verstraete, W. (2005). Process engineering of biological waste gas purification. In H. J. Jordening & J. Winter (Eds.), *Environmental biotechnology: Concepts and applications*, (pp. 409-425). Wiley – VCH Verlag GmbH & Co, KGaA – Weinheim, Germany.

Weber, F. J., & Hartmans, S. (1992). Biological waste gas treatment with integrated adsorption for the treatment of fluctuating concentrations. In A. T. Dragt., & J. Van Ham (Eds.) *Biotechniques for air pollution abatement and odour control policies*, (pp. 125-130). Amsterdam, The Netherlands: Elsevier.

Widrow, B., & Sterns, S. D. (1985). *Sterns adaptive signal processing*. Englewood Cliffs, NJ: Prentice Hall.

Zhang, Q., & Stanley, S. J. (1997). Forecasting raw-water quality parameters for the North Saskatchewan River by neural network modelling. *Water Research*, *31*, 2340–2350. doi:10.1016/S0043-1354(97)00072-9

ADDITIONAL READING

Drossu, R., & Obradovic, Z. (1996). Rapid design of neural networks for time series prediction. *IEEE Computational Science & Engineering*, *3*, 78–89. doi:10.1109/99.503317

Huken, M., & Stragge, P. (2003). Recurrent neural networks for time series classification. *Neurocomputing, 50*, 223–235. doi:10.1016/S0925-2312(01)00706-8

Igelnik, B., Tabib-Azar, M., & LeClair, S. R. (2001). A net with complex weights. *IEEE Transactions on Neural Networks, 12*, 236–249. doi:10.1109/72.914521

Jin, Y., Veiga, M. C., & Kennes, C. (2005). Effects of pH, CO_2 and flow pattern on the autotrophic degradation of hydrogen sulphide in a biotrickling filter. *Biotechnology and Bioengineering, 92*, 462–471. doi:10.1002/bit.20607

Kennes, C., Cox, H. H. J., Doddema, H. J., & Harder, W. (1996). Design and performance of biofilters for the removal of alkylbenzene vapours. *Journal of Chemical Technology and Biotechnology (Oxford, Oxfordshire), 66*, 300–304. doi:10.1002/(SICI)1097-4660(199607)66:3<300::AID-JCTB495>3.0.CO;2-9

Kennes, C., Jin, Y., & Veiga, M. C. (2006). Fungal and dechlorinating biocatalysts in waste gas treatment. In P. N. L. Lens., C. Kennes., P. Le Cloirec., & M. A. Deshusses (Eds.) *Waste Gas Treatment for Resource Recovery*, pp. 277-301, London, UK, IWA Publishing Co.

Kingdon, J. (1997). *Intelligent systems and financial forecasting*. New York: Springer-Verlag.

Langenhove, H. V., Wuytz, E., & Schamp, N. (1986). Elimination of hydrogen sulphide from odorous air by a wood bark biofilter. *Water Research, 20*, 1471–1476. doi:10.1016/0043-1354(86)90109-0

Leson, G., & Winer, A. M. (1991). Biofiltration: an innovative air pollution control technology for VOC emissions. *Journal of the Air & Waste Management Association, 41*, 1045–1054.

Lin, G., & Chen, L. (2005). Time series forecasting by combining the radial basis function network and the self-organizing map. *Hydrological Processes, 19*, 1925–1937. doi:10.1002/hyp.5637

McNevin, D., & Barford, J. (2000). Biofiltration as an odour abatement strategy. *Biochemical Engineering Journal, 5*, 231–242. doi:10.1016/S1369-703X(00)00064-4

Meng, Z., Yang, Q., Yip, P. C., Eyink, K. G., Taferner, W. T., & Igelnik, B. (1998). Combined use of computational intelligence and materials data for on-line monitoring of MBE experiments. *Engineering Applications of Artificial Intelligence, 11*, 587–595. doi:10.1016/S0952-1976(98)00024-4

Rene, E. R., Arulneyam, D., & Swaminathan, T. (2004). Biofiltration. In Pandey, A. (Ed.), *Concise Encyclopedia of Bioresource Technology* (pp. 31–39). NY: Haworth Press.

Rene, E. R., Murthy, D. V. S., & Swaminathan, T. (2005). Performance evaluation of a compost biofilter treating toluene vapors. [Wasserman, P.D.]. *Process Biochemistry, 40*, 2771–2779. doi:10.1016/j.procbio.2004.12.010

KEY TERMS AND DEFINITIONS

Biodegradation: The process of breaking down complex organic substrates (pollutants) into simpler compounds using microorganisms.

Elimination Capacity: The amount of pollutant removed in a biological treatment equipment per unit bed volume, usually represented as g m^{-3} h^{-1}.

Back Propagation Algorithm: A set of learning rules in a generalized feed – forward network, where the error term propagates backward during training, looking for a global minimum of the error function in weight space using the method of gradient descent.

Multilayer Perceptron (MLP): MLP refers to a simple network of interconnected neurons. These neurons perceptron computes a single output from multiple inputs by forming a linear combination according to its input weights and then possibly putting the output through some nonlinear activation function. A typical MLP consists of one input layer, one or more hidden layer and an output layer.

Network Internal Parameters: Refers to a set of internal parameters of the back propagation algorithm that can be adjusted to improvise the speed of training and convergence. These include epoch size, learning rate, momentum, activation function, error function and initial weight distribution.

Section 3
Concepts

Chapter 11
Motivated Learning for Computational Intelligence

Janusz A. Starzyk
Ohio University at Athens, USA

ABSTRACT

This chapter describes a motivated learning (ML) method that advances model building and learning techniques required for intelligent systems. Motivated learning addresses critical limitations of reinforcement learning (RL), the more common approach to coordinating a machine's interaction with an unknown environment. RL maximizes the external reward by approximating multidimensional value functions; however, it does not work well in dynamically changing environments. The ML method overcomes RL problems by triggering internal motivations, and creating abstract goals and internal reward systems to stimulate learning. The chapter addresses the important question of how to motivate an agent to learn and enhance its own complexity? A mechanism is presented that extends low-level sensory-motor interactions towards advanced perception and motor skills, resulting in the emergence of desired cognitive properties. ML is compared to RL using a rapidly changing environment in which the agent needs to manage its motivations as well as choose and implement goals in order to succeed.

INTRODUCTION

While we still do not know the mechanisms needed to build them, the design of intelligent machines is likely to revolutionize the way we live. Researchers around the world work to solve this highly challenging task. Artificial neural networks (ANN) modeled on networks of biological neurons are successfully used for classification, function approximation, and control. Yet a classical ANN learns only a single

DOI: 10.4018/978-1-60960-551-3.ch011

task for which it is trained, requires extensive training effort and close supervision during learning. The reinforcement learning (RL) method stimulates development of learning through interaction with the environment; however, state-based value learning that is in the core of any implementation of RL, is typically useful for simple systems with a small number of states working in slowly changing environments. Learning effort and computational cost increases significantly with the environmental complexity, so that optimal decision making in a complex environment is still intractable by means of reinforcement learning.

The overall goal of this chapter is to address the key issues facing development of cognitive agents that interact with a dynamically changing environment. In such an environment, typical reinforcement learning works poorly as the approximated value function changes, thus more extensive training does not translate into more successful operation. The main purpose of this chapter is to introduce a learning strategy that recognizes the environment's complexity, and captures it in the network of interdependent motivations, goals, and values that the machine learns while interacting with the hostile environment. The method is inspired by human learning, in which the external reward is not the only motivation to succeed, and actions taken are not just to maximize this reward, but lead to a deeper understanding of complex relations between various objects and concepts in the environment.

The method described in this chapter is known as motivated learning (ML), where internal motivations, created either by the external reward or other motivations, may dominate over the externally set goals (and rewards). In reinforcement learning, the machine does not always try to maximize its reward and sometimes performs random moves. This abandonment of the optimum policy is a part of its learning strategy. The random moves are used to explore the environment to perhaps improve its value system, but as the learning progresses, the machine follows the optimum policy more often, trying to maximize the total reward received. In motivated learning this abandonment of the optimum policy that maximizes the external reward is deliberate and is driven by the need to satisfy internally set objectives. In the process, the machine learns new perceptions, improves sensory-motor coordination, and discovers complex relations that exist in the environment. By relating its actions to changes they cause in the environment, a ML machine builds complex motivations and a system of internal rewards that help it to operate in this environment.

ML produces embodied intelligence (EI) agents that develop internal motivations, set their own goals and build internal reward systems. By providing an agent with an internal drive to learn, set its own objectives, and evaluate the success of its actions, motivated learning may lead to intelligent behavior. A ML agent receives reinforcement from the environment for its most primitive objectives and uses it to develop a complex system of motivations and internal goals, and learns actions to implement these goals. ML is better equipped to handle complexities of the environment, thus it delivers better performance in a hostile environment with complex rules. However, its main advantage is that it produces a system of values related to various, previously unknown to it, concepts in the environment without receiving explicit reward for this learning. As a result, it resembles human learning, where internal motivations lead to creation of advanced concepts and intelligent behavior.

This chapter first defines scalable models of intelligent systems, and then characterizes the main issues in building intelligent models that await solutions. Next a need is discussed for a mechanism that yields reactionary low-level sensory-motor interactions and naturally extends these interactions towards building complex pathways of higher-level relations between sensory inputs and motor outputs. The following section addresses the issue of motivation for a machine to develop its abilities and to learn.

It will be demonstrated how this brings about advanced perception and motor skills and results in the emergence of desired properties.

The subsequent section discusses how the machine can define its higher-level goals and learn to build proper representations of sensory-motor interactions to support these goals. These abstract goals will be related to predefined primitive goals; however they will not be directly represented at the design stage. Instead, they will emerge through a learning process to efficiently handle the built-in goals in an unknown, dynamically changing environment. Because these abstract goals are internally generated, only the machine "knows" if and when they are accomplished. This changes the dynamics of the learning process. ML, with its goal creation (GC) mechanism, improves an agent's ability to perceive useful objects. Thus an agent may improve its cognitive complexity by introducing new concepts and relating them to already familiar concepts. It also helps the agent to learn useful motor skills, thus increasing its ability to interact with environment.

Internal goals are created by the machine based on their relations to externally specified objectives and other internal goals. Thus the machine learns causal relations between its internal goals and externally reinforced ones. By learning how to satisfy the external goals, the machine learns to anticipate an outcome of its action. It will be illustrated how, by using the anticipated reward signal, the machine plans to implement externally set objectives. The machine can also change the planned set of actions, if the conditions in the environment indicate that the chosen ones cannot be successfully completed. This can be done, for instance, by blocking the selected action if the machine observes that a resource needed to complete this action cannot be found in the environment at a given time. Such anticipatory planning and action selection mechanism in the ML systems will be discussed and its activation will be illustrated.

As different goals compete for the machine's attention, the machine needs to decide which goal to address. Yet, there is no central command center to manage goals, since embodied intelligence uses many parallel processes to represent its actions, goals and sensory inputs. In this chapter it will be described how the machine manages various tasks to implement these goals in a dynamically changing environment. It will be also shown how a goal can be pursued in such a system in spite of distractions and interruptions that switch the machine's attention to analyze the disturbance or to address other goals that became more important in a given situation.

Learning complex goals may require the implementation of several subgoals. Such a strategy is effectively implemented in hierarchical RL (Bakker, 2004). This is different from learning how to implement the higher level goals that characterize ML. For instance earning money is a higher level goal that may be created when a machine needs to buy food, and may require the ML machine to create a concept of money. However, earning money is not a subgoal necessary for buying food, thus it is not a subject of hierarchical RL. A mechanism that yields such higher level goals will be discussed.

A separate section will illustrate the development process that intertwines the building of an abstract hierarchy of goals, features and skills. This process provides a motivation for the machine to act and learn, and is responsible for increasing the complexity of the machine's actions. It will be shown how this development and learning process modifies a machine's behavior, and the efficiency of the motivated learning and the reinforcement learning mechanisms will be compared. This chapter concludes with a summary of the proposed approach to revamping the idea of motivated learning, stressing necessary extensions of the existing approaches.

BACKGROUND FOR MOTIVATED LEARNING

Proposed by Hans Moravec (Moravec, 1984, pp. 215-224) and popularized by Rodney Brooks (Brooks, 1991a, pp. 139–159), embodied intelligence brought revolutionary changes to the design of autonomous robots and revived hopes for development of natural intelligence in machines. The subsumption architecture proposed by Brooks (Brooks, 1986, pp.77–84) uses hierarchical layers of behavioral modules, where lower layer modules are subordinate to higher levels and the design is bottom up from simpler to more complex goals. The modules coordinate sensory-motor interactions leading to predesigned skills of increasing complexity. This type of architecture is good for real time robotics, where multiple parallel sensory-motor paths control the robot's behavior. There is no central control or built-in representation of the environment structured in this architecture. Individual modules are designed gradually, layer after layer, using simple, data driven finite state machines. Although this architecture provides fast parallel operation and coordination of multiple concurrent processing units, it requires a designer's effort to build the hierarchy of modules – a task that is increasingly difficult as a machine's organization becomes more advanced and its operation less understood.

The Reinforcement Learning (RL) mechanism is related to the way animals and humans learn (Bakker, 2004, pp. 438-445). Based only on occasional pain and pleasure signals, RL agents must find out how to interact with their environment to maximize their expected reward. In reinforcement learning (Sutton, 1984), values are associated with the machine's states and actions to maximize total reward from the environment. However, when the environment is complex, this state based approach to learning of the value function takes a lot of effort and training data. Another problem is that reinforcement learning suffers from the credit assignment problem, which means that it is not able to properly reward or punish a machine's actions (Sutton, 1984), (Fu & Anderson, 2006). O'Reilly proposed a Primary Value and Learned Value (PVLV) scheme implementing Pavlovian conditioning (O'Reilly, 2007, pp. 31–49) to directly associate the stimuli and the reward, as an alternative to the temporal-differences (TD) used in traditional reinforcement learning. While this alleviated some concerns about credit assignment and had better biological justification than temporal difference, it did not remove the major restrictions of reinforcement learning in complex and changing environments.

Hierarchical reinforcement learning (Currie, 1991, pp. 49-86), (Kaelbling, 1993, pp. 167–173) was an attempt to improve reinforcement learning in structured environments. First, the hierarchy was provided by the designer and the complex task was subdivided for faster learning. In (Singh, 1992, pp. 323-340) a manager program selects sub-managers and assigns them their subtasks. State-action values are learned separately by managers and sub-managers in their corresponding domains. Dayan (Dayan & Hinton, 1993) proposed a similar organization consisting of a hierarchy of managers responsible for learning individual subtasks. It was demonstrated that this simplifies the reinforcement learning effort and increases its efficiency (Parr & Russell, 1998). Although the learning of value functions is performed automatically, organization of the hierarchy, and determination of the internal states, requires a designer's effort. Bakker and Schmidhuber took this hierarchical approach a step further by providing subgoal discovery and subpolicy learning at different levels of hierarchy (Bakker & Schmidhuber, 2004, pp. 438-445). In their work, a hierarchy structure is determined automatically by the system that identifies subgoals for the machine. The system is stimulated to learn subgoal organization by local rewards provided by a higher level policy in a fashion similar to the one used in advantage learning (Harmon & Baird, 1996). RL assumes that the current input tells the agent everything it needs to know about the environment. This is often unrealistic. If we want to develop machines with learning abilities similar to that of humans, then we must go beyond the reactive mappings used in RL.

An important question was raised by Pfeifer and Bongard – how to motivate a machine to do anything, and in particular to develop its own abilities to perceive and act (Pfeifer & Bongard, 2007). What mechanism can be used to direct an agent to explore its environment and learn new concepts and skills?

According to Pfeifer, an agent's motivation should emerge from the developmental process. Steels suggested equipping an agent with self-motivation (Steels, 2004, pp. 231-242) based on the idea of "flow" experienced by people when they outperform their current ability level. This "flow" is used as motivation for further development. Intrinsic motivations were proposed in developmental robotics based on curiosity-driven exploration, novelty, and surprise studied previously in psychology (White, 1959, pp. 297–333) and neuroscience (Schultz, 2002, pp. 241-263). Schmidhuber used these ideas to develop artificial curiosity in robots for autonomous exploratory behavior and learning of the unknown environment (Schmidhuber, 1991). Based on the curiosity principle, Oudeyer (Oudeyer et al., 2007) presented an intrinsic motivation system used to drive a robot in a continuous noisy inhomogeneous environment to self-organize its behavior. Also, active learning (Cohn, 1996, pp. 129–145), (Hasenjager & Ritter, 2002, pp. 137–169) using these ideas, maximizes the expected information gain and improves the learning speed by concentrating the machine's exploration on the cases where uncertainty of the internal model is the largest. In active learning, a machine can achieve higher learning efficiency by actively choosing the data from which it learns.

The big question is what to do next? How to move forward in developing concepts and models for machine intelligence? In particular, how to motivate a machine to act and enhance its intellectual abilities, how to improve its learning efficiency, how to suggest a mechanism for structural self-organization, from which higher level perceptions and skills could evolve through the machine's interaction with its environment. Finally, how do we design a machine that is capable not only of implementing given goals, but also of creating them and deciding which to pursue, and of doing so in a changing environment and in spite of distractions and unforeseen difficulties. In this chapter, I try to answer some of these questions by describing the motivated machine learning scheme, which yields machines that derive their motivations from external and internal pain signals and create their own goals.

In contrast to classical reinforcement learning, where the reinforcement signals come from the outside environment, the motivated learning mechanism generates internal reward signals associated with abstract motivations and goals accomplished by the machine. The machine's actions are followed by the internal assessments of how well the internally set objectives are satisfied, and based on these assessments an internal system of motivations, goals and skills is built. At the same time, internal motivations address specific goals rather than new unpredictable situations that characterize curiosity based learning. Yet, at any given time, when an agent does not have specific goals, it uses artificial curiosity to explore the environment. These explorations help the agent to learn its goal driven actions. However, not all unlearned experiences are worth learning. According to Schmidhuber's theory of surprise, novelty, interestingness, and attention, curious agents are interested only in learnable but yet unknown regularities.

NEED FOR MOTIVATED LEARNING

The biological brain is both an inspiration and a model for the development of intelligence in machines. We cannot build the brain, but we can try to make structures that exhibit similar activation of perceptions, memories, and motor control when exposed to similar signals from the environment. Learning based on intrinsic motivations is obtained when the machine learns how to act by observing the results of its actions and correcting them in such a way as to minimize the error between the obtained and the expected results. By exploring the environment, the machine learns what is there and how its actions affect the environment. Yet, rather than learning all its observations, the machine focuses on those that differ from what it already knows and, therefore, can predict. It is desirable that intrinsic motivation should lead to a learning strategy that is task independent. Using this strategy the machine will be able to learn a hierarchy of skills that can later be applied to specific tasks that it will need to do (Barto et al., 2004). This kind of intrinsic motivation can be based on surprise, novelty (Huang & Weng, 2002), or a learning process (Kaplan & Oudeyer, 2004).

The Problem with Curiosity Based Intrinsic Motivations

To some degree, intrinsic motivations that trigger curiosity based learning can be compared to the exploratory stage in reinforcement learning. In reinforcement learning, a machine occasionally explores the state-action space, rather than performing an optimum action in the task of maximizing its rewards. However, without proper control of these explorations, a machine may not develop its abilities or even develop a destructive behavior (Oudeyer et al., 2007, p. 267). Intrinsic motivations can also select actions that yield a maximum rate of reduction of the prediction error, which improves learning when the machine tries to improve on one kind of activity (e.g. specialized moves for a selected task). However, the problem is that switching between tasks may provide the maximum rate of error reduction and such action could be selected for learning based on the maximum rate of reduction of the prediction error. This would be counterproductive and would reduce progress in learning desired activities.

The Intelligent Adaptive Curiosity (IAC) method, that implements intrinsic motivations for developmental robotics, motivates machines to maximize their learning progress (Oudeyer et al., 2007, p. 269). It divides the state-action space into regions based on clustering of learned exemplars stored in the machine's memory under supervision of a higher level learning mechanism. This organization prevents the machine from learning rapidly in situations that are too easy or too difficult, improving its learning in continuous, unstructured state-action spaces. While the IAC method removes some of the problems of curiosity based intrinsic motivation, it leads to learning without purpose. Anything that is interesting to learn and improves the agent's motor skills will be tried out, and the machine will guide itself to generate optimum developmental sequences. While this approach is useful for an early stage of robot development, it does not stimulate learning of specific skills that may be required for an expert level performance.

According to Weng, machine learning methods that measure the performance of a system on a predefined task, are not suited for developmental robots (Weng, 2004). Yet, the strength of curiosity based method that is beneficial in the early stage of machine learning, may become its weakness once a machine needs to perform specific tasks and needs to specialize in what to learn. In complex systems with multi-goal operation, there may be simply too many interesting things to learn and the organization of motivations and goals needs external fine tuning. Thus, it may be useful to combine curiosity based learning with goal oriented learning in a novel and self-organizing way.

In hierarchical reinforcement learning (HRL) with subgoal discovery, subgoals are equivalent to desired and useful observations obtained by clustering input data (Bakker, 2004). In this approach, high level policies discover subgoals and relate them to an overall learning objective. This minimizes the designer's effort and leads to automatic learning of the goal hierarchy. Low-level policies learn how to implement individual subgoals by learning low-level value functions in local subspaces of the sensory-motor space. HRL aims at using high-level observations to optimize the subgoals and manage their real time use. System limitations include the large number of parameters and the proper identification of useful subgoals. Although HRL with subgoal discovery awards a machine for discovery of useful subgoals (using small internal rewards), it implements the main idea of reinforcement learning. As such, it is based on maximization of total reward for externally set objectives, and it inherits RL inability to set and pursue higher level goals. Thus its development is constrained.

How to Address this Problem?

An important question facing researchers in autonomous machine learning is how can intrinsic motivations be defined to provide lifetime, task-independent yet goal oriented learning? While learning must yield task-independent cumulative knowledge, to be an efficient learner the machine must use task driven exploration, accumulation, and generalization of knowledge. Active learning strategy does not seem to fit the bill, since the learning experiments must be prescribed even if the machine autonomously decides which of them to select.

The combination of curiosity based learning with HRL subgoal discovery does not provide a natural switching mechanism between useful subgoals and curiosity, and will not yield natural intelligence. On one hand, curiosity based machines will gather general knowledge about the world in a random fashion, and therefore, will limit efficient reuse of prior knowledge for higher level skills and concept development. On the other hand, goal driven subgoal discovery will limit the machine's interest in whatever knowledge it acquires to prespecified objectives. While robot designers may claim efficiency of such solutions, what they will get, as a result of applying such methods, is a well designed, well controlled, and predictable robot, not an intelligent machine.

What we may need to implement an intelligent machine is a goal driven mechanism that will motivate a machine to improve its understanding of the environment and to set and choose abstract goals related to its system of values, a mechanism that is different from aimless search and discovery (typical for curiosity based learning), and is different from relentless pursuit of the externally set objectives and related external rewards (typical for reinforcement learning).

MOTIVATED LEARNING METHOD

Neurocognitive Model

Before describing the proposed motivated learning, let us consider a biologically inspired model for cognitive processing. We need this model to justify and describe basic operating principles of biologically inspired motivated learning. The model reflects current theories in cognitive neuroscience about the organization and function of various brain regions, and how brain activities relate to cognition (Baars & Gage, 2007). The model involves collaboration of concurrent processing within central executive, reward and subconscious processing blocks, episodic and semantic memory, and interaction with sensory and motor pathways. Figure 1 represents a simplified diagram of such a model showing major collaborating blocks.

In this model the central executive block is spread between several functional units without clear boundaries or a single triggering mechanism. It is responsible for coordination and selective control of other units. This block interacts with other units for performing its tasks. Its tasks include cognitive perception, attention, motivation, goal creation and goal selection, thoughts, planning, learning, supervision and motor control, etc. For this purpose, it needs the ability to dynamically select and direct execution of programs that govern attention, cueing, episodic memory, and action monitoring. In addition, the central executive can activate semantic memory and control emotions.

The central executive directs cognitive aspects of machine control and learning experiences but its operation is influenced by competing signals representing motivations, desires, and attention switching that are not necessarily cognitive or consciously realized. The central executive does not have any clearly identified decision making center. Instead, its decisions are a result of competition between signals that represent memories, motivations, pains, and desires. At any moment, competition among these signals can be interrupted by attention switching signals. Such signals constantly vary in intensity as a result of internal stimuli (e.g., hunger) or externally presented and observed opportunities. Thus, the fundamental mechanism that directs the machine in its action is physically distributed as competing signals are generated in various parts of machine's mind. Further, it is not fully cognitive, since, before a winner is selected, the machine does not interpret the meaning of the competing signals.

Central executive cognition is predominantly sequential, as a winner of the internal competition is identified and serves as an instantaneous director and focus of attention of the cognitive thought process, until it is replaced by another winner. Once a winner of the internal competition is established, the central executive provides cognitive interpretation of the result, providing top down activation for perception, planning, internal thought or motor functions. It is this cognitive realization of internal processes that results in the central executive's decisions concerning what is perceived, planning of how to respond, internal talk, and what to do, that we associate with a conscious experience and a continuous train of such experiences constitutes consciousness.

A critical block, that influences operation of the central executive, contains mostly subconscious processing of primitive and abstract pain signals related to internal and external rewards and learned systems

Figure 1. Organization of cognitive processing

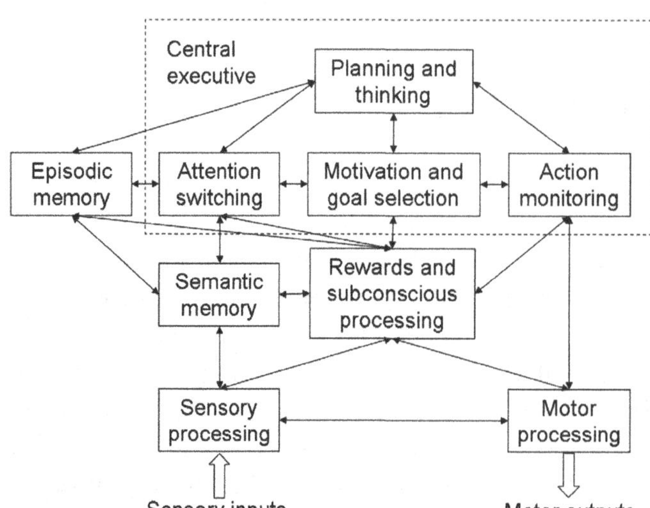

of values. This block is functionally related to a large number of regulatory organs in the brain such as the anterior cingulate cortex (responsible for reward anticipation, empathy and emotion), the amygdala (responsible for emotional associations), the ventral tegmental area (managing reward, motivation and addiction) and the hypothalamus (metabolic processes and pain signals), or the substantia nigra and basal ganglia (responsible for reward, addiction, motor control and learning). Within this block, reward signals that govern learning are processed or generated. This block may cue episodic and semantic memories, switch attention, provide motivations, help to select goals, and interact with action monitoring. Many cognitive operations of the central executive are influenced and triggered by subconscious processing in this block related to rewards, emotions, and pain signals that motivate the machine.

The model for cognitive processing presented in this section model is in agreement with the model proposed by Dehaene, Kerszberg, and Changeux (1998) a "neuronal model of a global workspace" and their hypothesis for how the integration of sensory inputs might take place in self-organizing structures of biological neurons. According to this hypothesis workspace neurons are globally interconnected in such a way that only one "workspace representation" can be active at any given time. They selectively activate or inhibit, through descending connections, the contribution of specific neurons in the sensory and motor pathways. The workspace activity is "a constant flow of individual coherent episodes of variable duration" controlled by attention and evaluation circuits (orbitofrontal cortex, anterior cingulate, hypothalamus, amygdala, ventral striatum, and mesocortical projections to prefrontal cortex).

Motivated Learning

The fundamental question is how to create a self-organizing mechanism that will use conscious and subconscious processing to trigger learning, motivate the machine, and manage its operations? The assumption made in motivated learning is that an intelligent machine must be able to learn how to avoid pain signals coming from the environment. The external pain signals may be predefined and wired to the centers that detect the level of this pain and are able to trigger a learning mechanism when such pain is either increasing (bad) or decreasing (good). For learning to take place, such pain must persist in various forms, so this requires a hostile environment. The machine's response to external pain signals constitutes goal oriented motivation to act. A machine's intelligence will develop to learn how to minimize this pain, and in the process of doing so, the machine will learn the rules of the environment.

To this end, an embodied intelligent agent is defined as follows:

Definition: *An Embodied Intelligence (EI) agent is a mechanism (biological, mechanical, or virtual) that learns how to reduce its pain signals in a hostile environment. Hostility of the environment is persistent and is expressed through perceived signals of pain. Pain signals are broadly defined and include desires, needs, aggression (towards the agent), insufficient resources, etc.*

Although learning can be governed through both reward and punishment signals, the second type of signal may be sufficient and unlike the first one will lead to stable systems. As an example of system instability consider that, given a choice, rats would electrically stimulate their reward centers in preference of food until they die (Baars & Gage, 2007, p. 383). It is also well known that drug abuse in humans (that stimulate their pleasure centers) may lead to their death. Thus pain, not gratification, will be chosen as the dominating stimuli for motivated learning. While we can always interpret the reduction of pain as a reward, from the system point of view, maximization of reward leads to different solutions than minimization of pain (negative signal). While the first one turns into a classical maximization problem and may produce unstable systems (with infinite reward), the second one will terminate once the negative pain signal is reduced below a specified threshold. Not only does pain reduction guarantee system stability, but what is equally important from the point of view of multi objective learning systems, it will provide a natural way of managing motivations and goal selection. Mathematically, it corresponds to solving a minimax problem, where the optimization effort is concentrated on the strongest pain signal and automatically switches to another objective once the dominant pain is reduced below other pain values. To guarantee system stability, any reward based learning should come with constraints on how much reward is accepted, temporarily desensitizing system to an additional reward. After reward exceeds a set threshold, sensitivity to this reward may gradually decrease and the perceived amount of reward will be small.

Pain, representing all types of discomforts, fear, panic, anger and pressures, is a common experience of all people and animals. On the most primitive level, people feel discomfort when they are hungry, so that they learn to eat and to search for food. Although, on more abstract levels, they may have different motives and higher-level goals, the primitive pains help them to develop these complex motivations and learn a system of values in order to learn skills useful for successful operation in their environments. Neurobiological study supports the suggestion that there are multiple regions of the brain involved in the pain system also known as the "pain matrix" (Melzack, 1990). Experiments using fMRI have identified that such a matrix includes a number of cortical structures, the anterior insula, cingulate and dorsolateral prefrontal cortices (Peyron, et al., 2000), and subcortical structures including the amygdala (Derbyshire, et al., 1997) and the thalamus and hypothalamus (Hsieh, et al., 2001). Two concurrent systems are identified in the pain matrix - the lateral pain system, which processes physical pains, and the medial pain system, which processes the emotional aspects of pain, including fear, stress, dread and anxiety (Tölle, et al., 1999). Physically harmful stimuli activate neurons in the lateral pain system, and the anticipation of pain activates the medial pain system inducing stress and anxiety. It has also been demonstrated that the anticipation of a painful stimulus can activate both pain systems (Porro, 2002). It has been widely accepted that pain has sensory-discriminative, affective, motivational, and evaluative components (Melzack, 1968). Thus pain can be used as a significant component of developmental experience. The work presented by (Mesulam, 1990) suggests that the cingulate cortex is the main contributor to a motivational network that interacts with a perceptual network in the posterior parietal cortex. In this work, it is proposed that the pain network is responsible for emergence of abstract motivations that lead to goal creation and learning, and affects attention, motor control, planning and sensory perception.

In order to govern machine's autonomous operation, a pain based mechanism capable of creating motivations and abstract goals for a machine to act, learn, and develop is suggested. A simple pain based goal creation system is explained next. It uses externally defined pain signals that are associated with primitive pains. The machine is rewarded for minimizing primitive pain signals. Yet, to prevent development of a cautious agent that is not willing to explore the environment, and thus stifle learning, the environment is inherently hostile to the agent. This means, that without a proper action by the agent, externally applied pain signals are gradually increasing, forcing the agent to respond and search for the appropriate solutions.

This model does not entirely exclude positive reward signals from playing a useful role in motivation, goal creation, and learning in intelligent systems. Neuroscience provides ample examples of reward pathways in mammalian brains, like dopaminergic neurons between ventral tegmental area (VTA) and nucleus accumbens in the forebrain or between VTA and orbitofrontal cortex (Panksepp, 1998). Dopamine is produced in anticipation of the reward signal and novel, unexpected events (Schultz, 2002). Similarly, liking and pleasurable experiences are related to GABA (gamma-amino butyric acid) neurotransmitter production and distribution of pleasure signals through the shell of nucleus accumbens, ventral pallidum, and brainstem parabrachial nucleus (Berridge, & Robinson, 2003). Such reward based motivation and learning can be made fully compatible with the presented pain based mechanism in which the strongest negative signal is selected as a winning signal. First, to make a reward system stable, the maximum reward will be limited. Then, by treating the maximum reward limit as a negative bias, we may treat lack of reward as a negative signal that can be minimized to zero when the reward reaches its maximum value. In this interpretation, both positive reward signals, and curiosity based learning are bounded between minimum and maximum values and are biased such that the maximum is set to zero. This will preserve a selection of the dominant (pain) signal as a singular motivation at any given moment of machine interaction with the environment.

Based on this mechanism, the system is motivated to act and learn, and importantly, introduces abstract concepts, and uses them to create higher order pain signals and abstract motivations. Internal reward signals reinforce the actions that lower both primitive and abstract pains. Thus, learning is focused on solving problems often set by the machine without intervention of a teacher. The machine progresses from the lower level goals towards more abstract goals automatically, provided that these abstract goals are warranted by more effective performance in the environment. The developed system of internal motivations, although initiated by externally regulated pain signals, has its own dynamics, with only an indirect relation to primitive motivations and rewards.

Organization of Motivation and Goal Creation System

This section describes the motivated learning method that is used by embodied intelligence agents to develop its skills, internal value system and cognitive abilities.

Definition: *Motivated learning (ML) is learning based on a self-organizing system of emerging internal motivations and goal creation in an embodied agent satisfying the following requirements:*

- The motivated learning mechanism creates higher level (abstract) motivations and sets goals based on dominating primitive and abstract pain signals.
- It generates internal rewards when a completed action triggered by a selected goal reduces the pain (primitive or abstract) associated with this goal.
- A goal is an objective that the agent intends to accomplish through action.
- ML applies to embodied intelligence agents working in a hostile environment.

An agent that uses motivated learning to develop its cognitive abilities will be called a Motivated Embodied Intelligence (MEI) agent. MEI agents share many similar properties with a special type of the rational software agents known as Belief-Desire-Intention (BDI) agents described by Rao & Georgeff (1995). Although the BDI software model is closely associated with intelligent agents, its main focus is choosing plans and their execution rather than programming of intelligent agents. On the other hand, MEI agents aim at development of intelligent agents and therefore do not assume prespecified plans or motivations other than those triggering the learning process (primitive pains).

The following discussion compares MEI to BDI agents:

- Like BDI, MEI agents develop a system of beliefs by observing the environment, learning its rules and recognizing the state of the environment using perception. These beliefs link perceptions to semantic knowledge about the environment, coded through a network of interconnections between perceptions, pain centers, goals and planned actions. However, since MEI is intended for neuronal network implementation, no formal syntax is used to represent knowledge and any inference and plans must be obtained through neural activations.
- Desires in the BDI agent correspond to motivations (primitive and abstract pains) in the MEI agent. These pains are competing for the agent's attention and typically are not realized unless one of them dominates. They participate in the MEI agent's goal switching mechanism.
- Goals that result from the winning pain signal and represent what the MEI agent wants to accomplish at any given time correspond to goals of the BDI agent. Only the winning pain signal motivates the MEI agent to act and can be recognized in a cognitive way by the agent's central executive as its goal, this is similar to adaptation of a single goal in a BDI agent.
- Intentions in a BDI agent are equivalent to selected (preferred) means and ways of implementing goals in a MEI agent. A preferred way of goal implementation is chosen by competition between various possible ways of satisfying the dominant pain, and depends on the environment condition (e.g. availability of resources) as well as the MEI agent's ability to perform the selected action. A MEI agent is an open-minded agent (as defined by Rao & Georgeff (1995)) that allows changes in the perceptions and motivations concerning actions.
- Finally, plans (sequences of learned actions) and events (external triggers and attention switching signals) in MEI agents correspond to plans and events in BDI agents. In a MEI agent, they will be learned and stored using neural networks structures capable of remembering sequences of actions and events. The requirement is to have these sequences stored in the episodic memory (similar in its function to hippocampus) or automated, subconscious motor sequences (as in cerebral cortex).

A significant difference is that while BDI agents try to choose proper actions and plans from set operations, its motivations are predetermined by the designers. Unlike a BDI agent, a MEI agent creates its own motivations to act and learns how to implement its goals.

Motivated learning needs a mechanism for creating abstract motivations and related goals. Once implemented, such a mechanism manages motivations, as well as selects and supervises the execution of goals. Motivations emerge from interaction with the environment, and at any given stage of development, their operation is influenced by competing pain and attention switching signals. Dominant motivations direct machine sensory-motor coordination and learning experiences. Pain signals and attention switching signals constantly vary in intensity as a result of the machine's interaction with the environment. Motivated learning uses external and internal rewards to learn, thus it may benefit from reinforcement learning techniques to learn how to attain a specific goal.

The motivation and goal creation system contains distributed pain detection and learning centers that the machine associates with its internally generated or externally applied pain signals through self-organization. Motivated learning builds internal representations of observed sensory inputs and links them to learned actions that are useful for its operation. If the result of the machine's action is not relevant to its current goal, no intentional learning takes place. This screening of what to learn is very useful since it protects machine's memory from storing insignificant observations, even though they are not predictable by the machine and may be of sufficient interest for curiosity based learning. Curiosity based learning still can take place in a ML system, when the system is not triggered by other motivations. However, it will play a secondary role to goal oriented learning.

A motivated learning mechanism develops a network of abstract pain detection and learning centers. These pain centers manage the pain signals and the competition between these pain signals results in motivation to act. The winning goals (removal of the most dominant pains) represent intentions of the machine. The machine learns the means to implement the goals by taking actions that reduce these pains. Eventually, a motivated learning machine discovers rules that govern the external environment. The rules in the environment are determined by and come from the environment. These are all kinds of rules that the environment enforces on the agent: for instance physical (like if you drop a tool it is going to fall to the ground) as well as societal rules (if you do not cooperate people may not be nice to you). These include rules related to abstract concepts, and complex relationships between such concepts, that may exist in the environment. The important fact is that neither the rules nor the related concepts are known to the machine a priori, and the machine's role is to discover these rules and use them to achieve its own objectives.

Notice, that initially, distributed pain detection and learning centers are not associated with any specific observations or goals. They are activated when local neurons to which they connect are selected through the self-organizing process to represent objects, goals, or actions that the machine finds useful (and associates them with specific pain reduction). Thus from the structural (neuronal network) point of view, no interpretation is possible (or desired) of what a particular pain detection and learning center represents as this can only be established through emerging learned properties.

Characteristics of the Motivation Mechanism

The basic motivation for a machine to act comes from a hostile environment that inflicts primitive pain to which the machine responds. The machine detects this pain, and if the pain dominates, it tries to act to lower the pain. The machine explores the environment and either discovers a way of lowering the dominant pain (preferred action) or another pain becomes stronger and switches the machine's attention to a more pressing issue. In this process, machines develop their ability to successfully operate in a given environment.

Eventually, if the machine cannot find the solution and pain reaches its maximum value, the machine has lost the battle for survival. This means that the environment was too harsh for the machine to learn how to solve the problem, or this problem was not solvable given the resources in the environment, or the machine was unable to perform needed action. For instance, if the machine does not have means to put-out the fire (no fire extinguisher) that started around it, and it cannot escape the fire (its legs got stuck), it will not survive when its body temperature rises too high.

At any given time, the machine suffers from the combination of different pains with different intensities. Pains vary over time, changing the effective motivation to act as the agent sets reduction of the strongest pain as its current goal. Each goal may require a unique approach both in terms of resources used and the type of action performed. If the machine finds a solution to the dominating pain, then the learned response becomes a mean to implement the goal, should a similar pain dominate in the future. From lower level goals, the machine builds more complex goals, and the same mechanism that was used in the lower levels is used to trigger the abstract pain and evaluate pain changes. This mechanism leads to the development of a complex system of drives, values, and concepts in a given environment.

At the lowest levels of the goal hierarchy, in initial stages of building stable perceptual representations and learning their meanings (and semantic associations with other representations) the responses that lover the primitive pain signals are not cognitive. They may be compared to learning reflexes, where semantic perception is not necessary to perform a desired action. However, as the machine responds in a desired way, it learns to associate perceptions and proper actions with pain reduction and, in the process, helps to establish internal representations of perceived sensory inputs. Thus conceptualization (input processing) and learning of desired response (goal implementation) are integrated, and the ML mechanism helps building stable representations of input signals, while simultaneously learning how to handle concepts that they represent.

The resulting organization of the motivated learning agent's "brain" is a function of the machine's ability to observe, learn, self organize its knowledge, and develop its motor functions and skills. It is also a function of changes taking place in the environment, and the complete history of the agent's interaction with this environment. Thus the agent's intelligence is a unique result of the entire learning process, and since no two agents may have exactly the same experiences in a natural environment, no two agents will develop exactly in the same way (except in an artificially simulated environment, where the changes in the environment can be exactly replicated). Therefore, embodied agents developing in a natural environment based on the motivated learning principle are unique beings.

Pain Detection and Learning Center

Pain based learning uses identical structural units capable of pain detection, evaluation and reinforcement learning, referred to as basic pain detection and learning centers. A simplified example of such a center is shown in Figure 2. It contains a pair of neurons responsible for pain detection (pain level neuron) and memory of the pain before the action took place (dual pain level neuron). Two simple comparators are used to detect a change in the pain level, and to reinforce learning. The pain detection and learning center is stimulated by the input pain signal that the machine needs to reduce. When the pain is reduced as a result of an action that involved a specific sensory-motor pair, then this action is reinforced and likely will be selected in future if a similar pain is detected. However, when the pain increases, such an action will be less likely to be selected in the future in response to this type of pain. Notice that the presented example of a pain detection and learning center illustrates only the idea of distributed, initially uncommitted processing units used in ML, and by no means is it the only or final implementation.

Primitive pain comes from the hostile environment, and it is assumed that such pain gradually increases, unless it is reduced by a proper action. This increasing pain stimulates the machine's action. Initially, actions are randomly selected, but with each unsuccessful try, the machine explores other actions. Upon a successful action, the learning center associated with this pain increases weights to the sensory-motor pair that reduces the pain, otherwise it reduces this weight. This association is shown symbolically as the excitation link between the pain neuron and the sensory-motor pair in Figure 2. The machine starts from the choice of action based on the most activated sensory-motor pair (known as a goal implementation neuron) with the strongest weights to given pain stimuli. The number of goal implementation neurons corresponds to the number of all sensory-motor pairs or their sequences, and this number is dynamically increasing with increasing complexity of the perceived concepts and learned motor skills that result from the developmental process. All goal implementation neurons and pain neurons are activated as a result of Winner-Take-All (WTA) competition between them, thus the machine

Figure 2. Basic pain detection and learning center

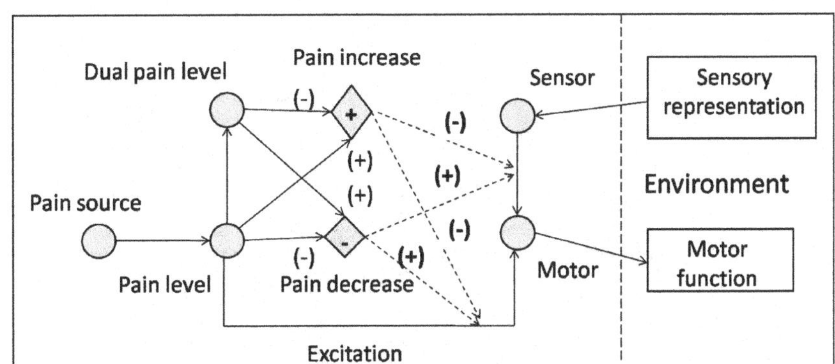

selects a dominant pain and responds to this pain with the best possible action that it has learned to lower such pain.

Although, it may happen that the external pain will be reduced without action taken by the machine, or in spite of an irrelevant action, gradually over a longer period of time, the machine will learn not to associate such an action with a specific pain.

Creation of Abstract Motivations and Abstract Goals

An abstract pain is created once the machine is unable to perform the action that resulted in the reduction of a lower level pain. For instance, if a machine needed a certain resource to alleviate its primitive pain, and the resource is not available or it is hard to find, this creates an abstract pain signal. This abstract pain motivates the machine to explore how to provide the missing resource. A similar organization of an abstract pain center is used to trigger this motivation, and the abstract pain signal may be related, for instance, to the amount of resource the machine needs in the environment. An abstract pain center is not stimulated from a physical pain sensor; an abstract pain for instance symbolizes insufficient resource that the machine needs to reduce the primitive pain, thus this pain signal is internally generated.

Suppose that an agent receives several "primitive" pain signals that indicate that he is "dirty", "thirsty", or "hungry" – these signals are generated by its sensors. Depending on which signal dominates the agent tries to lower this pain. If, for example, the agent is thirsty, he can learn that drinking water lowers this primitive pain. However, when there is no more water, he cannot alleviate this pain. Therefore, the agent develops an abstract pain related to the lack of water. Once created, this pain center will compete with all other pains for attention, independently of the original primitive pain that was responsible for its creation. Thus, an abstract pain leads to a new learned motivation that may direct an agent to perform certain actions independently from its primitive pains (motivations). For example, an agent may not be thirsty, and yet, if there is no water, he will look for it whenever this abstract pain "lack of water" will dominate.

Motivated by this new abstract pain, the agent needs to learn how to overcome it. It may find out that it can draw water from the well. Thus, it learns a new concept (the well) and is able to recognize the well as something related to its needs (specifically lack of water). It also learns a new useful action "drawing the water from the well", and it associates this action with means to remove the abstract pain of not having water (its abstract goal). It also expects that, after performing this action (drawing water from the well), it will get water. This expectation will be useful for future action planning as well as to

Figure 3. Creation of abstract pain signals

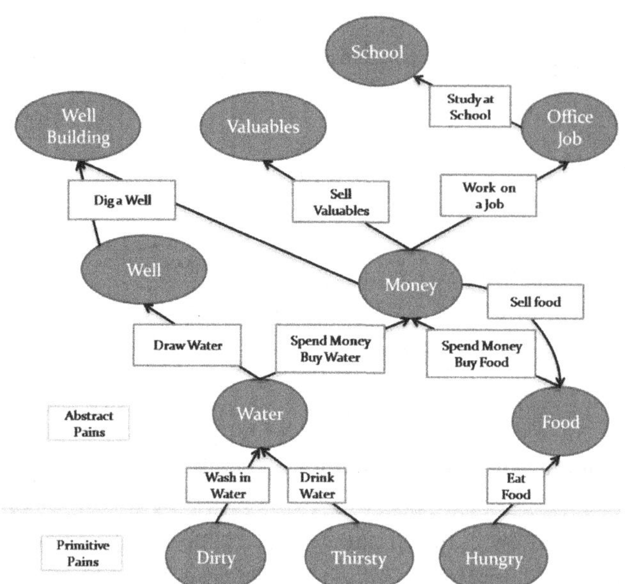

learn new concepts and to aid in their perception. At the same time, another higher level pain (and motivation to remove this pain) develops related to the possibility of drawing water from the well. Thus, if the well it was exploiting dries out, or the agent no longer can access this well, it may need to learn to overcome this pain, for instance by digging a new well. This process of building network of motivations (and abstract goal creation) is illustrated using Figure 3.

The network of motivations can be expanded both vertically (towards a higher abstraction level) as well as horizontally (on the same abstraction level). For instance, rather than drawing water from the well, an agent may learn that it is easier to buy water. Thus it develops an alternative way to accomplish this goal (get water). This will lead to an understanding of a new concept (money) and new abilities (buying water). Related to this will be another abstract pain of not having enough money, and related means to get rid of this pain (like selling food, working in an office, selling valuables, or digging a well). While some may point to new higher order motivations (like finishing school to get a good job), others may point to motivations previously developed both on a higher level (digging a well) or lower level (selling food).

Notice, that in the presented scheme, some goals may provide a circular path. For example, lack of food was an abstract pain developed through the action of eating food to satisfy hunger. An abstract goal resulting from the lack of food could be to earn money (to buy food), and yet selling food may be motivated by lack of money. Thus, a learning network must be able to detect and avoid using such circular solutions. In the proposed motivated learning scheme, this is accomplished by blocking the circular goals through inhibitory, unsuccessful action neurons (not shown on Figure 3 for the lack of space).

The machine is motivated by competing pain signals to act and to discover new ways of improving its interaction with the environment. By doing so, the machine not only learns complex relationships between concepts, resources, and actions; it also learns limitations of its own embodiment, and effective ways of using and developing its motor abilities. The machine learns to associate its motivations with goals that lead to deliberate actions. It learns the meaning of concepts and objects, and relations among objects, learns to perform new actions and to expect results of its actions. This builds up complex motivations and higher level goals as well as the means for their implementation. Based on competing pain signals, the machine chooses which actions to execute to satisfy its goals and manage the goal priorities at any given time.

Figure 3 was given only as illustration of complex interdependencies that an intelligent agent (in this case a human) may need to learn to be successful given the set of primitive pain signals. Typically machines are not thirsty, dirty or hungry, but they may have different predefined input signals treated as primitive pains, for instance low fuel level, low tire pressure, or dangerous exposure to heat, in addition to designer set objectives like a need to deliver a product on time, find the way home etc.

The following describes basic steps of pain based motivations, learning, and the goal creation algorithm.

Motivated Learning and Goal Creation Algorithm

1. Select a dominant pain signal through winner-take-all competition between pain centers.
   a. If no pain signals exceeds a prespecified threshold, wait until one does or perform a curiosity based action.
2. Set reduction of the dominant pain signal as the current goal.
   a. The current goal motivates machine to act.
3. Chose one of the previously learned actions that will most likely satisfy the current goal.
   a. If none left go to 6.
4. Check if this action can be executed in current environment conditions. If no go to 3.
5. Execute the learned action.
   a. If it resulted in lowering the dominant pain
      i. Increase the interconnection weights between the winning pain center and this action and increase the weight for the abstract pain associated with this action.
      ii. Go to 1.
   b. If the performed action did not lower the dominant pain
      i. Decrease the interconnection weights between the winning pain center and this action and decrease the weight for abstract pain associated with this action.
      ii. Go to 3.
6. Perform goal oriented exploration and try new actions.
   a. If a new action resulted in lowering the dominant pain
      i. Increase the interconnection weights between the winning pain center and this action and create a new abstract pain related to inability to perform this action.
      ii. Go to 1.
   b. If a new action did not lower the dominant pain repeat 6.

It is now widely recognized that humans, from their very onset, constantly and actively explore the environment (see Changeux, J.P., 2004). This is compatible with need based as well as curiosity based exploration. In motivated learning, an agent's ability to act on the environment is in agreement with affordances as presented in Gibson's ecological approach to perception (Gibson, 1979). In Gibson's affordances: action in the environment is in relation to the agent's motor capabilities and is independent of his experience, knowledge, or perception. In addition, an affordance either exists or it does not exist thus a desired behavior may be performed only if the opportunity presents itself in the environment.

The motivated learning approach may be combined with and will benefit from curiosity based learning. The curiosity will simply inform the machine about new discoveries (useful or not), while motivated learning will focus the search for specific objectives (increasing the effectiveness of learning). However, unlike reinforcement learning, designer of ML machine does not give these objectives to the machine. Motivations to accomplish them come from within the machine and the machine awards itself for satisfying these objectives.

Discovery of new ways to accomplish specific objectives makes learning more efficient than curiosity based discovery, and gives the machine freedom to decide how to approach a given problem. This brings the machine a step forward towards natural intelligence.

SIMULATION EXPERIMENTS

In order to illustrate motivated learning and to compare ML with RL, a simulated environment was designed and applied to two agents that were using ML, and RL respectively, for their development. Both agents interact with the environment by using the same type of sensory inputs, external pain signals, and motor actions. The external pain is reduced once a machine performs a specific action. In this system, the machine's action changed the environment by modifying the availability of various resources. In a general learning environment, ML can be used for both sensory concept building, motor control, and goal driven learning, however, in this experiment both sensory inputs and motor outputs are symbolic to focus on developmental process, which does not limit validity of the obtained results.

Two types of simulation experiments were designed to compare the effectiveness of motivated learning and reinforcement learning. In the first one, the resources in the environment change gradually with the probability of a resource observed on a symbolic input declining with the number of times that this resource was used given as:

$$P\left(sensor = true\right) = \frac{1}{1 + \dfrac{uses}{rate}} \tag{1}$$

where the "*rate*", that represents the rate of resource utilization, was set around 20 for all hierarchical levels. This is an easier environment, since the agent may restore a necessary resource by chance even without learning necessary dependencies.

In the second environment, the probability of resource availability declined rapidly and was described by:

$$P\left(sensor = true\right) = \exp\left(-\frac{uses}{rate}\right) \tag{2}$$

In this case, the learning agent has a small window of opportunity to learn proper interaction (to replenish missing resources) after which, needed resources are very difficult to find.

Motivated learning interacts with the environment and is informed about the quality of its actions by an external pain signal. This pain signal is a foundation for setting internal abstract pains and goals to remove these pains. Likewise, RL is rewarded by reduction of the external pain signal. A simple linear hierarchy of resource dependencies was used to describe the environmental complexity. For instance, if the lowest level pain signal is hunger and eating food reduces this primitive pain, then food is a resource required to perform the necessary action. However, by eating food, the food supply in the environment is reduced, so reduction of the food supply triggers the internal abstract pain signal. If buying food can restore the food supply, then money is a resource required to perform the necessary action on the second level of hierarchy. However, by spending money, available money is reduced; so reduction of the money at hand triggers the internal abstract pain signal on the next level of hierarchy. If working for money can restore the money supply, then finding a job is required to perform the necessary action on the third level of hierarchy, etc.

CASE I

In case I, both RL and ML agents were tested on gradually changing environments, governed by equation (1), using several levels of hierarchy to observe the simulation time and the pain signals. Q-learning (Sutton, R. S., & Barto, A. G., 1998) was used to implement the RL agent. In all tests, ML was 20-100 times faster than RL. While RL was able to learn the complexity of the environment with 6 levels of

Figure 4. Primitive pain and resource utilization count in RL at various levels of hierarchy

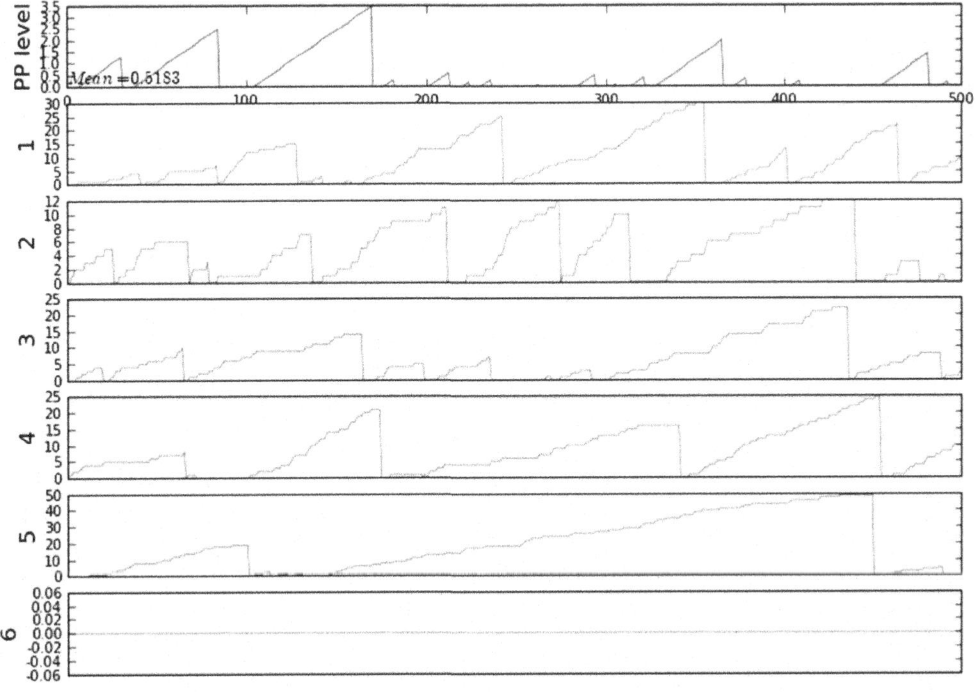

hierarchy, it took considerably more steps than ML to do so. At every step the primitive pain signal would increase by 0.1 unless the pain was removed by a proper action.

Figure 4 shows the average primitive pain level PP and resource utilization on levels 1-6 for the RL agent. The agent could restore resources while managing the maximum pain to be within 3.5. Since the RL agent does not create internal goals, resource utilization is shown to compare how both agents learn to manage external resources, and the larger resource utilization values indicate worse performance.

Figure 5 shows similar results for the ML agent. We can see that in less than 150 iterations the ML agent learned to properly manage all the resources in the environment and minimized its pain thereafter. During the learning period, the ML agent also showed smaller average pain PP than the RL agent. In addition, as soon as the needed resource was utilized (and abstract pain associated with this resource dominated) the ML agent took proper action to restore the resource, while the RL agent did this in a haphazard way (as seen in Figure 4), leading to larger average pain and larger resource utilization values.

In a more complex environment, with a larger number of hierarchical levels of resource dependencies, initially, RL seems to manage its external pain at lower levels than ML. Figure 6 shows the combined results for the average pain signal of both agents in several experiments with environments of various levels of dependencies between resources - from 6 to 18 levels of hierarchy. The average pain was calculated separately in the initial learning period before ML converged to a solution (convergence point CP), and after that point. The rightmost row shows the average primitive pain values in the ML agent before the CP, and the next row shows its pain values after the CP. The third row from the right shows average primitive pain values in the RL agent before the CP, and the fourth row shows its pain values after the CP.

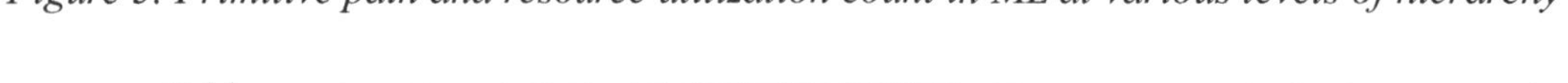

Figure 5. Primitive pain and resource utilization count in ML at various levels of hierarchy

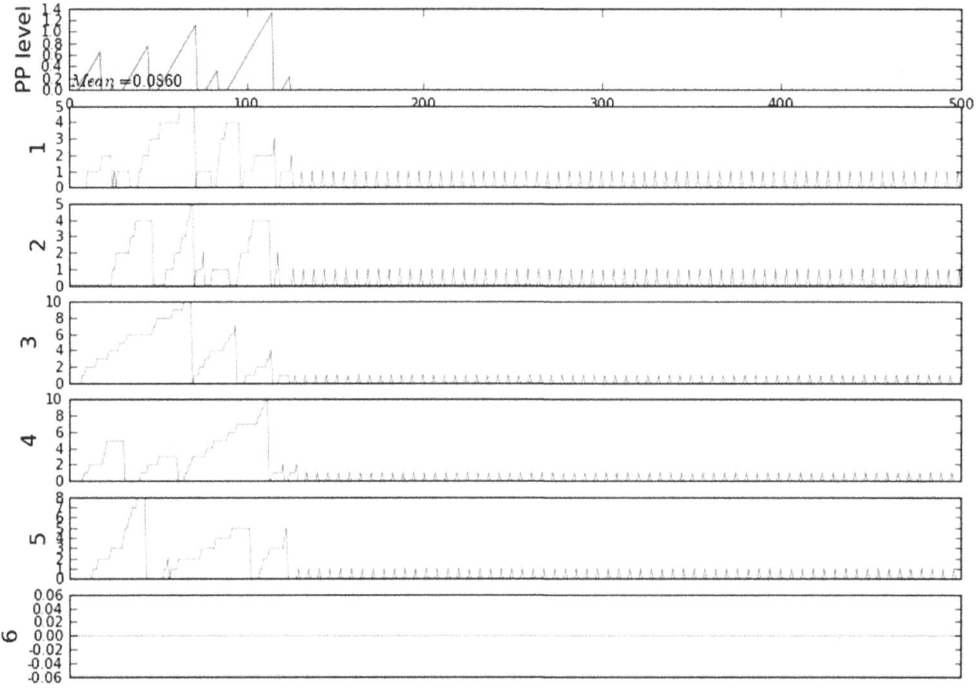

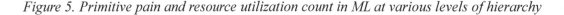

As we can see, the RL agent minimizes its primitive pain better in the initial phase (at least in the first 16 levels of hierarchy), however after the CP, ML reduced its average pain, while RL pain is gradually increasing. This indicates that RL did not properly learn the complexities of the environment and either converges to a higher level pain than ML in easier environments with smaller number of hierarchy levels, or the pain signal starts to diverge in more complex environments.

CASE II

In case II, both methods were tested in rapidly changing environments described by equation (2) using 10 levels of hierarchy to observe the average pain signals. RL initially outperformed ML as in case I. However, after the CP that was around 500 iterations in ML, RL slowly diverges, with a complete breakdown after 1100 iterations, when its pain started to increase linearly (logarithmically on the exponential pain scale presented in Figure 7). ML clearly shows that it can manage its external pain on the low level after the CP.

COMPARING MOTIVATED LEARNING AND REINFORCEMENT LEARNING

As demonstrated by the simulation experiments, motivated learning equips a machine to interact with complex and progressively hostile environments better than reinforcement learning. The machine gradually becomes both a better learner and a better actor. However, to develop in an optimum way, it requires gradually increasing complexity of the environment. The environment must initially be easier and give opportunity for the agent to learn before it becomes more hostile and demanding. This kind of scheme is what is needed for developmental robotics, and very much resembles conditions for the developmental processes in humans.

Figure 6. Primitive pain in ML and RL at various environments

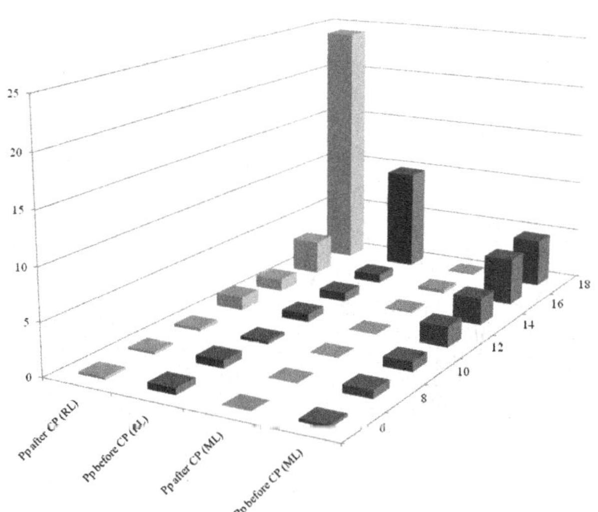

Although the learning process was triggered and continues to respond to primitive pain signals, to a large extent, a more developed ML machine responds to its internally generated motivations and goals. These goals may be different from those set by the designer. The machine may choose to pursue a higher level goal, even if it may have means and know how to implement lower level objectives. Since the decision as to which goal to pursue is based on the strength of various pain signals, at any time an abstract pain may dominate and the machine will perform actions to address this pain. Thus, a machine must be properly guided (perhaps with special incentives that it will find rewarding) to perform useful actions, without being forced to do so. This is definitely not what an RL machine will do, as it always pursues its prespecified goals. The RL machine may learn to perform subgoals only if they serve to accomplish a prespecified goal as was discussed in hierarchical reinforcement algorithms (Bakker & Schmidhuber, 2004).

RL can use artificial curiosity to explore and to learn a hierarchy of subgoals. However, all the steps it will perform respond to major goals set by the designer, and are just steps on the way to accomplish these goals. These, at best, can be considered as subgoals to a predetermined goal. None of these subgoals can be a separate goal by itself, and can be performed only if they were triggered by a need to perform a goal - as intermediate steps to accomplish the goal.

Contrariwise, the ML machine may search for a solution to an abstract goal, even if it can accomplish the goal set by its designer. However, it is doing this to learn complex relations in the environment that are relevant to its ability to perform designer specified goals. So, it is ready to use this knowledge if needed when the environmental conditions change for the worse. It is true that curiosity based learning can provide the machine with similar knowledge; however, the probability of randomly discovering the knowledge that is relevant to the machine's goals is very low.

Figure 7. Primitive pain in ML and RL at a rapidly changing environment

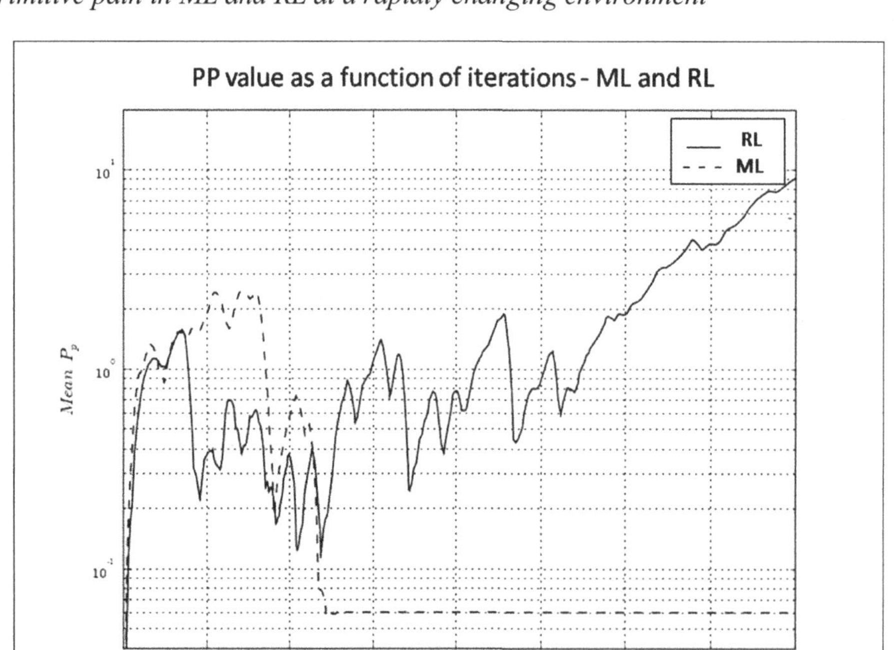

Table 1 presents major differences between general RL and ML methods. RL learns a value function for a specified goal (for which it receives an external reward). ML learns many value functions not only for the externally specified goal but also for all internal motivations and abstract goals. Since all externally provided rewards are observable from the environment, the RL machine can be fully optimized. This was demonstrated in the work by Hutter, where he showed theoretical proof for the existence of an optimal reinforcement learning agent (Hutter, 2001, pp. 225-238). To the contrary, ML cannot be optimized since its internal states are unknown to the environment; in particular, the environment cannot observe the total amount of reward the ML agent receives.

Once optimized, the RL agent is predictable, which is not the case with ML. In classical RL objectives are set by the designer, while in ML, at any given time, the machine may set and pursue new objectives that are not set or understood by the designer or may not be even known to him. These objectives change dynamically with changing motivations, are not predictable at the beginning of learning, and are fully dependent not only on the external reward and pain signals, but also on the whole learning experience.

RL solves basically an optimization problem for maximizing the reward, while a pain (negative reward) based ML solves a minimax problem. The difference is significant. Maximization may lead to destructive behavior and does not provide a natural switching mechanism for managing competing goals. Minimax leads to a multi-objective solution with a natural switching mechanism as discussed in the text. RL is always active, since the system tries to maximize the reward, while ML may rest when it does not experience any pain above a prespecified threshold value. Finally, the higher efficiency of ML over RL was demonstrated on a number of examples, in which the environment changes quickly, with complex dependencies between resources that require machine's awareness about these changes.

Thus, in a changing environment, it is no longer most productive to maximize the reward based on classical RL rules (like QV learning (Wiering, M. A., 2005), hierarchical reinforcement learning, temporal difference, etc.). The machine must show vigilance towards changes in the environment that may affect its future performance. Although ML and RL are different, ML may benefit from using efficient RL algorithms in its exploratory search for a solution to a specific problem (goal). It is the system that governs machine motivations and selects corresponding goals that differentiate them the most.

Table 1. Comparison between reinforcement learning and motivated learning

Reinforcement Learning	Motivated Learning
Single value function	Multiple value functions
Measurable rewards – can be optimized	Internal rewards – cannot be optimized
Predictable	Unpredictable
Objectives set by designer	Sets its own objectives
Maximizes the reward – potentially unstable	Solves minimax problem – always stable
No internal motivations and goal selection	Internal motivations and goal selection
Always active	Acts only when needs or wants to
Learning effort quickly increases with environment complexity	Learns better in complex environment than reinforcement learning

FUTURE RESEARCH DIRECTIONS

More research is required to develop and document the concept of the motivated learning method. One of these future steps is to test motivated learning on typical reinforcement learning benchmarks with large dimensionality of the state/action spaces possibly combining ML with hierarchical RL to learn how to efficiently implement subgoals. Any form of reinforcement learning, e.g. hierarchical reinforcement learning with subgoal discovery, can be used in such a combined learning process. Other mechanisms of learning relations between conditional signals and reward can be used to build motivations and establish new goals. For instance, the Pavlovian learning scheme proposed by O'Reilly is a viable alternative to temporal difference used in reinforcement learning (O'Reilly et all. 2007) and can be used to benefit ML.

CONCLUSION

Motivated learning provides a new learning paradigm for the development of autonomous, cognitive machines. It is based on a pain driven mechanism to create internal motivations to act and learn. It develops internal representations and skills based on an internal reward system that emerges from its successful interaction with the environment. In this chapter, it was compared with reinforcement learning both in terms of conceptual differences and computational efficiency. Motivated learning may be combined with reinforcement learning for a solution to a specific goal, and with curiosity based search to enhance its knowledge about the environment. However, ML is better focused than curiosity based learning and more efficient than reinforcement learning. Moreover, it provides a natural mechanism that governs machine motivations, select goals, and learns/selects actions to satisfy these goals. The proposed approach enriches a machine's learning by providing a natural mechanism for developing goal oriented motivations, dynamical selection of goals and autonomous control needed for machine intelligence.

REFERENCES

Baars, B. J., & Gage, N. M. (2007). *Cognition, brain, and consciousness*. Academic Press.

Bakker, B., & Schmidhuber, J. (2004). Hierarchical reinforcement learning based on subgoal discovery and subpolicy specialization. In F. Groen, N. Amato, A. Bonarini, E. Yoshida, & B. Kröse (Eds.), *Proceedings of the 8th Conference on Intelligent Autonomous Systems*, (pp. 438-445). Amsterdam, The Netherlands.

Barto, A., Singh, S., & Chentanez, N. (2004). Intrinsically motivated learning of hierarchical collections of skills. *Proceedings of the 3rd International Conference on Development Learning*, (pp. 112–119). San Diego, CA.

Berridge, K. C., & Robinson, T. E. (2003). Parsing reward. *Trends in Neurosciences*, *26*(9), 507–513. doi:10.1016/S0166-2236(03)00233-9

Brooks, R. (1986). *Asynchronous distributed control system for a mobile robot.* SPIE Conference on Mobile Robots, (pp. 77–84).

Brooks, R. A. (1991). Intelligence without representation. *Artificial Intelligence*, *47*, 139–159. doi:10.1016/0004-3702(91)90053-M

Changeux, J. P. (2004). *The physiology of truth.* Cambridge, MA & London, UK: Harvard University Press.

Cohn, D., Ghahramani, Z., & Jordan, M. (1996). Active learning with statistical models. *Journal of Artificial Intelligence Research*, *4*, 129–145.

Currie, K. W., & Tate, A. (1991). O-Plan: The open planning architecture. *Artificial Intelligence, 52*(1), 49-86. ISSN: 0004-3702

Dayan, P., & Hinton, G. E. (1993). Feudal reinforcement learning. In Hanson, S. J., Cowan, J. D., & Giles, C. L. (Eds.), *Advances in neural information processing systems, 5*. San Mateo, CA: Morgan Kaufmann.

Dehaene, S., Kerszberg, M., & Changeux, J. P. (1998). A neuronal model of a global workspace in effortful cognitive tasks. *Proceedings of the National Academy of Sciences of the United States of America*, *95*(24), 14529–14534. doi:10.1073/pnas.95.24.14529

Derbyshire, S. W. G., Jones, A. K. P., Gyulai, F., et al. (1997). Pain processing during three levels of noxious stimulation produces differential patterns of central activity. *Pain, 73*, 431–445., Amsterdam, The Netherlands: Elsevier. ISSN 0304-3959

Fu, W.-T., & Anderson, J. R. (2006). Solving the credit assignment problem: Explicit and implicit learning with internal and external state information. *Proceedings of the 28th Annual Conference of the Cognitive Science Society*. Hillsdale, NJ: LEA.

Gibson, J. (1979). *An ecological approach to visual perception*. Boston, MA: Houghton Mifflin.

Harmon, M. E., & Baird, L. C. (1996). *Multi-player residual advantage learning with general function approximation. Technical report*. Wright-Patterson Air Force Base.

Hasenjager, M., & Ritter, H. (2002). Active learning in neural networks. Berlin, Germany: *Physica-Verlag GmbH*, Physica-Verlag Studies In Fuzziness and Soft Computing Series, (pp. 137–169).

Hsieh, J. C., Tu, C. H., & Chen, F. P. (2001). Activation of the hypothalamus characterizes the acupuncture stimulation at the analgesic point in human: A positron emission tomography study. *Neuroscience Letters*, *307*, 105–108. doi:10.1016/S0304-3940(01)01952-8

Huang, X., & Weng, J. (2002). Novelty and reinforcement learning in the value system of developmental robots. *Proceedings of the 2nd International Workshop on Epigenetic Robotics: Modeling Cognitive Development in Robotic Systems*.

Hutter, M. (2001). Towards a universal theory of artificial intelligence based on algorithmic probability and sequential decisions. *Proceedings of the 12th European Conference on Machine Learning* (ECML-2001), (pp. 226-238).

Kaelbling, L. P. (1993). *Hierarchical reinforcement learning: Preliminary results*. (pp. 167–173). ICML-93, San Francisco, CA: Morgan Kaufmann.

Kaplan, F., & Oudeyer, P.-Y. (2004). Maximizing learning progress: An internal reward system for development. In Lida, F., Pfeifer, R., Steels, L., & Kuniyoshi, Y. (Eds.), *Embodied artificial intelligence* (pp. 259–270). Springer-Verlag. doi:10.1007/978-3-540-27833-7_19

Melzack, R. (1990). Phantom limbs and the concept of a neuromatrix. *Trends in Neurosciences, 13*, 88–92. doi:10.1016/0166-2236(90)90179-E

Melzack, R., & Casey, K. L. (1968). Sensory, motivational, and central control determinants of pain. In Kenshalo, D. R. (Ed.), *The skin senses* (pp. 423–439). Springfield, IL: C.C. Thomas.

Mesulam, M. M. (1990). Large-scale neurocognitive networks and distributed processing for attention, language, and memory. *Annals of Neurology, 28*, 597–613. doi:10.1002/ana.410280502

Moravec, H. P. (1984). Locomotion, vision and intelligence. In Brady, M., & Paul, R. (Eds.), *Robotics research, 1* (pp. 215–224). Cambridge, MA: MIT Press.

O'Reilly, R. C., & Frank, M. J. (2006). Making working memory work: A computational model of learning in the prefrontal cortex and basal ganglia. *Neural Computation, 18*(2), 283–328. doi:10.1162/089976606775093909

O'Reilly, R. C., Frank, M. J., Hazy, T. E., & Watz, B. (2007). PVLV: The primary value and learned value Pavlovian learning algorithm. *Behavioral Neuroscience, 121*(1), 31–49. doi:10.1037/0735-7044.121.1.31

Oudeyer, P.-Y., Kaplan, F., & Hafner, V. (2007). Intrinsic motivation systems for autonomous mental development. *IEEE Transactions on Evolutionary Computation, 11*(2), 265–286. doi:10.1109/TEVC.2006.890271

Panksepp, J. (1998). *Affective neuroscience: The foundations of human and animal emotions*. New York, NY: Oxford University Press.

Parr, R., & Russell, S. (1998). Reinforcement learning with hierarchies of machines. In *Advances in Neural Information Processing Systems, 10*. MIT Press.

Peyron, R., Laurent, B., & Garcia-Larrea, L. (2000). Functional imaging of brain responses to pain. A review and meta-analysis. *Neurophysiologie Clinique, 30*, 263–288. doi:10.1016/S0987-7053(00)00227-6

Pfeifer, R., & Bongard, J. C. (2007). *How the body shapes the way we think: A new view of intelligence. The MIT Press*. Bradford Books.

Porro, C. A., Baraldi, P., & Pagnoni, G. (2002). Does anticipation of pain affect cortical nociceptive systems? *The Journal of Neuroscience, 22*, 3206–3214.

Rao, A. S., & Georgeff, M. P. (1995). BDI-agents: From theory to practice. *Proceedings of the First International Conference on Multiagent Systems* (ICMAS'95), (pp. 312-319).

Schmidhuber, J. (1991). Curious model-building control systems. *Proceedings International Joint Conference on Neural Networks*, (pp. 1458–1463). Singapore.

Schultz, W. (2002). Getting formal with dopamine and reward. *Neuron, 36*, 241–263. doi:10.1016/S0896-6273(02)00967-4

Singh, S. P. (1992). Transfer of learning by composing solutions for elemental sequential tasks. *Machine Learning, 8*, 323–340. doi:10.1007/BF00992700

Steels, L. (2004). *The autotelic principle*. In (LNAI 3139), (pp. 231-242).

Sutton, R. S. (1984). *Temporal credit assignment in reinforcement learning.* Unpublished doctoral dissertation, University of Massachusetts, Amherst, MA.

Sutton, R. S., & Barto, A. G. (1998). *Reinforcement learning: An introduction.* Cambridge, MA: MIT Press.

Tölle, T. R., Kaufmann, T., & Siessmeier, T. (1999). Region-specific encoding of sensory and affective components of pain in the human brain: A positron emission tomography correlation analysis. *Annals of Neurology, 45*, 40–47. doi:10.1002/1531-8249(199901)45:1<40::AID-ART8>3.0.CO;2-L

Weng, J. (2004). Developmental robotics: Theory and experiments. *International Journal of Humanoid Robotics, 1*(2), 199–236. doi:10.1142/S0219843604000149

White, R. (1959). Motivation reconsidered: The concept of competence. *Psychological Review, 66*, 297–333. doi:10.1037/h0040934

Wiering, M. A. (2005). QV(lambda)-learning: A new on-policy reinforcement learning Algorithm. In D. Leone (Ed.), *Proceedings of the 7th European Workshop on Reinforcement Learning* (pp. 17-18).

ADDITIONAL READING

Audi, R. (2001). *The Architecture of Reason: The Structure and Substance of Rationality.* Oxford University Press.

Brand, P., & Yancey, P. (1993). *The Gift of Pain: Why We Hurt and What We Can Do About It.* Zondervan Publishing House.

Brooks, R. A. (1991b). Intelligence without reason, *Proc. 12th Int. Joint Conf. on Artificial Intelligence*, pp. 569-595, Sydney, Australia.

Legg, S., & Hutter, M. (2006). A Formal Measure of Machine Intelligence," *Proc. 15th Annual Machine Learning Conference of Belgium and The Netherlands,* pp.73-80.

Maes, P. (1990). Situated agents can have goals, pp. 49-70. *Robotics and Autonomous Systems*, 6.

Maturana, H. R., & Varela, F. J. (1980). *Autopoiesis and Cognition - The Realization of the Living* (*Vol. 42*). Boston Studies in the Philosophy of Science.

McCarthy, J., Minsky, M. L. & Shannon, C. E. (1955). *A proposal for the Dartmouth Summer Research Project on Artificial Intelligence.* Harvard University, N. Rochester, Aug. 31.

Moore, G. E. (1993). *Principia Ethica.* Cambridge: Cambridge University Press, 1903; Revised edition with "Preface to the second edition" and other papers, ed. T. Baldwin, Cambridge: Cambridge University Press.

Pfeifer, R., & Scheier, C. (1999). *Understanding Intelligence.* Cambridge, MA: MIT Press.

Rolls, E. T. (1989). Functions of neuronal networks in the hippocampus and neocortex in memory. In *Neural models of plasticity: experimental and theoretical approaches* (pp. 240–265). San Diego: Academic Press.

Si, J., & Wang, Y. (2001). On-Line Learning Control by Association and Reinforcement. *IEEE Transactions on Neural Networks*, *12*(2), 264–276. doi:10.1109/72.914523

Steels, L. (2003). Intelligence with Representation. *Philosophical Transactions: Mathematical, Physical and Engineering Sciences*, vol. 361, no. 1811, pp. 2381- 2395.

Steels, L. (2007). The symbol grounding problem is solved, so what's next? In De Vega, M., Glennberg, G., & Graesser, G. (Eds.), *Symbols, embodiment and meaning*. New Haven: Academic Press.

Stewart, J. (1993). Cognition without neurons: Adaptation, learning and memory in the immune system. *CC-AL*, *11*, 7–30.

Stout, A., Konidaris, G., & Barto, A. (2005). Intrinsically Motivated Reinforcement Learning: A Promising Framework For Developmental Robot Learning. *Proc. of the AAAI Spring Symp. on Developmental Robotics.*

Turing, A. M. (1950). Computing Machinery and Intelligence. *Mind*, *59*(236), 433–460. doi:10.1093/mind/LIX.236.433

Varela, F. J. Thompson, E. T. & Rosch, E. (1992). *The Embodied Mind: Cognitive Science and Human Experience*. Cambridge, MA: The MIT Press.

Walter, W. G. (1951). A Machine That Learns. *Scientific American*, *185*(2), 60–63.

Walter, W. G. (1961). *The Living Brain,* Duckworth, London, 1953, republished by Penguin, Harmondsworth, UK.

Wehner, R. (1987). Matched Filters - Neural Models of the External World. *Journal of Comparative Physiology. A, Neuroethology, Sensory, Neural, and Behavioral Physiology*, *161*, 511–531. doi:10.1007/BF00603659

Yellon, D. M., Baxter, G. F., & Marber, M. S. (1996). Angina reassessed; pain or protector? *Lancet*, *347*, 1159–1162. doi:10.1016/S0140-6736(96)90613-3

KEY TERMS AND DEFINITIONS

Artificial Curiosity: Learning based on exploration, novelty and surprise.
Autonomous Agents: Systems interacting with environment.
Computational Intelligence: Computational methods for intelligent machines.
Goal Creation: Mechanism to create abstract goals.
Machine Learning: Learning based on the input data.
Motivated Learning: Machine learning with internal motivations.
Pavlovian Learning: Associative learning based on conditional stimuli.
Reinforcement Learning: Reward based learning of state/action values.

Chapter 12
Topological Coding in the Hippocampus

Yuri Dabaghian
University of California at San Francisco, USA

Anthony G. Cohn
University of Leeds, UK

Loren Frank
University of California at San Francisco, USA

ABSTRACT

The brain constructs internal representations of the external world, and one essential element of efforts to understand neural processing focuses on understanding the nature of these internal representations. This chapter examines the currently available experimental evidence concerning the physiological and cognitive mechanisms of space representation in humans and in animals, and in particular, on the role of the hippocampus. The hippocampus is essential for the ability to navigate through space, and hippocampal neurons tend to fire in specific subregions of an animal's environment. At the same time, it is not clear how the hippocampal representation of space is best described in terms of well-established mathematical definitions of space, nor is it clear whether the hippocampal representation is sufficient to construct a mathematical space. This chapter shows that, using only the times of spikes from hippocampal place cells, it is possible to construct a topological space, and it is argued that the hippocampus is specialized for computing a topological representation of the environment. Based on this observation, the chapter discusses the possibility of a constructive neural representation of a topological space.

BACKGROUND

The task of space perception and spatial orientation is one of the most fundamental tasks faced by animals. An animal plans and executes essentially every aspect of its behavior in the context of the space that it experiences through neural activity in its brain. Currently, there exists a significant amount of

DOI: 10.4018/978-1-60960-551-3.ch012

data concerning the mechanisms of spatial encoding based on cognitive experiments and electrophysiological recordings from human, primate and rodent (notably rat's) brain. These experiments suggest that the complete representation of the spatial environment appears as a result of a complex association of several complementary types of spatial information computed in different parts of the brain, which are involved in a complex neurophysiological interaction (Andersen, Synder, Bradley, & Xing, 1997; Burgess, Jeffery, & O'Keefe, 1999). A fundamental conceptual challenge in understanding the neurophysiological principles of space perception is the task of interpreting the patterns of neuronal activity in the brain as equivalent to a particular aspect of the spatial realm. This was recognized as early as 1895-1902 in the works of H. Poincaré (Poincaré, 1895), and E. Mach (Mach, 2004), who pointed out that spatial cognition and the cognitive basis of geometry are provided by the brain's ability to build its own internal "representative" (Poincaré, 1895; Poincaré, 1898), or "physiological" (Mach, 2004),space. The analysis of the physiological organization of the sensory inputs known at the turn of the last century allowed them to make a number of interesting observations about the nature of various sensory (i.e. visual, tactile etc.) spaces. The current level of knowledge about the neurophysiology of spatial information processing as well as the mathematical concepts that can be used for interpreting the results of experimental observations are far more advanced, which allows for a much more detailed study of the phenomenon of representative space. Here we ask the following question: in what sense is it possible to define and to construct a space, as a physical and as a mathematical object, given the semantics of the neuronal system, i.e. the parameters of the spiking activity of neurons? We focus on currently available experimental results concerning the neural activity in the hippocampus – a brain area essential for spatial cognition (O'Keefe & Nadel, 1978; Hassabis, Kumaran, Vann, Maguire, 2007; Morris, Moser, Reidel, Martin, Sandin, Day, O'Carroll, 2003). Numerous experiments have shown that if the hippocampus is partially or completely damaged or impaired, the animal loses its full ability to solve many spatial navigation tasks, especially tasks based on following sequences of cues and on retrieving sequential (episodic) memories (Sharp, 2002), (Eichenbaum & Cohen, 2001; Kesner, Gilbert & Barua, 2002). The exact nature of the spatial information represented in the hippocampus remains somewhat unclear.

We propose an approach to hippocampal data analysis that allows us to not only describe many important aspects of the representative space and to match them with the properties of the environment. In addition, we address the deeper question of how can the neuronal firing patterns have spatial properties, i.e. in what sense a space can be build constructively out of neuronal activity. The goal of this enterprize is to understand, in a formal mathematical sense, the elements of the mental representation of space.

NEURONAL SPATIAL MAPS

Electrophysiological experiments examine the statistical correlations between patterns of neural activity and various external sensory and behavioral parameters. This approach led to the discovery that pyramidal cells in the rat hippocampus become active only when the animal is located in a relatively small portion of the environment and remain basically silent elsewhere (O'Keefe & Dostrovsky, 1971). Hence these cells (called "place cells", *PC*) highlight a certain system of regions (called "place fields", *PF*), and define a system of spatial "tags" via their firing activity. This place specific activity led to the hypothesis that the *PC*s encode a qualitative representation of the environment which has been referred to as "cognitive map" by O'Keefe and Nadel (O'Keefe & Nadel, 1978) and that this representation serves as one of the key elements of a rat's spatial awareness.

The standard approach to understanding place cell activity has been to measure the activity of place cells, either singly or in ensembles, and relate their firing to the experimenter's measurements of the animal's position, velocity, etc. (Sharp, 2002; Burgess, Jeffery, & O'Keefe, 1999). This approach has shown that the collection of *PF*s appears to cover the animal's environment (Wilson and McNaughton, 1993) and knowing the positions of relatively few (about 30) *PF*s in a small (about 1 m across) environment, one can predict the rat's location at any time with an impressive accuracy based on the current pattern of the activity of its *PC*s (Jensen & Lisman, 2000; Frank, Brown & Wilson, 2000), (Wilson & McNaughton, 1993). Although establishing correlations between the neuronal activity and the external parameters is crucial for identifying the basic properties of the spatial maps, the animal's spatial representation, here after referred to as "representative space", *R*, clearly depends on brain's internal ability to extract information about the spatial pattern from the spiking activity, i.e. on the ability to view the temporal pattern of neural network outputs as a reflection of the spatial pattern of the firing fields.

This suggests that certain spatial properties of the information processing in the hippocampus and in other space representing brain areas (Wiener & Taube, 2005), (Burgess, Jeffery, & O'Keefe, 1999) can be established as an intrinsic quality of the temporal structure of their spiking activities or a quality of the correlations between their spiking activities, rather than as characteristics of the correlations with the externally observed parameters. Such an autonomous interpretation of the neural space representation task is central for the following discussion.

SPACE RECONSTRUCTION EXPERIMENT

Current data suggest that the task of space representation involves a variety of different computations that integrate sensory information into several complementary spatial representations (Wiener & Taube,

Figure 1 The spike trains produced by 7 hypothetical place cells (PCs) (a) and a schematic representation of the corresponding place fields (PFs) (b) in an open field environment. The trajectory of the animal is shown by the dashed line. Notice that the overlaps between the spike trains are consistent with the overlap pattern between the PFs. The color shade of the PFs encodes the firing rate ranging from the background (fair shade) to highest level (dark shade).

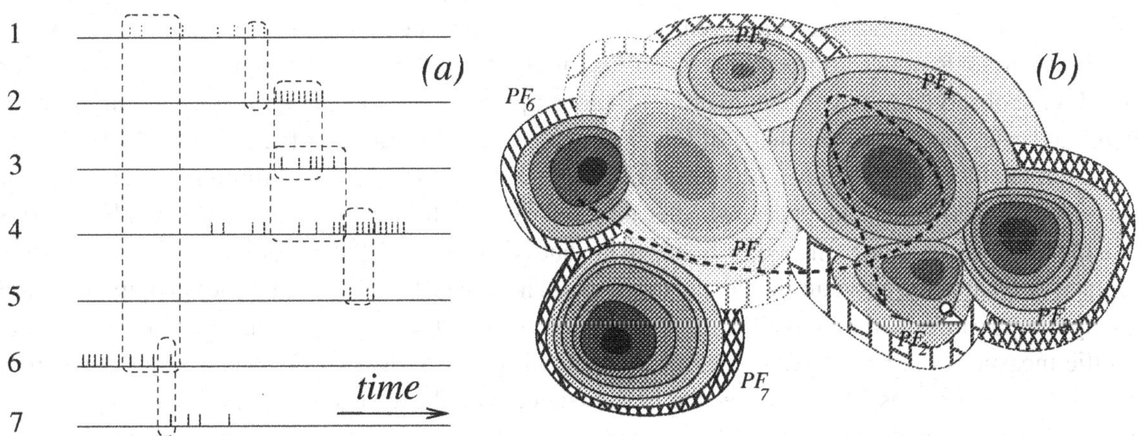

2005), (Burgess, Jeffery, & O'Keefe, 1999). Our ultimate goal is to understand the mathematical properties of these spatial representations, and thus it is important to note that, from the mathematical point of view, the colloquial term "space" implies a complex assembly of several mathematical structures (Dubrovin, Novikov, & Formenko, 1992), that must be coherently brought together to produce the familiar realm of space. These structures include: (1) Topological order, i.e. the relationships of adjacency and spatial connectivity, spatial interior, boundary, closure, which allow the most general and a highly abstract representation of the notion of spatial continuity;(2) A one structure – the possibility to define whether directions are parallel, and to establish the notion of "inbetweenness" giving a geometry with equivalence of regions under "slant" distortions. Going beyond affine structure, it is possible to extend expressiveness further, without establishing a full metric, e.g. by measuring directions qualitatively, using a discrete and coarse measure on angles between relative directions. (3) Metric information – a quantitative description of various spatial scales via a topologically consistent distance measure between objects. To address the question about what information can be extracted from the *PC* activity by the downstream neurons, and to address the nature of the spatial information encoded in the *PF*s, it will be convenient in the following discussion to refer to the following

Space Reconstruction thought Experiment (SRE)

Imagine an animal that is running in a certain arena, not directly observed by the experimenter. The experimenter receives the real time signals from the electrodes that are implanted into the animal's hippocampus, and is free to analyze the recorded information in any way in order to extract from it as much information as possible about the characteristics of the arena and about the navigational task faced by the animal. Question: how much would the experimenter be able to deduce about the geometrical and spatial properties of the environment based on the *PC* activity and which of the potential analysis algorithms are sufficiently robust and can be biologically implemented? For example, let us consider the SRE task in the simple case of a rat running on a linear (*1D*) track. After observing the *PC* signals for a sufficiently long time, the observer in the thought experiment described above may notice that there is a linear order to the time intervals in which hippocampal cells are active. If the experimenter interprets this order as spatial, he will conclude that the environment is linear. In more complex (*2D* or *3D*) environments the correspondence to the spatial order is less direct, however a careful analysis of the firing activity of a sufficient number of cells (for more detailed discussion see Sections VI and IX) will lead to the conclusion that the temporal pattern of spikes is consistent with a possible ordering of regions in a space, i.e. that the firing events can serve as a consistent system of spatial location labels.

It is important to notice however, that given *PF* variability, this system of spatial location tags a priori provides the observer only with spatial order relationships and does not contain in itself the information about the scale, the size or the shape of the environment. For example, in the case of a SRE analysis of a *1D* track, there are no known properties of place fields that would allow, through a mere observation of the *PC* activation sequences, whether the track is straight or bent (i.e. whether it is I-shaped or U-shaped or C-shaped or S-shaped or J-shaped), what is the scale of the environment, i.e. how long is the track or what is the curvature scale of its sections. Thus, in order to produce a more complete spatial description, the information about the location sequence and about the *PF*s must be associated with a specific measure of scale. For example, the increase of the firing frequency level as the rat is getting closer to the center of its *PF*, would need to be associated with the measure of animal's size, speed, etc., that are a priori unknown to SRE observer. This suggests that the information contained in the *PF* partitions alone is generally insufficient to represent the full extent of spatial relationships, e.g. the observed sizes of the *PF*s themselves, the distances or the angles between *PF*s or between the external cues. In order to obtain such characteristics, the *PC* data must be complemented by additional information, e.g. rat's speed, the direction and the duration of straight runs and turns, etc. Hence the analysis of the *PC* activity suggests the hypothesis that the information that can be extracted most robustly from the hippocampal neural activity represents the topological arrangement of the locations, i.e. the topology of the representative space.

STABILITY WITH RESPECT TO GRADUAL CHANGES

The above claim about the topological representation of information in the hippocampus was made based on the fact that certain geometrical information (distances, angles) does not seem to be encoded directly in *PC* activity. Given that an affine or metric representation of space would also allow for an extraction of topological information, we can ask whether there is any benefit to a representation that does not appear to explicitly represent angles or spatial scales. In other words, why might the hippocampus primarily represent topological information? One benefit of such a representation is that it is invariant to a number of affine and metric transformation. In particular, the strong version of the topological hypothesis predicts that if *PF* layout in slowly "morphing" familiar environments should remain stable. This means in particular, that if the whole set of sensory stimuli, including the objects embedded in the space, change coherently, so that the mutual spatial order between every set of sensory cues is preserved, then the *PF*s should generally maintain their relative positions with respect to external cues and each other, although the exact location of *PF*s and the shapes of *PC*'s activity distribution profiles may change. At the same time, transformations that rapidly alter the space or distort its topology of the space should produce some form of remapping where the relative order of *PC* firing changes. There are experimental data that address both of these conditions and provide support for this hypothesis. In studies where the topology of the environment is preserved, the shape of the environment is gradually altered and the positions of the *PF*s from the same *PC*s are recorded before and after the transformation (Sharp, 2002; Gothard, Skaggs, & McNaughton, 1996; Gothard, Skaggs, Moore, & McNaughton, 1996; Gothard, Hoffman, Battaglia, & McNaughton, 2001; Redish, Rosenzweig, Bohanick, McNaughton, & Barnes, 2000; O'Keefe & Burgess, 1996). The results show that indeed, if the changes are sufficiently smooth, the positions of the *PF*s follow continuously the change of the geometry of the environment, i.e. they are not in fact anchored to a specific area of the environment but drift continuously in the physical space without changing the original relative activity structure. More importantly, although the geometry alteration is typically achieved by moving local cues, the responses of the *PF*s are not local. Instead, they are highly correlated across the whole environment. For example, according to experiments of Gothard et. al (Gothard, Skaggs, & McNaughton, 1996; Gothard, Skaggs, Moore, & McNaughton, 1996; Gothard, Hoffman, Battaglia, & McNaughton, 2001) the overall pattern of the *PF*s on a linear track shifts coherently in response to stretches or compressions of the track (Figure 2). Not only the *PF*s located next to the moving end respond by shifting, but also the rest of them, all along the track, shift accordingly to their distance to the moving end. The overall response pattern of *PF*s is as if they were drawn on an elastic sheet that can stretch or compress with the shifts of parts of the environment. Further, studies that have been used to argue for a geometric representation in the hippocampus (Burgess & O'Keefe, 1996), are also consistent with the topological hypotheses, in that manipulations of the size of the environ-

Figure 2. Schematic representation of the elastic stretch of the PF layout reported in (Gothard, Skaggs, Moore, & McNaughton, 1996). The rat shuttles between the points A and B where it gets a chocolate reward. As the box A is moved towards B, so that the space available for navigation shrinks, the PF structure contracts as a whole, that includes the PF next to the moving box A and the PFs away from it.

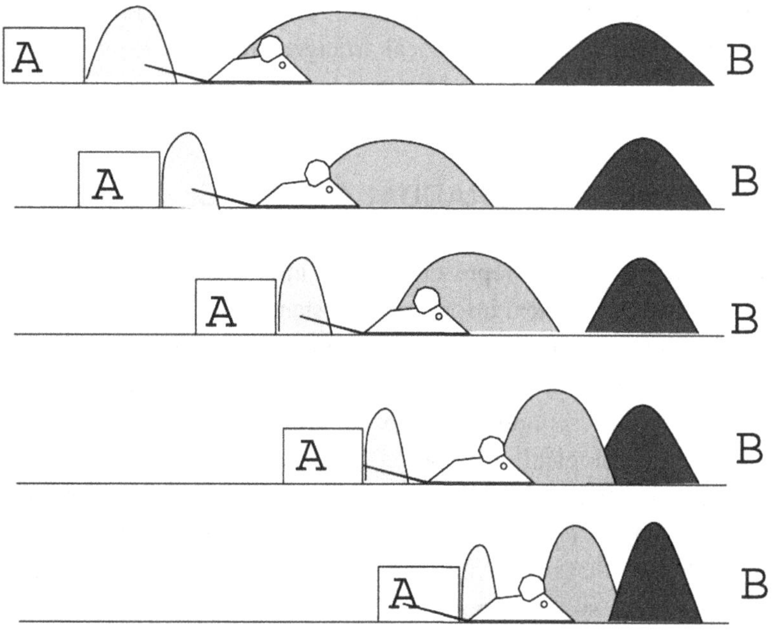

ment led to stretching or shrinking of individual fields but preserved the relative order of place fields. Other studies that have examined responses to geometrically complex and fast spatial transformations have shown that the hippocampal map can break into several maps coded by a separate groups of cells that are bound to different sets of objects or parts of the environment, thus forming a particular reference frame (Gothard, Skaggs, Moore, & McNaughton, 1996; Muller, 1996). In experiments (Gothard, Skaggs, Moore, & McNaughton, 1996) in which the walls of the environment were rotating while the floor and some objects scattered on it were static (which produces "shearing" of the space on the scale comparable to the size of the arena (Sharp, 2002; Muller, 1996)), the hippocampal representation also undergoes a complex transformation. Some place fields disappear, while a subgroup of *PF*s may remain bound to the walls (wall frame) and another subgroup of *PF*s remain floor (Gothard, Skaggs, Moore, & McNaughton, 1996) or object (Sharp, 2002; Skaggs & McNaughton, 1996; Muller, 1996) bound. Thus, the changes in the hippocampal representation of space reflect the shearing of the relationships between cues and spatial locations. From the point of view of the hippocampal network analysis, these results suggest that there exists a certain regime of structural stability of the hippocampal system due where it does not undergo a major restructuring in order to track slow, topologically consistent spatial variations. Indeed, if the relative order of the *PC* activity is encoded in a stable state of the network that is preserved throughout continuous spatial transformations, then the same sequences of *PC* activations are projected onto the morphing environment and therefore are observed as shifting *PF*s that preserve their relative order. Hence from the point of view of the neural network dynamics, the hypothesis about topological representation of spatial information is equivalent simply to a certain degree of stability of the configurations.

In the latter case if the mutual order of the *PF*s does not change then from the point of view of the SRE observer, the hippocampal network is encoding the same set of the relationships thus providing a certain invariant discretized representation of the behaviorally relevant spatial information, i.e. a map of topological nature. Overall, the above arguments suggest that *PF*s code for the topological information in the conventional mathematical sense in at least in two aspects – as a consistent collection of places that supplies topological information in static SRE experiments, which (as a matter of empirical coincidence) also has the "elastic grid" properties. These arguments suggest that the basic underlying assumption in the hippocampal SRE analysis should be that the *PC* activity is associated with a topological spatial structure and hence the analysis of the *PC* activity should focus on extracting the topological information about the representative space.

TOPOLOGICAL ANALYSIS OF SPACE CODING

A topological viewpoint on *PC* encoding activity opens broad perspectives for interpreting the *PC* activity patterns. If the *PC* activity is associated with the neighborhoods U_i of a topolodical space X, then thetemporal structure of the *PC* activity must be consistent with all possible spatial relationships between the neighborhoods of X. Since the topological structure of a space can be deduced from the properties of its coverings by local "neighborhoods" U_i (Novikov, 1996), this suggests that the topological properties of the representative space can be revealed by careful analysis of *PC* firing activity. Mathematically, the task of establishing a global arrangement of locally defined structures over a topological space X is a well defined problem that in its most general form is addressed in the so-called sheaf theory (Godement, 1964; Swan, 1964). The concept of a sheaf captures the idea of associating the local information with the spatial structure of a topological space as a whole 1, and provides a general framework for analyzing different types of information associated with the topological structure of the space. In the SRE context, the structures associated with neighborhoods are the firing patterns of cell populations, such as the firing rates of *PC*s, or of the head direction cells that specify the animal's angular orientation at different locations (Wiener & Taube, 2005; Sargolini, Fyhn, Hafting, McNaughton, Witter, Moser, & Moser, 2006), or of the cells in the parietal cortex that encode e.g. the animal's motion states, such as running straight or turning (Burgess, Jeffery, & O'Keefe, 1999; Nitz, 2006). From the perspective of the hippocampal topology reconstructing task, the SRE goal is to define the structure of the topological basis of the representative space based on the *PC* firing information, i.e. to integrate the local *PC* information into a global topological characteristic of the representative space as a whole. One of the fundamental applications of this theory is an algorithm for specifying the topology of the space based on the properties of the simplest topological construct associated with it – its covering by a set of regions (Novikov, 1996). In particular, one can consider coverings generated by the *PF*s. Let us assume that for a given set of k cells the *PF*s produce a complete covering of the environment, X:

$$\bigcup_i PF_i = X. \quad (1)$$

It is well known from algebraic topology (Novikov, 1996), that with a given set of the regions $U_1,\ldots, U_n$, covering the environment, one can associate the following multidimensional polytope (simplex) also called the "nerve" N of the covering 2: the vertexes $\sigma_i^{(0)}$ of the simplex correspond to the individual regions U_i, the edges $\sigma^{(1)}_{i_1 i_2}$ correspond to overlapping regions, $U_{i_1} \cap U_{i_2} \neq \varnothing$, the two dimensional simplexes (facets) $\sigma^{(2)}_{i_1 i_2 i_3}$ correspond to triple intersections $U_{i_1} \cap U_{i_2} \cap U_{i_3} \neq \varnothing$, etc. In general, *k*– simplexes $\sigma^{(k)}_{i_1 i_2 \ldots i_{k+1}}$ correspond to nonempty intersections $U_{i_1} \cap U_{i_2} \cap \ldots \cap U_{i_{k+1}} \neq \varnothing$ (Figure 3 (a)). The topological properties of the space can be revealed via the structure of the space of linear functions on the simplexes, the so-called cochains, $\alpha^k \left(\sigma^{(k)}_{i_1 i_2 \ldots i_{k+1}} \right)$, taking values in a properly selected set of coefficients *F*, e.g. 0 and 1 (Novikov, 1996; Zomorodian, 2005). In the mathematical theory of sheaves, the consistency of this and similar constructions is established by using the region restriction operation i_{UV} that restricts the sheaf structures associated with a region *U* to its subregion *V* and hence allows relating the simplexes of different dimensionality (Novikov, 1996; Swan, 1964). The resulting algebraic structure defines the set of topological invariants that uniquely characterize the topology of the simplex – the Čech cohomologies of the covering, $H^q \left(N \left\{ U_i \right\} \right)$. A basic result from the algebraic topology states that in case if *X* is a manifold and if the covering is such that all $U_{i_1} \cap \ldots \cap U_{i_{k+1}}$'s are contractible, e.g. small convex regions in the metric of *X*, then the nerve of the covering is homologically equivalent to *X*, $H^* \left(N \left\{ U_i \right\} \right) = H^* \left(X \right)$, so the topological (cohomological) characteristics of the covering are identical to the topological characteristics of the manifold itself. In the case of the SRE analysis, this whole construction can be implemented in terms of the temporal sequences of the *PC* spike trains. In such "temporal" context, the regions are defined in terms of the firing regimes of *PC* populations. Specifically, a region *U* is understood as a collection of the firing activity states of *n PC*s, $c_1, c_2, \ldots, c_n$, in which the firing probability $f^{(c)}$ of each cell lays within certain pre-specified bounds: $\theta_1 < f^{(c)} < \theta_2$. By main SRE assumption this collection of activity regimes corresponds (extends in terminology of (Sambin, 2003; Dabaghian, Cohn, & Frank, 2007)) to a region *U* in the representative space *R*, *U*=ext(*a*). It will be

Figure 3. (a) A cover simplex (nerve) generated by a covering of a plane environment by 7 PFs. (b) The corresponding "temporal" simplex formed by temporal overlap patterns between the firing regimes of the PCs.

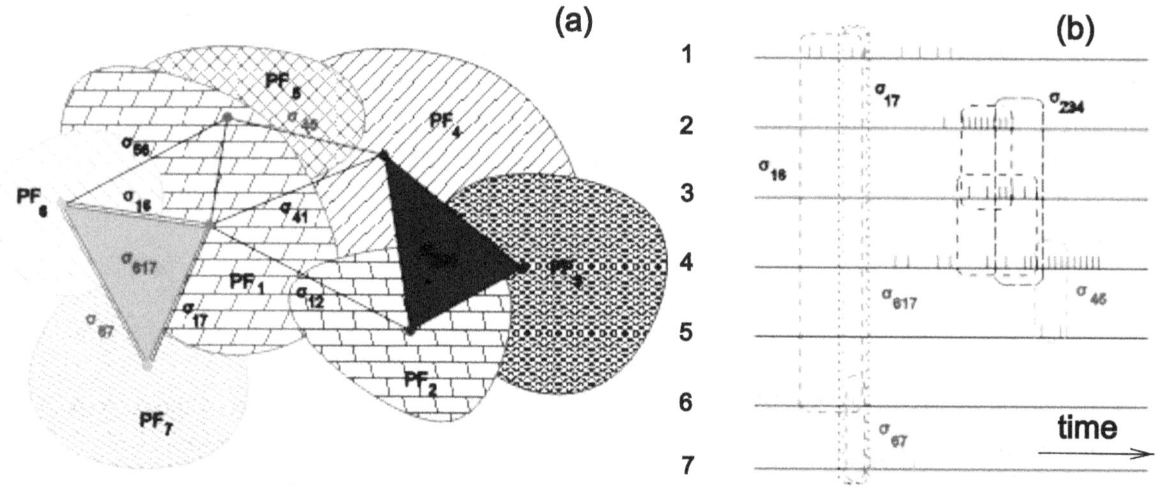

shown below that the basic topological relationships, such as the union, the inclusion and the intersection of the regions can be obtained immediately in terms of the properties of the firing rate intervals for the individual cells. As a result, this approach allows interpreting the temporal structure of the firing activity regimes as a spatial structure. In particular, it allows building the "temporal" covering of the representative space directly in terms of the firing activities of the *PC*s without referring to the externally observed geometrical features of the *PF* (including *PF* convexity, which can be understood as a topological property (van de Vel, 1993)) or the behavior of the rat.

The resulting structure can be put in the form of a "temporal simplex" shown on Figure 3 (b) that carries the same topological information as the conventional spatial covering simplex shown on Figure 3. The vertexes of such simplex are generated by the peaks of activity of *PC*s, the *1D* edges by the temporal overlap of *PC* activity, $PF_{c_1} \cap PF_{c_2} \neq \varnothing$, the *2D* facets by the coactive triples of *PC*s $PF_{c_1} \cap PF_{c_2} \cap PF_{c_3} \neq \varnothing$, etc. The restriction operator i_{UV} can also be understood in the "temporal" context. For example, for a region $V = PF_1 \cap PF_2$ contained in $U = PF_1$, the restriction operator i_{UV} from *U* to *V* corresponds to selecting the rat position states in which the firing rates of both cells simultaneously exceed selected thresholds. Clearly, for any three nested neighborhoods $W \subset V \subset U$, the restriction from *U* to *V* and then to *W* and the direct restriction from *U* to *W*, will yield the same result, i.e. $i_{VW} \circ i_{UV} = i_{UW}$. Since the restriction operation does not depend on the restriction sequence, the firing rate of the whole *PC* population can be extended in a unique way to form a continuous, global firing rate function (Novikov, 1996; Godement, 1964; Swan, 1964), which agrees with all the local firing rates f_i. This means that it is possible to produce a global description of the space in terms of the *PC* population firing rates, and in particular, it is possible to produce a global topological characterization of the representative space in terms of well defined topological invariants. This simple result can be used to identify the topology of the environment in the SRE context using different, a priori unrelated partitions of the space by the *PF*. It enables the SRE observer to establish mathematically several important (albeit biologically simple) properties of the neuronal spatial representation. For example, it allows concluding that the topology of the rat's representative space coincides with the topology of the environment defined via explicitly observed *PF* coverings, i.e. to argue that the topology observed by the experimenter is equivalent to the topology of the rat's own representative space. The fact that the same topological characterization of the environment can be achieved using the *PF* covering generated by deferent rats, shows that the representative spaces of deferent animals are mutually consistent on topological level so they can be mapped one onto another. This construction also indicates that the topology of the environment is represented through the restrictions on the possible *PC* coactivity patterns and that every order of overlap (pairwise, triple, etc.) carries information about the environmental topology. It also predicts, that for different environments, different orders of *PF* overlaps are essential for representing the topological information. Since the nontrivial topological characterization of the plane environments is given by their fundamental group $\pi_1(X)$ (that coincides with $H^{(1)}(X)$), the topological information on *2D* surfaces is essentially represented already in the pairwise coactivity relationships. For the *3D* case (as e.g. in (Knierim, McNaughton, & Poe, 2000)) space representing computations and animal's navigational strategies must include triple overlaps between the *PF*s, which reflects the computational complexity of *3D* spatial navigation. The possibility to specify the topology of the representative space using different *PF* partitions is also significant in view of the so-called remapping events, (Sharp, 2002; Fuhs, Van Rhoads, Casale, McNaughton, & Touretzky, 2005). Experimental evidence shows that if the objects placed in the environment or its geometry change significantly or abruptly, then the hippocampal network configuration loses its stability and transitions into a different state $S^{(j)} \neq S^{(i)}$, in which the observed *PF*s pattern is entirely different. For example, if large (compared to the size of the arena) barriers are added or removed, so that the navigational routes available to the rat change significantly, then the *PF* partition of the environment can change not only in the vicinity of the barrier, but also in the rest of the arena (Sharp, 2002; Fuhs, Van Rhoads, Casale, McNaughton, & Touretzky, 2005). A simple example of remapping is provided by the violation of the linear order of *PF*s on a *1D* track following the abrupt changes of the track configuration, in contrast with the orderly stretch observed in (Gothard, Skaggs, Moore, & McNaughton, 1996). Such abrupt scrambling of the *PF* order is qualitatively different from the organized response to the external changes, in which the quasi-topological order of the *PF*s is preserved. Nevertheless, since both pre- and post-remapping *PF* layouts cover the same environment (1), they define the simplex of the same cohomological type, which shows that the topology of the representative space is not violated in remappings. Certainly, the possibility to compute correct topological invariants depends crucially on the quality of the covering, i.e. on the availability of a sufficient number of the *PF*s. Usually the environments in which the behavior of a rat is studied have geometrically simple form, so it is assumed for simplicity that the environment is covered by a sufficient number of *PF*s. In case if the geometry of the environment is complex, the derivation of the correct cohomological characteristics becomes a more subtle problem (Zomorodian, 2005; de Silva, & Ghrist, 2006; González Díaz, & Real, 2003), that can be helped by the local analysis of the spatial relationships encoded by the *PF*s (Dabaghian, Cohn, & Frank, 2007). It will be shown below (see Section IX) that topological description in terms of the *PF*s can be sufficiently detailed to include the qualitative features of the environment, such as track junctions and other distinguishing features in the space are typically explicitly coded by the CA1 place cells. In the context of the topological space coding hypothesis, these features effectively play the role of spatial singularities and "marked points" that limit the topological plasticity of the representative space.

GENERAL TOPOLOGY OF THE REPRESENTATIVE SPACE

The above analysis shows that given a sufficient number of the *PF*s, it is possible to solve the hippocampal SRE task – to give a topological description of the space based only on the *PC* spike trains produced in a stable hippocampal configuration. However, the task of describing the representative space can be understood in a broader context. Since the ultimate question is to understand how does the representative space, as a separate mathematical object, emerge out of the coherent *PC* activity patterns, the task is not only in providing its descriptive topological classification of the space a whole, but also in building it constructively, as a single gestalt that embodies all possible topological relationships between all the regions that exist in it and that constructively defines the continuity of memory structures and sensory inputs. This implies studying not just a few regions that can together cover the space, and whose overlapping relationships lead to its global algebraic topological indexing, but in effect describing the complete set of all possible regions U_i that can be constructively specified using the neural activity patterns of the entire active *PC* population, and hence to explain in what sense this whole assembly of spatial relationships may equal to the topological basis of the representative space. To formalize this picture one can start by defining the regions in terms of the firing regimes of *PC*s. As mentioned above, the construction of the topological representative space in the hippocampal SRE is founded on the assumption that any continuous succession of the *PC* activity regimes, $a = \bigcup_t a(t)$ in a stable configuration of the network corresponds to a region *U* in the representative space *R*. For a single cell *c*, a region *U*(*c*) can be defined via a collection of this *PC*'s firing activity states in which its firing probability exceeds a certain threshold value θ_1, or lies below θ_2, or both, $\theta_1 < f^{(c)} < \theta_2$, or in general, it is defined by a system of threshold intervals, $U^{(C)} = ext(a)$, where $a^{(c)} = \left\{ f^{(c)} \mid f^{(c)} \in \cup_i I_i^{(c)}, I > \left[\theta_{i_1}, \theta_{i_2} \right] \right\}$.

The union, the inclusion and the intersection of the regions defined by a can be obtained immediately in terms of the properties of the firing rate intervals. For example, $U_{I_1}^{(c)} = \text{ext}\left(I_1\right)$ is a subregion of $V_{I_2}^{(c)} = \text{ext}\left(I_2\right), U_{I_1}^{(c)} \subseteq V_{I_2}^{(c)}$, if $I_1 \subset I_2$. So in terms of the firing threshold intervals, the SRE assumption is that for any cell *c*, a single connected and populated threshold interval corresponds to a connected region in the representative space. It is clear that since general systems of threshold intervals can be reduced to unions of connected components, $I_i^{(c)}$, every region $U^{(c)}$ can be considered as a formal union of basic regions defined as extensions of connected firing threshold intervals. For a multiple cell population, $C = \bigcup_{i=1}^{n} c_i$, a region is defined by a continuous succession of activity regimes of each of *n* cells. For example, a region $U^{(c)}$=ext(a) can be defined as a combination of states in which every cell fires simultaneously above the corresponding threshold, so that $a = a^{(c_1)} \wedge a^{(c_2)} \wedge \ldots \wedge a^{(c_n)}$, where $a^{(c_i)} = \left\{ f^{(c_i)} \mid f^{(c_i)} > \theta_i \right\}$ or as a set of states in which the firing rates of at least one cell exceeds the corresponding threshold from the set at all times, $a = a^{(c_1)} \vee a^{(c_2)} \vee \ldots \vee a^{(c_n)}$, etc. The union, the inclusion and the intersection of the regions can be defined immediately via the corresponding union, inclusion and intersection of the firing rate intervals Ii of the corresponding individual cells in the population.

Mathematically, the intuition that the set of all possible activity regimes of the *PC*s define the topology of the representative space implies that they define an approximation to the topology base of the representative space. In general topology (Bourbaki, 1961), a set of neighborhoods B_i forms a topology base, if every topological neighborhood can be formed as a union of elements B_i. It is also known that a topology base generates a unique topology for which they actually forms a base, which is the intersection of all topologies on *X* containing this base (Bourbaki, 1961). A necessary condition satisfied by the base regions B_i is that for any two overlapping elements B_1 and B_2, $U = B_1 \cap B_2$, there is another base element $B_3 \in U$ (Figure 4), so given a finite covering of *X* with the regions U_i, $X = \cup_i U_i$, it is possible to generate a topology base by completing the set $\{U_i\}$ with all the regions that are produced by all the finite intersections $U_i \cap U_j \cap \ldots \cap U_k$. By construction, such system of regions will be closed under the intersection operation so it can serve as a topology base (Figure 4). The simplest cover of the representative space available to the SRE observer is the *PF* cover of the environment. The intersection closure of *n* observed *PF*s that satisfy the definition of cover (1) generates an explicit approximation to the topology base $B^{(n)}$ of the representative space. Hence the topology $\mathfrak{O}^{(n)}$ produced by this base can be considered as a finitary approximation to the topology of the representative space, similarly to how the nerve of the same covering approximates its algebraic topological properties. The larger the number of the *PF*s available to the SRE observer, the better (the finer) is the place field topology $\mathfrak{O}^{(n)}$. A set of finer approximations to the topology of the representative space that is also directly accessible biologi-

Figure 4. Diagram for the topology neighborhoods generated by the covering shown on Figure 3. The base regions generated by the PFs and their intersections are shown with solid lines, dotted lines represent some of the regions generated by unions of the base elements

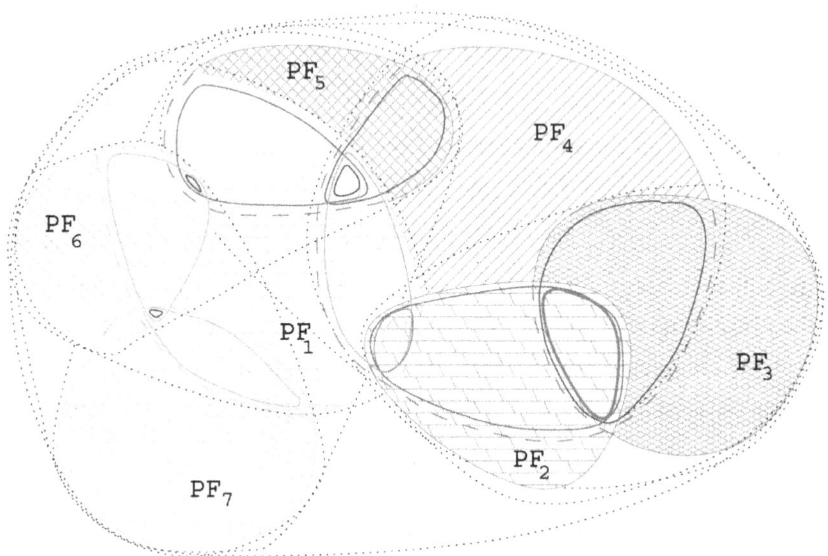

cally is generated by the set of regions defined by all possible levels of activity of *PC*s. Indeed, for a given cell *c*, consider a set of the regions $B_i^{(c)} = \mathrm{ext}\left(I_i^{(c)}\right)$ for a nested system of threshold intervals $I_1^{(c)} \supset I_2^{(c)} \supset I_3^{(c)} \supset \ldots$. For example, one can consider the intervals $I_1^{(c)} \supset I_2^{(c)} \supset I_3^{(c)} \supset \ldots$, i.e. by the regions marked by progressively higher levels of firing rates, so that each successive region $B_i^{(c)}$ lies closer to the center of the corresponding *PF*. From the point of view of the SRE observer, the intersection closure of this set is the base of the minimal topology $\mathfrak{O}^{(\max)}$ in which the firing rates of cell populations are continuous (see below). Importantly, the neighborhoods of the pointfree topology $\mathfrak{O}^{(3)}$ constructed here can be "filled" with points and hence be considered as the topology on a concrete, i.e. point based, topological space. The required points ("elementary locations") are formed by the atomic (i.e. invariant under the intersections) elements of the base (Sambin, 2003; Dabaghian, Cohn, & Frank, 2007). The resulting topological space *X* was proposed as the mathematical object that serves as a constructive topological model of the representative space *R* (Sambin, 2003; Dabaghian, Cohn, & Frank, 2007).

REPRESENTATIVE SPACE AND SPATIAL INFORMATION

The experimental arguments in support of the idea that the hippocampus provides a quasitopological frame for the representative space come from studying the collective *PF* activity, which shows that the behavior of the ensemble of the *PF*s can be better understood at the level of the properties of the representative space as a whole, rather than an assembly of individual "location tags". The properties of the *PF*s indicate that an external observer can describe the *PC* activity topologically and build a qualitative quasi-topological space that reflects the internal structure of the animal's environment. However, the statement that the hippocampal activity provides the "topology" for rat's activity implies more than a mere availability or completeness of the information about animal's possible locations. Having a set of space tags is not necessarily equivalent having an internal "space", in the same way as having a database of postal addresses does not amount to having a spatial map that permits spatial navigation and orientation (Mackintosh, 2002; Redish, 2001). An alternative to possessing an emergent internal representative space produced by the neural computations might be e.g. a database of ordered links that are not necessarily geometrized or geometrizable (analyzing the database of links between French internet websites will not lead to reconstructing the geographic map of France). The emergence of a space whose topology is represented by the succession of the neuronal activity regimes would imply, firstly, that the system is capable of producing a neural representation of places or regions and to compute topological relationships between them, such as intersection, inclusion, etc. Secondly, it would imply that the transitions between the population activity regimes of *PC*s and of other cells that encode spatial information are continuous in the topology defined by the order of the *PF*s, so that the patterns of cell activity are internally topologically consistent. The important conceptual difference between a mere collection of *PF*s and a holistic space that emerges from it is traditionally addressed in mereotopology (Cohn & Varzi, 2003). In the context of mereology and mereotopology, the emergence of a space *R* can be understood as a statement that although the *PF*s originally served as the primary building blocks for constructing *R*, it is ultimately the space *R* that should be considered as the primary object, in the context of which its parts, in particular the original collection of the *PF*s, are secondary. Although the emergent *R* certainly incorporates all the original *PF*s as its regions, it does not reduce to them uniquely. Further computations, that may involve associating additional spatial (e.g. metrical) and non-spatial information with so-constructed topological space (see below), as well as planning and spatial reasoning in *R* (see Section IX), can equally use the simplest base elements (i.e. the *PF*s encoded by separate *PC* activity regimes) as well as any other regions, encoded by more complex *PC* population activities. It is also assumed that spatial computations involving all these regions should be continuous in the *PC* defined topology. The transformation required for such a reorganization of spatial information processing can be achieved by a simple neural network computation that "fuses" the *PF* regions and provides equal neuronal activity representation for all (or, behaviorally, a sufficient number of) regions that exist in the emerging space *R*. A simple example of a network that uses just the first 3 *PF*s from the covering illustrated in Figure 3 and Figure 4 and encodes the full set of regions of the corresponding topology $\mathcal{O}^{(3)}$ shown in Figure 5. In this simple case, in addition to the regions $U_i=PF_i$, $i=1,2,3$, encoded by the cells c_i, there are 2 additional base regions $U_{1\wedge 2}=U_1\cap U_2$ and $U_{2\wedge 3}=U_2\cap U_3$ and the 3 regions obtained as unions of the base elements, $U_{1\vee 2}=U_1\cup U_2$, $U_{2\vee 3}=U_2\cup U_3$ and $U_{1\vee 2\vee 3}=U_1\cup U_2\cup U_3$. The base regions $U_{1\wedge 2}$ and $U_{2\wedge 3}$ are encoded by the activity of the cells b_1 and b_2 that receive excitatory connections from the PCs c_i and inhibitory connections from auxiliary cells g_1, g_2 and g_3. These inhibitory cells are in turn inhibited by c_i and we assume that any activity of c_i is sufficient to suppress the corresponding g_i while any activity of each cell g_i suppresses the activity of b_j, so the latter fires only if both of its inhibitors are quiet. This happens only if the animal is in the region $U_1\cap U_2$, so the activity of b_1 corresponds to the region $U_{1\vee 2}$. The regions $U_{1\vee 2}$, $U_{2\vee 3}$, $U_{3\vee 1}$ and $U_{1\vee 2\vee 3}$ are encoded correspondingly by the activity of cells a_1, a_2, a_3 and d_1 that receive pure excitatory connections directly from the PCs. Assuming that any activity of any of the cells c_i is sufficient to fire the cells a_i, d_1, then their activity will encode regions $U_{1\vee 2}$, $U_{2\vee 3}$, $U_{3\vee 1}$ and $U_{1\vee 2\vee 3}$. Hence, all the regions contained in the topology $\mathcal{O}^{(3)}$ PF are now represented similarly by the activity of the neurons in the bottom, "read off", layer of the network. By construction, the possible sequences of neuronal activities in this layer exhaust the topological relationships between the regions of $\mathcal{O}^{(3)}$, so in this sense the network of Figure 5 realizes the topology $\mathcal{O}^{(3)}$ constructively. The extent to which the hippocampal map can serve as the topological basis of the space representing neuronal activity throughout the brain, is determined by the range of the characteristics of neural activities that are continuous in this topology. Therefore, the task is to provide a context in which the local characteristics of neuronal activity can be considered as localizations of a certain global pattern, in such a way that the transitions between local activity regimes can be internally characterized as "continuous". Mathematically, this implies that certain local functions h of neuronal activity (for specificity, we will assume that neuronal activity is defined by the firing rates f_i, so $h_i = h_i(f)$, can be obtained as restrictions of some global function ν, that is defined over the whole representative space R, to a particular region $U_i \in R$, so that $h(f_i) = \nu(U_i)$.

The consistency of this construction for ν is ensured by the following requirements that must be satisfied by any two regions U, $V \in R$

1. $\nu(U \cup V) + \nu(U \cap V) = \nu(U) + \nu(V)$
2. $\nu(U) \leq \nu(V)$ for $U \subset V$ and
3. $\nu(\cup_{i \in I} U_i) = \sup_{i \in I} \nu(U_i)$ for every "nested" family of open sets U_i indexed by $i \in I$ (van de Vel, 1993).

Figure 5. (a) A network N that computes the topology structure generated by just the first three PFs that were shown in Figure 3, and the topology shown in Figure 4. The inhibitory connections are shown by dashed and excitatory by solid lines. The result of the computation are for convenience of illustration represented by the activity of the separate layer of cells r_i, $i = 1, \ldots, 8$, which can also be understood as the "input" cells of another network that interacts with N. (b) A diagram of the open set topology computed by N. The "atomic" regions $x_1 = U_1 \setminus U_{1\wedge 2}$, $x_2 = U_{1\wedge 2}$, $x_3 = U_2 \setminus (U_{1\wedge 2} \cup U_{2\wedge 3})$, $x_4 = U_{2\wedge 3}$ and $x_5 = U_3 \setminus U_2$ can be understood as the "points" of the concrete topological space that in this case models the representative space R.

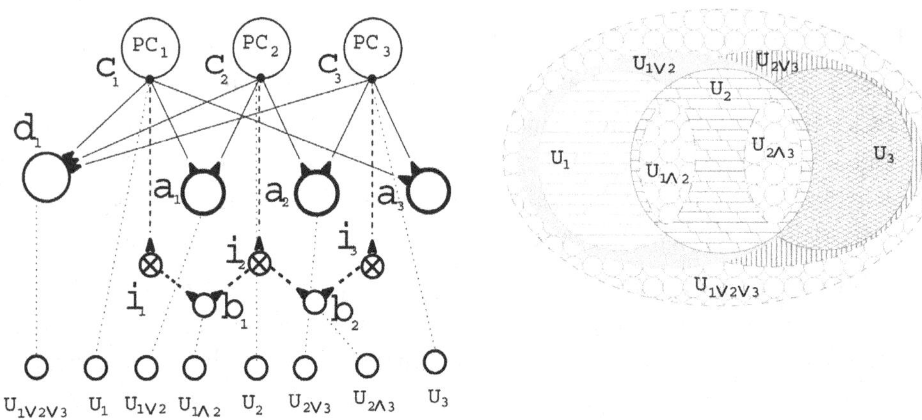

It can be shown that so defined global function ν is consistent with topology of R (hence it is continuous). Such functions are known in mathematics as continuous valuations (van de Vel, 1993; Klain & Rota, 1997). Since valuations are defined globally over the representative space *R*, they provide the required context in which the separate regions marked by individual cells' activities are bound together into single spatial gestalt. Hence the idea of "internal continuity" of neuronal activity can now be formally expressed as the requirement that the characteristics of neuronal activity should form continuous valuations over the topology defined by the hippocampal *PC*s. As an illustration, it is easy to construct a continuous valuation over the space shown on Figure 5 (b) in terms of the firing rates of read off layer cells' in the network of Figure 5 (a).

The simplest continuous valuation is given by the step function $h_i(f) = \Theta(f) = \nu(U_i)$ that simply marks continuous succession of the animal's presence in the corresponding regions. Alternative continuous valuations may be provided by the outputs of the networks coupled with *N*. In general, for any given *PF* topology there exists its own set of continuous characteristics of neural activity and vice versa – a particular function of neural activity can be considered as continuous only in special topologies, which can be computationally implemented in the networks of special architecture. These restrictions provide a possibility of experimental and numerical model testing of the topological coding hypothesis, for example, by verifying whether the characteristics of neuronal activity in other space coding regions of the brain (e.g. the head direction cells, the parietal cortex cells) that are coupled with the hippocampus, form continuous valuations in the *PC* topology. The specific algorithmic, computational and especially the experimental verifications of the topological coding hypothesis, of further navigational and spatial reasoning strategies based on the topological interpretation of the hippocampal spatial maps represents a separate matter of research. However, the arguments and constructions laid out in the preceding sections suggest a number of predictions that can be addressed experimentally:

1. The hippocampal SRE observer should be able to extract the topological information, e.g. to distinguish topologically different environments based on the temporal structure of the *PC* code (see below for the discussion of possible analyses algorithms). Given the variability and a certain degree of stochasticity of neuronal activity, this prediction emphasizes availability and robustness of topological information in the hippocampus. On the other hand, identifying an environment's shape based on the *PC* spike recordings alone should require additional assumptions about the geometry of the *PF*s.
2. The robustness of the topological information contained in the *PF* is guaranteed within a particular set of the parameters characterizing the *PC* population activity, such as the firing rates, *PF* sizes, etc (Dabaghian, Memoli, Frank, & Carlsson, 2010). The parameters observed experimentally in stable states of hippocampal activity in well learned environments should not violate these limitations.
3. Changing the geometrical proportions of the environment (slowly compared to the time scales of animal's navigational behavior) should leave the relative order of the *PC* firing unchanged: if the environment changes its spatial configuration (e.g. stretches or bends) sufficiently slowly, then the *PF*s will follow this change in the sense of (Gothard, Skaggs, Moore, & McNaughton, 1996; Gothard, Hoffman, Battaglia, & McNaughton, 2001), so the order of the firing sequences should remain invariant. It is clear that the spatial and temporal scale of the transformations is restricted due to the finite span of the receptive fields and the characteristic time constants of the *PC*s' plasticity

mechanisms. To emphasize that the topological regime is stable only within a certain finite range of parameters, the hippocampal mapping will sometimes be referred below as quasi-topological.

4. Since the cells involved in encoding a particular spatial frame are associated between themselves rather than with the places in the environment, they should not fire out of mutual order without compromising the stability of the map. For example, if two sections of the environment are swapped or moved apart, then the *PF*s that were associated with the moving parts should not follow them separately, leaving the rest of the *PF*s stable in their original positions. Instead, the map should either deform as a whole, or the entire set of *PF*s should "remap" and re-stabilize in a new global configuration.
5. There is a group of experiments where animals are exposed to two different environments (usually a square and a cylinder) and place cells are recorded as the two environments are morphed into one another (Leutgeb, Leutgeb, Treves, Meyer, Barnes, McNaughton, et al, 2005; Leutgeb, Leutgeb, Treves, Moser, & Moser, 2004; O'Keefe & Burgess, 1996). The outcomes of these experiments appear to depend critically on the specific animal training protocol, but it is clear that given sufficient experience, the place cells come to distinguish between topologically identical but geometrically distinct arenas. We suggest that this may be due to the conflict between the more geometrical representations carried in areas such as parietal cortex (Nitz, 2006; Qin, McNaughton, Skaggs & Barnes, 1997), and entorhinal grid cells (Sargolini, Fyhn, Hafting, McNaughton, Witter, Moser, & Moser, 2006) and the topological representation in the hippocampus. Thus, while the hippocampus would tend to preserve a topologically consistent representation when possible, inputs that are inconsistent with that representation will, over the course of days of experience, push the hippocampus toward remapping where the relative ordering of *PF*s change.
6. The previously mentioned coherent behavior of the *PF*s strongly suggests that *PC* activity should always be considered in the context of the global state of the network. This suggests that as long as the system remains in the same state, one should observe the same sequences of *PC* activations, whether they are driven by an external sensory input or by the internal network dynamics. In other words, network should "replay" the correct (direct or reversed) *PC* activation sequences both during the navigational activity (even if the environment is continuously deformed) or outside of it, in wake (Foster, & Wilson, 2006) and in asleep (Wilson & McNaughton, 1994; Skaggs & McNaughton, 1996; Louie & Wilson, 2006) animals. Sequentially correct patterns of activity should be "pinged" during short time spontaneous activity of the network known as "ripples" and sharp waves.
7. The characteristics of neuronal activity in the hippocampus and in the other space representing brain areas should form continuous valuations in the *PC* defined topology. Having now elucidated the mathematical aspects "topological coding hypothesis" and suggested how it might be tested empirically, we will discuss mathematical theories of spatial reasoning that enable the practical use of the outlined spatial coding mechanisms and its implementation in biological networks.

QUALITATIVE SPACE REPRESENTATION: RCC

The drawback of the mathematical formalisms used above for describing the topological properties of the space provide an insight into the overall topological structure of the representative space however they do not necessarily provide a framework for a biologically plausible analysis of the current, local

PC firing activity patterns that can serve as the actual basis of the local spatial planning, navigation and in general for spatial reasoning. For example, many of the environments used in experimental studies, such as the **U** track or the **W** track are topologically trivial contractible manifolds that are characterized by the same (trivial) algebraic invariants. However, from the biological point of view these two environments possess important qualitative features that require entirely different spatial reasoning for navigation. This suggests that more refined methods for topological description of the representative space are required. Fortunately, there exists a variety of qualitative space representation (QSR) methods (Cohn, & Hazarika, 2001), which provide practically useful, biologically plausible and conceptually complete approximate representations of space that include local topological information analysis. The reasoning techniques within different QSRs provide case specific formal languages and logical systems that include the notion of spatial proximity and other necessary spatial relationships. These languages can provide a complete description of arbitrarily complex spatial reasoning schemes used for navigating, spatial planning and establishing spatial (in)consistencies, which have been studied in a number of mathematical (Randell, Cui, Cohn, 1992; Cohn, Bennett, Goodday & Gotts, 1997; Cohn, & Hazarika, 2001) as well as applied contexts, such as organizing geographical databases, robotics, artificial intelligence, object recognition, etc. (e.g. (Egenhofer, Al-Taha, 1992; Escrig & Toledo, 1998; Fernyhough, Cohn & Hogg, 2000)) and including some bio-applications (Cohn, 2001; Donnelly, Bittner, & Rosse, 2006; Dabaghian, Cohn, & Frank, 2007). A simple example of qualitative spatial reasoning is provided by the above analysis of a linear sequence of PFs on a linear track that allows the SRE observer to conclude that the space the rat has explored is linear and how many ends it has. If the cell population activity patterns are always consistent with a simple linear (direct or reversed) sequence $a_1, a_2, \ldots, a_n$, then the SRE observer can conclude that the track is linear. The violations of the linear order via $a_1 \to a_n$ or $a_n \to a_1$ transitions would signify that the track is circular, while presence of "forking" sequences signals branching arms of the track, etc. In its most general form, 1D reasoning is addressed by the so-called Allen Interval Calculus relations reasoning calculus (Allen, 1983).

A practically convenient QSR method for describing topological spaces is provided by a pointfree method called the Region Connection Calculus (RCC) (Randell, Cui, Cohn, 1992; Cohn, Bennett, Goodday & Gotts, 1997; Cohn, & Hazarika, 2001; Gotts, Goodday, & Cohn, 1996) that can be used for studying the quasitopological space that emerges due the hippocampal PC activity. In its general form, the RCC method unifies several QSR schemes that are based on a single primitive, binary, reflexive and symmetric connectivity relation $C(x, y)$ (region x connects with region y), that relate every two regions of space. In the context of the SRE analysis, $C(x, y)$ can be evaluated directly as the coactivity of the cell populations above the corresponding threshold levels (similarly to Figure 3 (b)); hence the RCC analysis can be used directly in the space reconstruction setup. Within each particular RCC formalism the spatial order is defined via a family of binary topological relations imposed on the regions that guarantee the consistency of the space constructed from them. One of the most widely used formulation of RCC (Randell, Cui, Cohn, 1992; Cohn, Bennett, Goodday & Gotts, 1997; Cohn, & Hazarika, 2001; Gotts, Goodday, & Cohn, 1996; Gotts, Goodday, & Cohn, 1996) defines 5 jointly exhaustive and pairwise disjoint (JEPD) binary topological relations between pairs of regions with soft boundaries known as RCC5.

In the SRE "temporal" analysis context, at any moment of time t and for any chosen firing frequency thresholds θ_i there exists only a finite number of spikes that define a region, so the regions and their boundaries are "soft". Hence every pair of PFs can be related to one another via the set of RCC5 relations shown on Figure 6: two PFs can be either discrete from one another (DR), or partially overlap

(PO), or one can be a proper part (PP) or an inverse proper part (PPi) of another or they can be equal (EQ).

The RCC5 based analysis of PF connectivity allows to capture the connectivity structure of the environment (Dabaghian, Cohn, & Frank, 2007), e.g. distinguish topologically between the W track and the U track by representing explicitly qualitative features of each case. For example, a qualitative feature that allows distinguishing the topological structure of the W track from to a U-shaped track in the SRE framework is the existence of 3 mutually disconnected PFs, labeled 1, 2 and 3 on Figure 7b, all of which can be reached by connected paths originating from PF 4. For the 5 connected basic regions of the W track shown on Figure 7 a) that cannot be divided into two discrete (DR) parts, the pairs (a, b) or (b, d) are contractible but (a, c) or (b, e) are not. Hence, the SRE observer can use these relations to identify the "topological" W track (i.e. the W (Figure 7 (a) or topologically identical spatial configuration).

As the statistical information about the PC firing accumulates with time, the regions associated with PFs become sharper and the RCC5 relations between regions may change. However, it can be shown (Randell, Cui, Cohn, 1992; Cohn, Bennett, Goodday & Gotts, 1997; Cohn, & Hazarika, 2001) that the RCC relationships between regions change in well defined sequence schemes called conceptual neighborhoods (Figure 8), which specify the logical order in which RCC relationships between the regions may develop.

Hence the RCC conceptual neighborhood analysis has the potential not only to follow the accumulation of data in static environments, but also to follow the changes in the PF configurations in dynamic environments and in the regime of smooth continuous transitions. As a result the SRE ob- server can use RCC to reason and to resolve the space reconstruction task not only in static (Dabaghian, Cohn, & Frank, 2007), but also in flexible tracks and arenas. The resulting logical language can be applied to in depth, intrinsic analysis of the *PC* information. Currently, there exists a number of phenomenological models that aim to explain the observed properties of the *PF* regions based on common qualitative relations between *PF*s and the geometrical features of the environment (the "geometric determinants") (Hartley, Burgess, Cacucci, & O'Keefe, 2000; Touretzky, Weisman, Fuhs, Skaggs, Fento & Muller, 2004).

However, the RCC topological calculus the analysis can be taken further: given a certain initial amount of information, such as e.g., the association of several PFs with some "geometric determinants",

Figure 6. Jointly Exhaustive Pairwise Disjoint relationships of RCC5. Dashed and dotted lines represent region boundaries in the RCC5 approach

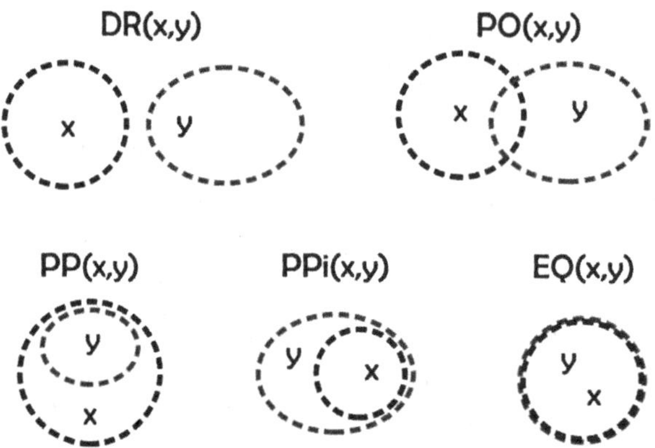

Figure 7. a) W track, with 5 basic connected component parts with crisp boundaries and 6 marked points (geometric determinants). b) A partition of a W track with 100 simulated PFs marked by different colors - regions with soft boundaries.

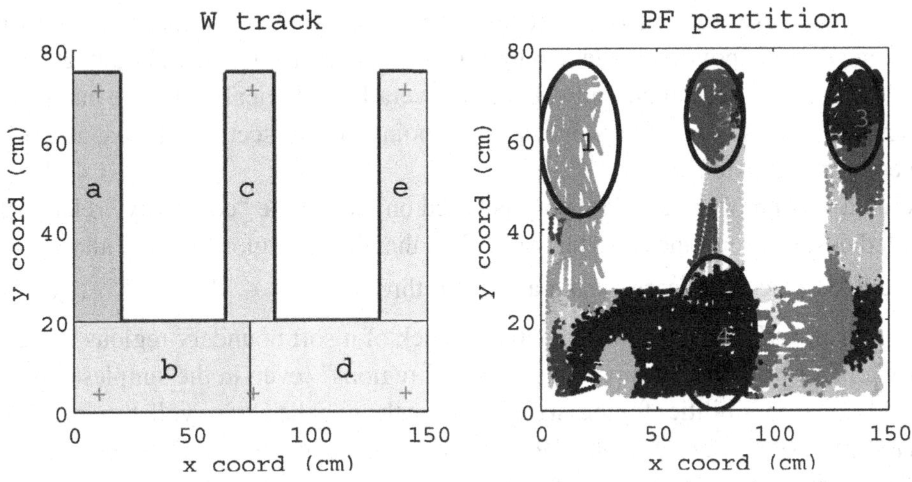

Figure 8. The immediate conceptual neighborhood structure of RCC5 – the possible sequences of gradual transformation of the binary JEPD relationships.

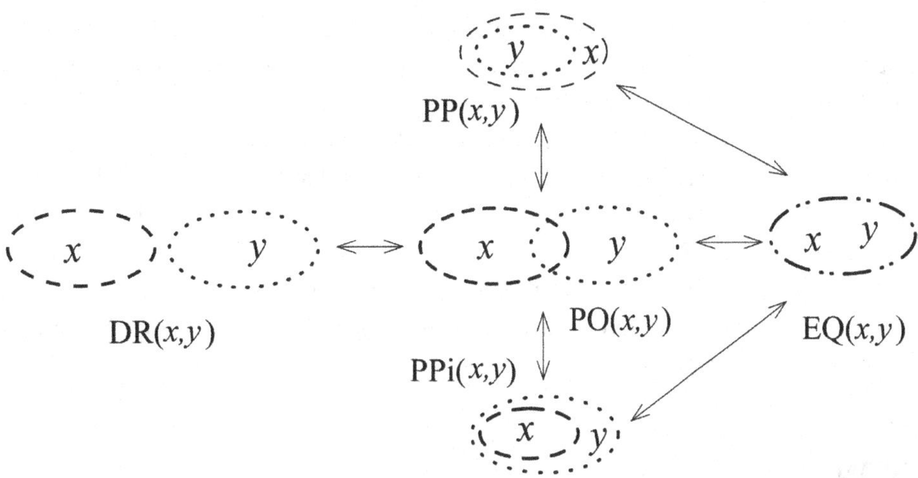

the SRE observer can reason logically, based on the spike information alone, about the sequence of PC activations in order to understand an animal's navigational strategies at the topological level, based on logical (arithmetical, mechanical) symbol manipulation, defined by the RCC logical calculus. Interestingly, these RCC relation- ships are also manifested at a cognitive level (Knauff, Ruah & Renz, 1997; Renz, Ruah, & Knauff, 2000). For example, RCC analysis could be used to decide whether the relationships encoded in the firing patterns actually permit the "spatial order" interpretation in the first place, i.e. it allows to check the hypothesis that the firing patterns of a certain collection of neurons can actually encode spatial relationships, in which co-firing of two cells represents the overlapping of the corresponding regions. This task can be conclusively tested using the RCC analysis in finite time that grows polynomially with the given number of "co-firing" relationships. Such an approach provides an interesting example of a mathematical (logical) identification of the computational nature of the receptive fields. Using the RCC5 formalism for the SRE topological analysis similarly to the RCC8 analysis of the W track mentioned above and other environments (Dabaghian, Cohn, & Frank, 2007), it becomes possible to identify and to reason not only about the overall topological structure, but also about more detailed structures such as the numbers of branching points, linear sections, loops, as well as possible paths in the environment, etc.

The described version of the RCC5 theory is based on the simple "coactivity" relationship $C(x, y)$. A more detailed description of the activities of the PFs that define regions x and y allows further development of the RCC5 theory. Clearly, using a set of n thresholds $f_{i,\alpha} \in \left[\theta_i^{(\min)}, \theta_i^{(\max)}\right]$, $\alpha = 1,..., n$, that mark different levels of PC activity will generate a stack of n soft boundary regions that are related to one another via PP or PPi relationships. This "stack of regions" (even in the simplest case n = 2) actually creates additional possibilities for the analysis within the so called "egg-yolk theory" (Cohn & Gotts, 1996; Cohn & Gotts, 1996; Cohn & Gotts, 1994; Lehman, & Cohn, 1994) and its generalizations, which describes vague regions using a formal "nested" structure – a representative "yolk" representing space that is definitely part of the region (for the yolk the threshold can be set sufficiently high) and the "white" between the yolk and the rest of the environment, representing space that may or may not be part of the PF. The threshold for the white (not-PFs) boundary can be set rather low to admit space that is not a part of the PF. Different egg-yolk versions of RCC5 with varying numbers of JEPD relationships (Cohn & Gotts, 1996) can be used for a specific logical analysis of a given PC data set. It should finally be mentioned that in general the RCC is more robust than other (e.g. the algebraic topology) methods used for topological analysis. For example, it can be applied to determine the structure of the environment in cases when the regions are multiply connected, however this case involves a more complicated analysis. From the point of view of the SRE analysis, it is also important that (see e.g. (Randell, Cui, Cohn, 1992; Cohn, Bennett, Goodday & Gotts, 1997; Cohn, & Hazarika, 2001; Gotts, Goodday, & Cohn, 1996) and the references therein) that the RCC relationships form predicates of a first-order logical system, which turns the spatial reasoning based on the PF information into a logical calculus, a formal mathematical theory, in which reasoning can be done based on formal logical symbol manipulation and be implemented in neural network computations.

CONCLUSION

The general question about the structure of the space representing neural computations across the brain is a fundamental problem that goes far beyond the hippocampus (Redish, & Touretzky, 1997). It is well established experimentally that different brain parts contain different types of spatially correlated neuronal populations. For example, the information about an animal's orientation, direction and duration of its travel is represented in the egocentric spatial frames in the parietal cortex (Andersen, Synder, Bradley, & Xing, 1997; Burgess, Jeffery, & O'Keefe, 1999). The head direction cells found in postsubiculum, retrosplenial cortex and the thalamus signal the instantaneous head direction of the animal regardless of the location of the animal in the environment (Wiener & Taube, 2005). Metric information is likely provided by proprioceptive (feedback from muscles and joints) and idiothetic (self motion) cues (Terrazas, Krause, Lipa, Gothard, Barnes, & McNaughton, 2005), based on visual, vestibular (McNaughton, Battaglia, Jensen, Moser, & Moser, 2006) sensory inputs. As for the hippocampus, which is functionally the highest associative level network in the brain (Banquet, Gaussier, Quoy, Revel, & Burnod, 2005; Lavenex, & Amaral, 2000), the arguments presented in this paper suggest that it supplies the most abstract representation of space – the allocentric topological map, that serves as a "locus" (Burgess & O'Keefe, 1996) of an animal's spatial awareness. The existence of a topological reference map stored in the brain may help the animal to track the small changes of the sensory input by putting them into an internal reference context, so that the animal does not have to evaluate anew every sensory configuration without recognizing patterns of continuous change. Biologically this is advantageous because an animal's survival may depend on its ability to extract salient changes in the environment from the relatively static surroundings as reliably as possible. On the other hand, from a mathematical point of view, a memory map that mediates spatial behavior can be considered as a separate mathematical space which we interpret as the topological basis of the representative space. Due to the specifics of its origins, such space possesses a number of exotic properties. For example, it is most adequately described not in terms of infinitesimal points, which is one of the most fundamental concepts of the standard geometry, topology and mathematical physics, but in terms of finite regions and therefore it is naturally understood in the framework of the constructive pointfree topology, such as Formal Topology (Dabaghian, Cohn, & Frank, 2007) and the pointfree topological reasoning methods such as RCC. In the familiar approach (Alexandroff, 1961; Bourbaki, 1961), a space is understood as a certain proximity, scale and affine structure defined on a set of "elementary locations" – the points of the space. In such an approach, the topological spatial structure emerges as a matter of associating subsets of points into a consistent system O of "neighborhoods". The consistency conditions (Kuratowski - Hausdorff axioms (Alexandroff, 1961; Bourbaki, 1961)) require that arbitrary unions and finite intersections of the subsets from O never produce subsets that lie outside of O. This guarantees that the chosen subsets can actually be considered as "proximity neighborhoods" in the conventional geometrical sense and that they generate a topological space structure on the original set of points. Interestingly, the proximity structure does not have to be applied to a set of infinitesimal elementary locations. Instead, the neighborhoods themselves can be understood the primary objects, so the proximity relationships are imposed on regions, rather than points. In such approaches (unified under the name "pointfree topology" (Johnstone, 1983; Johnstone, 1991; Whitehead, 1929), or alternatively by the term "mereotopology" (Cohn & Varzi, 2003)) points are secondary abstractions, produced by intersections of a sufficient number of regions. The analysis of the topological connections between the regions in point-free spaces reveals a particular structure of logical and algebraic relationships between them that define the spatial organization. So in the pointfree approach, the topological space emerges from a logical/algebraic structure imposed on the regions (Johnstone, 1983; Johnstone, 1991; Weil, 1938; Whitehead, 1929; Sambin, 2003; Vickers, 1989), which fits very well the needs of describing the neuronal spatial maps. A second important property of the representative space is that it is finitary, since it is generated in finite time, through finite network computations based on the activity of a finite number of the *PC*s. As a result, the representative space appears as a qualitative, finite approximation to the idealized Euclidean space. This suggests that the subsequent spatial information processing is founded in qualitative region-based spatiotemporal reasoning schemes that provide coarse, qualitative versions of the standard set-theoretic or abstract pointfree space computations. Such qualitative spatial representation techniques have a number of potential biological advantages. For example, it may often be impossible for the animal to know when and how its navigational task may change; hence its behavioral decisions must be made based on spatial encodings which do not precisely determine spatial location mechanisms (Cohn & Gotts, 1996; Hazarika, & Cohn, 2001). It is nevertheless clear that having a perfectly correct but vague solution to a fuzzily posed task is biologically more effective than spending time on producing computationally costly and certainly inaccurate precise answer.

Clearly, the principles of the spatial information representation and processing reflect the general structure of memory organization. Hence it is significant, in view of the topological coding hypothesis, that the hippocampus is known to be largely responsible for sequence coding on a variety of different time scales, which includes the cognitive and the behavioral level. At the cognitive level, structural coherence of the hippocampal memories is manifested in such phenomena as episodic memory, i.e. the ability to put a specific memory into the context of preceding and succeeding events (see Figure 9), as well as the ability to produce complete memory sequences from a single structured input (Eichenbaum, 2004). This is also manifested in a spatial context, where it has been shown (Kesner, Gilbert & Barua, 2002.; Agster, Fortin, & Eichenbaum, 2002; Dusek & Eichenbaum, 1997; Eichenbaum, 2004; Fortin, Agster, & Eichenbaum, 2002; Jensen & Lisman, 2005; Melamed, Gerstner, Maass, Tsodyks, & Markam, 2004; Wallenstein, Eichenbaum, Hasselmo, 1998) that the behavioral performance of humans and animals with hippocampal lesions in goal-directed navigation sequence tasks is significantly reduced compared to the control organisms. This reaffirms that the hippocampus is involved in organizing the memory elements (e.g. the memories of spatial locations) into a globally structured context. Taken together, these arguments suggest a certain unifying view on the hippocampal functioning, namely that the hippocampus produces a sequentially consistent memory representation map of the environmental features, navigational cues and behaviorally relevant memories – in short for the topological arrangement of memory elements. In a spatial con- text, this type of spatial representation implies topological mapping of the environment and allows building a constructive model of the representative space.By construction, this space is consistent with the animal's behavior, which makes it possible to speculate that it may provide a topological basis for animal's spatial perception and spatial cognition.

Figure 9. A schematic representation of the episodic memory elements according to (Eichenbaum, 2004). Each episode or its part may be retrieved as a part of several memory sequences.

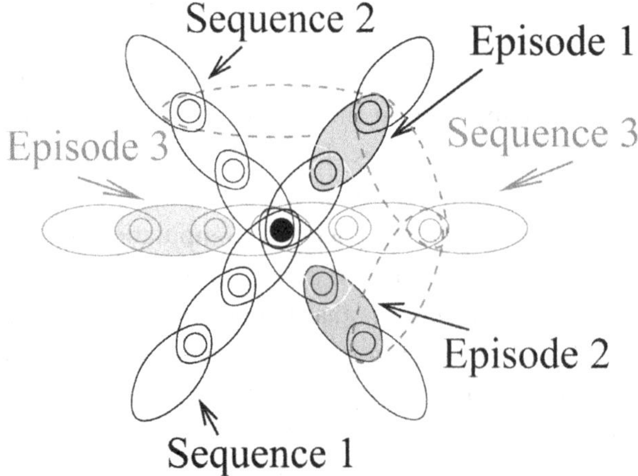

ACKNOWLEDGMENT

We are grateful to S. Cheng and A. Babichev for numerous discussions and valuable comments. The work was supported in part by the Sloan and Swartz foundation, by the NIH grant number F32 NS054425-01 and the UK EPSRC.

REFERENCES

Agster, K., Fortin, N., & Eichenbaum, H. (2002). The hippocampus and disambiguation of overlapping sequences. *The Journal of Neuroscience, 22*, 5760–5768.

Alexandroff, P. (1961). *Elementary concepts of topology*. New York, NY: Dover Publications.

Allen, J. F. (1983). Maintaining knowledge about temporal intervals. *Communications of the ACM, 26*(11), 832–843. doi:10.1145/182.358434

Andersen, R., Snyder, L., Bradley, D., & Xing, J. (1997). Multimodal representation of space in the posterior parietal cortex and its use in planning movements. *Annual Review of Neuroscience, 20*, 303–330. doi:10.1146/annurev.neuro.20.1.303

Banquet, J.-P., Gaussier, P., Quoy, M., Revel, A., & Burnod, Y. (2005). Hierarchy of associations in hippocampo-cortical systems: Cognitive maps and navigation strategies. *Neural Computation, 17*(6), 1339–1384. doi:10.1162/0899766053630369

Bourbaki, N. (1961). *Topologie générale*. Paris, France: Hermann.

Brown, E. N., Barbieri, R., Ventura, V., Kass, R. E., & Frank, L. M. (2001). The time-rescaling theorem and its application to neural spike train data analysis. *Neural Computation, 14*, 325–346. doi:10.1162/08997660252741149

Burgess, N., Jeffery, K., & O'Keefe, J. (Eds.). (1999). *The hippocampal and parietal foundations of spatial cognition*. Oxford University Press.

Burgess, N., & O'Keefe, J. (1996). Cognitive graphs, resistive Grids, and the hippocampal representation of space. *The Journal of General Physiology, 9*(107), 659–662. doi:10.1085/jgp.107.6.659

Cohn, A. G. (2001). Formalising bio-spatial knowledge. In C. Welty and B. Smith (Eds.), *Proceedings of the 2nd International Conference FOIS'01* (pp. 198–209). New York, NY: ACM.

Cohn, A. G., Bennett, B., Gooday, J. M., & Gotts, N. (1997b). RCC: A calculus for region based qualitative spatial reasoning. *GeoInformatica, 1*, 275–316. doi:10.1023/A:1009712514511

Cohn, A. G., Bennett, B., Goodday, J. M., & Gotts, N. (1997a). Qualitative spatial representation and reasoning with the region connection calculus. *GeoInformatica, 1*(3), 1–44. doi:10.1023/A:1009712514511

Cohn, A. G., & Gotts, N. M. (1994). Spatial regions with undetermined boundaries. *Proceedings of Gaithesburg Workshop on GIS*. New York, NY: ACM.

Cohn, A. G., & Gotts, N. M. (1996). Representing spatial vagueness: A mereological approach. In L. C. Aiello, J. Doyle & S. Shapiro (Eds.), *Proceedings of the 5th Conference on Principles of Knowledge Representation and Reasoning* (pp. 230–241). Burlington, MA:Morgan Kaufmann.

Cohn, A. G., & Gotts, N. M. (1996). The egg-yolk representation of regions with indeterminate boundaries. In P. Burrough & A. Frank (Eds.), *Proceedings, GISDATA Specialist Meeting on Geographical Objects with Undetermined Boundaries* (pp. 171-187). New York, NY: Francis Taylor.

Cohn, A. G., & Hazarika, S. M. (2001). Qualitative spatial representation and reasoning: An overview. *Fundamenta Informaticae, 46*(1-2), 1–29.

Cohn, A. G., & Varzi, A. (2003). Mereotopological connection. *Journal of Philosophical Logic, 32*, 357–390. doi:10.1023/A:1024895012224

Dabaghian, Y., Cohn, A. G., & Frank, L. (2007a). *Neural activity in the hippocampus in the framework of formal topology*. 3d Workshop on Formal Topology, Padova, Italy.

Dabaghian, Y., Cohn, A. G., & Frank, L. (2007b). Topological maps from signals. *Proceedings of the 15th ACM GIS conference.* New York, NY: ACM

Dabaghian, Y., Memoli, F., Frank, L., & Carlsson, G. (2010). *Topological robustness of the hippocampal spatial map.*

de Silva, V., & Ghrist, R. (2006). Homological sensor networks. *The International Journal of Robotics Research, 25*(12), 1205–1222. doi:10.1177/0278364906072252

Donnelly, M., Bittner, T., & Rosse, C. (2006). A formal theory for spatial representation and reasoning in biomedical ontologies. *Artificial Intelligence in Medicine, 36*(1), 1–27. doi:10.1016/j.artmed.2005.07.004

Dubrovin, B. A., Novikov, S. P., & Fomenko, A. T. (1992). *Modern geometry*. Berlin, Germany: Springer.

Dusek, J., & Eichenbaum, H. (1997). The hippocampus and memory for orderly stimulus relations. *Proceedings of the National Academy of Sciences of the United States of America, 94*, 7109–7114. doi:10.1073/pnas.94.13.7109

Egenhofer, M. J., & Al-Taha, K. K. (1992). *Theories and methods of spatio-temporal reasoning in geographic space (LNCS 639)* (pp. 196–219). Springer-Verlag.

Eichenbaum, H. (2004). Hippocampus: Cognitive processes and neural representations that underlie declarative memory. *Neuron, 44*(11), 109–120. doi:10.1016/j.neuron.2004.08.028

Eichenbaum, H., & Cohen, N. (2001). *From conditioning to conscious recollection*. London, UK: Oxford University Press.

Escrig, M. T., & Toledo, F. (1998). *Qualitative spatial reasoning: Theory and practice-application to robot navigation. Frontiers in AI and Applications, 47*. Amsterdam, The Netherlands: IOS Press.

Fenton, A., Csizmadia, G., & Muller, R. (2000). Conjoint control of hippocampal place cell firing by two visual stimuli. *The Journal of General Physiology, 116*, 191–221. doi:10.1085/jgp.116.2.191

Fernyhough, J., Cohn, A. G., & Hogg, D. (2000). Constructing qualitative event models automatically from video input. *Image and Vision Computing, 18*, 81–103. doi:10.1016/S0262-8856(99)00023-2

Fortin, N., Agster, K., & Eichenbaum, H. (2002). Critical role of the hippocampus in memory for sequences of events. *Nature Neuroscience, 5*(5), 458–462.

Foster, D., & Wilson, M. (2006). Reverse replay of behavioural sequences in hippocampal place cells during the awake state. *Nature, 440*, 680–683. doi:10.1038/nature04587

Frank, L., Brown, E., & Wilson, M. (2000). Trajectory encoding in the hippocampus and entorhinal cortex. *Neuron, 27*(10), 169–178. doi:10.1016/S0896-6273(00)00018-0

Fuhs, M., Van Rhoads, S., Casale, A., McNaughton, B., & Touretzky, D. (2005). Influence of path integration vs. environmental orientationon place cell remapping between visually identical environments. *Journal of Neurophysiology, 94*(4), 2603–2616. doi:10.1152/jn.00132.2005

Godement, R. (1964). *Topologie algébrique et théorie des faisceaux*. Paris, France: Hermann.

González Díaz, R., & Real, P. (2003). Computation of cohomology operations on finite simplicial complexes. *Homology. Homotopy and Applications, 5*(2), 83–93.

Gothard, K., Hoffman, K., Battaglia, F., & McNaughton, B. (2001). Dentate gyrus and CA1 ensemble activity during spatial reference frame shifts in the presence and absence of visual input. *The Journal of Neuroscience, 21*, 7284–7292.

Gothard, K., Skaggs, W., & McNaughton, B. (1996). Dynamics of mismatch correction in the hippocampal ensemble code for space: Interaction between path integration and environmental cues. *The Journal of Neuroscience, 16*(24), 8027–8040.

Gothard, K. M., Skaggs, W. E., Moore, K. M., & McNaughton, B. L. (1996). Binding of hippocampal CA1 neural activity to multiple reference frames in a landmark-based navigation task. *The Journal of Neuroscience, 16*(2), 823–835.

Gotts, N. M., Gooday, J. M., & Cohn, A. G. (1996). A connection based approach to common-sense topological description and reasoning. *The Monist, 79*(1), 51–75.

Hartley, T., Burgess, N., Cacucci, F., & O'Keefe, J. (2000). Modeling place fields in terms of the cortical inputs to the hippocampus. *Hippocampus, 10*, 369–379. doi:10.1002/1098-1063(2000)10:4<369::AID-HIPO3>3.0.CO;2-0

Hassabis, D., Kumaran, D., Vann, S., & Maguire, E. (2007). Patients with hippocampal amnesia cannot imagine new experiences. *Proceedings of the National Academy of Sciences of the United States of America, 104*, 1726–1731. doi:10.1073/pnas.0610561104

Hazarika, S. M., & Cohn, A. G. (2001). *Taxonomy of spatio-temporal vagueness: An alternative egg-yolk interpretation*. COSIT/FOIS Workshop on Spatial Vagueness, Uncertainty and Granularity, Maine, USA.

Jensen, O., & Lisman, J. (2000). Position reconstruction from an ensemble of hippocampal place cells: Contribution of theta phase coding. *Journal of Neurophysiology, 83*(5), 2602–2609.

Jensen, O., & Lisman, J. (2005). Hippocampal sequence-encoding driven by a cortical multi-item working memory buffer. *Trends in Neurosciences*, *28*(2), 67–72. doi:10.1016/j.tins.2004.12.001

Johnstone, P. T. (1983)... *Bulletin of the American Mathematical Society*, *8*, 41–53. doi:10.1090/S0273-0979-1983-15080-2

Johnstone, P. T. (1991)... *Research and Exposition in Mathematics*, *18*, 85–107.

Kesner, R., Gilbert, P., & Barua, L. (2002). The role of the hippocampus in memory for the temporal order of a sequence of odors. *Behavioral Neuroscience*, *116*, 286–290. doi:10.1037/0735-7044.116.2.286

Klain, D., & Rota, G.-C. (1997). *Introduction to geometric probability*. London, UK: Cambridge University Press.

Knauff, M., Rauh, R., & Renz, J. (1997). *A cognitive assessment of topological spatial relations: Results from an empirical investigation*. (LNCS 1329), (pp. 193-206).

Knierim, J., McNaughton, B., & Poe, G. (2000). Three-dimensional spatial selectivity of hippocampal neurons during space flight. *Nature Neuroscience*, *3*, 209–210. doi:10.1038/72910

Lavenex, P., & Amaral, D. (2000). Hippocampal-neocortical interaction: A hierarchy of associativity. *Hippocampus*, *10*, 420–430. doi:10.1002/1098-1063(2000)10:4<420::AID-HIPO8>3.0.CO;2-5

Lehmann, F., & Cohn, A. G. (1994). The egg/yolk reliability hierarchy: Semantic data integration using sorts with prototypes. *Proceedings of the Conference on Information Knowledge Management*. (pp. 272-279). ACM Press.

Leutgeb, J., Leutgeb, S., Treves, A., Meyer, R., Barnes, C., & McNaughton, B. (2005). Progressive transformation of hippocampal neuronal representations in morphed environments. *Neuron*, *48*, 345–358. doi:10.1016/j.neuron.2005.09.007

Leutgeb, S., Leutgeb, J., Treves, A., Moser, M., & Moser, E. (2004). Distinct ensemble codes in hippocampal areas CA3 and CA1. *Science*, *305*, 1295–1298. doi:10.1126/science.1100265

Louie, K., & Wilson, M. A. (2001). Temporally structured replay of awake hippocampal ensemble activity during rapid eye movement sleep. *Neuron*, *29*(1), 145–156. doi:10.1016/S0896-6273(01)00186-6

Mach, E. (2004). *Space and geometry. The Monist, 18*. New York, NY: Dover.

Mackintosh, N. J. (2002). Do not ask whether they have a cognitive map, but how they find their way about. *Psicológica (Valencia)*, *23*, 165–185.

McNaughton, B., Battaglia, F., Jensen, O., Moser, E., & Moser, M.-B. (2006). Path integration and the neural basis of the cognitive map. *Nature Reviews. Neuroscience*, *7*, 663–678. doi:10.1038/nrn1932

Melamed, O., Gerstner, W., Maass, W., Tsodyks, M., & Markram, H. (2004). Coding and learning of behavioral sequences. *Trends in Neurosciences*, *27*(1), 11–14. doi:10.1016/j.tins.2003.10.014

Morris, R. G. M., Moser, E. I., Riedel, G., Martin, S. J., Sandin, J., Day, M., & O'Carroll, C. (2003). Elements of a neurobiological theory of the hippocampus: The role of activity-dependent synaptic plasticity in memory. *Philosophical Transactions of the Royal Society of London. Series B, Biological Sciences*, *358*(1432), 773–786. doi:10.1098/rstb.2002.1264

Muller, R. (1996). A quarter of a century of place cells. *Neuron*, *17*, 979–990. doi:10.1016/S0896-6273(00)80214-7

Nitz, D. (2006). Tracking route progression in the posterior parietal cortex. *Neuron*, *49*, 747–756. doi:10.1016/j.neuron.2006.01.037

Novikov, S. P. (Ed.). (1996). *Topology I: General survey*. New York, NY: Springer-Verlag.

O'Keefe, J. (1999). Do hippocampal pyramidal cells signal non-spatial as well as spatial information? *Hippocampus*, *9*(4), 352–364. doi:10.1002/(SICI)1098-1063(1999)9:4<352::AID-HIPO3>3.0.CO;2-1

O'Keefe, J., & Burgess, N. (1996). Geometric determinants of place cell plasticity. *Nature*, *381*, 425–428.

O'Keefe, J., & Dostrovsky, J. (1971). The hippocampus as a spatial map: Preliminary evidence from unit activity in the freely-moving rat. *Brain Research*, *34*, 171–175. doi:10.1016/0006-8993(71)90358-1

O'Keefe, J., & Nadel, L. (1978). *The hippocampus as a cognitive map*. London, UK: Oxford.

Poincaré, H. (1895). L'espace et la géométrie. *Revue de Metaphysique et de Morale*, *3*, 631–646.

Poincaré, H. (1898). Des fondements de la géométrie. *The Monist*, *9*, 1–43.

Qin, Y.-L., McNaughton, B. L., Skaggs, W. E., & Barnes, C. A. (1997). Memory reprocessing in corticocortical and hippocampo-cortical neuronal ensembles. *Philosophical Transactions of the Royal Society of London, Series B*, *352*, 15–25. doi:10.1098/rstb.1997.0139

Randell, D. A., Cui, Z., & Cohn, A. G. (1992). A spatial logic based on regions and connection. *Proceedings of the 3rd International Conference on Knowledge Representation and Reasoning*, (pp. 165-176). San Mateo, CA: Morgan Kaufmann.

Redish, A. (2001). The hippocampal debate: are we asking the right questions? *Behavioural Brain Research*, *127*(1), 81–98. doi:10.1016/S0166-4328(01)00356-4

Redish, A., Rosenzweig, E., Bohanick, J. D., McNaughton, B. L., & Barnes, C. A. (2000). Dynamics of hippocampal ensemble activity realignment: Time versus space. *The Journal of Neuroscience*, *20*(24), 9298–9309.

Redish, A., & Touretzky, D. (1997). Cognitive maps beyond the hippocampus. *Hippocampus*, *7*(1), 15–35. doi:10.1002/(SICI)1098-1063(1997)7:1<15::AID-HIPO3>3.0.CO;2-6

Renz, J., Rauh, R., & Knauff, M. (2000). *Towards cognitive adequacy of topological spatial relations*. (LNCS 1849), (pp. 184–197). Springer.

Sambin, G. (2003). Some points in formal topology. *Theoretical Computer Science*, *305*(1-3), 347–408. doi:10.1016/S0304-3975(02)00704-1

Sargolini, F., Fyhn, M., Hafting, T., McNaughton, B., Witter, M., Moser, M., & Moser, E. (2006). Conjunctive representation of position, direction, and velocity in entorhinal cortex. *Science, 312*, 758–762. doi:10.1126/science.1125572

Sharp, P. E. (Ed.). (2002). *The neural basis of navigation*. Boston, MA: Kluwer Academic.

Skaggs, W., & McNaughton, B. (1996). Replay of neuronal firing sequence in rat hippocampus during sleep following spatial experience. *Science, 271*, 1870–1873. doi:10.1126/science.271.5257.1870

Swan, R. G. (1964). *The theory of sheaves*. Chicago, IL: University of Chicago Press.

Terrazas, A., Krause, M., Lipa, P., Gothard, K., Barnes, C., & McNaughton, B. (2005). Self-motion and the hippocampal spatial metric. *The Journal of Neuroscience, 25*(35), 8085–8096. doi:10.1523/JNEUROSCI.0693-05.2005

Touretzky, D., Weisman, W., Fuhs, M., Skaggs, W., Fenton, A., & Muller, R. (2004). Deforming the hippocampal map. *Hippocampus, 15*(1), 41–55. doi:10.1002/hipo.20029

van de Vel, M. (1993). *Theory of convex structures*. Amsterdam, The Netherlands: North Holland Publishers.

Vickers, S. (1989). *Topology via logic*. London, UK: Cambridge University Press.

Wallenstein, G., Eichenbaum, H., & Hasselmo, M. (1998). The hippocampus as an associator of discontiguous events. *Trends in Neurosciences, 21*(8), 317–323. doi:10.1016/S0166-2236(97)01220-4

Weil, A. (1938). *Sur les espaces à structure uniforme et sur la topologie générale. Publications de l'Institute Mathématique de l'Université de Strasbourg*. Paris, France: Hermann.

Whitehead, A. N. (1929). *Process and reality: An essay in cosmology*. New York, NY: Macmillan.

Wiener, S. I., & Taube, J. S. (Eds.). (2005). *Head direction cells and the neural mechanisms underlying directional orientation*. Boston, MA: MIT Press.

Wilson, M., & McNaughton, B. (1993). Dynamics of the hippocampal ensemble code for space. *Science, 261*, 1055–1058. doi:10.1126/science.8351520

Wilson, M., & McNaughton, B. (1994). Reactivation of hippocampal ensemble memories during sleep. *Science, 265*, 676–679. doi:10.1126/science.8036517

Zomorodian, A. (2005). *Topology for computing*. London, UK: Cambridge.

ENDNOTES

1 According to (Swan, 1964), "Sheaf is effectively a system of local coefficients over a space *X*."

2 The term "nerve" here is purely mathematical and has nothing to do with the uses of the word "nerve" in physiology and neuroscience.

Chapter 13
Knowledge Representation as a Tool for Intelligence Augmentation

Auke J.J. van Breemen
Radboud University, The Netherlands

Jozsef I. Farkas
Radboud University, The Netherlands

Janos J. Sarbo
Radboud University, The Netherlands

ABSTRACT

The goal of Intelligence Augmentation (IA) is the development of tools that improve the efficiency of human intelligence. To this end, the authors of this chapter introduce a model of human conceptualization on the basis of a cognitive theory of information processing and a Peircean theory of signs. An account of two experiments is provided. The first concerns conceptualization by individuals, and the second describes how problem elicitation was approached by a team of participants. A preliminary analysis of the results shows that the proposed model is congruent with multi channel and multi purpose human information processing. This implies that the cognitive model can be used as a model for knowledge representation in various fields of human-computer interfacing such as computer aided problem solving and problem elicitation.

INTRODUCTION

Intelligence Augmentation (IA) research aims at the development of tools that improve the efficiency of human intelligence. This form of enhancement contrasts with Artificial Intelligence (AI), whereby intelligence would be produced in an entirely artificial form. According to D.C. Engelbart (1962, p.1),

DOI: 10.4018/978-1-60960-551-3.ch013

"by 'augmenting human intellect' we mean increasing the capability of a man to approach a complex problem situation, to gain comprehension to suit his particular needs, and to derive solutions to problems".

Due to the importance of man in problem solving, computer systems augmenting intelligence demand a 'human-compatible' formal model of knowledge representation (KR). Important characteristic properties of human KR are flexibility (for adjustments) and portability (knowledge in one domain can be directly used in another domain). Experience with static, fact-based KR in past decades has shown that it is inflexible and non-portable. We believe that process-based, dynamical KR offers better perspectives. An illustration of the differences between static and dynamic KR may be found in natural language (NL) processing. Traditional (static) language modeling, characterized by large formal grammars and relatively small lexicons is not robust against modifications. By separating static and dynamic aspects of language symbols, respectively, in a lexicon (which is apt for modification) and a relational process (which can be invariantly used), dynamic modeling enables a more robust alternative (Sarbo, Farkas & van Breemen, 2007).

A philosophically informed dynamic view of KR has been introduced in (Breemen & Sarbo, 2009). The most important conclusion of this work is that the processes of perception and cognition can be modeled in the same way. We grounded our model in the theory of the American philosopher, C.S. Peirce (1839-1914) for two reasons. On the first hand, Peirce's sign theory (cf. semiotics) provides a unique classification of signs and sign aspects. On the other, his category theory enables categorical classification to be applied recursively hence it enables the development of ontological specification in a systematic fashion.

Here we start with a recapitulation and definition of our cognitively based, semiotically inspired model of KR that complies with those philosophical considerations. This model of knowledge representation models conceptualization as a process. A characteristic property of all processes, including conceptualization, is their teleological, goal-driven character. Such a goal is the generation of an appropriate response to the input problem. In practice this comes down to the generation of a response that is appropriate from a certain point of view as, for instance, when the response is mathematically well-formed (in the case of a mathematical problem).

Since in conceptualization it is only the final interpretation that really is of interest, intermediate representations can be considered as expressions of the input from the perspective of their contribution to the (desired) result. Such intermediate interpretations can be associated with Peircean sign aspects (Peirce, 1931-58). On the basis of the dependency and subservience relations between different sign aspects that are identified by Peirce, we suggest that intermediate representations can be ordered in a dependency structure.

The focus of this chapter is on an application of our theory of IA in human conceptualization. We will consider two fields: problem solving (Bruner, 1966) and problem elicitation (Krogstie, Sindre & Jorgensen, 2006). Utterances generated during problem solving and problem elicitation can be associated with sign aspects and ordered accordingly. Following this line of thinking, the quality of a conceptualization process can be characterized by the relation between the structure induced by the generated sign aspects, and the dependency structure defined by Peirce. In our first experiment, the quality of conceptualization is determined statistically. As an analysis of conceptualization by teams of participants can be more complex, in the second experiment we restricted our focus to a qualitative analysis of contiguous segments of a single process. Ontology specification is beyond the scope of this paper. An illustration of such a definition of syntactic symbols may be found in (Sarbo, Farkas & van Breemen, 2007).

TOWARDS A MODEL OF CONCEPTUALIZATION

Process Model

Human conceptualization can be characterized by an interaction, between an input stimulus and the observer, and the generation of an explanatory response: why this input is occurring to us. For instance, if we, see a traffic light to switch from green to red, our reaction can be "Stop!". A model of information processing underlying response generation can be the following (Sarbo, Farkas & van Breemen, 2007). See also Figure 1. Below, square brackets are used to indicate that an entity is not yet interpreted as a sign; no bracketing or the usual bracket symbols indicate that some interpretation is already available.

The input stimulus is affecting the observer occurring in some state. By denoting the qualia representing that state and the input stimulus, by q_s and q_e, respectively, the input of information processing can be defined by the collection of qualia or the *'primordial soup'*: $[q_s, q_e, C]$. Here, "C" stands for the memory information (memory response qualia) or the *context* triggered by q_s and q_e. In order to generate a response, the brain/mind as an interpreting system has (1) to sort out the input qualia in the primordial soup (cf. *sorting*; $[q_s]$, $[q_e]$, $[C]$), (2) to represent them separately from each other (cf. *abstraction*; q_s, q_e), (3) to complement them with memory information (cf. *complementation;* (q_s,C), (q_e,C)), and (4) to establish a relation between them (cf. *predication*; $(q_s,C)–(q_e,C)$). For an in-depth analysis of the 'primordial soup' see the Jamesian based research program "Empirical Modelling" (Beynon, Russ & McCarty, 2006).

An example for the input can be the qualia of the appearing red light (q_e), affecting us when we are in a state of moving (q_s). In context, red light can associated with "warning" and moving with "stopping" ([C]). The relation between the input qualia can be paraphrased by the expression: "The appearing red light is a warning for stopping moving" or, briefly, "Stop!".

Although the above model of information processing can be plausible, it may not enable us to interpret it as a meaning generation process. In order to associate the events of the model with an element of meaning, first we need to delve into a theory of conceptualization which is the subject of the next section.

Received View of Ontology

A domain specific ontology is a generalization of 'individual' conceptualizations. According to the Tractatus logico-philosophicus (Wittgenstein, 1922), truth preserving conceptualization ought to restrict

Figure 1. A model of cognitive information processing. A horizontal line stands for an interaction between interpretation moments

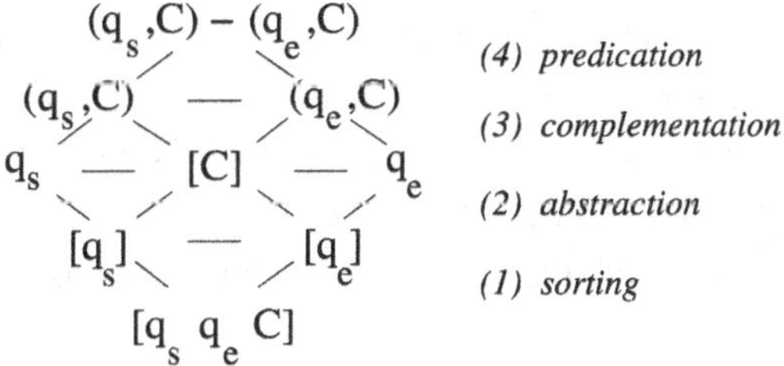

itself to a specification of entities coverable by statements of fact. This view is also adopted in computer science. Gruber (2008) nicely illustrates this point when he writes:

In the context of computer and information sciences, an ontology defines a set of representational primitives with which to model a domain of knowledge or discourse. [...] In the context of database systems, ontology can be viewed as a level of abstraction of data models, analogous to hierarchical and relational models, but intended for modeling knowledge about individuals, their attributes and their relationship to other individuals.[1]

It must be admitted that Wittgenstein intended to cover all of reality while Gruber modestly states that ontology in computer science is a technical term. The background scheme of thinking, however, is the same: propositions form the key entrance to ontological thinking. But what if the formation of the proposition is the true ground on which to base the most general ontology?

In the Philosophical Investigations, (Wittgenstein, 1971) shifts from a detached view to a more inside perspective. The meaning of an expression no longer depends solely on the pictured facts: instead meaning is determined by the role the expression plays in the language game in which it figures. Uttering a sentence is like doing a move in a game of chess. Using language is rule governed. Learning language is learning to do the right moves and picturing facts is only one of the families of games, that has to be sub-divided according to its variant forms on top of that.

Peircean Ontology

A shift from a static to a dynamic view of the world is an essential element of modern ontology. According to Peirce, our understanding of phenomena is marked by three categeories which he called Firstness (being), Secondness (existence) and Thirdness (reality, lawfullness or mediation)[2]. Because whatever appears requires a certain shock or contrast, it may be said that the appearance must be distinguished from the *event* of appearing, for the latter requires two elements which by themselves must be said to be mere ‘possibles’. Thus the appearance of red undoubtedly requires ‘red’ though this red does not *really* appear unless it is *perceived.* Thus the firstness of pure red appears only in the event of the perception consisting in the interaction of the perceiver and the perceived. And thus, the appearance in the event of appearing constitutes the aspect of Secondness. But the perception, to the extent that it is the merely brute fact of meeting, appears only insofar as it reveals itself as this particular perception, for instance the perception of this color red. Thus, in order to appear as perception, the perception must do so according to the rule that when this sort of event occurs, it appears as the perception of red. It is the rule governing the appearance that constitutes Thirdness. It tells us in what respect the appearance as event reveals the ‘possible’ elements of Thirdness.

The most original feature of Peirce’s analysis is that it shows that in everything cognizable all three categories are involved: respectively an aspect of reality which is not related to anything but itself (Firstness), an aspect of contrast (Secondness), and an aspect of mediation (of gluing together) (Thirdness). The dynamic version of the doctrine is that every event (which is the element of Secondness) involves some possible qualities (Firstness) and some aspect of order (Thirdness). On the basis of the above dependency and subservience relations, the three categories can be arranged in a structure. See Figure 2.

Sign Aspects and Interpretant Aspects

Every phenomenon, as far as it can be cognized, is of the nature of a sign. According to Peirce, a sign always consists of a complexus of the three categories. By recursively applying his categorical schema, this time to the three categories of signs, Peirce concluded that signs can be analyzed in nine sign aspects. Peirce writes:

A Sign, or Representamen, is a First which stands in such a genuine triadic relation to a Second, called its Object, as to be capable of determining a Third, called its Interpretant, to assume the same triadic relation to its Object in which it stands itself to the same Object.

As a First, a sign can be a quality (qualisign), an event (sinsign), or a rule-like habit (legisign). As a Second, it can represent its object through a relation of similarity (icon), by pointing in the direction of the object (index) or, by expressing a conventional property involved in it (symbol). As a Third, it can mediate its object to an interpreting agent through expressing the sign's object as a possible (rheme), an actually existent (dicent) or, a proposition (argument, proposition interpreted as in 'something proposed'). On the basis of the dependencies and subservience relations, between them, the nine sign aspects can be arranged in a structure. See Figure 2. Note the difference between interpretant, for instance, a thought sign, and interpreter, which is an interpreting system.

A sign only functions as a sign if it is interpreted. Following our assumption that for each sign aspect there must exist a corresponding interpretant aspect, in (Breemen & Sarbo, 2009) we have shown that Peirce's theory of interpretants can be completed in a structure consisting in nine interpretant aspects. See also Figure 3. We skip details and directly illustrate the nine interpretant aspects with an example.

An Example of the Nine Interpretant Aspects

We leave our earlier example of the appearing red light and proceed with the running example of the first experiment described later in this paper. Assume the sign to be the diagram, as shown in Figure 5, perceived as a collection of impressions (perceived qualities). In addition, assume that the interpreter is primed with the question: "area(*A*)=*2**area(*B*); *x=?*". The nine interpretant aspects can be explained as follows.

1. The impressions get sorted out as a form (mental energetic interpretant; icon) and settle as a singularity (physical energetic interpretant; sinsign).
2. Since it is a familiar *iconic* singularity the form is recognized as an instance of a typical geometrical problem (rule; legisign). Since it is a *singular* icon out of any context at this stage, all kinds of

Figure 2. Peirce's categories and their involvement relation. A lower category is involved in a higher one.

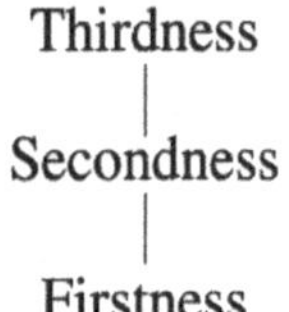

interpretations become possible such as the form as a sign of an affine transformation, a computation of area, and so on (immediate interpretant; rheme).

3. As the interpretation of the diagram is embedded in the specific context of the mathematical question, a conventional meaning of the legisign is developed (convention; symbol). Through the connection with knowledge contained in the interpreting system about known geometrical operations, the conventional meaning gets embedded in an understanding of the diagram as a sign of a certain geometrical operation to be applied on this occasion (dynamical interpretant; dicent). For instance, "the pair of diagonals of *A* divides it in four equal triangles (dicent), "a pair of equal triangles can be combined in a quadrangle through rotation" (symbol). Here, "diagonal" refers to background knowledge about quadrangles (index).
4. This dynamical interpretant is, again through a connection with what is contained in the interpreting system, placed under a rule of habit that covers this kind of case and a response is generated ("*A* contains two pairs of equal triangles; by means of rotation a pair of equal triangles of *A* can be combined in a quadrangle satisfying the desired goal; therefore we should apply this operation" (normal interpretant; argument).

Figure 3. Peirce's sign aspects (left) and their mundane terms (right). Firstness, Secondness and Thirdness are categories;First, Second and Third are categorical aspects.

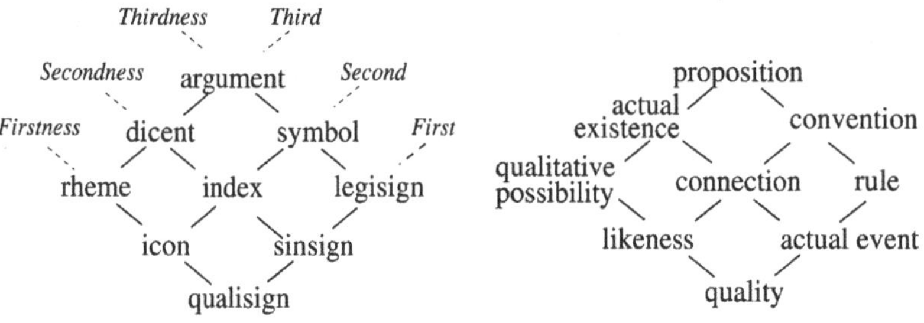

Figure 4. Peirce's interpretant aspects and associated sign aspects

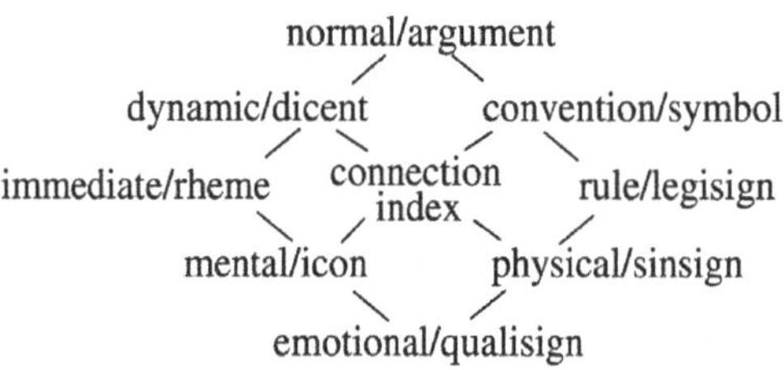

Figure 5. A geometrical problem

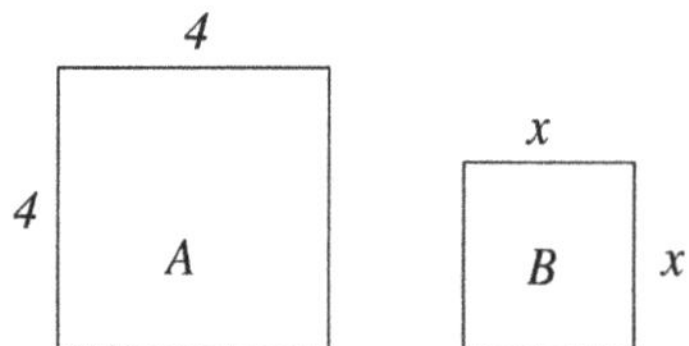

Process Model Revisited

The model of information processing introduced earlier in sect. "Process model" can be shown to be conform to the above classification of interpretant aspects. An important difference between the two models lies in the assumption, taken on behalf of the process model, that intermediate representations (cf. interpretation moments) arise via interactions between a state and an effect, in the context of background state and effect qualities. Through the interaction between state and effect, a change/contrast arises. That change is eventually interpreted as an event. In this chapter we merge the two models in a single one (see Figure 6). Interpretation proceeds in four stages. Below we refer to positions in the process model (cf. interpretation moments) by their Peircean sign aspects given in quotation marks, e.g. 'icon'.

1. In *sorting*, 'raw' qualities of an interaction ('qualisign') perceived by the interpreting system are sorted out in a state ('icon') and effect ('sinsign'), which are in focus, and background or context qualities ('index'), which are complementary (i.e. not in focus).
2. In the subsequent operation, *abstraction*, comprising the interaction between 'icon' and 'sinsign', the input qualities are abstracted into types, through matching with existing prototype concepts. This obtains a representation of the input in the 'rheme' (abstract state) and 'legisign' positions (abstract effect) (Smith, Osherson, Rips & Keans, 1988).
3. In *complementation*, the interaction between 'rheme' and 'index', and between 'index' and 'legisign' are represented by expressions in the 'dicent' and 'symbol' positions, respectively. This operation could be called contextualization, by virtue of the use of prototypical information provided by the 'index'. Contextualization is comparable to lexical access and semantic interpretation (Margolis & Laurence, 1999).
4. Finally, in *predication*, the interaction of 'dicent' and 'symbol' is represented by a hypothetical proposition ('argument') about the relation between the co-occurring state and effect qualities of the input interaction. If the hypothesis drawn does not fit or even is disconfirmed, either new complementation is searched for in the context or another focus is taken on the input qualities ('qualisign').

Note the correspondence between the above four stages, the four steps of interpretation, and the four levels of the model of information processing introduced in previous sections. As conceptualization is expressible as sign interpretation, in Figure 6 we have in front of us the blueprints of a procedure under-

Figure 6. Peirce's sign aspects as an interpretation process (horizontal lines represent interactions between interpretation moments)

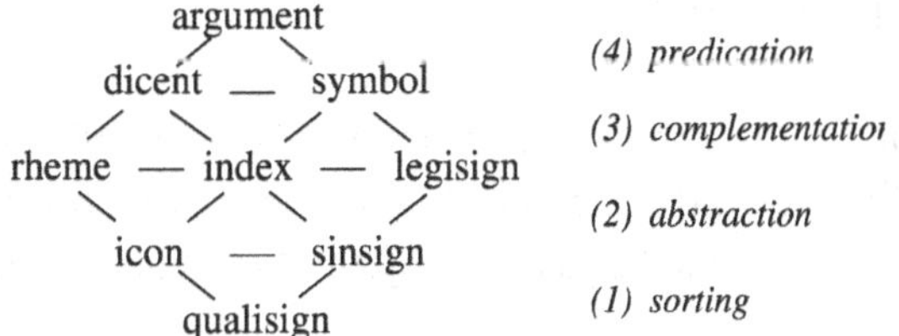

lying conceptualization as a process. Through its relation with the Peircean sign aspects, this procedure can be called a meaningful model of information processing.

In the experiments described later in this chapter the input consists in natural language utterances. How such utterances can be mapped to sign aspects that eventually yield the output, is illustrated in the next section with the analysis of a sample text. A full scale linguistic interpretation of the utterances is beyond our current goal. A formal definition of our process model as a syntactic parser may be found in (Sarbo & Farkas, 2002).

Cognitive Theoretical Background

Besides being grounded in Peircean semiotics, our process model is informed by cognitive theories of conceptualization as well. According to Piaget, learning and cognitive processes are adaptive 'tools' aiding man in its interaction with its environment. Focusing on cognitive development, Piaget defined four different stages in child development (Rigter, 1996):

1. *Sensory-motor phase.* Objects and object characteristics are learned and recognized through perception and motor manipulation; this knowledge is stored as concepts or abstract representations of object characteristics (e.g., sweet).
2. *Pre-operational phase.* Percepts are explained through reasoning. It is assumed that the most salient concept properties are included into interpretations.
3. *Concrete operational phase.* Learning that different points of view are possible.
4. *Formal operational phase.* Reasoning without preceding perception, development of abstract reasoning and hypothesizing.

A similar definition of conceptualization is due to Mead (1934, 1974), distinguishing cognitive activity in four phases: (1) impulse, (2) perception, (3) manipulation, (4) consummation. We assume that a 'fully developed' cognitive system amalgamates the processes and operations specified above and that these are effective in concept formation. Our model extends these notions and builds a bridge towards Intelligence Augmentation.

Sample Conceptualization Process

The running example of this section is a text found in (Huibers, 1996). In this fragment (see Figure 7), the author explains his conception of 'Information Retrieval Systems' as given in Figure 7 and depicted in Figure 8. The utterances in Figure 7 can be analyzed in sign aspects, as follows. Below, utterances are referred to by their sequence number and abbreviations, as shown in Figure 7. Sign aspects are assigned to utterances on the basis of their contribution to the desired result ('argument'). The results of the analysis are recapitulated in Figure 9.

1. *there are several document-bases (sev-docb)*:='icon'. The postulation (*are*) of *sev-docb* as constituent entities, not as qualitatively possible ones (rheme), nor as such entities in context (dicent). The hypothesis immediately above can be justified by the fact that, besides (2), *sev-docb* has no later references in the text.

Figure 7. A sample text defining the concept 'Information Retrieval Systems'

nr.	string	abbreviation
1.	*There are several document-bases.*	*sev-docb*
2.	*Each document-base contains*	*each-docb*
	different types of information.	*dt-of-info*
3.	*There are various types of users and*	*vt-of-users*
	there are vast differences between	
	their information needs	*vdiff-ineeds*
4.	*There are various kinds of search-tasks,*	*vk-of-st*
	or stated differently,	
	there are several ways in which	*sev-ways*
5.	*a user can be satisfied with*	*canb-satf*
	the returned information.	*ret-info*

Figure 8. An illustration of the underlying phenomenon

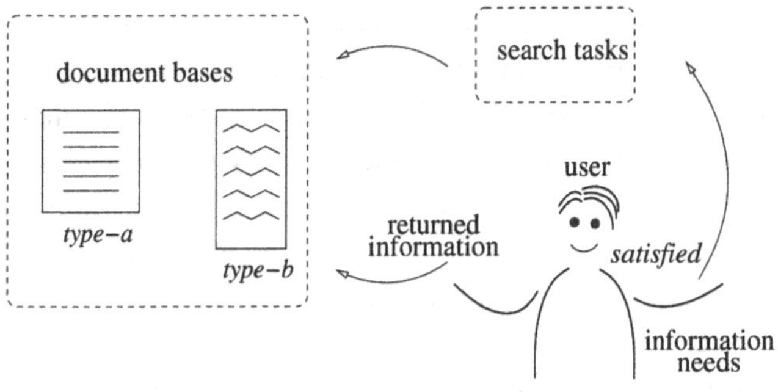

Figure 9. Interpretation moments as sign aspects

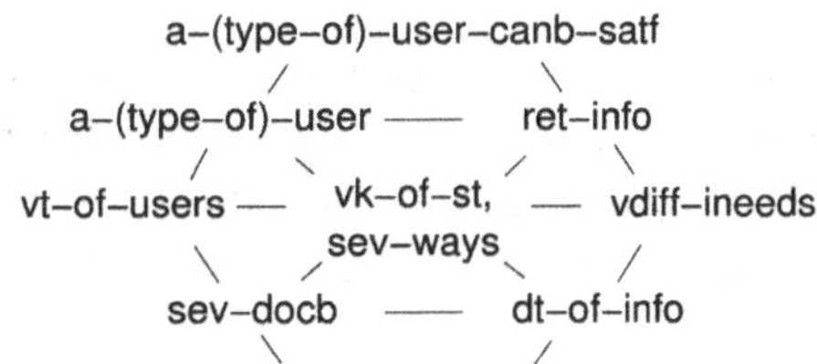

2. *different types of information (dt-of-info)*:='sinsign'. An expression of *dt-of-info* as an appearing new property of *docb* (cf. actual event). By means of the adjective *different*, this sinsign lays the ground for an interpretation of its relative difference with *each* (icon), as a legisign.
3. *there are various types of users (vt-of-users)*:='rheme'. An expression of existent entities (*are*). The later anaphoric reference to *users*, by *their*, in *vdiff-ineeds*, enables *vt-of-users* to be interpreted as an expression of a range of possibilities ('of what type can users be'). Following the dependencies

between the Peircean sign aspects, the interpretation of *vt-of-users* in the rheme position implies a representation of *users* in the icon position, enabling *users* and *docb* to be synonymously interpreted as constituents of 'Information Retrieval Systems' (their synonymous meaning is represented by *sev-docb*).

4. *there are vast differences between their information needs (vdiff-ineeds)*:='legisign'. A generalization of the single event, *dt-of-info*, in the rule governing this type of events, represented by *information-needs.* This is made possible by the relative difference between the icon and sinsign, marked by *each* and *several* on the one hand, and *different-types-of* on the other. The hypothesis immediately above is confirmed by the rule-like compatibility of *vast differences* (as an effect) and *information needs* (as its object), expressed by *vdiff-ineeds*. Due to the dependencies between the Peircean sign aspects, the interpretation of *vdiff-ineeds* as a legisign implies the interpretation of *vast differences* and *between* in the sinsign position. Note that this interpretation of the expressions is already involved in the interpretation of *dt-of-info.*
5. *there are various kinds of search-tasks (vk-of-st)*:='index'. As there is no reference to *vk-of-st* later in text, this symbol may not represent information which is in focus. For this reason, *vk-of-st* cannot be interpreted as a rheme or dicent expression of the input either. According to the preferred interpretation, *vk-of-st* is representing an event, not by explaining it in any way, but only pointing in its direction. Due to the dependencies between the Peircean sign aspects, an interpretation of *vk-of-st* as an index expression implies the existence of complementary qualities (qualisign position). Hence these qualities must be involved in the rheme and legisign expressions as well.
6. *there are several ways (sev-ways)*:='index'. By virtue of the coordinator, *or stated differently*, and the complementation by *in which...*, also the above symbol can be interpreted as an indexical expression of complementary qualities. Note the complementary perspectives conveyed by the expressions *vk-of-st* and *sev-ways*. This is typical for the index position.
7. *a user (a-user)*:='dicent'. An expression of *vt-of-users* in context (more precisely, *a-(type-of)-users*), representing users demanding *various-kinds-of-search-tasks*.
8. *returned information (ret-info)*:='symbol'. From a syntactic point of view, the predicate (symbol position) is defined by the phrase *can be satisfied with the returned information*. The complement (*ret-info*) can be interpreted as a representation of the nested phenomenon, 'information returning'. Following this line of thinking, *can be satisfied with (canb-satf)* is interpreted as a representation of an interaction between *ret-info* and *a-(type-of)-user*, hypothetically expressing the goal of 'Information Retrieval Systems' (argument position). Note that *ret-info* can be a representation of the conventional meaning of *vdiff-ineeds* in context, expressed by a combination of different *information needs* and *search tasks*, that may correctly be called 'information returning'.

Qualisigns can appear only when they are involved. Following this assumption of Peircean semiotics, expression in the qualisign position are omitted.

In order to test our hypothesis that conceptualization proceeds along the lines of our model, we conducted a couple of experiments. In the experiments the input is defined in natural language. By lack of space, an analysis of the utterances in sign aspects cannot be given in full extent. A more detailed account of this mapping may be found in (Couwenberg, 2007) and (Klomp, 2008).

FIRST EXPERIMENT: PROBLEM SOLVING

In the first experiment we focused on individual conceptualization. Twenty-eight pupils from a primary school in Nuland, The Netherlands, took part in this test. The age range was 11-12 years. The pupils were asked to solve a mathematical problem, as described by Plato (427-347 BC). See also Figure 5. In his dialog the *Meno*, he raises the question how to determine the length of the sides of a square which is half as large as a given square (Plato, 1871). We chose this problem because its solution is straight forward, as outlined in (Magnani, 2001). At the same time the problem is complex enough to furnish the experimenters with data. Although the pupils already learned to compute squares, they rated the problem as difficult. According to the teachers, the participating pupils were not familiar with the problem since it was not a part of their Math course. Regarding their cognitive development in this domain, 8th graders are similar to adults (Delfos, 2000). The sample problem was chosen because many IA applications are targeting the respective population.

It is plausible to assume that with complex problems the outlined conceptualization process is recursively used whereby the propositions formed at the end of one process serve as input for the next run. Per run, one proposition is generated. Each run is delimited by the identification (naming) of a relation (e.g. "Square *A* is larger than square *B*").

The process is driven by the goal to formulate a fitting proposition. In solving a problem, the number of embedded analyses (cf. recursion) can be affected by three parameters:

- What is in focus (always a contiguous segment of input qualities).
- Input complexity (number of propositions used for describing the phenomenon in focus).
- Internal context (relevant knowledge of the world).

These are the sources of inter- and intra variability in interpretation. By the given problem, with a generally accepted solution, it is possible to determine in advance the goal governing the entire conceptualization process. Exploiting the thinking-out-loud method in the process of solving a complex mathematical problem, it is possible to gather verbal reports containing utterances reflecting the interpretation process. Utterances can be coded and ordered as sign aspects. The degree of match with the dependency structure specified by our model can be statistically determined. But do note that the same utterance very well may function as another sign aspect if the goal of conceptualization is different.

Method

The test is supervised. If the hypothesis by the participants is disconfirmed by the experimenter, the experimenter may help shifting focus by the participant, from seeing the diagram as a problem to seeing it more as a solution, for instance, by drawing the participant's attention to the existence of diagonals in a quadrangle. To this end, the experimenter can make use of additional material. Background knowledge about diagonals is assumed to be available by the pupils. Note that by shifting focus, the instructor is not providing extra information with respect to the original problem.

In the experiment, verbalizations by the participants were recorded and transcribed during problem solving. Subsequently, verbal utterances were coded into the nine sign aspects. The use and the order of the stages of sign interpretation were determined on the basis of the prevailing sign aspects. This way, we were able to determine whether the observed conceptualization unfolds according to the stages specified by our model. This method is rather coarse in that verbalizations need not be entirely synchronous with the actual cognitive processing. We assume that the nine types of sign aspects are 'tied' to the respective operations of the model (e.g. 'icon', 'sinsign', 'index' - *sorting*, 'rheme', 'legisign' - *abstraction*, etc.).

Procedure and Materials

The experiment was conducted using a standard protocol. All sessions were videotaped. The time intervals needed to solve the problem were registered by the experimenter using a stop watch. The setting was an empty classroom; a familiar work surrounding for 8th graders. The experiment was conducted individually. The experimenter was seated in an L-setting with respect to the pupil in order to avoid a suggestion of a 'leadership role' to the experimenter since this may affect the pupils' level of commitment to solving the problem. The experiment was conducted during regular school time. The experimenter was instructed not to interfere with the process of solving the problem unless this is indicated in the protocol. Each session started with the experimenter giving an instruction about the task and the procedure. The recordings contained on average 75 verbal utterances. Instruction: "First of all, you will receive a card with a drawing on it. The drawing expresses a geometrical problem. Your task is to uncover the problem and to find its solution. While doing this I would like you to say everything you are thinking about this problem."

This is called 'thinking-out-loud' method. Subsequently, the participants were handed over the drawing (see Figure 5) and the session started. It was determined in advance in which situations the experimenter would interfere and how: If a participant was stuck with (part of) the problem (operationalized as inactive for 20 seconds) or if he/she made a mistake, the experimenter prompted him/her to try again and solve the problem or to try and correct the error. Some types of errors were anticipated upon which were already described in Plato's Meno. They indeed occurred in the pilot study. Additional material used in the experiments is displayed in Figure 10. This material was provided, if needed, in different orders assigned randomly.

Coding Procedure

All transcribed verbal utterances were first assessed for their contribution to the solution of the input problem. Two kinds of codes were assigned: (1) contributes to the solution of the problem; (2) 'side-tracking' or 'errors' like wrong perception/representation/interpretation of the problem, wrong assumptions, and logical errors. For the former kind of utterances a coding system was developed with sign aspects and examples specified. In order to validate the coding system two experts independently coded a sample of verbal protocols. The degree in which the interpretation process in solving the problem is congruent

Figure 10. Additional material used in the experiments

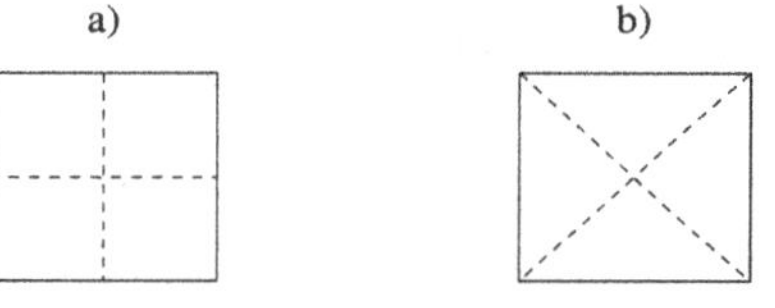

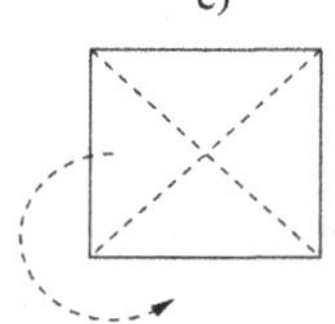

with the conceptualization process as specified by our model was determined on the basis of prevalence of 'correctly' formed output argument aspects, i.e. 'arguments' preceded by conceptualizations (cf. interpretation moments) from any of the preceding processing stages in the order specified by our model.

Analyses

The inter-rater reliability of the coding system was determined using Cohen's Kappa, and means and standard deviations (SD) were computed using Statistical Package for the Social Sciences, version 14 (SPSS 14).

Results

The inter-rater reliability for the coding criteria was high (Cohen's Kappa = 0,924). In total, 1690 verbal utterances were coded. Average percentage of task related utterances was M=79% (SD=17.07). Average percentage of utterances classifiable into sign aspects was 84 (SD=10.5). Average percentage of congruent 'arguments' was 42 (SD=37.81).

Discussion

Our preliminary results show a high level of congruence of concepts comprising verbal reports with the concept types specified in our model. Moreover, also the order of concept formation as inferred from verbal reports is congruent with the order of processing stages specified in our model.

Human conceptualization can be fast. In order to get hold of the unfolding interpretation process we introduced a task that, by virtue of its complexity, forces problem solving to be split into stages. In the first stage, subjects are typically stuck at a trivial interpretation of their input (e.g. "There is a mathematical problem"). In this stage, conceptualizations from the lower part of the process model (see Figure 6) are dominantly produced. The subsequent stages are more difficult and often re-focusing is needed in order to proceed in solving the problem. At the same time, conceptualizations of higher level sign aspects are generated (see Figure 6). The findings suggest that solving the problem is effective if the interpretation process proceeds as suggested in our model.

SECOND EXPERIMENT: PROBLEM ELICITATION

In the second experiment we concentrated on team-wise conceptualization. To this end we analyzed an actual elicitation process at the Dutch software firm Sogeti Nederland B.V. In this process, three clients assisted by a professional elicitator were involved in the specification of a problem with the clients' database system. The entire elicitation process, that took 4 hours, was recorded and transcribed. Since in this experiment we had access to data from a single process, statistical analysis was not possible. However, the elicitation process was complex and we could test our hypothesis, that conceptualization, if successful, proceeds along the lines of our process model, by considering an analysis of a number of nested sub-processes of conceptualization. An example is provided in the next section.

Individual conceptualization differs from co-operative conceptualization in two aspects. One of them is the use of the context ('index'). In individual conceptualization the context consists in prototypical information possessed by the interpreter about objects in the world. This is opposed to conceptualization processes by teams, in which a context comprising shared information about the common input problem is gradually developed by the participants. Another difference is the assumption of a shared, uniform representation of knowledge (a use of identical sign aspects) by the participants. As conceptualization is necessarily individual, establishing a common conceptualization of the input problem assumes that concepts generated by individual processes can be merged through coordination.

Sample Problem Elicitation

A problem with the clients' application software, '*myAssignment*', instigated the elicitation process. The goal of *myAssignment* is to provide adequate information to employees, managers and client(s), about assignments and, most importantly, about communication between the participants of a project. The elicitation process was conducted in a separate room, in a usual setting, without intervention by the observer whose only task was to operate the fixed camera.

A sample elicitation session is displayed in Figure 11. The goal of this session is the disclosure of missing functionalities in *myAssignment*. Utterances of the sample text are interpreted from the perspective of *this* goal. In the analysis below, interjections are omitted. Note that interjections do have functions such as expressing doubt, agreement and alike. The results of the analysis are recapitulated in Figures12-13.

1. *logical steps*:='icon', *no overview*:='sinsign'. Peter admits that in the current application he is missing (cf. event) steps that he finds logical (cf. state).

Figure 11. A sample elicitation session (Peter (Pe) and Caroline (Ca) are clients, Robert (Ro) is elicitator)

1. (Pe) What, what I miss, ehh, in the current application ... is that ehh ... that I have an overview, ehh ... of the steps that I find most logical.
(Ca) Hmm, hmm (with approval)
2. (Pe) What already happened.
(Ca) Yes.
(Pe) And ehh ... what turned out to be the result.
3. (Ca) History.
4. (Pe) Yes, history ...
(Ca) Yes.
(Pe) ... went that, that, ehh, that description of the assignment to the ehh... employee?
5. (Pe) For, I think I see a check mark of that application ...
(Ca) Yes.
6. (Pe) But I do not get a confirmation of anything, of ehh ...
(Ca) No.
(Pe) whether it, ... it has been sent.
7. (Pe) And I also do not know if it has been worked out by the employee.
(Ro) Hmm, hmm.
(Pe) Do you, ehh...?
8. (Ca) No, no I only know it because they tell me, like "Hi, I consulted and reached agreement and ehh ... that ehh ... "
9. (Ca) Yes of course, in the end you can read it off from the date of the last update, but you do not get ...
(Pe) O.K.
10. (Ca) ... an automatic mail or, or a mutation. For it is impossible to see what has been changed in the brief.
(Pe) OK.
11. (Ca) So, I also miss the history, like ehh ... what was the initial assignment.

Figure 12. Elicitation by a team of participants (utterances are labelled by their sequence number as shown in Figure 11)

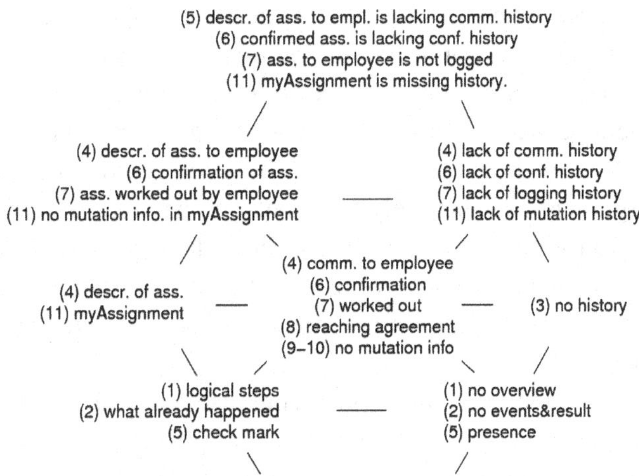

Figure 13. Nested conceptualization process

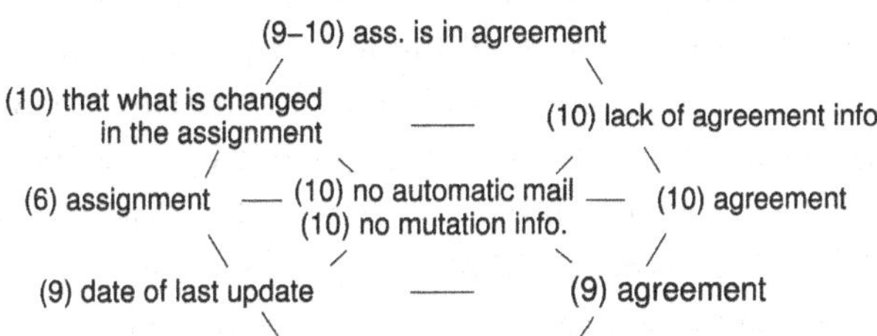

2. *what already happened*:='icon', *no events and result*:='sinsign'. Peter refines his judgment, by paraphrasing his earlier concepts.
3. *no history*:='legisign'. Finally, Caroline recognizes the habitual concept of '*no history*', in the instance ('*no overview*') and corresponding form ('*logical steps*') suggested by Peter.
4. *description of assignment*:='rheme'; *communication to employee*:='index'. Similarly so, Peter recognizes an abstract concept involved in the input problem: 'description of the assignment'. He also refers to 'communication' towards the '*employee*'. As that concept is not further explained in this session (nor in the encompassing text), it must refer to background information. From the fact that Peter is expressing his 'doubt' in a proposition about the input problem (*description of assignment to employee is lacking communication history*:= 'argument') we conclude that all less developed sign aspects must be generated as well, such as the 'lack of a communication history': *lack of communication history*:= 'symbol' and, the 'description of the assignment' communicated to the employee: *description of assignment to employee*:= 'dicent'.
5. *check mark*:='icon'; *presence*:='sinsign'. Peter is justifying his conclusion, by referring to a possible 'presence' (cf. effect) of 'check marks' (cf. state), in *myAssignment.*
6. *confirmation*:='index'. Peter's doubt is related to his question about the existence of a conventional logging of 'confirmations' and, corresponding 'confirmed assignments': *confirmation of assignment*:= 'dicent'; *lack of confirmation history*:= symbol'.

7. *working out*:='index'. Peter doubts, if logging is actually 'worked out' by the employee. The appearance of this background information enables a re-evaluation of all more developed interpretation moments: *assignment worked out by employee*:= 'dicent'; *lack of logging history*:= 'symbol'.
8. *reaching agreement*:='index'. Caroline admits having the same doubts as Peter has. She points out that the employee, not the application software is providing her with information about reaching agreement with the client. According to her, a lack of logging is what is meant by 'missing communication history'. Hereby she is referring to 'reaching agreement' as a nested process: *assignment is in agreement*:= 'argument', degenerately represented by a pointer: *reaching agreement*:= 'index', in the encompassing conceptualization process. By introducing a new 'index' expression, Caroline shows her interpretation of a common term involved in the generation of Peter's conclusion (note that a generation of the 'dicent' and 'symbol' positions is coordinated by the context ('index'), in the interpretation process).

9. and 10. Caroline is further elaborating on her conceptualization of the nested process. In 9. she pinpoints: date of last update:= 'icon'; agreement:= 'sinsign'. In 10. she introduces: no automatic mail, no mutation information:= 'index'; lack of agreement information:= 'symbol'. By making use of dependencies between the sign aspects and, the assumption that 'agreement' (cf. effect) must be related to an 'assignment', enables the nested conceptualization process to be completed: assignment:= 'rheme'; agreement:= 'legisign'; that what is changed in the assignment:= 'dicent'

11. *changing*:='index'.Through a proposition of the nested process, the element of a 'no mutation information' is inherited in the index position of the encompassing conceptualization process. The appearance of this information as an index expression, this time not as a sign of doubt, but as one of a hypothesis, triggers a re-evaluation of all more developed input sign aspects. Assuming 11. is providing a conclusion of the conceptualization process so far, it follows that the subject of the process Caroline is referring to (although not explicitly mentioning) must be the application program itself: *myAssignment*:= 'rheme'; *no mutation information in myAssignment*:= 'dicent'; *lack of mutation history*:= 'symbol'. She concludes: *myAssignment is missing history*:= 'argument'.

By introducing new conceptualizations for already existing ones that have identical sign aspects, the participants of the process make an attempt to coordinate their individual conceptualization processes with such processes by the others.

Discussion

The above example illustrates that conceptualization by a team of participants is congruent with our model. A preliminary analysis of the entire recorded text shows the possibility for a similar result (Klomp, 2008).

A practical conclusion that can be drawn from this experiment is the following. If the participant(s) of an elicitation process are all aware of the stages that their conceptualization process has to go through, then meta-level information about the process (what is the current stage and which stages do follow) can be used to control the process on object-level. In other words, the dependency structure of sign aspects can be used as pigeon-holes during the generation of a solution for a problem.

A rough analysis of the second experiment reveals that approximately 63% of the entire text is effectively contributing to concepts generated by the elicitation process. The remaining text is either redundant or not relevant for the problem in focus. In a workshop following the experiment the participants of the elicitation process have been instructed about the nine sign aspects. After a 15-20 minute introduction they were able to use the new information and comprehend their elicitation process from a higher-level perspective. This gives hope that efficiency on object-level could be improved by making use of meta-level information about the process. Further research is needed to unveil the effects of such a combined use of information in elicitation processes.

FUTURE RESEARCH DIRECTIONS

Our future research aims at the further development of our applied as well as of our theoretical results. This involves a more refined analysis of the data obtained by the Meno-experiment. We are in particular interested in the role played by goals and subgoals during problem solving and in the question how hierarchies of (sub)goals can be modeled and eventually used for a characterization of different conceptualization strategies. We also plan a new experiment that capitalizes on the use of object- and meta-level information in co-operative problem elicitation projects. The goal of this line of research is to validate our conjecture that a combined use of the two kinds of information can improve the efficiency of conceptualization.

In our theoretical research we try to expand our computational model to Peirce's most expanded, but unfinished sign classification. This classification is better known as the *Welby classification* because the ideas are made public mainly by Peirce's correspondence with lady Welby, a member of the Signific circle. The main difference between Peirce's 1903 classification, the classification we work with, and the Welby classification concerns the attention paid to quantification and modality in the latter. As a result the three sign relations, yielding nine sign aspects and ten sign types is expanded to ten relations, yielding thirty sign aspects and 66 possible sign types. Following the conclusion of Morand (2004) that the small classification is the kernel of the Welby classification, we try to show that on the basis of Peirce's nine sign aspects a computational model can be defined for the expanded classification as well.

CONCLUSION

We have shown that our model can be used to analyze concept formation in human problem solving, either individually or in teams. This means that the model is highly congruent with human information processing. This suggests that individual and team-wise conceptualization are in principle the same. Being a formal model, it can be used in a wide range of IA-applications such as computer supported tutoring and human-computer interfacing. A typical way to proceed would be to determine the goal that must be served and fill the sign aspects positions with what is needed to realize that goal. Note that in most cases, subordinate processes are needed. Such nested processes always appear through the index position that, by coordinating the interpretation moments, ties together the whole process of interpretation. However, more experiments are needed in order to explore the features of the model more extensively.

REFERENCES

Beynon, M., Russ, S., & McCarty, W. (2006). Human computing–modelling with meaning. [Oxford University Press.]. *Literary and Linguistic Computing, 21*(2), 141–157. doi:10.1093/llc/fql015

Breemen, A. van, & Sarbo, J. (2009). The machine in the ghost: The syntax of mind. *Signs – International Journal of Semiotics*, 135-184.

Bruner, J. (1966). *Toward a theory of instruction*. Harvard University Press.

Couwenberg, M. (2007). *Analyse van ontwikkeling van kenniselementen.* Master Thesis. Nijmegen, The Netherlands: Radboud Universiteit.

Delfos, M. (2000). *Luister je wel naar mij? Gespreksvoering met kinderen tussen vier en twaalf.* Amsterdam, The Netherlands: Uitgevereij SWP.

Engelbart, D. (1962). *Augmenting human intellect: A conceptual framework.* (Summary Report No. AFOSR-3233). Menlo Park, CA: Stanford Research Institute.

Gruber, T. (2008). Ontology. In *Encyclopedia of database systems*. Springer Verlag.

Huibers, T. (1996). *An axiomatic theory for information retrieval*. Doctoral dissertation, University of Nijmegen.

Klomp, E. (2008). *Conceptualisatie in een requirements development proces.* Master Thesis. Nijmegen, The Netherlands: Radboud Universiteit Nijmegen.

Krogstie, J., Sindre, G., & Jorgensen, H. (2006). Process models representing knowledge for action: A revised quality framework. *European Journal of Information Systems*, *15*, 91–102. doi:10.1057/palgrave.ejis.3000598

Magnani, L. (2001). *Abduction, reason, and science: Processes of discovery and explanation*. New York, NY: Kluwer Academic/Plenum Publishers. doi:10.1007/978-1-4419-8562-0

Margolis, E., & Laurence, S. (1999). *Concepts: Core readings*. Cambridge, MA: MIT Press.

Mead, G. H. (1938, 1972). *The philosophy of the act.* Chicago, IL: University of Chicago Press.

Morand, B. (2004). *Logique de la conception-figures de sémiotique générale d'après Charles S. Peirce. Collection L'ouverture philosophique, Paris, Éditions L'Harmattan. Peirce, C. (1931-58). Collected papers of Charles Sanders Peirce*. Cambridge, MA: Harvard University Press.

Plato. (1871). *Meno*. Translation of Benjamin Jowett Retrieved February 15, 2010, from http://classics.mit.edu/Plato/meno.html

Rigter, J. (1996). *Het palet van de psychologie, Stromingen en hun toepassingen in de hulpverlening.* Bussum, The Netherlands: Uitgeverij Coutinho.

Sarbo, J., & Farkas, J. (2002). A linearly complex model for knowledge representation. In U. Priss & D. Corbett (Eds.), *Conceptual structures: Integration and interface (ICCS'2002)* (Vol. 2193, pp. 20–33). Borovets, Bulgaria: Springer Verlag.

Sarbo, J., & Farkas, J. (2003). Logica Utens. In de Moor, A., & Ganter, B. (Eds.), *Using conceptual structures* (pp. 43–56). Dresden, Germany: Shaker Verlag.

Sarbo, J., Farkas, J., & van Breemen, A. (2007). Natural grammar. In Gudwin, R., & Queiroz, J. (Eds.), *Semiotics and intelligent system development* (pp. 152–175). Hersey, PA: Idea Group Publishing.

Smith, E., Osherson, D., Rips, L., & Keans, M. (1988). Combining proto-types: A selective modification model. *Cognitive Science, 12*(4), 485–527. doi:10.1207/s15516709cog1204_1

Wittgenstein, L. (1922). *Tractatus logico-philosophicus*. London, UK: Routledge and Kegan Paul.

Wittgenstein, L. (1971). *Philosophische Untersuchungen*. Frankfurt, Germany: Suhrkamp.

ADDITIONAL READING

Bergman, M. (2004). *Fields of Signification; Explorations in Charles S. Peirce's Theory of Signs* (No. 6). PhD Thesis, Philosophical Studies from the University of Helsinki.

Bush, V. (1945). As We May Think. *Atlantic Monthly, 176*(1), 1–8.

Chandler, D. (2002). *Semiotics: the basics*. London: Routledge. doi:10.4324/9780203166277

Davis, R., Shrobe, H., & Solovits, P. (2009). What is a knowledge representation? *AI Magazine, 14*(1), 17–33.

Deacon, T. (1997). What makes the human brain different? *Annual Review of Anthropology, 26*, 337–357. doi:10.1146/annurev.anthro.26.1.337

Debrock, G. (1998). Peirce's categories and the Importance of Secondness. In J. van Brakel & M. van Heerden (Eds.), Proc. of the International Symposium on Peirce, *C.S. Peirce: Categories to Constantinople*. Leuven, Belgium: Leuven University Press.

Fitzgerald, J. (1966). *Peirce's Theory of Signs as Foundation for Pragmatics*. The Hague: Mouton.

Fodor, J. (1998). *Concepts: Where cognitive science went wrong*. Oxford: Clarendon Press.

Gärdenfors, P. (2000). *Conceptual spaces: the geometry of thought*. Cambridge, MA: The MIT press.

Goldstone, R. L. J. S., D. Landy. (2008). *A well grounded education: The role of perception in science and mathematics*. In Symbols, embodiment, and meaning (pp. 327-355). Oxford Press.

Harnad, S. (1987). *Categorical Perception: The groundwork of cognition*. Cambridge: Cambridge University Press.

Hookway, C. (1985). *Peirce* London: Routledge and Kagan Paul plc.

Jackendoff, R. (1983). *Semantics and Cognition*. Cambridge, MA: The MIT press.

Kaptelinin, V., & Nardi, B. (2006). *Acting with Technology: Activity Theory and Interaction Design*. Cambridge, MA: The MIT press.

Liszka, J. (1996). *A General Introduction to the Semeiotic of Charles Sanders Peirce*. Bloomington, Indianapolis: Indiana University Press.

Liu, K. (2000). *Semiotics in information systems engineering*. Cambridge, UK: Cambridge University Press. doi:10.1017/CBO9780511543364

Mackay, D. (1987). *The organization of perception and action: A theory for language and other cognitive skills*. New York: Springer Verlag.

Mayhew, D., & Siebert, D. (2004). Ontology: The discipline and the tool. In G. Buchel, B. Klein, & T. Roth-Berghofer (Eds.), *Proceedings of the first workshop on philosophy and informatics* (pp. 57-64). Cologne (Germany).

McCarty, W. (2005). *Humanities computing. Houndmills*. Basingstoke: Palgrace Macmillan. doi:10.1057/9780230504219

Penrose, R. (1989). *The Emperor's New Mind*. Oxford, UK: Oxford University Press.

Ransdell, J. (2003). *The relevance of Peircean semiotic to computational intelligence augmentation*. S.E.E.D. Journal (Semiotics, Evolution, Energy, and Development), 3, (pp. 5-36).

Rosch, E. (1978). Principles of of categorization. In Rosch, E., & Lloyd, B. (Eds.), *Cognition and categorization*. Hillsdale, NJ: Lawrence Erlbaum.

Sarbo, J., & Farkas, J. (2002). A linearly complex model for knowledge representation. In U.Priss & D. Corbett (Eds.), *Conceptual structures: Integration and interfaces (ICCS'2002)* (Vol. 2193, pp. 20{33). Borovets (Bulgaria): Springer Verlag.

Short, T. L. (2004). The Development of Peirce's Theory of Signs. In Misak, C. J. (Ed.), *The Cambridge compendium to Peirce*. Cambridge, UK: Cambridge University press. doi:10.1017/CCOL0521570069.009

Short, T. L. (2007). *Peirce's Theory of Signs*. Cambridge, UK: Cambridge University press. doi:10.1017/CBO9780511498350

Skagestad, P. (1993). *Thinking with Machines: Intelligence augmentation*, Evolutionary Epistemology, and Semiotic. *Journal of Social and Evolutionary Systems, 16*(2), 157–180. doi:10.1016/1061-7361(93)90026-N

Skagestad, P. (1996). The Minds Machines: the Turing Machine, the Memex, and the Personal Computer. *Semiotica, 111*(3/4), 217–243. doi:10.1515/semi.1996.111.3-4.217

Solso, R. (1988). *Cognitive Psychology*. New York: Harcourt Brace Jovanovich.

Souza, C. (2005). *The semiotic engineering of human-computer interaction (acting with technology)*. Cambridge, MA: MIT Press.

Sowa, J. (2000). *Knowledge Representation: Logical, Philosophical, and Computational Foundations*. Pacific Grove, CA: Brooks Cole Publishing Co.

Thagard, P. (1993). *Computational Philosophy of Science*. Cambridge, MA: MIT Press.

Thomson, E. F. V. d, & Rosch, E. (1991). *The Embodied Mind*. Cambridge (MA): MIT Press.

van Breemen, A., & Sarbo, J. (2007). Sign Processes and the Sheets of Semeiosis (Ss). In K. Liu (Ed.), *10th International Conference on Complexity in Organisational and Technological Systems (ICOS)* (pp. 89-98. Sheffield (UK).

Zeman, J. (1977). Peirce's Theory of Signs. In Seboek, T. A. (Ed.), *A Perfusion of Signs*. Bloomington: Indiana University Press.

KEY TERMS AND DEFINITIONS

Intelligence Augmentation: A field of research aiming at increasing the capability of a man to approach a complex problem situation, to gain comprehension to suit his particular needs, and to derive solutions to problems.

Interpretation: A translation of input to an informed response, by an (interpreting) agent.

Ontology: The study of being qua being (philosophy). In computer science, ontology refers to (i) an inventory of all types of entities in a domain, (ii) an inventory of the mode of being of the representational primitives.

Problem Elicitation: A process that tries to control co-operative interpretation in complex situations.

Process: Can be characterized by three conditions: (i) one event initiates a sequence and another terminates it, (ii) every event that contributes to the sequences yielding the terminating event is regarded as part of the process and (iii) the terminating event governs which events make up the sequence.

Semiotics: A general theory of all possible kinds of signs, their modes of signification, of denotation, and of information; and their whole behavior and properties, so far as these are not accidental.

Sign: Traditionally equated with what we know as the sign vehicle (the sign as an object). In Peircean semiotics the concept of sign is much more encompassing since the relation of the 'vehicle' with its object(s) and interpretant(s) are included.

ENDNOTES

1 See: http://tomgruber.org/writing/ontology-definition-2007.htm

2 We obtained the association of the category Firstness with being, Secondness with existence and Thirdness with reality from C. Schuyt (personal communication, 1991)

Chapter 14
Data Discovery Approaches for Vague Spatial Data

Frederick E. Petry
Naval Research Laboratory, USA

ABSTRACT

This chapter focuses on the application of the discovery of association rules in approaches vague spatial databases. The background of data mining and uncertainty representations using rough set and fuzzy set techniques is provided. The extensions of association rule extraction for uncertain data as represented by rough and fuzzy sets is described. Finally, an example of rule extraction for both types of uncertainty representations is given.

INTRODUCTION

Data mining or knowledge discovery generally refers to a variety of techniques that have developed in the fields of databases, machine learning (Alpaydin, 2004) and pattern recognition (Han & Kamber, 2006). The intent is to uncover useful patterns and associations from large databases. For complex data such as that found in spatial databases (Shekar & Chawla, 2003) the problem of data discovery is more involved (Lu et al., 1993; Miller & Han, 2009).

Spatial data has traditionally been the domain of geography with various forms of maps as the standard representation. With the advent of computerization of maps, geographic information systems (GIS) have come to fore with spatial databases storing the underlying point, line and area structures needed to support GIS (Longley et al., 2001). A major difference between data mining in ordinary relational databases (Elmasri & Navathe, 2010) and in spatial databases is that attributes of the neighbors of some object of interest may have an influence on the object and therefore have to be considered as well. The explicit location and extension of spatial objects define implicit relations of spatial neighborhood (such

DOI: 10.4018/978-1-60960-551-3.ch014

as topological, distance and direction relations), which are used by spatial data mining algorithms (Ester et al 2000).

Additionally when wish to consider vagueness or uncertainty in the spatial data mining process (Burrough & Frank 1996; Zhang & Goodchild, 2002), an additional level of difficulty is added. In this chapter we describe one of the most common data mining approaches, discovery of association rules, for spatial data for which we consider uncertainty in the extraction rules as represented by both fuzzy set and rough set techniques.

BACKGROUND

Data Mining

Although we are primarily interested here in specific algorithms of knowledge discovery, we will first review the overall process of data mining (Tan, Steinbach & Kumar, 2005). The initial steps are concerned with preparation of data, including data cleaning intended to resolve errors and missing data and integration of data from multiple heterogeneous sources. Next are the steps needed to prepare for actual data mining. These include the selection of the specific data relevant to the task and the transformation of this data into a format required by the data mining approach. These steps are sometimes considered to be those in the development of a data warehouse (Golfarelli & Rizzi, 2009), i.e., an organized format of data available for various data mining tools. There are a wide variety of specific knowledge discovery algorithms that have been developed (Han & Kamber, 2006). These discover patterns that can then be evaluated based on some interestingness measure used to prune the huge number of available patterns. Finally as true for any decision aid system, an effective user interface with visualization / alternative representations must be developed for the presentation of the discovered knowledge.

Specific data mining algorithms can be considered as belonging to two categories - descriptive and predictive data mining. In the descriptive category are class description, association rules and classification. Class description can either provide a characterization or generalization of the data or comparisons between data classes to provide class discriminations. Association rules are the main focus of this chapter and correspond to correlations among the data items (Hipp et al., 2000). They are often expressed in rule form showing attribute-value conditions that commonly occur at the same time in some set of data. An association rule of the form $X \rightarrow Y$ can be interpreted as meaning that the tuples in the database that satisfy the condition X also are "likely" to satisfy Y, so that the "likely" implies this is not a functional dependency in the formal database sense. Finally, a classification approach analyzes the training data (data whose class membership is known) and constructs a model for each class based on the features in the data. Commonly, the outputs generated are decision trees or sets of classification rules. These can be used both for the characterization of the classes of existing data and to allow the classification of data in the future, and so can also be considered predictive.

Predictive analysis is also a very developed area of data mining. One very common approach is clustering (Mishra et al., 2004). Clustering analysis identifies the collections of data objects that are similar to each other. The similarity metric is often a distance function given by experts or appropriate users. A good clustering method produces high quality clusters to yield low inter-cluster similarity and high intra-cluster similarity. Prediction techniques are used to predict possible missing data values or distributions of values of some attributes in a set of objects. First, one must find the set of attributes relevant to the attribute of interest and then predict a distribution of values based on the set of data similar to the selected objects. There are a large variety of techniques used, including regression analysis, correlation analysis, genetic algorithms and neural networks to mention a few.

Finally, a particular case of predictive analysis is time-series analysis. This technique considers a large set of time-based data to discover regularities and interesting characteristics (Shasha & Zhu., 2004). One can search for similar sequences or subsequences, then mine sequential patterns, periodicities, trends and deviations.

Uncertainty Representations

In this section we overview the uncertainty representations we will use for data discovery in spatial data, specifically rough sets and fuzzy set similarity relationships.

Rough Set Theory

Rough set theory, introduced by Pawlak (Pawlak, 1984; Polkowski, 2002) is a technique for dealing with uncertainty and for identifying cause-effect relationships in databases as a form of database learning. Rough sets involve the following:

U is the universe, which cannot be empty,
R is the indiscernability relation, or equivalence relation,
A = (U,R), an ordered pair, is called an approximation space,
$[x]_R$ denotes the equivalence class of R containing x, for any element $x \in U$, elementary sets in A - the equivalence classes of R, definable set in A - any finite union of elementary sets in A.

Therefore, for any given approximation space defined on some universe U and having an equivalence relation R imposed upon it, U is partitioned into equivalence classes called elementary sets which may be used to define other sets in A. Given that $X \subseteq U$, X can be defined in terms of definable sets in A as below:

lower approximation of X in A is the set $\underline{R}X = \{x \in U \mid [x]_R \subseteq X\}$
upper approximation of X in A is the set $\overline{R}X = \{x \in U \mid [x]_R \cap X \neq \varnothing\}$.

Another way to describe the set approximations is as follows. Given the upper and lower approximations $\overline{R}X$ and $\underline{R}X$, of X a subset of U, the R-positive region of X is $POS_R(X) = \underline{R}X$, the R-negative region of X is $NEG_R(X) = U - \overline{R}X$, and the boundary or R-borderline region of X is $BNR(X) = \overline{R}X - \underline{R}X$. X is called R-definable if and only if $\underline{R}X = \overline{R}X$. Otherwise, $\underline{R}X \neq \overline{R}X$ and X is rough with respect to R. In Figure 1 the universe U is partitioned into equivalence classes denoted by the squares. Those elements in the lower approximation of X, $POS_R(X)$, are denoted with the letter P and elements in the R-negative region by the letter N. All other classes belong to the boundary region of the upper approximation.

Figure 1. Example of a Rough Set X

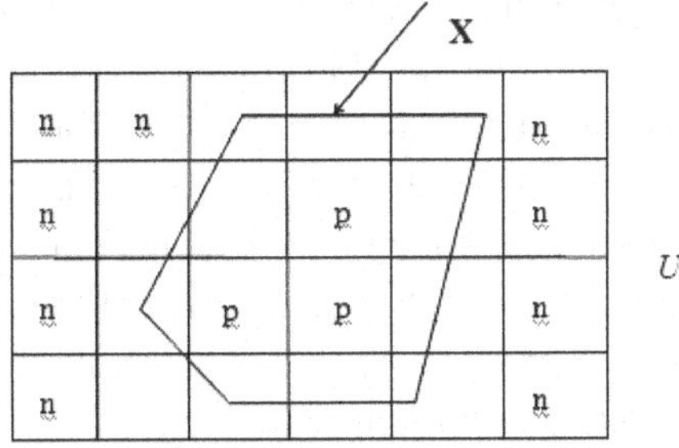

Fuzzy Set Theory

Fuzzy set theory is approach in which the elements of a set belong to the set to varying degrees known as membership degrees. Conventionally we can specify a set C by its characteristic function, $Char_C(x)$. If U is the universal set from which values of C are taken, then we can represent C as

$$C = \{x \mid x \in U \text{ and } Char_C(x) = 1\}$$

This is the representation for a crisp or non-fuzzy set. For an ordinary set C the range of $Char_C(x)$ are just the two values: {0, 1}. However for a fuzzy set A we have a range of the entire interval [0,1].

That is, for a fuzzy set the characteristic function takes on all values between 0 and 1 and not just the discrete values of 0 or 1 representing the binary choice for membership in a conventional crisp set. For a fuzzy set the characteristic function is often called the membership function and denoted $\mu_A(x)$.

One fuzzy set concept that we employ particularly in databases is the similarity relation, S(x, y), denoted also as xSy. For given domain D this is a mapping of every pair of values in the particular domain onto the unit interval [0,1], which reflects the level of similarity between them. A similarity relation is reflexive and symmetric as a traditional identity relation. However, special forms of transitivity are used So a similarity relation has the following three properties, for x, y, z ∈ D (Zadeh, 1970; Buckles & Petry, 1982):

1. **Reflexive:** $s_D(x, x) = 1$
2. **Symmetric:** $s_D(x, y) = s_D(y, x)$
3. **Transitive:** $s_D(x, z) \geq Max_y(Min[s_D(x, y), s_D(y, z)])$: (T1)

This particular max-min form of transitivity is known as T1 transitivity. Another useful form is T2, also known as max-product:

3'. Transitive: $s_D(x, z) = Max_y([s_D(x, y) * s_D(y, z)])$: (T2)

where * is arithmetic multiplication. An example of a similarity relation satisfying T2 transitivity is:

$$s_D(x, y) = e^{-\beta * |y-x}$$

where β > 0 is an arbitrary constant and x, y ∈ D.

So we can see that are different aspects of uncertainty dealt with in fuzzy set or rough set representations. The major rough set concepts of interest are the use of an indiscernibility relation to partition domains into equivalence classes and the concept of lower and upper approximation regions to allow the distinction between certain and possible, or partial, inclusion in a rough set. The indiscernibility relation allows us to group items based on some definition of 'equivalence' as it relates to the application domain.

A complementary approach to rough set uncertainty management is fuzzy set theory. Instead of the "yes-maybe-no" approach to belonging to a set, a more gradual membership value approach is used. An object belongs to a fuzzy set to some degree. This contrasts with the more discrete representation of uncertainty from indiscernibility relations or rough set theory

VAGUE QUERYING FOR SPATIAL DATA MINING

Here we describe the management of uncertainty in the data-mining query. Such a query develops the relation or table on which to apply the data mining algorithm is applied similar to the approach of GeoMiner (Koperski & Han, 1995; Han et al., 1997). The issue of concern is the form of the resultant relation obtained from the querying involving the spatial data and the representation of uncertainty. We will describe this for both fuzzy set and rough set approaches..

A crucial aspect of the query for the formulation of the data over which the data mining algorithm will operate is the selection of a spatial predicate that identifies the specific spatial region or area of interest (AOI). This is closely related to the property that causes objects of interest to cluster in space, which is the so-called first law of geography: "Everything is related to everything else but nearby things are more related than distant things" (Tobler, 1979). A common choice for this is some distance metric such as a NEAR predicate; however, other spatial predicates such as the topological relationships contains or intersects could also be used.

Let us consider an SQL form of a query:

```
SELECT Attributes A, B
                    FROM Relation X
                    WHERE
                         (X.A = α and NEAR (X.B, β))
                    AT Threshold Levels = M, N
```

Since we are considering approximate matching of the spatial we must specify for each of such predicates the threshold degree of matching below which the data will not appear in the resultant relation.

Fuzzy Set Querying Approach

To match the values in the query, we have for the attribute A, a spatially related attribute, a similarity table of its domain values, and for B, a spatial attribute such as location, the NEAR predicate can be evaluated. Since these values may not be exact matches, the intermediate resultant relation R_{int} will have to maintain the degree of matching. The final query results are chosen based on the values specified in the threshold clause. Results for attribute A are based on the first value M and similarly those for B

Table 1. The intermediate result of the SQL form query

RES_{int}	
A	**B**
$<a_1, \mu_{a1}>$	$<b_1, \mu_{b1}>$
$<a_2, \mu_{a2}>$	$<b_2, \mu_{b2}>$
$<a_3, \mu_{a3}>$	$<b_3, \mu_{b3}>$
……	……
$<a_i, \mu_{ai}>$	$<b_i, \mu_{bi}>$

are based on N. The level values are typically user specified as linguistic terms that correspond to such values (Petry, 1996). The intermediate step of the query evaluation is shown below as

In the table a_i is a value of A from X, and μ_{ai} is the similarity, *sim*, of a_i and α

$$\mu_{ai} = sim\ (a_i, \alpha)$$

For example, let the domain be soil types and if a_i = loam and α = peat then the similarity might be

sim (loam, peat) = 0.75

and if the threshold level value N in the query were lower than.75, we could possibly retain this in the final relation as the value and membership

< loam, 0.75 >

Similarly for the location attribute, where b_i = (13.1, 74.5) and β = (12.9, 74.1), we might have

< (13.1, 74.5), 0.78 >

if the coordinates (in some measure) are "near" by a chosen fuzzy distance measure

$$\mu_{near} = \text{NEAR}\ ((13.1, 74.5), (12.9, 74.1)) = 0.78.$$

Figure 2 shows an example of a fuzzy NEAR function that might be used here to represent:

" within a distance of about 5 kilometers or less."

Such a fuzzy function can be represented generally parameterized by inflection points, a,b, on a membership function F_{μ} (x, a, b) as shown below:

Figure 2. Fuzzy Membership Function for Distance

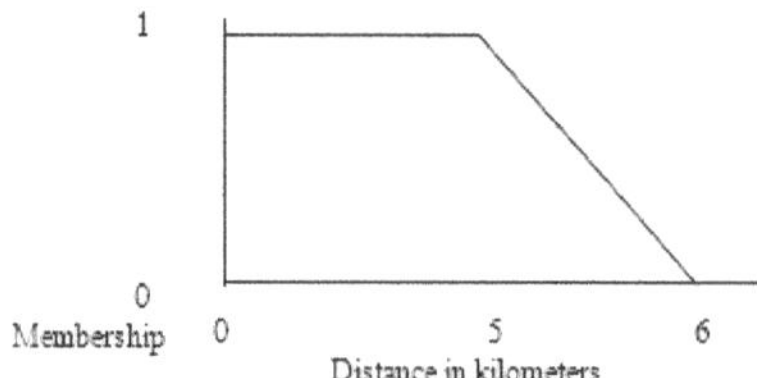


```
        F μ (x, a, b) =
1.          1                  x ≤ a
2.        (b-x) / (b-a)            a ≤ x < b
3.          0                x ≥ b
```

Specifically then using this representation, the fuzzy membership function in Figure 2 is:

$F_{\mu}(x, 5, 6)$

Now in the final resultant relation, rather than retaining these individual memberships, the data mining algorithm will be simplified if we formulate a combined membership value. Thus the final result is obtained by evaluating each tuple relative to the threshold values and assigning a tuple membership value based on the individual attribute memberships combined by the commonly used min operator. So the tuple $< a_i, b_i, \mu_t >$ will appear in the final result relation **RES** if and only if

$(\mu_{ai} > M)$ and $(\mu_{bi} > N)$

and the tuple membership is

$\mu_t = \min(\mu_{ai}, \mu_{bi})$

If the rows (tuples) 1 and 3 from R_{int} are such that the memberships for both columns are above their respective thresholds, then these are retained. However for tuple 2, let it be the case that $\mu_{a2} > M$, but the second attribute's membership is $\mu_{b2} < N$. Then this tuple will not appear in the final result relation

Rough Set Querying Approach

For a rough set approach predicates such as NEAR will be formulated as rough selection predicates as previously done in rough querying of crisp databases (Beaubouef & Petry, 1994). Spatial predicates for the rule discovery query can be made more realistic and effective by a consideration of vague regions and their spatial relationships. Consider the NEAR predicate in the query of the previous example. Several possibilities exist for defining predicates for such a spatial relationship in which application dependency of terms and parameters have to be taken into account (Clementini & DeFelice, 1997). Although the definition of "near" is subjective and determined by a specialist investigating the data and doing the actual data mining, we can still make some general observations about nearness that should apply in all cases.

Table 2. The final result relation of the SQL format query using threshold values

RES		
A	**B**	μ_t
a_1	b_1	Min ($\mu_{a1,}$ μ_{b1})
a_3	b_3	Min ($\mu_{a3,}$ μ_{b3})
......	......	
a_i	b_i	Min ($\mu_{ai,}$ μ_{bi})

Figure 3. Overlap of positive regions

If the lower approximations of two vague regions X and Y intersect (Beaubouef & Petry, 2004), they are definitely near, i.e.

$\underline{R}X \cap \underline{R}Y \neq \varnothing$

This can be restated as: if the positive regions of the two vague regions overlap, then they are considered near. In this case, the positions of the upper approximation regions are irrelevant. Figure 3 illustrate several of these cases: Let region X be the first "egg" (dashed line) and Y second (dotted line) in each pair. The "yolk of the egg" is lower approximation and the upper approximation is the outer part. So for example in the figure on the left the yolks – positive regions- completely overlap. The other two show some degree of overlaps of the positive regions illustrating the nearness of X and Y.

We should also consider the possibility that two vague regions are near if their lower approximations are within a prescribed distance of each other. This might be represented in several ways including measuring the distances of the centroids of the certain regions, using the distances between minimum bounding rectangles, or by simply comparing the distances between all points on the edges of the boundaries. For example, two towns might not be overlapping if they are separated from each other by a river. However, we would still want to say that they are near based on the ground distance measured between them. Depending on the application there could be different distance measures. If the distance measure was road distance and there were no bridges or ferries across the river in say, under than 20 kilometers, we would no longer consider the towns to be near.

Incorporating some of these points discussed, we can give a more general form of a NEAR predicate as needed for both the lower and then upper approximation:

```
Positive region (lower approximation)
NEAR (X,Y)   = True            if RX ∩ RY ≠ Ø,  (h =1) OR
                             if DISTANCE (RX,RY) < (N1),  (h = c)
```

```
 Boundary region
NEAR (X,Y)   = True          if DISTANCE (RX,RY) < (N2), (h=1) OR
                          if RX ∩ RY ≠ Ø, (h = d)
```

DISTANCE would have been defined previously based on various criteria as we have discussed. N1 and N2 are the specific distance thresholds entered by the user. The term h can be considered as a certainty factor for the matching in the predicate, with c and d being user/expert provided parameters. This factor could then be maintained for each tuple in the query result **RES** and act as a weighting factor for the rough support count for each value in apriori algorithm to be described in the next section. There could also be additional terms added to the NEAR predicate depending on the application. For example if one wanted to be sure to include the possible regions' (upper approximations) distance as a factor for inclusion in the boundary result of the query then we could include the term:

```
 If DISTANCE(RX, RY) < (N3), (h = e)
```

The result of a query is then:

RES = { $\underline{R}$T, $\overline{R}$T }

$\overline{R}$

ASSOCIATION RULES

Association rules capture the idea of certain data items commonly occurring together and have been often considered in the analysis of a "market basket" of purchases. For example, a delicatessen retailer might analyze the previous year's sales and observe that of all purchases 30% were of both cheese and crackers and, for any of the sales that included cheese, 75% also included crackers. Then it is possible to conclude a rule of the form:

Cheese → Crackers

This rule is said to have a 75% degree of confidence and a 30% degree of support. A retailer could use such rules to aid in the decision process about issues such as placement of items in the store, marketing options such as advertisements and discounts and so forth. In a spatial data context an analysis of various aspects of a certain region might produce a rule associating soils and vegetation such as:

Sandy soil → Scrub cover

that could be used for planning and environmental decision makers.

This particular form of data mining is largely based on the Apriori algorithm developed by Agrawal (Agrawal et al 1993). Let a database of possible data items be

$D = \{d_1, d_2, \ldots d_n\}$

and the relevant set of transactions (sales, query results, etc.) are

$R = \{T_1, T_2, \ldots\}$

where $T_i \subseteq D$. We are interested in discovering if there is a relationship between two sets of items (called itemsets) X_j, X_k; X_j, $X_k \subseteq D$. For such a relationship to be determined, the entire set of transactions in R must be examined and a count made of the number of transactions containing these sets, where a transaction T_i contains X_m if $X_m \subseteq T_i$. This count, called the support count of X_m, $SC_R(X_m)$, will be appropriately modified in the case of fuzzy set and rough set representations..

There are then two measures used in determining rules: the percentage of T_i's in R that contain both X_j and X_k (i.e. $X_j \cup X_k$) - called the support s if T_i contains X_j then T_i also contains X_k – called the *confidence* c.

The support and confidence can be interpreted as probabilities:

$s – \text{Prob}(X_j \cup X_k)$ and

$c – \text{Prob}(X_k \mid X_j)$

We assume the system user has provided minimum values for these in order to generate only sufficiently interesting rules. A rule whose support and confidence exceeds these minimums is called a strong rule.

The overall process for finding strong association rules can be organized as a 3 step process:

1. Determine frequent itemsets –commonly done with variations of the Apriori algorithm
2. Extract strong association rules from the frequent itemsets
3. Assess generated rules with interestingness measures.

The first step is to compute the frequent itemsets F which are the subsets of items from D, such as {d2, d4, d5}. The support count SC_R of each such subset must be computed and the frequent itemsets are then only those whose support count exceeds the minimum support count specified. This is just the product of the minimum support specified and the number of transactions or tuples in R. For a large database this generation of all frequent itemsets can be very computationally expensive. The Apriori algorithm is an influential algorithm that makes this more computationally feasible. It basically uses an iterative level-wise search where sets of k items are used to consider sets at the next level of k+1 items. The Apriori property is used to prune the search as seen in the discussion below.

After the first and more complex step of determining the frequent itemsets, the strong association rules can easily be generated. The first step is to enumerate all subsets of each frequent itemset F: f_1, f_2, …f_i… Then for each f_i, calculate the ratio of the support count of F and f_i, i.e.

$SC_R(F) / SC_R(f_i)$

Note that all subsets of a frequent itemset are frequent (Apriori property) and so the support counts of each subset will have been computed in the process of finding all frequent itemsets. This greatly reduces the amount of computation needed.

If this ratio is greater than the minimum confidence specified then we can output the rule

$f_i \rightarrow \{ F - f_i \}$

The set of rules generated may then be further pruned by a number of correlation and heuristic measures.

Extensions to Fuzzy and Rough Spatial Association Rules

Fuzzy Rules

We are now prepared to consider how to extend approaches to generating association rules to process the form of the fuzzy data we have developed for the spatial data query. Fuzzy data mining for generating association rules has been considered by a number of researchers. There are approaches using the SETM (Set-oriented mining) algorithm (Shu et al., 2001) and other techniques (Bosc & Pivert, 2001) but most have been based on the important Apriori algorithm. Extensions have included fuzzy set approaches to quantitative data (Zhang, 1999; Kuok et al., 1998), hierarchies or taxonomies (Chen et al., 2000; Lee, 2001), weighted rules (Gyenesei, 2000) and interestingness measures (de Graaf et al., 2001). Our extensions most closely follow that of Chen (Chen et al., 2000).

Recall that in order to generate frequent itemsets, we must count the number of transactions T_j that support an itemset X_j. In the ordinary Apriori algorithm one simply counts the occurrence of a value as 1 if in the set, or if not in the set - 0. Here, since we have obtained from the query a membership degree for the values in the transaction, we must modify the support count SC_R. To achieve this we will use the Σ Count operator which extends the ordinary concept of set cardinality to fuzzy sets (Yen & Langari, 1999).

Let A be a fuzzy set, then the cardinality of A is obtained by summation of the membership values of the elements of A:

$$\text{Card}(A) = \Sigma \text{ Count}(A) = \Sigma \mu_A(y_i);\ y_i \in A$$

Using this the fuzzy support count for the set X_j becomes:

$$FSC_R (X_j) = \Sigma \text{ Count } (X_j) = \Sigma\mu_{T_i} ;\ X_j \subseteq T_i$$

Note that membership of T_i is included in the count only all of the values of the itemset X_j are included in the transaction, i.e. it is a subset of the transaction.

Finally to produce the association rules from the set of relevant data R retrieved from the spatial database, we will provide our extension to deal with the resulting frequent itemsets. For the purposes of generating a rule such as $X_j \rightarrow X_k$ we can now extend the ideas of fuzzy support and confidence as

$$FS = FSC_R (X_j \cup X_k) / | R |$$
$$FC = FSC_R (X_j \cup X_k) / FSC_R (X_j)$$

Rough Set Rules

In this case since the query result R is a rough set, we must again modify the support count SC_T. So we define the rough support count, RSC_R, for the set X_j, to count differently in the upper and lower approximations:

$$RSC_R\ (X_j) = \Sigma\ W\ (X_j);\ X_j \subseteq T_i$$

$$\text{where} \quad W\ (X_j) = \begin{cases} 1 \text{ if } T_i\ \varepsilon \underline{R}T \\ a \text{ if } T_i\ \varepsilon\ \overline{R}T,\ 0 < a < 1. \end{cases}$$

The value, a, can be a subjective value obtained from the user depending on relative assessment of the roughness of the query result T. For the data mining example of the next section we could simply choose a neutral default value of a = ½. Note that W (X_j) is included in the summation only if all of the values of the itemset X_j are included in the transaction, i.e. it is a subset of the transaction.

Finally as in the fuzzy set case above we have rough support and confidence as follows:

$$RS = RSC_R\ (X_j \cup X_k) / |\ R\ |$$

$$RC = RSC_R\ (X_j \cup X_k) / RSC_R\ (X_j)$$

SPATIAL DATA MINING EXAMPLE

We now consider a data mining example involving a spatial database that could be used, for example, in industrial plant location planning. Here we would like to discover relationships between attributes that are relevant for providing guidance in the planning and selection of a suitable plant site. There may be several possible counties in the region that are under consideration for plant location and we will assume that smaller cities are of interest for this particular industry's operation since they would have sufficient infrastructure, but none of the congestion and other problems typically associated with larger cities. Transportation (airfields, highways, etc.), water sources for plant operation (rivers and lakes) and terrain information (soils, drainage, etc.), in and to an extent of about five kilometers surrounding the city are of particular interest for the site selection.

Fuzzy Spatial Representation

The first step we must then take to discovering rules that may be of interest in a given county is to formulate an SQL query as we have described before using the fuzzy function NEAR (Figure 2) to represent those objects within about 5 kilometers of the cities. We will use the fuzzy function of Figure 4 to select the cities with a small population.

```
SELECT City C, Road R, Railroad RR, Airstrip A, Terrain T
FROM County 1
WHERE ([NEAR (C.loc, R.loc), NEAR (C.loc, RR.loc),
  NEAR (C.loc, A.loc), NEAR (C.loc, T.loc)]
and C.pop = Small)
AT Threshold Levels =.80,.75,.70
```

Figure 4. Fuzzy Membership Function for Small City

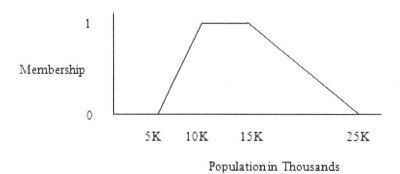

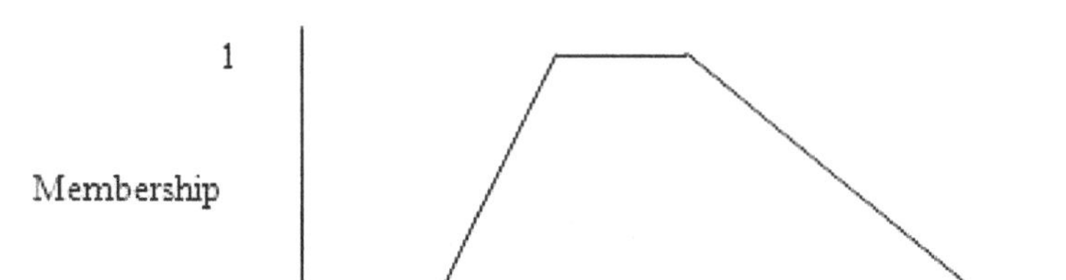

Table 3. The final result of the example query – **R**

City	Roads	Railroads	Airstrips	Terrain	μ_t
A	Hwy.10	RRx	None	Good	0.89
B	{Hwy.5,Hwy.10}	None	A2	Fair	0.79
F	Hwy.6	RRx	None	Good	0.92
...	...	...	...	...	...

We evaluate for each city in a selected county the locations of roads, railroads and airstrips using the NEAR fuzzy function. The terrain attribute value is produced by evaluation of various factors such as average soil conditions (e.g. firm, marshy), relief (e.g. flat, hilly), coverage (fields, woods), etc. These subjective evaluations are then combined into one membership value which is used to provide a linguistic label based on fuzzy functions for these. Note that the evaluation for terms such as "good" can be context dependent. For the purpose of development of a plant an open and flat terrain is suitable whereas for a recreational park a woody and hilly situation would be desirable.

Each attribute value in the intermediate relation then has a degree of membership. The three threshold levels in the query are specified for the NEAR, Small and the terrain memberships. The final relation **R** is formulated based on the thresholds and the overall tuple membership computed as previously described.

In **R** the value "None" indicates that for the attribute no value was found NEAR – within the five kilometers. For such values no membership value is assigned and so μ_t is just based on the non-null attribute values in the particular tuple.

Now in the next step of data mining we generate the frequent itemsets from **R** using the fuzzy support count. At the first level for itemsets of size 1(k=1), airstrips are not found since they do not occur often enough in **R** to yield a fuzzy support count above the minimum support count that was pre-specified. The level k=2 itemsets are generated from the frequent level 1 itemsets. Here only two of these possibilities exceed the minimum support and none above this level, i.e. k=3 or higher. This gives us the following table of frequent itemsets:

From this table of frequent itemsets we can extract various rules and their confidence. Rules will not be output unless they are strong – satisfy both minimum support and confidence. A rule produced from a frequent itemset satisfies minimum support by the manner in which frequent itemsets are generated, so

Table 4. The frequent itemsets found for the example.

k	Frequent Itemsets	Fuzzy Support Count
1	{Road Near}	11.3
1	{Good Terrain}	10.5
1	{Railroad Near}	8.7
2	{Road Near, Good Terrain}	9.5
2	{Good Terrain, Railroad Near}	7.2

it only necessary to use the fuzzy support counts from the table to compute the confidence. The "small city" clause that will appear in all extracted rules arises because this was the general condition that selected all of the tuples that appeared in query result R from which the frequent itemsets were generated.

Let us assume for this case that the minimum confidence specified was 85%. So, for example, one possible rule that can be extracted from the frequent itemsets in Table 4 is:

If C is a small <u>city</u> and has good <u>terrain</u> nearby then there is a <u>road</u> nearby with 90% confidence.

Since the fuzzy support count for {Good Terrain} is 10.5 and the level 2 itemset {Road Near, Good Terrain} has a fuzzy support count of 9.5, the confidence for the rule is 9.5 / 10.5 or 90%. Since this is above the minimum confidence of 85%, this rule is strong and will be an output of the data mining process.

If we had specified a lower minimum confidence such as 80% we could extract (among others) the rule:

If C is a small <u>city</u> and has a <u>railroad</u> nearby then there is good <u>terrain</u> nearby with 83% confidence.

Since the fuzzy support count for {Railroad Near} and {Railroad Near, Good Terrain} are 8.7 and 7.2, the confidence is 7.2 / 8.7 or 83% and so this rule is also output.

Rough Set Spatial Representation

Now we will consider this example using rough set techniques. We will make use of some rough predicates as has been done in rough querying of crisp databases (Beaubouef & Petry, 1994) using SMALL for population size of city and NEAR for relative distances between cities. We might roughly define SMALL, for example, to include in the lower approximation all cities that have a population < 8000, and in the upper approximation those cities that have a population < 50000. NEAR would include all distances that are < 5 kilometers for the lower approximation, and then all distances that are < 8 kilometers in the upper approximation, for example. We use a sample query similar to the previous one as:

```
SELECT City C, Road R, River RV, Airstrip A, Drainage D
FROM County 1
WHERE ((SMALL (C.pop) and [NEAR(C.loc, R.loc), NEAR(C.loc, RV.loc), NEAR
(C.loc, A.loc), NEAR(C.loc, D.loc) ])
```

Table 5. **R***: Rough results from spatial query*

City	County	Roads	Rivers	Airstrips	Drainage
A	1	Hwy 1	Oak	None	Good
B	1	{Hwy 5, Hwy 7}	None	A 1	Fair
C	1	Hwy 28	Sandy	None	Good
D	1	Hwy 10	Black	A 2	Acceptable
E	{ 1, 2}	Hwy 33	Black	None	Good
F	1	Hwy 2	{Sandy, Pearl }	A 3	Desirable

There are several potential issues related to drainage. For some plant operations a poor drainage of adjacent terrain might be unacceptable because of pollution regulations in the county under consideration. For other plants that do not produce wastewater discharges, the drainage situation is not as important. Depending on the specific plant being planned, the various drainages of terrains suitable for the purpose would be entered and a qualitative category for the terrain desirability taken into account. Assume the following rough resultant table **R** is Table 5.

Attribute values for drainage quality may have been partitioned by the following equivalence relation: {[POOR, UNACCEPTABLE],[FAIR, OK, ACCEPTABLE], [GOOD, DESIRABLE], [EXCELLENT]}. In table 5, the lower approximation region contains data for four cities (A, B, C, D). Cities E and F appear in the boundary region of the upper approximation result. These are results that do not match lower approximation certain results exactly based on our query and the definition of predicates, but do meet the qualifications for the boundary, or uncertain region. For example, CITY E is part of counties 1 and 2, and CITY F might be 7 kilometers from HWY 2, rather than within 5 kilometers, which would place it in the lower approximation.

As for the fuzzy set case we can generate the frequent itemsets from the relation **R** in Table 5 using the rough support count. A frequent itemsets table very similar to Table 4 for fuzzy sets will then result. As before we specify a minimum confidence such as 80%. This means we could obtain a rule such as:

If there is a <u>river</u> *closely located to a small* <u>city</u> *C then it is likely that there is good* <u>terrain</u> *near with 83% confidence.*

This would follow if the rough support count for {River Near} and {River Near, Good Terrain} was for example 8.5 and 7.0, in which case the rough confidence is RC = 7.0 / 8.5 or 82.4% for this rule.

CONCLUSION AND FUTURE DIRECTIONS

The use of data mining has become widespread in such diverse areas as marketing and intelligence applications. The integration of data discovery with GIS (Geographic Information Systems) allows extensions of these approaches to include spatially related data, greatly enhancing their applicability but incurring considerable complexity.

In this chapter we have described data discovery for spatial data using association rules. To permit uncertainty in the discovery process, vague spatial predicates based on fuzzy set and rough set techniques were presented. Finally examples of these approaches for industrial plant sites planning using typical association rules of interest were illustrated.

A number of topics that are now of current research can enhance future direction in data mining of vague spatial data. There are several recent approaches to uncertainty representation that may be more suitable for certain applications and forms of spatial data. Type-2 fuzzy sets have been of considerable recent interest (Mendel & John, 2002). In these as opposed to ordinary fuzzy sets in which the underlying membership functions are crisp, here the membership function are themselves fuzzy. Intuitionistic sets (Atanassov, 1999) are another generalization of a fuzzy set. Two characteristic functions are used for capturing both the ordinary idea of degree of membership in the intuitionistic set as well as the degree of non-membership of elements in the set and can be used in database design (Beaubouef & Petry, 2007). Combinations of the concepts of rough set and fuzzy set theory (Nanda & Majumdar, 1992) have also been proposed and can be used in modeling some of the complexities found in spatial data.

Closer integration of data mining systems and GIS can assist users in effective rule extraction from spatial data. The visual presentations would aid in the specification of imprecise spatial predicates and their corresponding thresholds. A user could utilize the GIS tools to experiment with a variety of spatial predicates and their thresholds to best represent the user's viewpoint and intuitions which are often very visually oriented. Additionally another issue for algorithms that generate association rules is that very large number of such rules are often produced. Deciding which rules are most valuable or interesting is an ongoing research topic (Hilderman & Hamilton, 2001; Tan et. al., 2002). By providing visual feedback of the spatial association rules, a user could more effectively prune the large set of potential rules.

ACKNOWLEDGMENT

We would like to thank the Naval Research Laboratory's Base Program, Program Element No. 0602435N for sponsoring this research.

REFERENCES

Agrawal, R., Imielinski, T., & Swami, A. (1993). Mining Association rules between sets of items in large databases. *Proceedings of the 1993 ACM-SIGMOD International Conference on Management of* Data (pp. 207-216). New York, NY: ACM Press.

Alpaydin, E. (2004). *Introduction to machine learning*. Boston, MA: MIT Press.

Atanassov, K. (1999). *Intuitionistic fuzzy sets: Theory and applications*. Heidelberg, Germany: Physica-Verlag.

Beaubouef, T., & Petry, F. (1994). *Rough querying of crisp data in relational databases*. Third International Workshop on Rough Sets and Soft Computing (RSSC'94), San Jose, California (pp. 34-41).

Beaubouef, T., Petry, F., & Ladner, R. (2007). Spatial data methods and vague regions: A rough set approach. *Applied Soft Computing*, 7, 425–440. doi:10.1016/j.asoc.2004.11.003

Bosc, P., & Pivert, O. (2001). On some fuzzy extensions of association rules. In *Proceedingsof IFSA-NAFIPS 2001* (pp. 1104–1109). Piscataway, NJ: IEEE Press.

Buckles, B., & Petry, F. (1982). A fuzzy representation for relational databases. *International Journal of Fuzzy Sets and Systems, 7*, 213–226. doi:10.1016/0165-0114(82)90052-5

Burrough, P., & Frank, A. (Eds.). (1996). *Geographic objects with indeterminate boundaries. GISDATA series* (*Vol. 2*). London, UK: Taylor and Francis.

Chen, G., Wei, Q., & Kerre, E. (2000). Fuzzy data mining: Discovery of fuzzy generalized association rules. In Bordogna, G., & Pasi, G. (Eds.), *Recent issues on fuzzy databases* (pp. 45–66). Heidelberg, Germany: Physica-Verlag.

Clementini, E., & DeFelice, P. (1997). Approximate topological relations. *International Journal of Approximate Reasoning, 16*, 173–204. doi:10.1016/S0888-613X(96)00127-2

de Graaf, J., Kosters, W., & Witteman, J. (2001). Interesting fuzzy association rules in quantitative databases. In *Principles of Data Mining and Knowledge Discovery (LNAI 2168)* (pp. 140–151). Berlin, Germany: Springer Verlag. doi:10.1007/3-540-44794-6_12

Elmasri, R., & Navathe, S. (2010). *Fundamentals of database systems* (6th ed.). Addison Wesley.

Ester, M., Fromelt, A., Kriegel, H., & Sander, J. (2000). Spatial data mining: Database primitives, algorithms and efficient and DBMS support. *Data Mining and Knowledge Discovery, 4*, 89–125. doi:10.1023/A:1009843930701

Golfarelli, M., & Rizzi, S. (2009). *Data warehouse design: Modern principles and methodologies*. McGraw Hill.

Gyenesei, A. (2000). *Mining weighted association rules for fuzzy quantitative items*. (TUCS Technical Report 346). Turku, Finland: Turku Center for Computer Science.

Han, J., & Kamber, M. (2006). *Data mining: Concepts and techniques* (2nd ed.). San Diego, CA: Academic Press.

Han, J., Koperski, K., & Stefanovic, N. (1997). GeoMiner: A system prototype for spatial data mining. In *Proceedings of the 1997 ACM-SIGMOD International Conference on Management of Data* (pp. 553-556). New York, NY: ACM Press.

Hilderman, R., & Hamilton, H. (2001). *Knowledge discovery and measures of interest*. Kluwer Academic Publishers.

Hipp, J., Guntzer, U., & Nakhaeizadeh, G. (2000). Algorithms for association rule mining- a general survey. *SIGKDD Explorations, 2*, 58–64. doi:10.1145/360402.360421

Koperski, K., & Han, J. (1995). Discovery of spatial association rules in geographic information databases. In *Proceedings of 4th International Symposium on Large Spatial Databases* (pp. 47-66). Berlin, Germany: Springer-Verlag.

Kuok, C., Fu, A., & Wong, H. (1998). Mining fuzzy association rules in databases. *SIGMOD Record, 27*, 41–46. doi:10.1145/273244.273257

Lee, K. (2001). Mining generalized fuzzy quantitative association rules with fuzzy generalization hierarchies. In [Piscataway, NJ: IEEE Press.]. *Proceedings of IFSA-NAFIPS, 2001*, 2977–2982.

Longley, P., Goodchild, M., Maguire, D., & Rhind, D. (2001). *Geographic Information Systems and science*. Chichester, UK: Wiley.

Lu, W., Han, J., & Ooi, B. (1993). Discovery of general knowledge in large spatial databases. In *Proceedings of Far East Workshop Geographic Information* Systems (pp. 275-289). Singapore: World Scientific Press.

Mendel, J., & John, R. (2002). Type-2 fuzzy sets made simple. *IEEE Transactions on Fuzzy Sets, 10*, 117–127. doi:10.1109/91.995115

Miller, H., & Han, J. (2009). *Geographic data mining and knowledge discovery* (2nd ed.). Chapman & Hall.

Mishra, N., Ron, D., & Swaminathan, R. (2004). A new conceptual clustering framework. *Machine Learning Journal, 56*, 115–151. doi:10.1023/B:MACH.0000033117.77257.41

Nanda, S., & Majumdar, S. (1992). Fuzzy rough sets. *Fuzzy Sets and Systems, 45*, 157–160. doi:10.1016/0165-0114(92)90114-J

Nguyen, H., & Walker, E. (2005). *A first course in fuzzy logic* (3rd ed.). Boca Raton, FL: CRC Press.

Pawlak, Z. (1984). Rough sets. *International Journal of Man-Machine Studies, 21*, 127–134. doi:10.1016/S0020-7373(84)80062-0

Petry, F. (1996). *Fuzzy databases: Principles and application*. Norwell, MA: Kluwer Academic Publishers.

Polkowski, L. (2002). *Rough sets*. Heidelberg, Germany: Physica Verlag.

Rigaux, P., Scholl, M., & Voisard, A. (2002). *Spatial databases with application to GIS*. San Francisco, CA: Morgan Kaufmann.

Shasha, D., & Zhu, Y. (2004). *High performance discovery in time series*. Springer.

Shekar, S., & Chawla, S. (2003). *Spatial databases: A tour*. Upper Saddle River, NJ: Prentice Hall.

Shu, J., Tsang, E., & Yeung, D. (2001). Query fuzzy association rules in relational databases. In [Piscataway, NJ: IEEE Press.]. *Proceedings of IFSA-NAFIPS, 2001*, 2989–2993.

Tan, P., Kumar, V., & Srivastava, J. (2002). Selecting the right interestingness measure for association patterns. *Proceedings of ACM SIGKDD International Conference on Knowledge Discovery in Databases*, (pp. 32-41). Edmonton, Canada.

Tan, P., Steinbach, M., & Kumar, V. (2005). *Introduction to data mining*. Boston, MA: Addison Wesley.

Tobler, W. (1979). Cellular geography. In Gale, S., & Olsson, G. (Eds.), *Philosophy in geography* (pp. 379–386). Dortrecht, Germany: Riedel.

Yen, J., & Langari, R. (1999). *Fuzzy logic: Intelligence, control and information*. Upper Saddle River, NJ: Prentice Hall.

Zadeh, L. (1970). Similarity relations and fuzzy orderings. *Information Sciences*, *3*, 177–200. doi:10.1016/S0020-0255(71)80005-1

Zhang, J., & Goodchild, M. (2002). *Uncertainty in geographical information*. London, UK: Taylor and Francis Pub.doi:10.4324/9780203471326

Zhang, W. (1999). Mining fuzzy quantitative association rules. In *Proceedings of IEEE International Conference on Tools with Artificial Intelligence* (pp. 99-102). Piscataway, NJ: IEEE Press.

KEY TERMS AND DEFINITIONS

Association Rule: A rule that capture the idea of certain data items commonly occurring together.

Data Mining: The process of applying a variety of algorithms to discover relationships from data files.

Fuzzy Set: A set in which an element can have a degree of membership in set.

Geographic Information System: A software system that provides a wide variety of tools to manipulate spatial data.

Itemsets: Sets of data items that occur in transactions such as sales.

Rough Set: A set specified by upper and lower approximations that are defined by indiscernability relations among the data.

Spatial Data: Geographic data that can be represented by points, lines or areas.

Chapter 15
Feature Selection and Ranking

Boris Igelnik
BMI Research, Inc., & Case Western Reserve University, USA

ABSTRACT

This chapter describes a method of feature selection and ranking based on human expert knowledge and training and testing of a neural network. Being computationally efficient, the method is less sensitive to round-off errors and noise in the data than the traditional methods of feature selection and ranking grounded on the sensitivity analysis. The method may lead to a significant reduction of a search space in the tasks of modeling, optimization, and data fusion.

INTRODUCTION

Feature selection and ranking (Perlovsky, 2001, pp. 97-100, 312-316) is an essential part of modeling. It can be used before modeling (preprocessing) and during this procedure in real time when a set of new patterns of data arrives (long-term updating). The purpose of feature selection and ranking is to determine what is a minimal set of inputs (features) to a modeled system that is sufficient for describing a system output (or outputs in case of multi-input/multi-output system). Therefore, a measure of change of the output when a particular input changes while the other inputs kept constant can be introduced as a measure of *meaning* of data in this case.

The traditional methods of feature selection and ranking (Zapranis & Refenes, 1999; Liu & Mutoda, 1998) are grounded on the sensitivity analysis and make use of the estimates of the partial derivatives of the output over the inputs. We argue that those estimates are very sensitive to round-off errors and noise. Additionally, if some an input is dependent on a subset of the inputs, then it is impossible, in general, keeping the inputs from the subset constant while changing this input. There exist many other references

DOI: 10.4018/978-1-60960-551-3.ch015

on feature selection and ranking, for example (Oja, Lampinen, 1994; Liu & Motoda, 2008; Jensen, Shen, 2008). None of them have main common features with the method described in this chapter.

We suggest another method for feature selection and ranking. This method consists of 3 phases. In phase 1 we get rid of dependent features using the expert knowledge and neural network modeling, in phase 2 we check if the removing of dependent features deteriorates the model significantly or not, and in phase 3 we rank remaining features, according to the measure of meaning of data. A subset of inputs, with a total sum of ranks less than a prescribed threshold, is temporarily removed. If the performance of the model with the reduced set of inputs changes insignificantly then this subset has been removed finally.

Since our measure of meaning is based on computation of a number of integrals, our ranks are much less sensitive to round-off errors and noise. More than that, since computation of the integrals is practically exact the accuracy of the rank computation equals approximately the accuracy of a model.

The accuracy of the model depends on the model design and the method of training and testing. We apply the CEA (Clustering Ensemble Approach) method, which is a combination of unsupervised and supervised learning. That method is especially good for treating large sets of timer-variant multidimensional data and for data fusion.

BACKGROUND

The CEA method (Igelnik et al., 1995-2003; Igelnik, 2009) was eventually developed for adaptive dynamic modeling of large sets of time-variant multidimensional data. It includes different neural network architectures both traditional (Haykin, 1994; Bishop, 1995) and not-traditional ones (Igelnik & Parikh, 2003a; Igelnik 2009). The latter are based on the use of splines (Prenter, 1975; Bartels et al, 1987) and have the basic functions with adaptively adjusted shape and parameters, while the former have fixed-shape basis functions and adaptively adjusted parameters. We do not utilize non-traditional architectures in this chapter, but make use of the traditional radial basis functions (RBF) architecture with the Gaussian activation function.

THE CEA METHOD

Basics of the CEA

The *CEA* method starts by dividing the whole data set available for learning in two sets, for learning and for validation, leaving 97% of the whole data for learning and 3% for validation. The training set uses 75% of learning data, while the testing set utilizes remaining 25%. The features of the objects of the data set are divided in the inputs and the outputs. The training set is used for optimization of the training mean squared error (MSE), while the testing set is used for optimizing the testing (generalization) MSE. Both optimizations are used to select the final learned model, which is validated on the validation set. The whole procedure of training consists of the following steps: (1) clustering; (2) building a set of *local neural nets*, using the *CEA* on each cluster; (3) building one *global net* from the set of local nets; 4) utilizing the global net for predictions; (5) short-term and long-term *updating* of relevant local nets and the *global net* on the basis of learning data. Short-term updating includes *updating* of one *local net* and *updating* of the *global net* and some cluster parameters. It is performed after each new pattern arrival. Long-term *updating* includes additionally updating of all *local nets* and complete re-clustering.

The *CEA* currently includes the following neural net architectures: nonlinear perceptron (NP) net, RBF net, complex weights net (CWN) (Igelnik et al., 2001a), and the Kolmogorov's spline net (KSN) (Igelnik & Parikh, 2003a). It is planned to include the Kolmogorov's spline complex net (KSCN) (Igelnik, 2009) in the *CEA* in the near future. Availability of a variety of modeling architectures, including currently the most efficient ones, favorably distinguishes the *CEA* from other existing modeling tools. But the *CEA* has several other distinguished features related to: (1) mitigating the "curse of dimensionality", avoiding a large size of a net and a large size of the learning set; (2) neural net training and testing stability; (3) dealing with *time-varying* data; and (4) treating data with different sets of inputs (data fusion). These features are considered in detail in the following subsections.

Clustering

Clustering can significantly reduce the size of the search space. Another advantage of clustering is that the training, testing and validation of a number of small local nets, trained separately on each cluster, could be made significantly faster than the training of one big net, built on the whole set. Thus, *clustering* is helpful in both coping with problems of the "curse of dimensionality" and increasing the speed of the algorithm by using smaller nets trained on smaller sets. The *clustering* algorithm makes patterns inside one cluster more similar to each other than the patterns belonging to different clusters, trying to minimize the following objective function

$$J_e = \sum_{i=1}^{c} \sum_{x \in C_i} \left\| x - m_i \right\|^2 \underset{C_i, m_i, n_i}{\rightarrow} \min,$$

where c is the number of clusters, m_i is the center of the cluster C_i, n_i is the number of patterns in the cluster C_i. In order to control the size of clusters, another objective function has been added

$$J_u = \sum_{i=1}^{c} \left(n_i - P / c \right)^2 \underset{n_i}{\rightarrow} \min,$$

where P is the total number of patterns. The final goal of *clustering* is to minimize the following objective

$$J = \lambda J_e + \mu J_u \underset{C_i, m_i, n_i}{\rightarrow} \min,$$

where λ and μ are nonnegative scaling coefficients satisfying the condition $\lambda + \mu = 1$.

The algorithm was developed and tested in (Igelnik, 2003b), and is based on dynamical version of the K-means clustering (Duda et al., 2001, pp. 548-550), with an advanced initialization step (Bradley & Fayyad, 1998; Duda et al., 2001, p.550), mitigating the deficiencies of the K-means algorithm. As to unknown number of clusters we follow a general leader-follow *clustering* strategy (Duda et al, 2001, pp. 562-563). This strategy suggests that initial number of clusters is found off-line by experimentation, while only a center of a cluster, closest to a new pattern being presented, is changed on-line. This is a part of short-term *updating* procedure in the *CEA* described below in this section. Clustering is related to (1) - (3) of *CEA* distinguished features, described above.

Building the Set of Local Nets and the Ensembles of the Local Nets

The general form of a *local net*, built by the CEA method, the following:

$$\tilde{f}_N\left(x,W\right) = w_0^{ext} + \sum_{n=1}^{N} w_n^{ext}\psi_n\left(x, w_n^{\text{int}}\right), \tag{1a}$$

where $\tilde{f}_N\left(x,W\right) \triangleq y_N = \left(y_1,\dots,y_D\right)$ is the multidimensional output, $x = \left(x_1,\dots,x_d\right)$ is the multi-dimensional input, $\left\{w_n^{ext}, n = 0,1,\dots,N\right\}$ is the set of external parameters, $\left\{w_n^{\text{int}}, n = 1,\dots,N\right\}$ is the set of internal parameters, W is the set of net parameters, which include both the external and internal parameters, $\left\{\psi_n,\ n = 1,\dots,N\right\}$ is the set of *basis functions* (nodes), and $N_{\max}$ is the maximal number of nodes ($1 \le N \le N_{\max}$), dependent on the class of application, time and memory constraints. The *basis functions* ψ_n are calculated in general for a net with real weights through superposition and summation of univariate functions as follows

$$\psi_n\left(x, w_n^{\text{int}}\right) = g_n\left[\sum_{i=1}^{d}\varphi_{ni}\left(x_i, w_{ni}^{\text{int}}\right)\right], \tag{1b}$$

where g_n and φ_{ni} are the univariate functions. In standard architectures, such as NP or RBF nets, the functions φ_{ni} are linear in x_i and in w_{ni}^{int} for NP nets and they are quadratic in the same arguments for RBF nets. The functions g_n, called the activation functions, are nonlinear univariate functions. They are chosen from a finite set of fixed form functions, such as the logistic function, the hyperbolic tangent, the Gaussian function, and so on, for standard architectures.

The process of building a learned net by the *CEA* has the following characteristics[1]. The *CEA* builds a set of (N+1) learned nets defined by equations (1) with the number of nodes N, $0 \le N \le N_{\max}$, starting from the net with N = 0, that is, building a net $\tilde{f}_0\left(x,\ W\right) = w_0^{ext}$. Nets for $N > 0$ are obtained from the learned net with (N – 1) nodes by a recursive step, going from a net with (N – 1) to a net with N nodes. For some integer K the *ensemble* of K candidate learned nets $\tilde{f}_{N,k}$, $k = 1,\dots,K$ with N nodes is obtained as follows. Keeping the internal parameters of learned net with (N – 1) nodes as a part of internal parameters of each member of the ensemble, an adaptive random number generator (ARG) generates the *ensemble* of internal parameters for N-th node. Therefore, all the internal parameters are defined for each member of the ensemble of nets with N nodes, and each member of the *ensemble* becomes a linear net. The optimal values of external parameters for each net $\tilde{f}_{N,k}$ from the ensemble $\left\{\tilde{f}_{N,k}, k = 1,\dots,K\right\}$ are obtained using the formulas of recursive linear regression (RLR) (Albert, 1972, p. 44). The RLR starts with N=0. For this case the net output is a constant, which optimal value can be calculated directly as

$$\tilde{f}_0(x,W) = \frac{1}{P_t}\sum_{p=1}^{P_t} y_p, \tag{2}$$

where $y_p, p = 1,...,P_t$ are the vector-values of the outputs in the training set, P_t is the number of patterns in the training set. For the purpose of further discussion of the *CEA* one has to introduce a design matrix P_N and its pseudo-inverse matrix P_{N+} (the pseudo-inverse matrix is a generalization of the inverse matrix for non-squared rectangular matrices) for a net with N nonlinear nodes

$$P_N = \begin{bmatrix} 1 & \psi_1(x_1, w_1) & \dots & \psi_N(x_1, w_N) \\ 1 & \psi_1(x_2, w_1) & \dots & \psi_N(x_2, w_N) \\ \dots & \dots & \dots & \dots \\ 1 & \psi_1(x_P, w_1) & \dots & \psi_N(x_P, w_N) \end{bmatrix}. \tag{3}$$

If the matrix P_{N-1} is known then the matrix P_N can be obtained by a recurrent equation

$$P_N = \begin{bmatrix} & \psi_N(x_1, w_N^{\text{int}}) \\ P_{N-1} & \psi_N(x_2, w_N^{\text{int}}) \\ & \dots \\ & \psi_N(x_P, w_N^{\text{int}}) \end{bmatrix}. \tag{4}$$

The matrix P_{N+} can be calculated by the following recurrent equations

$$P_{N+} = \begin{bmatrix} P_{N-1,+} - P_{N-1,+} p_N k_N^T \\ k_N^T \end{bmatrix}, \tag{5a}$$

$$p_N = \left[\psi_N(x_1, w_N^{\text{int}}), \dots, \psi_N(x_{P_t}, w_N^{\text{int}})\right]^T, \tag{5b}$$

$$k_N = \frac{p_N - P_{N-1}P_{N-1,+}p_N}{\left\|p_N - P_{N-1}P_{N-1,+}p_N\right\|^2} \text{ if } p_N - P_{N-1}P_{N-1,+}p_N \neq 0. \tag{5c}$$

In order to start using formulas (4) and (5) for recurrent calculation of the matrices P_N and P_{N+} through the matrices P_{N-1} and $P_{N-1,+}$, and the vector-column p_N, the initial conditions are defined as

$$P_0 = \Big[\underbrace{1,1,\ldots,1}_{P_t \text{ times}}\Big]^T, \; P_{0+} = \Big[\underbrace{1/P_t, 1/P_t, \ldots, 1/P_t}_{P_t \text{ times}}\Big]. \tag{6}$$

Then formulas (4), (5) are applied in the following order for $N = 1$. First the one-column matrix p_1 is computed by (5b). Then the matrix P_0 and the matrix p_1 are used to compute the matrix P_1 in formula (4). After that the one-column matrix k_1 is computed by formula (5c), using P_0, P_{0+} and p_1. Finally, the matrix P_{1+} is computed by formula (5a). That completes computation of P_1 and P_{1+} using P_0 and P_{0+}. The external parameters and the values of the model output for the training set are determined as

$$w^{ext} = P_{N+}y, \quad \tilde{y} = P_N w^{ext}, \tag{7}$$

where $w^{ext} = \left[w_0^{ext}, w_1^{ext}, \ldots, w_N^{ext}\right]^T$ is the $(N+1)\times D$ matrix of the values of external parameters for a net with N nodes, $\tilde{y} = \left[\tilde{f}_N\left(x_1^t, W\right), \ldots, \tilde{f}_N\left(x_{P_t}^t, W\right)\right]^T$ is the $P_t \times D$ matrix of the values of the net training outputs for a net with N nodes. After training of all linear nets with N nodes included in the ensemble is completed, the *CEA* computes the training MSEs for these nets. At the end of this recursive step, the unique net $\tilde{f}_N\left(x, W\right)$ with the minimal training MSE in the ensemble is selected, and the testing MSE is determined for this net. Calculation of the testing/validation MSE for this optimal net uses formulas (7) with the only difference: the matrix P_N is calculated by the formula (3) where the values of the net training inputs $x_p, p = 1, \ldots, P_t$ are replaced by the values of generalization/validation inputs and the number of training inputs P_t is replaced by the number of generalization/validation ones.

The process of building *local nets* through *ensemble* of nets was first considered in (Igelnik & Pao, 1995), where a close connection between training and testing of a *neural net* and approximate calculation of multiple integrals was shown. The idea of utilizing the *ensemble* of randomly selected nets was considered in (Igelnik & Pao, 1995), since it was known, that the most efficient way of calculating multiple integrals is through stochastic, or quasi-stochastic methods (Stroud, 1971; Niederreiter, 1978).

Optimizing the Number of Nodes

A special procedure uses the set of testing errors for determining the optimal number of nodes. This procedure finds the global minimum of the testing MSE $e_{N,g}(testMSE_N)$ and selects the learned net with the number of nodes $N_{opt} = \arg \min\limits_{0 \le N \le N_{\max}} \left(e_{N,g}\right)$.

Using smallest possible nets is the way of increasing stability of training and testing, and at the same time decreasing running time of modeling algorithms.

Filters for New Basis Functions and New Data

The RLR is a recursive process, when having a net with N *basis functions* defined by equation (1a), one adds a new basis function ψ_{N+1} from the ensemble in order to obtain a net with $N+1$ *basis functions*.

The adding of a new *basis function*, as a rule, increases the instability of learning, which has to be compensated by an increase of information about data provided by the new *basis function*. However, this increase will be insignificant, if the vector $p_{N+1} = \left(\psi\left(x_1, w_{N+1}^{\text{int}}\right), \ldots, \psi\left(x_P, w_{N+1}^{\text{int}}\right)\right)$, where $x_1,\ldots,x_P$ are input parts of the patterns from the training set, is too close to the linear space $L\left(p_0, p_1, \ldots, p_N\right)$ spanned by the vectors-columns $p_0, p_1, \ldots, p_N$, forming the design matrix $P_N = \left[p_0, p_1, \ldots, p_N\right]$. To avoid such a situation, the RLR computes absolute value of the sine of the angle between the vector p_{N+1} and space $L\left(p_0, p_1, \ldots, p_N\right)$, and rejects p_{N+1}, if this value is less than some small number $\eta > 0$. If value of η is not small enough, then the rejections will occur too often, leading to a significant increase of running time. From the other hand, too small values of η may result in a situation when rejections never occur. For power applications the value $\eta = 10^{-7}$ worked well. This value may be a reasonable starting point for other applications.

The filter of *basis functions* described above increases computational stability of training and testing in RLR.

The space $L\left(p_0, p_1, \ldots, p_N\right)$ can be considered as spanned by vector-rows

$$q_p = \left(1, \psi\left(x_p, w_1^{\text{int}}\right), \ldots, \psi\left(x_p, w_N^{\text{int}}\right)\right), p = 1, \ldots, P.$$

There exist formulas in RLR (Albert, 1972, pp.126, 127), allowing for recursive computing of a net with *N basis functions* trained on the set $\left\{x_1, \ldots, x_P, x_{P+1}\right\}$ from a net with same *N basis functions* trained on the set $\left\{x_1, \ldots, x_P\right\}$. It seems plausible, that patterns x_{P+1} too close to $L\left(p_0, p_1, \ldots, p_N\right)$ will add relatively small information to:

the training set $\left\{x_1, \ldots, x_P\right\}$ and can be filtered out by a procedure similar to procedure of filtering out unacceptable *basis functions*.

The work on justification of such a filter is in progress. If successful such a filter can be applied for choosing a pattern to remove in the short-term *updating*, and, therefore, keeping size of a training set bounded without significant loss of information for learning.

Training with Noise

One additional measure for validation, mitigating to some degree the effect of choosing the validation set from the same total set of data used for learning, is training (testing, validation) with noise (Breiman, 1996, 1999). That means, that every output value *y* is replaced by the sum *y+n,* where *n* is a simulated Gaissian noise with the zero mean and standard deviation equal to the standard deviation of the data used for training, or testing, or validation. The training with noise reduces time of learning compared to traditional cross-validation method (Stone, 1974) at least by an order of magnitude, without making worse the performance.

Global Net. For each cluster c=1,…,C a learned net $\mathcal{N}_c\left(x_c\right)$ has been built. The following equation gives a simple model of a *global net*

$$\mathcal{N}\left(x, w\right) = w_0 + \sum_{c=1}^{C} w_c \mathcal{N}_c\left(x_c\right) \exp(-\left\|x - \tilde{m}_c\right\|^2 / 2\sigma_c^2), \tag{8}$$

where N is the global net, $\mathcal{N}_c$ is a *local net* related to cluster c, C is the number of clusters, x_c is a vector of inputs to $\mathcal{N}_c$, x is the union of all x_c, $\tilde{m}_c$ is the input part of the cluster-center of c, $\|x - \tilde{m}_c\|$ is the distance between points x and $\tilde{m}_c$, σ_c is the intra-distance for a cluster c, $c = 1,\ldots,C$ (the intra-distance is defined as the shortest distance of a pattern, not belonging to cluster c, to the cluster-center $\tilde{m}_c$). The vectors x_c can be replaced by the vector x, if equation (8) is used before feature selection and ranking. Then the chosen features in different clusters can be different, that is why notation x_c for different clusters is utilized in equation (8). Another reason for choosing the notation x_c is a possible use of a *global net* for data fusion. In this case the different sets of cluster inputs are related to the different input sensors, while the *global* net combines them for common outputs. Cluster-centers and intra-distances are updated before *updating* the global net. Thus, the only unknown parameters with numerical values established during the learning are the parameters $w_0, w_1, \ldots, w_C$. Therefore, the *global net* is a linear net. The training of the *global net* can be performed by the RLR on the total training set and can be done fast (usually value of C is significantly less than the value of N_{max}, and there is no need for generating *ensembles*).

The *global net* plays important role in the CEA by: (1) expanding areas of reliable prediction around the clusters; (2) allowing for treating not perfect clustering, with intersecting clusters; (3) eliminating possible discontinuity of a model on the borders of clusters; (4) treating the local nets with different sets of inputs.

Updating the Model by the CEA

When a new pattern of data arrives the model is subjected to a short-term *updating* that include: determining the cluster-center $\tilde{m}_{\breve{c}}$ closest to the new pattern; temporarily including new pattern in the training part of the cluster $\breve{c}$; excluding one of the old patterns from the cluster training set (at random or by other strategy); *updating* the parameters $\tilde{m}_c$, σ_c; retraining the local net $\mathcal{N}_{\breve{c}}\left(x_{\breve{c}}\right)$; retraining the global net $\mathcal{N}\left(x, w^{ext}\right)$. Long-term updating includes additionally re-clustering and retraining of all local nets.

The CEA Implementation

The previous subsections described numerous features of the *CEA* and could make an impression of its excessive complexity. But the only complexity (not excessive at all for moderately experienced programmer) of *CEA* is in programming. The following example illustrates a *CEA* application in power industry. In this example dynamic updating of the set of training data was applied, using as a validation set as a source of new on-line data. The learning set was extracted from the set of historical data, which played the role of the total set. The results of updating are presented in Table 1. They demonstrate that the updating was successful. In this example, the total number of patterns and numbers of patterns for training, testing, and validation equal to 3450, 2504, 843, and 103, respectively, the dimension of input equals to 34, the dimension of output (content of nitrogen oxides in the atmosphere due to power generation) equals to 1, the number of clusters equals to 10. The *CEA* program was running on PC with

Table 1.

Error	Training	Testing	Validation
MSE	8.35E-05	8.65E-05	8.9E-05
MAE	0.0064	0.0066	0.0069
RMAE	2.216%	2.25%	2.33%
STD RAE	2.12%	2.06%	1.67%
Running time for:	Long-term retraining = 20 sec		Short-term retraining = 2 sec.

Pentium-4 processor, 2.66 GHZ and was written in C/C++. Following notations are used in the Table1: MSE-mean squared error, MAE -mean absolute error, RMAE-relative MAE, STD- standard deviation.

It should be mentioned that in this example performance of the *CEA*, measured in RMAE was 2 times better, and running time was 5 times better than for a traditional method of modeling time-variant data based on the Kalman filtering (Lewis, 1986; Brown & Hwang, 1997; Haykin, 2001). It can be claimed in general that advantages of the *CEA* in performance, running time, and stability of training and testing, far outweigh some difficulties in its programming.

CEA APPLICATION FOR FEATURE SELECTION AND RANKING

Feature selection is the process of finding the minimal set of inputs to a system, which determine its output. The suggested approach is an alternative to an approach popular in engineering (Zapranis & Refenes, 1999, pp. 79-85), utilizing estimates of partial derivatives of the system output over its inputs. However, the estimates of partial derivatives as the ratio of two small quantities are sensitive to both, noise and round-off errors. Alternatively, in the first stage of the suggested approach one is attempting to get rid of features correlated to other features. Some approaches to the first stage, using visualization and expert knowledge, are discussed in (Igelnik, 2003b, 2003c) and will not be considered in this chapter. A sketch of the ranking procedure (second stage of approach) is given below.

An algorithm of input feature selection and ranking, according to the input feature influence on the output, has been implemented and tested. This algorithm has three phases. In the first phase one has to get read of the dependent features. This phase is significantly based on the expert experience in guessing what feature depends on a number of other features. The direct learning of a suggested dependency tests this guess. After phase 1 all dependent features should be excluded. The phase 2 includes the learning of an output versus reduced set of independent features, using the CEA method. The phase 3 contains the ranking of independent features according to their influence on the output. The results of learning a neural net model are used for calculation of the variance of the output when only a particular input varies, while other inputs are kept constant. The rank of a particular input then is calculated as the ratio of the particular input variance to the sum of all input variances, multiplied by 100 (expressed in percents of the total variance). The features with smallest ranks can be removed in the end of Phase 3 if their removal does not deteriorate the performance of the learning output algorithm significantly.

Phase 1, resulting in elimination of dependent features, is not only important for this specific algorithm of feature selection and ranking, but it is also important in control for the stage of optimization. Indeed the optimization is typically performed in the rectangular area of the domain of input features.

The existence of mutually dependent features will exclude many points from the rectangular, making some optimization solutions actually infeasible. Phase 2 is common for many feature selection algorithms using neural networks (Liu & Motoda, 1998). Phase 3 was not described in the public literature on feature selection, except in (Igelnik, 2003c). It should be stressed that the proposed in that work feature selection and ranking algorithm was not implemented, tested and analyzed at the time of its publication. In Phase 3 a learned model of the plant output versus reduced (after excluding dependent input features) set of inputs was used to calculate variances of the features by explicitly computing multidimensional integrals involved in those calculations. The computed variances were the basis for calculations of the feature ranks. This ranking procedure has the following advantages over the currently existing feature selection algorithms: (1) allows for varying only one input at a time, keeping other inputs constant; (2) allows for estimating ranks in any rectangular sub-area of the input feature space in the computationally efficient manner; (3) using integrals instead of estimates of partial derivatives reduces an influence of round-off errors and noise.

An example of a power plant dataset is utilized in the subsequent subsections.

Eliminating Dependent Features

The learning of all dependences was made by the CEA. Some statistics is shown below:

1. Number of patterns equals to 1506;
2. Number of training patterns equals to 1086;
3. Number of testing patterns equals to 373;
4. Number of validation patterns equals to 47;
5. Number of inputs equals to 34;
6. Number of outputs equals to 1 (NOX);
7. Number of clusters equals to 9;

First of all one should differ the dependencies due to real dynamics of the plant with disturbances due to measurement errors, failure of sensors or devices, and similar unwanted reasons. Secondly one should take into account that the neural network control comes after the DCS (distributed control system). Let us illustrate this by the example. The author of this chapter, inspecting the data, paid attention that the inputs in the group of A_Mill_Amps, B_Mill_Amps, and C_Mill_Amps in many cases drop their values to unusually low numbers. They do it in the rather regular periods and one mill at a time. Consulted by an expert the author of this chapter learned that DCS does it deliberately in response to ups and downs in the input MWT (megawatts). So this is not a result of some device or sensor failure. Therefore, the guess that the MWT may be a function of inputs A_Mill_Amps, B_Mill_Amps, and C_Mill_Amps is justified. To check this guess the supposed dependency MWT = *f*(A_Mill_Amps, B_Mill_Amps, C_Mill_Amps) was learned on the data. Figure 1 illustrates the results of the learning, where the actual MWT and predicted MWT are shown as the functions of a pattern from the validation set.

The quantitative results of learning are presented in Table 2.

Since training, testing, and validation RMAE are all just slightly more than 2.5% the hypothesis that MWT is a function of three mills amperes is perfectly justified. Therefore, MWT should be excluded from the list of input features as a feature dependent on some other features in the list. The last conclusion is very important because inclusion of MWT in the list of controllable inputs (which is a common

Figure 1. Actual and predicted MWT as the functions of a pattern from validation set

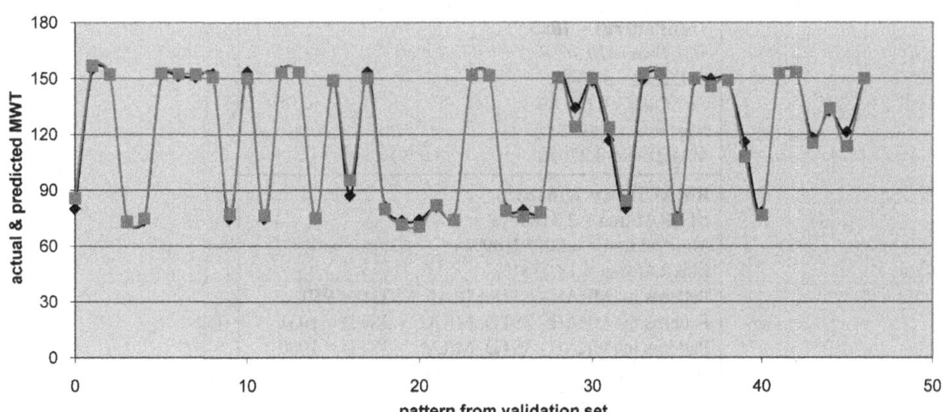

practice) will cause a problem in the optimization step leading sometime to unfeasible optimization solutions.

Other possible dependencies may include dependencies between O2 and different groups of inputs, such as groups of inputs, characterizing properties of mills: (Ampr) A_Mill_Ampr, B_Mill_Ampr, and C_Mill_ Amps; (SucDmprs) 1_A_Mill_Suc_Dmpr, 1_B_Mill_Suc_Dmpr, and 1_C_Mill_Suc_Dmpr; (ExhDP) 1_A_Mill_ExhDP, 1_B_Mill_ExhDP, and 1_C_Mill_ExhDP; the group related to flows: (Flow) 1_A_TC_Air_Flow and 1_B_TC_Air_Flow; the group of OFA inputs: (OFA) 1_N_1_3_OFA, 1_N_2_3_OFA, 1_S_1_3_OFA, and 2_S_1_3_OFA; and the group of 18 inputs related to secondary air (denoted as SA group). There possible also dependencies between inputs inside each group.

Full search for all hidden dependencies may involve a lot of computational time. Fortunately there are some general recommendations, which restrict the time of search to a reasonable amount. These recommendations are:

1. Start work on modeling with visual inspection of a data set indicating any unusual patterns;
2. Detect patterns obtained due to instrumentation or device failure or during repair (will be discussed elsewhere);
3. Remove or include with some corrections patterns detected in 2, due to some strategy (will be discussed elsewhere);
4. Represent in the model basic groups of variables;
5. Guessing dependency between inputs leads to a positive decision, if the testing and validation RMAE are not greater than 2.5%, and to the negative decision if these errors are greater than 7%;
6. Do not remove the inputs, which are part of a group, either remove or keep the entire group;
7. The number of inputs depends on the number of patterns in the data set, for power data the number of inputs should be in the range of 20-50 for datasets in the range of 1000-5000 patterns;
8. Dropping an input or a group of inputs as a rule lead to deterioration of the performance, check if reduced model deteriorates unacceptably in performance by running the reduced model;
9. Dropping an input or a group of inputs may lead to improvement of the performance if the number of inputs too high for a given number of patterns in the data set.

Table 2. Results of learning of MWT = f (MillsAmprs)

TranPatterns = 1083
MSETran = 10.2658
STDTran = 3.20403
varAOutT = 1171.49
RSqTran = 0.991237
MAETran = 2.27078
RMAETran = 2.18188%
STDRAEtran = 2.31886%
MinRAEtran = 0.00750109%
MaxRAEtran = 18.3531%
Patterns in (MRAE - STD, MRAE + STD) = 950
Patterns in (MRAE - 2STD, MRAE + 2STD = 1031
Patterns in (MRAE - 3STD, MRAE + 3STD = 1060
GenPatterns = 376
MSEGen = 14.1113
STDGen = 3.75645
varAOutG = 1147.08
RSqGen = 0.987698
MAE_Generalization = 2.72354
RMAEGen = 2.62923%
STDRAEgen = 2.93063%
MinRAEgen = 0.0122959%
MaxRAEgen = 19.1705%
Patterns in (MRAE - STD, MRAE + STD) = 329
Patterns in (MRAE - 2STD, MRAE + 2STD = 354
Patterns in (MRAE - 3STD, MRAE + 3STD = 368
TotalValPatterns = 47
MSEVal = 10.9301
MAEVal = 2.2508
RMAEVal = 2.12905%
STD of RAE = 2.30486%
Minimum RAE = 0.0053074%
Maximum RAE = 8.90005%
Patterns in (RMAE - STD, RMAE + STD) = 39
Patterns in (RMAE - 2STD, RMAE + 2STD = 43
Patterns in (RMAE - 3STD, RMAE + 3STD = 47

Summarizing the recommendations, one can say that the requirement to represent the basic groups and the upper bound on the number of inputs dramatically reduce the time for search of possible dependencies between inputs. It should be mentioned as well that the notion of dependent and independent features is relative in practice. We did not define how to classify supposed dependencies if the testing and validation errors are outside the range between 2.5% and 7%. This is a fuzzy situation when, with some probability, one can accept either way of classification. It is also clear that the numbers, 2.5% and 7%, cannot be strictly justified.

Phase 2: Learning Dependency between NOX and Reduced Set of Input Features

This was done with use of CEA. The results of learning are presented in the table 3.

Comparing the results obtained by the CEA with those obtained by the Back Propagation (BP) method has shown that the training MSE was lower while the testing MSE was significantly higher in the BP case. The ratio of testing MSE to training MSE was 15.20 in the BP case, while the ratio of test-

Table 3. Results of learning NOX versus the set of 34 input features

GeneralTranInfo TranPatterns = 1086 *MSETran = 0.000739587* STDTran = 0.0271953 varAOutT = 0.00684838 *RSqTran = 0.892006* MAETran = 0.0208311 **RMAETran = 5.02739%** STDRAEtran = 4.52578% MinRAEtran = 0.00224171% MaxRAEtran = 38.4204% Patterns in (MRAE - STD, MRAE + STD) = 873 Patterns in (MRAE - 2STD, MRAE + 2STD = 1049 Patterns in (MRAE - 3STD, MRAE + 3STD = 1066
GeneralGenInfo GenPatterns = 373 *MSEGen = 0.000765128* STDGen = 0.0272605 varAOutG = 0.00652985 RSqGen = 0.882826 MAE_Generalization = 0.0258748 **RMAEGen = 6.30243%** STDRAEgen = 5.45419% MinRAEgen = 0.0162076% MaxRAEgen = 46.9535% Patterns in (MRAE - STD, MRAE + STD) = 301 Patterns in (MRAE - 2STD, MRAE + 2STD = 362 Patterns in (MRAE - 3STD, MRAE + 3STD = 366
GeneralValInfo TotalValPatterns = 47 *MSEVal = 0.000800958* MAEVal = 0.0217617 **RMAEVal = 5.29176%** STD of RAE = 4.69951% Minimum RAE = 0.145246% Maximum RAE = 22.6741% Patterns in (RMAE - STD, RMAE + STD) = 32 Patterns in (RMAE - 2STD, RMAE + 2STD = 45 Patterns in (RMAE - 3STD, RMAE + 3STD = 46

ing to training MSE in CEA was 1.03 only. A huge difference between results in training and testing using the BP algorithm and those obtained by CEA can be explained as follows: the BP algorithm has no systematic way for choosing right number of neural net nodes, while the CEA has it.

Phase 3: Feature Ranking and Possible Further Removal of Excessive Features

A specific type of neural net architecture, the RBF net with Gaussian activation function $g(t) = e^{-t^2/2}$, was used in this chapter to allow for explicit calculation of involved complex multidimensional integrals. This architecture is described by the following equation

$$y = a_0 + \sum_{n=1}^{N} a_n e^{-w\sum_{i=1}^{d}(x_i - c_{ni})^2/2}, \tag{9}$$

where y is the neural net output; $x = (x_1, \ldots x_d)$ is the set of neural net inputs; d is the number of neural net inputs; N is the number of neural net nonlinear nodes; w is a manually adjusted parameter of the neural net (the value of this parameter was adjusted to $w = 0.4$ for Gallagher data); a_n, $n = 0, 1, \ldots N$ are the external parameters of the neural net; c_{ni}, $n = 1, \ldots N$, $i = 1, \ldots d$ are the internal parameters of the neural net.

The variances of the one-dimensional input components form the basis for calculation the ranks. Let denote $x_{-i} = (x_1, \ldots x_{i-1}, x_{i+1}, \ldots x_d)$ the set of all one-dimensional input components with excluded component x_i. Obviously the output of the net $y(x)$ can be represented in the form $y(x_{-i}, x_i)$. First the set of variances

$$\mathrm{var}_i(x_{-i}) = \int_0^1 \left[y(x_{-i}, x_i) - \int_0^1 y(x_{-i}, x_i)\, dx_i \right]^2 dx_i,\ i = 1, \ldots d. \tag{10}$$

These variances represent average squared fluctuation of the output from its average value when the component x_i varies between 0 and 1, while the rest of the components x_{-i} are fixed. To complete the estimation of the influence of a particular input on the output the variances $\mathrm{var}_i(x_{-i})$ should be averaged in the multidimensional unit cube $I^{d-1} = [0,1]^{d-1}$ leading to the set of variances

$$Var_i = \int_{I^{d-1}} \mathrm{var}_i(x_{-i})\, dx_{-i},\ i = 1, \ldots d. \tag{11}$$

Then the feature ranks, expressed in percents of the total variance

$$Var = \sum_{i=1}^{d} Var_i, \tag{12}$$

are defined as

$$rank_i = \frac{Var_i}{Var} * 100,\ i = 1, \ldots d. \tag{13}$$

The key formula for obtaining ranks has been derived in the Appendix this chapter and is as follows

$$Var_i = \sum_{n=1}^{N}\sum_{m=1}^{N} a_n a_m \prod_{j=1}^{d} \left\{ \frac{\sqrt{\pi}}{w} \left[\Phi\left(w\sqrt{2}\left(1 - \frac{c_{nj} + c_{mj}}{2}\right)\right) + \Phi\left(w\sqrt{2}\,\frac{c_{nj} + c_{mj}}{2}\right)\right] e^{-\frac{w^2}{4}(c_{nj} - c_{mj})^2} \right\} * \\ \left\{ 1 - \frac{2\sqrt{\pi} e^{\frac{w^2}{4}(c_{ni} - c_{mi})^2}}{w} \frac{\left[\Phi(w(1 - c_{ni})) + \Phi(wc_{ni})\right]\left[\Phi(w(1 - c_{mi})) + \Phi(wc_{mi})\right]}{\left[\Phi\left(w\sqrt{2}\left(1 - \frac{c_{ni} + c_{mi}}{2}\right)\right) + \Phi\left(w\sqrt{2}\,\frac{c_{ni} + c_{mi}}{2}\right)\right]} \right\},\ i = 1, \ldots d, \tag{14}$$

where

$$\Phi(x) = \frac{1}{\sqrt{2\pi}} \int_0^x e^{-t^2} dt \tag{15}$$

is the Laplace function. The Laplace function cannot be calculated through finite number of elementary functions explicitly. Fortunately, there exists very accurate approximate formula (Derenzo, 1977)

$$\begin{aligned} &\Phi(x) \approx 0.5 - 0.5 \exp\left[-\frac{(83x + 351)x + 562}{703 / x + 165}\right], \text{ if } 0 \leq x \leq 5.5, \\ &\Phi(x) \approx 0.5 - 0.5\sqrt{2 / \pi}\frac{1}{x}\exp\left[-x^2 / 2 - 0.94 / x^2\right], \text{ if } x \geq 5.5. \end{aligned} \tag{16}$$

The relative accuracy of both formulas is not worse than 0.042%. Practically the second formula is excessive since if $x > 5.5$ than $\Phi(x) \approx 0.5$ with the absolute accuracy 10^{-7}. In some parts of the program for feature ranking another method of calculating approximate values of the Laplace function was applied. This method is based on the approximate representation of the integrand e^{-t^2} as $e^{-t^2} \approx 1 + \sum_{i=1}^{I} \left(-t^2\right)^i / i!$ (value of I determines accuracy of approximation) and following integration of the right side of the Eq.(16).

The ranking of features can be used for a possible further removal of excessive input features. Suppose the input groups are arranged in the descent order of ranks. Let z input groups in the bottom of a table sum to 5% of the total variance, while remaining $(d - z)$ input features sum to 95%. Then these z input groups can be removed. To check this removal the neural net should run with reduced set of features. If RMAE in testing and validation increase not more than by 0.5% than removal is justified. If this increase is more than 1% in either testing or validation then the removal is rejected.

The ranks are calculated using either the whole data set, therefore using a 33-dimensional unit cube, or just for one point of this cube, which was chosen as the center of the cube, the point $x^{(0)} = \underbrace{(0.5, 0.5, \ldots 0.5)}_{33 \text{ times}}$. The results for 3 selected clusters are shown in the three right columns of Tables 4, 5, and 6.

Determining ranking over clusters assumes that different sets of inputs can be used for different clusters. This strategy has not been implemented yet in CEA. That is why it is interesting to describe distribution of the group ranks for the whole data set. This distribution can be obtained by summing group ranks GR_{jc}, $j = 1, \ldots, NumGr$, $c = 1, \ldots NumClust$, (where *NumGr* is the number of groups, *NumClust* is the number of clusters) for each cluster, multiplied by the weight w_c. The cluster weights are calculated as follows

$$w_c = \frac{numPat_c}{\sum_{c=1}^{numClust} numPat_c}, \ c = 1, \ldots numClust, \tag{17}$$

where $numPat_c$ is the number of patterns in the cluster c, $c = 1, \ldots numClust$. Thus the ranks of the groups of inputs GR_j, $j = 1, \ldots numGr$ over the whole data set are calculated as follows

Table 4. Cluster 1, # patterns = 168, # of NN nodes = 10

Ranking over the whole set			Ranking at one point		
Number	**Group of inputs**	**Rank (%)**	**Number**	**Group of inputs**	**Rank (%)**
1	SA	42.35	1	SA	41.57
2	O2	25.95	2	O2	26.68
3	Amps	14.61	3	Amps	14.59
4	Flow	8.81	4	Flow	8.22
5	OFA	4.46	5	OFA	4.17
6	ExhDP	2.87	6	ExhDP	2.84
7	SucDmpr	1.95	7	SucDmpr	1.93

Table 5. Cluster 2, # patterns = 325, # of NN nodes = 8

Ranking over the whole set			Ranking at one point		
Number	**Group of inputs**	**Rank (%)**	**Number**	**Group of inputs**	**Rank (%)**
1	O2	42.56	1	O2	43.66
2	SA	38.51	2	SA	36.30
3	OFA	9.18	3	OFA	10.62
4	Amps	4.54	4	Amps	4.86
5	ExhDP	2.75	5	ExhDP	2.40
6	SucDmpr	1.76	6	SucDmpr	1.54
7	Flow	0.70	7	Flow	0.62

$$GR_j = \sum_{c=1}^{numClust} w_c GR_{jc}, j = 1, \ldots, numGr, \qquad (18)$$

Calculations of the group ranks of inputs by the formula (18) give the results shown in the table 7. Analyzing the results of ranking some important conclusions can be made:

1. There are two groups of the inputs, SA (secondary air) and O2 (oxygen) that are responsible for over 70% of the output;
2. Other groups making 25-30% of the contribution to the output are also important;
3. Therefore, the problem of predicting NOX is essentially multidimensional, one cannot restrict himself by a few number of inputs;
4. Ranks are substantially depends on clustering, the clustering greatly decreases the search space, For example a cluster having in each dimension the range of the half of the range of the whole set has the volume equal $1/2^{34}$ of the volume of the whole set. The rough estimate of the last number says that the volume of the cluster is less than 0.00000000001 * (the volume of the whole set)! Decreasing the volume of the search space is the main problem in modeling and optimization affecting the reliability of using these both procedures for predicting results on the unknown data;

Table 6. Cluster 7, # patterns = 86, # of NN = 21

Ranking over the whole set			Ranking at one point		
Number	**Group of inputs**	**Rank (%)**	**Number**	**Group of inputs**	**Rank (%)**
1	SA	83.96	1	SA	85.39
2	OFA	10.52	2	OFA	9.97
3	O2	1.98	3	O2	1.43
4	ExhDP	1.33	4	ExhDP	1.10
5	Amps	1.17	5	SucDmpr	0.85
6	SucDmpr	0.66	6	Amps	0.69
7	Flow	0.38	7	Flow	0.47

Table 7. Ranks of the groups of inputs for the whole set in the descending order of ranks

Number of the group	Rank of the group (%)	Title of the group
1	49.93	SA
2	25.43	O2
3	8.06	Amps
4	6.63	OFA
5	3.91	ExhDP
6	3.22	SucDmpr
7	3.01	Flow

5. Surprisingly, results of ranking obtained for one point and for the whole data set are quite close. That says that the values of the predicted neural net output will not be terribly different (on average) than the target output values when predictions will be made in the whole range of the inputs change, not only in the area close to the collected in advance data. This partially can be explained by the work of the algorithm for selecting the number of neural net nodes.

The results of ranking fit the expert knowledge in the field (although the experts, as a rule, exaggerate the role of the oxygen).

The novelty of this approach is in the use of the approximate model. While traditional ranking uses partial derivatives for measuring sensitivity of the output that increases the round-off errors and noise in the data, this approach uses integrals over the model. The latter approach decreases noise and round-off errors.

CONCLUSION

The suggested approach to feature selection and ranking may lead to a significant reduction of the search space with insignificant loss in modeling performance. It also refutes, to some degree, a common believe that neural networks are "black box" models. The neural networks are mathematically defined models with good analytical properties. In particular one can integrate them and get an essential result for applications.

FUTURE RESEARCH DIRECTIONS

The author of this chapter plans for the future research the following:

1. Expanding the feature selection and ranking algorithm suggested in this chapter to all neural network architectures available in the CEA, both traditional and not-traditional;
2. Expanding the data fusion capability of the CEA to information fusion;
3. Building a general adaptive model of noise;
4. Incorporating in the CEA some features of intellect (Hawkins, 2004), in particular making the CEA a hierarchical method. This is supposed to do with an aid of the subsequent compressions of data;
5. Analyzing and making use, where possible, of other approaches to computational modeling and simulating of intellect.

REFERENCES

Albert, A. (1972). *Regression and the Moore-Penrose pseudoinverse*. New York, NY: Academic Press.

Bartels, R. H., Beatty, J. C., & Barsky, B. A. (1987). *An introduction to splines for use in computer graphics and geometric modeling*. San Mateo, CA: Morgan Kaufmann Publishers, Inc.

Bishop, C. M. (1995). *Neural networks for pattern recognition*. New York, NY: Oxford University Press.

Bradley, P. S., & Fayyad, U. M. (1998). *Refining initial points for K-means clustering*. In 15th International Conference on Machine Learning (pp. 91-99). Los Altos, CA: Morgan Kaufmann.

Breiman, L. (1996). Bagging predictors. *Machine Learning, 24*(1), 123–140. doi:10.1007/BF00058655

Breiman, L. (1999). Combining predictors. In Sharkey, A. (Ed.), *Combining artificial neural nets: Ensemble and modular multi-net systems* (pp. 31–50). London, UK: Springer.

Brown, R. G., & Hwang, P. Y. C. (1997). *Introduction to random signals and applied Kalman filtering*. New York, NY: John Wiley & Sons.

Derenzo, S. E. (1977). Approximations for hand calculators using small integer coefficients. *Mathematics of Computation, 31*(137), 214–225. doi:10.1090/S0025-5718-1977-0423761-X

Duda, R. O., Hart, P. E., & Stork, D. G. (2001). *Pattern classification*. New York, NY: JohnWiley & Sons, Inc.

Hawkins, J., & Blakeslee, S. (2004). *On intelligence*. New York, NY: Henry Holt and Company.

Haykin, S. (1994). *Neural networks, a comprehensive foundation*. New York, NY: IEEE Press.

Haykin, S. (Ed.). (2001). *Kalman filtering and neural networks*. New York, NY: John Wiley & Sons. doi:10.1002/0471221546

Igelnik, B. (2000). Some new adaptive architectures for learning, generalization, and visualization of multivariate data. In Sincak, P., & Vascak, J. (Eds.), *Quo Vadis computational intelligence? New trends and approaches in computational intelligence* (pp. 63–78). Heidelberg, Germany & New York, NY: Physica-Verlag.

Igelnik, B. (2001b). Method for visualization of multivariate data in a lower dimension. In *SPIE Visual Data Exploration and Analysis VIII, 4302*, 168-179. San Jose, CA.

Igelnik, B. (2003b). *Visualization of large multidimensional datasets in a lower dimension*. (SBIR Phase I Final Report #0232775, NSF).

Igelnik, B. (2003c). *Visualization of large multidimensional datasets in a lower dimension*. (SBIR Phase II Proposal, #0349713, NSF).

Igelnik, B. (2009). Kolmogorov's spline complex network and adaptive dynamic modeling of data. In Nitta, T. (Ed.), *Complex-valued neural networks* (pp. 56–78). Hershey, PA: IGI Global. doi:10.4018/9781605662145.ch003

Igelnik, B., & Pao, Y.-H. (1995). Stochastic choice of basis functions in adaptive function approximation and the functional-link net. *IEEE Transactions on Neural Networks*, *6*(6), 1320–1329. doi:10.1109/72.471375

Igelnik, B., Pao, Y.-H., & LeClair, S. R. (1996). *An approach for optimization of a continuous function with many local minima*. In 30th Annual Conference on Information Sciences and Systems, 2 (pp. 912-917). Department of Electrical Engineering, Princeton University, Princeton, NJ.

Igelnik, B., Pao, Y.-H., LeClair, S. R., & Shen, C. Y. (1999). The ensemble approach to neural network learning and generalization. *IEEE Transactions on Neural Networks*, *10*(1), 19–30. doi:10.1109/72.737490

Igelnik, B., & Parikh, N. (2003a). Kolmogorov's spline network. *IEEE Transactions on Neural Networks*, *14*(3), 725–733. doi:10.1109/TNN.2003.813830

Igelnik, B., Tabib-Azar, M., & LeClair, S. (2001a). A net with complex weights. *IEEE Transactions on Neural Networks*, *12*(2), 236–249. doi:10.1109/72.914521

Jensen, R., & Shen, Q. (2008). *Computational intelligence and feature selection. Rough and fuzzy approaches*. Piscataway, NJ: IEEE Press. doi:10.1002/9780470377888

Lewis, F. L. (1986). *Optimal estimation*. New York, NY: John Wiley & Sons.

Liu, H., & Motoda, H. (1998). *Feature selection for knowledge discovery and data mining*. Boston, MA: Kluwer Academic Publishers.

Liu, H., & Motoda, H. (2008). *Computational models of feature selection*. Boca Raton, FL: Chapman & Hall/CRC, Taylor & Francis Group.

Niederreiter, H. (1978). Quasi-Monte Carlo methods and pseudorandom numbers. *Bulletin of the American Mathematical Society*, *84*, 957–1041. doi:10.1090/S0002-9904-1978-14532-7

Oja, E., & Lampinen, J. (1994). Unsupervised learning in feature selection. In Zurada, J. M., Marks, R. J., & Robinson, C. J. (Eds.), *Computational modeling imitating life* (pp. 13–22). Pscataway, NJ: IEEE Press.

Perlovski, L. I. (2001). *Neural networks and intellect*. New York, NY: Oxford University Press.

Prenter, P. M. (1975). *Splines and variational methods*. New York, NY: John Wiley & Sons.

Stone, M. (1974). Cross-validatory choice and assessment of statistical predictions. *Journal of the Royal Statistical Society. Series B. Methodological*, *36*(1), 11–147.

Stroud, A. H. (1971). *Approximate calculation of multiple integrals*. Englewood Cliffs, NJ: Prentice-Hall.

Zapranis, A. D., & Refenes, A.-P. (1999). *Principles of neural model identification, selection and adequacy*. London, UK: Springer.

ADDITIONAL READING

Adamatzky, A. (2001). *Computing in nonlinear media and automata collectives*. Bristol, UK: Institute of Physics Publishing. doi:10.1887/075030751X

Batchelor, B. G., & Whelan, P. F. (1997). *Intelligent vision systems for industry*. New York: Springer.

Bekey, G. A. (2005). *Autonomous robots: from biological inspiration to implementation and control*. Cambridge, MA: The MIT Press.

Bekey, G. A. (2008). *Robotics: state of the art and future challenges*. Hackensack, NJ: World Scientific Publishing. doi:10.1142/9781848160071

Cloete, I., & Zurada, J. M. (Eds.), *Knowledge-based engineering*. Cambridge, MA: The MIT Press.

Feng, J. (Ed.). (2004). *Computational neuroscience: a comprehensive approach*. Boca Raton, FL: Chapman & Hall/CRC.

Freeman, W. J. (2000). *How brains make up their minds*. New York: Columbia University Press.

Goertzel, B., & Pennacin, C. (Eds.). (2007). *Artificial general intelligence*. Berlin, Heidelberg: Springer-Ferlag. doi:10.1007/978-3-540-68677-4

Gorodetsky, V. (Eds.). (2007). *Autonomous intelligent systems: agents and data mining*. Berlin, Heidelberg: Springer-Ferlag. doi:10.1007/978-3-540-72839-9

Haikonen, P. O. (2003). *The cognitive approach to conscious machines*. Charlottersville, VA: Imprint Academic.

Haikonen, P. O. (2007). *Robot brains*. Hoboken, NJ: John Wiley & Sons, Inc.doi:10.1002/9780470517871

Kolman, E., & Margaliot, M. (2009). *Knowledge-based neurocomputing: a fuzzy logic approach*. Berlin, Heidelberg: Springer-Ferlag.

Mataric, M. J. (2007). *The robotics primer*. Cambridge, MA: The MIT Press.

O'Reilly, R. C., & Munakata, Y. (2000). *Computational explorations in cognitive neuroscience*. Cambridge, MA: The MIT Press.

Perlovsky, L. (2007). Symbols: integrated cognition and language. In Gudvin, R., & Queiroz, J. (Eds.), *Semiotics and intelligent systems development*. Hershey, PA: Idea Group Publishing.

Priami, C. (2009). Algorithmic systems biology. *Communications of the ACM, 52*(5), 80–88. doi:10.1145/1506409.1506427

Wang, Y. (Ed.). (2009). *Novel approaches in cognitive informatics and natural intelligence*. Hershey, PA: IGI Global.

Wilkinson, D. J. (2006). *Stochastic modelling in systems biology*. Boca Raton, FL: Chapman & Hall/CRC.

KEY TERMS & DEFINITIONS

Basis Functions: The terms of a linear weighted sum in the neural net representation of a multidimensional function.

Computational Methods: Computational methods for intelligent machines.

Data Fusion: Combining the different models, built for a given dataset, in one model with a goal of increasing the modeling performance.

Feature Ranking: The quantitative measuring of the influence of one feature, from a selected set of features, on the output, given that all other features are kept constant.

Feature Selection: The selection of a minimal subset of the given set of features (inputs) that determine the output of a system.

Neural Networks: Adaptive nonlinear modeling tools using representation of a multidimensional function as a linear weighted sum of the nonlinear superpositions of the linear sums of one-dimensional functions.

Time-Variant Data: The data with the characteristics changing in time.

ENDNOTE

1 Possible dependency of a characteristic of a particular local net from a number of local nets is omitted in notations.

APPENDIX: DERIVATION OF EQUATION (14)

$$\begin{aligned}
&\operatorname{var}_i(x_{-i}) = \int_0^1 \left\{ \sum_{n=1}^{N} a_n \left[\varphi_n(x) - \int_0^1 \varphi_n(x)\, dx_i \right] \right\}^2 dx_i = \\
&\int_0^1 \sum_{n=1}^{N} a_n \left[\varphi_n(x) - \int_0^1 \varphi_n(x)\, dx_i \right] \sum_{m=1}^{N} a_m \left[\varphi_m(x) - \int_0^1 \varphi_m(x)\, dx_i \right] dx_i = \\
&\int_0^1 \sum_{n=1}^{N} \sum_{m=1}^{N} a_n a_m \varphi_{n1}(x_{-i}) \varphi_{m1}(x_{-i}) \left[\varphi_{n2}(x_i) - \int_0^1 \varphi_{n2}(x_i)\, dx_i \right] \left[\varphi_{m2}(x_i) - \int_0^1 \varphi_{m2}(x_i)\, dx_i \right] dx_i = \\
&\sum_{n=1}^{N} \sum_{m=1}^{N} a_n a_m \varphi_{n1}(x_{-i}) \varphi_{m1}(x_{-i}) \int_0^1 \left\{ \left[\varphi_{n2}(x_i) - \int_0^1 \varphi_{n2}(x_i)\, dx_i \right] \left[\varphi_{m2}(x_i) - \int_0^1 \varphi_{m2}(x_i)\, dx_i \right] \right\} dx_i
\end{aligned} \tag{A1}$$

$$\begin{aligned}
&\varphi_n(x) = \prod_{i=1}^{d} g\left(w\left(x_i - c_{ni}\right)\right), \\
&\varphi_{n1}(x_{-i}) = \prod_{j=1,\, j \neq i}^{d} g\left(w\left(x_j - c_{nj}\right)\right),\ \varphi_{n2}(x_i) = g\left(w\left(x_i - c_{ni}\right)\right).
\end{aligned} \tag{A2}$$

One easily obtains that

$$\begin{aligned}
&\int_0^1 \left\{ \left[\varphi_{n2}(x_i) - \int_0^1 \varphi_{n2}(x_i)\, dx_i \right] \left[\varphi_{m2}(x_i) - \int_0^1 \varphi_{m2}(x_i)\, dx_i \right] \right\} dx_i = \\
&\int_0^1 \varphi_{n2}(x_i) \varphi_{m2}(x_i)\, dx_i - \int_0^1 \varphi_{n2}(x_i)\, dx_i \int_0^1 \varphi_{m2}(x_i)\, dx_i.
\end{aligned} \tag{A3}$$

Substituting (A3) in (A1) yields

$$\operatorname{var}_i(x_{-i}) = \sum_{n=1}^{N} \sum_{m=1}^{N} a_n a_m \varphi_{n1}(x_{-i}) \varphi_{m1}(x_{-i}) \left[\int_0^1 \varphi_{n2}(x_i) \varphi_{m2}(x_i)\, dx_i - \int_0^1 \varphi_{n2}(x_i)\, dx_i \int_0^1 \varphi_{m2}(x_i)\, dx_i \right] \tag{A4}$$

Substituting (A2) and (A4) in (3) one obtains

$$Var_i = \sum_{n=1}^{N}\sum_{m=1}^{N} a_n a_m \left[\prod_{j=1,\, j\neq i}^{d} \int_0^1 \varphi_{n2}(x_j)\varphi_{m2}(x_j)\,dx_j\right]\left[\int_0^1 \varphi_{n2}(x_i)\varphi_{m2}(x_i)\,dx_i - \int_0^1 \varphi_{n2}(x_i)\,dx_i \int_0^1 \varphi_{m2}(x_i)\,dx_i\right]$$

$$= \sum_{n=1}^{N}\sum_{m=1}^{N} a_n a_m \left[\prod_{j=1}^{d} \int_0^1 \varphi_{n2}(x_j)\varphi_{m2}(x_j)\,dx_j\right]\left[1 - \frac{\int_0^1 \varphi_{n2}(x_i)\,dx_i \int_0^1 \varphi_{m2}(x_i)\,dx_i}{\int_0^1 \varphi_{n2}(x_i)\varphi_{m2}(x_i)\,dx_i}\right].$$

Calculations of $\int_0^1 \varphi_{n2}(x_i)\,dx_i \int_0^1 \varphi_{m2}(x_i)\,dx_i$ and $\int_0^1 \varphi_{n2}(x_i)\varphi_{m2}(x_i)\,dx_i$ yield:

$$\int_0^1 \varphi_{n2}(x_i)\,dx_i \int_0^1 \varphi_{m2}(x_i)\,dx_i = \int_0^1 e^{-\frac{w^2(x_i-c_{ni})^2}{2}}\,dx_i \int_0^1 e^{-\frac{w^2(x_i-c_{mi})^2}{2}}\,dx_i =$$

$$\frac{2\pi}{w^2}\left[\Phi\left(w(1-c_{ni})\right)+\Phi\left(wc_{ni}\right)\right]\left[\Phi\left(w(1-c_{mi})\right)+\Phi\left(wc_{mi}\right)\right], \tag{A5}$$

$$\int_0^1 \varphi_{n2}(x_i)\varphi_{m2}(x_i)\,dx_i = \int_0^1 e^{-\frac{w^2}{2}\left[(x_i-c_{ni})^2+(x_i-c_{mi})^2\right]}\,dx_i = \int_0^1 e^{-w^2\left[\left(x_i-\frac{c_{ni}+c_{mi}}{2}\right)^2+\left(\frac{c_{ni}-c_{mi}}{2}\right)^2\right]}\,dx_i =$$

$$\frac{\sqrt{\pi}}{w} e^{-w^2\left(\frac{c_{ni}-c_{mi}}{2}\right)^2}\left[\Phi\left(\sqrt{2}w\left(1-\frac{c_{ni}+c_{mi}}{2}\right)\right)+\Phi\left(\sqrt{2}w\frac{c_{ni}+c_{mi}}{2}\right)\right]. \tag{A6}$$

$$Var_i = \sum_{n=1}^{N}\sum_{m=1}^{N} a_n a_m \prod_{j=1}^{d}\left\{\frac{\sqrt{\pi}}{w}\left[\Phi\left(w\sqrt{2}\left(1-\frac{c_{nj}+c_{mj}}{2}\right)\right)+\Phi\left(w\sqrt{2}\,\frac{c_{nj}+c_{mj}}{2}\right)\right]e^{-\frac{w^2}{4}(c_{nj}-c_{mj})^2}\right\}*$$

$$\left\{1-\frac{2\sqrt{\pi}e^{\frac{w^2}{4}(c_{ni}-c_{mi})^2}}{w}\frac{\left[\Phi\left(w(1-c_{ni})+\Phi(wc_{ni})\right)\right]\left[\Phi\left(w(1-c_{mi})+\Phi(wc_{mi})\right)\right]}{\left[\Phi\left(w\sqrt{2}\left(1-\frac{c_{ni}+c_{mi}}{2}\right)\right)+\Phi\left(w\sqrt{2}\,\frac{c_{ni}+c_{mi}}{2}\right)\right]}\right\},\ i=1,\ldots d, \tag{A7}$$

Chapter 16
Brain-Like System for Audiovisual Person Authentication Based on Time-to-First Spike Coding

Simei Gomes Wysoski
Auckland University of Technology, New Zealand

Lubica Benuskova
University of Otago, New Zealand

Nikola Kasabov
Auckland University of Technology, New Zealand

ABSTRACT

The question of the neural code, or how neurons code information about stimuli, is not definitively answered. In addition to experimental research, computational modeling can help in getting closer to solving this problem. In this chapter, spiking neural network architectures for visual, auditory and integrated audiovisual pattern recognition and classification are described. The authors' spiking neural network uses time to first spike as a code for saliency of input features. The system is trained and evaluated on the person authentication task. The chapter concludes that the time-to-first-spike coding scheme may not be suitable for this difficult task, nor for auditory processing. Other coding schemes and extensions of this spiking neural network are discussed as the topics of the future research.

INTRODUCTION

Artificial information processing systems, despite enormous effort, still struggle to deliver general and reliable solutions, comparable with the performance of the brain. The core of the problem is that we still do not understand the neural code. The brain is a gigantic network of interconnected neurons. Research

DOI: 10.4018/978-1-60960-551-3.ch016

Figure 1. Neuron and its basic input-output behaviour. (A) Incoming pulses evoke the postsynaptic potential (PSP), which is the sum (Σ) of many (thousands) of synaptic PSPs. (B) Output pulses are released when the total PSP reaches the firing thresholdϑ. (C) Perceptron model. Note the innovations proposed over the years: changeable input weights **W**, *different activation functions f, and inputs/outputs with real numbers representing mean firing frequencies of spike trains.*

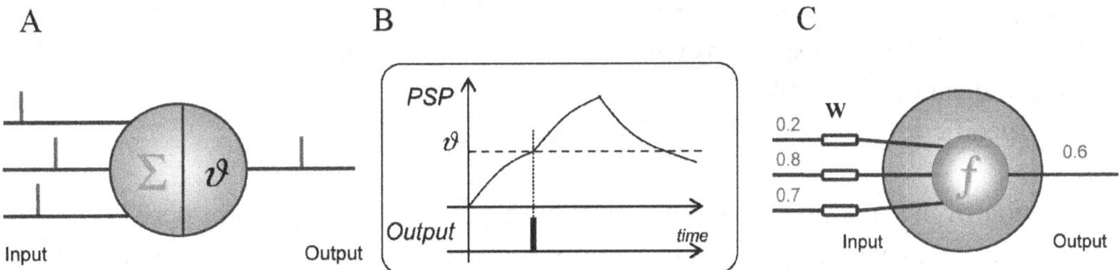

on the brain information processing has acquired enough evidence to suggest that biological neurons transmit information using short electrical discharges generated by electrochemical activity. Output signals of neurons have constant amplitudes (~100 mV) and short duration (~1ms). Therefore they are commonly referred as pulses or spikes. Neurons in the brain send messages to each other by spikes. The big scientific question nowadays is: how are the properties of a stimulus encoded in the individual and ensemble responses of neurons? In other words, *how are messages encoded in spikes*? To be able to answer this question will be of tremendous importance in understanding and modeling human intellect.

The typical behaviour of a neuronal unit can be roughly described as follows: an incoming pulse (received by a dendrite or soma) increases the inner potential of a neuron, which is called a postsynaptic potential (PSP). When the inner potential at a neuronal soma reaches a certain threshold, the neuron outputs a spike (through the axon). Figures 1A and 1B illustrate this process.

A wide range of models describing the functional behaviour of a single neuron has been proposed, e.g., integrate-and-fire, integrate-and-fire with leakage, spike response model, Izhikevich model (Gerstner & Kistler, 2002; Izhikevich, 2003). In the majority of models, a neuron is represented with three parts: dendrites, responsible for collecting signals from other neurons; soma, the summation unit, and axon, from which signals are released. Most of these attempts model information processing at a somatic level and consider the spiking characteristic as a means of communication between neurons (Gerstner & Kistler, 2002). These neuron models come in opposition to the perceptron model (Rumelhart & McClelland, 1996), which enables input/output communication using real numbers (Figure 1C).

While the perceptron enables the units to process only rate-based information, spiking neurons enable richer processing patterns. A sequence (train) of spikes emitted by a given neuron in response to stimulus may contain information based on different coding schemes. Frequency or rate coding is a traditional coding scheme assuming that information about the stimulus is contained in the output firing rate of the neuron. This has led to the idea that a neuron transforms information about a single input variable (the stimulus strength) into a single continuous output variable (the firing rate) as in the perceptron. Many artificial neural network models use this idea. However, a number of neurobiological studies have found that the temporal resolution of the neural code is on a millisecond time scale (Abeles & Gat, 2001; Hopfield, 1995; Izhikevich, 2006; Reece, 2001; Thorpe, Fize, & Marlot, 1996; Villa, Tetko, Hyland, & Najem, 1999). This indicates that precise spike timing is a significant element in neural coding. For example, time to first spike after the stimulus onset, or precisely timed temporal patterns of spikes or the relative timing of spikes with respect to an ongoing brain oscillation, are candidates for temporal codes. The interplay between the dynamics of the stimulus and the encoding neural dynamics makes the identification of a temporal code difficult. Therefore, besides the neurobiological experimental line of research, computational simulations and modeling studies can contribute to the search for the neural code.

In this chapter we describe our results on an integrated brain-like audiovisual pattern recognition model that uses the time to first spike as an information coding principle. We have evaluated the system on the person authentication problem.

The main specific contributions of this chapter are:

1. Description of the spiking neural network (SNN) architecture to perform person authentication through the processing of signals from auditory and visual modalities. The integrative architecture combines opinions from individual modalities within a supramodal layer, which contains neurons sensitive to multiple sensory inputs. An additional feature that increases biological relevance is the crossmodal coupling of modalities, which effectively enables a given sensory modality to exert direct influence upon the processing areas related to other modalities. This integrated model was introduced by Wysoski, Benuskova and Kasabov (2008b, 2010).
2. Description of adaptive online learning procedure for audiovisual pattern recognition. This online learning procedure which enables the system to change its structure by creating and/or merging neuronal maps of spiking neurons was introduced and evaluated by Wysoski, Benuskova and Kasabov (2006, 2008b) for visual SNN and adapted for the auditory SNN in (Wysoski, Benuskova and Kasabov 2007).
3. Summary of experimental evaluation of the SNN architecture that integrates sensory modalities on a person authentication problem, and comparison with the results from studies using similar experimental setup but different techniques. By comparing our model with artificial systems based on mathematical and statistical principles, we can show how far we can get in pattern recognition task with time-to-first-spike coding scheme.
4. Description and discussion of the limitations of the time-to-first-spike coding scheme and directions for future research.

BACKGROUND

Several theoretical and computational models of the visual system are based on the Hubel's and Wiesel's experimental findings on directionally selective and complex cells placed in a hierarchical visual pathway (Hubel & Wiesel, 1962) for the purpose of pattern recognition (Fukushima & Miyake, 1982; Mel, 1998; Riesenhuber & Poggio, 1999). Fukushima and Miyake (1982) proposed the Neocognitron, which processes information with rate-based neural units in a pioneering attempt to create a network in which the information is processed through several areas resembling the visual system. A new type of model for object recognition based on computational properties found in the brain cortex was described by Riesenhuber and Poggio (1999). This model uses hierarchical layers similar to the Neocognitron and processing units based on MAX-like operation, to define the postsynaptic response, which results in relative position- and scale-invariant features. This biologically motivated hierarchical method has been carefully analyzed by Serre et al., (2007) on several real-world datasets, extracting shape and texture properties. Their analysis encompassed invariance on single object recognition and recognition of multiple objects in complex visual scenes (e.g. leaves, cars, faces, airplanes, motorcycles). The method showed comparable performance with benchmark algorithms, like the constellation models, hierarchical SVM-based face detection, and systems that use Ullman et al's fragments and GentleBoost.

In the same way, Mel (1998) applies purely feed-forward hierarchical pathways to perform feature extraction, now integrating colour, shape, and texture. The hierarchical architecture enables the extraction of 102 features that are combined in a nearest-neighbour classifier. For a constrained visual world, the features demonstrated to be relatively insensitive to changes in the image plane and object orientation, fairly sensitive to changes in object scale and non rigid deformation, and highly sensitive to the quality of the visual objects. Kruger et al describes a rich set of primitive features that include frequency, orientation, contrast transition, colour and optical flow, which are integrated following semantic attributes (Kruger, Lappe, & Worgotter, 2004). Each attribute in practice, has a confidence level, which can be adapted according to visual context information.

Further in the attempt to explore the brain's way of processing, experimental results from neurobiology have led to the investigation of a third generation of neural network models which employ spiking neurons as computational units. Matsugu et al. (2002) utilized a hybrid of a convolutional and a spiking neural network (SNN) for face detection tasks. In this hierarchical network, local patterns defined by a set of primitive features are represented in the timing structure of pulse signals. The training method used standard error back-propagation algorithm for the bottom feature-detecting layer. The model implements hierarchical pattern matching by temporal integration of structured pulse packets. The packet signal represents intermediate or complex visual features (like an eye, nose, corners, a pair of line segments, etc.) that constitute a face model. As a result of the spatio-temporal dynamics, the authors achieved size and rotation invariant internal representation of objects. Endowed with a rule-based algorithm for facial expression classification, this hybrid architecture achieved robust facial expression recognition together with robust face detection (Matsugu et al., 2003).

Hopfield (1995) proposed a model and learning algorithm for spiking neurons to realize Radial Basis Functions (RBFs) where spatial-temporal information is presented based on the timing of single spikes, i.e., not in a rate-based fashion. Natschlager and Ruf implemented this idea, by defining the pattern not only by the sequence of input spikes, but also by the exact firing time (Natschlager & Ruf, 1998; Natschlager & Ruf, 1999). In these works, an input pattern representing a spatial feature is encoded in the temporal domain by one spike per neuron. It has also been shown how simple it is to modify the system to recognize sequences of spatial patterns by allowing the occurrence of more than one spike per neuron. Other conclusions of these works include: (a) even under the presence of noise (in terms of spatial deformation or time warping) the recognition can be undertaken; and (b) an RBF neuron can be used to perform a kind of feature extraction, i.e., a neuron can be designed to receive excitation/inhibition from a subset of features and be insensitive to others.

Maciokas, Goodman and Harris Jr. (2002) went down to the level of ion channels to describe a model of an audiovisual system that reproduces the responses of the GABAergic cells. Audio features were extracted using Short Term Fourier Transform and represented in tonotopic maps. The visual information of lip movement was extracted using Gabor filters. The two main results described in his work are: (a) the accurate model of diverse firing behaviours of GABAergic cells; and (b) proof that a large-scale network of the cortical processing preserves information in audiovisual modalities using an entropy measure. Though, no attempts to rigorously test the classification abilities of the network have been made.

All models that use one spike per neuron or time-to-first-spike refer directly or indirectly to Thorpe, Fize and Marlot (1996). They suggested that in order to be coherent with the time measured in psychophysical experiments on fast perceptual classification, the information processing mechanisms can afford to have neurons exchanging only one or a few spikes. The time between information acquisition and the cognitive response is too short to have rate-based neuronal encoding, since the information needs to travel sequentially over several tens of different compartments located in distinct brain areas. Thus, the information needs to be sparsely encoded and, highly complex cognitive activities are reached through a complex wiring system that connects neuronal units. As an output of this work, the authors proposed a multi-layer feed-forward network (SpikeNet) using fast integrate-and-fire neurons that can successfully track and recognize faces in real time (Delorme et al., 1999; Delorme & Thorpe, 2001). Coding of information in this model is based on the so-called rank order coding, where the first spike is the most important. It has been shown that using rank order coding and tuning the scale sensitivity according to the statistics of the natural images can lead to a very efficient retina coding strategy, which is compared to image processing standards like JPEG (Perrinet & Samuelides, 2002). We use these ideas in our model and extend them to auditory and audiovisual modality in order to explore the power and limits of time-to-first-spike coding principle.

Auditory system has a completely different organization compared to the visual system and also the processing stages and principles are different from the visual system. Robert and Eriksson (1999) proposed a biologically plausible model of the auditory periphery to simulate the response to complex sounds. The model basically reproduces the filtering executed by the outer/middle ear, basilar membrane, inner hair cells, and auditory nerve fibers. The purpose of Robert and Eriksson's model is to facilitate the understanding of signal coding within the cochlea and in the auditory nerve as well as analyse sound signals. The outputs of the inner hair cells and auditory nerve fibers are properly represented with trains of spikes. This model has been used in (Eriksson & Villa, 2006) to simulate the learning of synthetic vowels by rats reported in (Eriksson & Villa, 2006a). In this latter work, based on experimental measurements, besides proving that rats are able to discriminate and generalize instances of the same vowel, it is further suggested that, similar to humans, rats use spectral and temporal cues for sound recognition.

An SNN model has been applied in sound localization (Kuroyanagi & Iwata, 1994) and in sound source separation and source recognition in (Iwasa et al., 2007). In (McLennan & Hockema, 2001) a simple SNN structure is proposed to extract the fundamental frequency of a speech signal online. The highlight of the latter system is that a Hebbian learning rule dynamically adjusts the behaviour of the network based on the input signal. Mercier & Seguier (2002) proposed the use of the Spatio-Temporal Artificial Neural Network model (STANN) based on spiking neurons on the speech recognition problem (recognition of digits on the Tulips1 dataset) (Movellan, 1995). STANNs were initially proposed to process visual information (Seguier & Mercier, 2001).

Holmberg et al. (2005) put stress on the importance of temporal and spectral characteristics of sound signals. The spectral properties are inherently represented with "rate-place code" during the transduction of the inner hair cells. Temporal information, on the other hand, provides additional cues, such as amplitude modulation and onset time. In the same work a multi-layer auditory model is presented, which emulates inner ear filtering, compression and transduction. The work mainly concentrates on using spiking neurons to model octopus neurons, which are neurons located at the cochlear nucleus. Octopus neurons enhance the amplitude modulations of speech signals and are sensitive to signal onsets. Preliminary experiments showed that the system performs in much the same way as Mel Frequency Cepstral Coefficients (MFCC) (Rabiner & Juang, 1993).

Rouat, Pichevar and Loiselle (2005) envisage the advantages of merging perceptual speech characteristics and biologically realistic neural networks. After a description of the perceptual properties of the auditory system and non-linear processing performed by spiking neural networks, a biologically inspired system to perform source separation on auditory signals is proposed. In the same work and in (Loiselle et al, 2005), a preliminary evaluation used SNN for recognition of spoken numbers. These works can be considered to be an extension of principles used in the SpikeNet for auditory domain, which is substantially modified below in this chapter.

There is strong experimental evidence showing that integration of sensory information occurs in the brain (Calvert, 2001; Ghazanfar et al, 2005; Kriegstein & Giraud, 2006; Kriegstein et al, 2005; Stein & Meredith, 1993) and a lot is known about the location in the brain where different modalities converge. A more conservative theory asserts that the integration occurs in *supramodal* areas that contain neurons sensitive to more than one modality, i.e., neurons that process different types of information (Ellis, Jones, & Mosdell, 1997). Nonetheless, behavioural observations and electrophysiological experiments have demonstrated the occurrence of another integrative phenomenon: *crossmodal* coupling, which is related to the direct influence of one modality to areas that intrinsically belong to other modalities (Calvert, 2001; Ghazanfar et al, 2005). Brunelli and Falavigna (1995) presented a system where two classifiers are used to process speech signals and three others to recognize visual inputs. MFCC and the corresponding derivatives are used as features, and each speaker is represented by a set of vectors based on Vector Quantization (VQ) (Rosenberg & Soong, 1987). A local template matching approach at the pixel level, where particular areas of the face (eyes, nose, and mouth) are compared with a previously stored data, is used for face authentication. The results of these individual classifiers are connected to the input of a new integrative module based on HyperBF networks (Poggio & Girosi, 1990). Attempting to further improve the performance of the multimodal systems, several methods propose adaptation of the fusion mechanisms (Chibelushi, Deravi, & Mason, 1999; Sanderson & Paliwal, 2002). See (Chibelushi, Deravi, & Mason, 2002) for an extensive and comprehensive list.

Maciokas, Goodman, & Harris Jr. (2002) applied brain like approaches to tackle the problem of integrating the visual information of lip movements with the corresponding speech generated by it. The proposed system uses a biologically realistic spiking neural network with 25.000 neurons placed in 10 columns and several layers. Tonotopic maps fed from Short Term Fourier Transform (STFT) with a neural architecture that resembles MEL scale filters are used for converting audio signals to spikes. Gabor Filters extract the lip movements. The encoding of three distinct sentences in three distinct spiking patterns was demonstrated. In addition, after using the Hebbian rule for training, the output spiking patterns were also distinguishable from each other.

Seguier and Mercier (2002) also describe a system for integrating lip movements and speech signals to present a one-pass learning with spiking neurons. The performance achieved is favourable to the integrated system, mainly when audio signals are deteriorated with noise. The system is intended to produce real-time results, therefore simple visual features are used and auditory signals are represented by 12 cepstral coefficients. Vector quantization is applied individually to extract vector codes, which are then encoded into pulses to be processed by the Spatio-Temporal Artificial Neural Network (STANN) (Mozayyani, Baig, & Vaucher, 1998; Vaucher, 1998).

Chevallier, Paugam-Moisy, and Lemaitre (2005) present a system based on SNN to be used in a robot capable of processing audiovisual sensory information in a prey-predator environment. In reality, the system is composed of several neural networks (prototype-based incremental classifier), one for each sensorial modality. A centralized compartment for data integration is implemented as a bidirectional associative memory. A network (also incremental) is used to perform the final classification (This architecture is described in detail in (Crepet et al., 2000)). Particularly interesting in the prey-predator implementation is the spike-based bidirectional associative memory used. As properly suggested by the authors, the implementation using spikes enables the flow of information over time. The integration of these streams of incoming data is also processed on the fly as soon as the data from different modalities are made available. Furthermore, the bidirectional associative memory implemented with the spiking mechanism enables the simulation of crossmodal interaction.

Kittler et al (1998), after providing a review, tries to find a common basis for the problem of combining classifiers through a theoretical framework. It is argued that most of the methods proposed so far can be roughly classified in one of the following types: product rule, sum rule, min rule, max rule, median rule and majority voting. After performing error sensitivity analysis on several combined systems, it is further suggested that the sum rule outperforms the other combination procedures. A more specific review of the speech-based audiovisual integration problem (speech and speaker recognition) is provided in (Chibelushi, Deravi, & Mason, 2002).

In (Yamauchi, Oota, & Ishii, 1999; Yamauchi et al., 2001) a self-supervised learning procedure is described that learns categories automatically by integrating sensory information. After training, the system is able to control the priority of the sensors based on the characteristics of input signals. Particularly interesting in this design is the use of two networks for each sensor (forward and backward network). In the forward network, weights are adjusted for mapping incoming sensor signals (input) to the output, whereas in the backward network weights are adjusted for mapping the output vector to input signal. The result of the backward network is an estimation of the input signal, which is used during the recognition phase as a confidence measure of the sensory input. With this approach, priority between sensors can be established, which demonstrated to increase the learning ability of categories based on unlabelled datasets.

Among all the systems mentioned above, whether using traditional techniques or brain-like networks, none of them demonstrated performance degradation of multimodal systems. On the contrary, the integration, in a synergistic way, achieves higher accuracy levels when compared with single modalities alone.

Further sections of this chapter present our attempt to process bimodal sensory information with a new architecture of fast spiking neurons where only the time to the first spike spike carries the information. Besides the inherent ability of the neurons to process information in a simple and fast way, the main property of the system is the ability to receive and integrate information from different modules online, as the information becomes available. The crossmodal connections, which we employ in our model, go beyond the architectures of current multimodal systems that are based traditionally on the decomposition and consequent recombination of modalities.

SPIKE-BASED AUDIOVISUAL SYSTEM FOR PERSON AUTHENTICATION

The basic neural unit in our model is the integrate-and-fire neuron model described in (Delorme, Perrinet, & Thorpe, 2001; Delorme & Thorpe, 2001). The neuron's excitation depends on the order of arrival of spikes and the postsynaptic potential (PSP) for neuron i at time t is calculated as

$$PSP(i,t) = \sum_{j} \text{mod}^{order(j)} w_{j,i} \tag{1}$$

where mod $\in (0, 1)$ is the modulation factor, j is the index for the incoming connection, $w_{j,i}$ is the synaptic weight of input from neuron j on neuron i, and $order(j)$ is the order of spike arrival from neuron j to neuron i. For instance, setting mod = 0.9 and considering $w_{i,j} = 1$, the first spike to arrive ($order\ (j) = 0$) changes the PSP by $0.9^{(0)} = 1$. The second spike ($order\ (j) = 1$) further influences the PSP by $0.9^{(1)} = 0.9$, the third spike by $0.9^{(2)} = 0.81$, and so on. An output spike is generated if

$$PSP(i,t) \geq PSP_{Th}(i) \tag{2}$$

where PSP_{Th} is the postsynaptic firing threshold. The main advantages of these neurons are that they are computationally very inexpensive and they boost the importance of the first pre-synaptic spikes. The network structure, where neurons are placed in grids forming neuronal maps and consequently, layers of maps, are introduced in the next sections and are dependent on the task.

Simplified Model of the Visual System

In the visual part of our system, the functional behaviour of retina, orientation selective cells and complex cells is modelled within several layers of spiking neurons. By complex cells in this context we mean neurons that are selective to the complex combination of orientations of edges. Only feed-forward connections are used and no adaptation at lower levels is applied (retina and orientation cells). Architecture, training and experimental evaluation of spiking neural network (SNN) for visual information processing was described in detail in (Wysoski, Benuskova, & Kasabov, 2008a) with some preliminary results reported in (Wysoski, Benuskova, & Kasabov, 2006). For the sake of completeness of this chapter, we will repeat the main points here. Thus, our SNN is composed of four layers of integrate-and-fire neurons (Figure 2).

In the first two layers (L1 and L2) there is no learning, they simply act as passive filters and time domain encoders. Neurons in L1 represent the contrast cells of the retina, enhancing the high contrast parts of a given image (high-pass filter). One neuron in each L1 neuronal map is allocated to each pixel of an image (receptive fields). Images normalized in size with height of 60 pixels and width of 40 pixels, were used in the experiments. L1 can have several pairs of neuronal maps, each pair tuned to a different frequency scale. Contrast cells are implemented through weighted connections between the receptive fields and the L1 neurons. Weights are computed with a two-dimensional difference of Gaussians, where different scales are chosen varying the standard deviation σ of the Gaussian curve G. Equation 3 describes the contrast filters, where g normalizes the sum of weight elements to zero and the maximum and minimum convolution values to [+1, -1]:

$$\nabla^2 G(x,y) = g\left(\frac{x^2 + y^2 - \sigma^2}{\sigma^4}\right) e^{-\left(\frac{x^2+y^2}{2\sigma^2}\right)} \tag{3}$$

Figure 2. Visual SNN architecture composed of four layers. Neurons in L1 and L2 are sensitive to image contrast and orientation, respectively. L3 has the complex cells, trained to respond to specific patterns. L4 accumulates opinions over different input frames over time

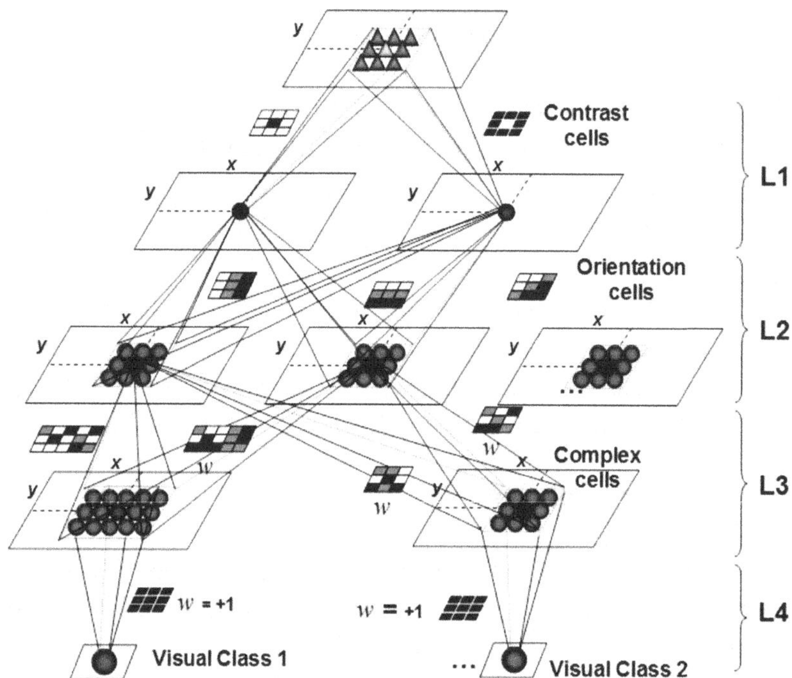

Output values of units in L1 are encoded to pulses in the time domain. High output values of the first layer are encoded with short time delay pulses whereas pulses with long delays are generated in the case of low output values, according to the rank order coding technique (Delorme, Perrinet, & Thorpe, 2001) (Figure 3). L1 basically prioritizes the pixels with high contrast, which are consequently processed first and have a higher impact on PSPs of neurons in the next layer.

The second layer (L2) is composed of eight orientation maps for each frequency scale, each one being selective to different directions (0°, 45°, 90°, 135°, 180°, 225°, 270°, and 315°). To compute the directionally selective filters the Gabor function is used:

$$\begin{aligned} G(x,y) &= e^{\left(\frac{x'^2+\gamma^2 y'^2}{2\sigma^2}\right)} \cos\left(2\pi\frac{x'}{\lambda}+\phi\right) \\ x' &= x\cos(\theta)+y\sin(\theta) \\ y' &= -x\sin(\theta)+y\cos(\theta) \end{aligned} \tag{4}$$

where φ is the phase offset, θ is the orientation [0,360], λ is the wavelength, σ is the standard deviation of the Gaussian factor of the Gabor function and γ is the aspect ratio, which specifies the ellipticity of the support of the Gabor function. These Gabor filters are normalized globally for each frequency scale, in such a way that neurons in L3 that have directionally selective cells as inputs can have PSPs that vary

Figure 3. Illustration of the Rank Order Coding. A hypothetical input signal is converted into pulses with delays inversely proportional to the signal's amplitude. That is, the stronger the input stimulation the sooner the neuron fires and vice versa

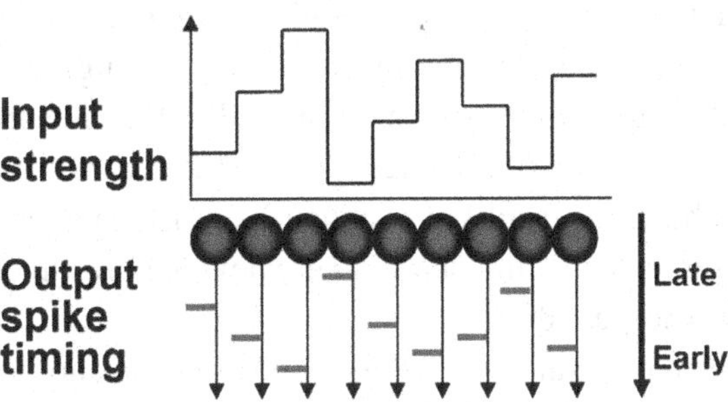

Figure 4. (A) Weights of ON and OFF contrast cells and weights of directionally selective cells applied to L1 and L2 respectively. (B) Example of neural activity when the network receives an input stimulus.

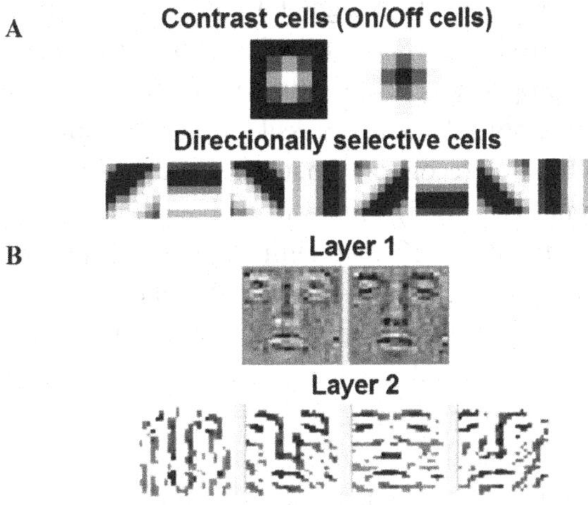

within that range [0, PSP_{max}], regardless of the scale of the filters. Depending on the task, these parameters can be subject of optimization as they are very sensitive and can affect the overall performance of the system. In the experiments presented in this chapter, contrast cells and directionally selective cells parameters have been tuned by hand. Two scales of On/Off cells (4 L1 neuronal maps) are used. In scale 1, the retina filters are implemented using a 3 x 3 Gaussian grid with $\sigma = 0.9$ and scale 2 uses a 5 x 5 grid with $\sigma = 1.5$. In L2, there are eight different directions in each frequency scale with a total of 16 neuronal maps. The directionally selective filters are implemented using Gabor functions with aspect ratio $\gamma = 0.5$ and phase offset $\varphi = \pi/2$. In scale 1 a 5 x 5 grid with a wavelength of $\lambda = 5$ and $\sigma = 2.5$ is used and in scale 2 a 7 x 7 grid with λ and σ set to 7 and 3.5, respectively. The modulation factor for the visual neurons was set to 0.995. Processing in the first two layers of the model visual system is illustrated in Figure 4.

In the third layer (L3), where the learning takes place, maps are trained to be sensitive to incoming excitation of more complex patterns. Neuronal maps are created or merged during learning, according to the online learning procedure described in the next section and in (Wysoski, Benuskova, & Kasabov, 2008a). An input pattern belongs to a certain class if a neuron in the corresponding neuronal map spikes first. There are lateral inhibitory connections between neuronal maps in the third layer L3, so that when a neuron fires in a certain map, other maps receive inhibitory pulses in the area centered in the same spatial position. Layer 4 (L4) has one neuronal map containing a single neuron for each pattern class. The L4 neuron of a given class is fed by the corresponding L3 neuronal maps. There are excitatory connections (typically $w = +1$) between neurons located close to the centre of L3 maps and the corresponding L4 neuron. In fact, L4 combines the results of a sequence of visual patterns, i.e. accumulates opinions from several frames. This layer and an online learning are new features in comparison with the original SpikeNet model (Delorme & Thorpe, 2001).

The connection weights between L3 and L4, in the simplest case, are not subject to learning. Excitatory connections with fixed amplitude can be used instead. In a more elaborate setup, connection weights with amplitude varying according to a Gaussian curve centred in the middle of each L3 map gives a sense of confidence regarding the L3 output spikes. This is because only the middle neuron in each L3 neuronal map is trained to respond optimally to a certain excitation pattern, decreasing in reliability as the neuron's location approach the map's extremities. However, independent of the choice of weights, the PSP thresholds for L4 neurons need to be assigned. L4 PSP thresholds can be trained using a global optimization algorithm, or alternatively, as was done in the following experiments, a simple heuristic that defines L4 PSP thresholds as a proportion p of the number of frames used for testing can be employed. With the inclusion of this simple procedure, it is possible to assess how many positive opinions from different visual frames are required to recognize a pattern successfully.

In terms of network dynamics (Figure 5), spikes of a given visual frame are propagated to L2 and L3 until any neuron belonging to any of L3 map emits the first output spike, which is consequently propagated to L4. If any neuron in L4 generates an output spike, the simulation is truncated and the frame is labelled to the corresponding class. The next frame follows. Otherwise, if there is no output spike in any L4 neuron or there are no spikes from L3, the next frame is propagated. The next frame starts to be propagated always only after resetting the PSPs and the order of arrival of spikes $order(i, j)$ in L2 and L3 neurons. On the other hand, L4 neurons retain their PSP levels and the order of arrival of spikes $order(i, j)$, to accumulate influences over consecutive frames, until a class is recognized with an L4 neuron output spike or until there are no more frames to be processed.

Learning of Visual Patterns

For the sake of a complete description of the model, we also summarize here the learning procedure presented in detail in (Wysoski, Benuskova, & Kasabov, 2008a). The learning procedure follows four sequential steps:

Propagate a sample $k = 1, \ldots, K$ of class C for training within L1 (retina) and L2 (directionally selective cells). Create a new map $Map_{C(k)}$ in L3 for sample k and train the weights using the equation:

$$\Delta w_{j,i} = \mathrm{mod}^{order(j)} \tag{5}$$

Figure 5. Spike propagation between layers. Visual excitation (frames f1, f2,..., fN) is propagated through L1, L2 to L3 until any L3 neuron generates an output spike (Δt_{fN}). L3 spikes are propagated to L4 and, if there is no output spike in any L4 neuron, L1, L2 and L3 neurons are reset to the rest potential. A new frame is then processed. The simulation is terminated when an L4 neuron spikes or there are no more frames to be processed.

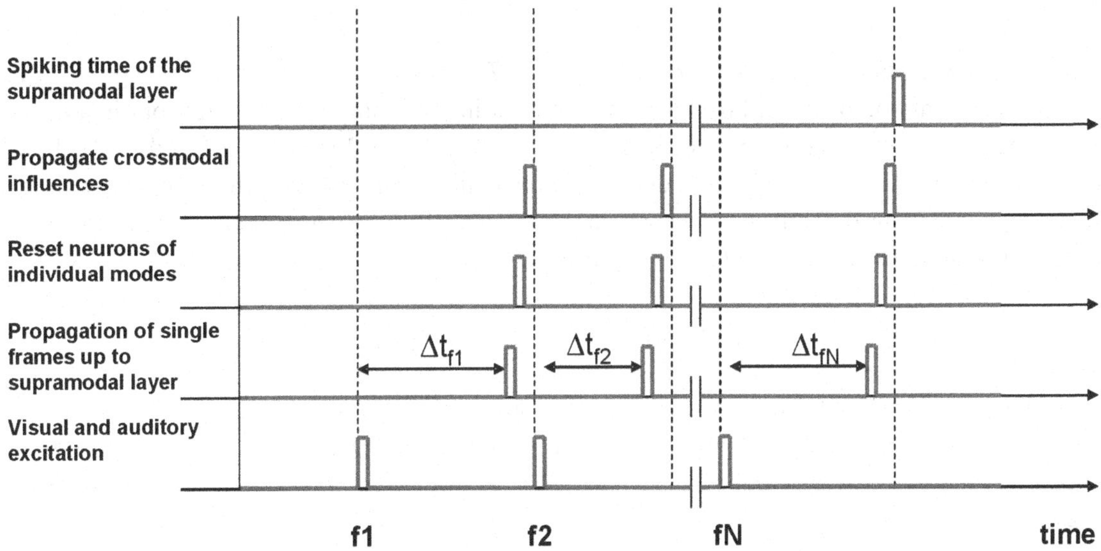

where $w_{j,i}$ is the weight between neuron j of L2 and neuron i of L3, mod $\in (0,1)$ is the modulation factor, *order(j)* is the order of spike arrival from neuron j to neuron i.

Firing thresholds (PSP_{Th}) of neurons in the map are calculated as a proportion $c \in [0,1]$ of the maximum postsynaptic potential (*PSP*) evoked in neurons in $Map_{C(k)}$, such that:

$$PSP_{threshold} = c\max(PSP) \tag{6}$$

The constant of proportionality c is a measure of similarity between a trained pattern and a sample to be recognized. If $c = 1$, for instance, only an identical sample of the training pattern evokes the output spike. Thus, c is a parameter to be optimized in order to satisfy the optimal requirements in terms of false acceptance rate (FAR) and false rejection rate (FRR).

Calculate the similarity between the newly created map $Map_{C(k)}$ and other maps belonging to the same class $Map_{C(K)}$. The similarity is computed as the inverse of the Euclidean distance between weight matrices. If one of the existing maps for class C has similarity greater than a chosen threshold $Th_{simC(K)} > 0$, merge the maps $Map_{C(k)}$ and $Map_{C(K\text{similar})}$ using arithmetic average as

$$W = \frac{W_{Map_{C(k)}} + N_{samples} W_{Map_{C(Ksimilar)}}}{1 + N_{samples}} \tag{7}$$

where matrix W represents the weights of the merged map and $N_{samples}$ denotes the number of samples that have already being used to train the respective map. The PSP_{Th} is updated in a similar fashion as:

$$PSP_{Th} = \frac{PSP_{Map_{C(k)}} + N_{samples} PSP_{Map_{C(Ksimilar)}}}{1 + N_{samples}} \tag{8}$$

Note that the learning procedure updates W and PSP_{Th} as well as enables map merging for each incoming sample during training. For this reason, presenting the samples to the network in a different order can potentially lead to different network structure as well as different final W and PSP_{Th}. In other words, samples presented in a different order could potentially form slightly different clusters (different numbers of output maps for a given class), which can in turn affect the performance of the network. The training can be summarized with the following pseudo-code:

```
For each sample in the training set
Create a new map in L3
Propagate the sample into the network through L1 and L2
Train the newly created map using Equation 5 and Equation 6
Calculate the similarity between resulting weight vectors of newly created map
and existent maps within L3
If similarity > Threshold
Merge newly created map with the most similar map using Equation 7 and Equa-
tion 8
```

The testing of the SNN-based multi-view face authentication system demonstrated:

1. The ability to adaptively learn from multiple frames as evaluated in (Wysoski, Benuskova, & Kasabov, 2008a). We showed that more training frames (different views) of a face increased the accuracy. A peak in performance was reached after five frames.
2. The ability of the system to accumulate opinions from several frames for decision-making. Further experiments in (Wysoski, Benuskova, & Kasabov, 2008a) demonstrated that the accumulation of opinion over more test frames (different from the training frames) increases accuracy. The accuracy level showed to flatten after five frames.

This was true for different combinations of numbers of training and testing faces taken from the VidTimit dataset. The best performance of our SNN in terms of Total Error (TE) = FAR + FRR (False Acceptance rate + False Rejection Rate) = 7.9%. In terms of correct classification, the best performance of our SNN on the test sets was 97%, which was comparable with the performance of a support vector machine and multilayer perceptron on the same training/resting set with the features extracted by means of PCA (more details in Wysoski, Benuskova, & Kasabov, 2008a). It seems that time-to-first spike coding works well for this type of the visual task, i.e. classification based on black-and-white 2D photographs.

Figure 6. Design of the auditory SNN that performs: (A) speech signal pre-processing, and (B) speaker authentication.

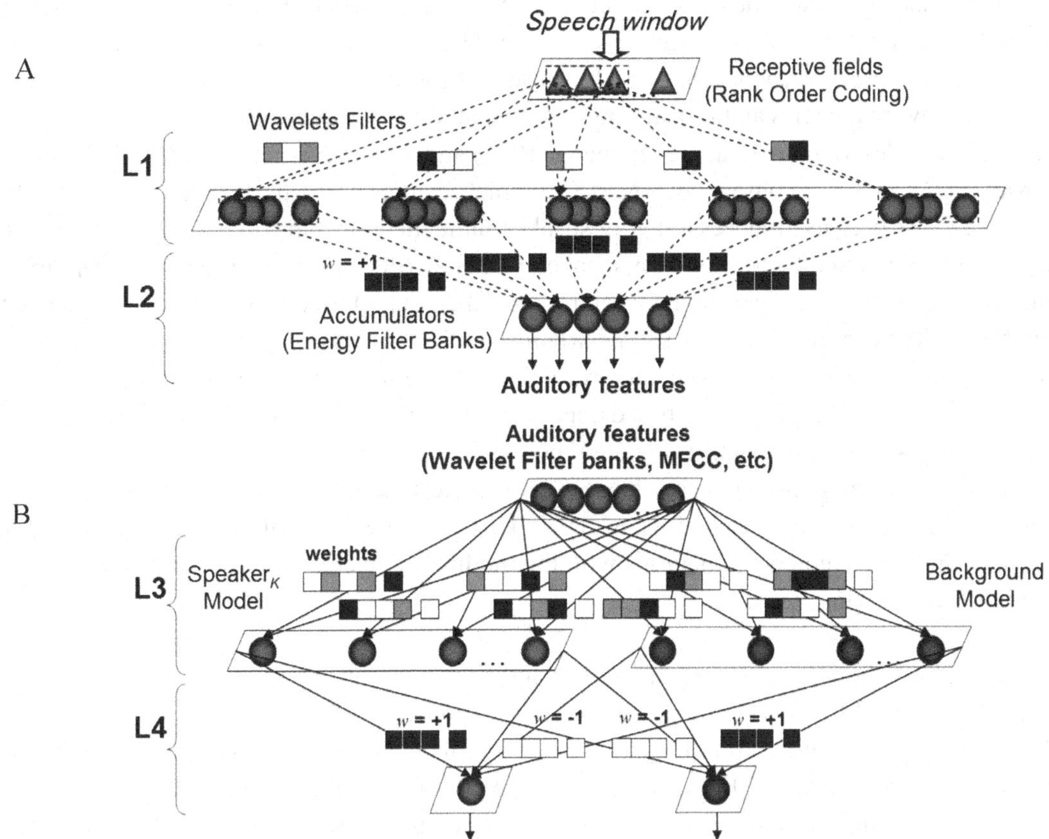

Simplified Model of the Auditory System

This section presents the design of a new network architecture based on fast spiking neurons performing feature extraction and recognition of speech signals. The network simulates the task of the inner hair cells of the cochlea, which perform the transduction of waves into spikes with tonotopically-organized ensembles. Features extracted from a functional model that resembles the characteristics of the human ear (Mel Frequency Cepstral Coefficients, MFCC) are used during the design and evaluation of the decision-making process for speech signals. In the experiments shown in this chapter, speech signals are sampled at 16 kHz, and features are extracted using standard MFCC with 19 MEL filter sub-bands ranging from 200 Hz to 7 kHz. A more elaborate design using tonotopic organization of the spiking neurons (wavelet-based) is proposed that amounts to the entire processing of sound signals being undertaken with spiking neurons. Architecture in Figure 6A is an extension of the auditory SNN (Figure 6B) for text-independent speaker authentication presented in (Wysoski, Benuskova, & Kasabov, 2007).

The systemic behaviour of the ensemble of inner hair cells is simulated with biologically inspired basic processing units (spiking neurons). However, note that this design does not aim to reproduce the activity of the inner hair cells in full detail. Sound signals are described with spectral characteristics.

Cochlear fibers are sharply tuned to specific frequencies (Kiang et al, 1965), which are commonly modelled with the Short Term Fourier Transform (STFT) or wavelets. STFT as a discrete mathematical method has intrinsic characteristics of being able to provide high spectral resolution of low frequency signals and low spectral resolution at high frequencies. This property does not affect the extraction of speech features for speech recognition. The Mel scale that forms the Mel filter banks also has sharply tuned filters at low frequencies and broadly tuned filters at higher frequencies.

Nonetheless, as described in (Rabiner & Juang, 1993) and the main object of research for Ganchev (2005), Mel filter banks and consequently MFCC, extract features particularly suitable for speech recognition. MFCC has been used successfully for speaker authentication, but it may occlude other features that can facilitate a unique description of a speaker. Ganchev (2005) further argues that capturing the uniqueness of the speaker may need higher spectral resolution at high frequency bands, at the same time requiring flexibility to precisely capture sharp variations in time. The same work explores in detail more general properties of wavelets when compared with STFT on the speaker recognition problem, and gives a comprehensive evaluation of wavelet-based approaches through a comparison with several variations of MFCC based systems and probabilistic neural networks.

In our design, for being more general than STFT, wavelets are used in a conceptual description of a speech signal pre-processing method using SNN. This pre-processing of speech signals with spiking units uses the integrate-and-fire neurons with the modulation factor described in Equation 1 and is composed of the following steps:

1. A pre-emphasis filter is applied to the speech signal;
2. The filtered signal is divided into small segments (frames);
3. Receptive fields convert each frame to the time domain using rank order coding. One neuron represents each frame position. From hereafter the processing is done through spikes;
4. Layer 1 (L1) neurons (see Figure 6) of the pre-processing network have weights calculated according to the wavelet mother function $\psi(t)$, for different scales s (expansion and compression of the wavelets) and different spatial shifts τ. The mother wavelet function is described as:

$$\psi_{s,\tau}(t) = \frac{1}{\sqrt{s}}\psi(\frac{t-\tau}{s}) \tag{9}$$

   In L1, the shape of the mother function, the number of scales and the number of shifts are parameters to be experimentally optimized.
5. Layer 2 (L2) neurons integrate the energy of different L1 filters representing spectral and spatial properties. This step resembles filter banks, where the numbers of banks and filter shapes are also subject to optimization. The output of L2 is a train of spikes that extracts spectral and spatial characteristics of an input frame that mimics wavelet computation.

Note that, despite of the filters in L1 being built using wavelet functions, due to the dynamics of the spiking neurons, more precisely, due to the non-linearity inserted during the computation of the *PSP*, the resultant features provide only a coarse representation of wavelet output. The advantage of this design is that the entire process (pre-processing stage and recognition) is done with the same basic processing units, i.e. spiking neurons.

The network architecture depicted in Figure 6B that was designed to perform classification of auditory patterns using spiking neurons includes two techniques that have already proven to be efficient in traditional methods (Gray, 1984; Reynolds, Quatieri, & Dunn, 2000). They are:

- creation of prototype vectors through unsupervised clustering, and
- adaptive similarity score (similarity normalization).

These techniques are implemented in Layer 3 (L3) and Layer 4 (L4). L3 is composed of two neuronal maps. One neuronal map has an ensemble of neurons trained by positive examples (prototypes). Each neuron in the neuronal map is created and/or merged and trained to respond optimally to different segments of the correct training utterances, i.e., different speech phones (minimal unit of speech segmentation). The second neuronal map in L3 is trained also adaptively with negative examples (background model). Several ways to represent background models that can be universal or unique for each class are described and analysed in (Bimbot et al, 2004).

Similar to L3, layer L4 has two neuronal maps representing the correct class and the background model. Each L4 neuronal map is composed of a single neuron. L3 and L4 are connected to each other as follows:

1. excitatory connections between neurons corresponding to neuronal maps with the same label, i.e., L3 correct class to L4 correct class and L3 background to L4 background, and;
2. inhibitory connections between neurons with differing neuronal map labels, i.e., L3 correct class to L4 background and L3 background to L4 correct class. Effectively, L4 neurons accumulate opinions of each frame of being/not being a speaker and being/not being the background.

The dynamic behaviour of the network is described as:

1. For each frame of a speech signal, features are generated by L1 and L2 layers.
2. The spikes are then propagated to L3 until any L3 neuron emits the first output spike, which is propagated to L4. If a neuron in L4 generates an output spike, the simulation is terminated. If not, the next frame is propagated.
3. Before processing the next frame, L3 PSPs and order of arrival of spikes $order(i, j)$ are reset whereas L4 neurons retain their PSPs, which are accumulated over consecutive frames, until an L4 output spike is generated.

The classification is completed when a neuron in L4 generates an output spike or all frames and all spikes in the network have been propagated. If the L4 neuron representing the correct class releases an output spike, the class is authenticated. The authentication fails in a case where no spikes occur in L4 after all frames have been processed or an L4 neuron representing background releases an output spike.

The authentication score of a class is calculated not only based on the similarity between a test sample and the correct class model, but on the relative similarity between the test sample and the class model and between the test sample and a background model. This normalization process is illustrated in Figure 7.

With this procedure, the variations between the train and test conditions are taken into account when computing similarity. Normalization in the similarity domain has already being extensively implemented in traditional methods of speaker verification and is currently found in most of state-of-the-art

Figure 7. Normalization in the similarity domain in a hypothetical two-dimensional space. Normalized similarity = Similarity$_1$ − Similarity$_2$.

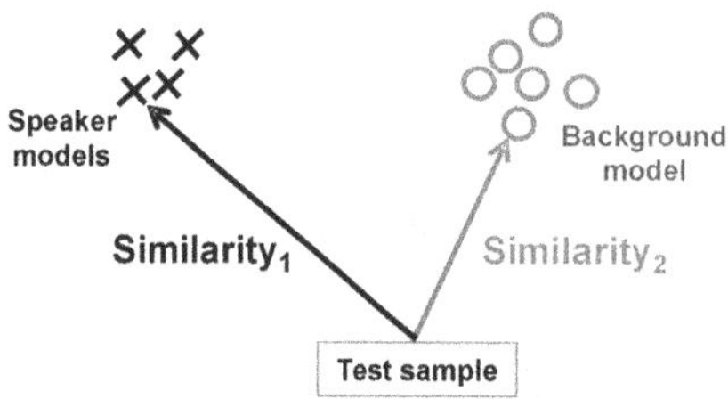

speaker authentication methods (Bimbot et al, 2004). In our experiments a SNN-based implementation, normalized similarity is computed allocating excitatory connections to neurons representing the speaker model and inhibitory connections to neurons representing the background model.

Learning of Auditory Patterns

Training is done on the synapses connecting L2 and L3 neurons. To update weights during training, the simple rule described in Equation 5 and Equation 6 is applied. For each training sample, the *winner-takes-all* approach is used, in such a way that only the neuron with the highest *PSP* value in L1 has its weights updated. The adaptive online procedure for training the network and creating new neurons is similar to the visual pattern recognition model and can be summarised with the following pseudo-code (see also (Wysoski, Benuskova, & Kasabov, 2007) for more details):

```
For each phrase sample in the training set
For each frame in a phrase
Create a new neuron
Propagate the frame into the network
Train the newly created neuron using Equation 5 and Equation 6
Calculate the similarity between weight vectors of newly created neuron and
existent neurons within the neuronal map
If similarity > Threshold
Merge newly created neuron with the most similar neuron using Equation 10 and
Equation 11
```

To merge a newly created neuron with an existing neuron, the weights W of the existing neuron n are updated calculating the average as

$$W = \frac{W_{new} + N_{Frames} W}{1 + N_{Frames}} \tag{10}$$

where N_{Frames} is the number of frames previously used to update the neuron in question. Similarly, the average is also computed to update the corresponding PSP_{Th}:

$$PSP_{Th} = \frac{PSP_{Thnew} + N_{Frames} PSP_{Th}}{1 + N_{Frames}} \tag{11}$$

In the computer simulations of the text-independent speaker authentication scenario, this adaptive learning procedure was used to create speaker codebooks. Neuronal maps representing background models were also introduced to achieve similarity normalization. Our SNN architecture from Figure 6B achieved the best TE ≈ 35% to authenticate 43 individuals from the VidTimit dataset uttering short-sentences (for details see Wysoski, Benuskova, & Kasabov, 2007). However, better level of performance was achieved with traditional Vector Quantization (VQ) model (TE ≈ 22%). Thus, it seems the time-to-first spike coding does not work so well for this type of auditory task, i.e. classification of individuals based on short utterances.

Audiovisual Integration

In this section we investigate the mechanisms of multimodal integration and its effect on the SNN performance. Integration of auditory and visual modalities is accomplished with a supramodal layer of spiking neurons and also by crossmodal connections (Figure 8).

During the recognition process, a supramodal layer integrates the result of individual modalities. In addition, if one single modality finalizes its process before others, crossmodal connections influence the decision of other modalities. In our system the sense of most trusted modality is obtained by faster processing time, i.e., when a signal is very similar to a previously learnt pattern, neurons are more activated. Consequently the output signal of a given modality is generated sooner. The sooner a given modality generates an output, the sooner other modalities receive the crossmodal influence. We show below that the integration of modes enhances the performance in several operating points of the system.

The dynamic behaviour is described as follows: each frame of the visual and auditory excitation (frames f1, f2,..., fN) are propagated through their corresponding modality architectures until the supramodal layer. Spikes of a given visual frame are propagated to L2 and L3 until a neuron belonging to a L3 map emits the first output spike, which is propagated to L4. L4 neurons accumulate opinions over several frames, whereas L1, L2 and L3 neurons are reset to their resting potential on a frame basis. The same occurs with auditory frames. Spikes are propagated to L1 neurons until a L1 neuron emits the first output spike, which is propagated to L2. L2 neurons accumulate opinions over several frames whereas auditory L1 neurons are reset to their resting potential before each frame is processed.

Each individual modality has its own network of spiking neurons as described in the previous sections. In general, the output layer of each modality is composed of neurons that authenticate/not authenticate a class (i.e. user) they represent when output spikes are released. The modality integration is implemented attaching a new layer to the output of the individual modalities. This layer (supramodal layer) represents the supramodal region and contains neurons that are sensitive to more than one modality (Stein & Meredith, 1993). In the simplest case, the supramodal layer contains two spiking neurons for each class label (i.e. for each user). Each neuron of these two neurons, representing a given class C in the supramodal layer, has incoming excitatory connections from the output of class C neurons of each individual modality. The two neurons have the same dynamics, yet different thresholds for spike generation (PSP_{Th}). For one neuron, the PSP_{Th} is set in such a way that an output spike is generated after receiving incoming spikes from any single modality (effectively it is a spike-based implementation of

Figure 8. Integrated audiovisual SNN. For the sake of picture clarity, the crossmodal connections are described in detail in text.

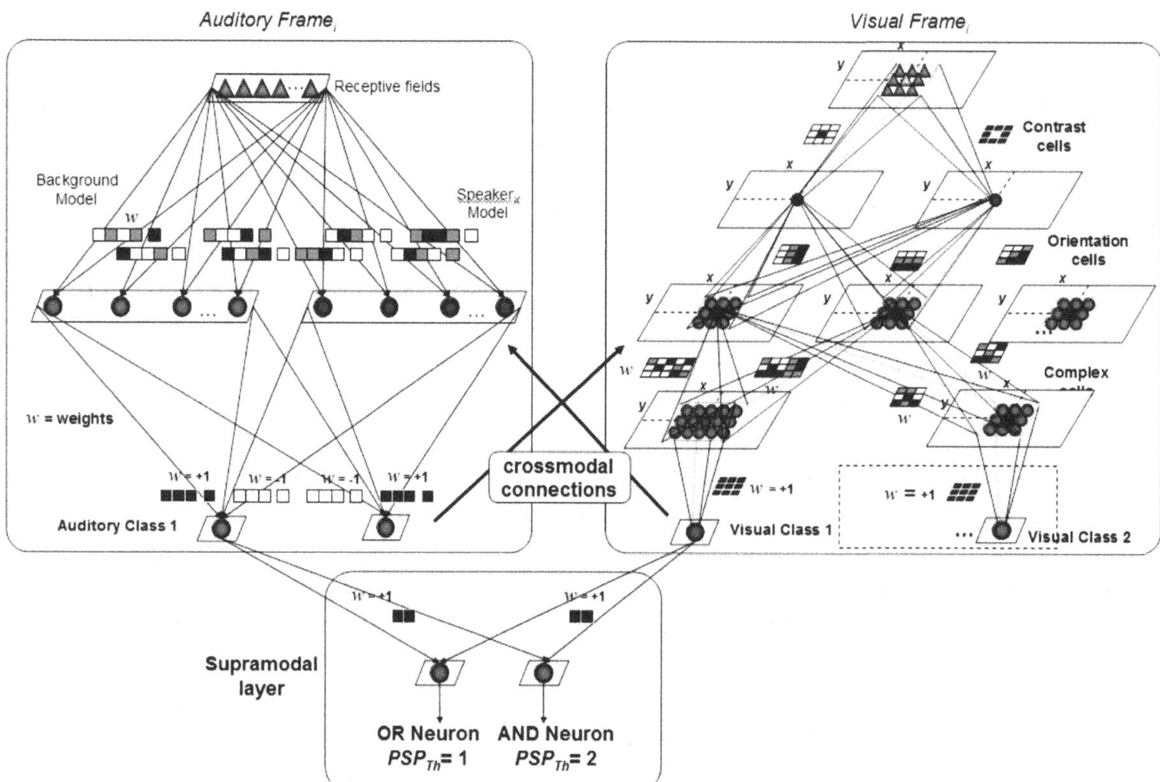

an OR gate). The other neuron has PSP_{Th} set so that incoming spikes from all individual modalities are necessary to trigger an output spike (AND gate). AND neuron maximizes the accuracy and OR neuron maximizes the recall.

In addition to the supramodal layer, a simple way to perform crossmodal coupling of modalities is designed. The crossmodal coupling is set as follows: when output neurons of an individual modality emit spikes, the spikes not only excite the neurons in the supramodal layer, but also excite/inhibit other modalities that still have ongoing processes. Effectively the excitation/inhibition influences the decision on other modalities, biasing (making it easier/more difficult) the other modality to authenticate/ not authenticate a pattern. Thus, both excitatory and inhibitory connections are implemented for the crossmodal coupling. With this configuration, the output of a given class C in one modality excites the class C neuronal maps in other modalities and inhibits all other classes $\hat{C} \neq C$ in other modalities.

In the integrated system, each modality is trained independently. In respect to learning rules, biological systems are capable of life-long functional and structural modifications, which enable learning of new tasks as well as memorization in an online fashion. When in training mode, the system automatically adds new classes, or further fine-tunes the training when new samples of a class are presented.

Evaluation

In this section we summarize simulation results of the integrated audiovisual model in terms of the False Acceptance Rate (FAR) and False Rejection Rate (FRR). More details about this experimental evaluation under different variations of the setup can be found in (Wysoski, Benuskova, & Kasabov, 2008b; Wysoski, Benuskova, & Kasabov, 2010). For the experimental evaluation of our integrated audiovisual SNN we used the VidTimit dataset. In the VidTimit dataset, video streams capture frontal view of individuals' faces while uttering predefined sentences. The dataset is composed of 10 streams of video (106 frames on average) from 43 different speakers, captured at 25 frames per second, recorded in 3 sessions. Individuals utter six sentences in the first session and two sentences in the second and third sessions. First, we evaluated the visual and auditory part of the model and then we evaluated the influence of various parameters of crossmodal interaction on the integrated system (see Figure 9). For this evaluation we used a subset of the VidTimit dataset. The setup for training was composed of six utterances from 10 individuals, whereas 12 individuals (10 that participated in the training stage and two completely unknown individuals) were used for testing. Different utterances have been used for training and testing for those individuals that participated in both training and test sets. Each of the 10 individuals had 4 attempts in the test in a total of 40 positive claims. Acting as impostors, two unknown individuals attempted to authenticate each of the 10 trained models four times, with a total of 2 x 4 x 10 = 80 impostor attempts (false claims). Five visual frames per second have been used whereas the speech samples have rate at 50 frames per second. The authentication threshold was set proportionally to the size of an utterance, that is 20% of the total number of frames needs to provide positive opinions, and only two visual frames were necessary to authenticate a person based on the face.

Figure 9, shows the performance on the test set of the integrated network for different values of crossmodal excitation. In Figure 9, each curve is built varying the auditory L1 PSP_{Th} and visual L3 PSP_{Th} in the range [0.5, 0.9] and [0.1, 0.5], respectively. These intervals for threshold values were arrived at experimentally. We can see in Figure 9 that crossmodal interactions for all chosen mutual excitation strengths improve the performance in terms of both FAR and FRR when compared to the results for isolated visual or auditory SNN, respectively. All the active crossmodal interactions are combined with the AND supramodal integration. Figure 9 also shows the supramodal AND and OR integration results for zero crossmodal interaction. It is clearly visible that AND integration works better for low FAR than any single modality and OR integration works better for low FRR than any single modality. The OR integration also works better for low FRR than the crossmodal integration. Thus, quite obviously the sole OR integration gives very low FRR accompanied with very high FAR.

To evaluate how our system compares with traditional (i.e. not based on spiking) methods, we chose the work of Sanderson & Paliwal (2002). Sanderson & Paliwal (2002) explored the integration of modalities using a combination of mathematical and statistical methods on the same VidTimit dataset. In a model of auditory system alone, they used MFCC features and Gaussian Mixture Model in a noise-free setup. Their auditory model reached minimal TE (total error) $\approx$ 22%. TE = FAR + FRR. Their visual system is reported to have the minimal TE $\approx$ 8% with features extracted using PCA and SVM for classification. After testing several adaptive and non adaptive systems to perform integration, the best performance was obtained with a new approach that builds the decision boundaries for integration with consideration of how the distribution of opinions are likely to change under noisy conditions. The accuracy with this integration reached TE $\approx$ 6% involving 35 users for training and 8 users acting as impostors. Despite some

Figure 9. Performance of auditory SNN, visual SNN and integrated audiovisual SNN for different values of crossmodal excitation VA and AV on the test set. VA = excitation strength from visual to auditory, AV = from auditory to visual. EER = equal error region. Each curve is built varying the auditory L1 PSP_{Th} and visual L3 PSP_{Th} in the range [0.5, 0.9] and [0.1, 0.5], respectively. AND and OR integration results are for zero crossmodal interaction and the active crossmodal interactions are combined with the AND supramodal integration.

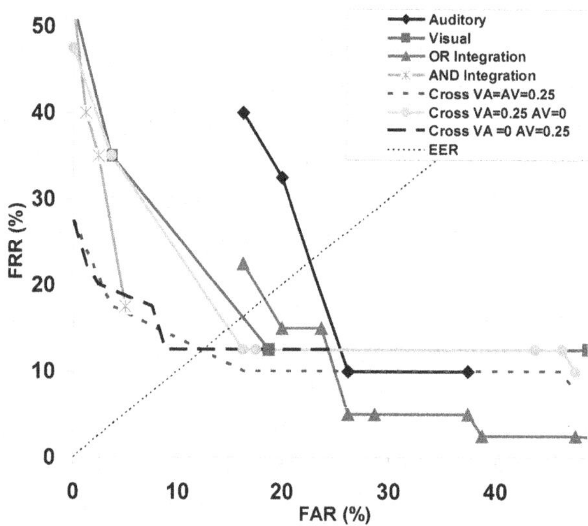

differences between our experimental setup, the results obtained by our brain-like model are clearly not as good as the results obtained by Sanderson and Paliwal (2002) as our TE was never lower than ≈22%.

Solutions and Recommendations

The overall result of testing of our integrated system suggests that the coding scheme of time to first spike may not be suitable for such a complex task like the audiovisual person authentication in general and for auditory processing in particular, because the FAR and FRR for auditory system are very high (see Figure 9). But without a computational model we would never be able to address such question. It is possible to perform the audiovisual person authentication based on time to first spike, but with quite high error rates. It would be interesting to have results with human subjects on the same task. In the next section we suggest a number of ways how to amend our model to improve its performance based on its many attractive features.

The experiments and results presented in this paper do not explicitly consider the effects of noise on the performance. However, in the previous work, the behaviour of ensembles of the same "integrate-and-fire" neuron models and rank order information encoding used here have been thoroughly investigated in the noise settings (Delorme & Thorpe, 2001). The system retained high accuracy (98% correct responses) even with input patterns corrupted with 30% of noise (Delorme & Thorpe, 2001). In addition, the experiments demonstrated high invariance with respect to the illumination levels when processing visual information, mainly because the system is based on the relative contrasts due to rank order coding. As the same principles of information processing remain in our visual system, we assume that a similar resistance to noise can be achieved. On the other hand, without an explicit testing, we cannot conclude that our model auditory system is resistant to noise and if so to what extent. This remains to be done.

In our experiments we have analyzed the accuracy of the system with a relatively low number of classes (up to 43 individuals). It is important to evaluate further the system with medium and large number of classes to better understand how the system will behave. We do not expect worsening of the performance thanks to our architecture and additive addition of new maps. We do expect slower processing due to the serial nature of our programs. Should the system work in parallel however, there will be no difference in processing time.

Basically in our system, each modality is trained independently. During the recognition process, a supra-modal layer integrates the result of individual modalities. In addition, if one single modality finalizes its process before others, crossmodal connections influence the decision of other modalities. In both works of Yamauchi et al (1999; 2001), two networks for each sensory modality (forward and backward network) are proposed. In the forward network, weights are adjusted for mapping income sensor signals (input) to the output, whereas in the backward network weights are adjusted for mapping the output to input signal. The result of the backward network is an estimation of the input signal, which is used during the recognition phase as a confidence measure of the sensory modality. With this approach, priority between sensors can be established, which demonstrated an increase in performance. This backward mechanism is not considered in our system. However, in our system the sense of most trusted modality is obtained by faster processing time, i.e., when a signal is very similar to a previously learnt pattern, neurons are more activated. Consequently the output signal of a given modality is generated sooner. The sooner a given modality generates an output, the sooner other modalities receive the crossmodal influence.

Under the multimodal pattern recognition perspective, our results show that the integration of modes enhances the performance in several operating points of the system. In our work, we have set up values of all parameters experimentally. To extract the best performance from the system more elaborate optimization procedures can be incorporated. However there are some fundamental facts, more important than parameter optimization, which need to be taken into account when trying to improve our system further. In the following we will discuss these fundamental issues in detail.

FUTURE RESEARCH DIRECTIONS

Striving to achieve simplicity yet biological plausibility, we have employed many simplifications and abstractions in our system. From the lower levels of sensory processing to the higher levels of cognition, a very simple model of spiking neurons was used. SNN inherently enables a close integration of feature extraction and decision-making modules as well as the integration of multiple modalities. This close integration is mainly possible because the processing time has a meaning in spiking neuron systems. In other words, with spiking neurons, the time a spike takes to travel from one neuron to another can be explicitly set up. Having the processing time of single units and the time spent in communication between units, the time taken by an area for processing can also be defined. This process can ultimately lead towards the simulation of an entire pathway where the information flows in a relevant time scale. The implication of achieving information processing where the time matters for pattern recognition is that it breaks the existing hard separation between feature extraction and classification. Features are propagated as soon as they are processed and they can arrive at different times in areas where classification is undertaken. Similarly, processing time in different modalities vary. Thus, the individual modalities asynchronously feed a global decision-making process. Alternatively, the buffer of working memory synchronizes the multimodal process. Computation with real processing time also enables the implementation of crossmodal connections between modalities, where one modality can influence others according to its partial opinions in time. This phenomena can effectively increase overall accuracy (as proved to be the case in the human brain) or make the decision-making process faster. However, in order to perform a realistic simulation of information processing where the processing time of different areas and pathways are biologically coherent, there are still some hurdles to overcome. Another challenge will be to incorporate color, stereo vision and/or movement into the system.

Crucially important is to explore other information coding schemes. In our design, only one information coding mechanism is evaluated, that is one spike per neuron where the highest importance is given to the first spike to arrive. Spiking time theory (in opposition to the spiking rate theory) was used in this work for the conceptual design and implementation of algorithms. In particular, a spiking neuron model was used that privileges early spikes and a constraint that enabled the occurrence of only one spike per neuron. Based on these assumptions, concrete models were implemented and validated. An extension to this design can be the reproduction of other patterns of spiking activity and thus other coding schemes. Although coding schemes utilized by the brain are still not clearly understood other spike-based coding mechanisms can be evaluated computationally. A good introduction to the issues related to the encoding of information in neuronal activity can be found in (Reece, 2001). As the traditional theory suggesting that information is transmitted by firing rates is proving gradually not to be universally valid, several independent neurophysiological experiments demonstrate the existence of spike-timing patterns in both single and in ensembles of neurons. For instance, in (Vaucher, 1998), *in vivo* measurements enabled prediction of rat's behaviour responses through the analysis of spatio-temporal patterns of neuronal activity. Izhikevich (2006) created the term "polychronization" to define the spatio-temporal behaviour of a group of neurons that are "time-locked" to each other, a term to distinguish it from synchronous or asynchronous spiking activity behaviour. Abeles (1982) first launched the term "synfire chains" to describe neuronal maps organized in a feed-forward manner with random connections between maps showing synchronous activity. This phenomenon has been experimentally verified in a series of independent works (Abeles & Gat, 2001) and computational models explored the storage and learning capabilities of this theory (Bienenstock, 1995; Gutig & Sompolinsky, 2006). Extending our design to be able to model synchronicity in processing will entail exploration of feedback connections and stability problems as so far only the feed-forward connections were employed.

One spike matters coding is based on experiments on ultra-fast perceptual classification of images into two categories (Thorpe, Fize, & Marlot; 1996). Person authentication studied in our model may be the task, which is beyond the one spike per neuron information coding. From all the coding schemes discussed, it is also reasonable to believe that different areas in the brain may utilize different coding schemes. If this is the case, combined approaches would be needed to better represent different information pathways.

In another direction, a future research could combine spiking neurons and dynamic logic (see chapter by Perlovsky & Ilin in this book). An important mind operation, according to dynamic logic, is a process "from vague to crisp", which could be implemented in the brain by gradual increase of coherence of neural firings (Perlovsky & Kozma, 2007).

CONCLUSION

In this chapter an integrated biologically inspired yet much simplified audiovisual pattern recognition system was described and critically evaluated. For the visual system, the functional behaviour of retina cells, directionally selective cells and complex cells are implemented with a two-dimensional grid of spiking neurons. By complex cells in this context we mean neurons that are selective to the combination of orientations. Only feed-forward connections are used and no adaptation at lower levels is applied. With respect to the auditory speaker recognition process, features extracted from a functional model that resembles the characteristics of the human ear (MFCC) are used during the design and evaluation of the decision-making process for speech signals. A more elaborate design using tonotopic organization of the spiking neurons (wavelet-based) is proposed that amounts to the entire processing of sound signals being undertaken with spiking neurons. The integration of modalities is also accomplished with spiking neurons. A supramodal area as well as crossmodal connections were used to process audiovisual features for person authentication. Different configurations of the integrated system clearly outperformed individual modalities. We investigated time-to-first-spike coding in our system. This coding works well for the visual model but not so well for our auditory model. Thus, the task of audiovisual person authentication and other more complex pattern recognition tasks may require feedback connections and other information coding schemes, like synchronicity or spatiotemporal patterns of spikes.

REFERENCES

Abeles, M. (1982). *Local cortical circuits: An electrophysiological study*. Berlin, Germany: Springer.

Abeles, M., & Gat, I. (2001). Detecting precise firing sequences in experimental data. *Journal of Neuroscience Methods, 107*, 141–154. doi:10.1016/S0165-0270(01)00364-8

Bienenstock, E. (1995). A model of neocortex. *Network (Bristol, England), 6*, 179–224. doi:10.1088/0954-898X/6/2/004

Bimbot, F. (2004). A tutorial on text-independent speaker verification. *EURASIP Journal on Applied Signal Processing, 4*, 430–451. doi:10.1155/S1110865704310024

Brunelli, R., & Falavigna, D. (1995). Person identification using multiple cues. *IEEE Transactions on Pattern Analysis and Machine Intelligence, 17*(10), 955–966. doi:10.1109/34.464560

Calvert, G. A. (2001). Crossmodal processing in the human brain: Insights from functional neuroimaging studies. *Cerebral Cortex, 11*, 1110–1123. doi:10.1093/cercor/11.12.1110

Chevallier, S., Paugam-Moisy, H., & Lemaitre, F. (2005). Distributed processing for modeling real-time multimodal perception in a virtual robot. *International Multi-Conference Parallel and Distributed Computing and Networks*, 393-398.

Chibelushi, C. C., Deravi, F., & Mason, J. S. D. (1999). Adaptive classifier integration for robust pattern recognition. *IEEE Transactions on Systems, Man, and Cybernetics - Part B, 29*(6), 902-907.

Chibelushi, C. C., Deravi, F., & Mason, J. S. D. (2002). A review of speech-based bimodal recognition. *IEEE Transactions on Multimedia, 4*(1), 23–37. doi:10.1109/6046.985551

Crepet, A., Paugam-Moisy, H., Reynaud, E., & Puzenat, D. (2000). *A modular neural model for binding several modalities*. International Conference on Artificial Intelligence, ICAI, (pp. 921-928).

Delorme, A., Gautrais, J., van Rullen, R., & Thorpe, S. (1999). SpikeNet: A simulator for modeling large networks of integrate and fire neurons. *Neurocomputing, 26-27*, 989–996. doi:10.1016/S0925-2312(99)00095-8

Delorme, A., Perrinet, L., & Thorpe, S. (2001). Networks of integrate-and-fire neurons using rank order coding. *Neurocomputing*, 38–48.

Delorme, A., & Thorpe, S. (2001). Face identification using one spike per neuron: Resistance to image degradation. *Neural Networks, 14*, 795–803. doi:10.1016/S0893-6080(01)00049-1

Ellis, H. D., Jones, D. M., & Mosdell, N. (1997). Intra- and inter-modal repetition priming of familiar faces and voices. *The British Journal of Psychology, 88*, 143–156.

Eriksson, J. L., & Villa, A. E. P. (2006). *Artificial neural networks simulation of learning of auditory equivalence classes for vowels*. International Joint Conference on Neural Networks, IJCNN, (pp. 1253-1260).

Eriksson, J. L., & Villa, A. E. P. (2006a). Learning of auditory equivalence classes for vowels by rats. *Behavioural Processes, 73*, 358–359. doi:10.1016/j.beproc.2006.08.005

Fukushima, K., & Miyake, S. (1982). Neocognitron: A self-organizing neural network model for a mechanism of visual pattern recognition. In Amari, S., & Arbib, M. A. (Eds.), *Competition and cooperation in neural nets* (pp. 267–285). Berlin/ Heidelberg, Germany: Springer-Verlag.

Ganchev, T. (2005). *Speaker recognition*. Unpublished doctoral dissertation, Dept. of Electrical and Computer Engineering, University of Patras, Greece.

Gerstner, W., & Kistler, W. M. (2002). *Spiking neuron models*. Cambridge, MA: Cambridge University Press.

Ghazanfar, A. A., Maier, J. X., Hoffman, K. L., & Logothetis, N. K. (2005). Multisensory integration of dynamic faces and voices in rhesus monkey auditory cortex. *The Journal of Neuroscience, 25*, 5004–5012. doi:10.1523/JNEUROSCI.0799-05.2005

Gray, R. M. (1984). Vector quantization. *IEEE Acoustics, Speech, and Signal Magazine*, 4-28.

Holmberg, M., Gelbart, D., Ramacher, U., & Hemmert, W. (2005). Automatic speech recognition with neural spike trains. *Interspeech*, 1253-1256.

Hopfield, J. J. (1995). Pattern recognition computation using action potential timing for stimulus representation. *Nature, 376*(6535), 33–36. doi:10.1038/376033a0

Hubel, D. H., & Wiesel, T. N. (1962). Receptive fields, binocular interaction and functional architecture in the cat's visual cortex. *The Journal of Physiology, 160*, 106–154.

Iwasa, K., Inoue, H., Kugler, M., Kuroyanagi, S., & Iwata, A. (2007). Separation and recognition of multiple sound source using pulsed neuron model. ICANN, (LNCS 4669), (pp. 748–757).

Izhikevich, E. M. (2006). Polychronization: Computation with spikes. *Neural Computation, 18*(2), 245–282. doi:10.1162/089976606775093882

Kiang, N. Y.-S., Watanabe, T., Thomas, E. C., & Clark, L. F. (1965). *Discharge patterns of single fibers in the cat's auditory nerve*. Cambridge, MA: MIT Press.

Kittler, J., Hatef, M., Duin, R. P. W., & Matas, J. (1998). On combining classifiers. *IEEE Transactions on Pattern Analysis and Machine Intelligence, 20*(3), 226–239. doi:10.1109/34.667881

Kruger, N., Lappe, M., & Worgotter, F. (2004). Biologically motivated multi-modal processing of visual primitives. *Interdisciplinary Journal of Artificial Intelligence the Simulation of Behaviors, AISB, 15*, 417–428.

Kuroyanagi, S., & Iwata, A. (1994). Auditory pulse neural network model to extract the inter-aural time and level difference for sound localization. *Transactions of IEICE, 4*, 466–474.

Loiselle, S., Rouat, J., Pressnitzer, D., & Thorpe, S. (2005). *Exploration of rank order coding with spiking neural networks for speech recognition*. International Joint Conference on Neural Networks, IJCNN, (pp 2076-2080).

Maciokas, J., Goodman, P. H., & Harris, F. C. Jr. (2002). *Large-scale spike-timing dependent-plasticity model of bimodal (audio/visual) processing*. Reno: Technical Report of Brain Computation Laboratory, University of Nevada.

Matsugu, M., Mori, K., Ishii, M., & Mitarai, Y. (2002). *Convolutional spiking neural network model for robust face detection*. International Conference on Neural Information Processing, ICONIP, (pp. 660-664).

Matsugu, M., Mori, K., Mitari, Y., & Kaneda, Y. (2003). Subject independent facial expression recognition with robust face detection using a convolutional neural network. *Neural Networks, 16*, 555–559. doi:10.1016/S0893-6080(03)00115-1

Mazurek, M. E., & Shadlen, M. N. (2002). Limits to the temporal fidelity of cortical spike rate signals. *Nature Neuroscience, 5*, 463–471.

McLennan, S., & Hockema, S. (2001) *Spike-V: An adaptive mechanism for speech-rate independent timing*. (IULC Working Papers Online 02-01).

Mel, B. W. (1998). SEEMORE: Combining colour, shape, and texture histogramming in a neurally-inspired approach to visual object recognition. *Neural Computation, 9*, 777–804. doi:10.1162/neco.1997.9.4.777

Mercier, D., & Seguier, R. (2002). *Spiking neurons (STANNs) in speech recognition*. 3rd WSES International Conference on Neural Networks and Applications. Interlaken.

Mozayyani, N., Baig, A. R., & Vaucher, G. (1998). *A fully neural solution for online handwritten character recognition*. International Joint Conference on Neural Networks, IJCNN, (pp. 160-164).

Natschlager, T., & Ruf, B. (1998). Spatial and temporal pattern analysis via spiking neurons. *Network (Bristol, England), 9*(3), 319–338. doi:10.1088/0954-898X/9/3/003

Natschlager, T., & Ruf, B. (1999). Pattern analysis with spiking neurons using delay coding. *Neurocomputing, 26-27*, 463–469. doi:10.1016/S0925-2312(99)00052-1

Perlovsky, L., & Kozma, R. (2007). *Editorial: Neurodynamics of cognition and consciousness* (Perlovsky, L., & Kozma, R., Eds.). Heidelberg, Germany: Springer Verlag. doi:10.1007/978-3-540-73267-9

Perrinet, L., & Samuelides, M. (2002). *Sparse image coding using an asynchronous spiking neural network.* European Symposium on Artificial Neural Networks, (pp. 313-318).

Poggio, T., & Girosi, F. (1990). Regularization algorithms for learning that are equivalent to multilayer networks. *Science, 247*, 978–982. doi:10.1126/science.247.4945.978

Rabiner, L., & Juang, B. (1993). *Fundamentals of speech recognition.* Prentice Hall.

Reece, M. (2001). Encoding information in neuronal activity. In Maass, W., & Bishop, C. (Eds.), *Pulsed neural networks.* MIT Press.

Reynolds, D. A., Quatieri, T. F., & Dunn, R. B. (2000). Speaker verification using adapted Gaussian mixture models. *Digital Signal Processing, 10*, 19–41. doi:10.1006/dspr.1999.0361

Riesenhuber, M., & Poggio, T. (1999). Hierarchical models of object recognition in cortex. *Nature Neuroscience, 2*(11), 1019–1025. doi:10.1038/14819

Robert, A., & Eriksson, J. L. (1999). A composite model of the auditory periphery for simulating responses to complex sounds. *The Journal of the Acoustical Society of America, 106*(4), 1852–1864. doi:10.1121/1.427935

Rosenberg, A. E., & Soong, F. K. (1987). Evaluation of a vector quantization talker recognition system in text independent and text dependent modes. *Computer Speech & Language, 2*(3-4), 143–157. doi:10.1016/0885-2308(87)90005-2

Rouat, J., Pichevar, R., & Loiselle, S. (2005). Perceptive, non-linear speech processing and spiking neural networks. In Chollet, G. (Eds.), *Nonlinear speech modeling (LNAI 3445)* (pp. 317–337). Berlin/Heidelberg, Germany: Springer-Verlag. doi:10.1007/11520153_14

Rumelhart, D. E., & McClelland, J. L.PDP Research Group. (1986). *Parallel distributed processing: Explorations in the microstructure of cognition.* Cambridge, MA: MIT Press.

Sanderson, C., & Paliwal, K. K. (2002). Identity verification using speech and face information. *Digital Signal Processing, 14*, 449–480. doi:10.1016/j.dsp.2004.05.001

Seguier, R., & Mercier, D. (2001). *A generic pretreatment for spiking neuron application on lipreading with STANN* (Spatio-Temporal Artificial Neural Networks). 5th International Conference on Artificial Neural Networks and Genetic Algorithms.

Serre, T., Wolf, L., Bileschi, S., Riesenhuber, M., & Poggio, T. (2007). Robust object recognition with cortex-like mechanisms. *IEEE Transactions on Pattern Analysis and Machine Intelligence, 29*(3), 411–426. doi:10.1109/TPAMI.2007.56

Stein, B. E., & Meredith, M. A. (1993). *The merging of the senses.* MIT Press.

Thorpe, S., Fize, D., & Marlot, C. (1996). Speed of processing in the human visual system. *Nature, 381*, 520–522. doi:10.1038/381520a0

Vaucher, G. (1998). An algebraic interpretation of PSP composition. *Bio Systems*, *48*, 241–246. doi:10.1016/S0303-2647(98)00077-X

Villa, A. E., Tetko, I. V., Hyland, B., & Najem, A. (1999). Spatiotemporal activity patterns of rat cortical neurons predict responses in a conditioned task. *Proceedings of the National Academy of Sciences*, USA, (pp. 1106-1111).

von Kriegstein, K., & Giraud, A. (2006). Implicit multisensory associations influence voice recognition. *PLoS Biology*, *4*(10), 1809–1820. doi:10.1371/journal.pbio.0040326

von Kriegstein, K., Kleinschmidt, A., Sterzer, P., & Giraud, A. (2005). Interaction of face and voice areas during speaker recognition. *Journal of Cognitive Neuroscience*, *17*(3), 367–376. doi:10.1162/0898929053279577

Wysoski, S. G., Benuskova, L., & Kasabov, N. (2006). *Online learning with structural adaptation in a network of spiking neurons for visual pattern recognition. ICANN06, (LNCS 4131)* (pp. 61–70). Berlin, Germany: Springer-Verlag.

Wysoski, S. G., Benuskova, L., & Kasabov, N. (2007). *Text-independent speaker authentication with spiking neural networks. ICANN07, (LNCS 4669)* (pp. 758–767). New York, NY: Springer-Verlag.

Wysoski, S. G., Benuskova, L., & Kasabov, N. (2008a). Fast and adaptive network of spiking neurons for multi-view visual pattern recognition. *Neurocomputing*, *71*(13-15), 2563–2575. doi:10.1016/j.neucom.2007.12.038

Wysoski, S. G., Benuskova, L., & Kasabov, N. (2008b). *Adaptive spiking neural networks for audiovisual pattern recognition. ICONIP'2007, (LNCS 4985)* (pp. 406–415). Berlin, Germany: Springer-Verlag.

Wysoski, S. G., Benuskova, L., & Kasabov, N. (2010). Evolving spiking neural networks for audiovisual information processing. *Neural Networks*..doi:10.1016/j.neunet.2010.04.009

Yamauchi, K., Oota, M., & Ishii, N. (1999). A self-supervised learning system for pattern recognition by sensory integration. *Neural Networks*, *12*(10), 1347–1358. doi:10.1016/S0893-6080(99)00064-7

Yamauchi, K., Takama, J., Takeuchi, H., Sugiura, S., & Ishii, N. (2001). Sensory integrating neural network with selective attention architecture for autonomous robots. *International Journal of Knowledge-Based Intelligent Engineering Systems*, *5*(3), 142–154.

ADDITIONAL READING

Burileanu, C., Moraru, D., Bojan, L., Puchiu, M., & Stan, A. (2002). On performance improvement of a speaker verification system using vector quantization, cohorts and hybrid cohort-world models. *International Journal of Speech Technology*, *5*, 247–257. doi:10.1023/A:1020244924468

Ghitza, O. (1988). Temporal non-place information in the auditory-nerve firing patterns as a front-end for speech recognition in a noisy environment. *Journal of Phonetics*, *16*, 109–124.

Gutig, R., & Sompolinsky, H. (2006). The tempotron: a neuron that learns spike timing-based decisions. *Nature Neuroscience*, *9*, 420–429. doi:10.1038/nn1643

Kasabov, N. (2007). *Evolving Connectionist Systems*. Springer-Verlag.

Maciokas, J. B. (2003). *Towards an understanding of the synergistic properties of cortical processing: a neuronal computational modeling approach*. PhD Thesis, University of Nevada.

Movellan, J. R. (1995). Visual speech recognition with stochastic networks. In Tesauro, G., Toruetzky, D., & Leen, T. (Eds.), *Advances in Neural Information Processing Systems 7* (pp. 851–858).

Shamma, S. A., Chadwick, R. S., Wilbur, W. J., Morrish, K. A., & Rinzel, J. (1986). A biophysical model of cochlear processing: intensity dependence of pure tone responses. *The Journal of the Acoustical Society of America*, *78*, 1612–1621. doi:10.1121/1.392799

Thorpe, S. (1990). Spike arrival times: a highly efficient coding scheme for neural networks. In Eckmiller, R., Hartman, G., & Hauske, G. (Eds.), *Parallel processing in neural systems* (pp. 91–94). Elsevier.

Tikovic, P., Vöros, M., Durackova, D. (2001) Implementation of a learning synapse and a neuron for pulse-coupled neural networks. *Journal of Electrical Engineering*, 52, 3-4, 68-73.

Viola, P., & Jones, M. J. (2001). Rapid object detection using a boosted cascade of simple features. *Proceedings of IEEE Computer Society Conference on Computer Vision and Pattern Recognition*, *1*, 511–518.

KEY TERMS AND DEFINITIONS

Brain-Like System: The system that is able to generalize and deal efficiently with novel stimuli. For instance, we can effortlessly recognize a familiar object under novel viewing conditions, or recognize a new object as a member of a familiar class. Sometimes it means also a system that mimics the architectural and/or functional organization of the brain.

Information Processing: The *change* of information in any manner detectable by an observer.

Intellect: Faculty of mind to think, acquire knowledge and to understand. In other words, it is the ability of mind to learn and reason or the mind capacity for knowledge and understanding.

Neural Code: How is sensory and other information represented in the brain, i.e. what is the relationship between the stimulus and the individual and ensemble neuronal responses.

Person Authentication: A process used to verify identity of a person (user).

Spike: A short electric pulse of constant amplitude, which is generated by a neuron when the total somatic postsynaptic potential gets bigger than the firing threshold.

Unsupervised Learning: Process of acquiring new knowledge or behavior, in which the learner is given only unlabeled examples.

Chapter 17
Modeling the Intellect from a Coordination Perspective

Lars Taxén
Linköping University, Sweden

ABSTRACT

Usually, models of the intellect take the individual mind and body as the point of departure and proceed outward towards the social and natural environment in which the individual is immersed. As a consequence, important social dimensions contributing to the epigenetic development of the individual are less articulated. This chapter suggests modeling the intellect from a more balanced perspective that recognizes both social and individual aspects–the coordination of actions. The author argues that co-ordination is made possible by certain innate dispositions called activity modalities: contextualization, spatialization, temporalization, stabilization, and transition. Consequently, a central task for modeling the intellect is to understand how perceptions received through sensory modalities are related to the activity modalities. To this end, the author proposes a research program for modeling the intellect, based on the concept of "activity" in the Russian Activity Theory and the activity modalities. Provisional arguments for the relevance of these modalities are discussed in three different realms associated with the intellect: the social, conceptual, and neural ones. The chapter is concluded with some preliminary research questions, pertinent for the research program.

INTRODUCTION

As stated in the introduction of this book, today the modeling and simulation of cognitive processes are a reality in areas such as pattern recognition, speech analysis and synthesis, robotics, information processing, etc. Usually, models of the intellect take – for good reasons – the individual as the point of departure and proceed outward towards her social and natural environment, which is typically concep-

DOI: 10.4018/978-1-60960-551-3.ch017

Figure 1. Situated action view of sensorimotor coordination (adapted after Clancey, 1993)

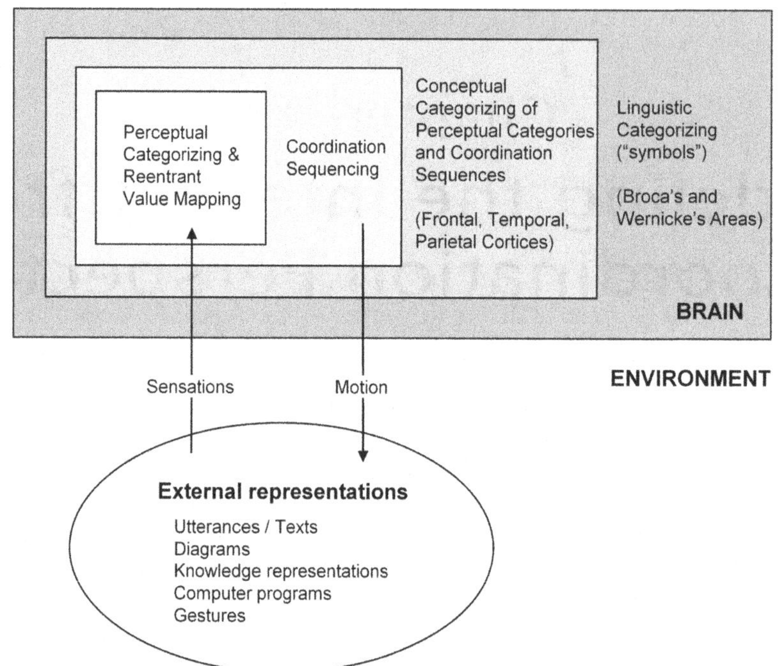

tualized (if at all) in terms like objects, actions, situation, relationships, culture, and the like. In short, the environment is seen as a more or less unproblematic background for modeling efforts. A typical example is given in Figure 1.

The subordinate role played by the environment is at first thought quite surprising. In daily life, it is immediately clear that our natural and social environment has a decisive influence on how we think and act. A human is definitely a social animal that could not survive in isolation: "No man is an island, entire of itself" (John Donne).

However, in a growing number of research programs, the environment is given more attention when inquiring into the intellect. Examples of such programs are "distributed cognition" (Hutchins, 1995; Hazlehurst, Gorman & McMullena, 2008), "situated cognition" (Brown, Collins, & Duguid, 1989; Clancey, 1993), and "extracortical organization of brain functions" (Kotik-Friedgut, 2006); a concept that originally was coined by Vygotsky (1997) and further developed by his apprentice Luria (1973). Moreover, the theory of cognition proposed by Maturana and Varela (e.g. Maturana & Varela, 1992; Prolux, 2008) has many features in common with the approach presented here. An example of neurological research approaching the same position is Changeux (1997; 2004), who strongly emphasizes the spontaneous, extrovert activity of the brain, and its epigenetic structuring from environmental influences.

The underlying figure of thought in these approaches is that the organization of the brain is inherently related to the environment:

If mind is socially constituted, then the field or locus of any individual mind must extend as far as the social activity or apparatus of social relations which constitutes it extends; and hence that field cannot be bounded by the skin of the individual organism to which it belongs. (Mead, 1974, p. 223)

If we accept this premise, investigating the environment might provide essential clues to how the brain works. This is, of course, not a trivial task. In this contribution the concept of *coordination* is chosen as the point of departure; the main reason being that coordination spans both individual and social realms. Actions can be performed individually, as when someone is chopping firewood. To succeed with this task, a sensorimotor coordination of learned chop-abilities, the movements of arm and legs, the swinging of the axe, and more, is necessary. Likewise, coordination is a prerequisite for individuals to interact socially with each other. Any task, where two or more people are jointly trying to achieve something, needs to be coordinated. Consequently, coordination may provide an entry point for more balanced inquiries where mind and activity are seen as a unity, rather than separate investigation domains.

This said and done, the concept of coordination needs to be articulated. Coordination is notoriously hard to narrow down (see e.g. Larsson, 1990; Malone & Crowston, 1994). A frequently referenced definition in the literature is: "Coordination is managing dependencies between activities" (Malone & Crowston, 1994, p. 91). This definition, however, introduces the additional problems of clarifying the meaning of "dependencies" and "activities". In addition, the link to the intellect needs to be defined.

I propose the following approach to tackle this problem. As a starting point, I will use of the notion of "activity" in Activity Theory (AT).[1] "Activity" (German: Tätigkeit; Russian: deyatel'nost') in the AT sense is quite distinct from the ordinary English term, and there is no precise translation of this concept into English. In short, activity can be considered as the minimal meaningful context in which individual actions make sense.

The second step is the idea that coordination of both individual and social actions can be characterized along certain dimension that I call the *activity modalities*. This construct was conceptualized over many years in my professional work at Ericsson™, a worldwide supplier of telecom systems. The modalities – *contextualization*, *spatialization*, *temporalization*, *stabilization*, and *transition* between contexts – stood out as crucial dimensions that had to be carefully managed in order to coordinate extremely complex development projects (see e.g. Taxén, 2009). I argue that the activity modalities represent innate dispositions for coordination that are ontogenetically manifested in all human activities. In order to act, humans (as well as other organisms equipped with a nervous system), need to develop coordinative capabilities in all modalities. Thus, percepts acquired through the sensory modalities and actions performed through activity modalities are inherently related to each other.

Since the activity modalities are assumed to be innate, these link between the environment and the mind. When the newborn infant starts to experience the world, epigenetic manifestations of the modalities will develop in the brain from interacting with the world. The manifested forms of the modalities are determined by the particular historical and cultural contexts in which the individual is born into and encounters during her lifetime. Thus, the origin of manifested modalities is truly social; something that was formulated by Vygotsky in his genetic law of development:

Every function in the child's cultural development appears twice: first, on the social level, and later, on the individual level; first, between people (interpsychological), and then inside the child (intrapsychological). (Vygotsky, 1978, p. 57)

In summary, I propose to view sensorimotor coordination as in Figure 2.

The environment of the individual is conceptualized as "activity" in the AT sense. Afferent sensory impressions in different sensory modalities are integrated into efferent capabilities for action according to the activity modalities. The relationship between mind and activity is seen as a dialectical one in the

Figure 2. An elaborated view of coordination

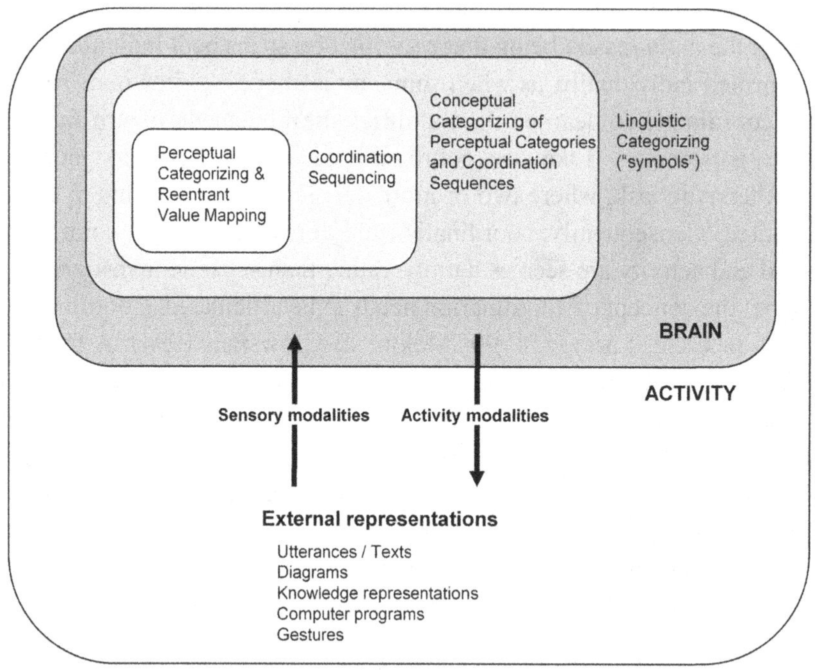

sense that our innate constitution of the mind is reflected in the activity, which in turn is reflected back into the ontogenetical constitution of the mind.

These provisional ideas need to be further investigated. To this end, the purpose of this chapter is to outline the contours of a research program based on the notions of "activity" and "activity modalities". The chapter is structured as follows. First, a thorough description of "activity" and "activity modalities" is given. Next, I discuss the unity between mind and activity, after which an epitome of a research program is suggested. I propose an analytical model of the intellect in three realms – the social, conceptual, and neural ones. This is followed by an analysis of the activity modalities in each realm, including some aspects of multi-modal integration of sensory modalities into a coherent, actionable percept of the environment. The contribution is concluded with some research questions pertinent to the research program.

THE ACTIVITY MODALITIES

The concept of activity, on which the idea of activity modalities is based, was first introduced by Leont'ev as a fundamental unit in his investigations of the early manifestations of the mind in the human evolutionary history:

I will call the process of activity the specific processes through which a live, that is, active relation of the subject to reality is realized, as opposed to other types of processes. (Leont'ev, 1981, in Kaptelinin & Nardi, 2006, p. 55)

Figure 3. Illustration of an activity (Bryant & Gay, 1883. Original wood engraving by E. Bayard)

A distinct feature of activities is that they cannot exist without *objects*: "Any activity of an organism is directed at a certain object; an 'objectless' activity is impossible" (ibid, p. 55).

Activity in this sense is equally applicable to every organism that engages in its immediate "life-sphere", whether they merely respond to signals like ticks, modify their environment like spiders, or use tools like apes using sticks to catch termites. The evolution of nervous systems in organisms enabled the mediation of activity by representations such as heeding calls warning for predators. However, the significance of these representations rarely stretches beyond the immediate situation in space and time that the organism encounters.

With the human mind, however, a qualitatively new level of the psyche is reached. Representations can signify situations beyond here and now: past times, future events, places far away, and so on. The survival of a human being is not solely determined by naturally given physical and biological things, such as the availability of food, shelter, etc., but also by the social reality the individual is born into. In particular, the individual must learn to master the language of its social milieu.

With the cultural dimension, activity becomes a social phenomenon in which humans fulfill social needs through the division of labor. Rather than having everyone doing all and the same tasks, the collective effort is distributed to different individuals, each proficient in performing a specific task. This implies that individual actions need to be *coordinated*.

In order to illustrate activity and the activity modalities, we may use the mammoth hunting scenery in Figure 3.

When looking at this scenery some things immediately come to mind. The mammoth is clearly the *object* around which everything else revolves: hunters, bows, arrows, actions, shouts, gestures, and so on. It is obvious that the hunters have to coordinate their actions; if every hunter attacked the mammoth one at a time, the result would be disastrous. There are also several perceivable *motives* for the hunt: the primary one presumably to get food. Related motives may be to get material for clothing, making arrowheads, and the like.

In order to coordinate their actions, the hunters must develop coordination capabilities in all activity modalities. To begin with, the *contextualization* modality refers to the fact that coordination requires a common understanding about the context around the mammoth. This context frames the purposefulness of individual actions. For example, it can be seen in the background of the illustration that some hunters, the beaters, have started a fire and make noises to scare the quarry away. The mammoth escapes in a direction where other hunters wait to circumvent the quarry and kill it. However, it is only in the light of the activity as a whole that the beaters' actions of scaring the quarry away make sense.

Second, a common sense of what is relevant in the context must be developed. Capabilities in the *spatialization* modality enable the actors to orient themselves in the same way as a map does. For example, the river is probably relevant since it is hinders the mammoth to escape in that direction. On the other hand, the fishes in the river are certainly irrelevant in this activity (they are of course relevant in a fishing activity).

Third, when the hunt starts, individual actions must be carried out in a certain order. Common capabilities developed in the *temporalization* modality enable the actors to synchronize individual actions. For example, the hunters must be in place before the beaters start making noises, the archers may shoot their arrows at a certain command, and so on.

Fourth, the archers cannot shoot their arrows in any way they like. If shooting in a wrong direction, other hunters may be hit rather than the mammoth. Gradually, after many successful and less successful mammoth hunts, a common understanding about how to perform appropriate mammoth hunting will evolve. Capabilities in this modality – *stabilization* – provide a common sense of the "taking for granted"; rules and norms indicating proper patterns of action that need not be questioned as long as they work.

Fifth, activities are not isolated. The brought-down quarry will be cut into pieces and prepared to eat. This is done in a cooking activity, which in turn has its particular motive (to still hunger) and object (which happens to be the same as for the hunting activity: the mammoth). Other related activities might be manufacturing weapons and weapon parts from the bones and the tusks of the mammoth. So, when several activities interact, certain issues must be resolved in the transition between activities, such as how to share the quarry among hunters and cooks, or deciding how many ready-made arrow heads will be returned for a certain amount of food. Such common understanding about how to coordinate different activities is developed in the *transition* modality. This modality is a direct consequence of contextualization since the emergence of contexts bring about a need for transition between those contexts.

An inherent part of activities in AT is that actions are always *mediated* by relevant means. The hunters make use of bows and arrows, the beaters use some kind of tools to make a fire, the assault of the mammoth is most certainly coordinated by gestures and shouts, and so on. The individual actors must of course learn how to use such means; both tools and specific mammoth-hunting terms, in order to become a resource in the mammoth hunting activity.

Although the modalities are treated here as separate, they are in fact strongly intertwined. For example, the stabilization modality will influence all other modalities since, over time, stable patterns concerning contexts, actions and transitions will be developed. Thus, rather than seeing the modalities as isolated, they should be regarded as different elements in a *dialectical unity*, where each modality influences and is influenced by all the others.

In summary, activities are molded by motives and objects towards which actions are directed. Actions are coordinated by evolving coordination capabilities in all activity modalities. In order to underline the importance of motives and objects for the formation of activities, I will refer to these in the following by initial capital letters: Motive and Object.

THE UNITY OF MIND AND ACTIVITY

In this section, I want to further explore the nature of actions. The most obvious aspect is that these are carried out in order to change something in the world. A man using an axe to chop logs obviously transforms logs into firewood suitable for the fireplace. Hence, actions have a *transformative* aspect. Furthermore, in order to chop logs, the movements of the hands and arms, the position of the legs in relation to the chopping block, the hitting angle of the axe towards the log, the velocity of the chop, and so on, need to be coordinated into one single, harmonious act. Thus, there is also a *coordinative* aspect of actions. This applies equally well to individual sensorimotor coordination of perceptions and movement of bodily parts, as to social coordination of individual acts. For analytical purposes, it is sometimes convenient to describe coordinative and transformative aspects of actions as two separate kinds (see e.g. Goldkuhl & Lind, 2008). However, actions, whether carried out in isolation or together with other, always have a transformative and coordinative facet. They are, in essence, two sides of the same coin.

Both transformative and coordinative actions are accomplished by the help of mediational means: "[Humans] always put something else between themselves and their Object of work" (Bødker & Bøgh Andersen, 2005, p. 362). A common characteristic of all means is that they must be *enacted*, a term coined by Weick:

The term 'enactment' is used to preserve the central point that when people act, they bring events and structures into existence and set them in motion. People who act in organizations often produce structures, constraints, and opportunities that were not there before they took action. (Weick, 1988, p. 306)

Enactment indicates that an "encounter" must take place between innate faculties in the brain/body, and potential, useful things in the environment. This encounter goes beyond mere passive learning:

Knowledgeability or knowing-in-practice is continually enacted through people's everyday activity; it does not exist "out there" (incorporated in external objects, routines, or systems) or "in here" (inscribed in human brains, bodies, or communities). Rather, knowing is an ongoing social accomplishment, constituted, and reconstituted in everyday practice. (Orlikowski, 2002, p. 252)

For analytical purposes it is convenient to apprehend the enactment process as two intertwined processes: *objectification* and *objectivation*. Objectification ("Vergegenständlichung"; Kosík, 1976), is efferent, reaches outwards, and is manifested externally as meaningful artifacts such as tools, institutions, organizations, language, etc. The second process, objectivation ("Objektivierung"; ibid, p. 131), is afferent, reaches inwards, and is manifested internally in terms of symbols, concepts, neural structures, etc., reflecting external manifestations. So, even if we regard objectivation and objectification as different processes, they are in essence two aspects of the one and same process in which humans enact a meaningful world by engaging in the externally given, physical and social world.

The objectivated and objectified manifestations are unique for each individual. However, in activities, the objectified artifacts are social in origin; they represent meaningful, common elements that make sense in the activity. This means that the same physical thing can be objectified in one activity and not in another. So, for example, a chain saw has a great potential to become objectified in a forestry activity, but hardly in a concert activity[2].

Figure 4. A guitar quartet in concert (Lars to the far right)

A Musical Example

Enactment of coordination brings about capabilities in all activity modalities. In order to make sense of this rather abstruse reasoning, it might be helpful to consider an example. Suppose a person, let's call him Lars, wants to play the guitar in a guitar quartet with the ultimate purpose of giving a concert. From the very moment Lars decides to do so, he becomes an actor in an activity where the Object is the concert (see Figure 4):

In order to carry out his part in this activity, Lars must be capable of playing scores such as the one in Figure 5.

The score is obviously a mediational means enabling the act of playing. The particular form and structure of the score have evolved since the 14th century when spacing and timing were brought together in the sheet music (Hoskin, 2004). Thus, everyone involved in playing, where this type of means is used, must enact the score into an objectified means for herself.

Learning to play means a long and arduous practice in which Lars enacts the notes and the guitar. This implies the coordination of the left and right hands, the reading of the score, the sitting position, and a number of other things. As time goes by, Lars and his guitar may eventually become so interweaved that they form a unity. The player becomes "one" with his instrument, as illustrated by the following quotation from the famous cellist Mstislav Rostropovich:

There no longer exist relations between us. Some time ago I lost my sense of the border between us.... I experience no difficulty in playing sounds.... The cello is my tool no more. (In Zinchenko, 1996, p. 295)

Thus, enactment is manifested as a "musical" objectification of the score and the guitar, and a "musical" objectivation in the brain and body.

Figure 5. A part of a score for an acoustic bass guitar

Several activity modalities can be observed in the score. First, there is an obvious *temporal* dimension manifested by the sequence of notes. Each note signifies a certain time interval as indicated by the stems and dots. By learning the temporal aspects of notes, capabilities along the *temporalization* modality are enacted. Correspondingly, the vertical positions of the notes relative to the staff indicate a spatial dimension (above, below, distance, etc.). This is a manifestation of the *spatialization* modality, which concerns how things are spatially related to each other.

Furthermore, the various signs in the score – the *mf* indicating mezzo forte, the ? signifying the F-clef, the # showing that the key is e-minor, etc. – are commonly understood signs representing norms that must be adhered to when playing. These norms have a stabilizing function; hence the *stabilization* modality is also present in the score.

Before anything can be played at all, the guitar must have built by a guitar maker. This is done in a quite different activity where the Object is the guitar. In order for a guitar to be playable, certain common understanding must exist between the player and the guitar maker. This understanding concerns elements like the distance between the frets, the string tensions, the size of the guitar, and much more. However, there is no need for player and guitar maker to agree upon all details in each their respective activity (in fact, this is not even possible). The elements that have to be agreed upon manifest the *transition* modality.

The coordination of the different players in the quartet is now made possible by a common score indicating how the different voices interact (see Figure 6).

Thus, social coordination of several actors presumes that each musician has enacted the music individually in a common way. As can be seen, the objectivated expression for social coordination is basically the same as for individual coordination, however with the additional objectification of aligning the individual voices on top of each other in order to achieve temporal and spatial coordination. It is also clear that the individual voices make sense only in the activity as a whole. Just playing one of the voices in isolation usually does not produce enjoyable results.

In summary, actions have a transactional and a coordinative facet, and make sense only in relation to the Motive and Object of the activity. Actions are mediated by means that must be enacted to become resources in the activity. Enaction brings about dialectically interrelated objectivated manifestations in the brain and objectified manifestations in the activity. Enaction of coordinative capabilities proceeds along the activity modalities. Thus, there is a fundamental unity between mind and activity:

[External] aids or historically formed devices are essential elements in the establishment of functional connections between individual parts of the brain, and that by their aid, areas of the brain which previously were independent become components of a single functional system. (Luria, 1973, p. 31; italics in original)

Figure 6. The common score

OUTLINING A RESEARCH PROGRAM

The ideas outlined above for modeling the intellect is, to the best of my knowledge, quite new and provisional in its current form, which means that they need to be further investigated. Since the scope of the approach is so encompassing, it might be pertinent to outline a research program for making inquiries into the intellect based on the activity modality construct. According to Lakatos (1974), scientists cannot constantly be engaged in debates regarding the basic assumptions and methods of a research program[3]. This would simply impede them to fully explore a certain line of inquiry. Lakatos calls the basic assumptions the "hard core" of the program. These are guarded from falsification by a "protective belt" of auxiliary hypotheses. As long as the hard core can be protected, the research program can be explored to its full potential. The moment the hard core cannot be sustained, the research program has to be abandoned.

The overall purpose of a research program based on the ideas presented in this contribution would be to investigate coordinative faculties of humans. How can we characterize coordination? Which are the innate cognitive and neural endowments of humankind that make coordination possible? What is specific for human coordination? Thus, other aspects of the intellect such as emotions, feelings, memory, and so on, will only be included if they have bearing on coordination. Following this idea, the "hard core" of a coordination research program may be stated as follows:

- The basic Unit of Analysis is "activity" in the Activity Theory sense.
- There are certain human, innate dispositions that enable coordination of actions.
- There is a dialectical unity between mind and activity. Innate dispositions influence the way we experience and constructs our environment, which in turn influences the epigenetic formation of our brains.

The "protective belt" would at least include the following hypothesis:

- Fundamental dimensions of coordination are captured by the activity modalities: contextualization, spatialization, temporalization, stabilization, and transition. Humans are endowed with innate dispositions for integrating sensations in various sensory modalities into an activity modality percept that enable the coordination of individual and social actions.

A MODEL OF THE INTELLECT

In order to proceed with the research program, a tentative model for the intellect is necessary. Such a model should preferably have both analytical and constructive qualities. It should be possible to state interesting research questions, to set up informative experiments, and to draw well grounded conclusions from the model. In addition, the model should have the potential to indicate principles for constructing equipments such as robots, artificial neural networks (ANNs), and other devices.

To this end, I will depart from a model proposed by Gärdenfors (2000). His knowledge interest is to model representations of the cognitive system for explanatory and constructive purposes such as developing ANNs. According to him, there are two dominant approaches for such models: the *symbolic* and the *connectionist* ones. In the symbolic approach, the brain is regarded as a Turing machine, which manipulates symbols according to certain rules; a representation that originated in the Artificial Intelligence (AI) area. The connectionist approach models the brain as a system of connected neurons that respond to stimuli of various kinds.

However, Gärdenfors claims that important aspects of the cognitive system, such as concept acquisition, i.e., how concepts are learnt and internalized, cannot be adequately captured by either one of these approaches. To this end, Gärdenfors proposes a third, intermediate level: the *conceptual* one. Thus, Gärdenfors ends up with three levels: the symbolic, conceptual and connectionist ones; providing a gradual transition from the outward interactions with the world towards the neural network in the brain.

The Gärdenfors' model is modified as follows. To begin with, I will use the notion of "realms" instead of "levels". "Level" indicates a hierarchical ordering; a conceptualization I want to avoid. In contrast, "realm" suggests separate domains of inquiry, which is more apt for the analysis of the activity modalities. In addition, I will conceive the symbolic level as a "social" realm, which is oriented towards the activity. Typically, this realm will be conceptualized in terms of symbols, signs, meaning, artifacts, and the like. A particular important element in this level is communication by linguistic and other means:

A word is a bridge thrown between myself and another. If one end of the bridge depends on me, then the other depends on my addressee. A word is territory shared by both addresser and addressee, by the speaker and his interlocutor. (Vološinov, 1986, p. 86)

Concerning the connectionist level, I retain the connectionist focus on the properties of neural network in the brain. However, I wish to name this realm "neural" in order to indicate a broader scope than just connections between neurons. The resulting model of inquiry is illustrated in Figure 7.

The activity modalities are investigated in three different realms, each indicating a certain area of investigation: that of neural networks, concepts acquisition, and social reality. As a consequence of this analytical separation, the transition between these realms must also be investigated. In the following sections, I will present some preliminary results substantiating the proposed model for the intellect.

Figure 7. The framing of a possible coordination research program

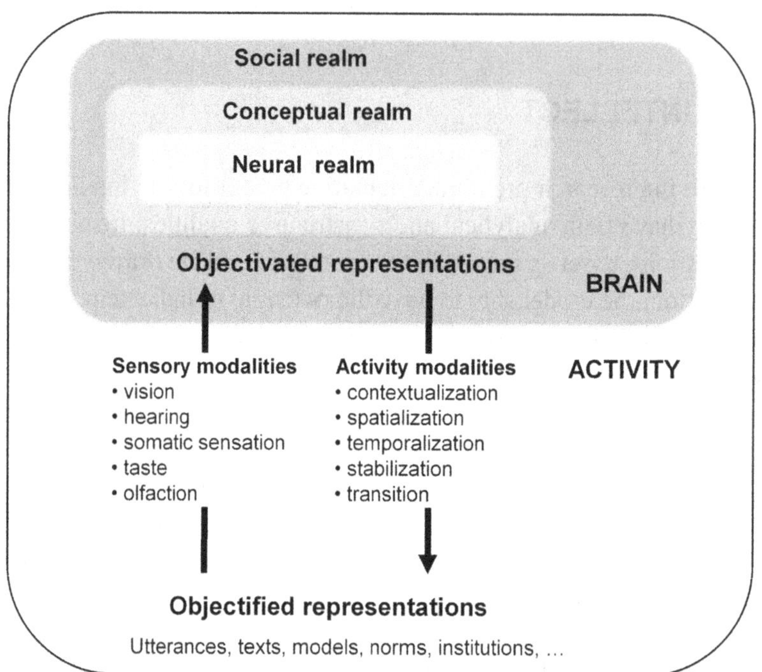

THE SOCIAL REALM

In order to analyze the social realm, I will use examples from Ericsson™ and references from the relevant literature. The reason for using Ericsson™ is that this is where the activity modalities were first conceived in my work with coordinating large and complex telecom projects. The means used – process models, product structures, business rules, information systems, etc. – stood out as different, yet tightly interrelated means that were profoundly important for the success of the projects. Gradually, the notion of activity modalities came up as a way to make sense of what seemed to be an incomprehensible complex, everyday reality. This process spanned more than fifteen years and is described in detail in Taxén (2009).

The Object and Motive

A natural point of departure for analyzing the social realm is to identify Objects and Motives; the determinants for the emergence, structure, and reason for an activity. In the case of mammoth hunting, the Object and Motive are straightforward: the visible mammoth and the need to get food. When humanity had learnt how to objectify symbols, other ways of conceptualizing the Object than direct perception became possible, such as images, drawings, models and the like.

If the Motive for an activity is to construct things that do not yet exist, symbolic means are the only possible way to perceive the Object. A striking illustration of this is the *anatomy*; a frequently used notation at Ericsson™ for visualizing complex telecom Objects. The anatomy is an illustration – preferably on one page – that shows *the dependencies between capabilities* in the system from start-up to

Figure 8. An illustration of an Object in the Ericsson™ development activity – a telecom processor (Reprinted from Taxén & Lillieskŏld, 2008. ©Elsevier. Used with permission)

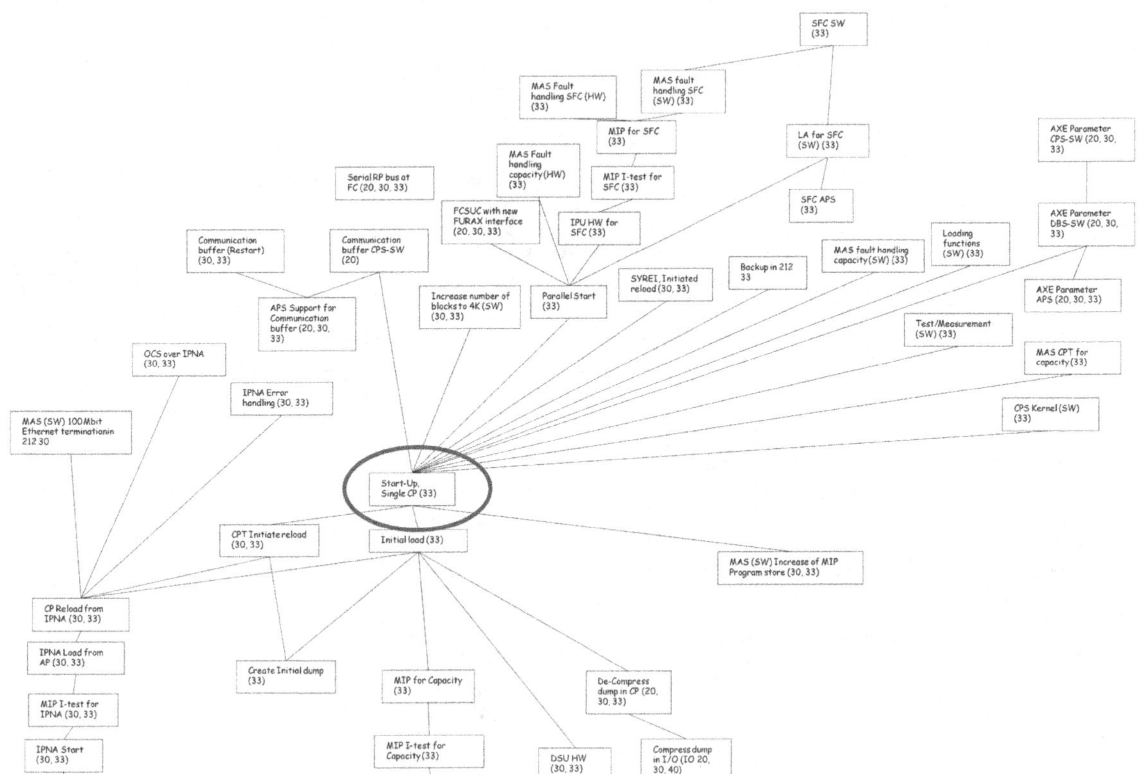

an operational system (see e.g. Adler, 1999; Jönsson, 2006; Taxén & Lillieskŏld, 2005; Taxén, 2009). Here, "capability" shall be understood as the ability of a certain system element to provide something that other system elements need. An anatomy for a telecom processor is shown in Figure 8.

The boxes, also called *anatoms*, (the details of which are less important here) should be read as capabilities provided by one or several modules in the system. The dependencies (lines) proceed from the bottom to the top of the anatomy. If a certain capability fails in the dependency chain, (for example, the encircled "Start-Up Single CP"), the whole system will fail. Since the system is developed and tested in the same order as the capabilities are invoked, the anatomy indicates, in a metaphorical sense, how the system "comes alive"; hence the term "anatomy".

The anatomy can be interpreted as a conceptualization of the Object in the activity of developing the telecom processor – a contemporary mammoth. Several Motives can be envisaged: making a profit by selling the system on a market, or simply providing communication capabilities. The gist of the anatomy is to create a common view of the Object as a means for coordinating activities. Since most parts of a telecom system are realized by software – which is not physically visible – an easy to apprehend image such as the anatomy is indispensible. Moreover, as a mediational means, the anatomy itself must be

Figure 9. Development activities defined for various parts of the product (Reprinted from Taxén & Lilliesköld, 2008. ©Elsevier. Used with permission)

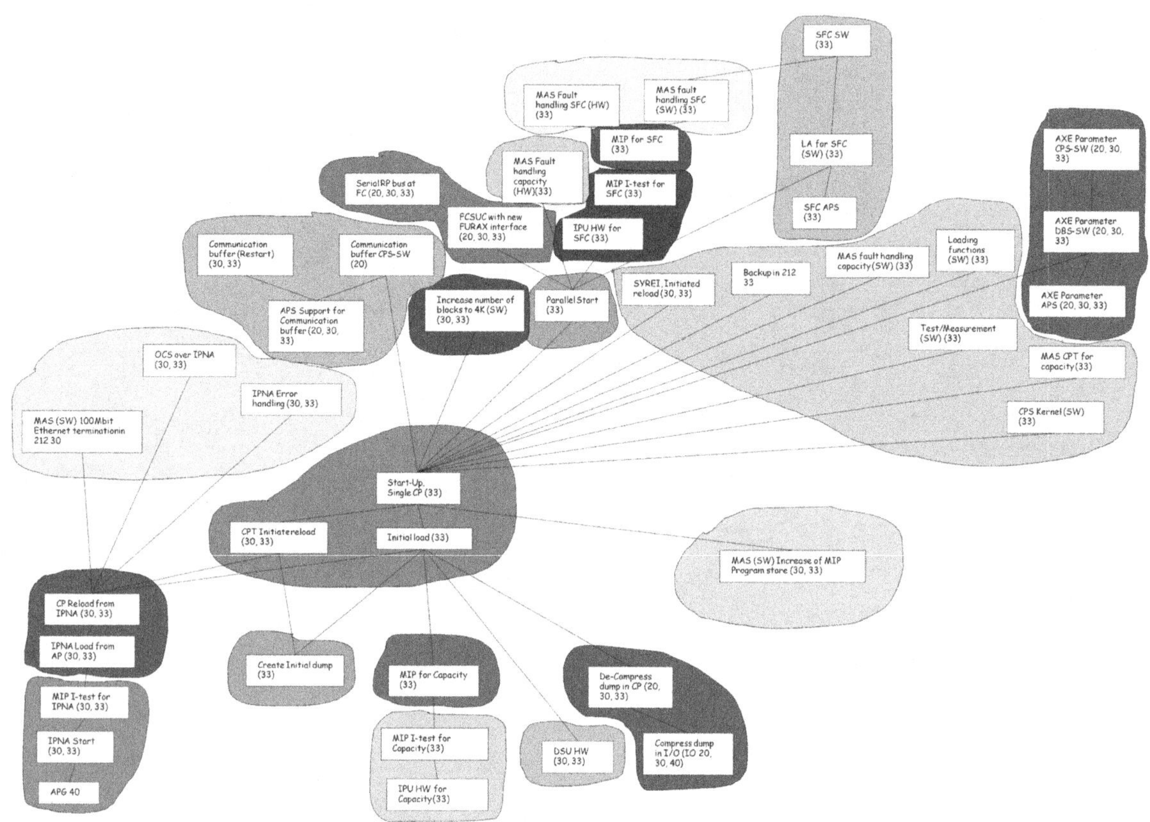

jointly developed by the actors in an objectivation – objectification process in order to become useful; the mammoth must come out of the fog, so to speak.

A telecom system is a complex product that consists of many different parts in which various technologies are utilized: software, hardware, mechanics, fiber optics, etc. This means that the overall activity must make use of other activities; each specialized to deliver a certain capability that the system needs. Each one of these activities has their own Object and Motive. In Figure 9, an illustration of various sub-activities for the telecom processor in Figure 8 is shown.

It can be seen that the dependencies between capabilities also define dependencies between activities. In this way it is easy to frame responsibilities in the overall activity. If, for example, the activity developing the "Start-Up Single CP" in the middle of the anatomy is delayed, all dependent activities will also be delayed. In essence, the anatomy is an ingenious way of visualizing the Object in order to facilitate coordination.

The Activity Modalities

The activity modalities can be observed in the social realm as follows.

Contextualization

It is evident that human action is dependent on the situation at hand. Certain things are attended in the foreground while other things remain unattended in the background. It appears that a capability to contextualize is innate:

Situated activity is not a kind of action, but the nature of animal interaction at all times, in contrast with most machines we know. This is not merely a claim that context is important, but what constitutes the context, how you categorize the world, arises together with processes that are coordinating physical activity. (Clancey, 1993, p. 95)

Although the notion of context is intuitively understandable, an unambiguous definition of context is less straightforward. In fact, there seems to be no common understanding of what context is and how it is used (Kofod-Petersen & Cassens, 2006). For our purposes we may regard "context" as the set of circumstances and conditions which surround and determine an idea, theory, proposition, or concept (Gershenson, 2002).

In language, contextualization is quite obvious. The same term, say "lie", has two quite different meanings depending on the context: "a statement that deviates from or perverts the truth" or "to be located or situated somewhere". An extreme proponent of contextuality is Vološinov:

The meaning of a word is determined entirely by its context. In fact, there are as many meanings of a word as there are contexts of its usage. (Vološinov, 1986, p. 79)

For Vološinov, verbal communication can never be understood and explained outside a connection with a concrete situation. None of our descriptions of the world is total, and new aspects can always be discovered. The way we describe something is not only determined by inherent qualities of the things, but also of how we relate to them and in what context. The color "blue", for example, means quite different things to a physicist and an artist.

From the organizational domain, we can illustrate contextualization by the life cycle of a product in a product development organization. From its inception to its disposal, the product passes through a number of different activities such as marketing, design, manufacturing, distribution, maintenance, and finally, scrapping (see Figure 10).

Although the product is recognized as a particular individual throughout its life cycle, it will be characterized differently in each of the contexts (Parsons, 1996). When marketed, properties like appearance, price, availability, etc., are relevant. When manufactured, the manufacturability of the product is in focus. When disposed, recycling and environmental concerns are emphasized, and so on.

Spatialization and Temporalization

In our daily life we have a strong sense of distinct spatial and temporal dimensions. Time is experienced as something qualitatively different from space:

Figure 10. The life cycle of a product

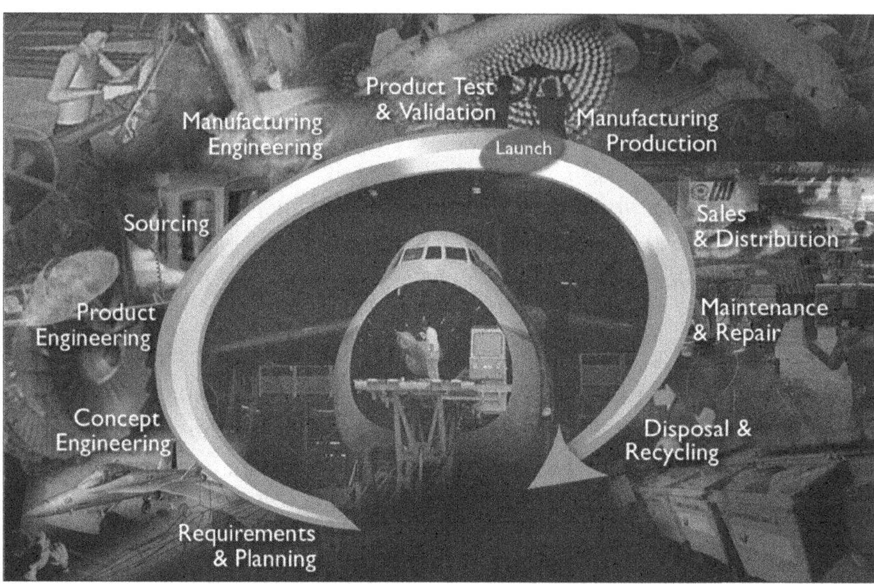

The world of everyday life is structured both spatially and temporally. [...]. Temporality is an intrinsic property of consciousness. The stream of consciousness is always ordered temporally. (Berger & Luckmann, 1991, p. 40)

Yet, even if we experience time and space as separate entities, we still find them closely intertwined:

Time and space provide contrasting perspectives on events. A temporal perspective highlights the sequence of transitions, the dynamic changes from segment to segment, things in motion. A spatial perspective highlights the sequence of states, the static spatial configuration, things caught still. Capturing the temporal and the spatial at once seems elusive; like waves and particles, the dynamic and the static appear to complement each other. (Zacks & Tversky, 2001, p. 19)

The complementary aspects of time and space can be illustrated by the sport of orienteering, where the goal is to run as quickly as possible from one control to another with the aid of a map and a compass. First, you have to orient yourself on the map. Where am I and where am I supposed to go? This act presumes a spatial capability; to literally orient oneself in the environment. The map can be seen as a spatial means supporting this task.

Next, I need to figure out a sequence of routes taking me from the start to the goal. This presumes a temporal capability; an ordering of events. First I will run towards the big stone along this path, then I cross the field aiming for the hill, then I run along the west side of the small marsh, and finally I head straight north to the goal. When I start on the first route I count my steps – a temporal dimension – and follow the direction of my compass – a spatial dimension. Now and then I check the map for a correspondence with the surrounding nature to make sure I am on the right track. Time and space are used interchangeably, and a capability to spatialize is needed to make sense of both the map and its "natural" correspondence.

In everyday life we can find an abundance of situations similar to the orienteering one. We constantly orient ourselves spatially and perform actions in an ordered manner. In doing so, we make use of various means devised to reflect one dominant modality, either spatiality or temporality such as maps, signposts, arrows, route descriptions, etc. (spatialization), and clocks, calendars, notification devices, etc. (temporalization).

Concerning language, we can see that spatialization and temporalization are at play in noun phrases ("$[_{NP}$ The boat that I saw coming into the harbor at nine o'clock] has just left") and verb phrases ("Mary $[_{VP}$ sent me a nice birthday present]"). Something is talked about and something happens. Spatialization and temporalization can also be recognized in speech act theory where the terms "locutionary" and "illocutionary" acts are used (e.g. Austin, 1962; Love, 1997; Searle, 1969). The locutionary or propositional act tells you something that you can understand or interpret within a context; what is talked about (spatialization). The illocutionary act is the act performed by saying something (temporalization).

In organizations, the enactment of spatial and temporal structures enables the coordination of activity[4]. Orlikowski & Yates expressed this in the following way:

People in organizations experience time through the shared temporal structures they enact recurrently in their everyday practices [...]. Whether implicitly or explicitly, people make sense of, regulate, coordinate, and account for their activities through the temporal structures they recurrently enact. (Orlikowski & Yates, 2002, p. 686)

Examples of spatial structures in the organizational context are information models, object-oriented models, data models, product structures, conceptual models, and the like. A concrete illustration of spatialization is given in Figure 11.

The image shows an information model for coordinating the development of the 3rd generation of mobile systems at Ericsson™ around year 2000. The model represents the common understanding of what actors in one activity considered relevant information elements for managing coordination. The enactment of this model, and its implementation in an information system, was a long and tedious process spanning several years. Only gradually, objectivated and objectified manifestations emerged (Taxén, 2009).

Likewise, examples of temporal structures in organizations are business process models, interaction diagrams, event diagrams, use cases, etc. In Figure 12, a temporal view of the activities in Figure 9, is shown.

The temporal view is important when discussing issues related to time such as delays, removing capabilities in order to finish on time, and the like. In fact, precisely the same things could be discussed based on Figure 9. However, since the temporal modality cannot be visualized in Figure 9, discussions about time issues are most likely aggravated using this image in comparison with Figure 12.

Stabilization

In every activity, a balance between order and disorder must be maintained:

Every social situation lives in order and disorder; every social situation holds a moment of order and a moment of disorder. (Nilson, 1976, p. 10, my translation)

Figure 11. An information model from Ericsson™

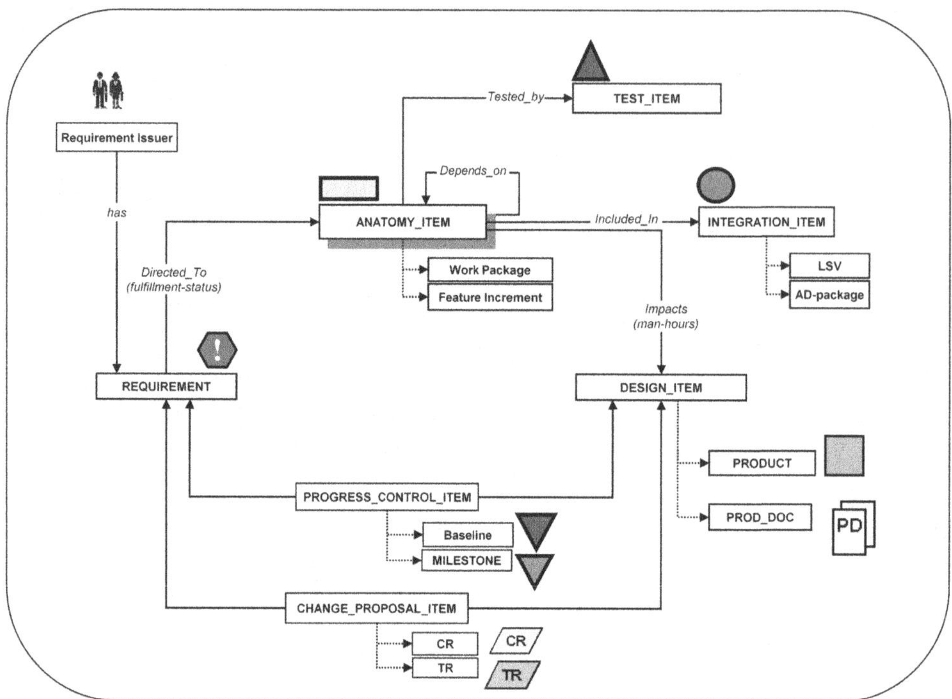

Balancing implies a certain level of stabilization that may be more or less comprehensive. A complete absence of stabilization brings about a state of chaos or disorder, while a complete coverage leads to petrification. At either end point, purposeful activity is impossible. Somewhere in between, rule coverage is optimal:

Upholding a balance means that elements, which distinguish valid actions from illegitimate ones, will be manifested in activities. Such elements, which has the function of "... reducing the infinite number of things in the world, potential or actual — to a moderate number of well-defined varieties" (March & Simon, 1958, p. 181), may originate from our physical environment. For example, violating norms preventing the consumption of lethal food or the falling off cliffs will result in death or serious diseases. Other stabilizing elements may be social conventions codified in religious or juridical norms.

Together, stabilization constitutes an *ideology*, that is, a wide-ranging system of beliefs in the activity that prescribes what phenomena are taken for real and which actions are considered valid. The ideology is manifested as common understanding about conventions, norms, values, habits, routines, rules, methods, standards, activity specific languages, etc., which enable a habitual performance of actions.

In communication, stabilization is evident in the grammar of a language. There are certain rules of composition that need to be enacted if utterances are to be intelligible; the syntax of the language has to be followed. Violating a rule in a "language game" in the Wittgensteinian sense means that an actor either does not understand the rule or deliberately chooses not to participate in the game:

Every stage in the development of a society has its own special and restricted circle of items which alone have access to that society's attention and which are endowed with evaluative accentuation by

Figure 12. Emphasizing the temporalization modality (Reprinted from Taxén & Lilliesköld, 2008. ©Elsevier. Used with permission)

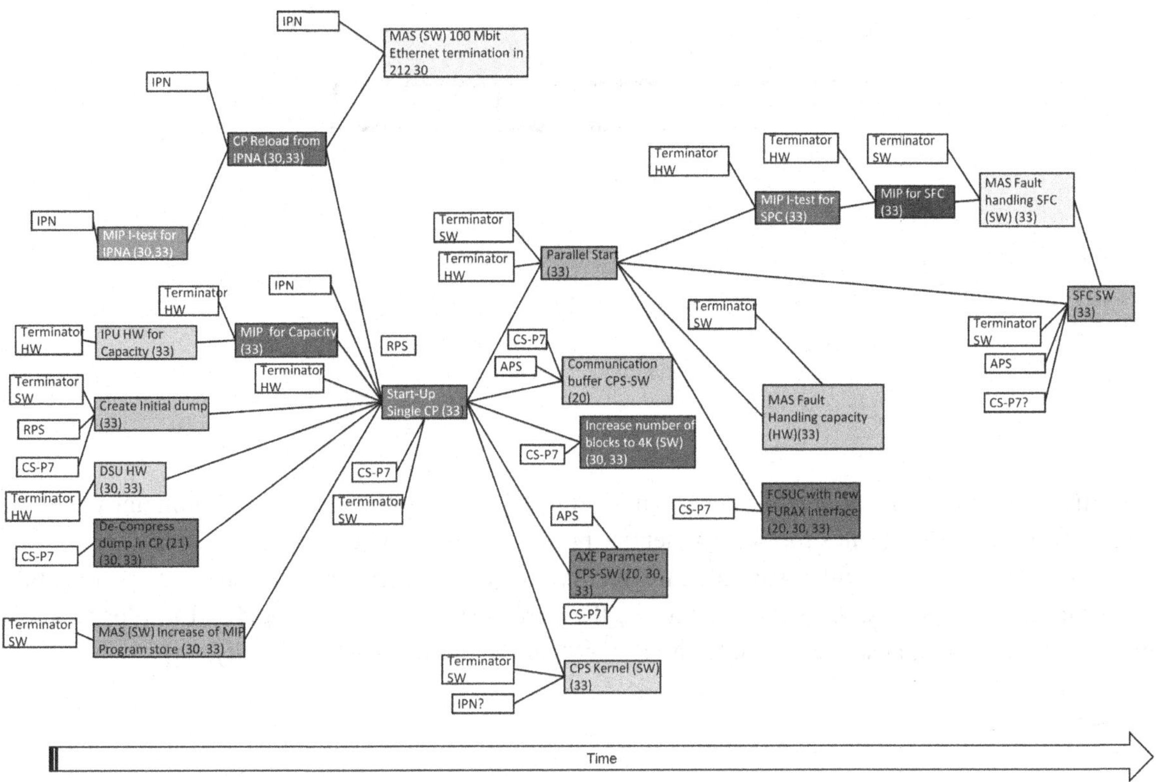

Figure 13. Balancing between chaos and petrification

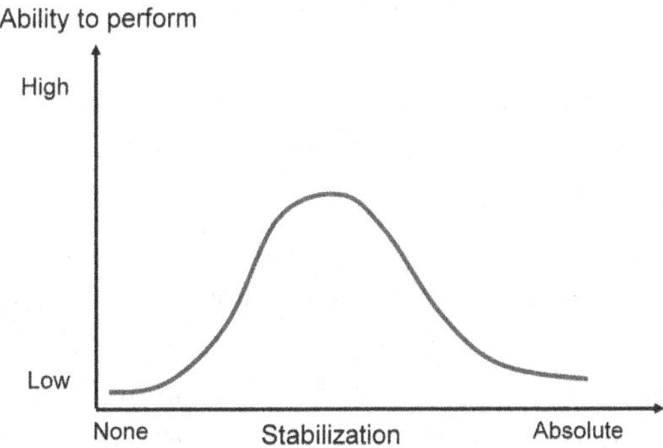

that attention. Only items within that circle will achieve sign formation and become objects in semiotic communication. (Vološinov, 1986, pp. 21-22)

In a large and distributed organization like Ericsson™, design centers around the world have certain autonomy to evolve locally in the manner they themselves find the best. At the same time, there must be some enterprise-wide common rules about how to approach customers, take heed for compulsory

Figure 14. Stabilizing elements at Ericsson™

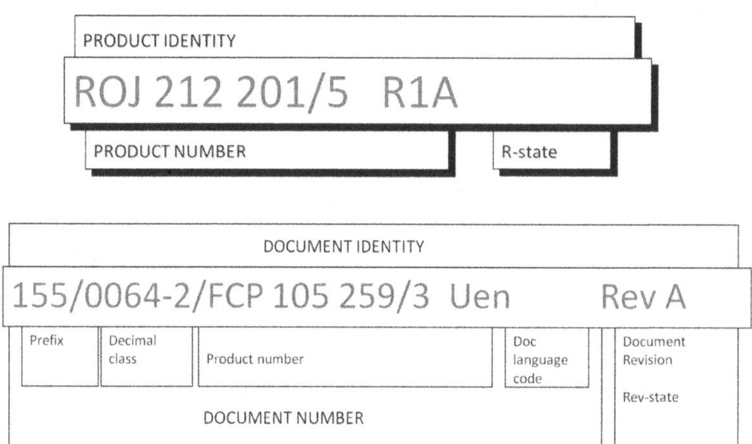

legislative norms, purchase materials, and so on. In Figure 14, two examples of such stabilizing elements at Ericsson™ are shown; rules for how to identify products and documents:

As can be seen, the particular way rules are manifested at Ericsson™ (and, for that matter, any other organization) is idiosyncratic. For most people, they are completely unintelligible. In order to make sense of these rules and use them, you have to enact them in the Ericsson™ activity.

Transition

Transition is, in short, the complement to contextualization. When an activity is "crystallized" around a certain Motive and Object, a sense of "insiders", common for those engaged in the activity, emerges. As a consequence, contextualization also produces "outsiders"; those who are not involved in the activity. Such actors may reside in other activities that might be needed in order to fulfill a common goal. This is where the transition modality becomes relevant[5].

As with the other modalities, we are surrounded by manifestations of transition in our daily life. Dictionaries, outlet adaptors, currency exchange tables, passport controls, gatekeepers, door keys, airlocks, etc., are all examples of transitional elements.

In organizations, we find an abundance of transitional elements such as contracts, agreements, interface specifications, mapping between different article codes, conversion between analog and digital signals, compilers for software languages, and so on. The division of labor raises the issue of how different organizational units shall work together. Differentiation and integration of work are opposites that somehow need to be reconciled (Lawrence & Lorsch, 1967). An example of this from Ericsson™ is shown in Figure 15.

The figure is an illustration of how four activities – Sales, Design, Hardware Design, and Supply – at Ericsson™ are coordinated in terms of development states. In particular, the figure shows how states in the activities HW Design and Design are mapped onto each other: PR- and DS1 are mapped to SC3 and SC4; PR1, PR2 and PRA to SC6; PRB to SC7. Such "mapping rules" between states in different activities are examples of organizational transitional elements.

Figure 15. An example of transition from Ericsson™

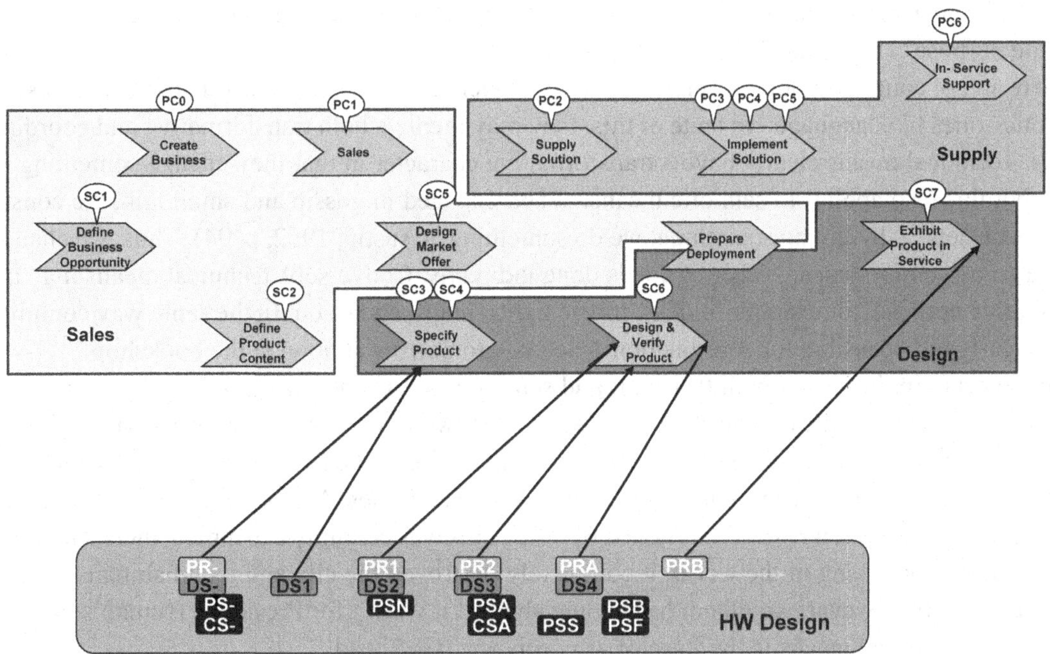

Mediation

The most obvious expression of mediation is the tool. Tools are intrinsic parts of humankind. When the hominids started to walk upright, the hands were set free for other purposes than support for moving around. This was a decisive step in the evolution from ape to man. It opened up for an intricate interplay between the human organism and her environment. Through hundreds of thousands of years of labor, the human hand evolved into a tool which is infinitely more sophisticated than that of any simian:

When the little child performs the perfect grip of the tweezers she starts her path as a tool maker; she becomes Homo faber, man as craftsman, the tool making animal. (Liedman, 2001, p. 180, my translation)[6]

The first tools were created and controlled by the hand, but the opposite is also valid: "... the hand is not only the organ of labor, it is also the product of labor" (Engels, 1954). The ability to produce tools played an important role for the increase of the brain and the low positioned larynx, which in turn were prerequisites for the development of language. The development of new tools goes hand in hand with the construction of a new language in order to use these tools, which in turn can give rise to new tools, etc. Hence, there is an intricate relationship between tools and language:

A tool is also a mode of language. For it says something, to those who understand it, about the operations of use and their consequences.... In the present cultural setting, these objects are so intimately bound up with intentions, occupations and purposes that they have an eloquent voice. (Dewey, 1991, p. 52, referred in Miettinen & Virkkunen, 2005, p. 443)

Thus, both tools and language are means by which actions are performed. Language "can be likened to a tool by which reality becomes tangible. 'Tools' thus become equivalent to every mean that is used for some purpose" (Liedman, 2001, p. 176, my translation).

There are, of course, obvious differences between "technical" means, such as hammers and axes, and "semiotic" ones like language[7]. In spite of this, they may mediate both transformative and coordinative actions. Technical means clearly have a transformative character in that they change something in the world, but this also applies to semiotic means. When engaged in gossip and small talk, we constantly use "speech acts": "by saying something, we do something" (Austin, 1962, p. 94). Thus, we change the world also by semiotic means, even if this is done indirectly. Conversely, technical means may have a coordinative purpose, for example, clocks, traffic lights, maps, and so on. In the same way communication is clearly indispensible for coordination: "See you tomorrow at noon at the bookshop!"

An important point is that both technical and semiotic means are intrinsically social in nature. For semiotic means this is quite obvious; you must be at least two individuals in order to communicate. It is of course possible to imagine technical means in solitary actions, like Robinson Crusoe on his island. In general though, technical means make sense only in social activities. A good example is the first atomic bomb that was dropped on Hiroshima August 6, 1945. This was certainly a technical means in the sense that it changed something in the world; it completely destroyed the city and its inhabitants. The dropping of the bomb, however, would not have come about if it wasn't for President Truman's ordering of the attack – a semiotic means in the form of a speech act: "Go ahead!"

Mediation and Activity Modalities

Mediational means are related the activity modalities as follows. To begin with, the capability of a means is context dependent. Consider, for example, the action of nailing. A hammer can be used to drive in nails, kill somebody or as a plummet by attaching a string to it. On the other hand, a hammer is utterly useless to cut down a tree. In spite of being the same physical object, the usefulness of the hammer is determined by the activity in which it is used.

What about spatialization and temporalization? Continuing with the hammer example, spatialization is at play when a carpenter frames a work situation in terms of placing the nail in the exact position on the plank, positioning himself in relation to the plank, judging the influence of other things in the situation that might intervene with his actions (such as the safety of the scaffold he might be standing on), and so forth. Temporalization is at work in laying out the order of actions: grasping the hammer, placing the nail, hitting the nail, replacing the hammer in the toolbox, etc.

Stabilization is present in the skill the carpenter has acquired in nailing. There is a preferred way of nailing that will be learnt and refined through repeated actions. It is all too well known what might happen with the thumb when an inexperienced person tries to hit the nail! Other manifestations of stabilization are, for example, rules that stipulate the wearing of safety glasses in order to avoid splinter, the wearing of safety lines when working on high altitudes, and so on. Stabilization is also present in standardization of nail sizes, quality classes of nails and hammers, and the like.

Transition is perceptible when the carpenter goes to the hardware store to buy more nails or a new hammer. He needs to explain his needs to the merchandiser, and he is dependent on other activities for producing the nails and transporting them to the store. Moreover, the payment of the merchandise is dependent on common understanding about the exchange value of the money used in the transaction.

Figure 16. A screen dump of an IS at Ericsson™

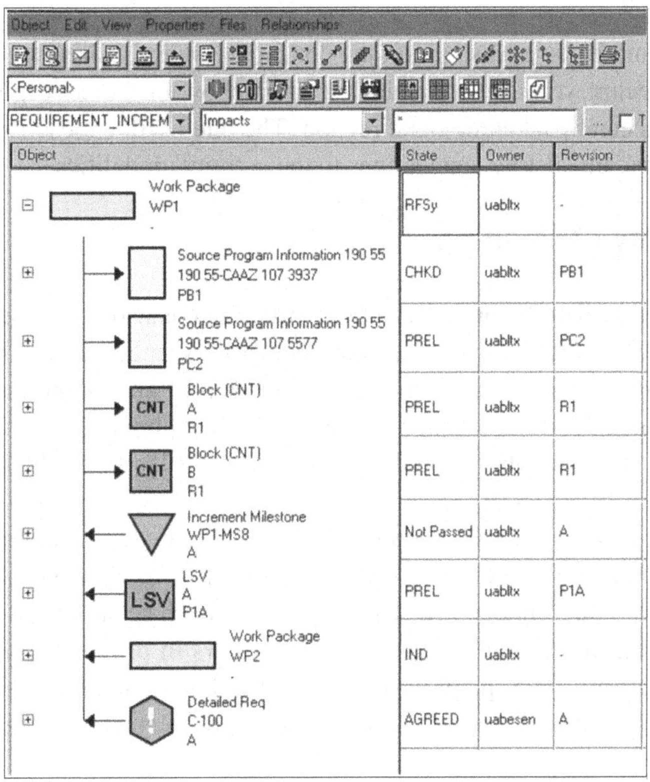

This simple example of nailing shows that the activity modalities and mediational means make up an indivisible whole. Means need to be enacted, i.e., they are literally useless unless an objectivation – objectification process has been effectuated. In this process, the individual and her means become so intertwined that it is more appropriate to talk about of "individual(s)-acting-with-mediational-means" rather than "individual(s)" alone when referring to the agent of action (Wertsch, 1991, p. 12).

A particular kind of mediational means is information systems (ISs), which are difficult to classify as either technical or semiotic in nature. From an activity modality point of view, however, an IS can be regarded as a coordinative artifact; a means to coordinate actions between actors in the same activity, or between different activities. An illustration of this is shown in Figure 16.

Contextualization is evident from the fact that the information shown is based on the context model in Figure 11. Only such items that are relevant in the context are visible in the IS. Spatialization is shown, among other things, in the relationships between items as indicated by the arrows. Temporalization can be noticed from the states of the items, since actions change the states. Stabilization is evident in the Ericsson™ specific way of naming items. Transition is not immediately visible in the image, since it shows the context of one activity only. However, when the information is passed on to other ISs, transitional means are needed to transfer the information.

THE CONCEPTUAL REALM

A suitable point of departure for investigating the conceptual realm is language. Language obviously belongs to the social realm; yet it must be anchored somehow in the conceptual and neural realms. Obviously, many routes can be taken in this direction. The one I will choose is Jackendoff's theory of meaning, which has some interesting connections to the activity modalities.

Jackendoff's Theory of Meaning

Chomsky (1965) suggested that the brain has a deep structure consisting of a set of rules operating on symbols from which the "surface" forms of sentences in various languages can be generated. Although explaining many features of language, such as the generation of an infinite number of different sentences from a finite number of rules, it failed to account for paraphrases, i.e., the profound similarities between sentences like "John bought the book from Bill" and "Bill sold the book to John" (O'Keefe & Nadel,1978, p. 395).

To this end, a number of researchers proposed other kinds of deep structures, based on some sort of conceptual network that code meaning through the interaction of elements (ibid, p. 398). One such structure was suggested by Jackendoff: "all sentences have a deep semantic structure that is analogous to the subset of sentences describing events or state of affairs in physical space" (Jackendoff, 1976, referred in O'Keefe & Nadel, 1978, p. 399). In other words, behind the multitude of different ways of talking about the world in various languages, there exists a deep structure that resembles the way all humans experience the world.

In his analysis, Jackendoff starts from the following questions (Jackendoff, 1983, p. 3):

- What is the nature of meaning in human language, such that we can talk about what we perceive and what we do?
- What does the grammatical structure of natural language reveal about the nature of perception and cognition?

According to Jackendoff, these two questions cannot be separated. He suggests that there is a single level of mental representation where linguistic, sensory and motor information are compatible: the *conceptual structure* (ibid, p. 17). Unless there is such a level, it would be impossible to use language to report sensory input. We could not speak about what we see, hear, touch, smell, etc. Likewise, linguistic information must be compatible at some level with information conveyed to the motor system. For example, a speech act like "Please close that window!" presumes an interaction of visual, linguistic and motor information.

Like Gärdenfors, Jackendoff claims that some kind of conceptual representation is needed as a bridge between the social realm and the neural realm. However, while Gärdenfors models the conceptual realm geometrically, Jackendoff proposes that the conceptual structure is characterized by a finite set of conceptual well-formedness rules that are universal and innate (ibid, p. 17). In order to explore the properties of these rules, two issues need to be addressed: What is the nature of the information that language conveys, and what is this information about? The first is concerned with sense or intention – the second with reference or extension.

Figure 17. Duck-rabbit (Wittgenstein, 1953; Kihlstrom, 2004)

These questions are approached from a discussion about what we see when we perceive something. From ambiguous figures like the famous Wittgensteinian "duck-rabbit" in Figure 17 it is clear that the brain overlays such figures with an organization that is not present in any physical sense.

There is no reason why this mechanism should be confined to the vision modality only. Thus, the world as we perceive and experience it is "unavoidably influenced by the nature of the unconscious processes for organizing environmental input. One cannot perceive the "'real world as it is'" (Jackendoff, 1983, p. 26). It follows that it is necessary to distinguish between the source of the environmental input and the world as experienced. Jackendoff calls the former the "real world" and the latter the "projected world". We have conscious access only to the projected world – the world as unconsciously organized by the mind. We can talk about things only insofar as they have achieved mental representation through these processes of organization. Hence, "information conveyed by language must be about the projected world" (ibid, p. 29). The information in the conceptual structure is the single level of mental representation onto which and from which all peripheral information is mapped. In this perspective, meaning is apprehended as the connection of sensory inputs to entities in the projected world.

In order to analytically distinguish the real world form the projected one, Jackendoff introduces a meta-language. References to the projected world are surrounded by # #. Entities in the conceptual structure, which give rise to the projected world, are designated in CAPITALS. Real-world entities are surrounded by * *[8].

Consider again Figure 17. By interacting with other people in an English speaking society, two entities in the conceptual structure are formed in the mind: RABBIT and DUCK. These are objectivated manifestations which have become associated with the real-world sensations *rabbit* and *duck*, for example, through audible spoken words, pointing to live animals, or visual drawings. The real-world electromagnetic radiation from the illustration in Figure 17 may be labeled *duck-rabbit*. This physical input on the retina is processed by the nervous system and mapped to either RABBIT or DUCK in the conceptual structure. From this structure, either the entity #rabbit# or #duck# may be projected into awareness. However, both projections cannot take place simultaneously. Thus, the same real-world input may give rise to different experiences in the projected world. If, for example, #duck# is projected, this entity may be transformed via correspondence rules to the linguistic and motor systems, resulting in the utterance "That is a duck!", possibly accompanied with a pointing gesture.

Consequently, the sense of the linguistic expression consists of expressions based on the conceptual structure. The reference of the expression takes place in the projected world, not the real-world. This view has far-reaching consequences. The traditional view of truth and reference as relations between statements and facts in the real-world cannot be upheld, since the direct connection between language and this world does not exist.

The single level of mental representation provided by the conceptual structure indicates that "semantic structures could be simply a subset of conceptual structures – just those conceptual structures that happen to be verbally expressible" (ibid, p. 19). Thus, the study of semantics and grammar of natural language should give evidence for the organization of the conceptual structure and the conceptual well-formedness rules.

Ontological Categories

An obvious feature of the projected world is that it includes #things# that have some kind of spatial and temporal integrity. These #things# are projected from a corresponding mental representation in the conceptual structure. Jackendoff calls a unitary piece of mental representation a *conceptual constituent* (ibid, p. 42). These are surrounded in the Jackendoff formalism with square brackets [ ]. Thus, in order to account for the fact that humans can perceive a #rabbit#, a corresponding conceptual constituent [RABBIT] must have been objectivated in the conceptual structure.

Utterances like "I have read that book (*pointing*)" relate linguistic and visual information. Such utterances are examples of what has been coined "pragmatic anaphora" (ibid, p. 48). It turns out that there is a set of different classes of pragmatic anaphora, which can be identified by different types of grammatical phrases. The utterance above is clearly about [THING]s, and the part "that book" can be identified as a noun phrase (NP). However, an utterance like "Your book is there (*pointing*)" is about a [PLACE], which is recognized by a prepositional phrase (PP). [PLACE] and [THING] are clearly of separate kinds. Such different types of basic categories are called *ontological categories*.

Through an elaborate linguistic discussion, Jackendoff identifies a set of ontological categories, which combine to perform meaning functions. The categories of prime interest here are as follows:

[THING]
[PLACE]
[PATH]
[EVENT]
[STATE]
[PROPERTY]
[DIRECTION]
[ACTION]

The semantic structure of a sentence is built from a hierarchical composition of the conceptual constituents, each belonging to an ontological category. These categories are realized by syntactically mapping them according to well-formedness rules to phrasal categories such as sentences (S), noun phrases (NP), verb phrases (VP), adjective phrases (AP), adverbial phrases (AdvP) and prepositional phrases (PP). For example, the sentence "John walked into the room" is mapped between syntactical and conceptual structures as follows:

Syntactic: $[_{S}\ [_{NP\ John}]\ [_{VP}$ walked $[_{PP}$ into $[_{NP}$ the room$]]]\ ]$.
Conceptual: $[_{Event}$ GO $([_{Thing}$ John$], [_{Path}$ TO $[_{Place}$ IN $[_{Thing}$ the room$]]])\ ]$.

In this way, Jackendoff tries to establish a connection between lexical categories and phrases used in different languages, and ontological categories common to all humans.

In later works, Jackendoff includes "thematic roles" as part of the conceptual structure (Jackendoff, 1990). A thematic role can then be seen as a relationship that ties a term with an event or a state, establishing a semantic relationship between a predicate (e.g. a verb) and an argument (e.g. the noun phrases) of a sentence. Examples of thematic roles are:

[AGENT] (The instigator of an action)
[ACTOR] (The willful instigator of an action)
[GOAL] (What the action is directed towards)

Jackendoff also discusses categorization as an essential aspect of cognition. Categorization refers to the ability to judge that a particular thing is or is not an instance of a specific category (Jackendoff, 1983, p. 77). The ability to categorize is indispensable for using previous experiences to guide the interpretation of new experiences. In order to discuss matters concerning categories and instances, Jackendoff refers to the thing being categorized as [TOKEN] and the category as a [TYPE]. The latter is the information that is created and stored when an organism learns a category.

Activity Modality Interpretation

How can the theory of Jackendoff be related to the activity modalities and the activity construct? First, it can be noted that some elements in the activity corresponds to ontological categories: "action" - [ACTION], "goal" - [GOAL], "actor" - [ACTOR]. Acting is represented by a binary function CAUSE with the structure $[_{\text{Event}}$ CAUSE $([_{\text{Thing}}\ x], [_{\text{Event}}\ y])]$, where x is the agent causing some event y. This means that the agent is not necessarily acting willfully as in the example "The wind blew the paper away". The case of an intentional actor is seen as a special case of [AGENT].

Contextualization

Contextualization implies establishing the extension of the activity. Only those #things# that are relevant with respect to the Motive and Object will become meaningful in the context. This means that different [PROPERTIES] can be associated with the same [THING] depending on the context (cf. Parsons, 1996).

Contextualization is inextricably related to the classification of [THINGS] into categories or [TYPES]. Our visual system simplifies a visual scene into foreground and background. Certain #things# enters into the circle of attention while other #things# remain unattended in the background (Jackendoff, 1983, p. 42).

There seems to be no direct correspondence in the conceptual structure to contextualization. However, the notion of [SEMANTIC FIELD] is used to describe a set of lexemes that are related in some way. For example, a [SEMANTIC FIELD] concerning air travel would include reservation, flight, travel, buy, price, cost, fare, rates, meal, plane, etc. This can be apprehended as a list of relevant [THINGS] in a context such as an activity with the motive of providing air travel services. A tentative suggestion would be that the contextualization, as an innate predisposition, engages a set of relevant conceptual constituents based on the Object and Motive in focus for an action; a suggestions that of course need to be reinforced by linguistic and neurological evidences.

Spatialization and Temporalization

In order to carry out actions, the actors need to know what kind of #things# are relevant in the activity. Spatialization manifests common understanding of these #things#, how they are characterized, how they are related to each other, and in what state or condition they are. Spatialization can be associated with the ontological categories as follows:

[THING]s are related to other [THING]s.
[THING]s have [PROPERTIES].
[THING]s have [STATE]s.
[DIRECTION]s provide orientation.

Temporalization can be associated to the conceptual structure as [EVENT]s which changes [STATE] s or [PROPERTIES] of [THING]s.

Stabilization

The ability to categorize is central to achieve stabilization. Stabilization affects [TYPE]s and [TOKEN] s in the conceptual structure and is constantly adjusted in interaction with the environment:

A processing model of cognition must include an active component that continually seeks to adjust and reorganize conceptual structure in an effort to maximize overall stability. (Jackendoff, 1983, p. 149)

Transition

It appears that there is no ontological category that directly corresponds to transition in the conceptual structure. Transition is however evident in, for example, conceptual constituents involved in translating different languages into each other (such as when [DOG] in English is mapped to the [HUND] in Deutsch).

Summing Up

In short, Jackendoff proposes that cognition emerges from a level of mental representation where language and sensory modalities are compatible. This level contains ontological categories such as [THING], [PLACE], [DIRECTION], [EVENT], etc. These categories characterize distinctions among major classes of #entities# we experience that the #world# consists of. The total set of ontological categories "must be universal: it constitutes one basic dimension along which humans can organize their experience, and hence it cannot be learned" (Jackendoff, 1983, p. 56).

The conceptual constituents can be regarded as "types" of concepts, derived from the ontological categories. These constituents correspond to the objectivated manifestations of actions carried out in a certain activity. For example, the conceptual constituent [WORK PACKAGE] found in the context model in Figure 11, is derived from the ontological category [THING]. When an actor focus on the image of a certain Work Package in Figure 16, the perception of the top yellow square (see Figure 18) indicated by WP1, is projected into consciousness as #WP1#; an exemplar of the conceptual constituent [WORK PACKAGE].

In order to perform meaningful actions on this information, an individual must have enacted a conceptual constituent [WORK PACKAGE] in her conceptual structure through lengthy and tedious interactions among actors in the activity.

Figure 18. A detail of Figure 16

THE NEURAL REALM

The point of departure for discussing the neural realm is a study by Jeffery, Anderson, Hayman, and Chakraborty (2004; JAHC in the following), who have proposed an architecture for the neural representation of what they call "spatial context".

According to JAHC, little is known about what constitutes contexts and how the brain represents them. In conditioning studies, it has been observed in that conditioning occurs between the unconditional stimuli (US) and background cues, or "context" of the experiment. The context is seen as a kind of conditional stimuli (CS) that influences the behavior of the laboratory animal. Contextual stimuli have been found to act like "occasion setters", i.e., stimuli that modulate other associations, such as the CS-US connection. The expression JAHC uses is that "contextual stimuli serve to 'gate' the relationship between a CS and US" (ibid, p. 202). Moreover:

That contextual stimuli are functionally different from other kinds of stimuli implies that they may be processed differently in the brain, and thus require a specialized processing apparatus. This raises the interesting question of where in the brain such an apparatus might exist, and how its representation of context is constructed. (ibid, p. 202)

JAHC approach this question by referring to the works of O'Keefe and Nadel (1978), who suggested a so called "'cognitive mapping system'; a set of brain structures including the hippocampus which collectively have been proposed as the site of a neural representation of place" (ibid, p. 202). O'Keefe & Nadel suggest that "the role of the hippocampus is to construct a spatial representation, or 'cognitive map', which an animal can use in spatially guided behaviors such as navigation" (JAHC, p. 203).

The cognitive mapping system is an attempt to understand how context cues might be sometimes part of the foreground of a situation, in which case they need to be attended by the animal in order to solve a problem; or sometimes part of the background and thus unattended to. Additional difficulties were posed by the fact that the same cues can alternatively be part of foreground or the background depending on the intentions and expectations of the animal. This leads JAHC to suggest that "Foreground and background stimuli do not therefore exist in a simple mutually exclusive relationship to each other, but rather in a more hierarchical relationship in which the context 'surrounds' or 'contains' the discrete (to-be-conditioned-to) stimuli" (ibid, p. 202).

Based on this, JAHC suggest that different kinds of information may be processed differently in the brain, contrary to more traditional views that learning is universal and indifferent with respect to the type of information. From this, JAHC continue to discuss "spatial context", by which they mean the subclass of contextual cues that serve to define an environment. In addition to spatial and featural stimuli, the spatial context includes also "non-physical aspects of the environment such as the intentions or expectations of the animal" (ibid, p. 203). Such stimuli "collectively define something more akin to a 'situation' or 'occasion' than simply an environment" (ibid, p. 203).

Activity Modality Interpretation

From the activity modality perspective several interesting observations can be made from the JAHC findings. First, it appears that there is a general acceptance about the role of the hippocampus in spatial behavior, which indicates a possible location in the brain for the spatialization modality. Second, the US, i.e., the primary focus of attention, may be interpreted as the Object towards which the animal takes action. The CS may be seen as a kind of symbolic association with the US, referring to the same Object.

Next, the notion of "spatial context" might be misleading. Contextualization and spatialization are two different things. The context is determined by the Object and Motive and thus, contextualization is primary with respect to the spatial structure of the context. If the context is changed due to a different Object or Motive, the spatial cues will change as well. Some cues will no longer be relevant; others may become relevant; and the characterization of cues may change. For example, a hungry bear may catch salmons in a river or feed on berries. Although the Motive is the same, the Object is different. Quite different contextual cues will become relevant depending on which Object is attended to. It follows that stimuli referring to the Object or Motive should not be regarded as "contextual" cues, since these are the determinants of the context.

Another observation is that spatialization is but one of the modalities constituting a context. Brain structures and processes for objectivation of Objects, Motives, temporalization, stabilization and transition must also be investigated. To begin with, psychological experiments indicate that "there are different retrieval patterns for objects and event concepts. The differences in the retrieval pattern [...] reflect significant differences in the underlying mental organizations and cognitive processes" (Chen, 2003, p. 966). This is also supported by neurophysiological findings:

Indeed, there are a broad range of behavioural, neuropsychological, and electrophysiological findings that support a dissociation between object knowledge in temporal cortex and action knowledge in parieto-frontal cortex. (Plaut, 2002, p. 631)

Another example is Greenfield, who quotes the neurophysiologist Ad Aertson:

[We] should distinguish between structural and anatomical connections on the one hand and functional or effective connectivity on the other. The former can be described as quasi-stationery, whereas the latter may be highly dynamic. (Greenfield, 1998, p. 217)

In their extensive work on space and the brain, O'Keefe and Nadel (1978) differ between maps and routes. Maps "represent the spatial relationships between the various things experienced in the environment" (ibid, p. 51), while routes provide instructions to get from one point to another. Routes imply goals which imply motivations (ibid, p. 83). From an activity modality point of view, maps are manifestations of spatialization, while routes are manifestations of both spatialization and temporalization. This is quite a different conceptualization as compared to the one proposed by O'Keefe and Nadel, which see maps and routes as two different means of getting around in the world (ibid, p. 80).

In any case, it appears that the brain is structured to distinguish between temporal and spatial information. There is evidence that certain brain regions are tuned to temporal aspects of action:

Temporal structure has a major role in human understanding of everyday events. Observers are able to segment ongoing activity into temporal parts and sub-parts that are reliable, meaningful and correlated with ecologically relevant features of the action. [...] a network of brain regions is tuned to perceptually salient event boundaries [...]. Activity within this network may provide a basis for parsing the temporally evolving environment into meaningful units. (Zacks et al., 2001, p. 651)

Another aspect of temporalization is simulation. According to Gärdenfors (2000), perceptions of advanced organisms are associated with a type of simulators in the brain, by which different types of actions can be anticipated before they are carried out[9]. The information from the sensory receptors is fed into the simulator and amended with other signals which might emerge from stored representations rather than sensory receptors. An interpretation of the situation is carried out, followed by relevant actions. Simulators presume a learning capability, which means that more complex nervous systems are involved than pure sensation processing.

Concerning stabilization, Greenfield (1998) describes how a group of neurons with relative long-lasting connections between them, may engage neuronal assemblies when a particular stimulus is reaching the brain. Depending on the size of the neuronal assembly, different forms of consciousness may arise. Small neuronal assemblies may result in a kind of consciousness that would be reactive to whatever crossed one's path without a lot of reflection and memories and thoughts. This form of consciousness appears in a child's perspective and in a schizophrenic person. On the other hand, abnormally large neuronal assemblies would have the opposite effect. The outside world would appear remote, grey and distant. This form of consciousness can be found in clinical depression. Thus it appears that a balance between the two extremes of chaos and petrification exist in a developed and healthy brain.

Mediation is not limited to tool-making beings. In Gibson's theory of perception (Gibson, 1979), both humans and animals relates to the environment through what he calls *affordances,* which stands for the "invitational" action-enabling qualities of a percepts or events[10]. This resonates well with the notion of objectification. Moreover, as with tools, affordances are also dependant on the activity modalities, for example, contextualization:

An affordance of a situation, crudely stated, is a way that a situation lends itself to being used. [...] We can change the affordances of an object merely by altering its context. [...]. An affordance, as we shall use the term then, is a dispositional property of a situation defined by a set of objects organized in a set arrangement, relativized to the action repertoire of a given agent. (Kirsh, 1995, p. 43)

Finally, all inquiries into the workings of the brain must take into consideration activity as the nexus of the epigenetic formation of the brain:

[The] neural structures and processes that coordinate perception and action are created during activity, not retrieved and rotely applied, merely reconstructed, or calculated via stored rules and pattern descriptions. (Clancey, 1993, p. 94, italics in original)

INTEGRATION

In order to experience and act in the world, vision, auditory, somatosensory, gustatory, and olfactory sensations must be integrated into a coherent representation of the environment:

[It is] understandable that evolution has provided multimodal sensory convergence in order to perform space-time integration on the multi-sensory percept, a Gestalt, not on its components prior to their assembly. (Freeman, 2004, p. 525)

In this context, at least two problems need to be addressed: how can we characterize the integrated percept, and how does the integration mechanism work? Again, an immense amount of research has been devoted to these issues[11]. Here, I will follow one line of reasoning suggested by Jean-Pierre Changeux (1997; 2004).

In the same way as Jackendoff, Changeux assumes that all humans share a basic set of concepts, or representations (Changeux, 2004, p. 48). This set is, as we saw, called ontological categories by Jackendoff, while Changeux refer to the basic set as *innate dispositions*. These make up a foundation from which the ontogenetic development of the individual proceeds. However, in contrast to previous opinions that the brain is a passive receptor of external stimuli, the brain actively produces representations that it projects onto the outside world:

The spontaneous activity of specialized sets of neurons causes the organism to constantly explore and test its physical, social, and cultural environment, to capture and register responses from it, and to compare them with its inner repertoire of stored memories. (ibid., p. 32)

Thus, from very early on, the brain is actively involved in probing and evaluating its immediate social and physical environment. This process results in semi-persistent impressions in the brain in the form of *pre-representations*:

Pre-representations (known also as "neural schemas" or preliminary categories) may be defined as dynamic, spontaneous, and transient states of activity arising from the recombination of preexisting populations of neurons. (ibid., p. 59)

Over time, validated pre-representations are stored in long-time memory, forming "the basis of the brain's ability to make sense of the world. They are, in short, the source of imaginative activity (ibid., p. 60)". Thus, through innate dispositions, the spontaneous activity of the brain and evaluation of external responses, individuals construct a meaningful world, which is created by individuals but inevitably dependent on the social milieu for its existence:

With the emergence of humankind, innate dispositions became enriched by the exploitation of epigenetic rules arising from interaction with the world, enlarging the brain's power to understand and act upon it, and ultimately creating a culture that could then be propagated and transmitted from one generation to the next. (ibid., p. 37)

As a consequence, pre-representations are central for integration of sensory modalities into an integrated percept. Dehaene, Kerszberg, and Changeux (1998) have proposed a "neuronal workspace hypothesis" for how the integration might take place. They identify two main computational spaces within the brain: a processing network composed of a set of parallel, distributed and functionally specialized processors; and a global *workspace*, consisting of a distributed set of cortical neurons that communicate with homologous neurons in other cortical areas through long-range excitatory axons (ibid, p. 14529). This architecture mimics computer systems consisting of a "central" processor that coordinates the processing of a number of "regional" processors, each specialized in particular tasks[12].

Dehaene, Kerszberg, & Changeux recognized five main types of "regional" processors: (1) perceptual circuits giving the workspace access to the present state of the external world; (2) motor programming circuits allowing the content of the workspace to be used to guide future intentional behavior; (3) long-term memory circuits providing the workspace with an access to past percepts and events; (4) Evaluation circuits allowing representations in the workspace to be associated with a positive or negative value; and (5) attention circuits allowing the workspace to mobilize its own circuits independently from the external world (ibid, p. 14530, see Figure 19):

Figure 19. The neuronal workspace (adapted after Dehaene, Kerszberg, & Changeux, 1998)

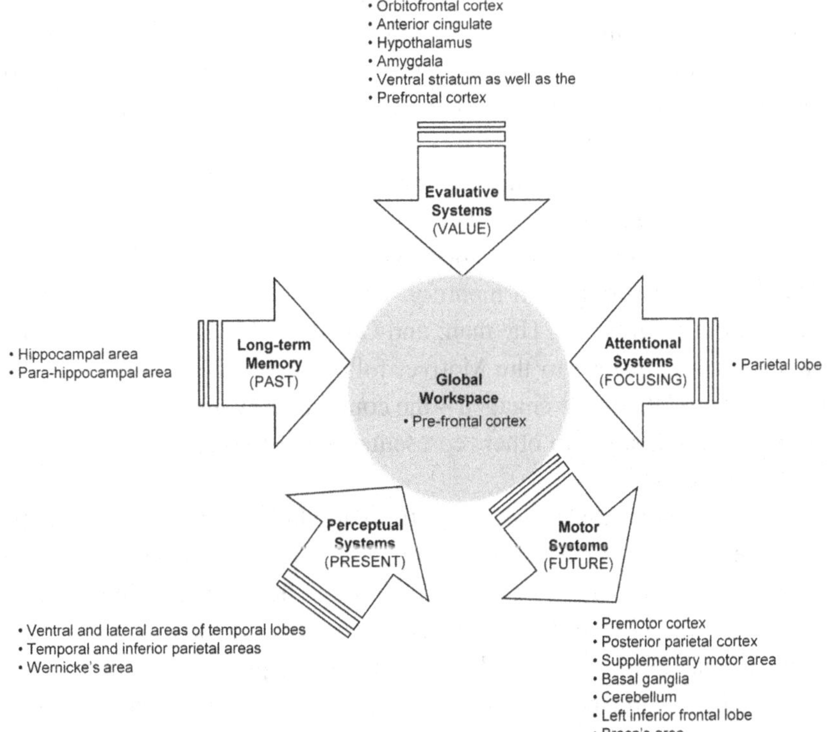

The workspace can, at each instant, contain only one active representation selected from the pre-selections in the long-term memory (cf. the "duck-rabbit" perception previously discussed). Selection can be triggered either from external stimuli provided through the perceptual system, or internally through the attentional system. The representation may remain active and resist changes in peripheral stimulation so long as the evaluative system receives positive reward signals (Changeux, 2004, p. 93). If attention is not sustained or reward signals become negative, the active representation may be revised or replaced by another.

The neuronal workspace hypothesis is corroborated by the newly discovered mirror neurons, which seem to play an important part for integration. Mirror neurons, unlike other sensory systems, appear to detect actions.

The receptors in the visual system respond to electromagnetic radiation, those in the auditory system to pressure waves, in the olfactory system to chemicals. But what physical stimuli carry information about actions?... Positioned as they are in association cortex, mirror neurons have access to information from other sensory systems... Clearly mirror neurons are responding to stimuli that have already been processed by other sensory systems... (Shapiro, 2009, p. 453)

Activity Modality Interpretation

A tentative interpretation of the neuronal workspace hypothesis from the activity perspective may proceed as follows. First, I propose that pre-representations for coordination can be conceptualized as objectivated manifestations of activity modalities. This means that a pre-representation will contain elements representing the Object, the Motive, contextual framing, spatial and temporal structures, stabilizing elements, and transitional elements. In other words, when interacting with the outside world, an individual creates persistent memories of entire situations – activities. Moreover, since pre-representations are epigenetic "elaborations" of innate endowments, it follows that some subset of these endowments corresponds to the activity modalities. This means that humans (and probably most nervous organisms) are predisposed to coordinate their actions according to these modalities.

The workspace is thus the integrating mechanism that "cross-couples" sensory modalities with activity modalities. The process is triggered by the attention of an Object, either in the form of perceived external stimuli or internally by spontaneous activation. A change in either Object or Motive will "load" another pre-representation from the long-term memory. This process may be guided by the "gating" mechanism proposed by Jeffery, Anderson, Hayman, and Chakraborty (2004). The evaluative system evaluates the representation with respect to the Motive, followed by actions effectuated through the motor systems. In acting, all modalities are engaged – the context, relevant stimuli, ordering of actions, habituated ways of acting, and transition to other representations if necessary. Figure 20 is an attempt to illustrate the integration process:

Besides the integration of sensory modalities into activity modalities, there exist other types of integration – cross-modal integration. In general, different modalities are engaged depending on what modality dominates a task. Vision has a higher spatial resolution, hence its dominance in spatially oriented tasks; whereas audition has a higher temporal resolution, hence its dominance in temporally oriented tasks (Shimojo & Shams, 2001, p. 506). However, there are plenty of evidences of integration across modalities. For example, vision may alter speech perception: the sound 'ba' tends to be perceived as 'da' when coupled with a visual lip movement associated with 'ga' (ibid, p. 506). Other examples

Figure 20. Integration of sensory modalities and activity modalities

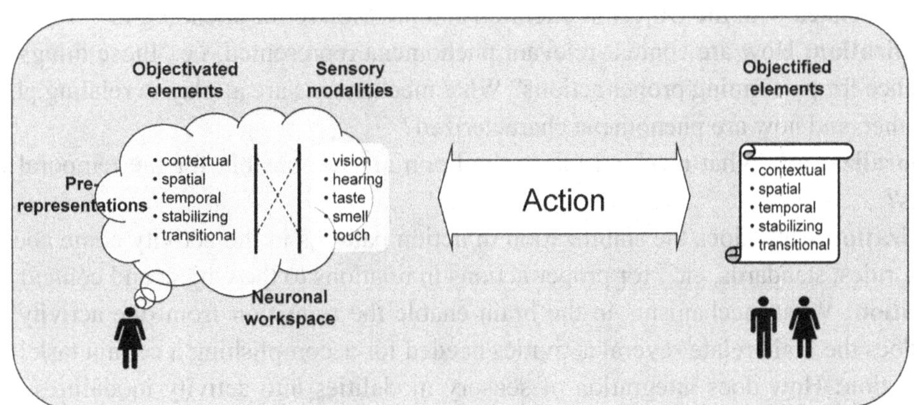

such as sound altering temporal aspects of vision, and vision altered by auditory or tactile sensations have also been reported (ibid, pp. 506-507).

Correspondingly, the activity modalities form an integrated, indivisible unit. For example, contextualization implies transition; the need to cross activities. Stabilization influences all other modalities in the sense that spatial, temporal, and transitional manifestations must acquire common understanding in the activity. Temporalization – the ordering of actions – presumes a spatial orientation:

I would like to focus on how [the narrative and the information processing modes of cognition] are being informed at a deep level by our basic concepts of space and time. I will propose that the information processing mode takes an inherently spatial approach to cognizing situations, and that the narrative mode takes an inherently temporal approach [...] both are needed [...]. (Boland, 2001, p. 14)

In the same way as sensory modalities, various activity modalities can be differently engaged depending on the nature of the activity. When coordinating actions in organizational contexts, it appears that mainly vision and hearing are utilized. This is, quite naturally, a consequence of the properties of mediational means used. Even so, the activity modalities must be seen as an integrated whole.

RESEARCH QUESTIONS

Based on the previous discussions, the following tentative research questions for further investigations can be formulated (without any particular prioritization):

- **The Object:** How are stimuli in various sensory modalities integrated into a coherent percept of an attended Object around which the activity is structured?
- **The Motive:** How is the Motive formed and evaluated with respect to the Object? How do the Object and Motive together determine the structure of the activity? As we saw, the same Object associated with different Motives gives rise to quite different activities.

- **Contextualization:** How are contexts of activities represented in the brain? The context is necessarily associated with the Object of attention and the Motive for attending it.
- **Spatialization:** How are context-relevant phenomena represented, i.e., those things that make a difference for performing proper actions? What mechanisms are at play in relating phenomena to each other, and how are phenomena characterized?
- **Temporalization:** What mechanisms in the brain are responsible for the temporal ordering of actions?
- **Stabilization:** How does the stabilization of action patterns in the activity come about? How do norms, rules, standards, etc., for proper actions in relations to the Object and context emerge?
- **Transition:** What mechanisms in the brain enable the transition from one activity to another? How does the brain relate several activities needed for accomplishing a certain task?
- **Integration:** How does integration of sensory modalities into activity modalities occur? What about cross-modality integration, both of sensory modalities and activity modalities?
- **The unity of mind and activity:** What mechanisms are responsible for the mutual constitution of mind and activity; what I have called the objectivation – objectification process?
- **Realm transitions:** How can we model transitions between the social, conceptual, and neural realms? I imagine that this research question will include issues like clustering of neurons into concepts and associations between such clusters.

CONCLUSION

In this contribution, I have outlined an approach towards modeling the intellect from a coordination point of view in three realms – the social, the conceptual, and the neural ones. The core of this approach is the activity modality construct, which I suggest is an organizing principle in all realms. These modalities represent fundamental, innate predispositions for coordinating actions. This means that we construct our social reality in such a way that it reflects the modalities. Thus, observation of objectified artifacts may provide clues into the architecture of the brain.

In a sense, the proposed model does not exhibit anything new. We are all familiar with expressions of context, space, time, norms and transition between various domains in our daily life. On the other hand, it is very hard to see what is right in front of us; "The aspects of things that are most important for us are hidden because of their simplicity and familiarity… we fail to be struck by what, once seen, is most striking and most powerful" (Wittgenstein, 1953, §125).

The activity modalities may indeed be interpreted in this manner. As with "duck" science, the modalities may provide alternative principles for investigating the intellect:

Knowing that some animal looks like a duck, walks like a duck, and quacks like a duck can be useful if one has a well-developed science of ducks. Using principles of duck science, researchers are in a better position to understand the behavior of a duckish creature than they would be if they had to begin their investigations from scratch. Of course, principles of duck science may in the end turn out not to be what's needed, but then that's worth knowing too. (Shapiro, 2009, p. 455)

If you know what to look for, it is likely that this will advance progress in research. Extant research has most probably provided answers to several of the issues discussed here. Thus, further investigations may be more a question about restructuring what is already known in line with the activity modalities. Even so, I maintain that the inclusion of such results in the larger picture of activity modalities is a valuable research contribution, well worth pursuing further in a research program.

REFERENCES

Adler, N. (1999). *Managing complex product development – three approaches*. EFI, Stockholm School of Economics.

Austin, J. L. (1962). *How to do things with words*. Oxford, UK: Oxford University Press.

Berger, P., & Luckmann, T. (1991). *The social construction of reality*. London, UK: Penguin Books.

Bødker, S., & Bøgh Andersen, P. (2005). Complex mediation. *Human-Computer Interaction, 20*, 353–402. doi:10.1207/s15327051hci2004_1

Boland, R. J. (2001). The tyranny of space in organizational analysis. *Information and Organization, 11*, 3–23. doi:10.1016/S0959-8022(00)00007-2

Brown, J. S., Collins, A., & Duguid, S. (1989). Situated cognition and the culture of learning. *Educational Researcher, 18*(1), 32–42.

Bryant, W. C., & Gay, S. H. (1883). *A popular history of the United States* (*Vol. I*). New York, NY: Charles Scribner's Sons.

Chalmers, A. F. (1976). *What is this thing called science?* St Lucia, Queensland: University of Queensland Press.

Changeux, J. P. (1997). *Neuronal man: The biology of mind*. Princeton, NJ: Princeton Univ. Press.

Changeux, J. P. (2004). *The physiology of truth*. Cambridge, MA & London, UK: Harvard University Press.

Chen, X. (2003, December). Object and event concepts: A cognitive mechanism of incommensurability. *Philosophy of Science, 70*, 962–974. doi:10.1086/377381

Chomsky, N. (1965). *Aspects of the theory of syntax*. Cambridge, MA: MIT Press.

Clancey, W. J. (1993). Situated action: A neuropsychological interpretation response to Vera and Simon. *Cognitive Science, 17*(1), 87–116. doi:10.1207/s15516709cog1701_7

Dehaene, S., Kerszberg, M., & Changeux, J. P. (1998). A neuronal model of a global workspace in effortful cognitive tasks. [PNAS]. *Proceedings of the National Academy of Sciences of the United States of America, 95*(24), 14529–14534. doi:10.1073/pnas.95.24.14529

Dewey, J. (1991). *Logic, the theory of enquiry. The later works of John Dewey*, vol. 12, J. A. Boydston (Ed.). Carbondale & Edwardsville, IL: Southern Illinois University Press.

Engels. F. (1954). *On the part played by labour in the transition from ape to man, dialectics of Nature*. Moscow, Russia: Foreign Languages Publishing House. Retrieved Jan 26, 2010, from http://www.marxists.org/archive/marx/works/1876/part-played-labour/index.htm

Freeman, W. J. (2004). How and why brains create meaning from sensory information. *International Journal of Bifurcation and Chaos in Applied Sciences and Engineering, 14*(2), 515–530. doi:10.1142/S0218127404009405

Gärdenfors, P. (2000). *Conceptual spaces: The geometry of thought*. Cambridge, MA: MIT Press.

Gärdenfors, P. (2000b). *How Homo became Sapiens: About the evolution of thinking*. Nora, Sweden: Nya Doxa.

Gershenson, C. (2002). *Contextuality: A philosophical paradigm, with applications to philosophy of cognitive science. University of Sussex*. UK: COGS.

Gibson, J. J. (1979). *The ecological approach to visual perception*. Boston, MA: Houghton Mifflin.

Goldkuhl, G., & Lind, M. (2008). Coordination and transformation in business processes: Towards an integrated view. *Business Process Management Journal, 14*(6), 761–777. doi:10.1108/14637150810915964

Greenfield, S. (1998). How might the brain generate consciousness? In Rose, S. (Ed.), *From brain to consciousness - essays on the new science of the mind* (pp. 210–227). London, UK: Penguin Books.

Hazlehurst, B., Gorman, P. N., & McMullena, C. K. (2008). Distributed cognition: An alternative model of cognition for medical informatics. *International Journal of Medical Informatics, 77*(4), 226–234. doi:10.1016/j.ijmedinf.2007.04.008

Hoskin, K. (2004). Spacing, timing and the invention of management. *Organization, 11*(6), 743–757. doi:10.1177/1350508404047249

Hutchins, E. (1995). *Cognition in the wild.* Cambridge, MA: MIT Press.

Jackendoff, R. (1976). Toward an explanatory semantic representation. *Linguistic Inquiry, 7*(1), 89–150.

Jackendoff, R. (1983). *Semantics and cognition*. Cambridge, MA: MIT Press.

Jackendoff, R. (1990). *Semantic structures*. Cambridge, MA: The MIT Press.

Jeffery, K. J., Anderson, M. J., Hayman, R., & Chakraborty, S. (2004). A proposed architecture for the neural representation of spatial context. *Neuroscience and Biobehavioral Reviews, 28*(2), 201–218. doi:10.1016/j.neubiorev.2003.12.002

Jones, K. S. (2003). What is an affordance? *Ecological Psychology, 15*(2), 107–114. doi:10.1207/S15326969ECO1502_1

Jönsson, P. (2006). *The anatomy-an instrument for managing software evolution and evolvability*. Second International IEEE Workshop on Software Evolvability (SE'06) (pp. 31–37). Philadelphia, Pennsylvania, USA. September 24, 2006.

Kaptelinin, V., & Nardi, B. (2006). *Acting with technology - activity theory and interaction design*. Cambridge, MA: The MIT Press.

Kihlstrom, J. F. (2004). *Joseph Jastrow and his duck-or is it a rabbit?* Retrieved June 6, 2010, from http://socrates.berkeley.edu/~kihlstrm/JastrowDuck.htm

Kirsh, D. (1995). The intelligent use of space. *Artificial Intelligence*, *73*(1–2), 31–68. doi:10.1016/0004-3702(94)00017-U

Kofod-Petersen, A., & Cassens, J. (2006). Using activity theory to model context awareness. In Roth-Berghofer, T. R., Schulz, S., & Leake, D. B. (Eds.), *Modeling and retrieval of context MRC 2005, (LNAI 3946)* (pp. 1–17). Berlin/ Heidelberg, Germany: Springer-Verlag. doi:10.1007/11740674_1

Kosík, K. (1976). *Dialectics of the concrete*. Dordrecht, The Netherlands: Reidel.

Kotik-Friedgut, B. (2006). Development of the Lurian approach: A cultural neurolinguistic perspective. *Neuropsychology Review*, *16*(1), 43–52. doi:10.1007/s11065-006-9003-9

Lakatos, I. (1974). Falsification and the methodology of scientific research programmes. In Lakatos, I., & Musgrave, A. (Eds.), *Criticism and the growth of knowledge* (pp. 91–196). London, UK: Cambridge University Press.

Larsson, R. (1990). *Coordination of action in mergers and acquisitions - interpretative and systems approaches towards synergy*. Dissertation No. 10, Lund Studies in Economics and Management, The Institute of Economic Research, Lund: Lund University Press.

Lawrence, P., & Lorsch, W. (1967). Differentiation and integration in complex organizations. *Administrative Science Quarterly*, *12*(1), 1–47. doi:10.2307/2391211

Leont'ev, A. N. (1981). *Problems in the development of the mind*. Moscow, Russia: Progress Publ.

Liedman, S.-E. (2001). *An eternal adventure – about the knowledge of humans*. Falun, Sweden: Albert Bonniers Förlag.

Love, N. (1997). Integrating Austin. *Language Sciences*, *19*(1), 57–65. doi:10.1016/0388-0001(95)00027-5

Luria, A. R. (1973). *The working brain*. London, UK: Penguin Books.

Malone, T., & Crowston, K. (1994). The interdisciplinary study of coordination. *ACM Computing Surveys*, *26*(1), 87–119. doi:10.1145/174666.174668

March, J. G., & Simon, H. A. (1958). *Organizations*. Cambridge, MA: Blackwell Publishers.

Maturana, H. R., & Varela, F. J. (1992). *The tree of knowledge: The biological roots of human understanding*. Boston, MA: Shambhala.

Mead, G. H. (1974). *Mind, self, and society: From the standpoint of a social behaviorist*. Chicago, IL: University of Chicago Press.

Merriam-Webster Online. (2008). Retrieved October 5, 2008, from http://www.merriam-webster.com/

Mesulam, M. M. (1998). From sensation to cognition. *Brain*, *121*(6), 1013–1052. doi:10.1093/brain/121.6.1013

Miettinen, R., & Virkkunen, J. (2005). Epistemic objects, artefacts and organizational change. *Organization*, *12*(3), 437–456. doi:10.1177/1350508405051279

Nilson, G. (1976). *Order/disorder: Studies in the conditions of love*. Göteborg, Sweden: Bokförlaget Korpen.

O'Keefe, J., & Nadel, L. (1978). *The hippocampus as a cognitive map*. Oxford, UK: Oxford University Press.

Orlikowski, W. (2002). Knowing in practice: Enacting a collective capability in distributed organizing. *Organization Science, 13*(3), 249–273. doi:10.1287/orsc.13.3.249.2776

Orlikowski, W., & Yates, J. (2002). It's about time: Temporal structuring in organizations. *Organization Science, 13*(6), 684–700. doi:10.1287/orsc.13.6.684.501

Parsons, J. (1996). An information model based on classification theory. *Management Science, 42*(10), 1437–1453. doi:10.1287/mnsc.42.10.1437

Plaut, D. C. (2002). Graded modality-specific specialization in semantics: A computational account of optic aphasia. *Cognitive Neuropsychology, 19*(7), 603–639. doi:10.1080/02643290244000112

Prolux, J. (2008). Some differences between Maturana and Varela's theory of cognition and constructivism. *Complicity: An International Journal of Complexity and Education, 5*(1), 11–26.

Searle, J. R. (1969). *Speech acts. An essay in the philosophy of language*. London, UK: Cambridge University Press.

Shapiro, L. (2009). Making sense of mirror neurons. *Syntheses, 167*(3), 439–456. doi:10.1007/s11229-008-9385-8

Shimojo, S., & Shams, L. (2001). Sensory modalities are not separate modalities: Plasticity and interactions. *Current Opinion in Neurobiology, 11*(4), 505–509. doi:10.1016/S0959-4388(00)00241-5

Taxén, L. (2009). *Using activity domain theory for managing complex systems*. Hershey, PA: IGI Global.

Taxén, L., & Lilliesköld, J. (2005). *Manifesting shared affordances in system development – the system anatomy*. ALOIS*2005, The 3rd International Conference on Action in Language, Organisations and Information Systems (pp. 28–47). 15–16 March 2005, Limerick: Ireland. Retrieved Feb 6, 2008, from http://www.alois2005.ul.ie/

Taxén, L., & Lilliesköld, J. (2008). Images as action instruments in complex projects. *International Journal of Project Management, 26*(5), 527–536. doi:10.1016/j.ijproman.2008.05.009

Vološinov, V. N. (1986). *Marxism and the language of philosophy*. London, UK: Harvard University Press.

Vygotsky, L. S. (1978). *Mind in society – the development of higher psychological processes. M. Cole, V. John-Steiner* (Scribner, S., & Souberman, E., Eds.). Cambridge, MA: Harvard University Press.

Vygotsky, L. S. (1981). The genesis of higher mental functions. In Wertsch, J. W. (Ed.), *The concept of activity in Soviet psychology*. Armonk, NY: M. E. Sharpe.

Vygotsky, L. S. (1997). *The collected works of L.S. Vygotsky, vol. 4, the history of the development of higher mental functions*. New York, NY: Plenum P.

Weick, K. E. (1988). Enacted sensemaking in crisis situations. *Journal of Management Studies*, *25*(4), 305–317. doi:10.1111/j.1467-6486.1988.tb00039.x

Wertsch, J. V. (1991). *Voices of the mind: A sociocultural approach to mediated action*. Cambridge, MA: Harvard University Press.

Wikipedia. (2008). *Homo faber*. Retrieved Jan 26, 2010, from http://en.wikipedia.org/wiki/Homo_faber

Wittgenstein, L. (1953). *Philosophical investigations*. Oxford, UK: Blackwell.

Zacks, J., & Tversky, B. (2001). Event structure in perception and conception. *Psychological Bulletin*, *127*(1), 3–21. doi:10.1037/0033-2909.127.1.3

Zacks, J. M., Braver, T. S., Sheridan, M. A., Donaldson, D. I., Snyder, A. Z., & Ollinger, J. M. (2001). Human brain activity time-locked to perceptual event boundaries. *Nature Neuroscience*, *4*(6), 651–655. doi:10.1038/88486

Zinchenko, V. (1996). Developing activity theory: The zone of proximal development and beyond. In Nardi, B. (Ed.), *Context and consciousness, activity theory and Human-Computer Interaction* (pp. 283–324). Cambridge, MA: MIT Press.

ENDNOTES

1. Activity Theory was an attempt to apply Marxian ideas to psychology in the early decades of the new socialist state, the Soviet Union. The front figure in this pioneering movement was the psychologist and semiotician L. S. Vygotsky (1896-1934) together with his collaborators A. N. Leont'ev (1903-1979) and A. R. Luria (1902-1977). For a good account of Activity Theory, see e.g. Kaptelinin & Nardi (2006).
2. Actually, in 1964 the Swedish composer and pianist Karl-Erik Welin used a chainsaw in a concert to cut off one of legs of the grand piano. It so happened that the saw bounced back and cut a gash in one of his own legs. In spite of this, he managed to finish the concert as the sirens of the ambulance drew nearer! However, this example of an objectified chainsaw in a concert activity is, to the best of my knowledge, quite unique.
3. See e.g. Chalmers (1976) for a comprehensive description of Lakatos' view on research programs.
4. For a thorough discussion of spacing and timing in organizations, see the special issue on this topic in Organization (2004, vol. 11, number 6).
5. The term "transition" is derived from the lexical definition "passage from one state, stage, subject, or place to another" (Merriam Webster, 2008).
6. Homo faber (Latin for "Man the Smith" or "Man the Maker"; in reference to the biological name for man, "Homo sapiens" meaning "man the wise") is a concept articulated by Hannah Arendt and Max Frisch. It refers to humans controlling the environment through tools (Wikipedia, 2008).
7. The terms "technical" and "semiotic" tools comes from Vygotsky (Vygotsky, 1981, p. 137, cited in Wertsch, 1991, p. 93).
8. Strictly speaking, Jackendoff does not indicate real-world entities in any particular way. However, for the discussion here, I have found it useful to introduce the *xxx* notation for clarity.

9 For example, a cat is capable of "simulating" a mouse behind a hole in the wall and sit waiting for hours for it to appear. A snake, on the other hand, does not have this capability. As soon as the prey disappears out of the snake's sensory range, the attention of the snake ceases. If the mouse suddenly appears again, the snake senses this as a new prey (Gärdenfors, 2000b, p. 45).

10 The concept of affordances is still discussed by scholars (see e.g. Jones, 2003).

11 A comprehensive overview is given by Mesulam (1998).

12 The core product at Ericsson™ for many years, the AXE switching system, has precisely this architecture. In noting this I am not suggesting that the brain works like a computer. Rather, it is the architectural likeness that is interesting.

Chapter 18
Information Processing by Chemical Reaction–Diffusion Media:
From Computing to Vision[1]

Nicholas G. Rambidi
Moscow State University, Russia

ABSTRACT

Chemical reaction-diffusion media represent information processing means fundamentally different from contemporary digital computers. Distributed character and complex nonlinear dynamics of chemical reactions inherent in the medium are the basis for large-scale parallelism and complex logical operations performed by the medium as primitives and equivalent to hundreds of binary fixed-point operations. Photo-sensitive catalysts controlling dynamics (modes of functioning) of the medium enable to easily perform input of initial data and output of computational results. It was found during the last decades that chemical reaction-diffusion media can be effectively used for solving artificial intelligence problems, such as image processing, finding the shortest paths in a labyrinth, and some other important problems that are at the same time problems of high computational complexity. Spatially non uniform control of the medium by physical stimuli and fabrication of multi level reaction-diffusion systems seem to be the promising way of enabling low cost and effective information processing devices that meet the commercial needs.

Biological roots and specific neural net architecture of reaction-diffusion media seem to enable simulating some phenomena inherent in the cerebral cortex, such as optical illusions.

INTRODUCTION

A lot of proposals have been considered during the past decades how to practically implement unique information processing mechanisms inherent in biological entities (see first ten items in reference list).

DOI: 10.4018/978-1-60960-551-3.ch018

And first of all, their capabilities to efficiently deal with complex logical problems that could hardly be effectively solved by contemporary digital computers in spite of tremendous progress in this field. One of the most promising attempts was information processing by distributed molecular and bio-molecular media. Nonlinear dynamics inherent in these media determines high logical complexity of primitive operations performed by the medium. It is this fundamental attribute, not the level of microminiaturization or high clock frequency typical of the contemporary digital computers, that leads to high computational power determined by high logical complexity of primitive operations performed by the medium. This unique feature together with large scale parallelism makes molecular and bio-molecular media attractive material for constructing information processing means. Because of biological roots they should be capable of effective solving artificial intellect problems that were during several last decades and are now of great importance for the understanding and control of complex dynamic systems. These systems - of biological, sociological, economic nature and many other important for the modern society, determine the everyday life of modern society.

Experimental investigations and numerical simulations of information processing capabilities of distributed systems have been performed beginning from the early seventies of the last century. They enabled to elucidate general principles and possible ways of its implementation. However this understanding has been changing during the several last years. Two basic points were responsible for these changes:

- elaboration of powerful wave theory of information processing (Serra, 1986; Young, 2002),
- tremendous increase in experimental technique for distributed chemical and biochemical media investigation.

This paper is designed to discuss information processing capabilities of chemical Belousov-Zhabotinsky type media based on new experimental results obtained lately and principles of mathematical morphology.

BACKGROUND

Complex Dynamic Systems and Artificial Intelligence Problems

Fantastic progress of information processing means during the second half of the last century was launched in the early forties based on the John von Neumann paradigm. General principles inherent in this paradigm proved to be indispensable for the elaboration of multipurpose computing systems that were capable of the optimal solving of different practically important tasks.

Priorities and needs of human society have been changing during the last fifty years. It has been recognized that understanding and control of complex dynamic systems were getting higher and higher priority in different fields of human activity. They embrace defense needs, processes in economics, social sciences, pollution control, biological and biotechnological applications and so on. All these problems could be reduced in general to:

1. Recognition of images, scenes, and situations that can be conditionally divided into a number of steps, such as:
    - classification of objects according to a definite set of features,
    - segmentation of objects into the smallest (for the chosen object) fragments,

   - recognition of the fragments in context, designing the image based on these fragments,
2. Investigation of the evolution of systems having complicated behavioral dynamics (for instance, problems of "predator-prey" type, dynamics of cell population etc.).
3. Choice of optimal (in some predetermined sense) structure or behavior of multifactor systems having complicated branching search trees ("traveling salesmen" type tasks, strategic and tactical decisions, games, including chess).
4. Control problems, that embrace:
   - continuous recognition of situations based on associative bounds,
   - continuous in general case choice of optimum strategy

(navigation systems for autonomous vehicles operating in a complex changing neighborhood, and other remote control devices could be designed based on these possibilities).

Remarkable feature of these problems is their biologically inspired origin. All of them, virtually, seem to be solved more efficiently by the human brain than by contemporary digital computers.

In the late 90s of the last century H. Moravek (1998) discussed perspectives of modern computers to match general intellectual performance of the human brain. Based on extrapolation of past trends and on examination of semiconductor technologies under development he concluded that the required hardware will be available in the 2020s. At the same time he mentioned, that "The most powerful experimental supercomputers in 1998, composed of thousands or tens of thousands of the fastest microprocessors and costing tens of millions dollars, can do a few million MIPS. They are within striking distance of being powerful enough to match human brainpower, but are unlikely to be applied to that end. Why tie up a rare twenty-million-dollar asset to develop one ersatz-human, when millions of inexpensive original-model humans are available? Such machines are needed for high-value scientific calculations, mostly physical simulations, having no cheaper substitute. AI research must wait for the power to become more affordable".

Here Moravec (1998) touched up the problem of the paramount importance. The point is that contemporary human activity needs material realizations of artificial intellect machines that should be simple enough and have high performance, easy to operate, and have low commercial mass production cost.

Problems considered here (understanding and control complex dynamic system) are known as artificial intelligence problems. Two significant features of them should be discussed.

High Computational Complexity

The world around us is complex. Complexity shows up in absolutely diverse fields of human activity beginning from complicated engineering designs up to sophisticated economic and social problems.

According to Casti (1979), the concept of complexity embraces three basic aspects.

"Static complexity represents essentially the complexity of the subsystems that realize the system, dynamic complexity involves the computational length required by the subsystems interconnection to realize the process, and control complexity represents a measure of computational requirements needed to keep the system behaving in a prescribed fashion."

Following Casti (1997) let us consider three basic hypostases of the complexity inherent in biomolecular systems capable of information processing. Given the biological background of the problems discussed, let us use the following terms:

- *Structural (static) complexity* of the system, that is essentially the complexity of the subsystems that realize the system,
- *Behavioral (dynamic) complexity* involves the computational length required by the subsystems interconnection to realize the process that determines the spatio-temporal evolution of the system performing an information processing operation,
- *Computational (control) complexity* of an algorithm describing information-processing operations performed, that represents a measure of computational requirements.

Several approaches to the quantitative definition of complexity are now in use. The notion of algorithmic complexity seems to be the most adequate for estimating complexity of the evolution of a dynamic system. (Yudin & Yudin, 1985; Klir, 1985). The algorithmic complexity of the process performed by a system, that is its behavioral complexity, is defined as minimal length of the assumed program from some set of them that describe the process adequately. It is possible also to introduce the notion of the structural complexity of the system itself, as complexity under fixed values of input parameters

The computational complexity of an algorithm describing the behavior of a system can be expressed as the dependence of computational capabilities (resources) which are necessary to simulate system behavior; i.e., a specific system characteristic called the problem size.

The computational complexity of a particular problem can be different depending on the type of machine used to solve it. The problem may scale differently for each type of machine.

During the second half of the last century the character of computational complexity of practically important problems was virtually of decisive importance for the choice of the paradigm used for the elaboration of new computing means. General principles of von Neumann approach proved to be indispensable for the elaboration of multipurpose digital computing systems that was capable of optimal solving different, mostly engineering projects. Mathematical and computational basis for these projects could be reduced mostly to the problems of rather low (polynomial) complexity. However for the couple of last decades, in essence, human society has had to face artificial intellect problems having high computational complexity. The point is now that, in spite of the tremendous progress of contemporary digital computers they did not prove to be efficient for solving these problems. And it is necessary to choose between two possibilities that will provide the most powerful route:

- to increase enormously the computational performance of contemporary digital semiconductor computers, or
- to elaborate information processing means fundamentally different from von Neumann ones and capable of solving efficiently, in the natural way problems of high computational complexity.

Biologically Inspired Roots of Artificial Intelligence Problems

Attempts to increase the computational performance of digitals computers was based during the last decades mainly on micro miniaturization of planar semiconductor IC's. Nowadays these devices are close to the physical limit as a result of the huge progress in this field. Therefore a lot of attempts to find the real alternative to semiconductor technology were performed. One of the most promising between them is biological paradigm based on mechanisms of information processing by bio-molecular and biological entities (see, for instance, Rambidi, 2003).

The first steps in this direction were made several decades ago. In early forties, nearly simultaneously with the advent of von Neumann paradigm McCulloch and Pitts (1943) offered a principally different approach to elaboration of information processing devices. According to the ideas of McCulloch and Pitts (1943) computational system is designed to be in a sense analogous to human brain. Simple processors (neurons) are constituent parts of the system and each of them is connected to all other processors in some definite manner. Computing capabilities of the system are defined by the predetermined complex structure of the system (that is by character of neuron connection), not by the stored program. Problems are solved by the system with very high degree of parallelism. At the same time the character of dynamics inherent in the system defines the storage of information and information processing capabilities of the system.

McCulloch and Pitts (1943) used two fundamental principles of information processing by biological entities laying in the basis of the neural net approach. They are:

- "all or none" mode of a single neuron activity, that is nonlinear dynamic mechanism,
- large-scale parallelism of neural connections in a neural net.

During the following decades (1950s-1970s) there was intense discussion on the information processing capabilities of those systems (see Rosenblatt, 1962). Principles to design neural nets capable of solving predetermined problem were analyzed in detail. Theoretical possibilities to train the net structure enable of optimal solving chosen problem were discussed.

Contemporary neurocomputers have proved to be a practical result of these theoretical investigations. Regretfully the theoretical basis of "hardware" development that is of material implementation of neural nets was not practically under consideration till now. And therefore designers of neural net devices used the most habitual, "making a road smooth" way - the utilization of planar semiconductor circuitry and technology, which proved to be fantastically suitable for the implementation of discrete von Neumann devices. It should be mentioned that there is virtually no alternative now to discrete circuitry and technology for the implementation of neural nets. It is easy to understand the roots of this situation. The point is that planar semiconductor technology supplanted all offered earlier realizations due to its manifest advantages.

Hardware implementation of neural nets based on semiconductor digital circuitry faces considerable and most likely principal difficulties, such as large-scale integration limits, functional and processing speed limits, and the "nightmare of interconnections". Typical semiconductor chip has rigid structure. Removing even one of its primitives (or changing its characteristics) makes in general case the chip disabled. Known biological systems capable of information processing (and having often neural net architecture) are built from initial molecular fragments different fundamentally from semiconductor primitives. One of the basic and probably the most important features is structural redundancy (Rambidi, 2003). Biopolymer enzyme molecules play important role in information processing by biological systems. The structure of enzyme molecule represents a combination of a functional molecular fragment and lengthy polypeptide tail. The remarkable property of this structure is that removing even rather big part of this tail leads to inessential small changes of enzyme function. In common case the redundancy is the basis for variation of object characteristics and selection. System built from such objects seems to be capable of learning and adaptive behavior. Structural and especially dynamic redundancy inherent in distributed reaction-diffusion media discussed below are fundamental features of biologically-inspired information processing.

Chemical Reaction-Diffusion Information Processing Media

Distributed continuous or discrete molecular and bio-molecular systems represent the most remarkable natural objects having high behavioral complexity and performing purposeful actions (see, for instance, Fleischer, 2005). It is these systems that have been considering during the last decades as promising bases for elaboration effective biologically inspired information processing means. Information is processed in each physical point of the medium (more exactly in some specific minimal volume, see below). Therefore large scale parallelism inherent in these systems could not be compared with parallelism of calculations performed even contemporary multi processor computers. As examples of such systems could be considered ants or bees colonies, performing complex intellectual actions, in spite of very simple behavior of single individual (Bonabeau, Dorigo, & Theraulaz, 2005) bacterial media where complex spatial distributions reveal spontaneously (Newell, 1977; Woodward et al., 1995), biochemical and chemical oscillating systems (Goldbetter, 1997).

Dynamics of distributed media could be described by the systems of partial differential equations showing local changes of medium components (u_i) in the process of its spatio-temporal evolution:

$$\frac{\partial u_i}{\partial t} = F_i\left(u_1, u_2, u_3 ... u_N\right) + \sum_j D_{ij} \Delta u_j$$

Here $F_i(u_1,u_2,u_3 \ldots u_N)$ defines local chemical dynamics of the medium components, the second term of the equation right side is responsible for the component diffusion.

The phase diagram corresponding to reaction-diffusion equations has a number of basins of attraction. Moving the point inside the space of the basin does not lead to quantitative changes of dynamic regime (that correspond to the moving to another basin of attraction). This feature can be defined as dynamic redundancy. In common case the redundancy could be considered as a basis for variation of object characteristics and selection. Systems built from such objects seem to be capable of learning and adaptive behavior.

Modes of reaction-diffusion medium functioning depend on the specificity of the $F_i(u_1,u_2,u_3 \ldots u_N)$ function. Nonlinear dynamics media seem to be the most promising for the information processing (Rambidi, 2003). Primitive operations performed by these media proved to be logically complex actions equivalent to tens or even hundreds of binary operations inherent in digital computer.

Belousov-Zhabotinsky Type Media

Belousov-Zhabotinsky type media are the most known chemical nonlinear reaction-diffusion systems (Field & Burger, (Eds.) 1985). The Belousov-Zhabotinsky reaction is the oxidation of some organic substance (malonic acid) by inorganic oxidizing agent (sodium or potassium bromate). Ions of transition metals (Fe or Ru mainly) are catalysts of the reaction. The principal scheme of the reaction corresponds to

$$C_3H_4O_4 + NaBrO_3 + H^+ \xrightarrow{Fe} C_3\,H_3BrO_4 + H_2O + CO_2$$

However the mechanism of the Belousov-Zhabotinsky reaction represents a set of intermediate stages. The real set of these stages is not known exactly till now. The most widely accepted model - Field-Korosh-Noyes (FKN) approximation (Field & Burger, 1985), contains 11 intermediate reactions and could be reduced to two kinetic equations that correspond to temporal evolutions of reaction inhibitor "u" ($HBrO_2$) and activator "v" (Fe^{3+} or Ru^{3+}):

$$\frac{\partial u}{\partial t} = \frac{1}{\varepsilon}\left[\frac{q-u}{q+u}\left(fv+\varphi\right)+u-u^2\right]+D_u\Delta u$$

$$\frac{\partial v}{\partial t} = u - v + D_v\Delta v$$

Here ε, q and f are constants defined by initial concentrations of the medium components and kinetic of intermediate reactions.

Neural Network Architecture of Belousov-Zhabotinsky Type Media

The important information processing feature of Belousov-Zhabotinsky type media that determine medium processing capabilities is neural network architecture.

Consider the simplest material version of chemical reaction-diffusion medium, namely flat thin pseudo two-dimensional layer of Belousov-Zhabotinsky reagent. To understand clearly information processing features of the system let us divide it into small cells with dimensions comparable to diffusion length l_D. It is determined as (Field & Burger, 1985):

$$l_D = (DT)^{1/2}$$

Here D is an average diffusion coefficient, T is a characteristic time of the dynamic process.

In a sense, the diffusion length is the distance where total intermixing of reaction components has taken place because of diffusion.

In this model:

1. Cells small by comparison with the diffusion length l_D can be considered as primitive processors representing chemical systems having point wise kinetics. If these cells are considered as independent stirred objects, trigger and oscillatory regimes should be inherent in them.
2. Cells are coupled because of diffusion. This coupling determines a number of complicated dynamic modes that could be displayed in experiment in thin layers and in a volume of the medium.
3. Changing the composition and temperature of the medium can provide control of excitable medium regimes. One powerful variant is based on using media containing light sensitive components.

In this case the composition of the medium can be easily changed by light illumination, with the degree of change being controlled by the amount of light exposure.

4. Generally speaking each cell is connected to each other cell of the medium due to diffusion coupling. Nonetheless this interaction is carried out with a time delay proportional to the distance between cells and the strength of the interaction decreases proportionally to this distance.

Let us mention that the above model (representing a system of cells coupled by diffusion) does not take into account that the media are uniform distributed systems. A more adequate model should be invariant to infinitesimal shifts of the cell system along the surface of the medium. In general case dynamics of distributed information processing media could be described by the system of integro-differential equations. They could not reduced to reaction-diffusion equations. However under some not too rigid assumptions these two models proved to be adequate.

Different approaches to describe such pseudo planar neural networks with lateral connections are known, starting with the pioneer work by McCulloch and Pitts (1943). A comprehensive review of neural net models has been done by Grossberg (1998).

Beginning from the late sixties, Grossberg launched a detailed investigation of biologically inspired neural networks. During the next three decades Grossberg with his collaborators have analyzed different aspects of neural network activity, including image processing capabilities. Based on psychobiological and neurobiological data Grossberg (1988) concluded that shunting on-center off-surround feedback networks display a number of remarkable image processing features. He has shown that shunting on-center off-surround feedback networks posses the key properties of:

- solving the noise-saturation dilemma,
- normalizing or conserving their total activity,
- being capable of absolutely stable short-time memory.

These neural networks proved to be capable of quenching noise (sharpening) or amplifying noise (broadening) of input signals, or of enhancing a signal's contour or the most intense fragments depending on the shape of $f(x)$ function.

Grossberg (1976) has also noted a dynamic analogy between shunting on-center off-surround feedback neural nets and reaction-diffusion systems, which were used by Gierer and Meinhardt (1972) for the description of the process of biological pattern formation.

Later this analogy was completely confirmed in experiment (Rambidi & Maximychev, 1997). Chemical basis of this analogy represents autocatalytic processes in small cells of the medium (on-center activation) and the sufficient increase of inhibitor diffusion coefficients in comparison with activator ones (off-center inhibition)

Neural network architecture of Belousov-Zhabotinsky media seems to explain specificity of primitive image processing operations produced by the medium, and similar to primitive operations of Grossberg neural nets (contour enhancement, sharpening and broadening of input signals).

Emerging Mechanisms of Information Processing

Information processing capabilities inherent in nonlinear chemical reaction-diffusion media may be thought of as mechanisms emerging at some level of multilevel complex dynamic system(Fenzi & Hofkirchner, 1997; Fleissner & Hofkirchner, 1996).

Initial level of the system dynamics is the kinetics of chemical reactions proceeding in the medium. Changes of the reaction component concentrations are defined by the initial composition of the medium, temperature and kinetic mechanisms. This is the lower level of the system dynamics. The set of dynamic modes inherent in the medium is the next dynamic level of the system. It is possible to describe it considering the medium as a whole and solving reaction-diffusion equations. Stirred Belousov-Zhabotinsky media (where diffusion term in kinetic equation is not valid) display bistability, stable stationary states (excitable modes), and concentration oscillations (Field & Burger, 1985). Diffusion increases sufficiently behavioral complexity of the medium. Trigger waves, moving concentration pulses, spirals, dissipative structures and other complex phenomena could be observed (Field & Burger, 1985).

These modes represent the basis for the next level of the system dynamics – interaction of reaction-diffusion modes. Principles of this interaction are specific enough and different from usual physical phenomena. Moving concentration pulses do not reflect from walls, for instance, but annihilate. The annihilation takes place also if pulses coincide. This level of system dynamics emerges based on mechanisms of previous levels, and, at the same time, could not be reduced to them. Such emergent mechanisms are typical for biological nonlinear dynamic systems and are caused by self-organization processes inherent in the media.

Thus three levels of dynamics could be considered as analogues of general definition offered in (Fleissner & Hofkirchner, 1996):

1. The level on which the elements of the system in question are interconnected. This is the level of the internal structure of the system (micro-level).
2. The level on which the system itself is in one state or in another. Compared to the structural level, the meso-level is focused.
3. The level on which the system exhibits its external behavior vis-à-vis its environment (macro-level).

Macro-level dynamics is responsible for the information processing by chemical reaction-diffusion media.

General Principles of Reaction-Diffusion Information Processing

Information processing means based on chemical nonlinear reaction-diffusion media are fundamentally different from contemporary digital von Neumann computers. Distributed character of the medium causes the large scale parallelism of information processing exceeded multiply the degree of parallelism even contemporary multi processor digital computer systems. Nonlinear dynamic mechanisms typical for chemical reaction-diffusion media lead to high logical complexity of primitive operations performed by the medium. Therefore the increase of the information processing power of reaction-diffusion device is determined by complication of the device dynamics that leads to the increase of primitive operation logical complexity, not by increase of computational speed (ultimate micro miniaturization).

MAIN FOCUS OF THE CHAPTER

Experimental Implementation of Reaction-Diffusion Information Processing Technologies

Chemical reaction-diffusion media of Belousov-Zhabotinsky type represent attractive starting material to elaborate information processing devices. They are stable, non-hostile reagents. Chemical substances used for preparation of these media are accessible and prices of them are reasonable. Furthermore the temperature range and temporal operation scale of the medium dynamics are convenient for investigation with available physical methods.

Information processing by chemical reaction-diffusion media should include several stages. The “macro-micro” interface should be used to input initial data into medium. It transforms macroscopical information (as a rule, optical image chosen for processing) into a non-uniform spatial distribution of chemical components corresponding to the input image.

Belousov-Zhabotinsky type media based on a light-sensitive catalyst are convenient for the input of initial information. The light-sensitive catalyst initiates a sequence of photochemical reactions under light illumination (Kadar, Amemia, & Showalter, 1997):

$$Ru^{+2} + h\nu \rightarrow {}^{*}Ru^{+2}$$
$${}^{*}Ru^{+2} + C_3H_3BrO_4 \rightarrow Ru^{+3} + Br^{-} + \text{organic products}$$
$$Ru^{+3} + C_3H_3BrO_4 \rightarrow Ru^{+2} + Br^{-} + \text{organic products}$$

The spatio-temporal evolution of the medium begins just after of input of initial data. The final state of the medium (or some intermediate one) represents the solution of the problem under consideration, that is the operation performed by the medium. The concrete content of the performed operation is determined by the state of the medium: its composition, temperature, exposure of light illumination.

It is important that light radiation could be used also for the control of the medium evolution. The dynamic mode of the initial process doesn’t change in the fields of the medium that are not illuminated during the process evolution. At the same time the initial process is killed in the fields where the medium is illuminated by the white light. It enables, for instance, to create obstacles of predetermined shape for concentration pulses spreading in the medium and so on.

The process of evolution of initial concentration distribution proceeds in the media due to chemical reactions and diffusion. The catalyst changes its electronic state in the course of reaction when the medium goes from one stable state into another. As a consequence, the reagent changes its color (from red to blue and vice versa) and it is easy to visualize the process and to observe its spatio-temporal evolution. Therefore the catalyst works also as a “micro-macro” interface bringing into correspondence the evolution of the chemical concentration distribution and optical (macro} image of the process evolution.

Operational Characteristics of the Reaction-Diffusion Processor

Experimental investigations discussed below were performed using the set up, that was sufficiently modified in comparison with their previous version (Rambidi, 2003). Optical tract of the set up was partly changed to add some additional operational modes and sources of extraneous light were carefully removed. Different designs of reaction-diffusion reactors based on polymeric materials were elaborated. As a result the quality of final images was greatly improved.

The computer-controlled Sanyo PLC-510M LCD video projector (VGA compatible, 270 ANSI lumens) was used for input of initial data. High uniformity of the background intensity of this projector improved the reliability of the experiment. At the same time the computer-controlled projector was indispensable for the elaboration of the technique suitable for image processing. A Mintron OS-045D video camera was used to record the steps of the image processing by the medium (0.02 lx sensitivity, 600 TV lines resolution). Digitized records of images were saved in the memory of the Pentium III PC. It was possible to write single frames and video clips using VidCap software. Different versions of closed reaction-diffusion reactor (based on a constant-temperature Petri dish 80-120 mm in diameter) were used. They embrace:

- a layer of liquid reagent containing light-sensitive catalyst $Ru(bpy)_3Cl_2$ of 0.5-1.5 mm thick used for preliminary investigations of image processing operations. It was shown in experiments that mode of the medium functioning, corresponding to initial composition of the reagent remained practically unchanged during 15-20 min.
- the medium where reaction catalyst was immobilized in thin (~ 0.2 mm thick) layer of solid silica gel covered aluminum foil (commercial plates for liquid chromatography were placed in the 0.0001 M solution of the catalyst for 50 min). All other chemical components of Belousov-Zhabotinsky reagent were in solution covered silica gel layer.
- the medium, where reaction catalyst was immobilized in the layer of silica hydro gel of 1.0-1.5 mm thick. The catalyst was included in the layer of silca hydro gel in the process of its formation. Other components of Belousov-Zhabotinsky reagent diffused through the layer and the reaction proceeds inside it.

Polymer based designs of the processors enable to avoid distortions of chemical component distribution in the layer because of mechanical pushes and vibrations, hydrodynamic processes and so on. It is possible also to use sufficiently more volume in comparison with liquid layer reactor) of Belousov-Zhabotinsky reagent. Therefore operating time of the closed reactor without changing initial mode of functioning was 1 -1.5 hours.

Light-sensitive media based on $Ru(bpy)_3Cl_2$ catalyst functioning in excitable and oscillating mode were used.

Initial compositions of the medium were:

excitable mode: H_2SO_4 – 0.3 M, $NaBrO_3$ – 0.4 M, malonic acid – 0.15 M, KBr – 0.07 M;
oscillating mode: H_2SO_4 – 0.6–0.8 M, $NaBro_3$ – 0.4 M, malonic acid – 0.15 M, KBr – 0.07 M.

Principal scheme of the set up for the investigation of the image processing capabilities of Belousov-Zhabotinsky media is shown in Figure 1. Four main modes of functioning were provided.

1. It was necessary to remove traces of previous experiments if the medium used repeatedly. Uniform visible light radiation of high intensity brings the processing medium to its initial state (Figure 1A).
2. An illumination of a thin planar layer of the medium by chosen optical image was used for the input of initial information. The direction of light was normal to the surface of the medium. The

Figure 1. Different operational modes of the experimental set up

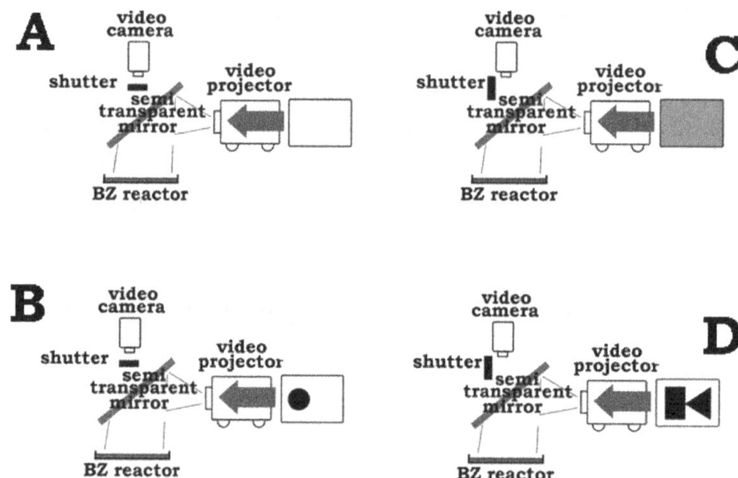

distribution of light intensity on the surface of the medium determined the initial distribution of reagent components stored in the medium. Semitransparent mirror used in the optical tract of the set up enabled to show and to check the process of the information input (Figure 1B).

3. The spatio-temporal evolution of the input image was recorded by video camera and safe in the computer memory. The illumination of the medium by uniform visible light is necessary to record this evolution because all sources of extraneous light were removed. The intensity of the illumination should be chosen carefully to be sufficient to record evolution of the input picture by video camera, and to be insufficient to change the dynamic mode of the light-sensitive medium used (Figure 1C).
4. It is important that light radiation could be used also for the control of the medium evolution. The dynamic mode of the initial process doesn't change in the fields of the medium that are not illuminated during the process evolution. At the same time the initial process is killed in the fields where the medium is illuminated by the white light of high intensity (Figure 1D). It enables, for instance, to create obstacles of predetermined shape for concentration pulses spreading in the medium and so on.

The software for numerical modeling of the image processing operations was elaborated and used together with experimental study. Field-Korosh-Noyes approximation (Field & Burger (Eds.), 1985) was used.

The software was designed as two independent modules. The first of them was used for the input of initial data and for the visualization of results of computations. The second performed calculations. Such software structure simplified the addition of the new data.

Modules were written using C++ programming language and were compilated by Microsoft Visual C++ 6.0. The size of the software is ~ 1 Mb.

Figure 2.

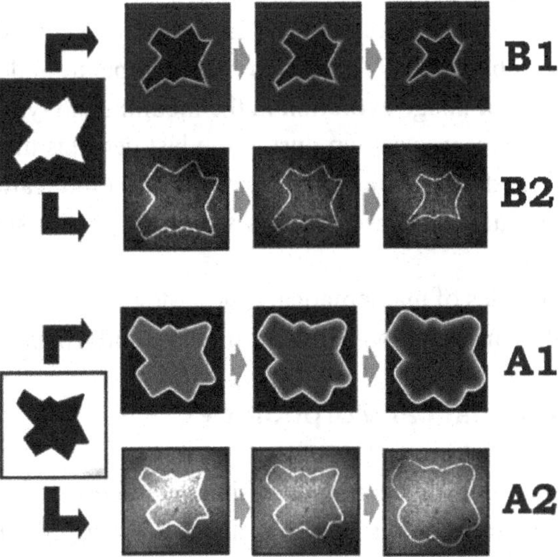

Image Processing by Chemical Belousov-Zhabotinsky Type Media

The foundations of image processing by chemical light-sensitive reaction-diffusion media was laid in pioneering studies performed by Lothar Kuhnert (1986, 1989). A little later the experimental work named "Information processing using light-sensitive waves" was published by Kuhnert, Agladze, Krinsky, (1989). It was important study that determined physical and chemical principles inherent in image processing by reaction-diffusion media. At the same time the information processing basis of this work was scanty enough. Detailed investigations of image processing capabilities in chemical light-sensitive reaction-diffusion media were performed in the beginning of nineties (see Rambidi (2003) and references therein). It was shown as result of these investigations that fundamental differences exist between:

- image processing of positive and negative images of initial pictures,
- responses of the medium to the light excitations and information processing operations based on these responses and performed by the medium,
- information processing of black and white pictures, pictures having several levels of brightness, and half-tone pictures.

To avoid vagueness in the following discussion let us define the positive image of a picture as image corresponding to typical picture inherent in human surroundings. If the notion of "typical picture" is uncertain (suppose in the case of geometrical figures, see, for instance, Figure 2, and Figure 6) let us define positive image as dark figure on the light background. Black and white and half-tone pictures will be used below. Images of these pictures could be considered as a set of optical density values D_i corresponding to each point of the picture ($0<D_i<D_\infty$, where D_∞ is a maximum value of the optical density). The negative image of the picture was defined as a set of inverted density values ($D_i^N = D_\infty - D_i$).

Let us mention here that methodological basis of image processing by reaction-diffusion media remains vague enough till now. The process of image evolution in the medium, not image processing, was considered virtually in the first investigation named "Image processing using light-sensitive chemical waves" and in the following publications. There were no attempts to understand how complete is the correspondence between modes of image evolution in the medium and typical image processing operations used in practice. Moreover, it was shown during the last decades that the behavioral complexity of chemical reaction media is high. Therefore chances exist that some features emerging in the process of image evolution could be artifacts. These features would be sooner sources of mistakes than real information for image analysis.

Let us try to use basic principles of mathematical morphology to realize what is the correspondence between details of image evolution in reaction-diffusion medium and typical image processing operations.

Some Remarks on Mathematical Morphology

The first attempts to simulate biological peculiarity of image processing were performed in the middle of the last century. One of the most known between them was the "cellular logic" approach (Unger, 1959) – the part of computational geometry, that represented the algebra of binary images, represented by matrices of binary numbers. Later, in the 60s Blum (1967) and Duda and Hart (1973) offered the "prairie fire" conceptions based on wave (parallel) principles of image processing. It is possible using this approach to excite, for instance, the wave in all points of arbitrary polygon contour and to measure the temporal dependence of the area of the figure determined by moving contour. This dependence enables to find the number of the polygon angles. It was shown later (Rambidi, Maximyzhev & Usatov, 1994) that Blum approach could be realized experimentally based on Belousov-Zhabotinsky media.

The important approach to considered problem – the theoretical basis and technique of image processing named "mathematical morphology?" was elaborated during the last decades (Sera, 1986; Young, 2002).

This modern computer oriented technique have been using successfully for solving different practical image processing problems.

Binary mathematical morphology operates complex two-dimensional (multi-dimensional in principle) objects defined in discrete space. Object "A" is a set of pixel satisfied to the condition:

```
A= {a | property (a) = TRUE}
```

In spite of numerical presentation of initial data the mathematical morphology operates images as a whole. Primitive operations of the mathematical morphology are dilation and erosion. Some notions are introduced additionally: together with object A structural element B is defined, which determine the character of the shape changes of object A at its border. In general case dilation

Dilation $A \oplus B = \left\{x : (\hat{B})_x \cap A \neq 0\right\}$

increases the image, and erosion

Erosion $A \Theta B = \left\{x : (B)_x \subseteq A\right\}$

decreases it.

Two basic operation of the mathematical morphology are defined based on these primitive operations (Figure 5): opening

Opening $A \circ B = (A \Theta B) \oplus B$

and closing

Closing $A \bullet B = (A \oplus B) \Theta B$

Detailed consideration shows that combined use of opening and closing operations enable to perform practically all basic image processing operations: contour enhancement, segmentation and so on.

Let us give several remarks important for the following discussion.

General feature of all these attempts to simulate biological route of image processing was that they were developed as numerical methods of information processing realized using traditional digital computers. It should be mentioned that there were also attempts to design specialized computing systems adapted to the considering image processing methods, in particular, to the cellular logic operations (see, for instance, Seibert & Waxman, 1989). Nevertheless none of them led to the practically and commercially important results, probably, because of the principal difference between digital methodology and biological information processing principles.

The main and principal difference in image processing by contemporary digital computers and biological objects consist in different representation of processing information. Instead of digitized images (sets of binary numbers) used by computers biological entities operates at all levels of image processing complex information modules (images).

Reaction-diffusion medium represents an image processing device different from digital means fundamentally. Initial data could be input into medium as natural complex fragments –images that processed by the medium without transformation them into digital form. They are virtually analog means, where some information processing features of specialized neural networks dynamically analogue to the cerebral cortex of the human brain are simulated.

Mechanisms of Image Processing by Belousov-Zhabotinsky Type Media

There are three basic modes of Belousov-Zhabotinsky media functioning: trigger, excitable and oscillating modes (see Mikhailov, 1994). Let us consider possibilities of image processing by the medium separately for each mode of functioning.

Excitable mode. Two operations of the contour enhancement of the input image could be considered as primitive ones for media functioning in the excitable mode. They could be defined as "contour$^{(+)}$" and "contour$^{(-)}$"and represent contour enhancement of the input image following by expanding (contour$^{(+)}$) or shrinking (contour$^{(-)}$) of the figure revealed (Figure 2). The choice between these operations is determined by the choice of the image form (negative or positive). Experimental results in this case coincide in all details with results of numerical simulations (Figure 2).

These primitive operations are adequate to dilation and erosion operations of the mathematical morphology. It is possible to reproduce also opening and closing operations, using contour$^{(+)}$ and contour$^{(-)}$

Figure 3. Basic mathematical morphology operations (A1: opening, A2: closing) and realization of them by light-sensitive Belousov-Zhabotinsky type medium (B1 and B2)

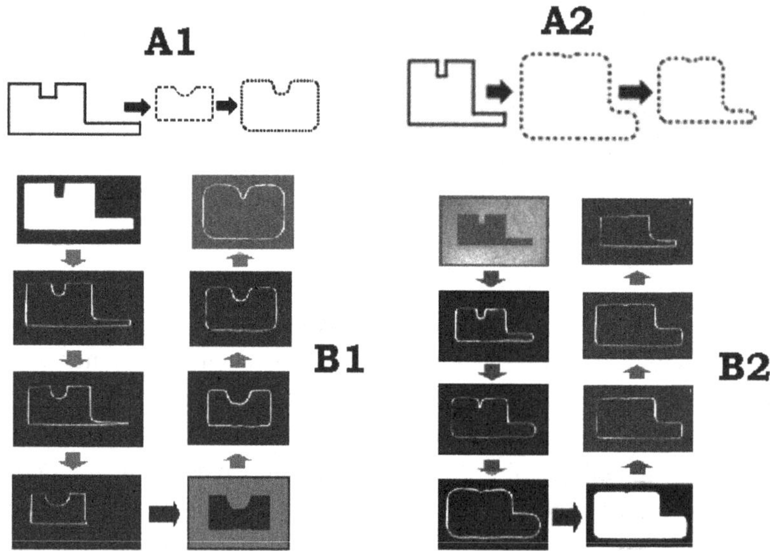

primitives of excitable medium (Figure 3). Therefore it is possible to conclude that reaction-diffusion medium can perform image processing operations typical for mathematical morphology. The contour$^{(+)}$ and contour$^{(-)}$ primitive operations (responses of the medium to the input of the image) enables to perform a lot of image processing operations based on these primitives:

- smoothing of immaterial features of the figure (enhancement its general shape) and segmentation of the figure (Figures 4 A,B),
- enhancement and removing of small features of the image (Figures 4 C,D).
- defect repair (Figure 4E),
- computing of the Voronoi diagram (Figure 5C).

Mention here that analogies considered should not bring to conclusion on detailed coincidence of reaction-diffusion and mathematical morphology operations. Reaction-diffusion technique is analogues virtually to the particular case of the mathematical morphology when the structural element is a circle. Nevertheless common general principles inherent in both of these approaches (first of all wave character of operations) and complex nonlinear dynamics of reaction-diffusion media seem to be the reasons why reaction diffusion media. could perform practically all mathematical morphology operations. At the same time the reaction-diffusion processor is the material device that operate images in a natural way do not transform them into digitized form.

The determination of the image skeleton could be performed by the medium functioning in the excitable mode in special cases of lengthy figures having thin fragments only (Figure 5A). In general case of arbitrary solid figure details of skeleton proves to be lost.

Figure 4. Image processing operations performed by Belousov-Zhabotinsky type medium

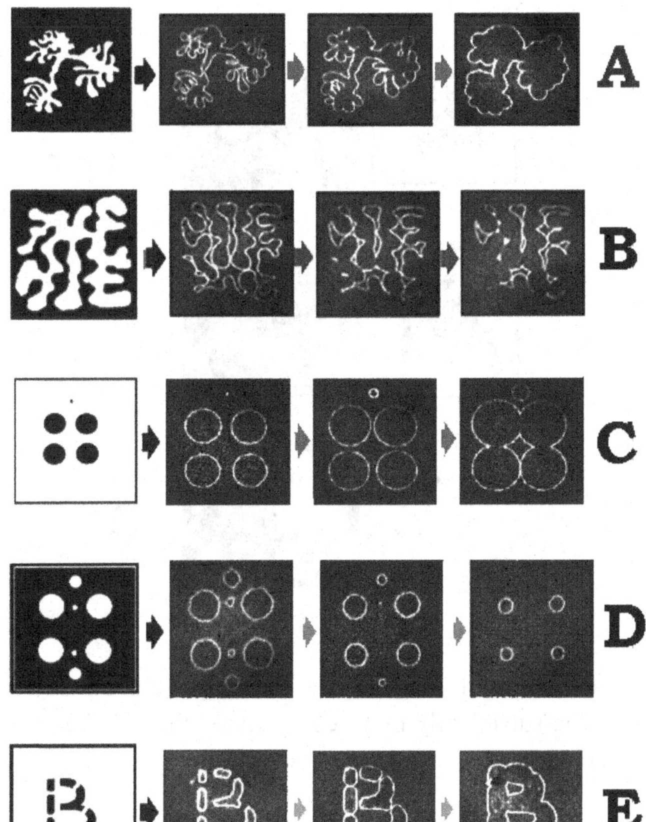

Attempts were performed also to use Belousov-Zhabotinsky type media functioning in the oscillating mode for processing half-tone images and images having several levels of brightness. However the sensitivity of the medium to details of the processed image was not satisfactory.

Inhibition (and deceleration) of chemical processes in a media under intense light illumination gives the possibility to control the process of input pattern evolution. Illumination of chosen fragments of the medium enables to exclude these fragments from the evolution *process* and to create predetermined configuration of the medium. This technique was used earlier (Rambidi (2003)) to simulate a chemical diode, a device offered by Agladze, Aliev and Yoshikawa (1996).

Trigger mode. Media functioning in the excitable mode does not give rise to possibility of skeleton determination in general case. Therefore an attempt was made to use Belousov-Zhabotinsky type media functioning in modes intermediate between excitable and trigger modes for skeleton determination. Concentration pulses become sufficiently broader in this case and the quality of the skeleton determined is better. Regretfully as far as the width of the pulse is broader, the sensitivity of the medium to the light radiation is less. Belousov-Zhabotinsky type medium in the trigger mode is not sensitive to the light radiation. This does not give the possibility to use optical input of information.

Numerical simulation was used to determine the skeleton of the arbitrary solid figure by the medium functioning in the trigger mode (Figure 5B). The quality of the skeleton proved to be satisfactory.

Figure 5. Experimental determination of (A) skeleton, (B) numerical simulation of skeleton, and (C) Voronoi diagram

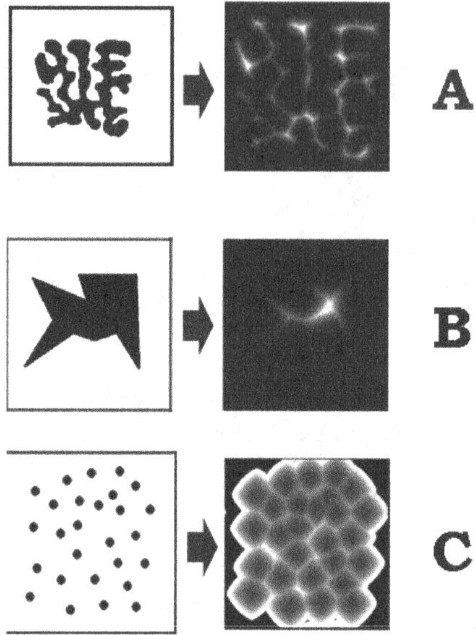

Oscillating mode. The evolution of images in the Belousov-Zhabotinsky type media functioning in oscillating mode proves to be sufficiently more complicated than in the case of excitable mode. The most remarkable phenomenon in this case is the dependence of the image evolution on exposure of input picture.

In general case if the exposure is small enough a positive black and white image is transformed by the medium into negative form, then the contour of the image reveals, and after the contour evolution the positive form of the image appears again. This complex evolution represents one period of image oscillation (Figure 6). The process considered is sensitive to light radiation and could be killed by intense illumination.

An increase of the exposure leads to new phenomenon. The image in the process of its input behaves as leading center emitting consecutively its contour every 20-30 seconds. The important feature of the process is that these moving contours have not removed even under intense light radiation. Mention that consecutive revealing of the contour system is similar to "mask effect" observed by Woodward et al (1995). If the illumination is switched off typical oscillations begin where all revealed contours take place (Figure 6). It is important that the medium after switching of radiation becomes sensitive to light radiation again.

The most interesting is the reversibility of oscillations and leading center modes during the same image evolution. This phenomenon is shown in Figure 7. In this case the exposure was chosen big enough for revealing two contours of the input image. After that the input image was switched off and spreading of revealed contours began under high level illumination. Several seconds after the illumination was changed to low level and oscillations of the image began. This process of changing high and low intensity levels following changes of dynamic modes (spreading pulses and oscillations) could be repeated several times. The intensity of high level illumination was determined by video projector characteristics (270 ANSI lumens), the intensity of low level was chosen equal to 30% of the initial illumination.

Figure 6. Temporal evolution of a black and white image (A) in the light-sensitive Belousov-Zhabotinsky type medium. Exposures: (B) 20 sec., (C) 40 sec., (D) 60 sec., (E) 90 sec.

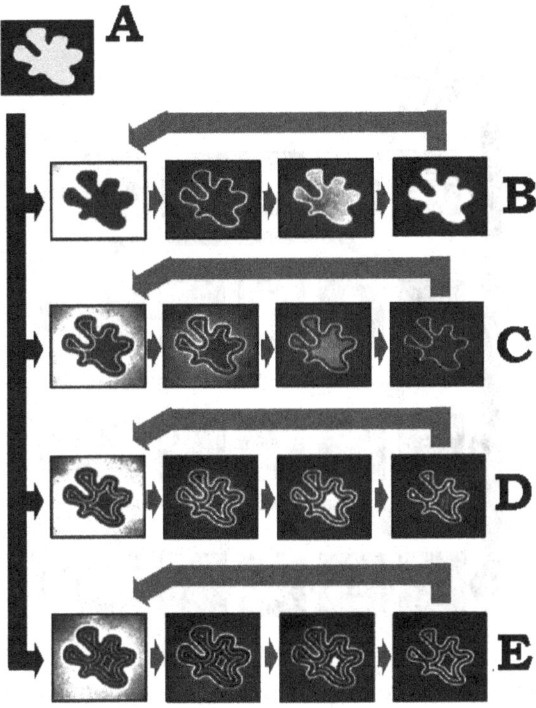

Figure 7. The process of consecutive changing contour spreading and oscillations in the light-sensitive Belousov-Zhabotinsky type medium, functioning in the oscillating mode

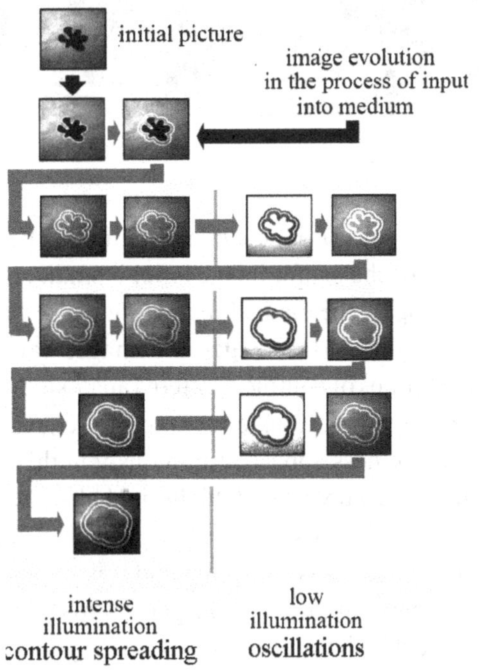

Figure 8. Temporal evolution of a half-tone image in the light-sensitive Belousov-Zhabotinsky type medium. Exposures: (A) 20 sec., (B) 40 sec., (C) 60 sec., (D) 90 sec.

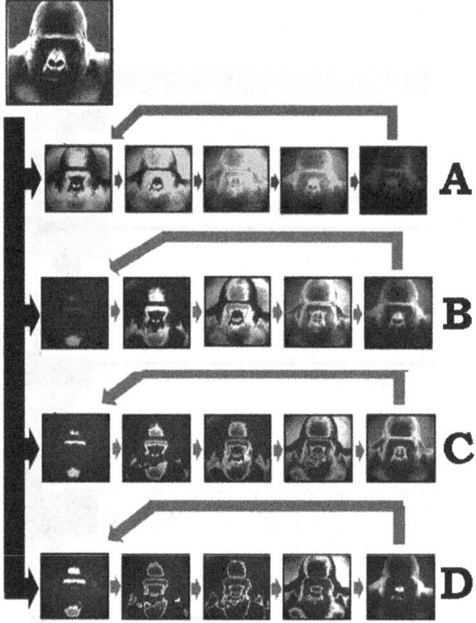

Figure 9. Detailed representation of the half-tone image evolution in the light-sensitive Belousov-Zhabotinsky type medium (between first and second slides of the case B in figure.10)

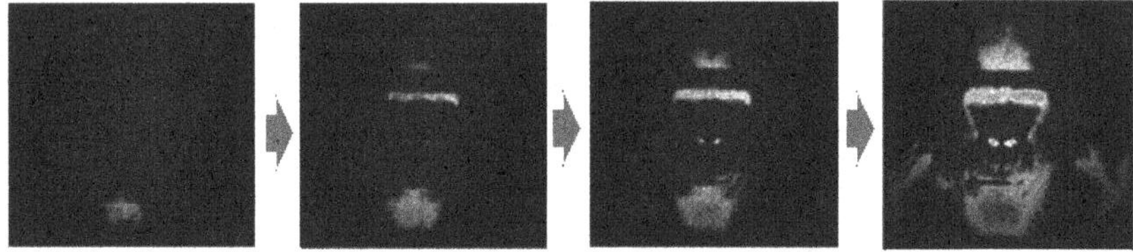

This consideration showed that results of image evolution in oscillating medium could be used for image processing only if the exposure chosen for image input is small enough. At the same time, in spite of this phenomenon image processing by the media functioning in oscillating mode seems to be of great importance, especially for processing half-tone images and images having several levels of brightness.

Considerable and notable possibilities of complex patterns analysis are opened in the case of half-tone images. In this case the positive image first transforms into the sequence of black and white negative images. Fragments of decreased brightness appear continuously in this sequence. After that, in general case, contours of fragments of the image reveal and the initial half-tone image is reconstructed (Figure 8). General phases of the evolution of images that were input using different exposures are shown in the Figure 8. Regretfully this representation is too rough and it is impossible to follow all details of the evolution. It is possible to show as an example, detailed part of this evolution (Figure 9) corresponding to the interval between first and second slides of Figure 10B. Easy to see that these data could be used to calculate histogram of the image brightness.

Figure 10. Processing of a pattern similar to multi-view aerial imagary by the light-sensitive Belousov-Zhabotinsky type medium

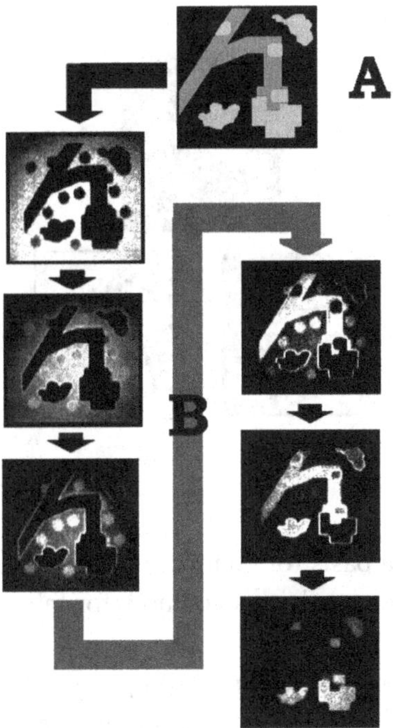

In general case one of the most important features of Belousov-Zhabotinsky type media is that these media seem to be a natural realization of the temporal sequence processor that transforms complex spatial distribution of data (half-tone pattern having fragments of different brightness) into temporal sequence of the distribution fragments. There are many different applications of these processors. One of them is processing patterns taken from aircrafts or satellites. Evolution of the model pattern similar to multi-view aerial imagery is shown in Figure 10. Easy to see how different fragments of the pattern having different brightness are singled out consecutively depending on the brightness of the fragments. Mention also another more practical example. An attempt to use mathematical morphology technique for urban road detection was performed lately by Zhang, Murai, and Baltsavias (1999). The urban map and results of preliminary detection of road network by mathematical morphology are shown in Figures 11A,B1. The detection of the road network by Belousov-Zhabotinsky type medium using the same urban map was done in our lab (Figure 11,B2). Easy to see, that these two road networks are in a good enough correspondence.

FUTURE RESEARCH DIRECTIONS

Potentialities for the Commercial Use

Experimental technique used now for material implementation of reaction-diffusion devices is, regretfully, in a primitive embryonic state. Therefore the laboratory-scale devices discussed above looks

Figure 11. The urban road detection by (B1) mathematical morphology, and light-sensitive (B2) Belousov-Zhabotinsky type medium using the same urban map (A)

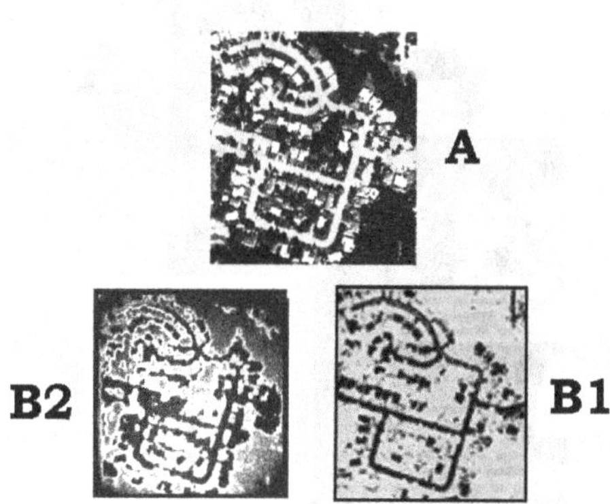

nowadays as beautiful toys, not as a basis for commercial. However the thorough analysis shows that reaction-diffusion media seem to be promising even now for fabrication of new effective information processing means.

Let us consider as an example one of the simplest operations – contour enhancement of arbitrary black and white image. The time of performing this primitive operation by Belousov-Zhabotinsky medium is about 1-5 sec. In the case of digital computer, if the shape of the image is not too complicated, it is possible to use resolution of the image about $10^3 \times 10^3$ points. Average time of floating point operation (multiplication) performed by Pentium III processor (600 MHz) is about 3×10^{-9} sec. Several (3-5) floating point operations in each point of the picture should be performed to calculate contour of the figure. Therefore the time of contour enhancement by digital computer is ~ 10^{-2} sec. that is much less than in the case of reaction-diffusion medium. However this time increases greatly if the resolution of the picture should be $10^4 \times 10^4$ – ~ 1 sec, or $10^5 \times 10^5$ – 100 sec.

The computational complexity of the object in this example is not high. Nevertheless the computational performances of reaction-diffusion medium and digital computer could be comparable. Given a problem of high computational complexity the performance of the reaction-diffusion medium could be sufficiently increased even by orders-of-magnitude.

The very important advantages of reaction-diffusion means should be simplicity and low commercial mass production costs. The material structure of reaction-diffusion devices is immeasurable simpler than VLSI. Therefore the technological basis for the fabrication of reaction-diffusion devices should be simpler and cheaper. The reaction-diffusion media are impurity tolerant in comparison with semiconductor devices. It leads to additional opportunities to decrease processing capabilities and cost.

Fields of Application

The progress of the human society faces more and more new challenges - simple, cheap, autonomous, massively deployed means capable to collect and store information, and to solve intellectual problems such as recognition, control and navigation. These systems should sense external stimuli and respond in real or near-real time. Important challenges embrace, for instance, the ocean shelf exploration. The nano satellite system deployment, military and dual-use applications such as mobile robots that work in dynamically changing environments. The real time for these systems is often ~ 0.1 – 1.0 sec. Moreover, the shelf-life of such means could be rather short.

Chemical and biochemical reaction-diffusion media seem to be an attractive basis for fabrication of these devices. They are capable of natural style performing of intellectual operations. Mention that information processing capabilities and problems that could be efficiently solved based on reaction-diffusion systems seem to be far from exhausted. A number of approaches could result in advanced powerful information processing means. Several possibilities could be mentioned which might be important for the future development reaction-diffusion information processing means. Promising theoretical and experimental investigations were performed during the last several years (see details in Rambidi, 2003) though most of them was not bound directly to information processing. However it should be reasonable to suppose that because of biological nature of the reaction-diffusion paradigm the biologically inspired principles would be indispensable to greatly broaden information processing capabilities. The most important between them seems to be the multi level organization of biological information processing. The understanding of the importance of multi level architecture was growing during the last years. And it is necessary to take the next step to realize, to choose, and to put together:

- practical problems most adequate to non von Neumann computing,
- to find multi level algorithms for solving these problems,
- to elaborate experimental technique to implement these algorithms.

Let us hope that it would be done in the nearest future. If successful, these efforts will create fundamentally new devices that rather supplement than compete with modern digital semiconductor computers broadening immensely the power of "information industry".

Routes for Understanding Brain Mechanisms: Simulation of Optical Illusions

Mammalian and especially human vision represent the most complicated and sophisticated phenomena of the brain activity. The pattern of the environmental reality is projected on the retinas of two eyes and after some transformations leaves the eye by way of the optic nerves. Crossing partly in chiasm visual information get to lateral geniculate nuclei and ultimately travel to primary visual cortex, where the whole volume of the visual information is collected. The visual cortex performs preliminary processing of the visual information: enhancing contours of the information fragments, borders between them, lines of definite directions and so on (Marr, 1982). Further interpretation of the environmental visual information represents complex psycho-biological process performed by the cerebral cortex.

The remarkable features of the human vision are receptive fields that could be of on-center of-surround or off-center on-surround type. First of them correspond to activation of neurons in the center of the field and inhibition at its border. The second corresponds to the opposite situation.

In the late sixties Grossberg (1976) offered the conception of specialized neural networks which includes specific features of receptive fields. This conception was used later (Grossberg, 1988) for understanding a lot of visual phenomena inherent in the brain activity.

Peculiarities of the human brain functioning leads often to the wrong perception of the neighborhood reality - illusions. There are a lot of them connected with ear and sense of touch. The most interesting illusions are the vision ones (Yudin & Yudin, 1985). All of them are determined more or less by the psychic factors. Nevertheless, some part of them seems to be understood at the level of neural dynamics of the visual cortex.

It was mentioned above that the remarkable feature of Belousov-Zhabotinsky type media is neural network architecture similar to the architecture of the Grossberg networks. This analogy was considered by Grossberg (1988), and investigated later (Rambidi, 2003) in experiment. In the basis of this phenomenon are nonlinear effects inherent in Grossberg networks and reaction-diffusion media. Reaction-diffusion media exhibits on-center activation because of autocatalytic reactions and off-center inhibition caused by the difference of activator and inhibitor diffusion coefficients.

Suppose that some optical illusions could be caused by nonlinear dynamics of the visual cortex, that is described by Grossberg neural approach. At the same time the dynamics of Grossberg neural nets could be simulated by Belousov-Zhabotinsky type media. Therefore it could be reasonable to see what will be the evolution of images that give rise to optical illusions caused by Belousov-Zhabotinsky medium.

Detailed investigation of the image processing capabilities of Belousov-Zhabotinsky type media showed that these media could perform complex enough operations. It could be supposed that nonlinear dynamics inherent in these media could be also the basis for understanding the mechanisms of optical illusions.

Experimental investigation of the image evolution was performed using excitable and oscillating modes of medium functioning.

Excitable mode. Evolutions of Kanizsa triangle and Kennedy figure are shown in v. It is possible to see that illusory images – triangle in the case of Kanizsa illusion and circle in the case of Kennedy figure, reveals distinctly as a result of image evolution. It is possible to see also in the Figure 12 that in the process of evolution of the black squares systems phantom dots between angles of squares appears. These features could be seen if to look intently at the picture.

Evolutions of a black square placed on the white background, contour of which spreads in the process of evolution, and white square on the black background, where contour shrinks, are shown in Figure 13. It could be compared to size perception illusion that is to the seeming difference in sizes of squares in initial image. The possible mechanism of the typography illusion (transformation of number "13" in to letter "B") is shown also in Figure 13.

Oscillating mode. Suppose that visual cortex having Grossberg neural architecture is able to function in a oscillating mode. This assumption does not contradict to the wave processes inherent into human brain and could be a basis for understanding mechanisms of some other illusions.

Let us consider in the case of Rubin bowl the image which is perceived as two black faces on the white background as positive form of the image. In the process of evolution this image oscillate between positive and negative form, which could be perceived more as black bowl on the white background (Figure 14A). Easiness of transition between these two forms of the image seems to open the possibility to explain the fact that this image could be perceived or as bowl or as two human faces.

The same situation arises in the case of saxophone player illusion where white man image with a saxophone on the black background could be defined as positive image. I this case the negative image is perceived subjectively more as woman face (Figure 14B).

Oscillating processes of the visual cortex could be considered also as possible explanation of after image illusion. The pattern giving rise to the vague associations only transforms in the process of evolution into recognizing face (Jesus Christ illusion, Figure 14C).

Figure 12. Simulation of optical illusions by light-sensitive Belousov-Zhabotinsky type medium: (A) Kanizsa triangle, (B) Kennedy figure, (C) phantom dots

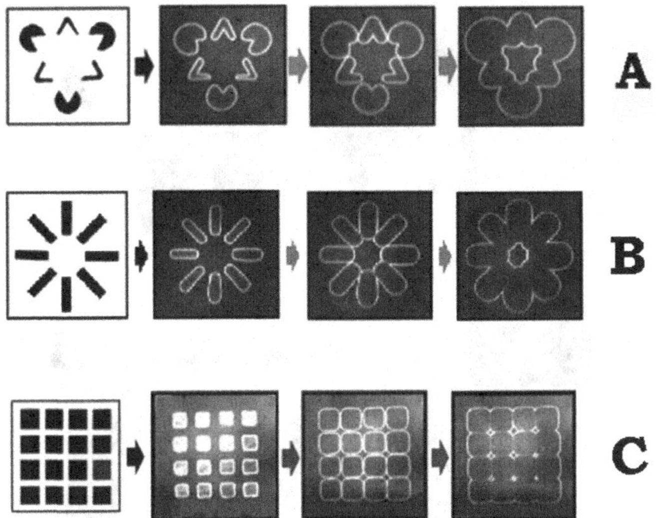

Figure 13. Simulation of optical illusions by light-sensitive Belousov-Zhabotinsky type medium: (A) white and black squares, (B) typogfaphy illusions

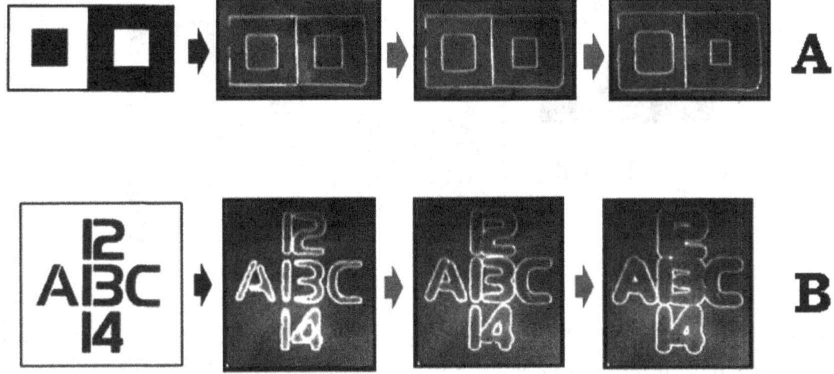

It should be mentioned that offered approach could be considered more as dynamic analogy than as mechanism explaining some of the optical illusions. These illusions seem to be considered as emerging effect erasing at the level higher than the level of neural net dynamics.

CONCLUSION

Prediction of the future represents often more of a complacent pastime than an activity producing useful results. Too many presently unknown factors might dramatically change contemporary seemingly reliable tendencies. That's why physical roots, possible mechanism at the molecular level and information processing potentialities of reaction-diffusion means were under comprehensive discussions during the

Figure 14. Simulation of optical illusions by light-sensitive Belousov-Zhabotinsky type medium: (A) Rubin bowl, (B) saxophone player illusion, (C) Jesus Christ illusion

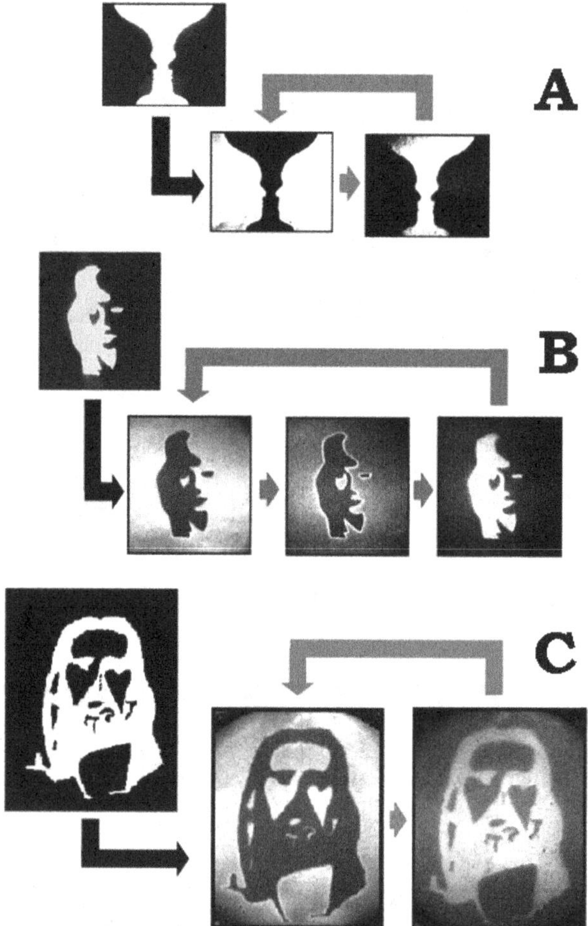

last couple of decades (see, for instance, Sienko et al., 2003; Adamatzky, 2005; Rambidi, 2007). At the same time two different in their nature experimental achievements produced lately seems to be important milestones in developing molecular computing.

The first of them was elaboration of a 160-kilobit molecular electronic memory patterned at 1011 bits per square centimeter. Green et al (2007) used [2]rotaxane molecules served as the data storage elements.

Bandyopadhyay and Acharia (2008) have realized parallel processing device using 2,3,5,6,tetramethyl-1-4-benzoquinone (DRQ) molecules. The processing device consisted of 17 identical DRQs wherein a single molecule simultaneously instructs 16 others, in 4^{16} possible ways. To test this parallel computer authors and their colleagues simulated two phenomena – electron diffusion and how cancer spreads in the body. This processing device similar in processing mechanisms to the reaction-diffusion means seems to be interesting example of future molecular computers.

REFERENCES

Adamatzky, A., De Lacy Costello, B., & Tetsuya, A. (2005). *Reaction diffusion computers*. Elsevier Science.

Agladze, K., Aliev, R. R., Yamaguchi, T., & Yoshikawa, K. (1996). Chemical diode. *Journal of Physical Chemistry, 100*, 13895–13897. doi:10.1021/jp9608990

Akagi, T., Okazaki, N., Yoshinobu, T., & Matsumura-Inoue, T. (2000). Comparative study of chemical waves and temporal oscillations in Ru(bpy)$_3$ catalyzed Belousov-Zhabotinsky reaction. *Chemical Physics Letters, 28*, 214–220. doi:10.1016/S0009-2614(00)00907-6

Bandyopadhyay, A., & Somobrata, A. (2008). 16-bit parallel processing in a molecular assembly. *Proceedings of the National Academy of Sciences of the United States of America, 105*, 3668–3672. doi:10.1073/pnas.0703105105

Blum, H. (1967). A transformation for extracting new descriptors of shape. In: *Symposium: Models for perception of speech and visual forms,* (Whaten-Dunn, W., Ed.), Cambridge, MA: MIT Press.

Bonabeau, E., Dorigo, M., & Theraulaz, G. (2005). *Swarm intelligence: From natural to artificial systems*. Retrieved from http://www.cs.virginia.edu/~evans/bio/slides/1

Casti, J. (1979). *Connectivity, complexity, and catastrophe in large-scale systems. Chichester, UK, New York, NY, Brisbane, Australia*. Toronto, Canada: John Wiley & Sons.

Conrad, M. (1974). *Molecular information processing in the central nervous system, part1: Selection circuits in the brain* (pp. 82–137). Berlin/Heidelberg, Germany, New York, NY: Springer Verlag.

Conrad, M. (1985). On design principles for a molecular computer. *Communications of the ACM, 28*, 464–480. doi:10.1145/3532.3533

Duda, R. G., & Hart, P. E. (1973). *Pattern classification and scene analysis*. New York, NY: John Wiley and Sons.

Fenzi, N., & Hofkirchner, W. (1997). *Information processing in evolutionary systems* (Schweitzer, F., Ed.). London, UK: Gordon and Breach.

Field, R. J., & Burger, M. (Eds.). (1985). *Oscillations and traveling waves in chemical systems*. New York, NY: Wiley-Interscience.

Fleischer, M. (2005). *Foundations of swarm intelligence: From principles to practice*. Retrieved from http://www.comdig2.de/Conf/C41SR/1

Fleissner, P., & Hofkirchner, W. (1996). Emergent information. *Bio Systems, 2-3*, 243–248. doi:10.1016/0303-2647(95)01597-3

Gierer, A., & Meinhardt, H. (1972). A theory of biological pattern formation. *Kybernetik, 12*, 30–39. doi:10.1007/BF00289234

Goldbetter, A. (1997). *Biochemical oscillations and cellular rhythms*. Cambridge, UK: Cambridge University Press.

Green, J. E., Jang Wook, C., Boukai, A., Bunimovich, Y., Johnston-Halperin, E., & Delonno, E. (2007). A 160-kilobit molecular electronic memory patterned at 1011 bits per square centimeter. *Nature*, *62*(445), 414–417. doi:10.1038/nature05462

Grossberg, S. (1976). On the development of feature detectors in the visual cortex with applications in learning and reaction-diffusion systems. *Biological Cybernetics*, *21*, 145–159. doi:10.1007/BF00337422

Grossberg, S. (1988). Nonlinear neural networks: Principles, mechanisms, and architectures. *Neural Networks*, *1*, 17–61. doi:10.1016/0893-6080(88)90021-4

Kadar, S., Amemia, T., & Showalter, K. (1997). Reaction mechanism for light sensitivity of the $Ru(bpy)_3^{2+}$ - catalyzed Belousov-Zhabotinsky reaction. *The Journal of Physical Chemistry A*, *101*, 8200–8206. doi:10.1021/jp971937y

Klir, G. J. (1985). Complexity: Some general observations. *Systems Research*, *2*, 131–140. doi:10.1002/sres.3850020205

Kuhnert, L. (1986). A new optical photochemical memory device in a light-sensitive chemical active medium. *Nature*, *319*, 393–394. doi:10.1038/319393a0

Kuhnert, L. (1986). Photochemische Manipulation von chemischen Wellen. *Naturwissenschaften*, *73*, 96–97. doi:10.1007/BF00365836

Kuhnert, L., Agladze, K. I., & Krinsky, V. I. (1989). Image processing using light-sensitive chemical waves. *Nature*, *337*, 244–247. doi:10.1038/337244a0

Marr, D. (1982). *Vision: A computational investigation into the human representation and processing of visual information*. New York, NY: W.H. Freeman and Company.

Masterov, A. V., Rabinovich, M. I., Tolkov, V. N., & Yakhno, V. G. (1988). Studies of regimes of autowaves and autostructures interaction in neural net like media. In Yakhno, V. G. (Ed.), *Collective dynamics of excitations and structure formation* (pp. 89–104). Gorkyi, Russia: Institute of Applied Physics of USSR Academy of Sciences.

McCulloch, W. J., & Pitts, W. (1943). A logical calculus of the ideas immanent in nervous activity. *The Bulletin of Mathematical Biophysics*, *5*, 115–133. doi:10.1007/BF02478259

Mikhailov, A. (1994). *Foundations of synergetics, 2nd revised edition*. Heidelberg, Germany, New York, NY, & London, UK: Springer Verlag.

Moravec, H. (1998). *When will computer hardware match the human brain?* Retrieved from http://www.transhumanist.com/volum1/moravec.htm

Newell, P. C. (1977). Aggregation and cell surface receptors in cellular slime molds in microbial interaction. In Reissig, J. L. (Ed.), *Receptors and recognition, series B*. Chapman and Hall.

Optical illusions. (1992). Retrieved from http://www.sandlotscience.com

Preston, K., Jr. (1981). *IEEE Transactions, PAM1-3,* 4.

Price, C. B., Wambacq, P., & Oosterlinck, A. (1990). Image enhancement and analysis with reaction-diffusion paradigm. *IEE Proceedings*, *137*, 135–145.

Rambdi,N. G.(2003). Chemical based computing and problems of high computational complexity. Reaction-diffusion paradigm.

Rambidi, N. G. (2003). Lure of molecular electronics–from molecular switches to distributed molecular information processing media. *Microelectronic Engineering*, *69*, 485–500. doi:10.1016/S0167-9317(03)00337-X

Rambidi, N. G. (2007). *Nanotechnology and molecular computers.* Moscow, Russia: FizMatLit.

Rambidi, N. G., & Maximychev, A. V. (1997). Molecular image-processing devices based on chemical reaction systems, 6: Processing half-tone images and neural network architecture of excitable media. *Advanced Materials for Optics and Electronics*, *7*, 171–182. doi:10.1002/(SICI)1099-0712(199707)7:4<171::AID-AMO300>3.0.CO;2-#

Rambidi, N. G., Maximychev, A. V., & Usatov, A. V. (1994). Molecular neural network devices based on non-linear dynamic media. *Bio Systems*, *33*, 125–137. doi:10.1016/0303-2647(94)90052-3

Rambidi, N. G., Zamalin, V. M., & Sandler, Y. M. (1988). Molecular information processing and problems of artificial intelligence. *Journal of Molecular Electronics*, *4*, S39.

Rosenblatt, F. (1962). *Principles of neurodynamics.* Washington, DC: Spartan.

Seibert, M., & Waxman, A. M. (1989). Spreading activation layers, visual saccades and invariant representation for neural pattern recognition system. *Neural Networks*, *2*, 9–12. doi:10.1016/0893-6080(89)90012-9

Serra, J. (1986). Introduction to mathematical morphology. *Computer Vision Graphics and Image Processing*, *35*, 283–305. doi:10.1016/0734-189X(86)90002-2

Sienko, T., Adamatzky, A., Rambidi, R., & Conrad, M. (Eds.). (2003). *Molecular computing.* Cambridge, MA; London, UK: The MIT Press.

Unger, S. H. (1959). Cellular logic. *Proceedings of IRE*, *40*(10).

Woodward, D. E., Tyson, R., Myerscough, M. R., Murry, J. D., Burdene, E. O., & Berg, H. C. (1995). Spatio-temporal patterns generated by Salmonella typhimurium. *Biophysical Journal*, *68*, 2181–2189. doi:10.1016/S0006-3495(95)80400-5

Young, N. (2002). Mathematical morphology. Retrieved from http://dmsun4bath.ac.uk/research/morphology/morphology.htm

Yudin, D. B., & Yudin, A. D. (1985). *The number and the thought.* Moscow, Russia: Znanie.

Zhang, C., Murai, S., & Baltsavias, E. (1999). *Road network detection by mathematical morphology.* Retrieved from http://www.photogrammetry.ethz.ch/general/persons/chunsun_pub/chunsun_paris99.pdf

ENDNOTE

1 The first version of this chapter was published in International Journal of Unconventional Computing (2005) together with S. G. Ulyakhin, D. E. Shishlov, V. A. Neganov, and A. S. Tsvetkov.

Section 4
Application of AI and CI Methods to Learning

Chapter 19
MLVQ: A Modified Learning Vector Quantization Algorithm for Identifying Centroids of Fuzzy Membership Functions

Kai Keng Ang
*Agency for Science, Technology and Research (A*STAR), Singapore*

Chai Quek
Nanyang Technological University, Singapore

ABSTRACT

The Learning Vector Quantization (LVQ) algorithm and its variants have been employed in some fuzzy neural networks to automatically derive membership functions from training data. Although several improvements to the LVQ algorithm have been proposed, problematic areas of the LVQ algorithm include: the selection of number of clusters, initial weights, proper training parameters, and forced termination. These problematic areas in the derivation of centroids of one-dimensional data are illustrated with an artificially generated experimental data set on LVQ, GLVQ, and FCM. A Modified Learning Vector Quantization (MLVQ) algorithm is presented in this chapter to address these problematic areas for one-dimensional data. MLVQ models the development of the nervous system in two stages: a first stage where the basic architecture and coarse connections patterns are laid out, and a second stage where the initial architecture is refined in activity-dependent ways. MLVQ determines the learning constant parameter and modifies the terminating condition of the LVQ algorithm so that convergence can be achieved and easily detected. Experiments on the MLVQ algorithm are performed and contrasted against LVQ, GLVQ, and FCM. Results show that MLVQ determines the number of clusters and converges to the centroids. Results also show that MLVQ is insensitive to the sequence of the training data, able to identify centroids of overlapping clusters, and able to ignore outliners without identifying them as separate clusters. Results using MLVQ algorithm and Gaussian membership functions with Pseudo Outer-Product Fuzzy Neural Network using Compositional Rule of Inference and Singleton fuzzifier (POPFNN-CRI(S)) on pattern classification and time series prediction are also provided to demonstrate the effectiveness of the fuzzy membership functions derived using MLVQ.

DOI: 10.4018/978-1-60960-551-3.ch019

1 INTRODUCTION

The main rationale in integrating fuzzy logic and neural networks in Neural Fuzzy Systems is to create a logical framework based on a linguistic model through the training and learning of the connectionist neural networks (Lin & Lee, 1996). Please refer to (Gupta & Rao, 1994) for the principles and architecture of fuzzy neural networks. The notion of linguistic variable in fuzzy set theory and fuzzy logic is extensively used in Neural Fuzzy Systems. The linguistic labels in each linguistic variable are usually defined as fuzzy sets with appropriate membership functions. These membership functions have to be predefined to enable fuzzy inference rules to map numerical data into linguistic labels.

Membership functions are usually predefined by human experts or experienced users. Several methods of automatically deriving membership functions from training data have been proposed and among these methods, the *Learning Vector Quantization* (LVQ) algorithm and its variants were employed in some fuzzy neural networks (Ang, Quek, & Pasquier, 2003; Li, Mukaidono, & Turksen, 2002; Lin, 1995; Zhou & Quek, 1996) to derive fuzzy membership functions. The use of LVQ in these fuzzy neural networks is not for pattern classification, but to utilise the centroids obtained from LVQ to derive Gaussian-shaped, triangular or trapezoidal-shaped membership functions for each individual dimension of the network's input and output. After the membership functions and fuzzy rules are derived, a supervised learning algorithm is often employed to fine-tune the rules and membership functions.

Although several improvements to LVQ have been proposed in (Kohonen, 1990), problematic areas of LVQ exists which include the selection of number of clusters, selection of initial weights, the selection of proper training parameters and the forced termination. Variants of LVQ were proposed in the literature to address some but not all of these problems, namely Soft Competition Scheme (SCS) (Yair, Zeger, & Gersho, 1992), Fuzzy Learning Vector Quantization (FLVQ) (Tsao, Bezdek, & Pal, 1994), Generalised Learning Vector Quantization (GLVQ) (Pal, Bezdek, & Tsao, 1993) and GLVQ-F (Karayiannis, Bezdek, Pal, Hathaway, & Pai, 1996).

The variants of LVQ in the literature did not address the selection of number of clusters, which is a crucial parameter in the determination of the number of linguistic labels for membership functions for fuzzy neural networks. The learning constant parameter in LVQ and its variants are usually decremented with time to force the termination of the training process. This guarantees termination, but not necessary converges to the means of the training data. The training parameters must also be varied from one data set to another to achieve good results. Furthermore, the final weights obtained after training are dependent on the initial weights and the sequence of the training data.

In contrast to LVQ and its variants, the *Fuzzy C-Means* (FCM) algorithm in (Bezdek, James C., 1981) has established convergence. FCM is a batch-learning optimisation algorithm that performs updates to the weights after iterating through the entire data set. Thus FCM is independent of the sequence of data (Bezdek, J. C., Hathaway, & Tucker, 1987). However, the iterative nature of FCM is computationally and memory intensive due to the large number of feature vectors involved (Cheng, Goldgof, & Hall, 1998), see (14) and (15). FCM is also unable to perform on-line learning since it is a batch-learning scheme (Rhee & Oh, 1996). Furthermore, the performance of FCM depends on a good choice of the weighting exponential m and the initial pseudo partition. Although guidelines are provided for a suitable choice for m (Choe & Jordan, 1992), however, this choice is still largely heuristic (Tsao et al., 1994).

This paper is organised as follows. Section 2 gives a review of clustering algorithms, mainly LVQ, GLVQ and FCM algorithms. See (Baraldi & Blonda, 1999) for more extensive review and assessment on clustering algorithms. Section 3 presents experimental results on these algorithms in the derivation

Figure 1. Structure of the LVQ clustering network

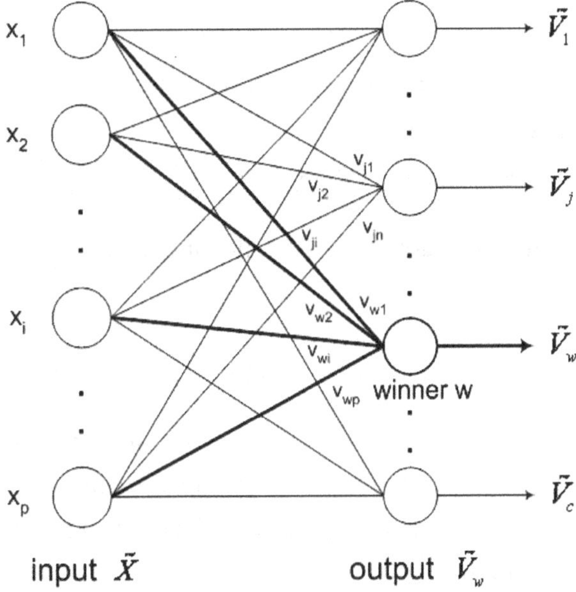

of centriods for an artificial experimental data set. Section 4 presents the Modified Learning Vector Quantization (MLVQ) algorithm and motivates the approach with the two-stage development process of our human nervous system. This section also illustrates how the algorithm determines the number of clusters, initial weights, selection of training parameters and how the optimal solution is obtained using the selected terminating condition. Section 5 presents further experimental results on the use of MLVQ with a fuzzy neural network, namely Pseudo Outer-Product Fuzzy Neural Network using Compositional Rule of Inference and Singleton fuzzifier (POPFNN-CRI(S)) (Ang et al., 2003) on existing data sets.

2 CLUSTERING ALGORITHMS

Learning Vector Quantization (LVQ) are unsupervised neural networks that determine the weights for cluster centres in an iterative and sequential manner (Kohonen, 1989). Figure 1 shows the structure of an LVQ network. This fundamental structure remains unchanged through the various improvements to the basic LVQ algorithm (Kohonen, 1990).

Each output neuron has a weight vector $\tilde{V}_j$ that is adjusted during learning. Given an input vector $\tilde{X}$, the neurons in the output layer compete among themselves. The winner w whose weight has the minimum distance from the input, updates its weights. The process is continued until the weights are forced to stabilise through the specification of a learning rate and an update neighbourhood factor that decrease with time. Hence asymptotic convergence of LVQ has not been theoretically established. The *Kohonen learning rule* used for training the network shown in Figure 1 is described in (1).

$$\tilde{V}_j^{(T+1)} = \begin{cases} \tilde{V}_j^{(T)} + \alpha^{(T)}(\tilde{X} - \tilde{V}_j^{(T)}) & \text{if } j = w \\ \tilde{V}_j^{(T)} & \text{if } j \neq w \end{cases} \quad (1)$$

where

$\tilde{X}$ = input data vector
$\tilde{V}_j$ = j^{th} cluster centre, also weight of competitive j^{th} neuron at iteration T
$\alpha^{(T)}$ = learning constant at iteration T
$\left\|\tilde{X} - \tilde{V}_j\right\|$ = Euclidean distance between the vectors $\tilde{X}$ and $\tilde{V}_j$

There are many versions of LVQ algorithm. The following describes a general one without neighbourhood update:

LVQ Algorithm

- **Step 1:** Given data set $\tilde{\mathbf{X}} = \left\{\tilde{X}_1, \tilde{X}_2, \ldots \tilde{X}_k, \ldots \tilde{X}_n\right\} \subset \mathbb{R}^p$, define c the number of clusters, ε the terminating criterion and T_{max} the maximum number of iterations.
- **Step 2:** Initialise T=0, weights $\tilde{\mathbf{V}} = \left\{\tilde{V}_1^{(0)}, \tilde{V}_2^{(0)}, \ldots \tilde{V}_j^{(0)}, \ldots \tilde{V}_c^{(0)}\right\}$ and learning constant $\alpha^{(0)}$.
- **Step 3:** For $T = 0..T_{max}$: For $k = 1..n$:
  a. Find winner w using (2).

$$\left\|\tilde{X}_k - \tilde{V}_w^{(T)}\right\| = \min_j\left(\left\|\tilde{X}_k - \tilde{V}_j^{(T)}\right\|\right) \quad \forall j = 1..c \tag{2}$$

  b. Update the weights of the winner with (3).

$$\tilde{V}_w^{(T+1)} = \tilde{V}_w^{(T)} + \alpha^{(T)}(\tilde{X}_k - \tilde{V}_w^{(T)}) \tag{3}$$

  End for k
  c. Compute $E^{(T+1)}$ using (4).

$$E^{(T+1)} = \left\|\tilde{\mathbf{V}}^{(T+1)} - \tilde{\mathbf{V}}^{(T)}\right\|^2 = \sum_{j=1}^{c}\left\|\tilde{V}_j^{(T+1)} - \tilde{V}_j^{(T)}\right\|^2 \tag{4}$$

  d. If $E^{(T+1)} \leq \varepsilon$ stop, else adjust learning rate $\alpha^{(T+1)}$ to satisfy (5) and (6).

$$\sum_{T=0}^{\infty}\alpha^{(T)} = \infty \tag{5}$$

$$\sum_{T=0}^{\infty}\left(\alpha^{(T)}\right)^2 < \infty \tag{6}$$

  End for T

One choice for the sequence of learning constants that satisfies (5) and (6) is given in (7).

$$\alpha^{(T+1)} = \lambda\alpha^{(T)} \tag{7}$$

where

λ = learning rate, $0<\lambda\leq 1$

Instead of updating only the winner's weights, the *Generalized Learning Vector Quantization* (GLVQ) proposed in (Pal et al., 1993) updates all weights depending on the degree of distance match to the winner nodes. The GLVQ algorithm defines the winner weights update for the kth input data set in (3) from LVQ step 3b using (8) and (9).

$$\tilde{V}_w^{(T+1)} = \tilde{V}_w^{(T)} + \alpha_i^{(T)}(\tilde{X}_k - \tilde{V}_w^{(T)})\left(\frac{D^2 - D + \left\|\tilde{X}_k - \tilde{V}_w^{(T)}\right\|}{D^2}\right) \tag{8}$$

$$\tilde{V}_j^{(T+1)} = \tilde{V}_j^{(T)} + \alpha_i^{(T)}(\tilde{X}_k - \tilde{V}_j^{(T)})\left(\frac{\left\|\tilde{X}_k - \tilde{V}_j^{(T)}\right\|}{D^2}\right) \swarrow\!\!\nearrow j \neq w \tag{9}$$

where

$$D = \sum_{j=1}^{c}\left\|\tilde{X}_k - \tilde{V}_j\right\|^2.$$

The GLVQ algorithm uses the learning constant update in (10).

$$\alpha^{(T)} = \alpha^{(0)}\left(1 - \frac{T}{T_{\max}}\right) \tag{10}$$

The *Fuzzy C-Means* (FCM) algorithm was developed (Bezdek, James C., 1981) to obtain fuzzy pseudo-partitions that minimises the objective function. A fuzzy pseudo-partition of a finite data set $\tilde{X}$ is defined in (11) and (12).

$$\sum_{j=1}^{c}\mu_j(\tilde{X}_k) = 1 \quad \forall k = 1..n \tag{11}$$

$$0 < \sum_{k=1}^{n}\mu_j(\tilde{X}_k) < n \quad \forall j = 1..c \tag{12}$$

where

c = number of clusters

n = number of data vectors
$\tilde{X} = \{\tilde{X}_1, \tilde{X}_2, \ldots \tilde{X}_k, \ldots \tilde{X}_n\}$ is a finite set of data
$P = \{ A_1, A_2, \ldots, A_c \}$ is a fuzzy pseudo-partition of X
$\mu_j(\tilde{X}_k)$ = Fuzzy membership of $\tilde{X}_k$ in the fuzzy set A_i

The objective function in FCM algorithm is given in (13) (Bezdek, James C., 1981).

$$J_m(P) = \sum_{k=1}^{n}\sum_{j=1}^{c}(\mu_j(\tilde{X}_k))^m \left\|\tilde{X}_k - \tilde{V}_j\right\|^2 \tag{13}$$

where

m = exponential value that influences the degree of fuzziness of the partition
$\tilde{X}_k$ = the kth data
$\tilde{V}_j$ = the jth cluster centre
$\left\|\tilde{X}_k - \tilde{V}_j\right\|$ = Euclidean distance between the vectors $\tilde{X}_k$ and $\tilde{V}_j$

A brief description of the FCM algorithm is given as follows.

FCM Algorithm

- **Step 1:** Define c as the number of clusters, m as the exponent weight and a small positive number ε as the terminating criterion.
- **Step 2:** Initialise T=0 and randomly initialize fuzzy pseudo-partition $P^{(0)}$.
- **Step 3:** Compute the cluster centres $\tilde{V}_1^{(T)}, \tilde{V}_2^{(T)}, \ldots \tilde{V}_j^{(T)}, \ldots \tilde{V}_c^{(T)}$ for $P^{(T)}$ using (14).

$$\tilde{V}_j^{(T)} = \frac{\sum_{k=1}^{n}(\mu_j(\tilde{X}_k))^m \tilde{X}_k}{\sum_{k=1}^{n}(\mu_j(\tilde{X}_k))^m} \quad \forall j=1..c \tag{14}$$

- **Step 4:** Update $P^{(T+1)}$ with (15).

$$\mu_i^{(T+1)}(\tilde{X}_k) = \left(\sum_{j=1}^{c}\left(\frac{\left\|\tilde{X}_k - \tilde{V}_i^{(T)}\right\|^2}{\left\|\tilde{X}_k - \tilde{V}_j^{(T)}\right\|^2}\right)^{\frac{1}{m-1}}\right)^{-1} \quad \forall i=1..c,\ k=1..n \tag{15}$$

If $\left\|\tilde{X}_k - \tilde{V}_i^{(T)}\right\|^2 = 0$, then $\mu_i^{(T+1)}(\tilde{X}_k) = 1$ and $\mu_j^{(T+1)}(\tilde{X}_k) = 0$ for $j=1..c, j \neq i$.

- **Step 5:** Compare $P^{(T+1)}$ with $P^{(T)}$ using (16).

Figure 2. Artificial experimental data set I

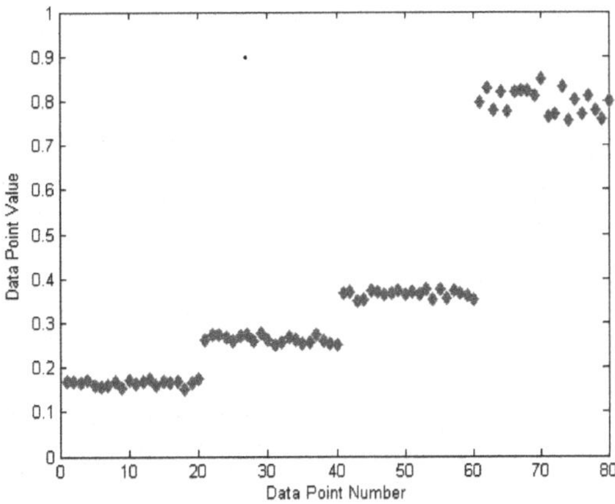

$$E = \left\| \mathrm{P}^{(T+1)} - \mathrm{P}^{(T)} \right\| = \sum_{j=1}^{c} \sum_{k=1}^{n} \left| \mu_j^{(T+1)}(\tilde{X}_k) - \mu_j^{(T)}(\tilde{X}_k) \right| \tag{16}$$

If $E>\varepsilon$ then $T=T+1$ and go to step 3. If $E\leq\varepsilon$ then stop.

3 EXPERIMENTS ON AN ARTIFICIAL EXPERIMENTAL DATA SET

An artificial one-dimensional experimental data set $X = \left\{x_1, x_2, \ldots x_k, \ldots x_n\right\} \subset \mathbb{R}$ is constructed to analyse the convergence of the LVQ algorithm. The data set is constructed using 4 normally distributed clusters with mean 0, variance 1 and standard deviation 1 containing 20 data points each. These 4 data sets are then scaled with a factor of [0.01, 0.01, 0.01, 0.025] and an offset of [0.175, 0.275, 0.375, 0.800] respectively into the experimental data set of 80 points. This experimental data set is purposely constructed to yield 3 clusters that are close together but distinguishable and 1 cluster that is far away from the other 3 clusters. The artificial experimental data set I is shown in Figure 2.

3.1 Experiment using LVQ with Forced Termination

The initial one-dimensional weights of LVQ $V = \left\{v_1^{(0)}, v_2^{(0)}, \ldots v_j^{(0)}, \ldots v_c^{(0)}\right\}$ are initialized using (17) to $V^{(0)}$= [0.2375 0.4122 0.5869 0.7616] in order to consistently partition the data set evenly instead of using random initialization. LVQ is then trained using the experimental data set I with parameters c=4, α=0.1, λ=0.9, a termination error factor ε=0.0005.

$$v_j = \min_k\left(x_k\right) + \frac{j - \frac{1}{2}}{c}\left(\max_k\left(x_k\right) - \min_k\left(x_k\right)\right) \; \forall k = 1..n, j = 1..c \tag{17}$$

Figure 3. Plot of (a) Error and Total error and (b) weights of LVQ trained on artificial experimental data set I using α=0.1, λ=0.9, ε=0.0005

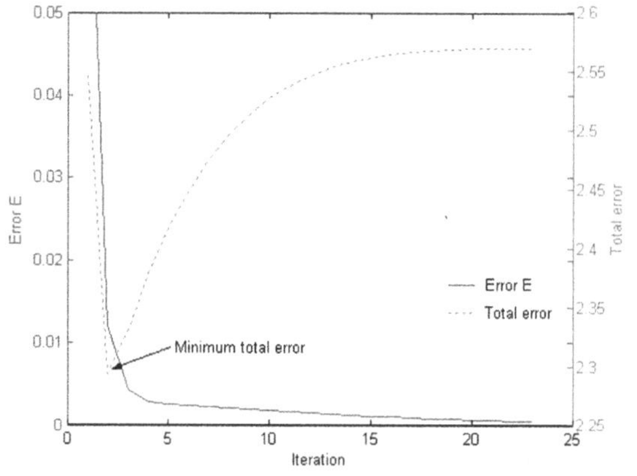

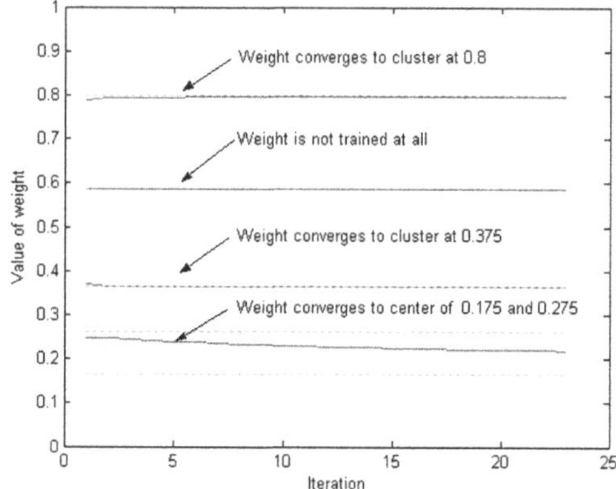

where

c = number of clusters
n = number of training data

Figure 3 shows the experimental results of the plot of error E and total error e of LVQ and its weights V during training, where E represents the error in (4) and e represents the total error between the data and the weights defined in (18). The training stopped after 23 iterations when $E<\varepsilon$ and the final total error obtained is e=2.5697. The final weights obtained are V= [0.1650, 0.3346, 0.5869, 0.7959] which shows a significant difference from the means of the data set.

$$e^{(T)} = \sum_{k=1}^{n} \left\| x_k - v_w^{(T)} \right\| \tag{18}$$

where

$$\left\| x_k - v_w^{(T)} \right\| = \min_j \left(\left\| x_k - v_j^{(T)} \right\| \right) \ \forall j = 1..c.$$

3.2 Experiment using LVQ with Unforced Termination

In another experiment, LVQ is trained using the same experimental data set I with parameters c=4 and ε=0.0005 but with different parameters α=0.0125 and λ=1.0. The training stopped after 25 iterations and the final total error obtained is e=2.5618. The final weights obtained are V=[0.2197 0.3646 0.5869 0.7979] which shows a significant difference from the means of the data set. Figure 4 shows the experimental results of the plot of error E and total error e of LVQ and its weights during training.

Figure 4. Plot of (a) Error and Total error (b) weights of LVQ trained on artificial experimental data set I using α=0.0125, λ=1.0, ε=0.00005

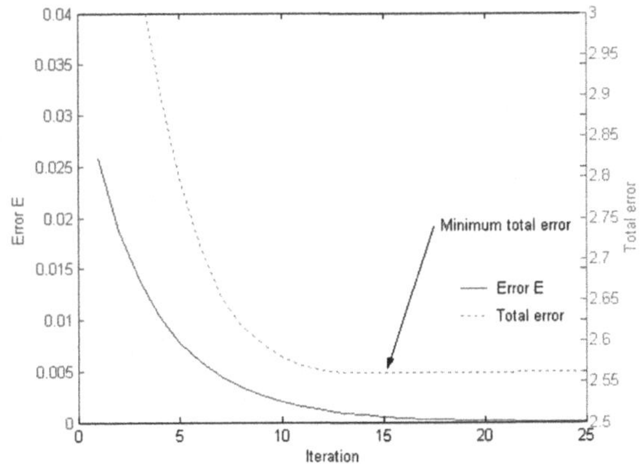

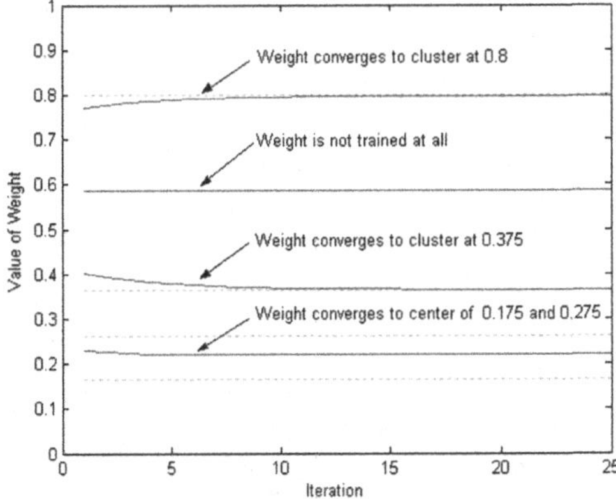

Comparing the results in Figures 3 and 4, the former shows LVQ trained using inappropriate training parameters as the total error increases rapidly after a minimum of total error is reached. The terminating condition of E<ε occurred in the training of LQV with both forced termination ($\lambda<1$) and unforced termination ($\lambda=1$) past the point where the minimum total error is reached. Figure 4b also shows that one of the weights is hardly changed throughout the training.

Generally, the following observations are made on the use of LVQ for the derivation of centroids for one-dimensional data set:

1. *Initialization*: LVQ requires a priori knowledge on the number of clusters and success depends heavily on the initial weights. Weights that are not properly intialized near the convex point of the data cluster will not converge to the center of the data cluster.
2. *Learning rate α and λ:* Different strategies of learning rate produces different results.
3. *Termination:* LVQ runs past its optimal solution in terms of the total error with both forced termination and unforced termination.

3.3 Experiment using GLVQ

In the next experiment, GLVQ is trained using the same artificial experimental data set I. To be consistent with the previous experiments, the initial weights of GLVQ are also initialized with (18) to $V^{(0)}$=[0.2375 0.4122 0.5869 0.7616]. GLVQ is then trained using the experimental data set I with parameters c=4, α=0.4, T=100, and a termination error factor ε=0.0005. The experiment using Euclidean D in (8) and (9) resulted in final weights that all converged to the same value of 0.2582. Better results are obtained when the distance D is modified to (19) for one-dimension data. Figure 5 shows the experimental results of the plot of error E and total error e of GLVQ and its weights V during training.

$$D = \sum_{j=1}^{c} \left| x - v_j \right| \tag{19}$$

Figure 5. Plot of (a) Error and total error; (b) weights of GLVQ trained on artificial experimental data set I using α=0.4, T=100, ε=0.0005

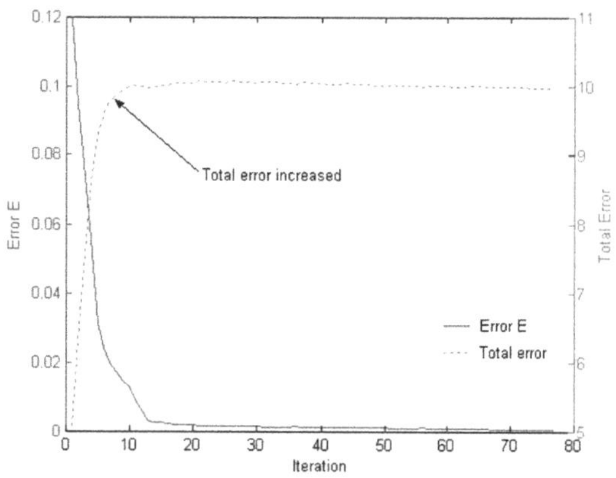

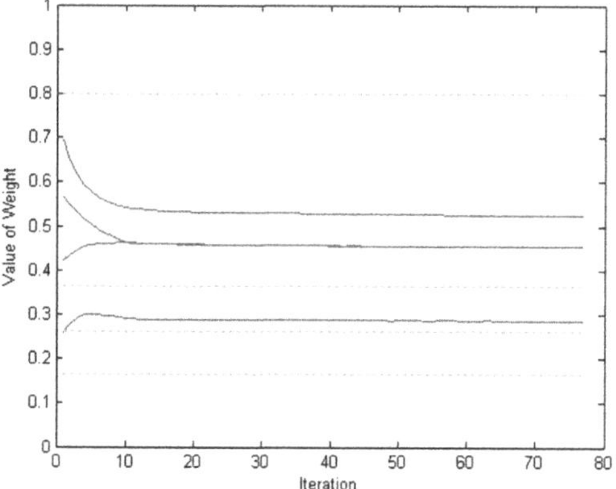

Comparing the results of Figures 4 and 5, GLVQ trained all the weight vectors whereas LVQ trained all but one weight vector. The weight vectors obtained from both algorithms are significantly different from the means of the data set. It was presented in (Karayiannis et al., 1996) that when $D<1$, GLVQ behaves opposite to what was desired, and a fix to GLVQ known as GLVQ-F algorithm was provided. Since the GLVQ-F algorithm uses a weights update equation that is similar to FCM, further experiments on GLVQ-F are not performed.

3.4 Experiment using FCM

In the next experiment, FCM is trained using the same artificial experimental data set I. Different runs of FCM give different results due to the random initialization of the FCM algorithm. Figures 6 and 7 shows the 2 different results obtained from FCM trained with the same experimental data using parameters m=2.0 and ε=0.0005.

In the former results, the training stops after 37 iterations with weights V=[0.1898 0.3495 0.7706 0.8206] that is significantly different from the means of data set. In the latter result, the training stops after 10 iterations with weights V=[0.1649 0.2626 0.3647 0.7988] that converges to the means of the data set. The probabilities of getting either the former or latter results are both 50% from 10 runs of the experiment. Comparing the very different experimental results in Figures 6 and 7 obtained from the FCM algorithm, the results show that the FCM algorithm is also sensitive to initialization. Convergence to the means of the one-dimensional artificial experimental data set is only achieved if the random initialization is suitable for convergence.

The artificial experimental data set I is purposely constructed to show the potential problem that surfaced in the derivation of centroids of one-dimensional data sets. Figure 8 shows a plot of the total and local cluster error of the artificial experimental data set. The results in Figures 3 and 4 show that 2 of the weights initialized to 0.3346 and 0.7959 trained using LVQ converged to 0.375 and 0.8 since when they fall within the convex surface of the respective local clusters. Although the weight that is initialized to 0.1650 falls within the convex surface of a local cluster, the absence of a weight initialized in the neighbouring cluster caused the weight to be trained to the means of two clusters. The weight

Figure 6. Plot of (a) Error and total error; (b) weights of FCM trained on artificial experimental data set I using m=2.0, ε=0.0005

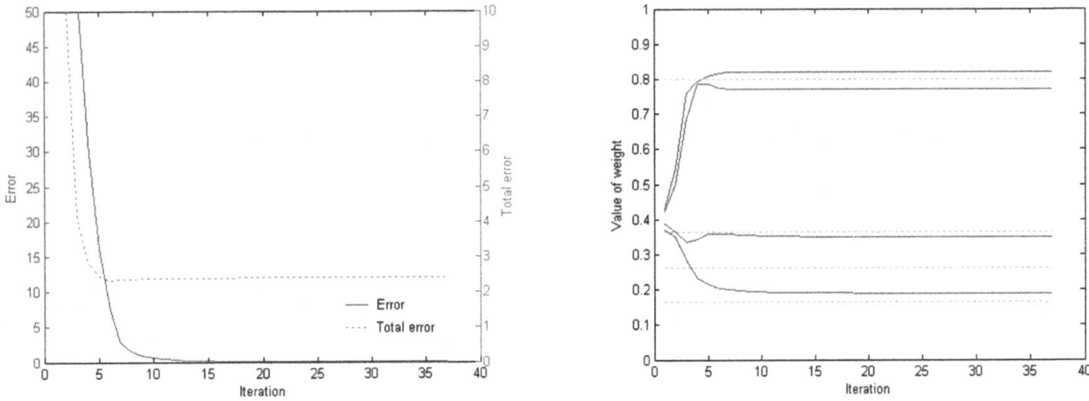

Figure 7. Plot of (a) Error and total error; (b) weights of another run of FCM trained on artificial experimental data set I using m=2.0, ε=0.0005

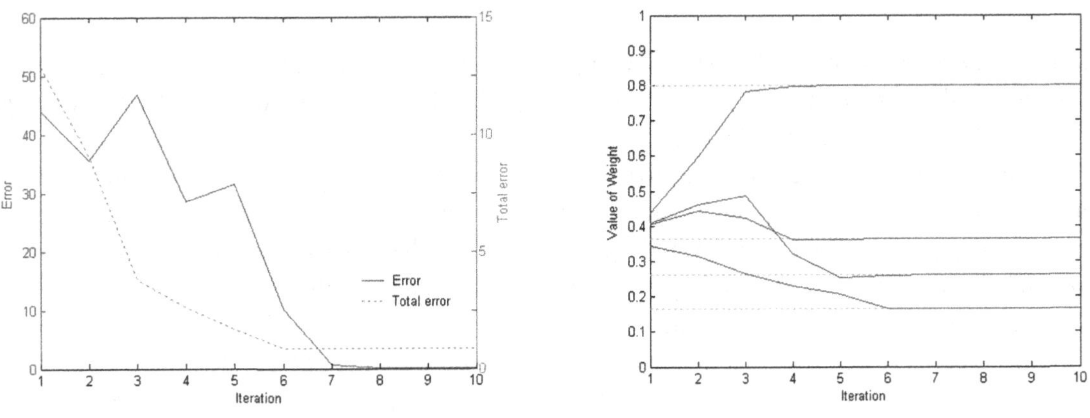

that is initialized to 0.5869 remains untrained because it falls outside the convex surface of all clusters. Therefore, the success of LVQ depends heavily on the initialization of weights.

4 MODIFIED LVQ

When we take a look at the distribution of the artificially generated experimental data set in Figure 2, we would be able to tell the number of clusters easily. The LVQ, GLVQ and FCM reviewed so far all require the a priori knowledge on the number of clusters. As illustrated in section 3, LVQ and GLVQ failed to converge to the centroids but FCM is able to converge to the centroids 50% of the time. However, FCM is much more computationally and memory intensive (Cheng et al., 1998) compared against LVQ. LVQ failed to converge because it depends heavily on the initialization of weights. This motivates the

Figure 8. Plot of total and local cluster error of artificial experimental data set

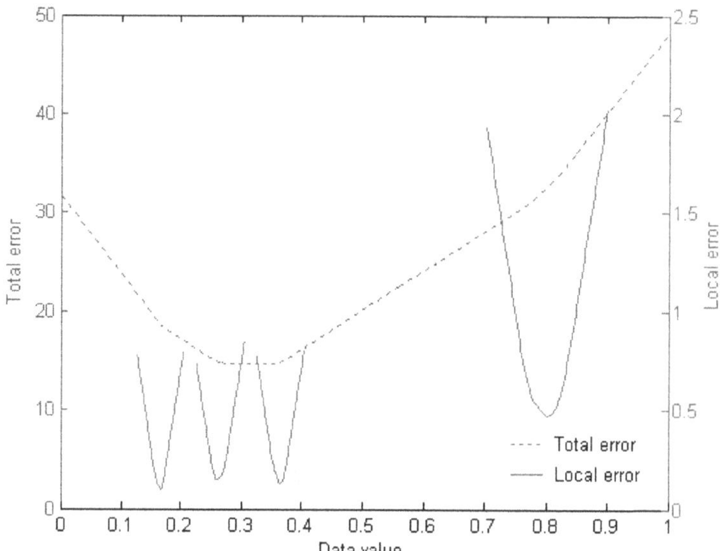

research to develop a modified LVQ that is computationally fast, able to automatically detect the number of clusters and initialize the weights in the convex surface of each local cluster so that it converges to the centroids of one-dimensional data.

Our matured brain is precisely wired to process sensory information into coherent patterns of activity that form the basis of our perception, thoughts and actions; but this precise wiring is not fully developed at birth (see chapter 60 in (Kandel, Schwartz, & Jessell, 1991)). The pattern of connections that emerges as a result of cell recognition events during prenatal development only roughly approximates the final wiring. This initially coarse pattern of connections is subsequently refined by activity dependant mechanisms that match precisely the pre-synaptic neurons. Thus the development of our nervous system proceeds in two overlapping stages. In the first stage, the basic architecture and coarse connections patterns are laid out without any activity-dependent processes. In the second stage, this initial architecture is refined in activity-dependent ways. Neural cell death is also an integral part of the development of the nervous system. A large overproduction of neurons is required to create the coarse pattern of connections. Active neurons stabilize through the uptake of trophic factors, whereas their unsuccessful competitors die. These findings in neuroscience inspired the idea of developing an algorithm with two overlapping stages similar to the development of our nervous system. The first stage creates the coarse pattern of neurons of architecture. Next, neurons that gather more trophic factors are identified and the rest removed. Now how should the initial coarse pattern look like, and what should be the trophic factor?

The Cerebellar Model Articulation Controller proposed in (Albus, 1975) is based on a neurophysiological model of the cerebellum. The CMAC modelled the high degree of regularity present in the organization of the cerebellar cortex (see chapter 41 in (Kandel et al., 1991)) and offers numerous advantages from the implementation point of view. A density-based clustering algorithm DBSCAN is proposed in (Ester, Kriegel, Sander, & Xu, 1996) that is designed to discover clusters of arbitrary shape. These two algorithms offered the insight of developing regularly spaced initial coarse pattern and using density as a torphic factor in the development of MLVQ for the discovery of clusters and weights initialization. A description of the Modified Learning Vector Quantization (MLQV) algorithm is given as follows:

MLVQ Algorithm

- **Step 1:** Initialize and select the algorithm parameters. Given data set $X = \{x_1, x_2, \ldots x_k, \ldots x_n\} \subset \mathbb{R}$, select the initial number of neurons, the pseudo potential threshold β, the terminating criterion ε and the maximum number of iterations T_{max}. Initialize the learning constant α=1/n, and the number of clusters c=0.
- **Step 2:** Construct the initial architecture with m regularly spaced neurons. Compute $\min_x$, $\max_x$ and gap_x using (20) to (22). Initialise all neuron weights $V = \{v_1^{(0)}, v_2^{(0)}, \ldots v_j^{(0)}, \ldots v_m^{(0)}\}$ and pseudo weights $V^P = \{v_1^P, v_2^P, \ldots v_j^P, \ldots v_m^P\}$ using (23).

$$\min_x = \min_k \left(x_k\right) \ \forall k = 1..n \tag{20}$$

$$\max_x = \max_k \left(x_k\right) \ \forall k = 1..n \tag{21}$$

$$gap_x = \frac{\max_x - \min_x}{m} \tag{22}$$

$$v_j^{(0)} = \min_x + \left(j - \tfrac{1}{2}\right)\left(gap_x\right),\ v_j^P = 0 \ \forall j = 1..m \tag{23}$$

- **Step 3:** Perform one-pass pseudo weight learning to discover density distribution of training data. For k=1..n:
  a. Due to the regularity of the initialized weights, the winner w can easily be found using (24).

$$w = \left\lfloor \frac{x_k - \min_x}{gap_x} \right\rfloor + 1 \tag{24}$$

  b. Find the distance D_w from the winner using (25).

$$D_w = x_k - v_w^{(0)} \tag{25}$$

  c. Determine runner-up neuron r using (26).

$$r = \begin{cases} w-1 & \text{if } \ D_w < 0 \text{ and } \left(w - 1\right) \geq 1 \\ \varnothing & \text{if } \ D_w = 0 \text{ or } \left(w - 1\right) < 1 \text{ or } \left(w+1\right) > m \\ w+1 & \text{if } \ D_w > 0 \text{ and } \left(w+1\right) \leq m \end{cases} \tag{26}$$

where ∅ represents the null value. r=∅ means there is no runner-up neuron, and this occurs when the distance to the winning neuron is 0 or the determined runner-up neuron r falls outside the range of 1 to m. Step 3c uses only one runner-up neuron and addresses the situation where no runner-up neuron can be found. Since this algorithm is generally applied to each individual dimension of the data, one runner-up neuron suffices.

d. Update pseudo weights of winner w and runner up r using (27) and (28).

$$v_w^p = \begin{cases} v_w^p + \left(1 - \frac{|D_w|}{gap_x}\right)\alpha & \text{if } r \neq \varnothing \\ v_w^p + \alpha & \text{if } r = \varnothing \end{cases} \tag{27}$$

$$v_r^p = v_r^p + \left(\frac{|D_w|}{gap_x}\right)\alpha \quad \text{if } r \neq \varnothing \tag{28}$$

End for k

- **Step 4:** Identify neurons with high trophic factors from their psuedo weights and remove the remaining neurons.

a. Initialise $V^{(1)}$=∅, i=∅, d=0.

For j=1..m:

b. Find the neuron with the highest pseudo weight using (29).

$$i = j,\ \ d = v_j^p \ \text{ if } \ v_j^p > (d + \beta) \tag{29}$$

where β is the selected pseudo potential threshold used to identify pseudo weight v_j^p that is significantly larger than d by the value β. This step 4b finds the neuron with the pseudo weight v_j^p that is larger than $d+\beta$ in the for loop above starting from neuron j=1 to m. Initially, d is initialized to 0, so if neuron i with pseudo weight $v_i^p \leq \beta$, then i=∅. In subsequent iterations, if neuron i with pseudo weight $v_i^p > \beta$ is found, then the value d is updated to $d = v_i^p$. This step then continues to find the neuron with pseudo weight $v_j^p > d+\beta$ in subsequent iterations from $j=i$ to m.

c. Identify neurons with high trophic factor that exhibit a characteristic drop in pseudo weight using (30) and assign weights of these neurons as $V^{(1)}$ and the number of neurons with high trophic factors as c.

$$v_i \in V^{(1)},\ c = c + 1,\ i = \varnothing \ \text{ if } i \neq \varnothing \text{ and } v_j^p < (d - \beta) \tag{30}$$

where β is the selected pseudo potential threshold used to identify pseudo weight v_j^p that is significantly lesser than d by the value β. If step 4b does not find the neuron with the pseudo weight

v_i^p that is larger than $d+\beta$, then $i=\varnothing$. If this is the case, then step 4.c assigns the weight v_i to $V^{(1)}$ if $v_i^p<(d-\beta)$.

d. Update lowest pseudo weight detected using (31)

$$d = v_j^p \text{ if } i = \varnothing,\ v_j^p < d \tag{31}$$

End for j

- **Step 5:** Iteratively refine the surviving neurons weights V^p using LVQ. For $T=1..T_{max}$

a. Initialise $e^{(1)}=0$.

For $k = 1..n$:

b. Find the winner w using (32).

$$\left\| x_k - v_w^{(T)} \right\| = \min_j \left(\left\| x_k - v_j^{(T)} \right\| \right) \ \forall j = 1..c, x_k \in X, v_j \in V^{(1)} \tag{32}$$

c. Update weights of the winner w with (33).

$$v_w^{(T+1)} = v_w^{(T)} + \alpha(x_k - v_w^{(T)}) \tag{33}$$

d. Compute $e^{(T+1)}$ using (34).

$$e^{(T+1)} = e^{(T)} + \left\| x_k - v_w^{(T)} \right\| \tag{34}$$

End for k

e. Compare $e^{(T+1)}$ and $e^{(T)}$ using (35).

$$\Delta e^{(T+1)} = e^{(T+1)} - e^{(T)} \tag{35}$$

f. If $\Delta e^{(T+1)} \leq \varepsilon$ stop

End for T

In MLVQ step 1, the learning constant is initialized using the number of training tuples n. In step 2, MLVQ models the first-stage development process of our nervous system by constructing an initial coarse connection pattern using a large overproduction of neurons without any activity-dependent processes. MLVQ constructs this initial architecture with m regularly spaced neurons that span the input space based on the concept of regularity in CMAC. Next in steps 3 and 4, MLVQ models the second-stage development process of our nervous system by identifying active neurons with high trophic factors. In step 3, MLVQ first performs a one-pass pseudo weight learning to obtain a density distribution of the training data. In step 4, the neurons whose pseudo weights form convex density peaks are identified as neurons with high trophic factors that survived while the remaining neurons are removed. These surviving neurons' weights then form the initial weights for further weight refinements in step 5. The operation of step 5 is fundamentally LVQ with a modification to the terminating condition so that convergence can be achieved and easily detected.

4.1 Results using the MLVQ Algorithm

In this experiment, the proposed MLVQ is trained using the same artificial experimental data set I with parameters α=0.0125 (selected from $1/n$ where n=80), β=0.025, m=20, ε=0.00005 and a maximum iteration of T=100. Figure 9 shows the plot of the V^p trained after executing MLVQ step 3 on the artificial experimental data set. After executing MLVQ step 4, the initial weights are identified from convex peaks of pseudo weights as $V^{(1)}$=[0.1677, 0.2725, 0.3773, 0.7616].

Figure 10 shows the experimental results of the change in total error Δe and total error e of MLVQ and its weights during training. The training stopped after 20 iterations and the final weights obtained are V=[0.2190 0.3645 0.5869 0.7979] which is significantly similar to the means of the data set.

Figure 9. Plot of pseudo weights after MLVQ step 3 trained with the artificial experimental data set I

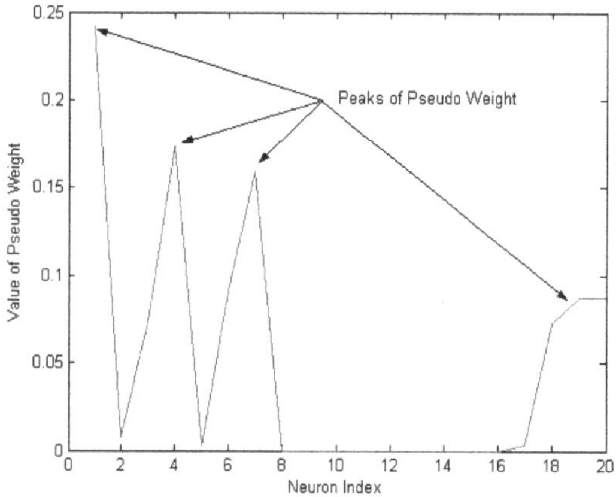

Figure 10. Plot of (a) Change in total error and total error (b) weights of MLVQ trained on artificial experimental data set I using α=0.0125, β=0.025, m=20, ε=0.00005 and T=100

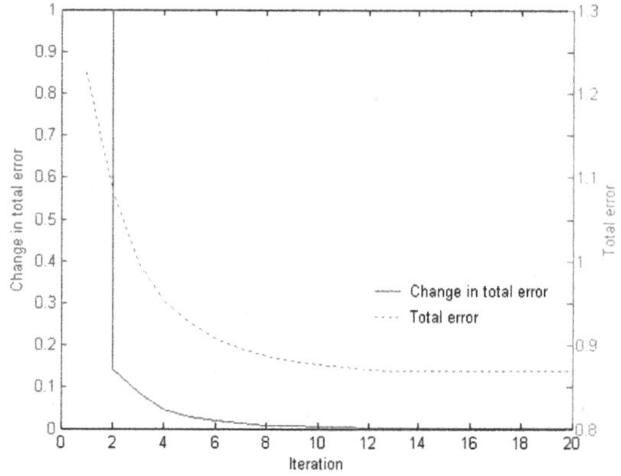

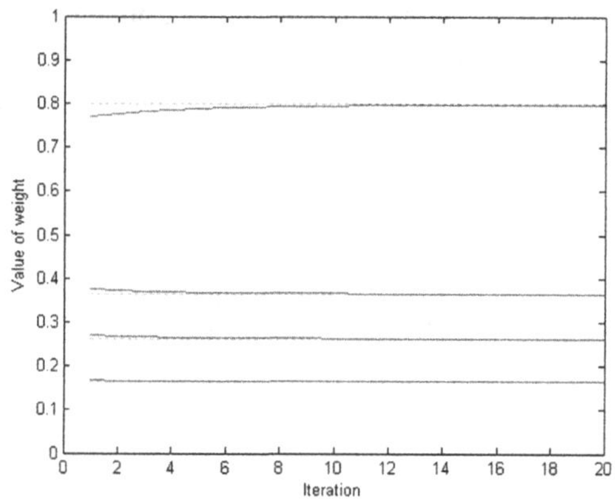

Comparing the results in Figures 3 and 10, the terminating condition of MLVQ which is change in total error $\Delta e < \varepsilon$ occurred at the point where the total error is at its minimum. However, the terminating condition of LVQ which is change in weight vector $E<\varepsilon$ occurred at the point where the total error is not at its minimum. This shows that the terminating condition of MLVQ stops the training at the optimal point but the terminating condition of LVQ does not stop the training at the optimal point. In addition, as MLVQ initializes the weights to the convex means of the training data, MLVQ terminates with a lesser total error of e=0.8688 whereas LVQ terminates with e=2.5697. To check whether the sequence of training data affects the convergence of MLVQ, further experiments were conducted with randomized sequences of the artificial experimental data set I. The randomized sequences are generated by several iterations of data point values exchanges with randomly selected data points. Figure 11 shows one of the randomized sequences of the artificial experimental data set I.

In this experiment, MLVQ is trained using the randomized sequence of the artificial experimental data I. Experimental results give a convergence to the weights V=[0.1649 0.2627 0.3646 0.7984] in 23 iterations, which is about the same weights V as shown in Figure 10b. Repeated experiments with different sequences are also performed. Although these repeated experiments converged in different number of iterations, they give consistent convergence to about the same weights. This shows that the convergence of MLVQ is not sensitive to the sequence of the training data.

Another experimental data set is constructed to further investigate the ability of MLVQ to detect the number of clusters of overlapped clusters, the sensitivity of MLVQ to magnitude of the data set and to outliners. The data set is constructed using 5 normally distributed clusters with mean 0, variance 1 and standard deviation 1 containing 200 data points each. These 5 data sets are all scaled with a factor of 0.5 and an offset of [2.0, 4.0, 6.0, 10.0, 12.0] respectively into the experimental data set of 1000 points. Next, 10 random outliners with values in the range of 0 to 20.0 are then added to the data set to for the artificial data set of 1010 points. The artificial experimental data set II is shown in Figure 12.

In the next experiment, MLVQ is trained using the artificial experimental data set II with parameters m=40, α=0.00099 (selected from 1/n where n=1010), β=0.025, ε=0.00005 and T=100. Figure 13 shows the plot of the pseudo weights V^p trained after executing MLVQ step 3 on the artificial experimental data set II.

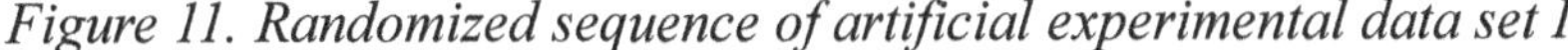
Figure 11. Randomized sequence of artificial experimental data set I

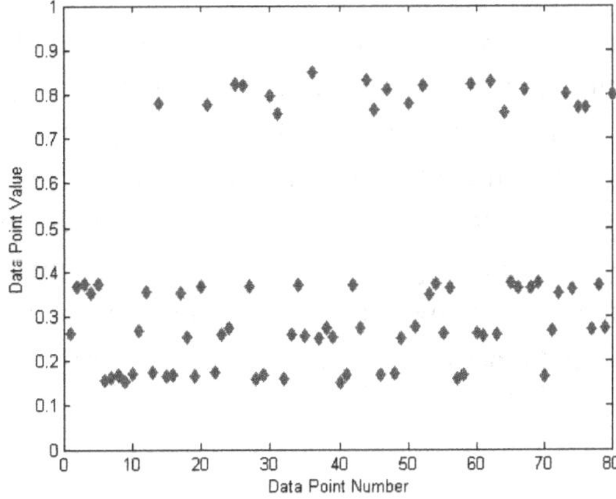

Figure 12. Artificial experimental data set II

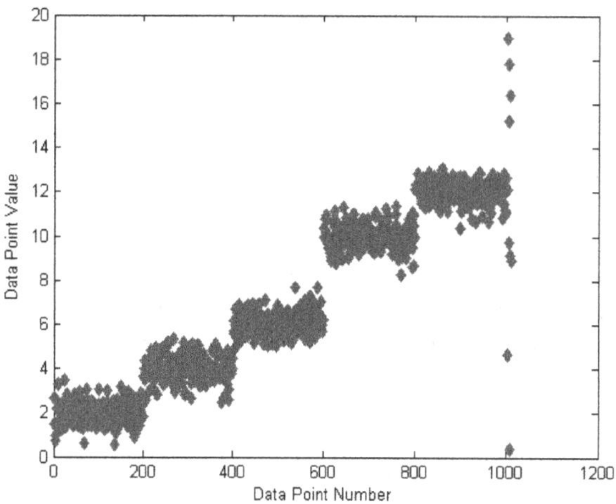

Figure 13. Plot of pseudo weights after MLVQ step 3 trained with artificial experimental data set II

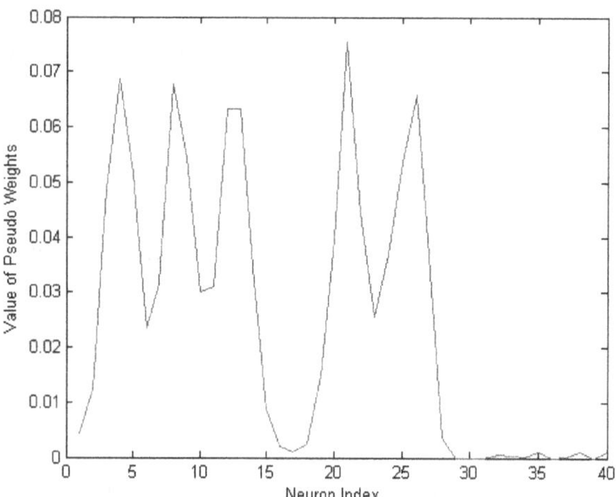

After executing MLVQ step 4, 5 convex peaks of pseudo weights are identified. Figure 14 shows the experimental results of the change in total error Δe and total error e of MLVQ and its weight V during training. The training stopped after 20 iterations and the final weights obtained are V=[1.9870 4.0128 6.0192 9.9480 12.1322] which is significantly similar to the means of the data set. This experimental results show that MLVQ is able to detect the number of clusters even when clusters overlapped. As the data point values of this data set is in the range of 0 to 20 compared against the range of 0 to 1 in artificial experimental data set I, the results show that MLVQ is not sensitive to the magnitude of the data set. Results also show that MLVQ did not mistakenly create additional clusters for outliners in the data set.

Figure 14. Plot of (a) Change in total error and total error (b) weights of MLVQ trained on artificial experimental data set II using α=0.00099, β=0.025, m=40, ε=0.00005 and T=100

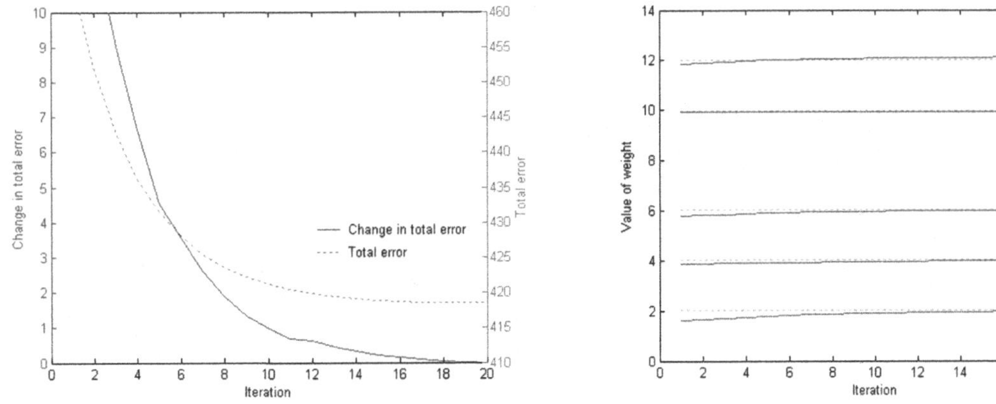

5 APPLICATION EXPERIMENTS

Further experiments were conducted to analyse the effectiveness of the centroids derived using MLVQ. The centroids derived were used to form Gaussian membership functions and results on clustering performance of POPFNN-CRI(S) (Ang et al., 2003) using these Gaussian membership functions are presented. The Gaussian membership functions are derived using (36) and (37) with the width parameter δ.

$$\mu(x_j) = e^{-\left(\frac{x-v_j}{\sigma}\right)^2} \tag{36}$$

$$\sigma = \delta\left(v_j - v_{closest}\right), \quad v_{closest} = \begin{cases} v_{j-1} \text{ if } \left|v_j - v_{j-1}\right| < \left|v_j - v_{j+1}\right| \\ v_{j+1} \text{ if } \left|v_j - v_{j-1}\right| > \left|v_j - v_{j+1}\right| \end{cases} \tag{37}$$

where

$\mu(x_j)$ = membership of x with respect to label j
δ = Gaussian membership width factor

5.1 Pattern Classification using Anderson Iris Data

Anderson's Iris data (Fisher, 1936) is used as the first experimental data set. This data set contains 50 vectors in R^4 for 3 classes of IRIS subspecies. The data set is available from (Frank & Asuncion, 2010) and has been used extensively to illustrate various clustering properties. Typical classification errors with the use of the entire data set for both training and evaluation for supervised clustering are 0-5 and for unsupervised clustering are 10-15 (Tsao et al., 1994). This data set is selected since membership functions derived from this data set are available for comparison (Ang et al., 2003) (Quek & Tung, 2001). In this experiment, MLVQ is trained using each individual input dimension of the data set with param-

Figure 15. Input Gaussian membership functions of Iris data set derived using MLVQ algorithm

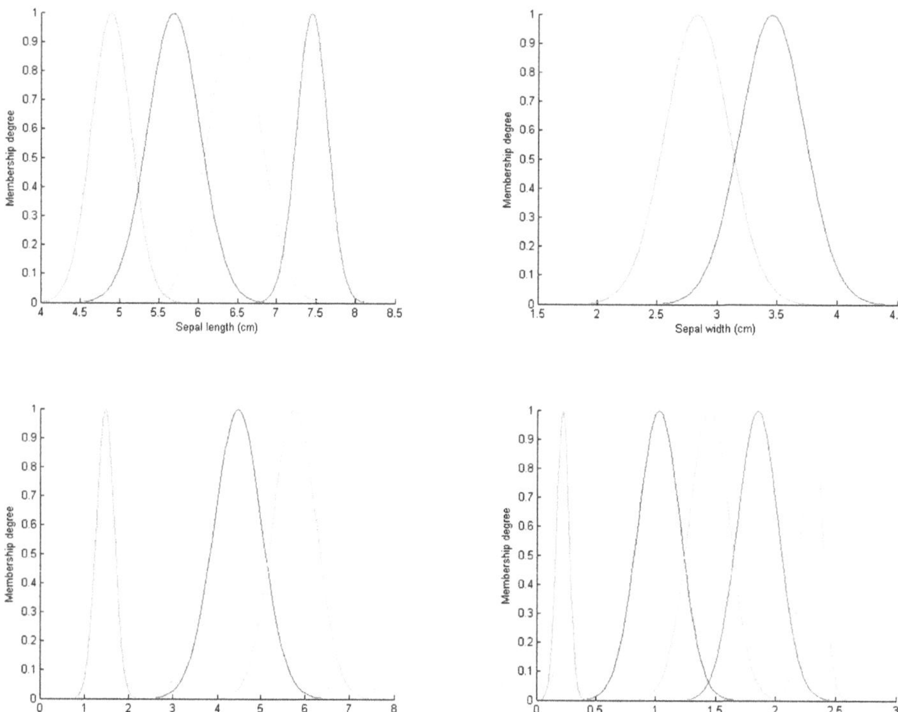

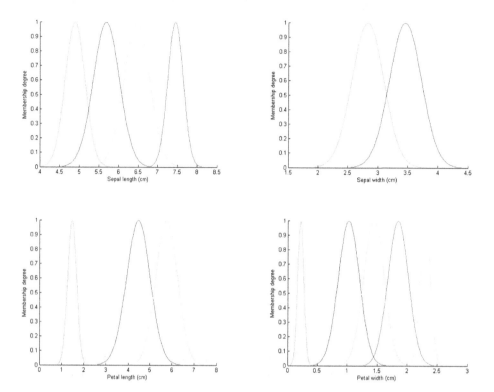

eters α=0.0067 (selected from $1/n$ where n=150), β=0.01, m=20, ε=0.00005 and a maximum iteration of T_{max}=100. Results obtained from after using MLVQ algorithm gives 4, 2, 3 and 5 centroids for each input and Gaussian membership functions are derived using δ=0.6. Figure 15 shows the membership functions derived for each individual input dimension.

The three classes of Iris subspecies are represented as Setosa=1, Versicolor=2 and Virginica=3 and singleton output membership functions are used as in (Ang et al., 2003). The POP learning algorithm (Quek & Zhou, 2001) is then used to derive the fuzzy rules based on the input and output membership functions. Figure 16 shows a plot of the classification results obtained against the Iris classes. The classification results from the POPFNN-CRI(S) give a range of values for classes 2 and 3 and a single value of 1 for class 1 because the nature of the Iris data set is such that class 1 can be linearly separated from the other two but classes 2 and 3 are not linearly separable from each other. To interpret the range of values obtained for classes 2 and 3, values less than 2.5 are considered classified as class 2 and values greater than 2.5 are considered classified as class 3. Classification results with value of 2.5 are considered unclassified. The results give 146 correctly classified patterns, 2 wrongly classified patterns and 2 unclassified patterns.

The membership functions for each individual input dimension of the Iris data set obtained in (Ang et al., 2003; Quek & Zhou, 2001) are restricted to the specified c=3 clusters. In contrast, the membership functions derived using MLVQ algorithm derives different number of clusters for each input from the training data. This gives the MLVQ algorithm a stronger advantage since the suitable number of clusters for each individual input dimension for a set of data may not be the same for all inputs.

Figure 16. Classification results of Iris data using POPFNN-CRI(S) with Gaussian input membership functions derived using MLVQ

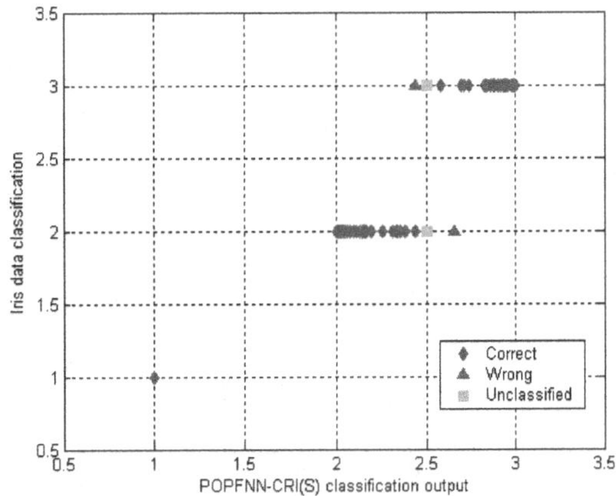

5.2 Time-Series Prediction using Mackey-Glass Differential Equation

The chaotic Mackey-Glass differential equation defined in (38) is used as the second experimental data set. Time series prediction is a very important practical problem with a diverse range of application from economic and business planning to signal processing and control. The prediction of future values of this series has been used extensively as a benchmark problem. This problem can be approached using recurrent fuzzy neural network with the problem formulated as given values $y(T-m)$, $y(T-m+1),\ldots,$ $y(T-1)$; determine $y(T-1+n)$ where m and n are fixed positive integers and T is the series index. There are several approaches to this problem. (Wang & Mendel, 1992) uses m=9 and n=1 and (Maguire, Roche, McGinnity, & McDaid, 1998) uses a range of m=6, m=9 and n=1, 2 and 4. In this experiment, the approach of m=6 and n=1 is used with τ=17 and an initial condition of $y(0)$=1.2. Figure 17 shows the first 1200 points of the experimental data set.

$$\frac{dy(t)}{dt} = \frac{0.2y(t-\tau)}{1+y^{10}(t-\tau)} - 0.1y(t) \tag{38}$$

The MLVQ algorithm is trained using 700 data points of each individual input and output dimension of the data set from T=6 to T=705 with parameters α=0.0014 (selected from $1/n$ where n=700), β=0.004, m=50, ε=0.00005 and a maximum iteration of T_{max}=100. Results obtained from after using MLVQ algorithm give 8 identical centroids for inputs $y(T\text{-}1)$, $y(T\text{-}2)$, $y(T\text{-}3)$ and outputs $y(T)$ and 7 identical centroids for inputs $y(T\text{-}4)$, $y(T\text{-}5)$, $y(T\text{-}6)$. Gaussian membership functions are derived using δ=0.6. Figure 18 shows the membership functions derived for each individual input and output dimensions. The POP learning algorithm is then used to derive the fuzzy rules based on the input and output membership functions. A further 300 untrained data points from T=706 to T=1005 is used as the test data set to assess the prediction results.

Figure 19 shows that the predicted and actual points of the untrained Mackey-Glass series test data set from T=706 to T=1005. The results show that the predicted and actual points are mostly similar

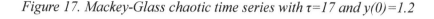

Figure 17. Mackey-Glass chaotic time series with τ=17 and y(0)=1.2

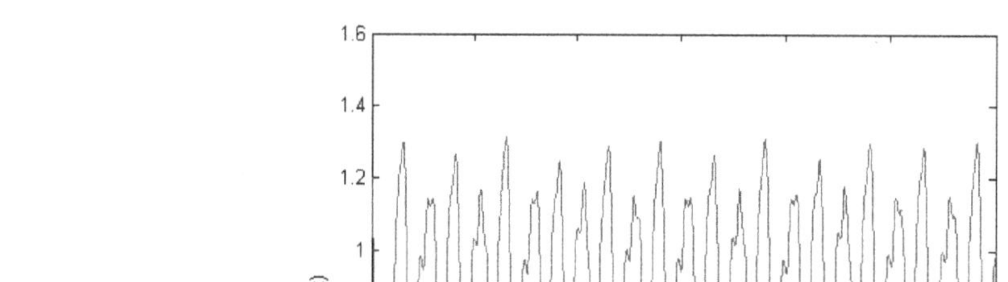

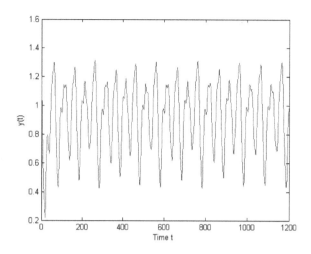

Figure 18. Input and Output Gaussian membership functions of Mackey-Glass data set derived using MLVQ algorithm

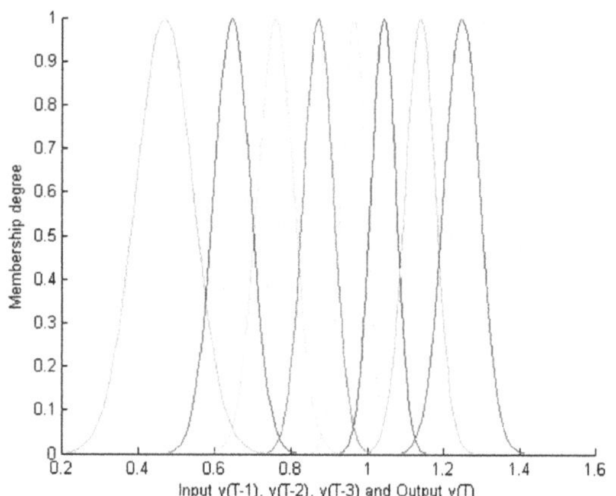

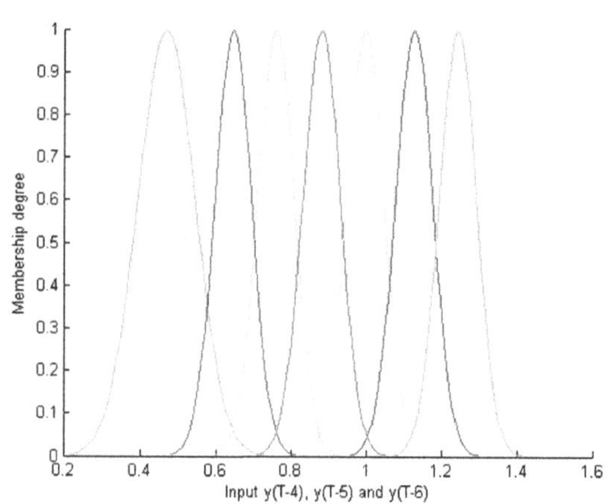

except for values greater than 1.25. The results are also evaluated in terms of the accuracy of the prediction using the Pearson product-moment correlation value (denoted as R^2) and root mean square error (denoted as RMSE). R^2=0.9886 and RMSE=0.0293 are obtained for this experiment. Since POPFNN-CRI(S) uses the Gaussian input and output membership function derived using the MLVQ algorithm and fuzzy rules derived using single-pass POP learning algorithm without further tuning of rules or membership function using back-propagation training, the results show that the membership functions obtained are effective in the area of time series prediction.

Figure 19. Predicted y(t) and actual y(t) of the Mackey-Glass series using POPFNN-CRI(S)

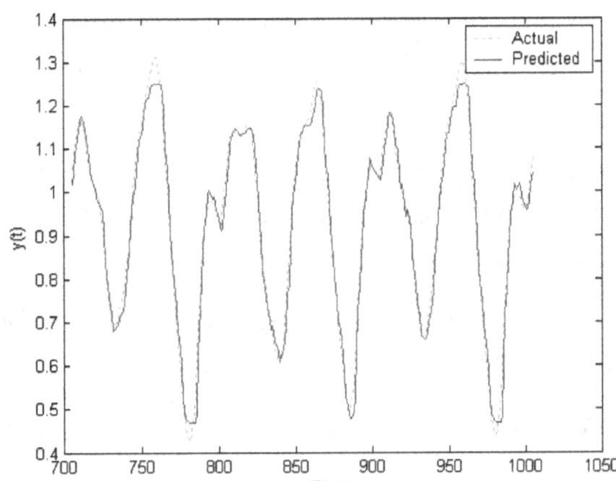

6 CONCLUSION

In this work, a Modified Learning Vector Quantization (MLVQ) algorithm is proposed to determine the cluster centers of training data for the derivation of fuzzy membership functions. Experimental results using LVQ, GLVQ and FCM on artificially generated one-dimensional data set show that these algorithms require a priori knowledge on number of clusters and they have difficulties in converging to the centroids of the training data. Experimental results on the same data set show that the MLVQ algorithm is able to determine the number of clusters and converge to the centroids of the training data. Further experiments on artificially generated experimental data sets show that the MLVQ algorithm is insensitive to the sequence and magnitude of the training data, able to correctly identify centroids of overlapped clusters and able to handle outliners without identifying them as clusters. Thus MLVQ is able to converge to the centroids of the training data, and addressed the problem associated with the selection of number of clusters, initial weight vectors, the sequence of training data, training parameters and the forced termination condition imposed on the LVQ algorithm using one-dimensional training data. Application results using POPFNN-CRI(S) on pattern classification of Anderson's Iris data and the prediction of Mackey-Glass chaotic time series are presented. The results show that the Gaussian membership functions derived using MLVQ are effective in the both areas.

POPFNN-CRI(S) (Ang et al., 2003) is a member of a class of fuzzy neural networks based on strong fuzzy logical inference (TVR, AARS, Yager) (Quek & Singh, 2005; Quek & Zhou, 1999; Zhou & Quek, 1996). The POP learning algorithm (Quek & Zhou, 2001) is used in this class of fuzzy neural network to objectively derive the fuzzy rules describing a problem domain. These POPFNN networks are self-organizing but suffer from offline clustering techniques that require a priori knowledge of number of clusters to derive the fuzzy membership functions. The proposed MLVQ algorithm is an initial attempt to merge the benefits of on-line CMAC with Fuzzy Neural Network to support online modeling of the decision making rules. Future work also includes the extension of the algorithm in clustering multi-dimension data sets with multi-centre clusters.

7 REFERENCES

Albus, J. S. (1975). A new approach to manipulator control: The Cerebellar Model Articulation Controller (CMAC). *Journal of Dynamic Systems, Measurement and Control. Transactions of the ASME, 97*, 270–277.

Ang, K. K., Quek, C., & Pasquier, M. (2003). POPFNN-CRI(S): Pseudo outer product based fuzzy neural network using the compositional rule of inference and singleton fuzzifier. *IEEE Transactions on Systems, Man and Cybernetics. Part B, 33*(6), 838–849.

Baraldi, A., & Blonda, P. (1999). A survey of fuzzy clustering algorithms for pattern recognition. *IEEE Transactions on Systems, Man and Cybernetics. Part B, 29*(6), 778–785.

Bezdek, J. C. (Ed.). (1981). *Pattern recognition with fuzzy objective function algorithms*. New York, NY: Plenum Press.

Bezdek, J. C., Hathaway, R. J., & Tucker, W. T. (1987). An improved convergence theory for the fuzzy c-means clustering algorithms. In Bezdek, J. C. (Ed.), *Analysis of fuzzy information* (*Vol. 3*, pp. 123–129). Boca Raton, FL: CRC Press.

Cheng, T. W., Goldgof, D. B., & Hall, L. O. (1998). Fast fuzzy clustering. *Fuzzy Sets and Systems, 93*(1), 49–56. doi:10.1016/S0165-0114(96)00232-1

Choe, H., & Jordan, J. B. (1992). *On the optimal choice of parameters in a fuzzy c-means algorithm*. IEEE International Conference on Fuzzy Systems, (pp. 349-354).

Ester, M., Kriegel, H.-P., Sander, J., & Xu, X. (1996). A density-based algorithm for discovering clusters in large spatial databases with noise. *Proceedings of 2nd International Conference on Knowledge Discovery and Data Mining (KDD-96)*, (pp. 226-231).

Fisher, R. A. (1936). The use of multiple measurement in taxonomic problems. *Annals of Eugenics, 7*, 179–188.

Frank, A., & Asuncion, A. (2010). *UCI machine learning repository*. Retrieved from http://archive.ics.uci.edu/ml

Gupta, M. M., & Rao, D. H. (1994). On the principles of fuzzy neural networks. *Fuzzy Sets and Systems, 61*(1), 1–18. doi:10.1016/0165-0114(94)90279-8

Kandel, E. R., Schwartz, J. H., & Jessell, T. M. (1991). *Principles of neural science* (3rd ed.). New Jersey: Prentice Hall.

Karayiannis, N. B., Bezdek, J. C., Pal, N. R., Hathaway, R. J., & Pai, P.-I. (1996). Repairs to GLVQ: A new family of competitive learning schemes. *IEEE Transactions on Neural Networks, 7*(5), 1062–1071. doi:10.1109/72.536304

Kohonen, T. (1989). *Self-organization and associative memory* (3rd ed.). Berlin, Germany & New York, NY: Springer-Verlag.

Kohonen, T. (1990). *Improved versions of learning vector quantization.* IJCNN International Joint Conference on Neural Networks, (pp. 545-550).

Li, R.-P., Mukaidono, M., & Turksen, I. B. (2002). A fuzzy neural network for pattern classification and feature selection. *Fuzzy Sets and Systems, 130*(1), 101–108.

Lin, C.-T. (1995). A neural fuzzy control system with structure and parameter learning. *Fuzzy Sets and Systems, 70*(2-3), 183–212. doi:10.1016/0165-0114(94)00216-T

Lin, C.-T., & Lee, C. S. G. (1996). *Neural fuzzy systems: A neuro-fuzzy synergism to intelligent systems.* Upper Saddle River, NJ: Prentice Hall.

Maguire, L. P., Roche, B., McGinnity, T. M., & McDaid, L. J. (1998). Predicting a chaotic time series using a fuzzy neural network. *Information Sciences, 112*(1-4), 125–136. doi:10.1016/S0020-0255(98)10026-9

Pal, N. R., Bezdek, J. C., & Tsao, E. C.-K. (1993). Generalized clustering networks and Kohonen's self-organizing scheme. *IEEE Transactions on Neural Networks, 4*(4), 549–557. doi:10.1109/72.238310

Quek, C., & Singh, A. (2005). POP-Yager: A novel self-organizing fuzzy neural network based on the Yager inference. *Expert Systems with Applications, 29*(1), 229–242. doi:10.1016/j.eswa.2005.03.001

Quek, C., & Tung, W. L. (2001). A novel approach to the derivation of fuzzy membership functions using the Falcon-MART architecture. *Pattern Recognition Letters, 22*(9), 941–958. doi:10.1016/S0167-8655(01)00033-2

Quek, C., & Zhou, R. W. (1999). POPFNN-AAR(S): A pseudo outer-product based fuzzy neural network. *IEEE Transactions on Systems, Man and Cybernetics. Part B, 29*(6), 859–870.

Quek, C., & Zhou, R. W. (2001). The POP learning algorithms: Reducing work in identifying fuzzy rules. *Neural Networks, 14*(10), 1431–1445. doi:10.1016/S0893-6080(01)00118-6

Rhee, H.-S., & Oh, K.-W. (1996). Unsupervised learning network based on gradient descent procedure of fuzzy objective function. *IEEE International Conference on Neural Networks, 3*, 1427-1432.

Tsao, E. C.-K., Bezdek, J. C., & Pal, N. R. (1994). Fuzzy Kohonen clustering networks. *Pattern Recognition, 27*(5), 757–764. doi:10.1016/0031-3203(94)90052-3

Wang, L.-X., & Mendel, J. M. (1992). Generating fuzzy rules by learning from examples. *IEEE Transactions on Systems, Man, and Cybernetics, 22*(6), 1414–1427. doi:10.1109/21.199466

Yair, E., Zeger, K., & Gersho, A. (1992). Competitive learning and soft competition for vector quantizer design. *IEEE Transactions on Signal Processing, 40*(2), 294–309. doi:10.1109/78.124940

Zhou, R. W., & Quek, C. (1996). POPFNN: A Pseudo Outer-product Based Fuzzy Neural Network. *Neural Networks, 9*(9), 1569–1581. doi:10.1016/S0893-6080(96)00027-5

Chapter 20
Outlier Detection in Linear Regression

A. A. M. Nurunnabi
University of Rajshahi, Bangladesh

A. H. M. Rahmatullah Imon
Ball State University, USA

A. B. M. Shawkat Ali
Central Queensland University, Australia

Mohammed Nasser
University of Rajshahi, Bangladesh

ABSTRACT

Regression analysis is one of the most important branches of multivariate statistical techniques. It is widely used in almost every field of research and application in multifactor data, which helps to investigate and to fit an unknown model for quantifying relations among observed variables. Nowadays, it has drawn a large attention to perform the tasks with neural networks, support vector machines, evolutionary algorithms, et cetera. Till today, least squares (LS) is the most popular parameter estimation technique to the practitioners, mainly because of its computational simplicity and underlying optimal properties. It is well-known by now that the method of least squares is a non-resistant fitting process; even a single outlier can spoil the whole estimation procedure. Data contamination by outlier is a practical problem which certainly cannot be avoided. It is very important to be able to detect these outliers. The authors are concerned about the effect outliers have on parameter estimates and on inferences about models and their suitability. In this chapter the authors have made a short discussion of the most well known and efficient outlier detection techniques with numerical demonstrations in linear regression. The chapter will help the people who are interested in exploring and investigating an effective mathematical model. The goal is to make the monograph self-contained maintaining its general accessibility.

DOI: 10.4018/978-1-60960-551-3.ch020

INTRODUCTION

With the remarkable development of computer and information technologies, the number of databases, as well as their volume, dimensionality and complexity grow rapidly, resulting in the analysis of outliers in heterogeneous structured data. When analyzing data, some observations are often occurred that are different from the majority. Generally such observations are called outliers. Sometimes, the outlying observations are not incorrect rather they are made under exceptional circumstances, or they belong to other population(s). So identification of outliers is often by itself the primary goal, without any intention of a regression model. Outlier detection has been suggested for numerous applications, such as credit and fraud detection, clinical trials, medical imaging, voting irregularity analysis, network intrusion, severe weather prediction, geographic information system, and other data mining tasks.

At the beginning, different methods were originally developed arbitrarily in individual fields, but now the systematic approaches are used for outlier detection from the full gamut of computer science and statistics. Machine learning community has shown growing interest in outlier detection. Kernel based methods (Breiman *et al.*, 1977; Terrell & Scott, 1992), distance-based methods (Knorr *et al.*, 2000; Angiulli *et al.*, 2006), density-based methods (Breunig *et al.*, 2000), support vector machines (Eskin *et al.*, 2002) and neural networks (Barron, 1993, 1994; Hawkins *et al.*, 2002) are used as outlier detection techniques. Interested readers are suggested to see the excellent survey by Hodge and Austin (2004). Igelnik (2009) shows neural networks can be efficiently utilized for dynamic modeling of time-variant data. Very recently Chiang *et al* (2010) observe the limitations of neural networks in real time water level predictions of sewerage systems. Although a non-linear model can sometimes provide accurate prediction result, linear methods are easy to interpret and have got well acceptance to the applied researchers. Linear regression is one of the most popular outlier detection techniques to the computer science and statistical community as well.

A good number of statistical measures have been proposed to study outliers and influence of individual observations in regression analysis. Two different but complementary remedies: robust regression and regression diagnostics with same objectives are well recognized to the statistics community. We make discussion of the most popular outlier detection techniques in linear regression. This is far from exhaustive, but we try to deal with the most popular techniques. Rest of the paper is arranged as in following order.

We briefly describe basics of linear regression, least squares estimation and the idea of unusual (outliers) observations in regression analysis. Classification of outliers is introduced, and consequences of outliers are shown by using a simulated data. We discuss a number of efficient graphical and numerical diagnostic measures. The measures are described and arranged sequentially according to the classification of unusual observations and their structural construction. We use the measures to serve their purposes and to show the efficiency through several artificial and well-referred data sets. Findings and future research issues are attached hereafter.

REGRESSION ANALYSIS AND LEAST SQUARES ESTIMATION

Regression analysis is a statistical technique, which helps us to investigate and to fit an unknown model, quantifies relations among observed variables in multifactor data. More specifically, regression analysis helps us understand how the typical value of the dependent variable changes when any one of the independent variables is varied, while the other independent variables are held fixed. Most commonly,

Table 1. Notion for the data used in regression analysis

Observation number	Response Y	Predictors			
		X_1	X_2	...	X_p
1	y_1	x_{11}	x_{12}	...	x_{1p}
2	y_2	x_{21}	x_{22}	...	x_{2p}
3	y_3	x_{31}	x_{32}	...	x_{3p}
⋮	⋮	⋮	⋮	⋮	⋮
n	y_n	x_{n1}	x_{n2}	...	x_{np}

regression analysis estimates the conditional expectation of the dependent variable given the independent variables. Chatterjee and Hadi (2006) point out; it is appealing because it provides a conceptually simple method for investigating functional relationship among variables.

To illustrate a regression model, let us consider, we have a dataset (sampled observations) as follows (in Table 1).

A regression model involves the independent variable(s) X with the dependent variable, Y. A regression model relates Y to a function of X and β, and the approximation is usually formalized as $E(Y \mid X) = f(X,\beta)$, where β may be a scalar (if dataset contains one independent variable) or a vector of length k. In linear regression, the model specification is that the dependent variable Y is a linear combination of the parameters (but need not be linear in the independent variables, X). The standard linear regression model stands by using this above data

$$Y = X\beta + \varepsilon, \tag{1}$$

where Y is an $n\times 1$ vector of response, X is an $n\times k$ ($n > k$; $k = p+1$) full rank matrix of independent (explanatory or regressor) variables including one constant predictor, β is a $k\times 1$ vector of unknown finite parameters to be estimated from the data, and ε is an $n\times 1$ vector of random (unobservable) errors. For the convenience of the study and analysis, we express the data and necessary components in vector and matrix notation,

$$y = \begin{bmatrix} y_1 \\ y_2 \\ y_3 \\ \vdots \\ y_n \end{bmatrix} X = \begin{bmatrix} 1 & x_{11} & x_{12} & \cdots & x_{1p} \\ 1 & x_{21} & x_{22} & \cdots & x_{2p} \\ 1 & x_{21} & x_{32} & \cdots & x_{3p} \\ \vdots & \vdots & \vdots & & \vdots \\ 1 & x_{n1} & x_{n2} & \cdots & x_{np} \end{bmatrix} \beta = \begin{bmatrix} \beta_0 \\ \beta_1 \\ \beta_3 \\ \vdots \\ \beta_p \end{bmatrix} \varepsilon = \begin{bmatrix} \varepsilon_1 \\ \varepsilon_2 \\ \varepsilon_3 \\ \vdots \\ \varepsilon_n \end{bmatrix}.$$

We can re-express the above model (Eq. 1) as scalar form,

$$y_i = x_i^T\beta + \varepsilon_i;\ i = 1, 2, \ldots, n, \tag{2}$$

where x_i and y_i are the *i*th values of explanatory and dependent variable. The method of least squares, minimizes the error sum of squares or equivalently finds the vector of LS estimators β, which minimizes

$$S(\beta) = \sum_{i=1}^{n} \varepsilon_i^2 = \varepsilon^T \varepsilon = (Y - X\beta)^T (Y - X\beta). \tag{3}$$

According to the LS principle, the least squares estimators must satisfy

$$\left.\frac{\delta S}{\delta \beta}\right|_{\beta} = 0 \Rightarrow -2X^T Y + 2X^T X\widehat{\beta} = 0, \tag{4}$$

where $\widehat{\beta}$ is the estimated values of the parameter vector β, which simplifies to

$$X^T X\widehat{\beta} = X^T Y. \tag{5}$$

Equation (5) is the least squares normal equation and is identical to Eq. (4). To solve the normal equation, premultiply both sides of Eq. (5) by $(X^T X)^{-1}$ and we get the least squares estimate of β as

$$\widehat{\beta} = \left(X^T X\right)^{-1} X^T Y. \tag{6}$$

The fitted regression model corresponding to the level of the regressor variable(s) is,

$$\widehat{Y} = X^T \widehat{\beta} = \widehat{\beta}_0 + \sum_{j=1}^{p} \widehat{\beta}_j x_j. \tag{7}$$

The properties of LS estimators and the statistical analysis are based on the following standard assumptions; (i) the sample must be representative of the population for the inference and prediction. (ii) ε is the vector of identically and independently distributed (*i.i.d.)* random disturbances, each of which follows normal distribution with mean 0 and variance σ^2 (*i.e.* the variance of the error is constant across observations, if not, weighted least squares or other methods might be used), (iii) the errors are uncorrelated, that is, the variance-covariance matrix of the errors is diagonal and each non-zero element is the variance of the error, (iv) explanatory variables are non-random and are assumed to be linearly independent of each other, (v) all observations are equally reliable and have approximately equal role in model building process and in influencing conclusions. These assumptions imply that the parameter estimates will be unbiased, consistent, and efficient in the class of linear unbiased estimators.

UNUSUAL OBSERVATIONS: OUTLIERS, HIGH-LEVERAGE POINTS AND INFLUENTIAL OBSERVATIONS

Observations are unusual in the sense that they are exceptional, they have extra role on model building process, or they may come from other population(s) and do not follow the pattern of the majority of

Figure 1. Scatter plot of artificial data

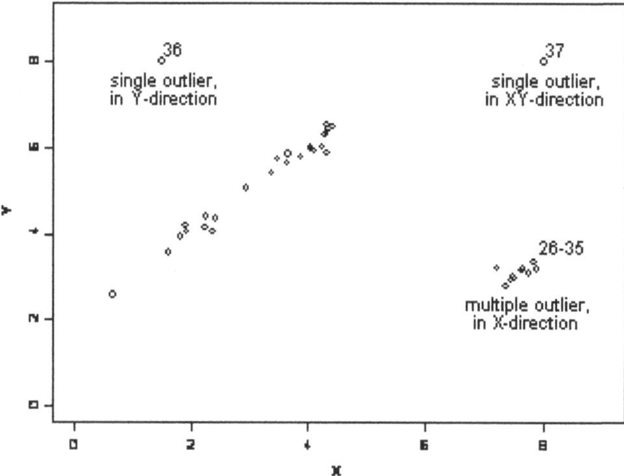

the data. Commonly in statistics, outlier is a synonym of unusual observation. The presence of unusual observations could make huge interactive problems in inference. Because some times they unduly influence the results of the analysis, and their presence may be a signal that the regression model fails to capture important characteristics of the data. What are outliers and what are the problems of outliers'? An interesting answer is found in the following quotation (see Barnett and Lewis, 1995).

In almost every true series of observations, some are found, which differ so much from the others as to indicate some abnormal source of error not contemplated in the theoretical discussions, and the introduction of which into the investigations can only serve … to perplex and mislead the inquirer.

Outlying observations do not inevitably 'perplex' or 'mislead'; they are not necessarily 'bad' or 'erroneous', and the experimenter may be tempted in some situations not to reject an outlier but to welcome it as an indication of new and important findings.

Outliers can pinpoint a change in the prediction process or in the experimental conditions. Especially, in regression analysis, we categorize unusual observations (outliers) into three: outliers, high leverage points and influential observations. While there are numerous definitions of outlier in statistics, machine learning and data mining literatures. Most of the outlier detection methods exist in statistics literature. Hadi *et al.* (2009)'s definition captures the spirit of the chapter: 'outliers are a minority of observations in a dataset that have different patterns from that of the majority observations in the dataset'. In the scale parameter context, by an outlier we mean an observation that is so much larger than the bulk of the observations that it stands out, and that there is doubt about it being from the proposed model. Outliers can be categorized into three ways (see Figure 1): (i) the deviation in the space of explanatory variable(s); deviated points in X-direction called leverage points, (ii) the change in the direction of response (Y) variable (outlier in Y-direction but not a leverage point is called vertical outlier) (iii) the other is deviated in both the directions (X and Y). Belsley *et al.* (1980) point out, "Influential observation is one which either individual or together with several other observations has a demonstrably larger impact on the calculated values of various estimates (coefficients, standard errors, t-values, etc) than is the case for most of the other observations".

Table 2. Artificial data

Index	Y	X	Index	Y	X	Index	Y	X
1	5.841576	3.670482	14	6.345323	4.310151	27	2.96462	7.512470
2	4.394134	2.258116	15	6.290046	4.305498	28	3.039794	7.475741
3	2.582207	0.671286	16	3.938996	1.819935	29	3.206224	7.217344
4	5.868199	4.336371	17	5.626811	3.64896	30	3.187115	7.648281
5	4.06286	2.367402	18	6.432413	4.365604	31	3.16522	7.610034
6	5.419333	3.388319	19	6.54014	4.327306	32	3.349946	7.824192
7	6.477101	4.432554	20	3.557845	1.609637	33	2.802016	7.354478
8	5.787768	3.875140	21	5.050812	2.943116	34	2.921835	7.446376
9	5.922375	4.122554	22	5.964297	4.051293	35	3.187675	7.876692
10	4.351615	2.409008	23	4.203484	1.898082	36	8.000000	1.500000
11	4.133598	2.230773	24	6.010955	4.042424	37	8.000000	8.000000
12	6.003132	4.238596	25	4.061444	1.918010			
13	5.745112	3.475461	26	3.092400	7.751916			

Consequences of Outliers in Linear Regression Model Estimation

To introduce with outliers, their consequences and detection procedures, now we consider an example. We simulate a dataset for simple linear regression for the specific understanding of outliers and graphical procedures. We generate 25 observations from the model

$$Y = \beta_0 + \beta_1 X + \varepsilon, \tag{8}$$

where x_i~Uniform (0.5, 4.5) and $y_i = 2 + x_i + \varepsilon_i$ where $\varepsilon_i \sim N\ (0, 0.2)$; $i = 1, 2, \ldots, 25$.

To create outliers, we generate 10 multiple outliers (cases 26-35) in X-direction, where X from Normal (7.5, 0.3) and Y from Normal (3.0, 0.3). For a single outlier in Y-direction, consider the 36th observation, and 37th observation is (8, 8). Table 2 contains the artificial dataset of 37 observations.

Figure 1, scatter plot (Y versus X) shows the indications of outliers (single and multiple) and regular observations.

We now apply the LS method for the artificial dataset and get the fitted model,

$$\hat{Y} = 5.6509 - 0.1902X, \tag{9}$$

validation of the parameters are shown in Table 3. Coefficient of determination $R^2 = 0.0808 \approx 8\%$ (approximately) that is sufficient to prove the poor performance of the LS fitted model. Moreover, residuals' normal quantile-quantile (QQ; Gnanadesikan and Wilk, 1968) plot (Figure 3) shows errors are non-normal, which means LS assumption is violated and LS estimation is not suitable for the dataset until the outliers are eliminated or refitted (if necessary).

Table 3. LS regression results (with and without outliers)

Observations deleted	Coefficients	Value	t-value	Pr(>|t|)	R^2
None	Intercept	5.6509	10.3973	0.0000	0.0808
	X	-0.1902	-1.7544	0.0881	
26-36	Intercept	2.0801	18.5061	0.0000	0.9743
	X	0.9739	29.5198	0.0000	

Figure 3. Residuals' normal QQ plot

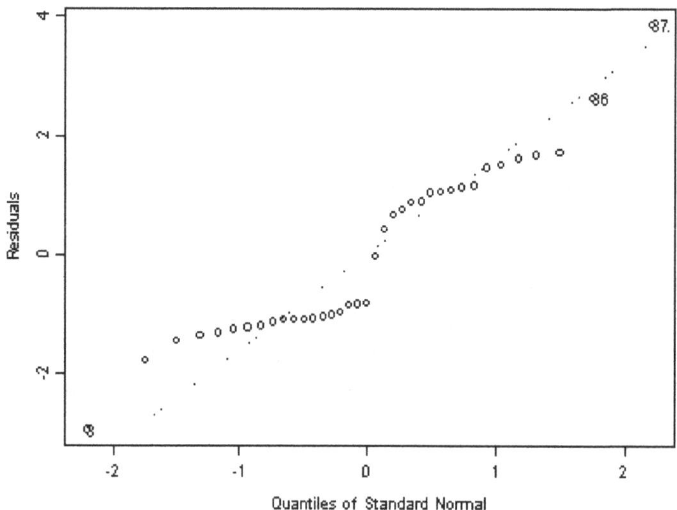

We know observations 26-35 are outliers; we discard the 11 observations and again apply LS method. We have the fitted model for the regular cases

$$\hat{Y} = 2.0801 + 0.9739X, \tag{10}$$

which finds that the parameters in Eq. (8) and the fitted model (Eq. 10) without outliers are approximately same

($\beta_0 = 2.0801 \approx 2$ *and* $\beta_1 = 0.9739 \approx 1$). We get the value of coefficient of determination (Chatterjee and Hadi, 2006) $R^2 = 0.9743 \approx 98\%$ (Table 3). We see the results of the fitted models (with and without outliers) in Table 3. Figure 2 shows that the LS lines are in reverse directions in presence of outliers and without the outliers.

Hence it is necessary to find proper and efficient diagnostic methods for detecting outliers prior to the final analysis and decision making.

Figure 2. Scatter plot Y vs. X, and LS fitted lines with and without outliers

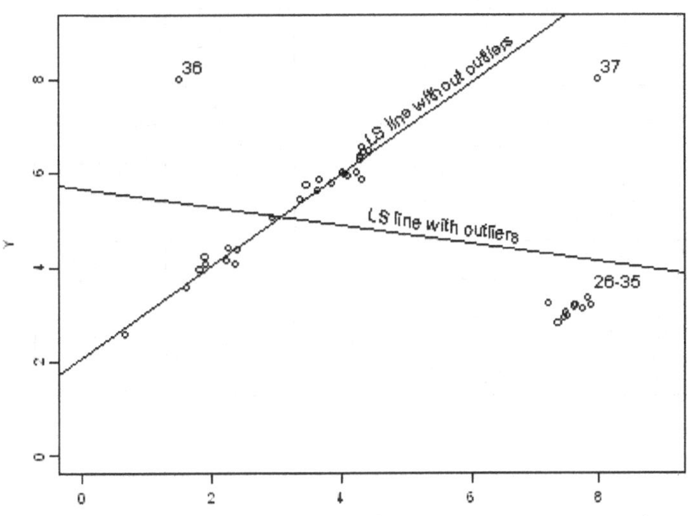

REGRESSION DIAGNOSTICS

Fox (1993) mention, 'Regression diagnostics are techniques for exploring problems that compromise a regression analysis and for determining whether certain assumptions appear reasonable'. We use the term 'regression diagnostics' to serve the purpose for outlier detection in a dataset. Stahel and Weisberg (1991) point, 'Rather than modifying the fitting method, diagnostics condition on the fit using standard methods to attempt to diagnose incorrect assumptions, allowing the analyst to modify them and refit under the new set of assumptions'. Field diagnostics is a combination of graphical and numerical tools. It is designed to detect and delete/refit (if necessary) the outliers first and then to fit the good data by classical (e.g., least squares) methods. The usual regression outputs clearly do not tell the whole story about the cause and/or effect of deviations from the assumptions of the model building process. Regression diagnostic can serve as the identification purpose of the deviations from the assumptions. So that the basic need of regression diagnostics is to identify the unusual observations in a data set.

Graphical Methods

Nobody can deny the importance of graphical methods in data analysis. Huber (1991) says, 'Eye-balling can give diagnostic insights no formal diagnostics will ever provide'. Chambers et al. (1983) emphasize by saying, 'There is no single statistical tool that is as powerful as a well-chosen graph'. Graphical displays in regression diagnostics can be classified into two complementary classes. One that is useful to get first idea about the data structure before performing a model, and the other type which are graphs after fitting a model. A lot of graphical techniques are now available in literature (Atkinson, 1985; Cook, 1998; Chatterjee & Hadi, 2006). Steam-leaf-display (Tukey, 1977), box plot (Tukey, 1977) and different scatter plots are common in outlier detection. Short descriptions about scatter plot and matrix plot are given here.

Table 4. Anscombe's Quartet: four data sets having same values of summary statistics

Index	Y1	X1	Y2	X2	Y3	X3	Y4	X4
1	8.04	10	9.14	10	7.46	10	6.58	8
2	6.95	8	8.14	8	6.77	8	5.76	8
3	7.58	13	8.74	13	12.74	13	7.71	8
4	8.81	9	8.77	9	7.11	9	8.84	8
5	8.33	11	9.26	11	7.81	11	8.74	8
6	9.96	14	8.1	14	8.84	14	7.04	8
7	7.24	6	6.13	6	6.08	6	5.25	8
8	4.26	4	3.1	4	5.39	4	12.5	19
9	10.84	12	9.13	12	8.15	12	5.56	8
10	4.82	7	7.26	7	6.42	7	7.91	8
11	5.68	5	4.74	5	5.73	5	6.89	8

Scatter (dot) plot is a display of data points on a two-dimensional space that shows the relationship between two variables. It can provide strength, shape, direction, relationship or presence of outliers in a dataset. We explain the importance scatter plot by using Anscombe (1973) well-known data sets. In this data, it has been constructed four data sets, each with a distinct pattern (having the same set of summary statistics; mean, median, standard deviation and correlation coefficients). The table and graphs are reproduced in Table 4 and Figure 4. The scatter plots in Figure 4 show: (a) a linear model may be reasonable, (b) presence of a nonlinear model, (c) indicates linear model (without the one in top right corner), and (d) indicates either an incomplete experimental design or a bad sample. Since the data sets having same summary statistics but the patterns are different in the figure, it needs extra care about the model and underlying assumptions to fit a regression model. A matrix plot is a kind of two-dimensional array of scatter plot which enables the user to see the pairwise relationships between variables. It contains all the pairwise scatter plots of the variables on a single page in a matrix format.

Numerical Measures

Despite the importance of graphical methods, numerical measures are inevitable in most of the situations. Graphical methods heavily depend on analyst's own interpretation and they are sometimes also clumsy and impossible (especially for multiple regression with a number of regressors) to tell the whole story and are failed to explore the insight of the data structure. Moreover, they cannot be easily compared objectively to more formal approaches.

Many nearest neighbor search algorithms have been proposed over the years; these generally seek to reduce the number of distance evaluations actually performed. Using an appropriate nearest neighbor search algorithm makes *k*-NN (k-nearest neighbor) (Nigsch *et al.,* 2006) computationally tractable even for large data sets. Another method, Grubbs' test (Grubbs, 1969) is based on statistical inference is popular for outlier detection to the machine learning community. Grubbs' test is particularly easy to follow, but it is evident that since the test is used to detect outliers in a univariate data set and based on normality assumption so, it is inefficient for identifying outliers in regression analysis.

Figure 4. Scatter plot of Anscombe (1973) quartet data with LS line

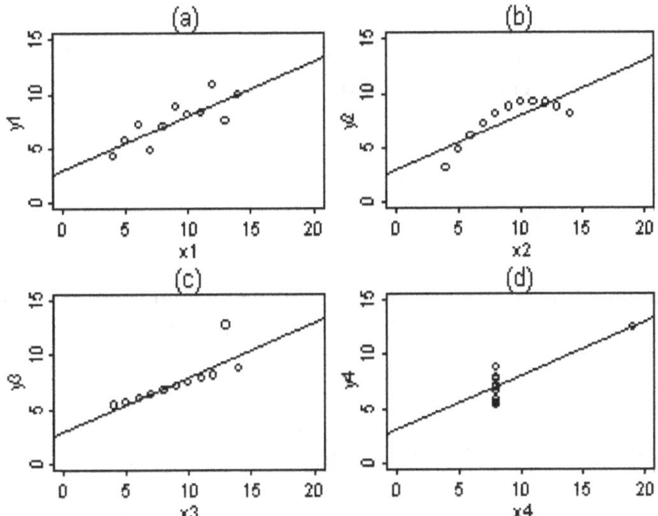

A bewilderingly large number of algorithms and methods have been proposed to find an effective technique for outlier, high-leverage points and influential observations detection in linear regression. The basic building blocks of regression diagnostics are residuals, leverage values, vector of forecasts and vector of estimated parameters.

Residuals Analysis

Chatterjee and Hadi (1988) point out, 'Residuals play an important role in regression diagnostics; no analysis is complete without a thorough examination of the residuals'. To assess the appropriateness of the model $Y = X\beta + \varepsilon$, it is necessary to ensure whether the assumptions about the errors are reasonable. The problem here is that the ε can neither be observed nor they can be estimated directly. This must be done indirectly using residuals. For the linear least squares, the vector of residual r can be written as

$$r = Y - \widehat{Y} = Y - X\widehat{\beta} = Y - HY = (I - H)\varepsilon, \tag{11}$$

where $H = X(X^T X)^{-1} X^T$ is the leverage (weight) matrix, and (*I-H*) is called the residual matrix (because applied it to *Y* produces the residuals).

In scalar form,

$$r_i = y_i - \widehat{y}_i = \varepsilon_i - \sum_{j=1}^{n} h_{ij}\varepsilon_j, i = 1, 2, \ldots, n \tag{12}$$

where h_{ij} is the *ij*-th element of *H*. Since the residuals do not have the same variance,

$$Var(r_i) = \sigma^2(1 - h_{ii}), \tag{13}$$

the ordinary residuals are not appropriate for diagnostic purpose; it is preferable to use a transformed version of the ordinary residuals. That is, instead of r_i one may use

$$f(r_i, \sigma_i) = \frac{r_i}{\sigma_i}, \tag{14}$$

where σ_i is the standard deviation of the i-th residual. Some special types of scaled residuals are given below.

Normalized Residuals

The i-th normalized residual is obtained by replacing σ_i in Eq. (14) by $\sqrt{r^T r}$ as

$$a_i = \frac{r_i}{\sqrt{r^T r}} \qquad i = 1, 2, \ldots, n \tag{15}$$

where r^T is the transpose of r.

Standardized Residuals

To overcome the problem of unequal variances, we standardize the i-th residual r_i by dividing it by its standard deviation (square root of the mean square for error).

Hence the i-th standardized residual is,

$$d_i = \frac{r_i}{\hat{\sigma}}. \tag{16}$$

Residuals have zero mean and approximate average variance, it is estimated by

$$i.e. \quad \hat{\sigma} = \sqrt{\frac{r^T r}{n-k}}, \tag{17}$$

where $\frac{\sum_{i=1}^{n}(r_i - \bar{r})^2}{n-k} = \frac{\sum_{i=1}^{n} r_i^2}{n-k} = \frac{SS_{\text{Res}}}{n-k} = MS_{\text{Res}} = \frac{r^T r}{n-k}$

Studentized Residuals

Standardized residual is also referred to an internal scaling of the residual because $\hat{\sigma}^2$ is an internally generated estimate of σ^2 obtained from the fitting of the model to all n observations. The internally Studentized residuals are defined by

$$e_i = \frac{r_i}{\hat{\sigma}\sqrt{1-h_{ii}}}, \; i = 1,2,\ldots,n \tag{18}$$

where $\sigma_i = \hat{\sigma}\sqrt{1-h_{ii}}$. Another approach would be to use an estimate of σ^2, based on a data set with the i-th observation deleted. This deleted scaled residual is referred as externally Studentized residual and defined as

$$e_i^* = \frac{y_i - x_i^T\hat{\beta}^{(-i)}}{\hat{\sigma}^{(-i)}\sqrt{(1-h_{ii})}} = \frac{r^{(-i)}}{\hat{\sigma}^{(-i)}\sqrt{1-h_{ii}}}, \quad i = 1,2,\ldots,n \tag{19}$$

where $\hat{\sigma}^{(-i)2} = \frac{1}{n-k-1}\sum_{j\neq i}(y_j - x_j{}^T\hat{\beta}^{(-i)})^2$.

After some simplifications, we get the relation between the external Studentized residuals and internal residuals as

$$e_i^* = e_i\sqrt{\frac{n-k-1}{n-k-e_i^2}}. \tag{20}$$

Under the usual assumptions, Ellenberg (1976) shows that externally Studentized residuals follow Student's t_{n-k-1} distribution. Behnken and Draper (1972), Davies and Hutton (1975), and Huber (1975) all of them recommend the external Studentized residuals as more appropriate than the standardized (internal Studentized) residuals for identifying outliers since the effect of i-th observation is more pronounced in the case of the former. Besides these, a number of residuals for outlier detection are available in the literature (Allen, 1974; Cook & Weisberg, 1982; Wu, 1986; Effron & Tibshirani, 1993; Shao & Tu, 1995).

Residuals plot are often more informative than their magnitude. They provide valuable information about the presence of outliers in addition about the adequacy of the model and /or the validity of the model assumptions. Some of the most commonly used residuals plots are: index plot of residuals, plot of residuals versus fitted values, plot of residuals versus explanatory variables and normal quantile-quantile (QQ) residuals plot.

Example

This example is appeared for the performance analysis of the different residuals.

Forbes' Data

The data is taken from Atkinson and Riani (2000), they use the data for outlier detection in simple linear regression. There are 17 observations on the boiling point ^{0}F at different Pressures, obtained from measurements at a variety of elevations in the Alps. We consider boiling point ^{0}F as explanatory variable and 100×log (pressure) as the response variable. We see in the scatter plot (Figure 5) that there is a strong

Figure 5. Scatter plot of 100×log pressure against boiling point for Forbes data

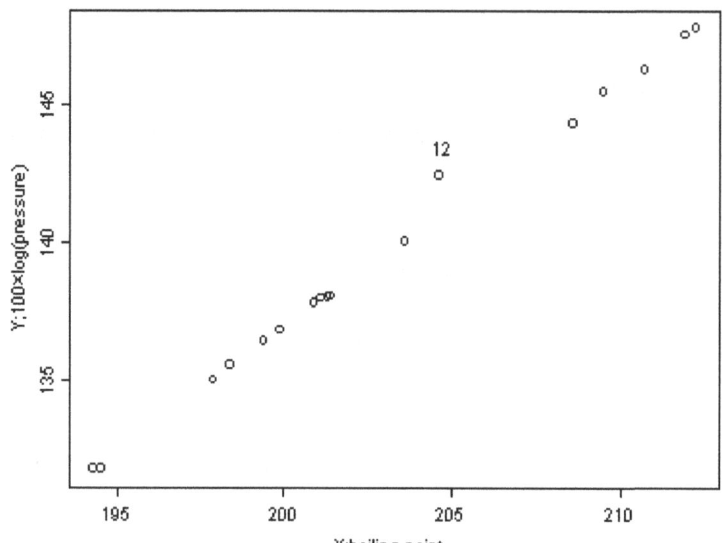

linear relationship between 100×log (pressure) and boiling point. A slightly longer glance reveals that one of the points (observation 12) lies off the line. The dataset, LS fitted values and residuals (LS residuals, LS standardized residuals, and LS Studentized residuals) are given in Table 5. Table shows, only the observation 12 has standardized and Studentized residuals exceed over the cut-off value |2.50| (because values generated by Gaussian distribution are rarely larger than 2.5 σ ; Debruyne *et al.*, 2006) *i. e.*, these two residuals identify the single (case 12) outlier in the dataset, but ordinary residuals fail to identify the outliers.

Index plots of three residuals, and different residuals versus fitted values are given in Figure 6. Every plot in Figure 6 show that observation 12 is clearly apart from the data. Figures 6 (c) and 6 (f) show the better performance of Studentized residuals comparing other two residuals.

Hat Matrix and Leverage Values

In this sub section, we will discuss some related quantities for measuring the leverage of a point. The leverage matrix $H = X(X^TX)^{-1}X^T$ determines many of the least squares results. The matrix H is sometimes called the hat matrix because it maps Y into $\widehat{Y}$ and sometimes called prediction matrix because it is the transformation matrix that applied to Y, produces the predicted values. An extensive discussion about H, and its roles and properties has been made in Chatterjee and Hadi (1988) and Atkinson and Riani (2000). Chatterjee and Hadi (1988) point, 'Examination of residuals alone is not sufficient for detecting unusual observations, especially those corresponding to high-leverage points. This can be seen from the property $0 \leq \left(h_{ii} + r_i^2 / r^T r\right) \leq 1$.

Observations with large h_{ii} tend to have small residuals and therefore go undetected in the usual plots of residuals'. Therefore, in addition to an examination of residuals it is necessary to examine leverage values to identify troublesome points.

Table 5. Forbes data with residuals

Observation Number	Y 100×Log (Pressure)	X Boiling Point (⁰F)	Fitted values ($\hat{y}_i$)	LS.res |2.50|	LS.Std.res |2.50|	LS.Stu.res |2.50|
1	131.79	194.5	132.037	-0.247	-0.725	-0.713
2	131.79	194.3	131.858	-0.067	-0.199	-0.193
3	135.02	197.9	135.081	-0.061	-0.171	-0.165
4	135.55	198.4	135.529	0.021	0.059	0.057
5	136.46	199.4	136.424	0.036	0.098	0.095
6	136.83	199.9	136.872	-0.042	-0.116	-0.112
7	137.82	200.9	137.768	0.052	0.143	0.139
8	138.00	201.1	137.947	0.053	0.146	0.141
9	138.06	201.4	138.215	-0.155	-0.423	-0.412
10	138.05	201.3	138.126	-0.076	-0.207	-0.200
11	140.04	203.6	140.185	-0.145	-0.395	-0.384
12	142.44	204.6	141.081	1.359	3.708	12.404
13	145.47	209.5	145.469	0.001	0.004	0.004
14	144.34	208.6	144.663	-0.323	-0.907	-0.901
15	146.30	210.7	146.543	-0.243	-0.705	-0.693
16	147.54	211.9	147.618	-0.078	-0.230	-0.223
17	147.80	212.2	147.886	-0.086	-0.258	-0.250

Figure 6. Residuals plots of Forbes data

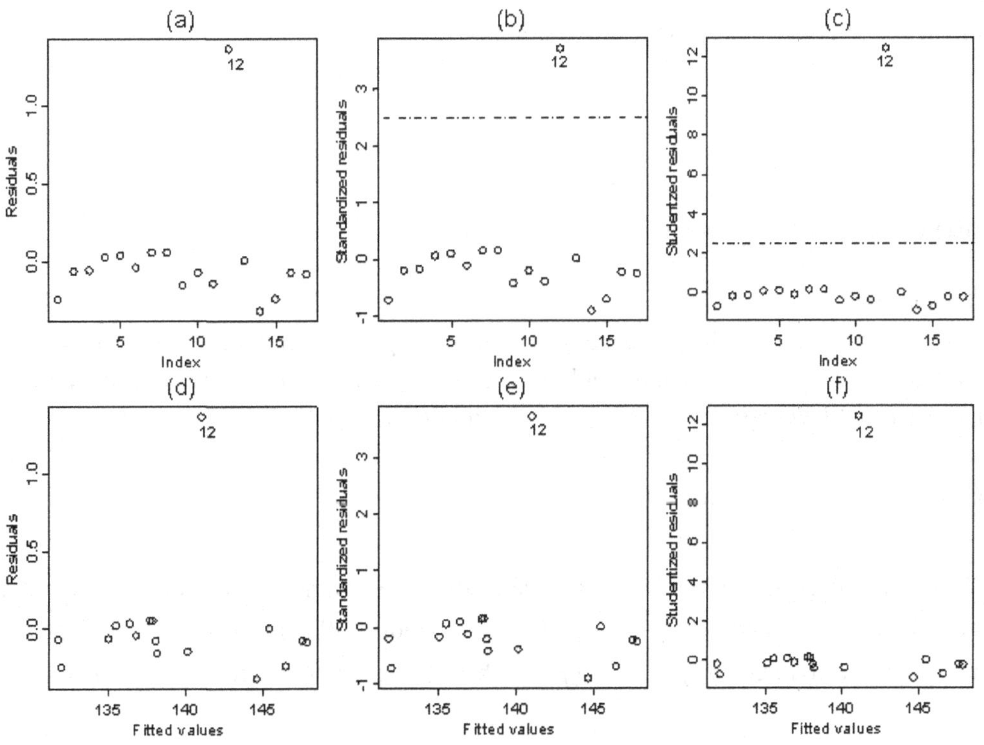

The diagonal elements of the hat matrix

$$h_{ii} = x_i^T \left(X^T X\right)^{-1} x_i,\ i = 1,2,...,n \tag{21}$$

play an important role in determining the fitted values, the magnitude of the residuals, and their variance-covariance structure. For these reasons, Hoaglin and Welsch in 1978 suggest the examination of both e_i^* (in Eq. 20) and h_{ii} (e_i^* for detecting outliers and h_{ii} for detecting high-leverage points that are potentially influential), and add, 'These two aspects of the search for troublesome data points are complementary; neither is sufficient by itself'. According to Hocking and Pendleton (1983), 'High-leverage points,...are those for which the input vector x_i is, in some sense, far from the rest of the data'. But the question here is "how far is far?" Some common cut-off points for h_{ii} are suggested as follows.

The reciprocal of h_{ii} can be thought of as the effective or equivalent number of observations that determine $\hat{y}_i$ (Huber, 1977; Huber, 1981). Huber (1981) suggests that points with

$$h_{ii} \geq 0.2\,,\ i = 1,2,...,n \tag{22}$$

be classified as high-leverage points.

Hoaglin and Welsch (1978) suggest that points with

$$h_{ii} \geq \frac{2k}{n},\ i = 1,2,...,n \tag{23}$$

and Vellman and Welsch (1981) suggest that points with

$$h_{ii} \geq \frac{3k}{n},\ i = 1,2,...,n \tag{24}$$

be classified as high-leverage points.

Hadi's Potential

Hadi (1992) mentions that in the presence of a high-leverage point the information matrix may breakdown and hence the observations may not have the appropriate leverages. He introduces a single case deletion measure of leverage named by potentials and defined as

$$p_{ii} = x_i^T (X^{(-i)T} X^{(-i)})^{-1} x_i\,, \tag{25}$$

where $X^{(-i)}$ is the data matrix with *i*-th case deleted. The relationship between p_{ii} (potential) and h_{ii} (leverage value) is established as $p_{ii} = h_{ii} / (1 - h_{ii})$. Hadi (1992) proposes a cut-off point to detect high-leverage points as $mean\,(p_{ii}) + c.SD.(p_{ii})$, where *c* is an appropriate chosen constant such as 2 or

3. Since mean and standard deviations (*SD*) are non-robust finally he suggests to change mean and *SD* by median and median absolute deviation (*MAD*) respectively. Mahalanobis distance (Mahalanobis, 1936), minimum covariance determinant and minimum volume ellipsoid; (Rousseeuw, 1985), Robust distance (Rousseeuw and van Zomeren, 1990) are also used to serve the purpose of high-leverage points diagnostics. Sometimes high-leverage points could be identified by graphical displays of h_{ii} such as index plot, stem-leaf -display, and/or box plot.

Influence Measures

Pregibon (1981) points out residuals, standardized residuals and leverage values are useful for detecting extreme points, but not for assessing their impact on various aspects of the fit. Influential observation (Belsley *et al.*, 1980) is another type of extreme point that has larger impact on various estimates and fit. To assess the impact of extreme points on fit we draw our attention to the influential cases. The general idea of influence analysis is to introduce small perturbations in the sample and see how these perturbations affect the model. It is to be noted that an outlier or a leverage point is not necessarily an influential observation and the converse is also true, that is an influential observation may not be an outlier or a leverage point (Chatterjee and Hadi, 1986). There are numerous influence measures of influence in the literature (Belsley *et al.,* 1980; Cook & Weisberg, 1982; Cook, 1986; Atkinson, 1985; Chatterjee & Hadi, 1988; Atkinson & Riani, 2000; Billor *et al.*, 2000; Pena, 2005). Among a large number of influence measures, the following are the most remarkable and popular to the practitioners.

Cook's Distance

Cook (1977, 1979) suggests a way for reducing the influence curve (Hampel *et al.*, 1986), using a measure of the squared distance between the least squares estimate based on all n points $\hat{\beta}$ and the estimate obtained by deleting the i-th point, say $\hat{\beta}^{(-i)}$. This distance measure can be expressed in general form as the Cook's distance (*CD*)

$$CD_i = \frac{\left(\hat{\beta}^{(-i)} - \hat{\beta}\right)^T M \left(\hat{\beta}^{(-i)} - \hat{\beta}\right)}{c}, \; i = 1, 2, \ldots, n. \tag{26}$$

The usual choice of M and c are $M = X^T X$ and $c = kMS_{\mathrm{Res}}$, so that Eq. (26) becomes

$$CD_i = \frac{\left(\hat{\beta}^{(-i)} - \hat{\beta}\right)^T X^T X \left(\hat{\beta}^{(-i)} - \hat{\beta}\right)}{kMS_{\mathrm{Res}}}, \; i = 1, 2, \ldots, n. \tag{27}$$

According to Bingham (1977), CD_i can be written as

$$CD_i = \frac{(\hat{Y} - \hat{Y}^{(-i)})^T (\hat{Y} - \hat{Y}^{(-i)})}{k\hat{\sigma}^2}, \; i = 1, 2, \ldots, n \tag{28}$$

and can also be rewritten as

$$CD_i = \frac{\sum_{j=1}^{n}(\hat{y}_j - \hat{y}_j^{(-i)})^2}{k\hat{\sigma}^2} \quad i = 1,2,...,n. \tag{29}$$

It is re-expressed by leverage values and internal Studentized residuals as

$$CD_i = \frac{e_i^2}{k}\left(\frac{h_{ii}}{1-h_{ii}}\right), \ i = 1,2,...,n. \tag{30}$$

The magnitude of CD_i is usually assessed by comparing it to $F_{\alpha,k,n-k}$ distribution (Cook and Weisberg, 1982). If $CD_i = F_{0.5,k,n-k}$, then deleting point i would move $\hat{\beta}^{(-i)}$ to the boundary of an approximate 50% confidence region (Cook and Weisberg, 1982) for β based on the complete data set. This is a large displacement and indicates that the least-squares estimate is sensitive to the i-th data point. Since $F_{0.5,k,n-k} \approx 1$, Cook and Weisberg (1982) suggest points to be influential for which $CD_i > 1$.

Difference in Fits (DFFITS)

Belsley *et al.* (1980) point out, the influence of the i-th observation on the predicted value can be measured by the change in the prediction at x_i when the i-th observation is omitted, relative to the standard error of, i.e.,

$$\frac{\hat{y}_i - \hat{y}_i^{(-i)}}{\hat{\sigma}^{(-i)}\sqrt{h_{ii}}} = \frac{x_i^T(\hat{\beta} - \hat{\beta}^{(-i)})}{\sigma^{(-i)}\sqrt{h_{ii}}} \quad i = 1,2,...,n. \tag{31}$$

Belsley *et al.* (1980) call this distance $DFFITS_i$, because it is the scaled difference between $\hat{y}$ *and* $\hat{y}^{(-i)}$. Using the results of Miller (1974) for $\hat{\beta}^{(-i)}$ and the external Studentized residual in Eq. (19), $DFFITS_i$ can also be re-expressed by leverage values and external Studentized residuals as

$$DFFITS_i = e_i^* \sqrt{\frac{h_{ii}}{1-h_{ii}}} \quad i = 1,2,...,n. \tag{32}$$

Belsley *et al.* (1980) suggest that any observation for which $|DFFITS_i| > 2 / \sqrt{k / n}$ warrants attention and is influential.

Hadi's Influence Measure

Hadi (1992) proposes an influence measure for i-th observation based on the idea that influential observation is an outlying observation in either the response or predictor variables, or both. He suggests the i-th influence measure as

$$H_i = \frac{h_{ii}}{1-h_{ii}} + \frac{k}{1-h_{ii}}\left(\frac{d_i^2}{1-d_i^2}\right),\ i = 1,2,\ldots,n \tag{33}$$

where $d_i = r_i \,/\, \sum_{i=1}^{n} r_i^2$; r_i is the i-th residual. He notices that CD_i and $DFFITS_i$ are multiplicative functions of the residual and leverage value, whereas H_i is an additive function, and H_i can best be examined graphically. The measure H_i does not focus on a specific regression result (residual or leverage), but it can be thought of as an overall general measure of influence.

The Potential-Residual (P-R) Plot

The potential-residual (P-R) plot is related to the leverage-residual (L-R) plot and is suggest by McCulloch and Meeter (1983) and Gray (1986). The P-R plot is introduced in Hadi (1992). It is a scatter plot of potential versus residual. We suggest here to make the scatter plot of Hadi's (1992) potential versus external Studentized residuals. The main usefulness of P-R plot is that they give the analyst a complete picture about leverage values and residuals individually as well as combined. It clears that some individual data points may be flagged as outliers, high-leverage points, or influential observations (see Figure 7 (d)).

Figure 7. Artificial data; (a) Scatter plot of response Y versus regressor Xs, and LS line with and without the outlier case 26 (b) Index plot of standardized residuals (c) Index plot of Studentized residuals (d) Scatter plot of potentials versus Studentized residuals (e) Index plot of CD and (f) Index plot of DFFITS

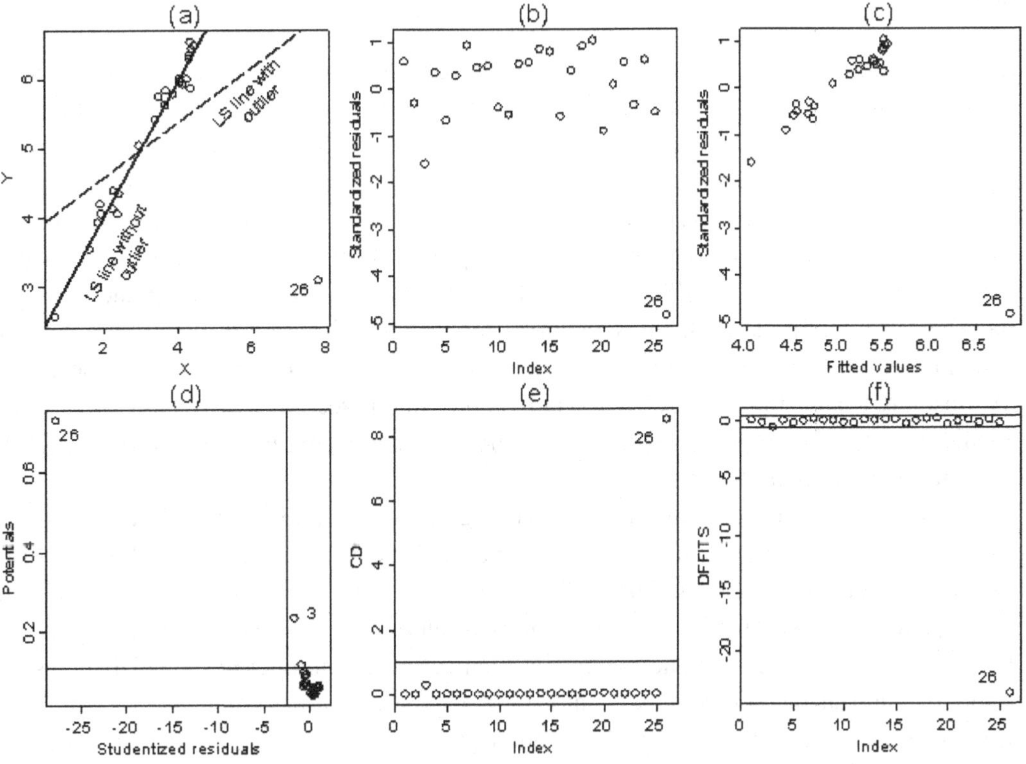

Example

Demonstration and analysis of single-case deletion diagnostic measures are given by an artificial data with single outlier (high-leverage point and influential observation).

Artificial Data with Single Outlier

We have the simulated dataset in Table 2; we consider only the first 26 observations (from Table 2) for the present example to demonstrate how the single case deletion measures identify high-leverage points and influential observations. We know, in Table 2 among the first 26 cases, 1-25 cases are generated as regular observations and the 26th one is created as an outlier, which lies in the group of outliers in X-direction. Table 6 contains different single measures for identifying any single unusual case (outlier, high-leverage point or influential observation). All the measures show that case 26 is an unusual comparing with reset of 25 regular cases.

We see that leverage values and potentials identify another point (case 3) as high-leverage point. We know in this dataset only one observation is outlier (high-leverage case), that proves high-leverage points are not always influential for the analysis because CD and DFFITS (see Table 6) do not consider it (case 3) as an influential case. Chatterjee and Hadi (2006) point out, 'Any point falling in one of these categories should be carefully examined for accuracy, relevancy, and special significance. Outliers should always be scrutinized carefully. Points with high-leverage values that are not influential do not cause problems. High-leverage points that are influential should be investigated because these points are outlying as far as the predictor variables are concerned and also influence the fit'. Plots in Figure 7 give us clear indications about high-leverage points and influential observations.

Group-Deletion Measures

All the aforementioned measures are based on single-case deletion, since they depend on single-case deletion so these are affected by masking and swamping in presence of multiple outliers (Atkinson, 1986). To quote Hadi and Simonoff (1993), 'Masking occurs when an outlying subset goes undetected because of the presence of another, usually adjacent subset. Swamping occurs when good observations are incorrectly identified as outliers because of the presence of another, usually remote subset of observations'. Thus, masking is a false negative decision and swamping is a false positive decision. Group-deletion methods are introduced to get the diagnostic measures that are free from masking and swamping phenomena. There is a multitude of diagnostics measures for identifying multiple outliers, high-leverage points and influential observations are now available in the literature (Ryan, 1997; Rousseeuw & Leroy, 2003; Atkinson & Riani, 2000; Chatterjee & Hadi, 2006). In this section we discuss generalized version of residuals, leverage values and influential measures for identifying multiple outliers, high-leverage values and influential observations.

A general approach to detect multiple unusual (irregular) observations is to delete a suspect group of observations at a time. The idea is to form a clean subset of the data that is presumably free of irregular observations, and then test the irregularity of the remaining points relative to the clean subset. Group deletion helps to reduce the maximum disturbance by deleting the suspect group of unusual cases at a time. It helps to make the data more homogeneous than before. Sometimes graphical displays like index plot, scatter plot and character plot of explanatory and response variables could give us some ideas about the influential observations, but these plots are not useful for higher dimension of regressors. There are

Table 6. Diagnostic measures for artificial data

Index	Std.res |2.50|	Stud.res |2.50|	h_{ii} (0.154)	p_{ii} (0.108)	CD_i (1.00)	$DFFITS_i$ |0.555|
1	0.588	0.580	0.040	0.042	0.007	0.118
2	-0.295	-0.290	0.065	0.070	0.003	-0.076
3	-1.593	-1.649	0.190	0.234	0.297	-0.498
4	0.355	0.349	0.056	0.059	0.004	0.085
5	-0.670	-0.662	0.060	0.064	0.014	-0.168
6	0.280	0.274	0.038	0.040	0.002	0.055
7	0.928	0.925	0.060	0.064	0.027	0.234
8	0.455	0.447	0.043	0.045	0.005	0.095
9	0.492	0.484	0.049	0.052	0.006	0.110
10	-0.397	-0.390	0.058	0.062	0.005	-0.097
11	-0.547	-0.539	0.066	0.071	0.011	-0.144
12	0.528	0.520	0.053	0.056	0.008	0.123
13	0.568	0.560	0.039	0.040	0.006	0.112
14	0.842	0.837	0.055	0.058	0.021	0.202
15	0.789	0.782	0.055	0.058	0.018	0.189
16	-0.586	-0.577	0.089	0.098	0.017	-0.181
17	0.383	0.376	0.040	0.041	0.003	0.077
18	0.908	0.905	0.057	0.061	0.025	0.223
19	1.030	1.032	0.056	0.059	0.031	0.251
20	-0.896	-0.892	0.104	0.116	0.046	-0.303
21	0.090	0.088	0.043	0.045	0.000	0.019
22	0.562	0.553	0.047	0.049	0.008	0.123
23	-0.347	-0.341	0.084	0.092	0.006	-0.103
24	0.612	0.603	0.047	0.049	0.009	0.134
25	-0.499	-0.491	0.083	0.091	0.011	-0.148
26	-4.827	-27.679	0.422	0.731	8.517	-23.666

some suggestions in the literature to use robust regression techniques, as for example, the least median of squares (LMS) or least trimmed of squares (LTS) (Rousseeuw, 1984), reweighted least squares (RLS) (see Rousseeuw and Leroy, 2003), block adaptive computationally-effective outlier nominator (BACON) (Billor *et al.,* 2000) or best omitted from the ordinary least squares (BOFOLS) (Davies *et al.,* 2004) for finding the group of suspect influential observations. Pena and Yohai (1995) introduce a method to identify influential subsets in linear regression by analyzing the eigen vectors (Searle, 1982) corresponding to the non-null eigen values (Searle, 1982) of an influence matrix. Clustering based backward-stepping methods (see Simonoff, 1991) are also suggested in this regard. In our proposed method, we try to find all suspect influential cases at the first step. Any suitable graphical display and/or robust regression techniques mentioned above can be used to flag the suspected group of influential cases.

We can assume that '*d*' observations among a set of *n* observations are suspected as irregular observations and to be deleted. We consider a set of cases 'remaining' (*n-d*) in the analysis by *R* and a set of cases 'deleted' by *D*. Without loss of generality, we assume that these observations are the last *d* rows of *X* and *Y*, we may rearrange the data matrix as

$$X = \begin{bmatrix} X_R \\ X_D \end{bmatrix}, \; Y = \begin{bmatrix} Y_R \\ Y_D \end{bmatrix}. \tag{34}$$

When a group of observations of size *d* is omitted, the vector of estimated coefficients $\widehat{\beta}^{(-D)}$, the vector of residuals and the vector of leverage values are defined respectively as

$$\widehat{\beta}^{(-D)} = \left(X_R^T X_R\right)^{-1} X_R^T Y_R, \tag{35}$$

$$r_i^{(-D)} = y_i - y_i^{(-D)} = y_i - x_i^T \widehat{\beta}^{(-D)} \tag{36}$$

and $h_{ii}^{(-D)} = x_i^T (X_R^T X_R)^{-1} x_i \quad .$ (37)

Generalized Studentized Residuals, Generalized Leverage Values and Generalized Potentials
Using the above results of group-deletion, Imon (2005) defines generalized Studentized residuals and generalized weights (leverage) as

$$t_i^* = \begin{cases} \dfrac{r_i^{(-D)}}{\widehat{\sigma}_{R-i}\sqrt{1 - h_{ii}^{(-D)}}} & for \quad i \in R \\ \dfrac{r_i^{(-D)}}{\widehat{\sigma}_R\sqrt{1 + h_{ii}^{(-D)}}} & for \quad i \in D \end{cases}, \tag{38}$$

and

$$h_{ii}^* = \begin{cases} \dfrac{h_{ii}^{(-D)}}{1 - h_{ii}^{(-D)}} & for \quad i \in R \\ \dfrac{h_{ii}^{(-D)}}{1 + h_{ii}^{(-D)}} & for \quad i \in D \end{cases}. \tag{39}$$

Imon (1996) also introduces generalized potentials for identifying multiple high-leverage points by using group-deletion idea for a dataset as

$$p_{ii}^{*} = \begin{cases} \dfrac{h_{ii}^{(-D)}}{1-h_{ii}^{(-D)}} \; for \quad i \in R \\ h_{ii}^{(-D)} \; for \quad i \in D \end{cases}. \tag{40}$$

Generalized DFFITS (GDFFITS)

Imon (2005) develops generalized DFFITS (*GDFFITS*) for the identification of multiple influential observations as

$$GDFFITS_{i} = \begin{cases} \dfrac{\widehat{y}_{i}^{(-D)} - \widehat{y}_{i}^{(-D-i)}}{\widehat{\sigma}^{(-D-i)}\sqrt{h_{ii}^{(-D)}}}, \quad i \in R \\ \dfrac{\widehat{y}_{i}^{(-D+i)} - \widehat{y}_{i}^{(-D)}}{\widehat{\sigma}^{(-D)}\sqrt{h_{ii}^{(-D+i)}}}, \quad i \in D \end{cases}, \tag{41}$$

where $\widehat{y}_{i}^{(-D+i)} = x_{i}^{T}\widehat{\beta}^{(-D+i)} = \widehat{y}_{i}^{(-D)} + \dfrac{h_{ii}^{(-D)}}{1+h_{ii}^{(-D)}} r_{i}^{(-D)}$, and $h_{ii}^{(-D+i)} = \dfrac{h_{ii}^{(-D)}}{1+h_{ii}^{(-D)}}$.

He re-expresses *GDFFITS* in terms of deletion residuals and leverages as

$$GDFFITS_{i} = \begin{cases} \sqrt{\dfrac{h_{ii}^{(-D)}}{1-h_{ii}^{(-D)}}} \; \dfrac{r_{i}^{(-D)}}{\widehat{\sigma}^{(-D-i)}\sqrt{1-h_{ii}^{(-D)}}} \quad for \quad i \in R \\ \sqrt{\dfrac{h_{ii}^{(-D)}}{1+h_{ii}^{(-D)}}} \; \dfrac{r_{i}^{(-D)}}{\widehat{\sigma}^{(-D)}\sqrt{1+h_{ii}^{(-D)}}} \quad for \quad i \in D \end{cases} \tag{42}$$

$$= \sqrt{h_{ii}^{*}}t_{ii}^{*} \quad \text{for } i = 1, 2, \ldots, n.$$

Imon (2005) suggests *i*-th observation is influential if

$$\left|GDFFITS_{i}\right| \geq 3\sqrt{k(n-d)}.$$

Measure (M_i)

Pena (2005) introduces a new statistic totally in a different way to measure the influence of observations. To quote him, 'instead of looking at how the deletion of a point or the introduction of same perturbation affects the parameters, the forecasts, or the likelihood function, we look at how each point is influenced by the others in the sample. That is, for each sample point we measure the forecasted change when each other point in the sample is deleted'. He outlines a procedure to measures how each sample point is being influenced by the rest of the data. He considers the vector

$$s_{i} = (\widehat{y}_{i} - \widehat{y}_{i}^{(-1)}, \ldots, \widehat{y}_{i} - \widehat{y}_{i}^{(-n)})^{T}, \tag{43}$$

where $\hat{y}_i - \hat{y}_i^{(-j)}$ is the difference between the *i*-th estimated value of *y* in presence of all observations and after *j*-th observation deleted. Pena (2005) defines his statistic for the *i*-th observation as

$$S_i = \frac{s_i^T s_i}{p\, V\left(\hat{y}_i\right)}, \qquad i = 1, 2, \ldots, n \tag{44}$$

where $V\left(\hat{y}_i\right) = \text{var}\,iance\left(\hat{y}_i\right) = \hat{\sigma}^2 h_{ii}$. Pena (2005) calls an observation influential for which

$$\left|S_i\right| \geq median\ (S_i) + 4.5\ MAD\ (S_i). \tag{45}$$

Nurunnabi *et al.* (2010) show, Pena's (2005) statistic is not efficient in presence of multiple influential cases. To get better result and as a remedy of masking and swamping effect they propose a two-step group deletion measure, M_i. At the first step, the measure tries to find out all suspect unusual cases by existing reliable robust and/or diagnostic methods. Then it forms a deletion-group (*D*) by the suspect cases. After the deletion of the suspect group (*D*), it at a time again deletes specific sample point from each of the observations one after another and measure the difference between the forecast ($\hat{y}_j^{(-D)}$) and ($\hat{y}_{j(i)}^{(-D)}$) that are with and without the specific one (*i*-th point) respectively. The corresponding vector of estimated coefficients when a group of observations indexed by *D* is omitted is denoted as $\hat{\beta}^{(-D)}$. The vector of difference between $\hat{y}_j^{(-D)}$ and $\hat{y}_{j(i)}^{(-D)}$ is

$$t_{(i)}^{(-D)} = \left(\hat{y}_1^{(-D)} - \hat{y}_{1(i)}^{(-D)}, \cdots, \hat{y}_n^{(-D)} - \hat{y}_{n(i)}^{(-D)}\right)^T \tag{46}$$

$$= (t_{1(i)}^{(-D)}, \ldots, t_{n(i)}^{(-D)})^T \tag{47}$$

and

$$t_{j(i)}^{(-D)} = \hat{y}_j^{(-D)} - \hat{y}_{j(i)}^{(-D)} \tag{48}$$

where $h_{ji} = x_j^T (X^T X)^{-1} x_i$, $r_i^{(-D)} = y_i - \hat{y}_i^{(-D)}$. Finally, they define the measure as a squared standardized norm

$$M_i = \frac{t_{(i)}^{(-D)T} t_{(i)}^{(-D)}}{kV\left(\hat{y}_i^{(-D)}\right)}, \tag{49}$$

where $V\left(\hat{y}_i^{(-D)}\right) = s^2 h_{ii}$ and $s^2 = \dfrac{r^{(-D)T} r^{(-D)}}{N - k}$.

It is re-expressed in terms of leverage and residuals as

$$M_i = \frac{1}{ks^2 h_{ii}} \sum_{j=1}^{N} h_{ji}^{\ 2} \frac{r_i^{(-D)2}}{(1-h_{ii})^2} . \tag{50}$$

The method identifies *i*-th observation as an influential point if it satisfies the rule

$$|M_i| \geq median(M_i) + 4.5MAD(M_i) , \tag{51}$$

where $MAD(M_i) = median\left\{\left|M_i - median(M_i)\right|\right\} / 0.6745$.

Generalized Potential-Residual (GPR) Plot

Generalized potential-residual (GPR) plot is as similar to the potential-residual (P-R) plot, it uses generalized version of potentials and residuals in case of potentials and Studentized residuals. This is a scatter plot of Imon's (1996) generalized potentials versus Imon's (2005) generalized Studentized residuals. This enables to give clear indication about multiple outliers and multiple high-leverage points in a same plot (see Figure 8(d)).

Examples

Here we consider two well-referred datasets from the diagnostic literature; one is Hawkin-Bradu-Kass (Hawkins *et al.*, 1984) artificial dataset to get prior idea about extreme cases, and the other is the Nitrogen in Lakes dataset (Atkinson & Riani, 2000).

Hawkins-Bradu-Kass Data

Hawkins, Bradu and Kass (Hawkins *et al.*, 1984) construct an artificial data set with three regressors containing 75 observations with 14 unusual observations among them first ten cases (1-10) are high leverage outliers and next four cases (11-14) are high leverage points. Most of the single case deletion techniques fail to detect these influential observations. Some of them identify four high leverage points wrongly as outliers. On the other hand, robust regression techniques like LMS and RLS identify outliers correctly, but they do not focus on the high leverage points (see Rousseeuw & Leroy, 2003).

We compute different influence measures for this data set. To avoid a lengthy table we include only the results of the first 14 cases in Table 7. Standardized and Studentized LS residuals identify high-leverage points; and leverage values and potentials identify three cases (12, 13 and 14) as high-leverage points. We observe from this table that Cook's distance identifies only one (case 14) as influential observation. DFFITS identifies seven observations (cases 2, 7, 8, 11, 12, 13 and 14) correctly but fails to detect the rest of the seven. Figure 8 (a, b, c) shows that the single case deletion methods are failed to proper identification of outlying observations. It is interesting to note that Pena's measure (see Nurunnabi *et al.*, 2010) identifies only one case 14 as influential. Now, we employ BACON (Billor *et al.*, 2000) algorithm to this data set, it flags the first 14 cases as suspects. We compute GDFFITS and M_i for the entire data set after the omission of the suspected 14 cases and observe that both the measures successfully separate the first 14 observations from the rest of the cases and hence the cases (1-14) can be declared as influential observations. Figure 8 (e, f) clearly supports each other in favor of GDFFITS and *Mi*.

Figure 8. Hawkins-Bradu-Kass data; (a) Index plot of standardized residuals (b) Standardized residuals versus fitted values (c) Potentials versus Studentized residuals (d) GPR plot; generalized potentials versus generalized Studentized residuals (e) Index plot of GDFFITS and (f) Index plot of M_i

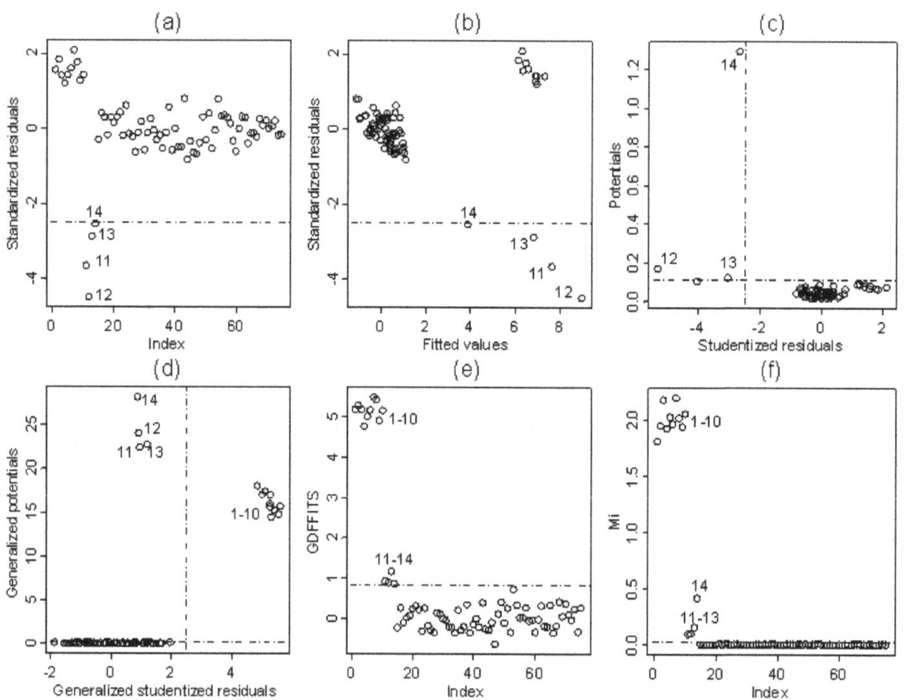

Table 7. Single and multiple case deletion diagnostic measures for Hawkins-Bradu-Kass data

Index	Std. residuals |2..50|	Stud. residuals |2..50|	h_{ii} (0.107)	Potentials (0.109)	CD (1.00)	DFFITS |0.462|	Generalized Studentized residuals |2..50|	Generalized potentials (0.192)	GDFFITS |0.849|	Mi (0.024)
1	1.55	1.57	0.063	0.067	0.040	0.406	5.353	14.464	5.177	1.806
2	1.83	1.86	0.060	0.064	0.053	0.470	5.442	15.223	5.272	1.945
3	1.40	1.41	0.086	0.094	0.046	0.430	5.319	16.967	5.169	2.176
4	1.19	1.19	0.081	0.088	0.031	0.352	4.889	18.015	4.759	1.924
5	1.41	1.42	0.073	0.079	0.039	0.399	5.145	17.381	5.003	2.026
6	1.59	1.61	0.076	0.082	0.052	0.459	5.314	15.611	5.151	1.964
7	2.08	2.13	0.068	0.073	0.079	0.575	5.647	15.705	5.475	2.194
8	1.76	1.79	0.063	0.067	0.052	0.464	5.589	14.817	5.410	2.015
9	1.26	1.26	0.080	0.087	0.034	0.372	5.040	17.034	4.899	1.937
10	1.41	1.42	0.087	0.095	0.048	0.439	5.308	15.974	5.149	2.053
11	-3.66	-4.03	0.094	0.104	0.348	-1.300	0.946	22.389	0.926	0.091
12	-4.50	-5.29	0.144	0.168	0.851	-2.168	0.902	24.026	0.884	0.099
13	-2.88	-3.04	0.109	0.122	0.254	-1.065	1.197	22.731	1.171	0.153
14	-2.56	-2.67	0.564	1.292	2.114	-3.030	0.872	28.158	0.857	0.417

Nitrogen in Lakes Data

This dataset is extracted from Atkinson and Riani (2000) as an example of multiple linear regression. There are 29 observations that have values with two explanatory variables and one response variable. The variables are:

- x_1: average influent nitrogen concentration,
- x_2: water retention time,
- y: mean annual nitrogen concentration.

The matrix plot in Figure 9 shows that there may be a linear relationship between y and x_1 without the 2 points (cases 10 and 23). In the same figure, scatter plot y versus x_2 reveals other 2 points (cases 2 and 22) are extreme to the rest of the dataset. We calculate both the single-case deletion and group-deletion diagnostic measures to show the effect of multiple outliers. In Table 8, we get LS standardized residuals and LS Studentized residuals do not identify any outlying cases. Three high leverage points are identified by leverage values (h_{ii}). Cook's distance (*CD*) identifies only one observation (23) and *DFFITS* identifies 3 observations (2, 16 and 23) as influential observations. That proves *CD* is affected by masking and *DFFITS* is affected by swamping respectively in presence of multiple outliers in the dataset. Atkinson and Riani (2000) make an extensive search and suspects 4 extreme cases (2, 10, 22, and 23), as we see in the matrix plot (Figure 9). Generalized potentials versus generalized Studentized residuals (GPR) plot (Figure 10 (d)) also gives clear indications about the extreme effect of the multiple outliers and high-leverage points. We calculate M_i with the deletion group containing the observation 2, 10, 22, and 23 as suspect cases. The Figure 10 (f) shows that three cases are influential in the data set. With the same suspect group, we calculate the *GDFFITS* values and find in Table 9 that the same 3 cases (2, 10 and 23) as influential observations by the values of *GDFFITS* and M_i.

ROBUST REGRESSION

Robust regression is another remedy for outlying observations, which wants to fit a regression to the majority of the data and then discover as those points that possess large residuals from the robust output. Among a good number of robust techniques, LMS, LTS, RWLS, MM and GMM (Huber, 1981; Hampel *et al.*, 1986; Rousseeuw & Leroy, 2003; Marona *et al.,* 2006) are the most well-known to the practitioners. To give a brief idea of the robust regression, we attach LMS, LTS, RWLS and MM -estimate. Though robust regression technique gives us better result as an alternative of LS, it has some deficiencies (i) The diversity of estimator types and the necessary choices of tuning constants are combined with a lack of guidance for these decisions (ii) The lack of simple procedures for inference or reluctance to use the straight forward inference based on asymptotic procedure. Here we have to take some help from the re-sampling techniques (Efron & Tibshirani, 1993) like 'bootstrapping' especially for small samples (iii) unfamiliarity with interpretation of results from a robust analysis.

Least Median of Squares (LMS) Regression

LMS is proposed by Hampel (1975) and further developed by Rousseeuw (1984). Instead of minimizing the sum of squared residuals, Rousseeuw proposes minimizing their median,

Figure 9. Matrix plot of nitrogen in Lakes data

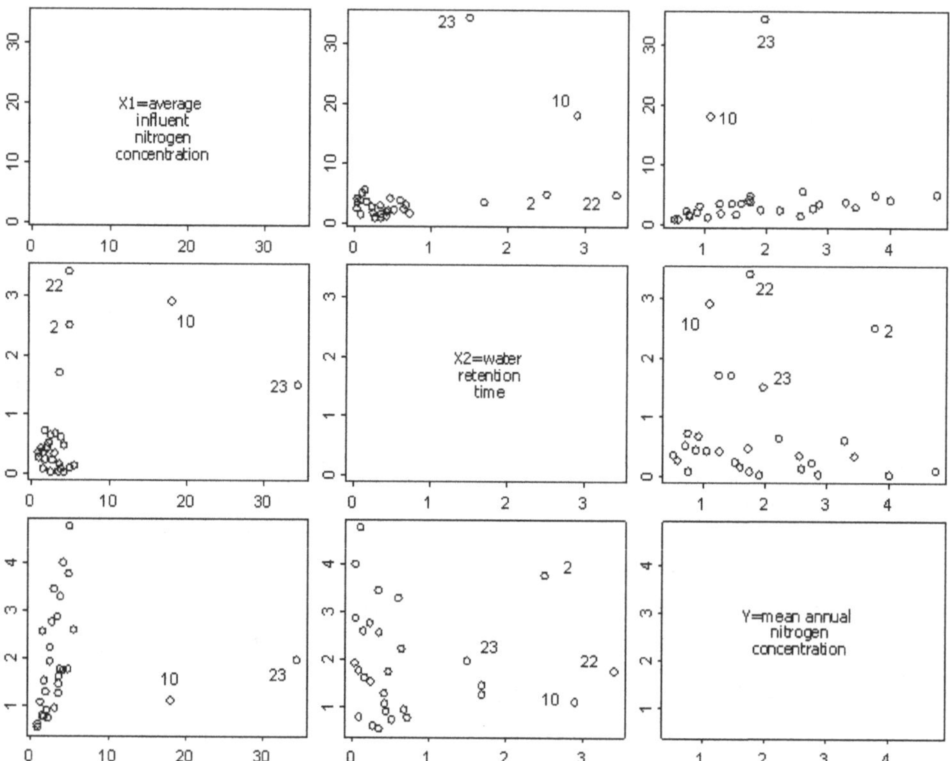

$$\text{minimize } r_i^2 \tag{52}$$

This estimator effectively trims almost the half ($n/2$) observations having the largest residuals, and uses the maximal residual value in the remaining set as the criterion to be minimized. Its breakdown point (Huber, 1981; Hampel *et al.*, 1986) is $\left(\lfloor n/2 \rfloor - p + 2/n\right)/n$ for p-dimensional data set *i.e.,* it attains maximum possible breakdown point 1/2 at usual models, but unfortunately it possesses poor asymptotic efficiency (Huber, 1981; Hampel *et al.,* 1986). In spite of that the family of LMS has excellent global robustness.

Least Trimmed Squares (LTS) Regression

LTS is introduced by Rousseeuw (1984) and is given as

$$\min_{\beta} \sum_{i=1}^{h} r_{i:n}^{\;2}, \tag{53}$$

Table 8. Single-case deletion diagnostic measures for nitrogen in Lakes data

Index	Fitted values	LS.reseiduals |2.50|	Std.residuals |2.50|	Stud. residuals |2.50|	h_{ii} (0.211)	potentials (0.093)	CD (1.00)	DFFITS |0.643|
1	2.044	0.55	0.49	0.48	0.058	0.061	0.005	0.119
2	1.634	2.14	2.07	2.22	0.200	0.250	0.357	1.110
3	1.919	-0.65	-0.57	-0.57	0.042	0.043	0.005	-0.118
4	1.740	-0.29	-0.27	-0.26	0.092	0.102	0.002	-0.084
5	1.928	1.36	1.20	1.21	0.035	0.037	0.018	0.232
6	1.901	-0.97	-0.86	-0.85	0.036	0.038	0.009	-0.165
7	1.998	-0.40	-0.35	-0.35	0.049	0.052	0.002	-0.079
8	1.739	-0.49	-0.44	-0.44	0.092	0.102	0.007	-0.140
9	1.954	1.50	1.32	1.34	0.041	0.043	0.025	0.279
10	1.850	-0.75	-0.78	-0.77	0.295	0.419	0.085	-0.500
11	2.015	-0.27	-0.24	-0.24	0.054	0.057	0.001	-0.056
12	1.903	-0.84	-0.75	-0.74	0.044	0.047	0.009	-0.160
13	1.918	-1.03	-0.91	-0.91	0.041	0.042	0.012	-0.187
14	1.968	0.79	0.70	0.69	0.046	0.048	0.008	0.151
15	1.945	-0.43	-0.38	-0.37	0.047	0.049	0.002	-0.083
16	2.038	2.73	2.44	2.72	0.058	0.061	0.121	0.672
17	1.892	0.33	0.29	0.28	0.038	0.040	0.001	0.057
18	1.922	-1.33	-1.18	-1.19	0.049	0.052	0.024	-0.271
19	1.907	-1.38	-1.22	-1.23	0.047	0.050	0.025	-0.275
20	1.996	-0.09	-0.08	-0.07	0.056	0.060	0.000	-0.018
21	2.032	1.98	1.77	1.85	0.059	0.063	0.065	0.462
22	1.481	0.26	0.30	0.29	0.415	0.710	0.021	0.247
23	2.435	-0.47	-0.98	-0.98	0.828	4.814	1.546	-2.152
24	1.921	0.63	0.56	0.55	0.044	0.047	0.005	0.120
25	1.965	-1.20	-1.06	-1.07	0.054	0.058	0.022	-0.256
26	1.908	-1.19	-1.05	-1.05	0.039	0.041	0.015	-0.213
27	1.959	-0.23	-0.20	-0.20	0.038	0.039	0.001	-0.039
28	2.016	0.84	0.75	0.75	0.057	0.060	0.011	0.183
29	1.863	-1.10	-0.98	-0.98	0.043	0.045	0.014	-0.206

where $r_{1:n}^2 \leq \cdots \leq r_{n:n}^2$ denotes the ordered squared residuals and h is to be chosen between $n/2$ and n. The LTS estimators search for the optimal subset of size h whose least squares fit has the smallest sum of squared residuals. Hence, the LTS estimate of β is then the least square estimate of that subset of size h. LTS has better statistical efficiency than LMS, because of its asymptotically normal property (Hossjer, 1994), whereas LMS has a lower convergence rate (Rousseeuw, 1984). It also fails to fit a correct model when large number of clustered outliers exits and with more than 50% outliers in the data. The

Figure 10. Nitrogen in Lakes data; (a) Index plot of standardized residuals (b) Standardized residuals versus fitted values (c) Potentials versus Studentized residuals (d) GPR plot; generalized potentials versus generalized Studentized residuals (e) Index plot of GDFFITS and (f) Index plot of M_i

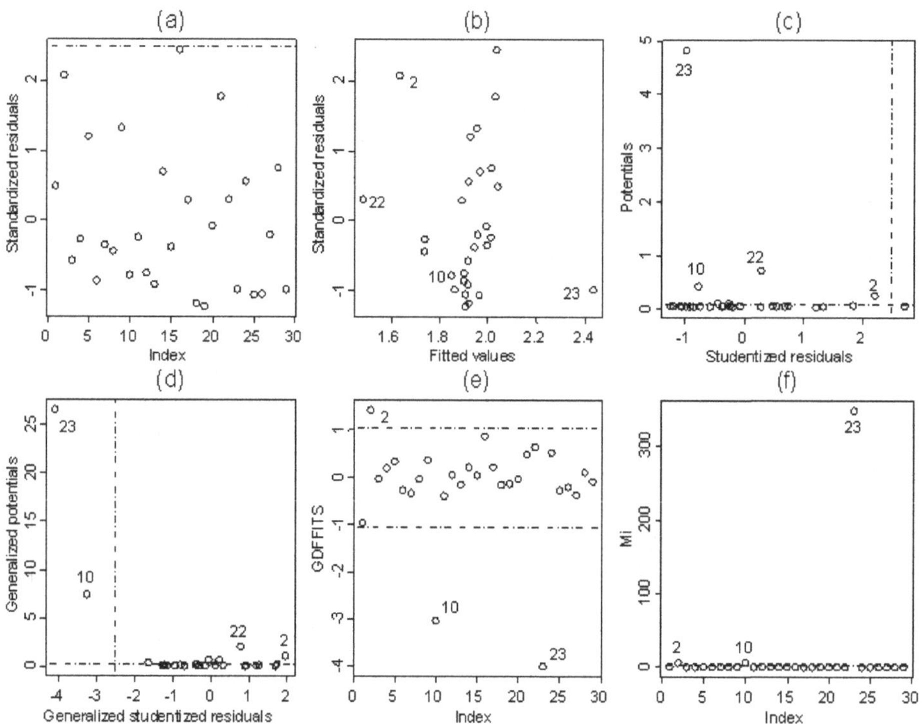

performance of this method has recently been improved by the FAST-LTS (Rousseeuw & Van Driessen, 1999) and Fast and robust bootstrap for LTS (Willems & Aelst, 2004).

Reweighted Least Squares (RLS) Regression

The basic principle of LMS and LTS is to fit the majority of the data, after which outliers may be identified as those points that lie far away from the robust fit; that is, the cases with large positive or large negative residuals. Rousseeuw and Leroy (2003) bring another idea to improve crude LMS and LTS solutions, apply a weighted least squares analysis based on the identification of outliers and use the following weights:

$$w_i = \begin{Bmatrix} 1 & if & \left| r_i / \hat{\sigma} \right| \leq 2.5 \\ 0 & if & \left| r_i / \hat{\sigma} \right| > 2.5 \end{Bmatrix}. \tag{54}$$

This means simply that the case i-th case will be retained in the weighted LS if its LMS residual is small to moderate, but disregarded if it is an outlier. Then they defined weighted least squares by

Table 9. Multiple-case deletion diagnostic measures for nitrogen in Lakes data

Index	Generalized Stud. residuals |2.50|	Generalized potentials (0.296)	GDFFITS |1.039|	Mi (0.140)	Index	Generalized Stud. residuals |2.50|	Generalized potentials (0.296)	GDFFITS |1.039|	Mi (0.140)
1	-1.631	0.352	-0.968	0.050	16	1.752	0.242	0.862	0.063
2	1.967	1.079	1.417	0.283	17	0.893	0.057	0.213	0.018
3	-0.153	0.063	-0.038	0.001	18	-0.397	0.164	-0.161	0.003
4	0.227	0.682	0.187	0.001	19	-0.366	0.162	-0.147	0.003
5	1.185	0.079	0.333	0.031	20	-0.133	0.085	-0.039	0.000
6	-1.155	0.059	-0.280	0.031	21	1.273	0.144	0.482	0.036
7	-1.231	0.079	-0.347	0.035	22	0.773	2.059	0.634	0.120
8	-0.051	0.679	-0.042	0.000	23	-4.074	26.572	-3.999	347.941
9	1.704	0.045	0.360	0.068	24	1.717	0.093	0.523	0.066
10	-3.241	7.425	-3.042	4.009	25	-0.786	0.126	-0.279	0.014
11	-1.265	0.101	-0.403	0.037	26	-0.934	0.053	-0.216	0.020
12	0.120	0.117	0.041	0.000	27	-1.202	0.101	-0.382	0.032
13	-0.694	0.057	-0.165	0.011	28	0.329	0.094	0.101	0.002
14	0.926	0.052	0.211	0.020	29	-0.308	0.100	-0.097	0.002
15	0.122	0.083	0.035	0.000					

$$\textit{minimize} \sum_{i=1}^{n} w_i r_i^2 . \tag{55}$$

Therefore, the RLS can be seen as ordinary LS on a reduced data set, consisting of only those observations that received a nonzero weight. The resulting estimator still possesses high breakdown point, but is more efficient in a statistical sense.

Robust MM Regression

S-PLUS (1997) computes a robust M-estimate (see Huber, 1981; Marona *et al.,* 2006) $\hat{\beta}$, which minimizes the objective function

$$\sum_{i=1}^{n} \rho\left(\frac{y_i - x_i^T \beta}{\hat{\sigma}}\right), \tag{56}$$

where $\hat{\sigma}$ is a robust scale estimate for the residuals and ρ is a particular optimal symmetric bounded loss function, described below.

Alternatively $\hat{\beta}$ is a solution of the estimating equation

$$\sum_{i=1}^{n} x_i \psi\left(\frac{y_i - x_i^T}{\hat{\sigma}}\right) = 0 \tag{57}$$

$\Psi = \rho'$ is a redescending (nonmonotonic) function. A key issue is that since ρ is bounded, it is non-convex, and the minimization above can have many local minima. Correspondingly, the estimating equation above can have multiple solutions. S-PLUS deals with this by computing highly robust initial estimates of $\hat{\beta}$ and $\hat{\sigma}$ with breakdown point 0.5, using the S-estimate approach described below, and computes the final estimate as the local minimum of the M-estimate objective function nearest to the initial estimate. We refer to an M-estimate of this type and compute in this special way as an MM-estimate, a term introduced by Yohai (1987). The key to obtaining a good local minimum of the M-estimation objective function, when using a bounded, non-convex loss function is to compute a highly robust initial estimate β^0. S-PLUS does this by using the S-estimate method introduced by Rousseeuw and Yohai (1984).

Examples

We give an example to demonstrate and show the performance of the group-deletion diagnostic measures and robust methods (LTS and LMS regression) in the same dataset.

Hertzsprung-Russell Diagram Data

Hertzsprung-Russsell diagram data (Rousseeuw and Leroy, 2003) is very well-known to the outlier diagnostic community, which contains 47 stars (observations) in the direction of Cygnus. The explana-

Figure 11. Scatter plot of Hertzsprung-Russell diagram data, LS line with and without outliers, LMS and LTS lines

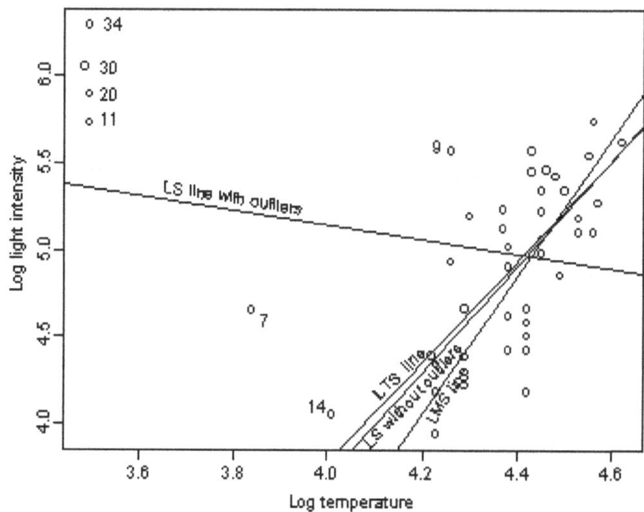

tory variable (X) is the logarithm of the effective temperature at the surface of the star and the dependent variable (Y) is the logarithm of its light intensity. Figure 11 is a scatter plot, log light intensity versus log temperature with LS (with and without outliers), LMS and LTS lines. Figure 11 shows that 4 stars (11, 20, 30 and 34) are clearly apart from the bulk of the stars. Two other stars (7 and 9) are also far from majority's direction. Rousseeuw and Leroy (2003) show that all the 6 stars (7, 9. 11, 20, 30, and 34) as outliers.

Since scatter plot in Figure 11 shows the presence of multiple outliers in the dataset, we calculate the group deletion diagnostic measures as well as the robust LTS and LMS residuals. In Table 10, columns 2 and 7 (LS standardized residuals) and columns 3 and 8 (LS Studentized residuals) show that there is no outlier in the dataset. But the generalized potential and generalized Studentized residuals identify the 7 cases (7, 9, 11, 14, 20, 30 and 34) as high-leverage points or outliers (see Figure 12(b)).

Table 10. Diagnostic and robust measures for Hertzsprung-Russell diagram data

Index	LS. Std.res |2.50|	LS.Stud.res |2.50|	G.Stud.res |2.50|	G.potentials (0.146)	Index	LS. Std.res |2.50|	LS.Stud.res |2.50|	G.Stud.res |2.50|	G.potentials (0.146)
1	0.435	0.431	1.244	0.027	25	0.066	0.065	0.529	0.026
2	1.500	1.522	1.061	0.070	26	-0.550	-0.546	-0.903	0.026
3	-0.184	-0.182	1.371	0.062	27	-0.645	-0.641	0.276	0.048
4	1.500	1.522	1.061	0.070	28	-0.149	-0.147	0.172	0.026
5	0.311	0.308	1.774	0.044	29	-1.182	-1.187	0.108	0.086
6	0.915	0.914	1.115	0.031	30	1.374	1.389	7.439	1.428
7	-1.026	-1.027	3.429	0.546	31	-1.009	-1.009	-1.255	0.026
8	0.660	0.656	-0.459	0.076	32	0.345	0.342	-0.881	0.070
9	0.962	0.961	3.120	0.058	33	0.477	0.473	0.490	0.029
10	0.238	0.235	0.917	0.027	34	1.852	1.906	7.883	1.397
11	0.748	0.744	6.822	1.397	35	-1.264	-1.272	-0.138	0.080
12	0.874	0.872	1.354	0.026	36	1.335	1.347	0.145	0.114
13	0.859	0.857	0.816	0.035	37	0.322	0.319	-0.60	0.054
14	-1.968	-2.035	1.157	0.386	38	0.477	0.473	0.490	0.029
15	-1.361	-1.375	-0.925	0.048	39	0.466	0.462	-0.359	0.054
16	-0.693	-0.689	-1.141	0.026	40	1.090	1.092	1.711	0.026
17	-1.980	-2.049	-1.357	0.080	41	-0.651	-0.646	-0.66	0.026
18	-1.411	-1.427	-2.330	0.026	42	0.190	0.188	0.014	0.029
19	-1.550	-1.576	-0.626	0.080	43	0.731	0.727	0.396	0.042
20	1.063	1.065	7.125	1.397	44	0.692	0.688	0.847	0.029
21	-1.147	-1.151	-0.565	0.048	45	1.131	1.135	0.545	0.064
22	-1.433	-1.450	-1.045	0.048	46	0.046	0.046	-0.224	0.029
23	-0.980	-0.980	-1.617	0.026	47	-0.837	-0.834	-1.379	0.026
24	-0.158	-0.156	-0.978	0.038					

Figure 12. Hertzsprung-Russell diagram data; (a) Standardized residuals versus fitted values (b)GPR plot; Generalized potentials versus generalized Studentized residuals (c) Index plot of LTS residuals (d) Index plot of LMS residuals (e) Index plot of GDFFITS, and (f) Index plot of M_i.

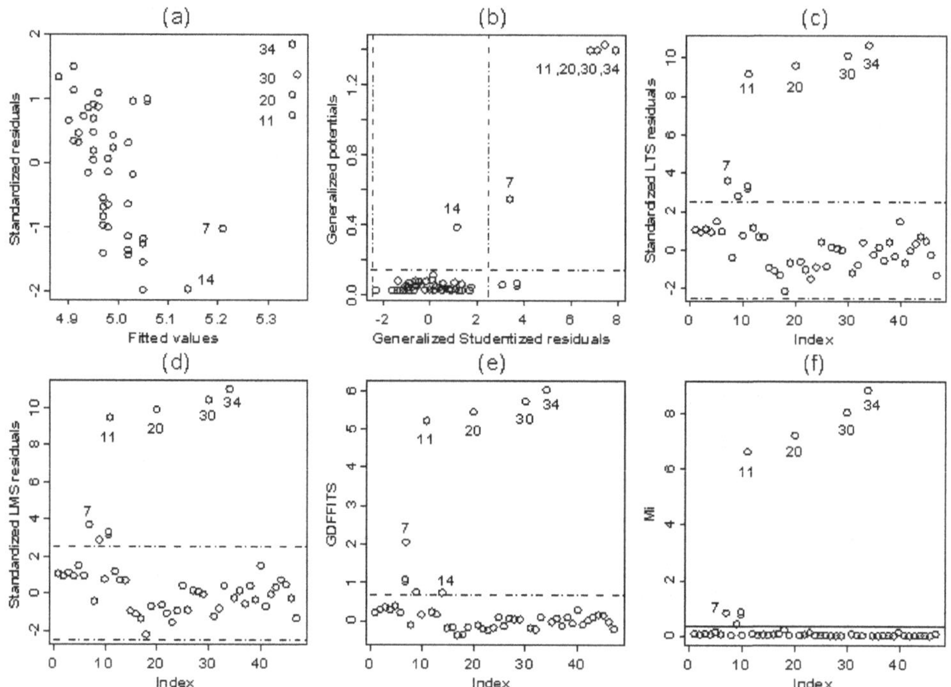

We calculate the values of M_i, considering the deletion group by the 6 suspected cases (7, 9, 11, 20, 30 and 34) that are identified from the scatter plot, single-case deletion measures and BACON algorithm. In Table 11, columns 3 and 8, the values of M_i support the index plot of M_i in Figure 12 (f). Considering same suspect observations we calculate *GDFFITS* and the values show that 7 observations (case 7, 9, 11, 14, 20, 30 and 34) are the influential in the dataset. At last we find the values of residuals from LTS and LMS in columns 4, 9 and 5, 10 respectively in Table 11. We find that the same six observations are identified by M_i as outliers.

Cement and Concrete Data

Our last example is a real data set of 1030 observations; taken from engineering literature (Yeh, 1998). This data set was assembled for concrete containing cement plus, fly ash, blast furnace, slag, and a superplasticizer. This data set is with total 1030 cases, 8 predictor (input) variables and one output variable. Variables are cement (X1), blast furnace Slag (X2), fly ash (X3), water (X4), superplasticizer (X5), coarse Aggregate (X6), fine aggregate (X7), age (Day 1~365; X8), and concrete compressive strength MPa (Y; output variable). Because of more than 3 dimensions (variables) we cannot show any initial plots before the diagnostics. Nurunnabi and Nasser (2009) show by Index plot of residuals and the residual versus fitted value plot that there is no indication of presence of outliers and even no indication of heterogeneity in the data set. They also show that the single case deletion diagnostic measures Cook's

Table 11. Diagnostic and robust measures for Hertzsprung-Russell diagram data

Index	GDFFITS |0.66|	Mi (0.221)	LTS.std. res |2.50|	LMS.std. res |2.50|	Index	GDFFITS |0.66|	Mi (0.221)	LTS.std.res |2.50|	LMS.std. res |2.50|
1	0.204	0.061	1.021	1.054	25	0.085	0.011	0.386	0.399
2	0.280	0.044	0.908	0.937	26	-0.144	0.032	-0.880	-0.908
3	0.340	0.071	1.074	1.109	27	0.060	0.003	0.125	0.129
4	0.280	0.044	0.908	0.937	28	0.028	0.001	0.067	0.069
5	0.371	0.121	1.456	1.503	29	0.032	0.000	-0.051	-0.053
6	0.195	0.049	0.937	0.967	30	5.705	8.053	10.077	10.405
7	2.038	0.824	3.576	3.692	31	-0.202	0.062	-1.208	-1.247
8	-0.126	0.008	-0.418	-0.432	32	-0.232	0.030	-0.792	-0.818
9	0.731	0.415	2.775	2.865	33	0.083	0.009	0.376	0.389
10	0.150	0.033	0.729	0.753	34	6.018	8.837	10.638	10.983
11	5.208	6.617	9.150	9.447	35	-0.039	0.001	-0.261	-0.270
12	0.220	0.072	1.142	1.179	36	0.049	0.001	0.125	0.129
13	0.154	0.026	0.676	0.698	37	-0.139	0.014	-0.561	-0.579
14	0.720	0.041	0.668	0.690	38	0.083	0.009	0.376	0.389
15	-0.202	0.033	-0.938	-0.968	39	-0.083	0.005	-0.348	-0.359
16	-0.182	0.051	-1.092	-1.128	40	0.277	0.116	1.461	1.508
17	-0.383	0.069	-1.324	-1.367	41	-0.106	0.017	-0.677	-0.699
18	-0.372	0.214	-2.155	-2.225	42	0.002	0.000	-0.049	-0.050
19	-0.176	0.015	-0.687	-0.709	43	0.081	0.006	0.309	0.319
20	5.440	7.219	9.575	9.886	44	0.144	0.028	0.695	0.718
21	-0.123	0.012	-0.619	-0.639	45	0.138	0.012	0.454	0.469
22	-0.228	0.042	-1.044	-1.078	46	-0.038	0.002	-0.261	-0.270
23	-0.258	0.103	-1.517	-1.566	47	-0.220	0.075	-1.305	-1.347
24	-0.191	0.038	-0.916	-0.945					

distance, *DFFITS*, and S_i (Pena, 2005) all are failed to identify outliers, but the deleted residuals versus deleted fitted values plot and the histogram of deleted residual show clear indications of the presence of heterogeneity. We apply LMS, LTS and MM robust methods and get 96 observations as outliers, we make deleted group by putting them at the end of the design matrix as our algorithms and the last 96 observations are deleted. We get that *GDFFITS* and M_i successfully identify 151 influential cases, including the above 96. Results from *GDFFITS* and M_i prove that 55 (151-96) cases were masked before. Figure 13 shows a comparative study for the outliers' indications for robust regression and regression diagnostics in a same frame.

FINDINGS AND FUTURE ISSUES

Successful identification of outliers in linear regression has a much close concern with regression diagnostics and robust regression. There is a lot of diagnostic statistics available both in regression diagnostics

Figure 13. Cement and Concrete data; (a)Index plot of standardized residuals (b)Index plot of standardized LMS residuals (c) Index plot of standardized LTS residuals (d) Index plot of standardized MM residuals (e) Index plot of GDFFITS and (f)Index plot of M_i

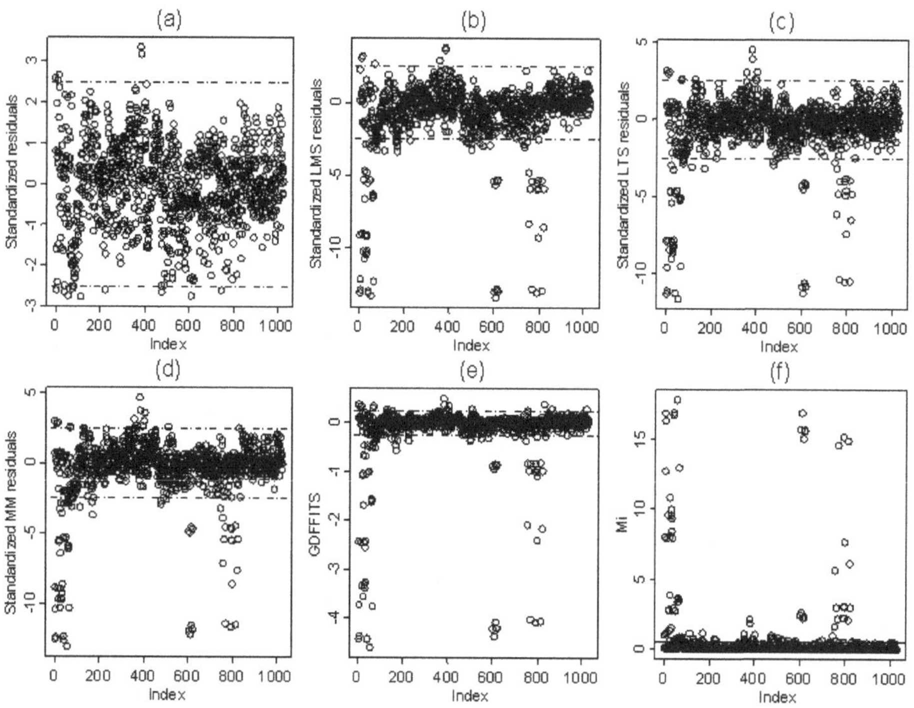

and robust regression. We see most of the times, specific one is not good for every situation. No such a significant guideline in literature to use them effectively. That is why it is problematic for practitioners to use the diagnostic measures efficiently. Only practice and knowledge of data analysis can make the user perfect. In regression diagnostics, graphical methods are not well suited with multiple linear regressions, because scatter plot is not very much effective for more than one explanatory variable. For numerical measures, single case deletion techniques are not sufficient for multiple outlier detection. They are frequently affected by masking and swamping phenomena. We find out the group deletion diagnostic methods that show better performance for identifying multiple outliers in linear regression. But multiple case (group) deletion techniques are sometimes impossible for combinatorial problems, especially for massive (high-dimensional and large) data sets. Robust techniques are not affected by combinatorial problem but they are much more depending on sophisticated mathematical knowledge. These are very computationally intensive and are not currently suitable for large data sets. The lack of simple procedure for inference makes reluctant to use robust regressions. At the beginning statisticians differ but now they recognize robust regression and regression diagnostics are two complementary approaches. We find out the group deletion diagnostic methods with robust regression show better performance for identifying outliers in linear regression. We use both of them for identifying irregular observations/outliers at a time.

Most of the existing methods are not efficient for large and high-dimensional data sets. There is no single universally applicable or generic outlier detection technique. Literature shows, only statistical approaches is not sufficient for outlier detection in real data sets. To fulfill the necessity, it is obvious that a full gamut of statistical (parametric and non parametric), neural and machine learning effort is needed. Additional research is also needed to find easily compatible and robust approach for large and high dimensional data that is to be efficient in data mining and similar applications.

REFERENCES

Allen, D. M. (1974). The relationship between variable selection and data augmentation and a method of prediction. *Technometrics, 16*, 125–127. doi:10.2307/1267500

Angiulli, F., Basta, S., & Pizzuti, C. (2006). Distance-based detection and prediction of outliers. *IEEE Transactions on Knowledge and Data Engineering, 18*(2), 145–160. doi:10.1109/TKDE.2006.29

Anscombe, F. J. (1973). Graphs in statistical analysis. *The American Statistician, 27*, 17–21. doi:10.2307/2682899

Atkinson, A. C. (1985). *Plots, transformations and regression*. Oxford, UK: Clarendon Press.

Atkinson, A. C. (1986). Masking unmasked. *Biometrika, 73*, 533–541. doi:10.1093/biomet/73.3.533

Atkinson, A. C., & Riani, M. (2000). *Robust diagnostic regression analysis*. London, UK: Springer.

Barnett, V., & Lewis, T. B. (1995). *Outliers in statistical data*. New York, NY: Wiley.

Barron, A. R. (1993). Universal approximation bounds for superpositions of a sigmoidal function. *IEEE Transactions on Information Theory, 39*, 930–944. doi:10.1109/18.256500

Barron, A. R. (1994). Approximation and estimation bounds for artificial neural networks. *Machine Learning, 14*, 115–133. doi:10.1007/BF00993164

Behnken, D. W., & Draper, N. R. (1972). Residuals and their variance patterns. *Technometrics, 14*, 101–111. doi:10.2307/1266922

Belsley, D. A., Kuh, E., & Welsch, R. E. (1980). *Regression diagnostics: Identifying influential data and sources of collinearity*. New York, NY: Wiley.

Billor, N., Hadi, A. S., & Velleman, F. (2000). BACON: Blocked adaptive computationally efficient outlier nominator. *Computational Statistics & Data Analysis, 34*, 279–298. doi:10.1016/S0167-9473(99)00101-2

Breiman, L., Meisel, W., & Purcell, E. (1977). Variable kernel estimates of multivariate densities. *Technometrics, 19*(2), 135–144. doi:10.2307/1268623

Breunig, M., Kriegel, H. P., Ng, R., & Sander, J. L. O. F. (2000). Identifying density-based local outliers. In *Proceedings of the 2000 ACM SIGMOD International Conference on Management of Data*, (pp. 93-104). New York, NY: ACM Press.

Chambers, J. M., Cleveland, W. S., Kleiner, B., & Tukey, P. A. (1983). *Graphical methods for data analysis*. Boston, MA: Duxbury Press.

Chatterjee, S., & Hadi, A. S. (1986). Influential observations, high leverage points, and outliers in regression. *Statistical Science*, *1*, 379–416. doi:10.1214/ss/1177013622

Chatterjee, S., & Hadi, A. S. (1988). *Sensitivity analysis in linear regression*. New York, NY: Wiley.

Chatterjee, S., & Hadi, A. S. (2006). *Regression analysis by examples*. New York, NY: Wiley. doi:10.1002/0470055464

Chiang, Y. M., Chang, L. C., Tsai, M. J., Wang, Y. F., & Chang, F. J. (2010). Dynamic neural networks for real-time water level predictions of sewerage systems–covering gauged and ungauged sites. *Hydrology and Earth System Sciences Discussions*, *7*, 2317–2345. doi:10.5194/hessd-7-2317-2010

Cook, R. D. (1977). Detection of influential observations in linear regression. *Technometrics*, *19*, 15–18. doi:10.2307/1268249

Cook, R. D. (1979). Influential observations in regression. *Journal of the American Statistical Association*, *74*, 169–174. doi:10.2307/2286747

Cook, R. D. (1986). Assessment of local influence. *Journal of the Royal Statistical Society. Series B. Methodological*, *48*(2), 133–169.

Cook, R. D. (1998). *Regression graphics: Ideas for studying regression through graphics*. New York, NY: Wiley.

Cook, R. D., & Weisberg, S. (1982). *Residuals and influence in regression*. London, UK: Chapman and Hall.

Davies, P., Imon, A. H. M. R., & Ali, M. M. (2004). A conditional expectation method for improved residual estimation and outlier identification in linear regression. *International Journal of Statistical Sciences, Special issue*, 191-208.

Davis, R. B., & Hutton, B. (1975). The effects of errors in the independent variables in linear regression. *Biometrika*, *62*, 383–391. doi:10.2307/2335377

Debruyne, M., Engelene, S., Hubert, M., & Rousseeuw, P. J. (2006). Robustness and outlier detection in chemomtrics. Retrieved on February 9, 2010, from wis.kuleuven.be/stat/robust/Papers/Robustness-CRAC.pdf

Efron, B., & Tibshirani, R. J. (1993). *An introduction to the bootstrap*. New York, NY: Wiley.

Ellenberg, J. H. (1976). Testing for a single outlier from a general regression. *Biometrics*, *32*, 637–645. doi:10.2307/2529752

Eskin, E., Arnold, A., Prerau, M., Portnoy, L., & Stolfo, S. (2002). A geometric framework for unsupervised anomaly detection: Detecting intrusions in unlabeled data. In Jajodia, S., & Barbara, D. (Eds.), *Applications of data mining in computer security, advances in information security*. Boston, MA: Kluwer Academic Publishers.

Fox, J. (1993). Regression diagnostics. In Beck, M. S. L. (Ed.), *Regression analysis* (pp. 245–334). London, UK: Sage Publications.

Gnanadesikan, R., & Wilk, M. B. (1968). Probability plotting methods for the analysis of data. *Biometrika*, *55*(1), 1–17.

Gray, J. B. (1986). A simple graphic for assessing influence in regression. *Journal of Statistical Computation and Simulation*, *24*, 121–134. doi:10.1080/00949658608810895

Grubbs, F. (1969). Procedures for detecting outlying observations in samples. *Technometrics*, *11*(1), 1–21. doi:10.2307/1266761

Hadi, A. S. (1992). A new measure of overall potential influence in linear regression. *Computational Statistics & Data Analysis*, *14*, 1–27. doi:10.1016/0167-9473(92)90078-T

Hadi, A. S., Imon, A. H. M. R., & Werner, M. (2009). *Detection of outliers, overview* (pp. 57–70). New York, NY: Wiley.

Hadi, A. S., & Simonoff, J. S. (1993). Procedures for the identification of outliers. *Journal of the American Statistical Association*, *88*, 1264–1272. doi:10.2307/2291266

Hampel, F. R. (1975). Beyond location parameters: Robust concepts and methods. *Bulletin of the International Statistics Institute*, *46*, 375–382.

Hampel, F. R., Ronchetti, E. M., Rousseeuw, P. J., & Stahel, W. A. (1986). *Robust statistics: The approach based on influence function*. New York, NY: Wiley.

Hawkins, D. M., Bradu, D., & Kass, G. V. (1984). Location of several outliers in multiple regression data using elemental sets. *Technometrics*, *26*, 197–208. doi:10.2307/1267545

Hawkins, S., He, G., Williams, H., & Baxter, R. (2002). Outlier detection using replicator neural networks. In *Proceedings of the 4th International Conference on Data Warehousing and Knowledge Discovery* (DaWaK02), Aix-en-Provence, France, (pp. 170-180).

Hoaglin, D. C., & Welsch, R. E. (1978). The hat matrix in regression and ANOVA. *The American Statistician*, *32*, 17–22. doi:10.2307/2683469

Hocking, R. R., & Pendleton, O. J. (1983). The regression dilemma. *Communications in Statistics Theory and Methods*, *12*, 497–527. doi:10.1080/03610928308828477

Hodge, V. J., & Austin, J. (2004). A survey of outlier detection methodologies. *Artificial Intelligence Review*, *22*, 85–106. doi:10.1023/B:AIRE.0000045502.10941.a9

Hossjer, O. (1994). Rank-based estimates in the linear model with high breakdown point. *Journal of the American Statistical Association*, *89*, 149–158. doi:10.2307/2291211

Huber, P. J. (1975). *Robustness and designs: A survey of statistical design and linear models*. Amsterdam, The Netherlands: North-Holland Press.

Huber, P. J. (1977). Robust covariances. In Gupta, S. S., & Moore, D. S. (Eds.), *Statistical decision theory and related topics* (pp. 165–191). New York, NY: Academic Press.

Huber, P. J. (1981). *Robust statistics*. New York, NY: Wiley.

Huber, P. J. (1991). Between robustness and diagnostics. In Stahel, W., & Weisberg, S. (Eds.), *Direction in robust statistics and diagnostics* (pp. 121–130). New York, NY: Springer-Verlag.

Igelnik, B. (2009). *Kolmogorov's spline complex network and adaptive dynamic modeling of data. Complex-valued neural networks: Utilizing high-dimensional parameters* (pp. 56–78). Hershey, PA: IGI-Global.

Imon, A. H. M. R. (1996). *Subsample methods in regression residual prediction and diagnostics*. Unpublished doctoral dissertation, University of Birmingham, UK.

Imon, A. H. M. R. (2005). Identifying multiple influential observations in linear regression. *Journal of Applied Statistics*, *32*, 73–90. doi:10.1080/02664760500163599

Knorr, M. E., Ng, T. R., & Tucakov, V. (2000). Distance-based outlier: Algorithms and applications. *The VLDB Journal*, *8*(3-4), 237–253. doi:10.1007/s007780050006

Mahalanobis, P. C. (1936). On the generalized distance in statistics. *Proceedings of the National Institute of Science of India*, *12*, 49–55.

Maronna, R. A., Martin, R. D., & Yohai, V. J. (2006). *Robust statistics: Theory and methods*. New York, NY: Wiley.

McCulloch, C. E., & Meeter, D. (1983). Discussion of outlier…s. *Technometrics*, *25*, 119–163. doi:10.2307/1268543

Miller, R. G. (1974). The Jackknife: A review. *Biometrika*, *61*, 1–15.

Nigsch, F., Bender, A., van Buuren, B., Tissen, J., Nigsch, E., & Mitchell, J. B. O. (2006). Melting point prediction employing k-nearest neighbor algorithms and genetic parameter optimization. *Journal of Chemical Information and Modeling*, *46*(6), 2412–2422. doi:10.1021/ci060149f

Nurunnabi, A. A. M., Imon, A. H. M. R., & Nasser, M. (2011). A diagnostic measure for influential observations in linear regression. *Communications in Statistics Theory and Methods*, *40*(7), 1169–1183. doi:10.1080/03610920903564727

Nurunnabi, A. A. M., & Nasser, M. (2009). Outlier detection by regression diagnostics in large data. In *Proceedings of International Conference on Future Computer and Communication*, 3-5 April, Kuala Lumpur, Malaysia, (pp. 246-250).

Pena, D. (2005). A new statistic for influence in linear regression. *Technometrics*, *47*, 1–12. doi:10.1198/004017004000000662

Pena, D., & Yohai, V. J. (1995). The detection of influential subsets in linear regression by using an influence matrix. *Journal of the Royal Statistical Society. Series B. Methodological*, *57*, 145–156.

Pregibon, D. (1981). Logistic regression diagnostics. *Annals of Statistics*, *9*, 977–986. doi:10.1214/aos/1176345513

Rousseeuw, P. J. (1984). Least median of squares regression. *Journal of the American Statistical Association*, *79*, 871–880. doi:10.2307/2288718

Rousseeuw, P. J. (1985). A regression diagnostic for multiple outliers and leverage points. *Abstracts in IMS Bulletin*, *14*, 399.

Rousseeuw, P. J., & Leroy, A. M. (2003). *Robust regression and outlier detection*. New York, NY: Wiley.

Rousseeuw, P. J., & van Driessen, K. (1999). A fast algorithm for the minimum covariance determinant estimator. *Technometrics*, *41*, 212–223. doi:10.2307/1270566

Rousseeuw, P. J., & van Zomeren, B. C. (1990). Unmasking multivariate outliers and leverage points. *Journal of the American Statistical Association*, *85*, 633–639. doi:10.2307/2289995

Rousseeuw, P. J., & Yohai, V. (1984). Robust regression by means of S-estimators. In Franke, J., Hardle, W., & Martin, R. D. (Eds.), *Robust and non-linear time series analysis* (pp. 256–272). New York, NY: Springer-Verleg.

Ryan, T. P. (1997). *Modern regression methods*. New York, NY: Wiley.

S-PLUS 4. (1997). *Guide to statistics*. Math Soft Inc., Seattle, Washington.

Searle, S. R. (1982). *Matrix algebra useful for statistics*. New York, NY: Wiley.

Shao, J., & Tu, D. (1995). *The jackknife and bootstrap*. New York, NY: Springer Verlag.

Simonoff, J. S. (1991). General approaches to stepwise identification of unusual values in data analysis. In Stahel, W., & Weisberg, S. (Eds.), *Robust statistics and diagnostics: Part II* (pp. 223–242). New York, NY: Springer-Verlag.

Stahel, W., & Weisberg, S. (1991). *Direction in robust statistics and diagnostics, (Preface)*. New York, NY: Springer-Verlag.

Terrell, G. R., & Scott, D. W. (1992). Variable kernel density estimation. *Annals of Statistics*, *20*(3), 1236–1265. doi:10.1214/aos/1176348768

Tukey, J. W. (1977). *Exploratory data analysis*. USA: Addision- Wesley.

Velleman, P. F., & Welsch, R. E. (1981). Efficient computing in regression diagnostics. *The American Statistician*, *35*, 234–242. doi:10.2307/2683296

Willems, G., & Aelst, S. V. (2004). *Fast and robust bootstrap for LTS*. Elsevier Science.

Wu, C. F. J. (1986). Jackknife, bootstrap, and other resampling methods in regression analysis. *Annals of Statistics*, *14*, 1261–1350. doi:10.1214/aos/1176350142

Yeh, I.-C. (1998). Modeling of strength of high-performance concrete using artificial neural networks. *Cement and Concrete Research*, *28*(12), 1797–1808. doi:10.1016/S0008-8846(98)00165-3

Yohai, V. J. (1987). High breakdown point and high efficiency robust estimates for regression. *Annals of Statistics*, *15*, 642–656. doi:10.1214/aos/1176350366

KEY TERMS AND DEFINITIONS

High-Leverage Point: Observations that are deviated in X-direction and do not follow the pattern of the majority of the data called high-leverage points.

Influential Observation: Influential observation is one which either individual or together with several other observations has a demonstrably larger impact on the calculated values of various estimates (coefficients, standard errors, t-values, etc) than is the case for most of the other observations.

Masking: Masking occurs when an outlying subset goes undetected because of the presence of another, usually adjacent, subset. Masking is a false negative decision.

Multiple Outliers: A group of outliers that are deviated from the majority of the observations in a dataset are called multiple outliers.

Outlier: Outliers are a minority of observation(s) in a dataset that have different patterns from that of the majority observations in the dataset.

Regression Analysis: Regression analysis is a statistical technique, which helps us to investigate and to fit an unknown model, quantifies relations among observed variables in multifactor data. In linear regression, the model specification is that the dependent variable is a linear combination of the parameters (but need not be linear in the independent variables).

Regression Diagnostic: Regression diagnostics are techniques for exploring problems that compromise a regression analysis and for determining whether certain assumptions appear reasonable. We use the term 'regression diagnostics' to serve the purpose for outlier detection in a dataset. It is designed to detect and delete/refit (if necessary) the outliers first and then to fit the good data by classical (e.g., least squares) methods.

Robust Regression: Robust regression, which wants to fit a regression to the majority of the data and then discover as those points that possess large residuals from the robust output.

Swamping: Swamping occurs when good observations are incorrectly identified as outliers because of the presence of another, usually remote subset of observations. Swamping is a false positive decision.

Chapter 21
Artificial Intelligence Techniques for Unbalanced Datasets in Real World Classification Tasks

Marco Vannucci
Scuola Superiore Sant'Anna, Italy

Valentina Colla
Scuola Superiore Sant'Anna, Italy

Silvia Cateni
Scuola Superiore Sant'Anna, Italy

Mirko Sgarbi
Scuola Superiore Sant'Anna, Italy

ABSTRACT

In this chapter a survey on the problem of classification tasks in unbalanced datasets is presented. The effect of the imbalance of the distribution of target classes in databases is analyzed with respect to the performance of standard classifiers such as decision trees and support vector machines, and the main approaches to improve the generally not satisfactory results obtained by such methods are described. Finally, two typical applications coming from real world frameworks are introduced, and the uses of the techniques employed for the related classification tasks are shown in practice.

DOI: 10.4018/978-1-60960-551-3.ch021

INTRODUCTION

When dealing with real world classification tasks it often happens to face problems related to unbalanced datasets. Although there is no prearranged rule for the definition of such datasets, they are characterized by a not uniform distribution of the samples in terms of the *class* variable which is also the one to be predicted by the classifier.

The effect of the class unbalance is, in most cases, very detrimental for the predictive performances of any classifier, in facts most of them, such as decision trees, neural networks and SVM, are designed to obtain optimal performances in terms of global errors (Estabrooks, 2000) thus, as a result, when coping with this kind of datasets they achieve good performance when classifying the most represented patterns while the others are practically ignored. In these cases the classification abilities of the predictors are compromised by several interacting factors. A part from rare cases where patterns belonging to different classes are clearly discernible and samples in the input space are easily separable, the little number of samples corresponding to infrequent events prejudices their correct characterization and makes the separation of the classes difficult for the classifier. Moreover in many real world problems the presence of noise in the data plays as well a detrimental role for the classifiers as it introduces further uncertainties.

Unbalanced datasets concern many real world problems. In the industrial framework malfunction detection databases are often unbalanced as when monitoring industrial processes most observations are related to the normal situations while the number of abnormal ones is represented only by a little percentage. In the same framework, in quality control tasks, the quantity of defective products is much lower than the number of those which have been produced without defects. A similar thing is observed in certain classification tasks in the medical field such as for instance in the diagnosis of breast cancer from the analysis of biopsy images: also in this case the dataset is unbalanced in favor of negative tests. Furthermore in the financial framework the fraud detection belongs to the same set of problems, in facts among the transactions constituting the database to be analyzed for the characterization of frauds a very high percentage of them corresponds to normal situations.

Another aspect to be considered when dealing with these kind of problems is that in certain fields, as those just cited, the rare events correspond to critical situations which should be identified as the different kinds of misclassification errors do not have the same relevance. In facts it is very important to detect a machinery malfunctioning in order to restore a normal situation in the production line by avoiding possible losses in terms of time and money; on the other hand it is not a big problem if a normal situation is misclassified as a malfunctioning, as a *false alarm* is generated, which would only lead to supplementary controls on the machinery without any substantial drawback. Similarly in the medical field the missed detection of a disease could bring to dreadful consequences while a false alarm simply to further medical exams.

Unfortunately most of these critical situations would not be identified by standard classifiers for the previously mentioned reasons, thus, in order to overcome this problem, many methods have been developed. Two different methodological approaches can be distinguished for dealing with unbalanced datasets: the *external* and *internal* ones. Internal approaches are based on the creation of new algorithms expressly designed for facing uneven datasets while the external ones exploit traditional algorithms but with suitably re-sampled databases in order to reduce the detrimental effect of unbalance.

Within this chapter the effect of unbalanced datasets in classification tasks will be described and analyzed; afterwards the main internal and external methods for coping with this problem will be presented and discussed together with some practical examples. Subsequently some case studies taken from real world applications will be described and finally conclusive remarks will be drawn.

CLASSIFICATION TASKS WITH UNBALANCED DATASETS

The detrimental effect of dataset imbalance on the predictive performances of standard classifiers can be observed in most of the datasets affected by such drawback. The performance reduction involves both the rate of overall correct classifications and the rate of rare events detected that – as it was previously mentioned – is a key issue for most applications and contributes to making the problem of the classification tasks with unbalanced datasets very critical.

The factors reducing these performance indexes are manifold and interacting. Among them the following ones are noticeable:

- little number of rare samples
- low separability of patterns
- the attitude of standard classifiers
- noise and outliers

The little number of samples belonging to rare classes makes the mission of the classifiers which have to characterize them by using a little number of information very hard. This aspect is particularly important if combined with the low separability of classes with respect to their location in the input space: in that case - due to the attitude of standard classifiers, which tend to maximize the overall performance – the task of the classifier will be more complicated as it will tend to not to separate patterns belonging to different classes. The presence of noise and outliers affects classifiers performance as well, due to the introduction of uncertainties in the dataset. All these factors mostly affect the classifier's performances in terms of generalization capabilities downgrading thus its operation on *real* problems when coping with unknown data.

Furthermore it must be emphasized that when coping with real world databases all these factors are very often observed; therefore large efforts in the improvement of techniques for classification purpose on these datasets are justified.

The effect of imbalance in datasets is independent with respect to the used classifier. In facts in literature are presented many comparative works (Estabrooks & Japkowicz, 2004) (Japkowicz, 2000) which show that unbalanced datasets produce the same effect in different frameworks and applications when faced with different methods. In particular the characteristics of the effect of unbalance in dataset have been studied in (Estabrooks & Japkowicz, 2004), which analyzes the predictive performance of decision trees trained by means of the C4.5 algorithm (Quinlan, 1993) on several datasets derived from real world applications or synthetically generated with different rates of rare events. In order to show within this paper this behavior, several tests have been performed on a well known database provided by the UCI Machine learning repository. Such dataset, the Wisconsin Breast Cancer Database (WBCDB), collects information concerning the analysis of biopsies conducted on patients suspected of breast cancer. From each analysis a set of features is extracted and is used to predict the presence (positive case) or the absence (negative case) of a tumor. This dataset contains 699 observations of which 34.5% correspond to positive examples. The tests performed aim at pointing out the effect of different degrees of unbalance in order to obtain general indications on classifiers behavior. In particular tests have been performed with subsets of the original datasets with the following ratios of positive/negative examples: 3:1, 2:1, 1:1, 1:2 (which corresponds more or less to the natural ratio), 1:3. The percentage of correct

Figure 1. Overall rate of patterns coming form the WBCDB with different degrees of imbalance (including the original rate labeled as "natural") correctly classified by means of C4.5 trained decision trees

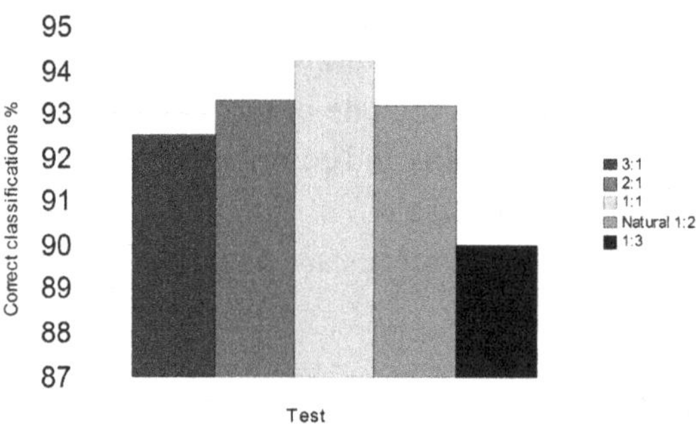

Figure 2. Rate of minority patterns (2a) and false alarms risen (2b) for patterns coming from the WBCDB with different degrees of imbalance. Classification performed by means of decision trees trained with the C4.5 algorithm

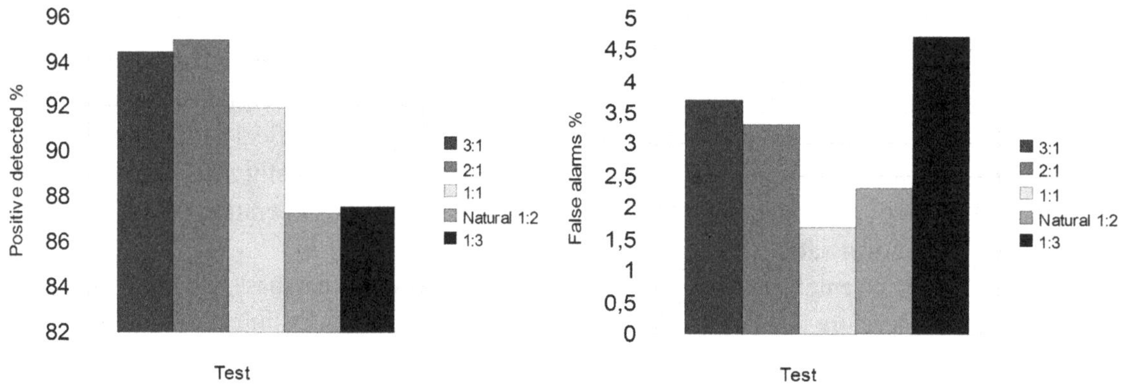

classifications obtained by decision trees trained by means of the C4.5 algorithm on the considered datasets are shown in Figure 1.

Together with the rate of correct classifications two other performance index have been taken into consideration: the rate of positive examples detected and the rate of false alarms. It must be highlighted that, due to the particular field of application of the classification task, the rate of positive detected is very important and its impact on the evaluation of a classifier clearly overcome the impact of false alarms rate. In Figure 2 these two latter performances are shown for the employed datasets. From the obtained results several consideration can be drawn:

- from Figure 1 it can be seen the detrimental effect of unbalanced datasets in terms of correct classifications. In particular, independently from the majority class, the more the dataset is unbalanced the lower is the performance. The same behavior is noticed on the rate of false alarms risen (Figure 2b).

- From Figure 2a it stands out that the rate of positive examples detected is related to their rate within the dataset. This behavior is in line with expectation as standard classifiers are oriented to the achievement of an overall optimal performance which corresponds to the correct classification of majority classes.

The results and consideration shown concerning the WBCDB are in line with those obtained for the other datasets analyzed in (Estabrooks & Japkowicz, 2004), thus it is possible to outline the general trend of the classification performance obtained by standard classifiers in presence of uneven datasets. In facts, in general, the more the dataset is unbalanced, the more performances are compromised, since the classifier tends to correctly classify the data belonging to the dominating classes, by ignoring the other ones. This effect is particularly important if the rare class corresponds to events whose identification is critical, because infrequent events tend not to be correctly spotted. Once the drawbacks deriving from unbalanced datasets have been focused, in the next paragraph, the most common techniques that have been developed in order to face this problem will be described.

TECHNIQUES AND ALGORITHMS FOR COPING WITH UNBALANCED DATASETS

As previously mentioned, there are two possible approaches for coping with the classifier's performances decrease due to unbalanced datasets: internal and external methods. The internal approaches are based on the development of new algorithms expressly designed for facing the problems related to unbalance in datasets. In this framework, together with new algorithms, there are standard algorithms which have been modified for this purpose. Internal methods can in certain cases solve the problem but they present the main drawback of being "algorithm- and problem-specific", in the sense that they are often designed to solve a specific problem by means of a specific method and therefore it is difficult and unfruitful to export the employed functionalities and ideas for solving other problems (Weiss & Kapouleas, 1990).

On the other hand, external approaches use unmodified versions of existing algorithms but they operate on the distribution of the dataset samples used for the training, by re-sampling the data and by trying this way to reduce the impact of data unbalance (Lewis & Gale, 1994)(Kubat & Matwin, 1997). By respect to internal methods, the external ones are more versatile as they do not require any change on the algorithms, although they are generally less efficient than the former ones.

In the following, both the approaches will be described and compared and their advantages and drawbacks will be analyzed.

External Methods

External methods are based on a number of operations that are executed on the distribution of positive (the rare ones) and negative (the frequent ones) examples in an unbalanced dataset in order to guide the classifier to learn the desired concept in a satisfactory way. This result is obtained by means of data re-sampling. There are two possible approaches to the re-sampling process, i.e. *oversampling* and *under-sampling,* which are both are directed toward the reduction of the imbalance rate of the dataset. Under-sampling techniques operate by removing from the dataset samples belonging to the more frequent classes until the desired ratio between positive and negative samples is reached. The selection of

Figure 3. Graphical representation of the creation of synthetic samples by means of the SMOTE algorithm: Circles represent majority patterns, grey triangles the minority patterns and white triangles the synthetically generated samples

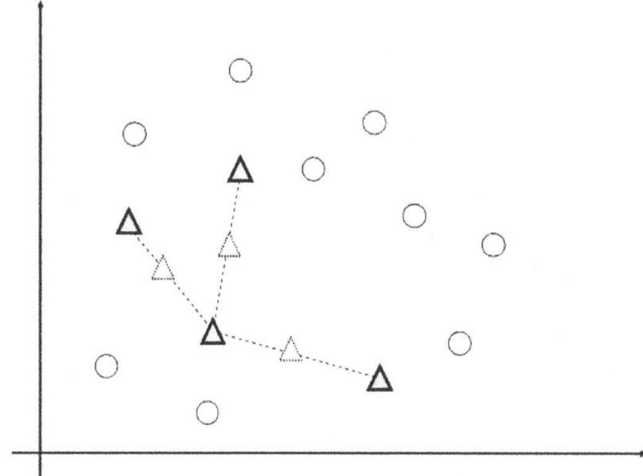

samples to be removed can be random or focused by removing only those samples lying on the extreme regions of the input space. This kind of focused under-sampling aims at the reduction of input space areas which for the classifier would correspond to negative patterns and to create a more specific concept of the corresponding class (Chawla, 2003).

A similar approach which makes extreme the concept of under-sampling can be found in (Japkowicz et al., 1995) and (Kubat et al., 1998) who build recognition-based learning classifiers using only samples drawn from the minority class. This method can obtain good results as it is able to characterize very well the interesting patterns; on the other hand, depending on the distribution of data, it can lead to the generation of a not negligible rate of false alarms.

Similarly oversampling methods are based on the addition of samples belonging to the minority class to the dataset. Also in this case such operation can be done by replicating random patterns that are present in the dataset or by replicating only those positive samples which lie on the boundary zones of the input space between positive and negative samples. This latter method is applied in order to spread the regions of the input space which the classifier will put into correspondence with the minority class and to limit eventual classification conflicts that standard classifiers would solve in favor of the majority class (Estabrooks, 2000).

A particular oversampling method which differs from the standard one is the SMOTE which is proposed in (Chawla et al., 2002). The main peculiarity of this method is that, instead of replicating positive samples as it happens with standard oversampling, new positive samples are synthetically created and appended to the database. In facts, the replication of minority patterns can lead the classifier to the creation of smaller and more specific input space areas devoted to the minority class. Replication do not add any further information to the dataset but only overbalance the decision metrics of the classifier. On the other hand the creation of new positive samples broadens the decision regions related to them. Synthetic data are created by SMOTE and placed in the input space where they likely *could* be; in particular the minority class is oversampled by taking each positive sample and inserting other positive samples along the lines connecting it to its positive neighbors as shown in Figure 3. Depending on the amount on synthetic samples required to reach the desired ratio between positive and negative samples, different numbers of neighbors are selected. In (Chawla et al., 2002) the efficiency of SMOTE is proven by using such technique coupled with different classification methods for solving well known classification problems.

The main drawback of the methods based on re-sampling is that there is no fix ratio between positive and negative samples obtained by under-sampling or oversampling which optimizes the performance of any classifier, thus this quantity must be found experimentally and is specific for any particular problem and employed classifier. In particular in (Estabrooks, 2000) several rates have been tested on real world and artificial problems in order to assess the behavior of various learners by respect to different ratios. Despite this latter aspect the efficiency of resampling methods has been proven (Japkowicz, 2000).

Between oversampling and under-sampling methods there is not an approach which outperforms the other; as a matter of fact their performance are related once again to the specific problem, classifier and dataset, thus in (Estabrooks, 2000) and (Ling & Li, 1998) a multiple resampling method which combines the two approaches is proposed. Both these methods use focused over and under-sampling and achieve good results.

Internal Methods

A diametrically opposing method with respect to re-sampling techniques for facing problems related to uneven datasets is represented by internal methods. Such group of methods is not based on the modification of the distribution of samples, but is rather characterized by the development of new techniques expressly designed to extract from the scarce information available on rare events all those features useful for their characterization. In many cases these techniques pay the sensitivity to rare patterns by performing a rather high rate of *false positive* errors but normally, due to characteristics of the practical applications, this behavior is tolerated.

The main reason for traditional classification methods fail when coping with unbalanced datasets is that ignoring rare samples is as penalized as ignoring frequent ones, thus classifier tend to focus their prediction to most probable events. In order to overcome this drawback by exploiting this intuition it is possible to train a classifier in order to award the detection of infrequent patterns. This operation can be done by using specific misclassifying cost matrix which determines the cost of any kind of possible classification error. The cost matrix can be created so as to compensate the class imbalance of the dataset by setting the cost of misclassifying a particular class inversely proportional to its frequency; otherwise cost can be assigned on the basis of application driven criteria which take into account users requirements.

Cost matrix is a general concept which can be used within most common classifiers, such as decision trees and neural networks. For instance it was used together with decision trees in the RCO method proposed in (Pazzani et al, 1994), where a cost matrix with high cost for underrepresented classes is used within a special metric employed during tree creation process which takes into account the error costs rather than the information gain measure which is traditionally used in ID3 (Quinlan, 1986) and C4.5 algorithms.

Another modified version of decision trees has been used in this framework in (Chawla, 2003). In such work a probabilistic version of the C4.5 algorithm was used, which modifies the mechanism for assigning to each leaf a class label. In the traditional version of the algorithm a leaf is labeled as corresponding to the positive class if the probability that it is a true positive leaf is higher than the probability that it is a false positive one, without taking into account the relative distribution of classes while in the mentioned work this information is taken into consideration and, together with the use of the SMOTE re-sampling method, leads to good results.

A similar procedure to the one applied with decision trees and involving the cost matrix was used with multilayer perceptrons neural networks and is described in (De Rouin et al., 1991). In that case a standard cost matrix was used but in the training process different learning rates were adopted and adapted to the relative frequencies of classes within the dataset. In the test carried out this change led to interesting results as it augmented the accuracy on the classification of the minority class.

Support vector machines (Boser et al., 1992) (SVM) have been widely used for solving classification problems with unbalanced dataset. Their classification capabilities have been deeply analyzed in (Akbani et al., 2004) where the effect of imbalance in the training dataset has also been discussed. In (Japkowicz & Shaju, 2002) they have been tested on a number of benchmarking problems and from those tests it stands out that such method is less affected that others by the imbalance of the classes. For this reason SVM have been often used as a starting point for the development of ad-hoc methods to cope with unbalanced datasets. In particular an evolution of SVM, the v-SVM proposed in (Scholkopf, 2000), have been used with good results with respect to other methods. v-SVM is a parametric version of SVM which, by means of the tuning of the so-called *v-parameter*, can control the performance of the support vectors better than traditional SVM. v-SVM can be used in order to recognize a single class patterns in a dataset as information on a single class are used for its training. Due to its peculiarity v-SVM can be employed to detect whether a pattern belongs to the rare ones by training it only with rare patterns; on the other hand the number of false positive could be quite high.

In (Yinggang & Qinming, 2006) work v-SVM are used within an algorithm which considers the distribution of the target classes and the types of errors committed by the classifier. Moreover this algorithm performs a re-sampling of the dataset in order to balance the sample distribution to an optimal level. From the artificial experiments carried out by exploiting this technique it stands out that the proposed algorithm performs well by correctly detecting the rare events.

v-SVM have also been used together with standard SVM in (Li et al., 2006). In such work the two SVM architectures have been used as an ensemble: v-SVM have been trained only by means of rare patterns in order to be able to detect them while SVM exploited a re-sampled version of the original dataset. Each one of the two SVM-based classifier are used on patterns to be classified then their responses are mixed by means of an average operator which considers the classes distribution. The proposed method has been tested both on an artificial dataset and on two real world benchmarking datasets (one is the WBCDB and the other is a Blood disorder data coming from the biomedical environment). From the results it emerges that the proposed ensemble of SVMs performs better than the approaches using only single SVM and obtain generally satisfactory results.

SVM have also been used coupled with SMOTE and with a cost matrix penalizing misclassification of positive samples. In facts in (Akbani et al., 2004) SMOTE and a specific cost matrix have been employed with the aim of forcing the boundary hyper-planes separating positive from negative patterns to be regular and to give more importance to the rare patterns by shifting the boundary far from them as shown in Figure 4.

In particular the cost matrix was expressly used for the placement of the boundary as far as possible from positive patterns samples while SMOTE re-sampling augmented the density of rare events with the effect of making that boundary well defined and characterized by a regular surface. This combination of methods, according to the performed tests on popular real datasets, leads to satisfactory results overcoming the results obtained by other methods.

A particular type of radial basis function (RBF) network has been used as well for solving the imbalanced datasets problem. Rectangular basis function networks (RecBF) proposed in (Berthold & Huber,

Figure 4. The learning boundary obtained by means of SVM without (left) and with (right) the use of the SMOTE algorithm. By using SMOTE the generated hyper-plane is more regular and gives more importance to the minority class

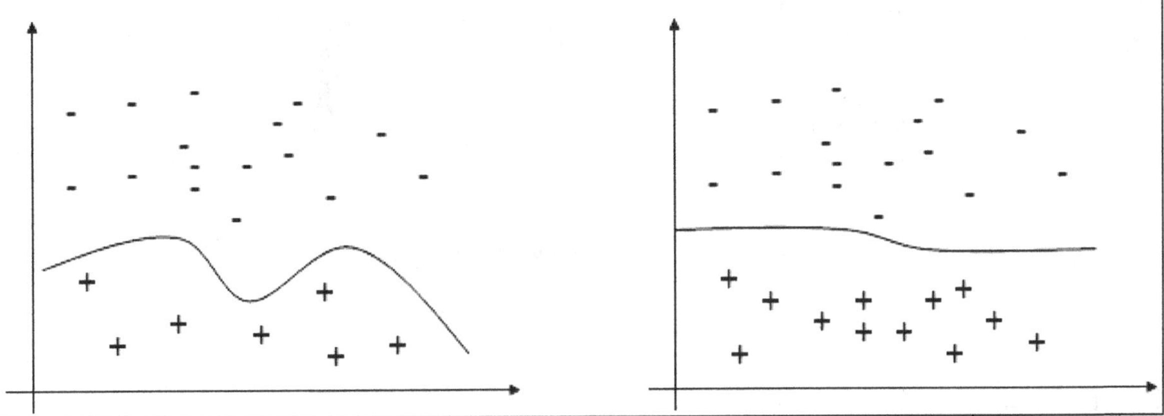

1995) exploit a special kind neurons in the hidden layer whose activation functions use hyper-rectangles. The basis functions used within this framework are related to the target classes of the dataset and the use of rectangles allows more precision in the detection of the boundary the input space regions reserved to each class. To each function two regions are associated: a core region which is the one where the membership degree of the zone to a certain class is unitary while the support region surrounds and contains the core region and corresponds to a lower membership to the class. In the training process several rectangular basis functions are created for each target class with the result that at the end of the process some functions will be devoted to the description of the minority classes. Due to these characteristics, RecBF have been used for coping with uneven dataset in the medical field in (Soler & Prim, 2007). RecBF are strictly related to association rules: in facts it is possible – due to the particular shape of the basis function – to put each basis function into relation with an association rule which gives the possibility of describing by means of natural language the result of the training process of RecBF as described in (Soler et al., 2006).

Boosting techniques have also been applied to uneven datasets: boosting consists in the fusion of a set of weak learners (classifiers which perform slightly better than random classifiers in the classification task). In the learning process weak learners are trained and progressively added to the strong learner. When new learners are added, their contribution to the strong classifier are weighted on the basis of their accuracy. In literature several works employed boosting techniques when learning from unbalanced datasets (Leskovec & Shawne-Taylor, 2003)(Guo & Viktor, 2004). In these works the basic approach is to award those learners which correctly detect the rare patterns by means of special error metrics considering such aspect. In (Guo & Viktor, 2004) a boosting method with these characteristics is tested on a very wide set of benchmarking problems achieving satisfactory results in line with those obtained by the other internal methods presented.

Figure 5. Picture describing the process flow for the introduced industrial application

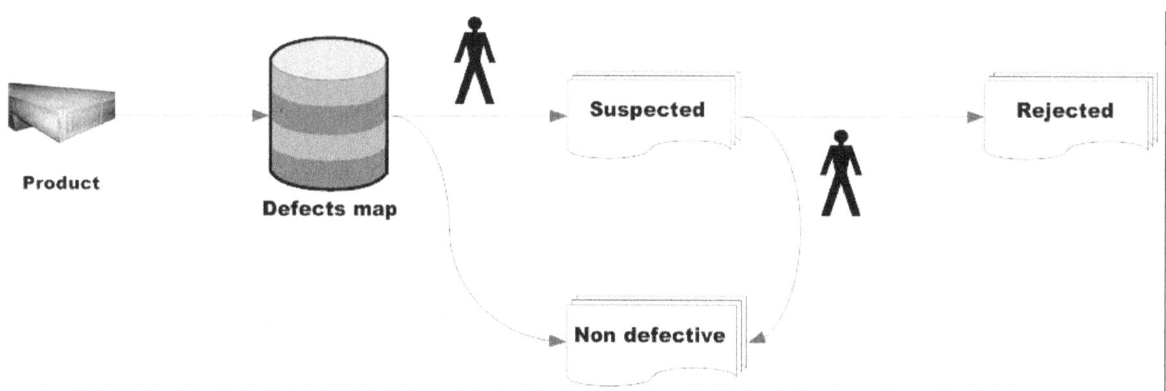

CASE STUDIES

In this section two case studies involving unbalanced datasets and faced by means of the some of the above mentioned techniques are presented. The proposed case studies are drawn from two real world frameworks which are often affected by data imbalance such as the industrial and the medical one. In particular one case study concerns the quality control procedures within the steel industry and the other one the prediction of major diseases in patients affected by diabetes.

Both the proposed problems are characterized by the presence of unbalanced datasets and by the necessity of correctly detecting the minority class which forced the experts to the design of ad-hoc architectures and algorithms granting a good performance from such point of view.

Surface Quality Control for Metallurgical Industry

In the steel industry when steel sheets are produced some surface controls on the sheets are necessary to verify the product quality and to avoid the presence of defects. This control is made by human operators which examine a map of possible defects created by an automatic vision system which collects several information concerning the possible defects spotted. Human operators on the basis these information and considering quantity, shape, extension and other factors concerning the spotted defects decides whether to discard or to accept the examined sheet.

Currently two human operators are devoted to this operation: the first one examines the defects map to point out those sheets which are suspected to be defective while the others are classified as non defective. The second operator examines the signaled sheets and decides among them which ones are to be discarded; the others are put into the market. The whole process (described in Figure 5) is very time consuming due to the high number of sheets processed and suspected to be defective which need a second control which thus represent the bottleneck of the whole process.

For these reasons, in order to speed-up the quality control, it was decided to use an automatic decision system to substitute the second human operator. The decision system will take as inputs the maps created by the vision system and then take the final decision.

The database collected by the vision system is unbalanced as the rate of defective sheets is lower than 20% and, due to the nature of the problem, the key goal of the decision system is to correctly detect as much defective sheets as possible otherwise a number of defective sheets would be put on the market with detrimental effects for the steel producer. On the other hand the generation of false alarms (sheets which are misclassified as defective) would not lead to serious consequences.

Due to the unbalance in the data traditional methods obtained not satisfactory results in the detection of defective steel sheets although the rate of overall correct classifications was high. An ad-hoc method based on a multilayer perceptron (MLP) feed-forward neural network was employed to improve the defective products detection rate. In particular the method proposed in (Vannucci et al., 2009) consists of a traditional MLP neural network with one single output neuron coupled with a threshold operator. The MLP neural network is trained exploiting the dataset formed by the vision system concerning suspected sheets. The so trained network has a real valued output o in the range *[0,1]* where *0* corresponds to non defective sheets and *1* to the defective ones. Due to the class distribution in the dataset the network output is strongly polarized to low values. The basic idea of the proposed system is to find a threshold t for which the network output will be post-processed so that values higher than t will be put into correspondence of defective products. The determination of t is calculated so as to meet the problem requirements that concerned a high rate of defective steel sheets detected. The value of t is thus determined on the basis of the performance obtained on the training set already used for the neural network training according to equation:

$$\varepsilon(t) = \left(\alpha\ UD(t)\ -\ FP(t)\right)\cdot\left(Corr(t)\ +\ \beta\ FP(t)\right)^{-1}$$

Where UD(t) is the rate of rare events detected, FP(t) the rate of false positive and Corr(t) of overall correct classifications for a candidate threshold t. In the formula α and β are two experimentally tuned parameters. It must be highlighted that the formula above works like a cost matrix improving the sensitivity of the system to rare patterns whose detection is supported.

The results obtained by the proposed methods, shown in table 1 in terms of overall correct classifications, rare events detected and false alarms, are satisfactory, in facts the method, compared to other standard approaches such as decision trees based on the C4.5 algorithm, SVM and MLP feed forward neural networks, outperforms their results in terms of percentage of rare patterns detected (+9% with respect the best performing one) and of rate of false alarms which is maintained very low. Such improvement of the detected defective sheets rate represents a considerable gain in terms of number of defective sheets which pass the second control and which could either be put into market of further checked.

Prediction of Diabetes due Diseases

The second case study here proposed comes from the medical field and concerns the prediction of diabetic nephropathy a common diabetic complication which damages kidney because of diabetes and is one of the main causes of death in people with diabetes.

Many studies have been carried out on this disease and many of them were aiming at the prediction of its occurrence for allowing doctors and patients to take the suitable countermeasures. The so far existing methods for such prediction are based on traditional statistical analysis such as regression and t-Student tests but further studies also tried to apply artificial intelligence techniques such as artificial neural networks and SVM but they did not lead to satisfactory results for several reasons among which the unbalance of the dataset.

Table 1. The results obtained by the tested methods on the industrial problem related to the detection of defective metal sheets.

Method	Correct	Unfr. Detected	False alarms
Decision tree (C4.5)	83%	68%	7%
MLP	72%	29%	4%
SVM	87%	65%	1.5%
Thresholded MLP	83%	77%	3%

Table 2. The performances obtained by the tested methods for the prediction of diabetic nephropathy in terms of overall accuracy and the balanced error rate

Method	Accuracy	BER
SVM linear	88.7%	0.5
SVM Gauss	89%	0.485
SVM linear + cost	89.5%	0.456
SVM Gauss + cost	89%	0.458

The missed detection of pattern related to the presence of the disease is strongly undesirable because it precludes the carrying out of any further check and care of the examined patient, thus the mission of any automatic classifier should be the detection of as much of these patterns as possible.

In (Baek Hwan et al., 2008) a method based on SVM with cost sensitive learning (Veropoulos et al., 1999) is proposed and compared to other traditional SVM methods. In particular in the mentioned work the training phase of SVM is modified so as to take into account the different error types and penalizing the missed detection of patterns corresponding to patients affected by diabetic nephropathy. This operation was done to improve the generalization capabilities of the classifier by placing the hyperplane far from the minority patterns by respect to the traditional approach. Several kind of SVM were tested on the problem: traditional SVM with linear and Gaussian kernel were employed both with and without cost sensitive learning. The results obtained by each of method are reported in Table 2. For the evaluation of the performance of each classifier two measures were taken into account: the first one, the accuracy, corresponds to the rate of correct classifications while the second one is more sensitive to the different kinds of possible errors although it does not completely concerns the rate of rare events detected. This latter measure called balanced error rate (BER) is the following:

$$\mathrm{BER} = \frac{1}{2}\left(\frac{\text{False negative}}{\text{positive}} + \frac{\text{False positive}}{\text{negative}} \right)$$

From the obtained results it stands out that the use of SVM with cost sensitive learning improved the performances of the classifiers most of all in terms of detection of rare patterns which is related to the BER value, in facts the classifier's configurations using this particular learning outperform the other approaches.

CONCLUSION

In this chapter the effect of target class imbalance in classification tasks is discussed together with the possible countermeasures which can be adopted to avoid the drawback they lead to. In particular by means of references to literature works and some test on suitable databases it was shown how unbalanced datasets influence the classification behavior of standard classification methods such as decision trees, support vector machines and neural networks. Traditional methods when coping to unbalanced datasets tend to exceed in classifying pattern as belonging to the majority class. This behavior is mainly due to the peculiar characteristics of the classifiers and of their learning processes.

Unbalanced datasets are frequent in real world applications and in many of them the main task of the classifier is the detection of infrequent patters such for instance failure detection within the industrial field or in fraud detection. By consequence the performances of standard methods in these frameworks are generally not acceptable.

In order to solve these problems several methods have been developed: some are based on the development of ad-hoc algorithms while others on the alteration of the training dataset in order to mitigate the effect of class imbalance. These methods, described within this chapter, generally achieve good results improving the detection rate of the rare events and maintaining high the rate of correctly classified patterns. Nevertheless these approaches are often bound to particular applications and datasets and a final solution to the problem still does not exist.

At the end of the chapter two typical applications coping with unbalanced datasets and coming from the real world are presented and the approaches used for their successful solution are described.

REFERENCES

Akbani, R., Kwek, S., & Japkowicz, N. (2004). Applying support vector machines to imbalanced datasets. In *Proceedings of 15th European Conference on Machine Learning*, Pisa, Italy, September 20-24, 2004.

Baek Hwan, C., Hwanjo, Y., Kwang-Won, K., Tae Hyun, K., In Young, K., & Sun, K. (2008). Application of irregular and unbalanced data to predict diabetic nephropathy using visualization and feature selection methods. *Artificial Intelligence in Medicine*, *42*(1), 37–53. doi:10.1016/j.artmed.2007.09.005

Berthold, M. R., & Huber, K. P. (1995). *From radial to rectangular basis functions: A new approach for rule learning from large datasets*. (Technical report, University of Karlsruhe, 1995).

Boser, B. E., Guyon, I. M., & Vapnik, V. N. (1992). A training algorithm for optimal margin classifiers. In D. Haussler (Ed.), *5th Annual ACM Workshop on COLT*, (pp. 144-152). Pittsburgh, PA: ACM Press.

Chawla, N. V. (2003). *C4.5 and imbalanced data sets: Investigating the effect of sampling method, probabilistic estimate, and decision tree structure*. Workshop on learning from imbalanced dataset II, ICML, Washington DC, 2003.

Chawla, N. V., Bowyer, K. W., Hall, L. O., & Kegelmeyer, W. P. (2002). SMOTE: Synthetic minority over-sampling technique. *Journal of Artificial Intelligence Research*, *16*, 321–357.

De Rouin, E., Brown, J., Fausett, L., & Schneider, M. (1991). Neural network training on unequally represented classes. In *Intelligent engineering systems through artificial neural networks* (pp. 135-141). New York, NY: ASME press.

Estabrooks, A. (2000). *A combination scheme for inductive learning from imbalanced datasets*. MSC thesis. Faculty of computer science, Dalhouise University.

Estabrooks, A., & Japkowicz, N. (2004). A multiple resampling method for learning from imbalanced dataset. *Computational Intelligence, 20*(1). doi:10.1111/j.0824-7935.2004.t01-1-00228.x

Guo, H., & Viktor, H. (2004). Learning from imbalanced data sets with boosting and data generation: The DataBoost-IM approach. *ACM SIGKDD Explorations Newsletter, 6*(1).

Japkowicz, N. (2000). The class imbalance problem: Significance and strategies. In *Proceedings of the 2000 International Conference on Artificial Intelligence (IC-AI'2000): Special track on inductive learning*, Las Vegas, Nevada.

Japkowicz, N., Myers, C., & Gluck, M. (1995). A novelty detection approach to classification. *Proceedings of the 14th Joint Conference on Artificial Intelligence (IJCAI-95),* (pp. 518-523).

Japkowicz, N., & Shaju, S. (2002). The class imbalance problem: A systematic study. *Intelligent Data Analysis*, *6*(5), 429–449.

Kubat, M., Holte, R., & Matwin, S. (1998). Machine learning for the detection of oil spills in satellite radar images. *Machine Learning, 30*, 195–215. doi:10.1023/A:1007452223027

Kubat, M., & Matwin, S. (1997). Addressing the curse of imbalanced data set: One-sided sampling. *Proceedings of the 14th Intl. Conference on Machine Learning*, Nashville, TN, (pp. 179-186).

Leskovec, J., & Shawe-Taylor, J. (2003). Linear programming boosting for uneven datasets. In *Proceedings of the 20th International Conference on Machine Learning (ICML-2003)*, Washington, DC.

Lewis, D., & Gale, W. (1994). Training text classifiers by uncertainty sampling. *Proceedings of the 7th ACM SIGIR Conference on Research and Development in Information Retrieval*, Dublin, 1994.

Li, P., Chan, K. L., & Fang, W. (2006). Hybrid kernel machine ensemble for imbalanced data sets. In *Proceedings of the 18th International Conference on Pattern Recognition*, (ICPR'06).

Pazzani, M., Marz, C., Murphy, P., Ali, K., Hume, T., & Brunk, C. (1994). Reducing misclassification cost. In *Proceedings of the 11th International Conference on Machine Learning*, (pp. 217-225).

Quinlan, J. R. (1986). Induction of decision trees. *Machine Learning, 1*, 81–106. doi:10.1007/BF00116251

Quinlan, J. R. (1993). *C4.5: Programs for machine learning*. Morgan Kaufmann Publishers.

Scholkopf, B. (2000). New support vector algorithms. *Neural Computation, 12*, 1207–1245. doi:10.1162/089976600300015565

Soler, V., Cerquides, J., Sabria, J., Roig, J., & Prim, M. (2006). Imbalanced datasets classification by fuzzy rule extraction and genetic algorithms. In *Proceedings of the 6th Conference on Data Mining* (ICDMW'06).

Soler, V., & Prim, M. (2007). *Rectangular basis functions applied to imbalanced datasets. (LNCS 4668)*. Springer.

Vannucci, M., Colla, V., Sgarbi, M., & Toscanelli, O. (2009). Thresholded neural networks for sensitive industrial classification tasks. In *Proceedings of International Work Conference on Artificial Neural Networks* (IWANN 2009). (LNCS 5517, pp. 1320-1327).

Veropoulos, K., Cristianini, N., & Campbell, C. (1999). Controlling the sensitivity of support vector machines. In *Proceedings of 16th International Joint Conference on Artificial Intelligence* (IJCAI'99) (pp. 55-60). San Francisco, CA: Morgan Kaufmann.

Weiss, S., & Kapouleas, I. (1990). An empirical comparison of pattern recognition, neural nets, and machine learning methods. In Shavlik, J. W., & Dietterich, T. G. (Eds.), *Readings in machine learning*. San Mateo, CA: Morgan-Kauffman.

Yinggang, Z., & Qinming, H. (2006). An unbalanced dataset classification approach based on-support vector machine. In *Proceedings 6th Congress on Intelligent Control and Automation*.

KEY TERMS AND DEFINITIONS

Classification: In the artificial intelligence framework, classification is the act of assigning to a pattern the belonging to an arbitrary class on the basis of predefined criteria.

Unbalanced Dataset: An unbalanced dataset is a collection of observations belonging to different classes whose distribution within the dataset is not uniform. There is no fixed rate of unbalancing for which a dataset can be defined unbalanced.

Decision Tree: Decision trees are a particular type of classifier exploiting the structure of a tree for performing a classification task: at each node of the tree a subset of the input pattern is analyzed in order to decide how to continue the exploration of the tree until a leaf of the tree is reached and a final decision is taken.

Artificial Neural Networks (ANN): Are sets of interconnecting artificial neurons which mimic the behaviour of real neurons. Artificial neural networks are used for solving many artificial intelligence tasks as they are able to approximate any kind of function.

Support Vector Machine (SVM): SVM is a widely used technique belonging to generalized linear classifiers based on supervised learning. SVM are employed in many regression and classification tasks.

Resampling: When coping with a dataset, resampling is the act of forming a new dataset selecting or replicating records from the original dataset with a particular criterium. Resampling is one of the main techniques employed for facing classification tasks with unbalanced datasets.

Missed Detection: In a classification framework where the main aim is the detection of a particular class a missed detection is generated if a pattern actually belonging to that class is not classified as belonging to it.

False Positive: In a classification framework where the main aim is the detection of a particular class a false positive is generated if a pattern is classified as belonging to that class but it actually does not belong to it.

Chapter 22
Ability of the 1-n-1 Complex-Valued Neural Network to Learn Transformations

Tohru Nitta
National Institute of Advanced Industrial Science and Technology (AIST), Japan

ABSTRACT

The ability of the 1-n-1 complex-valued neural network to learn 2D affine transformations has been applied to the estimation of optical flows and the generation of fractal images. The complex-valued neural network has the adaptability and the generalization ability as inherent nature. This is the most different point between the ability of the 1-n-1 complex-valued neural network to learn 2D affine transformations and the standard techniques for 2D affine transformations such as the Fourier descriptor. It is important to clarify the properties of complex-valued neural networks in order to accelerate their practical applications more and more. In this chapter, the behavior of the 1-n-1 complex-valued neural network that has learned a transformation on the Steiner circles is demonstrated, and the relationship the values of the complex-valued weights after training and a linear transformation related to the Steiner circles is clarified via computer simulations. Furthermore, the relationship the weight values of the 1-n-1 complex-valued neural network learned 2D affine transformations and the learning patterns used is elucidated. These research results make it possible to solve complicated problems more simply and efficiently with 1-n-1 complex-valued neural networks. As a matter of fact, an application of the 1-n-1 type complex-valued neural network to an associative memory is presented.

INTRODUCTION

In recent years there has been a great deal of interest in complex-valued neural networks whose weights, threshold values, and input and output signals are all complex numbers, and their applications such as telecommunications, speech recognition and image processing (Hirose, 2003, 2006; Nitta, 2008, 2009).

DOI: 10.4018/978-1-60960-551-3.ch022

The application field of the complex-valued neural network is wider than that of the real-valued neural network because the complex-valued neural network can represent more information (phase and amplitude) than the real-valued neural network (Hara & Hirose, 2004; Buchholz & Bihan, 2008; Mandic, Javidi, Goh,, Kuh & Aihara, 2009; Tanaka & Aihara, 2009), and the complex-valued neural network has some inherent properties such as the ability to learn 2D affine transformations (the ability to transform geometric figures) and the orthogonal decision boundary (Nitta, 2008).

In this chapter, we will clarify the properties of the 1-*n*-1 complex-valued neural network through learning of a transformation on the Steiner circles. As a result, it is shown that two learning patterns are sufficient for the learning ability of 2D affine transformation of a complex-valued neural network. The linear transformation on the Steiner circles is the simplest among linear transformations. That is the reason why we chose the linear transformation on the Steiner circles. Furthermore, we will elucidate the relationship the weight values of the 1-*n*-1 complex-valued neural network learned a transformation on the Steiner circles or 2D affine transformations and the learning patterns used. As a consequence, it is learned that a complex-valued neural network conducts learning so that the rotation component of the learned complex function is mainly reflected as the sum of the phases of weights. Furthermore, an application of the 1-*n*-1 type complex-valued neural network to an associative memory is presented where the knowledge obtained in this chapter is utilized effectively.

BACKGROUND

Neural Network

A brief overview of neural networks is given.

In the early 1940s, the pioneers of the field, McCulloch and Pitts, proposed a computational model based on a simple neuron-like element (McCulloch & Pitts, 1943). Since then, various types of neurons and neural networks have been developed independently of their direct similarity to biological neural networks. They can now be considered as a powerful branch of present science and technology.

Neurons are the atoms of neural computation. Out of those simple computational neurons all neural networks are build up. An illustration of a (real-valued) neuron is given in Figure 1. The activity of neuron n is defined as:

$$x = \sum\nolimits_m W_{nm} X_m + V_n, \qquad (1)$$

where W_{nm} is the real-valued weight connecting neuron n and m, X_m is the real-valued input signal from neuron m, and V_n is the real-valued threshold value of neuron n. Then, the output of the neuron is given by $f(x)$. Although several types of activation functions f can be used, the most commonly used are the sigmoidal function and the hyperbolic tangent function.

Neural networks can be grouped into two categories: feedforward networks in which graphs have no loops, and recurrent networks where loops occur because of feedback connections. A feedforward type network is made up a certain number of neurons, arranged in layers, and connected with each other through links whose values determine the weight of the connections themselves. Each neuron in a layer is connected to all of the neurons belonging to the following layer and to all of the neurons of the preceding

Figure 1. Real-valued neuron model. Weights W_{nm}, $m = 1,\ldots, N$ and threshold V_n are all real numbers. The activation function f is a real function

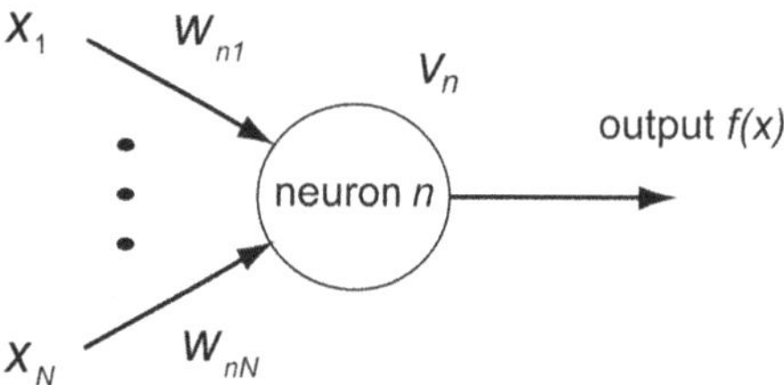

Figure 2. Complex-valued neuron model. Weights W_{nm}, $m = 1,\ldots, N$ and threshold V_n are all complex numbers. The activation function f_C is a complex function

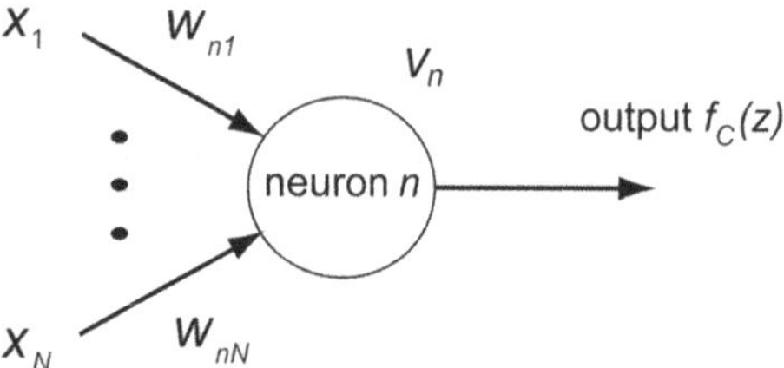

layer. However, there are no weights among neurons in the same layer. The feedforward network can be trained using a certain learning rule to achieve the desired mapping of the input data so as to match the desired target at the network output. The most popular learning rule is the back-propagation learning algorithm (Rumelhart, Hinton, & Williams, 1986). It is well-known that the feedforward neural network can generalize unlearned input data. The characteristic is called the generalization property.

Complex-Valued Neural Network

In this section, we will describe a multi-layer feedforward complex-valued neural network model used in this chapter.

We will first describe a complex-valued neuron model (Figure 2). The input signals, weights, thresholds and output signals are all complex numbers. The activity Y_n of neuron n is defined as:

$$Y_n = \sum\nolimits_m W_{nm} X_m + V_n, \tag{2}$$

where W_{nm} is the complex-valued weight connecting neuron n and m, X_m is the complex-valued input signal from neuron m, and V_n is the complex-valued threshold value of neuron n. To obtain the complex-valued output signal, convert the activity value Y_n into its real and imaginary parts as follows.

$$Y_n = x + iy = z, \tag{3}$$

where i denotes $\sqrt{-1}$. The activation function is as follows:

$$f_C(z) = f_R(x) + i f_R(y) \tag{4}$$

where $f_R(u) = 1/(1+\exp(-u))$ and is called the sigmoid function. It is obvious that $0 < \mathrm{Re}[f_C], \mathrm{Im}[f_C] < 1$. Note also that $f_C(z)$ is not holomorphic, because the Cauchy-Riemann equations do not hold:

$$\frac{\partial f_C(z)}{\partial x} + i\frac{\partial f_C(z)}{\partial y} = (1 - f_R'(x)) f_R(x) + i(1 - f_R(y)) f_R(y) \neq 0, \tag{5}$$

where $z = x + iy$.

The networks used in the chapter will have 3 layers. We will use w_{ml} for the weight between the input neuron l and the hidden neuron m, v_{nm} for the weight between the hidden neuron m and the output neuron n, θ_m for the threshold of the hidden neuron m, and γ_n for the threshold of the output neuron n. Let I_l, H_m, O_n denote the output values of the input neuron l, the hidden neuron m, and the output neuron n, respectively. Let also U_m and S_n denote the internal potentials of the hidden neuron m and the output neuron n, respectively. That is, $U_m = \sum_l w_{ml} I_l + \theta_m$, $S_n = \sum_m v_{nm} H_m + \gamma_n$, $H_m = f_C(U_m)$ and $O_n = f_C(S_n)$. Let $\delta^n = T_n - O_n$ denote the error between the actual pattern O_n and the target pattern T_n of output neuron n.

Next, we describe a complex-valued back-propagation learning algorithm (Complex-BP) for the three-layered complex-valued neural network described above (Nitta, 1997). For a sufficiently small learning constant (learning rate), $\varepsilon > 0$, the weights and the thresholds should be modified according to the following equations.

$$\Delta v_{nm} = \overline{H_m} \Delta\gamma_n, \tag{6}$$

$$\Delta\gamma_n = \varepsilon\left(\mathrm{Re}[\delta^n](1 - \mathrm{Re}[O_n])\mathrm{Re}[O_n] + i\,\mathrm{Im}[\delta^n](1 - \mathrm{Im}[O_n])\mathrm{Im}[O_n]\right), \tag{7}$$

$$\Delta w_{ml} = \overline{I_l} \Delta\theta_m, \tag{8}$$

$$\begin{aligned}\Delta\theta_m = {} & \varepsilon[(1 - \mathrm{Re}[H_m])\mathrm{Re}[H_m]\textstyle\sum_n(\mathrm{Re}[\delta^n](1 - \mathrm{Re}[O_n])\mathrm{Re}[O_n]\mathrm{Re}[v_{nm}] \\ & + \mathrm{Im}[\delta^n](1 - \mathrm{Im}[O_n])\mathrm{Im}[O_n]\mathrm{Im}[v_{nm}]) \\ & - i(1 - \mathrm{Im}[H_m])\mathrm{Im}[H_m]\textstyle\sum_n(\mathrm{Re}[\delta^n](1 - \mathrm{Re}[O_n])\mathrm{Re}[O_n]\mathrm{Im}[v_{nm}] \\ & - \mathrm{Im}[\delta^n](1 - \mathrm{Im}[O_n])\mathrm{Im}[O_n]\mathrm{Re}[v_{nm}])],\end{aligned} \tag{9}$$

where $\bar{z}$ denotes the complex conjugate of a complex number z.

Estimation of 2D Affine Transformations by Fourier Descriptors

Motion estimation (i.e., the computation of the motion parameters of objects) plays an important and central role in image processing. Wang et al. proposed a technique using the DFT (discrete Fourier transform), which estimates general 2D motion (2D affine transformation), including translation, rotation, and scaling (Wang & Clarke, 1990). Parameters of the motion between two frames are obtained by calculation (not learning) of the object's FDs (Fourier descriptors) in the two frames where FD is a Fourier transform derived from the contour of an object. Oirrak et al. also developed an algorithm using FDs to estimate the motion parameters (Oirrak, Daoudi, & Aboutajdine, 2002). In addition to translation, rotation and scaling, their algorithm allowed the estimation of the stretching that caused shape distortion.

Learning of 2D Affine Transformations by Complex-Valued Neural Networks

Neural networks have been applied to various fields actively by reason that neural networks have adaptability and generalization ability. In what follows a technique based on complex-valued neural networks that learns 2D affine transformation is described, which has adaptability and generalization ability as inherent nature.

One of the inherent properties of the complex-valued neural networks is an ability to learn 2D affine transformations (an ability to transform geometric figures): the 1-*n*-1 three-layered complex-valued neural network trained with the Complex-BP algorithm, a complex-valued version of the usual real-valued back-propagation learning algorithm (Rumelhart, Hinton, & Williams, 1986), can transform geometric figures, e.g. rotation, similarity transformation and parallel displacement of straight lines, circles, etc. (Nitta, 1997).

Only an illustrative example on a *rotation* is given below (Figure 3). In the computer simulation, a 1-6-1 three-layered complex-valued neural network was used, which transformed a point (x,y) into (x', y') in the complex plane. The experiment consisted of two parts: a training step, followed by a test step. The training step consisted of learning a set of (complex-valued) weights and thresholds, such that the input set of (straight line) points (indicated by black circles in Figure 3) gave as output, the (straight line) points (indicated by white circles) rotated counterclockwise over 90° around the origin. Input and output pairs were presented 1,000 times in the training step. These complex-valued weights and thresholds were then used in a test step, in which the input points lying on a straight line (indicated by black triangles) would hopefully be mapped to an output set of points lying on the straight line (indicated by white triangles) rotated counterclockwise over 90° around the origin. The actual output test points of the Complex-BP network did, indeed, lie on the straight line (indicated by white squares). It appears that the complex-valued network has learned to generalize the transformation of each point z_k $(= r_k \exp[i\theta_k])$ into $z_k \exp[i\alpha]$ $(= r_k \exp[i(\theta_k + \alpha)])$, i.e., the angle of each complex-valued point is updated by a complex-valued factor $\exp[i\alpha]$, however, the absolute length of each input point is preserved.

Mathematical analysis has indicated that a Complex-BP network which has learned a 2D affine transformation has the ability to generalize that transformation with an error which is represented by the

Figure 3. Rotation of a straight line. A black circle denotes an input training point, a white circle an output training point, a black triangle an input test point, a white triangle a desired output test point, and a white square an output test point generated by the complex-valued neural network. (© 1997, Elsevier. Used with permission.)

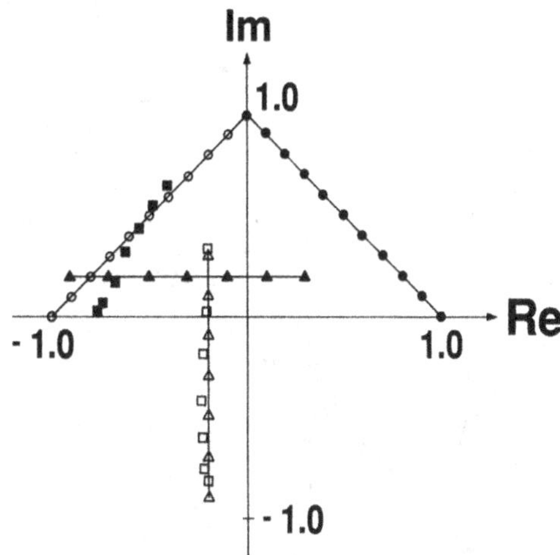

sine of the difference between the argument of the test point and that of the training point. This mathematical result has agreed qualitatively with simulation results (Nitta, 1997).

Note that although the 2D affine transformation that the Complex-BP network learned in the example described above was a *linear* transformation, the 1-n-1 complex-valued neural network can also learn *nonlinear* transformations of 2D figures (Nitta, 2008). For example, the 1-n-1 complex-valued neural network can learn two types of 2D affine transformations as described below. Figure 4 shows how the training points mapped onto each other. Those points lying northeast of the border line mapped onto points along the same line, but with a scale reduction factor of 2. Those points lying southwest of the border line mapped onto points along the same line, but with a scale reduction factor of 10. That is, we used two types of training patterns: similitude ratios 0.5 and 0.1. In the test step, by presenting the points lying on the outer circle (indicated by black triangles in Figure 4), the actual output points (indicated by white squares) took the pattern as shown in the figure. It appears that this complex-valued network has learned to generalize the reduction factor α as a function of the angle θ, i.e., $z_k (= r_k \exp[i\theta_k])$ is transformed into $\alpha(\theta_k) z_k (= \alpha(\theta_k) r_k \exp[i\theta_k])$, where $\alpha(\theta_k) \approx 0.5$ for θ_k northeast of the border line, and $\alpha(\theta_k) \approx 0.1$ for θ_k southwest of the border line. Angles, however, are preserved for each input point.

Applications of the Ability to Learn 2D Affine Transformations

In this section, two applications of the ability to transform geometric figures of the complex-valued neural network are given.

Figure 4. Two similarity transformations: 0.1 and 0.5 similitude ratios. The circles, triangles, and squares (black or white) have the same meanings as in Figure 3. (© 2008, Elsevier. Used with permission.)

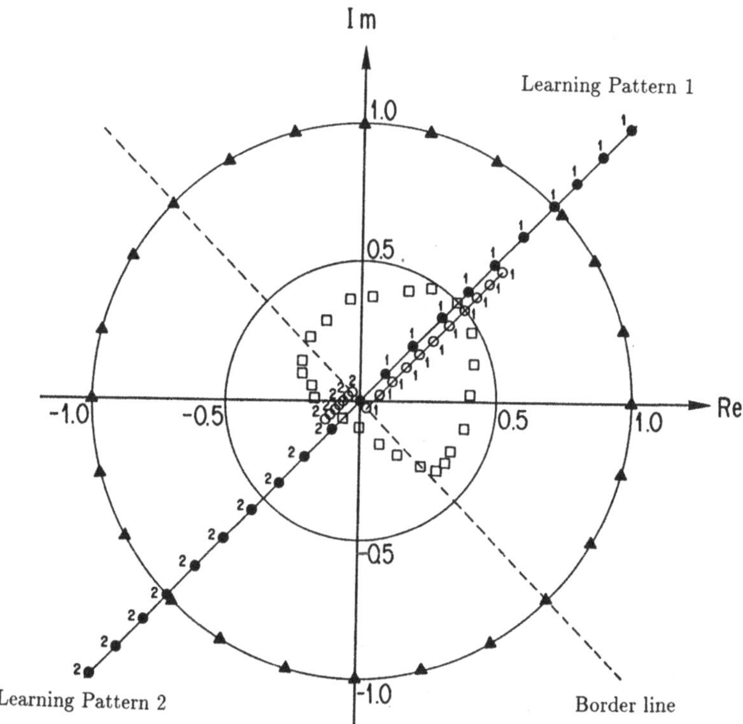

Estimation of Optical Flows

The motion vector field calculated from images, called *optical flow*, is effectively used to estimate how the object moves in a three-dimensional space in computer vision (Aggarwal & Nandhakumar, 1998; Horn & Schunck, 1981). Methods for estimating motion from optical flows include a method that obtains the optimum solution by using several flow vectors to solve motion equations (Adiv, 1986; Subbarao, 1989; Tsai & Huang, 1984). However, this method has some problems, for example, it is time consuming, and solutions for actual images cannot easily be obtained. Then, in order to solve such problems, a method for the interpretation of motion utilizing the complex-valued neural network is proposed (Miyauchi, Seki, Watanabe, & Miyauchi, 1993; Watanabe, Yazawa, Miyauchi, & Miyauchi, 1994). Since neural networks are generally far less affected by noises and the calculation time required after learning is small, they are suitable for the interpretation of motion.

The optical flow frequently cannot be obtained for the entire frame in the real world: some optical flow vectors are missing and the optical flow is partially defined (Figure 5). Then, the optical flow normalization network (called *OF normalization network*) was proposed for normalizing the sparse optical flow, which is a 1-n-1 three-layered complex-valued neural network (Miyauchi, Seki, Watanabe, & Miyauchi, 1993). As described above, the OF normalization networks have the ability to transform geometric figures. Thus, by having the OF normalization network learn the starting point (x,y) of each vector (u,v) of the optical flow as a point before conversion and the terminal point $\left(x', y'\right) = \left(x+u, y+v\right)$

Figure 5. An optical flow in the real world. Some optical flow vectors are missing

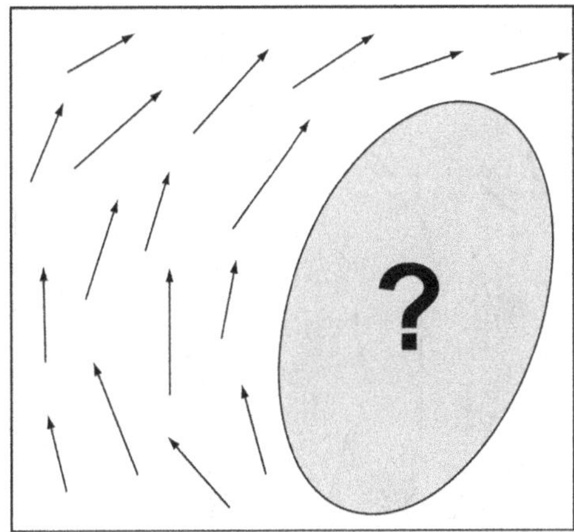

Figure 6. The way for giving an optical flow vector to the OF normalization network

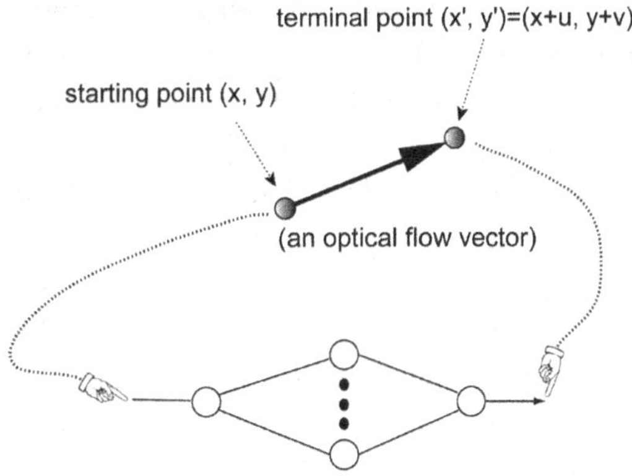

as a point after conversion, it is possible to have the OF normalization network estimate a complex function F, to describe the optical flow (Figure 6). After leaning, the OF normalization network is expected to output a value of the estimated complex function F at all points on the entire frame. By providing points aligned in an $n \times n$ lattice format to the learned OF normalization network as starting points, the final points can be obtained, resulting the generation of a normalized $n \times n$ optical flow (Figure 7).

Miyauchi et al. showed in the experiments that the OF normalization network worked well for real images (128 pixels×128 pixels).

Construction of Fractals

Next, the application of 1-n-1 complex-valued neural networks for constructing fractals is described.

The Iterated Function System (IFS) is a method for constructing fractal images. IFS consists of groups of two or more 2D affine maps including contraction maps. Repetitive mapping using IFS always results in integral orbits converging into an attractor that is inherent to the IFS regardless of the initial input value, and the resultant exclusively determined attractor is characteristically a fractal image. Image encoding

Figure 7. An optical flow normalized by the OF normalization network. The optical flow vectors are defined for the entire frame

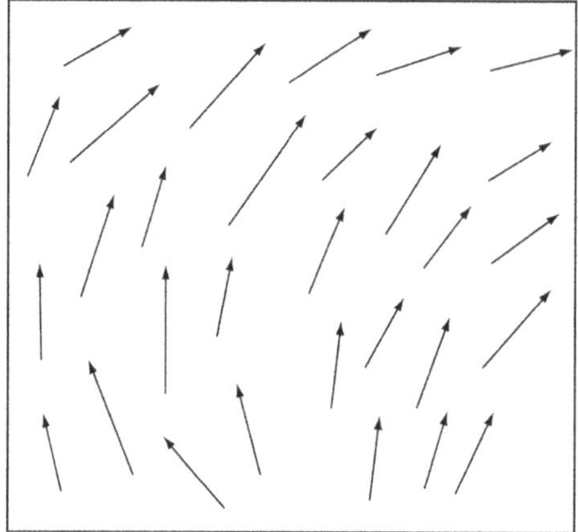

using this IFS theory has been investigated in studies on image encoding using fractals (Barnsley, Ervin, Hardin, & Lancaster, 1986; Jacquin, 1992). Fractal encoding using the IFS theory involves extracting elements that can be approximated by fractals and identifying the IFS that has an attractor similar to the extracted image elements. The inverse operation of identifying IFS can be solved by using the complex moment method and methods that use genetic algorithms (GA). However, these methods require long computation time, and so various measures have been devised.

Miura et al. proposed using the complex-valued neural network learned mappings as IFS for constructing a fractal image (Miura & Aiyoshi, 2003). The generalization ability of complex-valued neural networks are likely to enable an original fractal image to be accurately reproduced from relatively few sample data on the characteristics of the image when input-output relationships can be obtained using the data as training signals. A method for composing IFS using complex-valued neural networks, and the ability of IFS to construct fractal images using complex-valued neural networks, are described below.

An IFS for constructing a fractal image consists of two or more 2D affine maps. Thus, finding a complex-valued neural network that is similar to the 2D affine maps enables an IFS to be approximately composed using the complex-valued neural network and thus a fractal to be constructed using the complex-valued neural network. When the complex-valued neural network can determine the input-output relationship that gives the affine maps only for a limited number of sample points, the complex-valued neural network can also design a fractal image that corresponds to the relationship.

IFS is defined with two or more 2D maps, which are expressed as:

$$G_n\left(x\right) = \beta_n x + \gamma_n, \tag{10}$$

for any $x \in \mathbf{C}$ where $\mathbf{C}$ denotes the set of complex numbers, $\beta_n, \gamma_n \in \mathbf{C}$ are constants, and their application probability χ_n (called *associated probability*). In this case, IFS is given by:

Figure 8. Circuit of the IFS using the complex-valued neural network

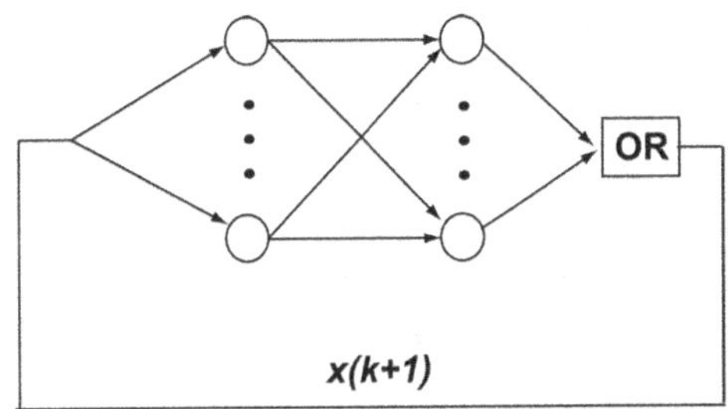

$$x(k+1) = \bigcup_{n=1}^{N} \{G_n(x(k)); \lambda_n\} \tag{11}$$

where the right side shows that one of $G_1(x(k)), \cdots, G_N(x(k))$ is selected with probability of $\lambda_1, \cdots, \lambda_N$, respectively. When $|\beta_n| < 1$ holds for any $n = 1, \cdots, N$, IFS is a contraction map. From the IFS theorem, which is an expanded form of the theorem of contraction maps, IFS has a single attractor, which is a self-similar fractal (Barnsley, Ervin, Hardin, & Lancaster, 1986).

The proposed method involves approximating an unknown IFS with complex-valued neural network by learning maps on a limited number of sample points, and then constructing a fractal image using the complex-valued neural network. First, an IFS of *N*th order is approximated by a complex-valued neural network of one input and *N* outputs. Training data is written as $\{(x_p, (G_1(x_p), \cdots, G_N(x_p))); p = 1, \cdots, P\}$, where x_p is a point on a 2D plane, and G_k is one of the affine maps that constitute the IFS. The learning parameter of the complex-valued neural network after learning is written as $\mathbf{w}^*$. Then, the *N* number of affine maps that are actualized by the complex-valued neural network, which learned the training data, can be written as $F_n(x; \mathbf{w}^*), n = 1, \cdots, N$. The probabilities at which the maps are applied are determined in advance as $\lambda_n, n = 1, \cdots, N$. Here,

$$x(k+1) = \bigcup_{n=1}^{N} \{F_n(x(k); \mathbf{w}^*); \lambda_n\} \tag{12}$$

is the iterated function system by the complex-valued neural network based on the training data. A schematic diagram of the process is shown in Figure 8.

Miura and Aiyoshi conducted the experiments using the fractal images: the Barnsley's fern and the snow crystal, and showed that even when very few sample points were used as training data, complex-valued neural network could reproduce the fractal with high precision when the complex-valued neural network could learn the sample points.

Steiner Circles

The Steiner circles are well known in connection with complex analysis (Ahlfors, 1979). The definition of the Steiner circles is given in the Definition 1.

Figure 9. Steiner circles

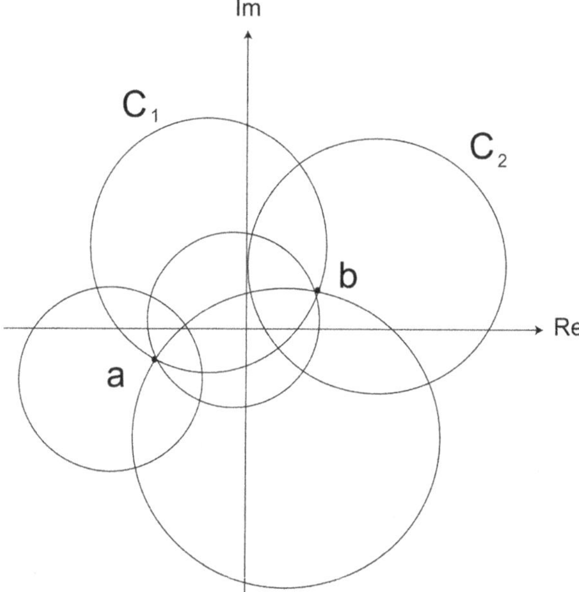

[Definition 1] Denote by C_1 the circles through *a*,*b*, and by C_2 the *circles of Apolonius* determined by *a* and *b* which are the loci of points whose distances from *a* and *b* have a constant ratio. The set formed by all the circles C_1 and C_2 is referred to as the *Steiner circles* determined by the limit points *a* and *b* (Figure 9).

The Steiner circles have the following property.

[Property 1] If a transformation $T: \mathbf{C} \to \mathbf{C}, z \mapsto w = T(z)$ carries a, b into *a*', *b*,' respectively, it can be written in the form

$$\frac{w - a'}{w - b'} = k\frac{z - a}{z - b}, \tag{13}$$

where $k \in \mathbf{C}$ is a constant. Then, the transformation *T* transforms the circles C_1 and C_2 of the Steiner circles with the limit points *a*, *b* into circles C'_1 and C'_2 of the Steiner circles with the limit points a', b' , respectively.

It is important to make clear how many training patterns are needed for learning 2D affine transformations using 1-*n*-1 complex-valued neural network when applying to real world problems. Actually, many learning patterns were used for a 2D affine transformation in the applications on the optical flows and the generation of fractals described above, some of which might be redundant. On the other hand, three distinct points in the extended complex plane $\mathbf{C} \cup \{\infty\}$ determines a linear transformation uniquely (Ahlfors, 1979), which carries circles into circles. It should be noted here that a linear transformation related to the Steiner circles is uniquely determined except $k \in \mathbf{C}$ in Eq. (13) just by two points in the complex plane. Thus, a linear transformation on the Steiner circles is the simplest among linear trans-

Table 1. Learning patterns used in the first experiment on a transformation of the Steiner circles

	Input	Output
Learning pattern 1	-0.59+0.52i	0.43+0.43i
Learning pattern 2	-0.69+0.32i	0.55+0.12i

formations in this sense. That is the reason why we focus on the linear transformation on the Steiner circles for clarifying the properties of the 1-n-1 complex-valued neural network.

LEARNING OF TRANSFORMATIONS ON THE STEINER CIRCLES

This section will demonstrate via computer simulations the behavior of the 1-n-1 complex-valued neural network for *Steiner circles*.

In the experiments, we got a 1-n-1 complex-valued neural network to learn the transformation T related to the Steiner circles (n is a natural number). The initial real and imaginary components of the weights and thresholds were chosen to be random numbers between -0.3 and + 0.3. The stopping criteria used for learning was

$$\sqrt{\sum_{p}\sum_{n=1}^{N}\left|T_n^{(p)}-O_n^{(p)}\right|^2}=0.01, \qquad (14)$$

where $T_n^{(p)}, O_n^{(p)}$ denote the desired (complex-valued) output value, the actual (complex-valued) output value of the output neuron n for the pattern p, i.e., the left side of Eq. (14) denotes the error between the desired output pattern and the actual output pattern; N denotes the number of neurons in the output layer. The presentation of one set of learning patterns to the neural network was regarded as one learning cycle. The learning rate used in the experiment was 0.1. Although the Complex-BP network generates a value z within the range $0 < \mathrm{Re}[z], \mathrm{Im}[z] < 1$, for the sake of convenience, we will present it in the tables and the figures given below as having a transformed value within the range $-1 < \mathrm{Re}[z], \mathrm{Im}[z] < 1$.

Table 1 shows a set of learning patterns used in the first experiment. The two points are mapped to the other two points. This means that the limit points of the Steiner circles are mapped to the limit points of the other Steiner circles. The input test patterns 1 to 4 are the four points on the circumference passing through the two the input learning points. The input test patterns 5 to 9 are the five points, each distance of which from the two input learning points has a constant ratio 1.0 (Table 2). Note that a straight line is regarded as a *circle* of the Steiner circles.

Figure 10 shows a simulation result using 1-10-1 complex-valued neural network where the learning stopped at the 80,800th cycle. In response to the four input test patterns 1 to 4, the output values from the complex-valued neural network lay approximately along the circumference passing through the two points of the output learning pattern. These patterns correspond to the circle C_1 described in Definition 1. The input test patterns 5 to 9 correspond to the circle C_2 described in Definition 1. In response to these input test patterns, the output values from the network reflect the ratio of the distances from the two

Table 2. Test patterns used in the first experiment on a transformation of the Steiner circles

	Input	Desired output
Test pattern 1	-0.75+0.42i	0.38+0.15i
Test pattern 2	-0.69+0.52i	0.33+0.32i
Test pattern 3	-0.52+0.42i	0.60+0.40i
Test pattern 4	-0.59+0.32i	0.65+0.24i
Test pattern 5	-0.79+0.5i	0.25+0.19i
Test pattern 6	-0.72+0.46i	0.36+0.23i
Test pattern 7	-0.64+0.42i	0.49+0.27i
Test pattern 8	-0.57+0.38i	0.60+0.31i
Test pattern 9	-0.49+0.34i	0.72+0.36i

limit points. The result suggests that the network learned the Steiner circles simply using two learning patterns. Assuming that the network could learn the holomorphic complex functions based on the given learning patterns, this behavior of the network is a natural result.

We used a set of learning patterns of the Table 3 and a set of test patterns of the Table 4 in the second experiment. Figure 11 shows a simulation result using 1-10-1 complex-valued neural network where the learning stopped at the 92,050th cycle. In response to the input test patterns, the output values from the network reflect the ratio of the distances from the two limit points.

The two experimental results described above suggest that the complex-valued neural networks have learned the transformation T (Eq. (13)). For the following reason, $k \in \mathbf{C}$, a constant, is presumed as $k = 1$ from the experimental results. By letting $k = 1$, the absolute values of both sides of Eq. (13) yield

$$\left|\frac{w - a'}{w - b'}\right| = \left|\frac{z - a}{z - b}\right|. \tag{15}$$

The right-hand side represents the ratio of distances between Points z and a and Points z and b, whereas the left-hand side expresses the ratio of distances between Points w and a' and Points w and b' : these ratios are equal, which agrees with the experimental results. Therefore, the presumption of $k = 1$ is considered valid.

Solving Eq. (13) for w yields

$$w = \frac{(a' - kb')z + (kab' - a'b)}{(1 - k)z + (ka - b)}. \tag{16}$$

This linear fractional transformation carries out rotation, similarity transformation, parallel displacement, and inversion. Inversion is a transformation that flips a figure. Especially when $k = 1$, Eq. (16) becomes

Figure 10. An example on the generalization ability of the complex-valued neural network for Steiner circles in the first experiment. The circles, triangles, and squares (black or white) have the same meanings as in Figure 3. (a) Input test patterns correspond to the circle C_1 of Definition 1. (b) Input test patterns correspond to the circle C_2 of Definition 1.

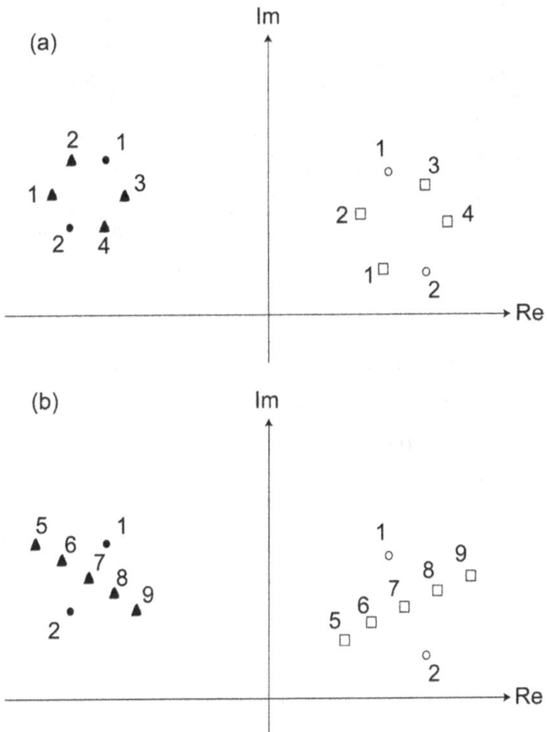

Table 3. Learning patterns used in the second experiment on a transformation of the Steiner circles

	Input	Output
Learning pattern 1	-0.40-0.40i	0.35-0.65i
Learning pattern 2	-0.35-0.60i	0.45-0.35i

$$w = \frac{a' - b'}{a - b} z + \frac{ab' - a'b}{a - b}, \tag{17}$$

which includes rotation, similarity transformation, and parallel displacement, but not inversion. In other words, Eq. (17) is 2D affine transformation. Consequently, it is considered after all that the complex-valued neural networks have learned 2D affine transformation.

Next, experiments using a real-valued neural network were conducted for comparison. The learning rate, the stopping criteria, and the initial values of weights and thresholds were set as identical values, as used in the experiments for a complex-valued neural network. First, we let a 2-7-2 real-valued neural network learn the learning patterns shown in Table 1. The real component of a complex number was

Table 4. Test patterns used in the second experiment on a transformation of the Steiner circles

	Input	Desired output
Test pattern 1	-0.48-0.50i	0.53-0.58i
Test pattern 2	-0.44-0.57i	0.55-0.45i
Test pattern 3	-0.28-0.51i	0.27-0.42i
Test pattern 4	-0.32-0.43i	0.25-0.55i
Test pattern 5	-0. 55-0.56i	0.68-0.57i
Test pattern 6	-0.46-0.53i	0.53-0.53i
Test pattern 7	-0.38-0.51i	0.41-0.50i
Test pattern 8	-0.27-0.47i	0.24-0.45i
Test pattern 9	-0.16-0.44i	0.07-0.40i

Figure 11. An example on the generalization ability of the complex-valued neural network for Steiner circles in the second experiment. The circles, triangles, and squares (black or white) have the same meanings as in Figure 3. (a) Input test patterns correspond to the circle C_1 of Definition 1. (b) Input test patterns correspond to the circle C_2 of Definition 1.

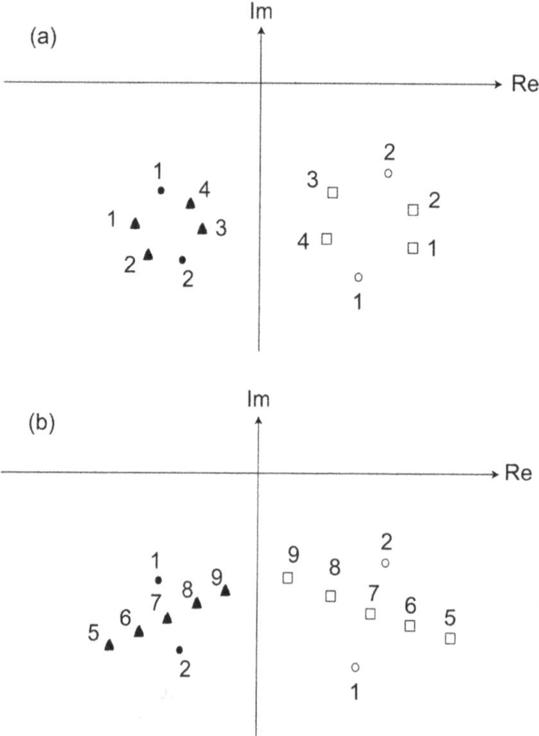

input into the first input neuron, and the imaginary component was input into the second input neuron. The output from the first output neuron was interpreted to be the real component of a complex number; the output from the second output neuron was interpreted to be the imaginary component. The learning

Figure 12. An example on the generalization ability of real-valued neural networks for Steiner circles. The circles, triangles, and squares (black or white) have the same meanings as in Figure 3. (a) Input test patterns correspond to the circle C_1 of Definition 1. 2-7-2 network was used. (b) Input test patterns correspond to the circle C_2 of Definition 1. 2-12-2 network was used.

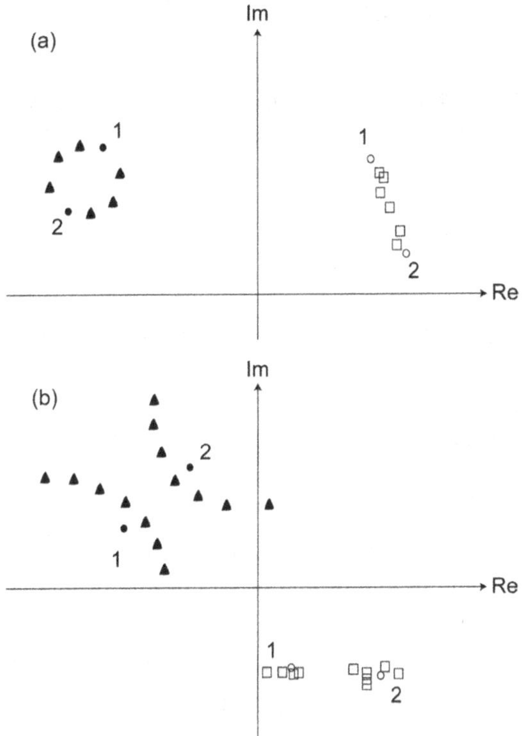

converged at the 115,350th iteration. A sequence of six points on a circle passing along two learning patterns was used as a test pattern, i.e., the test pattern for circle C_1. Figure 12(a) shows the experimental result. The real-valued neural network never output any point equivalent to circle C'_1 of Steiner circles.

We also let a 2-12-2 real-valued network learn learning patterns shown in Table 5. Learning converged at the 60,450th iteration. Then, test patterns for circle C_2 was given. However, the real-valued neural network did not output any point equivalent to circle C'_2 of Steiner circles (Figure 12(b)).

Next, the generalization ability of a complex-valued neural network on the transformation of Steiner circles T was analyzed quantitatively. We let a 1-n-1 complex-valued neural network learn the learning patterns of Table 1 (n = 1 ,..., 10). Other experimental conditions are the same as those described at the beginning of this section. Four test patterns, listed as 1–4 in Table 2, were used. We conducted 100 trials with the initial values of weight and threshold changed. The average and standard deviation of the generalization error were evaluated. The generalization error is defined using the following equation:

$$\sqrt{\sum_p \left| D^{(p)} - O^{(p)} \right|^2}, \tag{18}$$

Table 5. Learning patterns used in the experiment on real-valued neural networks

	Input	Output
Learning pattern 1	-0.52+0.37i	0.16-0.30i
Learning pattern 2	-0.23+0.61i	0.49-0.35i

Figure 13. Generalization ability of the 1-n-1 complex-valued neural network for Steiner circles (n = 1 ,..., 10) in the first experiment

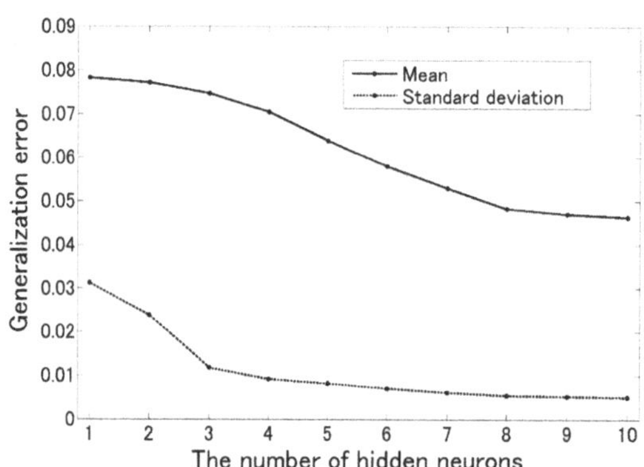

where $D^{(p)}$ and $O^{(p)}$ respectively represent the desired output pattern and the actual output of an output neuron to Pattern p. Figure 13 depicts the experimental result. The generalization error decreased monotonously as the number of hidden neurons increased. Generalization error converged mostly until the number of hidden neurons reached eight.

The same experiment was conducted using the learning patterns of Table 3 and the test patterns 1-4 of Table 4. The result resembles the experimental result obtained using the learning patterns presented in Table 1 (Figure 14).

RELATIONSHIP BETWEEN LEARNING PATTERNS AND WEIGHT VALUES

This section investigates the relationship between learning patterns about a 2D affine transformation that a 1-n-1 complex-valued neural network learned, and the values of the weights after learning.

Steiner Circles

As the preceding section described, a complex-valued neural network learned the transformation of Steiner circles T as a 2D affine transformation. Therefore, the weight values after completion of learning in the experiments of the transformation of Steiner circles T using a complex-valued neural network performed in the preceding section were investigated.

In the first experiment, using the learning patterns listed in Table 1, it is presumed that a complex-valued neural network learned the following function of a complex variable:

Figure 14. Generalization ability of the 1-n-1 complex-valued neural network for Steiner circles (n=1,...,10) in the second experiment

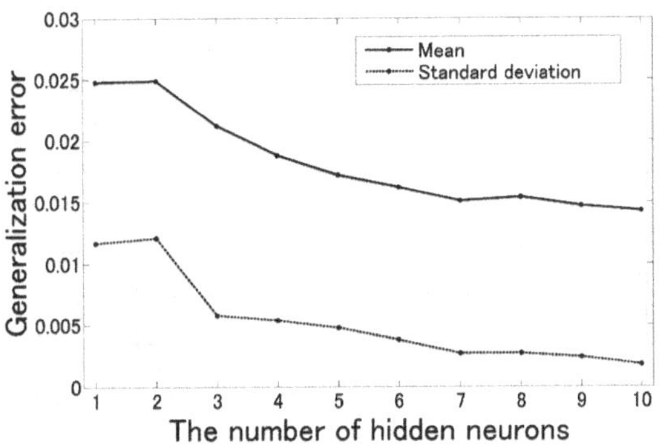

$$f(z) = 1.46e^{48i}z + 1.66e^{20i}. \tag{19}$$

This is obtained easily by substituting learning patterns into Eq. (17). The weights of a 1-n-1 complex-valued neural network used in the experiments are described hereinafter as follows for convenience. Let w_k be the weight between an input neuron and a hidden neuron k, and let v_k be the weight between the hidden neuron k and an output neuron (k = 1, ..., n). We conducted 100 trials in the experiment for a 1-n-1 complex-valued neural network. The following values after termination of learning were calculated as

$$\overline{\angle w_k + \angle v_k} \ (k = 1,\ldots,n), \tag{20}$$

where $\angle z$ expresses the phase of weight z. The value of Eq. (20) was computed for 1–10 of the number of hidden neurons n. In addition, $\overline{u}$ is the average of u over performed trials: Eq. (20) represents the average of the sum of the phases of weights $\angle w_k + \angle v_k$ over 100 trials. Table 6 presents experimental results, which indicate a concentration at around 50°. Then the following value was calculated.

$$\frac{\sum_{k=1}^{n} \overline{\angle w_k + \angle v_k}}{n}. \tag{21}$$

Eq. (21) is the average of Eq. (20) with respect to the number of hidden neurons n, and expresses the value of sum of phases of weights $\angle w_k + \angle v_k$ as the whole network. Figure 15 shows the result. The values of Eq. (21) were 49–55°. Consequently, Table 6 and Fig. 15 suggest that the average of the sum of the phases of weights is near 48°, the phase of rotation component of the learned complex function (Eq. (19)). The absolute values of weights and thresholds turned out to have no relevance with the learned complex function.

In the second experiment using the learning patterns of Table 3, it is presumed that a complex-valued neural network learned the following complex function:

$$f(z) = 1.53e^{148i}z + 0.97e^{239i}. \tag{22}$$

Table 6. Average of the sum of the phases of weights $\angle w_k + \angle v_k$ over 100 trials in the first experiment on the transformation of Steiner circles T using a 1-n-1 complex-valued neural network. The unit is degree.

The number of hidden neurons	**1**	**2**	**3**	**4**	**5**	**6**	**7**	**8**	**9**	**10**
$\overline{\angle w_k + \angle v_k}$ $(k = 1, \ldots, 10)$	53	44	44	44	44	42	42	42	42	39
		55	51	50	49	47	46	46	46	45
			54	52	51	49	49	48	48	47
				74	52	52	51	50	49	49
					57	54	52	51	50	50
						72	54	53	51	51
							72	55	53	52
								58	56	54
									76	58
										67

Figure 15. Average of Eq. (20) with respect to the number of hidden neurons n, $\frac{\sum_{k=1}^{n} \overline{\angle w_k + \angle v_k}}{n}$, in v first experiment

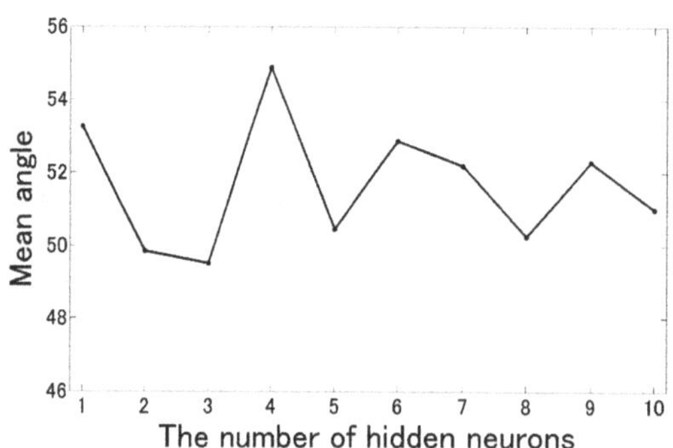

Table 7 and Figure 16 present values of Eqs. (20) and (21). The value of Eq. (20) is approximately 150°, whereas that of Eq. (21) is within 146–152°. The average of the sum of phases of weights $\overline{\angle w_k + \angle v_k}$ is near 148°, the phase of rotation components of the learned complex function (Eq. (22)), as in the first experiment. Again, the absolute values of weights and thresholds have no relevance with the learned complex function, as was true in the first experiment.

Simple Learning Patterns

Transformation of Steiner circles that a complex-valued neural network learned in the preceding section is a slightly complicated transformation of rotation, similarity transformation, and parallel displacement combined. The next investigation is how a learning pattern of one kind about simple rotation, similar-

Table 7. Average of the sum of the phases of weights $\overline{\angle w_k + \angle v_k}$ over 100 trials in the second experiment on the transformation of Steiner circles T using a 1-n-1 complex-valued neural network. The unit is degree

The number of hidden neurons	1	2	3	4	5	6	7	8	9	10
$\overline{\angle w_k + \angle v_k}$ $(k = 1, \ldots, 10)$	147	136	137	138	136	131	131	129	129	130
		164	144	142	141	140	139	138	138	138
			156	152	145	143	143	142	141	141
				177	154	147	146	145	144	143
					175	155	151	149	147	146
						166	156	154	152	149
							168	157	155	153
								171	158	156
									172	160
										177

Figure 16. Average of Eq. (20) with respect to the number of hidden neurons n, $\frac{\sum_{k=1}^{n} \overline{\angle w_k + \angle v_k}}{n}$, in the second experiment

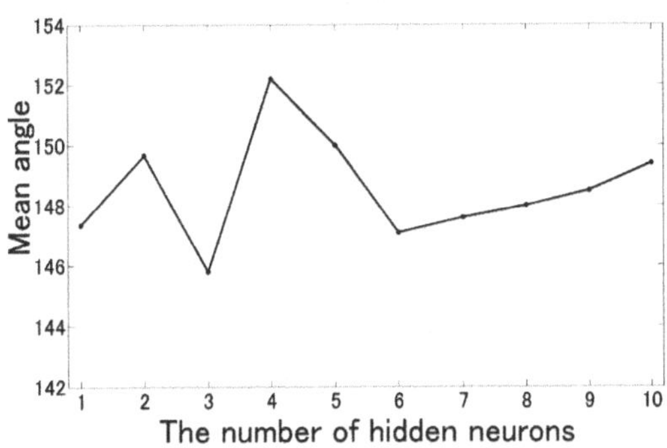

ity transformation, and parallel displacement is reflected in the values of weights. This section adopts a 1-1-1 complex-valued neural network, the simplest three-layered network. Experimental conditions are the same as those presented in the preceding section. The weights and thresholds of a 1-1-1 complex-valued neural network used in the experiment are hereinafter described as follows for convenience. Let w be the weight between an input neuron and a hidden neuron, and let v be the weight between a hidden neuron and an output neuron. Let θ and γ respectively signify the thresholds of a hidden neuron and an output neuron.

Learning patterns of three kinds shown in Table 8 were prepared, and learning was done separately. Learning patterns of the cases 1, 2 and 3 respectively represent 30, 60, and 90° of rotation. Presumably,

Table 8. Learning patterns used in the experiment on one kind about simple rotation

		Input	Output
Case 1 (30° of rotation)	Learning pattern 1	-0.40i	0.20-0.35i
	Learning pattern 2	-0.20i	0.10-0.17i
Case 2 (60° of rotation)	Learning pattern 1	0.50	0.25+0.43i
	Learning pattern 2	0.25	0.13+0.22i
Case 3 (90° of rotation)	Learning pattern 1	-0.30+0.30i	-0.30-0.30i
	Learning pattern 2	-0.15+0.15i	-0.15-0.15i

Table 9. Experimental results on one kind about simple rotation

		$\overline{\angle w + \angle v}$
Case 1 (30° of rotation)	Mean	29.81°
	Standard deviation	0.93°
Case 2 (60° of rotation)	Mean	60.65°
	Standard deviation	0.56°
Case 3 (90° of rotation)	Mean	89.99°
	Standard deviation	0.38°

a complex-valued neural network learns the following complex functions with the learning patterns of the three cases of Table 8, as

$$f(z) = e^{30i} z, \tag{23}$$

$$f(z) = e^{60i} z, \tag{24}$$

$$f(z) = e^{90i} z. \tag{25}$$

Actually, 100 trials were performed for a 1-1-1 complex-valued neural network in the experiment. The following value was determined after completion of learning:

$$\overline{\angle w + \angle v} . \tag{26}$$

Table 9 presents experimental results, which indicate about 30, 60, and 90° respectively for the cases 1, 2, and 3. The standard deviation is also small: the average of sum of phases of weights $\overline{\angle w + \angle v}$ is near the phase of rotation components of complex functions (Eqs. (23)–(25)).

Table 10. Learning patterns used in the experiment on one kind about simple similarity transformation

		Input	Output
Case 1 (reduction of 1/2)	Learning pattern 1	0.50+0.50i	0.25+0.25i
	Learning pattern 2	0.25+0.25i	0.13+0.13i
Case 2 (enlargement to twice)	Learning pattern 1	-0.10+0.25	-0.20+0.50i
	Learning pattern 2	-0.16+0.40	-0.32+0.80i

Table 11. Experimental results on one kind about simple similarity transformation

		$\overline{\angle w + \angle v}$ (degrees)
Case 1 (reduction of 1/2)	Mean	-0.28
	Standard deviation	0.49
Case 2 (enlargement to twice)	Mean	-6.8
	Standard deviation	0.36

Next, the experiment on similarity transformation was conducted. Table 10 shows learning patterns. The case 1 is reduction of 1/2, and the case 2 is an enlargement to twice. A complex-valued neural network is considered to learn the following complex functions with the learning patterns of the two cases in Table 10.

$$f(z) = \frac{1}{2} z, \tag{27}$$

$$f(z) = 2z. \tag{28}$$

We conducted 100 trials for a 1-1-1 complex-valued neural network in the experiment. The value of Eq. (26) was computed after completion of learning.

Table 11 presents the experimental results. Both cases 1 and 2 gave a value near 0°: the average of sum of phases of weights $\overline{\angle w + \angle v}$ is near the phase of rotation components of complex functions (Eqs. (27) and (28)). No relevance was apparent between the absolute values of weights and learning patterns.

Finally, an experiment was conducted on parallel displacement. Table 12 shows the learning pattern, which moves a distance of 0.6 rightward in parallel with the real axis. A complex-valued neural network is considered to learn the following complex function:

$$f(z) = z + 0.6. \tag{29}$$

We conducted 100 trials for a 1-1-1 complex-valued neural network in the experiment. The value of Eq. (26) and the following value after completion of learning were computed as

Table 12. Learning patterns used in the experiment on one kind about simple parallel displacement

	Input	Output
Learning pattern 1	-0.50-0.20i	0.10-0.20i
Learning pattern 2	-0.20-0.40i	0.40-0.40i

Table 13. Experimental results on one kind about simple parallel displacement

$\overline{\angle w + \angle v}$	Mean	1.22
	Standard deviation	4.15
$\overline{\|\theta - \gamma\|}$	Mean	0.51
	Standard deviation	0.07

$$\overline{|\theta - \gamma|}. \tag{30}$$

Table 13 shows the experimental results. The value of Eq. (26) is near 0°, whereas that of Eq. (30) is near 0.6. Consequently, results revealed that *the sum of phases of weights* and *difference between the amplitude of threshold of a hidden neuron and that of the output neuron* contribute to learning in this case.

Subsequently, we investigated how a training pattern of one type reflects in weights using a 1-n-1 complex neural network (n = 2, ..., 5) with multiple hidden neurons. The training pattern employed is the training patterns of the case 3 in Table 8 (rotation of 90°). Other experimental conditions are the same as those described in the preceding section. Hereinafter, the weights of a 1-n-1 complex-valued neural network used in the experiment are described as follows. Let w_k be the weight between an input neuron and a hidden neuron k, and v_k be the weight between a hidden neuron k and an output neuron (k = 1, ..., n).

We conducted 100 trials for the 1-n-1 complex-valued neural network in the experiment, and the values of Eqs. (20) and (21) were computed. Table 14 presents the experimental results. The average of the sum of the phases of weights $\overline{\angle w_k + \angle v_k}$ is near 90° over k (k = 1, ..., n). Moreover, the value of Eq. (21) was about 90° in all cases. These experimental results suggest that a single hidden neuron suffices as a training pattern of one type about rotation, although other hidden neurons are redundant.

Complicated Learning Patterns

This section investigates how training patterns of two types are reflected in weights. Training patterns used for the present study are related to rotations of 60° and 90° (the cases 2 and 3 in Table 8). A complex-valued neural network is presumed to learn the following complex functions simultaneously:

$$f(z) = e^{60i}z, \tag{31}$$

$$f(z) = e^{90i}z. \tag{32}$$

Table 14. Experimental results on one kind about simple rotation using a 1-n-1 complex-valued neural network (n = 2, ..., 5)

		$\overline{\angle w_k + \angle v_k}$					$\frac{\sum_{k=1}^{n} \overline{\angle w_k + \angle v_k}}{n}$
1-2-1 network	Mean	80.84	96.35				88.60
	Standard deviation	9.08	6.31				
1-3-1 network	Mean	79.22	89.10	105.62			91.30
	Standard deviation	7.88	3.35	17.67			
1-4-1 network	Mean	78.00	87.35	92.11	103.74		90.30
	Standard deviation	14.68	4.09	4.14	29.25		
1-5-1 network	Mean	77.81	84.70	89.80	94.85	115.38	92.50
	Standard deviation	14.54	5.34	3.71	4.06	49.51	

Table 15. Experimental results on two types about rotations of 60° and 90° using a 1-n-1 complex-valued neural network (n = 1, ..., 5)

		$\overline{\angle w_k + \angle v_k}$				
1-1-1 network	Mean	79.76				
	Standard deviation	6.93				
1-2-1 network	Mean	47.34	106.10			
	Standard deviation	7.43	9.34			
1-3-1 network	Mean	49.93	82.84	104.87		
	Standard deviation	11.21	16.33	9.28		
1-4-1 network	Mean	44.38	77.73	95.46	112.95	
	Standard deviation	11.94	13.60	12.86	8.82	
1-5-1 network	Mean	38.57	65.94	82.83	97.97	119.39
	Standard deviation	9.81	15.03	14.99	9.31	26.16

Other experimental conditions are the same as those introduced in the preceding section. Hereinafter, the weights of a 1-n-1 complex-valued neural network used in the experiment are described as follows (n = 1, ..., 5). Let w_k be the weight between an input neuron and a hidden neuron k, and v_k be the weight between a hidden neuron k and an output neuron (k = 1, ..., n).

We conducted 100 trials in the experiment; from them, the value of Eq. (20) was computed. Table 15 shows the experimental result. There were trials that did not converge by the termination of learning at 5 million times (18 of 100 trials with a single hidden neuron did not converge). The averages of sum of phases of weights $\overline{\angle w_k + \angle v_k}$ were roughly divisible into two types, near 60° and near 90°. These experimental results suggest that two hidden neurons suffice for training patterns of two types related to rotation, although other hidden neurons are redundant. The average of the sum of phases of weights with a single hidden neuron was 79.76°, which was incidentally near 75°, a value of the sum of 60° and 90° divided by 2.

DISCUSSION

Learning of the Linear Transformation on Steiner Circles

Transformation of Steiner circles is linear fractional transformation, which can flip a 2D figure. However, the experimental result implies that a complex-valued neural network performed learning of 2D affine transformation through learning of transformation of Steiner circles: a complex-valued neural network conducts learning without inversion. As described in the section for a complex-valued neural network, three or more training patterns were used in the experiment of learning ability of 2D affine transformation. However, it is thought that just two training patterns are sufficient for a complex-valued neural network to learn 2D affine transformation.

The average of generalization error in each network was evaluated with the number of hidden neurons changed from 1 to 10 in the experiment on learning the transformation of Steiner circles T. The average of generalization error and standard deviation dropped monotonously as the number of hidden neurons increased. An appropriate number of hidden neurons is presumed to be necessary so that a given complex function be approximated with sufficient accuracy.

Relationship between Learning Patterns and Weight Values

The values of weights after completion of learning in the experiments of the transformation of Steiner circles T using a complex-valued neural network were examined. The result revealed that the sum of phases of weights approached a value near the phase of rotation component of the complex function that was learned. Nitta conducted an experiment using only training patterns centered at the origin (rotation and similarity transformation) (Nitta, 1997). The condition of *centered at the origin* is meaningless in the case of parallel displacement. For example, learning was performed with training patterns presented in Figure 3. In that case, a complex-valued neural network is assumed to have learned the following complex function.

$$f(z) = e^{90i}z \,. \tag{33}$$

This complex function rotates an input pattern 90° counterclockwise around a center at the origin. The learning patterns used in the experiments about the transformation of Steiner circles conducted in this study are not centered at the origin, but are learning patterns assuming more general 2D affine transformation including the learning patterns presented in Figure 3. Consequently, the results revealed the behavior of a 1-n-1 complex neural network that has learned the more general learning patterns, including the case of reference (Nitta, 1997). An experiment described in the literature (Nitta, 1997) used a learning pattern comprising about 11 points: much more than 2. However, as discussed above, it is shown that two learning patterns suffice. Accordingly, it is considered that the interim sequence of points played only a supplementary role.

Next, using a 1-1-1 complex-valued neural network — the simplest three-layered network — it is investigated how a learning pattern of one kind about simple rotation, similarity transformation, and parallel displacement is reflected in the values of weights. The result shows that the phase of rotation component of a complex function, which a learning pattern is presumed to express, is reflected mainly in the sum of phases of weights of a complex-valued neural network. Moreover, this study investigated how a training pattern of one type is reflected in weight using a 1-*n*-1 complex neural network with multiple hidden neurons. The result suggests that a single hidden neuron is sufficient for learning a pattern of one type about rotation around the origin, and that other hidden neurons are redundant. Furthermore, results show how learning patterns of two types would reflect in weights. Results show the ability of two pieces to be sufficient as the number of hidden neurons, and that other hidden neurons are redundant for the learning pattern about rotations of two types.

APPLICATION TO ASSOCIATIVE MEMORY

In this section, a possibility of using the 1-*n*-1 type complex-valued neural network as an associative memory is suggested where the knowledge obtained in this chapter is utilized effectively.

The approaches based on complex-valued neural networks for storing gray-scale images have been proposed (Jankowski, Lozowski, & Zurada, 1996; Lee, 2001, 2003, 2009). The neuron state can assume one of K complex values, equally spaced on the unit circle. Each phase angle corresponds to a gray level. The complex-valued multistate Hopfield associative memories called CVHAM (Jankowski, Lozowski, & Zurada, 1996) is an auto-associative memory that stores complex-valued prototype vectors $X^k,\ k = 1,\cdots,m$ where m is the number of the prototype vectors and $X^k = (x_1^k\ x_2^k \cdots x_N^k)^T$. The learning algorithms of conventional CVHAMs include: generalized Hebb rule (Jankowski, Lozowski, & Zurada, 1996), gradient descent learning rule (Lee, 2001, 2003), energy design method (Müezzinoğlu, Güzeliş, & Zurada, 2003), and the generalized projection rule (Lee, 2009).

As described in Section, *Learning of 2D Affine Transformations by Complex-Valued Neural Networks*, the 1-*n*-1 complex-valued neural network can generalize two 2D affine transformations such as two similitude ratios. It could be regarded as the capability of a complex-valued associative memory on 2D affine transformations, which is different in quality from the CVHAM described above. In what follows, a complex-valued associative memory on 2D affine transformations using 1-*n*-1 type complex-valued neural network is illustrated with computer simulations.

In the experiments, we used a 1-2-1 complex-valued neural network to learn two types of rotation angles. It should be noted that the number of hidden neurons is two, which means that the research result in Section, *Relationship Between Learning Patterns and Weight Values*, was effectively utilized: two hidden neurons suffice for training patterns of two types related to rotation. Figure 17 shows that the first experimental result on the recall of rotation angles where the training patterns were related to the two rotation angles 45° and 90°. The 1-2-1 complex-valued neural network could recall the rotation angles: the test points (six black triangles 1-6) around the input training points related to the rotation angle 45° were rotated counterclockwise over about 45° around the origin, and the test points (six black triangles 7-12) around the input training points related to the rotation angle 90° were rotated counterclockwise over about 90° around the origin. Figure 18 shows that the second experimental result on the recall of rotation angles where the training patterns were related to the two rotation angles 15° and 90°. It should

Figure 17. The first experimental result on the recall of rotation angles. (a) Training patterns related to the two rotation angles 45° and 90°. (b) Test patterns and the actual output patterns generated by the 1-2-1 complex-valued neural network. The circles, triangles, and squares (black or white) have the same meanings as in Figure 3

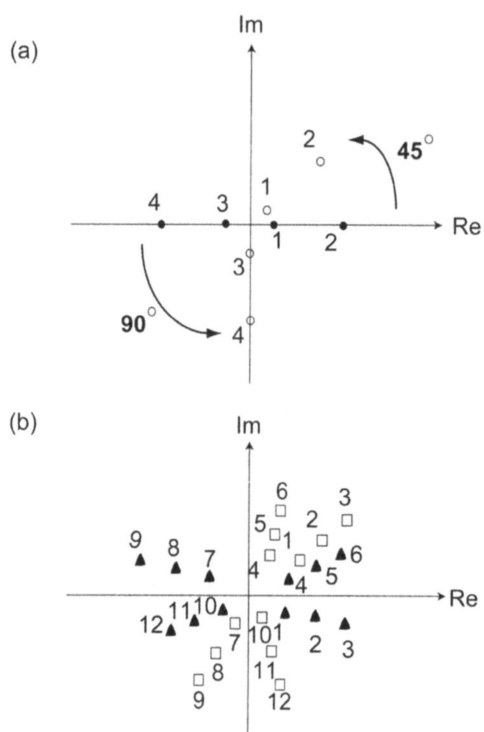

also be noted that the number of training points is two, which means that the research result in Section, *Learning of Transformations on the Steiner Circles*, was effectively utilized: just two training patterns are sufficient for a complex-valued neural network to learn 2D affine transformation.

CONCLUSION

We let a 1-*n*-1 three-layered complex-valued neural network learn the transformation about Steiner circles or simple 2D affine transformation, and evaluated it using simulations. The results suggest the following. (1) Two learning patterns are sufficient for the learning ability of 2D affine transformation of a complex-valued neural network. (2) A complex-valued neural network conducts learning so that the rotation component of the learned complex function is mainly reflected as the sum of the phases of weights. These research results make it possible to solve complicated problems more simply and efficiently with 1-*n*-1 complex-valued neural networks. As an example, an application of the 1-*n*-1 type complex-valued neural network to an associative memory was presented where the knowledge obtained in this chapter were utilized effectively.

Figure 18. The second experimental result on the recall of rotation angles. (a) Training patterns related to the two rotation angles 15° and 90°. (b) Test patterns and the actual output patterns generated by the 1-2-1 complex-valued neural network. The circles, triangles, and squares (black or white) have the same meanings as in Figure 3

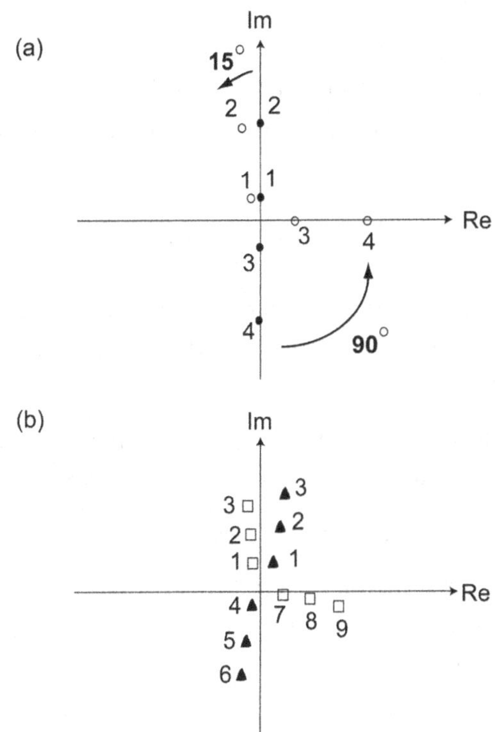

FUTURE RESEARCH DIRECTIONS

Results suggest that a single hidden neuron suffices for a learning pattern about rotation of 90°, and that other hidden neurons are redundant. Further experimentation is necessary to amplify this experimental result to determine whether a single hidden neuron is sufficient to learn a learning pattern of one kind about simple rotation, similarity transformation, or parallel displacement, whereas other hidden neurons are redundant. It will be necessary also to evaluate the generalization ability in that case. This argument also applies to the issue of whether N hidden neurons are sufficient to learn N patterns related to simple rotation, similarity transformation, or parallel displacement by amplifying the experimental result of learning about a rotation of 60° and 90°.

It is considered uncertain whether the values of weights after learning is relevant to a learning pattern in the case of an ordinary real-valued neural network. Meanwhile, information related to phase reflects in weights after learning in the case of a complex-valued neural network, which suggests that a network after learning might provide meaningful information corresponding to the field of application.

There exist many things other than optical flows, which can be represented with two-dimensional vector fields. For example, a volute of a galaxy, and some directions in which robots are navigated and so on. We believe that the ability to transform geometric figures of the complex-valued neural network will play an active role in various fields.

ACKNOWLEDGMENT

The author wishes to thank Prof. Y. Hirai, University of Tsukuba, for valuable comments about the weight values after training, and the Editor and the anonymous reviewers for valuable comments.

REFERENCES

Adiv, G. (1986). Determining three-dimensional motion and structure from optical flow generated by several moving objects. *IEEE Transactions on Pattern Analysis and Machine Intelligence*, *7*(4), 384–401. doi:10.1109/TPAMI.1985.4767678

Aggarwal, J. K., & Nandhakumar, N. (1998). On the computation of motion from sequences of images - a review. *Proceedings of the IEEE*, *76*(8), 917–935. doi:10.1109/5.5965

Ahlfors, L. V. (1979). *Complex analysis*. McGraw-Hill, Inc.

Barnsley, M. F., Ervin, V., Hardin, D., & Lancaster, J. (1986). Solution of an inverse problem for fractals and other sets. *Proceedings of the National Academy of Sciences of the United States of America*, *83*, 1975–1977. doi:10.1073/pnas.83.7.1975

Buchholz, S., & Bihan, N. L. (2008). Polarized signal classification by complex and quaternionic multi-layer perceptrons. *International Journal of Neural Systems*, *18*(2), 75–85. doi:10.1142/S0129065708001403

Hara, T., & Hirose, A. (2004). Plastic mine detecting radar system using complex-valued self-organizing map that deals with multiple-frequency interferometric images. *Neural Networks*, *17*(8-9), 1201–1210. doi:10.1016/j.neunet.2004.07.012

Hirose, A. (Ed.). (2003). *Complex-valued neural networks*. Singapore: World Scientific Publishing. doi:10.1142/9789812791184

Hirose, A. (2006). *Complex-valued neural networks. Studies in Computational Intelligence, 32*. Springer-Verlag.

Horn, B. K. P., & Schunck, B. G. (1981). Determining optical flow. *Artificial Intelligence*, *17*, 185–203. doi:10.1016/0004-3702(81)90024-2

Jacquin, A. E. (1992). Image coding based on a fractal theory of iterated contractive image transformations. *IEEE Transactions on Image Processing*, *1*(1), 18–30. doi:10.1109/83.128028

Jankowski, S., Lozowski, A., & Zurada, J. M. (1996). Complex-valued multistate neural associative memory. *IEEE Transactions on Neural Networks*, *7*(6), 1491–1496. doi:10.1109/72.548176

Lee, D.-L. (2001). Improving the capacity of complex-valued neural networks with a modified gradient descent learning rule. *IEEE Transactions on Neural Networks*, *12*(2), 439–443. doi:10.1109/72.914540

Lee, D.-L. (2003). Complex-valued neural associative memories: Network stability and learning algorithms. In Hirose, A. (Ed.), *Complex-valued neural networks: Theories and applications* (pp. 29–55). World Scientific. doi:10.1142/9789812791184_0003

Lee, D.-L. (2009). Image reconstruction by the complex-valued neural networks: Design by using generalized projection rule. In Nitta, T. (Ed.), *Complex-valued neural networks: Utilizing high-dimensional parameters* (pp. 236–255). Hershey, PA: Information Science Reference. doi:10.4018/9781605662145.ch010

Mandic, D. P., Javidi, S., Goh, S. L., Kuh, A., & Aihara, K. (2009). Complex valued prediction of wind profile using augmented complex statistics. *Renewable Energy, 34*(1), 196–210. doi:10.1016/j.renene.2008.03.022

McCulloch, W. S., & Pitts, W. H. (1943). A logical calculus of the ideas immanent in nervous activity. *The Bulletin of Mathematical Biophysics, 5*, 115–133. doi:10.1007/BF02478259

Miura, M., & Aiyoshi, E. (2003). Approximation and designing of fractal images by complex neural networks. *EEJ Transactions on Electronics. Information Systems, 123*(8), 1465–1472.

Miyauchi, M., Seki, M., Watanabe, A., & Miyauchi, A. (1993). Interpretation of optical flow through complex neural network. *Proceedings of International Workshop on Artificial Neural Networks*, Barcelona, (LNCS 686), (pp. 645-650). Springer-Verlag.

Müezzinoğlu, M. K., Güzeliş, C., & Zurada, J. M. (2003). A new design method for the complex-valued multistate Hopfield associative memory. *IEEE Transactions on Neural Networks, 14*(4), 891–899. doi:10.1109/TNN.2003.813844

Nitta, T. (1997). An extension of the back-propagation algorithm to complex numbers. *Neural Networks, 10*(8), 1392–1415. doi:10.1016/S0893-6080(97)00036-1

Nitta, T. (2008). Complex-valued neural network and complex-valued back-propagation learning algorithm. In Hawkes, P. W. (Ed.), *Advances in imaging and electron physics* (*Vol. 152*, pp. 153–221). Amsterdam, The Netherlands: Elsevier.

Nitta, T. (Ed.). (2009). *Complex-valued neural networks: Utilizing high-dimensional parameters* (p. 504). Hershey, PA: Information Science Reference.

Oirrak, A. E., Daoudi, M., & Aboutajdine, D. (2002). Estimation of general 2D affine motion using Fourier descriptors. *Pattern Recognition, 35*(1), 223–228. doi:10.1016/S0031-3203(01)00019-X

Rumelhart, D. E., Hinton, G. E., & Williams, R. J. (1986). *Parallel distributed processing* (*Vol. 1*). Boston, MA: The MIT Press.

Subbarao, M. (1989). Interpretation of image flow: A spatio-temporal approach. *IEEE Transactions on Pattern Analysis and Machine Intelligence, 11*(3), 266–278. doi:10.1109/34.21796

Tanaka, G., & Aihara, K. (2009). Complex-valued multistate associative memory with nonlinear multilevel functions for gray-level image reconstruction. *IEEE Transactions on Neural Networks, 20*(9), 1463–1473. doi:10.1109/TNN.2009.2025500

Tsai, R. Y., & Huang, T. S. (1984). Uniqueness and estimation of three-dimensional motion parameters of rigid objects with curved surfaces. *IEEE Transactions on Pattern Analysis and Machine Intelligence*, *6*(1), 13–27. doi:10.1109/TPAMI.1984.4767471

Wang, Q., & Clarke, R. J. (1990). Use of Fourier descriptors for the estimation of general motion in image sequences. *Electronics Letters*, *26*(22), 1877–1878. doi:10.1049/el:19901207

Watanabe, A., Yazawa, N., Miyauchi, A., & Miyauchi, M. (1994). A method to interpret 3D motions using neural networks. *IEICE Transactions on Fundamentals of Electronics, Communications and Computer Sciences. E (Norwalk, Conn.)*, *77-A*(8), 1363–1370.

ADDITIONAL READING

Aizenberg, I. N., Aizenberg, N. N., & Vandewalle, J. (2000). *Multi-Valued and Universal Ninary Neurons*. Boston: Kluwer Academic Publishers.

Arena, P., Fortuna, L., Muscato, G., & Xibilia, M. G. (1998). *Neural Networks in Multidimensional Domains, Lecture Notes in Control and Information Sciences. 234*. Springer.

Mandic, D. P., & Goh, V. S. L. (2009). *Complex Valued Nonlinear Adaptive Filters*. John Wiley & Sons, Ltd.doi:10.1002/9780470742624

Schreier, P. J., & Scharf, L. L. (2010). *Statistical Signal Processing of Complex-Valued Data*. Cambridge University Press.

KEY TERMS AND DEFINITIONS

Artificial Neural Network: A network composed of artificial neurons. Artificial neural networks can be trained to find nonlinear relationships in data.

Complex Number: A number of the form $a + ib$ where a and b are real numbers, and i is the imaginary unit such that $i^2 = -1$. a is called the *real part*, and b the *imaginary part*.

Back-Propagation Algorithm: A supervised learning technique used for training neural networks, based on minimizing the error between the actual outputs and the desired outputs.

Complex-Valued Neural Network: An artificial neural network whose learnable parameters are complex numbers. Complex-valued neural network can learn complex-valued patterns in a natural way.

Steiner Circles: A family of circles consisted of the two subfamilies. The first subfamily consists of the circles through the limit points of the Steiner circles a and b. The second subfamily consists of the *circles of Apolonius* with respect of a and b.

Affine Transformation: A transformation consists of a linear transformation followed by a translation.

Generalization Ability: An ability to generalize unlearned input patterns.

Compilation of References

Abeles, M. (1982). *Local cortical circuits: An electrophysiological study*. Berlin, Germany: Springer.

Abeles, M., & Gat, I. (2001). Detecting precise firing sequences in experimental data. *Journal of Neuroscience Methods*, *107*, 141–154. doi:10.1016/S0165-0270(01)00364-8

Adamatzky, A., De Lacy Costello, B., & Tetsuya, A. (2005). *Reaction diffusion computers*. Elsevier Science.

Adiv, G. (1986). Determining three-dimensional motion and structure from optical flow generated by several moving objects. *IEEE Transactions on Pattern Analysis and Machine Intelligence*, *7*(4), 384–401. doi:10.1109/TPAMI.1985.4767678

Adler, N. (1999). *Managing complex product development – three approaches*. EFI, Stockholm School of Economics.

Aggarwal, J. K., & Nandhakumar, N. (1998). On the computation of motion from sequences of images - a review. *Proceedings of the IEEE*, *76*(8), 917–935. doi:10.1109/5.5965

Agladze, K., Aliev, R. R., Yamaguchi, T., & Yoshikawa, K. (1996). Chemical diode. *Journal of Physical Chemistry*, *100*, 13895–13897. doi:10.1021/jp9608990

Agster, K., Fortin, N., & Eichenbaum, H. (2002). The hippocampus and disambiguation of overlapping sequences. *The Journal of Neuroscience*, *22*, 5760–5768.

Aguado, D., Ribes, J., Montoya, T., Ferrer, J., & Seco, A. (2009). A methodology for sequencing batch reactor identification with artificial neural networks: A case study. *Computers & Chemical Engineering*, *33*, 465–472. doi:10.1016/j.compchemeng.2008.10.018

Ahlfors, L. V. (1979). *Complex analysis*. McGraw-Hill, Inc.

Akagi, T., Okazaki, N., Yoshinobu, T., & Matsumura-Inoue, T. (2000). Comparative study of chemical waves and temporal oscillations in $Ru(bpy)_3$ catalyzed Belousov-Zhabotinsky reaction. *Chemical Physics Letters*, *28*, 214–220. doi:10.1016/S0009-2614(00)00907-6

Akbani, R., Kwek, S., & Japkowicz, N. (2004). Applying support vector machines to imbalanced datasets. In *Proceedings of 15th European Conference on Machine Learning*, Pisa, Italy, September 20-24, 2004.

Albert, A. (1972). *Regression and the Moore-Penrose pseudoinverse*. New York, NY: Academic Press.

Albus, J. M. (2001). *Engineering of mind: An introduction to the science of intelligent systems*. New York, NY: Wiley.

Aleboyeh, A., Kasiri, M. B., Olya, M. E., & Aleboyeh, H. (2008). Prediction of azo dye decolorization by UV/H_2O_2 using artificial neural networks. *Dyes and Pigments*, *77*, 288–294. doi:10.1016/j.dyepig.2007.05.014

Alexandroff, P. (1961). *Elementary concepts of topology*. New York, NY: Dover Publications.

Allen, R. (2001). Artificial intelligence and the evidentiary process: The challenges of formalism and computation. *Artificial Intelligence and Law*, *9*, 99–114. doi:10.1023/A:1017941929299

Allen, J. F. (1983). Maintaining knowledge about temporal intervals. *Communications of the ACM*, *26*(11), 832–843. doi:10.1145/182.358434

Allen, D. M. (1974). The relationship between variable selection and data augmentation and a method of prediction. *Technometrics*, *16*, 125–127. doi:10.2307/1267500

Amari, S., Chen, T., & Cichocki, A. (1997). Stability analysis of learning algorithms for blind source separation. *Neural Networks*, *10*, 1345–1351. doi:10.1016/S0893-6080(97)00039-7

Andersen, R., Snyder, L., Bradley, D., & Xing, J. (1997). Multimodal representation of space in the posterior parietal cortex and its use in planning movements. *Annual Review of Neuroscience*, *20*, 303–330. doi:10.1146/annurev.neuro.20.1.303

Angiulli, F., Basta, S., & Pizzuti, C. (2006). Distance-based detection and prediction of outliers. *IEEE Transactions on Knowledge and Data Engineering*, *18*(2), 145–160. doi:10.1109/TKDE.2006.29

Anscombe, F. J. (1973). Graphs in statistical analysis. *The American Statistician*, *27*, 17–21. doi:10.2307/2682899

Antani, S., Long, L. R., & Thoma, G. R. (2004). Content-based image retrieval for large biomedical image archives. In *Proceedings of 11th World Congress on Medical Informatics (MEDINFO)*, (pp. 829-833).

Antania, S., Kasturi, R., & Jain, R. (2002). A survey on the use of pattern recognition methods for abstraction, indexing and retrieval of images and video. *Pattern Recognition*, *35*(4), 945–965. doi:10.1016/S0031-3203(01)00086-3

Araki, M. (1996). Stability concepts - PID control. In H. Unbehausen (Ed.), *Control systems, robotics, and automation*. Kyoto, Japan: Encyclopedia of Life Support Systems (EOLSS).

Atkinson, A. C. (1985). *Plots, transformations and regression*. Oxford, UK: Clarendon Press.

Atkinson, A. C. (1986). Masking unmasked. *Biometrika*, *73*, 533–541. doi:10.1093/biomet/73.3.533

Atkinson, A. C., & Riani, M. (2000). *Robust diagnostic regression analysis*. London, UK: Springer.

Austin, J. L. (1962). *How to do things with words*. Oxford, UK: Oxford University Press.

Baars, B. J., & Gage, N. M. (2007). *Cognition, brain, and consciousness*. Academic Press.

Bäck, T., Hammel, U., & Schwefel, H.-P. (1997). Evolutionary computation: Comments on the history and current state. *IEEE Transactions on Evolutionary Computation*, *1*(1), 3–16. doi:10.1109/4235.585888

Baek Hwan, C., Hwanjo, Y., Kwang-Won, K., Tae Hyun, K., In Young, K., & Sun, K. (2008). Application of irregular and unbalanced data to predict diabetic nephropathy using visualization and feature selection methods. *Artificial Intelligence in Medicine*, *42*(1), 37–53. doi:10.1016/j.artmed.2007.09.005

Bailón, L., Nikolausz, M., Kästner, M., Veiga, M. C., & Kennes, C. (2009). Removal of dichloromethane from waste gases in one-and two-liquid-phase stirred tank bioreactors and biotrickling filters. *Water Research*, *43*, 11–20. doi:10.1016/j.watres.2008.09.031

Bakker, B., & Schmidhuber, J. (2004). Hierarchical reinforcement learning based on subgoal discovery and subpolicy specialization. In F. Groen, N. Amato, A. Bonarini, E. Yoshida, & B. Kröse (Eds.), *Proceedings of the 8th Conference on Intelligent Autonomous Systems*, (pp. 438-445). Amsterdam, The Netherlands.

Baluja, S., Sukthankar, R., & Hancock, J. (2001). Prototyping intelligent vehicle modules using evolutionary algorithms. In Dasgupta, D. (Ed.), *Evolutionary algorithms in engineering applications* (pp. 241–258). New York, NY: Springer.

Bandyopadhyay, A., & Somobrata, A. (2008). 16-bit parallel processing in a molecular assembly. *Proceedings of the National Academy of Sciences of the United States of America*, *105*, 3668–3672. doi:10.1073/pnas.0703105105

Bankman, I. N. (Ed.). (2008). *Handbook of medical image processing and analysis*. Boston, MA: Academic Press.

Banquet, J.-P., Gaussier, P., Quoy, M., Revel, A., & Burnod, Y. (2005). Hierarchy of associations in hippocampo-cortical systems: Cognitive maps and navigation strategies. *Neural Computation*, *17*(6), 1339–1384. doi:10.1162/0899766053630369

Bar, M., Kassam, K., Ghuman, A., Boshyan, J., Schmid, A., & Dale, A. (2006). Top-down facilitation of visual recognition. *Proceedings of the National Academy of Sciences of the United States of America*, *103*, 449–454. doi:10.1073/pnas.0507062103

Barnden, J. A. (2001). Uncertain reasoning about agents' beliefs and reasoning. *Artificial Intelligence and Law*, *9*, 115–152. doi:10.1023/A:1017993913369

Barnett, V., & Lewis, T. B. (1995). *Outliers in statistical data*. New York, NY: Wiley.

Barnsley, M. F., Hurd, L. P., & Anson, L. F. (1993). *Fractal image compression*. AK Peters Massachusetts.

Barnsley, M. F., Ervin, V., Hardin, D., & Lancaster, J. (1986). Solution of an inverse problem for fractals and other sets. *Proceedings of the National Academy of Sciences of the United States of America*, *83*, 1975–1977. doi:10.1073/pnas.83.7.1975

Barron, A. R. (1993). Universal approximation bounds for superpositions of a sigmoidal function. *IEEE Transactions on Information Theory*, *39*, 930–944. doi:10.1109/18.256500

Barron, A. R. (1994). Approximation and estimation bounds for artificial neural networks. *Machine Learning*, *14*, 115–133. doi:10.1007/BF00993164

Barsalou, L. W. (1999). Perceptual symbol systems. *The Behavioral and Brain Sciences*, *22*, 577–660.

Bar-Shalom, Y., & Fortmann, T. (1988). *Tracking and data association*. San Diego, CA: Academic Press, Inc.

Bartels, R. H., Beatty, J. C., & Barsky, B. A. (1987). *An introduction to splines for use in computer graphics and geometric modeling*. San Mateo, CA: Morgan Kaufmann Publishers, Inc.

Barto, A., Singh, S., & Chentanez, N. (2004). Intrinsically motivated learning of hierarchical collections of skills. *Proceedings of the 3rd International Conference on Development Learning*, (pp. 112–119). San Diego, CA.

Baruch, I. S., Georgieva, P., Barrera-Cortes, J., & de Azevedo, S. F. (2005). Adaptive recurrent neural network control of biological wastewater treatment. *International Journal of Intelligent Systems*, *20*, 173–193. doi:10.1002/int.20061

Bay, S. D. (1999). Nearest neighbor classification from multiple feature subsets. *Intelligent Data Analysis*, 3.

Bay, H., Ess, A., Tuytelaars, T., & Gool, L. V. (2008). Speeded-Up Robust Features (SURF). *Computer Vision and Image Understanding*, *110*(3), 346–359. doi:10.1016/j.cviu.2007.09.014

Beard, R., Saridis, G., & Wen, J. (1997). Approximate solutions to the time-invariant Hamilton-Jacobi-Bellman equation. *Automatica*, *33*(12), 2159–2177. doi:10.1016/S0005-1098(97)00128-3

Behnken, D. W., & Draper, N. R. (1972). Residuals and their variance patterns. *Technometrics*, *14*, 101–111. doi:10.2307/1266922

Bellman, R. E. (1957). *Dynamic programming*. Princeton, NJ: Princeton University Press.

Bellman, R. (1961). *Adaptive control processes*. Princeton, NJ: Princeton University Press.

Belsley, D. A., Kuh, E., & Welsch, R. E. (1980). *Regression diagnostics: Identifying influential data and sources of collinearity*. New York, NY: Wiley.

Benedetti, M. G., Catani, F., Leardini, A., Pignotti, E., & Giannini, S. (1998). Data management in gait analysis for clinical applications. *Clinical Biomechanics (Bristol, Avon)*, *13*(3), 204–215. doi:10.1016/S0268-0033(97)00041-7

Bennett, K., & Embrechts, M. (2003). An optimization perspective on kernel partial least squares regression. In J. Suykens, G. Horvath, C. M. S. Basu, & J. Vandewalle (Eds.), *Advances in learning theory: Methods, models and applications*, volume 190 of *NATO Science III: Computer & Systems Sciences* (pp. 227–250). Amsterdam, The Netherlands: IOS Press.

Berger, P., & Luckmann, T. (1991). *The social construction of reality*. London, UK: Penguin Books.

Berlyne, D. E. (1960). *Conflict, arousal, and curiosity*. New York, NY: McGraw-Hill. doi:10.1037/11164-000

Berridge, K. C., & Robinson, T. E. (2003). Parsing reward. *Trends in Neurosciences*, *26*(9), 507–513. doi:10.1016/S0166-2236(03)00233-9

Berthold, M. R., & Huber, K. P. (1995). *From radial to rectangular basis functions: A new approach for rule learningfrom large datasets*. (Technical report, University of Karlsruhe, 1995).

Beynon, M. J. (2005a). A novel technique of object ranking and classification under ignorance: An application to the corporate failure risk problem. *European Journal of Operational Research*, *167*, 493–517. doi:10.1016/j.ejor.2004.03.016

Beynon, M. J. (2005b). A novel approach to the credit rating problem: Object classification under ignorance. *International Journal of Intelligent Systems in Accounting Finance & Management, 13*, 113–130. doi:10.1002/isaf.260

Beynon, M. J., Jones, L., & Holt, C. A. (2006). Classification of osteoarthritic and normal knee function using three-dimensional motion analysis and the Dempster-Shafer theory of evidence. *IEEE Transactions on Systems, Man, and Cybernetics. Part A, Systems and Humans, 36*(1), 173. doi:10.1109/TSMCA.2006.859098

Beynon, M., Russ, S., & McCarty, W. (2006). Human computing–modelling with meaning. [Oxford University Press.]. *Literary and Linguistic Computing, 21*(2), 141–157. doi:10.1093/llc/fql015

Beynon, M., Curry, B., & Morgan, P. (2000). The Dempster-Shafer theory of evidence: An alternative approach to multicriteria decision modelling. *OMEGA - International Journal of Management Science, 28*(1), 37–50.

Bi, J., Bennett, K., Embrechts, M., Breneman, C., & Song, M. (2003). Dimensionality reduction via sparse support vector machines. *Journal of Machine Learning Research, 3*, 1229–1243. doi:10.1162/153244303322753643

Bielefeldt, A. R. (2001). Activated sludge and suspended growth bioreactors. In Kennes, C., & Veiga, M. C. (Eds.), *Bioreactors for waste gas treatment* (pp. 215–254). Dordrecht, The Netherlands: Kluwer Academic Publisher.

Bienenstock, E. (1995). A model of neocortex. *Network (Bristol, England), 6*, 179–224. doi:10.1088/0954-898X/6/2/004

Billor, N., Hadi, A. S., & Velleman, F. (2000). BACON: Blocked adaptive computationally efficient outlier nominator. *Computational Statistics & Data Analysis, 34*, 279–298. doi:10.1016/S0167-9473(99)00101-2

Bimbot, F. (2004). A tutorial on text-independent speaker verification. *EURASIP Journal on Applied Signal Processing, 4*, 430–451. doi:10.1155/S1110865704310024

Bishop, C. (2006). *Pattern recognition and machine learning*. Singapore: Springer.

Bishop, C. M. (2006). *Pattern recognition and machine learning. Springer Science + Business Media*. LLC.

Bishop, C. M. (1995). *Neural networks for pattern recognition*. New York, NY: Oxford University Press.

Blanchard, G., & Krämer, N. (2010). *Kernel partial least squares is universally consistent*. Thirteenth International Conference on Artificial Intelligence and Statistics (AISTATS), Sardinia, Italy.

Blum, A., & Langley, P. (1997). Selection of relevant features and examples in machine learning. *Artificial Intelligence, 1-2*, 245–271. doi:10.1016/S0004-3702(97)00063-5

Blum, H. (1967). A transformation for extracting new descriptors of shape. In: *Symposium: Models for perception of speech and visual forms,* (Whaten-Dunn, W., Ed.), Cambridge, MA: MIT Press.

Bødker, S., & Bøgh Andersen, P. (2005). Complex mediation. *Human-Computer Interaction, 20*, 353–402. doi:10.1207/s15327051hci2004_1

Boland, R. J. (2001). The tyranny of space in organizational analysis. *Information and Organization, 11*, 3–23. doi:10.1016/S0959-8022(00)00007-2

Bonabeau, E., Dorigo, M., & Theraulaz, G. (2005). *Swarm intelligence: From natural to artificial systems*. Retrieved from http://www.cs.virginia.edu/~evans/bio/slides/1

Boser, B. E., Guyon, I. M., & Vapnik, V. N. (1992). A training algorithm for optimal margin classifiers. In D. Haussler (Ed.), *5th Annual ACM Workshop on COLT*, (pp. 144-152). Pittsburgh, PA: ACM Press.

Boser, B., Guyon, I., & Vapnik, V. (1992). *A training algorithm for optimal margin classifiers*. 5th Annual ACM Workshop on COLT, Pittsburgh, PA, ACM Press.

Bouabdallah, S., & Siegwart, R. (2007). *Full control of a quadrotor*. IEEE/RSJ International Conference on Intelligent Robots and Systems, (pp. 153–158).

Bourbaki, N. (1961). *Topologie générale*. Paris, France: Hermann.

Bradley, A. (1997). The use of the area under the ROC curve in evaluation of machine learning algorithms. *Pattern Recognition, 30*(7), 1145–1159. doi:10.1016/S0031-3203(96)00142-2

Bradley, P. S., & Fayyad, U. M. (1998). *Refining initial points for K-means clustering*. In 15th International Conference on Machine Learning (pp. 91-99). Los Altos, CA: Morgan Kaufmann.

Brameier, M., & Banzhaf, W. (2001). A comparison of linear genetic programming and neural networks in medical data mining. *IEEE Transactions on Evolutionary Computation*, *5*, 17–26. doi:10.1109/4235.910462

Brattka, V. (2004). *Du 13-ième problème de Hibert à la théorie des réseaux de neurones: aspects constructifs du théorème de superposition de Kolmogorov*. Paris, France: Editions Belin.

Braun, J., & Griebel, M. (2007). On a constructive proof of Kolmogorov's superposition theorem. *Constructive Approximation*, *30*(3), 653–675. doi:10.1007/s00365-009-9054-2

Breemen, A. van, & Sarbo, J. (2009). The machine in the ghost: The syntax of mind. *Signs – International Journal of Semiotics*, 135-184.

Breiman, L. (1996). Bagging predictors. *Machine Learning*, *24*(1), 123–140. doi:10.1007/BF00058655

Breiman, L., Meisel, W., & Purcell, E. (1977). Variable kernel estimates of multivariate densities. *Technometrics*, *19*(2), 135–144. doi:10.2307/1268623

Breiman, L. (1999). Combining predictors. In Sharkey, A. (Ed.), *Combining artificial neural nets: Ensemble and modular multi-net systems* (pp. 31–50). London, UK: Springer.

Brest, J., Žumer, V., & Maučec, M. S. (2006). *Self-adaptive differential evolution algorithm in constrained real-parameter optimization*. IEEE Congress on Evolutionary Computation, Vancouver, BC, Canada

Breunig, M., Kriegel, H. P., Ng, R., & Sander, J. L. O. F. (2000). Identifying density-based local outliers. In *Proceedings of the 2000 ACM SIGMOD International Conference on Management of Data*, (pp. 93-104). New York, NY: ACM Press.

Brooks, R. A. (1991). Intelligence without representation. *Artificial Intelligence*, *47*, 139–159. doi:10.1016/0004-3702(91)90053-M

Brooks, R. (1986). *Asynchronous distributed control system for a mobile robot*. SPIE Conference on Mobile Robots, (pp. 77–84).

Brown, E. N., Barbieri, R., Ventura, V., Kass, R. E., & Frank, L. M. (2001). The time-rescaling theorem and its application to neural spike train data analysis. *Neural Computation*, *14*, 325–346. doi:10.1162/08997660252741149

Brown, R. G., & Hwang, P. Y. C. (1997). *Introduction to random signals and applied Kalman filtering*. New York, NY: John Wiley & Sons.

Brown, J. S., Collins, A., & Duguid, S. (1989). Situated cognition and the culture of learning. *Educational Researcher*, *18*(1), 32–42.

Brunelli, R., & Falavigna, D. (1995). Person identification using multiple cues. *IEEE Transactions on Pattern Analysis and Machine Intelligence*, *17*(10), 955–966. doi:10.1109/34.464560

Bruner, J. (1966). *Toward a theory of instruction*. Harvard University Press.

Bryant, W. C., & Gay, S. H. (1883). *A popular history of the United States* (*Vol. I*). New York, NY: Charles Scribner's Sons.

Buchholz, S., & Bihan, N. L. (2008). Polarized signal classification by complex and quaternionic multi-layer perceptrons. *International Journal of Neural Systems*, *18*(2), 75–85. doi:10.1142/S0129065708001403

Burgess, N., Jeffery, K., & O'Keefe, J. (Eds.). (1999). *The hippocampal and parietal foundations of spatial cognition*. Oxford University Press.

Burgess, N., & O'Keefe, J. (1996). Cognitive graphs, resistive Grids, and the hippocampal representation of space. *The Journal of General Physiology*, *9*(107), 659–662. doi:10.1085/jgp.107.6.659

Calvert, G. A. (2001). Crossmodal processing in the human brain: Insights from functional neuroimaging studies. *Cerebral Cortex*, *11*, 1110–1123. doi:10.1093/cercor/11.12.1110

Cao, F., Lisani, J.-L., Morel, J.-M., Musé, P., & Sur, H. (2008). *A theory of shape identification*. (LNCS 1948). Springer.

Carpenter, H., & Talley, N. (2000). The importance of clinicopathological correlation in the diagnosis of inflammatory conditions of the colon. *The American Journal of Gastroenterology*, *95*, 234–245. doi:10.1111/j.1572-0241.2000.01924.x

Carpenter, G., & Grossberg, S. (1987). A massively parallel architecture for a self-organizing neural pattern recognition machine. *Computer Vision Graphics and Image Processing*, *37*, 54–115. doi:10.1016/S0734-189X(87)80014-2

Carson, C., Belongie, Se., Greenpan, H., & Jitendra, M. (2002). Blobworld: Image segmentation using expectation-maximization and its application to image querying. *IEEE Transactions on Pattern Analysis and Machine Intelligence*, *24*(8). doi:10.1109/TPAMI.2002.1023800

Carter, M., Lobo, A., & Travis, S. (2004). Guidelines for the management of IBD for adults. *British Society of Gastroenterology*, *53*, 1–16.

Castano, R., Manduchi, R., & Fox, J. (2001). *Classification experiments on real-world texture.* Paper presented at the Third Workshop on Empirical Evaluation Methods in Computer Vision, Kauai, Hawaii.

Casti, J. (1979). *Connectivity, complexity, and catastrophe in large-scale systems. Chichester, UK, New York, NY, Brisbane, Australia.* Toronto, Canada: John Wiley & Sons.

Castillo, P., Dzul, A., & Lozano, R. (2004). Real-time stabilization and tracking of a four-rotor mini rotorcraft. *IEEE Transactions on Control Systems Technology*, *12*(4), 510–516. doi:10.1109/TCST.2004.825052

Chalmers, A. F. (1976). *What is this thing called science?* St Lucia, Queensland: University of Queensland Press.

Chambers, J. M., Cleveland, W. S., Kleiner, B., & Tukey, P. A. (1983). *Graphical methods for data analysis*. Boston, MA: Duxbury Press.

Chambolle, A. (2004). An algorithm for total variation minimization and applications. *Journal of Mathematical Imaging and Vision*, *20*, 89–97. doi:10.1023/B:JMIV.0000011321.19549.88

Chan, T., Esedoglu, S., & Nikolova, M. (2006). Algorithms for finding global minimizers of image segmentation and denoising models. *SIAM Journal on Applied Mathematics*, *66*, 1632–1648. doi:10.1137/040615286

Chang, C.-C., Li, Y.-C., & Lin, C.-H. (2008). A novel method for progressive image transmission using block wavelets. *International Journal of Electronics and Communication*, *62*(2), 159–162. doi:10.1016/j.aeue.2007.03.008

Chang, C.-C., & Lin, C.-J. (2010). *LIBSVM: A Library for Support Vector Machines*. Taipei, Taiwan: Department of Computer Science, National Taiwan University.

Chang, C., & Lin, C. (2003). *LIBSVM: A library for support vector machines*. Retrieved on 5 September, 2004, from http://www.csie.ntu.edu.tw/~cjlin/libsvm

Changeux, J. P. (2004). *The physiology of truth.* Cambridge, MA & London, UK: Harvard University Press.

Changeux, J. P. (1997). *Neuronal man: The biology of mind.* Princeton, NJ: Princeton Univ. Press.

Changeux, J. P. (2004). *The physiology of truth.* Cambridge, MA & London, UK: Harvard University Press.

Chapelle, O., & Vapnik, V. (2002). Choosing multiple parameters for support vector machines. *Machine Learning*, *46*(1-3), 131–159. doi:10.1023/A:1012450327387

Chapelle, O., & Keerthi, S. (2008). Multi-class feature selection with support vector machines. *Proceedings of American Statistical Association.*

Chatterjee, S., & Hadi, A. S. (1986). Influential observations, high leverage points, and outliers in regression. *Statistical Science*, *1*, 379–416. doi:10.1214/ss/1177013622

Chatterjee, S., & Hadi, A. S. (1988). *Sensitivity analysis in linear regression.* New York, NY: Wiley.

Chatterjee, S., & Hadi, A. S. (2006). *Regression analysis by examples*. New York, NY: Wiley. doi:10.1002/0470055464

Chau, T. (2001a). A review of analytical techniques for gait data, part 1: Fuzzy, statistical and fractal methods. *Gait & Posture*, *13*(1), 49–66. doi:10.1016/S0966-6362(00)00094-1

Chau, T. (2001b). A review of analytical techniques for gait data, part 2: Neural network and wavelet methods. *Gait & Posture*, *13*(2), 102–120. doi:10.1016/S0966-6362(00)00095-3

Chawla, N. V., Bowyer, K. W., Hall, L. O., & Kegelmeyer, W. P. (2002). SMOTE: Synthetic minority over-sampling technique. *Journal of Artificial Intelligence Research*, *16*, 321–357.

Chawla, N. V. (2003). *C4.5 and imbalanced data sets: Investigating the effect of sampling method, probabilistic estimate, and decision tree structure*. Workshop on learning from imbalanced dataset II, ICML, Washington DC, 2003.

Chee, Y.-K. (1999). Survey of progressive image transmission methods. *International Journal of Imaging Systems and Technology*, *10*(1), 3–19. doi:10.1002/(SICI)1098-1098(1999)10:1<3::AID-IMA2>3.0.CO;2-E

Cheikhrouhou, I., Djemal, K., Masmoudi, D. S., Maaref, H., & Derbel, N. (2008). *New mass description in mammographies. IEEE International Workshops on Image Processing, Theory, Tools and Applications (IPTA08), November 23*. Tunisia: Sousse.

Cheikhrouhou, I., Djemal, K., Masmoudi, D. S., Derbel, N., & Maaref, H. (2007). Abnormalities description for breast cancer recognition. *IEEE International Conference on E-medical Systems*, (pp. 199-205). October, Fez, Morocco.

Chen, H., Sun, M., & Steinbach, E. (2009). Compression of Bayer-pattern video sequences using adjusted chroma subsampling. *IEEE Transactions on Circuits and Systems for Video Technology*, *19*(12), 1891–1896. doi:10.1109/TCSVT.2009.2031370

Chen, Q., Zhao, J., Chaitep, S., & Guo, Z. (2009). Simultaneous analysis of main catechins contents in green tea (Camellia sinensis) by Fourier transform near infrared reflectance (FT-NIR) spectroscopy. *Food Chemistry*, *113*(4), 1272–1277. doi:10.1016/j.foodchem.2008.08.042

Chen, S. H., Jakeman, A. J., & Norton, J. P. (2008). Artificial intelligence techniques: An introduction to their use for modelling environmental systems. *Mathematics and Computers in Simulation*, *78*, 379–400. doi:10.1016/j.matcom.2008.01.028

Chen, X. (2003, December). Object and event concepts: A cognitive mechanism of incommensurability. *Philosophy of Science*, *70*, 962–974. doi:10.1086/377381

Chevallier, S., Paugam-Moisy, H., & Lemaitre, F. (2005). Distributed processing for modeling real-time multimodal perception in a virtual robot. *International Multi-Conference Parallel and Distributed Computing and Networks*, 393-398.

Chiang, Y. M., Chang, L. C., Tsai, M. J., Wang, Y. F., & Chang, F. J. (2010). Dynamic neural networks for real-time water level predictions of sewerage systems–covering gauged and ungauged sites. *Hydrology and Earth System Sciences Discussions*, *7*, 2317–2345. doi:10.5194/hessd-7-2317-2010

Chibelushi, C. C., Deravi, F., & Mason, J. S. D. (2002). A review of speech-based bimodal recognition. *IEEE Transactions on Multimedia*, *4*(1), 23–37. doi:10.1109/6046.985551

Chibelushi, C. C., Deravi, F., & Mason, J. S. D. (1999). Adaptive classifier integration for robust pattern recognition. *IEEE Transactions on Systems, Man, and Cybernetics - Part B*, *29*(6), 902-907.

Choi, D. J., & Park, H. (2001). A hybrid artificial neural network as a software sensor for optimal control of a wastewater treatment process. *Water Research*, *35*, 3959–3967. doi:10.1016/S0043-1354(01)00134-8

Chomsky, N. (1965). *Aspects of the theory of syntax*. Cambridge, MA: MIT Press.

Chomsky, N. (1981). Principles and parameters in syntactic theory. In Hornstein, N., & Lightfoot, D. (Eds.), *Explanation in linguistics: The logical problem of language acquisition*. London, UK: Longman.

Chou, M.-S., & Huang, J.-H. (1997). Treatment of methylethylketone in air stream by biotrickling filters. *Journal of Environmental Engineering*, *123*, 569–576. doi:10.1061/(ASCE)0733-9372(1997)123:6(569)

Chou, M.-S., & Wu, F. H. (1999). Treatment of toluene in an air stream by a biotrickling filter packed with slags. *Journal of the Air & Waste Management Association*, *49*, 386–398.

Churavy, C., Baker, M., Mehta, S., Pradhan, I., Scheidegger, N., Shanfelt, S., et al. (2008). Effective implementation of a mapping swarm of robots. *IEEE Potentials*, 28-33.

Clancey, W. J. (1993). Situated action: A neuropsychological interpretation response to Vera and Simon. *Cognitive Science*, *17*(1), 87–116. doi:10.1207/s15516709cog1701_7

Cohn, D., Ghahramani, Z., & Jordan, M. (1996). Active learning with statistical models. *Journal of Artificial Intelligence Research*, *4*, 129–145.

Cohn, A. G., Bennett, B., Gooday, J. M., & Gotts, N. (1997b). RCC: A calculus for region based qualitative spatial reasoning. *GeoInformatica*, *1*, 275–316. doi:10.1023/A:1009712514511

Cohn, A. G., Bennett, B., Goodday, J. M., & Gotts, N. (1997a). Qualitative spatial representation and reasoning with the region connection calculus. *GeoInformatica*, *1*(3), 1–44. doi:10.1023/A:1009712514511

Cohn, A. G., & Hazarika, S. M. (2001). Qualitative spatial representation and reasoning: An overview. *Fundamenta Informaticae*, *46*(1-2), 1–29.

Cohn, A. G., & Varzi, A. (2003). Mereotopological connection. *Journal of Philosophical Logic*, *32*, 357–390. doi:10.1023/A:1024895012224

Cohn, A. G. (2001). Formalising bio-spatial knowledge. In C. Welty and B. Smith (Eds.), *Proceedings of the 2nd International Conference FOIS'01* (pp. 198–209). New York, NY: ACM.

Cohn, A. G., & Gotts, N. M. (1994). Spatial regions with undetermined boundaries. *Proceedings of Gaithesburg Workshop on GIS.* New York, NY: ACM.

Cohn, A. G., & Gotts, N. M. (1996). Representing spatial vagueness: A mereological approach. In L. C. Aiello, J. Doyle & S. Shapiro (Eds.), *Proceedings of the 5th Conference on Principles of Knowledge Representation and Reasoning* (pp. 230–241). Burlington, MA:Morgan Kaufmann.

Cohn, A. G., & Gotts, N. M. (1996). The egg-yolk representation of regions with indeterminate boundaries. In P. Burrough & A. Frank (Eds.), *Proceedings, GISDATA Specialist Meeting on Geographical Objects with Undetermined Boundaries* (pp. 171-187). New York, NY: Francis Taylor.

Conrad, M. (1974). *Molecular information processing in the central nervous system, part1: Selection circuits in the brain* (pp. 82–137). Berlin/Heidelberg, Germany, New York, NY: Springer Verlag.

Conrad, M. (1985). On design principles for a molecular computer. *Communications of the ACM*, *28*, 464–480. doi:10.1145/3532.3533

Cook, R. D. (1977). Detection of influential observations in linear regression. *Technometrics*, *19*, 15–18. doi:10.2307/1268249

Cook, R. D. (1979). Influential observations in regression. *Journal of the American Statistical Association*, *74*, 169–174. doi:10.2307/2286747

Cook, R. D. (1986). Assessment of local influence. *Journal of the Royal Statistical Society. Series B. Methodological*, *48*(2), 133–169.

Cook, R. D. (1998). *Regression graphics: Ideas for studying regression through graphics*. New York, NY: Wiley.

Cook, R. D., & Weisberg, S. (1982). *Residuals and influence in regression*. London, UK: Chapman and Hall.

Cortes-Rello, E., & Golshani, F. (1990). Uncertain reasoning using the Dempster-Shafer method: An application in forecasting and marketing management. *Expert Systems: International Journal of Knowledge Engineering and Neural Networks*, *7*(1), 9–18. doi:10.1111/j.1468-0394.1990.tb00159.x

Couwenberg, M. (2007). *Analyse van ontwikkeling van kenniselementen.* Master Thesis. Nijmegen, The Netherlands: Radboud Universiteit.

Cover, T. M., & Hart, P. E. (1967). Nearest neighbor pattern classification. *IEEE Transactions on Information Theory*, *13*(1), 21–27. doi:10.1109/TIT.1967.1053964

Cox, H. H. J., & Deshusses, M. A. (2001). Biotrickling filters. In Kennes, C., & Veiga, M. C. (Eds.), *Bioreactors for waste gas treatment* (pp. 99–131). Dordrecht, The Netherlands: Kluwer Academic Publisher.

Crepet, A., Paugam-Moisy, H., Reynaud, E., & Puzenat, D. (2000). *A modular neural model for binding several modalities*. International Conference on Artificial Intelligence, ICAI, (pp. 921-928).

Cristianini, N., & Shawe-Taylor, J. (2000). *Support vector machines and other kernel based learning methods*. Cambridge, UK: Cambridge University Press.

Cristianini, N., & Campbell, C. (1998). Dynamically adapting kernels in support vector machines. *Proceedings of the 1998 conference on Advances in neural information processing systems,* vol. 11.

Curds, C. R., & Cockburn, A. (1970). Protozoa in biological sewage-treatment processes-I. A survey of the protozoan fauna of British percolating filters and activated-sludge plants. *Water Research, 4*, 225–236. doi:10.1016/0043-1354(70)90069-2

Currie, K. W., & Tate, A. (1991). O-Plan: The open planning architecture. *Artificial Intelligence, 52*(1), 49-86. ISSN: 0004-3702

Cybenko, G. (1989). Approximation by superposition of a sigmoidal function. *Mathematically Controlled Signals. Systems, 2*, 303–314.

Dabaghian, Y., Cohn, A. G., & Frank, L. (2007a). *Neural activity in the hippocampus in the framework of formal topology*. 3d Workshop on Formal Topology, Padova, Italy.

Dabaghian, Y., Cohn, A. G., & Frank, L. (2007b). Topological maps from signals. *Proceedings of the 15th ACM GIS conference.* New York, NY: ACM

Dabaghian, Y., Memoli, F., Frank, L., & Carlsson, G. (2010). *Topological robustness of the hippocampal spatial map*.

Dahlkamp, H., Kaehler, A., Stavens, D., Thrun, S., & Bradski, G. (2006). *Self-supervised monocular road detection in desert terrain.* Paper presented at the The Robotics Science and Systems Conference.

Dai, H., & MacBeth, C. (1997). The application of back-propagation neural network to automatic picking seismic arrivals from single-component recordings. *Journal of Geophysical Research, 102*, 105–113. doi:10.1029/97JB00625

Damasio, A. (1995). *Descartes' error: Emotion, reason, and the human brain*. New York, NY: Avon.

Dangcong, P., Yi, W., Hao, W., & Xiaochang, W. (2004). Biological denitrification in a sequencing batch reactor. *Water Science and Technology, 50*, 67–72.

Daniel, M. (2006). On transformations of belief functions to probabilities. *International Journal of Intelligent Systems, 21*, 261–282. doi:10.1002/int.20134

Davies, P., Imon, A. H. M. R., & Ali, M. M. (2004). A conditional expectation method for improved residual estimation and outlier identification in linear regression. *International Journal of Statistical Sciences, Special issue*, 191-208.

Davis, R. B., & Hutton, B. (1975). The effects of errors in the independent variables in linear regression. *Biometrika, 62*, 383–391. doi:10.2307/2335377

Dayan, P., & Hinton, G. E. (1993). Feudal reinforcement learning. In Hanson, S. J., Cowan, J. D., & Giles, C. L. (Eds.), *Advances in neural information processing systems, 5*. San Mateo, CA: Morgan Kaufmann.

De Rouin, E., Brown, J., Fausett, L., & Schneider, M. (1991). Neural network training on unequally represented classes. In *Intelligent engineering systems through artificial neural networks* (pp. 135-141). New York, NY: ASME press.

de Silva, V., & Ghrist, R. (2006). Homological sensor networks. *The International Journal of Robotics Research, 25*(12), 1205–1222. doi:10.1177/0278364906072252

Deacon, T. (1998). *The symbolics species: The co-evolution of language and the brain*. W.W. Norton & Company.

Debruyne, M., Engelene, S., Hubert, M., & Rousseeuw, P. J. (2006). Robustness and outlier detection in chemomtrics. Retrieved on February 9, 2010, from wis.kuleuven.be/stat/robust/Papers/RobustnessCRAC.pdf

Dehaene, S., Kerszberg, M., & Changeux, J. P. (1998). A neuronal model of a global workspace in effortful cognitive tasks. [PNAS]. *Proceedings of the National Academy of Sciences of the United States of America, 95*(24), 14529–14534. doi:10.1073/pnas.95.24.14529

Delfos, M. (2000). *Luister je wel naar mij? Gespreksvoering met kinderen tussen vier en twaalf.* Amsterdam, The Netherlands: Uitgeverelj SWP.

Dellana, S. A., & West, D. (2009). Predictive modelling for wastewater applications: Linear and nonlinear approaches. *Environmental Modelling & Software, 24*, 96–106. doi:10.1016/j.envsoft.2008.06.002

Delorme, A., Gautrais, J., van Rullen, R., & Thorpe, S. (1999). SpikeNet: A simulator for modeling large networks of integrate and fire neurons. *Neurocomputing, 26-27*, 989–996. doi:10.1016/S0925-2312(99)00095-8

Delorme, A., Perrinet, L., & Thorpe, S. (2001). Networks of integrate-and-fire neurons using rank order coding. *Neurocomputing*, 38–48.

Delorme, A., & Thorpe, S. (2001). Face identification using one spike per neuron: Resistance to image degradation. *Neural Networks, 14*, 795–803. doi:10.1016/S0893-6080(01)00049-1

Deming, R., & Perlovsky, L. (2007). Concurrent multi-target localization, data association, and navigation for a swarm of flying sensors. *Information Fusion, 8*(3), 316–330. doi:10.1016/j.inffus.2005.11.001

Deming, R., Schindler, J., & Perlovsky, L. (2009). Multi-target/multisensor tracking using only range and doppler measurements. *IEEE Transactions on Aerospace and Electronic Systems, 45*(2). doi:10.1109/TAES.2009.5089543

Deming, R. (1998). Automatic buried mine detection using the maximum likelihood adaptive neural system (MLANS). *Proceedings of the 1998 IEEE ISIC/CIRA/ISAS Joint Conference.* Gaithersburg, MD.

Deming, R., Schindler, J., & Perlovsky, L. (2007). *Concurrent tracking and detection of slowly moving targets using dynamic logic*. 2007 IEEE Int'l Conf. on Integration of Knowledge Intensive Multi-Agent Systems: Modeling, Evolution, and Engineering (KIMAS 2007). Waltham, MA.

Deming, R., Schindler, J., & Perlovsky, L. (2007). *Track-before-detect of multiple slowly moving targets.* IEEE Radar Conference 2007. Waltham, MA.

Dempster, A. P. (1967). Upper and lower probabilities induced by a multiple valued mapping. *Annals of Mathematical Statistics, 38*, 325–339. doi:10.1214/aoms/1177698950

Derbyshire, S. W. G., Jones, A. K. P., Gyulai, F., et al. (1997). Pain processing during three levels of noxious stimulation produces differential patterns of central activity. *Pain, 73*, 431–445., Amsterdam, The Netherlands: Elsevier. ISSN 0304-3959

Derenzo, S. E. (1977). Approximations for hand calculators using small integer coefficients. *Mathematics of Computation, 31*(137), 214–225. doi:10.1090/S0025-5718-1977-0423761-X

Descartes, R. (1989). *The passions of the soul: Les passions de lame*. Indianapolis, IN: Hackett Publishing Company.

Devinny, J. S., Deshusses, M. A., & Webster, T. S. (1999). *Biofiltration for air pollution control.* Boca Raton, FL: Lewis Publisher.

Dewey, J. (1991). *Logic, the theory of enquiry. The later works of John Dewey*, vol. 12, J. A. Boydston (Ed.). Carbondale & Edwardsville, IL: Southern Illinois University Press.

Dierks, T., & Jagannathan, S. (2010). Output feedback control of a quadrotor UAV using neural networks. *IEEE Transactions on Neural Networks, 21*(1), 50–66. doi:10.1109/TNN.2009.2034145

Djemal, K., Puech, W., & Rossetto, B. (2006). Automatic active contours propagation in a sequence of medical images. *International Journal of Image and Graphics, 6*(2), 267–292. doi:10.1142/S0219467806002252

Djemal, K. (2005). *Speckle reduction in ultrasound images by minimization of total variation.* IEEE International Conference on Image Processing, ICIP'05, Volume 3, (pp. 357–360). September, Genova, Italy. ISBN: 0-7803-9134-9

Djemal, K., Bouchara, F., & Rossetto, B. (2002). *Image modeling and region-based active contours segmentation.* International Conference on Vision, Modeling and Visualization VMV'02 (pp. 363-370). November, Erlangen, Germany. ISBN: 3-89838-034-3

Djemal, K., Chettaoui, C., & Maaref, H. (2005). *Shapes description for cells sickle illness recognition.* IEEE International Conference on Systems, Signals & Devices, Communication and Signal Processing, volume 3, March, Sousse, Tunisia.

Djouak, A., Djemal, K., & Maaref, H. (2007). Image recognition based on features extraction and RBF classifier. *Journal Transactions on Signals, Systems and Devices. Issues on Communication and Signal Processing, 2*(3), 235–253.

Donnelly, M., Bittner, T., & Rosse, C. (2006). A formal theory for spatial representation and reasoning in biomedical ontologies. *Artificial Intelligence in Medicine, 36*(1), 1–27. doi:10.1016/j.artmed.2005.07.004

Downing, N., Clark, D., Hutchinson, J., Colclough, K., & Howard, P. (2001). Hip abductor strength following total hip arthroplasty: A prospective comparison of the posterior and lateral approach in 100 patients. *Acta Orthopaedica Scandinavica, 72*(3), 215–220. doi:10.1080/00016470152846501

Dreier, M. E. (2007). *Introduction to helicopter and tiltrotor flight simulation. AIAA Education Series*. AIAA.

Du, D., Simon, D., & Ergezer, M. (2009). *Oppositional biogeography-based optimization*. IEEE Conference on Systems, Man, and Cybernetics (pp. 1035-1040). San Antonio, TX: IEEE.

Dubrovin, B. A., Novikov, S. P., & Fomenko, A. T. (1992). *Modern geometry*. Berlin, Germany: Springer.

Duda, R. O., Hart, P. E., & Stork, P. (2003). *Pattern classification and scene analysis*. New York, NY: Wiley.

Duda, R. O., Hart, P. E., & Stork, D. G. (2001). *Pattern classification*. New York, NY: JohnWiley & Sons, Inc.

Duda, R. G., & Hart, P. E. (1973). *Pattern classification and scene analysis*. New York, NY: John Wiley and Sons.

Dusek, J., & Eichenbaum, H. (1997). The hippocampus and memory for orderly stimulus relations. *Proceedings of the National Academy of Sciences of the United States of America, 94*, 7109–7114. doi:10.1073/pnas.94.13.7109

Eberhart, R. C., Kennedy, J., & Shi, Y. (2001). *Swarm intelligence*. San Mateo, CA: Morgan Kauffman.

Edelman, G. M., & Tononi, G. (1995). *A universe of consciousness: How matter becomes imagination*. New York, NY: Basic Books.

Efron, B., & Tibshirani, R. J. (1993). *An introduction to the bootstrap*. New York, NY: Wiley.

Egenhofer, M. J., & Al-Taha, K. K. (1992). *Theories and methods of spatio-temporal reasoning in geographic space (LNCS 639)* (pp. 196–219). Springer-Verlag.

Egmont-Petersen, M., de Ridder, D., & Handels, H. (2002). Image processing with neural networks-a review. *Pattern Recognition, 35*(10), 2279–2301. doi:10.1016/S0031-3203(01)00178-9

Eichenbaum, H. (2004). Hippocampus: Cognitive processes and neural representations that underlie declarative memory. *Neuron, 44*(11), 109–120. doi:10.1016/j.neuron.2004.08.028

Eichenbaum, H., & Cohen, N. (2001). *From conditioning to conscious recollection*. London, UK: Oxford University Press.

Elías, A., Ibarra-Berastegi, G., Arias, R., & Barona, A. (2006). Neural networks as a tool for control and management of a biological reactor for treating hydrogen sulphide. *Bioprocess and Biosystems Engineering, 29*, 129–136. doi:10.1007/s00449-006-0062-3

Ellenberg, J. H. (1976). Testing for a single outlier from a general regression. *Biometrics, 32*, 637–645. doi:10.2307/2529752

Ellis, G. (2000). *Control system design guide*. San Diego, CA: Academic Press.

Ellis, H. D., Jones, D. M., & Mosdell, N. (1997). Intra- and inter-modal repetition priming of familiar faces and voices. *The British Journal of Psychology, 88*, 143–156.

Embrechts, M., & Ekins, S. (2007). Classification of metabolites with kernel-partial least squares (K-PLS). *Drug Metabolism and Disposition: the Biological Fate of Chemicals, 35*(3), 325–327. doi:10.1124/dmd.106.013185

Embrechts, M., Bress, R., & Kewley, R. (2005). Feature selection via sensitivity analysis with direct kernel PLS. In Guyon, I., & Gunn, S. (Eds.), *Feature extraction*. New York, NY: Springer.

Embrechts, M., Szymanski, B., & Sternickel, K. (2004). Introduction to scientific data mining: Direct kernel methods and applications. In Ovaska, S. (Ed.), *Computationally intelligent hybrid systems: The fusion of soft and hard computing* (pp. 317–362). New York, NY: John Wiley.

Endsley, M. R. (1995). Toward a theory of situation awareness in dynamic systems. *Human Factors*, 32–64. doi:10.1518/001872095779049543

Engelbart, D. (1962). *Augmenting human intellect: A conceptual framework.* (Summary Report No. AFOSR-3233). Menlo Park, CA: Stanford Research Institute.

Engels. F. (1954). *On the part played by labour in the transition from ape to man, dialectics of Nature.* Moscow, Russia: Foreign Languages Publishing House. Retrieved Jan 26, 2010, from http://www.marxists.org/archive/marx/works/1876/part-played-labour/index.htm

Ergezer, M., Simon, D., & Du, D. (2009). *Oppositional biogeography-based optimization.* IEEE Conference on Systems, Man, and Cybernetics (pp. 1035-1040). San Antonio, TX: IEEE.

Eriksson, J. L., & Villa, A. E. P. (2006a). Learning of auditory equivalence classes for vowels by rats. *Behavioural Processes, 73*, 358–359. doi:10.1016/j.beproc.2006.08.005

Eriksson, J. L., & Villa, A. E. P. (2006). *Artificial neural networks simulation of learning of auditory equivalence classes for vowels.* International Joint Conference on Neural Networks, IJCNN, (pp. 1253-1260).

Escrig, M. T., & Toledo, F. (1998). *Qualitative spatial reasoning: Theory and practice-application to robot navigation. Frontiers in AI and Applications, 47.* Amsterdam, The Netherlands: IOS Press.

Eskin, E., Arnold, A., Prerau, M., Portnoy, L., & Stolfo, S. (2002). A geometric framework for unsupervised anomaly detection: Detecting intrusions in unlabeled data. In Jajodia, S., & Barbara, D. (Eds.), *Applications of data mining in computer security, advances in information security.* Boston, MA: Kluwer Academic Publishers.

Estabrooks, A., & Japkowicz, N. (2004). A multiple resampling method for learning from imbalanced dataset. *Computational Intelligence, 20*(1). doi:10.1111/j.0824-7935.2004.t01-1-00228.x

Estabrooks, A. (2000). *A combination scheme for inductive learning from imbalanced datasets.* MSC thesis. Faculty of computer science, Dalhouise University.

Estévez, E., Veiga, M. C., & Kennes, C. (2005). Biodegradation of toluene by the new fungal isolates *Paecilomyces variotii* and *Exophiala oligosperma. Journal of Industrial Microbiology & Biotechnology, 32*, 33–37. doi:10.1007/s10295-004-0203-0

Fan, H.-Y., & Lampinen, J. (2003). A trigonometric mutation operation to differential evolution. *Journal of Global Optimization, 27*, 105–129. doi:10.1023/A:1024653025686

Fawcett, T., & Provost, F. (2001). Robust classification for imprecise environments. *Machine Learning Journal, 42*(3), 203–231. doi:10.1023/A:1007601015854

Fawcett, T. (2003). *ROC graphs: Notes and practical considerations for data mining researchers.* (Technical Report HPL-2003-4, Hewlett Packard), Palo Alto, CA.

Feldman, J. A., & Ballard, D. H. (1982). Connectionist models and their properties. *Cognitive Science, 6*, 205–254. doi:10.1207/s15516709cog0603_1

Fenton, A., Csizmadia, G., & Muller, R. (2000). Conjoint control of hippocampal place cell firing by two visual stimuli. *The Journal of General Physiology, 116*, 191–221. doi:10.1085/jgp.116.2.191

Fenzi, N., & Hofkirchner, W. (1997). *Information processing in evolutionary systems* (Schweitzer, F., Ed.). London, UK: Gordon and Breach.

Fernando, T. M. K. G., Maier, H. R., & Dandy, G. C. (2009). Selection of input variables for data driven models: An average shifted histogram partial mutual information estimator approach. *Journal of Hydrology (Amsterdam), 367*, 165–176. doi:10.1016/j.jhydrol.2008.10.019

Fernyhough, J., Cohn, A. G., & Hogg, D. (2000). Constructing qualitative event models automatically from video input. *Image and Vision Computing, 18*, 81–103. doi:10.1016/S0262-8856(99)00023-2

Field, R. J., & Burger, M. (Eds.). (1985). *Oscillations and traveling waves in chemical systems.* New York, NY: Wiley-Interscience.

Fillion, C., & Sharma, G. (2010). Detecting content adaptive scaling of images for forensic applications. In N. Memon, J. Dittmann, A. Alattar & E. Delp III (Eds.), *Proceedings of SPIE-IS&T Electronic Imaging,* vol. 7541.

Fisher, R. A. (1925). *Statistical methods for research workers.* Edinburgh, UK: Oliver and Boyd.

Fleischer, M. (2005). *Foundations of swarm intelligence: From principles to practice.* Retrieved from http://www.comdig2.de/Conf/C41SR/1

Fleissner, P., & Hofkirchner, W. (1996). Emergent information. *Bio Systems, 2-3*, 243–248. doi:10.1016/0303-2647(95)01597-3

Fleming, P. J., & Purshouse, R. C. (2002). Evolutionary algorithms in control systems engineering: A survey. *Control Engineering Practice*, 1223–1241. doi:10.1016/S0967-0661(02)00081-3

Fontanari, J. F., & Perlovsky, L. I. (2007). Evolving compositionality in evolutionary language games. *IEEE Transactions on Evolutionary Computation, 11*(6), 758–769..doi:10.1109/TEVC.2007.892763

Fontanari, J. F., & Perlovsky, L. I. (2008). How language can help discrimination in the neural modeling fields framework. *Neural Networks, 21*(2-3), 250–256. doi:10.1016/j.neunet.2007.12.007

Fortin, N., Agster, K., & Eichenbaum, H. (2002). Critical role of the hippocampus in memory for sequences of events. *Nature Neuroscience, 5*(5), 458–462.

Foster, D., & Wilson, M. (2006). Reverse replay of behavioural sequences in hippocampal place cells during the awake state. *Nature, 440*, 680–683. doi:10.1038/nature04587

Fox, J. (1993). Regression diagnostics. In Beck, M. S. L. (Ed.), *Regression analysis* (pp. 245–334). London, UK: Sage Publications.

Frank, L., Brown, E., & Wilson, M. (2000). Trajectory encoding in the hippocampus and entorhinal cortex. *Neuron, 27*(10), 169–178. doi:10.1016/S0896-6273(00)00018-0

Freeman, W. J. (2004). How and why brains create meaning from sensory information. *International Journal of Bifurcation and Chaos in Applied Sciences and Engineering, 14*(2), 515–530. doi:10.1142/S0218127404009405

Fu, W.-T., & Anderson, J. R. (2006). Solving the credit assignment problem: Explicit and implicit learning with internal and external state information. *Proceedings of the 28th Annual Conference of the Cognitive Science Society*. Hillsdale, NJ: LEA.

Fuhs, M., Van Rhoads, S., Casale, A., McNaughton, B., & Touretzky, D. (2005). Influence of path integration vs. environmental orientationon place cell remapping between visually identical environments. *Journal of Neurophysiology, 94*(4), 2603–2616. doi:10.1152/jn.00132.2005

Fukushima, K., & Miyake, S. (1982). Neocognitron: A self-organizing neural network model for a mechanism of visual pattern recognition. In Amari, S., & Arbib, M. A. (Eds.), *Competition and cooperation in neural nets* (pp. 267–285). Berlin/ Heidelberg, Germany: Springer-Verlag.

Ganchev, T. (2005). *Speaker recognition*. Unpublished doctoral dissertation, Dept. of Electrical and Computer Engineering, University of Patras, Greece.

Ganesh, R., Balaji, G., & Ramanujam, R. A. (2006). Biodegradation of tannery wastewater using sequencing batch reactor-respirometric assessment. *Bioresource Technology, 97*, 1815–1821. doi:10.1016/j.biortech.2005.09.003

Garcia, J. A., Rodriguez-Sanchez, R., & Fdez-Valdivia, J. (2005). Emergence of a region-based approach to image transmission. *Optical Engineering (Redondo Beach, Calif.), 44*(6). doi:10.1117/1.1928268

Garcia-Ochoa, F., & Castro, E. G. (2001). Estimation of oxygen mass transfer coefficient in stirred tank reactors using artificial neural networks. *Enzyme and Microbial Technology, 28*, 560–569. doi:10.1016/S0141-0229(01)00297-6

Gärdenfors, P. (2000). *Conceptual spaces: The geometry of thought*. Cambridge, MA: MIT Press.

Gärdenfors, P. (2000b). *How Homo became Sapiens: About the evolution of thinking*. Nora, Sweden: Nya Doxa.

Garson, G. D. (1991). Interpreting neural-network connection weights. *Artificial Intelligence Expert, 6*, 47–51.

Gershenson, C. (2002). *Contextuality: A philosophical paradigm, with applications to philosophy of cognitive science. University of Sussex*. UK: COGS.

Gerstner, W., & Kistler, W. M. (2002). *Spiking neuron models*. Cambridge, MA: Cambridge University Press.

Ghazanfar, A. A., Maier, J. X., Hoffman, K. L., & Logothetis, N. K. (2005). Multisensory integration of dynamic faces and voices in rhesus monkey auditory cortex. *The Journal of Neuroscience, 25*, 5004–5012. doi:10.1523/JNEUROSCI.0799-05.2005

Ghorbel, F., Derrode, S., Mezhoud, R., Bannour, M. T., & Dhahbi, S. (2006). Image reconstruction from a complete set of similarity invariants extracted from complex moments. *Pattern Recognition Letters, 27*(12), 1361–1369. doi:10.1016/j.patrec.2006.01.001

Giacinto, G., Roli, F., & Didaci, L. (2003). Fusion of multiple classifiers for intrusion detection in computer networks. *Pattern Recognition Letters*.

Gibson, J. J. (1979). *The ecological approach to visual perception*. Boston, MA: Houghton Mifflin.

Gierer, A., & Meinhardt, H. (1972). A theory of biological pattern formation. *Kybernetik*, *12*, 30–39. doi:10.1007/BF00289234

Girosi, F., & Poggio, T. (1989). Representation properties of networks: Kolmogorov's Theorem is irrelevant. *Neural Computation*, *1*(4), 465–469. doi:10.1162/neco.1989.1.4.465

Gnanadesikan, R., & Wilk, M. B. (1968). Probability plotting methods for the analysis of data. *Biometrika*, *55*(1), 1–17.

Godement, R. (1964). *Topologie algébrique et théorie des faisceaux*. Paris, France: Hermann.

Golbraikh, A., & Tropsha, A. (2002). Beware of q2! *Journal of Molecular Graphics & Modelling*, *20*, 267–276. doi:10.1016/S1093-3263(01)00123-1

Goldberg, D. (1989). *Genetic algorithms in search, optimization, and machine learning*. Reading, MA: Addison-Wesley.

Goldbetter, A. (1997). *Biochemical oscillations and cellular rhythms*. Cambridge, UK: Cambridge University Press.

Goldkuhl, G., & Lind, M. (2008). Coordination and transformation in business processes: Towards an integrated view. *Business Process Management Journal*, *14*(6), 761–777. doi:10.1108/14637150810915964

Gonzalez, R. C., & Woods, R. E. (2005). *Digital image processing*. Reading, MA: Addison-Wesley.

González Díaz, R., & Real, P. (2003). Computation of cohomology operations on finite simplicial complexes. *Homology. Homotopy and Applications*, *5*(2), 83–93.

Gothard, K., Hoffman, K., Battaglia, F., & McNaughton, B. (2001). Dentate gyrus and CA1 ensemble activity during spatial reference frame shifts in the presence and absence of visual input. *The Journal of Neuroscience*, *21*, 7284–7292.

Gothard, K., Skaggs, W., & McNaughton, B. (1996). Dynamics of mismatch correction in the hippocampal ensemble code for space: Interaction between path integration and environmental cues. *The Journal of Neuroscience*, *16*(24), 8027–8040.

Gothard, K. M., Skaggs, W. E., Moore, K. M., & McNaughton, B. L. (1996). Binding of hippocampal CA1 neural activity to multiple reference frames in a landmark-based navigation task. *The Journal of Neuroscience*, *16*(2), 823–835.

Gotts, N. M., Gooday, J. M., & Cohn, A. G. (1996). A connection based approach to common-sense topological description and reasoning. *The Monist*, *79*(1), 51–75.

Grandvalet, Y., & Canu, S. (2002). Adaptive scaling for feature selection in SVMs. *Proceedings of the 2002 conference on Advances in neural information processing systems*, vol. 15.

Gray, J. B. (1986). A simple graphic for assessing influence in regression. *Journal of Statistical Computation and Simulation*, *24*, 121–134. doi:10.1080/00949658608810895

Gray, R. M. (1984). Vector quantization. *IEEE Acoustics, Speech, and Signal Magazine*, 4-28.

Green, J. E., Jang Wook, C., Boukai, A., Bunimovich, Y., Johnston-Halperin, E., & Delonno, E. (2007). A 160-kilobit molecular electronic memory patterned at 1011 bits per square centimeter. *Nature*, *62*(445), 414–417. doi:10.1038/nature05462

Greenfield, S. (1998). How might the brain generate consciousness? In Rose, S. (Ed.), *From brain to consciousness - essays on the new science of the mind* (pp. 210–227). London, UK: Penguin Books.

Griffiths, P. E. (1998). *What emotions really are: The problem of psychological categories*. Chicago, IL: University Of Chicago Press.

Grossberg, S. (1988). *Neural networks and natural intelligence*. Cambridge, MA: MIT Press.

Grossberg, S., & Levine, D. (1987). Neural dynamics of attentionally modulated pavlovian conditioning: Blocking, inter-stimulus interval, and secondary reinforcement. *Psychobiology*, *15*(3), 195–240.

Grossberg, S. (1976). On the development of feature detectors in the visual cortex with applications in learning and reaction-diffusion systems. *Biological Cybernetics, 21*, 145–159. doi:10.1007/BF00337422

Grossberg, S. (1988). Nonlinear neural networks: Principles, mechanisms, and architectures. *Neural Networks, 1*, 17–61. doi:10.1016/0893-6080(88)90021-4

Grubbs, F. (1969). Procedures for detecting outlying observations in samples. *Technometrics, 11*(1), 1–21. doi:10.2307/1266761

Gruber, T. (2008). Ontology. In *Encyclopedia of database systems*. Springer Verlag.

Guenard, N., Hamel, T., & Moreau, V. (2005). Dynamic modeling and intuitive control strategy for an X4-flyer. *International Conference on Control and Automation, 1*, 141–146.

Gujer, A., Henze, M., Mino, T., & van Loosdrecht, M., & IAWQ Task Group on Mathematical Modelling for Design and Operation of Biological Wastewater Treatment. (1999). Activated sludge model no. 3. *Water Science and Technology, 39*, 183–193. doi:10.1016/S0273-1223(98)00785-9

Guo, B., Gunn, S., Damper, R. I., & Nelson, J. (2008). Customizing kernel functions for SVM-based hyperspectral image classification. *IEEE Transactions on Image Processing, 17*(4), 622–629. doi:10.1109/TIP.2008.918955

Guo, H., & Viktor, H. (2004). Learning from imbalanced data sets with boosting and data generation: The DataBoost-IM approach. *ACM SIGKDD Explorations Newsletter, 6*(1).

Guyon, I., & Elisseeff, A. (2003). An introduction to variable and feature selection. *Journal of Machine Learning Research, 3*, 1157–1182. doi:10.1162/153244303322753616

Hadi, A. S. (1992). A new measure of overall potential influence in linear regression. *Computational Statistics & Data Analysis, 14*, 1–27. doi:10.1016/0167-9473(92)90078-T

Hadi, A. S., Imon, A. H. M. R., & Werner, M. (2009). *Detection of outliers, overview* (pp. 57–70). New York, NY: Wiley.

Hadi, A. S., & Simonoff, J. S. (1993). Procedures for the identification of outliers. *Journal of the American Statistical Association, 88*, 1264–1272. doi:10.2307/2291266

Hagan, M., & Menhaj, M. (1994). Training feedforward networks with the Marquardt algorithm. *IEEE Transactions on Neural Networks, 5*(6), 989–993. doi:10.1109/72.329697

Hall, D. L., & Llinas, J. (2001). *Handbook of multisensory data fusion*. CRC Press LLC.

Ham, F., & Kostanic, I. (2001). *Principles of neurocomputing for science and engineering*. New York, NY: McGraw Hill.

Hampel, F. R. (1975). Beyond location parameters: Robust concepts and methods. *Bulletin of the International Statistics Institute, 46*, 375–382.

Hampel, F. R., Ronchetti, E. M., Rousseeuw, P. J., & Stahel, W. A. (1986). *Robust statistics: The approach based on influence function*. New York, NY: Wiley.

Han, L., Embrechts, M., Szymanski, B., Sternickel, K., & Ross, A. (2006). Random forests feature selection with K-PLS: Detecting ischemia from magnetocardiograms. European Symposium on Artificial Neural Networks, Bruges, Belgium.

Hara, T., & Hirose, A. (2004). Plastic mine detecting radar system using complex-valued self-organizing map that deals with multiple-frequency interferometric images. *Neural Networks, 17*(8-9), 1201–1210. doi:10.1016/j.neunet.2004.07.012

Harmon, M. E., & Baird, L. C. (1996). *Multi-player residual advantage learning with general function approximation. Technical report*. Wright-Patterson Air Force Base.

Hartley, T., Burgess, N., Cacucci, F., & O'Keefe, J. (2000). Modeling place fields in terms of the cortical inputs to the hippocampus. *Hippocampus, 10*, 369–379. doi:10.1002/1098-1063(2000)10:4<369::AID-HIPO3>3.0.CO;2-0

Hasenjager, M., & Ritter, H. (2002). Active learning in neural networks. Berlin, Germany: *Physica-Verlag GmbH*, Physica-Verlag Studies In Fuzziness and Soft Computing Series, (pp. 137–169).

Hassabis, D., Kumaran, D., Vann, S., & Maguire, E. (2007). Patients with hippocampal amnesia cannot imagine new experiences. *Proceedings of the National Academy of Sciences of the United States of America, 104*, 1726–1731. doi:10.1073/pnas.0610561104

Hassoun, M. H. (1995). *Fundamentals of artificial neural networks*. Cambridge, MA: MIT Press.

Hastie, T., Tibshirani, R., & Friedman, J. (2003). *The elements of statistical learning: Data mining, inference, and prediction*. New York, NY: Springer.

Hawkins, J., & Blakeslee, S. (2004). *On intelligence*. New York, NY: Henry Holt and Company.

Hawkins, D. M., Bradu, D., & Kass, G. V. (1984). Location of several outliers in multiple regression data using elemental sets. *Technometrics, 26*, 197–208. doi:10.2307/1267545

Hawkins, S., He, G., Williams, H., & Baxter, R. (2002). Outlier detection using replicator neural networks. In *Proceedings of the 4th International Conference on Data Warehousing and Knowledge Discovery* (DaWaK02), Aix-en-Provence, France, (pp. 170-180).

Haykin, S. (1999). *Neural networks-a comprehensive foundation*. New York, NY: Macmillan.

Haykin, S. (Ed.). (2001). *Kalman filtering and neural networks*. New York, NY: John Wiley & Sons. doi:10.1002/0471221546

Hazarika, S. M., & Cohn, A. G. (2001). *Taxonomy of spatio-temporal vagueness: An alternative egg-yolk interpretation*. COSIT/FOIS Workshop on Spatial Vagueness, Uncertainty and Granularity, Maine, USA.

Hazlehurst, B., Gorman, P. N., & McMullena, C. K. (2008). Distributed cognition: An alternative model of cognition for medical informatics. *International Journal of Medical Informatics, 77*(4), 226–234. doi:10.1016/j.ijmedinf.2007.04.008

He, W., Wang, Z., & Jiang, H. (2008). Model optimizing and feature selecting for support vector regression in time series forecasting. *Neurocomputing, 72*(1-3), 600–611. doi:10.1016/j.neucom.2007.11.010

Hebb, D. (1949). *Organization of behavior*. New York, NY: J.Wiley & Sons.

Hecht-Nielsen, R. (1987). Kolmogorov's mapping neural network existence theorem. *Proceedings of the IEEE International Conference on Neural Networks,* (pp. 11-13). New York.

Hedar, A.-R., & Fukushima, M. (2003). Minimizing multimodal functions by simplex coding genetic algorithm. *Optimization Methods & Software, 18*(3), 265–282.

Higgins, I. J., & Burns, R. G. (1975). *The chemistry and microbiology of pollution* (pp. 55–105). London, UK: Academic Press.

Hirose, A. (Ed.). (2003). *Complex-valued neural networks*. Singapore: World Scientific Publishing. doi:10.1142/9789812791184

Hirose, A. (2006). *Complex-valued neural networks. Studies in Computational Intelligence, 32*. Springer-Verlag.

Hoaglin, D. C., & Welsch, R. E. (1978). The hat matrix in regression and ANOVA. *The American Statistician, 32*, 17–22. doi:10.2307/2683469

Hocking, R. R., & Pendleton, O. J. (1983). The regression dilemma. *Communications in Statistics Theory and Methods, 12*, 497–527. doi:10.1080/03610928308828477

Hodge, V. J., & Austin, J. (2004). A survey of outlier detection methodologies. *Artificial Intelligence Review, 22*, 85–106. doi:10.1023/B:AIRE.0000045502.10941.a9

Hoffmann, G. M., Huang, H., Wasl, S. L., & Tomlin, C. J. (2007). *Quadrotor helicopter flight dynamics and control: Theory and experiment*. AIAA Guidance, Navigation, and Control Conference.

Holmberg, M., Gelbart, D., Ramacher, U., & Hemmert, W. (2005). Automatic speech recognition with neural spike trains. *Interspeech*, 1253-1256.

Hong, S. H., Lee, M. W., Lee, D. S., & Park, J. M. (2007). Monitoring of sequencing batch reactor for nitrogen and phosphorus removal using neural networks. *Biochemical Engineering Journal, 35*, 365–370. doi:10.1016/j.bej.2007.01.033

Hopfield, J. J. (1995). Pattern recognition computation using action potential timing for stimulus representation. *Nature, 376*(6535), 33–36. doi:10.1038/376033a0

Hopfield, J. (1982). Neural networks and physical systems with emergent collective computational abilities. *Proceedings of the National Academy of Sciences of the USA, 9*, (p. 2554).

Horn, B. K. P., & Schunck, B. G. (1981). Determining optical flow. *Artificial Intelligence, 17*, 185–203. doi:10.1016/0004-3702(81)90024-2

Hoskin, K. (2004). Spacing, timing and the invention of management. *Organization, 11*(6), 743–757. doi:10.1177/1350508404047249

Hossjer, O. (1994). Rank-based estimates in the linear model with high breakdown point. *Journal of the American Statistical Association, 89*, 149–158. doi:10.2307/2291211

Hsieh, J. C., Tu, C. H., & Chen, F. P. (2001). Activation of the hypothalamus characterizes the acupuncture stimulation at the analgesic point in human: A positron emission tomography study. *Neuroscience Letters, 307*, 105–108. doi:10.1016/S0304-3940(01)01952-8

Hsu, C. W., & Lin, C. J. (2002). A comparison method for multi class support vector machines. *IEEE Transactions on Neural Networks, 13*, 415–425. doi:10.1109/72.991427

Huang, S., & Wu, T. (2010). Integrating recurrent SOM with wavelet-based kernel partial least squares regressions for financial forecasting. *Expert Systems with Applications, 37*(8), 5698–5705. doi:10.1016/j.eswa.2010.02.040

Huang, J., Kumar, S. R., Mitra, M., Zhu, W.-J., & Zabih, R. (1997). Image indexing using color correlograms. In *Proceedings of IEEE Computer Society Conference on Computer Vision and Pattern Recognition*, (pp. 762–768).

Huang, X., & Weng, J. (2002). Novelty and reinforcement learning in the value system of developmental robots. *Proceedings of the 2nd International Workshop on Epigenetic Robotics: Modeling Cognitive Development in Robotic Systems.*

Hubel, D. H., & Wiesel, T. N. (1962). Receptive fields, binocular interaction and functional architecture in the cat's visual cortex. *The Journal of Physiology, 160*, 106–154.

Huber, P. J. (1975). *Robustness and designs: A survey of statistical design and linear models*. Amsterdam, The Netherlands: North-Holland Press.

Huber, P. J. (1981). *Robust statistics*. New York, NY: Wiley.

Huber, P. J. (1977). Robust covariances. In Gupta, S. S., & Moore, D. S. (Eds.), *Statistical decision theory and related topics* (pp. 165–191). New York, NY: Academic Press.

Huber, P. J. (1991). Between robustness and diagnostics. In Stahel, W., & Weisberg, S. (Eds.), *Direction in robust statistics and diagnostics* (pp. 121–130). New York, NY: Springer-Verlag.

Huibers, T. (1996). *An axiomatic theory for information retrieval*. Doctoral dissertation, University of Nijmegen.

Hussain, M. (1999). Review of the applications of neural networks in chemical process control–simulation and online implementation. *Artificial Intelligence in Engineering, 13*, 55–68. doi:10.1016/S0954-1810(98)00011-9

Hutchins, E. (1995). *Cognition in the wild*. Cambridge, MA: MIT Press.

Hutter, M. (2001). Towards a universal theory of artificial intelligence based on algorithmic probability and sequential decisions. *Proceedings of the 12th European Conference on Machine Learning* (ECML-2001), (pp. 226-238).

Hwang, W.-J., Hwang, W.-L., & Lu, Y.-C. (1999). Layered image transmission based on embedded zero-tree wavelet coding. *Optical Engineering (Redondo Beach, Calif.), 38*(8), 1326–1334. doi:10.1117/1.602174

IEEE. (1985). (IEEE standard 754-1985 for Binary Floating-point Arithmetic). *SIGPLAN, 22*(2), 9–25.

Igelnik, B., Pao, Y.-H., & LeClair, S. R. (1999). The ensemble approach to neural-network learning and generalization. *IEEE Transactions on Neural Networks, 10*(1), 19–30. doi:10.1109/72.737490

Igelnik, B., Tabib-Azar, M., & LeClair, S. R. (2001). A net with complex weights. *IEEE Transactions on Neural Networks, 12*(2), 236–249. doi:10.1109/72.914521

Igelnik, B., & Pao, Y.-H. (1995). Stochastic choice of basis functions in adaptive function approximation and the functional-link net. *IEEE Transactions on Neural Networks, 6*(6), 1320–1329. doi:10.1109/72.471375

Igelnik, B., Tabib-Azar, M., & LeClair, S. (2001a). A net with complex weights. *IEEE Transactions on Neural Networks, 12*(2), 236–249. doi:10.1109/72.914521

Igelnik, B. (2009). Kolmogorov's spline complex network and adaptive dynamic modeling of data. In Nitta, T. (Ed.), *Complex-valued neural networks* (pp. 56–78). Hershey, PA: IGI Global. doi:10.4018/9781605662145.ch003

Igelnik, B. (2000). Some new adaptive architectures for learning, generalization, and visualization of multivariate data. In Sincak, P., & Vascak, J. (Eds.), *Quo Vadis computational intelligence? New trends and approaches in computational intelligence* (pp. 63–78). Heidelberg, Germany & New York, NY: Physica-Verlag.

Igelnik, B. (2001b). Method for visualization of multivariate data in a lower dimension. In *SPIE Visual Data Exploration and Analysis VIII, 4302*, 168-179. San Jose, CA.

Igelnik, B. (2003b). *Visualization of large multidimensional datasets in a lower dimension.* (SBIR Phase I Final Report #0232775, NSF).

Igelnik, B., Pao, Y.-H., & LeClair, S. R. (1996). *An approach for optimization of a continuous function with many local minima.* In 30th Annual Conference on Information Sciences and Systems, 2 (pp. 912-917). Department of Electrical Engineering, Princeton University, Princeton, NJ.

Ilin, R., & Perlovsky, L. (2010). Cognitively inspired neural network for recognition of situations. *International Journal of Natural Computing Research.*

Ilse, C., & Meyer, C. (1998). The idea behind Krylov methods. *The American Mathematical Monthly, 105*, 889–899. doi:10.2307/2589281

Imon, A. H. M. R. (2005). Identifying multiple influential observations in linear regression. *Journal of Applied Statistics, 32*, 73–90. doi:10.1080/02664760500163599

Imon, A. H. M. R. (1996). *Subsample methods in regression residual prediction and diagnostics.* Unpublished doctoral dissertation, University of Birmingham, UK.

Infante, P. F., Rinsky, R. A., Wagoner, J. K., & Young, R. J. (1997, July 9). Leukemia in benzene workers. *Lancet*, 76–78.

Iruthayarajan, M. W., & Baskar, S. (2009). Evolutionary algorithms based design of multivariable PID controller. *Expert Systems with Applications*, 9159–9167. doi:10.1016/j.eswa.2008.12.033

Iwasa, K., Inoue, H., Kugler, M., Kuroyanagi, S., & Iwata, A. (2007). Separation and recognition of multiple sound source using pulsed neuron model. ICANN, (LNCS 4669), (pp. 748–757).

Izhikevich, E. M. (2006). Polychronization: Computation with spikes. *Neural Computation, 18*(2), 245–282. doi:10.1162/089976606775093882

Jackendoff, R. (2002). *Foundations of language: Brain, meaning, grammar, evolution.* New York, NY: Oxford Univ Press.

Jackendoff, R. (1976). Toward an explanatory semantic representation. *Linguistic Inquiry, 7*(1), 89–150.

Jackendoff, R. (1983). *Semantics and cognition.* Cambridge, MA: MIT Press.

Jackendoff, R. (1990). *Semantic structures.* Cambridge, MA: The MIT Press.

Jacobs, C., Finkelstein, A., & Salesin, D. (1995). Fast multiresolution image querying. In *Proceedings of SIGGRAPH.*

Jacquin, A. E. (1992). Image coding based on a fractal theory of iterated contractive image transformations. *IEEE Transactions on Image Processing, 1*(1), 18–30. doi:10.1109/83.128028

Jain, A. K., Mao, J., & Mohiuddin, K. M. (1996). Artificial neural networks: A tutorial. *IEEE Computer, 29*, 31–44.

Jankowski, S., Lozowski, A., & Zurada, J. M. (1996). Complex-valued multistate neural associative memory. *IEEE Transactions on Neural Networks, 7*(6), 1491–1496. doi:10.1109/72.548176

Japkowicz, N., & Shaju, S. (2002). The class imbalance problem: A systematic study. *Intelligent Data Analysis, 6*(5), 429–449.

Japkowicz, N. (2000). The class imbalance problem: Significance and strategies. In *Proceedings of the 2000 International Conference on Artificial Intelligence (IC-AI'2000): Special track on inductive learning*, Las Vegas, Nevada.

Japkowicz, N., Myers, C., & Gluck, M. (1995). A novelty detection approach to classification. *Proceedings of the 14th Joint Conference on Artificial Intelligence (IJCAI-95)*, (pp. 518-523).

Jeffery, K. J., Anderson, M. J., Hayman, R., & Chakraborty, S. (2004). A proposed architecture for the neural representation of spatial context. *Neuroscience and Biobehavioral Reviews*, *28*(2), 201–218. doi:10.1016/j.neubiorev.2003.12.002

Jenkins, D., Richard, M. G., & Daigger, G. T. (1993). *Manual on the causes and control of activated sludge bulking and foaming*. Boca Raton, FL: Lewis Publishers.

Jensen, O., & Lisman, J. (2000). Position reconstruction from an ensemble of hippocampal place cells: Contribution of theta phase coding. *Journal of Neurophysiology*, *83*(5), 2602–2609.

Jensen, O., & Lisman, J. (2005). Hippocampal sequence-encoding driven by a cortical multi-item working memory buffer. *Trends in Neurosciences*, *28*(2), 67–72. doi:10.1016/j.tins.2004.12.001

Jensen, R., & Shen, Q. (2008). *Computational intelligence and feature selection. Rough and fuzzy approaches*. Piscataway, NJ: IEEE Press. doi:10.1002/9780470377888

Jin, Y., Veiga, M. C., & Kennes, C. (2006a). Development of a novel monolith bioreactor for the treatment of VOC–polluted air. *Environmental Technology*, *27*, 1271–1277. doi:10.1080/09593332708618744

Jin, Y., Veiga, M. C., & Kennes, C. (2006b). Performance optimization of the fungal biodegradation of α-pinene in gas-phase biofilter. *Process Biochemistry*, *41*, 1722–1728. doi:10.1016/j.procbio.2006.03.020

Jin, Y., Veiga, M. C., & Kennes, C. (2007). Co-treatment of hydrogen sulphide and methanol in a single-stage biotrickling filter under acidic conditions. *Chemosphere*, *68*, 1186–1193. doi:10.1016/j.chemosphere.2007.01.069

Jin, Y., Veiga, M. C., & Kennes, C. (2008). Removal of methanol from air in a low–pH trickling monolith bioreactor. *Process Biochemistry*, *43*, 925–931. doi:10.1016/j.procbio.2008.04.019

John, G. H., & Langley, P. (1995). Estimating continuous distributions in Bayesian classifiers. In *Proceedings of the 11th Conference on Uncertainty in Artificial Intelligence*.

Johnstone, P. T. (1983)... *Bulletin of the American Mathematical Society*, *8*, 41–53. doi:10.1090/S0273-0979-1983-15080-2

Johnstone, P. T. (1991)... *Research and Exposition in Mathematics*, *18*, 85–107.

Jolles, B., & Bogoch, E. (2004). Posterior versus lateral surgical approach for total hip arthroplasty in adults with osteoarthritis. *Cochrane Database of Systematic Reviews*, *1*, CD003828.

Jones, L., Beynon, M. J., & Holt, C. A. (2006). An application of the Dempster-Shafer theory of evidence to the classification of knee function and detection of improvement due to total knee replacement surgery. *Journal of Biomechanics*, *39*(13), 2512–2520. doi:10.1016/j.jbiomech.2005.07.024

Jones, L., & Holt, C. A. (2008). An objective tool for assessing the outcome of total knee replacement surgery. *Proceedings of the Institution of Mechanical Engineers (IMechE), Part H: J. Engineering in Medicine*, *222*(H5), 647–655. doi:10.1243/09544119JEIM316

Jones, L., Holt, C. A., & Beynon, M. J. (2008). Reduction, classification and ranking of motion analysis data: An application to osteoarthritic and normal knee function data. *Computer Methods in Biomechanics and Biomedical Engineering*, *11*(1), 31–40. doi:10.1080/10255840701550956

Jones, K. S. (2003). What is an affordance? *Ecological Psychology*, *15*(2), 107–114. doi:10.1207/S15326969ECO1502_1

Jönsson, P. (2006). *The anatomy-an instrument for managing software evolution and evolvability*. Second International IEEE Workshop on Software Evolvability (SE'06) (pp. 31–37). Philadelphia, Pennsylvania, USA. September 24, 2006.

Josephson, B. (1997). *An integrated theory of nervous system functioning embracing nativism and constructivism*. International Complex Systems Conference. Nashua, NH.

Jung, C. (1971). Psychological types. In *The collected works, v.6, Bollingen Series XX.* Princeton, NJ: Princeton University Press.

Kadar, S., Amemia, T., & Showalter, K. (1997). Reaction mechanism for light sensitivity of the $Ru(bpy)_3^{2+}$ -catalyzed Belousov-Zhabotinsky reaction. *The Journal of Physical Chemistry A*, *101*, 8200–8206. doi:10.1021/jp971937y

Kadyrov, A., & Petrou, M. (2001). *The trace transform and its applications. IEEE Transactions on Pattern Analysis and Machine Intelligence* (pp. 811–828). PAMI.

Kaelbling, L. P. (1993). *Hierarchical reinforcement learning: Preliminary results*. (pp. 167–173). ICML-93, San Francisco, CA: Morgan Kaufmann.

Kant, I. (1943). *Critique of pure reason (trans. J.M.D. Meiklejohn)*. New York, NY: Willey Book.

Kaplan, F., & Oudeyer, P.-Y. (2004). Maximizing learning progress: An internal reward system for development. In Lida, F., Pfeifer, R., Steels, L., & Kuniyoshi, Y. (Eds.), *Embodied artificial intelligence* (pp. 259–270). Springer-Verlag. doi:10.1007/978-3-540-27833-7_19

Kaptelinin, V., & Nardi, B. (2006). *Acting with technology - activity theory and interaction design*. Cambridge, MA: The MIT Press.

Kecman, V. (2001). *Learning and soft computing: Support vector machines, neural networks, and fuzzy logic models (complex adaptive systems)*. Cambridge, MA: The MIT Press.

Kennes, C., Montes, M., Lopez, M. E., & Veiga, M. C. (2009). Waste gas treatment in bioreactors: Environmental engineering aspects. *Canadian Journal of Civil Engineering, 36*, 1–9. doi:10.1139/L09-113

Kennes, C., Rene, E. R., & Veiga, M. C. (2009). Bioprocesses for air pollution control. *Journal of Chemical Technology and Biotechnology (Oxford, Oxfordshire), 84*, 1419–1436. doi:10.1002/jctb.2216

Kennes, C., & Veiga, M. C. (2004). Fungal biocatalysts in the biofiltration of VOC polluted air. *Journal of Biotechnology, 113*, 305–319. doi:10.1016/j.jbiotec.2004.04.037

Kennes, C., & Veiga, M. C. (2001). Conventional biofilters. In Kennes, C., & Veiga, M. C. (Eds.), *Bioreactors for waste gas treatment* (pp. 47–98). Dordrecht, The Netherlands: Kluwer Academic Publisher.

Kesner, R., Gilbert, P., & Barua, L. (2002). The role of the hippocampus in memory for the temporal order of a sequence of odors. *Behavioral Neuroscience, 116*, 286–290. doi:10.1037/0735-7044.116.2.286

Kiang, N. Y.-S., Watanabe, T., Thomas, E. C., & Clark, L. F. (1965). *Discharge patterns of single fibers in the cat's auditory nerve*. Cambridge, MA: MIT Press.

Kihlstrom, J. F. (2004). *Joseph Jastrow and his duck-or is it a rabbit?* Retrieved June 6, 2010, from http://socrates.berkeley.edu/~kihlstrm/JastrowDuck.htm

Kim, Z. W., & Nevatia, R. (1999). Uncertain reasoning and learning for feature grouping. *Computer Vision and Image Understanding, 76*(3), 278–288. doi:10.1006/cviu.1999.0803

Kim, J. O. (2003). Degradation of benzene and ethylene in biofilters. *Process Biochemistry, 39*, 447–453. doi:10.1016/S0032-9592(03)00093-1

Kimmel, R., & Bruckstein, A. M. (2003). Regularized Laplacian zero crossings as optimal edge integrators. *International Journal of Computer Vision, 53*, 225–243. doi:10.1023/A:1023030907417

Kirsh, D. (1995). The intelligent use of space. *Artificial Intelligence, 73*(1–2), 31–68. doi:10.1016/0004-3702(94)00017-U

Kittler, J., Hatef, M., Duin, R. P. W., & Matas, J. (1998). On combining classifiers. *IEEE Transactions on Pattern Analysis and Machine Intelligence, 20*(3), 226–239. doi:10.1109/34.667881

Klain, D., & Rota, G.-C. (1997). *Introduction to geometric probability*. London, UK: Cambridge University Press.

Klir, G. J. (1985). Complexity: Some general observations. *Systems Research, 2*, 131–140. doi:10.1002/sres.3850020205

Klomp, E. (2008). *Conceptualisatie in een requirements development proces*. Master Thesis. Nijmegen, The Netherlands: Radboud Universiteit Nijmegen.

Knauff, M., Rauh, R., & Renz, J. (1997). *A cognitive assessment of topological spatial relations: Results from an empirical investigation*. (LNCS 1329), (pp. 193-206).

Knierim, J., McNaughton, B., & Poe, G. (2000). Three-dimensional spatial selectivity of hippocampal neurons during space flight. *Nature Neuroscience, 3*, 209–210. doi:10.1038/72910

Knorr, M. E., Ng, T. R., & Tucakov, V. (2000). Distance-based outlier: Algorithms and applications. *The VLDB Journal*, *8*(3-4), 237–253. doi:10.1007/s007780050006

Koch, C., & Segev, I. (1998). *Methods in neuronal modeling: From ions to networks*. Cambridge, MA: MIT Press.

Kofod-Petersen, A., & Cassens, J. (2006). Using activity theory to model context awareness. In Roth-Berghofer, T. R., Schulz, S., & Leake, D. B. (Eds.), *Modeling and retrieval of context MRC 2005, (LNAI 3946)* (pp. 1–17). Berlin/ Heidelberg, Germany: Springer-Verlag. doi:10.1007/11740674_1

Kohonen, T. (1988). *Self organization and associative memory*. Berlin, Germany: Springer-Verlag.

Köppen, M., & Yoshida, K. (2005). Universal representation of image functions by the Sprecher construction. *Soft Computing as Transdisciplinary Science and Technology*, *29*, 202–210. doi:10.1007/3-540-32391-0_28

Köppen, M. (2002). *On the training of a Kolmogorov network*. (LNCS 2415), (pp. 140-145).

Kosík, K. (1976). *Dialectics of the concrete*. Dordrecht, The Netherlands: Reidel.

Kotik-Friedgut, B. (2006). Development of the Lurian approach: A cultural neurolinguistic perspective. *Neuropsychology Review*, *16*(1), 43–52. doi:10.1007/s11065-006-9003-9

Krasnopolsky, V. M., & Chevallier, F. (2003). Some neural network applications in environmental sciences. Part II: Advancing computational efficiency of environmental numerical models. *Neural Networks*, *16*, 335–348. doi:10.1016/S0893-6080(03)00026-1

Krogstie, J., Sindre, G., & Jorgensen, H. (2006). Process models representing knowledge for action: A revised quality framework. *European Journal of Information Systems*, *15*, 91–102. doi:10.1057/palgrave.ejis.3000598

Kruger, N., Lappe, M., & Worgotter, F. (2004). Biologically motivated multi-modal processing of visual primitives. *Interdisciplinary Journal of Artificial Intelligence the Simulation of Behaviors, AISB*, *15*, 417–428.

Kruk, M., Osowski, S., & Koktysz, R. (2007). Segmentation and characterization of glandular ducts in microscopic colon image. *Przeglad Elektrotechniczny*, *84*, 227–230.

Kubat, M., Holte, R., & Matwin, S. (1998). Machine learning for the detection of oil spills in satellite radar images. *Machine Learning*, *30*, 195–215. doi:10.1023/A:1007452223027

Kubat, M., & Matwin, S. (1997). Addressing the curse of imbalanced data set: One-sided sampling. *Proceedings of the 14th Intl. Conference on Machine Learning*, Nashville, TN, (pp. 179-186).

Kuhnert, L. (1986). A new optical photochemical memory device in a light-sensitive chemical active medium. *Nature*, *319*, 393–394. doi:10.1038/319393a0

Kuhnert, L. (1986). Photochemische Manipulation von chemischen Wellen. *Naturwissenschaften*, *73*, 96–97. doi:10.1007/BF00365836

Kuhnert, L., Agladze, K. I., & Krinsky, V. I. (1989). Image processing using light-sensitive chemical waves. *Nature*, *337*, 244–247. doi:10.1038/337244a0

Kuncheva, L. (2004). *Combining pattern classifiers: Methods and algorithms*. New Jersey: Wiley. doi:10.1002/0471660264

Kurkova, V. (1991). Kolmogorov's theorem is relevant. *Neural Computation*, *3*, 617–622. doi:10.1162/neco.1991.3.4.617

Kurkova, V. (1992). Kolmogorov's theorem and multilayer neural networks. *Neural Networks*, *5*, 501–506. doi:10.1016/0893-6080(92)90012-8

Kuroyanagi, S., & Iwata, A. (1994). Auditory pulse neural network model to extract the inter-aural time and level difference for sound localization. *Transactions of IEICE*, *4*, 466–474.

Lagunas, M. A., Pérez-Neira, A., Najar, M., & Pagés, A. (1993). *The Kolmogorov signal processor*. (LNCS 686), (pp. 494-512).

Lakatos, I. (1974). Falsification and the methodology of scientific research programmes. In Lakatos, I., & Musgrave, A. (Eds.), *Criticism and the growth of knowledge* (pp. 91–196). London, UK: Cambridge University Press.

Lalonde, J.-F., Vandapel, N., Huber, D., & Hebert, M. (2006). Natural terrain classification using three-dimensional ladar data for ground robot mobility. *Journal of Field Robotics*, *23*, 839–861. doi:10.1002/rob.20134

Larsson, R. (1990). *Coordination of action in mergers and acquisitions - interpretative and systems approaches towards synergy*. Dissertation No. 10, Lund Studies in Economics and Management, The Institute of Economic Research, Lund: Lund University Press.

Lavenex, P., & Amaral, D. (2000). Hippocampal-neocortical interaction: A hierarchy of associativity. *Hippocampus, 10*, 420–430. doi:10.1002/1098-1063(2000)10:4<420::AID-HIPO8>3.0.CO;2-5

Lawrence, P., & Lorsch, W. (1967). Differentiation and integration in complex organizations. *Administrative Science Quarterly, 12*(1), 1–47. doi:10.2307/2391211

Leake, R. J., & Liu, R. W. (1967). Construction of sub-optimal control sequences. *SIAM Journal on Control and Optimization, 5*(1), 54–63. doi:10.1137/0305004

Ledoux, J. (1998). *The emotional brain: The mysterious underpinnings of emotional life*. New York, NY: Simon & Schuster.

Lee, E. Y. (2003). Continuous treatment of gas-phase trichloroethylene by Burkholderia cepacia G4 in a two-stage continuous stirred tank reactor/trickling biofilter system. *Journal of Bioscience and Bioengineering, 96*, 572–574. doi:10.1016/S1389-1723(04)70151-6

Lee, D.-L. (2001). Improving the capacity of complex-valued neural networks with a modified gradient descent learning rule. *IEEE Transactions on Neural Networks, 12*(2), 439–443. doi:10.1109/72.914540

Lee, D.-L. (2003). Complex-valued neural associative memories: Network stability and learning algorithms. In Hirose, A. (Ed.), *Complex-valued neural networks: Theories and applications* (pp. 29–55). World Scientific. doi:10.1142/9789812791184_0003

Lee, D.-L. (2009). Image reconstruction by the complex-valued neural networks: Design by using generalized projection rule. In Nitta, T. (Ed.), *Complex-valued neural networks: Utilizing high-dimensional parameters* (pp. 236–255). Hershey, PA: Information Science Reference. doi:10.4018/9781605662145.ch010

Lehmann, C., Koenig, T., Jelic, V., Prichep, L., John, R., & Wahlund, L. (2007). Application and comparison of classification algorithms for recognition of Alzheimer's disease in electrical brain activity (EEG). *Journal of Neuroscience Methods, 161*(2), 342–350. doi:10.1016/j.jneumeth.2006.10.023

Lehmann, F., & Cohn, A. G. (1994). The egg/yolk reliability hierarchy: Semantic data integration using sorts with prototypes. *Proceedings of the Conference on Information Knowledge Management*. (pp. 272-279). ACM Press.

Leni, P.-E., Fougerolle, Y. D., & Truchetet, F. (2008), Kolmogorov superposition theorem and its application to multivariate function decompositions and image representation. In *Proceedings of IEEE Conference on Signal-Image Technology & Internet-Based System* (pp. 344–351). IEEE Computer Society Washington, DC, USA.

Leni, P.-E., Fougerolle, Y. D., & Truchetet, F. (2009b). *Kolmogorov Superposition Theorem and wavelet decomposition for image compression*. (LNCS 5807), (pp. 43-53).

Leont'ev, A. N. (1981). *Problems in the development of the mind*. Moscow, Russia: Progress Publ.

Leskovec, J., & Shawe-Taylor, J. (2003). Linear programming boosting for uneven datasets. In *Proceedings of the 20th International Conference on Machine Learning (ICML-2003)*, Washington, DC.

Leutgeb, J., Leutgeb, S., Treves, A., Meyer, R., Barnes, C., & McNaughton, B. (2005). Progressive transformation of hippocampal neuronal representations in morphed environments. *Neuron, 48*, 345–358. doi:10.1016/j.neuron.2005.09.007

Leutgeb, S., Leutgeb, J., Treves, A., Moser, M., & Moser, E. (2004). Distinct ensemble codes in hippocampal areas CA3 and CA1. *Science, 305*, 1295–1298. doi:10.1126/science.1100265

Levine, D. S., & Perlovsky, L. I. (2008). Neuroscientific insights on biblical myths: Simplifying heuristics versus careful thinking: scientific analysis of millennial spiritual issues. *Zygon. Journal of Science and Religion, 43*(4), 797–821.

Lewis, F. L., & Syrmos, V. (1995). *Optimal control* (2nd ed.). New York, NY: Wiley.

Lewis, F. L. (1986). *Optimal estimation*. New York, NY: John Wiley & Sons.

Lewis, D., & Gale, W. (1994). Training text classifiers by uncertainty sampling. *Proceedings of the 7th ACM SIGIR Conference on Research and Development in Information Retrieval*, Dublin, 1994.

Li, S., Fevens, T., & Krzyzak, A. (2006). Automatic clinical image segmentation using pathological modeling, PCA and SVM. *Engineering Applications of Artificial Intelligence, 19*, 403–410. doi:10.1016/j.engappai.2006.01.011

Li, Y., Sundararajan, N., & Saratchandran, P. (2000). Analysis of minimal radial basis function network algorithm for real-time identification of nonlinear dynamic systems. *IEE Proceedings. Control Theory and Applications, 147*(4), 476–484. doi:10.1049/ip-cta:20000549

Li, G., He, Z., An, T., Zeng, X., Sheng, G., & Fu, J. (2008). Comparative study of the elimination of toluene vapours in twin biotrickling filters using two microorganisms Bacillus cereus S1 and S2. *Journal of Chemical Technology and Biotechnology (Oxford, Oxfordshire), 83*, 1019–1026. doi:10.1002/jctb.1908

Li, P., Chan, K. L., & Fang, W. (2006). Hybrid kernel machine ensemble for imbalanced data sets. In *Proceedings of the 18th International Conference on Pattern Recognition*, (ICPR'06).

Liedman, S.-E. (2001). *An eternal adventure – about the knowledge of humans*. Falun, Sweden: Albert Bonniers Förlag.

Liguang, M., Yanrong, C., & Jianbang, H. (2008). Biomedical image storage, retrieval and visualization based-on open source project. *IEEE Congress on Image and Signal Processing, 3*(27-30), 63-66.

Lim, J.-H., & Chevallet, J.-P. (2005). *A structured learning approach for medical image indexing and retrieval*. In CLEF Workhop, Working Notes Medical Image Track, Vienna, Austria, 21–23 September.

Lin, C.-Y., Yin, J.-X., Gao, X., Chen, J.-Y., & Qin, P. (2006). *A semantic modeling approach for medical image semantic retrieval using hybrid Bayesian networks*. Sixth International Conference on Intelligent Systems Design and Applications (ISDA'06), vol. 2, (pp. 482-487).

Lindgren, F., Geladi, P., & Wold, S. (1993). The kernel algorithm for PLS. *Journal of Chemometrics, 7*, 45–49. doi:10.1002/cem.1180070104

Lipson, P., Grimson, E., & Sinha, P. (1997). Configuration based scene classification and image indexing. In *Proceedings of the IEEE Computer Society Conference on Computer Vision and Pattern Recognition*, (pp. 1007–1013).

Liu, H., & Motoda, H. (2008). *Computational methods of feature selection*. London, UK: Chapman.

Liu, S., & Wang, W. (1999). A study on the applicability on multicomponent calibration methods in chemometrics. *Chemometrics and Intelligent Laboratory Systems, 45*, 131–145. doi:10.1016/S0169-7439(98)00097-5

Liu, H., & Motoda, H. (1998). *Feature selection for knowledge discovery and data mining*. Boston, MA: Kluwer Academic Publishers.

Liu, H., & Motoda, H. (2008). *Computational models of feature selection*. Boca Raton, FL: Chapman & Hall/CRC, Taylor & Francis Group.

Liu, Y., Lazar, N., Rothfus, W., Dellaert, F., Moore, A., Schneider, J., & Kanade, T. (2004). Semantic based biomedical image indexing and retrieval. In *Trends and advances in content-based image and video retrieval*.

Livingstone, D. J., Manallack, D. T., & Tetko, I. V. (1997). Data modelling with neural networks: Advantages and limitations. *Journal of Computer-Aided Molecular Design, 11*, 135–142. doi:10.1023/A:1008074223811

Loiselle, S., Rouat, J., Pressnitzer, D., & Thorpe, S. (2005). *Exploration of rank order coding with spiking neural networks for speech recognition*. International Joint Conference on Neural Networks, IJCNN, (pp 2076-2080).

Lomolino, M. V., Riddle, B. R., & Brown, J. H. (2009). *Biogeography*. Sunderland, MA: Sinauer Associates.

Louie, K., & Wilson, M. A. (2001). Temporally structured replay of awake hippocampal ensemble activity during rapid eye movement sleep. *Neuron, 29*(1), 145–156. doi:10.1016/S0896-6273(01)00186-6

Love, N. (1997). Integrating Austin. *Language Sciences, 19*(1), 57–65. doi:10.1016/0388-0001(95)00027-5

Lucas, C., & Araabi, B. N. (1999). Generalisation of the Dempster-Shafer theory: A fuzzy-valued measure. *IEEE Transactions on Fuzzy Systems*, *7*(3), 255–270. doi:10.1109/91.771083

Luria, A. R. (1973). *The working brain*. London, UK: Penguin Books.

Mach, E. (2004). *Space and geometry. The Monist, 18*. New York, NY: Dover.

Maciokas, J., Goodman, P. H., & Harris, F. C. Jr. (2002). *Large-scale spike-timing dependent-plasticity model of bimodal (audio/visual) processing*. Reno: Technical Report of Brain Computation Laboratory, University of Nevada.

Mackintosh, N. J. (2002). Do not ask whether they have a cognitive map, but how they find their way about. *Psicológica (Valencia)*, *23*, 165–185.

Madsen, S., Ritter, M. A., Morris, H. H., Meding, J. B., Berend, M. E., Faris, P. M., & Vardaxis, V. G. (2004). The effect of total hip arthroplasty surgical approach on gait. *Journal of Orthopaedic Research*, *22*, 44–50. doi:10.1016/S0736-0266(03)00151-7

Magnani, L. (2001). *Abduction, reason, and science: Processes of discovery and explanation*. New York, NY: Kluwer Academic/Plenum Publishers. doi:10.1007/978-1-4419-8562-0

Mahalanobis, P. C. (1936). On the generalized distance in statistics. *Proceedings of the National Institute of Science of India*, *12*, 49–55.

Maier, H. R., & Dandy, G. C. (1998a). The effect of internal parameters and geometry on the performance of back-propagation neural networks: An empirical study. *Environmental Modelling & Software*, *13*, 193–209. doi:10.1016/S1364-8152(98)00020-6

Maier, H. R., & Dandy, G. C. (1998b). Understanding the behaviour and optimising the performance of back-propagation neural networks: An empirical study. *Environmental Modelling & Software*, *13*, 179–191. doi:10.1016/S1364-8152(98)00019-X

Maier, H. R., & Dandy, G. C. (2000). Neural networks for the prediction and forecasting of water resources variables: A review of modelling issues and applications. *Environmental Modelling & Software*, *15*, 101–124. doi:10.1016/S1364-8152(99)00007-9

Maier, H. R., & Dandy, G. C. (2001). Neural network based modelling of environmental variables: A systematic approach. *Mathematical and Computer Modelling*, *33*, 669–682. doi:10.1016/S0895-7177(00)00271-5

Maliyekkal, S. M., Rene, E. R., Swaminathan, T., & Philip, L. (2004). Performance of BTX degraders under substrate versatility conditions. *Journal of Hazardous Materials*, *B109*, 201–211. doi:10.1016/j.jhazmat.2004.04.001

Malone, T., & Crowston, K. (1994). The interdisciplinary study of coordination. *ACM Computing Surveys*, *26*(1), 87–119. doi:10.1145/174666.174668

Mandic, D. P., Javidi, S., Goh, S. L., Kuh, A., & Aihara, K. (2009). Complex valued prediction of wind profile using augmented complex statistics. *Renewable Energy*, *34*(1), 196–210. doi:10.1016/j.renene.2008.03.022

Manduchi, R. (2006). Learning outdoor color classification. *IEEE Transactions on Pattern Analysis and Machine Intelligence*, *28*(11), 1713–1723. doi:10.1109/TPAMI.2006.231

Manjunath, B. S., & Ma, W. Y. (1996). Texture features for browsing and retrieval of image data. *IEEE Transactions on Pattern Analysis and Machine Intelligence*, *18*(8), 837–842. doi:10.1109/34.531803

March, J. G., & Simon, H. A. (1958). *Organizations*. Cambridge, MA: Blackwell Publishers.

Margolis, E., & Laurence, S. (1999). *Concepts: Core readings*. Cambridge, MA: MIT Press.

Markiewicz, T., Wisniewski, P., Osowski, S., Patera, J., Kozlowski, W., & Koktysz, R. (2009). Comparative analysis of the methods for accurate recognition of cells in the nuclei staining of the Ki-67 in neuroblastoma and ER/PR status staining in breast cancer. *Analytical and Quantitative Cytology and Histology Journal*, *31*, 49–63.

Markiewicz, T., & Osowski, S. (2005). *OLS versus SVM approach to learning of RBF networks*. International Joint Neural Network Conference, Montreal, (pp. 1051-1056).

Maronna, R. A., Martin, R. D., & Yohai, V. J. (2006). *Robust statistics: Theory and methods*. New York, NY: Wiley.

Marr, D. (1982). *Vision: A computational investigation into the human representation and processing of visual information*. New York, NY: W.H. Freeman and Company.

Marraval, D., & Patricio, M. (2002). Image segmentation and pattern recognition. In Chen, D., & Cheng, X. (Eds.), *Pattern recognition and string matching*. Amsterdam, The Netherlands: Kluwer.

Marsili-Libelli, S. (1981). Optimal design of PID regulators. *International Journal of Control*, *33*(4), 601–616. doi:10.1080/00207178108922945

Masterov, A. V., Rabinovich, M. I., Tolkov, V. N., & Yakhno, V. G. (1988). Studies of regimes of autowaves and autostructures interaction in neural net like media. In Yakhno, V. G. (Ed.), *Collective dynamics of excitations and structure formation* (pp. 89–104). Gorkyi, Russia: Institute of Applied Physics of USSR Academy of Sciences.

Masters, T. (1995). *Advanced algorithms for neural networks: A C++ sourcebook*. New York, NY: John Wiley & Sons.

Masters, T. (1993). *Practical neural network recipes in C*. San Diego, CA: Academic Press.

Mataric, M., & Cliff, D. (1996). Challenges for evolving controllers for physical robots. *Robotics and Autonomous Systems*, 67–83. doi:10.1016/S0921-8890(96)00034-6

Matsugu, M., Mori, K., Mitari, Y., & Kaneda, Y. (2003). Subject independent facial expression recognition with robust face detection using a convolutional neural network. *Neural Networks*, *16*, 555–559. doi:10.1016/S0893-6080(03)00115-1

Matsugu, M., Mori, K., Ishii, M., & Mitarai, Y. (2002). *Convolutional spiking neural network model for robust face detection*. International Conference on Neural Information Processing, ICONIP, (pp. 660-664).

Maturana, H. R., & Varela, F. J. (1992). *The tree of knowledge: The biological roots of human understanding*. Boston, MA: Shambhala.

Mazurek, M. E., & Shadlen, M. N. (2002). Limits to the temporal fidelity of cortical spike rate signals. *Nature Neuroscience*, *5*, 463–471.

McCulloch, W. J., & Pitts, W. (1943). A logical calculus of the ideas immanent in nervous activity. *The Bulletin of Mathematical Biophysics*, *5*, 115–133. doi:10.1007/BF02478259

McCulloch, C. E., & Meeter, D. (1983). Discussion of outlier...s. *Technometrics*, *25*, 119–163. doi:10.2307/1268543

McCulloch, W. S., & Pitts, W. H. (1943). A logical calculus of the ideas immanent in nervous activity. *The Bulletin of Mathematical Biophysics*, *5*, 115–133. doi:10.1007/BF02478259

McFarland, B., & Osborne, G. (1956). Approach to the hip: A suggested improvement on Kocher's method. *The Journal of Bone and Joint Surgery. British Volume*, *36*(3), 364–367.

McLennan, S., & Hockema, S. (2001) *Spike-V: An adaptive mechanism for speech-rate independent timing*. (IULC Working Papers Online 02-01).

McNaughton, B., Battaglia, F., Jensen, O., Moser, E., & Moser, M.-B. (2006). Path integration and the neural basis of the cognitive map. *Nature Reviews. Neuroscience*, *7*, 663–678. doi:10.1038/nrn1932

Mead, G. H. (1974). *Mind, self, and society: From the standpoint of a social behaviorist*. Chicago, IL: University of Chicago Press.

Mead, G. H. (1938, 1972). *The philosophy of the act*. Chicago, IL: University of Chicago Press.

Mel, B. W. (1998). SEEMORE: Combining colour, shape, and texture histogramming in a neurally-inspired approach to visual object recognition. *Neural Computation*, *9*, 777–804. doi:10.1162/neco.1997.9.4.777

Melamed, O., Gerstner, W., Maass, W., Tsodyks, M., & Markram, H. (2004). Coding and learning of behavioral sequences. *Trends in Neurosciences*, *27*(1), 11–14. doi:10.1016/j.tins.2003.10.014

Melzack, R. (1990). Phantom limbs and the concept of a neuromatrix. *Trends in Neurosciences*, *13*, 88–92. doi:10.1016/0166-2236(90)90179-E

Melzack, R., & Casey, K. L. (1968). Sensory, motivational, and central control determinants of pain. In Kenshalo, D. R. (Ed.), *The skin senses* (pp. 423–439). Springfield, IL: C.C. Thomas.

Mercier, D., & Seguier, R. (2002). *Spiking neurons (STANNs) in speech recognition*. 3rd WSES International Conference on Neural Networks and Applications. Interlaken.

Merriam-Webster Online. (2008). Retrieved October 5, 2008, from http://www.merriam-webster.com/

Mesulam, M. M. (1990). Large-scale neurocognitive networks and distributed processing for attention, language, and memory. *Annals of Neurology*, *28*, 597–613. doi:10.1002/ana.410280502

Mesulam, M. M. (1998). From sensation to cognition. *Brain*, *121*(6), 1013–1052. doi:10.1093/brain/121.6.1013

Metcalf & Eddy Inc. (2003). *Wastewater engineering: treatment and reuse* (4th ed.). New York, NY: McGraw-Hill.

Meyer, D., Leisch, F., & Hornik, K. (2003). The support vector machine under test. *Neurocomputing*, *55*, 169–186. doi:10.1016/S0925-2312(03)00431-4

Meystel, A. (1995). *Semiotic modeling and situational analysis*. Bala Cynwyd, PA: AdRem.

Miettinen, R., & Virkkunen, J. (2005). Epistemic objects, artefacts and organizational change. *Organization*, *12*(3), 437–456. doi:10.1177/1350508405051279

Mikhailov, A. (1994). *Foundations of synergetics, 2nd revised edition*. Heidelberg, Germany, New York, NY, & London, UK: Springer Verlag.

Miller, R. M., Itoyama, K., Uda, A., Takada, H., & Bhat, N. (1997). Modelling and control of a chemical waste water treatment plant. *Computers & Chemical Engineering*, *21*, 947–952.

Miller, R. G. (1974). The Jackknife: A review. *Biometrika*, *61*, 1–15.

Mingzhi, H., Ma, Y., Jinquan, W., & Yan, W. (2009). Simulation of a paper mill wastewater treatment using a fuzzy neural network. *Expert Systems with Applications*, *36*, 5064–5070. doi:10.1016/j.eswa.2008.06.006

Minsky, M. (1988). *The society of mind*. Cambridge, MA: MIT Press.

Miura, M., & Aiyoshi, E. (2003). Approximation and designing of fractal images by complex neural networks. *EEJ Transactions on Electronics. Information Systems*, *123*(8), 1465–1472.

Miyauchi, M., Seki, M., Watanabe, A., & Miyauchi, A. (1993). Interpretation of optical flow through complex neural network. *Proceedings of International Workshop on Artificial Neural Networks*, Barcelona, (LNCS 686), (pp. 645-650). Springer-Verlag.

Mjalli, F. S., Al–Asheh, S., & Alfadaza, H. E. (2007). Use of artificial neural network black-box modelling for the prediction of wastewater treatment plants performance. *Journal of Environmental Management*, *83*, 329–338. doi:10.1016/j.jenvman.2006.03.004

Moon, B. S. (2001). An explicit solution for the cubic spline interpolation for functions of a single variable. *Applied Mathematics and Computation*, *117*, 251–255. doi:10.1016/S0096-3003(99)00178-2

Moore, A. T. (1959). The Moore self-locking Vitallium prosthesis in fresh femoral neck fractures: A new low posterior approach (the southern exposure). In: *AAOS. Instructional Course Lectures*, *16*, 309–321.

Moral, K., Aksoy, A., & Gokcay, C. F. (2008). Modelling of the activated sludge process by using artificial neural networks with automated architecture screening. *Computers & Chemical Engineering*, *32*, 2471–2478. doi:10.1016/j.compchemeng.2008.01.008

Morand, B. (2004). *Logique de la conception-figures de sémiotique générale d'après Charles S. Peirce. Collection L'ouverture philosophique, Paris, Éditions L'Harmattan. Peirce, C. (1931-58). Collected papers of Charles Sanders Peirce*. Cambridge, MA: Harvard University Press.

Moravec, H. P. (1984). Locomotion, vision and intelligence. In Brady, M., & Paul, R. (Eds.), *Robotics research, 1* (pp. 215–224). Cambridge, MA: MIT Press.

Moravec, H. (1998). *When will computer hardware match the human brain?* Retrieved from http://www.transhumanist.com/volum1/moravec.htm

Moreno, L., Piñeiro, J., Sanchez, J., Mañas, S., Merino, J., Acosta, L., & Hamilton, A. (1994). Using neural networks to improve classification: Application to brain maturation. *Neural Networks*, *8*(5).

Morris, R. G. M., Moser, E. I., Riedel, G., Martin, S. J., Sandin, J., Day, M., & O'Carroll, C. (2003). Elements of a neurobiological theory of the hippocampus: The role of activity-dependent synaptic plasticity in memory. *Philosophical Transactions of the Royal Society of London. Series B, Biological Sciences*, *358*(1432), 773–786. doi:10.1098/rstb.2002.1264

Mozayyani, N., Baig, A. R., & Vaucher, G. (1998). *A fully neural solution for online handwritten character recognition*. International Joint Conference on Neural Networks, IJCNN, (pp. 160-164).

Müezzinoğlu, M. K., Güzeliş, C., & Zurada, J. M. (2003). A new design method for the complex-valued multistate Hopfield associative memory. *IEEE Transactions on Neural Networks*, *14*(4), 891–899. doi:10.1109/TNN.2003.813844

Muller, R. (1996). A quarter of a century of place cells. *Neuron*, *17*, 979–990. doi:10.1016/S0896-6273(00)80214-7

Nakamura, M., Mines, R., & Kreinovich, V. (1993). Guaranteed intervals for Kolmogorov's theorem (and their possible relation to neural networks). *Interval Computations*, *3*, 183–199.

Nash, J. E., & Sutcliffe, J. V. (1970). River flow forecasting through conceptual models part 1 — a discussion of principles. *Journal of Hydrology (Amsterdam)*, *10*, 282–290. doi:10.1016/0022-1694(70)90255-6

Natschlager, T., & Ruf, B. (1998). Spatial and temporal pattern analysis via spiking neurons. *Network (Bristol, England)*, *9*(3), 319–338. doi:10.1088/0954-898X/9/3/003

Natschlager, T., & Ruf, B. (1999). Pattern analysis with spiking neurons using delay coding. *Neurocomputing*, *26-27*, 463–469. doi:10.1016/S0925-2312(99)00052-1

Nees, M. (1993). Approximation versions of Kolmogorov's superposition theorem, proved constructively. *Journal of Computational and Applied Mathematics*, *54*, 239–250. doi:10.1016/0377-0427(94)90179-1

Newell, A. F. (1983). Intellectual issues in the history of artificial intelligence. In *The study of information*. New York, NY: J. Wiley.

Newell, P. C. (1977). Aggregation and cell surface receptors in cellular slime molds in microbial interaction. In Reissig, J. L. (Ed.), *Receptors and recognition, series B*. Chapman and Hall.

Newman, D., Hettich, S., Blake, C., & Merz, C. (1998). *UCI repository of machine learning databases*.

Nicol, C., Macnab, C. J. B., & Ramirez-Serrano, A. (2008). *Robust neural network control of a quadrotor helicopter*. IEEE Canadian Conference on Electrical and Computer Engineering, (pp. 1233–1238).

Niederreiter, H. (1978). Quasi-Monte Carlo methods and pseudorandom numbers. *Bulletin of the American Mathematical Society*, *84*, 957–1041. doi:10.1090/S0002-9904-1978-14532-7

Nigsch, F., Bender, A., van Buuren, B., Tissen, J., Nigsch, E., & Mitchell, J. B. O. (2006). Melting point prediction employing k-nearest neighbor algorithms and genetic parameter optimization. *Journal of Chemical Information and Modeling*, *46*(6), 2412–2422. doi:10.1021/ci060149f

Nilson, G. (1976). *Order/disorder: Studies in the conditions of love*. Göteborg, Sweden: Bokförlaget Korpen.

Nitta, T. (1997). An extension of the back-propagation algorithm to complex numbers. *Neural Networks*, *10*(8), 1392–1415. doi:10.1016/S0893-6080(97)00036-1

Nitta, T. (Ed.). (2009). *Complex-valued neural networks: Utilizing high-dimensional parameters* (p. 504). Hershey, PA: Information Science Reference.

Nitta, T. (2008). Complex-valued neural network and complex-valued back-propagation learning algorithm. In Hawkes, P. W. (Ed.), *Advances in imaging and electron physics* (*Vol. 152*, pp. 153–221). Amsterdam, The Netherlands: Elsevier.

Nitz, D. (2006). Tracking route progression in the posterior parietal cortex. *Neuron*, *49*, 747–756. doi:10.1016/j.neuron.2006.01.037

Novikov, S. P. (Ed.). (1996). *Topology I: General survey*. New York, NY: Springer-Verlag.

Nurunnabi, A. A. M., Imon, A. H. M. R., & Nasser, M. (2011). A diagnostic measure for influential observations in linear regression. *Communications in Statistics Theory and Methods*, *40*(7), 1169–1183. doi:10.1080/03610920903564727

Nurunnabi, A. A. M., & Nasser, M. (2009). Outlier detection by regression diagnostics in large data. In *Proceedings of International Conference on Future Computer and Communication*, 3-5 April, Kuala Lumpur, Malaysia, (pp. 246-250).

O'Keefe, J. (1999). Do hippocampal pyramidal cells signal non-spatial as well as spatial information? *Hippocampus*, *9*(4), 352–364. doi:10.1002/(SICI)1098-1063(1999)9:4<352::AID-HIPO3>3.0.CO;2-1

O'Keefe, J., & Burgess, N. (1996). Geometric determinants of place cell plasticity. *Nature*, *381*, 425–428.

O'Keefe, J., & Dostrovsky, J. (1971). The hippocampus as a spatial map: Preliminary evidence from unit activity in the freely-moving rat. *Brain Research*, *34*, 171–175. doi:10.1016/0006-8993(71)90358-1

O'Keefe, J., & Nadel, L. (1978). *The hippocampus as a cognitive map*. London, UK: Oxford.

Oh, Y.-S., & Bartha, R. (1997). Removal of nitrobenzene vapors by trickling air biofilter. *Journal of Industrial Microbiology & Biotechnology*, *18*, 293–296. doi:10.1038/sj.jim.2900384

Oirrak, A. E., Daoudi, M., & Aboutajdine, D. (2002). Estimation of general 2D affine motion using Fourier descriptors. *Pattern Recognition*, *35*(1), 223–228. doi:10.1016/S0031-3203(01)00019-X

Oja, E., & Lampinen, J. (1994). Unsupervised learning in feature selection. In Zurada, J. M., Marks, R. J., & Robinson, C. J. (Eds.), *Computational modeling imitating life* (pp. 13–22). Pscataway, NJ: IEEE Press.

Optical illusions. (1992). Retrieved from http://www.sandlotscience.com

Oram, A. (2001). *Peer-to-peer: Harnessing the power of disruptive technologies*. Sebastopol, CA: O'Reilly Media.

O'Reilly, R. C., & Frank, M. J. (2006). Making working memory work: A computational model of learning in the prefrontal cortex and basal ganglia. *Neural Computation*, *18*(2), 283–328. doi:10.1162/089976606775093909

O'Reilly, R. C., Frank, M. J., Hazy, T. E., & Watz, B. (2007). PVLV: The primary value and learned value Pavlovian learning algorithm. *Behavioral Neuroscience*, *121*(1), 31–49. doi:10.1037/0735-7044.121.1.31

Orlikowski, W. (2002). Knowing in practice: Enacting a collective capability in distributed organizing. *Organization Science*, *13*(3), 249–273. doi:10.1287/orsc.13.3.249.2776

Orlikowski, W., & Yates, J. (2002). It's about time: Temporal structuring in organizations. *Organization Science*, *13*(6), 684–700. doi:10.1287/orsc.13.6.684.501

Ortony, A., & Turner, T. (1990). What's basic about basic emotions? *Psychological Review*, *97*, 315–331. doi:10.1037/0033-295X.97.3.315

Osowski, S., & Markiewicz, T. (2007). Support vector machine for recognition of white blood cells in leukemia. In Camps-Valls, G., Rojo-Alvarez, J. L., & Martinez-Ramon, M. (Eds.), *Kernel methods in bioengineering, signal and image processing* (pp. 93–123). Hershey, PA: Idea Group Publishing. doi:10.4018/9781599040424.ch004

Otsu, N. (1979). A threshold selection method from grey-level histograms. *IEEE Transactions on Systems, Man, and Cybernetics*, *9*, 62–66. doi:10.1109/TSMC.1979.4310076

Ottengraf, S. P. P., & Diks, R. M. M. (1991). Promising technique-process technology of biotechniques. *LUCHT*, *4*, 135–144.

Oudeyer, P.-Y., Kaplan, F., & Hafner, V. (2007). Intrinsic motivation systems for autonomous mental development. *IEEE Transactions on Evolutionary Computation*, *11*(2), 265–286. doi:10.1109/TEVC.2006.890271

Panksepp, J. (1998). *Affective neuroscience: The foundations of human and animal emotions*. New York, NY: Oxford University Press.

Papamarkos, N., Atsalakis, A. E., & Strouthopoulos, C. P. (2002). Adaptive color reduction. *IEEE Transactions on Systems, Man, and Cybernetics*, *32*(1), 44–56. doi:10.1109/3477.979959

Parhami, B. (2000). *Computer arithmetic: Algorithms and hardware designs*. Oxford, UK & New York, NY: Oxford University Press.

Park, Y.-M., Choi, M.-S., & Lee, K. Y. (1996). An optimal tracking neuro-controller for nonlinear dynamic systems. *IEEE Transactions on Neural Networks*, *7*(5), 1099–1110. doi:10.1109/72.536307

Park, S., Won, D. H., Kang, M. S., Kim, T. J., Lee, H. G., & Kwon, S. J. (2005). *RIC (robust internal-loop compensator) based flight control of a quad-rotor type UAV*. IEEE/RSJ International Conference on Intelligent Robots and Systems, (pp. 3542–3547).

Parr, R., & Russell, S. (1998). Reinforcement learning with hierarchies of machines. In *Advances in Neural Information Processing Systems, 10*. MIT Press.

Parsons, J. (1996). An information model based on classification theory. *Management Science*, *42*(10), 1437–1453. doi:10.1287/mnsc.42.10.1437

Parzen, E. (1962). On estimation of a probability density function and mode. *Annals of Mathematical Statistics*, *33*, 1065–1076. doi:10.1214/aoms/1177704472

Pazzani, M., Marz, C., Murphy, P., Ali, K., Hume, T., & Brunk, C. (1994). Reducing misclassification cost. In *Proceedings of the 11th International Conference on Machine Learning*, (pp. 217-225).

Pena, D. (2005). A new statistic for influence in linear regression. *Technometrics*, *47*, 1–12. doi:10.1198/004017004000000662

Pena, D., & Yohai, V. J. (1995). The detection of influential subsets in linear regression by using an influence matrix. *Journal of the Royal Statistical Society. Series B. Methodological*, *57*, 145–156.

Penrose, R. (1994). *Shadows of the mind*. Oxford, UK: Oxford University Press.

Perlovski, L. I. (2001). *Neural networks and intellect*. New York, NY: Oxford University Press.

Perlovsky, L. (1998). Conundrum of combinatorial complexity. *IEEE Transactions on Pattern Analysis and Machine Intelligence*, *20*(6). doi:10.1109/34.683784

Perlovsky, L., & Deming, R. W. (2007). Neural networks for improved tracking. *IEEE Transactions on Neural Networks*, *18*(6), 1854–1857. doi:10.1109/TNN.2007.903143

Perlovsky, L. I. (2004). Integrating language and cognition. *IEEE Connections*, *2*(2), 8–12.

Perlovsky, L. I. (2009). Musical emotions: Functions, origin, evolution. *Physics of Life Reviews*, *7*(1), 3–31.

Perlovsky, L. I. (2010). (in press). Intersections of mathematical, cognitive, and aesthetic theories of mind. *Psychology of Aesthetics, Creativity, and the Arts*. doi:10.1037/a0018147

Perlovsky, L. I., & Ilin, R. (2010). (in press). Neurally and mathematically motivated architecture for language and thought. *The Open Neuroimaging Journal*.

Perlovsky, L. I., & McManus, M. M. (1991). Maximum likelihood neural networks for sensor fusion and adaptive classification. *Neural Networks*, *4*(1), 89–102. doi:10.1016/0893-6080(91)90035-4

Perlovsky, L. I. (2006). Symbols: Integrated cognition and language. In Gudwin, R., & Queiroz, J. (Eds.), *Semiotics and intelligent systems development* (pp. 121–151). Hershey, PA: Idea Group. doi:10.4018/9781599040639.ch005

Perlovsky, L., & Kozma, R. (2007). *Editorial: Neurodynamics of cognition and consciousness* (Perlovsky, L., & Kozma, R., Eds.). Heidelberg, Germany: Springer Verlag. doi:10.1007/978-3-540-73267-9

Perlovsky, L. (1987). *Multiple sensor fusion and neural networks*. DARPA Neural Network Study.

Perlovsky, L. (1996). Mathematical concepts of intellect. *Proceedings, World Congress on Neural Networks* (pp. 1013-16.). San Diego, CA: L. Erlbaum Assoc.

Perlovsky, L. (1999). Emotions, learning, and control. *Proceedings of the International Symposium on Intelligent Control, Intelligent Systems & Semiotics*, (pp. 131-137). Cambridge, MA.

Perlovsky, L. I., Bonniot-Cabanac, M.-C., & Cabanac, M. (2010). *Curiosity and pleasure*. IEEE World Congress on Computational Intelligence (WCCI'10), Barcelona, Spain.

Perlovsky. (2001). *Neural networks and intellect*. New York, NY: Oxford Univerity Press.

Perrinet, L., & Samuelides, M. (2002). *Sparse image coding using an asynchronous spiking neural network*. European Symposium on Artificial Neural Networks, (pp. 313-318).

Peyron, R., Laurent, B., & Garcia-Larrea, L. (2000). Functional imaging of brain responses to pain. A review and meta-analysis. *Neurophysiologie Clinique*, *30*, 263–288. doi:10.1016/S0987-7053(00)00227-6

Pfeifer, R., & Bongard, J. C. (2007). *How the body shapes the way we think: A new view of intelligence. The MIT Press*. Bradford Books.

Piaget, J. (1981). *The psychology of the child (trans. H. Weaver)*. Basic Books.

Plato. (1871). *Meno*. Translation of Benjamin Jowett Retrieved February 15, 2010, from http://classics.mit.edu/Plato/meno.html

Plaut, D. C. (2002). Graded modality-specific specialization in semantics: A computational account of optic aphasia. *Cognitive Neuropsychology*, *19*(7), 603–639. doi:10.1080/02643290244000112

Poggio, T., & Girosi, F. (1990). Regularization algorithms for learning that are equivalent to multilayer networks. *Science*, *247*, 978–982. doi:10.1126/science.247.4945.978

Poincaré, H. (1895). L'espace et la géométrie. *Revue de Metaphysique et de Morale*, *3*, 631–646.

Poincaré, H. (1898). Des fondements de la géométrie. *The Monist*, *9*, 1–43.

Polat, K., & Günes, S. (2006). Automated identification of diseases related to lymph system from lymphography data using artificial immune recognition system with fuzzy resource allocation mechanism (fuzzy-airs). *Biomedical Signal Processing and Control*.

Porro, C. A., Baraldi, P., & Pagnoni, G. (2002). Does anticipation of pain affect cortical nociceptive systems? *The Journal of Neuroscience*, *22*, 3206–3214.

Pregibon, D. (1981). Logistic regression diagnostics. *Annals of Statistics*, *9*, 977–986. doi:10.1214/aos/1176345513

Prenter, P. M. (1975). *Splines and variational methods*. New York, NY: John Wiley & Sons.

Preston, K., Jr. (1981). *IEEE Transactions, PAMI-3*, 4.

Price, C. B., Wambacq, P., & Oosterlinck, A. (1990). Image enhancement and analysis with reaction- diffusion paradigm. *IEE Proceedings*, *137*, 135–145.

Prolux, J. (2008). Some differences between Maturana and Varela's theory of cognition and constructivism. *Complicity: An International Journal of Complexity and Education*, *5*(1), 11–26.

Pu, A., & Hung, Y. (1995). Use of artificial neural networks: Predicting trickling filter performance in a municipal wastewater treatment plant. *Environmental Management and Health*, *6*, 16–27. doi:10.1108/09566169510085126

Qin, Y.-L., McNaughton, B. L., Skaggs, W. E., & Barnes, C. A. (1997). Memory reprocessing in cortico-cortical and hippocampo-cortical neuronal ensembles. *Philosophical Transactions of the Royal Society of London, Series B*, *352*, 15–25. doi:10.1098/rstb.1997.0139

Quinlan, J. R. (1986). Induction of decision trees. *Machine Learning*, *1*, 81–106. doi:10.1007/BF00116251

Quinlan, J. R. (1993). *C4.5: Programs for machine learning*. Morgan Kaufmann Publishers.

Rabiner, L., & Juang, B. (1993). *Fundamentals of speech recognition*. Prentice Hall.

Rambdi, N. G. (2003). Chemical based computing and problems of high computational complexity. Reaction-diffusion paradigm.

Rambidi, N. G. (2003). Lure of molecular electronics–from molecular switches to distributed molecular information processing media. *Microelectronic Engineering*, *69*, 485–500. doi:10.1016/S0167-9317(03)00337-X

Rambidi, N. G., & Maximychev, A. V. (1997). Molecular image-processing devices based on chemical reaction systems, 6: Processing half-tone images and neural network architecture of excitable media. *Advanced Materials for Optics and Electronics*, *7*, 171–182. doi:10.1002/(SICI)1099-0712(199707)7:4<171::AID-AMO300>3.0.CO;2-#

Rambidi, N. G., Maximychev, A. V., & Usatov, A. V. (1994). Molecular neural network devices based on non-linear dynamic media. *Bio Systems*, *33*, 125–137. doi:10.1016/0303-2647(94)90052-3

Rambidi, N. G., Zamalin, V. M., & Sandler, Y. M. (1988). Molecular information processing and problems of artificial intelligence. *Journal of Molecular Electronics*, *4*, S39.

Rambidi, N. G. (2007). *Nanotechnology and molecular computers*. Moscow, Russia: FizMatLit.

Randell, D. A., Cui, Z., & Cohn, A. G. (1992). A spatial logic based on regions and connection. *Proceedings of the 3rd International Conference on Knowledge Representation and Reasoning*, (pp. 165-176). San Mateo, CA: Morgan Kaufmann.

Rao, S. (2009). *Engineering optimization: Theory and practice*. New York, NY: Wiley.

Rao, A. S., & Georgeff, M. P. (1995). BDI-agents: From theory to practice. *Proceedings of the First International Conference on Multiagent Systems* (ICMAS'95), (pp. 312-319).

Rasmussen, C. (2002). *Combining laser range, color, and texture cues for autonomous road following*. Paper presented at the International Conference on Robotics & Automation, Washington, DC.

Redish, A. (2001). The hippocampal debate: are we asking the right questions? *Behavioural Brain Research*, *127*(1), 81–98. doi:10.1016/S0166-4328(01)00356-4

Redish, A., Rosenzweig, E., Bohanick, J. D., McNaughton, B. L., & Barnes, C. A. (2000). Dynamics of hippocampal ensemble activity realignment: Time versus space. *The Journal of Neuroscience*, *20*(24), 9298–9309.

Redish, A., & Touretzky, D. (1997). Cognitive maps beyond the hippocampus. *Hippocampus*, *7*(1), 15–35. doi:10.1002/(SICI)1098-1063(1997)7:1<15::AID-HIPO3>3.0.CO;2-6

Reece, M. (2001). Encoding information in neuronal activity. In Maass, W., & Bishop, C. (Eds.), *Pulsed neural networks*. MIT Press.

Rene, E. R., Kim, S. J., & Park, H. S. (2008). Experimental results and neural prediction of sequencing batch reactor performance under different operational conditions. *Journal of Environmental Informatics*, *11*, 51–61. doi:10.3808/jei.200800111

Rene, E. R., López, M. E., Veiga, M. C., & Kennes, C. (2010a). Steady- and transient-state operation of a two-stage bioreactor for the treatment of a gaseous mixture of hydrogen sulphide, methanol and α-pinene. *Journal of Chemical Technology and Biotechnology (Oxford, Oxfordshire)*, *85*, 336–348. doi:10.1002/jctb.2343

Rene, E. R., López, M. E., Veiga, M. C., & Kennes, C. (2010b). Performance of a fungal monolith bioreactor for the removal of styrene from polluted air. *Bioresource Technology*, *101*, 2608–2615. doi:10.1016/j.biortech.2009.10.060

Rene, E. R., Maliyekkal, S. M., Swaminathan, T., & Philip, L. (2006). Back propagation neural network for performance prediction in trickling bed air biofilter. *International Journal of Environment and Pollution*, *28*, 382–401. doi:10.1504/IJEP.2006.011218

Rene, E. R., Veiga, M. C., & Kennes, C. (2009). Experimental and neural model analysis of styrene removal from polluted air in a biofilter. *Journal of Chemical Technology and Biotechnology (Oxford, Oxfordshire)*, *84*, 941–948. doi:10.1002/jctb.2130

Rene, E. R., Veiga, M. C., & Kennes, C. (2010). Biodegradation of gas-phase styrene using the fungus *Sporothrix variecibatus*: Impact of pollutant load and transient operation. *Chemosphere*, *79*, 221–227. doi:10.1016/j.chemosphere.2010.01.036

Renz, J., Rauh, R., & Knauff, M. (2000). *Towards cognitive adequacy of topological spatial relations*. (LNCS 1849), (pp. 184–197). Springer.

Reynolds, D. A., Quatieri, T. F., & Dunn, R. B. (2000). Speaker verification using adapted Gaussian mixture models. *Digital Signal Processing*, *10*, 19–41. doi:10.1006/dspr.1999.0361

Riedmiller, M., & Braun, H. (1993). *A direct adaptive method for faster backpropagation: Learning the RPROP algorithm*. Paper presented at the IEEE International Conference on Neural Networks (ICNN).

Riesenhuber, M., & Poggio, T. (1999). Hierarchical models of object recognition in cortex. *Nature Neuroscience*, *2*(11), 1019–1025. doi:10.1038/14819

Rigter, J. (1996). *Het palet van de psychologie, Stromingen en hun toepassingen in de hulpverlening*. Bussum, The Netherlands: Uitgeverij Coutinho.

Ritter, M. A., Albohm, M. J., Keating, E. M., Faris, P. M., & Meding, J. B. (1995). Comparative outcomes of total joint arthroplasty. *The Journal of Arthroplasty*, *10*(6), 737–741. doi:10.1016/S0883-5403(05)80068-3

Robert, A., & Eriksson, J. L. (1999). A composite model of the auditory periphery for simulating responses to complex sounds. *The Journal of the Acoustical Society of America*, *106*(4), 1852–1864. doi:10.1121/1.427935

Rogers, L. L., & Dowla, F. U. (1994). Optimization of groundwater remediation using artificial neural networks with parallel solute transport modelling. *Water Resources Research*, *30*, 457–481. doi:10.1029/93WR01494

Rosenberg, A. E., & Soong, F. K. (1987). Evaluation of a vector quantization talker recognition system in text independent and text dependent modes. *Computer Speech & Language*, *2*(3-4), 143–157. doi:10.1016/0885-2308(87)90005-2

Rosenblatt, F. (1962). *Principles of neurodynamics*. Washington, DC: Spartan.

Rosipal, R., & Trejo, L. (2001). Kernel partial least squares regression in reproducing kernel Hillbert spaces. *Journal of Machine Learning Research*, *2*, 97–128. doi:10.1162/15324430260185556

Rouat, J., Pichevar, R., & Loiselle, S. (2005). Perceptive, non-linear speech processing and spiking neural networks. In Chollet, G. (Eds.), *Nonlinear speech modeling (LNAI 3445)* (pp. 317–337). Berlin/ Heidelberg, Germany: Springer-Verlag. doi:10.1007/11520153_14

Rousseauw, J., du Plessis, J., Benade, A., Jordann, P., Kotze, J., Jooste, P., & Ferreira, J. (1983). Coronary risk factor screening in three rural communities. *South African Medical Journal*, *64*, 430–436.

Rousseeuw, P. J. (1984). Least median of squares regression. *Journal of the American Statistical Association*, *79*, 871–880. doi:10.2307/2288718

Rousseeuw, P. J. (1985). A regression diagnostic for multiple outliers and leverage points. *Abstracts in IMS Bulletin*, *14*, 399.

Rousseeuw, P. J., & Leroy, A. M. (2003). *Robust regression and outlier detection*. New York, NY: Wiley.

Rousseeuw, P. J., & van Driessen, K. (1999). A fast algorithm for the minimum covariance determinant estimator. *Technometrics*, *41*, 212–223. doi:10.2307/1270566

Rousseeuw, P. J., & van Zomeren, B. C. (1990). Unmasking multivariate outliers and leverage points. *Journal of the American Statistical Association*, *85*, 633–639. doi:10.2307/2289995

Rousseeuw, P. J., & Yohai, V. (1984). Robust regression by means of S-estimators. In Franke, J., Hardle, W., & Martin, R. D. (Eds.), *Robust and non-linear time series analysis* (pp. 256–272). New York, NY: Springer-Verleg.

Rubio, G., Herrera, L., Pomares, H., Rojas, I., & Guillén, A. (2010). Design of specific-to-problem kernels and use of kernel weighted k-nearest neighbors for time series modeling. *Neurocomputing*, *73*(10-12), 1965–1975. doi:10.1016/j.neucom.2009.11.029

Rumelhart, D. E., & McClelland, J. L.PDP Research Group. (1986). *Parallel distributed processing: Explorations in the microstructure of cognition*. Cambridge, MA: MIT Press.

Rumelhart, D. E., Hinton, G. E., & Williams, R. J. (1986). Learning internal representations by error propagation. In D. E. Rumelhart, J. L. McClelland & the PDP Research Group (Eds.), *Paralled distributed processing. Explorations in the microstructure of cognition. Volume 1: Foundations*, (pp. 318-362). Cambridge, MA: The MIT Press.

Russell, S., & Norvig, P. (1995). *Artificial intelligence: A modern approach*. New York, NY: Prentice–Hall.

Ryan, T. P. (1997). *Modern regression methods*. New York, NY: Wiley.

Safranek, R. J., Gottschlich, S., & Kak, A. C. (1990). Evidence accumulation using binary frames of discernment for verification vision. *IEEE Transactions on Robotics and Automation*, *6*, 405–417. doi:10.1109/70.59366

Said, A., & Pearlman, W. A. (1996). A new fast and efficient image codec based on set partitioning in hierarchical trees. *IEEE Transactions on Circuits and Systems for Video Technology*, *6*(3), 243–251. doi:10.1109/76.499834

Salomon, D. (2007). *Data compression: The complete reference*. New York, NY: Springer-Verlag.

Sambin, G. (2003). Some points in formal topology. *Theoretical Computer Science, 305*(1-3), 347–408. doi:10.1016/S0304-3975(02)00704-1

Sanderson, C., & Paliwal, K. K. (2002). Identity verification using speech and face information. *Digital Signal Processing, 14*, 449–480. doi:10.1016/j.dsp.2004.05.001

Sarbo, J., & Farkas, J. (2003). Logica Utens. In de Moor, A., & Ganter, B. (Eds.), *Using conceptual structures* (pp. 43–56). Dresden, Germany: Shaker Verlag.

Sarbo, J., Farkas, J., & van Breemen, A. (2007). Natural grammar. In Gudwin, R., & Queiroz, J. (Eds.), *Semiotics and intelligent system development* (pp. 152–175). Hersey, PA: Idea Group Publishing.

Sarbo, J., & Farkas, J. (2002). A linearly complex model for knowledge representation. In U. Priss & D. Corbett (Eds.), *Conceptual structures: Integration and interface (ICCS'2002)* (Vol. 2193, pp. 20–33). Borovets, Bulgaria: Springer Verlag.

Sargolini, F., Fyhn, M., Hafting, T., McNaughton, B., Witter, M., Moser, M., & Moser, E. (2006). Conjunctive representation of position, direction, and velocity in entorhinal cortex. *Science, 312*, 758–762. doi:10.1126/science.1125572

Sartre, J. P. (1984). *Existentialism and human emotions.* Citadel Press, Reissue edition.

Sastry, C. S., Pujari, A. K., Deekshatulu, B. L., & Bhagvati, C. (2004). A wavelet based multiresolution algorithm for rotation invariant feature extraction. *Pattern Recognition Letters, 25*, 1845–1855. doi:10.1016/j.patrec.2004.07.011

Schmidhuber, J. (1991). Curious model-building control systems. *Proceedings International Joint Conference on Neural Networks*, (pp. 1458–1463). Singapore.

Scholkopf, B., & Smola, A. (2002). *Learning with kernels.* Cambridge, MA: MIT Press.

Scholkopf, B. (2000). New support vector algorithms. *Neural Computation, 12*, 1207–1245. doi:10.1162/089976600300015565

Schölkopf, B., & Smola, A. (2002). *Learning with kernels.* Cambridge, MA: MIT Press.

Schultz, W. (2002). Getting formal with dopamine and reward. *Neuron, 36*, 241–263. doi:10.1016/S0896-6273(02)00967-4

Sclaroff, S., & Pentland, A. (1995). Modal matching for correspondence and recognition. *IEEE Transactions on Pattern Analysis and Machine Intelligence, 17*(6), 545–561. doi:10.1109/34.387502

Searle, J. R. (1969). *Speech acts. An essay in the philosophy of language.* London, UK: Cambridge University Press.

Searle, S. R. (1982). *Matrix algebra useful for statistics.* New York, NY: Wiley.

Seguier, R., & Mercier, D. (2001). *A generic pretreatment for spiking neuron application on lipreading with STANN* (Spatio-Temporal Artificial Neural Networks). 5th International Conference on Artificial Neural Networks and Genetic Algorithms.

Seibert, M., & Waxman, A. M. (1989). Spreading activation layers, visual saccades and invariant representation for neural pattern recognition system. *Neural Networks, 2*, 9–12. doi:10.1016/0893-6080(89)90012-9

Serra, J. (1986). Introduction to mathematical morphology. *Computer Vision Graphics and Image Processing, 35*, 283–305. doi:10.1016/0734-189X(86)90002-2

Serrano, N., Savakis, A. E., & Luo, J. (2004). Improved scene classification using efficient low-level features and semantic cues. *Pattern Recognition, 37*, 1773–1784. doi:10.1016/j.patcog.2004.03.003

Serre, T., Wolf, L., Bileschi, S., Riesenhuber, M., & Poggio, T. (2007). Robust object recognition with cortex-like mechanisms. *IEEE Transactions on Pattern Analysis and Machine Intelligence, 29*(3), 411–426. doi:10.1109/TPAMI.2007.56

Shafer, G. A. (1976). *Mathematical theory of evidence.* Princeton, NJ: Princeton University Press.

Shafer, G., & Srivastava, R. (1990). The Bayesian and belief-function formalisms: A general perspective for auditing. In Shafer, G., & Pearl, J. (Eds.), *Readings in uncertain reasoning.* San Mateo, CA: Morgan Kaufman Publishers Inc.

Shao, J., & Tu, D. (1995). *The jackknife and bootstrap*. New York, NY: Springer Verlag.

Shapiro, L. (2009). Making sense of mirror neurons. *Syntheses, 167*(3), 439–456. doi:10.1007/s11229-008-9385-8

Sharp, P. E. (Ed.). (2002). *The neural basis of navigation*. Boston, MA: Kluwer Academic.

Shetty, K. V., Nandennavar, S., & Srinikethan, G. (2008). Artificial neural network model for the prediction of steady state phenol biodegradation in a pulsed plate bioreactor. *Journal of Chemical Technology and Biotechnology (Oxford, Oxfordshire), 83*, 1181–1189. doi:10.1002/jctb.1892

Shimojo, S., & Shams, L. (2001). Sensory modalities are not separate modalities: Plasticity and interactions. *Current Opinion in Neurobiology, 11*(4), 505–509. doi:10.1016/S0959-4388(00)00241-5

Shouche, S. P., Rastogi, R., Bhagwat, S. G., & Sainis, J. K. (2001). Shape analysis of grains of Indian wheat varieties. *Computers and Electronics in Agriculture, 33*(1). doi:10.1016/S0168-1699(01)00174-0

Sienko, T., Adamatzky, A., Rambidi, R., & Conrad, M. (Eds.). (2003). *Molecular computing*. Cambridge, MA; London, UK: The MIT Press.

Sietsma, J., & Dow, R. J. F. (1998). *Neural net pruning - why and how?* In IEEE International Conference on Neural Networks (ICNN - 1988), 1, (pp. 325-333).

Simon, D. J. (2008). Evolutionary biogeography-based optimization. *IEEE Transactions on Evolutionary Computation, 12*(6), 702–713. doi:10.1109/TEVC.2008.919004

Simonoff, J. S. (1991). General approaches to stepwise identification of unusual values in data analysis. In Stahel, W., & Weisberg, S. (Eds.), *Robust statistics and diagnostics: Part II* (pp. 223–242). New York, NY: Springer-Verlag.

Singer, R. S. (1974). Derivation and evaluation of improved tracking filters for use in dense multitarget environments. *IEEE Transactions on Information Theory, 20*, 423–432. doi:10.1109/TIT.1974.1055256

Singh, K., Basant, N., Malik, A., & Jain, G. (2010). Modelling the performance of up-flow anaerobic sludge blanket reactor based wastewater treatment plant using linear and nonlinear approaches—a case study. *Analytica Chimica Acta, 658*, 1–11. doi:10.1016/j.aca.2009.11.001

Singh, S. P. (1992). Transfer of learning by composing solutions for elemental sequential tasks. *Machine Learning, 8*, 323–340. doi:10.1007/BF00992700

Skaggs, W., & McNaughton, B. (1996). Replay of neuronal firing sequence in rat hippocampus during sleep following spatial experience. *Science, 271*, 1870–1873. doi:10.1126/science.271.5257.1870

Skodras, A., Christopoulos, C., & Ebrahimi, T. (2001). The JPEG 2000 still image compression standard. *IEEE Signal Processing Magazine, 18*(5), 36–58. doi:10.1109/79.952804

Smith, J. R., & Chang, S. F. (1996). Tools and techniques for color image retrieval. *In SPIE Proceedings. Storage and Retrieval for Image and Video Databases, 2670*, 426–437.

Smith, E., Osherson, D., Rips, L., & Keans, M. (1988). Combining proto-types: A selective modification model. *Cognitive Science, 12*(4), 485–527. doi:10.1207/s15516709cog1204_1

Smith, J. R., & Chang, S. F. (1996). VisualSEEk: A fully automated content-based image query system. *Proceedings of ACM Multimedia,* Boston MA, (pp. 87–98).

Soille, P. (2003). *Morphological image analysis, principles and applications*. Berlin, Germany: Springer.

Soler, V., & Prim, M. (2007). *Rectangular basis functions applied to imbalanced datasets. (LNCS 4668)*. Springer.

Soler, V., Cerquides, J., Sabria, J., Roig, J., & Prim, M. (2006). Imbalanced datasets classification by fuzzy rule extraction and genetic algorithms. In *Proceedings of the 6th Conference on Data Mining* (ICDMW'06).

Sorial, G. A., Smith, F. L., Suidan, M. T., Biswas, P., & Brenner, R. C. (1995). Evaluation of trickle bed biofilter media for toluene removal. *Journal of the Air & Waste Management Association, 45*, 801–810.

Specht, D. F. (1990). Probabilistic neural networks. *Neural Networks, 3*, 109–118. doi:10.1016/0893-6080(90)90049-Q

S-PLUS 4. (1997). *Guide to statistics*. Math Soft Inc., Seattle, Washington.

Sprecher, D. A. (1965). On the structure of continuous functions of several variables. *Transactions of the American Mathematical Society, 115*(3), 340–355. doi:10.1090/S0002-9947-1965-0210852-X

Sprecher, D. A. (1996). A numerical implementation of Kolmogorov's superpositions. *Neural Networks, 9*(5), 765–772. doi:10.1016/0893-6080(95)00081-X

Sprecher, D. A. (1997). A numerical implementation of Kolmogorov's superpositions II. *Neural Networks, 10*(3), 447–457. doi:10.1016/S0893-6080(96)00073-1

Sprecher, D. A., & Draghici, S. (2002). Space-filling curves and Kolmogorov superposition-based neural networks. *Neural Networks, 15*(1), 57–67. doi:10.1016/S0893-6080(01)00107-1

Stahel, W., & Weisberg, S. (1991). *Direction in robust statistics and diagnostics, (Preface)*. New York, NY: Springer-Verlag.

Steels, L. (2004). *The autotelic principle*. In (LNAI 3139), (pp. 231-242).

Stein, B. E., & Meredith, M. A. (1993). *The merging of the senses*. MIT Press.

Stone, M. (1974). Cross-validatory choice and assessment of statistical predictions. *Journal of the Royal Statistical Society. Series B. Methodological, 36*(1), 11–147.

Storn, R., & Price, K. (1997). Differential evolution–a simple and efficient heuristic for global optimization over continuous spaces. *Journal of Global Optimization, 11*, 341–359. doi:10.1023/A:1008202821328

Stricker, M., & Dimai, A. (1997). Spectral covariance and fuzzy regions for image indexing. *Machine Vision and Applications, 10*(2), 66–73. doi:10.1007/s001380050060

Stricker, M., & Swain, M. (1994). *Capacity and the sensitivity of color histogram indexing.* (Technical Report, 94-05, University of Chicago).

Stroud, A. H. (1971). *Approximate calculation of multiple integrals*. Englewood Cliffs, NJ: Prentice-Hall.

Štruc, V., & Pavesić, N. (2009). Gabor-based kernel partial-least squares discrimination for face recognition. *Informatica, 20*, 115–138.

Subbarao, M. (1989). Interpretation of image flow: A spatio-temporal approach. *IEEE Transactions on Pattern Analysis and Machine Intelligence, 11*(3), 266–278. doi:10.1109/34.21796

Sung, G.-Y., Kwak, D.-M., & Lyou, J. (2010). Neural network based terrain classification using wavelet features. *Journal of Intelligent and Robotic Systems.*

Sutton, R. S., & Barto, A. G. (1998). *Reinforcement learning: An introduction (adaptive computation and machine learning)*. The MIT Press.

Sutton, R. S., & Barto, A. G. (1998). *Reinforcement learning: An introduction.* Cambridge, MA: MIT Press.

Sutton, R. S. (1984). *Temporal credit assignment in reinforcement learning.* Unpublished doctoral dissertation, University of Massachusetts, Amherst, MA.

Suykens, J., Gestel, T., Brabanter, J., Moor, B., & Vandewalle, J. (2003). *Least squares support vector machines*. Singapore: World Scientific Publishing Company.

Swain, M., & Ballard, D. (1991). Color indexing. *International Journal of Computer Vision, 7*(1), 11–32. doi:10.1007/BF00130487

Swan, R. G. (1964). *The theory of sheaves*. Chicago, IL: University of Chicago Press.

Swets, J., Dawes, R., & Monahan, J. (2000, October). Better decisions through science. *Scientific American*, 82–87. doi:10.1038/scientificamerican1000-82

Syu, M. J., & Chen, B. C. (1998). Back-propagation neural network adaptive control of a continuous wastewater treatment process. *Industrial & Engineering Chemistry Research, 37*, 3625–3630. doi:10.1021/ie9801655

Takashi, I., & Masafumi, H. (2000). Content-based image retrieval system using neural networks. *International Journal of Neural Systems, 10*(5), 417–424. doi:10.1016/S0129-0657(00)00032-6

Tanaka, G., & Aihara, K. (2009). Complex-valued multistate associative memory with nonlinear multilevel functions for gray-level image reconstruction. *IEEE Transactions on Neural Networks, 20*(9), 1463–1473. doi:10.1109/TNN.2009.2025500

Taubman, D., & Marcellin, M. (2001). JPEG2000. In *Image compression fundamentals, standards and practice*. Kluwer Academic Publishers.

Taxén, L. (2009). *Using activity domain theory for managing complex systems*. Hershey, PA: IGI Global.

Taxén, L., & Lilliesköld, J. (2008). Images as action instruments in complex projects. *International Journal of Project Management*, *26*(5), 527–536. doi:10.1016/j.ijproman.2008.05.009

Taxén, L., & Lilliesköld, J. (2005). *Manifesting shared affordances in system development – the system anatomy*. ALOIS*2005, The 3rd International Conference on Action in Language, Organisations and Information Systems (pp. 28–47). 15–16 March 2005, Limerick: Ireland. Retrieved Feb 6, 2008, from http://www.alois2005.ul.ie/

Terrazas, A., Krause, M., Lipa, P., Gothard, K., Barnes, C., & McNaughton, B. (2005). Self-motion and the hippocampal spatial metric. *The Journal of Neuroscience*, *25*(35), 8085–8096. doi:10.1523/JNEUROSCI.0693-05.2005

Terrell, G. R., & Scott, D. W. (1992). Variable kernel density estimation. *Annals of Statistics*, *20*(3), 1236–1265. doi:10.1214/aos/1176348768

Thompson, M. (1966). *Manual of photogrammetry*. Falls Church, VA: American Society of Photogrammetry.

Thorpe, S., Fize, D., & Marlot, C. (1996). Speed of processing in the human visual system. *Nature*, *381*, 520–522. doi:10.1038/381520a0

Thrun, S., Montemerlo, M., Dahlkamp, H., Stavens, D., Aron, A., & Diebel, J. (2006). Stanley: The robot that won the DARPA grand challenge. *Journal of Field Robotics*, *23*(9), 661–692. doi:10.1002/rob.20147

Tian, H., Tian, X., Deng, X., & Wang, P. (2009). *Soft sensor for polypropylene melt index based on adaptive kernel partial least squares*. Control and Instruments in Chemical Industry.

Tölle, T. R., Kaufmann, T., & Siessmeier, T. (1999). Region-specific encoding of sensory and affective components of pain in the human brain: A positron emission tomography correlation analysis. *Annals of Neurology*, *45*, 40–47. doi:10.1002/1531-8249(199901)45:1<40::AID-ART8>3.0.CO;2-L

Touretzky, D., Weisman, W., Fuhs, M., Skaggs, W., Fenton, A., & Muller, R. (2004). Deforming the hippocampal map. *Hippocampus*, *15*(1), 41–55. doi:10.1002/hipo.20029

Tsai, R. Y., & Huang, T. S. (1984). Uniqueness and estimation of three-dimensional motion parameters of rigid objects with curved surfaces. *IEEE Transactions on Pattern Analysis and Machine Intelligence*, *6*(1), 13–27. doi:10.1109/TPAMI.1984.4767471

Tu, J. (1996). Advantages and disadvantages of using artificial neural networks versus logistic regression for predicting medical outcomes. *Journal of Clinical Epidemiology*, *49*, 1225–1232. doi:10.1016/S0895-4356(96)00002-9

Tukey, J. W. (1977). *Exploratory data analysis*. USA: Addision- Wesley.

Unger, S. H. (1959). Cellular logic. *Proceedings of IRE*, *40*(10).

Valenti, M., Bethke, B., Fiore, G., How, J. P., & Feron, E. (2006). *Indoor multi-vehicle flight testbed for fault detection, isolation, and recovery*. AIAA Guidance, Navigation and Control Conference.

van de Vel, M. (1993). *Theory of convex structures*. Amsterdam, The Netherlands: North Holland Publishers.

Vannucci, M., Colla, V., Sgarbi, M., & Toscanelli, O. (2009). Thresholded neural networks for sensitive industrial classification tasks. In *Proceedings of International Work Conference on Artificial Neural Networks* (IWANN 2009). (LNCS 5517, pp. 1320-1327).

Vapnik, V. (1998). *Statistical learning theory*. New York, NY: Wiley.

Vapnik, V. (1995). *The nature of statistical learning theory*. Springer-Verlag.

Vapnik, V. (1998). *Statistical learning theory*. New York, NY: John Wiley & Sons.

Vasilevskiy, A., & Siddigi, K. (2002). Flux maximizing geometric flow. *IEEE Transactions of PAMI*, *24*, 1565–1578.

Vaucher, G. (1998). An algebraic interpretation of PSP composition. *Bio Systems*, *48*, 241–246. doi:10.1016/S0303-2647(98)00077-X

Veiga, M. C., & Kennes, C. (2001). Parameters affecting performance and modeling of biofilters treating alkylbenzene-polluted air. *Applied Microbiology and Biotechnology, 55*, 254–258. doi:10.1007/s002530000491

Velleman, P. F., & Welsch, R. E. (1981). Efficient computing in regression diagnostics. *The American Statistician, 35*, 234–242. doi:10.2307/2683296

Veropoulos, K., Cristianini, N., & Campbell, C. (1999). Controlling the sensitivity of support vector machines. In *Proceedings of 16th International Joint Conference on Artificial Intelligence* (IJCAI'99) (pp. 55-60). San Francisco, CA: Morgan Kaufmann.

Vickers, S. (1989). *Topology via logic*. London, UK: Cambridge University Press.

Villa, A. E., Tetko, I. V., Hyland, B., & Najem, A. (1999). Spatiotemporal activity patterns of rat cortical neurons predict responses in a conditioned task. *Proceedings of the National Academy of Sciences*, USA, (pp. 1106-1111).

Vološinov, V. N. (1986). *Marxism and the language of philosophy*. London, UK: Harvard University Press.

von Kriegstein, K., & Giraud, A. (2006). Implicit multisensory associations influence voice recognition. *PLoS Biology, 4*(10), 1809–1820. doi:10.1371/journal.pbio.0040326

von Kriegstein, K., Kleinschmidt, A., Sterzer, P., & Giraud, A. (2005). Interaction of face and voice areas during speaker recognition. *Journal of Cognitive Neuroscience, 17*(3), 367–376. doi:10.1162/0898929053279577

Vygotsky, L. S. (1978). *Mind in society – the development of higher psychological processes. M. Cole, V. John-Steiner* (Scribner, S., & Souberman, E., Eds.). Cambridge, MA: Harvard University Press.

Vygotsky, L. S. (1981). The genesis of higher mental functions. In Wertsch, J. W. (Ed.), *The concept of activity in Soviet psychology*. Armonk, NY: M. E. Sharpe.

Vygotsky, L. S. (1997). *The collected works of L.S. Vygotsky, vol. 4, the history of the development of higher mental functions*. New York, NY: Plenum P.

Walker, J. H., Garrett, S. M., & Wilson, M. S. (2006). The balance between initial training and lifelong adaptation in evolving robot controllers. *IEEE Transactions on Systems, Man, and Cybernetics, 36*(2), 423–432. doi:10.1109/TSMCB.2005.859082

Wallenstein, G., Eichenbaum, H., & Hasselmo, M. (1998). The hippocampus as an associator of discontiguous events. *Trends in Neurosciences, 21*(8), 317–323. doi:10.1016/S0166-2236(97)01220-4

Wang, T., Huang, H., Tian, S., & Xu, J. (2010). Feature selection for SVM via optimization of kernel polarization with Gaussian ARD kernels. *Expert Systems with Applications, 37*(9), 6663–6668. doi:10.1016/j.eswa.2010.03.054

Wang, Q., & Clarke, R. J. (1990). Use of Fourier descriptors for the estimation of general motion in image sequences. *Electronics Letters, 26*(22), 1877–1878. doi:10.1049/el:19901207

Warner, B., & Misra, M. (1996). Understanding neural networks as statistical tools. *The American Statistician, 50*, 284–293. doi:10.2307/2684922

Watanabe, A., Yazawa, N., Miyauchi, A., & Miyauchi, M. (1994). A method to interpret 3D motions using neural networks. *IEICE Transactions on Fundamentals of Electronics, Communications and Computer Sciences. E (Norwalk, Conn.), 77-A*(8), 1363–1370.

Watkins, C., & Dayan, P. (1992). Q-learning. *Machine Learning, 8*, 279–292. doi:10.1007/BF00992698

Watkins, C. (1989). *Learning from delayed rewards*. Unpublished doctoral dissertation, Cambridge University, Cambridge, England.

Waweru, M., Herrygers, V., Langenhove, H. V., & Verstraete, W. (2005). Process engineering of biological waste gas purification. In H. J. Jordening & J. Winter (Eds.), *Environmental biotechnology: Concepts and applications*, (pp. 409-425). Wiley – VCH Verlag GmbH & Co, KGaA – Weinheim, Germany.

Weber, F. J., & Hartmans, S. (1992). Biological waste gas treatment with integrated adsorption for the treatment of fluctuating concentrations. In A. T. Dragt., & J. Van Ham (Eds.) *Biotechniques for air pollution abatement and odour control policies*, (pp. 125-130). Amsterdam, The Netherlands: Elsevier.

Weick, K. E. (1988). Enacted sensemaking in crisis situations. *Journal of Management Studies, 25*(4), 305–317. doi:10.1111/j.1467-6486.1988.tb00039.x

Weil, A. (1938). *Sur les espaces à structure uniforme et sur la topologie générale. Publications de l'Institute Mathématique de l'Université de Strasbourg*. Paris, France: Hermann.

Weiss, S., & Kapouleas, I. (1990). An empirical comparison of pattern recognition, neural nets, and machine learning methods. In Shavlik, J. W., & Dietterich, T. G. (Eds.), *Readings in machine learning*. San Mateo, CA: Morgan-Kauffman.

Weng, J. (2004). Developmental robotics: Theory and experiments. *International Journal of Humanoid Robotics, 1*(2), 199–236. doi:10.1142/S0219843604000149

Wertsch, J. V. (1991). *Voices of the mind: A sociocultural approach to mediated action*. Cambridge, MA: Harvard University Press.

Whatling, G. M., Dabke, H. V., Holt, C. A., Jones, L., Madete, J., Alderman, P. M., & Roberts, P. (2008). Objective functional assessment of total hip arthroplasty following two common surgical approaches: The posterior and direct lateral approaches. *Proceedings of the Institution of Mechanical Engineers (IMechE), Part H: J. Engineering in Medicine, 222*(H6), 897–905. doi:10.1243/09544119JEIM396

White, R. (1959). Motivation reconsidered: The concept of competence. *Psychological Review, 66*, 297–333. doi:10.1037/h0040934

Whitehead, A. N. (1929). *Process and reality: An essay in cosmology*. New York, NY: Macmillan.

Whittaker, R. (1998). *Island biogeography*. New York, NY: Oxford University Press.

Widrow, B., & Sterns, S. D. (1985). *Sterns adaptive signal processing*. Englewood Cliffs, NJ: Prentice Hall.

Wiener, S. I., & Taube, J. S. (Eds.). (2005). *Head direction cells and the neural mechanisms underlying directional orientation*. Boston, MA: MIT Press.

Wiering, M. A. (2005). QV(lambda)-learning: A new on-policy reinforcement learning Algorithm. In D. Leone (Ed.), *Proceedings of the 7th European Workshop on Reinforcement Learning* (pp. 17-18).

Wikipedia. (2008). *Homo faber*. Retrieved Jan 26, 2010, from http://en.wikipedia.org/wiki/Homo_faber

Willems, G., & Aelst, S. V. (2004). *Fast and robust bootstrap for LTS*. Elsevier Science.

Wilson, M., & McNaughton, B. (1993). Dynamics of the hippocampal ensemble code for space. *Science, 261*, 1055–1058. doi:10.1126/science.8351520

Wilson, M., & McNaughton, B. (1994). Reactivation of hippocampal ensemble memories during sleep. *Science, 265*, 676–679. doi:10.1126/science.8036517

Wittgenstein, L. (1922). *Tractatus logico-philosophicus*. London, UK: Routledge and Kegan Paul.

Wittgenstein, L. (1971). *Philosophische Untersuchungen*. Frankfurt, Germany: Suhrkamp.

Wittgenstein, L. (1953). *Philosophical investigations*. Oxford, UK: Blackwell.

Wold, S., Sjōlstrōm, M., & Erikson, L. (2001). PLS-regression: A basic tool of chemometrics. *Chemometrics and Intelligent Laboratory Systems, 58*, 109–130. doi:10.1016/S0169-7439(01)00155-1

Wold, H. (1975). Path with latent variables: The NIPALS approach. In Balock, H. M. (Ed.), *Quantitative sociology: International perspectives on mathematical and statistical model building* (pp. 307–357). New York, NY: Academic Press.

Wold, H. (1996). Estimation of principal components and related models by iterative least squares. In Krishnaiah, P. (Ed.), *Multivariate analysis* (pp. 391–420). New York, NY: Academic Press.

Woodward, D. E., Tyson, R., Myerscough, M. R., Murry, J. D., Burdene, E. O., & Berg, H. C. (1995). Spatio-temporal patterns generated by Salmonella typhimurium. *Biophysical Journal, 68*, 2181–2189. doi:10.1016/S0006-3495(95)80400-5

Wu, C. F. J. (1986). Jackknife, bootstrap, and other resampling methods in regression analysis. *Annals of Statistics*, *14*, 1261–1350. doi:10.1214/aos/1176350142

Wysoski, S. G., Benuskova, L., & Kasabov, N. (2006). *Online learning with structural adaptation in a network of spiking neurons for visual pattern recognition. ICANN06, (LNCS 4131)* (pp. 61–70). Berlin, Germany: Springer-Verlag.

Wysoski, S. G., Benuskova, L., & Kasabov, N. (2007). *Text-independent speaker authentication with spiking neural networks. ICANN07, (LNCS 4669)* (pp. 758–767). New York, NY: Springer-Verlag.

Wysoski, S. G., Benuskova, L., & Kasabov, N. (2008a). Fast and adaptive network of spiking neurons for multi-view visual pattern recognition. *Neurocomputing*, *71*(13-15), 2563–2575. doi:10.1016/j.neucom.2007.12.038

Wysoski, S. G., Benuskova, L., & Kasabov, N. (2008b). *Adaptive spiking neural networks for audiovisual pattern recognition. ICONIP'2007, (LNCS 4985)* (pp. 406–415). Berlin, Germany: Springer-Verlag.

Wysoski, S. G., Benuskova, L., & Kasabov, N. (2010). Evolving spiking neural networks for audiovisual information processing. *Neural Networks*..doi:10.1016/j.neunet.2010.04.009

Yamauchi, K., Oota, M., & Ishii, N. (1999). A self-supervised learning system for pattern recognition by sensory integration. *Neural Networks*, *12*(10), 1347–1358. doi:10.1016/S0893-6080(99)00064-7

Yamauchi, K., Takama, J., Takeuchi, H., Sugiura, S., & Ishii, N. (2001). Sensory integrating neural network with selective attention architecture for autonomous robots. *International Journal of Knowledge-Based Intelligent Engineering Systems*, *5*(3), 142–154.

Yeh, I.-C. (1998). Modeling of strength of high-performance concrete using artificial neural networks. *Cement and Concrete Research*, *28*(12), 1797–1808. doi:10.1016/S0008-8846(98)00165-3

Yinggang, Z., & Qinming, H. (2006). An unbalanced dataset classification approach based on-support vector machine. In *Proceedings 6th Congress on Intelligent Control and Automation.*

Yohai, V. J. (1987). High breakdown point and high efficiency robust estimates for regression. *Annals of Statistics*, *15*, 642–656. doi:10.1214/aos/1176350366

Young, N. (2002). Mathematical morphology. Retrieved from http://dmsun4bath.ac.uk/research/morphology/morphology.htm

Yudin, D. B., & Yudin, A. D. (1985). *The number and the thought*. Moscow, Russia: Znanie.

Zabell, S. L. (2007). On student's 1908 article 'The probable error of a mean'. *Journal of the American Statistical Association*, *103*(481), 1–7. doi:10.1198/016214508000000030

Zacks, J., & Tversky, B. (2001). Event structure in perception and conception. *Psychological Bulletin*, *127*(1), 3–21. doi:10.1037/0033-2909.127.1.3

Zacks, J. M., Braver, T. S., Sheridan, M. A., Donaldson, D. I., Snyder, A. Z., & Ollinger, J. M. (2001). Human brain activity time-locked to perceptual event boundaries. *Nature Neuroscience*, *4*(6), 651–655. doi:10.1038/88486

Zadeh, L. (1997). Information granulation and its centrality in human and machine intelligence. [Gaithersburg, MD.]. *Proceedings of the Conference on Intelligent Systems and Semiotics*, *97*, 26–30.

Zapranis, A. D., & Refenes, A.-P. (1999). *Principles of neural model identification, selection and adequacy*. London, UK: Springer.

Zhang, H., Wei, Q., & Luo, Y. (2008). A novel infinite-time optimal tracking control scheme for a class of discrete-time nonlinear systems via the greedy HDP iteration algorithm. *IEEE Transactions on Systems, Man, and Cybernetics. Part B, Cybernetics*, *38*(4), 937–942. doi:10.1109/TSMCB.2008.920269

Zhang, Q., & Stanley, S. J. (1997). Forecasting raw-water quality parameters for the North Saskatchewan River by neural network modelling. *Water Research*, *31*, 2340–2350. doi:10.1016/S0043-1354(97)00072-9

Zhang, C., Murai, S., & Baltsavias, E. (1999). *Road network detection by mathematical morphology*. Retrieved from http://www.photogrammetry.ethz.ch/general/persons/chunsun_pub/chunsun_paris99.pdf

Zinchenko, V. (1996). Developing activity theory: The zone of proximal development and beyond. In Nardi, B. (Ed.), *Context and consciousness, activity theory and Human-Computer Interaction* (pp. 283–324). Cambridge, MA: MIT Press.

Zomorodian, A. (2005). *Topology for computing*. London, UK: Cambridge.

About the Contributors

Boris Igelnik received M.S. degree in electrical engineering from the Moscow Electrical Engineering Institute of Communication, M. S. degree in mathematics from the Moscow State University, and Ph.D. degree in Electrical Engineering from the Institute for Problems of Information Transmission, Academy of Sciences USSR, Moscow, Russia and the Moscow Electrical Engineering Institute of Communication. He is Chief Scientist at the BMI Research, Inc., Richmond Heights (Cleveland), OH, USA and Adjunct Associate Professor at Case Western Reserve University, Cleveland, OH, USA. His current research interests are in the areas of computational and artificial intelligence, digital signal processing, adaptive control, and computational models of intellect. Boris Igelnik is a Senior Member of IEEE.

* * *

A. B. M. Shawkat Ali is currently working as a senior lecturer with the School of Computing Sciences, Central Queensland University, Australia. He holds a PhD in Information Technology from Monash University, Australia on Statistical Learning Theory: Support Vector Machine. He is an author and editor of two Data Mining books published by Thomson and IGI-Global and has published over 70 book chapters, journals and conferences paper in the area of Data Mining, Bioinformatics, Telecommunications and Sensor Networking. He has served as the PC Chair DMAI 2008, 2009 and also PC member for many international conferences such as IEEE and ACS. He is an Editor-in-Chief of the International Journal of Emerging Technologies in Sciences and Engineering. He is also a Senior Member of the world largest professional organization IEEE.

Kai Keng Ang received the B.A.S.c degree (with first class honors) and the M.Phil degree in Computer Engineering from Nanyang Technological University, Singapore in 1997 and 1999 respectively. He was a senior software engineer with Delphi Automotive Systems Singapore Pte Ltd working on embedded software for automotive engine controllers from 1999 to 2003. He started working towards his Ph.D. degree in the Centre for Computational Intelligence, School of Computer Engineering, Nanyang Technological University from 2003 onwards, and has been awarded the Singapore Millennium Foundation Ph.D. Scholarship in 2005. He is currently a senior research fellow with the Institute for Infocom Research, Agency for Science, Technology and Research, Singapore. His research interests include Computational Intelligence, machine learning, pattern recognition and signal processing of which he has published several papers.

Lubica Benuskova is currently a Senior Lecturer at the Department of Computer Science, University of Otago, New Zealand. She is also an Associate Professor at the Faculty of Mathematics, Physics and Informatics at Comenius University in Bratislava, Slovakia. Her research interests are in the areas of computational neuroscience, cognitive science, neuroinformatics and computational intelligence. She is the first author of the book Computational Neurogenetic Modeling written together with Prof. Kasabov.

Malcolm J. Beynon is Professor of Uncertain Reasoning in Business/Management in Cardiff Business Cardiff at Cardiff University (UK). He gained his BSc and PhD in pure mathematics and computational mathematics, respectively, at Cardiff University. His research areas include the theoretical and application of uncertain reasoning methodologies, including Dempster-Shafer theory, fuzzy set theory and rough set theory. Also the introduction and development of multi-criteria based decision making and classification techniques, including the Classification and Ranking Belief Simplex. He has published over 160 research articles. He is a member of the International Rough Set Society, International Operations Research Society and the International Multi-Criteria Decision Making Society.

Auke van Breemen, Nijmegen, the Netherlands, is an independent research professional. His current research interests are in information processing, knowledge representation, and semiotic analysis of design processes.

Silvia Cateni was born in Cascina in 1977. She obtained the master degree in telecommunication engineering in 2005 from Università degli studi di Pisa. In 2005 she joined the Steel and Industrial Automation Division within the PERCRO laboratory of Scuola Superiore S.Anna where she is currently a researcher involved in several projects focused on industrial automation. Her research field includes artificial intelligence, data analysis, mathematical modeling and simulation. She is the author of several papers in the field of artificial intelligence and industrial automation.

Valentina Colla was born in La Spezia in 1970. She obtained her Master Degree In Engineering from the University of Pisa in June 1994 and her PhD in Robotics from Scuola Superiore Sant'Anna of Pisa in January 1998. In the same institution from 1998 until 2000 She was post-doctoral research fellow and She developed research work in the application of neuro-fuzzy control techniques to robotic and mechatronic systems. From 2000 until 2008 She was researcher at Scuola Superiore Sant'Anna and in this institution She is currently Technical Research Manager. Since 2002 she coordinates a research group with PERCRO laboratory that develops applied research in the field of industrial automation, with a special focus on steelmaking industry. She has been also professor of Applied Mechanics at the Faculty of Engineering of the University of Florence. Her research interests include mathematical modeling of industrial processes, modeling and control of industrial robots and machine tools and application of artificial intelligence techniques for optimization and control of industrial processes and manufacturing procedures.

Anthony Cohn Anthony Cohn is Professor of Automated Reasoning at the University of Leeds, UK where he is presently Director of the Institute for Artificial Intelligence and Biological Systems. He holds BSc and PhD degrees from the University of Essex. He now leads a research group working on Knowledge Representation and Reasoning with a particular focus on qualitative spatial/spatio-temporal reasoning. His current research interests range from theoretical work on spatial calculi and spatial ontologies, to cognitive vision, modelling spatial information in the hippocampus, integrating utility data recording the location of underground assets and detection of archaeological residues using remote sensing. He has been Chairman/President of the UK AI Society SSAISB, the European Coordinating Committee on AI (ECCAI), KR inc, the IJCAI Board of Trustees and is presently Editor-in-Chief of the AAAI Press, Spatial Cognition and Computation, and Artificial Intelligence. He is a Fellow of ECCAI, AAAI, AISB, the BCS, and the IET.

Yuri Dabaghian is a Research Assistant in the Department of Physiology at the University of California, San Francisco. Dr. Dabaghian obtained his Master's degree at the Landau Institute for Theoretical Physics in Moscow, Russia and his PhD in theoretical and mathematical physics at the University of Rhode Island. He did research in the field of Quantum Chaos and Spectral Theory. His current research interests lay in the field of neuronal representation of spatial information, computational neuroscience, computational geometry and topology, data analysis.

Khalifa Djemal received the diploma degree in Optical, Image and Signal processing in 1999 from the National School of Physics at the University of Marseille, France and the PhD in Image and signal processing, 2002, from the University of Toulon, France. Since 2003, he is Associate Professor at the Electrical Engineering department of the Institute of Technology at the University of Evry Val d'Essonne, France. He works now within T.A.D.I.B team of the IBISC Laboratory. His current research interests are in the areas of image and data processing (Restoration, Segmentation, Clustering and CBIR). Dr. Djemal chaired the International Conference on Image Processing Theory, Tools and Applications IPTA, in 2008 and 2010, and also International Workshop on Medical Image Analysis and Description for Diagnosis Systems, MIAD, in 2009 and 2010. He was the chair of some special sessions in number of conferences. He acted as technical chairman for a number of conferences. He is a reviewer for a number of international journals and conferences.

Mark J. Embrechts (S'74–M'81) received the M.S. degree in electrical engineering from the University of Leuven, Belgium, and the M.S. and Ph.D. degrees in nuclear engineering from Virginia Polytechnic Institute and State University, Blacksburg, in 1977, 1978, and 1981, respectively. After working as a Postdoctoral Fellow at Los Alamos National Laboratory, Los Alamos, NM, as a graduate student and postdoctoral staff member (1980 to 1983) he joined the Department of Nuclear Engineering, Rensselaer Polytechnic Institute, Troy, NY, in 1983. He is currently an Associate Professor in the Department of Decision Sciences and Engineering Systems and also Associate Professor in the Information Technology Program at Rensselaer Polytechnic Institute. He has published more than 150 conference and journal papers and coauthored *Exchange Rate Theory* (Oxford, U.K.: Basil Blackwell, 1993). His current areas of interest relate to neural networks, evolutionary computing, fuzzy logic, data mining, data fusion, text mining, and applications of soft computing to data mining, biotechnology, and molecular drug design.

Jozsef I. Farkas received his B.S. and M.S. degrees in Chemistry and Physics at Jozsef A. University of Szeged, Hungary and Ph.D. degree at the Radboud University, Nijmegen, the Netherlands. His current research interests are in cognitive aspects of knowledge representation.

Yohan D. Fougerolle received the MS degree in electrical engineering from the University of Burgundy, Dijon, France, in 2002, and the Ph.D from the same university in 2005. Since 2007, he is an assistant professor in the department of Electrical Engineering, at the University of Burgundy, Le Creusot, France. His research interests include 3D digitization, solid modeling, surface reconstruction, and image processing.

Loren Frank, PhD is an Assistant Professor in the Department of physiology and a member of the Keck Center for Integrative Neuroscience at the University of California, San Francisco. Dr. Frank did his PhD work in systems and computational neuroscience at M.I.T. and a post-doctoral fellowship in statistics and neuroscience at Harvard University and Massachusetts General Hospital. His laboratory uses a combination of techniques, including multielectrode recording, behavioral manipulations and optogenetic circuit manipulation to study the neural bases of learning, memory and decision making.

Long Han is Front Office quantitative Analyst at Constellation Energy Commodities Group. He received his Ph.D. in Decision Sciences and Engineering Systems from Rensselaer Polytechnic Institute in 2007. Prior to his Ph.D. study, he worked at Tokyo Japan as a lead software engineer after he received his B.S. and M.S. from ZheJiang University in China in 1997, and 2000 respectively. His research interests cover the broad area of Data mining and Computational Intelligence with current focus on quantitative analysis of financial/energy data.

Cathy Holt is a Senior Lecturer in Biomechanics in the Institute of Medical Engineering and Medical Physics, Cardiff School of Engineering, Cardiff University (UK). She gained her BEng and PhD in Mechanical Engineering at Cardiff University. Her research areas include the application of three-dimensional motion capture and analysis to medical applications including orthopaedic biomechanics and soft tissue mechanics and the promotion of cross-disciplinary studies to advance medical engineering applications. She is the Biomechanics, Motion Analysis and Rehabilitation Team Leader for the Arthritis Research UK Biomechanics and Bioengineering Centre awarded to Cardiff University in 2009. It is a multidisciplinary research centre dedicated to exploring and quantifying the links between human joint function, loading, biology, pain and inflammation. She has published over 100 research publications, proceedings and abstracts and is a member of the European and International Societies of Biomechanics.

Roman Ilin is a Computer Scientist at the Air Force Research Laboratory, Hanscom Air Force Base. He received a doctorate degree in Computer Science from the University of Memphis, Memphis, TN. His research interests include target tracking and characterization, multi-sensor data fusion, reinforcement learning, artificial neural networks, and approximate dynamic programming.

A. H. M. Rahmatullah Imon was born in Rajshahi, Bangladesh in 1967. He graduated with Honors in Statistics in 1987 and obtained his M.Sc. in Statistics in 1988 from the University of Rajshahi. He got his PhD in Mathematics and Statistics from the University of Birmingham, U.K. in 1996. Dr. Imon began his academic career as a Lecturer at the University of Rajshahi in 1992 and was promoted to a Full Professor position in 2004. He joined the Department of Mathematical Science, Ball State University in fall, 2008 and has been serving this department since then. Dr. Imon's areas of specialization are Regression Diagnostics, and Robust Regression and Outlier Detection. Dr. Imon has published 70 research articles in refereed journals and proceedings of international conferences. He got several awards for his outstanding academic records and research. He has been an elected member of the International Statistical Institute since 2005.

Nikola Kasabov is the Founder and Director of the Knowledge Engineering and Discovery Research Institute (www.kedri.info) at the Auckland University of Technology (AUT) in Auckland, New Zealand. He is also a Chair of Knowledge Engineering at the School of Computing and Mathematical Sciences at AUT. Prof. Kasabov is a leading expert in computational intelligence and knowledge engineering and has published more than 420 papers, books and patents in the areas of neural and hybrid intelligent systems, bioinformatics and neuroinformatics, speech-, image and multimodal information processing. He is a Fellow of IEEE, Fellow of the Royal Society of New Zealand, current President of the International Neural Network Society (www.inns.org) and a Past President of the Asia-Pacific Neural Network Assembly (www.apnna.net).

Christian Kennes, PhD, is Professor of Chemical Engineering at the University of La Coruña, since 1996. Among his recent teaching activities, he has been involved in courses on Advanced Chemical Engineering, Wastewater Treatment, Air Pollution Control Technologies and Air Quality. He did also work as a Faculty member at the University of Santiago de Compostela, just before joining the University of La Coruña, after spending some time in different research laboratories in Belgium, France, United States and The Netherlands. His research work pertains to environmental biotechnology, waste gas treatment, wastewater treatment and bioconversion processes. He is author or co-author of close to one hundred scientific papers, books and book chapters and editor of the book ''*Bioreactors for Waste Gas Treatment*'' published by Kluwer Academic Publishers.

Robert Koktysz was born in Poland in 1960. He received the medical doctor degree from Military Medical University, Lodz, Poland in 1996. Currently he is employed at the Department of Clinical Pathology, Military Institute of Medicine, Warsaw, Poland. His research interest is in pathology of the digestive system, breast cancer research, morphometry, and mathematical methods applied in pathology.

Michal Kruk was born in Poland in 1980. He received the M.Sc. and Ph.D. degrees from Warsaw University of Technology, Warsaw, Poland in 2004, and 2008 in electrical and computer engineering, respectively. Currently he is an Assistant Professor (adiunkt) at the University of Life Sciences, Warsaw, Poland. His research interests are in the areas of artificial intelligence, biomedical engineering and mathematical methods applied in biomedical signal and image processing.

Jaroslaw Kurek was born in Poland in 1980. He received the M.Sc. and Ph.D. degrees from Warsaw University of Technology, Warsaw, Poland in 2004, and 2008 in electrical and computer engineering, respectively. Currently he is an Assistant Professor (adiunkt) at the University of Life Sciences, Warsaw, Poland. His research interests are in the areas of artificial intelligence and mathematical methods applied in signal and image processing.

Jong-Soo Lee has received his BS in electrical engineering in 1973 from Seoul National University, Korea and his M.Eng in 1981 and Ph.D in 1985 from Virginia Polytechnic Institute and State University, USA. He is currently working in the area of multimedia at the University of Ulsan, Korea.

Pierre-Emmanuel Leni received in 2007 the master degree in electrical engineering from the University of Burgundy in Dijon, France. He is currently pursuing a Ph.D. degree in the same university, at the Le2i laboratory, UMR CNRS 5158, in Le Creusot, France. His research interests include functional representation, and image processing, particularly image compression.

Artem A. Lenskiy has received the BS degree in computer and information science and the MS degree in digital signal processing and data mining from Novosibirsk State Technical University, Russia. He received the PhD degree in electrical engineering from University of Ulsan, Korea in 2010. Prior coming to Korea in 2005, he was a lecturer and a head of IT laboratory. His current research interests include machine learning algorithms, computer vision and self-similar, fractal processes.

Frank L. Lewis, Fellow IEEE, Fellow IFAC, Fellow U.K. Institute of Measurement & Control, PE Texas, U.K. Chartered Engineer, is Distinguished Scholar Professor and Moncrief-O'Donnell Chair at University of Texas at Arlington's Automation & Robotics Research Institute. He obtained the Bachelor's Degree in Physics/EE and the MSEE at Rice University, the MS in Aeronautical Engineering from Univ. W. Florida, and the Ph.D. at Georgia Tech. He works in feedback control, intelligent systems, and sensor networks. He is author of 6 U.S. patents, 209 journal papers, 328 conference papers, 12 books, 41 chapters, and 11 journal special issues. He received the Fulbright Research Award, NSF Research Initiation Grant, ASEE Terman Award, and Int. Neural Network Soc. Gabor Award 2008. Received Outstanding Service Award from Dallas IEEE Section, selected as Engineer of the year by Ft. Worth IEEE Section. Listed in Fort Worth Business Press Top 200 Leaders in Manufacturing. He was appointed to the NAE Committee on Space Station in 1995. He is an elected Guest Consulting Professor at both South China University of Technology and Shanghai Jiao Tong University. Founding Member of the Board of Governors of the Mediterranean Control Association. Helped win the IEEE Control Systems Society Best Chapter Award (as Founding Chairman of DFW Chapter), the National Sigma Xi Award for Outstanding Chapter (as President of UTA Chapter), and the US SBA Tibbets Award in 1996 (as Director of ARRI's SBIR Program).

Estefania M. López, is a doctoral student at the Department of Chemical Engineering, University of La Coruña, Spain. Estefania focuses her research in improving bioreactor performance for the treatment of odorous pollutants from pulp and paper industry. She also applies ANNs for performance prediction in biotrickling filters.

Paul Lozovyy was born in Ukraine and moved to the United States in 1998 when he was 12 years old. He is a fluent speaker and writer in three languages (Ukrainian, Russian, and English). After high school he worked as a painter while attending community college. His interests led him to electronics and to Cleveland State University (CSU), where he is currently working on his B.S. degree in electrical engineering with emphases in control systems and power systems. Paul has been an active member of the IEEE since 2008, and is currently the treasurer of the CSU student branch of the IEEE. He is also a member of the International Council on Systems Engineering (INCOSE). His work in robotics as a research assistant at CSU involves evolutionary algorithms, programming, and controls.

Hichem Maaref is Professor at the University of Evry Val d'Essonne within the laboratory IBISC. Since 2001, he is the head of the team "Processing and Analysis of Data and Images - Biometrics". His research works concern mainly the methods of pattern recognition for applications to images analysis, sensorial fusion and autonomous robot navigation.

Mohammed Nasser is now Professor at Department of Statistics, University of Rajshahi. He got Honours and M.Sc degree in Statistics from Jahangirnagar University, Bangladesh and did his Ph.D degree on *"Continuity and Differentiability of Statistical Functionals; Its Relation to Robustness in Boostrapping"* at Research Centre for Mathematical and Physical Sciences, Chittagong University, Bangladesh. He is the founder chairman of Diagnostic Robust Resampling Statistics and Data Mining (DRRSDM) research group that has members working in five national-international universities and research organizations. He has already published more than forty articles in national and international journals in statistics, mathematics and sociology. His current research interest is in Mathematics of Kernel Methods, Bioinformatics, Robust Estimation and Globalization. He is a life member of both Bangladesh Statistical Society and Bangladesh Mathematical Society, and editorial board members of three national journals.

Tohru Nitta received the B.S. degree in mathematics, M.S. and Ph.D. degrees in information science from University of Tsukuba, Japan, in 1983, 1985, and 1995 respectively. From 1985 to 1990, he was with NEC Corporation and engaged in research on expert systems. He joined the Electrotechnical Laboratory, Agency of Industrial Science and Technology, Ministry of International Trade and Industry in 1990. He is currently a Senior Research Scientist in National Institute of Advanced Industrial Science and Technology (former Electrotechnical Laboratory), Japan. He was also with Department of Mathematics, Graduate School of Science, Osaka University as an Associate Professor from 2000 to 2006, and as a Professor from 2006 to 2008 (additional post). His research interests include complex adaptive systems such as neural networks.

A. A. M. Nurunnabi (1972-) received B. Sc (Hons) and M.Sc. in Statistics from the Department of Statistics, University of Rajshahi, Bangladesh in 1997 and 1998. He achieved M. Phil. in Statistics from the same department in 2008. He started his profession as a lecturer and later served as Principal at IMIT, Dhaka. He served (2003-2009) as an assistant professor at School of Business, Uttara University. He is working as a research fellow with the Diagnostics Robust Resampling Statistics and Data Mining (DRRSDM) research group, Rajshahi University. He has authored more than 30 research articles in referred journals and conference proceedings. His recent research interests are outlier detection, data mining, machine learning, bioinformatics, and pattern recognition. He is the member of several national and international statistical, computer sciences and engineers' association. He has edited a journal and reviewed a good number of journal and conference papers in diverse fields.

Stanislaw Osowski was born in Poland in 1948. He received the M.Sc., Ph.D., and habilitate doctorate (Dr.Sc.) degrees from Warsaw University of Technology, Warsaw, Poland, in 1972, 1975, and

1981, respectively, all in electrical engineering. Currently he is a professor of electrical engineering at the Institute of the Theory of Electrical Engineering, Measurement and Information Systems, Warsaw University of Technology and also at Military University of Technology. His research and teaching interest are in the computational intelligence, neural networks and biomedical signal and image processing.

Leonid Perlovsky is a Visiting Scholar at Harvard University, and Principal Research Physicist and Technical Advisor at the Air Force Research Laboratory, where current projects include signal processing, cognitive algorithms, modeling of the mind, languages, and cultures. He served as Chief Scientist at Nichols Research, a $0.5 B high-tech organization, leading the corporate research in intelligent systems and neural networks; as professor at Novosibirsk University and New York University. He participated as a principal in several commercial startups developing language learning search engines, biotechnology, and financial predictions. He has delivered invited keynote plenary talks and tutorial lectures worldwide, published more than 330 papers, 10 book chapters, and three books: "Neural Networks and Intellect," Oxford University Press, 2001 (currently in the 3rd printing), and two books by Springer in 2007. Dr. Perlovsky serves as Chair and Program Chair for conferences on Computational Intelligence. He chairs IEEE Boston Computational Intelligence Chapter, serves on the Board of Governors of International Neural Network Society, on Editorial Boards of six professional journals, including IEEE "Transactions on Neural Networks," "Natural Computations," and Editor-in-Chief for "Physics of Life Reviews," which he originated together with the late Nobel Laureate I. Prigogine. He has received prestigious awards including the 2007 Gabor Award, the top engineering award given by the International Neural Network Society, and the 2007 McLucas Award, the top scientific award from the Air Force.

Frederick E. Petry received BS and MS degrees in physics and a Ph.D. in computer science from Ohio State University in 1975. He is currently a computer scientist in the Naval Research Laboratory, Stennis Space Center Mississippi and was on the faculty of University of Alabama in Huntsville, Ohio State University and Tulane University. Dr. Petry has over 300 scientific publications including 130 journal articles/book chapters and 8 books written or edited. He is an associate editor of *IEEE Transactions on Fuzzy Systems* and several other journals and has been general chairperson of several international conferences. He is an IEEE Fellow, Fellow of the International Fuzzy Systems Association and an ACM Distinguished Scientist. In 2002 he was chosen as the outstanding researcher of the year in Tulane University School of Engineering and received the Naval Research Laboratory's Berman Research Publication awards in 2004 and 2008.

Chai Quek received the B.Sc. degree in electrical and electronics engineering and the Ph.D. degree in intelligent control from Heriot Watt University, Edinburgh, Scotland. He is an associate professor and a member of the Centre for Computational Intelligence, formerly the Intelligent Systems Laboratory and the Assistant Chair at the School of Computer Engineering, Nanyang Technological University. His research interests include intelligent control, intelligent architectures, AI in education, neural networks, fuzzy neural systems, neurocognitive informatics and genetic algorithms. C. Quek is a Senior Member of IEEE and a member of the IEEE Technical Committee on Computational Finance.

Nicholas George Rambidi is professor and chair of Polymer and Cristal Physics at Physics Department, Moscow State University (MSU). He received BS in 1954, Ph.D. in 1959, and Dr. S. (Doctor of

Science), all in Physical Chemistry, at MSU. Prof. Rambidi is a member of Russian Academy of Natural Science and International Academy of Informatics. He is on the Editorial Boards of the NeuroComputer, BioSystems, and International Journal of Unconventional Computing. Prof. Rambidi teaches courses of Quantum Chemistry and Physical and Chemical Bases of Nanotechnology at Physics Department, MSU. His research interests are in the areas of nonlinear phenomena exhibited by physical and chemical reaction-diffusion systems, based on structured polymer matrices; design and construction of complex systems having behavioral complexity; information processing capabilities of the complex polymer-based nonlinear dynamic systems; general principles of biocomputing and structure and dynamics of molecular and biomedical species.

Eldon R. Rene, PhD, is a "Juan de La Cierva" post–doctoral researcher at the Department of Chemical Engineering, University of La Coruña, Spain. His research focuses on the development of biosystems for waste air and wastewater purification. He also works with expert systems and artificial neural network by integrating the developed models to existing biological treatment systems. He has ten years of research experience in waste – gas treatment, desalination, SBR technology, and Eco – Industrial Parks, amongst others.

Alexander Ross is a Biomedical Engineer with a Ph.D. and M.S.in Biomedical Engineering from Rensselaer Polytechnic Institute and a B.S. in Electrical Engineering from the State University of New York at Binghamton. Alex joined a Fortune 500 medical device company in 2007 after developing medical device equipment for several years at CardioMag Imaging. In his multiple roles, Alex leads the development of new medical device platforms from concept through new product introduction, manages global project teams, and develops intellectual property strategies for new technologies. Alex gives seminars on biomedical engineering for local Universities and professional societies and is an active reviewer for several IEEE and IoP journals. Additionally, he is a Senior Member of the Institute of Electrical and Electronics Engineers, a certified Project Management Professional (PMP) with the Project Management Institute, and a full member of the Sigma Xi research society.

Janos J. Sarbo received Ph.D. degree in Electrical Engineering at the Technical University of Budapest, Hungary in 1985. Since 1986 he has been working at the Computer Science Department of the Radboud University in Nijmegen, the Netherlands. The focus of his research is in the formal conceptual analysis. Recently Dr. Sarbo entered the area of the definition of a cognitively based model of knowledge representation and its semiotic interpretation.

Mirko Sgarbi was born in Grosseto in 1972. He obtained his Master Degree In Engineering from the University of Pisa in July 2000. He has been Junior Researcher at Scuola Superiore Sant'Anna, where he joined the Steel and Industrial Automation Division (SIAD) of PERCRO laboratory in 2002. Since 2010 he is research cooperator in the same laboratory and he is involved in several projects in the field of industrial automation. His research interests mainly concern the application of soft computing algorithms in steel industry and the design and development of software tools for simulation of manufacturing processes with machine tools and robots. He is also expert in the application of Artificial Intelligence techniques for image processing and he is involved in projects related to quality control through artificial vision systems.

Dan Simon received a B.S. degree from Arizona State University (1982), an M.S. degree from the University of Washington (1987), and a Ph.D. degree from Syracuse University (1991), all in electrical engineering. He worked in industry for 14 years at Boeing, TRW, and several small companies. His industrial experience includes work in the aerospace, automotive, agricultural, biomedical, process control, and software fields. In 1999 he moved from industry to academia, where he is now a professor in the Electrical and Computer Engineering Department at Cleveland State University. His teaching and research involves embedded systems, control systems, and computer intelligence. He has published over 70 refereed conference and journal papers, and is the author of the text "Optimal State Estimation" (John Wiley & Sons, 2006).

Karsten Sternickel, After receiving his Ph.D. in physics in 2001 Dr. Sternickel moved to the US and worked as Research Scientist for Cardiomag Imaging Inc., a medical device manufacturer. Major milestones accomplished include obtaining the first FDA approval ever for a magnetocardiograph and successful application for research grants on which he served as Principal Investigator. He presented and published the results and filed patent applications. In 2004 he became a Project Leader and contributed to the companies' successful IPO in December 2005. In 2006 Dr. Sternickel joined Pharmaceutical Research Associates (PRA) International, a contract research organization, as Project Manager and has since been responsible for managing multiple projects on various indications including Parkinson's Disease, Epilepsy, inflammatory bowel disease and Cardiovascular Diseases.

Petru Emanuel Stingu obtained the Bachelor's Degree in Automatic Control and Computer Engineering at the Gheorghe Asachi Technical University of Iasi, Romania. He is working as a research assistant at the Automation & Robotics Research Institute of the University of Texas at Arlington where he obtained the M.Sc in Electrical Engineering in 2008 and is currently pursuing his PhD degree. His research interests include Approximate Dynamic Programming, adaptive control, control of distributed systems, and general theory of nonlinear systems with a focus on applications for complex systems such as unmanned air or ground vehicles.

Boleslaw K. Szymanski is the Claire and Roland Schmitt Distinguished Professor at the Department of Computer Science and the Director of the ARL Social and Cognitive Networks Academic Research Center at the Rensselaer Polytechnic Institute. He received his Ph.D. in Computer Science from National Academy of Sciences in Warsaw, Poland, in 1976. Dr. Szymanski published over three hundreds scientific publications and is the Editor-in-Chief of Scientific Programming. He is a foreign member of the National Academy of Science in Poland, an IEEE Fellow and a member of the IEEE Computer Society, and Association for Computing Machinery for which he was National Lecturer. He received the Wiley Distinguished Faculty Award in 2003 and the Wilkes Medal of British Computer Society in 2009. His research interests cover the broad area of distributed and parallel computer systems and algorithms with current focus on wireless and sensor networks.

Lars Taxen received his M. Sc. Form the Royal Institute of Technology in 1968. Between 1968 and 2003 he was employed at the Ericsson Telecommunication Company, where he held several positions related to hardware and software design. From 1995 he was engaged in the development and implementation of incremental development methods for large, globally distributed software development projects.

In parallel with his work at Ericsson he did research in this area at Linkoping University, Sweden, where he became a Ph. D. in 2003 and a n associate professor in 2007. The experiences from Ericsson and his research results were reported in the book "Using Activity Domain Theory for Managing Complex Systems", published by Information Science Reference in 2009. In addition, he has published in various conference proceedings and journals. He is now active as a researcher and consultant.

George Thomas is a junior undergraduate with a major in electrical engineering at Cleveland State University. His experience in industry includes designing a remote data acquisition system for solar power plant installations. His work in the academic research field involves robotics and embedded systems, PID and fuzzy logic control systems, distributed computation, and heuristic optimization methods such as genetic algorithms and biogeography-based optimization. His interests include most fields associated with electrical engineering and computer science, open source methodologies that disseminate technical work and knowledge freely to the public, and ultimately, engineering projects to benefit humanity.

Frédéric Truchetet was born in Dijon, France, on October 13, 1951. He received the master degree in physics at Dijon University, France, in 1973 and a Ph.D. in electronics at the same University in 1977. He was for two years with Thomson-CSF as a research engineer. He is currently "Professeur des Universités" in Le2i, UMR CNRS 5158, vice president of the Université de Bourgogne and expert/advisor for French Ministry of Research. His research interests are focused on image processing for artificial vision inspection and particularly on wavelet transform, multiresolution edge detection and image compression. He has authored and co-authored more than 200 international publications, three text books and holds two patents. He is a member of IEEE, SPIE, Chairman of SPIE's conference on optics and photonics and member of numerous technical committees of international conferences in the area of computer vision.

Marco Vannucci was born in Pontedera in 1976. He got the master degree in computer science in 2001 from Pisa University and the Ph.D. in engineering from Scuola Superiore S.Anna in 2006. He is currently junior researcher within the PERCRO laboratory of Scuola Superiore S.Anna where he is involved in several projects in the field of industrial automation and he focused its interest on the exploitation of artificial intelligence techniques in the industrial framework. His research activity includes simulation, mathematical modeling, artificial intelligence and robotics. He is the author of numerous papers in the field of artificial intelligence and industrial automation.

Maria C. Veiga, PhD, is a Professor at the Department of Chemical Engineering, University of La Coruña, Spain. She is the leader of the "Environmental Engineering" – group, that focuses on research topics mainly related to environmental biotechnology, biological and advanced oxidation treatment of industrial wastewaters. She regularly undertakes industry – sponsored research projects and to her scientific merit, she has published over fifty scientific manuscripts in SCI journals. She is one of the main organizers of the International Conference on ′′Biotechniques for Air Pollution Control′′, conducted every odd numbered year.

Gemma Whatling is a Cardiff Academic Fellow at the School of Engineering and School of Healthcare Studies, Cardiff University. She gained her First Class Honours MEng degree in Medical Engineering and PhD in Mechanical Engineering at Cardiff University. She works in the Biomechanics, Motion Analysis and Rehabilitation Team for the Arthritis Research UK Biomechanics and Bioengineering Centre at Cardiff University. Her research focuses on lower limb biomechanics, classification of osteoarthritic joints and recovery following surgical procedures, patient specific predictive modelling and fluoroscopy based image registration of natural and replaced joints. She is active in public engagement activities, is a member of the Women into Science, Engineering and Construction (WISE) in Wales Committee and a STEM Ambassador for Wales (STEMNET). She has published over 50 research publications, proceedings and abstracts, is a member of the European Society of Biomechanics and Associate Member of the Institution of Mechanical Engineers.

Simei Gomes Wysoski received his PhD at Auckland University of Technology, New Zealand, in 2008. He got his M.E. degree in Electrical and Computer Engineering from Nagoya Institute of Technology, Japan, in 2003, and B.E. in Electrical Engineering from the Federal University of Parana, Brazil, in 2000. His current interests include the use of brain-like neural networks for pattern recognition, evolving connectionist systems and computational modelling of brain functions.

Index

A

B

J

K

L

M

Q

R

S